30°E   45°E   60°E

Black Sea

Caspian Sea

Aral Sea

Aras River

Amu Darya (Oxus River)

Toros Dağlari

Kuhha-ye Zagros

Reshteh-ye Alborz

Hindu Kush

Cyprus

Tigris River

Mesopotamia

Euphrates River

Dasht-e Kavor
(Salt Desert)

Iranian Plateau

Jordan River

Syrian Desert

Dasht-e Lut
(Sand Desert)

Dead Sea

Sinai

Nafud

Persian Gulf

Nile River

Najd

Gulf of Oman

al-Hijaz

Red Sea

Nubian Desert

Arabian Peninsula

Atbara River

al-Rub al-Khali

Arabian Sea

Blue Nile River

Gulf of Aden

Socotra

Nile River

INDIAN OCEAN

N

For Reference

Not to be taken from this room

0   200   400 mi.

0   200   400 km

ENCYCLOPEDIA OF THE

MODERN MIDDLE EAST & NORTH AFRICA

SECOND EDITION

EDITOR IN CHIEF

Philip Mattar
United States Institute of Peace

ASSOCIATE EDITORS

Charles E. Butterworth
University of Maryland

Neil Caplan
Vanier College, Montreal, Canada

Michael R. Fischbach
Randolph-Macon College, Ashland, Virginia

Eric Hooglund
Institute for Palestine Studies, Washington, DC

Laurie King-Irani
University of Victoria, British Columbia, Canada

John Ruedy
Georgetown University

CONSULTANT EDITOR

Don Peretz
State University of New York

ENCYCLOPEDIA OF THE
MODERN
MIDDLE EAST &
NORTH AFRICA
SECOND EDITION

VOLUME 4

Shammar – Zurayk
Index

Philip Mattar

EDITOR IN CHIEF

MACMILLAN REFERENCE USA

An imprint of Thomson Gale, a part of The Thomson Corporation

THOMSON
GALE

Detroit • New York • San Francisco • San Diego • New Haven, Conn. • Waterville, Maine • London • Munich

THOMSON
GALE

The Encyclopedia of the Modern Middle East and North Africa, 2nd Edition

Philip Mattar

LIBRARY OF CONGRESS CATALOGING-IN-PUBLICATION DATA

Encyclopedia of the modern Middle East and North Africa / edited by Philip Mattar.— 2nd ed.
    p. cm.
        Includes bibliographical references and index.
        ISBN 0-02-865769-1 (set : alk. paper) — ISBN 0-02-865770-5 (v. 1 : alk. paper) — ISBN 0-02-865771-3 (v. 2 : alk. paper) — ISBN 0-02-865772-1 (v. 3 : alk. paper) — ISBN 0-02-865773-X (v. 4 : alk. paper)
        1. Middle East—Encyclopedias. 2. Africa, North—Encyclopedias. I. Mattar, Philip, 1944-

DS43.E53 2004
956'.003—dc22   2004005650

This title is also avalable as an e-book.
ISBN 0-02-865987-2 (set)
Contact your Gale sales representative for ordering information.

Printed in the United States of America
10 9 8 7 6 5 4 3

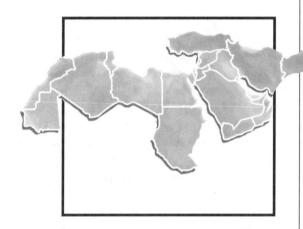

S

(*Continued*)

SHAMMAR

See TRIBES AND TRIBALISM: SHAMMAR

SHAMMAS, ANTON
[1950–]

Israeli Palestinian novelist, poet, journalist, translator, and nonfiction writer.

Anton Shammas was born to a Christian family in Fassuta, Galilee; he defines himself as an atheist, as a Palestinian citizen of Israel, and as one who identifies with Islamic culture. He studied art history and English and Arabic literature at Hebrew University of Jerusalem from 1968 to 1972, edited the literary journal *al-Sharq* from 1970 to 1975, and produced Arabic television shows in Israel from 1976 to 1986 at the same time that he worked as a freelance journalist.

Shammas writes in Hebrew and English, and his works are characterized by an attempt to challenge the definition and test the tolerance of the Israeli discourse from within the Hebrew language. His highly praised first novel *Arabeshot* (1986; *Arabesques,* 1988) was written in Hebrew and deals with the residents of his native village and, more specifically, with the Shammas family. Interwoven with their lives are historical events and associations that highlight the conditions of the Arabs residing in Israel.

He moved to the United States in 1987 and has been teaching at the University of Michigan since 1988.

See also HEBREW UNIVERSITY OF JERUSALEM.

Bibliography

Fischbach, Michael R. "Anton Shammas." In *Encyclopedia of the Palestinians,* edited by Philip Mattar. New York: Facts On File, 2000.

Shammas, Anton. *Arabesques,* translated from the Hebrew by Vivian Eden. New York: Harper & Row, 1988.

ANN KAHN
UPDATED BY MICHAEL R. FISCHBACH

SHAPIRA, HAYYIM MOSHE
[1902–1970]

Israeli political leader; active in the Ze'irei ha-Mizrahi Zionist movement.

Born in Russia, Hayyim Moshe Shapira studied at the Grodno Yeshiva in Russia and at the Hildesheimer Rabbinical Seminary in Berlin. He attended the fourteenth Zionist Congress and later was elected to the Zionist General Council as a representative of ha Po'el ha-Mizrahi. In 1925, he emigrated to Palestine, where he became a leader in the Zionist Executive.

After the Anschluss of Austria and Germany in 1938, Shapira went to evacuate Austrian Jews to Palestine. Throughout his life, he sought to facilitate the emigration of religious Jews to Israel. From the time the state of Israel was proclaimed in 1948 until his death, Shapira was a minister in the Israeli cabinet as part of the National Religious party.

BRYAN DAVES

SHARABATI, AHMAD AL-
[1905–]

Syrian politician.

Ahmad al-Sharabati, the son of nationalist Damascene merchant Uthman al-Sharabati, studied engineering at the American University of Beirut and at the Massachusetts Institute of Technology. He started his career by running a tobacco factory for his father and later became involved in the import trade, especially of motor vehicles. His political career started in the early 1930s when he joined the National Action League, a pan-Arabist movement that was anticommunist. Harassed by the French Mandatory authorities in Syria, Sharabati fled to Transjordan (now Jordan), where he stayed for several years. In 1943, he became a member of the Syrian parliament, running as a nationalist. In 1945, he became minister of education and then minister of national economy in the ministry of Faris al-Khuri. After his resignation from the cabinet that year, in 1946 he was appointed minister of national defense in the cabinet of Jamil Mardam. In 1948 he resigned as a result of the poor performance of the Syrian army in the Arab-Israel War. In 1951, he was implicated in a conspiracy against Adib Shishakli, the military ruler in Syria, and was sentenced to two years and four months in prison.

Bibliography

Khoury, Philip. *Syria and the French Mandate: The Politics of Arab Nationalism, 1920–1945.* Princeton, NJ: Princeton University Press, 1987.

Seale, Patrick. *The Struggle for Syria: A Study of Post-War Arab Politics, 1945–1958.* New Haven, CT: Yale University Press, 1987.

ABDUL-KARIM RAFEQ

SHA'RAWI, HUDA AL-
[1879–1947]

Egyptian feminist.

A native of Minya, Huda al-Sha'rawi was born to a prominent and prosperous politician-landowner and a Circassian mother. She was raised in an elite household, where domestic life was still centered on the cloistered *harim* (harem), although transitionally so during the late nineteenth century. She describes this experience in her memoirs, dictated to her secretary during the 1940s but published only in 1981; this section of the memoir has appeared in English as *Harem Years.* Sha'rawi grew up studying with tutors at home, as was typical for elite girls of the time, and was taught in Arabic, Persian, Turkish, and French. Her marriage to her much older cousin and guardian, Ali Sha'rawi, also a prominent politician, was arranged by the family and took place when she was thirteen. Some seven years later she managed to obtain a separation. Her interest in women's issues developed gradually out of her experiences and her awareness of women's activism in Europe. She was one of the founders of the 1914 Intellectual Association of Egyptian Women. As a wealthy patron as well as an organizer, she was active in charity organizing, a province open to upper-class women. But Sha'rawi was unusual in moving from behind-the-scenes work into a highly visible, public political role. She spearheaded the Wafdist Women's Central Committee (1919) and was a leader of the famous first women's nationalist demonstration in March 1919. However, disagreement over women's appropriate political roles and particularly over whether women's demands should be admitted to discussions leading to the Egyptian constitution caused a rift with the Wafd, Egypt's nationalist party. Sha'rawi went on to found, with a group of women, al-Ittihad al-nisa'i al-Misri (Egyptian Feminist Union; EFU) in 1923. She presided over it until her death. The EFU founded two journals, the French-language *L'Egyptienne* (1925), for which Sha'rawi wrote editorials, and *al-Misriyya* in Arabic over a decade later (1937), when a broader audience fueled the need for a journal in the indigenous language. Sha'rawi's writing appeared here, too, though she probably played less of a role in the journal. Sha'rawi and two colleagues attended the 1923 International Women Suffrage Alliance in Rome and was responsible for a famous symbolic moment when, on her return, she publicly lifted her veil at Cairo's main railway station. She gradually became more involved in regional and international feminist organizing, becoming vice president of the International Alliance of Women for Suffrage and Equal Citizenship in 1935 and leading a move to found the Arab Feminist Union in 1945.

> See also ARAB FEMINIST UNION; CIRCASSIANS; EGYPT; EGYPTIAN FEMINIST UNION; GENDER: GENDER AND EDUCATION; GENDER: GENDER AND LAW; GENDER: GENDER AND POLITICS; WAFDIST WOMEN'S CENTRAL COMMITTEE.

Bibliography

Badran, Margot. *Feminists, Islam, and Nation: Gender and the Making of Modern Egypt.* Princeton, NJ: Princeton University Press, 1995.

Shaarawi, Huda. *Harem Years: The Memoirs of an Egyptian Feminist (1879–1924),* translated, edited, and introduced by Margot Badran. London: Virago, 1986; New York: Feminist Press, City University of New York, 1987.

DAVID WALDNER
UPDATED BY MARILYN BOOTH

SHA'RAWI, MUHAMMAD MUTWALLI AL-
[1911–1998]

Egyptian cleric.

Muhammad Mutwalli al-Sha'rawi was born in Daqadus, Egypt, in 1911. He originally wanted to devote his career to farming, but his father encouraged him to study in Cairo. In 1937 he joined the faculty of Arabic language of al-Azhar. He was active in student politics and served time in jail. Sha'rawi came to prominence as a cleric during the presidency of Anwar al-Sadat. He was famous for his utilization of modern media (television, audio- and videocassettes, pamphlets, and books) to disseminate his religious message. He was a firm believer in Islamic fundamentalism, but did not address political questions directly for fear of embarrassing his friend and protector, Sadat. He served as minister of Waqf from 1976 to 1978, but he was more famous

for his televised religious sermons. As minister, he was behind the establishment of the Faysal Bank, the first Islamic bank in Egypt. Sha'rawi never wavered from his loyalty to Sadat, which led his critics to accuse him of serving as the "sultan's cleric." Sha'rawi has been credited (or blamed) for convincing a few well-known Egyptian actresses and singers—most famously, Shadya and Shams al-Barudi—to veil themselves and withdraw from show business.

> See also SADAT, ANWAR AL-.

Bibliography

Sha'rawi, Muhammad Mutwalli. *How Allah Provides.* Cairo: Dar At-Taqwa, 1995.

AS'AD ABUKHALIL

SHAREF, ZE'EV
[1906–1984]

Israeli political leader.

Having emigrated from Romania in 1924, Ze'ev Sharef became secretary of the central committee of the Haganah. After Israeli statehood he served in various capacities in the government, including as secretary of the political department of the Jewish Agency, secretary of the Emergency Committee and the National Administration (which established the Israeli civil service), and secretary of the Cabinet from 1948 to 1957.

Sharef played a unique role in Israeli history by transporting the Proclamation of Statehood from the Jewish National Fund Building (where it was typed) to David Ben-Gurion at the Tel Aviv Museum on the afternoon the State of Israel was declared, 14 May 1948. After Ben-Gurion read the Proclamation Sharef read out the names of the members of the National Council to sign the document.

From 1948 to 1957 Sharef was the first secretary of the Israeli government. From 1957 to 1959 he was director general of the Prime Minister's Office. He served as director of state revenues, and administrator of the Weizmann Institute. From 1965 to 1974 he was a member of the Knesset, serving as minister of commerce and industry in 1966, as minister of finance in 1968, and as minister of housing from 1969 to 1974.

Bibliography

Jerusalem Center for Public Affairs. "Israel's Early Diplomatic Struggles: From the Debates of the First Knesset." In *Glossary of Israeli Parties and Personalities—1948–1981*. Available from <http://www.jcpa.org/art>.

Jewish Agency for Israel, Department for Jewish Zionist Education. "Israel & the UN: A Resolution of Support, About the Declaration of Independence." Available from <http://www.jajz-ed.org.il>.

Sharef, Ze'ev. *Three Days*, translated by Julian Louis Meltzer. Garden City, NY: Doubleday, 1962.

Wohlgelernter, Elli. "One Day that Shook the World." *Jerusalem Post* (30 April 1998).

BRYAN DAVES
UPDATED BY GREGORY S. MAHLER

SHARETT, MOSHE
[1894–1965]

Israel's first foreign minister and second prime minister.

Moshe Sharett was born Moshe Shertok. His family migrated from Russia to Palestine in 1906. He attended school in Herzliyya and Tel Aviv, and after graduating in 1913, he entered the University of Istanbul to study law. When World War I broke out, he was drafted into the Turkish army.

At the end of the war, Sharett attended the London School of Economics, graduating in 1924. He returned to Palestine and became a journalist; from 1929 to 1931 he was editor of *Davar*, a daily newspaper in Tel Aviv.

In 1931 Sharett became political secretary of the Jewish Agency Executive. In 1935 he was named director of its political department, and began laying the foundations for what was later to become Israel's Ministry of Foreign Affairs. Sharett had a long-time working partnership with David Ben-Gurion in the Jewish Agency Executive, and after 1948, in Israel's first cabinets.

In 1946 he participated unofficially in talks in London to negotiate Zionist goals. Sharett was a representative of the Jewish Agency in the 1947 negotiations with the United Nations (UN) Special Committee on Palestine. He sought UN support for the creation of an independent state for the Jews in Palestine. In December 1947 he was among Jewish leaders lobbying for American support in the UN.

Moshe Sharett (1894–1965) in the 1950s. Sharett was an influential member of the Zionist movement and played an important role in the creation of the state of Israel in 1948. He was Israel's first foreign minister, and in January 1954 became the second man to serve as premier. © BETTMANN/CORBIS. REPRODUCED BY PERMISSION.

In May 1948, Sharett (who had hebraized the name Shertok at the time of the creation of the state of Israel) was named foreign minister in the Jewish provisional administration. In that capacity he negotiated support for Israel's statehood with U.S. Secretary of State George Marshall.

Once the state of Israel was in existence, Sharett became its first foreign minister, a position he held until 1956. In that post he emphasized that proceeds from the sale of lands belonging to absentee Arabs would be applied to a fund to resettle the refugees elsewhere, not to repatriate them in Israel. He argued that the problems of the Palestinian refugees were just like the problems of refugees around the world. In that sense, there was no legal precedent requiring their repatriation to the lands they had occupied before the war.

In March 1949, Sharett introduced the "principle of nonidentification" to indicate that Israel would not be aligned with either the East or the West. Israel's intention was to work with all nations to develop peaceful links and support for its existence. By 1951, however, it had become clear that the Soviet Union would support the Arab bloc against Israel, and Israel's foreign policy became clearly aligned with the West.

Prime Minister Ben-Gurion resigned in December 1953, and Sharett became prime minister. In June 1955 his cabinet was overturned by the withdrawal of the General Zionist Party from the coalition. He remained as acting prime minister until the scheduled elections for the third Knesset took place. After the elections, Ben-Gurion returned to the prime ministership with a new cabinet in November 1955.

In 1956 tensions increased between Ben-Gurion and Sharett over the appropriate response to Egypt's actions in and around the Suez Canal. Sharett argued that Israel should act with great restraint, while Ben-Gurion was in favor of a more provocative strategy. When Ben-Gurion felt that the tensions were growing too great, he asked for Sharett's resignation as foreign minister in June 1956, replacing him with Golda Meir.

See also BEN-GURION, DAVID; JEWISH AGENCY FOR PALESTINE; KNESSET; MEIR, GOLDA; NEWSPAPERS AND PRINT MEDIA: ISRAEL.

Bibliography

Ben-Gurion, David. *Israel: A Personal History,* translated by Nechemia Meyers and Uzy Nystar. New York: Funk and Wagnalls, 1971.

Sachar, Howard M. *A History of Israel: From the Rise of Zionism to Our Time,* 2d edition. New York: Knopf, 1996.

Sheffer, Gabriel. *Moshe Sharett: Biography of a Political Moderate.* Oxford and New York: Clarendon Press, 1996.

GREGORY S. MAHLER

SHARI'A

Arabic for "the trodden path leading to a water hole." In Islam, the regulations of God's law as transmitted through a prophet; the dominant law in Islamic societies.

Muslims, Christians, and Jews each have "a law (*shir'a*) and a normative way to follow," the Qur'an attests (verse 48). In the Middle Ages, Islamic discourse referred not only to this strict definition of *Shari'a* as law but also to all that which Allah has revealed—whether it pertained to actual religious practice or to belief. In Islam, those aspects relating to practice belong to the province of law (*fiqh*); those that concern belief belong to theology (*ilm al-kalam or ilm al-tawhid*). Law, however, depends on theology, since the contents and validity of law rest on textual sources, whose divine origins and truth are known. Furthermore, all sciences that are used to attain a knowledge of law and theology are considered *Shari'a* sciences, even if their subject matter is not legal or theological. Therefore, the Arabic language, *hadith* (verbal statements of Prophetic traditions), exegesis (interpretations), and even logic are deemed *Shari'a*—even if designating logic this way has always been controversial.

The use of the term *Shari'a* has actually, in practice, been restricted to the realm of law, and particularly to those aspects that bear upon the conduct of the individual in both worldly and religious matters. *Shari'a* may be equated, therefore, with *fiqh* in both its components: (1) positive law (*furu*) and (2) legal theory (*usul*). Positive law delineates legal obligations, ranging from rituals to personal and penal law; contracts; sales; hunting; and more. Legal theory demonstrates how positive law is derived through legal reasoning and interpretation, which results in the law stipulating the legal and moral responsibility thrust upon Muslims.

The legal and moral elements in the *Shari'a* are evident in the individual rulings classified in accordance with five norms (*ahkam*): (1) the obligatory (*wajib*), (2) the recommended (*mandub*), (3) the permissible or indifferent (*mubah*), (4) the prohibited (*haram*), and (5) the repugnant (*makruh*). The obligatory represents an act whose performance entails reward and whose omission entails punishment. It is commonly divided into those acts that are binding on all and those that are binding on the Muslim community as a whole but which are discharged once a sufficient number of individuals perform them. The recommended act requires a reward for performance but does not involve a punishment for omission. In the permissible, both omission and commission are equally legitimate. The prohibited is an act that entails punishment upon commission. The repugnant act is rewarded when omitted but not punished when committed.

The nature of reward and punishment supports the permeating moral element in Islamic law. Reward is always bestowed in the hereafter; punishment—in rituals and in several other spheres of the law—is nothing but divine punishment to be meted out at the resurrection. As a comprehensive system of law, imbued with religious mores, the rules of the *Shari'a* are not always enforceable.

As a system of legal rights and obligations that governs public and private life, *Shari'a* has always been the dominant law in Islamic societies. No doubt secular organs of justice, such as the early and medieval *mazalim* courts and the *qanun* of the Ottoman Empire, have always supplemented *Shari'a*; however, their jurisdiction was confined mainly to administrative and penal law, and they were, more often than not, run by *Shari'a* judges and jurists.

Judges and jurisconsults (muftis) have played the central role of developing *Shari'a* since the first century of Islam. Immediately after the death of the Prophet Muhammad in 632 C.E., the Qur'an provided the main source of the law that may be considered Islamic. To be sure, customary Arabian law and the later Umayyad dynasty's administrative practices supplemented Qur'anic legislation, but these were not yet imbued with a religious character. The Prophet's *sunna* (his utterances and idealized practice as expressed in *hadith*) was to gain importance as a source of law only gradually. It was not until the end of Islam's first century (c. 700 C.E.) that his *sunna* became a source of law, supplementing the Qur'an and the still prevailing popular and administrative practices of the Umayyads. Islam's second century (ending c. 800 C.E.) witnessed a gradual yet definite process whereby these practices were idealized as the consensus of the geographical schools—a consensus seen to reflect the ideal practice of the Prophet Muhammad and the early caliphs who succeeded him. Thus imbued with a religious element, these practices, expressed through verbal statements of *hadith*, were gradually and constantly projected back to the earlier generations until they have come to be connected with the Prophet himself. By the beginning of Islam's third century (the ninth century C.E.), the process of back-projection was virtually completed, and the law, now elaborated to its fullness, was recognized to have been exclusively derived from the Qur'an and the *sunna* and sanctioned by the authoritative instrument of consensus (*ijma*).

By the eighth and ninth centuries, the body of *Shari'a* law was elaborated by a variety of legal schools, ranging from those that resorted to free reasoning and expediency in elaborating their positive law—such as the Hanafi school of law—to those standing on the other end of the spectrum, such as the Zahiris, who interpreted the texts literally. Such radical tendencies and their schools, including the Zahiri, soon disappeared; but liberal tendencies were not sufficient to bring the Hanafi school to extinction. Nevertheless, they had to be rationalized and modified to be admitted by mainstream jurisprudence. A classical example of this process of adjustment may be seen in the concept of *istihsan*, which represented to the eighth-century Hanafis a means of formulating law on the basis of practical considerations, without being restricted by the imperatives of the religious texts. Whereas problems of law solved by *istihsan* were largely accepted, even in later centuries, the procedure of *istihsan* had to be, and indeed was, restructured by the likes of Dabusi and Sarakhsi—this was based on the proposition that the *sunna* and the Qur'an were the ultimate sources of the law and that no human intervention can be allowed in the unraveling of divine law.

The Sunni schools of law thus came finally to acknowledge a common legal theory, though differences among them continued to exist—partly as a reflection of the legacy they inherited from their early development within differing geographical schools. Be that as it may, in addition to the Shi'a schools, only four Sunni schools survive and they provide, in effect, a comprehensive system of *Shari'a*.

Shari'a continued to dominate the life of Muslims until the nineteenth century, when, because of influences and pressures from the West, changes in the law were deemed necessary. Formally, the most notable legal change was the introduction of the code system, which was foreign to *Shari'a*, a law based on interpretation of religious doctrine. Substantively, several attempts were made to wholly substitute European codes for a number of *Shari'a* laws. Thus, during the Ottoman Empire, commercial and penal codes based on their French counterparts were promulgated in 1850 and 1858, respectively. A more important codification of this period was the Mejelle (1876), which represented the first attempt ever to codify Islamic law. Selectively codified, Hanafi law was restricted to contracts, some

torts, and a law of procedure. The last part, however, was soon replaced by the Code of Civil Procedure (1880), again based on French law.

A more drastic set of reforms was adopted in
Egypt in 1875. In addition to new penal, commercial, and procedural codes based on French law, a
new court structure was introduced. It incorporated
into the Egyptian court system the Mixed Courts,
with a majority of non-Egyptian judges, one of
whom presided over the bench.

In 1917, the first attempt at reforming family
law was made by the Ottomans, without resorting to
European codes. It promulgated the *Ottoman Law of
Family Rights,* which regulated matters of personal status and was based on a comprehensive amalgama-
tion of legal doctrines belonging to the Maliki,
Shafiʿi, and Hanbali schools of law, and sometimes
weak authorities from the Hanafi school. One of the
main concerns in this promulgation was the improvement of the legal status of married women.

Legal reforms, introduced by national legislation, have become an ongoing process in the Muslim states since the beginning of the twentieth
century (based on Sunni and Shiʿite principles). In
these reforms, *Shariʿa* law was to some extent preserved in the area of family matters, but even here
it was applied in a new system of courts and administered through a modern law of procedure.
With these sweeping changes, the officials of the traditional court virtually disappeared, and the traditional role of the qadi (judge) has been drastically
diminished.

See also FIQH; HADITH; HANAFI SCHOOL OF
LAW; HANBALI SCHOOL OF LAW; MALIKI
SCHOOL OF LAW; MIXED COURTS; MUHAM-
MAD; QANUN; QURʾAN; SHAFIʿI SCHOOL OF
LAW.

Bibliography

Anderson, Norman. *Law Reform in the Muslim World.* London: Athlone Press, 1976.

Fyzee, A. A. *Outlines of Muhammadan Law,* 2d edition. London and New York: Oxford University Press, 1955.

Khadduri, Majid, and Liebesny, Herbert J., eds. *Law in
the Middle East.* Washington, DC: Middle East Institute, 1955.

Schacht, Joseph. *An Introduction to Islamic Law.* Oxford and
New York: Clarendon, 1982.

Schacht, Joseph. *The Origins of Muhammadan Jurisprudence.* Oxford: Clarendon, 1953.

Smith, Wilfred Cantwell. "The Concept of Shariʿa
among Some Mutakallimun." In *Arabic and Islamic
Studies in Honor of Hamilton A. R. Gibb,* edited by George
Makdisi. Cambridge, MA: Harvard University Press,
1965.

WAEL B. HALLAQ

SHARIʿATI, ALI
[1933–1977]

*Iranian Islamic ideologue, whose lectures and writings
on secularly educated youth helped prepare the way for
the Islamic Revolution of 1978/79.*

Ali Shariʿati was born in the village of Mazinan in
northeastern Iran but soon moved with his father,
Mohammad Taqi Shariʿati, a reformist cleric of Islam, to the city of Mashhad. There he attended high
school and teachers' training college as well as pursuing a religious education under the aegis of his
father. He then began working as a teacher, studying at the same time at the Mashhad Faculty of Letters and beginning his long career of oppositional
activity; his first arrest came in 1957. After a year's
delay, he was permitted to travel to Paris in 1960
for his doctoral studies. While in France, he came
under the influence of scholars and thinkers, such
as Louis Massignon and Jacques Berque, became
politically involved in the struggle for Algerian independence and the organization of Iranian students in Europe, and, most importantly, acquired
the ideological orientation that was essential to his
thought.

Immediately on his return to Iran in 1964,
Shariʿati was arrested and detained for several
months before being allowed to take up a post at the
University of Mashhad. His tenure there was short-
lived, and it was outside the academic environment
that he exercised the greatest influence. Moving to
Tehran, he began lecturing on Islam in a variety of
settings, most importantly the Hosayniyeh-ye Er-
shad, a modernist religious institution established
in 1969 that attracted large crowds to its functions.
Shariʿati's name became virtually synonymous with
the institution, and when it was closed by the government in 1973, he was arrested for a third time.
Released in 1975, he spent two years under house
arrest in his native village before being allowed to

leave for England. He died there on 19 June 1977, soon after his arrival, under circumstances that led to widespread suspicion of involvement by the Iranian secret police. His body was taken to Damascus for burial.

Central to Shari'ati's understanding and presentation of Islam were an emphasis on the social and civilizational functions of religion; an impatience with the niceties and abstractions of traditional Iranian Islamic culture; and a bold if often unconvincing use of themes and terms eclectically derived from non-Islamic sources. His legacy has been varyingly assessed in postrevolutionary Iran, being sometimes denounced for its syncretic nature and its implicitly anticlerical message.

Bibliography

Shari'ati, Ali. *On the Sociology of Islam,* translated by Hamid Algar. Berkeley, CA: Mizan Press, 1979.

HAMID ALGAR

SHARIATMADARI, KAZEM
[1904–1986]

One of Iran's most important clerics.

Ayatollah Sayyid Kazem Shariatmadari, born in Azerbaijan, was a *marja al-taqlid* (source of emulation) from 1962 until his death in 1986.

Ayatollah Shariatmadari was not inclined to political activism. But throughout the Pahlavi period, the scholars affiliated with his Center for Islamic Study and Publication rivaled Ayatollah Ruhollah Khomeini's more activist followers. Shariatmadari was briefly imprisoned in 1963, following the June uprisings. In general, he viewed the Pahlavi regime as dictatorial and favored restoration of constitutional rule in Iran. With the triumph of the Islamic Revolution in 1979, Shariatmadari again called for restraint and the rule of law, denouncing the revolutionary tribunals and summary executions of the early days of the revolution. He also confronted the regime on the issue of a referendum to decide the form of the post-Pahlavi state. Rather than a simple vote of yes or no on an Islamic republic, Shariatmadari, as well as most secular parties, supported at the least a choice between an Islamic, democratic, or just simple and plain republic. Shariatmadari

was also associated with the Islamic People's Republican party (IPRP), the main contender to Khomeini's Islamic Republican party. The IPRP favored collective rule of the *ulama* (Islamic clergy), a more democratic constitution, and an elected rather than an appointed assembly of experts empowered to draft the constitution of the nascent Islamic republic. The IPRP was dissolved in 1980, over the first presidential elections, a victory for Khomeini and the Islamic Republican party.

Shariatmadari continued to oppose the excesses of the Khomeini regime and, in 1982, was implicated in a coup against the Islamic republic, organized by Sadeq Qotbzadeh, was stripped of his title of *marja al-taqlid,* and was placed under house arrest, where he remained a marginal player in the political life of his country until his death in 1986.

See also KHOMEINI, RUHOLLAH; MARJA AL-TAQLID; PAHLAVI, MOHAMMAD REZA; QOTBZADEH, SADEQ.

Bibliography

Akhavi, Shahrough. *Religion and Politics in Contemporary Iran: Clergy-State Relations in the Pahlavi Period.* Albany: State University of New York Press, 1980.

Bakhash, Shaul. *The Reign of the Ayatollahs: Iran and the Islamic Revolution,* revised edition. New York: Basic Books, 1990.

NEGUIN YAVARI

SHARIF

An Arabic word that literally means "noble" or "illustrious," especially by virtue of one's lineage.

In the first few centuries of the Muslim era, *sharif* (pl., *ashraf* or *shurafa*) was used to refer to members of the prominent Arab families that made up the typically landed aristocracy of the expanding Muslim domains. Much like its rough equivalent *sayyid,* however, use of *sharif* as an honorific was gradually limited to scions of the clan of the prophet Muhammad (that is, the Banu Hashim), and eventually was further restricted to Muhammad's direct descendants through his grandsons Hasan and Husayn. In Mecca, Medina, and their environs, the custom developed of applying the title *sharif* almost exclusively to descendants of Hasan, with *sayyid* referring to descendents of Husayn. Under Ottoman rule the senior member of the Arabian sharifs was recognized as the semiautonomous governor of Mecca and the keeper of its sacred sanctuary.

See also MUHAMMAD.

SCOTT ALEXANDER

SHARIF, AZIZ
[1904–]

Iraqi politician.

Born in Ana and educated at Baghdad Law College, Aziz Sharif founded the People's Party in 1943 and subsequently joined the Communist Party. He was a candidate member of its central committee (1958–1963), and secretary-general of the Partisans of Peace, a pro-Soviet umbrella organization. Sharif was minister of justice under the Baᶜth government (1970–1971) and a key intermediary in the Baᶜth-Kurdish negotiations. Sharif served as minister without portfolio until 1976.

MARION FAROUK-SLUGLETT
UPDATED BY MICHAEL R. FISCHBACH

SHARIF-EMAMI, JAᶜFAR
[1910–1998]

Iranian prime minister and statesman.

Jaᶜfar Sharif-Emami was the son of Hajj Mohammad Hasan (known as Sharif), a member of the religious establishment who worked as an aide to Sayyid Mohammad Emami, the leader of Friday prayers in Tehran. Sharif-Emami attended college in Germany and worked at the Railroad Office of the Ministry of Roads. In 1943 the British forces accused him of belonging to a German fifth column in Iran and incarcerated him for one year. He was elected to the senate as a deputy from Tehran in 1953 and became minister of industries and mines in 1957 and prime minister in 1960. In 1961 he was made head of the Pahlavi Foundation, the largest corporation in the country; he amassed a great fortune in that capacity. In 1962 he also was appointed speaker of the senate. It was widely believed that Sharif-Emami led the German Freemasonry Lodge in Iran. In an effort to quell the Islamic Revolution by choosing a leader with some degree of credibility with the clerical establishment, Mohammad Reza Shah Pahlavi reappointed him premier in August

1978. Sharif-Emami failed in his mandate, however, and the military government of General Gholam Reza Azhari was declared in November 1978. Sharif-Emami left Iran in 1979 and died in New York on 16 June 1998.

Bibliography

Ladjevardi, Habib, ed. *Memoirs of Jafar Sharif-Emami, Prime Minister of Iran (1960–1961 & 1978)*. Cambridge, MA: Center for Middle Eastern Studies, Harvard University Press, 1999.

NEGUIN YAVARI

SHARIFIAN DYNASTIES

Rulers of Morocco since the sixteenth century, when the modern principle was first established that they be sharifs—descendants of the prophet Muhammad, founder of Islam.

The cult of the Sharif was introduced in Morocco under Idris II in the early ninth century but went into abeyance. Sharifism became established in Morocco as a response to the crises of the sixteenth century—occasioned by Christian efforts to extend the *reconquista* (reconquest) of the Iberian Peninsula into Morocco; large-scale tribal migrations in North Africa; the fragmentation of the Moroccan polity following the decline of the Merinid dynasty; the rise of regional Sufi powers; and the conquest of Algeria in 1517 by the Ottoman Empire.

Both the Saᶜdians (1548–1641) and the Alawi (1668–present) were Alids, and traced their descent to Muhammad through his son-in-law Ali, but they were Sunni rather than followers of Shiᶜism. Both assembled powerful political coalitions that combined tribal solidarities, rural Sufism, and Sharifism. Both rose to power after first securing control over southern Morocco and then conquered the cities and Atlantic plains. Both were responses to the long-term crisis of legitimization caused by the fragmentation of Islam's power in the Maghrib (North Africa) and al-Andalus (Iberian province) and especially to the threat posed by the Spanish and Portuguese, who had driven the Moors from the Iberian Peninsula and unified their countries under Catholic monarchs.

The Saᶜdians emerged in the period 1514–1548 as opponents of the Portuguese in southern Morocco and revivers of Islam. Under Muhammad al-Shaykh, they defeated the reigning Wattasids, conquered Fez and Marrakech, and stabilized Morocco's frontiers at roughly their present borders. Under Ahmad al-Mansur (1578–1603), the state was reorganized along Ottoman principles, including notably a force of musketeers, financed by the production of sugar for export on royal estates. The conquest of Timbuktu in 1591 briefly gave Morocco direct access to the salt and gold of the sub-Saharan zone. With the help of an alliance with Elizabethan merchant adventurers, the Saʿdians were able to defeat the Iberians and confine them to a few coastal enclaves. Following the death of Ahmad in 1603, the Saʿdians went into a long decline, as the result of dynastic conflict, a resurgence of Iberian threat, and the reemergence of regional power centers of which the *zawiya* (community) of Dila in the Middle Atlas mountains and the Andalusian corsair republic of Sala were the most important.

The rise of the Alawis, cousins of the Saʿdians, took place under Muhammad al-Sharif and Rashid, who were able to defeat the Dila Marabouts and assert their control over Morocco by 1668. The consolidator of the dynasty was Ismaʿil (1672–1727), a remarkable ruler who by incessant warfare and systematic organization was able to bring the disparate regions of the state under control. Ismaʿil restructured the army around a contingent of musket-wielding black slaves, defeated the Sufi brotherhoods, and imposed a system of heavy taxation. He expelled foreign occupiers, notably the Spanish from Larache and the British from Tangier. Henceforth, Moroccan sultans styled themselves as "Commander of the Faithful," an implicit claim to the caliphate otherwise also claimed by the Ottomans. Following Ismaʿil's death, however, the army revolted, and power once again fragmented.

After the turbulent reign of Abdullah, who was deposed five times between 1727 and 1757, the state was reorganized under Muhammad III (1757–1790), the architect of "modern," that is, precolonial, Morocco. By de-emphasizing the tax on agricultural produce and increasing trade (and thus customs revenues), Muhammad III provided an alternate basis for the state finances without disturbing the potentially volatile rural populations. The port of Essaouira was founded in 1767 to place the foreign trade of the Atlantic coast of Morocco under government control.

By emphasizing the religious aspects of his leadership as sultan, caliph, and sharif, Muhammad III sought to counter the reassertion of the maraboutic forces in the countryside. By constant diplomatic negotiation with foreign powers and constant bargaining with local authorities, he devised a precarious balance for the Moroccan state. Its dependence upon foreign commerce made it vulnerable to foreign intervention, however, while the absence of a strong army deprived it of any means to reassert its control over the population.

Under Sulayman (1792–1822) and Abd al-Rahman ibn Hisham (1822–1859), Morocco entered into a precolonial phase, increasingly dependent upon foreign trade and increasingly vulnerable to European pressure, notably signing after 1856 a series of treaties granting most-favored nation status to leading European powers. In retaliation for Moroccan support of the Algerian resistance leader Abd al-Qadir, Moroccan ports were shelled by the French navy, and a Moroccan army was defeated at Isly in 1844. A war with Spain in 1859–1860 over the city of Tetuan was settled only after Morocco agreed to pay a sizable indemnity and make other concessions.

Hassan I (1873–1894) sought to reverse the decline, with mixed results. His military and administrative reforms failed to survive his death, although his adroit diplomacy managed to buy time for Morocco in the face of rising European imperialist ambitions. His successors Abd al-Aziz and Abd al-Hafid also sought to introduce needed reforms and to play off the European powers, but with less success. The Moroccan Question (1900–1912) marks a period of increase in European rivalries over Morocco. In 1912 the Treaty of Fes with France and the Spanish–Moroccan accords marked the formal end of Moroccan independence.

The protectorates of France and Spain lasted from 1912 to 1956. During this period, Moroccan sultans Mulay Youssef (1912–1927) and Muhammad V (1927–1961) were formally incorporated into the French colonial administration, their titles confirmed, but their powers largely alienated to the European occupiers and their local Moroccan agents through a factional delegation. With the rise of nationalism in the 1930s and 1940s, Muhammad V began increasingly to show his sympathy for the nationalists. In 1946 he publicly broke with the French and assumed leadership of the nationalist movement.

Since 1956, independent Morocco has continued to be governed by the Alawite dynasty. The present sultan, Hassan II, assumed power in 1961 upon the death of his father.

See also ABD AL-AZIZ IBN AL-HASSAN; ABD AL-HAFID IBN AL-HASSAN; ABD AL-QADIR; ABD AL-RAHMAN IBN HISHAM; ALAWI; ALAWITE DYNASTY; FES, TREATY OF (1912); HASSAN I; HASSAN II; MOROCCAN QUESTION; MUHAMMAD; MUHAMMAD V; SUFISM AND THE SUFI ORDERS; SULEIMAN, MULAY; YOUSSEF, MULAY.

Bibliography

Abun-Nasr, Jamil M. A History of the Maghrib, 2d edition. Cambridge, U.K., and New York: Cambridge University Press, 1975.

Julien, Charles André. History of North Africa, translated by John Petrie. New York: Praeger, 1970.

Laroui, Abdullah. The History of the Maghrib, translated by Ralph Manheim. Princeton, NJ: Princeton University Press, 1977.

Pennell, C. R. Morocco since 1830: A History. New York: New York University Press, 2000.

EDMUND BURKE III

SHARIF OF MECCA

The local, hereditary rulers of Mecca from about 965 to 1916.

Although the sharifs never enjoyed complete independence from distant powers, their remoteness from the imperial capitals of Cairo and Constantinople (now Istanbul) helped them maintain effective rule in Mecca, as did their claimed descent from the prophet Muhammad. The last sharif, Husayn ibn Ali (1852–1931), tried to establish an independent Arabian kingdom, leading the Arab Revolt in 1916 against the Turks in the Hijaz, but he was overthrown by the Saudis in 1925. Founder of the modern Arab Hashimite dynasty, Husayn died in Amman, the capital of his son Abdullah, then ruler of Transjordan (now Jordan). His third son, Faisal I, founded the royal line of Iraq.

See also ABDULLAH I IBN HUSSEIN; ARAB REVOLT (1916); FAISAL I IBN HUSSEIN; HASHIMITE HOUSE (HOUSE OF HASHIM); HUSAYN IBN ALI.

Bibliography

De Gaury, Gerald. Rulers of Mecca. London: Harrap, 1951.

KHALID Y. BLANKINSHIP

SHARIF, OMAR
[1932–]

Egyptian movie star.

The son of a wealthy merchant of Lebanese descent, Omar (also Umar) Sharif was born Michel Chalhoub on 10 April 1932. Educated at Victoria College in Alexandria, he converted from Christianity to Islam and changed his name to Omar Sharif before making his Egyptian film debut in The Blazing Sun in 1953. Between 1953 and 1958, he appeared in twenty-four Arabic-language films. On the set of his first film, Sharif became bored during the long pauses between his scenes and took up the game of bridge to while away the time. Sharif became internationally known after playing a lead role in the film Lawrence of Arabia, a part for which he received an Academy Award nomination for best supporting actor. Sharif has appeared in many English-language films, including Doctor Zhivago and Funny Girl. He won the Golden Lion lifetime achievement award for fifty years in films in 2003 after a comeback in the film Mr. Ibrahim, in which he plays the role of an old Arab man in Paris who adopts a young Jewish boy. He also pursued his interest in bridge, becoming one of the world's leading authorities on the game and authoring several books on the subject.

Bibliography

Katz, Ephraim. The Film Encyclopedia. New York: Crowell, 1979.

DAVID WALDNER
UPDATED BY ROXANNE VARZI

SHARJAH

One of seven shaykhdoms making up the United Arab Emirates.

Sharjah is the third largest emirate in the United Arab Emirates (U.A.E.), with an area of 1,000 square miles. Seventy-five percent of its 400,000 inhabitants (2001 estimate) live in the capital city of the same name on the Persian Gulf coast, just north of Dubai. Three exclaves on the Gulf of Oman coast—Dibba, Kalba, and Khor Fakkan—belong to Sharjah and make it the only one of the seven emirates to share borders with all the others. It has the extreme summer heat and aridity of its neighbors, but agriculture is possible in the Dhayd Oasis and in the exclave territories.

In the late-eighteenth and early nineteenth centuries Sharjah and its northern neighbor, Ra's al-Khayma, formed the most powerful state of the lower Gulf under the al-Qasimi family, which is still the ruling clan in each emirate. The al-Qasimi state was defeated by Britain in an 1819 naval battle. Subsequently, the al-Qasimi ruler signed the General Treaty of Peace (1820), which began the process by which the area became a protectorate of Britain. During the 1840s and 1850s the al-Qasimi gradually were eclipsed by the Banu Yas tribal confederation of Abu Dhabi—then, as now, led by the Al Nahayyan family. Following the death of Shaykh Sultan bin Saqr al-Qasimi, one of his sons set up an "independent" state at Ra's al-Khayma; this state formally split from Sharjah in 1869, but it did not gain formal British recognition as a separate emirate until 1921.

Sharjah enjoyed moderate prosperity in the early twentieth century, boosted by the presence of a Royal Air Force base from the 1930s until 1955. In the early 1950s Sharjah's creek became silted, and with the decline of maritime commerce, it lost its position of importance in the lower Gulf. In 1971, on the eve of independence, Britain pressured Sharjah to agree to shared sovereignty with Iran of the island of Abu Musa. This agreement precipitated a coup attempt in Sharjah (1972) during which the ruler, Shaykh Khalid ibn Muhammad, was killed.

Oil and gas discoveries in 1973 and 1980 brought prosperity, as did the development of several factories in a specially created industrial zone in the western part of Sharjah city. Sharjah also has developed a successful tourist industry. Reflecting the academic bent of the ruler, who holds a doctorate from Exeter University, Sharjah leads the U.A.E. in the development of arts, literature, and museums.

See also ABU MUSA ISLAND; QASIMI FAMILY OF SHARJAH, AL-; UNITED ARAB EMIRATES.

Bibliography

Hooglund, Eric, and Toth, Anthony B. "United Arab Emirates." In *Persian Gulf States: Country Studies,* edited by Helen Chapin Metz. Washington, DC: Library of Congress, 1994.

Peck, Malcolm C. *The United Arab Emirates: A Venture in Unity.* Boulder, CO: Westview Press, 1986.

MALCOLM C. PECK
UPDATED BY ERIC HOOGLUND

SHARM AL-SHAYKH

Strategic town opposite Tiran island, near the southern tip of the Sinai Peninsula.

The cove and town of Sharm al-Shaykh control maritime access to the Strait of Tiran from the Gulf of Aqaba. In 1954 Egypt fortified the cove to block Israeli shipping from the port of Elat, but in the Arab–Israel War (1956) Israel captured it along with the rest of the peninsula. The United States later persuaded Israel to withdraw its forces in return for assurances of free passage through the Tiran Strait. When the Sinai was restored to Egyptian control in 1957, the United Nations Emergency Force was based at Sharm al-Shaykh until 1967, when Egypt asked it to leave. Its removal was one of the events precipitating the 1967 Arab–Israel War. Occupied by Israel during that conflict, the site became the Israeli naval and air base of Ophira. Restored to Egypt in 1982, the town has become a major tourist resort and frequently serves as the site of high-profile meetings of Middle Eastern and world leaders, notably the Antiterrorism Summit of 1996 and one phase of the Israeli-Palestinian negotiations in 2000.

See also AQABA, GULF OF; ARAB–ISRAEL WAR (1956); ARAB–ISRAEL WAR (1967); TIRAN, STRAIT OF.

Bibliography

Fry, Michael, and Hochstein, Miles. "The Forgotten Middle East Crisis of 1957: Gaza and Sharm el Sheikh." *International History Review* 15 (1993): 46–83.

ZACHARY KARABELL
UPDATED BY ARTHUR GOLDSCHMIDT

SHARON, ARIEL

[1928–]

Israeli prime minister and army commander.

Ariel Sharon was born on 27 February 1928 into a family of stubbornly independent pioneer farmers in Kfar Malal. He joined the Haganah in 1945 and took part in the 1948 Arab–Israel War as a platoon commander and intelligence officer. He served in Jerusalem and the northern Negev, making his mark as an inspirational leader. In 1952 he formed Unit 101, a special commando force geared for unconventional retaliatory operations in enemy territory. In 1953 it raided the Palestinian village of Qibya, destroying forty-five houses and killing sixty-nine villagers, half of them women and children. Unit 101 set the standard for the elite commando units of the Israel Defense Force (IDF). In 1954 it was integrated into the paratroop regiment, with Sharon as commander. In 1956 he was appointed to command a paratroop corps, which executed Israel's defense strategy of inflicting retaliatory blows more severe than the original provocations.

Sharon's performance as military strategist during the 1956 Arab-Israel War earned him a reputation as one of IDF's most brilliant field commanders. At the same time, his activism made him a controversial figure and drew criticism from his superiors. He disobeyed orders and sent paratroopers into the Mitla Pass, deep in the Sinai desert. This ended disastrously, with thirty-eight Israelis dead. As a major general commanding an armored division during the 1967 Arab-Israel War, Sharon revealed a new talent for orchestrating huge, set-piece battles. In 1969 he was appointed chief of the Southern Command. He ruthlessly demolished thousands of homes in Gaza refugee camps to open roads for antiterror patrols, and deported hundreds of young men to Jordan and Lebanon. The number of sabotage attacks dropped dramatically.

Sharon retired from the army in June 1972 after he recognized that he was not going to be promoted chief of the general staff. He entered politics as a member of the Liberal party and was influential in merging it with the right-wing Herut and two smaller parties to form the Likud. He was called back to military service for the 1973 Arab–Israel War, during which he led Israeli forces in penetrating Egyptian defenses to cross the Suez Canal. During

Israeli prime minister Ariel Sharon (b. 1928) is a veteran of the Israeli military and achieved his first seat in government in 1973. He was elected prime minister in a special election on 6 February 2001. © AP/WIDE WORLD PHOTOS. REPRODUCED BY PERMISSION.

this period, in a bitter dispute with the military high command over tactics, he was accused of insubordination but was not relieved of his command. Elected in December 1973 to the Knesset, he resigned after a year to accept an emergency appointment with the IDF. From June 1975 to March 1976, he served as Prime Minister Yitzhak Rabin's special adviser on terrorism. He founded a new political party, Shlomzion, which gained two Knesset seats in the 1977 elections. Shortly thereafter, he rejoined the Likud, which had won the elections, and was appointed minister of agriculture.

Sharon spearheaded Jewish settlement expansion in the occupied territories. Yet he supported returning Sinai to Egypt under the 1979 peace treaty and initiated and administered the destruction of the Jewish settlements there. In 1981 he was appointed defense minister in Menachem Begin's government. He planned and led Israel's invasion of Lebanon, which began in June 1982, and was accused of extending the war's objectives far beyond those originally approved by the government. The war destroyed the Palestine Liberation Organization's infrastructure and drove its leaders into exile in Tunis, but it left Israeli troops mired in guerrilla warfare in Lebanon for the next eighteen years. The Kahan Commission concluded that Sharon was culpable for not preventing the slaughter of hundreds of Palestinians by Israel's Lebanese Christian allies at the Sabra and Shatila refugee camps. As a consequence, he was forced to resign the defense ministry but allowed to remain in the cabinet. In 1984, and again in 1988, he was appointed industry and trade minister in a National Unity government. From 1990 to 1992 he served as housing and construction minister under Yitzhak Shamir and as chairman of the ministerial committee on immigration and absorption. After the collapse of the Soviet Union, he built homes for hundreds of thousands of immigrants.

When the Likud returned to office, Benjamin Netanyahu appointed Sharon national infrastructure minister in 1996, and foreign minister two years later. Following the election of Labor's Ehud Barak as prime minister in May 1999, Sharon succeeded Netanyahu as Likud leader. His visit to the Temple Mount in Jerusalem in September 2000 sparked Muslims riots, which grew into a second, more bloody, Palestinian intifada.

Sharon was elected prime minister in February 2001 following the collapse of Barak's peace policy and his failure to control the violence. After a suicide bomber killed thirty Jews celebrating Passover in a Netanya resort hotel in March 2002, Sharon invaded and reoccupied West Bank cities, destroying buildings and killing and capturing hundreds of Palestinian fighters. Although the bloodshed continued, albeit on a reduced scale, the voters endorsed his aggressive strategy and confirmed him in the premiership by a landslide in January 2003. Sharon declared the Palestinian leader Yasir Arafat "irrelevant" and isolated him in the ruins of his Ramallah headquarters.

Under United States pressure, Arafat appointed Mahmud Abbas as the first Palestinian prime minister. Sharon opened negotiations with him and accepted a "performance-based road map to a permanent two-state solution," drafted by the United States, the European Union, Russia, and the United Nations. Abandoning his earlier contention that "Jordan is Palestine" and that the Jews had a right to all of the land west of the River Jordan, Sharon surprised many observers when he labeled the West Bank and Gaza territories as "occupied" and declared that Israel could not go on ruling 3.5 million Palestinians. After Abbas was replaced by Ahmad Qurai, Sharon gave the new prime minister a chance to prove that he could curb the Palestinian militias and bring the two sides back to the negotiating table. Sharon showed himself more pragmatic than his party, but his premiership was shadowed by police investigations of alleged financial irregularities.

See also ABBAS, MAHMUD; AQSA INTIFADA, AL-; ARAFAT, YASIR; BEGIN, MENACHEM; HAGANAH; ISRAEL; ISRAELI SETTLEMENTS; KAHAN COMMISSION (1983); LIKUD; QURAI, AHMAD SULAYMAN; SABRA AND SHATILA MASSACRES.

Bibliography

Benziman, Uzi. *Sharon: An Israeli Caesar,* translated by Louis Rousso. New York: Adama, 1985.

Miller, Anita; Miller, Jordan; and Zetouni, Sigalit. *Sharon: Israel's Warrior-Politician.* Chicago: Academy Chicago, Olive, 2002.

Sharon, Ariel (with David Chanoff). *Warrior: The Autobiography of Ariel Sharon,* 2d Touchstone edition. New York: Simon & Schuster, 2001.

YAAKOV SHAVIT
UPDATED BY ERIC SILVER

SHARQI FAMILY, AL-

Ruling family of Fujayra, one of the members of the United Arab Emirates.

Fujayra's ruling family's Sharqiyyin tribe inhabits the Hajjar Mountains and the coastal region of the Shimailiyya district on the Gulf of Oman. The current ruler's family, the Sharqi, came to power in 1876 with the accession of Hamad ibn Abdullah al-Sharqi, who was part of the Qasimi tribal federation that ruled Sharjah. In 1902 the ruler declared independence from Sharjah and was recognized by the other emirates, but not by Britain. Hamad's son Muhammad continued the family's rule and its insistence on independence, which the British finally recognized in 1952. The current ruler, Hamad ibn Muhammad al-Sharqi, came to power in 1974 after his father's death. Born in 1948, he was educated at Mons Military Academy and Hendon Police College.

See also FUJAYRA.

Bibliography

Abdullah, Muhammad Morsy. *The United Arab Emirates: A Modern History.* New York: Barnes and Noble; London: Croom Helm, 1978.

Heard-Bey, Frauke. *From Trucial States to United Arab Emirates: A Society in Transition.* New York: Longman, 1982.

Reich, Bernard, ed. *Political Leaders of the Contemporary Middle East and North Africa: A Biographical Dictionary.* Westport, CT: Greenwood Press, 1990.

M. MORSY ABDULLAH
UPDATED BY ANTHONY B. TOTH

SHARQI, HAMAD IBN MUHAMMAD AL-

See SHARQI FAMILY, AL-

SHAS

See ISRAEL: POLITICAL PARTIES IN

SHASHILIK

See FOOD: SHASHILIK

SHATT AL-ARAB

The narrow waterway that forms the southern border between Iran and Iraq.

The Shatt al-Arab, or Arvandrud in Persian, provides Iraq with its only means of access to the Persian Gulf. Issues of joint sovereignty over the waterway have long been a source of contention between Iran and Iraq. In 1975 Mohammad Reza Shah Pahlavi of Iran and Vice President Saddam Hussein of Iraq signed the Algiers Agreement, which demarcated the *thalweg* (middle) line along the Shatt al-Arab as the border between the two states. In September 1980 Iraq launched an offensive against

the Islamic Republic of Iran, declaring one of its intentions to be the restoration of the Shatt al-Arab to sole Iraqi sovereignty. Hostilities were brought to an end in 1988, but a peace agreement remains to be signed between the two countries. UN Resolution 598 has not been implemented other than to establish a cease-fire; sovereignty of and navigation rights in the Shatt al-Arab remain unresolved. Since Iraq's massive defeat at the hands of the United States in the Gulf War of 1991, borders have reverted to the 1975 demarcations, albeit unofficially.

See also ALGIERS AGREEMENT (1975).

Bibliography

Sirriyeh, Hoseyn. "Development of the Iraqi–Iranian Dispute, 1847–1975." *Journal of Contemporary History* 20, no. 3 (1985): 483–492.

NEGUIN YAVARI

SHA'UL, ANWAR
[1904–1984]

Iraqi Jewish writer and journalist.

Anwar Sha'ul was born into a Jewish family in the city of al-Hilla in southern Iraq; they moved to Baghdad when he was in his early teens. He studied at the Alliance Israélite Universelle and later obtained a law degree. Between 1924 and 1938 he was a journalist, first editing the Jewish weekly *al-Misbah* (The lantern) and in 1929 launching his own weekly magazine, *al-Hasid* (The reaper).

Sha'ul's knowledge of foreign languages enabled him to translate literary works from English and French. A volume of original and translated fiction appeared in 1922 under the title *al-Hisad al-Awwal* (The first harvest). It was followed in 1955 by *Fi Ziham al-Madina* (In the crowded city) and in 1956 by a volume of poetry, *Hamasat al-Zaman* (Whispers of time).

Sha'ul stayed in Iraq after the mass exodus of its Jewish community in 1951 and 1952. In 1971 he left Baghdad and settled in Kiron, near Tel Aviv. In 1981 he published his collected poetry in *Wa Bazagha Fajr Jadid* (And a new dawn has risen). He also published an autobiography, *Qissat Hayati fi Wadi al-Rafidayn* (My life in Mesopotamia), in 1980.

Bibliography

Somekh, Sasson. "Lost Voices: Jewish Authors in Modern Arabic Literature." In *Jews among Arabs: Contacts and Boundaries,* edited by Mark R. Cohen and Abraham L. Udovitch. Princeton, NJ: Darwin Press, 1989.

SASSON SOMEKH

SHAWA, LAILA

[1940–]

Palestinian artist and illustrator.

A native of Gaza, Laila Shawa (Layla Shawwa) is an oil painter, a silk-screen artist, and an illustrator of children's books who has also done sculpture. She studied in Cairo, at two arts academies in Rome, and in Austria with Oskar Kokoschka. She has also worked on United Nations children's art programs in Gaza. Shawa's famous silk-screen installation *Walls of Gaza* (1992–1995) exemplifies her ongoing interest in political struggle and oppression, and in children who live with war and deprivation. Her photographs of children and graffiti-laden walls in Gaza are juxtaposed on large panels to make the viewer confront the effects of conflict and violence on generations of children. Other works examine breast cancer as a metaphor for other eruptions and invasions, such as the 1991 Gulf War, and atomic bombs, linking the body with the land—a strategy adopted by other Palestinian artists. Shawa's paintings on a variety of subjects, including the restrictions on Middle Eastern women, are reminiscent of Henri Rousseau in style and color. Her works have been exhibited throughout the Middle East, in England, and in the United States.

See also ART; GENDER: GENDER AND EDUCATION.

Bibliography

Ali, Wijdan. *Modern Islamic Art: Development and Continuity.* Gainesville: University Press of Florida, 1997.

Lloyd, Fran, ed. *Contemporary Arab Women's Art: Dialogues of the Present.* London: Women's Art Library, 1999.

Shawa, Laila. Available at <http://www.lailashawa.com>.

Shawa, Laila. *Laila Shawa Works 1964–1996.* Cyprus: MCS Publications, 1997.

JESSICA WINEGAR

SHAWARMA

See FOOD: SHAWARMA

SHAW COMMISSION

A British commission of inquiry into a 1929 disturbance in Palestine.

A commission of inquiry, led by Sir Walter Shaw, was sent to Palestine by the British government to investigate the August 1929 Western Wall Disturbances, which caused the deaths of 249 Jews and Arabs. The commission's report, issued in March 1930, stated that the fundamental cause of the political violence was "the Arab feeling of animosity and hostility towards the Jews consequent upon the disappointment of their political and national aspirations and fear for their economic future." The Palestinians feared that by "Jewish immigration and land purchases they may be deprived of their livelihood and placed under the economic domination of the Jews." The commission's report called for an explicit policy regulating land and immigration that would have, in effect, curtailed the Zionist program in Palestine. The British government, however, postponed consideration of any change in policy until after another commission, which it appointed in May 1930 under Sir John Hope-Simpson, had studied land settlement, immigration, and development.

See also WESTERN WALL DISTURBANCES.

Bibliography

Palestine Government. *A Survey of Palestine for the Information of the Anglo-American Committee of Inquiry.* 2 vols. Jerusalem, 1946. Reprint, Washington, DC: Institute for Palestine Studies, 1991.

Smith, Charles D. *Palestine and the Arab-Israeli Conflict,* 4th edition. Boston: Bedford/St. Martin's, 2001.

PHILIP MATTAR

SHAWQI, AHMAD

[1868–1932]

Foremost Arab neoclassical poet.

In the course of his poetic career of forty years, Ahmad Shawqi both renovated the language of Arabic poetry and endowed it with the genre that had been missing in it, namely, the verse drama. After receiving a thorough Arabic and Islamic education in Cairo, he was sent by Khedive Tawfiq to France, where he spent three years, 1891 to 1893, during which he immersed himself in French literature, especially the Romantic Trio: Alfred de Musset, Lamartine, and Victor Hugo. This was the decisive influence on Shawqi—his window into Western literary art, through which he was able to rejuvenate modern Arabic poetry.

On his return to Egypt, he became in 1893 the court poet of Khedive Abbas Hilmi II. This marked the first phase of his poetic career, which lasted until 1914, when the First World War broke out. During this period, he composed odes on the khedive and the Alawi Dynasty and on Egyptian history, and he emerged as the poet of Islam and the Islamic Caliphate (then the Ottoman Empire). He also wrote a number of historical novels, perhaps inspired by his model, Victor Hugo. In 1898 he published his collected poems as a *diwan* titled *al-Shawqiyyat,* and this immediately established his reputation as the leading poet of his generation in the entire Arab world.

In 1914 his patron, the khedive, was deposed by Britain, and Shawqi was sent into exile. He chose Spain, where he spent the second phase of his poetic career, four years (1915–1919) in Barcelona, devoting his time to reading and contemplation. These four years witnessed the composition of splendid odes in which he remembered the glories of Spanish Islam.

The third phase of Shawqi's poetic career began in 1919 on his return to Egypt and lasted until his death in 1932. Shawqi was free from involvement with the court and court life, and with the abolishment of the caliphate in 1924, he became more interested in Arab nationalist aspirations, especially in Egypt and Syria, which inspired his memorable odes with pan-Arab overtones. It was also in this period that he composed his verse dramas, the most striking of which are *Majnun Layla* and *Masra Cleopatra.*

Shawqi did not limit his themes to the Arab and Islamic world. He is the poet of the Mediterranean par excellence and of pharaonic Egypt. His odes on both, hardly known in Europe and the United States, stand well in comparison with the best in world literature. Four years before his death, his preeminence as a poet was recognized when delegates from the Arab world travelled to Cairo, fêted him, and saluted him as *Amir al-Shuʿara* ("Prince of Poets").

See also LITERATURE: ARABIC.

Bibliography

"The Arab Mirror." In *Napoleon: One Image, Ten Mirrors,* edited by John Hirsh and Roberto Severino. Washington, DC: Georgetown University, 2002.

Shawqi, Ahmad. *Al-Mawsuʾa al-Shawqiyya,* vols. 1–9, edited by I. al-Abyari, Dar al-Kitab al-Arabi. Beirut: 1994–1995.

IRFAN SHAHÎD

SHAYKH

A general title of respect.

The term *shaykh* (also sheikh), can be applied to an elderly man, a tribal chief, a ruler of a shaykhdom along the Persian Gulf, a village chief, a religious scholar, a senator, or a Sufi master. The early caliphs were known as shaykhs. Shaykh al-Islam was the title given to the chief *mufti* (jurist) of the Ottoman Empire, who had direct access to the sultan and served as the highest-ranking legal administrator.

See also SHAYKH AL-ISLAM.

MARILYN HIGBEE

SHAYKH AL-ISLAM

Honorary title for Muslim jurists.

Shaykh al-Islam (literally, Elder of Islam) is an honorific title that has been historically applied to prominent Muslim jurists, theologians, and spiritual masters in recognition of outstanding knowledge and/or piety. In the early medieval period (c. 800–1200), the title was quasi-official and conferred on an elite few through acclamation by disciples or peers. Over time, however, the title was adopted by certain highly trained jurists (that is, muftis, or "jurisconsults"), who could legitimately claim the authority to issue a formal legal opinion *(fatwa).* In fact, although the more elitist, quasi-official usage of this title has continued into the modern period (particularly in the form of posthumous conferral), the later medieval and early modern periods witnessed an increasingly widespread attachment of the title to official positions in state-controlled judicial administrations.

The office of Shaykh al-Islam seems to have reached its apex as part of the Ottoman imperial establishment. By the time of Süleyman I (ruled 1520–1566), the chief jurisconsult of Constantinople (now Istanbul) was designated as the unique Shaykh al-Islam and recognized as the highest-ranking and most powerful member of the extensive imperial judiciary with exclusive direct access to the sultan himself. In 1916, however, the Committee for Union and Progress transferred much of the power of the former Ottoman Shaykh al-Islam to a secular Ministry of Justice, and by 1924 the new Turkish republic completely abolished the office. It is important to note that the office of Shaykh al-Islam has been much more widely and systematically instituted in Twelver Shiʿa contexts than in Sunni contexts. It was first introduced into the Iranian Shiʿite judicial system by the Safavid Shah Abbas I (ruled 1588–1629) and remains today the official title of the presidents of municipal religious courts in the Shiʿa communities of Iran and the former Soviet Union.

See also COMMITTEE FOR UNION AND PROGRESS; SHAYKH.

Bibliography

Gilsenan, Michael. *Recognizing Isla: Religion and Society in the Modern Middle East.* London and New York: Tauris, 2000.

Wheeler, Brannon M. *Teaching Islam.* New York: Oxford University Press, 2003.

SCOTT ALEXANDER

SHAYKH, HANAN AL-

[1945–]

Arab writer.

Hanan al-Shaykh is undisputedly one of the most important Arab women writers at the beginning of the twenty-first century. Born and raised in Lebanon, al-Shaykh first distinguished herself by writing prose fiction that exposed some of the repressive patriarchal traditions of her society. She did so by introducing characters, often women, who unabashedly explored themselves, their families, and their communities. She faced brief periods of censorship and occasional negative reviews. Although some of her fiction is set in the broader Arab world, two of her most prominent novels are situated in Lebanon

during the Civil War of 1975 through 1990. Al-Shaykh has become an important voice in critical studies of the war itself. The renowned *Hikayat Zahra* (The Story of Zahra, 1980) is a relentless psychosexual drama that manages, primarily through its complex protagonist, to narrate an insane society in violent civil disarray. Al-Shaykh's stark imagery and gripping plot mesmerized readers. Her follow-up novel, *Barid Bayrut* (Beirut blues, 1992), structured as a series of letters by another memorable female protagonist, extends the depiction of the Lebanese wars and fortifies the ideology of nonpartisanship, as every militia, army, confessional (religious/ethnic), and national group is subject to critique and to ridicule. Al-Shaykh's focus is on nuanced reactions, complex relationships, and multiple points of view. Her war novels offered new ways of imagining Lebanon in this destructive era.

Al-Shaykh spent her early school years in Lebanon and Egypt and later lived in Saudi Arabia. Since the early 1980s, she has lived in London and has participated in local productions of her experimental plays. One of her publications, *Only in London* (2001), explores some of the issues of Arab émigrés in Europe. With a keen sense of humor and a fresh Arabic writing style, al-Shaykh's works have extended the possibilities for Arab women writers. Because of good translations into English and other languages, Al-Shaykh's readership is growing outside the Arab world.

See also GENDER: GENDER AND EDUCATION; LEBANESE CIVIL WAR (1958); LEBANESE CIVIL WAR (1975–1990); LEBANON; LITERATURE: ARABIC.

Bibliography

Cooke, Miriam. *War's Other Voices: Women Writers on the Lebanese Civil War.* Cambridge, U.K.: Cambridge University Press, 1988.

Salem, Elise. *Constructing Lebanon: A Century of Literary Narratives.* Gainesville: University Press of Florida, 2003.

Zeidan, Joseph. *Arab Women Novelists: The Formative Years and Beyond.* New York: New York University Press, 1995.

ELISE SALEM

SHAYKHI

Follower of Shaykh Ahmad al-Ahsaʿi (1753–1826), a Twelver Shiʿite Islamic thinker who emphasized the esoteric and intuitional aspects of the religion.

Shaykh Ahmad cultivated followers in al-Hasa in eastern Arabia, Bahrain, and Iraq, as well as in Yazd and Kermanshah in Iran. A separate school of Shiʿism did not coalesce around his name until after his death, when he was succeeded by Sayyid Kazim Rashti (d. 1844) in Karbala; for a time, esoteric Shaykhism offered a challenge to the scholastic orthodoxy of the Usuli school.

After Rashti's death, though many Shaykhis became Babis, important Shaykhi communities continued to exist in the Persian Gulf, and in Kerman and Tabriz. The Tabriz Shaykhis diminished their doctrinal and ritual differences with the majority Usuli school, and played a progressive role during Iran's Constitutional Revolution (1905–1911). The Kerman Shaykhis, led by the Qajar noble Karim Khan Kermani (1810–1871) and his descendants, remained esoteric. Some among the Qajar nobility, as well as Mozaffar al-Din Shah (r. 1896–1906), converted to this school. Kerman Shaykhism proved conservative and often was supported by local governors. This privileged position helped to provoke Shaykhi-Usuli riots in 1905.

In the twentieth century Shaykhism became marginalized as a Shiʿite sect and Shaykhis suffered persecution under the Islamic Republic of Iran after 1979. Shaykhi communities persist in Kerman and elsewhere. The Ihqaqi family (based in Kuwait but originally from Tabriz) now produces most Shaykhi publications and claims many followers in southern Iraq. The movement also has been prominent in recent decades in Pakistan, where debates have raged over its orthodoxy and a Shaykhi Institute was founded in Faisalabad.

See also BABIS.

Bibliography

Amir-Moezzi, Mohammad Ali. "An Absence Filled with Presences: Shaykhiyya Hermeneutics of the Occultation." In *The Twelver Shiʿa in Modern Times: Religious Culture and Political History,* edited by Rainer Brunner and Werner Ende. Boston; Leiden, Netherlands: Brill, 2001.

Bayat, Mangol. *Mysticism and Dissent: Socioreligious Thought in Qajar Iran.* Syracuse, NY: Syracuse University Press, 1982.

Cole, Juan R. I. "Casting Away the Self: The Mysticism of Shaykh Ahmad al-Ahsaʾi." In *The Twelver Shiʿa in*

Modern Times: Religious Culture and Political History, edited by Rainer Brunner and Werner Ende. Boston and Leiden, Netherlands: Brill, 2001.

Naqvi, Syed Hussain Arif. "The Controversy about the Shaykhiyya Tendency among Shiʿa ʿUlamaʾ of Pakistan." In *The Twelver Shiʿa in Modern Times: Religious Culture and Political History,* edited by Rainer Brunner and Werner Ende. Boston and Leiden, Netherlands: Brill, 2001.

JUAN R. I. COLE

SHAZAR, SHNEOUR ZALMAN
[1898–1974]

Third Israeli president.

Shneour Zalman Shazar's last name is actually an acronym for Shneour Zalman Rubashov, his original name. Shazar was born in Minsk, Russia, and raised in Stabsty where he was educated in a Habad Heder, a Lubovitch Hasidic school. He joined the Poʿalei Zion (Labor Zionist) movement in 1905. In 1911, Shazar went to Palestine for the first time and worked on Kibbutz Merhavia, but he did not emigrate there until 1924. He became a member of the Secretariat of the Histadrut (General Federation of Labor) and was on the editorial board of its newspaper, *Davar*.

In 1947, he served as a member of the Jewish Agency delegation to the United Nations. After statehood Shazar ran and was elected on the MAPAI (Labor) list for the Knesset in 1949 and served there until 1957. He was appointed to be the minister of education and culture in 1949, and two years later he became a member of the executive of the Jewish Agency. In 1963 he was elected Israel's third president, to succeed Yizhak Ben-Zvi, and served two terms.

See also BEN-ZVI, YIZHAK; HISTADRUT; ISRAEL: POLITICAL PARTIES IN; JEWISH AGENCY FOR PALESTINE; KNESSET; LABOR ZIONISM; NEWSPAPERS AND PRINT MEDIA: ISRAEL.

Bibliography

Winer, Gershon. *The Founding Fathers of Israel.* New York: Bloch, 1971.

BRYAN DAVES

SHAZLI, SA'D AL-DIN AL-
[1922–]

Egyptian military officer and opposition politician.

Sa'd al-Din al-Shazli (also Shadhili, Shazly) was educated at Cairo University and the Military and Staff colleges in Cairo, and received training at the infantry school at Fort Benning in the United States. Shazli was chief of staff of Egyptian armed forces during the 1973 Arab–Israel War. Al-Shazli broke with President Anwar al-Sadat over Sadat's 1977 peace initiative with Israel, and was sent as ambassador to the United Kingdom and to Portugal. In 1978, he called for the overthrow of Sadat. In 1980, he went into exile in Algeria, where he formed an opposition party. Al-Shazli has published books on military strategy and the Arab–Israeli conflict.

See also ARAB–ISRAEL WAR (1973); SADAT, AN-WAR AL-.

Bibliography

El Shazly, Saad. *The Arab Military Option.* San Francisco, CA: American Mideast Research, 1986.

El Shazly, Saad. *The Crossing of the Suez.* San Francisco, CA: American Mideast Research, 1986.

DAVID WALDNER

SHEKEL

Name of Israeli currency.

The word *shekel* derives from biblical times, when coins were called shekels. *Shekel* was the term used by leaders of the Zionist movement to denote the price of membership. For the purpose of designating this cost of membership, attendees at the First Zionist Congress pegged the shekel to a fixed rate of certain major Western currencies.

Until 1970, the Israeli currency was called the lira or pound. In 1984, following a steep devaluation, the name of the currency was changed to the new Israeli shekel (NIS).

BRYAN DAVES

SHENHAR, YITZHAK
[1902–1957]

Hebrew writer.

Yitzhak Shenhar was born in Ukraine and became active in the ha-Halutz movement before moving to Palestine in 1921. He published his first poetry in 1924 and held a number of manual labor jobs until he began his literary career. In the 1930s, he worked as a writer, editor, and translator for the Schocken publishing house. He wrote short stories and poems about the life of Jews in Eastern Europe and in Palestine.

BRYAN DAVES

SHENOUDA III
[1923–]

Patriarch of the Coptic Orthodox Church.

Few Coptic patriarchs have had as much experience in both secular and ecclesiastical affairs prior to their election as Shenouda III. Born near Asyut and originally named Nazir Jayyid, he graduated from Cairo University in 1947 and fought in the 1948 Arab-Israel War. He earned a bachelor of divinity degree in 1950 from the Coptic Orthodox Theological Seminary. He became a leader in the lay-dominated Sunday School movement, editing its monthly magazine, and took holy orders in 1954. Within the church, he was successively a monk, a secretary to Cyril VI, and a bishop. He became a professor of Old Testament studies at the Coptic Seminary and the editor of its journal. Elected patriarch in 1971, Shenouda is the highest-ranking cleric of the Coptic Orthodox Church, the Middle East's largest Christian denomination. He has traveled frequently to North America, Europe, and Australia in order to maintain contact with expatriate Copts worldwide.

Shenouda was among the more than 1,500 Egyptians who were accused by President Anwar al-Sadat in September 1981 of extremist religious activity. Exiled and replaced by a council of five bishops, Shenouda fled to the desert monastery of Anba Bishoi in Wadi Natrun, northwest of Cairo. The reasons for his arrest and exile were unclear. Although religious turmoil had increased in the late 1970s and early 1980s (mainly instigated by Muslims opposed to Sadat's peace treaty with Israel), the president's charges, including those against Shenouda, could not be proven. Some Copts and Muslims punished by Sadat were active in religious professions and thus superficially gave credence to his allegations, but others had secular occupations—lawyers, writers, journalists, broadcasters, politicians—and appear to have been guilty only of disagreeing with the president.

Sadat's actions may have been a delayed response to Shenouda's September 1977 protest against the proposed imposition of Islamic law (shariʿa) in Egypt. The proposal would have made apostasy—in this case, conversion from Islam—a capital offense. Shenouda had feared that the law would discriminate against Egyptian Christians and other non-Muslims. He succeeded temporarily, for Sadat's recommendation was withdrawn, only to be reintroduced in 1980. Because Muslim fundamentalists then unleashed a murderous round of terror against the Copts, Shenouda ordered a series of demonstrations that enraged many Muslims and caused them to accuse the patriarch of engaging in politics. Sadat turned down Shenouda's repeated requests for a meeting, and so in 1981 the patriarch refused to accept the government's Easter greeting, humiliating Sadat, who may have taken revenge by the September arrest. Some Copts believed that Shenouda's dismissal was a political move to balance Sadat's incarceration of many Muslims. Another possible explanation is that, during a 1980 meeting between Sadat and U.S. president Ronald Reagan in Washington, D.C., a group of Coptic expatriates staged a protest, which Sadat wrongly blamed on Shenouda.

The censure of Shenouda for "sectarian sedition" was both ironic and unfortunate. Although he had vigorously defended the Coptic Church and struck back against Muslim fundamentalists, he has never been antagonistic toward Islam per se. Throughout his career, he has been sympathetic to Muslim causes and to Egyptian national interests. Some of his theological writings, particularly his major 1967 work al-Khalas fi al-Mafhum al-Urthuduksi (Salvation in Orthodox understanding), are as critical of aspects of Protestantism as of Islamic fundamentalism. Shenouda has specifically denounced the intrusion of religion as a divisive force in political affairs. One result of his historic meeting with the Roman Catholic Pope Paul VI in May 1973 (the first visit by an Egyptian pope to his Roman counterpart since 325 C.E.) was a joint statement of concern about the Palestinian problem. In May 1986 Shenouda sent a

representative to the funeral of a leader of the Muslim Brotherhood.

Shenouda's plight improved slowly after Sadat's assassination in October 1981. However, in 1983 an administrative court upheld Sadat's actions against Shenouda and ordered the Coptic Orthodox Church to hold a new papal election; only in January 1985 did a decree from President Husni Mubarak allow Shenouda to regain his office.

Shenouda reaffirmed his policy against politicizing religion by opposing an initiative by the Ibn Khaldun Center to host a conference in 1994 on minorities in the Arab world and efforts by the U.S. Congress in 1997 to pass legislation that would have barred aid to Egypt as long as it allowed discrimination against Copts. He attacked Israel's administration of Christian holy places and vowed not to visit Jerusalem until it was freed from Jewish control. He also condemned U.S. policy toward Iraq. Generally, his strategy has been to align Egypt's Copts closely with their Muslim counterparts in the interest of preserving national unity. He received UNESCO's prize for tolerance in October 1995. He is a past president of the World Council of Churches and headed for many years the Middle Eastern Council of Churches.

See also CHRISTIANS IN THE MIDDLE EAST; COPTS; SADAT, ANWAR AL-.

Bibliography

Abu-Saif, Leila. *Middle East Journal: A Woman's Journey into the Heart of the Arab World.* New York: Scribner, 1990.

Fernandez, Alberto M. "The Coptic Orthodox Salvation Theology of Anba Shenouda III." M.A. thesis, University of Arizona, 1983.

Goldschmidt, Arthur, Jr. "Shinuda III, al-Baba." In *Biographical Dictionary of Modern Egypt,* edited by Arthur Goldschmidt, Jr. Boulder, CO: Lynne Rienner, 2000.

Hirst, David, and Beeson, Irene. *Sadat.* London: Faber and Faber, 1981.

Pennington, J. D. "The Copts in Modern Egypt." *Middle Eastern Studies* 18 (1982): 158–179.

"Shenouda III." In *Coptic Encyclopedia.* New York: Macmillan, 1991.

Tincq, Henri. "Siege Mentality Grips the Copts of Egypt." *Guardian.* 21 February 1988.

DONALD SPANEL
UPDATED BY ARTHUR GOLDSCHMIDT

SHEPHEARD'S HOTEL

British gathering place in Cairo from 1841 to 1952.

In 1841 a British farmer's son named Samuel Shepheard built Shepheard's Hotel in Cairo. As Britain became more involved with the finances of khedival Egypt and especially after the establishment of an informal British protectorate in 1882, Shepheard's became the center of British social life in Cairo. Renovated in 1891, 1899, 1904, 1909, and 1927, the hotel was famous for its opulence.

British officers and administrators often retired to the bar at Shepheard's at the end of the day, and the Moorish Hall attracted tourists from Europe and America. After World War II, the relationship between Britain and Egypt deteriorated and, on Saturday, 26 January 1952, riots erupted in Cairo, which led to the destruction of numerous British and foreign establishments. Singled out by the crowd for particular attention was Shepheard's Hotel. The hotel was destroyed in an explosion, and although rebuilt on another site in 1957, it never regained its former stature.

Bibliography

Hopwood, Derek. *Egypt: Politics and Society, 1945–1990,* 3d edition. London and New York: Routledge, 1987.

ZACHARY KARABELL

SHESHBESH

One of several names for a board game, known in the West as backgammon, played with two dice and thirty pieces (fifteen per side).

Sheshbesh pieces are usually black for one player and white for the other. The origins of the game are obscure; while some experts argue for its invention in Persia, others suggest that it originated in southwest Asia. In 1927, Sir Leonard Wooley discovered a board game in the ruined city of Ur that was marked off into elaborately inlaid squares (twenty in all) accompanied by two sets of dice and two sets of discs, seven white and seven black. This places sheshbesh variants in Sumeria as early as 2600 B.C.E. Although it is not known how this game was played, experts assume that movement of the pieces over the board was governed by rolling the dice. The Ur game appears somewhat related to modern ludo, which in turn is related to backgammon.

The traditional game consists of balancing the elements of skill and chance while playing on a board marked with twenty-four chevrons in alternating colors of black and white. The pieces, fifteen to a player, are arranged on the trays according to a specific pattern, or are held off the board. Entry or movement begins according to the roll of the dice. The pieces move the full distance around the board in a race to the home tray, and are then borne off. Most commonly, players try to prevent and delay one's opponent from bearing off. If a hit has been made the player will attempt to block the entry of the piece by making homes—covering a chevron with a minimum of two pieces. Sheshbesh is known by a large variety of names. These include *takht-e nard* in Iran, *plakato* and *tawali* in Greece, *tric-trac* in France and Germany, tables *reales* in Italy and Spain, *mahbusa, yahudiyya farahjiyya,* or *tawlat al-zahr* in Syria and Arabia, and *bula* in Egypt.

Bibliography

Grosvenor, N. *Modern Backgammon.* New York: Holt, 1928.

CYRUS MOSHAVER

SHIBERGHAN

City in northern Afghanistan.

The capital of the Afghan province of Jowzjan, Shiberghan is located approximately 80 miles west of Mazar-e Sharif. The city has about 30,000 inhabitants, but the number is only a rough approximation. The official 1979 census showed a population of 19,000, but by 2003 estimates held that it might be as high as 40,000. Most of Shiberghan's population is Uzbek, although the city also has a sizable Turkmen and Tajik population. After natural gas was discovered in 1931, Shiberghan was developed with Soviet aid into a modern city. The city became a focal point in the battle between the Taliban and Afghanistan's Northern Alliance. Shiberghan is the location of a prison used by the Northern Alliance, and it has been alleged that several hundred Taliban and al-Qaʿida prisoners were killed at the prison.

Bibliography

Adamec, Ludwig. *Historical Dictionary of Afghanistan,* 2d edition. Lanham, MD: Scarecrow Press, 1997.

GRANT FARR

SHID, NAHID

[1953–]

Iranian lawyer.

Nahid Shid was born in 1953. She graduated from Tehran University law school and pursued religious education with Ayatollah Mar'ashi-Najafi. She has been an attorney since 1980, specializing in women's affairs, employment, and social insurance. She also is an expert at the Social Welfare organization and a consultant at the High Council of the Cultural Revolution. She initiated several amendments to the insurance law and divorce law, especially the principles of *ojrat-ol misl* and the reevaluation of dowry. The amendment to *ojrat-ol misl*, which was promulgated in 1993, stipulates that when a man files for divorce his wife can ask to be compensated for the housework she did during the marriage. The change to dowry, promulgated in 1996, stipulates that the amount of dowry should be calculated according to its current value, taking into account inflation. Shid argues that most religious laws should be changed because they are based on secondary principles and do not take account of social change. She maintains that blood money cannot be functional in a society in which women are medical doctors, university professors, and the like, and concludes that blood money should be the same for men and women. She presented her candidacy for the Fifth Parliament elections (1996) but was disqualified by the Council of Guardians.

Bibliography

Interview with Nahid Shid. *Zanan* 5, no. 28 (March 1996): 18–19.

AZADEH KIAN-THIÉBAUT

SHIDYAQ, AHMAD FARIS AL-

[1804–1887]

Lebanese writer, linguist, and literary critic who played a leading role in the Arabic literary revival of the mid-to-late nineteenth century.

A Maronite who converted to Protestantism in 1826 after witnessing the Maronite clergy's persecution of his brother As'ad, Faris al-Shidyaq was sent to Egypt by the American Protestant missionaries in Lebanon so that he could pursue his studies in Cairo. From 1834 to 1848, he taught at the American Protestant mission school in Malta, undertook a new Arabic translation of the Bible, and edited the publications of the American press there. For several years afterward, he traveled widely through Europe and the Near East, and worked as editor of the official Tunisian journal *al-Ra'id al-Tunisi* between 1854 and 1860. He converted to Islam during his stay in Tunis and adopted the name Ahmad Faris. In 1860, he relocated to Istanbul at the invitation of the Ottoman authorities. While there, he undertook his most important project: the publication of the Arabic-language newspaper *al-Jawa'ib,* a mouthpiece for Ottomanism which soon became a leading forum for the discussion of the political and cultural issues of the time and can be considered a pioneer of modern Arabic journalism. In addition to the many pieces of literary criticism that he wrote for this journal and others, Ahmad Faris al-Shidyaq is also remembered for his own writings in prose and verse and for his travel writing. A writer whose influence was felt throughout the region, he was one of the architects of modern literary Arabic.

See also OTTOMANISM.

Bibliography

Salibi, Kamal. *The Modern History of Lebanon.* New York: Praeger, 1965.

Sharabi, Hisham. *Arab Intellectuals and the West: The Formative Years, 1875–1914.* Baltimore, MD: Johns Hopkins Press, 1970.

GUILAIN P. DENOEUX

SHIHABI, ZLIKHA AL-

[1903–1992]

Palestinian women's activist.

Zlikha (also Zulaykha) Ishaq al-Shihabi was born in Jerusalem and educated at the Sisters of Zion School there. Her education was supplemented by private lessons. In 1929 she was a member of the Arab Women's Executive Committee, which convened the Palestine Arab Women's Conference in Jerusalem, and directed the Palestinian women's movement during the Mandate period. Shihabi was elected president of the Arab Women's Union (AWU) in Jerusalem in 1937, a position she held until her death. In the 1940s the AWU founded a sports club with its own playground and tennis courts, and in 1946 it opened a clinic near Bab

al-Zahira, a gate of the Old City of Jerusalem. She represented Palestinian women and spoke at the Eastern Women's Conference on Palestine (Cairo, 1938), and the Arab Women's Conference (Cairo, 1944), as well as other international conferences. In 1964 she was president of the preparatory committee that founded the General Union of Palestinian Women in Jerusalem, which was subsequently banned by both the Jordanian authorities and then the Israeli government after Jerusalem was captured in 1967. Because of her political activities the Israelis deported Shihabi to Jordan in 1969, but she managed to return to Jerusalem after a few months and continued her work with the AWU there until her death.

See also GAZA STRIP; GENDER: GENDER AND LAW; GENDER: GENDER AND POLITICS; GENERAL UNION OF PALESTINIAN WOMEN'S COMMITTEES (GUPWC); JERUSALEM; PALESTINE; PALESTINE LIBERATION ORGANIZATION (PLO); WEST BANK.

Bibliography

Fleischmann, Ellen. *The Nation and Its "New" Women: The Palestinian Women's Movement, 1920–1948.* Berkeley: University of California Press, 2003.

Kawar, Amal. *Daughters of Palestine: Leading Women of the Palestinian National Movement.* Albany: State University of New York Press, 1996.

ELLEN L. FLEISCHMANN

SHI'ISM

Branch of Islam that traces its leadership to Ali ibn Abi Talib, cousin of Muhammad.

The Shi'a constitute the largest Islamic community after the Sunnis, numbering close to 90 million worldwide. Iran is the only predominantly Shi'ite country; significant Shi'ite minorities exist in Iraq, India, Pakistan, Afghanistan, Yemen, Kuwait, Bahrain, eastern Saudi Arabia, Lebanon, and various Western countries. Shi'ism rests on a belief that the right of succession to political and religious leadership of the community belongs solely to the prophet Muhammad's cousin, Ali ibn Abi Talib, and his progeny. The Prophet was first succeeded by three of his companions—Abu Bakr, Umar, and Uthman—who ruled successively (632–656). Ali's rule (656–661) was almost immediately contested by Mu'awiyya, who succeeded him and founded the Umayyad dynasty. Upon Mu'awiyya's death, Ali's son Husayn revolted against Yazid, the successor and son of Mu'awiyya. For the followers of Ali, Husayn's death in battle at Karbala became symbolic of the hostility between them and those linked with Sunni Islam. The battle, especially the martyrdom of Husayn, continues to be commemorated by Shi'a.

Origins

The assassination of Uthman in 656 opened a split in the Islamic community. Soon after the accession of Ali to the caliphate, Mu'awiya, governor of Syria, kinsman of Uthman, and among the last generation of companions of the Prophet, declared his opposition to Ali's leadership. His opposition soon gained support among tribal groups in Syria and Mesopotamia. In response, Ali moved the Islamic capital to Kufa (in southern Iraq) and engaged Mu'awiya in a protracted rivalry that ended in an armistice known as *al-Tahkim*, which left Mu'awiya sovereign in Syria, Egypt, and northern Mesopotamia, while Ali ruled the Arabian peninsula and the east. Those who supported Ali were known as *Shi'at Ali* (the partisans of Ali); hence the name Shi'ism. Ali was assassinated in 661; subsequently, Mu'awiya consolidated his rule over the territories formerly under Ali and moved to make the line of political succession that of his family, the Umayyads. Since Ali's martyrdom the city of al-Najaf, where he is buried, has become a place of pilgrimage for Shi'a.

Ali had two sons, Hasan and Husayn (or Hussein), from his marriage to the Prophet's daughter, Fatima. They quickly inherited Ali's leadership and attracted the loyalty of the Shi'a. Exasperated by the political deadlock, Hasan abandoned his claim to succession, leaving Mu'awiya free to extend his control. Mu'awiya was succeeded in 680 by his son Yazid, who lacked the political acumen of his father. Yazid's hereditary route to power upset an Islamic community accustomed to having a strong consultative element in political election and viewing senior companions of the Prophet as worthier candidates to rule.

In 680 the residents of Kufa invited Husayn, who lived in Medina, to assert his right to succeed his father, and they pledged to support him. Husayn left Medina with his family and close associates, but before he could reach Kufa, an Umayyad force attacked and killed him and most of his family. This unprovoked attack on the youngest of the Prophet's grandchildren increased opposition to the Umayyads.

The cause of Shi'ism then expanded to include other branches of the larger family of the Prophet, the Banu Hashim, or Hashimites. There were a number of Hashimite revolts, primarily in Iraq and the east. Pivotal revolts were those of Zayd ibn Ali ibn al-Husayn in Kufa (743), and of his son Yahya in Transoxiania. Zayd's movement formed an early current of Shi'ism that espoused political activity to further the Alid cause, and did not restrict the imamate to one particular branch of the Alid family. (The Zaydi sect still survives in Yemen.)

In 750 a broadly based movement originating in Khorasan toppled the Umayyad caliphate. Succession to the caliphate passed to the Abbasids, a Hashimite branch named after Abbas, an uncle of the Prophet. Feeling betrayed, the Alids staged several revolts, the most notable of which was the one in Medina by Muhammad al-Nafs al-Zakiyya (762), a descendant of Hasan. By then, however, the Abbasids had consolidated their control.

Theology

Shi'ism originated as a political movement supporting the rights of Ali to the caliphate. Since leadership in the early Islamic community was associated to a great extent with religious merit, Ali was considered the rightful ruler not only because of his early conversion to Islam and close family ties to the Prophet, but also because of his religious knowledge. Shi'ite tradition states that the Prophet always referred to Ali as the preeminent expert on spiritual matters among his companions, and that at Ghadir Khumm, Muhammad reportedly declared to his companions that Ali was his *waliyy* (rightful and trusted successor) and blessed him with special prayers. The earliest concrete evidence of Shi'ism as a spiritual sect, however, did not appear until the 750s or 760s. In the era immediately following the revolution, a divergence emerged among those supporting the cause of Ali's family. Shi'ism came to be associated increasingly with descendants of Husayn, and in particular, the sixth descendant, Ja'far al-Sadiq.

The Abbas Mosque, located in Kerbala, Iraq. © AFP/CORBIS. REPRODUCED BY PERMISSION.

Although little historical fact is known about Ja'far al-Sadiq, it is generally believed that it was during his time that the rudiments of Shi'ite theology were first formed. These consisted of the beliefs that the imam (presumably from the Husaynid line) holds the secrets of religious knowledge (*ma'rifa*), that he has the authority to pass on this knowledge to a designated successor through a process of investment known as *wasiyya*, and that the followers of the imam must not challenge the authority of the established state in support of the Alid imamate until the imam declares the historically assigned time for such a political revolution. From the time of Ja'far al-Sadiq, the Shi'a became closely clustered around the line of his descendants. However, a significant division took place within his lifetime. Ja'far's son Isma'il was supposed to be the spiritual successor to his father, and thus began to attract followers. Either because Isma'il died during his father's lifetime or because during his last years Ja'far decided to transfer the succession to another of his

The Hussein Mosque, located in Kerbala, Iraq. © CHARLES & JOSETTE LENARS/CORBIS. REPRODUCED BY PERMISSION.

sons, Musa, another group began to recognize Musa as his only successor.

This latter group continued to recognize the transmission of the authority of the imamate in a line of twelve successors, the last of whom, a child, is believed to have disappeared in the city of Samarra in 873. Shi'a believe that the last of the twelve imams will one day reveal himself as the leading religious and political guide (the Mahdi), reestablish his leadership over the whole Islamic community, and usher in an age of justice and righteousness. Recognition of twelve descendants of Ali as imams led to this larger Shi'ite community being known as Twelver (also Itha'ashar) Shi'a, or Imamis. The other group, which refused to accept Musa as successor and maintained its religous loyalty to Isma'il, the seventh imam, is hence known as Isma'ilis, or Seveners. Like the Twelvers, some Isma'ilis believe in occulation (ghayba), but they consider Isma'il to be the vanished imam destined to usher in a righteous age.

The Growth of Shi'ism

In the late ninth century competing Shi'ite missions emerged. For some time, Isma'ili da'wa (mission, propaganda) had its strongest support in North Africa, where it was the religious affiliation of the Fatimid dynasty (909–1171), which came to rule North Africa, Egypt, Hijaz, and Syria. Establishing the city of Cairo (969) as their capital, the Fatimids hoped to turn Egypt into the center of Isma'ili propaganda, and for this purpose they founded al-Azhar seminary. The Fatimids' religious enterprise had little

success because the majority of their subjects adhered to Sunni schools of thought; Isma'ilism became the ideology of the state and of a minority in society. Elsewhere in the Islamic world, the Buyid dynasty, which ruled Iran and Iraq between 932 and 1062, declared its loyalty to Shi'ism but chose to follow the Twelver branch. Although Shi'ism did not become the religious affiliation of the majority under Buyid rule, the dynasty did much to promote it. For example, Husayn's murder was commemorated with public ceremonies on the tenth of Muharram, the events at Ghadir Khumm were celebrated, and steps were taken to protect Shi'ism.

The next stage of substantial elaboration of Twelver Shi'ite thought occurred in the sixteenth century under the Safavid dynasty in Iran. Until their arrival, Iran had been primarily a Sunni region. Locked in a mortal conflict with two Sunni dynasties—the Ottomans to the west and the Uzbeks in Transoxiania to the east—Isma'il al-Safawi (1494–1524), founder of the dynasty, found it politically helpful to underline the ideological particularity of his government by adopting Shi'ism as the state religion. At the time, Safavid Shi'ism consisted largely of an affiliation to Sufi movements in Azerbaijan. Under Safawi's successor, Tahmasp (1524–1576), however, the state moved toward a more institutional and hierarchical structure guided by a clergy and an established law, rather than by the esoteric propensity of Sufi masters. This change fostered the alliance between the state and the clergy, the latter bolstering the legitimacy of the state and the former supporting Shi'ite propaganda. The Safavids sought to make Shi'ism the law of the land and the only religious affiliation in society. Under Abbas I (1588–1629) they built theological seminaries and attracted renowned scholars from Iraq, southern Lebanon, and Bahrain to help systematize Shi'ite learning. Sunni Islam was all but eliminated in the Safavid territories.

Shi'ite Scholars and Differences with Sunnism

The idea of the occultation of the imam deprived Shi'ism of binding authority in spiritual matters. This inevitably called for the presence of religious scholars who could guide the community. Kufa was the earliest center of Shi'ite thought, and in later times Qom in Iran emerged as a preeminent center of Shi'ite learning. Among the most prominent of scholars in Qom were Abu Ja'far al-Kulayni (d. 941) and Ibn Babawayh al-Saduq (d. 991). Noted scholars in the later theological schools of Baghdad were Shaykh al-Mufid (d. 1022) and Sharif Murtada Alam al-Huda (d. 1067). The greatest Shi'ite scholar, however, was perhaps al-Majlisi (d. 1699), who contributed the most toward changing a Sufi form of Shi'ism to a dogmatic and formal legislative form. Beginning in the nineteenth century there was a debate between two main currents in Shi'ism: the Akhbari, which seeks to establish Shi'ite jurisprudence on the authority of tradition (akhbar), and the Usuli, which emphasizes the primacy of rationalist principles (usul) and the need to exercise ijtihad (reasoned speculation). Since the debate has been resolved in favor of the Usuli current in the twentieth century, the authority of the mujtahid (expert scholar capable of exercising reasoned speculation) has taken on greater importance. Although Shi'a and Sunnis agree on core matters of ritual, dogma, and law, they differ on details. Whereas Sunnis, for instance, permit the occasional practice of wiping the foot covering with water (al-mash ala al-khuffayn) during ablution, Shi'a reject the practice. The institution of temporary marriage (mut'a), accepted under Shi'ite law, is rejected in Sunnism. The most prominent area of difference, however, remains historical. The Shi'a's rejection of the caliphate of the first successors to the Prophet—viewed as equals according to Sunni historical reading—and their insistence on the sole right of Ali ibn Abi Talib to the succession has long formed the most visible difference between the two communities.

See also AKHBARI; AZHAR, AL-; ISLAM; ISMA'ILI SHI'ISM; KARBALA; MAHDI; MUHAMMAD; NAJAF, AL-; SUNNI ISLAM; USULI; ZAYDISM.

Bibliography

Algar, Hamid. Religion and State in Iran, 1785–1906: The Role of the Ulama in the Qajar Period. Berkeley: University of California Press, 1980.

Arjomand, Said Amir. Authority and Political Culture in Shi'ism. Albany: State University of New York Press, 1988.

Arjomand, Said Amir. The Shadow of God and the Hidden Imam: Religion, Political Order, and Societal Change in Shi'ite Iran from the Beginning to 1890. Chicago: University of Chicago Press, 1984.

Chelkowski, P. J. Ta'ziyeh: Ritual and Drama in Iran. New York: New York University Press, 1979.

Dabashi, Hamid. Theology of Discontent: The Ideological Foundation of the Islamic Revolution in Iran. New York: New York University Press, 1993.

Daftary, Farhad. The Isma'ilis: Their History and Doctrines. Cambridge, U.K.: Cambridge University Press, 1990.

Keddie, Nikki. Religion and Politics in Iran: Shi'ism from Quietism to Revolution. New Haven, CT: Yale University Press, 1983.

Momen, Moojan. An Introduction to Shi'i Islam. New Haven, CT: Yale University Press, 1985.

Moosa, Matti. Extremist Shi'ites: The Ghulat Sects. Syracuse, NY: Syracuse University Press, 1988.

Sachedina, A. A. Islamic Messianism: The Idea of the Mahdi in Twelver Shi'ism. Albany: State University of New York Press, 1981.

TAYEB EL-HIBRI
UPDATED BY ROXANNE VARZI

SHILLUK

Non-Muslim Sudanese people.

The Shilluk are a linguistic group belonging to the Western Nilotic subgroup of the Eastern Sudanic branch of the Nilo-Saharan family. They are concentrated along the west bank of the White Nile in southern Sudan. Because Shilluk political organization is centered around the king (reth), the Shilluk have experienced greater unity than other tribes in the region. Enjoying access to good agricultural land along the Nile, the Shilluk are more settled than other tribes and rely more on cultivation and fishing than on cattle raising. The Shilluk numbered about 150,000 persons according to the 1983 census.

Bibliography

Voll, John Obert. Historical Dictionary of the Sudan. Metuchen, NJ: Scarecrow Press, 1978.

DAVID WALDNER

SHILOAH, REUVEN
[1909–1959]

Israeli intelligence official, strategist, and diplomat.

Born Reuven Zaslani in Jerusalem, Shiloah served in the SHAI (the Haganah intelligence service) in the 1930s and worked with the Jewish community in Iraq. He headed the Arab section of the political department of the Jewish Agency under Moshe Shertok (Sharett). He was liaison officer with British and U.S. intelligence services during World War II. Shiloah held many secret meetings with King Abdullah of Transjordan before and after the 1948 war.

He was the first director of the political department of the Israeli Foreign Ministry and headed the Israeli delegation to the Lausanne peace talks in 1949. He was also the first head of the Mossad (1949–1952), but was worn down by the disastrous collapse of the Israeli spy network in Iraq, by a serious road accident, and by constant feuding with Isser Harel, the first head of the Shin Bet and Shiloah's successor as Mossad chief.

Shiloah resigned his chairmanship of the intelligence services coordinating committee to serve under ambassador Abba Eban as a minister at the Israeli embassy in Washington, D.C. (1953–1957). While there he forged close ties with the U.S. intelligence community.

As a senior adviser to Golda Meir, the foreign minister, Shiloah was instrumental in forging Israel's "periphery doctrine" of responding to the Cold War and Nasserism by seeking closer links with non-Arab regimes such as Turkey, Iran, and Ethiopia. He attempted but failed to establish an Israeli relationship with NATO. Shiloah was widely described as a workaholic; this trait contributed to his poor health and his premature death.

See also EBAN, ABBA (AUBREY); HAREL, ISSER; MOSSAD; SHIN BET.

Bibliography

Black, Ian, and Morris, Benny. *Israel's Secret Wars: A History of Israel's Intelligence Services.* New York: Grove Press, 1991.

Eshed, Haggai. *Reuven Shiloah: The Man Behind the Mossad.* London: Frank Cass, 1997.

IAN BLACK

SHIM'UN, MAR
[1908–1975]

Patriarch of the Assyrian (Nestorian) community.

Ishai Mar Shim'un XXIII was born in the Ottoman Empire (now Turkey) and educated in England in the 1920s. In 1918 and 1919, some 20,000 Assyrians (Nestorians) who had fled southeastern Turkey were settled in Iraq by the British authorities. Fearing the consequences of British withdrawal in 1932, the Mar Shim'un attempted to set up a separate enclave for his people with himself as politico-spiritual leader. The Assyrians were told that they should either become assimilated as Iraqis or leave, and in a confrontation between the community and the Iraqi army in August 1933, at least 600 Assyrians were killed. The Mar Shim'un left Iraq, eventually reaching the United States; though he returned briefly to Iraq in 1970, he died in the United States in 1975.

See also ASSYRIANS.

PETER SLUGLETT

SHIN BET

Israel's General Security Service (G.S.S. or Shabak), responsible for preventing hostile activity.

The Shin Bet was created in 1948 to counter espionage, subversion, and sabotage. Its early preoccupations were Soviet-bloc espionage and monitoring Israel's Arab minority. Its first head was Isser Harel, who was succeeded by Amos Manor in 1954.

The Shin Bet expanded greatly after the 1967 war, becoming the leading civilian agency for controlling the Palestinians in the newly occupied territories, recruiting informers and collaborators and working with the Mossad to penetrate resistance groups such as al-Fatah and the Popular Front for the Liberation of Palestine.

The Shabak affair (1984–1986) brought unwelcome exposure of Shin Bet practices. Two Palestinians who hijacked an Israeli bus were said by the authorities to have died during the rescue. Photographs showed them leaving the bus alive, and it became clear that they had been deliberately killed by Shin Bet personnel while in custody. Israel's attorney general recommended that Avraham Shalom, head of the Shin Bet, be dismissed, but amid accusations of a cover-up, President Chaim Herzog pardoned Shalom and eleven other Shin Bet officers. A new committee investigated Shin Bet procedures, including interrogation methods that some human-rights experts said constituted torture.

The Shin Bet struggled to cope with the Palestinian uprising after 1987 and saw its effectiveness weakened when Israel withdrew from the Gaza Strip and large parts of the West Bank after the Oslo Accords. Its reputation was damaged by its failure to prevent the assassination of Yitzhak Rabin by a right-wing Jew in 1995 and by the Palestinian suicide bombings that accompanied the second intifada that began in 2000.

See also HAREL, ISSER; MOSSAD; SHILOAH, REUVEN.

Bibliography

Black, Ian, and Morris, Benny. *Israel's Secret Wars: A History of Israel's Intelligence Services.* New York: Grove Press, 1991.

Raviv, Dan, and Melman, Yossi. *Every Spy a Prince.* Boston: Houghton Mifflin, 1990.

JULIE ZUCKERMAN
UPDATED BY IAN BLACK

SHIRAZ

Ancient city and provincial capital in southwestern Iran.

Shiraz, the capital of Fars, probably dates back to Achemenid times (c. 550–330 B.C.E.). During the Sassanian dynasty (c. 226–642 C.E.), it developed into an important commercial center and military base, a position it has retained for more than 1,300 years. During the medieval period, two of Iran's greatest poets, Sa'di and Hafez, lived in the city. Shiraz flourished in the late eighteenth century as the capital of the Zand dynasty (1750–1794).

During the nineteenth century Shiraz was an important center for the distribution of foreign trade, much of which passed through the Persian Gulf port of Bushehr (Bushire), about 125 miles west of the city. The development of ports in Khuzestan in the early twentieth century, and especially the building of the Trans-Iranian Railway, which bypassed both Shiraz and Bushehr, led to the decline of this trade. Beginning in the 1930s, however, modern industries were developed in Shiraz, initially textile factories, but increasingly more diversified manufacturing after 1965. Industrialization brought a major influx of rural migrants, and the city's population increased nearly sixfold in 40 years, from 179,000 in 1956 to 1,053,000 by 1996.

Bibliography

Fisher, W. B. "Physical Geography." In *The Cambridge History of Iran,* vol. 1, edited by W. B. Fisher. Cambridge, U.K.: Cambridge University Press, 1968.

NEGUIN YAVARI
UPDATED BY ERIC HOOGLUND

SHIRAZI, MIRZA HASAN
[1815–1897]

Nineteenth-century Iranian cleric.

Born in Shiraz to a well-established clerical family, Mirza Hasan Shirazi embarked on vigorous religious training that took him first to Isfahan and then Iraq. He has become most notable for a religious decree (*fatwa*) in 1892 against the use of tobacco. The decree read as follows: "In the name of God the merciful, the usage of tobacco in any way is equal to denouncing God and fighting against the divinely guided messianic leader [that is, the Mahdi, the Imam of the Age]." Shirazi's decision to issue such a proclamation is said to have stemmed from the allocation of exclusive rights of tobacco production and sales to the British by Naser al-Din Shah and his prime minister. The effect of the decree was that the government was forced to annul its agreement with the British. It is said that even the wives of the shah refused to use and serve tobacco during the period of the decree.

See also TOBACCO REVOLT.

Bibliography

Algar, Hamid. *Mirza Malkum Khan: A Study in the History of Iranian Modernism.* Berkeley: University of California Press, 1973.

FARHAD ARSHAD

SHIRAZ UNIVERSITY

A private university established in 1956 in Shiraz, Iran.

The Pahlavi University of Shiraz, Iran, was established by a special law passed by the parliament in 1956 as a nongovernment university under the trust of the king, the queen, and the crown prince. Its name was changed to Shiraz University after the 1979 Iranian Revolution. It began with nine colleges or faculties and by 1977 had 648 faculty members and 5,129 students. It was one of the first Middle Eastern universities created on the U.S. model, offering courses in English and including among its faculty a number of foreigners. Its curriculum includes courses in literature, natural sciences, medicine, agriculture, and engineering. It had 12,600 students and 360 teachers in 2002.

PARVANEH POURSHARIATI

SHISH KEBAB

See FOOD: SHISH KEBAB

SHITREET, BEKHOR
[1897–1967]

Israeli Mizrahi leader.

Bekhor Shitreet (also Shitrit) was born in Tiberias into a family that had emigrated from Morocco to Palestine in the eighteenth century. He was educated as a rabbi and taught Hebrew, Arabic, and French in the Alliance (French) school system in Tiberias. An organizer of the police force set up in Palestine by the British in 1919, he later was a police commander in lower Galilee and head of the Tel Aviv police force in 1927. After the founding of the State of Israel in 1948, he was elected to the Knesset as a member of the MAPAI party and served as minister of police. During his lifetime Shitreet sought to improve relations between religious minorities in Israel.

See also ISRAEL: POLITICAL PARTIES IN; KNESSET.

BRYAN DAVES

SHLONSKY, AVRAHAM
[1900–1973]

Hebrew poet, literary critic, editor, and translator.

Avraham Shlonsky was the main leader and proponent of modern Hebrew poetry in the evolving Jewish community of British mandatory Palestine and the State of Israel. Born in 1900 in the tsarist Ukraine, he was sent at age thirteen by his Zionist parents to study at the prestigious Herzliya Gymnasia (high school) in Tel Aviv, but had to return to Russia during World War I. In 1921 he emigrated to Palestine and joined a new kibbutz and for a while worked as

a *halutz* (pioneer) in road paving, construction, and agriculture. His early poems appeared in 1922, and he was soon drawn to the burgeoning cultural life in Tel Aviv. During a visit to Paris, Shlonsky was influenced by modern French poetry, especially by the symbolists and the expressionists, but also by the Russian avant-garde poetry that flourished during the Russian Revolution and in the early days of the Soviet Union.

During the 1920s Shlonsky became a leading figure in the literary revolt against the rhetorical-didactic style of Hayyim Nahman Bialik, the towering and authoritative king of early Hebrew and Zionist poetry. Shlonsky edited the literary pages of *Davar*, the daily paper of the labor movement, and from 1926 edited *Ketuvim* (Writings) and from 1933 *Turim* (Columns), the literary journals of the rebellious young opposition to the literary establishment. In the late 1930s he became active in the Marxist left wing of the labor movement (ha-Shomer ha-Tzaʿir and later MAPAM), founded its *Sifriyat ha-Poʿalim* (Workers Library) publishing house, and edited the party's literary supplements and journals. In the late 1940s and early 1950s Shlonsky edited *Orlogin*, the home for what was then called Progressive Culture, which sympathized with the Soviet Union in the Cold War. During the 1950s he was active in the Moscow-influenced World Peace Movement, but after the revelations of Stalin's antisemitic tendencies Shlonsky became critical of the attitude of the Soviet regime toward the Jews and Zionism.

Shlonsky was acclaimed for his agility with the Hebrew language. Beside his influential "serious" poetry, he was widely admired for his light poetry, satires, and children's verse. A prolific translator, he introduced the young Hebrew-speaking generation to the world classics (Shakespeare, Molière, Romain Rolland, De Coster) and in particular to Russian poetry and prose (Pushkin, Gogol, Chekhov, Mayakovsky, and Tolstoy). In addition to the nine major collections of poetry that he published, Shlonsky also translated more than seventy major European works into Hebrew. In 1967 Shlonsky was awarded the prestigious Israel Prize. He died in 1973.

See also BIALIK, HAYYIM NAHMAN; LITERATURE: HEBREW; NEWSPAPERS AND PRINT MEDIA: ISRAEL.

Bibliography

Burnshaw, Stanley, Carmi, T., and Spicehandler, Ezra, eds. *The Modern Hebrew Poem Itself,* updated edition. Cambridge, MA: Harvard University Press, 1989.

Spicehandler, Ezra. "The Fiction of the 'Generation of the Land.'" In *Israel: The First Decade of Independence,* edited by S. Ilan Troen and Noah Lucas. Albany: State University of New York Press, 1995.

MORDECHAI BAR-ON

SHOCHAT, MANYA

[1879–1961]

Leading Zionist pioneer, advocate for Russian Jewry, feminist, mother of the kibbutz movement, and founder of the League of Arab-Jewish Rapprochement.

Born near Grodno, Russia, Manya Wilbushevitz Shochat (also Shohat) reacted to the Kishinev pogrom of 1903 by distancing herself from the Russian revolutionary movement in favor of Jewish self-defense and nonrevolutionary socialist movements. For supporting an attempt to assassinate the Russian interior minister, Shochat was imprisoned. She persuaded the secret police to release her, then fled when her police contact fell from office. Arriving in Ottoman Palestine in 1904, Shochat established the first collective, Kibbutz Sejera, and was a founding member of the Jewish self-defense movement, Ha-Shomer. She undertook a number of overseas fundraising missions on behalf of Palestinian Jewish workers and Russian Jewry and attempted to foster dialogue with local Arabs while also smuggling arms to Jewish communities, which led to her arrest by the Turkish authorities. Under the British Mandate in Palestine, Shochat was prominent in the kibbutz movement and the newly established Haganah (Jewish defense force). After rioting resulted in the death of Jews across the country in 1929, she helped to found the small League of Arab-Jewish Rapprochement while continuing to support Jewish immigration and defense efforts—a combination she pursued through the subsequent war, believing that respect could win peace while survival demanded self-reliance.

See also HAGANAH; HA-SHOMER.

Bibliography

Ben-Zvi, Rahel Yanait. *Before Golda: Manya Shochat: A Biography,* translated by Sandra Shurin. New York: Biblio Press, 1989.

Bernstein, Deborah, ed. *Pioneers and Homemakers: Jewish Women in Pre-State Israel.* Albany: State University of New York, 1992.

Shepherd, Naomi. *A Price below Rubies: Jewish Women as Rebels and Radicals.* Cambridge MA: Harvard University Press, 1993.

GEORGE R. WILKES

SHORFA

North African title for all descendants of the prophet Muhammad.

In Morocco, since the rule of the Idrisid dynasty, descent from the prophet Muhammad became a source of legitimacy for establishing political power. All the founders of the religious brotherhoods claimed such origin to gain authority and credit among disciples. A genealogical tree linking the shorfa to the Prophet would assess the claim. The Sa'di (sixteenth century) and Alawi (seventeenth century to the present) dynasties that ruled or have ruled Morocco are considered shorfa dynasties.

See also ALAWI; IDRISIDS; SHARIF.

RAHMA BOURQIA

SHUF

Region of Lebanon.

The Shuf is the district (*qada*) located in southern Lebanon between the Jizzin and al-Matn districts, and between the Mediterranean Sea and the Biqa valley. It has more than 220 towns. The main city is the predominantly Druze town of Ba'aklin, which was, for a while, the seat of government for the Ma'nids. The Shuf was made part of the governorate of Mount Lebanon because a sectarian balance between Maronite Christians and Druze was desired. Historically, the electoral battles in the region were between the candidates of Kamal Jumblatt and those of Camille Chamoun, but the presence of a number of sects in the region forced both leaders to seek support among nonaligned sects to win the election. For example, the Shuf had a Sunni Muslim seat, and even the Maronite Chamoun had to field a Sunni candidate to win the election. Druze leader Walid Jumblatt has been demanding the division of the Mount Lebanon governorate into two sections to achieve a degree of sectarian parity. He does not feel he should have to seek support among the Maronites, who constitute a majority in the northern part of the governorate. By the early 2000s, however, Jumblatt—whose traditional pro-Syrian stance had shifted—began making political alliances with Christian candidates.

See also BIQA VALLEY; CHAMOUN, CAMILLE; JUMBLATT, KAMAL; JUMBLATT, WALID.

Bibliography

AbuKhalil, As'ad. *Historical Dictionary of Lebanon.* Lanham, MD: Rowman and Littlefield, 1998.

AS'AD ABUKHALIL
UPDATED BY MICHAEL R. FISCHBACH

SHUFMAN, GERSHON
[1880–1972]

Hebrew writer.

Born in Belorussia, Gershon Shufman received a traditional Yeshiva education and taught himself Hebrew and Russian. In 1902, he enlisted in the Russian army, which coincided with the publication of his first collection of short stories. From 1913 to 1938 he lived in Austria and from there emigrated to Palestine. His brief articles and short stories are his best literary creations. They describe life in Galicia, Austria, and in Israel, and focus on day-to-day experiences that, in turn, reflect reality.

Shufman's writings are considered forerunners of modern Hebrew literature. A four-volume revised version of his collected works appeared between 1946 and 1952, and a fifth volume was added in 1960. He received the Israel Prize for literature in 1957.

ANN KAHN

SHUKRI, MOHAMMAD
[1935–]

Moroccan novelist.

Mohammad Shukri was born in Beni Shiker in the Nadhor region of Morocco. He learned to read and write only at the age of twenty. He lives in Tangier.

Shukri's first autobiographical novel, *al-Khubz al-Hafi Sira Riwa'iyya, 1935–1956* (For bread alone), details his difficult childhood and stirs the admiration of the reader for his efforts to overcome his circumstances. The extreme realism of Shukri's writings, reproducing the life of hunger, theft, drugs, and prostitution he experienced or observed around him, delayed the publication of his novel in Arabic for many years—the English translation by Paul Bowles, *For Bread Alone* (1973), appeared first. Shukri's collection of short stories *Majnun al-Ward* (1979; Enamored of roses) depicts city life in Morocco with the same harsh realism and a camera-eye technique; the words are even more poignant than the situations they describe, and have a stronger impact on the reader.

The second volume of Shukri's autobiography, *Zaman al-Akhta* (The time of mistakes) was published in 1992; its fourth edition has a different title, *Al-Shuttar* (2000; Streetwise). Abandoning the fictionalized narrative of *For Bread Alone,* Shukri stays closer to reality made vibrant through the use of the present tense, and the forthrightness in speech that characterized his earlier book reappears. Autobiographical information also figures in Shukri's fiction works such as *al-Suq al-Dakhili* (1985; The inner market), where he evokes with his usual blunt and uninhibited style the intimate details of day and night life in Tangier.

Shukri's oeuvre extends beyond the novel. His account of Jean Genet and Tennessee Williams's visit to Tangier was later translated into French by Mohammed el-Ghoulabzouri under the title *Jean Genet et Tennessee Williams à Tangier* (1992). His literary assessment of his contemporary Arab and Western authors (as well as his own work) is found in *Ghiwayat al-Shahrur al-Abyad* (1998; The seduction of the white sparrow). Shukri has also published two plays, *al-Talqa al-Akhira* (1980; The last bullet) and *al-Sa'ada* (1994; Happiness).

See also LITERATURE: ARABIC, NORTH AFRICAN.

Bibliography

Allen, Roger. "Shukri, Muhammad." In *Encyclopedia of Arabic Literature,* edited by Julie Scott Meisami and Paul Starkey. London and New York: Routledge, 1998.

Williams, Malcolm, and Watterson, Gavin, trans. *Anthology of Moroccan Short Stories.* Tangier, Morocco: King Fahd School of Translation, 1995.

AIDA A. BAMIA

SHULTZ, GEORGE

[1920–]

U.S. secretary of state, 1982 to 1989.

George Shultz was born in New York City on 13 December 1920. He earned an economics B.A. from Princeton in 1942, and a Ph.D. from the Massachusetts Institute of Technology (MIT) in 1949. During World War II he joined the Marine Corps Reserve. Shultz pursued an academic career at MIT, as a member of the U.S. Senate staff, and at the University of Chicago. In the late 1960s he started his political career as secretary of labor and then director of the Office of Management and Budget.

While secretary of the treasury in the administration of U.S. president Richard Nixon, George Shultz was confronted with the Oil Crisis. During a business career he established a solid economic knowledge of the Middle East. Following Alexander Haig as the second secretary of state of the administration of Ronald Reagan, Shultz had to tackle the aftermath of the Iranian Revolution and the Israeli invasion within the Lebanese civil war. His time in office as secretary of state was marked by the final stages of the Cold War, from a deterioration of relations up to the beginning of the U.S.–Soviet honeymoon in the short period before the collapse of the Soviet Union.

Despite Israeli–U.S. tensions that flared over the Reagan Plan, which linked Palestinian self-rule with Jordan, and escalated during the Lebanon invasion and the Pollard spy case, bilateral relations between Israel and the United States were largely improved as—due to the political wills of Shultz and Reagan—Israel was declared a strategic ally.

The Iran-Contra Affair and the clandestine U.S. involvement in the anti-Soviet resistance in Afghanistan were not shaped by Shultz. New approaches in engaging an Arab-Israeli peace process were only possible shortly after his term in office, when the end of the Cold War and the Kuwait crisis profoundly reshaped the political landscape of the Middle East.

See also ARAB–ISRAEL WAR (1982); REAGAN, RONALD.

Bibliography

Shultz, George P. *Turmoil and Triumph: My Years as Secretary of State.* New York: Charles Scribner's Sons, 1993.

OLIVER BENJAMIN HEMMERLE

SHUMAYYIL, SHIBLI

[1850–1917]

Syrian medical scholar and intellectual.

Born in Syria to a Christian family, Shibli Shumayyil was one of the first graduates of the Syrian Protestant College's medical school in Beirut. He completed his medical studies in Paris and settled in Egypt to practice medicine and write numerous articles on medicine and on social and scientific theories. He was particularly influenced by Charles Darwin, using the evolutionist's ideas to formulate his ideas on the unity of being and natural laws in human society. He denounced despotism as unnatural and false. Also influenced by the thought of philosophers Herbert Spencer and Ludwig Büchner, Shumayyil criticized nationalism and all forms of exclusive solidarity because they divided human society. He preached universalism and liberalism and so gave measured support to the Young Turk movement. Like his contemporary, the Lebanese Farah Antun, Shumayyil sought the theoretical basis for a secular state that would promote a society where Christians and Muslims would be equal.

Bibliography

Hourani, Albert. *Arabic Thought in the Liberal Age, 1789–1939.* Cambridge, U.K., and New York: Cambridge University Press, 1983.

ELIZABETH THOMPSON

SHUQAYRI, AHMAD

[1908–1980]

Diplomat, activist, and first head of the Palestine Liberation Organization.

Ahmad Shuqayri was a Palestinian born in Tibnin, Lebanon, while his father, the Islamic judge Shaykh As'ad Shuqayri, was living there in exile. Ahmad returned to the family's home town of Acre in 1916. After studies there and in Jerusalem, he entered the American University of Beirut in 1926 but was expelled by French Mandate authorities the following year for Arab nationalist activities. Following his return to Palestine, he studied law and wrote for a newspaper; after graduating from college, he went to work in the law offices of the nationalist figure Awni Abd al-Hadi and became involved in the pan-Arab nationalist Istiqlal Party. During the 1930s,

Shuqayri put his legal skills to work on behalf of Palestinians charged by the British with security offenses. He fled Palestine for Cairo following the end of the Palestine Arab Revolt, returning only at the end of World War II. During the late 1940s, he was appointed head of the Arab Higher Committee's Arab Information Office in Washington and later headed the central Arab Information Office in Jerusalem. He fled to Lebanon during the 1948 fighting.

In exile, Shuqayri rose to become a leading Arab diplomatic figure during the 1950s and early 1960s. He served in the Syrian delegation to the United Nations from 1949 to 1950 before being appointed assistant general secretary of the League of Arab States (Arab League) from 1950 to 1957. He then served the government of Saudi Arabia as minister of state for UN affairs and as its UN representative until he was dismissed in 1963 for disagreeing with the Saudis over Egyptian intervention in the first Yemeni Civil War. Shuqayri began to play a major role in Palestinian nationalist affairs in September 1963, when he was asked to serve as the representative of Palestine at the Arab League. At the Arab summit of January 1964, he was asked to begin investigating the possibility of creating a uniquely Palestinian organization. That February, Shuqayri called for the convening of a Palestine National Council in East Jerusalem. At that meeting the Palestine Liberation Organization (PLO) was created, with Shuqayri as its head. The PLO sought to mobilize Palestinians politically and militarily. It established offices in several Arab countries and worked to raise men to serve in the PLO's fighting force, the Palestine Liberation Army, brigades of which were attached to the armies of Syria, Iraq, and Egypt.

Shuqayri and the PLO remained close to Egyptian president Gamal Abdel Nasser and the Arab regimes. Far from a revolutionary organization, the PLO consisted of conservatives and nationalists willing to work with the regimes in liberating Palestine in coordination with overall Arab strategies toward Israel. Younger Palestinian militants, such as those in the al-Fatah organization, believed instead in a policy of independent, guerrilla-style struggle. Israel's massive defeat of Arab forces during the Arab–Israel War of June 1967 rendered the policies of the Arab states and the PLO bankrupt in the eyes

of many Palestinians. For them, Shuqayri's elegant and sometimes heated rhetoric about liberation contrasted starkly with his failure and that of the established Arab elites. Associated with Nasser and the catastrophe of defeat, and facing criticism for his administration of the PLO, Shuqayri resigned on 24 December 1967.

He lived thereafter in Cairo until his opposition to the 1978 Camp David Accords prompted him to leave Egypt and move to Tunisia. He died in Amman, Jordan, while receiving medical treatment there on 25 February 1980, and was buried in the Jordan Valley just across the cease-fire line from his native country.

See also ABD AL-HADI FAMILY; ARAB HIGHER COMMITTEE (PALESTINE); ARAB–ISRAEL WAR (1967); CAMP DAVID ACCORDS (1978); FATAH, AL-; ISTIQLAL PARTY: PALESTINE; LEAGUE OF ARAB STATES; NASSER, GAMAL ABDEL; PALESTINE LIBERATION ORGANIZATION (PLO); PALESTINE NATIONAL COUNCIL; SHUQAYRI FAMILY.

Bibliography

Cobban, Helena. *The Palestinian Liberation Organization: People, Power, and Politics.* Cambridge, U.K.: Cambridge University Press, 1984.

Lesch, Ann Mosely. *Arab Politics in Palestine, 1917–1939: The Frustration of a Nationalist Movement.* Ithaca, NY: Cornell University Press, 1979.

MICHAEL R. FISCHBACH

SHUQAYRI, AS'AD AL-

See SHUQAYRI FAMILY

SHUQAYRI FAMILY

Prominent Palestinian family from Acre.

In the late nineteenth century, the Shuqayris emerged among the elites of Acre, one of the fastest-growing Palestinian cities of the time. They were landowners, Ottoman administrators, and religious officials. The family's prominence continued into the twentieth century. As'ad Shuqayri (1860–1940), mufti of Acre, served on the Shari'a Inquiries Court at Istanbul and as mufti for the Fourth Army during World War I. Opposed to the anti-Zionist movement, As'ad sold several hundred *dunums* of the family's land near Haifa to Zionists in the 1930s.

The family was associated with the Nashashibi-led National Defense party. Another member of the family, Dr. Anwar al-Shuqayri (?–1939), was assassinated by members of the opposing Husayni party in 1939. As'ad's son Ahmad Shuqayri (1908–1980), a lawyer, edited the newspaper *Mir'at al-Sharq* for two years and was a founder of the Istiqlal Party in 1931. In the 1940s Ahmad became known as a feisty nationalist, taking on several leading political roles. In the 1950s he represented Syria and Saudi Arabia at the United Nations and in the 1960s was chosen Palestinian delegate to the Arab League. He founded the Palestine Liberation Organization (PLO) in 1964.

See also ISTIQLAL PARTY: PALESTINE; SHUQAYRI, AHMAD.

Bibliography

Khalaf, Issa. *Politics in Palestine: Arab Factionalism and Social Disintegration, 1939–1948.* Albany: State University of New York Press, 1991.

Mandel, Neville J. *The Arabs and Zionism before World War I.* Berkeley University of California Press, 1976.

Muslih, Muhammad Y. *The Origins of Palestinian Nationalism.* New York: Columbia University Press, 1988.

ELIZABETH THOMPSON

SHURA

A consultative council.

The first recorded *shura* in Islamic history was called by Caliph Umar in 644 to choose his successor. The choice of later caliphs, although usually designated by their predecessor, was customarily ratified by a *shura* of family members and political leaders. The *shura* soon became generalized as an Islamic tradition of leaders consulting members of a community or family and asking them to reach consensus on troublesome issues.

The term *shura* has been used throughout the Middle East in the nineteenth and twentieth centuries to confer traditional legitimacy on a variety of modern representative councils. The Ottomans applied the term to many of the administrative councils created by the nineteenth-century Tanzimat reforms. Political groups in twentieth-century Arab states, particularly around the Gulf, have based their demands for representative bodies on injunctions in the Qur'an that men should conduct their affairs through *shura*, or consultation, with others.

Bibliography

Lapidus, Ira M. *A History of Islamic Societies,* 2d edition. Cambridge, U.K., and New York: Cambridge University Press, 2002.

Peterson, J. E. *The Arab Gulf States: Steps toward Political Participation.* New York: Praeger, 1988.

ELIZABETH THOMPSON

SHUSTER, W. MORGAN
[1877–1960]

Financial adviser to Persia in the early twentieth century.

W. Morgan Shuster, an American publisher, financier, and lawyer, was born in Washington, D.C. After attending Columbia College and Law School, Shuster worked for the War Department and the Cuban Customs Service from 1898 to 1901. He then served in a variety of posts in the Philippines from 1901 to 1909, after which he became a banker. From May 1911 to January 1912, he was treasurer general and financial adviser in Persia (now Iran). In 1915 Shuster became president of the Century Corporation in New York City, a post he held until 1933 when he became the president and chief executive officer of Appleton-Century-Croft. In an effort to rationalize Persia's finances, the Majles (legislature) hired Shuster upon the recommendation of the U.S. State Department and with the consent of Russia. Described by some as lacking in tact and courtesy, Shuster immediately organized a Treasury Gendarmerie to collect taxes, some from prominent Russian officials. Shuster chose Major C. B. Stokes, a devoted friend of Persia and former British military attaché, to head this new treasury police force. The Russian legation opposed this appointment, leading the British to post Stokes to India. Shuster's successful opposition to the Russian-supported restoration of Muhammad Ali as shah earned him additional enmity from that quarter.

The British also viewed Shuster's activities as hostile to Anglo-Russian understandings regarding

Persia, dating from the agreement of 1907. This opposition came to a head in November 1911 when Shuster ordered the confiscation of property owned by the former shah's brother, Shoa al-Saltana, then living in exile in Russia. The Russian consul general, claiming that Saltana's assets were owed to the Russian bank, sent an armed force often Russian-trained Persian cossacks to prevent Shuster from taking control of the property. Shuster responded with a larger force. This led to the Russian demand of 5 November for an apology; Persia apologized, but then Russia demanded Shuster's removal. For a time the Majles rejected this demand, and Persian nationalists attacked Russian troops in Tabriz and Rasht. There was also a boycott of Russian goods and the assassination of a pro-Russian minister. Russia responded with force, hanging a number of nationalists and sending troops to Tehran. In early December, the Majles again rejected the demand of Shuster's removal, but it finally yielded to Russian pressure and that of the powerful Bakhtiari tribe on 20 December. Shuster left Persia in January 1912 to pursue his other interests.

Bibliography

Shuster, W. Morgan. *The Strangling of Persia: A Story of the European Diplomacy and Oriental Intrigue that Resulted in the Denationalization of Twelve Million Mohammedans—A Personal Narrative.* New York: Century, 1912; reprint, Washington, DC: Mage Publishers, 1987.

DANIEL E. SPECTOR

SHUTTLE DIPLOMACY

See GLOSSARY

SIB, TREATY OF (1920)

Treaty between the sultanate and imamate in Oman.

A British-mediated undertaking signed 25 September 1920, by the rival sultanate and imamate governments in Oman. Ending seven years of warfare, it recognized both regimes' mutual autonomy and initiated a peace lasting until 1955. Subsequently, it was used unsuccessfully to justify the creation of a fully independent imamate in Oman's interior.

Bibliography

Landen, Robert G., *Oman since 1856: Disruptive Modernization in a Traditional Arab Society.* Princeton, NJ: Princeton University Press 1967.

ROBERT G. LANDEN

SIDARA

See GLOSSARY

SIDERA, ZINEB
[1963–]

London-based multimedia artist of Algerian origin.

Sidera's video installations and photographic work center on displacement and exile; they draw on her own experience being born in France to immigrant Algerian parents and moving to Britain. She trained at the Slade School of Art, Central Saint Martin's School of Art, and Royal College of Art in England, where she lives and works. Women, the veil, the gaze, and memory are some of the themes that emerge in her artistic exploration of the shifting subject positions that are part of the immigrant and exile experience, especially among Muslim and Arab women living in the West. Like many other artists from Arab countries living in exile, Sidera is particularly concerned with capturing the personal and political paradoxes and contradictions of living within and between cultures and finds the veil a useful way to do so. In many of her works, she examines the ways in which veiling has carried multiple meanings—from the history and legacy of the Algerian encounter with French colonialism to its place within individual and family life. Sidera also explores what she has called "the veiling of the mind"—the process of censorship and self-censorship within individuals and societies. Through photographs of herself veiled and veiling, or photographs of her own gaze (marked off by obscuring the edges of the work as if it were being seen by a veiled viewer), she challenges stereotypes of the submissive veiled woman while at the same time showing how the veil becomes a sign of backwardness and a vehicle of submission. The ambiguous meanings of visible and invisible veiling are a metaphor for her own restless experience of migration and exile, and for the complicated questions she has encountered therein.

See also ALGERIA: OVERVIEW; ART.

Bibliography

Lloyd, Fran, ed. *Contemporary Arab Women's Art: Dialogues of the Present.* London: WAL, 1999.

Lloyd, Fran, ed. *Displacement and Difference: Contemporary Arab Visual Culture in the Diaspora.* London: Saffron Books, 2001.

JESSICA WINEGAR

SIDON

Syrian seaport city.

Sidon (in Arabic, Sayda, Saida, or Sayida) was an ancient Mediterranean seaport city founded by the Phoenicians during the third millennium B.C.E. and ruled in turn by Assyrians, Babylonians, Persians, Alexandrian Greeks, Syrian Seleucids, Egyptian Ptolemys, Romans, Arabs, Crusaders, and Ottomans. Located on the coast of present-day southwestern Lebanon, its name derives from *sayd* (*fishing* in Semitic languages), referring to murex marine snail (*Murex brandaris*) fishing, from which the famous purple dye was extracted. Sidon is mentioned in ancient writings, including the Egyptian Amarna letters, inscriptions in the city of Ugarit, and in Homer's *Iliad*. The city's golden age was during the seventeenth century C.E., under Amir Fakhr al-Din II, when Sidon became a dynastic capital and a center for the dyeing and silk industries. Fakhr al-Din built castles, gardens, and inns to house foreign tradesmen. During this period, religious coexistence among Christians and Muslims was marked, and it is still reflected in Sidon's Great Mosque of Umar and the Maronite church, whose foundations date to Roman times. Rebuilt after a disastrous 1837 earthquake, Sidon remains a commercial, fishing, and agricultural market center for citrus fruit and vegetables. A petroleum refinery plant, light industry, and fishing provide important sources of livelihood for Sidon's 140,000 inhabitants (as of 2000), the majority of whom are Sunni Muslims.

GEORGE E. IRANI
UPDATED BY CHARLES C. KOLB

SIDQI, BAKR
[1885–1937]

Iraqi soldier and government official.

Bakr Sidqi carried out the first military coup in the period between the two world wars in the Arab Middle East. Sidqi fought in the Ottoman army in World War I and joined the Iraqi army in 1921. In August 1933, he gained national prominence as the commander of an army unit that killed some six hundred Assyrian villagers in Sumayl.

Sidqi's ruthlessness and decisiveness in putting down the Rumaytha Rebellion in 1935 served to enhance his prestige further. At the same time, he formed a secret alliance between himself and Yasin al-Hashimi's main rivals, Jama'at al-Ahali, the Ahali Group, led principally by Hikmat Sulayman. This culminated in a coup d'état, organized by Sidqi and Sulayman, which forced Yasin's government out of office on 29 October 1936. Sulayman became prime minister and appointed a largely Ahali or pro-Ahali cabinet, while Sidqi remained the power behind the regime. However, Sidqi's dictatorial style gradually lost him the confidence of al-Ahali, most of whom had resigned by May 1937. By this time, Sidqi had also managed to alienate many of his colleagues in the army, who organized his assassination at Mosul in northern Iraq on 11 August 1937.

See also AHALI GROUP; HASHIMI, YASIN AL-; SULAYMAN, HIKMAT.

PETER SLUGLETT

SIDQI, ISMA'IL
[1875–1949]

Egyptian politician and prime minister.

Isma'il Sidqi was born into a bourgeois family in Alexandria. His father was a high government official. Sidqi graduated from the School of Law in Cairo, and began a career in government. He was a colleague of Sa'd Zaghlul, the leader of the Wafd party favoring autonomy for Egypt, and was exiled with the other Wafdists in 1919, but soon broke with Zaghlul and joined the Liberal Constitutionalist party in 1924.

When King Fu'ad dismissed the Wafd government in 1930, Sidqi was asked to form a new government. Sidqi quickly renounced his membership in the Liberal Constitutionalist party, suspended parliament, instituted press censorship, and abrogated the 1923 constitution, replacing it with a more conservative constitution. He next formed his own political party, al-Shaʿb (The People), which he used to run in the 1931 elections. The Wafd and other liberal parties boycotted these elections in protest of Sidqi's autocratic rule. Throughout Sidqi's term as prime minister, there were frequent protest by nationalist politicians demanding the restoration of the 1923 constitution. Sidqi's policies, combined with the effects of the 1929 depression, made his rule very unpopular in Egypt, but the lack of unity among his opponents kept him in office.

By 1933, King Fu'ad felt that he had sufficiently weakened the Wafd and strengthened his own power that he could rule without Sidqi. Sidqi stepped down in September of 1933 and immediately joined the National Front, which called for the reinstatement of the 1923 constitution.

In February of 1946, Sidqi was again invited to form a government, which lasted until December of 1946, when he resigned on the grounds of bad health. During this year, Sidqi conducted negotiations with Britain about troop withdrawals. These negotiations were widely condemned by nationalists, particularly with regard to the threat to Egypt's position in the Sudan.

DAVID WALDNER

SIDRA, GULF OF

A body of water on the coast of Libya.

The Gulf of Sidra is located on the Mediterranean cost of Libya. Its coastline, 310 miles (500 km) of barren desert, forms an important geographical boundary between Libya's two major populated areas: Tripolitania, the western coastal region that shares many historical features with the Maghrib, and Cyrenaica, the eastern coastal region that has been more closely associated with the Arab states of the Middle East. This gulf then provides an important dividing line for the culture of the Maghrib and that of the Mashriq.

See also MAGHRIB.

STUART J. BORSCH

SILK

Fiber taken from the wrapping of silkworm cocoons.

Silk became an important textile product and luxury commodity in the Middle East from antiquity. Silk textiles came into the Middle East by trade from India and China. While Indian and Arab merchants sailed the Indian Ocean, Chinese merchants sent the fine cloth along the famous 4,000 mile (6,400 km) Silk Road—through central Asia and northern Iran to Europe. (Except for a few traders, rarely did any travel more than a short distance of the entire route.)

In the sixth century C.E., the Byzantines smuggled Chinese silk cocoons to Istanbul to begin their own mulberry groves and silkworm industry. Lebanon, Iran, and Iraq cultivated mulberry trees and silkworms as well. Parts of the Ottoman Empire, Bursa and Mount Lebanon, were important centers of silk-cocoon farming, and their fine silk textiles were loomed throughout the empire for both trade and imperial use. In the late nineteenth and early twentieth centuries, many Middle Eastern silk weavers lost their trade because of French intervention during the mandate period and the appearance of increasingly inexpensive silk goods that were being produced in the industrialized nations and in Asia for world markets.

See also OTTOMAN EMPIRE; TEXTILE INDUSTRY; TRADE.

Bibliography

Owen, Roger. *The Middle East in the World Economy, 1800–1914.* London and New York: Methuen, 1981.

Quataert, Donald. "The Silk Industry of Bursa, 1880–1914." In *Contributions à l'histoire economique et sociale de l'empire ottoman.* Louvain, Belgium: Editions Peeters, 1983.

"Silk Route." *Encyclopedia of Asian History.* 4 vols. New York: Scribner; London: Collier Macmillan, 1988.

ELIZABETH THOMPSON

SILVER, ABBA HILLEL
[1893–1963]

American Jewish leader.

Abba Hillel Silver was born in Lithuania. He was brought to the United States as a small child and raised in New York City's Yiddish-speaking immigrant milieu. He later studied at the University of Cincinnati and the Hebrew Union College, the seminary of U.S. Reform Judaism. In 1917, Silver assumed the pulpit of The Temple—Tifereth Israel in Cleveland, Ohio, a position he maintained until his death.

During the 1930s, Silver was among the first U.S. Jewish leaders to denounce the Nazi Party in Germany, and he joined with Rabbi Stephen S. Wise in organizing a countrywide anti-Nazi boycott. With the escalation of violence against the Jews of Central Europe, Silver emerged as a spokesman for U.S. Zionism's militant camp. He publicly challenged the Franklin Roosevelt administration to do more to intervene on behalf of European Jews. After the outbreak of World War II, he emerged as U.S. Zionism's undisputed leader.

Silver brought energy and vigor to Zionist lobbying efforts in Washington, D.C., during the 1940s. He campaigned tirelessly for bipartisan support of a Jewish state in postwar Palestine and skillfully deployed U.S. Jewry's political leverage to advance Zionist interests. His efforts to increase public pressure on the Roosevelt and Harry S. Truman administrations marked a dramatic shift in U.S. Jewish policymaking.

MIA BLOOM
UPDATED BY MARK A. RAIDER

SIMAVI, SEDAT
[1896–1953]

Turkish newspaper and magazine publisher.

Sedat Simavi, born in Istanbul, was the son of a governor of Samsun and was descended on both sides of his family from grand viziers of the Ottoman Empire. After graduating from Galatasaray Lycée, he worked as a teacher for a few years, then in 1917 made two of Turkey's earliest films, *The Claw* and *The Spy.* He began his publishing career in 1916, with magazines like the political-humor weekly *Hande* and, in 1919, the slick, progressive monthly women's magazine *Inci.* Simavi published a variety of popular magazines between 1918 and 1939 on women, fashion, health, humor, and cinema.

Simavi is best known for founding the daily newspaper *Hürriyet,* in 1948. The first of the boulevard-type newspapers, emphasizing slick style, sensation, and personal stories, it reached a circulation of

30,000 in its first year and by the 1950s was Turkey's largest paper (it had supported the winner—the new Democrat party—in the 1950 elections). While *Hürriyet*'s circulation approached 700,000 in the 1970s, it declined in the 1980s to about 450,000, with stiff competition from newer newspapers like Sabah and the Simavi-owned *Günaydin.* After Simavi's death, his son Erol became editor of the paper. With other family members, including grandson Sedat Simavi, he heads a publishing empire that includes several top daily newspapers and magazines.

See also HÜRRIYET.

Bibliography

Özkök, Ertuğrul. "The Turkish Press, 150 Years of Controversy." In *The Transformation of Turkish Culture,* edited by Günsel Renda and C. Max Kortepeter. Princeton, NJ: Kingston Press, 1986.

ELIZABETH THOMPSON

SINAI PENINSULA

Triangular peninsula between the Mediterranean and Red seas.

The Sinai is the desert area of northeast Egypt that forms the land bridge between Africa and Asia. In the north it is a flat and sandy dune sheet. Rugged mountains, including the al-Tih Plateau and Egma Escarpment as well as Sinai Massif surrounding Gabal Musa, dominate the central and southern regions. The peninsula is bordered on the east by the State of Israel and the Gulf of Aqaba and on the west by the Suez Canal and the Gulf of Suez. To the north it is bordered by the Mediterranean and in the south it comes to a point extending into the Red Sea. The Sinai is hot year round: it has average highs of about 90°F (32°C) and average lows of about 60°F (15°C), but temperatures tend to be lower in the mountains of the south.

The term *Sinai* is an ancient one, derived possibly from the name of the Semitic moon god Sin. The peninsula has generally come under Egyptian domination since ancient times. According to the Bible, it was the area in which the Israelites wandered for forty years after their deliverance from slavery in Egypt, and the site of Mount Sinai, where Moses received the Ten Commandments. During the reign of the Byzantine Emperor Justinian (527–565), the Eastern Orthodox Monastery of Saint Catherine was built at the foot of the legendary Mount Sinai, known as Gabal Musa (Mount Moses), in central Sinai. It remains an important attraction for pilgrims and tourists.

During the Middle Ages, the area was settled primarily by nomadic Bedouin tribes and loosely controlled by successive empires. It fell under the Ottoman Turks from 1517 until 1840. After Muhammad Ali broke with the Ottoman Empire, the Treaty of London gave Muhammad Ali control over Egypt, but the Sinai remained under Ottoman administration. The British Colonial Office exerted its own rule over Egypt from 1882 and clashed with the Ottomans over specific areas of the Sinai. They managed to establish the eastern boundary as a line from al-Arish or Rafah to Aqaba. A line from Rafah to Aqaba became the southern boundary of the British Mandate territory of Palestine from 1922 to 1948. It remained the international border between Egypt and the new state of Israel from 1949 through June 1967, when Israel occupied the Sinai. During Israel's occupation, Jewish settlements were established in the Sinai, two major air force bases were constructed, and the Alma Oil Field was discovered and developed.

Under the 1978 Camp David Accords, phased Israeli withdrawals were undertaken in 1980 and 1982. The territory of Sinai was divided between four demilitarized zones, three in Egypt and one on the Israeli side of the border. Under the Egypt-Israel Peace Treaty of 1979, the Multinational Force and Observers (MFO), headquartered in the area of al-Gorah in northeast Sinai, has been established to observe and verify force reductions in the eastern zone, and to ensure free navigation through the Strait of Tiran.

The Sinai is now primarily divided between the two Egyptian governorates of North and South Sinai, with portions of the region abutting the Suez Canal attached to the governorates of Bur Sa'id, Ismailiyya, and Suez. The population of the peninsula was estimated at about 38,000 in 1948, mainly Bedouin; it had grown to about 140,000 by 1970, with the development of petroleum and manganese deposits plus the influx of Palestinian refugees. By 1994 the population of the peninsula had grown to approximately 270,000. Aggressive plans for resettlement and development of the region, most importantly the Salam Canal project in the north, have contributed to a rapidly increasing population base.

Along the northeastern coast of North Sinai is the city of al-Arish, the largest settlement in the Sinai with a population of well over 75,000. Along the southern coasts, several small resorts have emerged as important local centers, including Taba, Nuwayba, and Dahab on the coast of the Gulf of Aqaba, and the port of Sharm al-Shaykh on the Red Sea coast at the extreme southern end of the peninsula. The latter has played host to several high-level negotiations and Middle East summits since the early 1990s. It is also renowned as a diving resort for its spectacular coral reef and variety of tropical fish. The environmental significance of the area was recognized with the creation of nearby Ras Muhammed National Park in 1983.

Bibliography

Greenwood, Ned H. *The Sinai: A Physical Geography.* Austin: University of Texas Press, 1997.

Saad el Din, Mursi; Taher, Ayman; and Romano, Luciano. *Sinai: The Site and the History.* New York: New York University Press, 1998.

Siliotti, Alberto. *Guide to Exploration of the Sinai.* Shrewsbury, U.K.: Swan Hill, 1994.

ELIZABETH THOMPSON
UPDATED BY PAUL S. ROWE

ŞINASI, İBRAHIM
[1826–1871]

Ottoman intellectual.

İbrahim Şinasi's father was an army officer for the Ottoman Empire, and Şinasi himself became an army scribe after completing elementary school. He learned French, and in 1849 he was sent to Europe by the leading Tanzimat reformer, Mustafa Reşid Paşa. There he was influenced by such luminaries as Ernest Renan and Albert Lamartine, but when he returned to Turkey, he was unable to advance in the government and devoted himself to literary endeavors. The author of several plays and books of poetry, he was also a prominent journalist and the editor of *Tasvir-i Efkar* (Description of ideas), which began in 1862 and acted as a clearinghouse for the liberal Young Ottoman ideas then in vogue. Like many of the Young Ottomans, Şinasi found himself at odds with the more autocratic Tanzimat officials of the day, including Ali Paşa and Fuad Paşa, and he was forced to leave Istanbul in 1864. He remained in Paris until his return to Istanbul shortly before his death.

Bibliography

Lewis, Bernard. *The Emergence of Modern Turkey,* 3d edition. New York: Oxford University Press, 2002.

Mardin, Serif. *The Genesis of Young Ottoman Thought: A Study in the Modernization of Turkish Political Ideas.* Princeton, NJ: Princeton University Press, 1962.

Shaw, Stanford J., and Shaw, Ezel Kural. *History of the Ottoman Empire and Modern Turkey.* 2 vols. Cambridge, U.K., and New York: Cambridge University Press, 1976–1977.

ZACHARY KARABELL

ŞIRKET-I HAYRIYE

Nineteenth-century Istanbul ferryboat company for the Bosporus Straits.

This was the first substantial joint-stock company established in the Ottoman Empire. It was founded in 1849 with two thousand shares and sixty thousand Turkish lire in capital with the support of Mustafa Reşid Paşa, one of the leaders of the mid-nineteenth-century reforms called Tanzimat. Created to provide ferry transport on the Bosporus in Istanbul, the company bought its boats for seven thousand Turkish lire each from a British company.

The company was promoted by Reşid Paşa as an example of new economic forms. To demonstrate the security of joint-stock companies, he encouraged several other government officials to invest in the ferryboat firm. Similar companies were soon founded in the 1850s, including the Bank-ı Osmani, the Aydin-İzmir Railroad, and Şirket-i Osmaniyyesi.

Bibliography

Lewis, Bernard. *The Emergence of Modern Turkey,* 3d edition. New York: Oxford University Press, 2002.

ELIZABETH THOMPSON

SIRRY, GAZBIA
[1925–]

Egyptian painter.

Gazbia Sirry (also Jadhbiya Sirri) is one of the most prominent and influential painters in Egypt. Sirry trained at the Faculty of Fine Arts in Cairo and received additional tutelage in Paris under Marcel Gromaire as well as at the Slade School of Art in London. A prolific painter as well as an art educator, she has held more than fifty solo exhibitions, received many prizes both in Egypt and abroad, and established a fund in her name to support young Egyptian artists. Throughout her career, she has been concerned with the fusion of the personal with the social or political, describing her work as embodying her "sensual relationship with color" and her "obsession with the human condition." Sirry was a member of the Group of Modern Art in the 1950s, which adopted the ideology of modernization. Sirry's contribution was to portray nationalist subjects (e.g., martyrdom against British occupation; peasant mothers) in a figurative style inspired by pharaonic representation and also international Expressionism. With the increasing problems of the Nasserist regime and the Arab defeat in the 1967 war, Sirry took on grim subjects such as imprisonment, grief, and racial discrimination. In the 1970s and 1980s, her concerns shifted to crowded urban environments and, in contrast, the sparse landscapes of the desert and the sea. The changes in Sirry's subjects and styles parallel the ebbs and flows in the general outlook of Egyptian intellectuals toward politics and society during her career.

See also EFFLATOUN, INJI; GENDER: GENDER AND EDUCATION.

Bibliography

El-Din, Mursi Saad. *Gazbia Sirry: Lust for Color.* Cairo: American University in Cairo Press, 1998.

Karnouk, Liliane. *Contemporary Egyptian Art.* Cairo: American University in Cairo Press, 1995.

JESSICA WINEGAR

SISCO, JOSEPH
[1919–]

U.S. diplomat at the heart of Henry Kissinger's shuttle diplomacy.

Educated in Illinois, Joseph Sisco gained his Ph.D. (University of Chicago) between periods of service in the army (1941–1945) and in the CIA (1950–1951). From 1951 to 1968 he worked at the State Department on UN affairs, then was appointed assistant secretary for Near East and South Asian affairs in 1968 and undersecretary of state for political affairs in 1974. By that time, Sisco was Secretary of State Henry Kissinger's key adviser on the Middle East, and third in seniority in the State Department. From 1968 to 1976 Sisco played a key role in attempts to mediate between Israel and neighboring Arab states, notably the series of interim peace settlements reached through U.S. *shuttle diplomacy*—a term Kissinger attributed to Sisco underscoring the role of American mediators flying between enemies that refuse to meet.

Sisco had not served in the Middle East and did not speak Arabic, and he began his term as assistant secretary for Near East affairs with a personnel reshuffle that some saw as marginalizing its "Arabist" diplomats. Both Arab and Israeli critics claimed that Sisco's attempts to forge realistic interpretations of UN Resolution 242 were biased, but the shuttles nevertheless proved crucial in the 1974 and 1975 disengagement agreements between Egypt and Israel.

Sisco later became a member of several company and university boards, president of American University, chairman of the American Academy of Diplomacy, and a partner in the management consultancy Sisco Associates. He coauthored a Trilateral Commission report on the peace process in 1981, and was a regular commentator on Mideast policy thereafter.

See also KISSINGER, HENRY.

Bibliography

American Enterprise Institute for Public Policy Research. *Middle East Negotiations: A Conversation with Joseph Sisco.* Washington, DC: Author, 1980.

Kissinger, Henry. *Years of Upheaval.* London: Phoenix, 1982.

Oren, Nissan. *Intellectuals in Politics.* Jerusalem: Magnes Press, 1984.

Sisco, Joseph. "Middle East—Progress or Lost Opportunity?" *Foreign Affairs* 61, 3 (1983): 611–640.

GEORGE R. WILKES

SISTAN AND BALUCHISTAN

Province in the southeast of Iran.

The formerly separate provinces of Sistan and Baluchistan united in 1959 to form one administrative unit (Baluchistan is also a contiguous Pakistani province). The region is fertile but has a hot, arid climate. The Helmand is the principal river and the source for agriculture in the region. Major cities include Zahedan (the capital), Zabol, and Iranshahr. Although each province has a separate but intertwined history, the ethnic groups residing in each are distinct. The population of Baluchistan is composed mainly of Baluchi tribespeople who speak Baluchi, a western Iranian language now heavily influenced by eastern regional languages. Standard Persian is more common in Sistan, but the eastern language known as Sistani is still spoken to some extent. According to the 1996 census, the population of the combined province was 1,722,579.

See also BALUCHISTAN.

Bibliography

Barthold, W. *An Historical Geography of Iran,* edited by C. E. Bosworth, translated by Svat Soucek. Princeton, NJ: Princeton University Press, 1984.

PARVANEH POURSHARIATI

SISTANI, ALI AL-

[1930–]

Leading Shi'ite cleric in Iraq.

The most senior Shi'ite cleric in Iraq by early 2004, Ali al-Husayni al-Sistani is actually an Iranian who, despite having lived in Iraq for decades, speaks Arabic with a heavy Persian accent. Al-Sistani was born in Mashhad, Iran, to a family of well-known Shi'ite religious figures. His father was Mohammad Baqir, and his grandfather was a famous cleric known as Sayyid Ali. Al-Sistani studied theology in Qom, Iran, and first traveled to al-Najaf, Iraq, in 1951 to continue his studies. He lived in al-Najaf for most of the rest of his life.

By 1960 he had been certified as a *mujtahid,* one of the few Shi'a permitted to interpret Islamic practice. Al-Sistani eventually obtained the rank of grand ayatullah (*ayatullah uzma*). After the death of Grand Ayatullah Abu al-Qasim al-Kho'i (1899–1992) in 1992, al-Sistani was the unquestioned leading Shi'ite in Iraq. He also became the sold surviving *marja al-taqlid* (source of imitation) for Shi'a worldwide.

The breakdown of security in Iraq following the American invasion in March 2003 led to the death of two potential rivals for influence among Iraq's Shi'a. Ayatullah Muhammad Baqir al-Hakim (1939–2003), leader of the Supreme Council for the Islamic Revolution in Iraq, returned from two decades of exile in Iran only to be killed in a massive bombing in al-Najaf in August 2003. Another potential rival was killed earlier in April 2003: Abd al-Majid al-Kho'i (1962–2003), son of the Grand Ayatullah Abu al-Qasim al-Kho'i.

The clear leading figure among Iraqi Shi'a by late 2003, al-Sistani was in a position to influence the United States' attempt to politically reconstruct the country. Unlike some of his contemporaries, including Iran's late Ayatollah Ruhollah Khomeini, with whom he studied when they were both young, al-Sistani called for maintaining the separation of politics and religion. Although he made it clear that he wanted U.S. forces to leave the country as soon as possible, he urged the Shi'a not to resist them. Since then he has pointedly refused to meet with U.S. government representatives, but has granted audiences to others from his secluded residence. It was his opinion that prompted the U.S. to allow the UN a greater role in Iraq's reconstruction as well as to allow a constitution to be written prior to elections (which he urged be held as soon as possible). Al-Sistani's influence was also what prompted a last-minute delay in the signing of the new, interim Iraqi constitution in early March 2004.

See also KHOMEINI, RUHOLLAH; MARJA AL-TAQLID; NAJAF, AL-; QOM; WAR IN IRAQ (2003).

MICHAEL R. FISCHBACH

SITRA

One of the thirty-three islands in the Bahrain archipelago.

Sitra lies in the Persian (Arabian) Gulf, just off the northeast corner of Bahrain, the main island, to which it is connected by a short bridge. On Sitra are located the petroleum loading terminal and tank farm belonging to the Bahrain Petroleum Company, as well as a small number of date palm gardens and a limited amount of cropland at the northern end of its eleven square miles (28 sq. km).

Bibliography

Clarke, Angela. *The Islands of Bahrain: An Illustrated Guide to Their Heritage.* Manama: Bahrain Historical and Archaeological Society, 1981.

FRED H. LAWSON

SITT

See GLOSSARY

SIVAS CONFERENCE (1919)

Convened (4–11 September 1919) to resist plans of the Triple Entente to dismember the Ottoman Empire; a significant step in the progression of events leading to the Turkish revolution.

The official communiqué issued by the Sivas Conference was the first Turkish declaration against the partitioning of lands under Ottoman sovereignty that had taken place when the Mudros Armistice was signed. The same document summoned the sultan to call for a general election and announced the creation of the Association for the Defense of the Rights of Anatolia and Rumelia, whose Representative Committee was designated to act as a provisional government in Anatolia until May 1920.

AHMET KUYAS

SIWA OASIS

Oasis in northwest Egypt.

The Siwa oasis, 186 miles (300 km) west of Marsa Matruh, had an estimated population of 23,000 in 2002. In ancient times Siwa was the seat of the oracle of Jupiter Ammon, visited by Alexander the Great in 331 B.C.E. It has historically served as both Egypt's western boundary and the easternmost area inhabited by Berbers. The spoken Siwan dialect is a Berber language heavily influenced by Arabic. In the nineteenth century it was one of the centers of the Sanusi Order, and some fighting took place there during World War I. The people of Siwa pride themselves on their differences from other Egyptians and their ability to resolve disputes without resort to bloodshed. The oasis is a center for date palm agriculture. Formerly isolated, it has become accessible by motor transport and is now being developed for tourism. Siwa is also the name of a town in the southern part of the oasis.

See also SANUSI ORDER.

Bibliography

Fakhry, Ahmed. *Siwa Oasis.* Cairo: American University in Cairo Press, 1990.

Sears, Constance S. "The Oasis of Siwa: Visited and Revisited." *Newsletter of the American Research Center in Egypt* 165 (spring/summer 1994): 1–10.

Souryal, Sam S. "Social Control in the Oasis of Siwa: A Study in Natural Justice and Conflict Resolution." *International Criminal Justice Review* 11 (2001): 82–103.

Vivian, Cassandra. *Siwa Oasis: Its History, Sites, and Crafts.* Ma'adi, Egypt, 1991.

ARTHUR GOLDSCHMIDT

SLAVE TRADE

The buying and selling of humans for servitude was an old tradition in the Middle East as in many other parts of the world.

Since antiquity, slavery was an integral part of the various societies that inhabited the Middle East. Men, women, and children were enslaved within these lands or imported into them from neighboring and faraway regions. From the early sixteenth to the early twentieth centuries, the Middle East was part of the Ottoman Empire, in which slavery was legal and the slave trade active. The traffic in slaves was substantially reduced toward the end of the nineteenth century, and slavery died out in most of the Middle East during the first decade of the twentieth. In certain parts of Arabia, the practice lingered on well into the second half of this century, and various forms of slavery continue to exist even today.

"Slavery" in Middle Eastern—and other—societies can be difficult to define. Some attempts to answer the question "who is a slave?" have resulted in "one whose labor is controlled and whose freedom is withheld," a person "in a state of legal and actual servility or [who is] of slave origins," or a "natally alienated and generally dishonored person" under "permanent, violent domination." In Islamic legal terms, slavery grants one person ownership over another person, which means that the owner has rights to the slave's labor, property, and sexuality and that the slave's freedoms are severely restricted. But in sociocultural terms, slavery sometimes meant high social status, or political power, for male slaves in the military and bureaucracy (Mamluks and *kuls*) and female slaves in elite harems. Even ordinary domestic slaves were often better fed, clothed, and protected than many free men and women. In any event, slavery was an important, albeit involuntary, channel of recruitment and socialization into the elite and a major—though forced—means of linking into patronage networks.

Slavery gradually became a differentiated and broadly defined concept in many Islamic societies since the introduction of military slaves into the Abbasid Caliphate in the ninth century. In the Ottoman Empire, military-administrative servitude, better known as the *kul* system, coexisted with other types of slavery: harem (quite different from Western fantasy), domestic, and agricultural (on a rather limited scale). While the latter types of slavery remained much the same until late in the nineteenth century, the *kul* system underwent profound changes.

From its inception, the *kul* system was nourished on periodical levies of the unmarried, able-bodied, male children of the sultan's Orthodox Christian subjects, mostly from the Balkans. This child levy was known as the *devşirme*. The children were reduced to slavery, converted to Islam, and rigorously socialized at the palace school into various government roles, carrying elite status. However, freeborn Muslims gradually entered government service, and the *kul* system evolved to accommodate this change. Ultimately, the child levy was abandoned during the seventeenth century, the palace school lost its monopoly on the reproduction of military-administrative slaves, and a new, *kul*-type recruitment-cum-socialization pattern came to prevail.

With the evolution of the *kul* system, the classification of *kuls* as slaves was gradually becoming irrelevant. Ottoman officials of *kul* origins and training held elevated, powerful positions with all rights, privileges, and honors, and cases in which the sultan confiscated their property or took their life became increasingly rare. Whereas *kuls* and non-*kuls* were subject to the sultan's "whims" to the same extent, the intimacy and mutual reliance of the master-slave relationship often provided the *kul* with greater protection than that enjoyed by free officials. Harem women of slave origins were in much the same predicament, playing a major role in the reproduction of the Ottoman elite. Toward the nineteenth century, the servility of persons in the *kul*/harem category becomes more a symbol of their high status and less a practical or legal disability. All that has led some scholars to question the very use of the term "slaves" for such men and women. In any event, the Hatt-i Serif of Gülhane of 1839 freed government officials from the last vestiges of servility attached to their status.

In the Ottoman Middle East, and with local modifications also in other Muslim societies, there was a continuum of various degrees of servility rather than a dichotomy between slave and free. At one end of that continuum were domestic and agricultural slaves, the "real slaves" in Ottoman society, while at the other were officeholders in the army and bureaucracy, with little to tie them to actual slavery. In between, but close to officeholders and far from domestic and agricultural slaves, came officials of slave origins (*kul*-type) and then harem ladies of slave origins.

The overwhelming majority of the slaves living in the Middle East during the Ottoman period were female, black, and domestic; they served in menial jobs in households across a broad social spectrum. A smaller number of white female slaves also worked in similar circumstances, as did a number of black and white male slaves. African male slaves were employed in the Red Sea, Persian/Arabian Gulf, and Indian Ocean as pearl divers, oarsmen, and crew members in sailboats, in Arabia as agricultural laborers (in date, coffee, and other plantations) and outdoor servants, and in Egypt as cotton pickers in the 1860s. African men were used as soldiers in scattered instances in Yemen and other parts of Arabia, as in Egypt where the experiment of Muhammad Ali Pasha to recruit Sudanese slave soldiers failed. *Kul* and harem slaves were a relatively small minority among Middle Eastern slaves in the nineteenth century.

At the time, a fairly steady stream of about eleven thousand to thirteen thousand slaves per year entered the region from central Africa and the Sudan, from western Ethiopia, and from Circassia, Abkhazia, and Georgia. They were brought in by caravan and boat via the Sahara desert routes, the Ethiopian plateau, the Red Sea, the Nile river valley, the Mediterranean, the Persian Gulf, the Black Sea, and the pilgrimage routes to and from Arabia. After raids, sales, and resales, they reached their final destinations in the great urban centers of the Middle East, where they were sold in markets or in private homes of slave dealers.

Whereas slaveholding was still legal at the beginning of the twentieth century, the slave trade into the region had already been prohibited by law for several decades. The traffic in Africans and Caucasians practically died down, although it would pick up from time to time on a small scale. Slavery was gradually being transformed into free forms of service-cum-patronage, such as raising freeborn children (mostly female) in the household, socializing them into lower- or upper-class roles—as talent and need determined—and later marrying them off and setting them up in life. Ottoman elite culture was articulating a negative attitude toward the practice and gradually disengaging from it on moral grounds. This was a significant development, given the fact that slavery enjoyed Islamic legitimacy and wide social acceptance in the Middle East and that, except for cases of cruelty and ill-usage, it was a matter over which no serious moral debate ever arose.

The profound change that occurred was part of a major reform program introduced into the Middle East during the nineteenth century. Much of this happened during the Tanzimat (loosely covering the 1830s to the 1880s), generally regarded as a period of change in many areas of Ottoman life, although it is not certain how deeply the reforms affected the over-whelming majority of the population or even the peripheral groups within the Ottoman elite. Visible changes in the army, the bureaucracy, the economy, law and justice, education, communication, transportation, and public health went along with the reinvigoration of central authority. This was the work of a strongly motivated, Ottoman-centered group of reformers, who implemented their own program and political agenda and were not merely the tools of Western influence. While the government came to possess more efficient means of repression, its reforms also sowed the seeds of political change, giving rise to a strong constitutional movement, although the extent to which Western ideas—not just technology and fashion—were assimilated into Middle Eastern culture is still under debate.

Having abolished slavery by the end of the first third of the nineteenth century, the powers of Europe now turned their zeal to slavery in the Americas. But in the 1840s, the British government and public opinion were already beginning to take an interest in the abolition of slavery in the Ottoman Middle East. Attempts to induce Istanbul to adopt measures to that effect soon proved futile. Instead—and as an alternative method that would ultimately choke slavery for want of supply—a major effort was launched to suppress the slave trade into the region. The essence of that long-term British drive was to extract from the Ottomans, on humanitarian grounds, edicts forbidding the trade in Africans and Caucasians. The implementation of such edicts was then carefully monitored by British diplomatic and commercial representatives throughout the Middle East and reported back to London. In turn, London would press Istanbul to enforce the edicts, and so on.

This pattern yielded the prohibition of the slave trade in the Gulf in 1847, the temporary prohibition of the traffic in Circassians and Georgians in 1854–1855, the general prohibition of the African slave trade in 1857, the Anglo-Egyptian convention for the suppression of the slave trade in 1877, and the Anglo-Ottoman one in 1880. The campaign reached its climax in the Brussels Act against the slave trade, which the Ottoman government signed in 1890. From the mid-1850s onward, Caucasian slavery and slave trade were excluded from the realm of Anglo-Ottoman relations. In that area, the Ottomans initiated some major changes, acting alone and according to their own views.

One of the most important factors that shaped Ottoman policy toward Caucasian slavery was the large number of Circassian refugees—estimates run from 500,000 to 1 million—who entered Ottoman territory from the mid-1850s to the mid-1860s. That Russian-forced migration contained about 10 percent unfree agricultural population, which put the question of non-African slavery into a different perspective. Increased tensions between refugee owners and slaves, at times causing violence and disturbance of public order, induced the Ottoman government in 1867 to design a special program for slaves who wished to obtain their freedom. Using an Islamic legal device, the government granted the slaves the land they were cultivating in order to purchase manu-mission from their own masters.

In 1882, the authorities moved further in the same method to facilitate the conscription of Circassian and Georgian slaves. Such a step was necessary because only free men could be drafted into the army. Measures were also taken from the mid-1860s onward to restrict the traffic in Circassian and Georgian children, mostly young girls. Thus, by the last decade of the nineteenth century, the trade in Caucasian slaves was considerably reduced. The remaining demand was maintained only by the harems of the imperial family and the households of well-to-do elite members. The imperial harem at the time contained about 400 women in a wide array of household positions quite different from those consigned to them by Western fantasy. Those harems also continued to employ eunuchs, and as late as 1903, the Ottoman family alone owned 194 of them. In the nineteenth century, a perceived decline occurred in their political influence, both as individuals and as a distinct corps in court politics. Whether officially abolished by the 1908 revolution, or only later by the new Turkish republic, Ottoman slavery died piecemeal, not abruptly, with the end of the empire.

Except for the issue of equality for non-Muslims, the call for the abolition of slavery was perhaps the most sensitive and culturally loaded topic processed in the Tanzimat period. Although it was rarely debated in the open, this was a matter of daily and personal concern, for both the public and private spheres of elite life were permeated by slaves on all levels. Faced with British diplomatic pressure to suppress the slave trade into the Middle East and with the zeal of Western abolitionism, Ottoman reformers and thinkers responded on both the political and the ideological planes. However, that response came when slavery was already on the wane, doomed to disappear with other obsolete institutions.

See also MAMLUKS; TANZIMAT.

Bibliography

Baer, Gabriel. "Slavery and Its Abolition." In *Studies in the Social History of Modern Egypt*, by Gabriel Baer. Chicago: University of Chicago Press, 1969.

Lewis, Bernard. *Race and Slavery in the Middle East: An Historical Enquiry*. New York: Oxford University Press, 1990.

Peirce, Leslie P. *The Imperial Harem: Women and Sovereignty in the Ottoman Empire*. New York: Oxford University Press, 1993.

Toledano, Ehud R. "The Imperial Eunuchs of Istanbul: From Africa to the Heart of Islam." *Middle Eastern Studies* 20, no. 3 (1984): 379–390.

Toledano, Ehud R. "Ottoman Concepts of Slavery in the Period of Reform (1830s to 1880s)." In *Breaking the Chains: Slavery, Bondage and Emancipation in Modern Africa and Asia*, edited by Martin A. Klein. Madison: University of Wisconsin Press, 1993.

Toledano, Ehud R. *The Ottoman Slave Trade and Its Suppression, 1840–1890*. Princeton, NJ: Princeton University Press, 1982.

Toledano, Ehud R. "Slave Dealers, Women, Pregnancy, and Abortion: The Story of a Circassian Slave-Girl in Mid-Nineteenth-Century Cairo." *Slavery and Abolition* 2, no. 1 (1980): 53–68.

EHUD R. TOLEDANO

SMILANSKY, MOSHE
[1874–1953]

Israeli author, peace advocate, and agricultural pioneer.

Moshe Smilansky was born in Kiev province in Russian Ukraine to a family of farmers. He emigrated to Palestine in 1891 and helped to found the Hadera settlement, farming in various places before settling in Rehovot in 1893. There he spent the remainder of his life as a citrus plantation owner, writer, and agricultural leader (heading the Histadrut ha-Ikarim, or Farmers' Association). A disciple of Ahad Ha-Am, he took issue with Theodor Herzl's political Zionism and sought coexistence with Arabs throughout his career, gaining prominence among the binationalists after the 1936 Arab uprising.

Smilansky's Hebrew stories depicting Arab life, written under the pseudonym Khawaja Musa, were collected in a single volume entitled *Benei Arav* (1964; Arab sons). Through his writing, Smilansky hoped to show the benefits of cooperation between Arabs and Jewish pioneers. His most famous works on the pioneers are the six-volume *Perakim be-Toledot ha-Yishuv* (1959; Chapters in the history of the Yishuv) and the four-volume *Mishpahat ha-Adamah* (1943–1953; Family of the soil). His works were highly criticized at the time, but have had greater impact on students of Hebrew literature since. His son is the noted writer S. Yizhar.

Bibliography

Domb, Risa. "The Arab in Fact and Fiction as Reflected in the Works of Moshe Smilansky (1874–1953)." *Jewish Quarterly* 29, no. 4 (1982): 3–7.

Ramras-Rauch, Gila. *The Arab in Israeli Literature*. Bloomington: Indiana University Press, 1989.

ANN KAHN
UPDATED BY GEORGE R. WILKES

SNEH, MOSHE
[1909–1972]

Israeli politician and statesman.

Born in Poland where he became an active Zionist, Moshe Sneh emigrated to Israel in 1940. He was active against British anti-Zionist policy, and was chief of the Haganah high command from 1941 to 1946. Between 1945 and 1946 Sneh was a member of the Jewish Agency's executive committee, but he resigned in 1946 when they decided to refrain from further sabotage against the British occupation forces in Palestine. He served as director of the Jewish Agency's European office from 1946 to 1947. Sneh was also a physician active in the Zionist movement in its early years, and later in the MAPAM party. From 1949 to 1965 he was a member of the Knesset from Maki, the Israeli communist party, and editor of its daily newspaper. In the Knesset Sneh advocated self-determination for the Palestinian nation and recognition of Palestinian rights to a state of their own. After being out of the Knesset from 1965 to 1969 he was reelected in 1969 and served until his death in 1972.

See also ISRAEL: POLITICAL PARTIES IN.

Bibliography

Ben-Gurion, David. *Israel: A Personal History*. New York: Funk and Wagnalls, 1971.

WALTER F. WEIKER
UPDATED BY GREGORY S. MAHLER

SOBOL, YEHOSHUA

[1939–]

Israeli playwright.

The plays of Yehoshua Sobol reflect common Israeli themes, including the Holocaust, the Zionist state-building enterprise, and the Arab-Israel conflict. A graduate of the Sorbonne in Paris, Sobol has worked as artistic director of the Haifa Municipal Theater since 1984, and most of his plays have premiered there. His most famous work is *Ghetto* (1984), one of three related plays about the Vilna ghetto. Other works include *Soul of a Jew* (1982), *The Days to Come* (1971), and *Shooting Magda*, or *The Palestinian Girl* (1985). Sobol has made it his artistic mission to explore the problematic roots of the Zionist project, as he did most forcefully in his 1977 production, *Night of the Twentieth*, and to show the consequences for both Jews and Arabs of succumbing to political interests rather than fulfilling nationalist ideals. Many of his later plays, such as *Kefar* (1996), have also probed the difficulties of trying to assimilate personal lives into paradigms created by historical developments. Looking at history as a way of examining contemporary Israeli society, Sobol is particularly interested in the intersection between the personal—even the emotional—and the political. His plays emphasize that while Zionist ideals could not extinguish personal desires, they did complicate the formation of strong, secure individual identities. *Almah* (1999) extends his focus on individual personality by meditating on the life of Alma Mahler Gropius Werfel and her torturous efforts to form an authentic, creative public life. Sobol's plays, always sensitive to the morally problematic compromises imposed upon by history and circumstance, have been produced all over the world and in many languages.

Bibliography

Abramson, Glenda. *Drama and Ideology in Modern Israel.* Cambridge, U.K.: Cambridge University Press, 1998.

Ben-Zvi, Linda, ed. *Theater in Israel.* Ann Arbor: University of Michigan Press, 1996.

Sobol, Yehoshua. *Ghetto,* translated from the Hebrew by Miriam Shlesinger. Tel Aviv: Institute for the Translation of Hebrew Literature, 1986.

Taub, Michael. *Israeli Holocaust Drama.* Syracuse, NY: Syracuse University Press, 1996.

Taub, Michael. *Modern Israeli Drama in Translation.* Portsmouth, NH: Heinemann, 1992.

JULIE ZUCKERMAN
UPDATED BY DONNA ROBINSON DIVINE

SOCIAL DEMOCRATIC PARTY OF AZERBAIJAN

Political party in Iranian Azerbaijan.

The Firqa-ye Ijtima'iyun-e Ammiyun (Social democratic party), also called *Mujahid,* was active mainly in Iranian Azerbaijan. It may have been an offshoot of the Adalat (Justice) party, a nominally social democratic, but actually anticolonial, organization formed in 1904/05 by Azerbaijanis in Baku (on the Caspian Sea) who were involved in the social democratic party Hümmet (Endeavor). Adalat was created for workers from Iran employed in the Baku petroleum industry.

In August or September 1906, members of the founding committee of the party established a "secret center" in Tabriz, then cells in Ardebil, Rasht, and Enzeli; these organizations apparently remained under the direction of a central committee in Baku. The party program demanded a constitution in Iran, ministerial responsibility to the Majles (Iran's legislature), establishment of universal suffrage, and civil liberties. It pointed to Qur'anic precedents and the example of "every civilized state of Europe and Asia."

The party was apparently suppressed around 1909 but served as a model to the later Communist Tudeh Party.

See also ADALAT PARTY; TUDEH PARTY.

Bibliography

Bayat, Mangol. *Iran's First Revolution: Shi'ism and Constitutional Revolution of 1905–1909.* New York: Oxford University Press, 1991.

Swietochowski, Tadeusz, and Collins, Brian C. *Historical Dictionary of Azerbaijan.* Lanham, MD: Scarecrow Press, 1999.

AUDREY L. ALTSTADT

SOCIAL DEMOCRATIC POPULIST PARTY

Center-left political party in Turkey, 1985 to 1998.

The Social Democratic Populist Party (Sosyal Demokrat Halkçi Partisi, or SHP) was formed in November 1985 as a result of the merger of two left-of-center parties, the Social Democratic Party (SDP), founded in 1983 by Erdal İnönü, and Necdet Calp's Populist Party, which also was founded in 1983. In the parliamentary elections of November 1983 the Populist Party had won the second largest number of seats in the Turkish Grand National Assembly. The SDP had been banned from participating in those elections, but the National Security Council did allow it take part in the 1984 local elections, and it emerged at the local level as the main opposition to the ruling Motherland Party of Turgut Özal. The Populist Party received less than 10 percent of the vote in the local elections and thus won no seats on the municipal councils, although it remained the main opposition to the Motherland Party within the National Assembly. Because they espoused a similar political ideology and appealed to the same voting constituency, the two parties joined to form the SHP. İnönü became the chair of the SHP, which presented itself as an heir to the Republican People's Party (CHP), which had been founded by his father, İsmet İnönü, and Mustafa Kemal Atatürk. In the 1991 parliamentary elections the SHP emerged as the third largest party in the National Assembly, with 88 seats. Subsequently, it joined with the True Path Party of Süleyman Demirel as the junior partner in a coalition government. The SHP's participation in this coalition became controversial because a small group of SHP deputies charged that the True Path Party sanctioned civil-rights abuses, especially in the Kurdish areas, and that these violations compromised democratic practices and also Turkey's chances for membership in the European Union. Most prominent among these dissidents was Deniz Baykal, who left the SHP in 1992 and announced that he was reactivating the CHP. Although several of its deputies in parliament defected to the CHP, the SHP remained in the coalition government until the 1996 parliamentary elections, when it lost many seats. Subsequently, the SHP entered into negotiations with the CHP and merged with it following the February 1997 "soft coup" by the military against the Refah Party–dominated coalition government of Prime Minister Necmeddin Erbakan.

See also ATATÜRK, MUSTAFA KEMAL; DEMIREL, SÜLEYMAN; ERBAKAN, NECMEDDIN; İNÖNÜ, ERDAL; MOTHERLAND PARTY; NATIONAL SE-CURITY COUNCIL (TURKEY); ÖZAL, TURGUT; REFAH PARTISI; REPUBLICAN PEOPLE'S PARTY (RPP); TRUE PATH PARTY; TURKISH GRAND NATIONAL ASSEMBLY.

Bibliography

Hooglund, Eric. "Government and Politics." In *Turkey: A Country Study*, edited by Helen Chapin Metz. Washington, DC: GPO for Library of Congress, 1996.

FRANK TACHAU
UPDATED BY M. HAKAN YAVUZ

SOCOTRA

Largest island of Yemen.

Measuring 1,200 square miles, Socotra (also Suqutra) Island is located in the Arabian Sea, about 500 miles from Aden and less than 200 miles from Somalia. The sparsely populated island has a mountainous interior and most of its population engages in farming or fishing; the most striking feature of this isolated place is its biodiversity and the great number of unique flora and fauna. The ruler of the Mahra Sultanate of Qishn and Socotra resided there under British rule during much of the nineteenth and twentieth centuries. The island became a part of South Yemen in 1967 and, with Yemeni unification in 1990, it became a part of the Republic of Yemen (ROY). Given its location near the sea lanes, Socotra was long thought to be of strategic value by Western imperial powers. During the latter half of the Cold War, South Yemen allowed the Soviet Union to maintain a submarine base and other military facilities there; Russia continues to maintain a modest naval presence. During the late 1990s there were rumors about a deal between the United States and the ROY over military facilities on the island, but the complicated, if not strained, relations between the two countries, beginning with the bombing of the U.S.S. *Cole* in Aden in 2000, squelched this talk. The considerable activities regarding Socotra now focus on its development as a tourist destination featuring and protecting its unique biodiversity.

See also YEMEN.

Bibliography

Miller, Anthony G., and Morris, M. J. *An Ethnoflora of the Socotra Archipelago*. Edinburgh: Royal Botanic Garden, 2004.

Wranik, Wolfgang. *A Field Guide to the Fauna of the Socotra Archipelago.* Rostock, Ger.: University of Rostock, 2004.

ROBERT D. BURROWES

SOHEYLI, ALI
[?–1954]

Iranian politician.

Ali Soheyli was born in Tabriz and studied at the military school in Tehran. After several cabinet positions, he was named minister of foreign affairs in 1937 and served three times as prime minister during the tenure of Mohammad Reza Shah Pahlavi. In 1947, because of pressure from the parliamentary faction loyal to Mohammad Mossadegh, Soheyli, a royalist, was put on trial. He was charged with mishandling of public funds, illegal intervention in elections in the south of the country, disrespect for the constitutional provision of free speech and a free press, and conspiracy against the nationalist government. After being acquitted of all charges, Soheyli resumed political activity as a minister without portfolio. Famous for his skill in handling foreign diplomats in Iran, he enjoyed amicable relations with both the Russian and the British legations in Tehran. In 1953, he sought appointment as prime minister but failed to get it. The shah appointed him ambassador to Britain, where he died of leukemia.

See also MOSSADEGH, MOHAMMAD; PAHLAVI, MOHAMMAD REZA.

NEGUIN YAVARI

SOKOLOW, NAHUM
[1859–1936]

Hebrew journalist, author, Zionist diplomat and leader.

Born and educated in Poland, Nahum Sokolow was a journalist for the Hebrew language newspaper *ha-Tzfira,* becoming editor in 1885. Sokolow published numerous books on the sciences, Hebrew literature, and the historical roots of Zionism, among other topics, writing in six languages. He was a strong supporter of Theodor Herzl and a principal spokesman for Zionism in eastern Europe. He was appointed secretary-general of the World Zionist Organization (WZO) in 1906, whereupon he established the WZO's official newspaper, *ha-Olam.*

In 1911 Sokolow was given the political portfolio on the Zionist Executive, and he traveled extensively as a diplomat for the Zionist cause, meeting with leaders throughout Europe and with Arab leaders in Lebanon and Syria. He chaired the committee that drafted the Balfour Declaration in 1917, and in 1919 led the Zionist delegation to the Paris Peace Conference. In 1929 he became chairman of the expanded Zionist Executive. At the 17th Zionist Congress in 1931, Chaim Weizmann was defeated in his reelection bid for the presidency of the WZO after a bitter challenge from Vladimir Jabotinsky and the Revisionists. Sokolow, a broadly respected Zionist leader, took Weizmann's place and was reelected president at the 18th Congress in 1933. When the Revisionists withdrew from the WZO in 1935, Weizmann resumed the presidency. Sokolow died in London the following year.

See also BALFOUR DECLARATION (1917); WEIZMANN, CHAIM; WORLD ZIONIST ORGANIZATION (WZO).

Bibliography

Laqueur, Walter. *A History of Zionism.* New York: Schocken, 2003.

PIERRE M. ATLAS

SOLTANI, ABDELLATIF
[1904–1983]

Islamic religious scholar in Algeria.

Shaykh Abdellatif Soltani was a highly respected, independent religious scholar and a staunch critic of the socialist orientation of the postindependence Algerian regime. Soltani was born in 1904 in Biskra, northeast of Algiers, and received a religious education at the Zaytouna mosque in Tunisia. He became closely associated with the Islamic reformer Abdelhamid Ibn Badis, the founder of the Association of Algerian Scholars, which was established in 1931 to promote Arabic and Islamic teachings and to reassert the Algerian identity. Soltani worked as an educator and as an imam in a number of mosques that became bastions of Islamic activism. He taught religious subjects to young Algerians, some of whom later became leaders of the Islamic Salvation Front, the main Islamic opposition party in Algeria.

In 1974 Soltani published a book, *Mazdaqism Is the Origin of Socialism,* that was published in Morocco and banned in Algeria, in which he scathingly criticized the country's ruling elite and secular intellectuals for their deviation from the true Islamic principles and for their adoption instead of foreign ideologies. He also criticized the regime for its intolerance of dissent and defended the country's scholars against attempts to marginalize them. His other two books were *Arrows of Islam* and *Toward Islamic Doctrine.*

Following the eruption of violent clashes in 1982 between Islamist and communist students at the main campus of the University of Algiers, Soltani, along with Abbasi al-Madani and Ahmed Sahnoun, issued a statement, "The Statement of Advice," in which they criticized the secular policies of the state and demanded the promotion of Islam in government and society. Soltani was placed under house arrest until his death in 1983.

See also ALGERIA; ARABIZATION POLICIES; BENDJEDID, CHADLI; BOUYALI, MOUSTAFA; FRONT DE LIBERATION NATIONALE (FLN); FRONT ISLAMIQUE DU SALUT (FIS); SAH-NOUN, AHMED.

Bibliography

Shahin, Emad Eldin. *Political Ascent: Contemporary Islamic Movements in North Africa.* Boulder, CO: Westview Press, 1998.

EMAD ELDIN SHAHIN

SOMIKH, ABDULLAH
[1813–1880]

Iraqi rabbi.

Somikh, one of the most venerated rabbinic authorities in Baghdad in the nineteenth century, was instrumental in renewing Jewish religious studies in that city. In 1840 he established its first modern rabbinic seminary, Bet Zilkha. He wrote a commentary on Shulhan Arukh and a number of volumes of responsa that often addressed problems arising from the incursion of technology and modern education into the life of the Mizrahi (Jews of Middle Eastern, North African, and Western Asian origin) —for instance, whether a telegraphic message can be used as evidence in a Torah court. Somikh often dealt with religious questions addressed to him by Iraqi Jews who had settled in India, China, and other Far Eastern nations. In the 1860s, when the Alliance Israélite Universelle was established in Baghdad, he sent his son to study there, ignoring the protestations of conservative rabbis who strongly disapproved of secular education. Somikh died in Baghdad during a plague epidemic.

See also ADOT HA-MIZRAH; ALLIANCE IS-RAÉLITE UNIVERSELLE (AIU).

Bibliography

Cohen, Hayyim J. *The Jews of the Middle East, 1860–1972.* New York: Wiley, 1973.

SASSON SOMEKH
UPDATED BY MICHAEL R. FISCHBACH

SONATRACH

Holding company for the state's interests in Algeria's hydrocarbon sector.

In the events leading up to the independence of Algeria in 1962, the French government attempted to create a number of arrangements for continued access to Algerian oil, which had been discovered in the Sahara regions of the country a few years earlier. As part of its strategy to put the proceeds from oil sales into industrialization, the government of Algeria formed SONATRACH (Société Nationale de Transport et de Commercialisation des Hydrocarbures). It was headed initially by Abdessalam Belaid, who would become the country's head of centrally guided industrialization—a strategy in which SONATRACH was seen as the financial cornerstone.

The initial difficulty faced by SONATRACH was that all production and marketing of hydrocarbons in the country had been geared toward the requirements of France's economy, a goal now incompatible with the socialist and inward-oriented new development strategy of the Algerian government. Initially restricted to pipeline development and marketing abroad in an effort to break the French monopoly, SONATRACH eventually branched out into all aspects of oil exploration, refining, and marketing, often entering into joint ventures with foreign oil companies for exploration and production. By the early 1970s SONATRACH had become a giant state enterprise and the single largest employer in the country. It not only exercised control over the recovery of oil but managed the major refineries in Algiers, Arzew, and Skikda, and it was the domestic distributor for Algerian oil. In addition, the state enterprise also controlled a large number of oil-related subsidiaries that fueled much of the country's industrialization drive.

Because Algeria was estimated to possess the fourth-largest gas reserves in the world, the Algerian government under President Houari Boumédienne (1965–1978) attempted to index the price of natural gas to that of petroleum. At the same time SONATRACH increased its exploration activities substantially, at a time when the world demand for Algerian natural gas was stagnant or declining. The strategy necessitated heavy investments, among other items, in liquefaction plants built on the Algerian coast, for which the country borrowed extensively on the international market, starting in the mid-1970s. Neither the indexing nor the investments proved sound decisions, and by the early 1980s SONATRACH was forced to renegotiate most of its major contracts and accept lower prices for its natural gas exports. By 1970 SONATRACH directly controlled an estimated 30 percent of Algerian oil production, which accounted for some 34 percent of the country's gross domestic product. By 1977, after a series of nationalizations that ended in 1971, its participation had increased to approximately 75 percent.

The death of President Boumédienne in 1978 brought to a halt the socialist experiment that Algeria had adopted after independence. The June 1980 party congress, guided by the new president, Chadli Bendjedid, stressed the need for increased privatization and liberalization in the Algerian economy. Bendjedid advocated a reorganization of the huge national enterprise to make it more competitive and efficient. A decentralization process thus began, and the giant company was divided into smaller companies, each of which would compete for clients.

Since the early 1990s international companies have been allowed to work in existing oil fields, but the state-owned company still controls the industry. A new hydrocarbon investment law was drafted in 1991, but SONATRACH's complete privatization stalled as it faced staunch opposition from trade

unions and, most important, from certain factions within the regime that resisted losing control over the most valuable resource of political and economic power in Algeria. As of 2003, SONATRACH continued to provide the Algerian economy with over 90 percent of its foreign currency revenues.

Bibliography

Entelis, John P. "Sonatrach: The Political Economy of an Algerian State Institution." *Middle East Journal* 53, no. 1 (1999): 9–27.

DIRK VANDEWALLE
UPDATED BY ANA TORRES-GARCIA

SOROUSH, ABDOLKARIM
[1944–]

Iranian religious reformer and author who became internationally known during the 1990s for his liberal interpretation of Islam.

AbdolKarim Soroush was born Farajollah Dabbagh in Tehran in 1944. After being educated at a religious high school and at Tehran University, he went to England for graduate studies in pharmacology and philosophy. Returning to Iran in 1979, he became a vocal advocate of the newly inaugurated Islamic Republic of Iran. Adopting the name *Soroush* (meaning angel, especially the archangel Gabriel, in Persian), he became a major promoter of Islamic ideology, mainly writing against and debating Marxists, who were seen as ideological rivals. In the early 1980s Soroush was involved in the Cultural Revolution, a project that imposed "Islamic" curricula on Iranian universities and purged them of dissidents—mostly leftist students and professors—many of whom were imprisoned or executed.

However, as the Islamic Republic faced mounting problems in its second decade, Soroush emerged as a leader in a movement of loyal dissidents calling themselves "religious intellectuals." In numerous books, essays, and public lectures, he argued against turning religion into a political ideology and urged that Islam was open to a plurality of interpretations. Eclectically drawing on philosophy of science, modern hermeneutics, rationalist theology, and mysticism, Soroush holds that humans are able to understand and appreciate revelation according to their rational faculties and cultural limitations. His constant challenge to the clergy's claim to binding religious authority thus prompts some to portray him as something of a Muslim "Protestant." Similarly, his controversial proposal for a "democratic religious government" is a challenge to the Shi'ite clergy's hold on political power in Iran.

Soroush's ideas gained further attention during the first presidential term of another "religious intellectual," Mohammad Khatami (1997–2001). However, during Khatami's second term (2001–present), the limitations of "Islamic democracy" as envisioned by Soroush and his like-minded colleagues became more evident as clerical hard-liners contained the movement to reform the Islamic Republic from within.

See also IRANIAN REVOLUTION (1979); KHATAMI, MOHAMMAD.

Bibliography

Boroujerdi, Mehrzad. *Iranian Intellectuals and the West: The Tormented Triumph of Nativism.* Syracuse, NY: Syracuse University Press, 1996.

Matin-asgari, Afshin. "Abdolkarim Sorush and the Secularization of Islamic Thought in Iran." *Iranian Studies* 30, nos. 1–2 (Winter–Spring 1997).

Vahdat, Farzin. *God and Juggernaut.* Syracuse, NY: Syracuse University Press, 2002.

Vala, Vakili. *Debating Religion and Politics in Iran: The Political Thought of Abdolkarim Sorush.* New York: Council on Foreign Relations, 1996.

AFSHIN MATIN-ASGARI

SOUSSE

Northeast coastal town in Tunisia on the Gulf of Hammamet.

Sousse (also Susa; ancient Hadrumetum) was founded as a Phoenician commercial post and became the center of Sousse province under French colonialism (after the protectorate of 1881). After the independence of Tunisia in 1956, it was made the center of the Sousse governorate. In 2002, its estimated population was 177,450. It is a busy port, handling mostly phosphates and olive oil, and the tourist trade centers on a well-preserved medieval Islamic fortress.

MATTHEW S. GORDON

SOUSTELLE, JACQUES
[1912–1990]

French statesman.

A faithful adherent of General Charles de Gaulle, Jacques Soustelle was governor-general of Algeria (1955–1956), where he combined social reforms with harsh repression of the Front de Libération Nationale (FLN; National Liberation Front). He broke with de Gaulle in 1960 over concessions to the FLN, and following the failed army coup of 1961, Soustelle left France under the threat of arrest because of his hard-line *pied noir* sympathies. He remained in exile until 1968.

See also DE GAULLE, CHARLES; FRONT DE LIBÉRATION NATIONALE (FLN).

Bibliography

Horne, Alistair. *A Savage War of Peace: Algeria 1954–1962,* revised edition. New York: Penguin, 1987.

ZACHARY KARABELL

SOUTH ARABIAN ARMED FORCES

Short-lived army of the Federation of South Arabia.

The armed forces of the ill-fated Federation of South Arabia were created by the merger of the Federal National Guard and the Federal Regular Army in mid-1967, on the eve of South Yemen's rushed independence. By this time, however, the national struggle had rendered these forces unreliable, and they were to play no real part in the collapse of the federation and the transfer of power from the British to the National Liberation Front (NLF).

ROBERT D. BURROWES

SOUTH ARABIAN LEAGUE

Group promoting independence of Britain's protectorates in southern Arabia.

The South Arabian League was the oldest (founded 1950) of the major nationalist groups created to change the status of Britain's possessions in southern Arabia. Its goal was to unite the various principalities of Aden and the Protectorate States into an independent state, to be called South Arabia.

The league's politics tended to be reformist and conservative, and it received much of its support from Saudi Arabia during the 1960s, when the conflict over the future of the protectorates and Aden became a major issue. In 1967, they became part of South Yemen.

See also YEMEN.

MANFRED W. WENNER

SOUTHEASTERN ANATOLIA PROJECT

A massive integrated regional development scheme for the Euphrates and Tigris river basins in Turkey (in Turkish, Güney Anadolu Projesi, or GAP).

The project area covers about 27,000 square miles (70,000 sq. km) in six provinces of the Anatolia region of Turkey, lying between the Anti-Taurus mountains and the border with Syria: Adiyaman, Diyarbakir, Gaziantep, Mardin, Sanliurfa, and Siirt. The project is designed to create economic, social, and spatial changes through the construction and integration of dams, hydroelectric power plants, and irrigation projects, and infrastructural improvements in transportation, health, education, and nonagricultural employment opportunities. Estimated completion is in 2013.

GAP is composed of thirteen subprojects, of which seven are on the Euphrates and six on the Tigris. These comprise fifteen dams, fourteen hydroelectric power stations, and nineteen irrigation projects. The completed project will also incorporate the already completed Keban Dam and will vastly increase the extent of irrigated land in what has been the most economically depressed region of Turkey. As of the early 1990s, only some 315,000 acres (about 127,000 ha) were irrigated in this region—or about 4 percent of the total irrigated land in Turkey. Upon completion, almost 5 million acres (some 2 million ha) will be irrigated. The project will also double Turkey's electrical output by generating 22 billion kilowatt-hours of electricity each year.

The World Bank refused to provide project loans until an agreement had been reached with Syria and Iraq on sharing the water of the two rivers. Because foreign currency has been in great shortage in Turkey, international contractors who had been awarded contracts were replaced by Turkish firms. Since Turkish firms have proven themselves capable of completing the project, international financial circles have been persuaded to make loans. In 1985, the Export-Import Bank of New York and Manufacturers-Hanover Trust lent Turkey 111 million U.S. dollars for the Atatürk Dam, and European banks are providing another 440 million dollars for equipment purchases.

GAP has caused friction with Turkey's neighbors. The Euphrates and Tigris rivers are important sources of water for both Syria and Iraq, and the governments of both countries have expressed reservations about the project. The official Turkish position is that year-long regulation of the flow of the rivers will increase the amount of water available to Syria and Iraq. In July 1984, Turkey and Iraq signed a protocol guaranteeing a minimum flow of 654 cubic yards (500 cu. m) per second, which did not include Syria. In July 1987, a similar agreement was signed with Syria, and further negotiations were held in March 1991. The agreements have not ended the political tensions created by GAP: Turkish forces stood guard in January of 1990 when the Euphrates river was cut to divert water into the reservoir for the Atatürk Dam, which reduced the flow of water into Syria and Iraq by 75 percent.

A number of problems have delayed completion of the project. Because the dam sites are located in remote mountainous areas, roads, worker accommodations, and other infrastructure services must be provided. There are also shortages of skilled labor and engineers. Finally, the reservoirs created by the two Karakaya and Atatürk dams alone will force the relocation of an estimated seventy thousand people, with more relocations to come in the future.

See also WATER.

Bibliography

Kolars, John R., and Mitchell, William A. *The Euphrates River and the Southeast Anatolia Development Project.* Carbondale: Southern Illinois University Press, 1991.

Pitman, Paul M., III. *Turkey: A Country Study,* 4th edition. Washington, DC: U.S. Government Printing Office, 1988.

DAVID WALDNER

SOUTH LEBANON ARMY

Israeli-supported militia in southern Lebanon.

Renegade Lebanese army Major Saʿd Haddad founded the Free Lebanon Militia (FLM) to combat the Palestine Liberation Organization (PLO) in southern Lebanon during Lebanon's civil war (1975–1990) and made common cause with Israel when it invaded Lebanon in March 1978 to drive PLO guerrillas away from the Israeli border. Israel withdrew from Lebanon in June 1978 and turned over to Haddad a buffer zone three to six miles (5 to 10 km) wide along the Lebanese side of the border. Israel funded and trained Haddad's renamed South Lebanon Army (SLA) in return for SLA efforts to prevent the return of elements hostile to Israel to the area.

Israel's 1982 invasion of Lebanon to rout the PLO deepened the relationship between the Israel Defense Force (IDF) and the SLA. Headquartered in Marjayoun, Lebanon, the SLA's twenty-five hundred fighters were Maronite Christians (40%) and Shiʿa Muslims (60%), although Christians predominated among the officers. Haddad died in January 1984 and General Antoine Lahad replaced him. In 1985 Israel withdrew from Lebanon, leaving behind a small force to advise the SLA. The rise of Hizbullah, a Shiʿite militia created to liberate southern Lebanon from Israel and its SLA client, provoked SLA-Hizbullah battles and drew IDF troops back into Lebanon. By the late 1990s IDF fatalities in Lebanon led to an Israeli grass-roots campaign for a unilateral withdrawal. When the IDF withdrew from Lebanon suddenly on 24 March 2000, the SLA disintegrated, and its members either surrendered to Hizbullah or to the Lebanese army, returned quietly to their villages, or sought emergency refuge, along with their families, in Israel. Military courts in Beirut sentenced hundreds of SLA members to prison terms ranging from months to years for collaborating with the enemy, while SLA commanders tried in absentia received death sentences. SLA families struggled to adjust to Israeli society; most returned to Lebanon or moved to other countries within several years of the SLA's collapse.

See also HADDAD, SAʿD; LAHAD, ANTOINE.

Bibliography

Hamizrachi, Beate. *The Emergence of the South Lebanon Security Belt: Major Saʿad Haddad and the Ties with Israel, 1975–1978.* New York: Praeger, 1988.

Schiff, Zeʾev, and Yaʾari, Ehud. *Israel's Lebanon War.* New York: Simon & Schuster, 1984.

ELIZABETH THOMPSON
UPDATED BY LAURA ZITTRAIN EISENBERG

SOUTH PERSIA RIFLES

British-organized paramilitary unit in Iran during World War I.

The South Persia Rifles was a largely indigenous, paramilitary force of about 8,000 men trained and paid by Britain. Its headquarters was in Shiraz, with secondary bases in Abadeh and Kerman. Britain dispatched Major (later Brigadier General) Sir Percy Molesworth Sykes (1867–1945) to southern Iran in 1916 to organize a military force to counter the presumed pro-German sentiments of the Swedish-officered gendarmerie in Fars and Kerman provinces. It thus could protect British interests—southern Iran was adjacent to British India—from perceived threats by agents of Germany, Britain's enemy during World War I (1914–1918). The reluctance of the Iranian government to recognize the South Persia Rifles encouraged the largest and most militarily powerful tribal confederation in southern Iran, the Qashqaʾi, to attack the force in May 1918. Sykes and his troops were besieged for several weeks at Shiraz before they finally defeated the Qashqaʾi tribesmen. Following the 1921 coup d'état in Tehran, Minister of War Reza Khan, the future Reza Shah Pahlavi, ordered the disbanding of the South Persia Rifles.

See also PAHLAVI, REZA.

Bibliography

Sykes, Percy Molesworth. *A History of Persia*, vol. 2, 2d edition. London: Macmillan, 1921.

JACK BUBON
UPDATED BY ERIC HOOGLUND

SPAIN AND THE MIDDLE EAST

The Kingdom of Spain, located in southwest Europe, has ties with the Middle East and North Africa that go back to the early medieval period.

Between 711 and 1492, the Iberian Peninsula witnessed the growth of several Islamic administrations, which ruled over a multiethnic and multireligious population in a space that would be known as *al-Andalus*. The arrival of Berber troops under Arab leadership in 711 was followed by the establishment of a governorate dependent on the Umayyad caliphate based in Damascus (711–756). With the onset of the Abbasid revolution in the east, the Umayyad Abd al-Rahman I established an independent emirate based in Cordova (756–929). In 929, Abd al-Rahman III proclaimed himself caliph and turned Cordova into the most important cultural and intellectual center of Western Europe (929–1008). Cordovese splendor lasted for a century, after which the Christian kingdoms of the north began pushing southward, conquering Muslim territory while taking advantage of the weakness of the petty kingdoms (1031–1086). An invasion by North African Berber tribes (Almoravids and Almohads; 1086–1232) temporarily halted the Christian advance. The Nasrid kingdom of Granada (1232–1492), last Muslim stronghold in the peninsula, fell in 1492 to the armies of the Catholic monarchs of Castile and Aragon, Isabella and Ferdinand. The monarchs decreed that Iberian Jews must either convert or be expelled; in 1502, Castilian Muslims were forced to convert to Christianity, and Aragonese Muslims were forced to do so in 1525. Zealous religious authorities were suspicious of the fidelity of new Christians (Jewish *conversos* and Muslim *moriscos*), who fell under the scrutiny of the Inquisition. Morisco rebelliousness against the abuses of the old Christian settlers led to the uprising of the Alpujarras (1568–1571). In 1609, Phillip III decreed the mass expulsion of the remaining *moriscos*. Throughout the sixteenth century, the rivalry between imperial Spain and the Ottoman Empire led to the Spanish occupation of several North African ports—Oran, Budjia, Algiers, Tripoli, and Tunis—under Charles V. The diminution of the rivalry with the Ottoman Empire, the economic crisis that affected the Spanish Empire in the seventeenth century, and Spain's colonial enterprise in the Americas put a hold on Spanish incursions in North Africa.

In 1859–1860, Spain waged war against Morocco. Franco-Spanish rivalry in North Africa led to the establishment of a Spanish protectorate in northern Morocco (1912–1956) and the Western Sahara (1884–1975); Spanish troops fiercely repressed the Berber liberation movement of the Rif region (1921–1927). After the Spanish Civil War (1936–1939), General Francisco Franco maintained an official policy of "friendship" toward Arab countries. In 1975, King Hassan II of Morocco organized the Green March toward Western Sahara and occupied the former Spanish protectorate. The signing of the Madrid Agreements (1975), in which Spain ceded the territory to Morocco and Mauritania, ignored the wishes of the inhabitants of the region and was opposed by POLISARIO; almost thirty years after the signing of the Madrid Agreements, the Saharan conflict is pending resolution under UN supervision. Upon joining the European Economic Community (E.E.C.) in 1986, Spain—then under a democratic socialist government—established diplomatic ties with Israel. In 1991, the socialist government supported the international coalition against Iraq. That same year, Spain hosted the Madrid Peace Conference. Subsequently, Spain became an important mediator in the Palestinian-Israeli conflict. Throughout the last quarter of the twentieth century, Spain and Morocco maintained a bitter contest over the sovereignty of the Spanish cities of Ceuta and Melilla and over fishing rights along the Moroccan coast.

Under the Conservative government of Prime Minister José María Aznar (1996–2003), Spain aligned itself with the policies of the United States. In the aftermath of the 11 September 2001 attacks on the United States, Aznar was a staunch ally of U.S. policies in the Middle East and became one of the international anchors of the war against Iraq in 2003. Despite widespread popular opposition—90 percent of the population opposed military intervention in Iraq—the Spanish government supported the U.S. occupation and stationed troops in the Diwaniyah region.

See also GREEN MARCH; POLISARIO; WAR IN IRAQ (2003); WESTERN SAHARA.

Bibliography

Castro, Américo. *The Structure of Spanish History.* Princeton, NJ: Princeton University Press, 1954.

Hess, Andrew. *The Forgotten Frontier: A History of the Sixteenth Century Ibero-African Frontier.* Chicago: University of Chicago Press, 1978.

Menocal, Maria Rosa. *The Ornament of the World: How Muslims, Jews, and Christians Created a Culture of Tolerance in Medieval Spain.* Boston: Little, Brown, 2002

VANESA CASANOVA-FERNANDEZ

SPANISH MOROCCO

Portions of northwest Africa held by Spain from the 1500s until 1975.

The presence of Spain along the coast of northwest Africa was initially manifested during the 1400s and 1500s—after centuries of Muslim rule in the Iberian Peninsula had been overturned by warfare and the Moors retreated to North Africa. The Mediterranean port cities of Melilla and Ceuta came under Spanish rule in 1496 and 1578, respectively, and remain so today, as do three tiny islands off the Mediterranean coast of Morocco. In the late nineteenth century, Spain joined the European scramble for overseas territories. Spain expanded its Ceuta and Melilla enclaves, asserted itself militarily in the Rif mountains, and temporarily occupied Tetuan in 1860; an 1860 treaty committed Morocco to ceding land along its southern coast for the establishment of Spanish fisheries, eventually resulting in Spain staking claim to Ifni. Further south, Spain established coastal trading stations at Villa Cisneros (Dakhla), Cintra, and Cape Blanca. In December 1884, a Spanish protectorate was declared along the Saharan coast, a claim recognized by the Berlin Conference in 1885.

Spanish holdings in both the north and south were expanded by three treaties between Spain and France, the last in 1912. Spain then nominally held full sovereignty over Saguia el-Hamra and Rio de Oro (Spanish Sahara, now Western Sahara), 102,703 square miles (266,000 sq km) of territory, below the twenty-seventh parallel, wedged in between the Atlantic Ocean and what are today the internationally recognized boundaries of Morocco, Algeria, and Mauritania. Implementation of Spanish authority came in stages: Control of Tarfaya, north of the twenty-seventh parallel, was taken in 1916; La Guera, in the extreme south of Rio de Oro, in 1920; the 580-square-mile (1,502 sq km) Ifni zone, between Tarfaya and Agadir, in 1934; and Smara, in the Saharan interior, also in 1934. Spanish Sahara and the Ifni and Tarfaya areas were governed be-

Part of the "Green March" moves into Spanish Morocco in November 1975. During the Green March, hundreds of thousands of Moroccan civilians marched across their border into Spanish Morocco at the behest of King Hassan II, as part of an effort to assert Morocco's claim to the territory. © ALAIN NOGUES/CORBIS SYGMA. REPRODUCED BY PERMISSION.

tween 1934 and 1958 as parts of Spanish West Africa, whose military governor was based in Ifni.

The Spanish protectorate in the north, established in 1912, was one-twentieth the size of the French zone. Tangier was made part of the Spanish zone from 1940 to 1945, but then reverted to its previous international regime. The Spanish zone's population in 1955, including Europeans, was about one million, nearly 10 percent of Morocco's total population. Economic resources were few and the area underwent little development, constituting an economic liability to Spain.

Spain was both a competitor and sometimes junior partner of France, often working in tandem politically and militarily—the latter during the Rif rebellion led by Muhammad ibn Abd al-Karim al-Khattabi from 1921 to 1926; in the southern campaigns in 1934; and again in 1957–1958 against the irregular Moroccan Army of Liberation, following Morocco's achieving independence in 1956. Nonetheless, Spanish rule was both weaker and often less dominating than that of France. Spain returned Tarfaya and its surroundings to Morocco in 1958 and the Ifni enclave in 1969.

Phosphates were first discovered in Spanish Sahara during the 1940s, and proved to be of high grade and large quantity. Exports began in the early 1970s. By 1975, exports stood at 2.6 million tons (2.36 million metric tons), the sixth largest in the world. In 1974, the Spanish presence numbered just over 26,000; a 1974 census of the native Sahrawi population counted 73,497 persons, most of whom had been sedentarized from their nomadic life.

In 1973, Spain decided to introduce internal self-government, to deflect international pressure for decolonization. But by mid-1974, following the collapse of Portugal's Africa empire, Madrid promised to implement United Nations calls for a referendum in the territory during the first half of 1975. In September 1975, Spain's foreign minister and POLISARIO representatives agreed on a mutual release of prisoners and the principle of an independent Sahrawi state in return for fishing and phosphate concessions to Spain. But following Morocco's Green March in the Western Sahara War, and with Spain's Generalissimo Francisco Franco on his deathbed, Spain, Morocco, and Mauritania signed a tripartite agreement in Madrid on 14 November 1975, administratively dividing the region into Moroccan and Mauritanian zones and setting up a transitional tripartite administration. The final Spanish departure from its Saharan colony came on 26 February 1975.

See also GREEN MARCH; KHATTABI, MUHAMMAD IBN ABD AL-KARIM AL-; POLISARIO; RIF WAR.

Bibliography

Hodges, Tony. *Western Sahara: The Roots of a Desert War.* Westport, CT: L. Hill, 1983.

Mercer, John. *Spanish Sahara.* London: Allen and Unwin, 1976.

Pennell, C. R. *Morocco since 1830: A History.* New York: New York University Press, 2000.

BRUCE MADDY-WEITZMAN

SPECIAL FORCES OF THE LEVANT

Military group under the French mandate in Lebanon.

After France gained control of Lebanon through the mandate from the League of Nations, it formed the Troupes Spéciales du Levant, which recruited Lebanese and Syrian soldiers and was commanded almost exclusively by French officers. It was devised to legitimize French police and military activities in the region and to give the impression of local rule. The percentage of officers who were Lebanese or Syrian increased over the years although the power of command and control remained in French hands. By 1945, 90 percent of the officers in the 14,000-strong Special Forces were Arabs.

During World War II, Lebanese Special Forces troops were ordered to fight on the side of the Vichy French against the British and Free French. When the Vichy forces in the Middle East surrendered in 1941, volunteers from the Special Forces were recruited by the Free French to fight actively in North Africa, Italy, and southern France. In 1945 three thousand Lebanese troops in the Special Forces formed the nucleus of the Lebanese Army.

AS'AD ABUKHALIL

SPHINX

Mythological human-headed lion carved from rock at the pyramids of Giza.

The Sphinx is 190 feet (27 m) long and 66 feet (20 m) tall at its highest. It probably represents the pharaoh Khafre (c. 2550 B.C.E.), whose pyramid is nearby. Arabs called it Abu al-Hawl, "father of terror." Like the pyramids, it has become a symbol of Egypt, first appearing on postage stamps in 1867 and replacing the bust of King Farouk (1936–1952) on coins in the 1950s.

Bibliography

Hassan, Selim. *The Sphinx: Its History in the Light of Recent Excavations.* Cairo: Government Press, 1949.

DONALD MALCOLM REID

SPRINZAK, JOSEPH
[1885–1959]

Israeli political leader.

Born in Moscow, Joseph Sprinzak was one of the founders of Tze'irei Zion in Russia (1905) and was a delegate to Zionist Congresses.

He began medical school at the American University in Beirut but then settled in Palestine in 1908, where he was an early activist in the Labor movement. He was a founder of the Histadrut and the MAPAI party and served in leadership positions in both organizations. Unanimously elected speaker of the first Knesset in 1949, he served in that capacity until his death. He also was acting president of Israel while Chaim Weizmann was ill and after Weizmann's death (1952), until the election of Yizhak Ben-Zvi.

See also HISTADRUT; ISRAEL: POLITICAL PARTIES IN.

Bibliography

Merhav, Peretz. *The Israeli Left: History, Problems, Documents.* San Diego, CA: A. S. Barnes, 1980.

BRYAN DAVES

SRVANTZIANTS, GAREGIN
[1840–1892]

Armenian ecclesiastical leader, ethnographer, and folklorist.

Garegin Srvantziants was born in Van and educated in local parochial schools. He became a teacher and was ordained a celibate priest in 1867. While assigned ecclesiastical responsibilities in Van, Erzurum, Bitlis, and Harput, he organized a number of schools and was the assistant prior of the Armenian monastery of Surp Karapet (Holy Precursor), one of the most hallowed sites of Armenian religious pilgrimage, at Moosh. After his investiture as a bishop in 1886, he was appointed prior of Surp Karapet. A fervent preacher and exponent of Armenian emancipation, he was removed from office and placed under surveillance in Istanbul.

Well before his confinement to the Ottoman capital, Srvantziants had published what in the aggregate may be considered the most important ethnographic data on the Armenians yet gathered at the time. As an associate of Mkrtich Khrimian, he had traveled with the later catholicos through the Armenian provinces in 1860 and 1861. Recognized much like his mentor for the kinship he felt with his own people, Srvantziants was instructed by the Armenian patriarch of Istanbul, Nerses Vazhapet-

ian, to investigate and report on the condition of the Armenian communities in eastern Anatolia after the Russian–Ottoman War of 1877 and 1878, while Khrimian prepared to plead the Armenian cause at the Congress of Berlin.

During these trips, and at all other opportunities, Srvantziants tirelessly recorded the folklore of the Armenian rustic population. He released the results of his expeditions in a series of works issued in the 1870s and 1800s. In *Grots u brots* (The written and the spoken, 1874), he published popular Armenian folk stories and traditions. In *Hnots yev norots* (From the old and the new, 1874), he published Armenian stories from manuscript records. *Manana* (Manna, 1876) included proverbs, riddles, songs, and epigraphs from the Van region. In *Hamov-hotov* (The flavorful and the colorful, 1884), he described the topography, climate, and monuments of Armenia. The most significant of his discoveries was the first cycle of what was later recognized as the Armenian national folk epic *Sasna Tsrrer* (The daredevils of Sasun), more popularly known by the name of its hero. Srvantziants recorded the section called "Sasuntsi Davit kam Mheri tur" (David of Sasun, or the Gate of Mher). Srvantziants also published important studies on the subjects he recorded and was elected an honorary member of the Imperial Academy of Antiquities in Saint Petersburg. He died in Istanbul.

See also BERLIN, CONGRESS AND TREATY OF; KHRIMIAN, MKRTICH; RUSSIAN–OTTOMAN WARS; VAZHAPETIAN, NERSES.

ROUBEN P. ADALIAN

STACK, LEE
[1868–1924]

Governor-general of the Sudan and sirdar (commander) of the Egyptian army.

Sir Lee Stack was assassinated in Cairo as part of an Egyptian nationalist campaign to gain complete independence from Great Britain. He had joined the Anglo-Egyptian army in the Sudan in 1899 (when it became an Anglo-Egyptian condominium after its conquest, 1896–1898). As governor-general, he contributed to the economic and political development of the Sudan.

Bibliography

Marlowe, John. *Anglo-Egyptian Relations, 1800–1956*, 2d edition. London: F. Cass, 1965.

OLES M. SMOLANSKY

STANHOPE, HESTER
[1776–1839]

English aristocrat and traveler.

Hester Stanhope was the eldest of three daughters of Charles, third earl of Stanhope, and Lady Hester Pitt, sister of William Pitt the Younger. She emerged in London society as hostess and private secretary to her uncle, the prime minister, and was known for her satiric tongue. After Pitt's death in 1803, dissatisfied with a quiet life in London, she tried Wales but left for the eastern Mediterranean in 1810. By 1818 she had settled in Lebanon, befriending the Druze Amir Bashir al-Shihabi, whom she later opposed. She built an elaborate manor with lush tropical gardens on a hilltop above the village of Jun (7 miles northeast of Sidon), where she maintained a large pool of servants and a camel caravan to supply the manor with drinking water. Known as *al-Sitt* (the lady), she was both imperious and generous to the local population; some believed her to have special spiritual powers. She seems to have had considerable influence, since Ibrahim Pasha, about to invade Ottoman Syria in 1832, is said to have wanted her to declare neutrality.

Stanhope visited mosques in Damascus dressed as a young male Arab and organized a lavish procession to Palmyra, where the Bedouin apparently called her "the second Queen Zenobia." To maintain her estate, she fell into heavy debt to local moneylenders, despite the pension the British government had given her after Pitt's death, and she died poor. She was buried on her estate but her remains were transferred to a British cemetery near Beirut in 1989. Not only her own memoirs but remembrances by Charles Kingslake and Alphonse de Lamartine enhanced her notoriety; early twentieth-century Arab feminists memorialized her as a negative exemplar.

See also BELL, GERTRUDE; COLONIALISM IN THE MIDDLE EAST; GENDER: GENDER AND EDUCATION.

Bibliography

Booth, Marilyn. *May Her Likes Be Multiplied: Biography and Gender Politics in Egypt.* Berkeley: University of California Press, 2001.

Haslip, Joan. *Lady Hester Stanhope: A Biography.* New York: Frederick A. Stokes, 1936.

Meryon, Charles Lewis, ed. *Memoirs of the Lady Hester Stanhope, As Related By Herself in Conversations with Her Physician, Comprising Her Opinions and Anecdotes of Some of the Most Remarkable Persons of Her Time*, 3 vols. London: H. Colburn, 1845.

Meryon, Charles Lewis, ed. *Travels of Lady Hester Stanhope, Forming the Completion of Her Memoirs, Narrated by Her Physician*, 3 vols. London: H. Colburn, 1846.

MARILYN BOOTH

STARK, FREYA
[1893–1993]

British author and explorer.

Born in Paris into an expatriate English family and raised largely in Italy, Freya Madeleine Stark moved to England in 1911 to study English and history at Bedford College. When World War I interrupted her studies, she returned to the Continent, where she volunteered as a nurse. After the war, Stark studied Arabic in London, followed by a more intensive course in the Levant. The Arab world became her passion, and in 1927 she began extensive travels in the region, publishing newspaper articles in the *Baghdad Times* and elsewhere about the Middle East.

Stark's visit to the remote castles of the Assassins in western Iran in 1930 and 1931 led to the publication of her first book, *The Valleys of the Assassins* (1934). It brought instant recognition, together with financial success; its photographic observations set the style for her future work. Stark next journeyed south to Arabia in 1935, which resulted in the publication of *The Southern Gates of Arabia* (1935), followed by *Winter in Arabia* (1940). Stark spoke English, French, German, and Italian in addition to Arabic, Persian, and Turkish. Her knowledge of languages greatly facilitated her travels across the eastern Mediterranean and over much of the Asian continent.

Stark's remarkable life spanned almost the entire twentieth century. She mapped remote regions of the Arab world, and her cartographic accomplishments were honored by the Royal Geographic Society. However, it is as an author that she is most remembered. Freya Stark was the most gifted and widely read female travel writer of her time. She published more than thirty books, most of which were highly personal travel adventures and many of which remain in print.

See also BELL, GERTRUDE; COLONIALISM IN THE MIDDLE EAST; GENDER: GENDER AND EDUCATION; STANHOPE, HESTER.

Bibliography

Geniesse, Jane Fletcher. *Passionate Nomad: The Life of Freya Stark.* New York: Random House, 1999.

Ruthven, Malise, ed. *Freya Stark in Southern Arabia.* Reading, U.K.: Garnet Publishing, 1995.

Stark, Freya. *The Southern Gates of Arabia: A Journey in the Hadhramaut.* New York: Modern Library, 2001.

Stark, Freya. *The Valleys of the Assassins and Other Persian Travels.* New York: Modern Library, 2001.

RONALD BRUCE ST JOHN

STAR OF NORTH AFRICA

The first Algerian political movement to call openly for independence.

The Star of North Africa, also known as the Etoile Nord-Africaine (ENA) was founded in 1926 in Paris by Hadj Ali Abd al-Qadir and Messali al-Hadj. With a base in the large Algerian immigrant community that was influenced by the Communist-dominated French labor movement, it also propounded a leftist social and economic agenda.

The movement was banned in 1929 but grew clandestinely until it reappeared in reorganized form in 1933. Messali al-Hadj returned to Algeria in the summer of 1936 to address the Algerian Muslim Congress that was designing a program of reforms within the Colonial framework. Before that audience, he became the first individual to speak openly of independence within Algeria itself. He then turned to organizing ENA cells across the country. Authorities in January 1937 banned the ENA. Its successor was the Parti du Peuple Algérien (PPA), which was outlawed, in its turn, in September 1939.

See also HADJ, MESSALI AL-.

JOHN RUEDY

STATE PLANNING ORGANIZATION (SPO)

Organization set up in Turkey in 1960 to administer national economic development.

Turkey first experimented with central planning in the 1930s, but with the focus only on industrialization. Between 1950 and 1960, the Democratic Party governments were criticized for their opposition to any kind of economic planning. The agricultural sector was virtually tax exempt. After the military intervention of May 1960, planning became a priority. Accordingly, the principle of indicative, not compulsory, planning was written into the 1961 constitution. The State Planning Organization (SPO) was created to draw up five-year plans covering all aspects of economic development, as well as long-term plans and annual programs. The institutional structure of the SPO was designed to create a degree of independence and security for the technical experts charged with preparing the plans and to facilitate cooperation between them and political authorities. The final authority was supposed to lie with the High Planning Council.

During the discussion of the first five-year plan, there were differences of opinion between planners and military bureaucrats. In contrast to the planners' liberal-productive conception of the state, the military bureaucrats remained loyal to an etatist patrimonial tradition that gave priority to social justice and full employment over economic growth and efficiency. With the transition to civilian rule in October 1961, the climate changed radically. The Justice Party viewed the SPO as a political tool of a military-cum-bureaucratic elite, to which they were opposed by both interest and instinct. Although the party had to implement the constitutional requirement, the party leadership was anxious to limit the planners' power.

After 1965 representatives of the private sector, who had been virtually excluded from the preparation of the first plan, were fully consulted on the second, which was to run from 1967 to 1972. The new constitution of 1982 endorsed planning, and a decree of 1984 reorganized the SPO and attached it to the office of the prime minister.

The SPO is headed by an undersecretary. It consists of eight departments: Economic Planning; Social Planning; Coordination; Priority Regional

Development; Relations with the European Union; Credit Allocation; Foreign Capital Investment; and Evaluation of Yearly Programs. The SPO also maintains permanent representatives in international economic organizations and major foreign capitals. In spite of its elaborate organizational structure and its constitutionally defined task, the state bureaucracy regards the suggestions and recommendations of the SPO as a hindrance to its administrative tasks.

The most important achievement of the SPO is the realization of the Southeastern Anatolia Project (GAP). This project is a multisector and integrated regional development effort approached in the context of sustainable development. The project covers nine administrative provinces established in the basin of the Euphrates and Tigris Rivers. The program envisages the construction of 22 dams and 19 hydraulic power plants and irrigation of 1.7 million hectares. The total cost is estimated at $32 billion (in 1997 prices). The GAP represents a major part of the Eighth Five-Year Development Plan (2001–2006). The SPO also is involved in the preparation of the pre-accession structural changes required by the European Union.

Bibliography

Hale, William. *The Political and Economic Development of Modern Turkey.* London: Croom Helm, 1981.

Milor, Vedat. "The Genesis of Planning in Turkey." *New Perspectives on Turkey,* 4 (1990): 1–30.

Pamuk, Şevket, and Owen, Roger. *A History of the Middle East Economies in the Twentieth Century.* Cambridge, MA: Harvard University Press, 1998.

NERMIN ABADAN-UNAT

STERN, ABRAHAM
[1907–1942]

Jewish underground leader during the British mandate of Palestine.

Abraham Stern (nicknamed Ya'ir) was born in Poland but spent many of his formative years in Russia. He moved to Palestine in 1924 where he studied Latin and Greek at Hebrew University and later began to study for his doctorate in Florence, Italy. Stern served in the Haganah starting in 1929 but broke off in 1931 to form the Irgun Zva'i Le'umi (IZL), through which he smuggled weapons into Palestine and established contacts with the Polish military. In 1934 he gave up his academic interests to devote himself fully to the underground.

Stern returned to Palestine in 1939, following the publication of the British White Paper, to organize resistance to the British. He was detained by the British for ten months, until his friends in the Revisionist movement arranged for his release. In 1940 he broke with the Irgun and its leader, David Raziel, and formed a new group, Lohamei Herut Yisrael, also known as Lehi, or the Stern Gang, because he did not feel the Irgun was militaristic enough. His ideological manifesto, "Eighteen Principles of Renaissance," included many controversial ideas, including that the new Zionist goals should be a land of Israel extending from the Nile to the Euphrates Rivers.

During World War II, unaware of the realities of the Holocaust, Stern sought links with Fascist Italy and Nazi Germany, although they did not result in anything. Stern, who appeared on British "wanted" posters for bank robbery and murder, was found and killed by British policemen in 1942.

See also HAGANAH; HOLOCAUST; IRGUN ZVA'I LE'UMI (IZL); LOHAMEI HERUT YISRAEL; WHITE PAPERS ON PALESTINE.

Bibliography

Heller, Joseph. *The Stern Gang: Ideology, Politics, and Terror.* London and Portland, OR: F. Cass, 1995.

JULIE ZUCKERMAN

STOCK MARKET

Middle Eastern stock markets are small and often closed to foreign investors.

The stock markets of the Middle East tend to remain relatively small relative to the respective economies of each country, and except in Turkey and Israel are not used by entrepreneurs to fund their operations.

Even in countries where economic liberalism is embedded in the economic life, such as Saudi Arabia, capital markets are heavily regulated and have not had any major influence in helping nongovernment firms raise capital from the public at large. Exchanges suffer from a lack of reliable information on and from the companies, insider trading is often a problem, and accounting practices are not reliable enough for private investors and funds to make adequate judgment on the value of the companies. Governments tend to interfere with the markets, either to limit their expansion through overregulation or to limit the losses in downtrends, as was the case in Kuwait in 1982. In most countries the markets have little depth and are closed to foreign investors. Since 1998 there have been some efforts to use the markets to improve privatization efforts. Foreign investors have been welcomed in some bourses, such as those of Egypt, Lebanon, and Israel. However, most other markets have limited foreigners to investment through small mutual funds managed by local banks, as in Saudi Arabia. The Saudi market has the largest capitalization of the Arab world, at about US$100 billion.

Bahrain

The market in Bahrain is still very small and highly regulated. However, it is beginning to open up to foreign investors if they reside in Bahrain. Each foreign investor is limited to a maximum 1 percent stake in a company. If markets become more deregulated in Bahrain and if Saudi Arabia—the main center for private industrial ventures—approves, this stock market could become an important place for Persian (Arabian) Gulf industries to raise capital.

Iran

In the liberalization of 1992 the Iranian stock market was expected to be the transmission belt between Iranian capital at home and abroad and the companies to be denationalized. Foreign capital was permitted to buy minority positions. However, the move toward liberalization seems to have stalled, and the market is not very active.

Israel

The Israeli stock exchange is located in Tel Aviv. It lists about 654 companies and has a capitalization of US$41 billion. The market is open to foreign investors. Technically, the market is quite advanced, with computer support similar to that of U.S. markets. However, volumes traded are relatively low, in the average range of $36 million per day in 2002. The market tends to be somewhat volatile due to the

---

Major stock markets within the Middle East, 2003

Country traded	Number of companies	Capitalization (in millions of U.S. $)
Israel	617	40,900
Turkey	262	33,800
Saudi Arabia	68	100,000
Kuwait	93	35,100
Jordan	76	1,664
Iran	324	65,000
Egypt	1,110	18,400

SOURCE: Zawya, online at http://www.zawya.com; Tehran Stock Exchange, online at http://www.tse.or.ir; Istanbul Stock Exchange, online at http://www.ise.org; Tel Aviv Stock Exchange, online at http://www.tase.co.il; *Middle East Economic Survey*; Saudi Arabian Monetary Agency, online at http://www.sama.gov.sa

TABLE BY GGS INFORMATION SERVICES, THE GALE GROUP.

---

low number of buyers and sellers. The progress of the markets is marked by the TASE index.

Jordan

The Jordanian market, which was started in 1977, is still small in terms of volume but has a good reputation among investors. Foreign investors need to be approved by the government, which greatly limits the liquidity of the shares and the potential growth of the market.

Kuwait

Until 1982 the Kuwaiti capital markets were the largest in the Middle East. After the crash of the Suq al-Manakh, the government enforced old regulations and introduced new ones. The number of brokers, the number of companies eligible to be traded, and the daily volumes are limited. The 1991 Gulf War, which caused many industrial companies to disappear, limited the number of tradable issues to the financial institutions. Kuwaiti-owned companies based in Bahrain and elsewhere in the Gulf also are traded. No foreigners are allowed to trade in Kuwaiti shares, except Gulf Cooperation Council nationals.

Saudi Arabia

Saudi Arabia, despite having the largest volume of shares traded in the Gulf, does not have a stock exchange or trading floor. All shares are exchanged

The Istanbul Stock Exchange was established in 1986 and is an autonomous organization that provides trading in equities, bonds and bills, revenue-sharing certificates, private sector bonds, foreign securities, real estate certificates, and international securities. © AP/WIDEWORLD PHOTOS. REPRODUCED BY PERMISSION.

and cleared through the banks. To have shares traded, companies must be registered as Sharikat al-Musahama, a registration somewhat similar to a U.S. Corporation C. To obtain this status, companies must be vetted by the Saudi Arabian Monetary Agency and, until 1992, also needed approval by the king. Only firms not involved in defense or oil are allowed to register. Thus, Saudi firms have a very difficult time raising money directly from the public through the stock market. No foreign capital is allowed to trade in Saudi shares, except in limited circumstances if originating from within the Gulf Cooperation Council. Since 11 September 2001, the Saudi stock market index has become more popular. The number of shares traded has increased from 691 million in 2001 to 1736 million in 2002. In an overall declining world market, TASI, the Saudi stock exchange index, increased 5.7 percent between 2001 and February 2003.

Turkey

The stock exchange in Turkey got its impetus from a 1989 law on investments. The law strongly restricts insider trading, provides for proper financial reporting by companies, and authorizes foreigners to invest. By 1993 the Turkish market had become one of the leading emerging markets, with investments from many U.S. and European mutual funds.

JEAN-FRANÇOIS SEZNEC

STORRS, RONALD
[1881–1955]

British colonial official.

After studying classics at Pembroke College, Cambridge, Ronald Storrs served as Lord Horatio Kitchener's Oriental secretary in Egypt prior to and during World War I. In this capacity, he met with Amir Abdullah ibn Hussein in April 1914, one of the Hashimites' early attempts to determine Britain's attitude toward their ambitions. Storrs later played an important role in the Anglo–Hashimite dialogue and the Arab Revolt, traveling from Egypt to the Hijaz on several occasions in 1916, including a journey with T. E. Lawrence, to cement Britain's relationship with the Hashimites.

In December 1917, Storrs was appointed the first military governor of Jerusalem after Allied troops entered the city. He believed that the role of Britain's military government in Palestine was simply to administer the country, not to introduce fundamental social or political changes. Britain, however, had pledged to support Zionist settlements in Palestine through the Balfour Declaration. In April 1918, Storrs formally received the Zionist commission, headed by Chaim Weizmann, which had traveled to Jerusalem to begin making arrangements for implementing the Balfour Declaration. He felt that the commission's dismay at the negative attitude displayed toward it and Zionism in general betrayed a fundamental naïveté about the Palestinians and their understanding of Zionism.

Palestinian nationalist frustrations were manifested in the Nabi Musa disturbances (April 1920). As governor of Jerusalem, Storrs subsequently dismissed the mayor of Jerusalem, Musa Kazim al-Husayni, for his role in the affair. Husayni went on to become the senior Palestinian nationalist figure in the 1920s, as head of the Arab Executive.

Storrs took an interest in cultural preservation in Jerusalem, forming the Pro-Jerusalem Society to restore historic monuments in the city. He arranged for Armenian artisans to produce tiles for the Islamic shrines at the Haram al-Sharif as part of these efforts.

Following the introduction of civil rule in Palestine in the mid-1920s, Storrs was Jerusalem's first civilian governor. After leaving service in Palestine, he became governor of Cyprus in 1926 and of Northern Rhodesia in 1932. He retired from colonial service in 1934.

See also ABDULLAH I IBN HUSSEIN; BALFOUR DECLARATION (1917); HARAM AL-SHARIF; HUSAYNI, MUSA KAZIM AL-; KITCHENER, HORATIO HERBERT; LAWRENCE, T. E.; NABI MUSA PILGRIMAGE; WEIZMANN, CHAIM.

Bibliography

Storrs, Ronald. *Orientations: The Memories of Sir Ronald Storrs.* London: Nicholson and Watson, 1943.

Wasserstein, Bernard. *The British in Palestine,* 2d edition. Oxford and Cambridge, MA: B. Blackwell, 1991.

MICHAEL R. FISCHBACH

STRAITS CONVENTION

International agreement, signed in 1841, on access to the Black Sea; it denied passage in peacetime to non-Ottoman warships through the Straits connecting the Mediterranean and Black seas.

Until 1774, when the Russian Empire under Catherine the Great acquired territory on the north shore of the Black Sea, there was no question concerning passage of ships between the Black and Mediterranean seas because the Black Sea was essentially an internal Ottoman sea. After 1774 access to the Straits presented a persistent problem in international affairs. Russia sought to ensure its right to passage while opposing similar rights for other maritime powers; Britain, in particular, wanted to restrict Russian access to the Mediterranean as a threat to its aspirations in the Levant. The Ottoman Empire considered its control of the Straits essential to its sovereignty and a guarantee of its security and independence.

The Straits Convention of 1841 resulted from internal Ottoman problems and imperial rivalries. The Ottoman Empire had been wracked by the aspirations of Greece for independence and the threat posed by Muhammad Ali of Egypt in his efforts to establish control over Syria and possibly to replace the Ottomans as head of the empire. Russia and most other European powers supported the Greek cause. France supported Muhammad Ali in hopes of reaping benefits as his ally. Russia wanted unhampered access to the Mediterranean and acknowledgment of its claim of protection over Christian Orthodox subjects of the Ottoman Empire. Britain and Austria-Hungary were suspicious of Russian designs.

Muhammad Ali originally supported the Ottomans in their struggle against the Greeks seeking independence; he sent his son Ibrahim ibn Muhammad Ali with an army to help the Ottomans subdue the Greeks in 1825. The venture was not successful, and by 1828 Ibrahim's army had withdrawn from Greece. Muhammad Ali then turned his attention to Syria in an attempt to expand his control of the eastern Mediterranean, launching an army led by Ibrahim against the Ottomans in the first Syrian war (1831–1833). France tacitly supported this effort; Britain, distracted by other international problems (particularly Belgium), did not; the Russians supported the Ottomans. Ibrahim's forces came within 150 miles of Constantinople, but in February 1833 Russia sent a naval force and troops to support the Ottoman defense of the city. France and Britain, fearing the prospect of Russian influence in the Ottoman Empire, called for mediation. The Convention of Kütahya (8 April 1833) conceded Ottoman Syria to Egypt but prevented Egyptian control of the empire as a whole. Because of its support, Russia retained its position as the Ottomans' principal ally. This was reflected in the Treaty of Hunkar-Iskelesi (8 July 1833), in which Russia and the Ottoman Empire pledged mutual support in any future conflict. The treaty also called for closure of the Straits to any naval forces threatening Russia.

The agreements of 1833 did not last long. In 1839 Sultan Mahmud II decided to deal with Muhammad Ali's threat by sending a military force against his son, Ibrahim, in Syria; thus began the second Syrian war. In spite of a force developed by Helmuth von Moltke of Prussia, the Ottomans were defeated at Nesib on 24 June and the Ottoman fleet defected to Egypt. Fearing that the breakup of the Ottoman Empire would not be in the best interests of Britain, Lord Palmerston, foreign minister and later prime minister, called for talks with Russia, Austria, and Prussia in London in 1840. In July the ambassadors of the four powers persuaded the Ottomans to recognize Muhammad Ali as hereditary pasha of Egypt and grant him control of Palestine (southern Syria) in return for a cease-fire within ten days. France, although now under a government more favorable to Britain, was noncommittal, and Muhammad Ali refused the compromise. The British, with help from Austria, occupied Beirut and Acre in October and November and helped the Ottomans defeat Ibrahim's forces in Syria. Muhammad Ali, no longer counting on French help, was forced to accept Egypt as a hereditary domain and return the Ottoman fleet to the control of Constantinople.

Russia, Austria, Prussia, Britain, and France then signed the Treaty of London on 13 July 1841, ratifying these agreements. Appended to the treaty was an agreement on the Straits question: "Warships of foreign powers have always been forbidden to enter the Straits of the Dardanelles and of the Bosporus." Lord Palmerston had succeeded in strengthening Britain's position in the Middle East, preventing France from gaining influence in Syria, and containing Russian advances in the Ottoman Empire. That empire was thus preserved for a time, its existence now guaranteed by the five major European powers. Muhammad Ali remained in control of Egypt, with special rights in the Sudan. Although all parties seemed to have gained something, the stage was set for continued jockeying for position in the Middle East.

See also HUNKAR-ISKELESI, TREATY OF (1833); IBRAHIM IBN MUHAMMAD ALI; KÜTAHYA, PEACE OF; MAHMUD II; MOLTKE, HELMUTH VON; MUHAMMAD ALI; PALMERSTON, LORD HENRY JOHN TEMPLE; STRAITS, TURKISH.

Bibliography

Arnakis, George G. *The Near East in Modern Times,* Vol. 1: *The Ottoman Empire and the Balkan States to 1900.* Austin, TX: Pemberton Press, 1969–1973.

Hurewitz, J. C. *Diplomacy in the Near and Middle East,* Vol. 1: *1535–1914.* Princeton, NJ: Van Nostrand, 1956.

DANIEL E. SPECTOR

STRAITS, TURKISH

A strategic 200-mile (320 km) natural waterway that joins the Black and Aegean seas.

Less than 30 percent of the length of the Straits—the Bosporus, starting in the Black Sea, and the

MAP BY XNR PRODUCTIONS, INC. THE GALE GROUP.

Dardanelles, ending in the Aegean—are natural straits; between them lies the inland Sea of Marmara. So long as the Black Sea was Ottoman and the only approaches flowed through the sultan's domain, he alone decided what ships might visit what parts of his realm. Foreign naval vessels did not enter Ottoman inland waters except on calls of courtesy or for repairs—unless in time of war they sought to breach the sultan's naval defenses. At the Straits and in the Ottoman-dominated river mouths of the Black Sea, attempting such a breach would have entailed over-whelming risks. The fact that at its southern end the Bosporus divided the imperial capital between Europe and Asia enhanced the Ottoman security planners' sensitivity to the movement of foreign vessels through the Straits. By the eighteen century, commercial ships arriving from the Mediterranean were permitted into the Sea of Marmara only as far as Constantinople. From that point north, all trade with Black Sea ports moved on Ottoman ships.

Once Russia captured primary river outlets to the Black Sea (such as the Dnieper and the Don—the latter connected to the Black Sea by the Sea of Azov), and thus could validly claim riparian status, the situation changed. The Treaty of Kuçuk Kaynarja, which in 1774 ended a six-year war with the

Ottoman Empire, opened all water lanes with outlets on the Black Sea to Russian commercial shipping. The Ottomans subsequently bestowed the privilege of free merchant navigation through the Straits upon other seafaring powers of Europe and even the United States. This was done by separate act for any Western state enjoying capitulatory (extraterritorial) privileges that requested it. The Ottoman government in 1822 notified all powers that "the passage of the Bosporus is closed to the ships of nations to whom the Porte never accorded the right of entry to . . . [the Black] sea." Not until the Treaty of Paris in 1856 was commercial freedom conferred on all flags.

The transit of war vessels was also resolved by international agreement, starting with the Straits Convention, signed in London on 13 July 1841. Article 1 expressed the sultan's firm resolve "to maintain . . . the principle . . . [whereby] it has . . . been prohibited for the Ships of War of Foreign Powers to enter the Straits . . .; and . . . so long as the Porte is at peace . . . [to] admit no foreign Ship of War into the said Straits." In the same article the powers of Europe pledged "to respect this determination." In Article 2 the sultan reserved "to himself . . . to deliver f[e]rmans [edicts] of passage for light vessels under flag of war . . . employed . . . in the services of the Missions of foreign powers."

The defeat in World War I of the Ottoman imperial government ended the 1841 agreement. Under the Armistice of Mudros in 1918, the victors (chiefly Britain, France, and Italy) imposed a naval occupation on the Sublime Porte, and in 1922 on its successor, the Republic of Turkey. The powers of Europe assumed the role of Straits traffic regulator until the ratification in 1923 of the Treaty of Lausanne. For a dozen years, an International Straits Commission oversaw the flow of all Straits traffic. In 1936 the Montreux Convention restored sovereign authority to the Republic of Turkey.

In conferences with Britain and the United States at Tehran in 1943 and at Yalta in 1945, the Soviet Union declared the Montreux Convention prejudicial to its security interests. It acknowledged that in wartime Turkey had acted with goodwill in defense of the Straits. Nevertheless, Moscow demanded revision of the 1936 convention to assure its warships free movement through the Straits at all times.

When the issue was reviewed at Potsdam in mid-1945, the Western powers agreed that each of the Big Three would hold talks with the Turkish government on revising the 1936 instrument "to meet present-day conditions." After a year of diplomatic exchanges, Moscow's insistence on sharing in the defense of the Straits led to a stalemate in August 1946. The Soviet Union refused to modify its demands, and Britain and the United States gave full support to Turkey. Seven months later, President Harry Truman promulgated the U.S. strategy for the global containment of the Soviet Union "and international communism" thereby marking the formal start of the Cold War.

See also CAPITULATIONS; LAUSANNE, TREATY OF (1923); MONTREUX CONVENTION (1936); STRAITS CONVENTION.

Bibliography

Hurewitz, J. C. The Middle East and North Africa in World Politics: A Documentary Record. 2 vols. New Haven, CT: Yale University Press, 1975–1979.

Hurewitz, J. C. "Russia and the Turkish Straits: A Revaluation of the Origins of the Problem." World Politics (July 1962): 605–632.

Shotwell, James Thomson, and Deák, Francis. Turkey at the Straits: A Short History. New York: Macmillan, 1940.

J. C. HUREWITZ

STRUMA

Ship on which Jewish World War II refugees died, in part because of Britain's wartime refugee policy.

In October 1941, the 180-ton Romanian coastal vessel Struma, which normally carried one hundred passengers, sailed for Haifa with almost one thousand Jewish refugees. The ship broke down at Istanbul on 16 December because of overloading, a leaking hull, and defective engines. Turkey would not permit the passengers to land without British certificates for Palestine, but the British refused to issue them.

Since the refugees could not go forward and could not return to Romania, the Struma remained in port for ten weeks. The British refused the appeal of the Jewish Agency to permit the refugees entrance to Palestine—if only for later transport to Mauritius, an island in the Indian Ocean. On 24

February, Turkey towed the *Struma* with its passengers out to sea, where six miles from shore it sank; it is not known whether it capsized, struck a mine, or was hit by a torpedo. Some 70 children, 269 women, and 428 men drowned—only 2 swam to safety.

This event became the symbol for the Jewish community in Palestine (the Yishuv) of Britain's unrelenting World War II policy toward the Jewish refugees of Nazi-occupied Europe.

See also YISHUV.

Bibliography

Morse, Arthur D. *While Six Million Died: A Chronicle of American Apathy.* New York: Random House, 1968.

Sachar, Howard M. *A History of Israel: From the Rise of Zionism to Our Time,* 2d revised and updated edition. New York: Knopf, 1996.

MIRIAM SIMON

STUDENTS IN THE LINE OF THE IMAM

An organization of Iranian students that held U.S. hostages for over one year.

Students in the Line of the Imam was a militant group formed after the Iranian Revolution (1979). It advocated radical policies that its members insisted were supported by the revolution's leader, Ayatollah Ruhollah Khomeini, whom they called *imam.* The group acquired domestic and international attention when it seized the U.S. embassy in Tehran in November 1979 and announced that captured U.S. diplomatic personnel would be held until the United States extradited the deposed shah, Mohammad Reza Pahlavi, to Iran for trial. This action began the most dramatic of regional hostage crises, one that would not be resolved for 444 days. During the crisis, the students pasted together shredded secret documents pertaining to U.S. policy that they found in the embassy compound. They published the U.S. documents in several volumes and also used the material in the documents to discredit moderate politicians mentioned in them. Although the Students in the Line of the Imam group gradually was relegated to the margins of Iranian politics after the hostage crisis was resolved in January 1981, several of its leaders subsequently played important roles. Abbas Abdi, for example, became an influential editor and champion of the reform movement in the 1990s. Maryam Ebtehar, media spokesperson for the Students in the Line of the Imam, became Iran's first woman vice president in 1997.

See also HOSTAGE CRISES; IRANIAN REVOLUTION (1979); KHOMEINI, RUHOLLAH; PAHLAVI, MOHAMMAD REZA.

Bibliography

Bakhash, Shaul. *The Reign of the Ayatollahs: Iran and the Islamic Revolution.* New York: Basic Books, 1986.

Iran Research Group. *Who's Who in Iran.* Meckenheim, Germany, 1990.

NEGUIN YAVARI
UPDATED BY ERIC HOOGLUND

SUARÈS FAMILY

Prominent Sephardic family, influential in Egyptian society and economy.

The Suarès family settled in Livorno, Italy, then went to Egypt during the first half of the nineteenth century. Menachem Suarès della Pegna settled in Alexandria while his brother Isaac settled in Cairo. In the mid-1870s Isaac's sons—Joseph (1837–1900), Félix (1844–1906), and Raphael (1846–1902)—created the Banque Suarès, which until 1906 served as mediator for European capital investment in Egypt. Given Raphael Suarès's connections with British industrial investors, he channeled British investments into such enterprises as the construction of the first Aswan Dam, the National Bank of Egypt, and the khedivial estates (*al-da'ira al-saniyya*). The Suarès family was not only involved in banking and finance but also transportation, establishing in Cairo the first public transportation company and building railway lines between Cairo and Helwan, Qina and Aswan. Members of the family owned real estate in the heart of Cairo where Suarès Square bore Félix Suarès's name (Maydan Suarès was renamed, in 1939, Maydan Mustafa Kamil).

One family member, Edgar Suarès, was involved with a major shareholders' company. Owing to his initiative, vast areas of land—several thousand *feddan* (a *feddan* is approximately one acre)—were purchased in Upper and Lower Egypt. Edgar Suarès reclaimed them and introduced modern irrigation facilities for large-scale agricultural development. He subsequently sold the land as small holdings to rural Egyptians at low prices and long-term credit. The Suarèses were not very active in Jewish communal affairs; only Edgar Suarès served very briefly as president of Alexandria's Jewish community during World War I. Their influence in Egyptian society and the economy declined after the 1930s.

Bibliography

Krämer, Gudrun. *The Jews in Modern Egypt, 1914–1952.* Seattle: University of Washington Press, 1989.

Mizrahi, Maurice. "The Role of Jews in Economic Development." In *The Jews of Egypt: A Mediterranean Society in Modern Times,* edited by Shimon Shamir. Boulder, CO: Westview Press, 1987.

MICHAEL M. LASKIER

SUBLIME PORTE

Residence/office of the Ottoman sultan.

In the Ottoman Empire, the sultan would appoint a grand vizier to head the government. Just as the prime minister of Great Britain resides at 10 Downing Street, the grand vizier of the Ottoman Empire lived and worked in the Sublime Porte. This term is a French translation of *al-Bab al-Ali,* which means literally "the High Door." In the nineteenth century, it became common to refer to the entire Ottoman government as "the Sublime Porte," as it is common today to refer to the U.S. government as "the White House."

Bibliography

Lewis, Bernard. *The Emergence of Modern Turkey,* 3d edition. New York: Oxford University Press, 2002.

ZACHARY KARABELL

SUDAN

A country in northeast Africa located south of Egypt on the Nile.

Known in the past as *bilad al-sudan* (the land of the black people), Sudan is the largest country in Africa, covering one million square miles. Its nearly thirty million residents, who live scattered across the wide expanse, differ along lines of ethnicity, language,

Omdurman is the largest city and chief commercial center of Sudan. It is located across the White Nile from Khartoum, the country's capital. © CORBIS. REPRODUCED BY PERMISSION.

and religion. The country's political instability is, in part, a result of this diversity. Moreover, given its geostrategic location astride the Nile, it has been vulnerable to foreign pressure.

Peoples

Sudan contains more than fifty ethnic groups, which are subdivided into at least 570 tribes. The principal groups in the north are Arab, Beja, Nuba, Nubian, and Fur. Nearly half the population identifies itself as Arab, generally meaning peoples who speak Arabic and reflect its cultural heritage. The Arabs along the northern and central Nile valley tend to dominate Sudanese political and economic life. The Beja, who comprise 6 to 7 percent of the population, are concentrated in the east along the Red Sea and coastal mountain ranges; they are Muslim but speak a distinct language. The Nuba, residing in the Nuba mountains of southern Kordofan, are 5 percent of the population and also speak their own

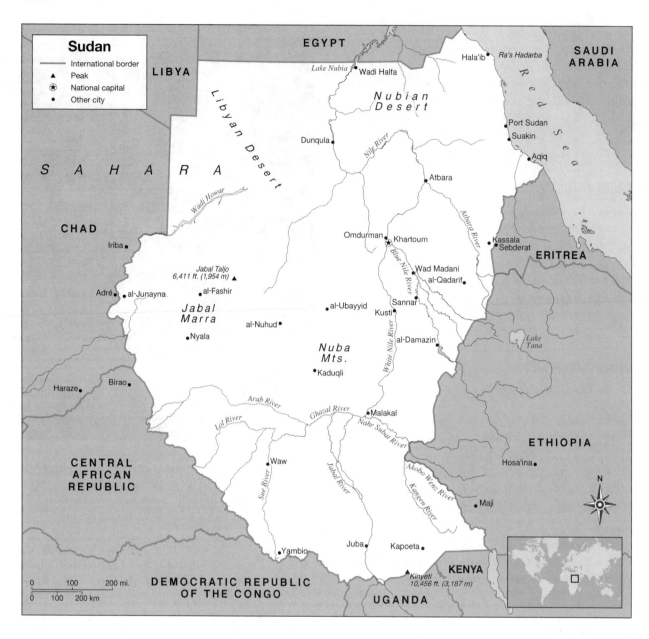

Sudan

- International border
- ▲ Peak
- ⊛ National capital
- • Other city

MAP BY XNR PRODUCTIONS, INC. THE GALE GROUP.

languages, not Arabic; some are Muslim, others Christian or adherents of traditional African religious beliefs. About 3 percent are Nubians, who traditionally lived along the northern reaches of the Nile, merging into Egypt. In the early 1960s, many Nubians were relocated to Khashm al-Ghirba in central Sudan when the construction of the Aswan High Dam flooded their homes. They speak their own ancient languages; they were early converts to Christianity but converted to Islam several centuries ago. The Fur, 2 percent of the population, live in the far west; like the Nubians, they have a tradition

of independent kingdoms. The Sultanate of Fur lasted from the fifteenth century until the early 1890s. Many other non-Arab peoples live in villages in the west, notably the Berti, Zaghawa, Borgu, and Massalit.

In the southern third of Sudan, the Dinka are 40 percent of the population, or 12 percent of the Sudanese as a whole. The Nuer are 5 percent of the whole Sudanese people, and the Shilluk are 1 percent. None of those groups are homogeneous, and they compete for territory, cattle, and trade routes.

The numerous groups that live in Equatoria, the southernmost area, differ in language, customs, and religion. Overall, the ethnic fragmentation in the south is greater than in the north.

In addition to those indigenous groups, 6 percent of the Sudanese are migrants from West Africa who settled in western and central Sudan in search of employment or on their way to or from Mecca, the most important site for Muslim pilgrims. Known by the pejorative term *fellata,* they lack many of the legal and economic protections accorded to full Sudanese citizens.

Language overlaps with ethnicity as a basic distinguishing trait among the Sudanese. Half the population speaks Arabic as its native tongue. At most, half the adults are literate (far fewer than that in the wartorn south and Nuba Mountains), and indigenous languages remain important. Arabic serves as the lingua franca among the educated classes in the north. Although residents of the south resisted learning Arabic and were taught English in the missionary schools, Arabic has made inroads there in recent decades.

Religion also divides the population—65 to 70 percent are Muslim, 20 to 25 percent follow traditional beliefs, and 5 to 10 percent are Christian. The north is overwhelmingly Muslim, with pockets of Christians in the Nuba Mountains and in urban areas. Many Muslims belong to the networks of Sufi *tariqas* (brotherhoods) that formed around holy men and serve economic, social, and political as well as religious functions. The brotherhoods cut across tribal and ethnic allegiances: For example, many Beja belong to the Khatmiyya order, which is led by the Arab riverain Mirghani family. Otherwise, most of the divisions reinforce cleavages, particularly the Arab/Muslim separation from the African/non-Muslim.

Geography and Economy

Sudan is predominantly rural, with a third of the population living in urban areas. (That share is growing as people flee famine in the outlying provinces.) Two-thirds of the labor force works in agriculture or herding, and a third of the gross national product was derived from agriculture until the advent of oil exports in 1999. Northern Sudan is largely flat savannah and desert where cattle,

Men in Rashayda build a mud hut. In many areas of Sudan, there is little building material to work with other than what nature has provided. Even some government facilities, such as immigration and customs centers, are wattle-and-daub structures. © CORBIS. REPRODUCED BY PERMISSION.

camels, and sheep are raised, sorghum and sesame are grown, and gum arabic is harvested. Meat and grains are sold in large amounts to oil-rich states in Arabia, and gum arabic is exported to Europe and the United States for use in soft drinks. Along the Blue and White Nile, south of Khartoum, cotton and peanuts are grown for export on large-scale agricultural holdings called *schemes.* Rains are heavier in the tropical south than in the north, but development in the south has been hampered by civil war and difficult conditions, such as the vast swamp known as the Sudd (barrier). The north suffers from severe deforestation: The forest cover diminished annually by one percent in the 1980s and 1990s due to overgrazing, charcoal burning, and drought.

Industry is based on agriculture, and its products are consumed within the country. Manufactures include sugar refining, flour milling, vegetable oil processing, canning, and textiles. Cement, tire, and cigarette production is also important for the domestic market.

There are substantial untapped deposits of copper and other minerals in Sudan. Chinese and French joint ventures export gold from the Red Sea Hills. Oil has now become the most important resource.

In 1979 the Chevron Oil Company discovered oil in Bentiu (Upper Nile) and Muglad (southern Kordofan). Extraction was blocked by the civil war that resumed in 1983. Chevron sold out its share to the Sudanese government in 1984. In the mid-1990s the government resumed exploration, utilizing the skills of a consortium of Canadian, European, Chinese, and Malaysian oil companies. Export began in August 1999, when the pipeline to Port Sudan was completed. Since then Sudan has become self-sufficient in oil. It exports increasing amounts of crude and refined oil, particularly to East Africa and Asia. The Canadian Talisman company sold its share to the Indian state oil company in 2002 after widespread protests by human-rights groups against the government's expulsion of Nuer from Upper Nile in order to ensure central control over this vital resource.

Oil exports have enabled Sudan to have a positive balance of trade for the first time in decades and to start to reduce its heavy debt burden. That burden is estimated at $23 billion, most of which is long in arrears. U.S. government sanctions, imposed in November 1997, ban U.S. companies from conducting transactions in Sudan, with the exception of those for gum Arabic.

Urban Areas

The urban population is centered in the Three Towns—Khartoum, Omdurman, and Khartoum North—which serve as the political and economic capital and together house at least 1.2 million people. Port Sudan (pop. 300,000), built by the British in 1910, remains the only port on the Red Sea, although efforts have been made to revive the historic port at Sawakin. Kassala (pop. 235,000) and Qadarif (pop. 190,000) are the main towns in the grain-growing east, and Wad Madani (pop. 220,000) is the capital of the cotton-growing Gezira area. In the west, al-Ubayyad (pop. 230,000) serves as the capital of Kordofan, and al-Fashir—on the border with Chad—is the capital of Darfur; both are important trading centers. Juba (pop. 115,000), the capital of Equatoria, was the capital of the south when it was unified from 1972 to 1983; it has been isolated from the surrounding countryside by the rebel forces of the Sudan Peoples Liberation Army (SPLA) since 1985.

History since 1821

The territory that now comprises Sudan was not unified until the Turco-Egyptian invasion of 1821, which imposed centralized control over most of the north relatively quickly. The Turco-Egyptian forces did not conquer Darfur until 1874 and never subdued the southern tribes. Their raiders seized gold, ivory, and slaves from the south, deeply alienating those African peoples.

The indigenous politico-religious movement called the Mahdiyya overthew the Turco-Egyptian government in 1885 and ruled until 1898. Muhammad Ahmad ibn Abdullah called himself the *mahdi* (messiah) in 1881, gathering his followers on Aba Island (White Nile) and later in Kordofan, from which he launched attacks against the Turco-Egyptian army. The mahdi died shortly afterward. His successor (*khalifa*) Abdullahi al-Ta'isha consolidated control over northern Sudan and attempted to seize territory from Ethiopia and Egypt. He established a religious-based government that continued to raid into the southern areas, seizing slaves and promoting Islam.

British forces, marching south from Egypt, overran the country in 1898 to 1899 and imposed the Anglo-Egyptian condominium. Messianic anti-colonial revolts broke out in the west and center, and were finally subdued in 1912. Sultan Ali Dinar was not defeated in Darfur until 1916. In the early 1920s nationalist outbreaks called for Sudan's independence, or for its linking with Egypt: Those two strands persisted in the northern nationalist movement until Egypt renounced its claim to Sudan in the 1950s. One enduring legacy of British rule was the virtual separation of the south from the north; from 1922 to 1946 the southern provinces and Nuba Mountains were isolated from the rest of the country. Meanwhile, considerable economic and educational development took place in the north, centered on the Gezira agricultural scheme (opened in 1925) and Gordon Memorial College (opened in 1903). In 1938 the graduates formed the Graduates Congress, which lobbied for independence during World War II. By then, several northern political parties also competed for influence. Britain established a legislative assembly in 1948; this led to self-government in 1952 and the election of the first parliament in the next year. Sudanization of the army and administration began in 1954. Those measures primarily benefited the north; the south was compelled to accept a subordinate position at the Juba Conference (1947) and hardly benefited from Sudanization.

When Sudan gained independence on 1 January 1956, parliamentary rule was established. The two leading religious orders—the Ansar and the Khatmiyya—predominated in the new governments, although secular nationalists, communists, and southerners gained token positions in the parliament. The democratic institutions had not had taken root by the time General Ibrahim Abbud instituted military rule on 17 November 1958. His rule lasted until November 1964, when a popular uprising led to a renewed democracy. That, too, proved unstable as the traditional politicians jockeyed for power, were challenged from the religious right by Hasan al-Turabi's Islamist Party, and failed to deal with the rebellion that had accelerated in the south during Abbud's era.

Young officers led by Muhammad Ja'far Numeiri launched a coup d'état on 25 May 1969 and crushed the traditional political groups. Numeiri turned against his left-wing allies in 1971 but mollified the south by granting regional autonomy in 1972. He instituted major economic development programs in the mid-1970s, backed by the party, the Sudan Socialist Union. Economic development remained hampered by poor planning, high-level corruption, and skyrocketing oil prices. In 1977 to 1978 Numeiri sought to widen his base of support by reconciling with the traditional and fundamentalist religious forces. That led to the gradual Islamization of the political system. Numeiri instituted Islamic criminal punishments in September 1983, which he enforced against widespread opposition by draconian emergency measures. By spring 1985 Numeiri's support was confined to Turabi's Islamic movement—northern secularists, the banned political forces, and the southerners (who resumed their civil war in 1983 under the banner of the Sudan People's Liberation Movement) actively sought to overthrow him.

In April 1985 a popular uprising led to a bloodless coup and the installation of a one-year Transitional Military Council. Elections were held in April 1986, and northern religious-oriented political movements won 85 percent of the seats. Turabi's National Islamic Front (NIF) won 20 percent of those seats. African (southern and Nuba) and northern secularist (communist) parties controlled only 15 percent of the parliamentary seats. Al-Sadiq al-Mahdi, leader of the Umma Party and

the Ansar religious order, became prime minister. Despite his pledges to institute a liberal government and to negotiate an end to the fighting, he failed to cancel Numeiri's Islamic laws. Instead, he announced that he would not enforce them in the south, a move that alienated the southerners as well as northern secularists. Mahdi's rival Muhammad Uthman al-Mirghani, leader of the Khatmiyya Sufi order and head of the Democratic Unionist Party (DUP), won acclaim for reaching an agreement with the SPLM to freeze the Islamic laws pending the convening of a constitutional conference. Mahdi and Turabi joined to force the DUP out of the government, but the senior army officers then compelled Mahdi to endorse Mirghani's agreement and negotiate with the SPLM.

On 30 June 1989, hours before the government could finalize the freezing of Islamic law, Brigadier Umar Hasan Ahmad al-Bashir overthrew the government. The coup d'état was orchestrated by Turabi's NIF, which vehemently opposed the annulment of Islamic law. Once again, constitutional institutions were banned: Bashir closed the parliament, banned political parties and trade unions, and shut down independent newspapers. The government accelerated the fighting in the south and in the Nuba mountains. The civil war was redefined as a jihad (holy war) against infidels and apostates. The regime instituted Islamic legal codes in 1991 and an Islamic constitution in 1999. In the late 1990s it reintroduced carefully controlled parliamentary elections and a direct presidential election, which Bashir won handily. In late 1999 Bashir and Turabi had a major falling-out after Turabi sought to sideline Bashir. Bashir, using his power as president and commander of the military and security services, decreed emergency rule and closed down the parliament. From early 2001 until late 2003, Bashir kept Turabi either in jail or under house arrest.

The political and trade union groups that had benefited from the short-lived parliamentary system formed the National Democratic Alliance (NDA) in October 1989. NDA members inside Sudan attempted to mount protests and petitions, which were crushed by the military regime. Most of the leaders fled into exile, from which they continued to try to overthrow the government and reinstitute democracy. The NDA attempted to mount military operations in eastern Sudan, but it lacked the strength to bring down the regime either militarily or politically. The government even attracted Mahdi back to Khartoum in 2000, but it failed to provide him with a significant political position.

Sudan Today

The geostrategic location of Sudan contributes to its sociopolitical instability. Located astride the Nile River, which flows north from Ethiopia and Uganda into Sudan and through Egypt to the Mediterranean Sea, Sudan has been the object of contention by those neighbors as well as external powers. Egypt cannot tolerate the presence of a hostile government in Khartoum, because the Egyptian economy depends on the Nile waters. Sudan and Egypt worry that Ethiopia might dam the Blue Nile and deprive them both of water. Sudan also borders the Red Sea, a major artery of international trade, and adjoins nine countries (Egypt, Libya, Chad, Central African Republic, Congo, Uganda, Kenya, Ethiopia, and Eritrea). Lacking the capacity to police its remote desert borders and its lengthy coast along the Red Sea, Sudan is vulnerable to incursion. Refugees from neighboring civil wars and famines find haven in Sudan, and hostile governments support rebellious Sudanese groups. Sudanese governments have meddled in the politics of such neighbors as Ethiopia, Chad, and Uganda, although those countries can easily undertake reprisals.

Some view Sudan as a *terra media,* lying between and linking Africa and the Arab world; others see it as lying on the fault line between the two peoples, torn between them and unable to unite. Nearly fifteen years after achieving independence, Sudan's national identity and political system are still violently contested.

See also ABBUD, IBRAHIM; ANSAR, AL–; BEJA; DINKA; KHARTOUM; KORDOFAN; NUBIANS; NUER; NUMEIRI, MUHAMMAD JA'FAR; OMDURMAN; SHILLUK; SUDANESE CIVIL WARS; TURABI, HASAN AL–; UMMA PARTY.

Bibliography

Abdel Rahim, Muddathir. *Imperialism and Nationalism in the Sudan.* Oxford, U.K.: Clarendon Press, 1969.

Bechtold, Peter K. *Politics in the Sudan: Parliamentary and Military Rule in an Emerging African Nation.* New York: Praeger, 1976.

Beshir, Mohamed Omer. *Revolution and Nationalism in the Sudan.* London: Rex Collings, 1974.

Khalid, Mansour. *The Government They Deserve: The Role of the Elite in Sudan's Political Evolution.* London: Kegan Paul, 1990.

Lesch, Ann M. *The Sudan: Contested National Identities.* Bloomington: Indiana University Press, 1998.

Lobban, Richard A., Jr.; Kramer, Robert S.; and Fluehr-Lobban, Carolyn. *Historical Dictionary of the Sudan,* 3d edition. Lanham, MD: Scarecrow Press, 2002.

Mahmoud, Fatima Babiker. *The Sudanese Bourgeoisie: Vanguard of Development?* London: Zed Books, 1984.

Voll, John Obert, and Voll, Sarah Potts. *The Sudan: Unity and Diversity in a Multicultural State.* Boulder, CO: Westview Press, 1985.

Woodward, Peter. *Sudan, 1898–1989: The Unstable State.* Boulder, CO: Westview Press, 1990.

ANN M. LESCH

SUDANESE CIVIL WARS

Two wars fought since the independence of Sudan in 1956.

There have been two prolonged civil wars in Sudan since independence in 1956. The first lasted from August 1955 to March 1972, and the second began in May 1983. Although both wars have been fought largely in the southern third of the country, their aims have diverged. The first aimed at independence, or at least autonomy for the south, whereas the second primarily aimed at restructuring the central political institutions and devolving power on marginalized areas. Secession is the fallback position should restructuring fail.

The background for the wars lay in the tension between north and south Sudan, the former largely Arabic speaking and Muslim and the latter home to diverse African peoples who adhered to traditional religions or converted to Christianity. Southern peoples had resisted Turco-Egyptian and Mahdist slave raids in the nineteenth century; the British did not manage to subdue them until the 1920s. Britain then imposed the Closed Districts Act (1925) and other measures that banned northern traders and Muslim preachers from the south and even banned Arab-style dress and the use of the Arabic language in government offices and schools. Britain failed to promote education and economic development in the south, leaving it far behind the north when the two parts were merged at independence under a centralized system that placed power in the hands of northerners. Many southerners felt that they had not gained independence but had, instead, exchanged one foreign ruler for another.

First Civil War, 1955–1972

The first civil war was triggered by the Torit mutiny (August 1955) of the Southern Defence Force and was heightened by the northern politicians' rejection of federalism. Under the parliamentary system (1956–1958), the south was marginalized politically. Under the military rule of General Ibrahim Abbud (1958–1964), the religious and ethnic norms that predominate in the north were imposed on the south: Arabic became the language of government and education, Islam was promoted and Christianity repressed, and increasingly harsh military means were used to quell the revolt. The return to civilian rule in late 1964 did not, in itself, end the conflict. Although the Roundtable Conference of March 1965 examined southern grievances, the ruling northern political parties still sought to establish an Islamic state, which was anathema to southerners and northern secularists. Only after Muhammad Jaʿfar Numeiri seized power in May 1969 was an effort made to recognize the inherent ethnic and religious diversity in Sudan and negotiate with the Anya-Nya rebels. The Addis Ababa Accord of 27 February 1972, which ended the first war, was implemented through the Regional Self-Government Act for the Southern Provinces (promulgated on 3 March 1972) and incorporated into the permanent constitution of 1973. The three southern provinces became one large region with its own regional assembly and High Executive Council (HEC). The south gained considerable autonomy in the social and economic fields. Religious discrimination was prohibited, and English was recognized as the principal language in the south because it had been the common language used in schools. Efforts were made to reintegrate the refugees who had fled the country during the seventeen years of fighting and to absorb the Anya-Nya into the regular armed forces.

Despite constitutional safeguards against altering provisions of the Addis Ababa Accord, Numeiri interfered continually in the implementation of the accord. At times, he dissolved the regional assembly, dismissed the HEC, and tried to prevent potential oil revenue from accruing to the south. Finally, he decreed on 5 June 1983 the redivision of the south into its three original provinces. That illegal action completed the dismemberment of the accord. By then, members of the absorbed Anya-Nya forces had engaged in sporadic mutinies, culminating in mutinies in Bor and Pibor in spring 1983. When Numeiri sent troops to crush the mutineers, they fled to the bush, where they were joined by Colonel John Garang de Mabior, head of the army research center in Khartoum.

Second Civil War, 1983

By midsummer 1983 Garang had molded the Sudan People's Liberation Army (SPLA) and its political wing, the Sudan People's Liberation Movement (SPLM) into a militant force that supported the continued unity of Sudan, but on a new basis, requiring proportional sharing of power among the various peoples and regions; special attention to the socioeconomic needs of the deprived east, west, and south; and nondomination by any one religious or racial group over the others. The SPLM gained support as Numeiri's policies led to economic ruin and his institution of Islamic law in September 1983 alienated a wide array of citizens. Numeiri's overthrow in April 1985 did not, however, end the rebellion. The transitional government (April 1985 to April 1986) and the elected government under Prime Minister al-Sadiq al-Mahdi (May 1986 through June 1989) failed to respond to the underlying demands of the SPLM and SPLA. The governments sought to modify, rather than annul, Islamic laws, and they treated the SPLM merely as a southern movement. Nonetheless, in spring 1989 the high command of the armed forces compelled the politicians to negotiate an accord with the SPLM that involved canceling Islamic laws until a constitutional conference could resolve the issue of the legal basis of rule. By then, the SPLA controlled nearly 90 percent of the countryside in the south and had made inroads into areas in the north. Fighting had spread into the Nuba Mountains and the southern Blue Nile Province, where the Ingessana people held economic and political grievances against their Arab overlords.

The Sudan People's Liberation Army fought for a unified Sudan during the country's second civil war. © AP/WIDE WORLD PHOTOS. REPRODUCED BY PERMISSION.

That effort to negotiate a solution was undermined abruptly by the coup d'état on 30 June 1989—the coup's leaders rejected the agreement to hold the constitutional conference and insisted that Islamic laws be retained. A comprehensive Islamic legal system was instituted in the north and the south was fragmented into ten provinces. After the coup, the SPLM aligned with the exiled opposition National Democratic Alliance in March 1990 and gained the support of the ousted high command of the armed forces in September 1990. The SPLM became the most militarily active element in the nationalist opposition to the Islamist military government. By 1991 the SPLA controlled nearly all the south. However, the fall of Mengistu's government in Ethiopia, which had provided essential support for the SPLA, deepened internal tensions inside the SPLA. Commanders in Upper Nile defected in August 1991, thereby enabling the armed forces to recapture many garrisons and to put the SPLA on the defensive.

Prospects for a negotiated solution seemed to vanish. At negotiations in Abuja, Nigeria, in 1992 and 1993, the SPLM proposed establishing a confederal system, just short of secession, but the government responded that "secession will come at the barrel of the gun" (Wondu and Lesch, p. 51). The Organization of African Unity's East African Intergovernmental Authority on Drought and Desertification (IGADD) initiated negotiations in 1994. IGADD called for the formation of a secular state in Sudan; absent a secular, democratic system, the south should have the right to secede. This position pleased the SPLM but infuriated the government in Khartoum. Only in 1997 did the government allow the issue of self-determination to be an agenda item in the negotiations. Soon after, Khartoum's incentive to negotiate diminished: The export of oil from Upper Nile, which began in August 1999, enabled the government to double its arms purchases within two years and establish military industries. The expulsion of the indigenous (largely Nuer) population from the oil fields area accelerated in the late 1990s and early 2000s. This deepened the already severe humanitarian crisis on the south.

After 11 September 2001, the government began to respond to U.S. pressure to negotiate. It reengaged in negotiations (the African body having been renamed the Intergovernmental Authority on Development—IGAD) and signed a potentially breakthrough accord with the SPLM at Machakos (Kenya) in July 2002. This accord called for the formation of a confederation between the north and south that would last for a transitional six years. Negotiations during the winter of 2002 to 2003 over the specifics of power and resource sharing and the relation of religion to the state remained acrimonious and it remained uncertain whether a fundamental accord was possible. The future status of the other marginalized areas also remained uncertain.

The two civil wars sought to deal with the underlying problem of Sudan—how to build unity in a multiethnic and multireligious country. The first war proposed regionalism as the means to give each community a degree of autonomy; the second war proposed restructuring power in the center so that regional autonomy could be secure. Sudanese politicians still grapple with that fundamental problem.

See also ABBUD, IBRAHIM; GARANG, JOHN; NU-
MEIRI, MUHAMMAD JAʿFAR; SUDAN.

Bibliography

Alier, Abel. *Southern Sudan: Too Many Agreements Dishonoured.* Exeter, U.K.: Ithaca Press, 1990.

Beshir, Mohammed Omer. *The Southern Sudan: Background to Conflict.* London: Hurst, 1968.

Deng, Francis. *War of Visions: Conflict of Identities in the Sudan.* Washington, DC: Brookings Institution Press, 1995.

Garang, John. *John Garang Speaks,* edited by Mansour Khalid. London: Kegan Paul, 1987.

Jok, Jok Madut. *War and Slavery in Sudan.* Philadelphia: University of Pennsylvania Press, 2001.

Lesch, Ann M. *The Sudan: Contested National Identities.* Bloomington: Indiana University Press, 1998.

Wondu, Steven, and Lesch, Ann. *Battle for Peace in Sudan: An Analysis of the Abuja Conferences, 1992–1993.* Lanham, MD: University Press of America, 2000.

ANN M. LESCH

SUDANESE WOMEN'S UNION

Women's-rights organization.

The Sudanese Women's Union (SWU), an affiliate of the Sudanese Communist Party and an heir of the Educated Girls' Association and the Association of Sudanese Women as well as other organizations of the 1940s, was founded in 1952. Its first executive committee was composed of Fatima Talib, Khalda Zahir, and Fatima Ahmed Ibrahim.

The SWU was active during the late nationalist period (1952–1956). It reached its zenith in 1965, when it had branches throughout the country and a successful monthly publication, *Sawt al-Marʾa* (Woman's voice), and had made gains in women's rights such as suffrage, equal pay, and maternity leave. In addition, its president, Fatima Ibrahim, was the first woman elected to parliament. Under Ibrahim's leadership, the SWU gained prominence as one of the largest and most effective women's organizations on the African continent, boasting some 15,000 members at its peak.

Political repression under successive military governments took a toll on the SWU. Ultimately,

with the Islamist military coup d'etat in 1989, the SWU was forced underground and Ibrahim into exile in London. Nonetheless, in the 1990s Amnesty International and the United Nations presented the SWU with human-rights awards for its history of struggle and its efforts in exile.

See also GENDER: GENDER AND LAW; GENDER: GENDER AND POLITICS; IBRAHIM, FATIMA AHMED; SUDAN; SUDANESE CIVIL WARS.

Bibliography

Fluehr-Lobban, Carolyn. "Women and Social Liberation: The Sudan Experience." In *Three Studies on National Integration in the Arab World.* North Dartmouth, MA: Association of Arab-American University Graduates, 1974.

Hale, Sondra. *Gender Politics in Sudan: Islamism, Socialism, and the State.* Boulder, CO: Westview Press, 1996.

Hall, Marjorie, and Ismail, Bakhita Amin. *Sisters under the Sun: The Story of Sudanese Women.* London: Longman, 1981.

Mahmoud, Fatima Babiker. *The Role of the Sudanese Women's Movement in Sudanese Politics.* Unpublished M.A. dissertation, University of Khartoum, 1971.

Niblock, Tim. *Class and Power in Sudan.* Albany: State University of New York Press, 1987.

Sanousi, Magda M. el-, and Amin, Nafissa Ahmed el-. "The Women's Movement, Displaced Women, and Rural Women in Sudan." In *Women and Politics Worldwide,* edited by Barbara Nelson and Najma Chowdhury. New Haven, CT: Yale University Press, 1994.

SONDRA HALE

SUDD

Great swamps of the Upper Nile.

Sudd (in Arabic, *sadd,* or barrier) was the word used by European and Arab merchants to describe the largest swamps in the world, which are situated on the Upper Nile in Sudan. It had prevented passage up the Nile River until 1841, when Salim Qapudan, acting on the orders of Muhammad Ali Pasha, viceroy of Egypt, was the first person to pass through its labyrinthine channels. Although open to navigation, the Sudd continues to present a formidable barrier to the passage of water from the equatorial lakes to Sudan and Egypt. Its size expands and contracts depending on the amount of water from the lakes, and its slope, only a few inches per mile, spreads any additional water across the Nilotic plain. The average annual amount of water flowing into the Sudd in the twentieth century is 33 billion cubic meters, of which only half, some 16 billion cubic meters, leaves the Sudd for Sudan and Egypt. In 1976 the French Compagnie de Constructions Internationales (CCI) began the excavation of the Jonglei Canal to permit water from the Lake Plateau to bypass the swamps. The excavation of the 225-mile canal past the Sudd threatened to disrupt the seasonal movement of livestock and the migrations of great herds of African wildlife. When the Sudan People's Liberation Movement/Army (SPLM/A), led by John Garang de Mabior, revolted against the Sudan government in May 1983, his forces terminated the canal's construction at mile 166. It has never been resumed.

See also NILE RIVER.

Bibliography

Collins, Robert. *The Nile.* New Haven, CT: Yale University Press, 2002.

Howell, Paul P.; Lock, M.; and Cobb, S. *The Jonglei Canal: Impact and Opportunity.* Cambridge, U.K.: Cambridge University Press, 1988.

ROBERT O. COLLINS

SUEZ CANAL

Channel built from 1856 to 1869 that links the Mediterranean Sea to the Red Sea.

Several early rulers of Egypt constructed canals for the passage of seagoing ships, usually linking the Nile River to the Gulf of Suez. The followers of Saint-Simon, the French utopian socialist (Claude Henri de Rouvray, Comte de Saint-Simon, 1760–1825), proposed building a canal linking the Mediterranean to the Red Sea in the early nineteenth century. The entrepreneur who actually carried out this scheme was Ferdinand de Lesseps, a former French diplomat who was on friendly terms with Muhammad Saʿid Pasha. As soon as Saʿid became Egypt's viceroy in 1854, de Lesseps described to him his plan for constructing and financing this waterway, which would be the largest public-works project in Egypt since the pyramids. Saʿid consented, but it took some time for de Lesseps to secure approval from the sultan of the Ottoman

The Suez Canal was inaugurated on 17 November 1869. The waterway, which extends one hundred miles and has been enlarged twice since its completion, is used to transport 41 percent of goods and cargo that reach the Persian/Arab Gulf ports and 14 percent of total world trade. © BETTMANN/CORBIS. REPRODUCED BY PERMISSION.

Empire and the European powers (Britain was strongly opposed to a canal that might imperil its defense of India) and to raise the necessary capital.

The construction cost, estimated at more than 450 million French francs (worth about $100 million at that time), was borne mainly by Egyptian taxpayers and by thousands of unpaid or underpaid Egyptian peasants who were forced into corvée labor until the European powers and the Ottoman government enjoined the Universal Maritime Suez Canal Company to stop this practice.

When the 100-mile waterway was opened in 1869, it was 30 feet deep and 100 feet wide, adequate for most oceangoing vessels at the time. It soon became a main trade route for steam-driven passenger and cargo ships because it reduced travel time between Europe and East Africa, South Asia, China, Japan, and the East Indies. The canal was supposed to be open to ships of all nations in war or peace, but Britain made sure that it was closed to shipping for Germany and its allies in both world wars, and Egypt barred its use to Israel and to other countries' ships carrying goods for Israel until 1975. The canal was administered by the Canal Company until it was nationalized by Egypt under Gamal Abdel Nasser in 1956. Since then it has been admin-

Suez Canal

	No. of transits		Net ship tonnage in thousands of tons	
	2000	2001	2000	2001
Tankers	2,563	2,764	105,237	117,014
Other vessels	11,578	11,222	333,725	339,099
Total	14,141	13,986	438,962	456,113

SOURCE: MEES 45:18, 6 May 2002.

TABLE BY GGS INFORMATION SERVICES, THE GALE GROUP.

istered by the Suez Canal Authority. It was closed from 1956 to 1967 and from 1967 to 1975 because of the Arab-Israel conflict.

The canal was enlarged from 1960 to 1964 and from 1975 to 1980 to accommodate larger oil tankers, which have become its main users; in 1992, it was 590 feet wide at its narrowest point and had a maximum draught of 53 feet. Transit time is now 15 hours, and 80 ships can transit per day. The Suez Canal is a major route for transport of crude oil from the Persian Gulf. In 2000 the northbound tankers from the Gulf carried 28.2 million tons of crude oil (about 580,000 barrels per day) and in 2001 28.8 million tons (about 592,000 barrels per day).

The transit rates are established by the Suez Canal Authority. They are computed to keep the canal transit fees attractive to shippers. For example, in January 2002, the fee for the transport of crude oil for very large tankers was $1.21 per ton above the first 30,000 tons. Such a rate would amount to approximately $190,000 for a 150,000-ton oil tanker.

See also LESSEPS, FERDINAND DE; NASSER, GAMAL ABDEL; SAʿID PASHA; SUEZ CRISIS (1956–1957).

Bibliography

Beatty, Charles. *De Lesseps of Suez.* New York: Harper, 1956.

Kyle, Keith. *Suez: Britain's End of Empire in the Middle East.* New York: I.B. Tauris, 2003.

Marlowe, John. *The Making of the Suez Canal.* London: Cresset Press, 1964.

Schonfield, Hugh J. *The Suez Canal in Peace and War.* Coral Gables, FL: University of Miami Press, 1969.

ARTHUR GOLDSCHMIDT
UPDATED BY JEAN-FRANÇOIS SEZNEC

SUEZ CANAL UNIVERSITY

Public university founded in Ismaʿilia, Egypt, in 1976.

Egypt's President Anwar al-Sadat (1970–1981) founded Suez Canal University as part of his plan to rebuild and symbolically reclaim the war-damaged Suez Canal cities. In 1975 he had reopened the canal, which had been blocked since the June 1967 Arab–Israel War. With five colleges in Ismaʿilyya and two each in al-Arish and Suez, the university has a teaching staff of 638, 12,312 undergraduates, and 1,588 graduate students.

Bibliography

Suez Canal University. Available from <http://www.suez.edu.eg>.

The World of Learning 2004. London, Europa Publications, 2004: pp. 492–93.

DONALD MALCOLM REID

SUEZ CRISIS (1956–1957)

The British and French challenging of Egyptian President Nasser's nationalization of the Suez Canal, also involving Israel, and ending in the achievement of control of the Canal by Egypt.

On 26 July 1956, before 100,000 Egyptians in the main square of Alexandria, Egyptian President Gamal Abdul Nasser announced his decision to nationalize the Suez Canal Company. This came as a rebuff to the recent withdrawal of the United States and Great Britain from their pledge to finance the construction of a high dam across the Nile River near Aswan. The Suez Canal lay formally under Egyptian sovereignty, but the implementation of these sovereign rights was regulated by an international convention agreed upon by Egypt and several maritime powers in 1888 in Constantinople. The revenue and daily administration of navigation through the canal were handled by an international company based in Paris and owned mainly by British and French shareholders. There was nothing illegal in the act of nationalization, since Nasser promised to compensate the shareholders faithfully and ensure there was no disruption of navigation. But Great Britain and France saw in Nasser's act a defiant blow to their prestige and political standing in the Middle East and North Africa.

Within hours the British and French decided jointly to make every effort, including the use of military action if necessary, to regain control of the Canal. They ordered their chiefs of staff to plan an invasion of Egypt. Under the command of British general Sir Charles Keightley and French admiral Pierre Barjot, a large force assembled in several Mediterranean ports and operative plans were laid out for an operation code-named "Musketeer." The U.S. administration, while in agreement on the need to ensure the international nature of the Canal, made clear from the outset its strong objection to the use of force for this purpose. Also, considering the support Nasser was allegedly giving to Arab rebels in Algeria, French public opinion supported its government's hard-lined intention. Public opinion in Britain, even within the ruling Conservative Party, was, however, divided.

In order to overcome these difficulties and save the time needed for the preparation of the military operation, some preliminary diplomatic measures had to be taken. While British Prime Minister Sir Anthony Eden and French Prime Minister Guy Mollet interpreted these measures as preparation of the military operation, American Secretary of State John Foster Dulles took them as an opportunity to calm his allies and forestall any resort to force. As expected, the Soviet Union and several "neutral" states led by India unequivocally supported Egypt's position. A conference was held between 18 and 23 August in London, at the end of which a resolution signed by eighteen of the participating maritime states was presented to President Nasser by Australian Prime Minister Sir Robert Menzies. The resolution demanded that Egypt agree to the empowerment of a new international agency that represented the interests of the canal users and took over the administration of canal affairs.

The French and British, having almost completed their military preparations, were ready to take the next diplomatic step of bringing the issue before the United Nations (UN) Security Council. But Dulles feared that such a move would lead to an impasse

and precipitate the use of force. He persuaded his allies and several other maritime states to convene once more on 19 September for a second conference in London. On 21 September the group announced the formation of a Suez Canal Users' Association (SCUA), which was supposed to deal with matters of finance and administration of the canal on a practical level and uphold the users' rights. But SCUA was stillborn, since in the meantime Nasser had replaced all the old company's navigators and arranged for uninterrupted operation of the canal under Egyptian management. Prudently, Nasser decided at this stage not to force the issue of payments for the passage in the canal, rendering SCUA nothing more than a paper declaration.

At the end of September Britain and France, becoming restless as their assembled invasion force began to exact a heavy burden, filed a formal complaint in the Security Council. Dag Hammarskjöld, the UN secretary-general, tried to mediate a compromise in private meetings with foreign secretaries Selwyn Lloyd (Great Britain), Christian Pineau (France), and Mahmud Fawzi (Egypt), and formulated a six-point draft proposal to be elaborated at a later stage. But France and Great Britain were not looking for a compromise in defeating Nasser. Despite the fact that the Security Council voted favorably on Hammarskjöld's "Six Points," Lloyd and Pineau insisted on another formal Security Council resolution that would condemn and nullify the nationalization act. This proposal was defeated by a Soviet veto and the council disbanded without a practical solution to the crisis.

From the British and French standpoint, by the middle of October 1956 all diplomatic measures were exhausted and the time was ripe for the "Musketeer" operation. But in view of the smooth operation of the canal, mounting opposition inside Britain, and repeated warnings of the American administration against the use of force, Eden procrastinated. It seemed that he had lost a clear and compelling casus belli.

From the beginning of the crisis the British, knowing of the warm relations developing between France and Israel over recent months, had insisted on a strict separation between their quarrel with Nasser and the Arab–Israeli conflict. Israel, Britain maintained, should be left outside the imbroglio. Despite having many grievances against Egypt and despite the disruption of the balance of power introduced in September 1955 by a huge Soviet-Egyptian arms deal, Israel preferred to concentrate all its energies on absorbing the large quantities of armaments acquired from France since the end of June. The French, on the other hand, whose part in "Musketeer" was to operate on the east bank the Canal, sought to examine the possibility of getting tactical assistance from Israeli forces, if they could press the Egyptians in the Sinai Peninsula from the east. By the end of September, recognizing Eden's hesitations, the French had begun to consider triggering the entire situation by inducing Israel to take the initiative and attack Nasser first.

Invited by the French, Golda Meir, Israel's minister of foreign affairs, together with General Moshe Dayan, the Israel Defense Force (IDF) chief of staff, and Shimon Peres, the director-general of the Ministry of Defense, arrived in Paris on 30 September for exploratory talks. The St. Germain Conference did not yield any definitive military plans, however, since the situation at the UN was not resolved and Britain's position remained unclear. Under the assumption that Israel might be invited at some point to participate in the war, further French armaments were rapidly shipped to Israel and a group of high-ranking French officers, headed by Major General Maurice Challe, proceeded to Tel Aviv to explore operations possibilities. Having become better acquainted with Israel's capabilities, Challe conceived a new plan: Israel would initiate an assault on the Sinai, and the French and British would issue an ultimatum to Israel and Egypt to withdraw so that French and British forces could occupy the canal and assure free and secure navigation. Assuming that Nasser would reject the demand, the road for "Musketeer" was open.

Eden was persuaded to join in this collusion, under the strict condition that it not look as if Great Britain had invited Israel's attack, and that Great Britain appeared to be reacting to a new situation provoked by Israel. Prime Minister of Israel David Ben-Gurion considered the proposal humiliating; he also did not trust the British intention to fulfill their share of the "scenario." To unravel the complex situation, a highly confidential meeting took place between 20 and 23 October at a small private villa in Sèvres, outside Paris. A series of meetings involving Ben-Gurion, Moshe Dayan, and Shimon Peres from Israel; Guy Mollet, Christian Pineau, and Maurice Bourges-Maunoury, the French minister of defense, and briefly also involving Selwyn Lloyd of Great Britain, took place. After the group reached agreement on slight changes in the Challe scenario, and the French assured Israel of military reinforcement, the Sèvres Protocol was signed by Ben-Gurion, Pineau, and Patrick Dean, a senior British official.

On 29 October, an Israeli parachute battalion was dropped east of the Mitla Pass, about forty miles east of Port Suez, and Israeli armor and infantry began to push west into the heart of Sinai. In accordance with the Sèvres Protocol, the next day an appeal was made jointly by the French and British governments demanding that the belligerent parties clear the canal zone. Israel, not intending to reach the banks of the canal anyway, acceded to the request. Nasser, as expected, declined. Thirty-six hours later, on the evening of 31 October, the British and French launched heavy air attacks on Egyptian airports and other military and supply installations, operating from their bases in Cyprus and from aircraft carriers off the shore of Egypt, and started the six-day naval voyage of their invasion forces from Malta, Toulon, and Algiers.

The thinly disguised deception and the unwarranted attack on Egypt incensed President Eisenhower who started, in concert with the Soviet Union and almost the entire international community, to put pressure on the colluding parties. Because British and French vetoes would be used to stymie the Security Council, a special emergency session of the General Assembly convened under the "Uniting for Peace" formula (which had been used during the Korean crisis in 1950). On 5 November French and British paratroopers dropped near the towns of Port Said and Port Tawfiq at the northern edge of the canal, while Israel had by this point already completed the conquest of the entire Sinai Peninsula. The landing from the sea of further troops the next day completed the capture of Port Saʿid, but their advance was arrested about thirty miles to the south. The mounting pressure of the UN, threats of the Soviet Union, and heavy pressure of public opinion in Great Britain opposing the war, were all factors that moved Eden to order a cease-fire.

Following a proposal devised by Lester Pearson, the Canadian minister of foreign affairs, the UN established a special Emergency Force (UNEF) under the command of Canadian general E. L. M Burns. The invading parties now succumbed to international pressure and withdrew their forces from the Canal on 22 December, assuming that UNEF would take responsibility for the management of the areas they evacuated. But, acting on their sovereign prerogatives, the Egyptians immediately took over those territories and UNEF moved eastward into Sinai to shadow the gradually retreating Israeli forces. By the middle of February 1957, after the IDF completed the evacuation of almost the entire peninsula, a crisis developed because Israel had hoped to hold on to the Gaza Strip and to the entrance to the Gulf of Aqaba (Elat) at Sharm al-Shaykh. Heavy American pressure and the threat of UN sanctions moved Ben-Gurion to withdraw Israeli forces to the old armistice demarcation lines by 6 March 1957. The UN force was newly deployed along the Egyptian side of the Egyptian-Israeli frontier, but the Egyptians refrained from returning to the Sinai Peninsula and the Gaza Strip with more than token forces. Both these measures put an end, at least for the following ten years, to the many frictions that had inflamed relations along those frontiers before the war, and left the Straits of Tiran open to Israeli navigation.

The 1956 Suez War is commonly considered a major blunder in modern international relations and a watershed leading to the final demise of British and French colonialism. Within a few years both Great Britain and France lost their positions in the Middle East and North Africa, and their status as first-rate powers waned while dependence on U.S. power grew. The Eisenhower Doctrine of January 1957 gave a symbolic imprimatur to the evolving new situation in the Middle East. The main winner of the entire affair was President Nasser, who not only achieved nationalization of the Suez Company and expelled the last vestiges of British presence along the canal, but also emerged as the uncontested leader of the Arab people and became, along with India's Jawaharlal Nehru and Yugoslavia's Josef Broz Tito, one of the outstanding leaders of the neutralist bloc of nations.

See also ARAB–ISRAEL WAR (1956); LONDON CONFERENCE (1956); SÈVRES PROTOCOL.

Bibliography

Bar-On, Mordechai. *The Gates of Gaza: Israel's Road to Suez and Back, 1955–1957.* New York: St. Martin's, 1994.

Burns, E. L. M. *Between Arab and Israeli.* London: G. G. Harrap, 1962.

Fawzi, Mahmoud. *Suez 1956, an Egyptian Perspective.* London: Shorouk International, 1986.

Golani, Motti. *Israel in Search of a War: The Sinai Campaign, 1955–1956.* Brighton and Portland, OR: Sussex Academic Press, 1998.

Kyle, Keith. *Suez.* London: Weidenfeld and Nicolson, 1991.

Love, Kennett. *Suez— The Twice-Fought War: A History.* New York: McGraw-Hill, 1969.

Lucas, W. Scott. *Divided We Stand: Britain, the US, and the Suez Crisis.* London: Hodder & Stoughton, 1991.

Nutting, Anthony. *No End of a Lesson: The Story of Suez.* London: Constable, 1967.

Pineau, Christian. *1956 Suez.* Paris: R. Laffont, 1976.

MORDECHAI BAR-ON

SUEZ–MEDITERRANEAN PIPELINE

Pipeline linking the Red and Mediterranean seas.

The Suez–Mediterranean Pipeline (SUMED) was opened in 1977. It consists of two pipelines 210 miles long and 42 inches in diameter. It has a capacity of 2.4 million barrels per day. SUMED allows the Persian Gulf oil-producing states to bypass the Suez Canal, which cannot accommodate tankers larger than 200,000 tons. The pipeline can provide an alternative route to Gulf exporters if the Suez canal is blocked, as happened in 1973. Half of the pipeline is owned by the Egyptian General Petroleum Company. The balance is divided among PETROMIN of Saudi Arabia, the Abu Dhabi Oil Company, and the Qatar General Petroleum Company.

SUMED is designed to allow easy transshipment and dispatch to numerous destinations with minimal disruption. It can transport different grades of crude oil with minimal contamination. The terminals at Ayn Sukhna, on the Red Sea, and at Sidi Krayr, near Alexandria, can accommodate both very small tankers and those over 500,000 tons. Many tankers too large to use the Suez Canal can unload a portion of their oil in Ayn Sukhna, sail through the canal, and reload in Sidi Krayr.

Seventy-three percent of the oil transported by SUMED is destined for Europe. The pipeline has more than forty clients. The main ones are the major oil companies, Arabian American Oil Company, and the National Iranian Oil Company.

See also PETROLEUM, OIL, AND NATURAL GAS; PETROMIN.

JEAN-FRANÇOIS SEZNEC

SUFISM AND THE SUFI ORDERS

Islamic mysticism.

The word *Sufi* is generally assumed to derive from *suf* (wool), in reference to the simple clothing of the early ascetic mystics. It refers to the practice and philosophical tradition in Islam that relates to spiritualism and mysticism.

Theological and Philosophical Basis

Mysticism in Islam has two distinct origins. The first is the Qur'an itself, which postulates an intensely personal and direct relationship between the individual and God. This fervent devotion was expressed in the early practice of Hasan al-Basri (d. 728) and the poetry of Rabi'a al-Adawiyya (d. 801) and gave rise to spiritual Sufism. Practiced by preachers who embraced a simple—almost ascetic—life, it also included celibacy and extensive religious worship and contemplation carried out individually or, more often, in a *halaqa*, or circle of devotees.

The second source is the mystical doctrines of other religious traditions, including gnosticism, Christianity, Zoroastrianism, and Hinduism, which converts to Islam brought into their new faith, giving rise to theosophical Sufism. These traditions had elaborate theosophical doctrines, at the heart of which lay the concept of the unity with the divine, the ultimate goal of the mystic. However, the principle of *tawhid* (divine unity), the cornerstone of orthodox Islamic belief, establishes God's absolute unity and absolute transcendence, thereby precluding any possibility of the creature joining with the Creator.

Theosophical Sufism eventually resolved this contradiction through the elaboration of a number

Idris I (1889–1983) became king of Libya in 1951, when the country declared its independence. He ruled until 1969, when he traveled to Turkey for medical treatment and Muammar al-Qaddafi overthrew the monarchy. © HULTON-DEUTSCH COLLECTION/CORBIS. REPRODUCED BY PERMISSION.

of paradoxical concepts that maintain at once unity and difference, annihilation of self into the divine (*fana*) and self-persistence (*baqa*), presence and absence, intoxication and sobriety. The analogy of seeing God in a mirror image of oneself is often used to explain this unity with the divine. The reinterpretation of *tawhid* as unity of being, according to which the mystic could claim unity with divine existence or attributes while preserving the transcendence of divine essence, allowed Sufism to claim adherence to fundamental orthodox Islamic dogma and gave Islamic mysticism its distinctive flavor.

On the basis of this new interpretation, divine truth (*haqiqa*) became the ultimate object of the Sufi gnosis, which was called *ma'rifa* (intuitive knowledge) to set it apart from the rational and exoteric discourse of the law; the law itself became secondary—either a mere step to reach unity with the divine or a hindrance that could be dismissed after a certain level of illumination. Knowledge of the divine

Iraqi Sufis practice a mystical form of Islam that focuses heavily on enlightening the soul through internal holiness, rather than external surroundings. Pictured is a group of Sufis praying at their shrine in Baghdad. © BENJAMIN LOWY/CORBIS. REPRODUCED BY PERMISSION.

nature was called *kashf* and was considered to be infallible, a characteristic that in orthodox Islam is attributed only to Prophetic revelation. The concept of the unity of being was tied to the Hellenistic understanding of God as a First Intellect from whose self-contemplation the world emanates, and that was reinforced by the Greek-inspired Muslim philosophers, who adopted that understanding against the dogma of the Muslim theological schools. The articulation of theosophical Sufism and its harmonization with the *shariʿa* (Islamic law) was carried out by Muhyi al-Din ibn al-Arabi (d. 1240), who systematized a sainthood hierarchy that culminated in a "seal of sainthood" parallel to the Qurʾanic "seal of prophecy" that he attributed to himself.

Although at first fought by the orthodox, this process of presenting the theosophical concepts in Islamic terms and justifying them through the esoteric interpretation of the Qurʾan eventually made Sufism legitimate. The process was furthered by the elaboration of a body of Sufi prophetic sayings (*hadith*) that justified Sufi practice (although that led to the elaboration of anti-Sufi *hadith*.) The full adherence by theosophical Sufism to the *shariʿa* and the nominal adherence to the concept of *tawhid* met the main legal requirement of the faith. In addition, the materialism that accompanied the economic, technological, and cultural expansion of the Islamic empire in Umawi and Abbassid times, as well as the tendency among literalist jurists and theologians to reduce the law and the faith to a numbing amalgam of rules and rituals, helped the spread of Sufism by causing a popular reaction against these trends. In the eleventh century, Abu Hamid al-Ghazzali (d. 1111), who dominated the orthodox movement with his powerful intellect, strongly defended the spiritual dimension in Sufism against the impoverished literalist views of its most vocal opponents and integrated it into the theological expression of the faith; and although he opposed the unity of being and the asceticism and withdrawal preached by some Sufis, the stature of al-Ghazzali helped validate Sufism. Sufism could now spread unimpeded in all its various expression, although any unambiguous claim of having achieved unity with the divine met with retribution or persecution from the orthodox theologians (as happened to Husayn bin Mansur al-Hallaj, executed for heresy in 922.)

Sufi Orders

Partly because orthodox resistance precluded its integration in the theological disciplines and partly because of its very nature, Sufism did not become an organized discipline and came to refer to anything from intense piety to specific devotional steps to mystical philosophy. Most often, however, a Sufi cell (called *tariqa* or *zawiya* or *ribat*) was formed around a teacher, and spiritual doctrine and practice could vary widely from one cell to another. Generally, the Sufi experience centers on a number of practices (including *dhikr* or recitation of the Qur'an, contemplation, prayer, singing, dancing, and fasting) prescribed by the Sufi shaykh, who determines the progress of the disciple through the *maqamat* (stages of spiritual development, codified by Dhu Nun, d. 859.) Sufism contributed greatly to Islamic art in poetry (that of Jalal al-Din al-Rumi, d. 1273, is the best known in the Muslim world as well as in the West) and in literature and music.

By the middle of the ninth century, Sufi orders had established schools throughout the Muslim world. Since any teacher could establish a cell, these were innumerable. However, the main Sufi schools established a *silsila* (chain) through which the master's teachings were transmitted from teacher to disciple, and a loose lineage was traced back either to Abu al-Qasim al-Junayd (d. 910) in the Arab world or to Abu Yazid al-Bistami (d. 874) in Central Asia and Iran. Within the Arab tradition, the Rifaʿiyya

(Ahmad al-Rifaʿi, d. 1182), became know for some wild practices and spread widely until overtaken in the fifteenth century by the Qadiriyya (Abd al-Qadir al-Jilani, d. 1166), whose orthodox bent and more flexible teachings became popular. Less famous because of its emphasis on strict mystical discipline was the Suhrawardiyya (al-Suhrawardi, d. 1168), which gained favor with the upper classes. Within Central Asia and Anatolia, were the Mawlawiyya (also Mevlevis; Jalal al-Din al-Rumi, d. 1258), an introspective order known for its use of chanting and its dancing dervishes, the nomadic Yasawiyya (Ahmad al-Yisavi, d. 1166), and the powerful and orthodox Naqshbandiyya (Muhammad Baha' al-Din al Naqshabandi, d. 1389), which was popular with the elite in India and Central Asia. Also popular in the Indian subcontinent was the Chishtiyya (Muʿin al-Din Chishti, d. 1236). In Africa, the Badawiyya in Egypt (Ahmad al-Badawi, d. 1276) and the Shadhiliyya (Abu al-Hassan al-Shadhili, d. 1258) had emerged from the Rifaʿiyya, though the latter was more insistent on following the Sunna (tradition of the Prophet) and discouraged asceticism. The Tijaniyya (Ahmad al-Tijani, d. 1815) became very active in fighting European colonization in Northern Africa in the nineteenth century. Amongst the Shiʿa, the most popular orders were the Safawiyya (Safiy al-Din, d. 1334), which originally had been a Sunni movement, and the Niʿmatullah (Niʿmatullah bin ʿAbdullah, d. 1431). The orders shared the same general structure, an initiation ceremony during which the disciple (or the affiliate) was inducted in a similar path, marked with individual and collective rituals that focused on total obedience to the Sufi master.

These orders contributed greatly to the spread of Islam and often served as social protest movements, through their association with craft and commercial guilds, against state authority and abuses of power. But the veneration of the saints and the belief in their power to perform miracles (a claim that was eventually sanctioned by orthodoxy) slowly degenerated in popular practice into a muddle of saint worship, fatalism, superstition, and magic and cultic practices. This was accentuated by the excesses of the more extreme Sufi organizations, which demanded profession of faith in the saints as part of the *shahada* (Muslim creed); other organizations allowed followers to use illicit substances and disregard the law in the pursuit of the loftier goal of achieving knowledge of the divine; still others preached extreme asceticism and withdrawal from the world. Such excesses had always met with strong disapproval from orthodox jurists, although all of the jurists accepted the spiritual dimension of Sufism, but it was not until the reform movements of the eighteenth century that a reaction against these excesses took place. Building on the criticism of theosophical Sufism by Taqiyy al-Din ibn Taymiyya, Muhammad ibn Abd al-Wahhab (d. 1792) introduced a strict return to the pristine sources of Islam, namely the Qur'an and the *Sunna* (the Prophet's tradition), and condemned the morally lax practices and quasi-worship of the saints and the Prophet that were practiced by Sufis.

In India and North Africa, reform was also under way, although for different reasons. The Sufi movements, whose active preaching had brought massive conversions to Islam in those areas, had adopted beliefs and practices from their converts that were at times clearly in opposition to Islamic belief and to the *shari'a.* Alarmed by this syncretism, Sufi masters including Muhammad al-Baqi Billah and Ahmad Sirhindi in India and Muhammad ibn Idris in North Africa initiated a move to restore orthodoxy and in the process reinterpreted the Sufi concepts and shifted their content from unity of being to unity of witnessing God (*wahdat al-shuhud*) and from a traditional Sufi path (*tariqa*) centered on a saint to a *tariqa Muhammadiyya* (the Prophet's *tariqa*) centered on the emulation of the Prophet through strict and active observation of the *shari'a.* But the threat that European colonialism posed to the Muslim movements transformed their efforts from religious and social reform to a national jihad against the invaders, which only hastened the disintegration of a Sufi worldview based on otherworldliness and ascetic withdrawal. Modern Muslim movements facing many of the same political challenges have generally been critical of Sufism and have espoused more and more a legalistic interpretation of the faith. However, despite the decline of the Sufi orders in recent history, many of the Sufi rituals and traditions survive today in individual and communal practice.

The Muslim world's understanding of its faith has constantly oscillated between the poles of excessive spiritualism and legalistic interpretation, although the existence of these poles has kept Islam from falling permanently into one or the other extreme, in the one case by preserving the spiritual dimension of the faith and preventing the reification of religious consciousness and in the other by grounding the faith in textual sources and moral activism. The great jurists and theologians have attempted to maintain a balance between these two dimensions of Islam, and despite opposition to certain elements in it, Sufism is generally seen as part of normal religious commitment. Thus, it was considered perfectly acceptable during the 1980s for the vice president of Cairo University, a noted scholar in Arabic-Islamic philosophy, to serve as the leader of Sufi circles in Egypt. Popular religion, however, has generally swung from one extreme to the other.

See also HADITH; MEVLEVI BROTHERHOOD; NAQSHBANDI; QADIRIYYA ORDER; QUR'AN; *SHARI'A;* SUNNA.

Bibliography

Nasr, Sayyed Hossein. *Three Muslim Sages: Avicenna, Suhrawardi, ibn Arabi.* Cambridge, MA: Harvard University Press, 1964.

Rahman, Fazlur. *Islam,* 2d edition. Chicago: University of Chicago Press, 1979.

Trimingham, J. Spencer. *The Sufi Orders in Islam.* Oxford: Clarendon, 1971.

MAYSAM J. AL FARUQI

SUISSA, ALBERT
[1959–]

Israeli author.

Suissa was born in Casablanca, Morocco, and emigrated to Israel in 1963. He grew up in Jerusalem, where he studied in an Orthodox school. Later he moved to Paris and studied mime, taught theater, and performed with a mime troupe. He now lives in Paris and Jerusalem.

Akud (The bound, 1990), Suissa's only book, consists of novellas that cumulatively form a variation of a bildungsroman. The protagonist is a child of an immigrant North African family uprooted and replanted on the outskirts of Jerusalem—for that matter, on the margins of Israeli society. Rich with ornamental details, fantasy, and ethnic authenticity, the novel relates the development of a child whose disintegrating family has had its very foundations undermined by its transplantation. Pitted against the slogans of Eastern European Zionism and mainstream Israeli culture, the impotence and irrelevance of the family is portrayed boldly. Both the original home and the new home seem to be driven by violence and oppression, which breed a devastating alienation. Suissa's language and the structure of the novel are arabesque in pattern and logic, baroque in style, and modern in psychological sensitivities.

Bibliography

Gover, Yerach. *Zionism: The Limits of Moral Discourse in Israeli Hebrew Fiction.* Minneapolis: University of Minnesota Press, 1994.

Shaked, Gershon, ed. *Hebrew Writers: A General Directory.* Israel: Institute for the Translation of Hebrew Literature, 1993.

ZVIA GINOR
DONNA ROBINSON DIVINE

SULAYMAN, HIKMAT
[1889–1946]

Iraqi government official.

Hikmat Sulayman held various senior administrative positions and ministerial posts in Iraq in the 1920s and 1930s. Associated first with Yasin al-Hashimi and Rashid Ali al-Kaylani, he fell out with them in 1935. His friendship with Bakr Sidqi led to his becoming prime minister after the latter's coup in October 1936, a post he held until Sidqi's overthrow in August 1937.

PETER SLUGLETT

SULAYMANIYA

Town in northeastern Iraq, capital of Iraqi Kurdistan.

A market town in Kurdistan, Iraq, 60 miles (96.5 km) east of Kirkuk, Sulaymaniya is bounded on the east and south by Iran. Its name was linked to Süleyman Paşa, *wali* of Baghdad when the town was founded in 1781. Surrounded by mountains, the town has cold winters and mild summers. It has archaeological sites (some in caves) that date to about fifty thousand years ago.

Most of the population are Kurds. Dokan Dam, 37 miles (60 km) northwest of the town, has a hydroelectric station.

Bibliography

Harris, George L. *Iraq: Its People, Its Society, Its Culture.* New Haven, CT: HRAF Press, 1958.

Hassani, Abdul Razzak, Al-. *The History of Modern Iraq.* Baghdad, 1980.

NAZAR AL-KHALAF

SULEIMAN, MULAY

Alawi sultan of Morocco, 1792–1822.

Heir to the badly divided government of his brother and predecessor, Mulay Yazid (ruled 1790–1792), Suleiman also faced provincial unrest and a weakened tax base. He brought much of coastal and central Morocco under *makhzan* control, although his capture and subsequent release by Berber forces in the central Atlas mountains in 1819 underscored the limits of the crown's control over large provinces of Morocco. Suleiman is also known for his bid to suppress popular Sufism and other local socioreligious activities. In the face of growing European pressures, Suleiman adopted a generally hostile and insular stance.

See also ALAWI; SUFISM AND THE SUFI ORDERS.

Bibliography

Burke, Edmund, III. *Prelude to Protectorate in Morocco: Precolonial Protest and Resistance, 1860–1912.* Chicago: University of Chicago, 1976.

Pennell, C. R. *Morocco since 1830: A History.* New York: New York University Press, 2000.

MATTHEW S. GORDON

SULH, KAZEM AL-
[1909–1977]

Lebanese politician, diplomat, and journalist; former ambassador to Iraq; member of parliament, 1960–1964.

Kazem al-Sulh (also al-Solh) was born into a prestigious Sunni family that was active in the Arab nationalist movement at the turn of the century. He emerged in the 1930s as one of the most articulate advocates of an independent, sovereign Lebanon that would be free from French control but would also remain separate from Syria. In defending the territorial boundaries that the French mandatory power had established, he went against the dominant opinion of people in his community, who still favored reintegrating into Syria those regions the French had annexed to Mount Lebanon in 1920.

Unlike many of his Muslim contemporaries, Kazem al-Sulh understood very early on that independence from France could only be gained by reaching out to moderate Christians, particularly Maronites. He argued that the Maronites would more easily loosen their ties to France and join the nationalist cause if they could be reassured that independence would not be followed by absorption into Syria, or by policies that would undermine Lebanon's political autonomy vis-à-vis other Arab countries. He aspired to create an independent Lebanon based on Muslim-Christian accommodation. It would be possible to achieve this goal, he believed, if the Sunnis agreed to a historic compromise: if they would shed their traditional demand for reunification with Syria in exchange for the Maronites' abandoning their call for a Christian Lebanon and renouncing French protection and interference in Lebanese affairs.

To promote these ideas, Kazem al-Sulh created a group called al-Nida al-Qawmi (The National Appeal), which attracted moderate Sunnis and became a political party in 1945. Although it never was able to develop a mass following, the group played an important role in mobilizing Sunni support for an independent Lebanon. It also strengthened the hand of Maronite leaders like Bishara al-Khuri who were arguing within their own communities for the very kind of cross-confessional compromise that Kazem al-Sulh and like-minded Sunni notables and intellectuals were advocating. Some measure of the influence of Kazem al-Sulh and groups such as al-Nida al-Qawmi can be gotten by noting that the aspirations they articulated were eventually embodied in the 1943 National Pact. Kazem and his brother Taki al-Din are usually credited with facilitating the conversion of their first cousin Riyad al-Sulh to the cause of an independent, sovereign Lebanon managed through a Maronite-Sunni partnership.

Although his ideas had a critical impact on the course of Lebanese history, Kazem al-Sulh played only a marginal role in post-independence Lebanese politics. Although he was a gifted writer and political thinker, he never was a particularly effective politician. By the late 1950s, al-Nida al-Qawmi had ceased to function, a victim to the rising tide of Arab nationalism. Kazem al-Sulh's politics had always been based on compromise, tolerance, and conciliation, and this approach had become increasingly inappropriate in the context of an Arab world that, caught in the ferment of the 1950s and 1960s, witnessed the radicalization of the Sunni masses. Kazem al-Sohl served as Lebanese ambassador to Iraq during the 1940s and 1950s, and he was criticized by pan-Arab intellectuals and politicians for the part it was alleged he played in designing the ill-fated Baghdad Pact. Thanks to Christian votes, he was elected a Sunni representative from Zahle to the parliament (1960–1964). Kazem al-Sulh ended his career as a relatively uninfluential politician, largely discredited within his own community.

See also BAGHDAD PACT (1955); NATIONAL PACT (LEBANON); SULH, RIYAD AL-.

Bibliography

Goria, Wader R. *Sovereignty and Leadership in Lebanon, 1943–1976*. London: Ithaca Press, 1985.

Hudson, Michael C. *The Precarious Republic: Political Modernization in Lebanon.* Boulder, CO: Westview Press, 1985.

Johnson, Michael. *Class and Client in Beirut: The Sunni Muslim Community and the Lebanese State, 1840–1985*. London: Ithaca Press, 1986.

GUILAIN P. DENOEUX

SULH, RASHID AL-
[1926–]

Lebanese politician; prime minister, 1974–1975 and 1992.

Rashid al-Sulh (also Solh), born into a minor branch of the prestigious Sunni Sulh family, was brought up in the house of former prime minister Sami al-Sulh. After studying at the College of the Christian Brothers and al-Maqasid College, he received his LL.B. from Saint Joseph University in Beirut and became a lawyer and a judge. Elected deputy for Beirut in 1964 and 1972, he inherited the political mantle of Sami al-Sulh following the latter's death in 1968. Considered a moderate among Sunni leaders in the 1970s, Sulh nevertheless developed a reputation as a champion of the working class and maintained a close relationship with Kamal Jumblatt. While still a relative newcomer among Sunni political bosses, he was chosen as prime minister by President Sulayman Franjiyya in October 1974; he held the premiership until May 1975, when he resigned. He thus presided over the outbreak of the Lebanese Civil War, which he was unable to prevent or stop. Before stepping down, Sulh denounced the inertia of Lebanon's society and the political and administrative corruption and nepotism that, he claimed, had thwarted the implementation of his reforms. He warned that unless the entire political system was overhauled, the country was headed toward political chaos and disintegration.

In May 1992, Sulh became prime minister again, following the demonstrations and riots that brought down the government of Umar Karami. He held the position until October, when he was replaced by Rafiq Hariri. During his short tenure, he was frequently criticized for subservience to Syria. In particular, his insistence on proceeding with parliamentary elections in the summer of 1992 alienated many Lebanese, who opposed the timing of these elections. Beirut's electorate severely punished him for this and other decisions that were seen as bowing to Syria's wishes. The electoral list he headed was soundly defeated by that led by Salim al-Hoss. Although he managed to win a seat in parliament, Sulh received the fewest votes (11,428) of any Sunni elected, and no other Sunni on his list was elected (three Armenian Orthodox candidates and one Armenian Catholic were).

See also FRANJIYYA, SULAYMAN; HARIRI, RAFIQ BAHAʾUDDIN AL-; HOSS, SALIM AL-; JUMBLATT, KAMAL.

Bibliography

Johnson, Michael. *Class and Client in Beirut: The Sunni Muslim Community and the Lebanese State, 1840–1985.* Atlantic Highlands, NJ: Ithaca Press, 1986.

GUILAIN P. DENOEUX
UPDATED BY MICHAEL R. FISCHBACH

SULH, RIYAD AL-

[1894–1951]

Lebanese politician; prime minister, 1943–1945 and 1946–1951.

Riyad al-Sulh (second from right) was the first prime minister of independent Lebanon. He played an instrumental role in ending French control of the region and in establishing Lebanon's sectarian political system. He is shown here at a meeting of the Arab League in Aley, Lebanon, 1947. © HULTON-DEUTSCH COLLECTION/CORBIS. REPRODUCED BY PERMISSION.

Riyad al-Sulh (also al-Solh) was born into a prominent Sunni family that had played a major role in the Arab nationalist movement during the last decades of the Ottoman Empire. Unlike many other aristocratic families in Beirut, whose concerns revolved around parochial issues, the Sulhs were known for their cosmopolitanism, sophistication, and wide-ranging contacts throughout the empire. His father, Rida, had served as governor (*mutasarrif*) in Salonika and in 1909 had been elected one of Beirut's two representatives in the Ottoman parliament at Constantinople.

Sulh studied law at the University of Istanbul and at St. Joseph University in Beirut. After World War I, he and his father were elected to the National Congress of Syria, which proclaimed Amir Faisal king of an independent Syria. Following the military defeat of Faisal by France in July 1920, and the establishment of Greater Lebanon two months later, he became a vocal opponent of France's mandate. Forced to flee Lebanon, he was sentenced to death in absentia and spent most of the 1920s in exile, primarily in Paris and Geneva, where he worked closely with other Arab nationalists. In 1929, Sulh was allowed to return to Lebanon after Emile Eddé intervened on his behalf with the government of Charles Dabbas. From then on, except for another brief period of exile in 1935, he lived in Beirut. By the early 1930s, he had become one of the most influential Arab nationalist politicians, despite France's efforts to contain his power.

In the late 1930s, Sulh was progressively converted to the concept of an independent Lebanon that would be free of France's control and separate from Syria. This position, which he adopted in part under the influence of his cousins Kazem al-Sulh and Taki al-Din al-Sulh, reflected the growing recognition among large segments of the Sunni community that their interests lay in the preservation of existing boundaries and an alliance with moderate Maronite leaders.

The outbreak of World War II made possible the Christian-Muslim alliance that Sulh had advocated. The war weakened France's influence and prestige in Lebanon and thus undermined those in the Maronite community, led by Eddé, who insisted on a Christian Lebanon closely aligned with France. By the same token, it strengthened the hand of those Maronites, led by Bishara al-Khuri and his Constitutional Bloc, who called for an independent and sovereign Lebanon based on Muslim-Christian accommodation. Taking advantage of this changing balance of power within the Maronite community and of active support for Lebanese independence by Britain and the United States, Khuri and Riyad al-Sulh formed an alliance that led the movement for an end to France's mandate.

After parliament elected him president of Lebanon in September 1943, Khuri immediately chose Sulh as his prime minister. The two quickly concluded the informal agreement known as the National Pact, which embodied the "historical compromise" between Muslims and Christians that they had supported for some time. Because of his role in the National Pact, which became the backbone of postindependence politics in Lebanon, Sulh can be regarded as one of the founding fathers of independent Lebanon. His pragmatism and tolerance made him ideally suited to play a leading role in designing a system based on interconfessional accommodation, while his charisma, dynamism, and political skills ensured that he could deliver the support of his community. His vision of a secular, sovereign Lebanon based on a cross-confessional understanding and open to the outside world continued to inspire generations of Lebanese politicians long after his death, and despite its shortcomings, it permitted Lebanon to experience several decades of political stability, remarkable economic growth, and rapid modernization. It is important to note that Sulh appears to have been aware of the limits of the political formula embodied in the National Pact, which called for the distribution of positions in the government and the bureaucracy among the country's various sects. He saw this confessional system as only a temporary expedient that would have to be eliminated in the long run. He once described political sectarianism as "an obstacle to national progress, impeding the representation of the national will and poisoning the good relations between diverse elements of the Lebanese population."

One of the first decisions of Sulh's government was to abrogate the parts of the 1926 constitution that limited Lebanon's sovereignty to the benefit of France. The mandate authorities responded by arresting Khuri, Sulh, and all but two members of the cabinet. Strikes and widespread demonstrations and riots ensued; together with pressure by Britain and the United States on the government of Free France, they forced the latter to reverse its policy and reinstate Khuri and Sulh on 22 November 1943. This date effectively marks the emergence of independent Lebanon.

Until the beginning of Khuri's second term in 1949, Sulh maintained a close working relationship with the president. Between 1943 and 1951, he headed six cabinets for a total of some sixty-five months. For most of his tenure as prime minister, he was involved in all important decisions and was widely seen as almost an equal of Khuri, for whom he was a precious ally because of the weight his opinions carried with the Sunni masses. Following Khuri's reelection, however, strains developed between the two men, largely as a result of the president's increasing tendency to bypass the cabinet and rely instead on a group of cronies, influence peddlers, and advisers headed by his brother Salim. Sulh resigned on 14 February 1951. He was assassinated on 16 July by a member of the Syrian Social Nationalist Party (SSNP), who killed him at the airport in Amman, Jordan, in revenge for Lebanon's 1949 execution of Antun Saʿada, the SSNP's founder and leader.

See also EDDÉ, EMILE; KHURI, BISHARA AL-; NATIONAL PACT (LEBANON); SULH, KAZEM

AL-; SULH, TAKI AL-DIN AL.; SYRIAN SOCIAL NATIONALIST PARTY.

Bibliography

Binder, Leonard, ed. *Politics in Lebanon.* New York: Wiley, 1966.

Goria, Wade R. *Sovereignty and Leadership in Lebanon, 1943–1976.* London: Ithaca Press, 1986.

Hudson, Michael C. *The Precarious Republic: Political Modernization in Lebanon.* Boulder, CO: Westview Press, 1985.

Johnson, Michael. *Class and Client in Beirut: The Sunni Muslim Community and the Lebanese State, 1840–1985.* London: Ithaca Press, 1986.

GUILAIN P. DENOEUX

SULH, SAMI AL-
[1890–1968]

Lebanese Muslim politician.

Sami al-Sulh (also al-Solh), born to a prominent Sunni Muslim family, studied in Beirut and earned a law degree from Istanbul. He went to France to obtain a doctorate in law but returned to Lebanon before completing his studies. He claimed that while in Istanbul he had joined Arab secret societies working against the government of the Ottoman Empire, but no documentation supports his claims. He is accused of having supported the Ottoman government when other educated Arabs were struggling for Arab independence. He was a judge from 1920 to 1942, and, with French support, he was appointed prime minister in 1942. He represented Beirut in the Chamber of Deputies from 1943 to 1960 and from 1964 to 1968 and was prime minister seven times between 1945 and 1958.

The most controversial aspect of al-Sulh's political career was his support for Camille Chamoun. During the 1958 civil war he refused to criticize Chamoun, opposing the tide of Muslim public opinion. Al-Sulh was seen as a weak prime minister who did not stand up to President Chamoun. Chamoun used al-Sulh as a token Muslim because al-Sulh did not object to Chamoun's pro-Western foreign policy. His close association with Chamoun earned him the wrath of the Muslim masses, and his house in Beirut was burned down. He fled Lebanon for several months, then settled in the predominantly Christian area of Beirut. Al-Sulh surprised all those who had prematurely written his political obituary by returning to public life in 1964 after winning a parliamentary seat from Beirut. Christian support in his district of course helped make his victory possible, but within a few years he was able to win the backing of some Muslims who had declared him a traitor in 1958. He spent the rest of his life defending his position in 1958, writing two memoirs to vindicate himself. He claimed that he never opposed President Gamal Abdel Nasser of Egypt, and that he was a staunch defender of the Palestinian cause. He blamed Nasser's supporters in Lebanon for the anti-Nasser reputation that was associated with his name after 1958.

Being the oldest deputy made al-Sulh president protem of the parliament. Members of the Christian establishment saw al-Sulh as demonstrating how Muslim politicians should conduct themselves. His support for Chamoun was viewed by the Phalange party, which supported him, as evidence of his patriotism. He was nicknamed Abu al-Faqir (Father of the Poor) because he championed the common people.

AS'AD ABUKHALIL

SULH, TAKI AL-DIN AL-
[1909–1988]

Lebanese journalist and politician.

A first cousin of Riyad al-Sulh, Taki al-Din al-Sulh (also al-Solh, Taqi al-Din or Takidedine) was born in Beirut and educated at the American University of Beirut, where he studied literature and history. During the 1930s, he worked as a journalist, literature teacher, and director of the Ministry of Information. With his brother Kazem, he founded the al-Nida al-Qawmi (The National Appeal), a group of moderate Sunni politicians and intellectuals who advocated a free and sovereign Lebanon, independent from the French and separate from Syria. A traditional, nonideological politician, al-Sulh proved either unwilling or unable to build a strong political machine and consequently did not develop a wide base of popular support. He nevertheless—because of his connection to a prestigious family—occupied several important political positions in the 1960s: he was a member of parliament (1964–1968) and a minister of the interior (1964–1965).

Al-Sulh's early career reached its zenith in July 1973 when President Sulayman Franjiyya called upon him to become prime minister. During his fifteen months in office, he was unable to prevent Lebanon's slide toward political disintegration. His tenure was marked by economic crisis and political turmoil, student and labor unrest, a growing rift between Muslims and Christians, repeated clashes between the Lebanese army and Palestinian commandos, and numerous Israeli raids in southern Lebanon. He resigned in September 1974 and was replaced by Sa'ib Salam, but served as prime minister again in 1980.

See also AMERICAN UNIVERSITY OF BEIRUT (AUB); FRANJIYYA, SULAYMAN; SALAM, SA'IB; SULH, RIYAD AL-.

Bibliography

Hudson, Michael C. *The Precarious Republic: Political Modernization in Lebanon.* Boulder, CO: Westview, 1985.

Salibi, Kamal S. *Crossroads to Civil War: Lebanon, 1958–1976.* Delmar, NY: Caravan Books, 1976.

GUILAIN P. DENOEUX
UPDATED BY MICHAEL R. FISCHBACH

SULTAN

Title implying political power; a king or sovereign, especially of a Muslim state.

The title of sultan came to prominence around 1000 C.E., after the political position of the caliphate (office of the leader of Islam) had eroded around the time of the establishment of the Seljuk sultanate. Turko–Iranian dynasts used the title as an equivalent of the Eurasian steppe title khan. Later, it was used generally in Islamic lands by many states large and small. In some cases, for example, in Persia (now Iran), from 1500 on, the term was further devalued to denote a governor, not even a petty ruler.

In the Ottoman Empire, sultan, along with *padishah* and khan, was one of the titles of the sovereign (for example, Sultan Süleyman Khan), as well as the other members of the ruling family. The ruler's sons and grandsons, who served as governors and thus shared political power in the steppe manner, were all styled sultan. In the case of the female members of the ruling house, the title followed the personal name of the main designation—for example, Hürrem Sultan, *valide sultan* (dowager queen), *khasseki sultan* (favorite consort), or Mihrimah Sultan, who was a princess. The sultanate of the Ottoman Empire was abolished in 1922, just before the Republic of Turkey was founded.

I. METIN KUNT

SULTAN AHMET MOSQUE

Ottoman mosque.

Popularly known as the Blue mosque because of the predominantly turquoise-colored faience tile panels that embellish its vast prayer hall, the mosque of Sultan Ahmet I (1590–1617) stands next to Istanbul's Hippodrome. Supporting a domed, cruciform superstructure and six slender minarets, it is the major work of the architect Sedefkar Mehmet Ağa.

Bibliography

Goodwin, Godfrey. *A History of Ottoman Architecture.* London: Thames and Hudson, 1971.

APTULLAH KURAN

SULTAN HASAN MOSQUE

One of the finest examples of Arab Egyptian architecture; situated below the citadel in Cairo.

Sultan Hasan mosque was built for the Mamluk Sultan Hasan al-Nasir in 1356–1363. The ground plan of the mosque takes the form of an irregular pentagon and occupies 9,450 square yards (7,800 sq m). It boasts a 267-foot (88 m) minaret in its south corner, the tallest in Cairo, and a massive main door at the north corner that is almost 85 feet (26 m) high. The exterior walls echo an ancient Egyptian temple, with large expanses of stone that are relieved by blind niches and double round arched windows. Stalactitic cornices, heavily restored, crown the facades. The mausoleum, which extends from the southeast wall, carries a 180-foot-high (55 m) dome of the Arab Turkish style that was almost completely rebuilt in the eighteenth century.

Bibliography

Berhens-Abuseif, D. *Islamic Architecture in Cairo: An Introduction.* Leiden, Netherlands, and New York: Brill, 1989.

Rogers, J. M. "Seljuk Influence in the Monuments of Cairo." *Kunst des Orients* 7 (1970–1971): 40 ff.

RAYMOND WILLIAM BAKER

SULTANI SCHOOLS

Ottoman intermediate schools.

Sultani lycées were higher secondary schools funded by the sultan's personal treasury. The first and most famous of these was Lycée Galatasaray (also called Mekteb-i Sultani), founded in 1868 in Istanbul and modeled on the French lycée. An 1869 educational reform law provided for one sultani lycée in each provincial capital. In an expansion of the humanist education offered at these schools, in 1908 ten former İdadi schools, whose curriculum had partly overlapped that of the lycées, were renamed sultani schools. By 1914 there were 8,380 students, mostly from elite backgrounds, enrolled in twenty-four sultani schools across the Ottoman Empire.

See also İDADI SCHOOLS.

Bibliography

Kazamias, Andreas M. *Education and the Quest for Modernity in Turkey.* Chicago: University of Chicago Press, 1966.

ELIZABETH THOMPSON

SUMUD

Principle adopted by the Palestinian national movement of clinging to the soil of the homeland.

The Sumud (Steadfastness) Fund was established at the Baghdad Arab Summit in 1978 to discourage Palestinian emigration from the territories occupied by Israel in 1967. The annual budget of $150 million was to be administered by the Joint Committee, composed of members from the Palestine Liberation Organization (PLO) and the government of Jordan. Funds were distributed to Palestinian leaders, trade unions, universities, newspapers, and cooperatives. Sumud paid unemployment benefits and pensions for retirees and granted interest-free housing loans. In the early 1980s, about $87 million per year was transferred to the occupied territories. Funds dried up in the mid-1980s as oil-rich Arab countries defaulted on their contributions.

In the late 1980s, the principle of *sumud* was revived in an altered form by Palestinian residents of the Gaza Strip, Golan Heights, and West Bank who resented their passive role as welfare recipients. Under the leadership of Dr. Hisham Awartani, an economist at al-Najah University in Nablus, *sumud* was transformed into a call for Palestinian residents to think and act for themselves.

See also BAGHDAD SUMMIT (1978); PALESTINE LIBERATION ORGANIZATION (PLO).

Bibliography

Benvenisti, Meron. *The West Bank Handbook: A Political Lexicon.* Jerusalem: Jerusalem Post, 1986.

Cobban, Helena. *The Palestinian Liberation Organisation: People, Power, and Politics.* Cambridge, U.K., and New York: Cambridge University Press, 1984.

Schiff, Ze'ev, and Ya'ari, Ehud. *Intifada: The Palestinian Uprising—Israel's Third Front,* translated by Ina Friedman. New York: Simon and Schuster, 1990.

Shehadeh, Raja. *Samed: Journal of a West Bank Palestinian.* New York: Adama Books, 1984.

ELIZABETH THOMPSON

SUNAY, CEVDET
[1899–1982]

Turkish military officer and politician; president of Turkey, 1966–1973.

Cevdet Sunay was born in Trabzon, the son of a village effendi in the Ottoman Empire. He attended the Küleli military high school and fought in Palestine in World War I. In the Turkish War of Independence (1921–1922), Sunay fought on the Maraş, Gaziantep, and Western fronts, finally chasing enemy armies to İzmir. He became a staff officer for the new Republic of Turkey in 1930, after completing studies at the War Academy; he was promoted to general in 1958. In 1961, he was appointed chief of staff, following the military coup, although he apparently did not play a direct role in the plot against Adnan Menderes.

Sunay resigned his office to become president of Turkey in 1966 in an alliance between the Justice party and military interests. He served as president through the 1971 coup, in which some observers said he played a key role. Sunay's presidency ended in 1973, when his bid for an extended term fell one vote short in the assembly. His term in office is associated with the continued penetration of the military into Turkish politics.

Bibliography

Lewis, Geoffrey. *Modern Turkey*, 4th edition. New York: Praeger, 1974.

ELIZABETH THOMPSON

SUN LANGUAGE THEORY

A 1930s movement that claimed Turkish was the mother of all languages.

H. F. Kvergic is credited with inventing this theory in 1935, although numerous others contributed to its general formulation. The theory draws its name from Kvergic's initial proposition that a Turkish man was first inspired to create language while looking at the sun. Others, such as Ibrahim Necmi Dilmen, presented charts of concept groups drawn from the sun—for example, light/beauty, fire/excitement, and motion/time. Supporters of the theory held that since Turks inhabited the so-called cradle of civilization, central Asia, their language was the origin for later languages, such as those of the Hittites, Arabs, and Europeans.

Although criticized for fantastic speculations, the theory attracted interest in the mid-1930s for several reasons. Some supporters, including Atatürk, used it to stem the drastic expurgation from the modern Turkish language of foreign words by language reformers. Supporters argued that since foreign words were derived from Turkish, they should remain in use. Others found in the theory justification for radical nationalist Turkist ideologies in their vaunting of the Turks' ancient heritage. They also used its link to the Hittites to establish a long history for the Turks in Anatolia. By World War II, interest in the theory faded, although Atatürk's support of it is occasionally evoked today by opponents of the direction of Turkish-language reform.

Bibliography

Lewis, Geoffrey. *Modern Turkey*, 4th edition. New York: Praeger, 1974.

ELIZABETH THOMPSON

SUNNA

Literally, trodden path, *meaning* norm *or* practice.

The *Sunna* refers to the divine physical and moral laws set out in the universe and in the Qur'an. How-ever, the term is used most commonly in reference to the example and customary practice of the prophet Muhammad. The Prophet's *Sunna* has more than one usage in Muslim tradition. As a technical term used in the *shari'a* (Islamic law), it refers to the binding rules derived from the Prophet's sayings, or *hadith*. The *Sunna* then represents the laws that can be extracted from the *hadith*. As such, it is the second most important source of law after the Qur'an. In a more general meaning, often used by jurists and theologians, the *Sunna* refers also to all the customs and habits of the Prophet, including his everyday life practices, that are not considered by the *shari'a* as obligatory. Hence the term *Sunna* is often used in the sense of *recommended* or *good practice*. Examples of this are the supererogatory prayers and fasting the Prophet performed over and above the prescribed rituals. These are referred to as *Sunna* prayers or *Sunna* fasting. Certain very strict Muslim movements make the nonbinding *Sunna* obligatory, and extreme Muslim parties have, at times, after seizing power, imposed it on all Muslims and made practices such as wearing beards mandatory, although the enforcement of any practice that is not legally binding is considered illegitimate in Islamic law.

See also HADITH; MUHAMMAD; QUR'AN; SHARI'A.

Bibliography

Kamali, Mohammad Hashim. *Principles of Islamic Jurisprudence*, revised edition. Cambridge, U.K.: Islamic Texts Society, 1991

SCOTT ALEXANDER
UPDATED BY MAYSAM J. AL FARUQI

SUNNI ISLAM

The largest branch in Islam, sometimes referred to as "orthodox Islam"; its full name is ahl al-Sunna wa al-jama'a *(the people of* Sunna *and consensus), and it represents about 90 percent of the world Muslim population.*

The Sunni movement can be identified in terms of its differences with the second largest division of Islam, the Shi'ite, with whom it shares the fundamental creed of Islam. After the death of the Prophet, the political issue of how leadership was to be chosen split the new community. The Shi'a of

Ali (literally, the party of Ali) insisted that the Prophet had intended for his cousin Ali to succeed him, while the majority of Muslims maintained that the caliph should be elected and did not have to belong to the Prophet's family. The Sunnis maintained that since the Prophet had not clearly designated a successor, his *Sunna* (example, custom), by which they were to abide (hence their name), mandated elections. Of course, the Shi'a also consider the *Sunna* of the Prophet as binding and second only to the Qur'an in authority, but they differ on the actual content of the *Sunna* in regard to the matter of the divinely appointed leaders from the Prophet's family (imams), who in their view are the legitimate rulers. In addition to the concept of divinely appointed leadership, the Sunnis also reject the notion of a *mahdi* (messiah) as an integral part of the creed, and they emphasize exoteric interpretation of the Qur'an over the esoteric approach followed by the Shi'a.

The Sunni Schools of Law

In addition to the Qur'an and the *Sunna* as primary sources of Islamic law, Sunni jurists also admit *ijma* (consensus) and *qiyas* (personal parallel reasoning) as legitimate sources for legal judgment. *Qiyas,* the fourth source of law, is a form of *ijtihad* (exercising personal judgment in legal interpretation). All schools of law generally admit *ijtihad,* but with different definitions and restrictions. At first, *ra'y* (personal opinion issued without justification) was exercised, but its unrestricted use was deemed too arbitrary and it was eliminated in favor of *qiyas,* a form of reasoning that identifies an *illah (ratio legis)* parallel or similar to another already established by the Qur'an or the *Sunna.*

Ijma, or consensus, constitutes the third source of law and it takes precedence over *qiyas.* There was disagreement among the Sunni schools of law as to the nature of consensus. While all jurists accept the consensus of the companions of the Prophet, the more liberal schools will also admit of the consensus of the schools of law at any given time. The more conservative schools will only accept a global community consensus, which cannot be easily achieved, so in effect the Sunni schools of law did build the legal system on the basis of juristic consensus. However, the right to dissent *(ikhtilaf)* was scrupulously maintained by all schools. In contrast, the Shi'a eschew *ijma* in favor of the *ijtihad* of the imam or his representative. That the Sunnis consider the law to be a matter of consensus (whether juristic or communal) is underscored in their name, *ahl al-Sunna wa al-jama'a.*

Over time, the various Sunni schools of law coalesced into four major schools: the Hanafi (founded by Abu Hanifa, d. 767), the Maliki (founded by Malik ibn Anas, d. 795), the Shafi'i (founded by Shafi'i, d. 820) and the Hanbali school (founded by ibn Hanbal, d. 855). The most widespread is the Hanafi, which was favored by various Muslim governments, most notably by the Ottomans, since it was not as strict as the other schools in its acceptance and use of less rigorous tools of legal interpretation. The Hanafis can be found throughout the Muslim world, while the Malikis are mostly found in Egypt and North Africa, the Shafi'is in Southeast Asia, and the Hanbalis in the Arabian Peninsula.

Historical and Modern Developments

Tensions between Sunnis and Shi'a (especially with the sectarian movements derived from the Shi'a, such as the Isma'ilis) were very high in early Muslim history as Shi'ite groups tried to destabilize the Sunni caliphate and ensure leadership to the followers of the imams. The problems subsided after the decisive victory of the Ayyubids over the Shi'ite regimes of Egypt and the Near East in the late twelfth century and the subsequent coming to power of the Ottoman Turks, who had always been staunch Sunnis. Tension still exists between local Sunni and Shi'ite groups, although most of it is due more to ethnic and tribal strife than to religious divisions, as can be seen in Lebanon and Pakistan. However, the rise among the Sunnis of strict reform movements (such as the Wahhabi movement), which came to oppose any deviation from their interpretation of the Islamic creed, has exacerbated existing tensions with the Shi'a in the Persian Gulf area and wherever Wahhabism has spread.

The theological and juristic views on which the four major Sunni schools agree are considered to form the core of orthodox Islam. Although some of these views have coalesced into dogma, others have been subject to changes of interpretation through the years. Specifically, the eventual reliance by

Sunni jurists on *taqlid* (imitation or continuation of established past consensus) led to a reification of thought and law that gave rise to reform movements in the eighteenth century. Taking a stand against past consensus and building on the thought of the Hanbali ibn Taymiyya, the reform movements (the Wahhabis of Arabia, the Sanusis of North Africa, and the followers of Sirhindi in India), rejected *ijma* and emphasized *ijtihad,* considering themselves *ghayr muqallidin* (against imitation) and underscoring the need for new thought in Islamic law. Today, however, and after most Muslim countries have adopted the secular constitutions imposed on them by colonial powers in the nineteenth and early twentieth centuries, the major concern of the various contemporary Sunni Muslim movements is how to restore Islamic law and make it compatible with the demands of modern life.

See also ISLAM; MUWAHHIDUN; SANUSI ORDER; SHIʿISM.

Bibliography

Kamali, Mohammad Hashim. *Principles of Islamic Jurisprudence.* Cambridge, U.K.: Islamic Texts Society, 1991.

Makdisi, George. *Religion, Law, and Learning in Classical Islam.* Aldershot, U.K.; Brookfield, VT: Variorum, 1991.

Rahman, Fazlur. *Islam,* 2d edition. Chicago: University of Chicago Press, 1979.

TAYEB EL-HIBRI
UPDATED BY MAYSAM J. AL FARUQI

SUPHI EZGI

[1869–1962]

Turkish composer and musicologist.

Suphi Ezgi was born in Istanbul and attended the Military Medical Academy. At the same time, he was studying music with Turkish masters like Dede Zekai. Between 1913 and 1920, Suphi Ezgi, along with Sadeddin Arel and Rauf Yekta Bey, created modern Turkish musicology. Suphi Ezgi was also an accomplished singer and tanbur player and composed more than seven hundred pieces. The most important of this fourteen books on musicology is the five-volume *Nazari ve ameli Türk musikisi* (Turkish music in theory and practice).

DAVID WALDNER

SUPREME MUSLIM COUNCIL

Muslim institution in Palestine, 1921–1948.

During Ottoman rule in Palestine (1516–1917), Muslim *waqf* (plural, *awqaf*) and *shariʿa* courts were headed by the Shaykh al-Islam, and in the nineteenth century they were administered by the Ministry of Awqaf in Constantinople (now Istanbul). The British occupation of Palestine, which started in 1917, severed all ties with Constantinople, and these Muslim institutions were placed under British officials. Palestinian Muslims were alarmed at the prospect of their religious affairs being controlled by a Christian power headed by Zionists: Sir Herbert Samuel, the first high commissioner, and Norman Bentwich, legal secretary in charge of the *awqaf* and *shariʿa* courts. The Muslims complained of religious discrimination and demanded control over their affairs. Anxious lest the 1921 anti-Zionist disturbances recur and wanting to provide the Palestinians with autonomous institutions that the Zionists were granted, Samuel proposed that the Muslim secondary electors to the last Ottoman parliament choose a higher body that would control the affairs of the Muslim community.

Samuel issued an order in December 1921 establishing a Supreme Muslim Council (SMC) constituted for "the control and management of Moslem awqaf and Shariʿa affairs in Palestine." It was to consist of a president and four members, two of whom were to represent the district of Jerusalem and the remaining two to represent the districts of Nablus and Acre. All were to be paid from government and *awqaf* funds. In the first election, held on 9 January 1922, the mufti of Jerusalem, Hajj Amin al-Husayni, was elected president; his budget was 50,000 British pounds.

Husayni initiated an Islamic cultural revival in Palestine in the 1920s. Through the SMC, he established an orphanage, supported schools, expanded welfare and health clinics, and renovated religious buildings. The most ambitious and impressive project was the renovation of the two dilapidated mosques within the Haram al-Sharif, the third holiest shrine of Islam. The restored structures enhanced the importance of Jerusalem in the Muslim and Arab worlds and asserted Jerusalem's centrality within Palestine. By the end of the decade, the mufti had consolidated his religious power and had increased his political influence throughout Palestine. He used his enhanced political position to advocate Palestinian self-determination. After he led the Palestine Arab Revolt (1936–1939), however, the British dismissed him and dissolved the SMC in 1937.

See also BENTWICH, NORMAN; HUSAYNI, MUHAMMAD AMIN AL-; PALESTINE ARAB RE-VOLT (1936–1939); SAMUEL, HERBERT LOUIS; SHARI'A; WAQF.

Bibliography

Mattar, Philip. *The Mufti of Jerusalem: Al-Hajj Amin al-Husayni and the Palestinian National Movement,* revised edition. New York: Columbia University Press, 1992.

Palestine Government. *A Survey of Palestine for the Information of the Anglo-American Committee of Inquiry.* Jerusalem, 1947. Reprint, Washington, DC: Institute for Palestine Studies, 1991.

PHILIP MATTAR

SURSOCK, LADY COCHRANE

Lebanese cultural official.

Yvonne, Lady Cochrane Sursock is the daughter of Alfred Bey Sursock, a Levantine aristocrat who came to Lebanon from Turkey at the beginning of the twentieth century, and Donna Maria Theresa Serra diCassano, daughter of Francesco Serra, seventh Duke of Cassano. She is the wife of Sir Desmond Cochrane, whom she married in 1946. She has played an active public role in Lebanon since her young adulthood, particularly in the arts. She was president of the committee and general manager of the Nicolas Sursock Museum in Beirut (1960–1966) and founder and president of the Association for the Protection of the Natural Sites and Ancient Buildings (APSAD; Association pour la protection des sites et anciennes demeures) in Lebanon (1960–2002). She is currently involved in projects to stem the exodus of Lebanese by rerooting them in their villages of origin and creating jobs in the fields of agriculture, textiles, and handcrafts. Lady Cochrane has been a pioneer in the protection of the environment and in developing Lebanese citizens' awareness of the unique architectural and cultural heritage of Lebanon.

See also ARCHITECTURE; ART; GENDER AND ED-UCATION; HARIRI, RAFIQ BAHA'UDDIN AL-;

LEBANESE CIVIL WAR (1958); LEBANESE CIVIL WAR (1975–1990); LEBANON.

MONA TAKIEDDINE AMYUNI

SURSUQ FAMILY

Prominent Lebanese landowning business family.

One of the wealthiest Greek Orthodox families in Beirut, the Sursuqs (also Sursock or Sursok) benefited from the 1858 Ottoman land reform to acquire large tracts of fertile land in northern Palestine. They were also bankers who controlled cotton and grain trade in Acre. The family was associated with controversial land sales to Zionists before and after World War I.

Various family members were active in Beirut politics before World War I, with Albert Sursuq a leading member of the Beirut Reform Society and Michel Sursuq a member of the Ottoman parliament. After the war, the family became a target of anti-Zionist criticism when their land sales to Jews in the Jezreel valley and at Lake Hula displaced hundreds of peasants. The family remained prominent among Beirut's Europeanized elite after World War II. In the 1960s, the family villa was turned into the Nicolas Sursuq Museum.

Bibliography

Abboushi, W. F. *The Unmaking of Palestine.* Wisbech, U.K.: Middle East and North African Studies Press; Boulder, CO: L. Rienner, 1985.

ELIZABETH THOMPSON

SUWAYDI FAMILY

Iraqi family prominent in religious affairs and politics.

The Suwaydi family of al-Karth district of Baghdad traces its origins to Abbas, the uncle of the Prophet Muhammad, whose descendants founded the Abbasid dynasty that ruled Baghdad from 750 to 1258. A well-known member was Shaykh Abdullah al-Suwaydi, a Sunni jurist who took part in the famous theological conference at al-Najaf in 1773 that sought to bring about reconciliation between the Sunni and Shi'a sects.

The Suwaydi family also has played a leading role in the affairs of modern Iraq. For example,

Yusuf Suwaydi (1854–1925), a *shar*ʿ*ia* (religious) judge, played a leading role in the Arab movement against the Ottoman Empire. He was imprisoned in 1913 and 1914 for his political activities and later released. He also was involved in the revolt against the British in 1920.

Two of Yusuf's children, Naji and Tawfiq, completed their legal training in Istanbul in the early part of the twentieth century and helped to draft Iraq's constitution. Both of them were elected deputy and senator, and both served as prime minister. Naji advocated pan-Arabism and resented British interference in Iraq. He participated in the 1941 uprising against the British. When the uprising failed, he was exiled to Rhodesia, where he died in 1945. Tawfiq was a pro-British activist. After the revolution of 1958, he was sentenced to life imprisonment but was released in 1962. Tawfiq moved to Lebanon where he died in 1968.

See also SUWAYDI, TAWFIQ AL-.

Bibliography

Khadduri, Majid. *Independent Iraq, 1932–1958: A Study in Iraqi Politics,* 2d edition. London and New York: Oxford University Press, 1960.

Longrigg, Stephen Hemsley. *Iraq, 1900 to 1950: A Political, Social, and Economic History.* London and New York: Oxford University Press, 1953.

AYAD AL-QAZZAZ

SUWAYDI, TAWFIQ AL-
[c. 1889–1968]

Iraqi politician.

Tawfiq al-Suwaydi, a pro-British moderate, was born in Baghdad to an influential Sunni family. His origins trace back to Abbas, the uncle of the Prophet Muhammed, whose descendants established the Abbasid dynasty that ruled Baghdad from 750 to 1258. Suwaydi attended school in Baghdad and studied law in Istanbul and France. He was elected to parliament and served in various government capacities: minister of education (1928), ambassador to Iran (1931), minister of justice (1935), and minister of foreign affairs (1934, 1937, 1941). Suwaydi was prime minister three times (1929, 1946, 1950). During his second term he legalized previously banned political parties. In his last term, he initiated negoti-

ations for a new oil agreement, established the Board of Development to improve economic conditions, and enacted a law permitting Iraqi Jews to leave the country, provided they gave up their citizenship and property. In the aftermath of the 1958 revolution, Suwaydi was sentenced to life imprisonment. In 1962 he was permitted to leave Iraq for Lebanon, where he died.

See also SUWAYDI FAMILY.

Bibliography

Khadduri, Majid. *Independent Iraq, 1932–1958: A Study in Iraqi Politics,* 2d edition. London and New York: Oxford University Press, 1960.

AYAD AL-QAZZAZ

SUWAYDIYA OIL FIELDS

Largest oil field in Syria, with a yearly output of 1 million tons (907,000 t).

The first Suwaydiya oil well was discovered toward the end of 1960 by the German company Concordia at a depth of 5,617 feet (1,712 m). This well is located southeast of Qarah Shuk in al-Jazira plateau in northeastern Syria. It was the second oil field to be discovered in Syria after the Qarah Shuk field, which was discovered in 1958 and contained nine wells. Between 1960 and 1962, the Concordia Company's field showed minimal progress. Three more wells were drilled in the Suwaydiya field, capable of production from the upper Cretaceous rock layer, with average depths of 5,000 feet (1,525 m). But the heaviness of the crude oil produced was discouraging, unless it was blended with lighter crudes from Iraq, in which case the Homs refinery could handle it. At that time, the Suwaydiya reserves were assessed at about 35 million tons (31.7 million t). The Suwaydiya fields were then thought capable of producing 12,000 barrels per day. In 1964, Concordia, which had begun a deep test-well a year earlier, had its license suspended when the Syrian government nationalized the oil industry. The Syrian Petroleum Authority, which was attached to the Ministry of Industry, undertook drilling with assistance from Soviet geophysicists and drillers.

In 1965, the Suwaydiya oil fields were considered commercial. Toward the end of 1974, a ministry for oil and mineral resources was established in Syria. It became responsible for concerting efforts with foreign oil companies for oil drilling, which has intensified since then. Compared with the Qarah Shuk, the Rumayla, and the Tayyim oil fields, the Suwaydiya fields are the largest, with an established reserve of 410 million tons (372 million t) and a yearly output of 1 million tons (907,000 t).

See also HOMS; PETROLEUM, OIL, AND NATURAL GAS; SYRIA.

Bibliography

Longrigg, Stephen H. *Syria and Lebanon under French Mandate.* London and New York: Oxford University Press, 1958.

ABDUL-KARIM RAFEQ

SUWAYHLI, RAMADAN AL-

[?–1920]

Tripolitanian nationalist.

Ramadan al-Suwayhli was a member of a prominent Arab family from the eastern Tripolitanian coastal town of Misurata. They opposed the interests of the other leading family, the Muntasirs.

Suwayhli had been tried and acquitted of murdering Abd al-Qasim Muntasir shortly after the Young Turk Revolution of 1908, when Tripolitania was part of the Ottoman Empire. Suwayhli had played a vital role in supporting the Ottomans against Italian and Sanusi incursions. After the Treaty of Ouchy (1912), which ended the war between Italy and the Ottoman Empire, Suwayhli sought an independent Tripolitania. He had been instrumental in founding the short-lived Tripolitanian republic in 1917, which had not been recognized by Italy but was tolerated (even after the laws of 1919, the *Legge Fondamentale,* when alternative administrative structures were established). Its members, including Ramadan al-Suwayhli, were paid large stipends by the Italian authorities until the structure of the republic collapsed. Italy then connived in Suwayhli's death, at the hands of the Muntasir family (who still held him responsible for Abd al-Qasim's murder) and Abd al-Nabi Bilhayr, leader of the Warfalla (who had fallen out with him concerning the republic).

See also MUNTASIR FAMILY; TRIPOLITANIA.

Bibliography

Anderson, Lisa S. "The Tripoli Republic, 1917–1922." In *Social and Economic Development of Libya,* edited by E. G. H. Joffe and K. S. McLachlan. Wisbech, U.K.: Middle East and North African Studies Press; Boulder, CO: Westview Press, 1982.

GEORGE JOFFE

SYKES, MARK

[1879–1919]

British soldier, orientalist, politician, and emissary.

An artistocrat, Mark Sykes first visited the Ottoman Empire as a boy and returned there as a Cambridge undergraduate. As an honorary consul in Constantinople who was sympathetic to the old Ottoman regime, he rode on horseback through many regions that the British would occupy after defeating the Turks in World War I. Sykes served as an officer in the Boer War. In two books and several articles, he revealed his preference for the religious, rural, and traditional elements of the East over the materialism and cosmopolitanism he so disliked in its cities. Sir Mark became a conservative member of Parliament in 1911.

After serving briefly on the Western front in World War I, Sykes was attached to the general staff of Lord Kitchener. Kitchener sent Sykes to the Middle East and India, where he found poor communication and little coordination among British officers and officials. To deal with these problems, he founded the Arab Bureau in Cairo after he returned to London and then made comprehensive plans for the postwar Middle East. Sykes advocated a large, loose Arab confederation under Husayn, the Sharif of Mecca, except for an international area around Jerusalem, holy to Christians, Muslims, and Jews. Sykes and his French counterpart, François Georges-Picot, negotiated a secret wartime agreement that was signed by tsarist Russia, but later repudiated by the Bolsheviks. Sykes was deeply impressed by Zionism in Russia, where he believed Jews would fight for Zion if not the tsar.

In the last two years of the war, when Sykes was attached to the War Cabinet Secretariat, he drafted various statements for the British entry into Jerusalem,

Baghdad, and Damascus that were in line with the anti-imperialism and self-determination favored by the United States, which had not declared war against the Turks. His third wartime mission to the Middle East failed to get any consensus among Arabs, Armenians, and Jews. Sykes then attended the peace conference at Paris, where he contracted influenza and died.

See also SYKES–PICOT AGREEMENT (1916).

Bibliography

Adelson, Roger. *Mark Sykes: Portrait of an Amateur.* London: Cape, 1975.

Fromkin, David. *A Peace to End All Peace: Creating the Modern Middle East, 1914–1922.* New York: H. Holt, 1989.

ZACHARY KARABELL
UPDATED BY ROGER ADELSON

SYKES, PERCY MOLESWORTH

See SOUTH PERSIA RIFLES

SYKES–PICOT AGREEMENT (1916)

World War I document of 1916 that would have divided the Middle East into British and French spheres.

The Sykes–Picot Agreement was one of the pivotal diplomatic documents of World War I concerning the Middle East. It was negotiated in secret at the end of 1915 by Sir Mark Sykes of Great Britain and Georges François Picot of France, with full knowledge by their respective foreign ministries. It provided for a partition of the Middle East into French and British spheres.

The French were to have direct control of Syria, Lebanon, and Cilicia plus a zone of influence extending east from Damascus and Aleppo through Mosul. The British were granted direct control of the Mesopotamian provinces (now Iraq) of Baghdad and Basra as well as a zone of influence extending from Basra to Palestine. Palestine was itself to be placed under international administration.

Under the subsequent Anglo–Russian–French Agreement of 1916, the Russians adhered to Sykes–

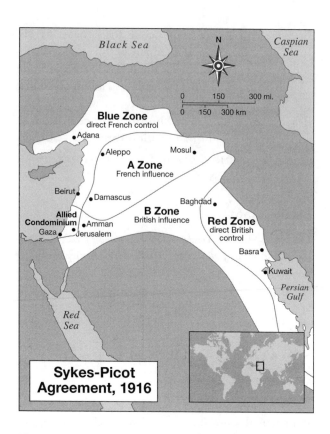

MAP BY XNR PRODUCTIONS, INC. THE GALE GROUP.

Picot after extensive discussions between Sykes and the Russian foreign minister, Sergei Sazanov. In return for their support, the Russians were granted direct control over much of eastern Anatolia. In a successful attempt at embarrassing the coalition, the terms of the Anglo–Russian–French Agreement were made public by the Bolsheviks in the spring of 1918. The Arabs claimed that Sykes–Picot contradicted promises made to them by the Hussein-McMahon Correspondence, and the Jews claimed that it contravened the Balfour Declaration. U.S. President Woodrow Wilson wished to annul Sykes–Picot, and even Sykes soon repudiated the agreement. Nonetheless, though the French renounced their claim to Mosul and Britain won control of Palestine, the Middle East treaties framed at the Paris Peace Settlements after World War I closely mirrored the Sykes–Picot Agreement.

See also BALFOUR DECLARATION (1917);
HUSAYN–MCMAHON CORRESPONDENCE
(1915–1916); PARIS PEACE SETTLEMENTS
(1918–1923); SYKES, MARK; WILSON,
WOODROW.

Bibliography

Anderson, Matthew S. *The Eastern Question.* New York: St. Martin's, 1966.

Fromkin, David. *A Peace to End All Peace.* New York: Henry Holt, 1989.

Hurewitz, J. C., ed. *The Middle East and North Africa in World Politics.* New Haven, CT: Yale University Press, 1979.

Khalidi, Rashid. *British Policy towards Syria and Palestine, 1906–1914: A Study of the Antecedents of the Hussein–the [sic] McMahon Correspondence, the Sykes–Picot Agreement, and the Balfour Declaration.* London: Ithaca Press, 1980.

ZACHARY KARABELL

The world-renowned Great Mosque was constructed in the eighth century, when Damascus was the seat of the Umayyad dynasty. Most Syrians are Sunnis, with far smaller numbers of other Muslims as well as a sizable minority of Christians, primarily Greek Orthodox and Armenian Gregorian. Islamic fundamentalists are active but not in a position of power; the socialist Ba'th Party violently suppressed an uprising of the Muslim Brotherhood in 1982. © CORBIS. REPRODUCED BY PERMISSION.

SYRIA

Formally, the Syrian Arab Republic (al-Jumhuriyya al-Arabiyya al-Suriyya).

Syria's 71,500 square miles include a narrow plain along the Mediterranean between Turkey to the north and Lebanon to the south, which contains the ports of Latakia and Tartus; fertile highlands between the capital, Damascus, and the border with Jordan, called the Hawran (Hauran); an extensive central plain, in which are situated the cities of Homs, Hama, and Aleppo; the Euphrates River valley, in which are the cities of al-Raqqa (Rakka) and Dayr al-Zawr; an eastern plateau bounded by Turkey to the north and Iraq to the east, whose major centers are al-Hasaka and al-Qamishli; and a large southeastern desert adjacent to Iraq and Jordan, whose oases contain the ruins of ancient fortifications and trading posts.

Syria has three major rivers. The largest, the Euphrates, enters from Turkey and is joined by the Khabur and the Balikh before crossing into Iraq southeast of Al Bu Kamal. The Euphrates system is regulated by the Euphrates Dam at Tabaqa, just west of al-Raqqa, which stores water for use in irrigation and power generation. Running south from mountains in the pre-1920 Syrian province of Iskenderun (now the Turkish province of Hatay), through the fertile Ghab basin and past the cities of Hama and Homs, is the Orontes river (Nahr al-Asi). The Yarmuk river, across which small irrigation dams were constructed during the 1980s, defines the border between Syria and Jordan. At current rates of use, Syria's groundwater reserves are expected to run dry by 2010, leaving the country entirely dependent on river water.

Population

The total population is estimated to be 17.6 million (2002) with Damascus and Aleppo the major population centers. Population growth averaged over 3 percent annually for much of the second half of the twentieth century but then slowed to 2.45 percent (2002). On the other hand, the death rate plunged from 21 deaths per 1,000 during the early 1950s to 5 per 1,000 in 2002. Several thousand Armenians moved to Syria from the Soviet Union in 1945–1946, and founded a sizable community in Aleppo. After the establishment of the state of Israel, virtually all of the Syrian Jewish population emigrated, and about 100,000 Palestinians fleeing Israel's takeover of the Galilee in 1948 ended up in camps on the fringes of Damascus.

Muslims make up 85–90 percent of the population; approximately 75 percent of this number are Sunnis, 13–15 percent are Alawis, about 1 percent are Isma'ilis, and less than 1 percent are Twelver Shi'ites. Some 3 percent of Syrians are Druze, a sect

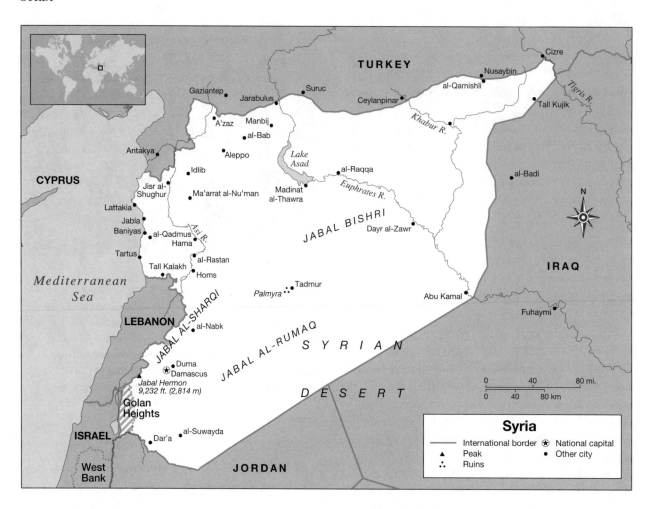

MAP BY XNR PRODUCTIONS, INC. THE GALE GROUP.

that follows a mixture of Christian and Shiʿa doctrines. Isolated pockets of Yazidis exist in the hills outside Aleppo and northeast of al-Qamishli. About 10 percent of the population are Christians, divided among at least a dozen sects. The Greek Orthodox and Armenian Gregorian communities are the largest and most influential.

Administration

Syria's governmental structure is highly centralized and strictly hierarchical, concentrating power primarily in the hands of the president and secondarily with the top leadership of the Baʿth party. This system was developed after March 1963, when military supporters of the Baʿth overthrew the parliamentary order that had reappeared following the dissolution of the union with Egypt in 1961. In November 1970, Gen. Hafiz al-Asad, minister of defense and head of the Baʿth party's military wing,

seized power. He served as head of state, commander in chief, and secretary-general of the Regional (Syrian) Command of the Baʿth until his death in June 2000. Shortly after coming to power, the new regime appointed a representative body, the People's Council, to draft a permanent constitution. This document, approved in March 1973, provides for a seven-year presidential term of office; it empowers the president to appoint and remove the vice presidents, the prime minister, and other cabinet ministers. In addition, it grants the president the authority to dissolve the People's Council and call national plebiscites to ratify legislative measures not adopted by the parliament. Upon the death of Hafiz al-Asad, his second son, Bashshar al-Asad, was elected president in July 2000.

Syria consists of thirteen provinces, each administered by a governor. Each governor is advised by a provincial council, one-fourth of whose members are appointed and the remainder of whom are elected by popular balloting. Since 1970, these councils have exercised little decision-making autonomy. Municipal councils provide public services, license businesses, and supervise the collection of local taxes. Each municipal council is headed by a mayor. Damascus city constituted a separate governorate until 1987, when it merged with the surrounding province of Damascus to form a single administrative unit.

Economy

Syria's economy expanded dramatically during the 1940s, due to a combination of restrictions on imports and heightened spending by British and French occupation forces. The Korean War perpetuated the boom by creating greater demand for Syrian cotton on world markets. Private enterprise provided the main impetus for economic growth until the union with Egypt in 1958, when state officials introduced an extensive program of land reform, nationalization of industry, and regulation of commercial transactions. The short-lived parliamentary regime that seceded from the union in 1961 attempted to resurrect the private sector, but the Ba'th-affiliated officers who overthrew the civilian regime in March 1963 gradually extended government control over most sectors of the economy. State intervention peaked with the nationalization of industry, banking, and trade that began in January 1965. Under the regime of Salah Jadid (1966–1970), extensive state control accompanied the establishment of a network of production and distribution cooperatives, state farms, and Ba'th-affiliated popular-front organizations.

By the end of the 1960s, Syria's public-sector enterprises were experiencing severe financial difficulties. The government responded by relaxing restrictions on the activities of private business, particularly in construction and trade. Private enterprise quickly moved into agriculture and manufacturing as well, supported both by the return of large amounts of local capital that had fled the country during the late 1950s and by an influx of investment from the oil-producing Arab Gulf states. Government spending jumped from around 29 percent of gross domestic product (GDP) in 1972 to some 37 percent of GDP in 1987. This rise was not matched by an increase in current revenues, resulting in large budget deficits. The shortfalls resulted primarily from sharp increases in military spending; by 1987, support for the armed forces accounted for 39 percent of total state outlays. With an imbalance of this magnitude sustainable only through heavy reliance on the Communist bloc and Arab oil states, the implosion of the Soviet Union during the early 1990s forced the Syrian government to take austerity measures.

The economy grew at a rate of more than 9 percent per year during the 1970s, slowed to around 2.2 percent during the 1980s, rebounded to more than 5 percent during the 1990s, and continued to grow at an annual rate of 2.5 to 3.5 percent during the early years of the twenty-first century. Income per capita was approximately $1,000 (2002). With the growth in population approximating 2.5 percent, the World Bank has estimated that Syria would need real economic growth of more than 5 percent to improve the welfare of its people. Major distortions contribute to the overall weak performance of the Syrian economy, including multiple exchange rate and exchange controls, restrictions on private sector activity, price controls, major agricultural subsidies, an inefficient state-owned financial system, and the dominance of state-owned enterprises.

The Syrian government implemented limited economic reforms after 2000, permitting Syrians to hold foreign currency and licensing the first public banks, an essential step in modernizing the state-dominated economy. However, the far-reaching economic reforms required to modernize the economy were put on hold for fear that widespread economic change could lead to calls for concomitant political reform and democratization. As a result, sweeping economic reform remains the number one priority in the Syrian domestic agenda.

Education

Since 1967, Syria's schools, technical institutes, and universities have been supervised by the Ministry of Education or the Ministry of Higher Education. Successive Ba'th regimes have expanded the education system, and have taken steps to reduce illiteracy by establishing adult and women's education programs. Elementary education is free and compulsory. Secondary education, which consists of three years of preparatory school and three years of high school, is free but not compulsory. The great majority of children attend public schools; several private schools in Damascus serve foreign nationals and the elite. The Ministry of Education regulates textbooks, curricula, and teacher certification.

Syria has four universities. The largest and most prestigious is Damascus University, founded in 1923, which had some 60,000 students by 2002. The University of Aleppo, chartered in 1958, serves around 30,000 students. Tishrin University in Latakia and al-Ba'th University in Homs offer limited curricula. The University of Aleppo operates a faculty of agriculture in Dayr al-Zawr. Technical institutes are scattered throughout the country. The language of instruction is Arabic, although English and French are required as second languages by many faculties.

History

Syria's modern history began with the end of the Egyptian occupation (1831–1840). After the reassertion of Ottoman control, European manufactured goods flooded the country, ruining the textile industry and leading urban merchants to invest in agricultural land. The trend toward private estate ownership was reinforced by the Ottoman land law of 1858, which allowed landholders to convert nominally state-owned communal lands in the villages into private property. At the end of the nineteenth century, French enterprises won numerous concessions in exchange for loans to the Ottoman authorities. French firms invested in ports, railroads, and highways, opening the cities of the interior to the outside world. As manufacturing continued to contract, to the evident benefit of Syria's well-connected minority communities, anti-Christian and anti-European riots, like the 1860 massacres in Damascus, erupted. These drew European governments into local politics, and growing outside interference generated rising disaffection with Ottoman authority among Syria's Arab elite.

During the 1890s, clubs advocating Syrian independence formed in Aleppo, Damascus, and Beirut. These coalesced into political parties after the 1908 revolution that brought the Committee of Union and Progress (CUP) to power in Constantinople (now Istanbul). Members of an underground CUP branch in Damascus led popular demonstrations in support of the coup, prompting prominent reli-

gious notables to form an organization of their own, the Muslim Union. Candidates sympathetic to the latter won the parliamentary elections of 1909. Liberal opponents of the CUP openly denounced the regime in Constantinople, setting the stage for new elections in 1912, which were rigged to ensure that only CUP supporters won seats in parliament.

Following the balloting, influential Syrian liberals emigrated to Cairo, where they formed the Ottoman Party of Administrative Decentralization to seek greater autonomy for the empire's Arabic-speaking provinces. The publication of its program accompanied widespread anti-CUP agitation orchestrated by secret societies including the Constantinople-based Qahtan society, the Paris-based Young Arab Society (al-Fatat), and the Iraq- and Syria-based Society of the Covenant (Jam'iyyat al-Ahd). The seeds of Arab nationalism germinated among these societies prior to World War I.

Nationalist sentiment blossomed during the war, and when Faisal I ibn Hussein of the Hijaz led an Arab army into Damascus in October 1918, he was welcomed as a liberator and Damascus declared itself an autonomous Arab administration for the whole of greater Syria. Faisal attempted to consolidate popular support by calling elections in mid-1919, but CUP sympathizers won most of the seats representing Damascus. Members of the Young Arab Society dominated the rest of the assembly, and in the fall of 1919 this organization formed the Committee of National Defense to resist Faisal's alleged willingness to capitulate to French demands. Faisal responded by forming the National Party, whose platform called for the establishment of a constitutional monarchy with French assistance. The assembly, led by Hashim al-Atasi of Homs, acclaimed Faisal king of an independent Syria. His acquiescence in the declaration led France to occupy Damascus in 1920, establishing a tutelary regime that governed the country for the next quarter-century.

After independence in 1946, the armed forces became a major means of advancement for Syria's minority communities, particularly poorer Alawis and Druze, who entered the military academy in rapidly growing numbers. There they encountered radical political ideas, including those of the Ba'th and the local communist party. Rising disaffection within the ranks prompted the military high com-

Markets remain a focus of life in Syria. Agriculture, like construction, trade, and manufacturing, has benefited from an influx of private capital since the 1960s. © CORY LANGLEY. REPRODUCED BY PERMISSION.

mand to champion social reform programs and solidarity with nationalists in neighboring Arab states. Popular and parliamentary discontent over Syria's defeat in Palestine persisted through the winter of 1948–1949, and in March 1949 a clique of commanders led by Col. Husni al-Zaʿim overthrew the elected government. Zaʿim abrogated the 1930 constitution, suppressed all political parties, and ruled by decree. That June he was assassinated by rival officers, who restored civilian rule and called for elections to a popular assembly to frame a new constitution. The assembly fragmented along regional lines, and in December a group of junior officers led by Col. Adib Shishakli seized power. Shishakli's regime adopted a revised constitution in 1950 but soon resorted to severe tactics to control the resurgent labor unions and peasant movement, and was ousted in 1954.

The new military-civilian coalition restored the 1950 constitution and held parliamentary elections, in which the Arab Baʿth Socialist party won a substantial number of seats. Leftist forces were unable to form a coalition cabinet, and the liberal People's party took over the government. This development sparked renewed militancy among workers and peasants, convincing the cabinet to implement wide-ranging agricultural and industrial reforms. Startled by the reforms, as well as by demands for greater change from the Baʿth and the communists, conservatives in parliament mobilized support for former President Shukri al-Quwatli, who won the presidency in 1955. By 1957 escalating tensions among pro–United States, pro-Egypt, and Syrian nationalist politicians led to a postponement of local elections while military intelligence officers uncovered an elaborate plot by agents of Iraq to undermine the government. These developments sent Chief of Staff Afif al-Bizri to Cairo to request immediate union with Egypt. In 1958 President Quwatli announced the creation of the United Arab Republic.

Downtown Damascus shows clear signs of Syria's efforts since the 1980s to modernize its economy, with some additional reforms taking effect after 2000. Many sectors of the economy, however, have long been run by the state; the country has been firmly under the centralized, hierarchical control of the Ba'th party, with the backing of the military, since 1963. © AP/WIDEWORLD PHOTOS. REPRODUCED BY PERMISSION.

Efforts to unify the two countries eventually provoked widespread unrest in Syria. When the cabinet nationalized and redistributed the assets of private enterprises during the summer of 1961, largely in response to problems in Egypt, merchants and tradespeople in Syria's cities agitated for dissolution of the union. A group of military officers and civilian politicians orchestrated secession that September. Over the next two years, Syria's politics consisted of jockeying among socialists, who favored continued state control over key sectors of the economy; large landholders and rich merchants, who advocated the restoration of private property and parliamentary rule; and moderates, including a wing of the Ba'th party led by Michel Aflaq, who supported maintaining a mixed economy. In 1962, a compromise government supported by the military high command took steps to dismantle the public sector and remove doctrinaire socialists from the

armed forces, moves that precipitated both resistance among Ba'th and communist officers and growing Islamist opposition. Spurred by threats to the position of radicals within the military and by burgeoning popular unrest, members of the military committee of the Ba'th carried out a coup in 1963, ushering in a period of Ba'th party–military rule.

Gen. Hafiz al-Asad, who played a major role in the 1963 coup, was promoted to commander of the air force in 1964, serving also as a senior leader in the Ba'thist military command. Mastering the survival techniques necessary in the factional politics plaguing Syria, he seized control of the government in November 1970, dismissing or purging opponents and initiating three decades of rule. Characterized by internal political stability and continuity, the Asad regime ushered in a new chapter in both domestic and foreign policies. On the domestic front, it stressed the need for reconciliation and national unity, built stable state institutions, and courted disenchanted social classes with measures of economic and political liberalization. At the same time, it tolerated no opposition, attacking the Muslim Brotherhood and viciously suppressing an uprising in Hama in February 1982. In addition to the army, the institutional pillars of the regime were a multilayered intelligence network, formal state structures, and revitalized Ba'th party congresses.

In foreign policy, the Asad regime succeeded in transforming Syria into a regional middle power out of all proportion to its size, population, and economic resources. The regime began by moving quickly to end Syrian isolation in the Arab world, focusing on Egypt, Jordan, and Saudi Arabia. Accepting UN Security Council Resolutions 242 and 338, it agreed to a May 1974 disengagement agreement with Israel in the wake of the 1973 Arab-Israel War, but then worked to kill the 1983 Israel-Lebanon accord. Syrian military power expanded steadily in this period; by 1986, it had a very large military force for a state of its size. Personal animosity, together with geopolitical rivalry and a Ba'th party schism, separated Asad's Syria from Saddam Hussein's Iraq. Syria sided with Iran during the Iran-Iraq War and adhered to the Western-led anti-Iraq coalition during the Gulf War. A new entente with Egypt, and Syria's subsequent involvement in the U.S.–sponsored Middle East peace process that started with the Madrid Conference in October 1991, led the Syrian government for the first time into face-to-face negotiations with Israel. Stalled in 1996, talks with Israel again foundered in 1999. However, the positions of the two protagonists were closer than ever before, and a future agreement seemed possible.

President Hafiz al-Asad died of natural causes on 10 June 2000 and was replaced by his son, Bashshar al-Asad, on 17 July 2000. Dual themes of continuity and change characterized the early policies of the new regime. Bashshar al-Asad cautiously promoted limited socioeconomic change to stimulate the economy and generate popular support, but delayed broader economic reforms out of fear they would cause political destabilization. In foreign affairs, he maintained his father's commitment to a just and lasting Middle East peace in which Syria would regain all occupied lands. However, the Israeli-Palestinian struggle, the U.S. occupation of Iraq, and Syria's uncertain place in the war on terrorism combined to limit Bashshar al-Asad's scope for regional and international initiatives.

See also AFLAQ, MICHEL; ASAD, BASHSHAR AL-; ASAD, HAFIZ AL-; BA'TH; DAMASCUS; HAMA; IRAN–IRAQ WAR (1980–1988); JADID, SALAH; MUSLIM BROTHERHOOD.

Bibliography

Batatu, Hanna. *Syria's Peasantry, the Descendants of Its Lesser Rural Notables, and Their Politics.* Princeton, NJ: Princeton University Press, 1999.

Deeb, Marius. *Syria's Terrorist War on Lebanon and the Peace Process.* New York: Palgrave Macmillan, 2003.

Hinnebusch, Raymond A. *Authoritarian Power and State Formation in Ba'thist Syria: Army, Party, and Peasant.* Boulder, CO: Westview Press, 1990.

Hinnebusch, Raymond A. *Syria: Revolution from Above.* London: Taylor & Francis, 2002.

Khoury, Philip S. *Syria and the French Mandate: The Politics of Arab Nationalism, 1920–1945.* Princeton, NJ: Princeton University Press, 1987.

Kienle, Eberhard, ed. *Contemporary Syria: Liberalization between Cold War and Cold Peace.* London: British Academic Press, 1994.

Longrigg, Stephen Hemsley. *Syria and Lebanon under the French Mandate.* New York; London: Oxford University Press, 1958.

Perthes, Volker. *The Political Economy of Syria under Asad.* New York; London: I. B. Tauris, 1995.

Pipes, Daniel. *Greater Syria: The History of an Ambition.* New York: Oxford University Press, 1990.

Seale, Patrick. *Asad: The Struggle for the Middle East.* Berkeley: University of California Press, 1995.

Seale, Patrick. *The Struggle for Syria: A Study of Post-War Arab Politics, 1945–1958.* New York; London: Oxford University Press, 1965.

Van Dam, Nikolaos. *The Struggle for Power in Syria: Politics and Society under Asad and the Ba'th Party.* New York; London: I. B. Tauris, 1996.

Wedeen, Lisa. *Ambiguities of Domination: Politics, Rhetoric, and Symbols in Contemporary Syria.* Chicago: University of Chicago Press, 1999.

FRED H. LAWSON
UPDATED BY RONALD BRUCE ST JOHN

SYRIAN DESERT

A huge stretch of mostly barren land covering parts of four countries: Syria, Iraq, Jordan, and Saudi Arabia.

Known in Arabic as *Badiyat al-Sham* after the nomadic bedouin (Badu, hence Badiya) who roam its parts in search of pasture, it is also known as the Greater Badiyat al-Sham (Badiyat al-Sham al-Kubra) because it extends between the desert of al-Nufud on the Arabian peninsula and the Euphrates river. Badiyat al-Sham covers about two-thirds—about 52,000 square miles (130,000 sq. km)—of the overall area of Syria. It is divided into two parts: the first, in the northeast, is called Badiyat al-Jazira, and the second, in the southeast, is called al-Shamiyya or Badiyat al-Sham, that is, the Syrian desert. This desert begins at the Syro-Jordanian border, skirts the frontier of settlement toward the north at a line east of Jabal Druze, al-Ghuta oasis of Damascus and its *marj* (meadow), then up along the Qalamun mountains, then east of al-Jabbul, the finally ends at Meskene on the Euphrates.

The Syrian desert, in turn, is divided into two parts, which differ in their surface structure. The first, a plateau in the southwest, is more elevated than the other part and also much drier. The part to the northeast starts at lower elevation in the south—2,208 feet (673 m)—and ends at 623 feet (190 m) in the north. This part is dry and has dry river channels (wadis) exposed to flooding. These wadis range in length from 93 to 186 miles (150–300 km) and in width from 0.3 to 0.6 miles (0.5 to 1 km). Annual precipitation in the Syrian desert does not exceed 5.85 inches (150 mm).

The few plants and animals of the Syrian desert are of the type that can withstand a subtropical climate. The nomads raise sheep and camels, and they move according to the seasons, from one region to the other across political frontiers seeking pasture. Phosphates, oil, and butane gas have been discovered in this desert, and modern network of roads and railways makes the exploitation of the desert much easier than before.

ABDUL-KARIM RAFEQ

SYRIAN SOCIAL NATIONALIST PARTY

Political party established in Lebanon in 1932 with the aim of uniting the Syrian nation.

Syrian Social Nationalist Party militia watch over the streets of Beirut. After decades of division and weakness, the radical party reached a more pragmatic accommodation with the Syrian government of Hafiz al-Asad in the 1980s. © SAMER MOHDAD/CORBIS. REPRODUCED BY PERMISSION.

The Syrian Social Nationalist Party (SSNP) was founded in Beirut by Antun Khalil Sa'ada, a Greek Orthodox intellectual, in November 1932. He served as the party's leader until his death in 1949, and the organization reflects his personality and ideas. The SSNP had a strong political influence on the twentieth-century history of the two states, Lebanon and Syria, where it was the most active. It was the first political party in the region to embrace radical, secular ideas which later had an impact on virtually every radical group organized in the two countries, especially the Ba'th Party. The SSNP offered minorities, particularly Greek Orthodox Christians, a vehicle for political action. Its ideology also influenced the development of Pan-Arabism, defining inter-Arab relations in the Levant.

The party's ideology, as defined by Sa'ada, was grounded in three related tenets: radical social reform along secular lines, fascist-style rituals and organization, and a Pan-Syrian doctrine. Best known for its Pan-Syrian approach, emphasizing Syrian history and culture but opposing Arab unity, the SSNP called for the creation of a "Greater Syria," encompassing Cyprus, Jordan, Lebanon, and Palestine, in addition to Syria. In one of his publications, Sa'ada wrote: "[The] Syrian homeland is that geographic environment in which the Syrian nation evolved. It has natural boundaries which separate it from other countries, extending from the Taurus range in the north-west and the Zagros in the northeast to the Suez Canal and the Red Sea in the south and including the Sinai peninsula and the Gulf of Aqaba, and from the Syrian Sea (Mediterranean) in the west, including the island of Cyprus, to the arch of the Arabian desert and Persian Gulf in the east. (This region is also called the Syrian Fertile Crescent, the island of Cyprus being its star.)" While this Pan-Syrian emphasis was the most prominent aspect of SSNP ideology, its appeal and influence also stemmed from its fascist qualities and emphasis on radical social reform.

Saʿada argued that Lebanon did not constitute a separate entity but was instead part of the Syrian nation. This philosophy led to clashes with Lebanese authorities. In 1949 Saʿada declared an armed revolt against the government and called on his supporters to carry weapons and attack police stations. With the help of Syrian leader Husni al-Zaʿim, Lebanese authorities retaliated and arrested Saʿada. He was executed in July 1949. Saʿada's death led to the overthrow of Zaʿim in Syria and to increased popularity for the SSNP in the 1950s. The killing of a major Baʿth party official and the adversarial relationship between SSNP members and Arab nationalists later caused the party to lose its support in Syria.

In the Lebanese upheaval of 1958, the SSNP allied itself with President Camille Chamoun against pro-Arab nationalist forces in Lebanon. Under attack in Syria, the leaders of the SSNP rightly feared that a victory of the government's opponents would close Lebanon to them. At the end of 1961, the SSNP was involved in an unsuccessful coup against the Lebanese government. As a result, the party was banned in Lebanon as well as in Syria. Many of the party leaders were arrested, and the other party members dispersed or left the organization.

During the Lebanese civil war (1975–1976), the SSNP regained some strength but remained a divided party. One faction retained Saʿada's original ideology. Another group, led by Inʿam Raad, believed it possible to combine Marxist doctrine with the ideology of the SSNP. This group also considered violence a legitimate means of achieving political aims. Raad and his group split from the original SSNP and joined the Lebanese National Movement. In September 1977 a third splinter of the SSNP was formed for the purpose of unifying the party.

Militia members of the Syrian Social Nationalist Party (SSNP) in Beirut, Lebanon, birthplace of the movement in 1932. The party, whose radical secular ideology is centered around the concept of a "Greater Syria," comprising not only Syria and Lebanon but also Cyprus, Jordan, Iraq, Kuwait, and Palestine. © SAMER MOHDAD/CORBIS. REPRODUCED BY PERMISSION.

Syrian president Hafiz al-Asad's government later co-opted Pan-Syrianism into what has been characterized as Syro-centric Arabism, and the Baʿth Party and SSNP cooperated as never before. Several factors helped to explain the reconciliation that took place. Asad grew up in a time and place in which SSNP ideology enjoyed great strength; the family of his wife had close ties to the party; and Asad saw practical, political advantage in accommodating the SSNP. Following decades of competition, they thus reached a mutually beneficial accommodation in which the SSNP became a client of the Syrian state. Even though it remained discredited in its pure, ideological form, a reborn, pragmatic Pan-Syrianism became more significant during the 1980s and after than at any time since the 1920s. For example, in the 1990 and 1994 elections, an SSNP member was elected to the Syrian parliament, albeit standing formally as an independent.

The Syrian Social Nationalist Party has had a profound impact on politics in Lebanon and Syria, introducing a variety of new ideas to the region, including the ideological party, fascist leadership, complete political secularism, and the destruction of existing borders between states. Its repeated challenges to the Lebanese state also served to undermine the power and prestige of the Beirut government. Finally, it led the way in the use of violence to destroy the existing political order, with virtually every radical group in the region adopting aspects of its program.

See also ASAD, HAFIZ AL-; PAN-ARABISM; RAAD, INᶜAM; SAᶜADA, ANTUN.

Bibliography

Pipes, Daniel. *Greater Syria: The History of an Ambition.* New York: Oxford University Press, 1990.

Suleiman, Michael W. *Political Parties in Lebanon: The Challenge of a Fragmented Political Culture.* Ithaca, NY: Cornell University Press, 1967.

RONALD BRUCE ST JOHN

SYRKIN, NACHMAN
[1867–1924]

Early Socialist Zionist.

Nachman (also spelled Nahman) Syrkin wrote a brochure in German, "The Jewish Problem and the Socialist Jewish State," under the pseudonym Ben Elieser, in Switzerland in 1898. The pamphlet was his considered opinion on solving the Jewish problem with Socialist Zionism. Born a Russian Jew who subsequently went to the West for an education, Syrkin drew on his experience of both Russian socialism and the misery and suffering of Russian Jewish life. He was one of the first to do so.

He attended the first Zionist Congress in 1897 and remained in the World Zionist Organization until 1905, when at the seventh Zionist Congress it was clear that the British offer of Uganda as a place for a Jewish state was impossible. He moved to the United States in 1907 to continue as an official of the Labor Zionist movement and worked as a territorialist (a member of Israel Zangwill's Jewish Territorial Organization [ITO], willing for the Jewish people to settle any unpopulated area). He also wrote and edited journals in Yiddish and Hebrew in support of his views.

Syrkin's socialism was utopian and ethical, not Marxist. At the base was his view that the common people would realize a Jewish state, not the successful or wealthy; and the state was necessary, since even a new socialist order would not integrate the Jewish minority. He reasoned that modern antisemitism was different from historical forms that had been unleashed in earlier eras, since it stemmed from dislocations of modernization.

Bibliography

Hertzberg, Arthur, ed. *The Zionist Idea: A Historical Analysis and Reader.* Philadelphia: Jewish Publication Society, 1997.

Syrkin, Marie, ed. *Nachman Syrkin: Socialist Zionist.* New York: Herzl Press, 1960.

DONNA ROBINSON DIVINE

SZOLD, HENRIETTA
[1860–1945]

Founder of Hadassah, the largest Jewish women's organization.

Henrietta Szold was the daughter of a modernist rabbi from Baltimore. After visiting Palestine in 1909, she resolved to bring modern medical care and hygiene to the area and to establish a healthcare system to meet the needs of the Jewish community there. Szold was the first director of the Youth Aliyah.

See also YOUTH ALIYAH.

Bibliography

Dash, Joan. *Summoned to Jerusalem: The Life of Henrietta Szold.* New York: Harper and Row, 1979.

Geller, L. D., ed. *The Henrietta Szold Papers in the Hadassah Archives, 1875–1965.* New York: Hadassah, 1982.

MIA BLOOM

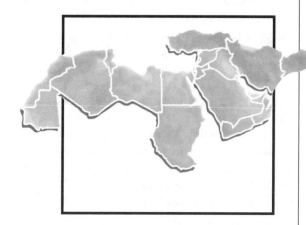

TABA

A piece of land disputed by Egypt and Israel.

Taba is a 250-acre patch of land that juts into the Gulf of Aqaba, a dozen miles south of Elat. When the Israeli and Egyptian governments finalized terms on 19 January 1982 for the return of the entire Sinai peninsula to Egypt, Israeli negotiators claimed that Taba should remain within Israel. They based their claim on alleged ambiguities in the physical description of Taba in the 1 October 1906 accord that demarcated the administrative border between Palestine and Egypt. Israel reinforced that claim by constructing two hotels, after spring 1982, within the Taba zone. Article 7 of the Egypt-Israel peace treaty of 1979 provided for mediation or arbitration of such differences if direct negotiations failed to resolve them. Egypt urged the formation of an international arbitration team, but the Israeli cabinet did not agree to the principle of arbitration until 13 January 1986. The membership and terms of the arbitration team were agreed upon by 12 September 1986. The three-person panel was empowered to decide on the location of the boundary pillars as of 1948, the end of the Palestine Mandate, and its rulings were final and binding on both parties. On 29 September 1988, the panel ruled in favor of Egypt. Israel evacuated Taba on 15 March 1989. Egyptian sovereignty was restored over Taba and over the hotels that Israel had constructed. However, Israelis could visit the enclave without obtaining an Egyptian visa, and Israel continued to supply Taba's water and electricity from Elat. The Taba accord was a rare example of the resolution of a contentious issue through judicial means.

Bibliography

Lesch, Ann M. "The Egyptian-Israeli Accord to Submit the Dispute over Taba to International Arbitration." In *The Middle East and North Africa: Essays in Honor of J. C. Hurewitz,* edited by Reeva S. Simon. New York: Middle East Institute, 1990.

ANN M. LESCH

TABA ACCORDS

See TABA; TABA NEGOTIATIONS (1995, 2001)

TABA NEGOTIATIONS (1995, 2001)

Two separate Israeli-Palestinians negotiations that led to an accord on interim arrangements in 1995, and to bridging differences on the final status issues in 2001.

The Taba resort in Egypt was the site of the Israeli-PLO negotiations that concluded with the Israeli-Palestinian Interim Agreement, West Bank–Gaza Strip, also known as the Taba Accords or Oslo II, which was signed in Washington, D.C., on 28 September 1995. The agreement dealt with such issues as civil affairs, economic relations, legal matters, the Palestinian election of an 88-member Palestinian Legislative Council, and security arrangements. The West Bank was divided into areas A, B, and C. In area A, Israel was to redeploy from six cities, whose overall security would be placed in Palestinian hands. In area B, Palestinian towns and villages, Israel would be responsible for security and the Palestinians for public order. In area C, unpopulated areas, Israel would maintain full control. Negotiations for permanent status of the territories were to begin in May 1996, but were delayed for four years.

Five years after the first Taba negotiations, President Bill Clinton convened a summit on 11 through 24 July 2000 at Camp David between Israeli Prime Minister Ehud Barak and PLO Chairman Yasir Arafat and their teams to negotiate the final status issues, but the parties failed to reach an agreement. More negotiations took place, especially at Bolling Air Force Base in December 2000; these ended on 23 December with Clinton issuing what became known as the Clinton proposals or parameters. These meetings and Clinton's intervention set the stage for the last Israeli-Palestinian meeting of the Oslo peace process, which took place at Taba between 21 and 27 January 2001.

Thanks to the Clinton proposals the two parties at Taba were able to narrow their differences on final status issues, though, since there was no official note taking, there are conflicting accounts about the extent of the progress. Both sides made unprecedented concessions. The Israelis reportedly agreed to withdraw from 100 percent of the Gaza Strip and 92 percent of the West Bank, coupled with a 3 percent land swap. The Palestinians accepted Israeli annexation of clusters of settlements but were seeking sovereignty over 98 percent so as to have maximum contiguity in the West Bank. These figures are in dispute, since both sides do not agree on how to calculate withdrawal percentage, especially on whether East Jerusalem, parts of the Jordan Valley, and other parts should count as part of the West Bank. When these parts are counted, the withdrawal figures are smaller than those cited above. On Jerusalem, the Palestinians conceded the Jewish Quarter, including the Western Wall, and Israel agreed to return noncontiguous parts of East Jerusalem. The parties discussed the return of 100,000 to 150,000 Palestinian refugees, out of some 3.7 million, to what is now Israel, but they remained apart on this and other issues.

While the Israeli offer was far-reaching, it was not enough for the Palestinians, because it would not have allowed for a contiguous capital in East Jerusalem, the settlement clusters that Israel wanted to annex would have reduced contiguity in the West Bank, and Palestinian inability to control their borders and air space would have negated Palestinian sovereignty. The two sides needed more time to bridge their differences, but time ran out. The negotiations were interrupted by the departure from office of Clinton on 20 January 2001, and by the defeat of Barak in the Israeli elections of 6 February 2001. But the narrowing of differences at Taba in 2001 had been significant and was hailed by several of the negotiators as representing the closest the two sides had ever come to an agreement.

See also CLINTON, WILLIAM JEFFERSON; OLSO ACCORD (1993).

Bibliography

Enderlin, Charles. *Shattered Dreams: The Failure of the Peace Process in the Middle East, 1995–2002.* New York: Other Press, 2002.

The Moratinos Document. Available at <http://disarm .igc.org/morotinosdocument1.htm>.

PHILIP MATTAR

TABAQA DAM

Dam on the Euphrates river built to irrigate Syria.

Started in 1968, the dam was finished in 1973 with Soviet assistance, at a total cost of US$600 million. It forms Lake Asad on the Euphrates, above Raqqa, Syria. It is intended to irrigate 1.5 million acres (640,000 ha) by the year 2005 and produce six hundred megawatts of electricity. By the mid-1980s, only about 187,500 acres (75,000 ha) were under irrigation and five of the eight power generators were not operating.

When all projects are completed, the dam will take seven billion cubic meters of the thirty billion cubic meters of water that once entered Iraq each year. Iraq complains of this and that the upstream irrigation projects lower Iraq's water quality by raising salinity levels. Turkey also has ambitious irrigation projects under way at Keban and Karababa, which will reduce Iraq's share to eleven billion cubic meters. Syria has protested to Turkey about excessive use of Euphrates water and tried in 1984 to block Arab oil states from making loans to Turkey for construction of the Karababa dam. No treaty exists for sharing the flow, thus this serious dispute has no foreseeable prospect of resolution.

Bibliography

Drysdale, Alasdair, and Blake, Gerald H. *The Middle East and North Africa: A Political Geography.* New York: Oxford University Press, 1985.

JOHN R. CLARK

TABATABA'I, MOHAMMAD
[1841–1920]

Persian religious scholar; one of the principal leaders of the Constitutional Revolution, 1905–1909.

Born in Karbala in 1841 to a family with illustrious scholarly antecedents, Mohammad Tabataba'i spent his early childhood in Hamadan in the care of Aqa Sayyed Mehdi, his paternal grandfather, before moving to Tehran, the capital, where his father, Sayyed Sadeq, was firmly established as a leading religious authority. There he studied jurisprudence with his father and other prominent scholars, philosophy with Mirza Abul-Hasan Jelve, and—most significant for his political activity in later years—ethics with Shaykh Hadi Najmabadi, many of whose opinions were regarded as subversively liberal. At the same time, through reading newspapers and closely questioning returning travelers, Tabataba'i began taking an interest in the affairs of Europe, which was atypical for the religious scholars of his time.

In 1882, Tabataba'i set out from Tehran with the intention of making the pilgrimage to Mecca.

He took a circuitous route, traveling via Russia, Anatolia, and Istanbul, meeting new scholars and men of state wherever he alighted, and he arrived in Mecca too late for the pilgrimage. Cholera was raging in the Hijaz, so he left promptly for the area that is now Iraq, where he joined the circle of the great scholar Mirza Hasan Shirazi in Samarra. He spent more than ten years with Shirazi, perfecting his command of Shi'ite jurisprudence and acting as the trusted adviser of his teacher in political matters. It was in this capacity that he was addressed a letter by the celebrated Jamal al-Din Asadabadi (Afghani), then resident in London, calling on him to make greater political use of Shirazi's prestige, which had been inaugurated by the Tobacco Revolt and boycott of 1891.

Despite the oppositional tendencies that Asadabadi correctly perceived in him, Tabataba'i's return to Tehran was due to an initiative of Naser al-Din Shah. The monarch wished to create in Tehran a counterweight to Mirza Hasan Ashtiani, a cleric whose prestige had grown considerably in the course of the tobacco boycott, and he accordingly suggested to Shirazi that he should send one of his prominent disciples to Tehran. Shirazi selected Tabataba'i, who arrived back in Tehran in the fall of 1893. His father had died almost a decade before, but Tabataba'i fell heir to his influence in the Iranian capital with little difficulty. The shah's expectations of Tabataba'i were disappointed; not only did he establish cordial relations with Mirza Hasan Ashtiani, but he also emerged as an implacable critic of the corruption and tyranny of the court. Indeed, in 1911 he claimed to have begun working for the cause of constitutional government immediately after his return from Samarra, preaching from the pulpit on the need for establishing a consultative assembly. On another occasion, he stated frankly that he and his colleagues in the clerical class had no direct acquaintance with the concept of constitutionalism, having learned of it from those with experience of Europe. During the decade leading up to the Constitutional Revolution he deepened both his understanding of constitutional government and his contacts with secular intellectuals working for the same goal.

The beginnings of the revolution may be dated to an alliance concluded by Tabataba'i with another leading cleric of Tehran, Sayyed Abdollah Behbahani, on 23 November 1905, initially for the purpose of obtaining the dismissal of Ayn al-Dowleh, the prime minister. Soon thereafter, the two clerics joined a group of bazaar merchants who had taken sanctuary in the Shah Mosque in Tehran to protest government policies. After Tehran's *imam jomeh* (the highest-ranking paid government-appointed cleric) had the group forcibly evicted from the mosque, Tabataba'i and the clerics led a migration of their colleagues and supporters to the shrine of Shah Abd al-Azim, south of Tehran, where they formulated the demand for an *adalat-khaneh* (house of justice) as a condition of their return. Their demand was formally accepted, and on 12 January 1906 Tabataba'i and Behbahani returned to the capital in triumph. Ayn al-Dowleh remained in office, however, and he stalled implementing the royal decree for convening a house of justice. The tensions that persisted between him and the constitutionalists led to a new and more significant migration of Tabataba'i, Behbahani, and their associates, this time to Qom, on 15 July 1906. They demanded the dismissal of Ayn al-Dowleh, in addition to the establishment of a consultative assembly. Their demands were accepted, and on 18 August 1906 Tabataba'i and Behbahani were able to reenter Tehran. Tabataba'i exercised great influence in the *majles* (assembly) that was convened soon thereafter, attempting to preserve the alliance of personalities and interests that had made possible the introduction of constitutional government. His success was limited, however, and the majles was in a state of chronic dissension when its debates were brought abruptly to an end by the royal coup of 23 June 1908. Tabataba'i was arrested and taken in chains to the garrison at Bagh-e Shah. After a spell of imprisonment, he lived in seclusion in Shemiran, north of Tehran, before being banished to Mashhad. He returned to Tehran on 24 August 1909, one month after the restoration of the constitution, but thereafter tired of direct political involvement. He spent the rest of his life in Tehran, with the exception of a journey in 1917 to the shrine cities of Iraq.

Tabataba'i stands out above all as the most prominent religious leader of his time to have understood fully and accepted the far-reaching implications of constitutionalism for Iranian society, recognizing, for example, that it required a modernization of the educational system. This broadness of outlook may have been connected to the Freemasons' affiliations he had inherited from his father, which led him also to join the Masonic Lodge Reveil de l'Iran, the first Iranian lodge officially affiliated to the Grand Orient of France.

See also AFGHANI, JAMAL AL-DIN AL-; SHIRAZI, MIRZA HASAN.

Bibliography

Browne, Edward. *The Persian Revolution of 1905–1909.* Cambridge, U.K.: Cambridge University Press, 1910.

Hairi, Abdul-Hadi. *Shiʿism and Constitutionalism in Iran.* Leiden, Netherlands: Brill, 1977.

HAMID ALGAR
UPDATED BY ERIC HOOGLUND

TABATABA'I, ZIYA
[c. 1889–1969]

Anglophile Iranian politician and journalist.

Born in Iran, in the southeastern city of Yazd, Ziya Tabataba'i began his public career as a journalist in Shiraz, publishing a series of newspapers—*Islam Sharq* (The east), and *Barq* (Lightning)—in which he supported the causes of constitutional government and social reform. He next moved to Tehran, where during World War I he published *Ra'd* (Thunder), a journal staunchly supporting British policy in Iran. This earned him favorable standing with the British, enabling him to act as a go-between for Iranian notables who wanted their checks cashed by the British-owned Imperial Bank of Persia, which in turn gained for him considerable influence in Tehran society. In 1919, Tabataba'i traveled to Baku (in Azerbaijan) to negotiate on behalf of Iran a political and commercial treaty with the temporarily independent states of the south Caucasus, taking advantage of the opportunity to impress other members of the delegation with his political acumen. In 1920 and 1921, he was active in the Anjoman-e Pulad (Steel Committee), a reformist political committee that was the offshoot of a similar organization established by the British in Isfahan and sought to bring together politicians and military officers to initiate change. At the same time, he maintained close links with the head of the British military mission in Iran. These relations with the British enabled him, together with Reza Khan (later Reza Shah

Pahlavi), then a commander of the Iranian Cossack Brigade, to launch a coup d'état on 21 February 1921, that resulted in the appointment of Tabataba'i as prime minister.

The real significance of this coup was that it marked the first stage in the rise of Reza Khan to supreme power and the replacement of the Qajar dynasty by the Pahlavis, and the premiership of Tabataba'i did not last long. He began energetically enough, banning newspapers hostile to his government and imprisoning many of the titled landowners for whom he nurtured a lifelong enmity. He then concluded a treaty of friendship with the Soviet Union and formally abrogated the already moribund Anglo-Iranian Agreement of 1919. His intention, as he privately informed the British minister in Tehran, was to "throw dust in the eyes of the Bolsheviks and native malcontents" (*Documents on British Foreign Policy, 1919–1939*, London, 1963, vol. 13, p. 731). However, differences soon arose. Over the objections of Tabataba'i, on 6 May 1921, Reza Khan succeeded in bringing the gendarmerie under the control of the Ministry of War and then, some two weeks later, in obtaining the dismissal of the British officers who had been seconded to the Iranian army. The swift erosion of Tabataba'i's position became fully apparent on 24 May, when most of the enemies he had had arrested were released without his permission; the following day he went into exile.

Tabataba'i spent the next nine years in Switzerland, moving in 1930 to Palestine, where he lived for thirteen years under the protection of the British mandate government. In the course of World War II Reza Khan was deposed by the Allies (1941), and in September 1943 Tabataba'i was able to return to Iran—in the face of strong objections from the Iranian court, the Soviet Union, and the United States, which were overcome only by the energetic representations of the British.

Embarking on the second half of his political career, Tabataba'i first aligned himself with the Patriotic Caucus (Fraksiun-e Mihan), a pro-British grouping in the Majles (Iran's legislature). Soon, however, he founded his own party, the Fatherland party (Hezb-e Vatan), which early in 1944 was reorganized along authoritarian lines and renamed the National Will party (Hezb-e Erade-ye Melli).

He launched yet another newspaper, *Ra'd-e Emruz* (Today's thunder), in which he denounced the remnants of the military dictatorship established by Reza Khan, the continued hold on national life of the landowning oligarchy, and the growing influence of the communist Tudeh party. Tabataba'i's views won him the support of many bazaar merchants and guild leaders, as well as some lesser-ranking religious scholars, but his National Will party did not contest parliamentary elections. Nonetheless, he was elected to the Majles as deputy from Yazd, under the auspices of the Patriotic Caucus. He opposed a whole series of prime ministers, including most notably Qavam al-Dowleh, who had him arrested for several months in 1946, probably to placate the Soviet Union, the patron of the Tudeh party. Despite his rooted aversion to the Tudeh party, Tabataba'i sided with it in 1948 when efforts were under way to wrest control of the army from the shah. This tactical alliance did not last long, and it was in part because of a growing dependence on the Tudeh party that Tabataba'i opposed the government of Mohammad Mossadegh from 1951 onward (his continued alignment with the British was, no doubt, a more important factor in this regard).

Tabataba'i appears to have withdrawn from active political involvement even before the royalist coup of August 1953 that restored full-fledged autocracy to Iran. He spent the remaining years of his life in the village of Sa'adatabad, dying there in 1969. Notwithstanding his earlier hostility to the Pahlavis, he is said to have become a trusted consultant of the shah during the last phase of his life, meeting with him regularly at least once a week.

See also PAHLAVI, REZA.

Bibliography

Abrahamian, Ervand. *Iran between Two Revolutions.* Princeton, NJ: Princeton University Press, 1982.

Avery, P. W. *Modern Iran.* New York: Praeger, 1965.

HAMID ALGAR

TABBULA

See FOOD: TABBULA

TABRIZ

Provincial capital in northwestern Iran.

Tabriz, the capital of East Azerbaijan, is Iran's fourth largest city, with 1,191,000 inhabitants according to the 1996 census. The city dates back to the Parthian period (approximately 238 B.C.E. to 224 C.E.). The Blue Mosque, built in the fifteenth century, and the Rubʿe Rashidi, constructed by the famous Mongol vizier Rashid al-Din Fazl Allah, are among its archaeological sites. In 1295 the Mongol ruler Ghazan Khan made Tabriz the capital of his empire. In the fourteenth century Tamerlane conquered Tabriz. The Safavid Shah Ismaʿil I made it his capital in 1501. At that time, Tabriz, with a population estimated at 250,000, was one of the world's largest cities. Most of the city was destroyed in the massive earthquake of 1721, which left it devastated, and according to some accounts, caused 80,000 to 100,000 casualties. In the Qajar period (between 1779 and 1925) Tabriz was the seat of the crown prince and a major military headquarters against the Russian frontier. During the Constitutional Revolution (1905–1911) it was a site of antigovernment activity, and Russians occupied the city from 1911 to 1917. Soviet troops occupied the city in 1941 and in 1945 supported the Autonomous Government of Azerbaijan, a secessionist movement headed by Jaʿfar Pishevari. The Soviets withdrew in 1946, and subsequently Iranian forces occupied Tabriz and put an end to Pishevari's government. As an important commercial center, Tabriz also played a prominent role in the revolution of 1979.

Tabriz is one of Iran's most important centers for manufacturing industries, producing chemicals, metals, machinery, and textiles. Hand-knotted carpets made in the city have had an international reputation for quality and design for more than a century. Agricultural products from the Tabriz region include wheat, barley, potatoes, and onions; this region is also a considerable producer of fruits and nuts exported from Iran. The variety of agricultural products has contributed to Tabriz becoming a major food-processing center.

See also AZERBAIJAN.

NEGUIN YAVARI

TABRIZ UNIVERSITY

University in Tabriz, Iran.

Established in 1949 as the University of Azerbaijan, the University of Tabriz had 5,187 students by 1970.

It includes schools of literature, agriculture, science, and engineering, as well as an institute for advanced studies. The faculty of literature and philosophy publishes a journal with a solid reputation. According to the university's own statistics, the total student population in 2002 exceeded 10,000, and the faculty numbers about 500, with some 900 administrative personnel.

PARVANEH POURSHARIATI

TAGGER, SIONEH
[1900–1988]

Israeli artist.

Sioneh Tagger was born at the turn of the century in Jaffa to Sephardic Jews who had settled there in the nineteenth century. Her parents helped to found the modern city of Tel Aviv. She studied art at the Herzliya Gymnasium in 1919/20 with a Russian sculptor, Joseph Constant, who introduced her to cubism and European modernism. In 1921 she moved to Jerusalem to study at Bezalel on condition that she live with her grandfather's family, who were religious people. Her works from this period include drawings of elderly Jews and "Oriental types" of Jews, as well as decorative metalwork and painting of miniatures. In 1924 she went to study in Paris, where she learned to build her drawings based on simple geometric structures. Tagger was influenced by several painters from the Jewish School of Paris, as well as by André Derain and Picasso, whose influence can be seen in *Clown* (1925) and *Harlequin* (1901). Later in life, Tagger painted on plexiglass, inspired by memories of glass paintings decorating quotations from the Qurʾan hanging in Arab homes in Jaffa (she, though, used Jewish themes).

JULIE ZUCKERMAN

TAHA, MAHMUD MUHAMMAD
[c.1909–1985]

Founder of the Republican Brotherhood.

Mahmud Muhammad Taha was born in Rufaʿa, in central Sudan, in either 1909 or 1911. He graduated from Gordon Memorial College (now the University of Khartoum) in 1936 and practiced agricultural engineering in the Gazira, where his interest in local and nationalist politics grew. Taha founded the New Islamic Mission or Republican Brotherhood in 1945. His first arrest was in 1946, for leading a demonstration for the release of a midwife detained for performing a circumcision on a young girl just after the British had outlawed the practice. Taha's point was that the colonial authorities had no legitimacy to legislate morality that could only change with the equality of women in society.

Taha was both theologian and political leader. The Republican Brotherhood movement was one of the many nationalist movements that agitated for the independence of Sudan from British colonialism. In addition, Taha's "second message" of Islam was among the earliest of the liberal Muslim reformist movements now called "progressive Islam." He argued for a scientific understanding in Islam rendering it capable of resolving the problems of modern life. He argued against the application of the *hadd* punishments of amputation for theft as a violation of *shari'a* and of Islam because their imposition presupposes a level of education and social justice that are lacking in today's society. He also argued for equal rights for women in marriage in Islamic law. The community of "Republicans," which included significant numbers of women, put into practice the egalitarian ideas of the movement. The movement was also notable for its emphasis on the rights of non-Muslims in predominantly Muslim Sudan, especially recognizing the oppressed southern masses whose resistance has been manifested in decades of protracted civil war.

Taha and the Republican movement opposed the imposition of *shari'a* as state law in September 1983 because it divided Muslims from the large non-Muslim Sudanese population and thus was contrary to national unity. They argued that non-Muslims should enjoy full rights as citizens and called for repeal of the "September laws." As a result of this protest, Taha was tried by the Islamist government of Ja'far Nimeiri for apostasy. He was found guilty and hanged by the regime on 18 January 1985.

See also GENDER: GENDER AND EDUCATION; GENDER: GENDER AND LAW; GENDER: GENDER AND POLITICS; NUMEIRI, MUHAMMAD JA'FAR; *SHARI'A*; SUDAN; SUDANESE CIVIL WARS.

Bibliography

Howard, W. Stephen. "Mahmoud Mohamed Taha." In *Historical Dictionary of the Sudan,* edited by Richard A. Lobban, Jr., Robert S. Kramer, and Carolyn Fluehr-Lobban. Lanham, MD: Scarecrow Press, 2002.

Taha, Mahmoud Mohammed. *The Second Message of Islam,* translated by Abdullahi Ahmed An-Na'im. Syracuse, NY: Syracuse University Press, 1987.

CAROLYN FLUEHR-LOBBAN

TAHA YASIN RAMADAN

See RAMADAN, TAHA YASIN

TAHINA

See FOOD: TAHINA

TAHIR, KEMAL
[1910–1973]
Turkish novelist.

The son of a naval officer, Kemal Tahir was born Ismail Kemalettin Demir in Istanbul and attended the prestigious Galatasaray Lycée (secondary school), though he did not graduate. In 1932, he began writing for newspapers and periodicals, as well as historical novels that glorified the Ottoman past. Between 1938 and 1950, he was imprisoned, along with the poet Nazim Hikmet, by the government of Turkey because of his ideological views and political convictions. During his incarceration, Tahir collected the observations of villagers who were in prison with him; he used these as the basis for a series of novels that authentically depicted the mentality, social structure, and mode of life in the villages of central Anatolia. He was released from prison in 1950 as part of a general amnesty.

Tahir's novels and his political-cultural theories influenced many Turkish authors, known collectively as Tahiris. His influence spread beyond the realm of literature into cinema, inspiring filmmakers to create films rooted in popular Turkish culture, not Western masterpieces. One of Tahir's last novels, *Mother State,* which took as its subject the founding of the Ottoman Empire in the thirteenth century, signaled a transition in Turkish literature from portraying social realities to searching for new models for change.

Bibliography

Ertop, Konur. "Trends and Characteristics of Contemporary Turkish Literature." In *The Transformation of Turkish Culture: The Atatürk Legacy,* edited by Günsel Renda and C. Max Kortepeter. Princeton, NJ: Kingston Press, 1986.

Halman, Talat Sait, ed. *Contemporary Turkish Literature: Fiction and Poetry.* Rutherford, NJ: Fairleigh Dickinson University Press, 1982.

DAVID WALDNER

TAHTAWI, RIFA'A AL-RAFI AL
[c. 1801–1873]

Egyptian writer and educator and the founder of the translation movement; precursor of modern Arab secular thought.

Rifa'a al-Rafi al-Tahtawi was born in Tanta, in upper Egypt, into a family of rural notables with a religious learning tradition, whose genealogy went back to al-Husayn ibn Fatima, grandson of the prophet Muhammad. In his early childhood, his family was exposed to pecuniary difficulties following the confiscation by Muhammad Ali of the *iltizamat* (tax farms).

Education

He was educated in al-Azhar in the traditional range of religious and linguistic studies, but was exposed there to the influence of the unconventional Shaykh Hasan al-Attar who advocated a broader out-look to *ilm* (knowledge) than the range to which al-Azhar was confined. His career was further inspired in Paris (1826–1831), where he was attached to the first mission of students from Egypt, initially as an imam (prayer leader) but soon as the mission's only translation student. Tahtawi read in a wide range of subjects, became acquainted with French liberal tradition, established direct contacts with leading French orientalists and noted the institutionalization of Arabic studies in L'Ecole Spéciale des Langues Orientales Vivantes. He also followed closely the 1830 revolution, studied the structure of the French political system and keenly observed Parisian social life and manners. He provided in great detail the first documented Arabic account of

modern encounters with Western life and society in his *Takhlis al-Ibriz fi Talkhis Bariz* (The extraction of gold in the summary of Paris, 1935).

Institutional Career

Tahtawi's institutional career thrived during the reigns of Muhammad Ali and Isma'il in two distinct and separate phases. In each phase, he held several positions, all at the same time. The first of these phases (1837–1849), started toward the end of Muhammad Ali's expansion of education and continued up to the large-scale closure of schools at the time of Abbas (1848–1854). During that phase, Tahtawi directed the newly established *Madrasat al-Alsun* (School of languages), then founded and headed *Qalam al-Tarjama* (Translation department) and became chief editor of *al-Waqa'i al-Misriyya* newspaper in 1842. The second phase (1863–1873), corresponds to the reign of Isma'il (1863–1879), during which new activity in translation and education was initiated. In this second phase, Tahtawi headed the reinstated Qalam al-Tarjama, participated in *Qumisyun al-Ta'lim* (a central commission for educational planning), and was chief editor of a new fortnightly (*Rawdat al-Madaris al-Misriyya*). He continued to hold these positions until his death in 1873. During the long interlude between these phases (1849–1863), a general trend of reductions in education, and hence translation, prevailed under Abbas (1848–1854) and Sa'id (1854–1863). Tahtawi, virtually exiled to the Sudan for four years (1850–1854), was kept from institutional channels of influence, not-withstanding a relatively short-lived assignment to run a new military school with wide-ranging departments from its opening in 1855 to its closure in 1860.

Educational Agenda and Influence

Tahtawi practically founded the translation movement in Egypt. Works translated by Tahtawi and his pupils into Arabic and Turkish number more than two thousand, many of them geared to a wide variety of educational and general policy requirements. As an educator, he was equipped to run an integrated syllabus of studies. When initial contractions in Muhammad Ali's military establishment forced retrenchments in education, several schools were amalgamated in 1842 into a single institute under Tahtawi's directorship. He ran in that expanded domain the first curriculum that offered a combination of Islamic studies—including law—and European studies, in an educational milieu which had been characterized by strict dualism. These orientations earned Tahtawi the resentment of the *ulama*, whose traditional positions (that is, as judges) were being threatened by his pupils. During the reign of Isma'il, Tahtawi cosubmitted a project *(Makatib al-Milla)* for the establishment of a new educational administration to promote and supervise an integrated syllabus in existing elementary schools of traditional learning *(Katatib)*, and to sponsor the opening of a network of similarly oriented government elementary schools.

Towards the end of his life, Tahtawi articulated prescriptive reformist views on knowledge, education and the political order in *Manahij al-Albab al-Misriyya fi Mabahij al-Adab al-Asriyya* (The paths of Egyptian minds to the joys of modern manners, 1869) and *al-Murshid al-Amin fi Tarbiyyat al-Banat wa al-Banin* (The honest guide in the upbringing of girls and boys, 1874). Within the context of a dominating traditional heritage, Tahtawi challenged traditional notions on knowledge and education in effective support for state-managed change. He preached that any branch of learning which contributed to human welfare fell within the realm of necessary ilm, that civilization had a material component acquired through adoption of rational sciences from advanced sources in Europe by appropriately prepared calibers, and that education should therefore be aimed at producing new men of knowledge capable of making such adoptions. On these premises, the existing state of al-Azhar *ulama* was criticized and education reforms were advocated, including girls' education, a call that coincided with the opening of the first girls' school in Egypt at the time of Isma'il.

Political Perspective

Tahtawi's prescriptions for political reform involved a blend of traditional Islamic and modern secular orientations. He referred to Egypt as a distinct and historically continuous entity, and perceived of the community in terms of a social and political order pertinent to a territorial nation *(watan)* whose members were bound by the common tie of nation-hood and were equally entitled to freedom of belief. He recognized that the social order could be organized on the basis of a man-made law equally

applied to all members in the national community *(al-jam'iyya)*, that the political order involved three distinct functional organs, including a legislative organ, and that its role in binding the community made it a necessity to include basic political education in schools' syllabi. But the inherent secular and liberal orientations were constrained by traditional premises and dimensions. Religion was maintained as a determinant within the political community by the perception that a common religious law was among the binding elements for a nation and by preaching equal civil rights of non-Muslims on an appeal to tolerance and justice based on *shari'a* (Islamic law) rather than on the implications of equality inherent in nation-hood. The absolute authority of the monarch was maintained by requiring that absolute obedience was due to him, that he was not held accountable to his subjects, and that the parliamentary organ's functions were only consultative and supportive. It is on the basis of his general exposure of the Arab mind to reform issues, rather than on the specific positions taken on each, that the origin of modern Arab secular thought is identified with Tahtawi.

Analysis of His Role

His role through state-sponsored institutions, as well as the congruence and timing of specific elements of his thought with specific policy measures, prompted a perception of him as an etatistic ideologue. The mix of reformist and conservative notions in his writings is interpreted accordingly by Israel Altman. Based on this perception, Tahtawi's thought is seen to have reflected a blend of vested interests in educational reform, intellectual commitment to the cause, and self-assertion vis-à-vis the Turco-Circassian bureaucratic superiors, all characteristic of Egyptian officials who participated in state reform policies between 1830 and 1880.

The Western influence on Tahtawi is generally emphasized. However, the contention that his thought was largely a process of acculturation to the West was recently challenged, and it was shown that Tahtawi's work involved "the reestablishment of direct contact with certain elements of classical Islamic [rationalist] tradition." The genuine and indigenous elements in Tahtawi's thought, and in the Arab "renascence" in general, are accordingly highlighted and emphasized.

Tahtawi produced over thirty publications of translations and original works, including Fénelon's *Les aventures de Télémaque* (1867), the first translation into Arabic of a work of Western literature. Among his other important original writings were two attempts made to simplify the teaching of Arabic grammar, the second of which, *al-Tuhfa al-Maktabiyya li-Taqrib al-Lughat al-Arabiyya* (The bookshelves' [or library's] Antique [*sic*] for the Simplification of Arabic Language, 1869) involved a departure from the prose-memorizing method applied then to the presentation of rules in a tabulated and systematic form. As chief editor of *al-Waqa'i al-Misriyya*, he introduced the newspaper article as a new genre of writing through various commentaries on current affairs. He wrote in serial form, in *Rawdat al-Madaris al-Misriyya*, the first sira (prophet's biography) in modern times, later published as *Nihayat al-Ijaz fi Sirat Sakin al-Hijaz* (The ultimate brief on the biography of the resident of Hijaz, 1876).

Notwithstanding the specific differences in interpreting his role and in classifying his political thought, Tahtawi's contributions to the policies and notions of cultural change, as well as his contributions to Arab secular thought, continue to be recognized. More than a century after Tahtawi's death, he remains relevant to contemporary endeavors. During Nasser's era, the widely circulating Egyptian daily *al-Ahram* used his words as epigraph for its opinion page: "Let the watan, the fatherland, be a place for our common happiness, which we build with freedom, intellect, and factories."

Bibliography

Altman, Israel. "The Political Thought of Rifa'a Rafi' at-Tahtawi, A Nineteenth Century Egyptian Reformer." Ph.D. diss., University of California at Los Angeles, 1976.

Cole, Juan R. "Rifa'a al-Tahtawi and the Revival of Practical Philosophy." *The Muslim World* 70 (1980): 29–46.

Heyworth-Dunne, J. "Rifa'a Badawi Rafi' at-Tahtawi: The Egyptian Revivalist." *Bulletin of the School of Oriental and African Studies* 9 (1937–1939): 961–967; and 10 (1939–1942): 399–415.

Husry, Khaldun S., Al- *Origins of Modern Arab Political Thought*. Delmar, NY: Caravan Books, 1980.

ABDEL AZIZ EZZELARAB

TA'IF ACCORD

Agreement ending the civil war in Lebanon, 1989.

In July 1989, the Arab Tripartite Committee (Morocco, Saudi Arabia, and Algeria) made recommendations to resolve Lebanon's civil war: expanded Lebanese sovereignty, a pullback of Syria's forces, and formalization of Syria and Lebanon's relationship with Israel. Syria promptly rejected them. In September, in the city of Ta'if, Saudi Arabia, representatives of the various Lebanese factions accepted a new National Unity charter. Under it, Syria would restrain Shi'ite groups backed by Iran in exchange for recognition of its dominance in Lebanon and the isolation of the Christian military figure Michel Aoun; vacant parliamentary seats would be filled by the new government before holding elections; Syria was empowered to become involved in reconstituting national governmental authority; redeployment of its forces left Syria firmly in control of territory strategically important for access to Beirut; and the governments of Syria and Lebanon were permitted to conclude secret agreements. The Ta'if Accord came under heavy criticism because several of its clauses were never implemented. Foremost was the issue of Syrian troops' presence in Lebanon. In 2002 and 2003, the Syrian regime implemented symbolic minor withdrawals from some areas in Lebanon, including Beirut. As of today, there are still more than 25,000 Syrian troops in Lebanon.

BRYAN DAVES
UPDATED BY GEORGE E. IRANI

TA'IF, AL-

A highland city in Saudi Arabia's al-Hijaz region.

Al-Ta'if is about 75 miles southeast of the holy city of Mecca. Although located on a sandy plain, it possesses plentiful water, making it an important agricultural center serving Mecca and Jidda. Many inhabitants are immigrants or the descendants of immigrants from throughout the Islamic world, especially Yemen, the Indian subcontinent, and central Asia. Al-Ta'if was the first city of al-Hijaz to fall to the Al Sa'ud in 1924, and the Ikhwan armies that first entered the city plundered it and massacred many of its inhabitants. It has long served as a summer residence for kings and wealthy Meccans, who are a mainstay of its economy, along with several Saudi military bases. Estimates in the early twenty-first century placed its permanent population at about 350,000, with a seasonal increase to 500,000. The nearby district of al-Shafa is a popular summer resort.

See also AL SAʿUD FAMILY; IKHWAN; SAUDI ARABIA.

Bibliography

Hogarth, David George. *Hejaz before World War I: A Handbook,* 1917. Reprint, New York: Oleander, 1978.

Peterson, J. E. *Historical Dictionary of Saudi Arabia,* 2d edition. Landover, MD: Scarecrow Press, 2003.

J. E. PETERSON

TA'IF, TREATY OF AL-

Treaty that concluded the 1933–1934 border war between Saudi Arabia and Yemen.

The treaty that ended the border war between Saudi Arabia and Yemen and set up a framework for peaceful relations was signed in al-Taʾif (Hijaz) in May 1934. After Saudi Arabia's occupation of the port city of Hodeida, Yemen—and under pressure from Great Britain and Italy, which were wary of the extension of Saudi Arabia's power nearer their colonies (Aden and Eritrea, respectively)—King Abd al-Aziz (Ibn Saʿud) and Imam Yahya agreed to settle the border issue. Yemen recognized Saudi Arabia's sovereignty over Asir and the towns of Najran and Jizan and agreed to pay Saudi Arabia an indemnity of 100,000 pounds sterling in gold. In exchange, Saudi Arabia evacuated its forces from Hodeidah and other areas of Yemen it had captured. The border area was to be demilitarized, and its demarcation was outlined from the Red Sea coast to just east of Najran; beyond that point it was undefined. A committee was to be established in order to work out the limits of tribal areas. In addition, the treaty called for the renewal of its terms in twenty years. Its terms were reaffirmed and expanded in a June 2000 international border treaty between the two countries.

See also ABD AL-AZIZ IBN SAʿUD AL SAʿUD; HODEIDA; YEMEN.

Bibliography

Tuson, Penelope, and Quick, Emma, eds. *Arabian Treaties, 1600–1960.* Volume 4. Slough, U.K.: Archives Editions, 1992.

F. GREGORY GAUSE III
UPDATED BY ANTHONY B. TOTH

TA'IZ

Province and largest city in the south of North Yemen.

Taʿiz Province is, along with Ibb Province, the heart of the Shafiʿi south of North Yemen. It embraces the Hujariyya region, and the city of Taʿiz is its soul. The southern uplands of Taʿiz Province, at a few thousand feet, have a more temperate climate and more rainfall than do the northern highlands, and the agriculture of the province has in the past supported a larger, denser population than that of provinces farther north. In the past, the city of Taʿiz was an important center of power in North Yemen, especially under the Rasulids from the mid-thirteenth to the mid-fifteenth centuries; more recently, Imam Ahmad insisted on residing there between 1948 and 1962. Linked since the late nineteenth century to British Aden by an increasing stream of workers, merchants, and students, and then linked through Aden to the outside world, Taʿiz became a part of world commerce and was in touch with the modern world and its ideas far more than was Sanʿa; by the 1940s, it had become the hotbed of modernist, republican, and even revolutionary ideas in the Yemen ruled by the imams. Thus, through the 1970s, Taʿiz was compared favorably to Sanʿa, and especially by many southerners.

By the 1980s, however, Sanʿa had outstripped it in size and political importance and Hodeida had outstripped it in commercial importance; its basic infrastructure—including electricity, water, and roads—was allowed to degrade. Still, Taʿiz remained in the 1990s and thereafter a major center of business and light industry; its links to Aden, and the new economic role of the latter, may enhance the position of Taʿiz in unified Yemen, or unification may lead to a bypassing of Taʿiz. In any case, the Taʿiz of old is no more. Within defining walls and highlighted by great whitewashed mosque minarets and domes, its back pressed against the cloud-topped mountain named Jabal Sabr, which towers over it, the old Taʿiz was a jewel of a small Arab Islamic city. The Taʿiz of today has burst its walls, and unattractive modern construction has replaced, crowded out, and hidden most of the old. The population of Taʿiz and the villages it has absorbed is about 700,000.

See also SANʿA; YEMEN; YEMEN ARAB REPUBLIC.

Bibliography

Burrowes, Robert. *Historical Dictionary of Yemen.* Lanham, MD: Scarecrow Press, 1995.

Carapico, Sheila. *Civil Society in Yemen: The Political Economy of Activism in Modern Arabia.* New York and Cambridge, U.K.: Cambridge University Press, 1998.

Dresch, Paul. *A History of Modern Yemen.* New York and Cambridge, U.K.: Cambridge University Press, 2000.

ROBERT D. BURROWES

TAJIKS

People of Central Asia; the original Iranian population of Afghanistan and historic Turkistan.

The Tajiks are Muslim people of Central Asia living in the countries of Afghanistan, Tajikistan, and Uzbekistan. Their population is thought to be about 10 million, with more living outside of Tajikistan than within. About 3.5 million live in Afghanistan. Although their history is not well known, Tajiks are thought to be the original inhabitants of Central Asia, perhaps the direct descendants of the ancient Aryans. Their language, Tajiki, is a dialect of Persian.

Tajiks in Afghanistan live primarily in the northern and western provinces, where they are mainly settled farmers and landowners. Most Tajiks in Afghanistan, like most Afghans, identify with their local village or valley and are not always aware of their ethnic name. In fact, *Tajik* is sometimes used to describe any Persian speaker in Central Asia, whether or not the people themselves so identify.

In Afghanistan the Tajiks played an important role in the civil war of the 1980s and 1990s, especially those in the Panjsher Valley. The famous Afghan resistance leader Ahmad Shah Masoud was a Panjsher Tajik.

Although historically the Tajiks have not played an important role in the governance of Afghanistan, their position changed after 11 September 2001. The Northern Alliance, which had strong Tajik leadership, took control of Afghanistan in November 2001. Tajiks occupied a number of key Afghan ministries in the government of Hamid Karzai, including foreign affairs and defense. They have continued to play a dominant role in the Karzai government.

See also AFGHANISTAN; KARZAI, HAMID.

Bibliography

Ewans, Martin. *Afghanistan: A New History.* London: Curzon Press, 2001.

GRANT FARR

TAJIN

See FOOD: TAJIN

TAKFIR WA AL-HIJRA, AL-

Egyptian Islamic fundamentalist organization.

Al-Takfir wa al-Hijra is one of the most notorious radical Egyptian fundamentalist organizations. Its real name is the Society of Muslims (Jamaʿat al-Muslimin). The group was formed in 1969 by Shukri Mustafa, who had been arrested in 1965 and served prison time with the influential Sayyid Qutb (an Egyptian who came to be considered the most radical fundamentalist thinker in the Arab world). Mustafa argued that the Egyptian society is living in a corrupt, decadent, and non-Islamic state of paganism (*jahiliyya*). His solution for the group was to withdraw itself from society and forge a new, purely Islamic society, in the unpopulated hinterland off the Nile River Valley. Though the group did spend some time living in caves, for most of its existence members lived in shared apartments in the poor neighborhood of Cairo. When the government arrested and detained several members in 1977, the organization responded by kidnapping, and ultimately murdering, a former minister for religious endowments. After a large-scale shootout with the police, several hundred members of the group were arrested and tried. Shukri Mustafa and four other leaders were sentenced to death, and others received prison sentences ranging from five to twenty-five years. Today, the group is considered to be part of the Arab Afghans and is led by Ahmad al-Jaza'iri.

At the ideological level, Mustafa delineates two stages for the organization: First, the stage of weakness (istidd'af), during which the group builds itself; and second, the stage of action (tamkin), during which the group attacks the jahili society. Hence the group's popular names al-takfir (excommunication) and al-hijra (migration). Furthermore, the group rejects mainstream doctrines accepted by traditional scholars and moderate fundamentalists. Thus, it does not believe in the validity of consensus (ijma) or independent reasoning (ijtihad)—it only believes in the literal validity of the Qur'an and the Sunna of the Prophet, which are the basis of constructing divine governance (hakimiyya) and destroying worldly paganism. The group adheres to a militant view of jihad (holy war) and makes the whole world its enemy; thus, the United States, the United Nations, and Israel as well as the Islamic states are viewed as illegitimate systems of government that should be toppled.

Bibliography

Kepel, Gilles. *Muslim Extremism in Egypt: The Prophet and Pharaoh.* Berkeley: University of California Press, 1985.

Moussalli, Ahmad. *Historical Dictionary of Islamic Fundamentalist Movements in the Arab World, Iran, and Turkey.* Lanham, MD: Scarecrow Press, 1999.

DAVID WALDNER
UPDATED BY AHMAD S. MOUSSALLI

TAKVIM-I VEKAYI

See NEWSPAPERS AND PRINT MEDIA: TURKEY

TALABANI, JALAL
[1934–]

Kurdish leader.

Leader of one of the two main Iraqi Kurdish political parties, Jalal Talabani was born in 1934 near Koi Sanjaq, in Iraqi Kurdistan. The son of a Qadiri (Sufi) *murshid* (teacher) belonging to a very famous Kurdish family, Talabani studied law in Baghdad. In 1962 he joined General Mustafa Barzani in the armed struggle of the Kurds against the Arabs. The bright leftist intellectual Talabani could not get along with the more traditional, conservative Barzani, and from 1966 until 1970 Talabani led a group of government mercenaries (*jash*) fighting against the Kurdistan Democratic Party (KDP). After the 11 March 1970 autonomy agreement between General Barzani and Iraq's then vice president Saddam Hussein, Talabani lived in exile in Beirut and Damascus. After the collapse of Barzani's movement (caused by the Algiers Agreement in March 1975), Talabani founded in 1977 the Patriotic Union of Kurdistan (PUK). Since then he has competed with Mas'ud al-Barzani (the general's son) for the leadership of the Iraqi Kurdish movement. After the Gulf War (1990–1991) and the formation of the Kurdish Autonomous Zone, Talabani shared power with Mas'ud al-Barzani from the elections of May 1992 until May 1994, when fighting resumed between the two leaders. In 1996 Talabani established his own Kurdish Regional Government in Sulaymaniyya. Since the Washington Agreement of September 1998, Talabani has coexisted with Barzani, and on 8 September 2002 he signed the agreement of Sari Rash, which paved the way for the first full session of the Kurdish Parliament on 4 October 2002 and the normalization of the relations between the KDP and PUK. In 2003, after the fall of Saddam Hussein, Talabani was appointed a member of the Iraqi Governing Council.

See also BARZANI FAMILY; KURDISH AUTONOMOUS ZONE; PATRIOTIC UNION OF KURDISTAN (PUK).

Bibliography

McDowall, David. *A Modern History of Kurds.* London: I. B. Tauris, 1996.

Randal, Jonathan C. *After Such Knowledge, What Forgiveness?: My Encounters with Kurdistan.* New York: Farrar, Straus, and Giroux, 1997.

CHRIS KUTSCHERA

TALAL IBN ABDULLAH
[1909–1972]

King of Jordan who, during his brief reign, encouraged democracy.

Talal ibn Abdullah assumed the duties of king at a critical period of transition in Jordan's history. When King Abdullah I ibn Hussein was assassinated

Talal ibn Abdullah, crown prince of Jordan, stands to the left of his father King Abdullah bin Al-Hussein in the Palace Gardens of Amman, Jordan, 1948. Talal became king on 5 September 1951 after the assassination of his father, but due to his poor mental health he was forced to abdicate in favor of his son on 11 August 1952. © BETTMANN/CORBIS. REPRODUCED BY PERMISSION.

on 20 July 1951, a group of Jordanian royalists determined that King Abdullah's chosen successor, his grandson Prince Hussein ibn Talal, was too young to govern. The only way to ensure the legitimacy of transition to Hussein was for Crown Prince Talal, who suffered from acute depression and paranoia, to be crowned king. The alternatives were either to crown Prince Na'if, the regent and Talal's half-brother, or to accede to some form of union with Iraq, in which case a member of the Iraqi branch of the Hashimite dynasty would succeed to the Jordanian throne. Hence, Talal was considered an interim figure, yet he became significantly more during his tenure.

On 5 September 1951, the cabinet proclaimed Talal king, and the newly elected parliament confirmed Talal on the throne on receipt of a medical report by Minister of Health Jamil Tutunji. Prince Na'if, the regent, flew to Switzerland to escort his brother home.

The most notable legacy of King Talal's brief reign was to transform Jordan into a true democracy. Under Talal's instructions, the veteran prime minister, Tawfiq Abu al-Huda, won a vote of confidence in parliament on 24 September 1951. A new constitution was promulgated, declaring the people the source of all power. Citizens were guaranteed individual liberty and equality before the law. The constitution was approved by the lower and upper houses and was signed by King Talal on 1 January 1952. It enshrined the freedom of opinion, the right to hold public meetings and form political parties and trade unions, the freedom of conscience and worship, compulsory free education, as well as the right to own property. The new constitution made the cabinet collectively and individually responsible to parliament. Ministers could be impeached. The king could dissolve parliament, but new elections had to be held within four months, otherwise the old parliament would be reinstated. According to Article 93, parliament could override the king's veto over legislation by a two-thirds majority. Parliament was empowered to ratify treaties and could assemble without being called to do so by the king, but the king could declare martial law by decree with the consent of the cabinet.

The king's foreign minister declared in September 1951 that Jordan was not seeking union with Iraq. In December 1951, the king visited Saudi Arabia and made clear his desire for good relations with the house of Sa'ud. He was skeptical of Western alliances, and in January 1952, he led Jordan into acceptance of the Arab Collective Security Pact.

Despite his popularity, after eight months the king's psychological troubles returned. While vacationing in Europe in May 1952, the cabinet transformed the Regency Council into a Crown Council, which exercised the powers of head of state for the rest of Talal's reign. On 11 August 1952, parliament deposed him and proclaimed Prince Hussein king. King Talal accepted gracefully. The duties of king were assumed by a Regency Council until Hussein came of age.

The deposed king moved to Egypt then took up residence in Turkey, where he died twenty years later. Talal was the first king of Jordan to graduate from the Royal Military College at Sandhurst, an English school, and while there had absorbed democratic ideals. Sir John Bagot Glubb recalls in his memoir, *A Soldier with the Arabs*: "The tragedy of King Talal seemed to be rendered more poignant by the fact that, apart from his insanity, he appeared so ideally fit to be king. . . . He was of acute intelligence, outstanding personal charm, faultless private morals, and inspired by a deeply conscious wish to serve his country and his people, with no selfish motives."

> *See also* ABDULLAH I IBN HUSSEIN; ABU AL-HUDA, TAWFIQ; GLUBB, JOHN BAGOT; HUSSEIN IBN TALAL.

Bibliography

Abidi, Aqil Hyder Hasan. *Jordan: A Political Study, 1948–1957.* New York: Asia, 1965.

Glubb, John Bagot. *A Soldier with the Arabs.* New York: Hodder and Staughton, 1957.

JENAB TUTUNJI

TALAT, MEHMET
[1874–1921]

Turkish statesman.

Born in Edirne, Mehmet Talat Bey became chief administrator of the telegraph and postal office in Salonika in the Ottoman Empire. There, he became part of the secret Committee for Union and Progress. After the Young Turk revolution, he went to Istanbul in December 1908 to assume a leading position in the Young Turk government, rising to minister of interior. After 1913 and until the Ottoman defeat in World War I, Talat Paşa, Enver Paşa, and Cemal Paşa comprised the unofficial triumvirate that controlled the Ottoman Empire. While Enver was a military leader and Cemal was famous for his ruthlessness, Talat was a sophisticated diplomat and a consummate politician. In February 1917, Talat became grand vizier and held that position until 8 October 1918, just before the armistice of Mudros, which signaled the Ottoman surrender to the Allies. On 2 November, three days after the armistice was signed, Talat left Istanbul on a German ship and was murdered in Berlin in 1921.

Bibliography

Lewis, Bernard. *The Emergence of Modern Turkey,* 3d edition. New York: Oxford University Press, 2002.

Ramsaur, E. E. *The Young Turks: Prelude to the Revolution of 1908.* Princeton, NJ: Princeton University Press, 1957.

Shaw, Stanford J., and Shaw, Ezel Kural. *History of the Ottoman Empire and Modern Turkey.* 2 vols. Cambridge, U.K., and New York: Cambridge University Press, 1976–1977.

ZACHARY KARABELL

TALEQANI, AZAM
[1943–]

Iranian advocate for women's rights, social justice, and democracy.

Azam Taleqani, daughter of the radical cleric Ayatollah Mahmud Taleqani, was born in 1943 in Tehran. She obtained her B.A. degree in Persian literature and was a schoolteacher and principal. She was politically active before Iran's Islamic Revolution and a political prisoner under the shah. After the revolution she was elected to the first parliament (1980–1984). Her quest for social justice led her to focus on the plight of women. In 1979 she founded the Iranian Islamic Women's Institute and started publishing a magazine, *Payam-i Hajar,* which has been closed down temporarily several times. Along with the members of her institute, she assists urban poor and rural women, providing them with legal advice, organizing conferences on women's problems, and creating jobs for women carpet weavers, tailors, and the like. *Payam-i Hajar* was the first journal to publish an article (in 1992) that refuted the legal basis of polygyny and men's superiority and proposed a new interpretation of the Qur'anic verse *al-Nisa* (Women) founded on Iranian social, demographic, and cultural realities. Taleqani registered to run as a candidate in the 1997 presidential elections in order to challenge the traditional views on women. She and seven other women candidates were disqualified by the Council of Guardians, which provided no reason for their disqualification. She also was disqualified in the 1999 municipal elections. She criticizes personal enrichment on the part of the power elite and the widening gap between the rich and the poor, and continues to advocate social justice and democracy.

AZADEH KIAN-THIÉBAUT

TALFA, ADNAN KHAYR ALLAH
[1940–1989]

Iraqi government official; relative of Saddam Hussein.

Adnan Khayr Allah Talfa was Saddam Hussein's brother-in-law and a maternal cousin; Saddam is married to Talfa's sister Sajida. Talfah was born in Tikrit and combined military and political careers in Iraq. In 1977, when still a colonel, through Saddam Hussein's pressure he became a member of the Regional Leadership of the Baʿth party and of the Revolutionary Command Council, as well as minister of defense. During the Iran–Iraq War (1980–1988), he played a major role in mediating between the civilian leadership and the military. In 1988 his relations with Saddam Hussein became strained through a family dispute. In May 1989 he was killed in a helicopter crash amid rumors of foul play on the part of Saddam.

See also HUSSEIN, SADDAM.

Bibliography

Baram, Amatzia. "The Ruling Political Elite in Baʿthi Iraq, 1968–1986." *International Journal of Middle East Studies* 21 (1989): 447–493.

AMATZIA BARAM

TALIʿA, AL-

See NEWSPAPERS AND PRINT MEDIA: ARAB COUNTRIES

TALIBAN

Islamic fundamentalist group in Afghanistan.

The Taliban appeared in Afghanistan in late 1994. In September 1996 they took Kabul and hanged Najibullah, Afghanistan's Soviet-sponsored president. Subsequently, they banned female access to education and employment, and imposed draconian Islamic laws that called for severe punishments, including the stoning to death of proven adulterers and the amputating of thieves' hands and feet. The Taliban's Islamic fundamentalism was a kind of transnational street force that had the potential to topple established governments through agitation, or to terrorize even much larger nations. Increasingly, fear of Islamic fundamentalism replaced the old dread of communism in the United States.

The term *taliban* is derived from the Persian and Pashtun plural of the Arabic word *talib* ("seeker of knowledge"). Before 1947, Afghan religious students studied in India, and when it was partitioned, they went to Pakistan. Their favorite *madrasa* in India was the Dar al-Ulum (House of Sciences) of the University of Deoband in Uttar Pradesh, which was established in 1862. It was known for its anti-Western orientation and stood for the independence of a united India. The Deoband Dar al-Ulum trained young, working- and lower-middle-class Muslims, who received a traditional religious education and joined the ranks of "big" and "small" mullahs in *masajid* (mosques).

Intellectually, the Taliban are heirs to the traditional affinity between the Deoband Dar al-Ulum and the Afghan *ulama* (Islamic scholars). After 1947, *ulama* in Pakistan established Houses of Science (Diyar al-Ulum) in all the provinces of Pakistan. The number of graduates of different levels of education from these institutions, especially from 1982 to 1987, was impressive. The Taliban leaders were the product of these theological seminaries. Their education is frozen in time: All Sunni theological institutions' curricula are based upon the curriculum established by the eighteenth-century scholar Mullah Nizam-ud-Din, who flourished during the period of Aurangzeb (d. 1707). This curriculum comprises:

1. Arabic grammar;
2. syntax;
3. rhetoric;
4. philosophy of logic;
5. dialectical theology *(ilm al-kalam)*;
6. Qurʾanic exegesis *(tafsir)*;
7. Islamic jurisprudence *(fiqh)*;
8. roots of Islamic jurisprudence *(usul al-fiqh)*;
9. accounts of sayings and deeds by the Prophet and immediate followers *(hadith)*; and
10. some mathematics.

The Taliban's educational system emphasized *taqlid,* the following of traditional Islam, which neglected modern scientific training. They divided the world into *Dar al-Islam* (the Muslim states, especially Saudi Arabia, the United Arab Emirates, and Pakistan, which had recognized their rule) and *Dar al-Harb* (the non-Muslim states, which were projected as the enemies of Islam and Muslims). This bifurcation of the world into external enemies and permanent friends generated an exceptionally intolerant mind-set, which distinguished the Taliban's educational system.

The Taliban's political structure was based, according to them, on that of the four "rightly guided" caliphs (632–662) who succeeded the prophet Muhammad. The Taliban were "committed to establishing an exemplary Islamic rule" for the world, and especially for the Muslim states. Emulating the early caliphate, the Taliban created a supreme council (Majles al-Shura) of twenty individuals. Almost 1,500 Sunni *ulama* who represented various ethnic tribes elected young Mullah Muhammad Omar *amir al-mu'minin* ("commander of the faithful"). The majority of the council members were Pashtuns; fourteen of them had suffered corporeal loss while fighting against the Soviet Union (Mullah Omar, for example, lost an eye). Because of the Pashtun ethnic origin of the Taliban, their jihad became a struggle for power against the Tajiks in the Panjsher Valley and the Uzbeks in the north.

During the 1980s, Osama bin Ladin established guerrilla warfare bases in Afghanistan against the Soviet Union. After the Soviet withdrawal from Afghanistan in 1989, bin Ladin turned his attention to the United States. On 11 September 2001 his terrorists attacked the World Trade Center in New York City and the Pentagon outside Washington, D.C. In retaliation, the United States invaded Afghanistan, eliminated the Taliban's rule, and destroyed bin Ladin's terror infrastructure.

See also AFGHANISTAN; BIN LADIN, OSAMA; DAR AL-ULUM; NAJIBULLAH; OMAR, MUHAMMAD (MULLAH); SUNNI ISLAM.

Bibliography

Kamal, Matinuddin. *The Taliban Phenomenon: Afghanistan, 1994–1997.* Oxford, U.K.: Oxford University Press, 1999.

Marsden, Peter. *The Taliban: War, Religion, and the New Order in Afghanistan.* London: Zed Books, 1998.

Rashid, Ahmed. *Taliban: Militant Islam, Oil, and Fundamentalism in Central Asia.* New Haven, CT: Yale University Press, 2000.

HAFEEZ MALIK

TALLAL, CHAIBIA
[1929–]

Moroccan painter.

Chaibia Tallal is a self-taught painter who was "discovered" and encouraged by Pierre Gaudibert, director of the Museum of Modern Art in Grenoble, France. She gained recognition in Europe and in the Arab world for her bright paintings, done in what has been called a naive style. Chaibia (who is known by her first name) was born in the village of Chtouka and came to the suburbs of Casablanca as a girl but counts her experience in the village as formative. Her memories of being unusual in her community, of making things with flowers and covering herself with them, and of a dream that motivated her to paint help explain how a woman who was not born into the urban life of art and intellectuals came to be an internationally celebrated artist. Chaibia is primarily a colorist who has been described as capturing the vibrancy of Moroccan life and landscape. Like Matisse's Moroccan work, her paintings feature human figures and flora and fauna rendered in expressive, often broad, brushstrokes and fields of rich color. Chaibia has exhibited throughout Europe, mainly in Paris, and also participated in the Havana Biennial. In 1984 one of her paintings served as the poster for the Contemporary Women's International Art Exhibition in France.

See also ART; GENDER: GENDER AND EDUCATION; MOROCCO.

Bibliography

Tallal, Chaibia. "My Life." In *Opening the Gates: A Century of Arab Feminist Writing,* edited by Margot Badran and Miriam Cook. Bloomington: Indiana University Press, 1990.

JESSICA WINEGAR

TALL AL-ZA'TAR REFUGEE CAMP

Refugee camp in East Beirut, Lebanon.

Built in 1950 by UNRWA (United National Relief and Works Agency for Palestinian Refugees in the Near East), Tall al-Za'tar's Palestinian and South Lebanese population exceeded thirty thousand refugees by the early 1970s. In perhaps the bloodiest battle of the Lebanese Civil War that started in

1975, members of the Christian Phalange laid siege to the camp 22 June 1976. Thousands of residents are believed to have been killed during the siege and the mass killings that followed the Phalangist victory 12 August. The remaining population of the camp was transferred to West Beirut. The Phalangists' intent is believed to have been the expulsion of all non-Christians, and particularly the Palestine Liberation Organization (PLO), from East Beirut. The Christian militias had largely avoided direct confrontations with the PLO until the Syrian army entered the war in Lebanon on the Christian side 31 May 1976. The PLO defended the camp for fifty-two days before it fell with the help of Syrian artillery.

See also PHALANGE.

Bibliography

Petran, Tabitha. *The Struggle over Lebanon.* New York: Monthly Review Press, 1987.

Smith, Pamela Ann. *Palestine and the Palestinians, 1876–1983.* New York: St. Martin's, 1984.

ELIZABETH THOMPSON

TALL, MUSTAFA WAHBI AL-
[1899–1949]

Jordan's most famous poet.

Mustafa Wahbi al-Tall's use of colloquial expressions in his poetry plus mentions of geographical places helped establish a unique Jordanian literary tradition in the Arabic language. Despite numerous positions in the government of Jordan, his populist politics and anti-establishment behavior landed him in prison or exile on several occasions. He is also the father of the Jordanian politician Wasfi al-Tall.

See also TALL, WASFI AL-.

Bibliography

Tall, Mustafa Wahbi. *Mustafa's Journey: A Verse of Arar, Poet of Jordan.* Irbid, Jordan: Yarmouk University Publications, 1988.

MICHAEL R. FISCHBACH

TALL, WASFI AL-
[1920–1971]

Prime minister of Jordan (1962–1963, 1965–1967, 1970–1971).

Wasfi al-Tall was born in Irbid, in northern Jordan. After being educated at the American University of Beirut, he served as an officer in Britain's army (1942–1945), then joined Jordan's civil service, rising to the rank of ambassador to Iraq (1961–1962). Tall was expelled from Baghdad for alleged subversive activities against the regime of Abd al-Karim Qasim; he was also channeling funds to the anti-Nasser Syrian Social Nationalist party in Lebanon.

Tall formed his first cabinet in January 1962 and embarked on an efficiency campaign in the civil service and attempted to promote economic development. He also launched a policy designed to show that Jordan was the true repository of Palestinian aspirations; it was a failure.

A Jordan–Saudi Arabia summit in August 1962 resulted in an agreement to coordinate foreign policy. When a coup took place in Yemen in October 1962, resulting in the proclamation of the Yemen Arab Republic, Jordan and Saudi Arabia backed the insurgents under Imam al-Badr. In November 1962, Tall supervised parliamentary elections in which political parties were banned. Ba'athist coups in Baghdad in February 1963 and in Damascus in March 1963 led Iraq and Syria to launch unity talks with Egypt. A shift in policy was required, so Tall resigned at the end of March.

In February 1965, Tall began his second term as prime minister. He helped King Hussein ibn Talal reactivate the entente with Saudi Arabia, and on 9 August 1965, a treaty was signed delimiting borders between the two countries. Jordan joined an alliance of Islamic states organized by Saudi Arabia and directed against Egypt, Syria, and Iraq.

Al-Fatah raids into Israel began. Under pressure from the Arab League, Jordan agreed to set up "summer camps for military training and moral guidance" for Palestinian recruits. In June 1966, King Hussein said there could be no cooperation with the Palestine Liberation Organization (PLO), and Tall prevented elections for the PLO National Council.

Tall closed the PLO office in Amman and expelled Ahmad Shuqayri, head of the PLO. In retaliation for an operation by al-Fatah guerrillas supported by Syria, Israel launched a raid against

Jordan, demolishing the village of Sammu on 13 November 1966. Residents of the West Bank and refugee camps hated Tall because of his disbanding of the National Guard, which had been stationed in frontier villages. Under the press law of 1 February 1967, instigated by Tall, all existing papers and periodicals were closed down, and newly licensed publications had to have 25 percent government ownership. Tall resigned in March 1967 and was appointed chief of the royal court, in which position he tried unsuccessfully to keep Jordan out of the Arab–Israel War of 1967.

Tall began his third term as prime minister on 26 September 1970. The following day, King Hussein and PLO chairman Yasir Arafat signed an agreement in Cairo that called for the withdrawal of Palestinian guerrillas from the cities but allowed them to continue the battle against Israel from the countryside. Tall and the military, however, devised a plan to drive the guerrillas out of Amman, Irbid, Jarash, and Ajlun. It was all over by 18 June 1971. In revenge, during a visit to Cairo in September 1971, Tall was assassinated by the Black September Group.

See also ARAB–ISRAEL WAR (1967); ARAFAT, YASIR; BLACK SEPTEMBER; FATAH, AL-; HUSSEIN IBN TALAL; JORDANIAN CIVIL WAR (1970–1971); LEAGUE OF ARAB STATES; PALESTINE LIBERATION ORGANIZATION (PLO); QASIM, ABD AL-KARIM; SHUQAYRI, AHMAD.

Bibliography

Amos, John W., II. *Palestinian Resistance: Organization of a Nationalist Movement.* New York: Pergamon, 1980.

Dann, Uriel. *King Hussein and the Challenge of Arab Radicalism: Jordan, 1955–1967.* New York: Oxford University Press in cooperation with the Moshe Dayan Center for Middle Eastern and African Studies, Tel Aviv University, 1989.

Iyad, Abu, with Rouleau, Eric. *My Home, My Land: A Narrative of the Palestinian Struggle,* translated by Linda Butler Koseoglu. New York: Times Books, 1978.

Lunt, James. *Hussein of Jordan: Searching for a Just and Lasting Peace.* New York: W. Morrow, 1989.

Susser, Asher. *On Both Banks of the Jordan: A Political Biography of Wasfi al-Tall.* Newberry Park, U.K., and Portland, OR: F. Cass, 1994.

JENAB TUTUNJI

TALMUD

The Jewish teachings of the sages.

The Pentateuch (*Torah*), Prophets (*Nevi'im*), and Hagiographa (*Ketuvim*) constitute the written law of Judaism. Over the years, that law was discussed, interpreted, and transferred. These teachings of the sages are known as the oral law. Eventually, the oral law (*torah she-b'al peh*) was written down and formed the basis of the Talmud. While *torah* refers only to the written law and *talmud* to the oral law, both terms essentially carry the same meaning: teaching or study. Since it is incumbent upon the children of Israel to follow the path of their ancestors, it is necessary for the Jewish people to continually teach and study the law until they understand and follow it completely.

Scholars differ as to when the Talmud began to be written down and whether it was based on notes or recorded upon its completion. It is generally accepted that Rabbi Yehuda ha-Nasi (170–219 C.E.) compiled and edited the first section of the Talmud, the Mishnayot (pl. of *mishna,* or teaching, to distinguish it from Torah) from a multitude of manuscripts, perhaps in different dialects and languages.

The Mishnayot are organized into six sections, or *sedarim,* each dealing with a particular subject. The sections are then subdivided into tracts (or *mesekhtot,* singular *mesekhta*) that deal with matters relating to those sections. The sections are: Seeds (or *Zera'im,* which includes laws relating to vegetables; offerings; tithes; and *shmitta,* the sabbatical year); Festivals (or *Mo'ed,* holidays; the Sabbath; and more general laws affected by the festivals); Women (or *Nashim,* including marriage and divorce); Damages (or *Nezikin,* laws of property; penalties; and morals); Sacred Things (or *Kodashim,* sacrifices; laws of the first born; and slaughtering); Purifications (or *Tohorot,* defilement and purification in general; and defilement of vessels, tents, and menstruating women).

The Mishnayot were imparted with a degree of sanctity that dictated that nothing could be added to or subtracted from them. Upon their completion, religious colleges were established in Palestine and Babylonia to explain their meaning and to extrapolate the laws that emanated from them. This task was complicated by contradictory Mishnayot and by the discovery of new texts that had not been incorporated in the Mishnayot. The body of knowledge that developed from the discussions and the explanations of the Mishna came to be called *Gemara* (Aramaic for *teaching*). The tractates of the Gemara are arranged like the sections of the Mishnayot. The Mishna opens the tractate and is followed by the Gemara. The Mishna and the Gemara together constitute the Talmud.

At the time of Rabbi Yehuda ha-Nasi's death, the Roman-dominated Middle East was characterized by political strife, which led many Jews to leave Galilee for Persian-ruled Babylon. The development of the Talmud continued there. The Palestinian Talmud, also known as the Jerusalem Talmud *(Talmud Yerushalmi),* was finalized in about 400 C.E. (although it might have been much later). The Babylonian Talmud *(Talmud Bavli,* which might have developed without its formulators knowing about the Jerusalem Talmud) was finalized in about 500 C.E. Although the Jerusalem Talmud includes more tracts (thirty-nine to the Babylonian's thirty-seven), it is considerably smaller (about one-fourth the size) and less elaborate, especially in the field of religious law *(Halakhah).* It is stronger in *Aggadah,* a collection of legends and stories, proverbs, parables, and mystic and veiled religious wisdom. The Babylonian Talmud, with its emphasis on religious law, became the dominant focus of study. This was partially determined by the political situation, which allowed the Jews in exile to study the Talmud to a greater degree than Jews could in Palestine. It is the Babylonian Talmud that continues to dominate today.

Talmudic rulings have served as the basis for religious law in Judaism throughout the generations. A vast rabbinic literature now exists based on discussions and analyses stemming from Talmudic discourse. Whereas elementary school education includes the study of the Pentateuch and Prophets, advanced religious education in higher *yeshivot* (Torah seminaries) concentrates on the study of the Talmud. Religious traditionalists reject the scientific approach to the study of the Talmud, which has developed in the university. Many similarly reject the desire of a small but increasing number of Orthodox women who wish to take part in intensive religious study, believing that only men are allowed to learn this sacred text.

Bibliography

Gilbert, Martin, ed. *The Illustrated Atlas of Jewish Civilization: 4,000 Years of Jewish History.* New York: Macmillan, 1990.

BENJAMIN JOSEPH
UPDATED BY EPHRAIM TABORY

TAMI

See ISRAEL: POLITICAL PARTIES IN

TAMIMAHS

Paramount shaykhs of larger Omani tribal groupings.

Tamimahs are selected from an elite family within the tribe, and their main functions are to resolve disputes and provide a focus of leadership among lineages within the tribe. The title implies complete or total authority to the extent that the bearer has the power to impose the death penalty on a tribesman, although this is rarely the case at the tribal level in Oman.

CALVIN H. ALLEN, JR.

TAMIMI, AMIN AL-
[1892–1944]

Palestinian politician.

Born to a Muslim family in Nablus, Palestine, Amin al-Tamimi studied in Istanbul, where he encountered Arab literary and political circles before World War I. After the war, he served as an adviser to the regime of the Syrian king, Faisal I ibn Hussein, in Damascus and joined delegations to Istanbul and to Lausanne in 1922 to seek Turkish support for Arab independence. He was a leader of the Nablus Muslim–Christian Association, and a member of the Supreme Muslim Council of the *mufti* (interpreter of the law of Islam) in Jerusalem from 1926 to 1938.

Tamimi went to Iraq in 1939 and participated in the 1941 Rashid Ali al-Kaylani revolt of pan-Arabism against Britain. The British then interned him in Rhodesia, where he died. He was proclaimed a martyr in the streets of Jerusalem. His son Adnan, an Iraqi citizen, was a United Nations official until 1983.

See also FAISAL I IBN HUSSEIN; KAYLANI, RASHID ALI AL-; PAN-ARABISM.

Bibliography

Hurewitz, J. C. *The Struggle for Palestine.* New York: Norton, 1950.

Porath, Yehoshua. *The Emergence of the Palestinian-Arab National Movement, 1918–1929.* London: Frank Cass, 1974.

Porath, Yehoshua. *Palestinian-Arab National Movement, 1929–1939: From Riots to Rebellion.* London and Totowa, NJ: Frank Cass, 1977.

ELIZABETH THOMPSON

TAMIR, SHMUEL
[1923–]

Israeli politician and attorney.

Shmuel Tamir was born in Jerusalem as Shmuel Katsnelson. He was influenced by the 1929 Hebron massacre, during which sixty Orthodox Jews were murdered by Arab rioters. The rioters were themselves reacting to a demonstration by Jews who demanded access to the Western Wall in Jerusalem, At age fifteen he joined Irgun Zva'i Le'umi. He was arrested in 1947 and deported to Kenya, where he was allowed to take his final law examinations. Returning to Israel after it became a state, he changed his name to Shmuel Tamir (his underground name) and was active in the Herut movement, where he was viewed as a natural heir to Menachem Begin.

He established a reputation as an outstanding attorney and was involved in some well-known cases, including the Kasztner trial in 1954, in which Reszo Kasztner brought suit against Malkiel Grunwald, who had accused Kasztner of being a traitor and causing the deaths of many Jews by negotiating with the Nazis. As Grunwald's attorney, Tamir framed the trial as being about Kasztner rather than Grunwald. The judge, Benjamin Halevi, accepted most of Tamir's arguments and accused Kasztner of having "sold his soul to the devil." Before the verdict was handed down, Kasztner was murdered by nationalist extremists who took Halevi's words literally. In the end, the court exonerated Kasztner on all charges except that he had helped Nazis escape from justice.

Tamir was a member of sixth through ninth Knessets, representing several different parties, including Gahal, the Free Center, Likud, and the Democratic Movement for Change. In 1977, when Tamir joined the Democratic Movement for Change, he was appointed minister of justice under Begin. In 1981, he left politics and returned to his legal practice.

See also BEGIN, MENACHEM; IRGUN, ZVA'I LE'UMI (IZL); ISRAEL: POLITICAL PARTIES IN; LIKUD.

Bibliography

Bell, J. Bowyer. *Terror out of Zion: Irgun Zvai Leumi, LEHI, and the Palestine Underground, 1929–1949.* New York: St. Martin's, 1977.

"Kasztner, Reszo." Museum of Tolerance. Available from <http://motlc.wiesenthal.com/text/x12/xm1230.html>.

Segev, Tom. *The Seventh Million: The Israelis and the Holocaust,* translated by Haim Watzman. New York: Hill and Wang, 1993.

JULIE ZUCKERMAN
UPDATED BY GREGORY MAHLER

TAMMUZ, BENYAMIN
[1919–1989]

Israeli novelist and journalist.

Benyamin Tammuz was born in Kharkov, in the Ukraine, and emigrated to Palestine in 1924. Throughout his life he worked for various newspapers, including *Haaretz.* Tammuz was a founding member of the Canaanite movement, which advocated the creation of a Hebrew, rather than a Jewish, state in Israel. This association undoubtedly influenced his earlier works, which were republished as *Angioxyl, Terufah Nedirah* (1973; A rare cure, 1981). He left the movement following a stay in Europe, which brought him into close contact with European Jews. Tammuz served as cultural attaché at the Israeli embassy in London in 1971.

In his works, Tammuz criticizes Israeli society's loss of soul and its lack of normalcy. *Requiem Le-Na'aman* (1978; Requiem for Na'aman, 1982) is considered his most forceful work. He deals with the seemingly intractable Arab-Israel conflict in his metaphorical *Ha-Pardes* (1971; The orchard, 1984) and in *Taharut Sehiya* (1952; Swimming race, 1953). In his *Mishlei Baqbuqim* (1975, Proverbs of bottles), Tammuz addresses Israel's lack of spirituality, while in *Pundaqo Shel Yirmiyahu* (1984, Jeremiah's inn), he satirizes the involvement of the ultra-orthodox in Israeli politics.

ANN KAHN

TAN

See NEWSPAPERS AND PRINT MEDIA: TURKEY

TANBURI CEMIL
[1871–1916]

Ottoman Turkish musician and composer.

Tanburi Cemil was born in Istanbul into a family of musicians. He enrolled in the Mulukhiyya but left before finishing his studies and began to study music. By his death at the age of forty-five, he was considered the foremost Turkish virtuoso. Although he was most well known for playing the *tanbur* (guitar), an instrument he had mastered as a child, Tanburi Cemil was equally proficient on the *kemençe* (a small three-stringed violin) and the *lavta* (lute). Tanburi Cemil's compositions, characterized by a refined sensitivity, are considered among the masterpieces of Turkish music. Among his best-known works are *Ferahfeza Saz Semaisi, Mahur Peşrevi, Muhayyer Saz Semaisi,* and *Hicazkar Saz Semaisi.*

DAVID WALDNER

TANER, HALDUN
[1916–1986]

Turkish writer.

The son of a university professor, Haldun Taner was born in Istanbul, where he attended Galatasaray Lycée. He studied political science at Heidelberg University in 1938 and later studied literature in Istanbul. He then taught literature and art history for a number of years at the Journalism Institute and at the Ankara Language, History, and Geography School. Taner became popular in the 1950s for his short stories about the urban middle class, which have been translated from Turkish into more than a dozen languages. He worked as a journalist and in 1960 became editor-in-chief of the Istanbul daily *Tercüman.*

Taner also made his mark in the theater world, joining a young generation of playwrights in the 1950s who addressed the tensions between traditional values and the demands of modern life. He drew on the epic traditions of Turkey for his play *The Ballad of Ali from Keshan,* which was also made into a film. He won a prize with Orhan Kemal in 1957 for their screenplay *Ferhat, the Mountain Lover.* Taner also founded a private theater, the Devekusu Kabare Tiyatrosu.

Bibliography

Renda, Günsel, and Kortepeter, C. Max, eds. *The Transformation of Turkish Culture.* Princeton, NJ: Kingston Press, 1986.

ELIZABETH THOMPSON

TANGIER, TREATY OF

Franco-Moroccan agreement of 10 September 1844.

The Treaty of Tangier followed the defeat of the Moroccan army at the Battle of Isly by a French force pursuing the Algerian resistance leader Abd al-Qadir, who had frequently sought refuge in Moroccan territory. The treaty obligated the Moroccan government to consider Abd al-Qadir an outlaw and to offer him no assistance.

See also ABD AL-QADIR.

KENNETH J. PERKINS

TANIN

See NEWSPAPERS AND PRINT MEDIA: TURKEY

TANPINAR, AHMED HAMDI
[1901–1962]

Turkish professor and author.

The son of a *qadi* (judge), Ahmed Hamdi Tanpinar was born in Istanbul and moved with his father to various cities of the Ottoman Empire. He graduated from the Antalya secondary school and studied at the Faculty of Literature, where he was a student of Yahya Kemal. After graduating in 1923, he taught at secondary schools, including the Fine Arts Academy, until 1939, when he was appointed professor of modern Turkish Literature at Istanbul University.

He wrote a major volume on post-Tanzimat-era Turkish literature, a monograph on Tevfik Fikret, and a series of critical essays.

Tanpinar also wrote poetry, novels, and short stories. In his novels, he studied the era from the Crimean War (1854) to World War II (1939), portraying developments within Turkish society and the fate of traditional ties in a modernizing society. In 1942, Tanpinar was elected to the parliament, representing Maraş.

Bibliography

Ertop, Konur. "Trends and Characteristics of Contemporary Turkish Literature." In *The Transformation of Turkish Culture: The Atatürk Legacy,* edited by Günsel Renda and C. Max Kortepeter. Princeton, NJ: Kingston Press, 1986.

DAVID WALDNER

TANTAWI, MUHAMMAD SAYYID AL-
[1928–]

Shaykh of al-Azhar.

Born in Suhaj in Upper Egypt, Muhammad Sayyid al-Tantawi earned a Ph.D. in Qur'anic Exegesis and *Hadith* (sayings of the Prophet) from al-Azhar University in 1966. In 1976 he became a professor; ten years later he became dean of the Islamic and Arabic Studies faculty and was appointed the grand mufti, Egypt's highest religious juristic authority. In 1996 he was appointed shaykh of al-Azhar, making him the forty-third shaykh of al-Azhar. Muslims seek his advice on new controversial matters.

As a mufti, Tantawi issued opinions representing the views of the government. His *fatawa* (legal opinions) have mostly been at odds with those of al-Azhar. But once he became shaykh of al-Azhar, he began oscillating between the opinions he issued as mufti and pronouncements more faithful to al-Azhar. He is under constant pressure from religious scholars to follow al-Azhar's conservative line of thinking. Many civil and human-rights organizations welcomed the appointment of this liberal shaykh to the top religious post in Egypt, but his *fatwa* prohibiting the boycott of U.S. goods brought about major protests by Christians as well as Muslims. The powerful and conservative Front for the

Scholars of al-Azhar, founded in 1946, had been critical of Tantawi since he became mufti, challenging him on his giving permission to deal with banks based on interest, his prohibition of suicide attacks committed by HAMAS in Palestine, his meeting the chief rabbi of Israel, and his reduction of secondary education to three years. He was able to get the government to dissolve the Front in 1998, and he fired many outspoken scholars from al-Azhar.

On the touchy issue of female circumcision, Tantawi, as the mufti, argued against its validity. However, as shaykh of al-Azhar he gave in to the Azharite establishment. Later, when the Ministry of Health banned the practice, Tantawi changed his view again. Also, as a mufti, Tantawi viewed the *hijab* (head cover) as a woman's choice, but as shaykh, he upheld the Azhar view that it was mandatory. But on the issue of organ transplants, he held to his original position, and promised to donate his own organs after his death. On the political level, when Tantawi became shaykh, his political views became more obvious. For instance, he asked Muslims to launch jihad (holy war) against Israel to prevent the Judaization of Jerusalem, and to defuse religious sectarian tensions in Egypt, he met with Pope Shenouda III and other Christian personalities. These changes of opinion seem to be the result of both political expediency and an attempt to serve the interests of the Egyptian government.

See also AZHAR, AL-.

AHMAD S. MOUSSALLI

TANZIMAT

Mid-nineteenth-century Ottoman reform movement.

The Tanzimat-i Hayriye (Auspicious Reorganization) was a series of governmental reforms between 1839 and 1876 that sought to centralize and rationalize Ottoman rule and capture more tax revenues for the military defense of the empire. The Tanzimat period is usually associated with particular personalities in the central government: the sultans Abdülmecit II and Abdülaziz, and the high-ranking bureaucrats Mustafa Reşid Paşa, Ali Paşa, and Fuad Paşa. The Tanzimat was preceded by earlier reform efforts since the eighteenth century, particularly by Abdülmecit I and Abdülaziz's father, Mahmud II, between 1808 and 1839. And it would be followed by reforms in the early reigns of Abdülhamit II and the Young Turks.

Order and Justice

The thirty-seven years of the Tanzimat period are significant in this long process for establishing the basic principles and the governmental apparatus of reform. The bywords of the movement were justice and order, which were seen as prerequisites to effecting substantial social and economic change. The major product of the movement was a huge increase in the power of the central state. The major edicts of the Tanzimat significantly enlarged the scope of government activity by creating new fiscal, legal, and administrative instruments. For example, the edict that inaugurated the Tanzimat, the 1839 Hatt-i Şerif of Gülhane, proposed replacing inefficient tax farms with a centralized revenue service and establishing a new imperial council, the Meclis-i Vala, to formulate and direct reform policy. Subsequent edicts sought to promote justice and confidence in government, such as those of 1840, 1850, and 1870 to 1876 that laid out uniform codes of law for commerce, civil transactions, and criminal cases. A series of provincial reforms culminating in the 1864 Vilayet Law regularized the structure of local government and strengthened lines of authority to Constantinople (now Istanbul). And in the capital itself, government was reorganized into formal departments and specialized ministries. During the Tanzimat period, the Ottoman state also began to intervene in society in new ways. The 1839 Gülhane edict and other laws expanded military conscription. And the state established new elite secular schools. The 1869 Regulation of Public Instruction introduced an empire-wide school system intended to produce bureaucrats and military officers at every level of government equipped with the skills necessary to implement policy.

Defense and International Affairs

But the Tanzimat was not solely a project of administrative reform. Its goals of order and justice were often ancillary to other, more immediate goals. The 1839 Gülhane edict was issued when the Ottomans were fighting to regain territory captured by Egypt in 1832. Greece had already won its independence in 1839, and in the Crimean War (1853–1856)

the Ottomans would again go to war with Russia. Hence, the 1839 edict would promise to continue the military buildup begun by Mahmud II to defend the empire from external threats. The military was reorganized in 1842 and 1869, producing a larger, more unified structure under the *serasker,* a combined chief of staff and war minister. And many other reforms were explicitly intended to raise more revenue for defense.

Tanzimat goals were further complicated by international affairs with the growing influence of France and England in the empire. The Ottomans sought European alliances for protection against Russian and Egyptian invasions. This alliance was bought at a price. For their own domestic reasons, and to further their interests in the empire, France and England pushed another set of often contradictory goals. While the Europeans advocated equal rights and democratic participation in the empire, they also acted to protect the privileges and separate status of non-Muslim millets. So, while the Gülhane edict and the 1856 Hatt-i Hümayun proclaimed equality of all citizens regardless of religion, and new secular courts were established to offset any prejudice in *shariʿa* (Islamic law) courts, in fact, society remained divided by religion in subcommunities with separate legal and social institutions.

Economic Concerns

Missing from the great initiatives of the Tanzimat was serious fiscal and economic reform. Roger Owen explains the neglect of economic reform thus: "Limited financial resources, the lack of competent administrators, the growing technological gap between Europe and the rest of the world, and the constraints imposed by Turkey's social structure and weakened international position all combined to set strict limits on the types of economic politics pursued" (Owen, p. 116). Restricted in their development of policy, the Ottomans were also plagued by the misfortune that they were attempting reform precisely during a period of economic boom in France and England.

The Tanzimat coincided with the first wave of industrial imperialism. France and England used their diplomatic influence in Constantinople to facilitate imperialist expansion at the expense of economic reform within the empire. For example, the

1838 Anglo-Turkish commercial convention, which preceded British support in fighting Egypt, promoted the spread of European imports in Ottoman markets. In the 1850s and 1860s, the British and French established new kinds of investment banks equipped to funnel domestic savings into overseas loans and projects. These banks played no small part in encouraging Ottoman indebtedness. The first foreign loan was taken out in 1854, for 3 million British pounds, to pay war expenses. Twenty years later, the Ottoman government would devote more than half of its budget to servicing foreign loans totaling 242 million British pounds.

The Tanzimat reforms had not yet produced a government apparatus capable of mounting an economic defense. For example, attempts to increase collection of taxes (and avoid foreign loans) faltered without trained personnel until well after 1859, when the Mekteb-i Mülkiye school to train bureaucrats was established. And although the 1858 land code sought to encourage more efficient exploitation of agriculture by promoting private land ownership, poor administration derailed it. In many areas, wealthy absentee landowners succeeded in registering large tracts of land, taking control away from the peasants who, if they had owned the land, might have found incentive to improve efficiency in cultivation. Instead, sharecropping discouraged investment in the land.

This is not to say that there was no effort at economic development, but rather that these efforts were overwhelmed by external factors. The Tanzimat period saw the first boom in building roads, ports, and other economic infrastructure that facilitated the transport of goods. But the tariff structure made the new transport more profitable to foreign traders than domestic merchants. While Ottoman exports increased nearly 500 percent between 1840 and the 1870s, these exports represented less than 10 percent of total production in the empire and were largely in the form of raw agricultural materials sent to England and France. In the meantime, the empire's terms of trade with Europe actually worsened. Ottoman industry, especially textiles, was undermined by unprecedented foreign competition. Although Ottoman officials established an industrial reform commission in the 1860s, they produced no significant industrial policy. So while Ottoman port cities boomed in this period, producing the first bloom of bourgeois culture, their wealth came from the profits of international trade, not from local production. The empire still relied overwhelmingly on an agricultural economy, and peasants remained as destitute as ever. And despite pockets of prosperity, the empire as a whole would sink so far into debt that it would declare bankruptcy in 1875.

It would be misguided, however, to conclude that the Tanzimat was the handmaiden of European imperialism. Older theories that it was primarily European pressure that forced the Tanzimat on the "sick man of Europe" have been substantially revised. Scholars like Shaw and Ortayli have suggested that the main impetus for reform came from bureaucrats, most prominently Mustafa Reşid Paşa, author of the 1839 edict. They acted from alarm at internal corruption and weakness, as well as from the desire to advance their own interests and protect their rights against the power of the sultan. Hence the 1839 edict abolished the sultan's right to confiscate property, commonly practiced on bureaucrats. Disenchanted bureaucrats led a second reform movement, the Young Ottomans, who in the 1860s and 1870s advocated liberalization and curtailment of the sultan's power. This led to a coup in 1876 that established a short-lived constitution and parliament.

European Influences and Internal Motivations

European influence, while not a primary motive of reform, was nonetheless significant. French and British diplomats repeatedly contributed to drafts of the various Tanzimat reform edicts, particularly those issued in times of war, as in the 1839 expulsion of the Egyptians and in 1856, at the end of the Crimean War. And Ottoman reformers often turned to European institutions for inspiration, as in the 1864 restructuring of provincial administration, the 1868 Council of State, and the 1869 Education Law, all modeled on French institutions.

Finally, a motive for reform came from the peoples of the empire. Dissatisfaction with Ottoman military weakness and a growing perception of alternatives to the current regime promoted unrest. This included not only the often cited Balkan nationalist movements, but smaller intermittent outbreaks, like the 1860 riots in Mount Lebanon and in Damascus that grew out of economic upheaval. Religious leaders, too, organized protest, as in the 1859 Küeli Incident in Constantinople. And religious minorities agitated against the oppressive and often corrupt rule of their state-sponsored patriarchs, leading to reform of the millets in the 1860s. Provincial notables used the local councils established in 1840 as a forum for protest and as a vehicle for negotiating the path of reform.

Design and Implementation of Efforts

In assessing the success of the Tanzimat, it is important to recognize that it was not a coherent, prefabricated plan; the Gülhane proclamation was not a blueprint. The Tanzimat took shape through efforts in Constantinople and in the provinces of Ottoman officials and notables to reconcile the many pressures on the empire. In Istanbul, the Meclĭs-Ĭ Vala, in concert with the grand vizier and sultan, had to weigh a variety of simultaneous and often conflicting interests, including military challengers like the Russians, Egyptians, and separatist movements in the Balkans; entrenched interests like those of landowners and the religious hierarchy; and the expanding aims of France and England. In the provinces, local representative councils and governors faced their own spectrum of interests to satisfy: landowners, *ulama* (Islamic clergy) who resented the new secular courts and schools, artisans hurt by European imports, and peasants who could not pay the new taxes.

Tanzimat goals were thus formulated and implemented through bargains made among opposing forces. Policy steered between the simultaneous aims of central control and provincial autonomy, between the ideal of a universal and equal Ottoman citizenry and reality of divisive religious social structures and nationalist particularisms, between the need to appease international challenges and the need to protect domestic interests, and between the efficacy of autocratic, top-down reform and the equally necessary participation of the public in effecting change.

Summary of Accomplishments

In the end, the reform program succeeded most in its goal of order: reorganizing the central and provincial bureaucracy, restructuring the military, and building infrastructure for trade and transport. Less auspicious was its progress toward justice; while

law codes were rationalized and venality in office reduced through improved salaries, economic inequalities increased and political participation remained minimal. The concentration of power in Constantinople lent itself to abuse. The Tanzimat period would conclude with a far more effective administrative and legal apparatus, but one that would be commandeered by an autocratic sultan, with the accession of Abdülhamit II in 1876. And in some ways, the Tanzimat was too little, too late. Efforts to strengthen the military and to integrate a population riven with religious and ethnic differences would not proceed quickly enough to avert the dismemberment of the Balkan provinces and the disastrous Russo-Turkish War of 1877/78.

The Tanzimat was, however, a bold and often impressive attempt to restructure the Ottoman polity; it simply did not have the time or opportunity by 1876 to effect significant social and economic change. Much of what the Tanzimat started, however, would bear fruit under Abdülhamit, who continued the Tanzimat's pursuit of order. And while Abdülhamit would leave behind other significant aspects of the Tanzimat, like justice and political participation, these would be taken up again with the rise of a new generation trained in the Tanzimat's schools and the 1908 constitutional revolution.

See also MILLET SYSTEM; YOUNG OTTOMANS.

Bibliography

Davison, Roderic H. *Reform in the Ottoman Empire, 1856–1876.* Princeton, NJ: Princeton University Press 1963.

Lewis, Bernard. *The Emergence of Modern Turkey,* 3d edition. New York: Oxford University Press, 2002.

Owen, Roger. *The Middle East in the World Economy, 1800–1914.* New York: Methuen, 1981.

Pamuk, Şevket. *The Ottoman Empire and European Capitalism, 1820–1913: Trade, Investment, and Production.* Cambridge, U.K., and New York: Cambridge University Press, 1987.

Shaw, Stanford J., and Shaw, Ezel Kural. *History of the Ottoman Empire and Modern Turkey,* Vol. 2: *Reform, Revolution, and Republic: The Rise of Modern Turkey, 1808-1975.* Cambridge, U.K., and New York: Cambridge University Press, 1977.

Thompson, Elizabeth. "Ottoman Reform in the Provinces: The Damascus Advisory Council,

1844–1845." *International Journal of Middle East Studies* 25, no. 3 (August 1993).

ELIZABETH THOMPSON

TAQLA, PHILIPPE
[1915–]

Lebanese politician and banker.

Philippe Taqla was born into a well-established Greek Catholic family with a long history of involvement in Lebanese politics. His father, Salim Taqla, was a minister in the cabinet that amended the Lebanese constitution and was, as a result, jailed by the French on 8 November 1943. He was released on 22 November 1943. A member of Bishara al-Khuri's Constitutional Bloc party, Philippe Taqla became a minister for the first time in 1946, the year his father died. In 1947, he was elected to parliament, and he held several ministerial positions between 1946 and 1952. His opposition to President Camille Chamoun (1952–1958) kept him out of power for several years, although he was again elected to parliament in 1957.

Under presidents Fu'ad Chehab (1958–1964) and Charles Hilu (1964–1970), he was minister of foreign affairs in eight separate cabinets, for a total of some fifty-seven months—a record by Lebanese standards. From 1965 to 1966, he was head of the Bank of Lebanon. In 1967, he became the permanent representative of Lebanon to the United Nations, and from 1968 to 1971 he was the ambassador to France. During his public career, which spanned the three decades from 1946 to 1976, he belonged to more cabinets than any other Lebanese politician except the late Prince Majid Arslan. From 1975 to 1976, he was a member of the Syrian-sponsored National Dialogue Committee, which unsuccessfully sought to put an end to the civil war that had just broken out. The war ended Taqla's public career. Since the end of the Lebanese civil war, Taqla has been serving on the board of one of Lebanon's largest commercial banks, BLOM Bank (Banque du Liban et d'Outre-Mer).

See also CHEHAB, FU'AD; CONSTITUTIONAL BLOC; HILU, CHARLES; KHURI, BISHARA AL-; LEBANESE CIVIL WAR (1975–1990); LEBANON.

Bibliography

Goria, Wade. *Sovereignty and Leadership in Lebanon, 1943–1976.* London: Ithaca Press, 1985.

Khazen, Farid el. *The Breakdown of the Lebanese State, 1967–1976.* London: I.B. Tauris, 1999.

Salameh, Ghassan. "Is a Lebanese Foreign Policy Possible?" In *Toward a Viable Lebanon,* edited by Halim Barakat. London: Croom Helm, 1988.

GUILIAN P. DENOEUX
UPDATED BY KHALIL GEBARA

TAQLID

See GLOSSARY

TARBUSH

See CLOTHING

TARHAN, ABDÜLHAK HAMIT
[1852–1937]

Turkish poet, diplomat, and politician.

Abdülhak Hamit Tarhan was born into a wealthy Istanbul family; his grandfather was physician to the sultan of the Ottoman Empire. He was privately tutored, then enrolled in a French school, and after a tour of Europe became one of the first Muslim students to enroll at Robert College (now part of Bosporus University). In 1871, he married into an aristocratic family and served in the empire's embassy in Paris. In 1878, his play *Nestren* was deemed subversive, and he was dismissed. In 1881, he was readmitted to the Ottoman foreign service and was posted abroad (in Paris, Bombay, London, and Belgium) until 1921. This was also his most active period of literary production. In 1922, he returned to Turkey, where he was soon elected to represent Istanbul in the new Turkish Grand National Assembly.

Tarhan was a major writer of the Tanzimat era. His participation in the *Servet-i Fünun* (Wealth of Sciences) movement, with its concern for technique and its valorization of art for its own sake, helped to prepare an environment for the flowering of modern literature in Turkey. The sheer extent of his output—the drama *Finten* is five hundred pages— is more remarkable than the quality of his prose, with its mixed meters and bombastic language. Tarhan is not widely read today.

Bibliography

Ertop, Konur. "Trends and Characteristics of Contemporary Turkish Literature." In *The Transformation of Turkish Culture: The Atatürk Legacy,* edited by Günsel Renda and C. Max Kortepeter. Princeton, NJ: Kingston Press, 1986.

Mitler, Louis. *Ottoman Turkish Writers: A Bibliographical Dictionary of Significant Figures in Pre-Republican Turkish Literature.* New York: P. Lang, 1988.

DAVID WALDNER

TARIKH TOLANA

The Afghan Historical Society.

Tarikh Tolana (Long History) is the Afghan name for the Historical Society of Afghanistan. Tarikh Tolana was founded in 1941 by Zahir Shah to promote the historical study of Afghanistan. Tarikh Tolana produced many publications, including the journals *Aryana* and *Afghanistan. Aryana* appeared in Pushto and Dari from 1942 to 1985, and *Afghanistan,* also in Dari and Pushto, from 1945 to 1975. The society later became part of the Afghan Academy of Science. The society fell into disarray as Afghanistan disintegrated in civil war in the 1980s and although it has never officially been disbanded, it no longer functions.

Bibliography

Adamec, Ludwig. *Historical Dictionary of Afghanistan,* 2d edition. Lanham, MD: Scarecrow Press, 1997.

GRANT FARR

TARIKI, ABDULLAH

[1919–]

Cofounder of the Organization of Petroleum Exporting Countries and prominent Saudi government minister during the 1950s and 1960s.

Born in 1919 in the Najd town of Zilfi and educated in Cairo and at the University of Texas, Abdullah Tariki was a prominent figure among Saudi Arabia's first generation of technocrats. He became head of the Directorate of Oil and Mining Affairs in 1955 and was instrumental in guiding Saudi domestic and international oil policies. In 1959, Tariki met with Juan Pablo Pérez Alfonso of Venezuela and representatives of Iran, Iraq, and Kuwait in order to establish a consultative commission designed to regulate oil prices, establish national companies, and oppose the fifty-fifty participation agreements with Western oil companies that characterized oil concessions of the day. This informal group coalesced into the Organization of Petroleum Exporting Countries (OPEC) on 14 September 1960, after Western oil companies initiated a price cut without consulting with nationals of the oil-producing countries.

Because of his opposition to the often overbearing and exploitative practices of U.S. oil companies in Saudi Arabia and his strong support for Arab nationalism, including that of Egypt's Gamal Abdel Nasser, Tariki's detractors called him "the Red Shaykh." In 1962, Crown Prince Faisal replaced him with Ahmad Zaki Yamani. From 1962 to 1976, Tariki remained politically active, writing articles and serving as a consultant for petroleum-producing countries, including Muammar al-Qaddafi's Libya. His nationalism and populism led him to denounce Western oil companies and urge Arabs to take full control over their natural resources so they could better advance their societies.

See also NASSER, GAMAL ABDEL; ORGANIZATION OF PETROLEUM EXPORTING COUNTRIES (OPEC); QADDAFI, MUAMMAR AL-.

Bibliography

Duguid, S. "A Biographical Approach to the Study of Social Change in the Middle East: Abdullah Tariki as a New Man." *International Journal of Middle East Studies* 1 (1970): 195–220.

Peterson, J. E. *Historical Dictionary of Saudi Arabia.* Metuchen, NJ: Scarecrow Press, 1993.

Yergin, Daniel. *The Prize: The Epic Quest for Oil, Money, and Power.* New York: Simon & Schuster, 1991.

LES ORDEMAN
UPDATED BY ANTHONY B. TOTH

TASHILHIT LANGUAGE

Berber dialect spoken in the south of Morocco.

The Berber language as a whole is composed of three dialects: Tashilhit, used in the region of Agadir and

Sous (southwest of Marrakech); Tamazight, widespread in the Middle Atlas and High Atlas mountains in the heart of Morocco; and Tarifit, spoken in the Rif, a region in the north of Morocco. *Tifinagh* is the name given to the writing of Tashilhit.

RAHMA BOURQIA

TAURUS MOUNTAINS

Major mountain chain of southern Turkey.

The Taurus chain is composed of several parallel limestone ranges rimming and reaching the Mediterranean, for about 930 miles (1,500 km), from Muğla in the west to Lake Van in the east. The summits often exceed 10,000 feet (3,000 m), the highest nonvolcanic peak being 12,323 feet (3,756 m)—the Aladağ—north of Adana. The average width of the range is 95 miles (150 km), and it forms a barrier to the Anatolian plateau but provides a valuable source of water for irrigation, forest products, and summer pasture. The most important pass is north of Tarsus, called the Cilician Gates. To the northeast is the extension of the range, called the Anti-Taurus.

Bibliography

Fisher, Sydney N. *The Middle East: A History,* 3d edition. New York: Knopf, 1979.

JOHN R. CLARK

TAX FARMING

Means of managing agrarian revenues, as well as of financing governmental programs.

Similar to the contemporary concept of privatization, tax farming is a poorly understood phenomenon in Middle Eastern history. It is often linked to the abuse of state power and debates on the institutional causes of the fall of premodern Islamic states. In essence, however, tax farming refers to any type of tax collection conducted by private individuals rather than salaried state personnel. These individuals acquire the right, often by auction, to collect a defined revenue for a specific period of time. From the Umayyads onward, Islamic states contracted out collection of taxes in proximate and more distant provinces. Tax farming allowed ad-

ministrators a degree of flexibility and an opportunity to strike a compromise between the old and the new. Indeed, the earliest Islamic administrators of Egypt awarded contracts to Copts and women. Although the powers of tax farmers were contingent on the type of revenue collected, the status of taxpayers, and the degree of state oversight, Islamic governments found ways to curb abuse and default of contract by requiring financial guarantors and subdividing responsibilities. As this form of collection falls under the legal notions of contract, Islamic lawyers usually separate the discussion of tax farming from the actual fiscal responsibilities of Muslim and non-Muslim subjects in terms of alms (*zakat*), tithes (*ushr*), and poll taxes (*jizya*).

There are few comprehensive studies of tax farming during the period between the Abbasids and the Mongols, though Middle Eastern states contracted out to private agents many types of taxes, both those that were Islamically recognized and those that were not. More than an institutional or legal question, tax farming may be regarded as a window on the evolving structure of premodern Islamic states and its relation to society. Because most of the Islamic schools of law regarded conquered land of non-Muslim populations (*kharaj*) to be, effectively, state land, tax farming was utilized alongside the *iqta* or tax fief, a form of resident administration, as an important means of managing agrarian revenues. Pending further research, one may speculate that the alternation between military and privatized forms of tax collection preceding and after the thirteenth-century Mongol invasions was not only the result of corruption of institutions or abuse of office, as the private auction of tax fiefs during the later Mamluk period in Egypt suggests, but also a means of coping with the dislocation of agrarian populations, greater demand for cash revenues, and changing land-use patterns.

Although the forms of tax farming in the Middle East after the sixteenth century have similar legal bases, the practices coincide with new worldwide trends, namely the escalating costs of warfare and expanding global trade. In the Ottoman Empire, for example, tax farming before the sixteenth century had been largely limited to certain commercial revenues and tariffs, and many of the tax farmers were non-Muslims. But as participants in the "gunpowder revolution" and the battle for Europe and

West Asia, the Ottomans required ever greater sources of cash to pay their infantries. Auctions of revenue contracts were a means of borrowing: They allowed the state to anticipate future tax receipts, albeit at a certain loss. Although the Ottoman state continued to administer many taxes directly, over the seventeenth century, many Muslim Ottoman officers and civilians bid for rights to collect taxes on the extensive crown and vizierial domains, tariffs, and manufacturing and tribal taxes, as well as to hold certain offices. A 1695 decree gave Muslim tax farmers the right to hold contracts for life (*malikane mukataa*) and to pass these holdings on to male heirs. Although this extensive use of tax farming produced many problems, it also reinforced the loyalty of Muslim tax farmers, if only by dint of self-interest, to the state, which awarded and recognized these rights.

Since the French Revolution, social scientists have tended to regard fiscal decentralization as one of the ancien régime's greatest evils as did the Ottoman state planners who tried to restrict and then eliminate tax farming in the early decades of the nineteenth century. Despite good intentions, Middle Eastern reformers were frustrated by chronic fiscal shortfalls and lack of administrative staff. No such compunctions about modern statecraft burdened the French colonial regime in Algeria, however. Well into mid-century, French imperialists continued to adapt an older tax-farming system to new political and fiscal purposes.

Bibliography

Cuno, Kenneth M. *The Pasha's Peasants: Land, Society, and Economy in Lower Egypt, 1740–1858.* Cambridge, U.K., and New York: Cambridge University Press, 1992.

Frantz-Murphy, Gladys. "Land Tenure and Social Transformation in Early Islamic Egypt." In *Land Tenure and Social Transformation in the Middle East,* edited by Tarif Khalidi. Beirut: American University of Beirut, 1984.

Johansen, Baber. *The Islamic Law on Land Tax and Rent.* London and New York: Croon Helm, 1988.

Morony, Michael G. "Land Holding and Social Change: Lower al-Iraq in the Early Islamic Period." In *Land Tenure and Social Transformation in the Middle East,* edited by Tarif Khalidi. Beirut: American University of Beirut, 1984.

Salzmann, Ariel. "An Ancien Régime Revisited: Privatization and Political Economy in the Eighteenth-Century Ottoman Empire." *Politics & Society* 21, no. 4 (1993): 393–423.

ARIEL SALZMANN

TCHERNICHOVSKY, SAUL
[1875–1943]

Hebrew poet, translator, and physician.

Saul Tchernichovsky (also Tsharnikhousky) was born in Mikhailovka, a village bordering on the Ukraine and Crimea. The most versatile of Hebrew poets, he was instrumental in the development, both in form and content, of Hebrew poetry. He published his first poem, *Ba-Halomi* (1892; In My Dream), at seventeen in the U.S. Hebrew paper *Ha-Pisgah*. His first book of poetry, *Hezyonot U-Manginot* (1898; Visions and Melodies), is romantic in style and deals with love and nature. From 1899 to 1906, he studied medicine in Heidelberg and Lausanne. During this period he wrote the first of his "Greek" poems— an indictment of Judaism's weakness vis-à-vis the vitality of Greek culture. The most powerful of these poems is *Lenokhah Pesel Apollo* (In the Presence of Apollo's Statue). In 1906 he returned to Russia, and until World War I, he held various positions as a doctor. The turbulent period in Russia following the war is described in his collection *Sonnetot Krim* (Crimean Sonnets). His *Lashemesh* (To the Sun), a series of sonnets written beginning in 1919, is in stark contrast to the surrounding darkness. In 1922 he left Russia but, failing to reach Palestine, he settled in Berlin where he translated such classical writers as Goethe, Molière, Shakespeare, and Homer. In 1929 he began to publish a ten-volume jubilee edition of his poetry, short stories, plays, and translations.

In 1931, at the invitation of Dr. A. M. Masie's family, Tchernichovsky arrived in Palestine to complete and edit a medical dictionary begun by the deceased doctor. The result was a trilingual work in Latin, English, and Hebrew, *Sefer Ha-Munahim Li-Refuah U-Lemadaei Ha-Tev'a* (1934, A Book of Terminologies in Medicine and the Natural Sciences). Tchernichovsky first resided in Tel Aviv and then moved to Jerusalem, where he wrote his final works of poetry. In 1937 he published *Kol Shirei Shaul Tcher-*

nichovsky (The Poems of Saul Tchernichovsky). In 1942 the Tel Aviv municipality established a prize in his name for translations of classics and world classical literature with Tchernichovsky as its first recipient. Once in Palestine, his poems became strongly nationalistic, and in the resettlement of Eretz Yisrael, he saw the redemption and rejuvenation of pre-exilic Judaism. He expressed all these sentiments in ballad form, such as in *Amma Dedhahaba* (1943; The Golden People). Tchernichovsky died after a long illness and was buried in Tel Aviv's old cemetery.

ANN KAHN

TEA

A drink for social occasions and after meals.

In the Middle East, tea is a popular drink brewed with the leaves and water in a kettle (although tea bags are becoming more common). Hot tea is strained into small glasses, often set in decorative metal holders, and served with various additions depending on region and personal taste. These include sugar, honey, lemon, apple flavoring, and mint. (Mint tea is also a very popular digestive drink; it is made solely from mint leaves of the genus *Mentha,* which grow throughout the Mediterranean region and Eurasia.)

Tea is imported to the Middle East from the Asian tea plantations of China, Japan, India, Sri Lanka, and islands of the East Indies. It is also cultivated along Iran's Caspian Sea coast and Turkey's Black Sea coast. Originally it came into the region by way of ancient caravan routes along the Silk Road (from China to Iran to the Black Sea and Constantinople) or ship routes from the South China Sea and the Indian Ocean into the Arabian Sea, the Persian Gulf, and the Red Sea.

Bibliography

Hartel, Herbert, et al. *Along the Ancient Silk Routes.* New York: Metropolitan Museum of Art, 1982.

CLIFFORD A. WRIGHT
UPDATED BY ERIC HOOGLUND

TEBU TRIBE

See TRIBES AND TRIBALISM: TEBU TRIBE

TECHNION-ISRAEL INSTITUTE OF TECHNOLOGY

Israeli university.

The Technion-Israel Institute of Technology, located in Haifa, was founded because of the lack of opportunities for technical studies for Jews in places such as Russia. This void meant that Jews were excluded from technical professions and pushed into urban commercial occupations. While the cornerstone was laid in 1912, World War I delayed the opening. The first classes were held in 1924. Hebrew became the language of instruction only after a long "language conflict" over whether German or Hebrew should be used.

There are faculties and departments in aeronautical engineering, agricultural engineering, architecture and town planning, chemical engineering, chemistry, civil engineering, electrical engineering, food and biotechnology, general studies, industrial and management engineering, materials engineering, mathematics, mechanical engineering, mechanics, nuclear sciences, physics, and teacher training. The number of undergraduate and graduate students enrolled in 1999/2000 was 12,700.

MIRIAM SIMON

TEHIYA

See ISRAEL: POLITICAL PARTIES IN

TEHRAN

Capital of Iran since the late eighteenth century.

In 1800, Tehran was a small city with an estimated population of 20,000; it was surrounded by twenty-foot mud walls with four gates. The wall was encircled by a moat, which was up to 40 feet wide and between 20 and 30 feet deep. Although several new buildings were constructed during the reign of Fath Ali Shah Qajar (1797–1834), the first major expansion of Tehran dates from the reign of Naser al-Din Shah (1848–1896), the third Qajar monarch. The old walls were pulled down, plans for an octagonal wall on a French model were followed, and twelve gates were built. New grounds were added to the city compound, as well as large boulevards and imposing public and private buildings, designed with many European features. The city had a small railway leading to a place of pilgrimage in the south, and the summer resorts in the Alborz Mountains in the north were developed and became popular with richer Tehranis. In 1852, a first census and a count of all the buildings were made, which show how small the city still was: It had only 12,772 buildings, 8,697 houses, and 4,220 shops. The second census, prepared in 1869, gave the population as 150,000.

Tehran's second phase of development dates to the reign (1926–1941) of Reza Shah Pahlavi, founder of the Pahlavi dynasty. The city was expanded outside its old walls, especially to the north and the northwest. A notable feature was the neoclassical buildings, designed mainly by European architects, especially exiles fleeing the Russian Revolution but also Iranians who had studied abroad. Houses began to be built facing outward, to the street, instead of inward, to the courtyard, and streets were planned for the passage of automobiles. The ornate gates, a special feature of old Tehran, were pulled down, as were many buildings of the Qajar dynasty period.

Tehran's third phase of development dates to the early 1950s, when a new generation of Iranian architects and technocrats, who had studied in U.S. universities, returned to erase many of the remaining features of the old city. Tehran began expanding rapidly and haphazardly, because of the petroleum industry, oil-induced construction, and the industrialization boom of the 1960s and 1970s. Between 1956 and 1976, the city's population tripled, from 1.5 million to 4.5 million. Despite the economic, political, and social upheavals caused by the Iranian Revolution (1979) and the Iran–Iraq War (1980–1988), Tehran's population continued to grow at an average annual rate of 3.5 percent from the mid-1970s to the late 1980s. Thereafter, population growth declined by about 1 percent per year within the city, but nearby towns and rural areas experienced rapid growth as they were developed as suburban communities to the east, south, and west of Tehran. According to the 1996 census, a total of 6,759,000 people lived in the city of Tehran; more than 1.3 million lived in suburbs, including the densely populated communities of Islamshahr and Karaj.

See also FATH ALI SHAH QAJAR; IRANIAN REVOLUTION (1979); IRAN–IRAQ WAR (1980–1988); NASER AL-DIN SHAH; PAHLAVI, REZA.

Bibliography

Adamec, Ludwig W., ed. *Historical Gazetteer of Iran*, Vol. 1, *Tehran and Northwestern Iran*. Graz, Austria: Akademische Drucku, 1976.

Ettehadieh, Mansoureh. "Patterns in Urban Development: The Growth of Tehran, 1852–1903." In *Qajar Iran: Political, Social and Cultural Change, 1800–1925*, edited by Edmund Bosworth and Carole Hillenbrand. Edinburgh, U.K.: Edinburgh University Press, 1983.

Firoozi, Ferydoon. "Tehran: A Demographic and Economic Analysis." *Middle Eastern Studies* 10, no. 1 (Jan. 1974): 60–67.

MANSOUREH ETTEHADIEH
UPDATED BY ERIC HOOGLUND

TEKELI, ŞIRIN
[1940–]

A feminist activist in Turkey.

Şirin Tekeli is the foremost feminist author and activist of second-wave feminism in Turkey. Born in 1944, she is the only child of two philosophy teachers. She received her high school education in Ankara and completed her college education in political science in Lausanne University, Switzerland. She studied the work of David Easton for her Ph.D. in political science in Istanbul University, where she was employed as an assistant professor. The thesis she wrote in 1978 for promotion to associate professor was on women's political participation, and prompted her feminist activism. Published in 1982 as a book called *Kadınlar ve Siyasal-Toplumsal Hayat* (Women and political-social life), this study was the first serious and comprehensive discussion of women's marginalization in sociopolitical life written in Turkish and from a predominantly Marxist perspective. Her interviews with Turkish women parliamentarians, which she included in the book, exposed their striking marginality and problems in political life. The book was widely read, moving beyond a narrow academic circle, and had immediate and long-lasting influence in shaping a feminist culture in Turkey.

Tekeli resigned from her position as an associate professor in 1981 and began her career as a feminist activist, translating and editing books. She engaged in organizing consciousness-raising groups and feminist publication circles in early 1980s and initiated the founding of the Kadın Eserleri Kütüphanesi ve Bilgi Merkezi (Women's Library and Information Center) and Mor Çatı Kadın Sığınağı (Purple Roof Women's Shelter) Foundations with her friends in 1990. She worked as a volunteer in the Women's Library between 1990 and 1996 and helped the institution develop into a vital organ of feminist dialogue. In 1997, she responded to the hunger strikes that were staged in prisons by deciding to work for women's entry into the parliament. She founded KADER, Kadın Adayları Destekleme ve Eğitme Derneği (Association to support and educate women candidates) in 1997 and served as its president between 1997 and 1999. The French government presented her with the award of *Officier* of *l'Ordre des Palmes Academiques* in 1996.

See also GENDER: GENDER AND LAW; GENDER: GENDER AND POLITICS; TURKEY; WOMEN'S LIBRARY AND INFORMATION CENTER.

YEŞIM ARAT

TEKKE

Local headquarters for Sufi orders.

Tekke is the Turkish word for the local meeting and living center of a Sufi fraternity. The Persian equivalent, *khangah,* is commonly used in most non-Turkic contexts, while *zawiya* (Arabic) functions as a distinctively North African synonym.

The late tenth and eleventh centuries saw a rise in the popularity of Sufi teachings and charismatic leaders, as well as the concurrent evolution of various Sufi organizations or "fraternities." As they expanded, these fraternities began to establish special living quarters for their members, as well as space for the various ritual, scholarly, and social service activities conducted by the local chapters of what gradually grew into international Sufi orders. In different contexts, either the state or private citizens endowed a vast network of tekke and khangah complexes designed to serve as regional headquarters for the fraternities. Many of these were composed of residence cells, a large kitchen-refectory

for members and guests, a Qur'an school for local youth, a library for advanced study, a tomb-shrine of a deceased spiritual master, and a mosque. Partly because the money used to endow tekkes and khangahs was often invested in local business and agriculture, a number of them throughout the late medieval and early modern Muslim world (c. 1200–1900) functioned as important economic, cultural, and political centers. In fact in some regions—particularly southern Asia, western North Africa, and the Balkans—tekkes and khangahs played a role in the Islamization of local peoples and cultures. Although the institution of the tekke generally flourished under Ottoman patronage, the stridently secularist vision of Mustafa Kemal Atatürk and his regime led to the 1925 closing of all the great Anatolian tekkes—including that of the Mevlevi Brotherhood (the famed "whirling dervishes") in Konya—and the subsequent abolishment of nearly all institutional Sufi activity in the new Turkish republic.

See also SUFISM AND THE SUFI ORDERS.

Bibliography

Trimingham, J. Spencer. *The Sufi Orders in Islam.* New York: Oxford University Press, 1998.

SCOTT ALEXANDER

TEL AVIV

Coastal city founded in Ottoman Palestine in 1909; capital of Israel, 1948–1950.

Tel Aviv is a sprawling metropolis surrounded by suburbs; it was the first city to be established by Jews in the modern era. As numerous Jewish settlers arrived in Palestine in the late nineteenth century, they had increasing difficulties finding accommodations at affordable prices in the overcrowded residential areas of Jerusalem and Jaffa. In both cities, Jews began to purchase land and build new suburbs.

Jaffa is adjacent to, and today part of, Tel Aviv because Ahuzat Bayit, the building society, purchased beachfront property and underwrote the construction of Tel Aviv's first sixty houses in 1909—initially intended as a new suburb of Jaffa. Important differences between this project and other suburbs could be immediately discerned. Architects and engineers helped design the arrangement of houses and streets; individual land grants were large; all connecting roads and streets were paved; and running water was supplied to each house. Ahuzat Bayit became the most spacious and comfortable suburb in all Palestine. The building society changed the name to Tel Aviv in 1910, marking both a biblical text (Ezekiel 3:15) where the name appears and mention in Nahum Sokolow's translation of Zionist leader Theodor Herzl's *Alteneuland* (The Old New Land). Initially planned as a residential suburb, all of Tel Aviv's first settlers worked in Jaffa. Many of Tel Aviv's founders had private capital; they owned businesses and worked in the free professions. Jewish engineers and contractors built the city's first houses with supplies furnished by Jewish factories. Symbol of the New Yishuv (Jewish community), Tel Aviv's relatively rapid expansion paused during World War I, but resumed and intensified during the British mandate (1923–1948).

Although Zionism stressed agricultural settlement, and donated funds subsidized the cost of collective and communal settlements, most immigrants chose to live in cities and many selected Tel Aviv. By 1935, the population had grown from 2,000 to 120,000 and Tel Aviv became the political, economic, and cultural center of the Jewish National Home. Factories and businesses stood alongside the Histadrut (Jewish Labor Federation) and military headquarters. Publishing firms, major newspapers, several dance and theater companies, the symphony, and an important museum were founded. Transport and roads radiated out to other cities and the countryside.

In May 1948, David Ben-Gurion proclaimed the independence of the State of Israel at a meeting held in the Tel Aviv Museum. In 1950, the commercial port city of Jaffa was incorporated with Tel Aviv, forming the twin city of Tel Aviv-Jaffa. Tel Aviv-Jaffa has benefited from Israel's rapid economic growth, today numbering more than 350,000 residents. (The population of Tel Aviv and its outskirts numbers 2.5 million.) The Histadrut headquarters no longer dominates the skyline or the city's economy. Art, music, and drama flourish in galleries and theaters, and there is an impressive array of shops, cabarets, and restaurants (both kosher and non-kosher). Much of Tel Aviv's cosmopolitan core now remains open on the Jewish Sabbath, presenting an urban profile that differs in scale and tone from that projected by Jerusalem.

Bibliography

Kark, Ruth. *Jaffa: A City in Evolution, 1799–1917,* translated by Gila Brand. Jerusalem: Yad Izhak Ben-Zvi Press, 1990.

Katz, Yossi. "Ideology and Urban Development: Zionism and the Origins of Tel Aviv, 1906–1914." *Journal of Historical Geography* 12 (1986): 402–424.

Orni, Efraim, and Elisha Efrat. *Geography of Israel,* 4th revised edition. Jerusalem: Israel Universities Press, 1980.

DONNA ROBINSON DIVINE

TEL AVIV UNIVERSITY

Israeli university.

In 1953 the city of Tel Aviv founded the university to meet the higher education needs of the populous, developing area.

The university offers programs in the arts and sciences within the nine faculties of engineering, exact sciences, humanities, law, life sciences, management, medicine, social sciences, and visual and performing arts, as well as schools of dental medicine, social work, education, and environmental studies. In 2002 the student population was approximately 26,000.

MIRIAM SIMON

TELEVISION

See RADIO AND TELEVISION

TEL HAI

Pioneer Jewish settlement in Palestine that became a national symbol.

Tel Hai is a Jewish settlement founded in 1918 in Galilee, on the northern frontier of Palestine, as an attempt to influence the drawing of the boundary between British and French colonial possessions. After the British gave up responsibility for Syria and Lebanon at the end of World War I, and before the French Mandate began, a hiatus in authority led to irregular warfare endangering Jewish settlements in the undefined upper Galilee/northern border area. Many Zionist leaders, among them Vladimir Ze'ev Jabotinsky, advised the small number of settlers at Tel Hai to withdraw because a reasonable defense could not be mounted. They remained, and six Jews died in the final attack in 1920, among them the military hero Yosef Trumpeldor, who had been sent to organize their defense. Tel Hai became a national symbol of the determination of Zionists to hold on to settlements at all costs and a metaphor for the principle that Jewish national life in Palestine required personal sacrifice.

See also TRUMPELDOR, YOSEF.

Bibliography

Zerubavel, Yael. "The Historic, the Legendary, and the Incredible: Invented Tradition and Collective Memory in Israel." In *Commemorations: The Politics of National Identity*, edited by John R. Gillis. Princeton, NJ: Princeton University Press, 1994.

Zerubavel, Yael. *Recovered Roots: Collective Memory and the Making of Israeli National Tradition.* Chicago: University of Chicago Press, 1995.

DONNA ROBINSON DIVINE

TELL

See GLOSSARY

TEMPLARS

German evangelical settlers in Palestine in the late nineteenth century.

The Temple Society (Tempelgesellschaft) was founded in the mid-nineteenth century in the Kingdom of Württemberg. Pietistic Evangelicals, the Templars criticized the church and decided at first to settle and found colonies and, later, to improve the land in Palestine as they awaited the imminent Kingdom of Heaven. They established a colony in Haifa in 1868 and brought modern European methods of agriculture. They also established the carriage trade from Jaffa to Jerusalem, exported wine, and established settlements in Jaffa, Haifa, Sarone (part of modern Tel Aviv), Jerusalem, Wilhelma, Galilen Bethlehem, and Waldheim. Individuals settled in Jerusalem and founded a Ger-

man colony there that, although denied official support by the German government, numbered some 1,200 people by 1914.

Deported as enemy aliens by the British from 1917 to 1918, as German nationals they kept a low profile after they were permitted to return during the Palestine Mandate. Their religious fervor had decreased by the third generation and, as Germans, many were receptive to National Socialism, even though there was no official advocacy of support for the Nazi Party. Many sympathetic members were allowed to join the party; they also enlisted their children in the Nazi Youth and disseminated Nazi propaganda. With the outbreak of World War II, there were approximately 1,500 Germans of Templar origin who were interned, and afterward they were repatriated to Germany in exchange for Palestinians who had fallen into German hands. Some were deported to Australia. In 1948 their property was taken over by the Israeli government and placed under the Guardian of German Property; it was later taken into account during the negotiations over Nazi Holocaust reparations conducted by the World Jewish Congress and the West German government.

See also GERMANY AND THE MIDDLE EAST; HAIFA; JAFFA; JERUSALEM; WEST GERMAN REPARATIONS AGREEMENT.

Bibliography

Carmel, Alex. "The German Settlers in Palestine and Their Relations with the Local Arab Population and the Jewish Community, 1868–1918." In *Studies on Palestine during the Ottoman Empire*, edited by Moshe Ma'oz. Jerusalem: Magnes Press, 1975.

Thalmann, Naftali. "Introducing Modern Agriculture into Nineteenth Century Palestine: The German Templers." In *The Land that Became Israel: Studies in Historical Geography*, edited by Ruth Kark. New Haven, CT: Yale University Press, 1990.

Yazbak, Mahmoud. "Templars as 'Proto-Zionists': The 'German Colony' in Late Ottoman Haifa." *Journal of Palestine Studies* xx, no. 112 (Summer 1999): 40–45.

REEVA S. SIMON
UPDATED BY MICHAEL R. FISCHBACH

TEMPLE, HENRY JOHN

See PALMERSTON, LORD HENRY JOHN TEMPLE

TEMPLE MOUNT AND HARAM AL-SHARIF

See HARAM AL-SHARIF

TEMPORARY MARRIAGE

See ZIWAJ MUT'A

TERAKKI

See NEWSPAPERS AND PRINT MEDIA: TURKEY

TERCÜMAN-I AHVAL

See NEWSPAPERS AND PRINT MEDIA: TURKEY

TERCÜMAN-I HAKIKAT

See NEWSPAPERS AND PRINT MEDIA: TURKEY

TERRORISM

Violence directed primarily and randomly against civilians with the aim of intimidating them, achieving political goals, or exacting revenge for perceived grievances.

Since the 11 September 2001 terrorist attacks that destroyed the twin World Trade Center skyscrapers in New York City and killed nearly 2,800 persons, terrorism arising out of conflicts in the Middle East has been a focus of international media attention. Concern about violence undertaken by groups and states it considered to be terrorists prompted the United States to declare a war on terrorism, two manifestations of which have been the wars in Afghanistan and Iraq. Despite this close association of terrorism with the Middle East, with the notable exception of the year 2001, the majority of terrorist incidents committed worldwide and the majority of victims of terrorism have been outside of or unrelated to political conflicts in the Middle East. Nevertheless, it is true that civilians somewhere in the Middle East have been victims of politically motivated violence every year since at least 1992.

Defining Terrorism

In trying to assess the significance of terrorism, the most difficult problem is the lack of an agreed-upon understanding of what the word *terrorism* means. Political scientists tend to restrict terrorism to acts of violence carried out by nonstate actors against civilians. Historians, sociologists, and experts in international humanitarian law, however, tend to use a broader definition that includes all premeditated acts of violence against civilians, whether carried out by nonstate political groups or by states. Governments—especially those confronting armed opposition groups—and the media generally use the political-science definition of terrorism, often expanding it to include violent acts against military as well as civilian victims. In contrast, the nonstate perpetrators of violence consider their actions to be legitimate forms of resistance to state terrorism aimed at suppressing self-determination, even though they may be directed against civilians (Kimmerling, p. 23). The notion of a legitimate right to resist state oppression is controversial, and no international legal convention addresses this matter. Nonstate groups generally cite the 1960 United Nations General Assembly Resolution on the Granting of Independence to Colonial Countries and Peoples as recognizing their right of resistance. Indeed, that resolution declares, "forcible resistance to forcible denial of self-determination . . . is legitimate," and it says that nonstate groups may receive external support from other governments.

Giving a measure of international legitimacy to resistance struggles has complicated the problem of defining terrorism because it essentially has become a political decision whether a nonstate actor is deemed a terrorist or a genuine national liberation movement fighting for independence from foreign control or occupation. During the Cold War rivalry between the Soviet Union and the United States (1947–1991), such decisions tended to be based more on ideological factors than on objective assessments of the goals and motives of particular nonstate groups. For example, the Soviet Union provided clandestine support for the South Yemen independence movement (1963–1967) and for the Dhufar liberation movement in Oman (1965–1971) primarily because both areas at the time were under the control of Britain, a major U.S. ally. Similarly, the United States provided covert assistance to the Kurds in Iraq (1970–1975) and the Mojahedin in Afghanistan (1979–1989) primarily because in both cases the nonstate groups were fighting for independence from Soviet client regimes. The Soviet Union and the United States condemned as

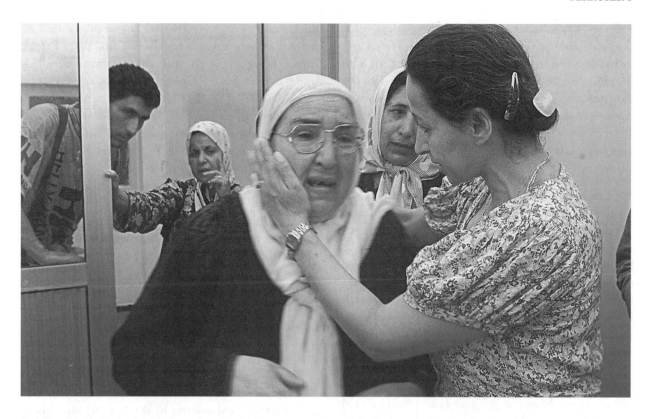

Social worker Farida Djefel (right) comforts Khalti Taous at the offices of the National Association for the Families of Terrorism Victims in Algiers, Algeria, in 1999. Taous's son, a policeman, was killed by suspected Islamic militants in 1994. © AP/WIDE WORLD PHOTOS. REPRODUCED BY PERMISSION.

terrorists those nonstate groups that were fighting against regimes the other country favored, and they praised as national resistance heroes those groups fighting against governments they opposed.

Over time, a special vocabulary of terrorism emerged. For instance, the term *state terrorism* came to be used for violent acts used by disfavored states to suppress resistance movements. The Soviet Union used this term to describe the policies of two U.S. allies: Israel, for the repression of Palestinians in the occupied West Bank and Gaza Strip after 1967; and Turkey, for the repression of its Kurdish minority after 1984. The United States, in turn, used *state terrorism* as early as the mid-1970s to describe the repressive domestic policies of states it considered to be Soviet allies, such as Iraq, Syria, and South Yemen. During the 1980s another term, *state sponsor of terrorism,* emerged to describe the support for nonstate groups provided by countries that clearly were not allied to either the Soviet Union or the United States. Iran and Libya were identified as the main state sponsors of terrorism, the former because

of its assistance after 1982 to Hizbullah in Lebanon. In the case of Libya, the United States accused that country of supporting Palestinian groups that targeted U.S. and Israeli interests in Europe and of assisting several terrorist groups operating in north and central Africa.

Origins of Terrorism in the Arab–Israel Conflict

The superpower rivalry in and rhetoric about the Middle East tended both to obscure the local origins of terrorism and to frustrate efforts to address the multifaceted consequences of violence. This problem is best revealed in the Arab–Israel conflict, which began in 1948 separately from but in tandem with the Cold War and still continues unresolved even though the superpower conflict has ended. One significant legacy of the Cold War relationship to the Arab–Israel conflict has been a great volume of partisan literature, especially in the years after the formation of the Palestine Liberation Organization (PLO) in 1964. The Israeli–Palestinian struggle over pre-1948 Palestine (which became Israel plus the territories of the Gaza Strip and the West Bank in 1948) is the core of the Arab–Israel conflict. The literature on this aspect of the conflict illustrates the controversies in trying to achieve any relatively objective consensus on what groups merit designation as terrorists and what kinds of violent acts constitute terrorism. For this reason, it is a useful case to study.

For nearly thirty years prior to the signing of the Oslo Accord in September 1993, the State of Israel proclaimed the PLO and the various Palestinian resistance groups that comprised its membership to be terrorist organizations. Inevitably, there emerged a body of writings that supported the Israeli position, not just in Israel but also in Europe and North America. Although some of these studies were sophisticated and scholarly analyses of the PLO's goals and methods, other accounts were merely polemical denunciations of PLO tactics. Beginning in 1968 and continuing for more than a decade, armed Palestinian groups known as *fidaʾiyyun* (guerrillas) carried out numerous, violent operations that resulted in the deaths of civilians. Many of their actions were sensational incidents that attracted considerable media attention—a PLO objective, as the guerrillas hoped publicity would further their cause. The several international airplane hijackings, for example, culminated in September 1970 (known as Black September) with the hijacking of four planes in as many days, precipitating a civil war between the PLO and the army of Jordan. Attacks on Israeli interests abroad culminated in the seizing of Israeli athletes as hostages at the 1972 Olympic games in Munich, an incident that left eleven athletes dead. Sporadic cross-border raids into Israel (from Jordan and Lebanon) culminated in the temporary seizure of buildings in the northern Israeli towns of Kiryat Shmona and Maʿalot (April and May 1974) and the deaths of thirty-eight civilians, including many children. Rather than winning sympathy for the Palestinians as the perpetrators expected, such incidents created and reinforced a public image of the PLO as a terrorist organization.

In contrast to the official Israeli and U.S. views, the PLO saw itself as a national liberation movement dedicated to achieving Palestinian rights and resisting what it termed Israeli state terrorism. Its fighters were lauded as heroes and martyrs, and its

operations against Israeli civilians were justified as defense of, or reprisals for, Israeli attacks on Palestinian refugee camps and assassinations of PLO leaders. The Soviet Union, the primary international backer of the PLO after 1968, tended to remain silent about many of the more sensational acts of violence by Palestinian guerrillas, but it continued to promote the PLO as a national liberation movement. Soviet support was especially significant after 1974 when Moscow encouraged diplomatic recognition of the PLO as the legitimate representative of the Palestinian people. Quite separate from the Soviet backing for the PLO, a few academic studies and advocacy articles appeared that were sympathetic to Palestinian claims and rights. Although these writings were scarcer than the volumes of pro-Israeli literature and never achieved a similar impact on the mainstream U.S. media, they did have some influence on intellectuals in Africa, Asia, and Europe.

The Israeli–PLO conflict affected both regional and international politics by the late 1970s. This is because the PLO used Lebanon, where a large number of Palestinian refugees had lived since 1948, as a base for operations against Israel throughout the 1970s, and Israel responded with retaliatory raids against what it termed "terrorist nests"—suspected PLO facilities in refugee camps. Many Lebanese and Palestinian civilians died in these raids, and their deaths were described officially as "collateral damage" in a larger operation against "terrorist infrastructure." The PLO condemned Israeli air strikes as further evidence of state terror and also cited them as justification for its own continuing attacks across the Lebanon-Israel border. The escalating cycle of attacks and reprisals contributed to the civil war in Lebanon (1975–1989) and also led to an Israeli invasion of southern Lebanon in 1978. Israeli forces occupied a 6-mile-wide security strip, ostensibly to prevent attacks into Israel; this occupation lasted until 2000. A second Israeli invasion of Lebanon in 1982 resulted in a war with the PLO, its forced withdrawal from Lebanon under international protection, and the Israeli occupation of Beirut and all of southern Lebanon. However, almost as soon as the threat from the PLO seemed to be contained, Israel faced a new source of terrorism that stemmed directly from its occupation of Lebanon (which lasted until 1985).

A Lebanese group, Hizbullah, was formed in late 1982 with the initial aim of expelling Israeli forces from Lebanon. Hizbullah's tactics, which included suicide bombings against French and U.S. military forces in 1983 and, beginning in 1984, the kidnapping of European civilians to use as hostages for the release of its members held in Israeli jails, earned it an international reputation as a terrorist organization. Hizbullah, however, neither sought nor received any support from the Soviet Union. Like the revolutionary government that assumed power in Iran in 1979, Hizbullah was equally hostile to Soviet and U.S. policies in the Middle East. Although its objectives were first and foremost political, Hizbullah also was inspired by its own interpretation of Shi'ite Islam. Its frequent use of religious rhetoric to explain or to justify its actions tended to alienate the Soviet Union even more than its direct criticisms did. Thus, Hizbullah became one of the first major nonstate groups in the Middle East to lack a superpower patron. Despite or perhaps because of this status, Hizbullah succeeded in establishing a permanent presence in Lebanon's politics and in becoming a nonstate group whose actions Israel neither could control nor ignore.

Meanwhile, the removal of the PLO to Tunisia did not end its political influence among Palestinians, and when an intifada (uprising) erupted in December 1987 among Palestinians living under Israeli occupation in the West Bank and Gaza Strip, the PLO gradually emerged as a main coordinating force for the resistance. New groups unaffiliated with the PLO also emerged during the intifada, principally HAMAS and Islamic Jihad. Unlike the PLO, which claimed to be inspired by secular ideas, HAMAS and Islamic Jihad cited religious ideals and percepts as at least partial justification for their resistance against Israeli rule. Concern about the increasing influence of groups such as HAMAS and Islamic Jihad may have prompted the leaders of Israel's Labor Party to begin negotiations with the PLO to end the long conflict. The political rapprochement between Israel and the PLO in 1993 not only was unexpected, but it also necessitated a re-evaluation of the negative ways each side had depicted the other. However, the years of intellectual and emotional investment in the terrorism paradigm made it difficult for some people on both sides to view formerly hated terrorists as legitimate partners in peace ne-

A 1999 wanted poster for Osama bin Ladin, leader of the al-Qa'ida terrorist network. The poster depicts the carnage from bombings of the U.S. embassies in Kenya and Tanzania on 7 August 1998, an act that the United States blamed on bin Ladin. The terrorist attacks of 11 September 2001 would bring far greater infamy to bin Ladin in the future. © CORBIS. REPRODUCED BY PERMISSION.

gotiations. Thus, from the outset of the Oslo peace process, some Israelis and Palestinians were skeptical of the agreement and even were determined to overturn it. The assassination of Israeli prime minister Yitzhak Rabin in November 1995 (by an Israeli opposed to the Oslo Accord) and the first suicide bombings undertaken in 1996 by HAMAS were significant terrorist incidents that led to multiple actions and reprisals that cumulatively undermined popular support for the peace process among both Israelis and Palestinians.

It was in this increasingly tense atmosphere that Israeli politician Ariel Sharon intervened in a manner that would have the effect (albeit at the time, unforeseen) of overturning the peace process. Sharon was one of those Israelis who distrusted and even opposed the Oslo Accord, and it is plausible that he never had changed his conviction that the PLO was a terrorist organization. When in September 2000 he led a group of Knesset members, under armed escort, into the Muslim religious complex in Jerusalem known as al-Haram al-Sharif, his intention was to assert Israeli sovereignty over a site that Jews claim is the Temple Mount—the location of their ancient temple destroyed by the Romans more than 2,000 years ago—and thus to prevent its possible return to Palestinian sovereignty, which had been proposed by some members of the Labor Party. The incident provoked clashes with Palestinian worshipers, and the next day Israeli police killed four protesting Palestinians as they emerged from Friday prayers at the al-Aqsa Mosque in al-Haram al-Sharif complex. The situation escalated rapidly as Palestinian policemen, in an effort to protect civilians, clashed with Israeli soldiers at checkpoints in the West Bank. The al-Aqsa intifada thus began, and subsequently its characteristic features included targeted assassinations of suspected Palestinian resistance leaders by Israel and retaliatory Palestinian suicide bombings at crowded civilian sites inside Israeli cities. By early 2001, Israel and its supporters were labeling all acts of violence from the Palestinian side as terrorism.

The U.S. "War on Terrorism"

Middle East terrorism, except for incidents such as the attack at the Munich Olympic games in 1972, generally has stayed within the region. However, Middle East–related terrorism acquired a global dimension with the 11 September 2001 attacks in the United States by nineteen members of the al-Qaʿida network. Al-Qaʿida is a political organization founded by Saudi Arabian national Osama bin Ladin, and its objectives after 1991 were to attack the United States and its interests because it viewed the U.S. government as the main sponsor of regimes that it defined as "unjust," oppressive, and illegitimate. Ironically, bin Ladin collaborated with U.S. officials during the 1980s when he and the United States shared the same goal of forcing the Soviet Union to withdraw its troops from Afghanistan. But when the United States dispatched troops to Saudi Arabia in 1990, bin Ladin viewed this development

as being no different from the situation of Soviet troops in Afghanistan—in both cases the army of an "imperialist" superpower occupying a weaker and Muslim country. Furthermore, the presence of U.S. military forces in Saudi Arabia meant that a non-Muslim army for the first time in more than 1,400 years was occupying the religiously sacred land in which were located Islam's two holiest sites, the cities of Mecca and Medina. Even though bin Ladin believed and practiced a very conservative interpretation of Sunni Islam, his primary objectives vis-à-vis the United States are political, not religious. Beginning with the bombing in the underground parking garage of the World Trade Center in 1993, persons close to his al-Qaʿida organization were implicated in several terrorist attacks. The most sensational incidents included suicide bombings outside the barracks housing U.S. military personnel in Saudi Arabia in 1996 and outside two U.S. embassies in East Africa in 1998. The 2001 attacks prompted the United States to declare a "war on terrorism," and the Taliban regime in Afghanistan became the first target because it provided sanctuary to al-Qaʿida and rejected requests for the extradition of bin Ladin and other leaders.

Its war on terrorism policy led the United States to focus on groups it designated as terrorist to an unprecedented extent. One consequence of this new preoccupation was that after 2001 Washington accepted the argument of Israeli prime minister Sharon that PLO chairman and Palestinian Authority president Yasir Arafat was condoning terrorist actions by groups such as HAMAS, Islamic Jihad, and his own Al-Fatah movement. When in spring 2002 the Israeli army reoccupied West Bank towns and villages that were supposed to be under the control of the Palestinian Authority, the United States effectively did not protest. Thus, the peace process between Israel and the PLO, seriously ailing since fall 2000, became an indirect but fatal casualty of the war on terrorism.

The war on terrorism is cause for concern among legal experts in the field of international humanitarian law, especially because states identified as sponsors of terrorism, such as Iraq, become legitimate targets for attack because they are thought to possess weapons of mass destruction that they might provide to terrorist groups. The experts believe that civilians, who have been the primary victims of violent conflicts since the early 1990s, will be the main victims again, and they cite statistics that demonstrate that this has been the case in both Afghanistan and Iraq.

The phenomenon of terrorism has prompted the drafting of several conventions, most notably the Rome Statute, that would make the intentional killing of civilians a war crime, no matter who is responsible (i.e., a government or a nonstate group). The intent is to criminalize violence against civilians so that individuals can be prosecuted. The European Union generally, and its member states such as Belgium specifically, have made the most progress in terms of accepting the idea that violence against civilians, whether undertaken by a state or nonstate organization, is terrorism and needs to be punished. Other states, including major countries such as China, Israel, Russia, and the United States, reject categorically the notion of state terrorism and insist that international laws pertaining to terrorism must limit definitions to nonstate groups that target civilians. Ultimately, one of the most effective ways of reducing terrorism is for states to identify and remove the causes that motivates terrorists, such as the denial of freedom and political participation, repressive political occupation, and poverty and despair.

See also AQSA INTIFADA, AL-; ARAFAT, YASIR; BIN LADIN, OSAMA; BLACK SEPTEMBER; FIDA'IYYUN; HAMAS; HIZBULLAH; HOSTAGE CRISES; ISLAMIC JIHAD; PALESTINE LIBERATION ORGANIZATION (PLO); POPULAR FRONT FOR THE LIBERATION OF PALESTINE; QA'IDA, AL-.

Bibliography

Davis, Joyce M. *Martyrs: Innocence, Vengeance, and Despair in the Middle East.* New York: Palgrave, 2003.

Falk, Richard. "Azmi Bishara, the Right of Resistance, and the Palestinian Ordeal." *Journal of Palestine Studies* 31, no. 2 (Winter 2002): 19–33.

Hirst, David. *The Gun and the Olive Branch: The Roots of Violence in the Middle East,* 3d edition. New York: Thunder Mouth's Press/Nation Books, 2004.

Picco, Giandomenico. *Man without a Gun: One Diplomat's Secret Struggle to Free the Hostages, Fight Terrorism, and End a War.* New York: Times Books/Random House, 1999.

Ron, James. *Frontiers and Ghettos: State Violence in Serbia and Israel.* Berkeley: University of California Press, 2003.

Shlaim, Avi. *The Iron Wall: Israel and the Arab World.* New York: Norton, 2000.

Stern, Jessica. *Terror in the Name of God: Why Religious Militants Kill.* New York: Ecco, 2003.

Victor, Barbara. *Army of Roses: Inside the World of Palestinian Women Suicide Bombers.* Emmaus, PA: Rodale, 2003.

ERIC HOOGLUND

TETUAN

Provincial capital of Morocco's northern Rif region.

Tetuan, with a population of about 466,000 (projection for 2001 based on 1994 census number of 363,813), was founded (1306–1307) by the Maranid sultan to serve as a base for attacks against Ceuta. It was destroyed by Henry III of Castile in 1400, and rebuilt around 1492. Tetuan was occupied by Spain on 6 February 1860, after they had defeated the Anjar tribesmen.

As the first part of Morocco to be occupied by Europeans in two centuries, Tetuan symbolized the threat from Christian Europe. Pressure by Britain and rethinking within Spain's leadership resulted in Spain's agreement to evacuate the city (2 May 1862) in return for a lower indemnity payment. In 1906, Spain was given responsibility for policing the port of Tetuan by a thirteen-nation conference called to maintain the balance of power between European states in Morocco, and to institute economic reforms and an open door policy. Three years later, Spain began its conquest of northern Morocco and built road links to Tetuan. It was made the capital of the Spanish protectorate in 1913, and remained so until Morocco attained independence in 1956 and Spain evacuated the area.

BRUCE MADDY-WEITZMAN

TEVFIK FIKRET

[1867–1915]

Ottoman Turkish poet and editor.

Tevfik Fikret, the son of a bureaucrat in the foreign service, was born Mehmet Tevfik in Istanbul. He studied literature at the prestigious Galatasaray lycée, where his teachers included Muallim Naci and Recaizade Mahmud Ekrem. At the age of fifteen, he published his first poetry in the newspaper *Tercüman-i Hakikat* under the name Nazmi. He entered the civil service but later resigned, drawing public attention when he donated his salary to the refugee commission, saying that it was "a disgrace to accept so much money for so little work." In 1896, he became the editor of *Servet-i Fünun*, the main journal of the new literary movement. At this time, he became known as Tevfik Fikret. Under the influence of the French Parnassian school, his pre-1901 poetry emphasizes art for its own sake, preferring form and technique over content, and poetry over prose. Generally written in the *aruz* meter, Fikret's poetry draws from scenes of everyday life, as in the poems "Hasta çocuk" (The sick child), "Balikçilar" (The fishermen), and "Bir içim su" (A drink of water). In 1899, Fikret became professor of literature at Robert College. Following the Young Turk Revolution in 1908, he joined with Hüseyin Cahit Yalçin in establishing the newspaper *Tanin* (The echo).

Bibliography

Mitler, Louis. *Ottoman Turkish Writers: A Bibliographical Dictionary of Significant Figures in Pre-Republican Turkish Literature.* New York: P. Lang, 1988.

Shaw, Stanford, and Shaw, Ezel Kural. *History of the Ottoman Empire and Modern Turkey,* Vol. 2: *Reform, Revolution, and Republic: The Rise of Modern Turkey, 1808–1975.* Cambridge, U.K., and New York: Cambridge University Press, 1977.

DAVID WALDNER

TEXTILE INDUSTRY

Production of fibers, filaments, and yarns used in making woven or knitted cloth for domestic or foreign trade is widespread in the Middle East.

The oldest textile materials produced and used in the Middle East—linen and wool—go back to remote antiquity. Cotton and silk, which originated in India and China, respectively, came into the region during the Roman Empire, in the early centuries of the Christian era. By the early Middle Ages, quantities of flax (for linen) were exported to Europe, chiefly from Egypt; of raw cotton from Syria and Egypt; of silk thread from Iran, Syria, and the Bursa

region (northwest Turkey); and of mohair from Turkey. Flax and silk fibers and fabrics were traded to Europe for many centuries, but flax was gradually produced in many European nations, and the silks of India, China, and Japan competed with Middle Eastern silks and cottons as well as with cottons from the newly colonized Americas and from India. In the nineteenth century, however, the introduction of long-staple cotton made Egypt an important producer, and in the twentieth century, Egypt was joined by Turkey, Syria, Sudan, and Israel. In the 1990s, the Middle East produced 75 percent of the world output of long-staple cotton but only about 8 percent of the total world output of all cottons.

Although the preeminence of the Middle East in the manufacture of handloomed textiles goes back to antiquity, by the late Middle Ages, European products—woolens, fine silks, and linens—were fine enough to be imported by the Middle East. Until the middle of the eighteenth century, the Middle East continued to export cotton cloth and yarn to Europe, but European protective tariffs soon restricted even that trade. With the Industrial Revolution, European machine-loomed fabrics overwhelmed Middle Eastern handmade products and local markets. The number of Middle Eastern handlooms and

Textiles are the major export for the Turkish economy. Pictured is a Turkish woman weaving a carpet. © JOSÉ F. POBLETE/ CORBIS. REPRODUCED BY PERMISSION.

their total output declined sharply; for example, in Bursa, output of cloth fell from 20,000 pieces in 1843 to 3,000 in 1863. In Aleppo and Damascus combined, the number of looms dropped from about 12,000 in the 1820s to some 2,500 in the 1840s. Middle Eastern weavers were able to recover by using improved looms, importing cheaper and better European yarns, concentrating on inexpensive products, and drastically reducing wages. Handcrafted fabrics continued to form a large proportion of the textile output until after World War II. In Syria, in the 1930s, there were some 40,000 handweavers, and in Egypt in the 1940s, some 50,000. In Turkey and Iran, carpetmaking was greatly stimulated by rising foreign demand, lower freights that reduced export costs, and some foreign capital investments in the industry. Just before World War I, in 1913, Turkey exported 1,500 tons of carpets, then worth three million U.S. dollars, but the subsequent world wars devastated the industry. Persian carpet exports in 1914 were then worth five million U.S. dollars, and by the 1950s Iran's rugweaving and carpetmaking employed some 130,000 people—with exports of 5,000 tons, then worth twenty-five million U.S. dollars, the carpets accounted for 16 percent of Iran's non-oil exports.

Mills

Textile factories, or mills, were first used in the Middle East in the 1830s, in the modernizing program of Muhammad Ali's Egypt. The mills exported large amounts of cotton textiles, but they did not survive his death. A few small factories were also set up in Turkey in the nineteenth century, and by World War I, several textile centers had been developed in Turkey—notably in Adana, İzmir, and in the Salonika region. Egypt also had cotton-spinning mills in Alexandria and Cairo. Iran had a small spinning mill in Tehran, but other unsuccessful mills had closed. In Syria, one small mill, founded in Damascus in the 1860s, was operating, but two others, in Beirut and Antioch, had failed. Some two hundred small silk-reeling factories were set up in Lebanon, with others in Bursa, İzmir, and other silk-growing regions of Turkey. In Iran, there was a mill in Gilan.

After World War I, the textile industry wove rayon as well as cotton and wool and expanded greatly, especially after the tariff reforms. Table 1

Middle East cotton industry in 1939				
	Spindles (thousands)	Power looms (thousands)	Output of yarn (thousands of metric tons)	Output of cloth (million square meters)
Egypt	250	15	24	100
Iran	188	4	—	—
Iraq	—	1	—	—
Lebanon	14	1	1	—
Palestine	12	2	1	4
Syria	10	4	1	—
Turkey	189	6	23	152
Total	**663**	**33**	**50**	**256**

SOURCE: United Nations, *Review of Economic Conditions in the Middle East, 1951-52* (New York, 1953).

TABLE BY GGS INFORMATION SERVICES, THE GALE GROUP.

shows the situation in the cotton industry in 1939, at the outbreak of World War II. By then, textile factories had been built in all the main towns and cities of the Middle East, and local production of cotton yarn and fabrics met 35 to 50 percent of total domestic demand within the larger countries.

During World War II, the region's textile industry expanded by about 50 percent, and the expansion continues—with several additional countries,

Middle East textile output in 1987					
	Cotton		Wool		Silk
	Yarn[2]	Fabrics[3]	Yarn[2]	Fabrics[3]	Fabrics[3]
Egypt	251	694	19	24	5
Iran[1]	88	140	16	26	—
Israel	16	—	4	—	—
Jordan	—	2	—	—	—
Syria	39	180	2	1	—
Turkey	332	399	51	27	1
Total	**726**	**1,415**	**92**	**78**	**6**
World	15,091	47,360	2,223	3,484	2,248

[1]1981
[2]In million metric tons
[3]In million square meters

SOURCE: United Nations. *Industrial Statistical Yearbook* (New York, 1988).

TABLE BY GGS INFORMATION SERVICES, THE GALE GROUP.

with diversification, and with improvement in quality, especially in the finishing processes. Foreign investments have been gradually taken over, and the industry is now owned mainly by the state or local citizens. Turkey, Israel, Egypt, and Lebanon now export significant textile lots to worldwide markets. The second table shows recent figures.

Bibliography

Issawi, Charles. *An Economic History of the Middle East and North Africa.* New York: Columbia University Press, 1982.

CHARLES ISSAWI

THAALBI, ABD AL-AZIZ
[1874–1944]

Tunisian political leader and founder of the Destour party.

Abd al-Aziz Thaalbi's father was a notary whose family had emigrated to Tunis following the French occupation of Algeria in 1830. During his studies at Zaytuna University, Thaalbi became conversant with Salafiyya concepts. For a year following his graduation from Zaytuna in 1895, he published a religious journal called *Sabil al-Rashid* (the Proper Path). When the French authorities suspended the journal, Thaalbi left the country and traveled in Libya, Egypt, and India until 1902. Soon after his return to Tunis, he was imprisoned by a beylical tribunal for making a reformist attack on the local saints, who formed an important part of popular religious practices. In 1904, he published, in both an Arabic and a French edition, *L'esprit libérale du Coran* (The liberal spirit of the Qur'an), which criticized the religious establishment. At this time, Thaalbi established links with the Young Tunisians. He became the editor of the Arabic edition of its newspaper, *Le Tunisien,* in 1909 and participated in all of its political activities until his expulsion from Tunisia in 1912. He returned to the country at the start of World War I.

At the end of the war, Thaalbi joined a delegation of former Young Tunisians that went to Versailles to petition the Allies for a relaxation of French control. Frustrated by France's unwillingness to make concessions, Thaalbi wrote *La Tunisie martyre* (Tunisia martyred) in early 1920. In this book, he stressed the need for restoration of the Tunisian constitution of 1861, the creation of an elected assembly and an independent judiciary, the development of education, and the safeguarding of individual liberties. He also urged that the establishment of the protectorate had stalled Tunisian development. Thaalbi was arrested and brought back to Tunisia. Upon his release in 1921, he assumed the leadership of a group of middle-class merchants, artisans, and lower level *ulama,* many of them formerly affiliated with the Young Tunisians, that had evolved into a political party, the Destour, based on the program elaborated in *La Tunisie martyre.*

In response to Destour demands, France introduced a series of limited reforms in 1922. Thaalbi guided Destour's rejection of these changes, arguing that they fell too far short of Tunisian requirements to merit consideration. The death in 1923 of the Tunisian ruler Nasir Bey, who had sympathized with Destour, and the growing impatience of the protectorate authorities with the party convinced Thaalbi that his political activism would not be tolerated much longer, and he fled the country in the same year.

After fourteen years of exile in Egypt, Iraq, and India, he returned in 1937, when the relative liberalism of the French Popular Front government created a more congenial atmosphere for the expression of nationalist grievances. By that time, however, the remnants of Thaalbi's Destour party had given way to the Neo-Destour, whose youthful, dynamic, and secular leaders had little use for Thaalbi or for the traditional Arab-Islamic values he stressed. Finding support among only a small segment of the population and encountering opposition from Neo-Destour militants who disrupted his public appearances, Thaalbi attempted to revive Destour but failed miserably, though the party survived in moribund form until his death in 1944.

See also SALAFIYYA MOVEMENT.

KENNETH J. PERKINS

THALWEG LINE

See GLOSSARY

THARTHAR PROJECT

Reservoir constructed in eastern Iraq to control flooding and provide irrigation.

The Wadi al-Tharthar is a vast natural depression forty-two miles (68 km) southwest of Samarra and one hundred miles (160 km) north of Baghdad between the Tigris and Euphrates rivers. The Iraqi Development Board, on the recommendation of the International Bank for Reconstruction and Development, created an enormous storage reservoir in the Wadi al-Tharthar depression to drain runoff from the Tigris and thereby protect Baghdad from flooding. Staged construction of the reservoir, the largest earth-moving project of its kind in the Middle East, began in 1952. A regulator built on the Tigris near Samarra diverted excess water into the reservoir, which was also connected by a channel with the Euphrates. By 1972, with a capacity of 110 billion cubic yards (85 billion cu. m) when filled to a height of 200 feet (60 m) above sea level, the water contained in the reservoir could be used to irrigate nearly half a million acres (200,000 ha) of land.

Bibliography

Salter, Lord. *The Development of Iraq: A Plan of Action.* London, 1955.

ALBERTINE JWAIDEH

THARWAT, ABD AL-KHALIQ

[1873–1928]

Egyptian politician.

A graduate of the School of Law in Cairo, Abd al-Khaliq Tharwat was one of the first Egyptian nationalist leaders and a founder of the Liberal Constitutionalist Party. His negotiations with Britain's high commissioner for Egypt, Edmund Allenby, led to the declaration of Egyptian independence from Britain in 1922. Tharwat supported the declaration, even though it guaranteed the maintenance of British influence in Egypt, because he believed that it made possible the drafting of a constitution and the establishment of parliamentary politics. He formed the first government following the declaration and helped to draft the post-independence constitution. Tharwat was opposed by Sultan Fu'ad, who objected to being reduced to a constitutional monarch, and by the Wafd party, which objected to the preservation of British control. Tharwat resigned as prime minister in November 1922. He formed a second ministry in April 1927, but again

confronted opposition from Fu'ad—who had taken the title of king in 1922—and the Wafd. He resigned in February 1928.

See also LIBERAL CONSTITUTIONALIST PARTY.

Bibliography

Sayyid-Marsot, Afaf Lutfi al-. *Egypt's Liberal Experiment, 1922–1936.* Berkeley: University of California Press, 1977.

DAVID WALDNER

THAWRA, AL- (IRAQ)

See NEWSPAPERS AND PRINT MEDIA: ARAB COUNTRIES

THAWRA, AL- (SYRIA)

See NEWSPAPERS AND PRINT MEDIA: ARAB COUNTRIES

THEATER

Overview of the region's numerous traditional and indigenous dramatic art forms and performances.

The Middle East comprises four regions: The Arab world (22 countries), Iran, Turkey, and Israel. This area did not know theater (in the Western sense of a space containing stage and auditorium, and dramas with the three unities of time, space, and plot) in its pre-modern periods. However, the whole region had numerous traditional and indigenous dramatic art forms and performances. Through colonialism and cultural exchanges with Europe in the early nineteenth century, theater as a space and a mode of writing and presenting found its way into the various Middle Eastern cultures. In the modern period, as a form of cultural identity, many Middle Eastern theater artists have tried to honor their traditional art forms and rituals by incorporating aspects of them with their stage events. This endeavor is a prevalent feature, and an ongoing trend, in Middle Eastern theater.

Arab Theater

The ancient Arab literary tradition did not encompass dramatic texts; however, the countries that constitute today's Arab world have always incorporated dramatic and mimetic arts within their performance and literary traditions. Among the various Arab performance arts that thrived throughout the premodern periods are *al-hakawati* (storytellers), dance, ritual reenactments, shadow plays, puppetry, poetry recitations, *maqama* (outdoor dramatic enactments in poetry and prose), street performance by traveling troupes called *al-muhabizun,* and *al-samir* (village gatherings that included dramatizations). Many of these art forms continue, albeit in a state of decline, but others have died away as a result of competing modern entertainment.

In the nineteenth century, contact with the European theatrical tradition through colonialism, educational exchanges, and translations sparked a theatrical movement in the Arab world. In 1848, the Lebanese writer Marun al-Naqqash (d. 1855) mounted in his own home performances of plays based on Molière's dramas as well as adaptations of tales from *A Thousand and One Nights.* This process was continued in Damascus by Abu Khalil al-Qabbani (d. 1902), whose attempts to stage dramatic performances aroused the opposition of the religious establishment. Al-Qabbani moved to Egypt, where artists were able to exercise more freedom.

In Egypt, Ya'qub Sanu (d. 1912), considered by many the father of Egyptian theater, formed a troupe of actors and in 1870 opened the first Egyptian playhouse under the auspices of the khedive. Sanu wrote and directed his own plays and introduced women to the Egyptian stage for the first time. His theater was an immediate success but was closed down by the authorities in 1873 on the grounds that his plays were politically subversive.

By the turn of the century, many theater troupes were presenting musicals, dramatic adaptations, and Arabizations of world drama, but no original plays in Arabic. A number of Egyptian poets wrote verse dramas; among them was the poet laureate of Egypt, Ahmad Shawqi. However, those plays were not stage successes, since their poetic merit exceeded their dramatic construction.

The towering figure of prose drama in Egypt and the Arab world is Tawfiq al-Hakim (1898–1986). His family sent him to France to obtain a doctorate in law. Instead, he spent his time there learning the Western theater tradition. When he returned to Egypt, he took up writing for the stage. His dearest wish was to establish a modern Egyptian dramatic tradition based on Western notions of the unity of space, time, and action. He spent five decades of his life working to enrich the Arab dramatic tradition, and enrich it he did. He wrote more than seventy plays of exceptional variety, experimenting with dramatic form and offering various dramatic styles. He also presented a variety of dramatic themes, some of which he categorized as the theater of ideas, the theater of social themes, and the theater of the absurd.

During the second half of the nineteenth century, many young playwrights emerged, theaters were built, and theater troupes were established around the Arab world. The 1960s is regarded as the golden age of Arabic theater for its impressive theatrical movement, which gave rise to great playwrights, actors, and directors throughout the region, including Nu'man Ashur, Yusuf Idris, Alfred Farag, Mikha'il Ruman, and Najib Surur in Egypt; Sa'dallah Wannus, Walid Ikhlassi, and Yusuf al-Ani in Syria and Iraq; Isam Mahfuz and Roger Assaf in Lebanon; and Izz al-Din al-Madani, Ahmad al-Ilj, and al-Tayyib al-Siddiqi in the Maghrib.

In Palestine, under the watchful eye of the Israeli armed forces, theater troupes like the Balalin and Hakawati have produced highly experimental dramas that comment on the plight of their fellow countrymen. Alongside the male dramatists, directors, and critics, a large number of Arab women have contributed to the modern Arab stage, including playwrights Fathiyya al-Assal, Nehad Gad, Andre Chided, and Nawal al-Saadawi; director Nidal al-Ashqar; and critic Nehad Selaiha.

Israeli Theater

The Israeli theater is essentially modern; whereas pre-1960s theater was heavily influenced by Russian social realism, in the 1960s it diverged and presented experimental drama. Until the early 1970s, most of the theatrical repertoire in Israel continued to be European classics and modern plays. However, in the 1970s and 1980s, playwrights focused more on the contemporary Israeli's predicament and identity. From the 1980s onward a shift became noticeable in the Hebrew stage, from a commitment to the ideology of the Jewish national

The courtyard and entrance to the Jerusalem Center for the Performing Arts in Jerusalem, Israel. © Dave G. Houser/Corbis. Reproduced by permission.

movement to debates over secularization and cultural identity.

After the 1948 war, two Israeli playwrights rose to prominence in the newly established state. In 1949, Moshe Shamir wrote *Hu Halah Basdot* (He walked in the fields), and Yigal Mossinsohn produced *Be'arvot Hanegev* (In the plains of the Negev). The first is a stage adaptation of a novel—a prevalent practice in late 1940s and 1950s Israel due to the limited number of playwrights. The second is a war story that tries to uphold the ideals of the new Israeli society; its success was based more on audience reaction then than on artistic excellence.

In the 1950s, Israeli theater focused on realism and produced plays concerned with the social realities of Israel after the 1948 war. One of the major themes that preoccupied dramatists was the realities of coexistence between early and new immigrants, and between Palestinians and Israelis. Some of the

playwrights who tackled these issues were Ephraim Kishon, Yigal Mossinsohn, and Hanoch Bar-Tov.

In the 1960s, Israeli theater departed from realism and created a non-mimetic experimental theater, opening itself to the influence of modern European drama as well as to new themes, forms, and theatrical devices. Using techniques from the Theater of the Absurd, Israeli playwrights set out to depict the grotesque and absurd in their society. Without reference to particulars, their criticism was conveyed through abstractions, symbolism, and distancing techniques. Among the most talented playwrights of that decade are Nessim Aloni (b. 1921), Ben-Zion Tomer (b. 1928), Yosef Bar-Yosef (b. 1933), and A. B. Yehoshua (b. 1936). Their efforts propelled Israeli theater away from a provincial outlook to universal themes.

In the 1970s, Israeli theater became self-reflective and began expressing doubts about the means of realizing the Zionist dream. For some, those were introspective years of self-reevaluation. Two new stars became the focus of the Israeli stage: Yehoshua Sobol (b. 1939) and Hanoch Levin (b. 1943). Sobol's writing style is naturalistic. Some of his earlier works are semifictitious and based on documentary material. Levin, on the other hand, is famous for his biting satire and tendency to break taboos. He continues to be one of the most provocative and controversial figures in Israeli theater.

The following decades show a variety of dramatic themes and approaches, from social and political disillusionment, as many Israelis call for an alternative to war, to fears about the demise of the Zionist dream. Common themes include nationhood, selfhood, and secularization. In addition, many theaters continue to present world classics and modern comedies. At the top of the list of thriving theater companies in Israel are the Habima (also ha-Bima), the Cameri, and the Haifa Municipal Theaters.

Persian Theater

Persian theater can be divided into three categories: traditional, which comprises ritual reenactments, puppetry, and improvised street theater; modern, which is primarily modeled on Western paradigms; and diasporic, which laments the separation from the homeland after the 1979 revolution.

The most famous traditional Persian theater is Ta'ziyeh, which encompasses cycles of passion plays intended not for entertainment but rather to console the devout Shi'ite population by reenacting the events that led to the martyrdom of their beloved imam (spiritual leader) Husayn, grandson of the Prophet. The house of Husayn in its entirety was decimated in the city of Karbala, in Iraq, by Mu'awiyah, the governor of Syria, who the Shi'a believe usurped the throne from Ali, Husayn's father, closest cousin and confidant of the Prophet. The suffering and death of this holy family is the central theme of elaborate mourning rites, in Iran and wherever there is a considerable Shi'ite population. Those rites take place on the tenth day of Muharram, the first month of the Islamic calendar.

Two categories of Ta'ziyeh plays deal with the tragic events of Karbala, and others refer to those events indirectly. However, those dealing with the martyrdom of Husayn and his family are the most popular and moving. Ta'ziyeh is written in verse by anonymous writers and its stagecraft is extremely simple, with virtually no scenery. Settings are indicated symbolically, and men play the women's roles. The most important component of these plays is the music: Players chant and sing, and musical instruments are used to heighten the mood. Although professional Ta'ziyeh players exist, the plays are frequently presented by amateurs as an act of piety.

By the turn of the twentieth century, and as a result of Western impact, Ta'ziyeh went into a decline. Today, there is a great deal of interest in the performance and study of Ta'ziyeh, both inside and outside of Iran.

During the early nineteenth century, Western drama found its way into Persian culture in the form of translations of European and Turkish plays. This was followed by a period of Persian dramatic and satirical composition that took reform as its main subject matter. During the first half of the twentieth century, a number of didactic dramas upholding the modernizing and educational efforts of Reza Shah Pahlavi were on the rise. Among the most popular playwrights of this period are Sayyed Ali Nasr (1893–1965), who founded and headed the Komedi-e Iran in 1918, and Sadegh Hedayat (1903–1951).

The second half of the twentieth century was characterized by severe censorship, which led playwrights to find refuge in symbolism, Theater of the Absurd, and psychological themes. Gifted playwrights emerged during this period and produced exciting works. Among them are Ali Nasirian, Gholamhossein Sa'edi (working under the pseudonym Gowhar Morad), and Bahram Beyzai.

After the 1979 revolution, a number of artists, disillusioned by the new regime, left the country with no intention of returning. Living in exile, they write dramas that are inherently Iranian and intensely nostalgic for the homeland. Among those is Parviz Sayyad, who continues to produce plays that have been categorized as theater of diaspora.

Turkish Theater

The first Western-style Turkish play performed in Istanbul was *Vatan yahut Silistre* (Fatherland), by Namik Kemal, in 1873. From that date onward theater in

Turkey following the Western paradigm was a vital element in the country's cultural life.

Turkey has been home to a wide array of popular performance arts and entertainments since the thirteenth century, including dances, peasant plays, pageants, rites, processions, mock fights, festival acts, acrobatics, mime, puppetry, marionette performances, clowning, juggling, and magic. The most dramatic and popular of all are the *meddahs* (who are panegyrists, storytellers, and comedians), *karagoz* (shadow plays), and *ortaoyunus* (improvised plays). *Meddahs* were solo performers who told traditional tales of heroism and religious narratives. *Karagoz,* have the longest history and continued to be practiced until the 1940s. They are being resurrected in many contemporary plays. They were essentially a one-man act. The presenter manipulated flat leather figures behind a linen screen and played all characters. *Ortaoyunu,* the indigenous Turkish theater-in-the-round, is the most mimetic premodern performance art form. It borrowed many of its basic plots and characters from the *karagoz,* and the actors performed in the middle of a circle of spectators. The characters were presented as stereotypes, depending on wordplay and comic situations. All three ancient art forms had declined severely by the early twentieth century due to competition from Western-style theater and cinema.

The second half of the nineteenth century introduced Western theater into Turkey. A number of local theater troupes were created, mainly by Armenians, and they presented European plays in both their original languages and in translation. The first Turkish play published was *Shair Evlenmesi* (The poet's marriage, in 1860), by Ibrahim Shinasi, and the first produced on stage was *Fatherland*. In spite of the quick strides that playwrights made by the late nineteenth century, severe censorship by the sultan slowed the progress of Turkish drama. However, theater was given new vigor in 1908 by an era of political freedom under a constitutional government. Until 1923, Turkish theater featured a variety of new naturalistic and satirical plays reflecting social problems and expressing a need for political reform. One of the most celebrated playwrights of that period was Abdulhak Hamit (1852–1937), who produced verse and history plays. In 1916, the government-subsidized City Theater in Istanbul was established; it remained a vital core of Turkey's theatrical scene until the 1950s.

With the founding of the Turkish Republic under Mustafa Kemal Atatürk, theater received greater government support and funding. Mushin Ertuğrul, artistic director of the City Theater, shaped the modern theater movement in Turkey by creating a children's theater, encouraging young playwrights, and establishing a network of regional theaters. In 1936 the State Conservatory for Music and Drama was inaugurated, and in the 1940s the State Opera. Since the 1960s Turkey has established twenty-six state theaters in sixteen provinces, and state theaters are continually opening in Istanbul. In the 1950s and 1960s a number of private theaters were established in both Istanbul and Ankara.

In the 1960s, a number of excellent playwrights contributed to the Turkish stage, including Turan Oflazoglu, Necati Cumali, Gunger Dilmen, and Haldun Taner. In the 1970s and 1980s, the varying strengths and weaknesses of the Turkish theatrical scene reflected the political and economic situation. During the following two decades Turkish theater witnessed a rising number of experimental plays by a younger generation wishing to explore new ground and possibilities.

See also HAKIM, TAWFIQ AL-; HEDAYAT, SADEGH; IDRIS, YUSUF; IKHLASSI, WALID; SAADAWI, NAWAL AL-; SAʿEDI, GHOLAMHOSSEIN; SANU, YAʿQUB; SHAMIR, MOSHE; SHAWQI, AHMAD; SOBOL, YEHOSHUA; TANER, HALDUN.

Bibliography

Allen, Roger. *An Introduction to Arabic Literature.* Cambridge, U.K.: Cambridge University Press, 2000.

And, Metin. *A History of Theatre and Popular Entertainment in Turkey.* Ankara: Forum Yayinlan, 1963.

And, Metin. *Karagoz: Turkish Shadow Theatre.* Ankara: Dost Yayinlari, 1975.

Badawi, Muhammad Mustafa. *Early Arabic Drama.* Cambridge, U.K.: Cambridge University Press, 1988.

Badawi, Muhammad Mustafa. *Modern Arabic Drama in Egypt.* Cambridge, U.K.: Cambridge University Press, 1987.

Ben-Zvi, Linda, ed. *Theater in Israel.* Ann Arbor: University of Michigan Press, 1996.

Chelkowsky, Peter, ed. *Ta'ziyeh, Ritual and Drama in Iran.* New York: New York University Press, 1979.

Gouryh, Admer. "Recent Trends in Syrian Drama." *World Literature Today* 60, No. 2 (spring 1986): 216–221.

Halman, Talat Sait, ed. *Modern Turkish Drama: An Anthology of Plays in Translation.* Minneapolis, MN: Bibliotheca Islamica, 1976.

Jaffery, Yunus, ed. *History of Persian Literature.* Delhi: Triveni, 1981.

Khozai, Mohamed A. al-. *The Development of Early Arabic Drama, 1847–1900.* London: Longman, 1984.

Offer, Rita. *Literature in Pre-Revolutionary Iran: Golshiri's Prose Fiction,* 1983.

Ricks, Thomas, ed. *Critical Perspectives on Modern Persian Literature.* Washington, DC: Three Continents, 1984.

Sayyad, Parviz. *Theater of Diaspora: Two Plays, The Ass and The Rex Cinema Trial,* edited by Hamid Dabashi. Costa Mesa, CA: Mazda, 1992.

Urian, Dan. *The Arab in Israeli Drama and Theater,* translated by Naomi Paz. Amsterdam: Harwood, 1997.

Urian, Dan. *The Judaic Nature of Israeli Theatre: A Search for Identity,* translated by Naomi Paz. Amsterdam: Harwood, 2000.

DINA AMIN

THEATER, ARAB

See THEATER

THEATER, ISRAELI

See THEATER

TIBERIAS

Town located on the eastern shore of Lake Tiberias (also referred to as the Sea of Galilee or Kinneret) in northern Israel.

The town of Tiberias was founded by Herod Antipas (c. 20 C.E.) and named for the Roman emperor Tiberius. It was an important center of Jewish learning, law, and religion from the second through fifth centuries. Over the course of its history, Tiberias was controlled by Arabs, Crusaders, and Ottoman Turks. Early Zionist pioneers set up kibbutzim in this area around the turn of the twentieth century. The city's population quadrupled after the establishment of the state of Israel in 1948. In the 1948 Arab-Israel War, fighting broke out with an Arab attack on Jews in the older sections of the town. Jewish fighters were able to push out their Arab adversaries, and eventually the Arab inhabitants fled.

Tiberias, which has a relatively warm climate in winter, is a favorite tourist site, featuring boating, lakefront hotels, and a hot springs spa. Its 2004 population was about 43,000, the majority of them immigrants from North African and Eastern European countries.

BRYAN DAVES

TIGRIS AND EUPHRATES RIVERS

River systems that join to drain into the Persian Gulf.

The Tigris (Arabic, *Shatt Dijla*; Turkish, *Dicle*) rises in a lake in the mountains north of Diyarbakir, in southeastern Turkey. It picks up major tributaries, the Zab rivers, downstream from Mosul, then the Diyala, just past Baghdad—flowing some 1,180 miles (1,900 km). It ends at the confluence of the Euphrates, in southeast Iraq, to form the Shatt al-Arab, which empties into the Gulf. With its short tributaries flowing directly from the mountains, it floods in April, about one month before the Euphrates, and with about 50 percent greater flow.

The Euphrates (Arabic, *Furat*; Turkish, *Firat*) also originates in Turkey, from a spring in the Taurus mountains. It flows for 1,740 miles (2,800 km), passing through northern Syria and providing that country with an important water source. In 1973, Syria completed construction of the large Euphrates Dam. From Syria, the Euphrates flows into Iraq, where it joins the Tigris.

Since the Sumerian era (3500 B.C.E.), canals have connected tributaries to the Tigris-Euphrates confluence area, although the lower course was farther west at that time. The capitals of great empires—Ashur, Nineveh, Seleucia, Ctesiphon, and Baghdad—were built on or near its banks. In 1990, Turkey completed the Atatürk Dam, the first of twenty-two dams, as well as a series of hydroelectric power stations, planned for the Tigris and Euphrates. Turkey's huge diversion of water may pose serious problems for countries such as Syria and Iraq. Most of Iraq's future irrigation schemes rely on Tigris water.

Bibliography

Shapland, Greg. *Rivers of Discord: International Water Disputes in the Middle East.* New York: St. Martin's, 1997.

JOHN R. CLARK

TIKRIT

Iraqi city on the Tigris River northwest of Baghdad, on the main road to Mosul.

Tikrit (also Takrit) is located in north-central Iraq, some 100 miles north-northwest of Baghdad. The fortress around which the city was built was constructed by a Sassanid Persian king as a border post against the Byzantines. The first dwellers of the city belonged to the Banu Iyad tribe of Christian Arabs, and its name is believed to have honored the tribal chief's daughter. It was conquered by Muslims in the mid-600s C.E. Tikrit's population is now mainly Sunni Arab, with some Kurds. The Kurdish Muslim hero Salah al-Din al-Ayyubi (Saladin, 1137–1193) was born in Tikrit.

With the decline in sales of *kalaks* (rafts of inflated skins), for which the city was noted, many people moved to Baghdad during the nineteenth century. Under the monarchy, some entered the military academy with the help of an influential Tikriti. After the 1968 coup by the Ba'th party, Tikritis became the single most powerful group in Iraq's senior officer corps and in the civilian flank of the party. Both Ahmad Hasan al-Bakr and Saddam Hussein were from Tikrit, so they invested large sums in modernizing the city. In 2003, its population numbered about 30,000.

See also BAKR, AHMAD HASAN AL-; BA'TH, AL-; HUSSEIN, SADDAM.

Bibliography

Batatu, Hanna. *The Old Social Classes and the Revolutionary Movements of Iraq: A Study of Iraq's Old Landed and Commercial Classes and of Its Communists, Ba'thists, and Free Officers.* Princeton, NJ: Princeton University Press, 1978.

AMATZIA BARAM
UPDATED BY MICHAEL R. FISCHBACH

TIKRITI FAMILIES

Iraqi families from Tikrit.

The Tikriti trace their origins to the city of Tikrit in Iraq. Tikrit is located on the Tigris River halfway between Baghdad and Mosul, and has a rich history that goes back to the Assyrian empire. The famous Muslim leader Saladin, who defeated the Crusaders, was born in Tikrit. In recent history, Tikrit was a small, sleepy town with a few thousand inhabitants.

The military coup of 1963 temporarily brought to power a few people who were born in Tikrit. Hasan al-Bakr, who became prime minister, and Hardan al-Tikriti, who became a defense minister, were born in Tikrit. The coup of 1968 brought to power more people from Tikrit, who controlled and shaped Iraqi politics from 1968 until the U.S. invasion of Iraq in March 2003.

The most prominent one was Saddam Hussein, who dominated Iraqi politics after 1968, and was born on 28 April 1937 in the small village of al-Awja, a village that belongs to the city of Tikrit. Like many other Tikritis, he belonged to the Al Abu Nasir tribe. He was vice president of Iraq until 1979, when he became president. He was removed from office when the United States invaded Iraq in 2003.

Hussein relied heavily on his immediate family, close relatives, and members of his tribe to govern the country, putting them into top positions in the bureaucracy, the armed forces, the police forces, and the local governments. In most cases, they were chosen mainly for their loyalty rather than for their skills and qualifications. During the Hussein regime, Tikrit was transformed into a large modern city with a university, modern facilities, and services. It also became the capital of the newly established province of Salah al-Din in the early 1980s.

See also BAKR, AHMAD HASAN AL-; HUSSEIN, SADDAM; TIKRIT; TIKRITI, HARDAN AL-.

Bibliography

Marr, Phebe. *The Modern History of Iraq,* 2d edition. Boulder, CO: Westview Press, 1985.

Tripp, Charles. *A History of Iraq.* Cambridge, U.K.: Cambridge University Press, 2000.

AYAD AL-QAZZAZ

TIKRITI, HARDAN AL-
[1925–1971]

Iraqi military officer and official of the Ba'th party.

Born in Tikrit to the family of a Sunni Arab police officer, Hardan al-Tikriti graduated from both flight and staff academies. He also joined the Ba'th party in 1961. After the Ramadan Revolution, from February to November 1963, he commanded the Iraqi air force. After the second Ba'thist coup of July 1968, he served as deputy commander in chief of the armed forces, deputy prime minister, minister of defense, and member of the Revolutionary Command Council. In 1970, after a power struggle with his two distant relatives, Ahmad Hasan al-Bakr and Saddam Hussein, he was dismissed from his posts and promoted to the ceremonial position of vice president. He was then formally dismissed and exiled. He was assassinated in Kuwait in 1971 by Hussein's agents.

See also BAKR, AHMAD HASAN AL-; BA'TH, AL-; HUSSEIN, SADDAM.

Bibliography

Batatu, Hanna. *The Old Social Classes and the Revolutionary Movements of Iraq: A Study of Iraq's Old Landed and Commercial Classes and of its Communists, Ba'thists, and Free Officers.* Princeton, NJ: Princeton University Press, 1978.

AMATZIA BARAM
UPDATED BY MICHAEL R. FISCHBACH

TIMAR

Land rights earned in exchange for service to the Ottoman state.

The *timar* system began under Murad I (1359–1389), who granted land rights as payment to his military officers. In the fifteenth and sixteenth centuries timars became the primary means of financing the Ottoman military. The typical timar holder was a provincial cavalry officer who contributed troops and supplies when called up for battle. He financed these through his timar, a state grant of nonhereditary rights over land, usually in the village where he lived. The officer kept a set amount of the tax revenue as his salary and delivered the remainder to the central state.

With economic and technological change in the late sixteenth and seventeenth centuries, tax farms gradually supplanted timars. The state confiscated timars from officers who died or could no longer afford to send troops, and reassigned them to no-

tables who would contract to collect taxes in exchange for monetary compensation. Although they contributed less and less to imperial tax revenues, timars continued to exist on a small scale through the nineteenth century.

Bibliography

Karpat, Kemal H. "The Land Regime, Social Structure, and Modernization in the Ottoman Empire." In *The Beginnings of Modernization in the Middle East: The Nineteenth Century,* edited by William R. Polk and Richard L. Chambers. Chicago: University of Chicago Press, 1968.

Keyder, Çağlar, and Tabak, Faruk, eds. *Landholding and Commercial Agriculture in the Middle East.* Albany: State University of New York Press, 1991.

ELIZABETH THOMPSON
UPDATED BY ERIC HOOGLUND

TINDOUF

A strategically important Saharan town in western Algeria, situated near large mineral deposits.

Tindouf is close to Algeria's borders with Mauritania, Morocco, and Western Sahara. It was an administrative outpost built largely by the French colonial government and became a political and economic hub in the years after Algeria gained independence from France in 1962. Rich deposits of phosphates and iron ore dominate the region, particularly at Gara Djebilet, 93 miles (150 km) to the southeast. Tindouf became the capital of the Western Saharan government-in-exile after Morocco's invasion of what was then the Spanish Sahara in 1975 and 1976. Both Algeria and Libya assisted POLISARIO (Frente Popular para la Liberación de Saguia el Hamra y Río de Oro) in its bid for an independent state, which froze relations between Algeria and Morocco throughout the 1980s and 1990s. Since then, oil and natural gas deposits discovered nearby have increased Tindouf's importance in regional politics and economic development. The Algerian government signed exploratory agreements with major European energy companies in the early 2000s for the Tindouf basin, and Morocco signed similar agreements with American energy companies for Western Sahara. This heightened competition over natural resources threatened what had been improving relations between Algeria and Morocco as well as the fragile cease-fire agreement between Morocco and POLISARIO.

The 1998 Algerian census estimated Tindouf's population at 27,000. However, this figure does not include the nearby refugee camps, which are estimated to house 180,000 Reguibat refugees from Western Sahara.

See also ALGERIA: OVERVIEW; ARAB MAGHREB UNION; POLISARIO; WESTERN SAHARA; WESTERN SAHARA WAR.

Bibliography

Hodges, Tony. *Western Sahara: The Roots of a Desert War.* Westport, CT: L. Hill, 1983.

DAVID GUTELIUS

TIRAN, STRAIT OF

A strategic strait connecting the Gulf of Aqaba and the Red Sea.

The Strait of Tiran is barely 2.5 miles wide at one point; it provides narrow passage for ships traveling from the Red Sea to the Jordanian port of Aqaba and the Israeli port of Elat. Near the coast of the Sinai Peninsula at the mouth of the strait are several islands, including Tiran and Sanafir, that Saudi Arabia permitted Egypt to claim in 1949. Egypt subsequently asserted that its territorial waters extended across the strait, and closed the passage to ships bound for Elat on two occasions as part of its political and military conflict with Israel. The first instance, in the early 1950s, was one of the reasons for Israel's attack on the Sinai in 1956. The second blockade was established in May 1967 and precipitated the 1967 War. Israel occupied the islands and reopened the straits to its ships after the war. As a result of the peace treaty between Egypt and Israel in 1979, the Strait of Tiran was recognized as an international waterway. Israel relinquished the islands to Egypt in 1982 as part of its withdrawal from the territories it had occupied in the Sinai in 1967.

See also SUEZ CRISIS (1956–1957).

Bibliography

Drysdale, Alasdair, and Blake, Gerald H. *The Middle East and North Africa: A Political Geography.* New York: Oxford University Press, 1985.

ANTHONY B. TOTH

TISHRIN

See GLOSSARY

TIWIZI

See GLOSSARY

TLAS, MUSTAFA

[1932–]

Syrian military officer and politician.

Born in al-Rastan, near Homs, Mustafa Abd al-Qadir Tlas attended Syria's military academy in Homs (1952–1954). Commissioned in the tank corps, he served in Egypt (1959–1961) during the period of the United Arab Republic.

Tlas joined the Ba'th Party in 1947. The Ba'thist military committee that overthrew Syria's government in 1963 brought him into its ranks after the coup. Tlas was granted important positions through which he proved his loyalty to the party and the military committee. He was elected to the Regional Council of the Ba'th Party in 1965 and headed courts trying persons accused of plotting against the regime, including the regime established following the 1964 anti-Ba'thist violence in Hama. As commander of the garrison at Homs in 1965, Tlas was associated with the "radical" faction of the Ba'th during the period of growing intra-Ba'thist friction. Removed from his post in December 1965 after trying to dismiss officers loyal to President Amin al-Hafiz, Tlas returned to the military after Salah Jadid's "radical Ba'th" coup in 1966.

Tlas's most important contribution in Syrian history, however, lies in his long-standing and loyal association with the powerful Ba'thist figure Hafiz al-Asad. Tlas and Asad studied together in the military academy and came from similar backgrounds. Although Tlas was a Sunni Muslim and Asad an Alawi, both were of humble village origins and both supported the secular, pan-Arab socialist ideology of the Ba'th. As Asad's confidant, Tlas quickly rose to high positions in the military and the regime. While defense minister, Asad appointed Tlas chief of staff and deputy defense minister (1968). When Ba'thist rivals tried to depose the two in 1970, Asad seized power, and he appointed Tlas defense minister in 1972. Tlas has been Syria's defense minister since then, overseeing tremendous growth in the size and technological sophistication of the nation's military through Soviet assistance in the 1970s and 1980s. In 1972, he attended staff training at Voroshilov Academy in Moscow. Elected to the Baʿth central committee in 1980, he remained a key member of the Asad regime until Asad's death in 2000, after which he continued as defense minister under Syria's new president, Asad's son Bashshar.

Tlas is known as an outspoken hard-liner in Syria's frosty relationship with the Palestine Liberation Organization (PLO) and its chairman, Yasir Arafat, since the mid-1970s. Tlas and Syria's military had assisted guerrillas from Arafat's al-Fatah movement in the 1960s and during the PLO's conflict with Jordan in 1970, but he became increasingly hostile to Arafat after Syria intervened against the PLO in Lebanon's civil war in 1976 and the bitter Syria–PLO relations that followed.

Tlas runs a publishing house, Dar al-Tlas, in Damascus, and has written numerous books on military science, literature, and other topics.

See also ALAWI; ARAFAT, YASIR; ASAD, BASHSHAR AL-; ASAD, HAFIZ AL-; BAʿTH, AL-; FATAH, AL-; HAFIZ, AMIN AL-; HAMA; HOMS; JADID, SALAH; PALESTINE LIBERATION ORGANIZATION (PLO); SUNNI ISLAM; UNITED ARAB REPUBLIC (UAR).

Bibliography

Batatu, Hanna. *Syria's Peasantry, the Descendants of Its Rural Notables, and Their Politics.* Princeton, NJ: Princeton University Press, 1999.

Seale, Patrick. *Asad: The Struggle for the Middle East.* Berkeley: University of California Press, 1988.

MICHAEL R. FISCHBACH

TLATLI, MOUFIDA
[1947–]

Tunisian film director, editor, and screenwriter.

Moufida Tlatli was born in 1947 in picturesque Sidi Bou Said, Tunisia. Following her graduation from the Institut des Hautes Etudes Cinématographiques (IDHEC) in Paris, Tlatli worked as a writer and production manager for the Office de la Radiodiffusion-Télévision Française (ORTF) from 1968 to 1972. Returning to Tunisia, Tlatli edited and wrote screen-

plays for a number of important Arab films, such as Allouache's *Omar Gatlato,* Ben Ammar's *Aziza,* Louhichi's *L'ombre de la terre,* and Boughedir's *Halfaouine.* Tlatli's own award-winning first film, *Les Silences du palais* (Samt al Qusur, 1994), which takes place on the eve of independence from the French in the 1950s, traces the systemic and internalized oppression suffered by generations of servant women working in the kitchens of the Bey's relatives. Like *Silences,* Tlatli's second film, *La saison des hommes* (2000), set on the island of Djerba, focuses on mothers and daughters confronting patriarchal traditions, now exacerbated by economic pressures that have made their husbands internal migrants who come home one month a year. Tlatli's rich, sensuous imagery, slow rhythms, and retrospective narrative structures translate unspoken feelings of isolation and desire into the body language of women who long to emancipate themselves—not from Tunisian men or Arab culture, but from the everyday practices and social systems, both local and global, that entrap them.

See also FILM; GENDER: GENDER AND EDUCATION.

LAURA RICE

TLEMCEN

City near the Moroccan border in eastern Algeria.

Situated on a high ridge of the Little Atlas mountains thirty miles (50 km) inland from the Mediterranean Sea, Tlemcen has a population of 155,000 (1998). The Almoravids founded Tlemcen in the eleventh century, on an ancient Berber, Phoenician, and Roman site. It was an important trade and political center in the Middle Ages, as capital of the Arab sultanate, and was Abd al-Qadir's capital from 1837 to 1842, when it came under French colonial rule. Tlemcen had received many of the Moors expelled from Spain after 1492. The city came under the Ottoman Empire in 1555 and was attached to Algeria in 1942.

LAURENCE MICHALAK

TLILI, MUSTAFA
[1937–]

Tunisian novelist.

Mustafa Tlili was born in Fériana, Tunisia. He attended the *madrasa* (traditional school) in his native city and later received a bilingual education at the Sorbonne, where he received a *diplôme d'études supérieurs de philosophie*. He also studied at the UN Institute for Training and Research and worked for almost thirteen years at the UN offices in New York. He moved to France in 1980, and he was made a Knight of the French Order of Arts and Letters.

Tlili has published four novels, all written in French. Each reflects in its own way the writer's preoccupation with life's meaning. He is determined to denounce corruption, especially among the aristocracy, whether in the Arabian Peninsula, as revealed in *Gloire des sables* (1982; Glory of the sands); in Paris, as described in *La rage aux tripes* (1975; Visceral anger); or in New York, as in *Le bruit dort* (1978; The noise sleeps). Tlili's fourth and last novel, *La montagne du lion* (1988; Lion mountain), centers on corruption in Tunisia. Tlili's language reflects a playful anger and humorous cynicism toward the upper classes of society.

In spite of Tlili's global outlook, he remains strongly linked to the Maghrib. His multilingual and multicultural background enhances his novels and reflects a new trend among Maghribi writers who write in French: Instead of being confined to two cultures—Arabic and French—as their predecessors were, they are expanding their horizons. With Tlili it is possible to speak of the beginning of the cultural liberation of the French-educated Maghribi writers.

See also LITERATURE: ARABIC, NORTH AFRICAN.

Bibliography

Jack, Belinda. *Francophone Literatures. An Introductory Survey.* New York: Oxford University Press, 1996.

Mortimer, Mildred, ed. *Maghrebian Mosaic.* Boulder, CO, and London: Lynne Rienner Publishers, 2001.

AIDA A. BAMIA

TOBACCO REVOLT

A popular rebellion (1891–1892) in Iran that defeated a tobacco monopoly granted to British interests.

One of the most controversial concessions that Iran's Qajar monarchy granted to foreign nationals in exchange for monetary compensation was a complete monopoly on the production, domestic sales, and export of tobacco. This was granted to Major G. F. Talbot of Britain and was registered in March 1890 as the Imperial Tobacco Corporation of Persia. Talbot agreed to pay 25,000 pounds immediately for the concession and to provide an annual payment of 15,000 pounds to the Imperial Treasury. This payment was to be accompanied by a 25 percent share of the net profits after deduction of a 5 percent shareholder's dividend. The arrangement was to be maintained for a period of fifty years.

Beginning in the spring of 1891 the implications of the monopoly became apparent to merchants and the Iranian population at large, the majority of whom consumed some form of tobacco on a daily basis, arousing nationalistic fervor. The void in leadership prompted the politicization of the intellectuals and the clergy. As the events of 1891 unfolded, the *ulama* (the clergy) successfully mobilized crowds against the government and its foreign policies. Under the leading *ulama,* protests began in Shiraz and Tabriz, principal market centers for domestic tobacco production, and then spread throughout the rest of the country. In Isfahan two leading *ulama,* Aqa Najafi and his brother Shaykh Muhammad Ali, pronounced the use of tobacco unclean as their followers took to the streets and broke all visible water pipes in the bazaars. In December the most prominent *mujtahid* (expert on Shiᶜite Islamic law), Mirza Muhammad Hasan Shirazi, who resided in Ottoman Iraq, issued a *fatwa* (legal opinion) forbidding all forms of smoking until the tobacco concession was abolished. Shops throughout the bazaars closed and smoking was completely abandoned, even in the shah's own palace.

The value of the shares paid to the Imperial Bank was reduced by 50 percent. On Christmas Day, placards were hung throughout the Isfahan bazaar threatening a jihad against Europeans. Three days later, the shah announced the conditional withdrawal of the tobacco concession and requested that the population resume smoking. The suspicious crowds awaited word from Shirazi that the *fatwa* had been rescinded, but it did not arrive. The agitated shah, Naser al-Din, sent a personal letter to Tehran's leading *mujtahid,* Mirza Hasan Ashtiani, demanding that he immediately resume smoking or leave the country. As the news of the shah's message spread through the capital, the enraged crowds occupied the streets surrounding the shah's palace.

Fearing for the safety of the shah, the government's troops opened fire on the rioters, killing seven people, including the *sayyid* who originally had led the crowds. With the help of the merchants, Ashtiani and other *ulama* sent a strong message to Naser al-Din Shah and his prime minister, Amin al-Soltan. Realizing the severity of the situation, the shah in January 1892 abolished the concession completely, agreed to pay compensation to the families of those killed, and pardoned all leaders of the revolt. Shirazi telegraphed a few days later to say that Muslims could resume smoking.

See also SHIRAZI, MIRZA HASAN.

Bibliography

Browne, Edward G. *The Persian Revolution of 1905–1909.* Cambridge, U.K.: Cambridge University Press, 1910.

Keddie, Nikki. *Religion and Rebellion in Iran: The Tobacco Protest of 1891–1892.* London: Frank Cass, 1966.

Keddie, Nikki. *Sayyid Jamal ad-Din al-Afghani.* Berkeley: University of California Press, 1972.

Lambton, Ann K. S. "The Tobacco Regie: Prelude to Revolution." *Studia Islamica* 23 (1965): 71–90; 119–157.

ROSHANAK MALEK
UPDATED BY ERIC HOOGLUND

TOBRUK

Small Libyan seaport west of the Egyptian border; scene of fierce fighting during World War II.

Tobruk had been occupied by General Erwin Rommel's Afrika Korps but fell to British forces under General Archibald Wavell on 22 January 1941 during World War II. In April 1941, Rommel's counteroffensive left Tobruk under siege until December, when it was retaken by the British. Rommel's drive into Egypt in May 1942 led to the surrender of 25,000 troops at Tobruk on 21 June, after a one-day assault. Tobruk remained in German hands until liberated by General Bernard Law Montgomery's Eighth Army, after Britain's successful conclusion to the battle of al-Alamayn in November 1942.

In the 1960s, port facilities in the town were expanded to provide links to nearby oil fields. The population of Tobruk in 2004 was estimated at 157,800.

Bibliography

Pitt, Barrie. *The Crucible of War.* London: Cassell, 2001.

DANIEL E. SPECTOR

TOMAN

See GLOSSARY

TOPKAPI PALACE

Governmental seat of the Ottoman Empire.

The New Palace (Saray-Cedid), now known as the Topkapi Palace (in reference to the eighteenth-century royal summer residence next to the seaside Cannon Gate), occupied the site of Byzantium's ancient acropolis in what was then the city of Constantinople (now Istanbul). Enclosed by protective walls, the Topkapi Palace stood in the middle of a vast woodland. It served for nearly four centuries as the principal center of governance for the entire Ottoman Empire.

The administrative functions of the government were located in the outer (*birun*) court of the fortress-palace, and the inner (*enderun*) court included space for the royal pavilions and the palace school. The quarters for the sultan's pages surrounded the inner court; the harem quarters were behind its northern wall, overlooking the section of Istanbul known as the Golden Horn.

The Topkapi Palace lost its importance when the court moved to the Dolmabahçe Palace in 1854. After that date, aside from certain ceremonial occasions involving the holy relics of Islam (kept in the privy chamber), it hardly ever was used. Since its renovation in the 1930s, the Topkapi Palace has been a museum.

Bibliography

Necipoğlu, Gülrü. *Architecture, Ceremonial, and Power: The Topkapi Palace in the Fifteenth and Sixteenth Centuries.* New York: Architectural History Foundation, 1991.

APTULLAH KURAN
UPDATED BY ERIC HOOGLUND

TOUMI, KHALIDA

[1958–]

One of the pioneers of the feminist movement in Algeria.

Khalida Toumi was known as Khalida Messaoudi before she reclaimed her maiden name. She was born in 1958 in Sidi Ali Moussa, a village in the Kabylie region, and entered the University of Algiers in 1977 to pursue a degree in mathematics. After graduating from the École Normale Supérieure, she taught mathematics until 1993. In 1981, she founded the Collectif féminin (Women's Grouping) not only to oppose the ministerial interdiction on Algerian women leaving the country unless accompanied by a male family member, but also to oppose state endorsement of the discriminatory Family Code, which the National Assembly eventually adopted in 1984. Following the adoption of this code, Toumi presided over the Association for Equality between Men and Women, founded by a group of Trotskyite militants. In 1985, she cofounded and became a member of the executive committee of the Algerian League of Human Rights. She later distanced herself from the Trotskyite militants and in 1990 founded the Independent Association for the Triumph of Women's Rights. She staunchly opposed Islamist ideology and endorsed cancellation of the January 1992 legislative elections, which the Islamic Salvation Front (FIS) was poised to win. She considered the FIS to display "absolutely all the classic ingredients of totalitarian populist movements." During the years of terrorism in Algeria, she traveled to Western countries to provide an anti-Islamist perspective. A member of the Rassemblement pour la Culture et la Démocratie (RCD), she won a seat in the assembly and served as the RCD's national vice president for human rights and women's issues. After profound disagreements with the RCD's president Said Sadi, she severed relations with the RCD in January 2001, at the peak of the crisis in her native Kabylie; she was subsequently expelled from the RCD. In May 2002, she became minister of culture and communication, as well as the government's spokesperson, the first woman ever to hold that job. Khalida Toumi has in recent years lost her credibility as a staunch proponent of democracy because of her loyalty to President Abdelaziz Bouteflika, harshly criticized today for his authoritarianism and alliance with Islamists. The independent press and most advocates of democracy do not wish to see Bouteflika re-elected in April 2004.

See also ALGERIA: OVERVIEW; GENDER: GENDER AND POLITICS; KABYLIA; RASSEMBLEMENT POUR LA CULTURE ET LA DÉMOCRATIE (RCD); SADI, SAID.

Bibliography

Messaoudi, Khalida, with Schemla, Elisabeth. *Unbowed: An Algerian Woman Confronts Islamic Fundamentalism,* translated by Anne C. Vila. Philadelphia: University of Pennsylvania Press, 1998.

YAHIA ZOUBIR

TOURISM

An economic and social activity that has widely varying manifestations in the Middle East and North Africa.

Since the rise of civilization, the Middle East has been rich in notable sights and sites, and people have been visiting them for millennia. The Great Pyramids, the Hanging Gardens of Babylon, and places of religious significance such as Jerusalem and Mecca were drawing visitors long before the invention of the word *tourism*. And while travel for the purpose of seeing religious sites or carrying out religious obligations may be rightly termed "pilgrimage," the social and economic effects of this sort of travel are essentially indistinguishable from travel for purely secular reasons. If one accepts a broad definition of tourism, then it has been going on for centuries, on a large scale, to the region's many religious destinations. If one defines tourism more narrowly, as secular travel for the purposes of sightseeing and leisure on a scale large enough to be economically significant, then tourism, especially by Europeans, became important in the region only in the second half of the nineteenth century, when transportation methods improved and leisure time increased along with disposable income.

Europe's interest in the region historically had a religious component: Its Christians and Jews were keenly aware of the Holy Land, and much of the literature of European travelers to Palestine is intertwined with religious themes. Colonialism also drove European curiosity. The French and British occupations of parts of Egypt brought a flood of information about the land of the pharaohs. And with

Tourists take in the sights of Istanbul. Tourism is Turkey's second-largest source of foreign currency earnings, bringing in approximately US$10 billion a year. Upwards of thirteen million people typically visit Turkey annually, though recent terrorist activity in the country has severely curtailed those numbers. © DAVID KEATON/CORBIS. REPRODUCED BY PERMISSION.

the coming of steamship travel and the wealth and leisure generated by the industrial revolution in Europe, tourism as an organized industry spread from Europe to the Middle East. The first tours of Egypt from England were organized by Thomas Cook in 1868, and the first editions of Baedeker's guides for Palestine, Syria, and Egypt were published a few years later, first in German and later in French and English.

Early tourists were drawn by the region's sites of religious and historical importance, and today many still flock to such world treasures as the Great Pyramids at Giza, the Blue Mosque of Istanbul, and

the old medina of Fez. As modern governments and private investors attempt to increase tourism revenues, they are adopting new strategies to attract visitors and keep them entertained. Egypt, Syria, Morocco, and some Persian Gulf countries have been developing waterfront resorts. Turkey, long a summertime destination for many Europeans, has begun to develop mountain areas for winter tourism. Bahrain expanded its International Exhibition Centre in 1999 and plans to construct facilities for international-caliber formula-one auto racing. Dubai, in the United Arab Emirates, has for years been hosting international tennis and golf tournaments. Several countries have built large exhibition and convention facilities, new sports venues, and a variety of resorts, from Tunisia's Saharan winter resorts to beach complexes on the Mediterranean, Red Sea, Persian Gulf, and Gulf of Oman and Indian Ocean coasts.

Turkey has the largest volume of annual tourist arrivals in the region, with about 11.6 million visitors recorded in 2001. Tunisia also has an active tourism sector, with an average of about 5 million visitors between 1999 and 2001. Morocco, where tourism is important in the country's development strategy, averaged more than 2 million arrivals between 1999 and 2001. Countries with the least tourist activity were Algeria, Iraq, Oman, Qatar, and Yemen.

The political and security situations in a country can have a markedly negative impact on tourism. Periods of prolonged conflict can cut the number of visitors drastically, even in places where tourism often is encouraged. For example, despite a highly developed and well-funded tourism infrastructure and an active Ministry of Tourism, tourist arrivals in Israel dropped from 2.3 million in 1999 to 1.2 million in 2001, due in large part to continuing violence. The fact that arrivals in Algeria, a country with tremendous tourist potential, numbered fewer than 200,000 between 1998 and 2000 can be attributed in large part to the unsettled security situation there. Violent groups sometimes attempt to make a political statement by attacking tourists or other foreigners. This was the case in Egypt when Islamists carried out a number of deadly attacks in the late 1990s. The government responded by increasing security measures, including the hiring of special "tourist police." In Yemen it has been the practice of some tribes to put pressure on the government by taking hostages, often foreign tourists. After the events of 11 September 2001, security became more perilous as the government, in cooperation with the United States, attempted to capture or kill al-Qaʿida members and sympathizers.

Bibliography

Compendium of Tourism Statistics, 2001 Edition. Madrid: World Tourism Organization, 2001.

ANTHONY B. TOTH

TRACHOMA

See DISEASES

TRADE

The geographical position of the Middle East has made the region part of far-flung trade networks, as both market and supplier, since antiquity.

The Middle East is the cradle of civilization, the place where agriculture and urban life are thought to have originated. The region was economically vibrant and a center of trade in early antiquity, and it connected far-flung markets across the Eastern Hemisphere during Roman times. The collapse of the Roman Empire fragmented governing institutions in northwestern Europe, dividing its markets from the rest of the world. The rise of Islam during the seventh century C.E. and its subsequent diffusion spread Arabic and a common legal system (*shariʿa*) across the southern Mediterranean and as far east as what now is Indonesia. Trade was reinvigorated and, following the Mongol conquest and consolidation in east and west Asia, overland trade between the Middle East and China along the Silk Road also thrived.

Trade before the Modern Period

Before the modern period, the Middle East exported mainly high-quality manufactured products to Europe and Africa, with which it generally enjoyed a trade surplus. Raw materials and manufactured products went to Asia but, like others trading with this region, Middle Eastern merchants often ran deficits with their east Asian partners.

The area around the Indian Ocean was a main market and supplier of goods to the Middle East.

Pepper and spices came from the East Indies and were re-exported as well as consumed locally. Teak for ship construction and other tropical woods were imported from India; porcelain and silk came from China. After silkworms were smuggled out of China during the sixth century C.E., the Middle East also became a producer and exporter of silk cloth. Arab and Iranian shipping dominated the Indian Ocean as far as the Straits of Malacca, where Chinese junks took over, sailing to Guangzhou (Canton) and other Chinese ports to sell carpets, linens, cotton and wool fabrics, metalwork, iron ore, pearls, and ivory.

Overland trade with the Baltic region went via the Volga and other Russian rivers. Along these routes, Middle Eastern traders exchanged manufactured goods for furs, wax, amber, and slaves. The ancient sea trade with East Africa expanded greatly with the spread of Islam and with the establishment of branches of family trading concerns by Arabs and Iranians down the East African coast. Middle Eastern traders exchanged cloth, glassware, weapons, and trinkets for Africa's wood, ivory, palm oil, and gold. Slaves were sent from Africa to the Middle East in large numbers, most remaining in the countries bordering the Red Sea and Persian Gulf, but some going as far as India and China. The trans-Sahara trade blossomed following the introduction of caravans between Egypt, North African ports, and tropical Africa, exchanging African gold, ivory, pepper, and slaves for salt, weapons, copper, textiles, glassware, and trinkets.

Trade with Europe eventually would come to dominate Middle Eastern exchange relations, but Europe's lagging development following the sack of Rome confined most European exports to the Middle East to raw materials such as wood, iron, furs, and slaves. In exchange, Europeans received the high-quality manufactures for which the Middle East had long been famous: glassware, metal goods, and fabrics. As corruption eroded Egypt's competitive position during the fourteenth century, manufactures brought by Venetian traders began to displace local products. During the first half of the sixteenth century, Portugal invaded and took control of the Indian Ocean trade, constructing fortifications in ports like Bahrain and charging protection rents to merchants for allowing their goods to pass. The Dutch then displaced the Portuguese from much of their empire, and Portuguese interference with

Dubai, the chief commercial center of the United Arab Emirates, boasts the world's largest man-made harbor, Jabal Ali Port. It is the most frequented port outside of the United States, with sixty-seven berths and an impressive dry-dock facility. © PETER BLAKELY/CORBIS SABA. REPRODUCED BY PERMISSION.

local shipping waned. Shipbuilding thrived in the Persian Gulf during the eighteenth century, and merchant families grew rich from pearling and long-distance trade. Gulf-based merchants carried a wide variety of goods—including live horses—east to South Asia and west to the African coast. Their predominance in their own region was challenged and gradually eroded during the nineteenth century. In mid-century, competition from British steam-powered ships began taking business from Arab shippers who relied on wind-powered dhows and boums. Near the end of the century, the British navy established protectorates over the smaller emirates near the mouth of the Gulf and soon dominated that sea.

During the nineteenth century, the terms of trade between the Middle East and Europe gradually shifted as Europeans penetrated Middle Eastern markets and pressed governments for changes favoring imports over articles produced locally. High value-added products (i.e., manufactured or processed goods rather than raw materials) increasingly came from Europe rather than being produced at home. For example, Morocco had been famous for its refined sugar, but its Middle Eastern markets were overtaken by sugar from southern Europe and by sugar from the New World that had been refined in Europe. A similar displacement occurred

later with respect to coffee. Manufactured goods were similarly displaced as fine silk and woolen fabrics, high-quality paper, and glass, which formerly had gone from the Middle East to Europe, began to flow from Europe to the Middle East. New European products, such as clocks, spectacles, and weapons, entered Middle Eastern markets without local competition. Although yarn exports to Europe continued until the end of the eighteenth century, it was clear by the time of the industrial revolution that the Middle East was becoming a peripheral actor in world trade, exporting mostly primary products and importing mostly manufactured and processed goods from the industrializing European core.

Shifting trade patterns accelerated during the nineteenth-century era of globalization, which ended with World War I. Total world trade rose from some $1.7 billion in 1800 to $42 billion in 1913. During this period, the share of world trade going to the Middle East was halved, falling from about 3 percent in 1800 to 1.5 percent in 1913. The slope of the upsurge in trade reflected European investment in steamships and railroads, and what economists like John Gallagher and Ronald Robinson called "the imperialism of free trade": in the name of open markets, Britain forced weaker trading partners to abolish monopolies and local trade regulations and to adopt low uniform tariffs on imports. Referred to as *capitulations,* these institutional changes ensured that the market effects of competition from an industrializing Europe on artisan production in the Middle East (and elsewhere) would not be moderated by the state. This virtually guaranteed that the region would be incorporated into the global trading system as a dependent exporter of raw materials: tobacco, dried fruits, and cotton from Turkey; silk and opium from Iran; wheat, barley, and dates from Syria and Iraq; silk from Lebanon; oranges from Palestine; and coffee beans from Yemen.

Foreign investment and loans were key elements changing the terms of trade and fostering trade dependency. Egyptian overinvestment in cotton production during the U.S. Civil War displaced local food production and, when cotton prices collapsed, increased Egypt's foreign debt. The protection of foreign creditors served as a justification for imposing on the Egyptian government a joint British-French commission in 1876. Britain used this

Sacks of figs being prepared for shipping from Smyrna. Turkey is one of the world's leading exporting countries of dried figs, raisins, and dried apricots. © UNDERWOOD & UNDERWOOD/CORBIS. REPRODUCED BY PERMISSION.

opportunity to take control of the Suez Canal and, in 1882, of Egypt itself. Trade deficits combined with heavy foreign borrowing caused the Ottoman Empire to declare bankruptcy in 1875 and, six years later, led to the establishment of the Ottoman Debt Commission. This essentially parallel ministry of finance represented the interests of the Ottoman Empire's creditors, and imposed an early version of conditionality (i.e., the surrender of control over fiscal policy to an agent of foreign creditors) to ensure that they would be repaid.

The Modern Period

The discovery of oil in Iran at the turn of the twentieth century confirmed the position of the Middle

East as a supplier of raw materials, defining its position in world trade for the next century. Competition between France and Britain for control of Iraqi oil influenced the way the defeated Ottoman Empire was divided into mandates governed by these two victors after World War I. During the interwar period, oil was found in Bahrain, Kuwait, and Saudi Arabia, while the Iraqi oil industry became the balance wheel regulating the development of production capacity in the region via the Red Line Agreement of 1928. During World War II, trade volume declined regionally and globally owing to blockades, dangers to shipping, and shut-in oil production. Afterward, the production and sale of petroleum came to dominate interregional trade. Starting in 1960, the Organization of Petroleum

Foreign trade of some Middle East Countries *

	1938	1948	1963	1977	1984	2000
Egypt						
Imports	190	700	900	4,800	10,300	14,010
Exports	150	600	500	1,700	3,200	4,641
Israel						
Imports	56	300	700	4,700	8,400	35,750
Exports	29	40	300	3,000	4,900	31,404
Turkey						
Imports	120	300	700	5,700	10,800	53,499
Exports	115	200	400	1,800	7,100	26,572
Iran						
Imports	—	200	500	13,800	11,500	14,296
Exports	—	500	900	24,200	13,200	28,345
Iraq						
Imports	50	—	300	3,900	19,900	n/a
Exports	—	—	800	9,700	9,800	n/a
Kuwait						
Imports	—	—	300	4,500	8,300	7,157
Exports	—	—	1,100	9,800	10,600	19,436
Saudi Arabia						
Imports	—	—	—	14,700	39,200	30,237
Exports	—	300	1,100	43,500	46,900	77,583
United Arab Emirates						
Imports	—	—	—	4,600	9,400	38,139
Exports	—	—	—	9,500	14,400	n/a
Total						
Imports	**400**	**1,500**	**4,300**	**58,500**	**123,400**	**179,687**
Exports	**400**	**1,500**	**5,700**	**106,000**	**119,700**	**268,495**
Middle East as percentage of the world						
Imports	1.6	2.4	2.6	5.2	6.2	2.9
Exports	1.7	2.6	3.7	9.4	6.3	4.4

* In millions of U.S. dollars, rounded.

SOURCE: United Nations, *Statistical Yearbook* (New York: United Nations, 1986); for 2000, United Nation, *Statistical Yearbook* (New York: United Nations, 2003), 667-677.

TABLE BY GGS INFORMATION SERVICES, THE GALE GROUP.

Exporting Countries (OPEC) struggled to reverse the unfavorable terms of trade that had beset its Middle Eastern members since the nineteenth century by halting and then reversing the incipient decline in real oil prices that threatened to erode oil-exporter income.

Oil exports altered economic positions intraregionally. Until 1948, Egypt and Turkey accounted for the majority of Middle Eastern trade. After that, the oil-producing countries captured an enormous proportion of total regional trade, especially exports. Attempts to foster intraregional trade through common markets and regional organizations such as the Gulf Cooperation Council mostly foundered on the shoals of economies deformed by dependent development—that is, development strategies em-

phasizing oil and gas production rather than goods and services aimed primarily at domestic and regional markets. Local industrial development also was affected by what is sometimes called "Dutch disease" (because the same situation affected Holland during the heyday of its exploitation of the riches of the East Indies), oil export–induced monetary inflation that decreased the competitiveness of local goods as compared to imports. Dutch disease makes domestic production uncompetitive, even at home, further discouraging economic diversification.

The Arab League trade boycott, imposed against Israel after its creation in 1948 and still in effect in a number of Arab countries, was another factor retarding the development of local industries in Arab countries; it also deprived Israeli farms and factories of a nearby market for their products and increased Israel's already massive dependence on foreign assistance. Together, these outcomes increased the power of government over civil society, both in Israel and in the Arab states, by diminishing the capacity of domestic business interests to exercise checks on the state. The boycott also aggravated a conflict that all the region's governments used to their advantage to discourage if not repress domestic dissent.

Middle Eastern trade oscillates in response to political crises and wars, many connected to the Arab–Israeli conflict. In general, crises tend to depress Middle Eastern oil exports, either through oil embargoes or as a result of war-induced oil price increases. For example, the global position of Arab oil exporters was gravely damaged by consumer efforts to find other sources of hydrocarbon imports following the 1973 Arab-Israel war and the Arab oil embargo, which enabled OPEC to raise crude oil prices to what then were unheard-of levels. Ten years later, the volume of oil exports from OPEC countries was half what it had been in 1973. (Oil income did not fall in proportion because of further oil price increases during that period.) Other conflicts, such as the revolution in Iran and the subsequent U.S. trade sanctions against it, and the three Gulf Wars in which Iraq was a major belligerent (1980–1988; 1990–1991; and 2003), also affected regional trade. The first Gulf War, between Iran and Iraq, was fought in part with oil exports. Iraqi exports were occasionally halted by Iranian attacks but Iraq continued to receive oil income from Saudi and Kuwaiti sales of oil from the former Neutral Zone. Meanwhile, Iran suffered under U.S. trade sanctions, which depressed its export income.

As regards the balance of trade overall, oil-exporting-country revenues usually have exceeded the cost of imported goods and services. Non-oil exporters, such as Egypt, Israel, Syria, Jordan, Yemen, and Turkey, ran trade deficits, some incurred to pay for oil imports. The deficits were covered by foreign aid and loans, leading to large foreign debts. These macro-level effects mask significant changes in non-oil-exporting economies. For most, the composition of exports has changed. Traditional raw-material exports like cotton and grain have declined owing to greater processing and consumption at home. A growing export trade in manufactured goods, such as high-tech equipment and finished textiles, is bringing new trade income to Israel, Turkey, Egypt, Syria, and Lebanon. On the import side, rising incomes from oil exports have trickled down to non-oil-exporting neighbors via labor migration and, prior to the collapse in oil prices in 1986, through intraregional foreign aid. This allowed imports of foodstuffs, durable consumer goods, industrial and transport machinery, and raw materials to rise.

The most disturbing component of Middle Eastern trade is armaments. Higher oil prices in the 1970s were offset by the aggressive marketing of weapons to Middle Eastern Muslim countries. The motives of arms buyers were diverse. Some, such as Iran, Iraq, and Saudi Arabia, sought arms from external patrons as a way to assert their political and religious authority in the region. Others felt themselves to be at a disadvantage as compared to their neighbors, especially Israel, with its virtually First World military industries and its ability to acquire weapons and advanced military technologies, mostly free, from the United States. The overall decline in the world economy following the 1973 Arab-Israeli war made trade-surplus oil exporters attractive targets of marketing efforts by arms exporters from throughout the world. Britain, France, China, and Russia joined the United States in building arms export markets in the Middle East. Beginning in the 1980s, when U.S. policy shifted toward greater marketization of supporting strategic industries by encouraging them to market weapons abroad, then expanding during the 1990s, following the collapse of the Soviet Union, even materials for so-called weapons of mass destruction became widely available for import into the Middle East and elsewhere.

See also GULF COOPERATION COUNCIL; ORGANIZATION OF PETROLEUM EXPORTING COUNTRIES (OPEC); RED LINE AGREEMENT.

Bibliography

Gallagher, John, and Robinson, Ronald. "The Imperialism of Free Trade." *Economic History Review*, 2d series, no. 6 (1953): 1–15.

Issawi, Charles. *An Economic History of the Middle East and North Africa.* New York: Columbia University Press, 1982.

Nitzan, Jonathan, and Bichler, Shimshon. *The Global Political Economy of Israel.* Sterling, VA; London: Pluto Press, 2002.

Schwartz, Herman M. *States Versus Markets: The Emergence of a Global Economy*. 2d edition. New York and Basingstoke, U.K.: Palgrave, 2000.

CHARLES ISSAWI
UPDATED BY MARY ANN TÉTREAULT

TRAD, PETRO

[1876–1947]

Lebanese politician.

Petro Trad was born to a Greek Orthodox family in Beirut and received a law degree from the University of Paris. Known for his eloquent presentations, he was one of a handful of wealthy lawyers who monopolized law practice in Beirut. Trad was also involved in politics; he was one of six signatories to a petition presented to the French Foreign Ministry in 1913 on behalf of Christian sects in Beirut, that demanded an end to Ottoman control of Syria (including Palestine and Lebanon) and called for a separate entity run by "French specialists." This petition so angered Cemal Paşa against Arabs in general and Christians in particular that he asked the War Council in Alayh to execute the six signatories. They fled Lebanon.

After the World War I, Trad returned to Beirut as an ally of the French and founded the League of Christian Sects, which comprised the elite of Beirut society and demanded a French mandate over Syria and Lebanon. His law firm attained fame throughout the region, partly because he would defend poor persons who could not afford his fees. He was elected deputy from Beirut in 1925, with both Arab and French support. Trad served in the parliament for much of the 1920s and 1930s, either elected or appointed by the French authorities. He was a member of the parliamentary committee that worked on the French-Lebanese treaty of 1936. The French rewarded his support by appointing him speaker of parliament in 1937, a post he held until September 1939.

Trad could not stay neutral in the political feud between the staunchly pro-French Emile Eddé and the moderately pro-French Bishara al-Khuri. In his memoirs al-Khuri accuses Trad of supporting Eddé. In fact, Trad believed that both al-Khuri and Eddé were incapable of winning the presidency. He promoted himself as a consensus candidate.

Trad became president by default. He was briefly appointed by the French government, to oversee the election of a new president by members of an appointed parliament. The election of al-Khuri made it clear to him that his chances of winning the presidency were nil. He died in Beirut.

See also CEMAL PAŞA; EDDÉ, EMILE; KHURI, BISHARA AL-.

AS'AD ABUKHALIL

TRANS-ARABIAN PIPELINE

Pipeline transporting crude oil from Saudi Arabia to the Mediterranean.

The Trans-Arabian Pipeline (Tapline) was constructed by the Arabian American Oil Company (ARAMCO) to carry crude oil from Abqaiq, Saudi Arabia, to the Mediterranean coast. As originally conceived during World War II, the line was to follow a great circular route running northwest through Saudi Arabia and Jordan, which would have located the Mediterranean terminus at Haifa, then part of the British Mandate of Palestine. The postwar conflict over the disposition of Palestine ended in the Arab–Israel War (1948) that put Haifa in the new state of Israel. Tapline's route, more than 1,000 miles long, was altered to run through Syria and site its western terminus a few miles south of Sidon, Lebanon.

The construction of Tapline was hastened by the end of the Red Line Agreement, which brought a new infusion of capital into ARAMCO as the result of the removal of the restriction preventing Standard Oil of New Jersey (now Exxon) and Socony Vacuum (now Mobil; both combined as Exxon Mobil) from joining the partnership then composed of SOCAL (now Chevron) and Texaco. Capital was not the only requirement in short supply. Steel was also scarce following the end of World War II, and its allocation was controlled by the U.S. government. A second important factor speeding the construction of Tapline was support from the administration of U.S. president Harry S. Truman, which regarded Middle Eastern oil as crucial to the success of the Marshall Plan.

When Tapline was built, it was the world's largest privately financed construction project. At the peak of construction, it employed more than sixteen thousand men. Towns were constructed at Qaysumah, Rafha, Badana, and Turayf, where the four main pumping stations in Saudi Arabia were located. Initial capacity was 320,000 barrels per day. In 1957 auxiliary pumping stations were installed, raising capacity to 450,000 barrels per day. Tapline's capacity in 2003 was 500,000 barrels per day.

Tapline increased ARAMCO's capacity to export crude oil and reduced its oil-transport expenses. This prompted the government of Saudi Arabia to demand 50 percent of Tapline's profits under the fifty-fifty profit-sharing agreement that governed oil production. ARAMCO argued that transport was not covered under the profit-sharing agreement and claimed that Tapline was not an affiliate of ARAMCO but a separate company. After years of negotiations, the company agreed in 1963 to pay Saudi Arabia half the difference, after costs were deducted, between the price of petroleum at Ra's Tannūrah and the price at Sidon. The agreement, retroactive to 1953, netted the government $93 million in arrears.

Tapline and other pipelines in the region not only reduce transport costs and increase oil-export capacity but also provide alternatives to shipping from the Persian Gulf or through the Suez Canal. However, pipelines have security problems. Syria halted the passage of oil through Tapline for twenty-four hours in October 1956 during the Arab–Israel War, and in Syria a tractor ruptured Tapline in May 1970, just as Libya was restricting the production of Occidental Petroleum during the early days of the "squeeze." This blocked the transit of 500,000 barrels of crude from Saudi Arabia to the Mediterranean, triggering an immediate threefold rise in oil-tanker rates. The vulnerability of Tapline was highlighted by several incidents of sabotage in 1973, including an armed attack on the Sidon terminal and attacks on the pipeline itself in Syria and in Saudi Arabia.

In order to counter some of the strategic liabilities of relying so heavily on Tapline for pipeline transport, Saudi Arabia constructed a 720-mile crude-oil pipeline, Petroline, from the eastern oil fields to Yanbu, on the Red Sea, in 1981. A parallel line, connected to a spur running from Iraq's southern oil fields, was constructed to enable Iraq

to export oil from Saudi Arabia during its war with Iran. This line was closed under United Nations sanctions following Iraq's invasion of Kuwait. The Saudis seized ownership in June 2001. Petroline, located entirely within Saudi Arabia, carried a maximum of 5 million barrels per day at its peak. In 2003 utilization was about half this capacity to accommodate the conversion of the line to carry natural gas. Like Tapline, Petroline increases the kingdom's export flexibility and demonstrates its commitment to a secure supply of hydrocarbon fuels to consumers.

See also ARABIAN AMERICAN OIL COMPANY (ARAMCO); PETROLEUM, OIL, AND NATURAL GAS; PETROLEUM RESERVES AND PRODUCTION; RED LINE AGREEMENT.

Bibliography

Nawwab, Ismail I.; Speers, Peter C.; and Hoye, Paul F.; eds. *ARMACO and Its World: Arabia and the Middle East.* Dhahran, Saudi Arabia: ARMACO Dhahran, 1980.

Yergin, Daniel. *The Prize: The Epic Quest for Oil, Money, and Power.* New York: Simon & Schuster, 1991.

MARY ANN TÉTREAULT

TRANS-IRANIAN RAILWAY

North-south railroad completed in 1938, which links Caspian ports in the north to Tehran and Persian/Arabian Gulf ports in the south.

The Trans-Iranian railway, one of the great engineering feats of the twentieth century, was commissioned by Reza Shah Pahlavi after his consolidation of power in Iran in 1925. Preliminary planning and construction efforts were contracted with KAMPSAX, a Scandinavian syndicate, in 1933. With the hub at Tehran, single tracklines were laid north and south through mountain and desert terrain to newly constructed ports on the Caspian Sea and Persian Gulf coasts. The 865-mile (1,392-km) railroad became operational in 1938, with 190 tunnels, totaling 47 miles (76 km), and traversing mountain passess higher than 7,000 feet (2,135 m).

The railway symbolized the new regime's goals of nationalism, independence, and modernization. To avoid foreign exploitation, particularly from English and Russian interests, it was financed by taxes on the popular subsistence items of tea and sugar. Ironically, during World War II, the railroad was commandeered by the Allies as a major supply route to the Soviet Union.

Bibliography

Millspaugh, Arthur C. *Americans in Persia.* Washington, DC: Brookings Institution, 1946.

JACK BUBON

TRANSJORDAN FRONTIER FORCE

Military group established to defend Palestine and Transjordan (1926–1948).

The Transjordan Frontier Force (TJFF) was organized by the high commissioner for Palestine to fulfill Britain's responsibility under terms of the mandate treaty. The TJFF should not be confused with the Arab Legion, from which it was entirely separate.

Confusion arose out of the TJFF's having a name identifying it with Transjordan but being a part of the imperial forces in Palestine and thus a Palestinian responsibility. In the end, the British treasury agreed to have Palestine pay five-sixths of the cost of the TJFF and Transjordan pay one-sixth, following the line of reasoning that security in Transjordan contributed to security in Palestine.

Further disagreement arose over the need for a force to undertake responsibilities many believed could be handled by the Arab Legion. The high commissioner for Palestine, Lord Plumer, considered that the frontiers with Syria and Saudi Arabia were vulnerable. The latter frontier was regarded as particularly open to the possibility of expansion efforts by Abd al-Aziz ibn Saʿud Al Saʿud, who had proclaimed himself king of the Hijaz in January 1926 and conceivably would seek to expand into areas controlled by the Hashimites, particularly Transjordan. The TJFF proved incapable of patrolling the desert of Transjordan and retired across the Jordan river to Palestine in 1930 when John Bagot Glubb created the Desert Mobile Force, which became the nucleus of the Arab Legion, and took over responsibility for the frontiers.

When the TJFF was formed, its recruits came from the disbanded Palestine gendarmeries, including noncommissioned officers and enlisted men who had had five years of experience. Some 70 percent of the recruits were Arabs from Palestine, mainly literate fallahin from the villages. In addition, there was a camel company of Sudanese enlisted men; it was replaced in 1933 by a mechanized unit. Some Jews and town Arabs served in administrative and technical services. Before 1935, about 25 percent of the force were Circassians.

The TJFF was under direct control of the high commissioner in Jerusalem, and above him the War Office in London. Non-British officers were not to attain command positions that gave them seniority over British personnel. Therefore, the officer corps and squadron commanders (majors or above) were British. Troop commanders (captains) and below included Palestinians, Syrians, Sudanese, Circassians, and a few Jews.

Initially the TJFF had three squadrons of two companies each, plus one camel company. In 1930, a mechanized company was added, bringing the total to eight companies. After the camel corps was replaced by a mechanized company, the TJFF consisted of three squadrons and two mechanized companies until the TJFF was disbanded.

All in all, there were some one thousand officers and men in the TJFF. Command headquarters, al-Zarqa, near Amman, was headed by a British lieutenant colonel. By 1935, there were twenty-four British officers in command of the TJFF: the commanding officer, seven majors, and sixteen captains. This complement remained more or less constant.

See also ABD AL-AZIZ IBN SAʿUD AL SAʿUD; ARAB LEGION.

Bibliography

Dann, Uriel. *Studies in the History of Transjordan, 1920–1949: The Making of a State.* Boulder, CO: Westview Press, 1984.

Vatikiotis, P. J. *Politics and the Military in Jordan: A Study of the Arab Legion, 1921–1957.* New York: Praeger, 1967.

JENAB TUTUNJI

TRANSPORT

Ships, caravans, railroads, and pipelines carry Middle Eastern goods to market.

Until the twentieth century, and in many places until the middle of that century, people, animals, and water were the primary modes of transport in the Middle East.

Shipping

Waterways are few and not always navigable, but coastal navigation has always been important. Of the various river systems, only two were navigable—the Nile and the Tigris and Euphrates system. All were used for irrigation as well as transport, and canal systems were built to extend their benefits. The Nile runs north through East Africa, emptying across a broad delta into the eastern Mediterranean Sea. The longest river in the world, it flows from Lake Victoria through Uganda, Sudan, and Egypt. Since the prevailing winds are northerly, boats without motors can sail upstream and float downstream. The Tigris and Euphrates rivers are less suited to navigation, since their currents are swifter, their levels vary, and they often change course before merging into the Shatt al-Arab, which drains into the Persian Gulf. Because of these means of access to the sea, both areas have long transported bulk goods by water and built seaports that accommodated goods from other coastal trading areas, such as Turkey and Syria. Since antiquity, the coastal people of the Mediterranean have traded, traveled, and warred among themselves over the riches of one another's lands.

Caravans

For the local movement of goods to rivers or seaports, and even for long-distance overland journeys, caravans were relied on. Caravans of mules and, especially, camels, took over from wheeled traffic at the end of the Roman era. Camel loads varied, generally ranging from 550 to 660 pounds; the speed of a caravan was 2.5 to 3 miles per hour; the usual daily stage was 15 to 20 miles. Caravans differed greatly in size, depending on need and the availability of people and animals: In 1820, before the Suez Canal was built, the Suez caravan had about 500 camels; in 1847, the Baghdad–Damascus caravan had some 1,500 to 2,000 camels; and the Damascus–Baghdad caravan, some 800 to 1,200. During the 1870s, some 15,000 pack animals made three round trips a year on the Tabriz–Trabzon route (Iran to Turkey), carrying the equivalent of the contents of seven or eight sailing ships each way. Boats and pack animals were adequate for the

After an agreement was negotiated between French engineer Ferdinand de Lesseps and the Egyptian government, construction of the Suez Canal began in 1859 and continued for ten years. The canal links two oceans and two seas, and transports 14 percent of total world trade. © Peter Turnley/Corbis. Reproduced by permission.

relatively small volume of traffic under traditional conditions before the advent of the industrial revolution and the expansion of European trade and imperialism into the Middle East.

Steamships

During the nineteenth century, transport was revolutionized. During the 1820s and 1830s, regular steamer lines linked the Middle East with Europe

In the 1830s, the East India Company began to use steamships to travel between Bombay and Suez. In these early days, ports were inadequate for loading and unloading, and cargo had to be ferried out to the ships in smaller boats. © Jack Fields/Corbis. Reproduced by permission.

across the Mediterranean, with Russia and Austria across the Black Sea, and with India through the Red Sea. Later, services were established in the Caspian Sea and the gulf. By the closing decades of that century, the bulk of the region's foreign trade was carried on steamships, and freight costs were drastically reduced. Starting in the 1830s, steam tugs and steamboats were used on the Nile and on the Euphrates, soon carrying a large portion of domestic trade. Since no port improvements had occurred since Roman times, the steamers were loaded and unloaded by lighters, which were boats used to carry cargo from ships to ports. The first modern port facilities were installed in Alexandria in 1818 (followed by later improvements), at Suez in 1866, in İzmir in 1875, in Aden in 1888, in Beirut in 1895, and in Istanbul in 1902. Except for Alexandria and Suez, all these harbors were built with European capital. The opening of the Suez Canal in 1869 by a French company was a major advance for world navigation.

Railroads

The first railway in the Middle East was begun in 1851, at British insistence, to link Alexandria with Cairo and Suez, speeding transport on the Mediterranean–India route. Like all Egypt's main lines, it was financed by the government. Soon after, British capital built two lines from İzmir in Turkey to the countryside. The Ottoman Empire, however, wanted a railroad that linked Istanbul with their provinces of Anatolia, Syria, and Iraq; following the completion of the Vienna–Istanbul line in 1888 (which became the Orient Express), it gave a concession to a German company for an Istanbul–Ankara line, later extended to Basra. This Berlin–Baghdad Railway aroused much international controversy, which was settled just before the outbreak of World War I. When the war ended in 1918, the line reached Aleppo in northern Syria, and a small stretch had been built in Iraq. Other foreign-owned short lines were built in Palestine, Lebanon, and Syria. The Hijaz Railroad (1903–1908), linking Damascus, in Syria, to Medina, in western Saudi Arabia (near Mecca), was financed by contributions from Muslims throughout the world. During World War I, the British army built extensive rail lines in Iraq and Palestine and put the Arabian section of the Hijaz railroad out of service. In Iran, the Russians built a line to Tabriz. After the war, Turkey doubled its mileage and Iran built a railroad between the Caspian Sea and the Persian Gulf. Since then, important lines have been built in Iran, Saudi Arabia, and Syria. Table I shows the length of rail lines built from 1870 to 2000. Rail service reduced both the time and costs of transport. On the Ankara–Istanbul route, the rate per ton-mile fell from 10 cents to 1 cent; on the Damascus–Beirut line, from 4.5 cents to 1.5 cents; the journey from Damascus to Cairo was reduced from 25 days to 18 hours. In some areas, telegraph lines accompanied or preceded the railroads.

Length of rail service (in kilometers)

Country	1870	1890	1914	1939	1948	1975	2000
Egypt	1,400	1,797	4,314	5,606	6,092	4,856	8,600
Iran	—	—	—	1,700	3,180	4,944	6,600
Iraq	—	—	132	1,304	1,555	2,203	2,000
Jordan	—	—	—	332	332	420	700
Lebanon	—	—	—	232	423	417	200
Palestine/Israel (as of 1948)	—	—	—	1,188	1,225	902	n.d
Saudi Arabia	—	—	800	—	—	612	700
Sudan	—	—	2,396	3,206	3,242	4,556	5,000
Syria	—	—	—	854	867	1,761	2,400
Turkey	230	1,443	3,400	7,324	7,634	8,138	10,300
Total	**1,630**	**3,240**	**11,042**	**21,746**	**24,550**	**28,809**	**36,500**

SOURCE: *The International Year Book and Statesmen's Who's Who, 2003.* East Grinstead, U.K.: CSA, 2002. *Africa South of the Sahara, 2003.* London: Europa Publications, 2002. *The Middle East and North Africa, 2003.* London: Europa Publications, 2002. *Statistical Yearbook 1999.* New York: United Nations, 2002.

TABLE BY GGS INFORMATION SERVICES, THE GALE GROUP.

Modern means of transport, as of 2003

	Paved Roads (thousands of km)	Passenger Motor Vehicles (thousands)	Commercial Motor Vehicles (thousands)	Ships (thousands of grt/tons)*	Airlines (millions of passenger/km)
Egypt	39.0	1,154	554	1,350	8,036
Iran	93.5	1,793	235	3,943	8,539
Iraq	39.9	773	323	240	20
Israel	16.5	1,460	371	611	12,418
Jordan	5.5	245	112	42	4,065
Kuwait	3.8	747	140	2,291	6,207
Lebanon	6.2	1,299	92	301	1,504
Saudi Arabia	47.3	2,762	2,340	1,133	18,820
Sudan	3.9	285	53	43	148
Syria	43.3	138	322	498	1,410
Turkey	62.6	4,539	1,590	5,896	n.d.
United Arab Emirates	3.3	346	89	746	15,633

* grt is gross registered tons
Note: The dates for the figures in this table range from 1993 to 2001. n.d. = no data available.

SOURCE: *The International Year Book and Statesmen's Who's Who, 2003.* East Grinstead, U.K.: CSA, 2002. *Africa South of the Sahara, 2003.* London: Europa Publications, 2002. *The Middle East and North Africa, 2003.* London: Europa Publications, 2002. *Statistical Yearbook 1999.* New York: United Nations, 2002.

TABLE BY GGS INFORMATION SERVICES, THE GALE GROUP.

Modern Services

From the mid-1900s on, the Middle East has been served by an extensive network of telegraph and telephone lines, which extend to all cities and towns, and to almost all villages. Computer, electronic mail, and Internet and fax services exist in main centers as well.

Modern roadways were first built during the late nineteenth century; except for those in northern Iran and Lebanon, they played no significant role in the transport system of the period. After World War I, and then again after World War II, they were greatly expanded and improved. Motor vehicles, which came to the Middle East before World War I, carry the bulk of inland transport. Air transport has a similar history: every country has its own airline and the region has become a hub of air traffic, connecting North America and Europe with Africa, India, and Asia.

Because of the Suez Canal, the Middle East plays an important part in world navigation. Just before Egypt nationalized the canal in 1956, it carried 13 percent of world shipping but 20 percent of oil tankers. The canal has been repeatedly enlarged and deepened to accommodate increasingly larger tankers and supertankers. During the 1990s, most petroleum producers maintained a large fleet of tankers, and oil-refining and consumer nations had sizeable merchant and tanker fleets; still, the share of the Middle East in world shipping was only 1 percent, and its share in world tankers only 3 percent. Nationalization of all transport facilities has been a fact of Middle Eastern life, beginning with Turkey's railways during the 1920s.

Oil has brought another form of transport to the region: pipelines. The first, opened in 1934, carried Iraq's oil to the Mediterranean. Since then, far longer and larger pipelines have been built to transport Saudi Arabian and Iraqi oil through Syria to the Mediterranean, as well as Iraqi oil through Turkey and Saudi Arabia. Many pipelines no longer operate due to various political conflicts. Oil-producing countries also have extensive networks of internal pipelines that transport crude petroleum to refineries.

See also BERLIN–BAGHDAD RAILWAY; HIJAZ RAILROAD; PERSIAN (ARABIAN) GULF; SHATT AL-ARAB.

Bibliography

American Automobile Manufacturers Association. *World Motor Vehicles Data.* Detroit, 1989.

Earle, Edward. *Turkey, the Great Powers, and the Bagdad Railway: A Study in Imperialism.* New York: Macmillan, 1923.

International Air Transport Association. *World Air Transport Statistics.* Montréal: Author, 1991.

Issawi, Charles. *An Economic History of the Middle East and North Africa.* New York: Columbia University Press, 1982.

Kark, Ruth. "The Pilgrimage to Budding Tourism: The Role of Thomas Cook in the Rediscovery of the Holy Land." *Travellers in the Levant: Voyagers and Visionaries,* edited by Sarah Searight and Malcolm Wagstaff. Durham, U.K.: Astene, 2001.

CHARLES ISSAWI
UPDATED BY ANTHONY B. TOTH

TRANS-TURKEY PIPELINE

Oil pipeline connecting fields in Iraq and Turkey.

The Iraq-Turkey pipeline connects the rich oil fields around Kirkuk, Iraq, to the Mediterranean port of Yumurtalik in Turkey. It consists of two parallel pipes, 584 miles (941 km) long (398 miles or 641 km in Turkey), with a total capacity of 14 million barrels of crude oil. The first line was opened in 1977; the second, in 1987. It is operated jointly by the national oil companies of Iraq and Turkey. Oil flows through the pipeline ceased in 1991, in accordance with UN sanctions against Iraq after its invasion of Kuwait.

NIYAZI DALYANCI

TREATY OF 1815

Agreement between the United States and the ruler of Algiers that ended U.S. annual tribute payments.

In 1815, after the *dey* (ruler) of Algiers had declared war on the United States and began to tolerate corsair attacks on American shipping in the Mediterranean Sea, Washington dispatched to the area a ten-ship squadron under the command of naval hero Stephen Decatur (1779–1820). Decatur's objective was to punish Algiers and to assert freedom of the seas for trade. Decatur defeated the Algiers fleet and threatened to bombard the city unless the dey signed a new treaty promising to protect American ships and seamen from corsairs. The treaty signed on 30 June 1815 abolished U.S. indemnity payments, freed all U.S. prisoners without any ran-

som, and granted U.S. ships trading privileges in ports that recognized the suzerainty of Algiers.

See also CORSAIRS.

Bibliography

Chidsey, Donald B. *The Wars in Barbary: Arab Piracy and the Birth of the United States.* New York: Crown, 1971.

ERIC HOOGLUND

TREATY OF PROTECTION (1886)

British treaty made with south Arabian rulers.

This formal treaty of friendship and protection between Britain and the rulers of Qishn and Socotra in 1886 was followed by similar treaties with the rulers of the other states along the southern coast of the Arabian Peninsula and with the major tribal shaykhs of the interior that were deemed crucial to the security and commerce of Aden. Designed to end growing threats posed by the Ottoman Turks in North Yemen and by other European imperial powers, these treaties were a major step toward the creation of the Aden Protectorates and the binding of Aden to the interior territories in modern times. The local rulers traded control of foreign policy for British protection and modest subsidies. Between 1886 and 1895, Britain signed treaties with the Aqrabis, Lower Aulaqis, Fadhlis, Hawshabis, Alawis, Lower Yafais, and some of the Wahidis.

ROBERT D. BURROWES

TRIBALISM

See TRIBES AND TRIBALISM

TRIBES AND TRIBALISM

This entry consists of the following articles:

ARABIAN PENINSULA
BUTAYNA TRIBE
DAWASIR TRIBE
FADAN KHARASA TRIBE
GUISH TRIBES
HASSANA TRIBE
MATAWIRAH TRIBE
MUNTAFIQ TRIBE
MURRAH, AL-

ARABIAN PENINSULA

In the peninsula, a tribe is a group defined by perceived descent from a common male ancestor.

The word *qabila* (tribe) refers not only to a kinship group but also to a status category: *qabili* families claim descent from one of two eponymous Arab ancestors, Adnan or Qahtan, and feel themselves to be distinct from and superior to the nontribal *khadiri*, freeborn people who cannot claim such descent. The *khadiri* included most of the tradesmen, artisans, merchants, and scholars of pre-oil Arabia.

People of *qabili* status divide themselves into superior and inferior tribes, with the former able to claim purity in blood and origin (*asl*). The most prominent of the superior tribes of Arabia are the Aniza, Shammar, Harb, Mustayr, Ajman, Dhafir, Banu Khalid, Banu Hajir, al-Murrah, Qahtan, Utayba, Dawasir, Sahul, Manasir, Banu Yas, Sibay, Qawasim, Banu Yam, Za'ab, and Banu Tamim. The main tribes considered inferior are the Awazim, Rashayda, Hutaym, Aqayl, and Sulubba. The Sulubba, who traveled the desert as tinkers and metalworkers in service to the more affluent bedouin, were at the bottom of the tribal social scale.

Marriage between individuals of *qabila* and *khadiri* status, and between individuals of superior and inferior tribes, is frowned upon. Since the *qabili* claim to status is dependent upon purity of descent through the paternal line, the children of such a marriage would suffer the taint of mixed blood and reflect on the status of the tribe as a whole. These status barriers to marriage are beginning to break down in contemporary Saudi Arabia as access to education and economic advantage have created new status categories, which are beginning to compete with tribal affiliation and are undermining its importance in the social hierarchy.

The proportion of the population of Saudi Arabia that claims a tribal affiliation is unknown. Nearly all nomadic people are organized in tribal associations, and in 1950 Saudi Arabia's nomadic population was estimated at 50 percent. Since, historically, branches of tribal groups have lived in agricultural settlements at least part of the year or were permanently settled in towns, an estimate (according to a study done in the late 1970s) that the proportion of the population who claim a tribal affiliation could be as high as 80 percent would seem reasonable. A more recent study, however, suggests that the bulk of the settled population in Najd were nontribal *khadiri*, many of whom intermarried with the *abd*, or black slaves. Since the major cities of the Hijaz—Jidda and Mecca—and the towns of the Persian (Arabian) Gulf have long attracted foreigners, it is likely that the proportion of the contemporary Saudi population claiming a tribal affiliation is far smaller.

Structurally, nomadic tribal groups are organized by patrilineal descent, which unites individuals in increasingly larger segments. The smallest functional unit is the *hamula* (lineage), which consists of three to seven generations of one family related through the paternal line. Since lineage members are patrilineal cousins, the *hamula* is also referred to as one's *ibn amm* (father's brother's son), or *ahl* (people). The residential unit within the lineage is the *bayt* (house or tent), usually consisting of members of a nuclear family, including wife or wives and children.

Members of a single lineage usually camp close to one another and herd their animals as a unit. The lineage shares joint responsibility for avenging wrongs suffered by its members and pays compensation for any caused by its members. Although tribes may differ in status, all lineages within a given tribe are considered equals. Water wells, aside from the newer deep wells drilled by the government, are held in common by lineages. Among nomads, lineage membership is the basis of summer camps, and all animals, though they are owned by individual households, bear the lineage's brand. In terms of social relationships, access to government bureaucracy, and economic well-being, connection with the lineage is the most important relationship for the individual member of a tribe.

Bedouin nomads gather to eat at a camp in the Sahara Desert of Tunisia. © CORBIS. REPRODUCED BY PERMISSION.

Above the level of lineage there are larger segments that together make up the tribe. The *fakhd* (thigh) consists of a number of lineages that together control pasture and wells in the tribal area, while the *ashira* (plural *asha'ir*) consisting of numerous *fakhds,* is the largest segment below the tribe. While the system allows lineages to locate themselves genealogically relative to other groups in the same tribe, in general the larger the tribal segment, the smaller its function in the daily life of the individual.

In eastern Arabia, there is a recognized division among tribal groups based on perceived origin: the Yamani (or Qahtani) who predominate in Oman are believed to have emigrated in ancient times from Yemen in the south, while the Adnani (or Nizari) tribes—settled in northern Oman, the Trucial coast, Bahrain, and Qatar—are believed to have come from the north and are considered racially less "pure" than those from the south. Most of the tribal groups in Qatar, despite their common origin, are also located throughout eastern Arabia. The ruling family

of the State of Qatar are the Al Thani, originally part of the Banu Tamim tribe of central Arabia who arrived in Qatar in the early seventeenth century. The Manasir, one of the most widespread tribes of eastern Arabia, are mostly bedouin and range from the al-Buraymi oasis across the United Arab Emirates to Qatar and al-Hasa in the west, with some residing in Sharjah and Ra's al-Khayma, and in the al-Shafra and al-Liwa oases in western Abu Dhabi. Some sections of the formerly powerful al-Na'im tribe of Oman reside in Qatar as well as in the rest of eastern Arabia. The Quabysat section of the Banu Yas Tribe tried unsuccessfully in the early twentieth century to settle at Khawar al-Udayd, a marshy inlet at the eastern base of the Qatar peninsula.

In Saudi Arabia, a new national consciousness to compete with tribal identities is starting to emerge as the centralized state undercuts tribal autonomy, sedentarization undermines the economic benefits of tribal organization, and children are exposed to a common government-imposed school curriculum. Tribal affiliation, however, especially for no-madic people, plays a pivotal role in relations between individuals and the central government. Since the mid-1980s, the central government has assumed the right to officially designate tribal leaders who may act as representatives on behalf of tribal members' interests. These leaders are expected to work through district amirs and governors and to deal with such issues as education, agricultural development, assis-tance in legal matters, transportation and commu-nication improvement, welfare and social assistance, and helping to attain citizenship privileges.

For many tribal groups such as the al-Murrah, the National Guards have institutionalized tribal solidarity and strengthened tribal ties to the central government. Membership in individual National Guards units is based on tribal affiliation, and lead-ership of each tribal unit can be synonymous with traditional tribal leadership. Through the National Guards, former nomads receive training and the potential for higher-level careers, instruction in military sciences, housing, and health and social ser-vices for dependents and families.

For those tribal people who continue to live as bedouins, the government also provides water taps; market areas in cities, towns, and villages that are used in marketing livestock; veterinary services; subsidized fodder; and buildings for storage. It has been estimated that only 5 percent of the Saudi pop-ulation today remain wholly nomadic.

Most tribes are affiliated with the House of Sa῾ud through marriage ties as the product of Ibn Sa῾ud's deliberate policy of cementing ties between himself and the tribal groups. Today the political alliance between tribe and state is being reinforced through marriage between tribal women and govern-ment officials as well as Saudi princes. Among the al-Sa῾ar bedouin in southern Arabia, for example, these marriages are encouraged by tribal leaders as a means of ensuring ongoing access to governmen-tal leaders.

See also ABD AL-AZIZ IBN SA῾UD AL SA῾UD;
AJMAN; AL THANI FAMILY; NAJD.

Bibliography

Anthony, John Duke. *Historical and Cultural Dictionary of the Sultanate of Oman and the Emirates of Eastern Arabia.* Metuchen, NJ: Scarecrow, 1976.

Dahlan, Ahmed Massan, ed. *Politics, Administration and Devel-opment in Saudi Arabia.* Jidda, Saudi Arabia: Dar al-Shorouq, 1990.

Dickson, Harold. *The Arab of the Desert.* London: Allen and Unwin, 1949.

Doughty, Charles. *Travels in Arabia Deserta.* Reprint, New York: Dover, 1980.

Hopkins, Nicholas. "Class and State in Rural Arab Communities." In *Beyond Coercion,* edited by Adeed Dawisha and I. Zartman. London and New York: Croom Helm, 1980.

Kingdom of Saudi Arabia. *Fifth Plan.* N.d.

ELEANOR ABDELLA DOUMATO

BUTAYNA TRIBE

One of two major factions within the Siba῾a (also Asbi῾a) tribe of Syria.

The Siba῾a is a major tribe of the Anaza confeder-ation of tribes. The other faction is al-Abda tribe. Both factions were divided into clans. Those clans spend the summer season north of al-Salamiyya in Syria, to the east of Hama, and also east of Homs.

The Siba῾a tribe as a whole numbered about 4,000 households *(bayt)* in the early 1930s. A *bayt* or *khayma* (tent) numbered about 5 persons, ac-cording to the Ottoman *Salname* (yearbook). Thus the Siba῾a would total 20,000 persons. It is not known what percentage of this total the Butayna tribe represented.

ABDUL-KARIM RAFEQ

DAWASIR TRIBE

A sharif tribe of central Saudi Arabia, centered in the Wadi al-Dawasir south of Riyadh.

The Dawasir are notable for their great success as landowners and oil contractors and for their main-tenance of tribal solidarity. The Al Sudayri family is the most famous to have come from the tribe; through it the tribe's influence has been felt through-out Saudi Arabia.

See also AL SUDAYRI FAMILY.

ELEANOR ABDELLA DOUMATO

FADAN KHARASA TRIBE

Kharasa is one of two factions of the Fadan, which is a major tribe in the Anaza confederation of tribes.

The other faction is the Fadan Wa'ad. The Kharasa numbered 1,500 *bayt* (household) or *khayma* (tent) in the early 1930s. According to the Ottoman *Salname,* which gives the size of the *khayma* as equal to about five persons, the total number of the Kharasa would have been 7,500 inhabitants. The Kharasa spread in the summer season along the Balikh and the Euphrates rivers in Syria; they are not allowed by the Syrian authorities to cross both rivers to the west. In winter, they go eastward into Iraq, especially during the years of drought. The Kharasa are divided into smaller clans, and they are on the whole warlike tribes.

ABDUL-KARIM RAFEQ

GUISH TRIBES

Tribes in the military service of the Makhzen in precolonial Morocco.

The most important of the Guish tribes were the Sherarda, Sheraga, and Udayay. Guish tribes were distinguished from the Naiba tribes, which were occasionally recruited to serve the Makhzen militarily. They lived on a plot of land offered by the sultan and did not pay taxes. Most of the administrators of the Makhzen were recruited from the Guish tribes.

RAHMA BOURQIA

HASSANA TRIBE

A major tribe of the Anaza confederation of Arab tribes who were known for their bravery.

In the second half of the eighteenth century, the Hassana tribe headed towards Syria from Najd, pushed by the Wahhabis. They reached the confines of Homs and Hama and clashed with the Mawali bedouin in control there. The weakened Mawali relinquished their positions and retreated towards Salamiyya and Ma'arrat al-Nu'man. The Hassana numbered 400 *bayts* (households), that is, about 2,000 persons (the *bayt* or the *khayma* [tent], according to the Ottoman *Salname,* included about five persons). The Hassana additionally had 300 *bayts* of followers.

ABDUL-KARIM RAFEQ

MATAWIRAH TRIBE

One of four major tribal confederations into which the Alawite community of Syria is divided.

The other three Alawite confederations are the Khayyatin, the Haddadin, and the Kalbiyya. Each of these confederations is made up of a number of clans, each of which carries a specific name. A case in point is the Numaylatiyya clan, which is part of the Matawirah tribe.

Bibliography

Khuri, Fuad. "The Alawis of Syria: Religion, Ideology and Organization." In *Syria, Society, Culture, and Polity,* edited by Richard Antoun and Donald Quataert. Albany: State University of New York Press, 1991.

ABDUL-KARIM RAFEQ

MUNTAFIQ TRIBE

A tribal confederation in southern Iraq.

Muntafiq designates a 300,000-member tribal confederation of settled, seminomadic, and nomadic tribes, including the Ajwad, Bani Malik, Bani Sa'id, Dhafir, and Jasha'am. They occupied the banks of the Euphrates from Chabaish to Darraji, and the Shatt al-Gharraf as far as Kut al-Hay. Led by the al-Sa'dun family, they were independent from the Ottomans, who relied upon them to defend lower Iraq against the Wahhabis and the Persians. Before and during the Mamluk period (1749–1831), they contested the court of Baghdad for power over Basra. After 1831, the policy of Iltizam, which required tribal shaykhs to collect government duties and revenues, eroded tribal relationships as the leaders demanded ever-increasing taxes on behalf of the government. When the Sa'dun became Ottoman landlords and government officials in 1870, reducing their tribes from landholders to tenants, the intense sense of betrayal further undermined their authority and weakened tribal power.

See also MAMLUKS; SA'DUN FAMILY, AL-.

Bibliography

Longrigg, Stephen Hemsley. *Four Centuries of Modern Iraq.* Oxford: Clarendon Press, 1925.

ALBERTINE JWAIDEH

MURRAH, AL-

A bedouin tribe of Saudi Arabia.

The al-Murrah inhabit the Empty Quarter (Rub al-Khali), southern Najd, south-central al-Hasa, and as far west as the Najran oasis. Considered to be a Sharif tribe (one claiming noble descent), they are renowned both for their utilization of the Empty Quarter for grazing camels and for skills of desert tracking, and have therefore been called the "nomads of the nomads." Although the majority still remain nomadic, in recent years al-Murrah households have begun to build permanent housing near traditional watering places, replacing camel herding with herding sheep and goats, and to derive part of their income from urban occupations and service in the Saudi National Guard.

See also RUB AL-KHALI; SHARIF.

ELEANOR ABDELLA DOUMATO

MUTAYR TRIBE

A tribe of northeastern Arabia.

The Mutayr cover an area that ranges from Kuwait in the north to al-Dahna, the sand belt in the south. The Mutayr were active in the Ikhwan movement in the first quarter of the twentieth century. Among the first to be induced to settle under the movement's influence, Mutayr tribespeople in 1912 built al-Artawiya, an Ikhwan settlement that achieved fame for its zealotry in attempting to create a religious community living by God's laws, and for trying to convert others to the same goal. Some of the Mutayr, such as Faysal al-Duwish, led the Ikhwan rebellion against King Ibn Saʿud in 1929/1930.

See also IKHWAN.

ELEANOR ABDELLA DOUMATO

QASHQAʾI

Turkic-speaking (western Oghuz Turkic) tribal people of the southern Zagros Mountains of southwestern Iran, in the vicinity of the city of Shiraz.

The Qashqaʾi form a historically important tribal confederacy that originated in the late eighteenth century. Until the 1960s, the majority of Qashqaʾi were nomadic pastoralists. In the 1990s, many Qashqaʾi continue to rely on nomadism (increasingly by motorized vehicles) for a livelihood. Many have settled in villages, some for part of the year, and agriculture plays an increasingly important economic role.

Qashqaʾi territory is ecologically rich and diverse. Low-altitude winter pastures near the Persian Gulf and high-altitude summer pastures to the north and northeast are separated by hundreds of miles, and the migrations of spring and autumn each last from two to three months. The people follow Shiʿism and numbered approximately 600,000 in 1990. The Qashqaʾi have a strong sense of ethnic and national-minority identity, especially because of periodic repression of them by Iranian state rulers.

Bibliography

Beck, Lois. *Nomad: A Year in the Life of a Qashqaʾi Tribesman in Iran.* Berkeley: University of California Press, 1991.

Beck, Lois. *The Qashqaʾi of Iran.* New Haven, CT: Yale University Press, 1986.

LOIS BECK

QURAYSH TRIBE

The tribe of the Prophet Muhammad and the leading tribe of Mecca in the Prophet's time.

Before being converted to Islam, the Quraysh provided the strongest opposition to Muhammad, because the monotheism preached by the Prophet appeared to undermine tribal wealth derived from the pilgrimage to the Kaʿba, then a house of idol-worship. In classical theory it was held that the leadership of the Muslim *umma* (community) should be held only by a descendant of the Quraysh tribe, and this idea has been used by political opposition groups in contemporary Saudi Arabia to challenge the legitimacy of the Al Saʿud family, who are of the Anaza tribe. It has also been used to strengthen the legitimacy of the Sharifian dynasty of Morocco, which claims descent from the Quraysh.

See also KAʿBA.

ELEANOR ABDELLA DOUMATO

SHAMMAR

A tribe of north-central Saudi Arabia.

The Shammar are a sharif tribe (a tribe claiming noble descent), centered in northern Najd in the region of Haʾil, Jabal Shammar, and the Nafud. The Shammar are led by the Al Rashid family, former rulers of Haʾil who captured Riyadh in 1891 and were ousted by Ibn Saʿud in 1902. Divided into four sections—Abda, Aslam, Al Sinjara, and Tuman—the Shammar tribe was primarily camel-herding bedouin. Some few lineages live in farming villages. Many of their lineages, including the ruling Al Rashid, were seminomadic, maintaining oasis gardens during part of the year and grazing their animals in the desert in the wake of winter rains. In the nineteenth century, the Al Rashid were active proponents of the Muwahhidun reform movement, though they opposed the extension of Al Saʿud family rule into their territory, encouraged Qurʾanic education for boys and girls, and required Friday attendance in the mosque by men. In the twentieth century, the Shammar intermarried with the Al Saʿud family and benefit today from the patronage of the ruling family, although they have been generally excluded from governing posts.

ELEANOR ABDELLA DOUMATO

TEBU TRIBE

Group of black Africans of unknown origin centered in the Tibesti mountains of the Sahara.

The Tebu are located in both southern Libya and northern Chad. Their language is part of the Nilo-Saharan family. The Tebu are Muslims, their form of Islam strongly influenced by the Libyan Sanusi movement of the nineteenth century. Their economy is a combination of pastoralism, farming, and date cultivation.

Bibliography

Metz, Helen Chapin, ed. *Libya: A Country Study,* 4th ed. Washington, DC: U.S. Government Printing Office, 1989.

STUART J. BORSCH

UTAYBA TRIBE

The most powerful tribe in central Arabia.

The Utayba (also Otayba) were wealthy in camels and horses, which were sold on the international market, and strong in arms. In nobility, the Utayba were second only to the Anaza tribe of the Al Saʿud, and they ranged from the eastern Hijaz to central Najd. In the nineteenth century, there were settled villages of Utayba as well as large, fully nomadic confederations. The Utayba joined the Ikhwan in the early years of the twentieth century, with some sections of the tribe settling in Artawiya and Ghatghat, the most fervent of the Muwahhidun religious settlements. The religious zealot who led the attempt to seize the Grand Mosque at Mecca in 1979, Juhaiman al-Utaybi, was a member of the Utayba.

ELEANOR ABDELLA DOUMATO

YAZIDIS

Kurdish tribe.

A Kurdish tribal group of nomadic clans numbering 60,000 to 70,000 persons indigenous to the area of northern Iraq (Mosul) and eastern Turkey (Diyarbekir), they practice a heterodox religion incorporating Islamic, Christian, Jewish, and pagan elements. These include baptism, dualism, the prohibition of certain foods, circumcision, fasting, pilgrimage, interpretation of dreams, and transmigration of souls. Though they possess two sacred books—*Kitab al-Jilwa* (Book of revelation) and *Mashaf Rash* (Black book)—written in Arabic, they are not accorded the status of Ahl al-Kitab (protected minority status).

The Yazidis (the name does not seem to be related to *Yazid* but probably to the Persian word *ized* or angel) refer to themselves as Dasin or Dawasin (possibly from the name of an old Nestorian diocese). They believe themselves to be a unique people; not, for instance, descended directly from Adam and Eve like the rest of humanity. They practice a form of dualism between God and the peacock angel, with whom Shaykh Adi (to whose tomb annual devotional pilgrimages are made) was united through transmigration. Figures of peacocks made of bronze or iron are ritual devotional objects. There is a hierarchy of clerics, tribal shaykhs, and lesser priests, headed by a religious chief shaykh and a lay leader, Mirza Beg.

Pejoratively labeled "devil worshipers" or associated with the Caliph Yazid, they were branded as heretics, and numerous unsuccessful attempts by Turks and Kurds were made to convert or completely annihilate them.

Bibliography

Held, Colbert C. *Middle East Patterns: Places, Peoples, and Politics,* 3d edition. Boulder, CO: Westview, 1994.

REEVA S. SIMON

YEMINI

Yemeni tribes, rather than being mere vestiges of the past, are vital forces that continue to play determinant roles in the political, social, and cultural spheres.

Despite the tendency to characterize the highlands of Northern Yemen as "tribal" and southern Yemen as "peasant," tribes and tribalism are part of the cultural, social, and political landscape of nearly all regions of Yemen, even the Tihama coast and Wadi Hadramawt. For centuries, however, what has distinguished the northern highlands from the other regions of the country is the importance of the tribe as a unit of identification and action and the great extent to which tribes can be mobilized and organized into larger confederations when the interests of the tribe or tribal system are at stake. Although many residents of the southern uplands and the Hadramawt claim a tribal lineage, this often seems to be less important as a basis of personal identity than does place of origin—a village, valley, or region—or some other attribute. By contrast, many men of the highlands define themselves primarily in terms of their tribes, and many of these northern highland tribes with their present names were in existence at least a thousand years ago.

The majority of tribesmen in most parts of Yemen are sedentary farmers who grow sorghum, but the sparsely populated arid land on the edge of the Rub al-Khali (Empty Quarter) and the Ramlat al-Sabatayn is home to nomadic tribes principally engaged in animal husbandry. These bedouin populations have declined in recent years, in part because they were forced to give up their traditional roles as guardians and pillagers of the old trade routes, and now constitute a tiny portion of the total population of unified Yemen.

ROBERT D. BURROWES

TRIPARTITE DECLARATION (1950)

Declaration issued by the United States, Britain, and France guaranteeing borders in Middle Eastern states.

On 25 May 1950 the United States, Britain, and France jointly issued the Tripartite Declaration, which guaranteed the territorial status quo determined by Arab–Israeli armistice agreements and stipulated close consultation among the three powers with a view to limiting the Arab–Israeli arms race. The aim of the Western powers was to contain the Arab–Israeli conflict in order to focus the attention of the states of the Middle East on anti-Soviet defense plans.

In June 1952 the Western powers set up the Near East Arms Coordinating Committee (NEACC), through which they coordinated their arms sales to all parties in the conflict. In fact, the United States sold virtually no arms in the Middle East, leaving those markets to Britain and France. Despite fierce Anglo-French competition, the NEACC functioned reasonably well for more than three years. Both Britain and France periodically withheld arms from the rivals in the Arab–Israeli dispute, primarily when those states took action that threatened British or French regional interests. The Czech arms deal of September 1955, by means of which the Soviet Union agreed to sell Egypt $250 million worth of modern weaponry, made irrelevant Western efforts to limit the flow of arms. In April 1956 France began to transfer large quantities of modern arms to Israel.

See also ARMS AND ARMAMENTS IN THE MIDDLE EAST.

Bibliography

Levey, Zach. *Israel and the Western Powers, 1952–1960.* Chapel Hill: University of North Carolina Press, 1997.

Safran, Nadav. *From War to War: The Arab–Israeli Confrontation, 1948–1967; A Study of the Conflict from the Perspective of Coercion in the Context of Inter-Arab and Big Power Relations.* New York: Pegasus, 1969.

Slonim, Shlomo. "Origins of the 1950 Tripartite Declaration on the Middle East." *Middle Eastern Studies* 23
(1987): 135–149.

ZACH LEVEY

TRIPARTITE TREATY OF ALLIANCE

*Agreement regulating Allied occupation of Iran during
World War II.*

Following the German invasion of the Soviet Union
in June 1941, the British and Soviet governments
jointly demanded that Iran, which bordered the
southern Soviet Union, expel an estimated 2,000
Germans working on various projects there. Dissatisfied with the pace of Iran's response, British and
Soviet military forces jointly invaded Iran on 25 August 1941, routed its armed forces within days, and
occupied the country. To harmonize the occupation
with the aims of the Atlantic Charter, which had
been promulgated by Britain and the United States
less than two weeks before the invasion, Britain and
the Soviet Union signed a Tripartite Treaty of Alliance with Iran on 29 January 1942. Under the
terms of this agreement, the Allies pledged to respect the territorial integrity, sovereignty, and political independence of Iran, and to withdraw all
their military forces from the country within six
months after the cessation of all hostilities.

Bibliography

Avery, Peter. *Modern Iran.* New York: Praeger, 1965.

ERIC HOOGLUND

TRIPOLI

City on the Mediterranean coast of northwest Libya.

Tripoli is the capital, largest city, and chief seaport
of Libya. The city was founded by the Phoenicians
on a small, rocky promontory. Known by the Romans as Oea, it formed (with Sabrata and Leptis
Magna) the *tripolis* (Greek, three towns) from which
its modern name derives. (In Arabic Tripoli is known
as *Tarablus al-Gharb*—Tripoli of the West—to distinguish it from Lebanon's Tripoli.) Tripoli owed its
preeminence to a fair harbor on the short sea route
to Malta, Sicily, and Italy; to good water supplies
and a moderately productive oasis and hinterland;

and to domination of the northern ends of the
shortest trade routes from the Mediterranean to
central Africa via Fezzan.

After a history of foreign and local rule, prosperity declined by the end of the nineteenth century
with the demise of Barbary Pirates and Mediterranean corsairing as well as the collapse of the trans-
Saharan trade system. In 1911, the population was
estimated at some 20,000, when Tripoli was the
prime objective of the Italian invasion. It remained
in Italian hands throughout the varying fortunes of
Italy's presence in Libya. Under Italian rule, and
especially during the post-1922 Fascist era, Tripoli
was developed outside the walled Old City and
acquired modern municipal services and the appearance of an Italian provincial town. In 1934, it
became the capital of the colony of Libya, combining Tripolitania and Cyrenaica. During World War
II, Tripoli fell, with little damage, to the invading
British Eighth Army in January 1943 and became
the seat of the British military administration that
ruled Tripolitania until Libya's UN-supervised independence in 1951. On independence, Tripoli became joint capital of the Libyan federal kingdom,
with Benghazi.

The oil boom of the 1950s and 1960s brought
commercial expansion and increased population,
with development into the outlying villages of the
oasis. Shantytowns—which housed migrants from
the countryside—proliferated on the outskirts. The
United States had a large air base at Wheelus (al-
Mallaha) to the east of the city, and the international airport was developed at the Royal Air Force
base at Idris, near Gasr ben Gashir to the south. After the 1969 revolution, Tripoli became the sole
capital of Libya and, following expulsion of its remaining Italian and Jewish communities, took on a
more overtly Arab and Muslim character. Shantytowns were cleared and large public-housing schemes
and commercial developments spread in a six-to-
ten mile (10–15 km) radius from the city center.
The population doubled between 1973 and 1984.

Attempts by the royalist regime to create a new
capital at Baida and move the central administration to the central Libyan oases did little to diminish
Tripoli's political, commercial, and social preeminence. It dominates one of Libya's main agricultural and industrial regions, and its port, airport,

and roads to Tunisia, Fezzan, and Cyrenaica make it a key communications and transshipment center.

In 1986 the United States bombed Tripoli because of Libya's involvement in international terrorism. Some of the city was destroyed. Its population in 2003 was estimated at 1,775,000.

Bibliography

Wright, John. *Libya*. New York: Praeger, 1969.

JOHN L. WRIGHT

TRIPOLI CONFERENCE (1977)

Conference of Arab leaders in Tripoli, Libya.

The Tripoli Conference was convened 2 December 1977 in response to Egyptian President Anwar Sadat's trip to Jerusalem the previous month. It established the Steadfastness and Confrontation Front to oppose Sadat's peace initiative toward Israel. The front was joined by all of the attending heads of state, from Libya, Syria, Algeria, and South Yemen, and by leaders of Palestine Liberation Organization (PLO) factions.

Iraq, which sent a minor delegate, refused to join. On 5 December, Sadat broke diplomatic relations with all countries that attended the conference. A second result of the conference was the brief reunion of feuding PLO factions under Syria's sponsorship.

Bibliography

Cobban, Helena. *The Palestinian Liberation Organisation: People, Power, and Politics.* Cambridge, U.K., and New York: Cambridge University Press, 1984.

ELIZABETH THOMPSON

TRIPOLI PROGRAMME (1962)

Document representing the first comprehensive endeavor to define an identity and direction for independent Algeria.

At the end of the Algerian War of Independence, the Tripoli Programme, one of the most important documents in modern Algerian history, was introduced,

the product of the meeting in Libya of Algeria's Front de Libération Nationale (National Liberation Front, FLN). This occasion in June 1962 marked the last time the wartime FLN convened before the intraelite conflict of that summer, which established the new government under Ahmed Ben Bella.

The program proposed a "socialist option" for Algeria's development. According to its chief authors, Redha Malek, Mohamed Bedjaoui, and Mohamed Benyahia, the quest for democracy necessitated class conflict and economic transformation. It projected the nationalization of foreign interests, the establishment of an industrial economy, and the inauguration of agricultural cooperatives. Stridently anticolonial, the program viewed the recently signed Evian agreements with France as neocolonialist. The Tripoli Programme was complemented in April 1964 by the Algiers Charter and by Algeria's National Charter (1976; 1986).

See also ALGIERS CHARTER.

PHILLIP C. NAYLOR

TRIPOLITANIA

A region in Libya.

The three historic North African regions of Tripolitania, Cyrenaica, and the Fezzan combine to make up the modern state of Libya, which is officially known as the Great Socialist People's Libyan Arab Jamahiriya. Tripolitania is the most populous of the three regions, with almost 80 percent of the country's five million people. It is located in the northwestern part of the country and covers an area of approximately 140,000 square miles (365,000 sq. km). Bordered on the north by the Mediterranean Sea, its boundaries stretch east to the Gulf of Sidra and Cyrenaica, west to Tunisia, and south into the Saharan Desert, where it adjoins the Fezzan.

In classical times, three ancient cities, Leptis Magna, Oea, and Sabratah, flourished on the northern coast of Tripolitania. Founded by Phoenician colonists, each was situated at the end of a long caravan route winding south into the heart of sub-Saharan Africa. All three cities enjoyed naturally safe harbors; lying at the end of ancient routes to the south, what began as primitive trading posts soon turned into flourishing caravan centers.

During the Roman period, Leptis Magna developed into one of the finest examples of an African city. A key factor in its development was its location on the Mediterranean Sea, sheltered by a promontory at the mouth of the Wadi Lebda, and near the relatively well watered hinterland of Tripolitania. Leptis, over time, became much more important as a commercial center than either Oea or Sabratah. Leptis Magna is the most impressive archaeological site in Tripolitania, and in Libya as well. The Severan Arch, erected in honor of a visit from Emperor Septimius Severus in 203 C.E., and the Hadrianic Baths complex are particularly noteworthy.

Tripolitania shares a common history and close ties with the Maghrib, the western Islamic world traditionally comprising Algeria, Morocco, and Tunisia. It is a part, both geographically and culturally, of the Maghrib and is sometimes included in descriptions of that region. Libyan migration from Tripolitania to Tunisia, in particular, has been commonplace for centuries. Cross-border migration was especially heavy during the Italian occupation, which began in 1911, as many Tripolitanians fled Libya to escape the Italian invaders. In consequence, many Tunisians are of Libyan descent, and related families are often found on opposite sides of the Libya–Tunisia border.

At the outset of the twentieth century, the Italian occupation of Libya stimulated political consciousness throughout Tripolitania. Consequently, it was from this region that the strongest impulses supporting unification with Cyrenaica and the Fezzan developed. The ill-fated Tripoli Republic, proclaimed in the fall of 1918, was the first republican government formally created in the Arab world. However, the creation of the Tripoli Republic, together with a declaration of independence and subsequent attempts to promote Libyan independence at the 1919 Paris Peace Conference, stirred little enthusiasm among the major powers of the world. By 1923 the Tripoli Republic had disintegrated.

Following World War II, a wide variety of political groups and parties were formed in Libya, and especially in Tripolitania. All of them favored a free and united Libya with membership in the Arab League. However, they differed widely in their choice of leadership for an independent Libya. When the foreign powers charged with determining Libya's future were unable to reach agreement, the traditional elites in Tripolitania, together with their peers in Cyrenaica and the Fezzan, agreed in 1950 to form a federal government, known as the United Kingdom of Libya, under the leadership of King Idris I. The monarchy was later replaced by a revolutionary government headed by Muammar al-Qaddafi in September 1969.

Located on the site of the ancient city of Oea, Tripoli is the capital of Tripolitania as well as the de facto capital of Libya. The area surrounding Tripoli as far south as the Jabal Nafusa is rich agricultural land with large groves of fruit and olive trees as well as date palms. Much of Libya's food comes from this region. South of the Jabal Nafusa, the desert begins, providing spectacular scenery most of the way to the Fezzan. Tripolitania also includes limited oil reserves and scattered iron ore deposits.

See also LIBYA; MAGHRIB; QADDAFI, MUAMMAR AL-; TRIPOLI.

Bibliography

Nelson, Harold D., ed. *Libya: A Country Study,* 3d edition. Washington, DC: U.S. Government Printing Office, 1979.

St John, Ronald Bruce. *Historical Dictionary of Libya,* 3d edition. Lanham, MD: Scarecrow Press, 1998.

Wright, John. *Libya: A Modern History.* Baltimore, MD: Johns Hopkins University Press, 1982.

RONALD BRUCE ST JOHN

TRUCIAL COAST

Colonial precursor of the United Arab Emirates.

The Trucial Coast was known to Europeans as the Pirate Coast in the late eighteenth and early nineteenth centuries, when the powerful federation of the Qawasim, operating primarily from the port of Ra's al-Khayma, ravaged shipping in the lower Persian (Arabian) Gulf. The government of British India sent several expeditions against them, finally subduing them in 1819. In the following year, Britain through the General Treaty of Peace, imposed a truce that condemned piracy and implied Britain's obligation to maintain peace in the Gulf. Subsequent treaties (truces) made the agreements more explicit, and the territories ruled by the shaykhs who were signatories to them became, in European usage, the Trucial Coast. The terms "Trucial States" and, confusingly, "Trucial Oman" were also used.

Fear of European rivals led Britain to establish "exclusive agreements" with these shaykhs in 1892. These engagements made Great Britain, through the colonial government in Delhi, responsible for the foreign relations of these shaykhdoms and, by implication, for their protection. The British, interested primarily in the security of the Gulf, kept their involvement on land to a minimum. Their intervention however, tended to freeze political relationships. This situation remained essentially unaltered until the interwar period, when the British government forced the rulers to deal only with prospecting oil companies of which it approved. Britain's simultaneous establishment of an air route across the Gulf began to open the area to the outside world, especially Sharjah, where an Imperial Airways airfield was established. Moreover, oil concession agreements created the need for the novel concept of fixed borders, which the British began to establish.

After World War II, Britain was much more fully involved in the affairs of the Trucial States. After 1947, with India's independence, the states became the responsibility of the Foreign Office in London. Britain's representative in the Trucial States was a permanent political officer assigned to Sharjah in 1948 (upgraded to political agent in 1953), and several state institutions were established. In 1951 the Trucial Oman Levies, a small force with British officers, was created to keep order in the Trucial States. Expanded and renamed the Trucial Oman Scouts in the mid-1950s, it became the nucleus of the United Arab Emirates, armed forces in 1971. In 1952 the Trucial States Council was created; though limited to a consultative role, it provided the first forum in which the rulers of the seven shaykhdoms could discuss common concerns. From 1965 until independence a Development Office, operating under the aegis of the Council, carried out infrastructure projects financed through a development fund to which Britain, Kuwait, Bahrain, Qatar, and Abu Dhabi contributed; Abu Dhabi carried the lion's share as its oil income expanded from the mid-1960s.

In December 1968, Britain's Labor government, beset by a balance-of-payments crisis, decided to withdraw military forces and relinquish responsibilities in the Gulf by the end of 1971. Though some of the rulers viewed Britain's withdrawal with alarm, Shaykh Zayid of Abu Dhabi and Shaykh Rashid of Dubai, the wealthiest of the seven Trucial States, agreed, as early as February 1968, to form a federation that would include Bahrain and Qatar. Despite British encouragement of this venture, it had foundered by early 1971. On 2 December 1971, a few months after Bahrain and Qatar had become separately independent, Sharjah, Umm al-Qaywayn, Ajman, and Fujayra joined Abu Dhabi and Dubai in the federation of the United Arab Emirates. In February 1972, Ra's al-Khayma belatedly joined the United Arab Emirates.

See also SHARJAH; UNITED ARAB EMIRATES.

Bibliography

Anthony, John Duke. *Arab States of the Lower Gulf: People, Politics, Petroleum.* Washington, DC: Middle East Institute, 1975.

Heard-Bey, Frauke. *From Trucial States to United Arab Emirates: A Society in Transition.* New York: Longman, 1982.

Peck, Malcolm C. *The United Arab Emirates: A Venture in Unity.* Boulder, CO: Westview Press, 1986.

MALCOLM C. PECK

TRUE PATH PARTY

A major centrist political party in Turkey from the late 1980s to the end of the 1990s.

The True Path Party (Doğru Yol Partisi, or DYP) was founded in 1983 by former members of the Justice Party. The military's National Security Council had banned former Justice Party chair Süleyman Demirel from active participation in politics until 1987; nevertheless, he was the behind-the-scenes driving force for the organization of the DYP. After his political activity ban had been lifted, Demirel became DYP's chair and led it to victory in the 1991 parliamentary elections. DYP won the largest number of seats, but not an absolute majority, and so formed a coalition government with the Social Democratic Populist Party (SHP). Upon the sudden death of President Turgut Özal in 1993, the Turkish Grand National Assembly voted for Demirel to be the new chief of state, and he resigned as the party's chair. DYP then chose Tansu Çiller as its leader, and she subsequently formed a new coalition government with SHP as Turkey's first woman prime minister. DYP lost its parliamentary plurality to the Refah Party in the 1995 elections. It formed a brief coalition with its rival, the Motherland Party, in early 1996, then joined Refah in a coalition from June 1996 to June 1997. Nevertheless, DYP's appeal continued to erode, and in the 1999 parliamentary elections it secured just 15 percent of seats. In the 2002 elections DYP fared even worse, receiving less than 10 percent of the overall nationwide vote and thus no seats in the parliament.

> See also ÇILLER, TANSU; DEMIREL, SÜLEYMAN; JUSTICE PARTY; MOTHERLAND PARTY; NATIONAL SECURITY COUNCIL (TURKEY); REFAH PARTISI; SOCIAL DEMOCRATIC POPULIST PARTY; TURKISH GRAND NATIONAL ASSEMBLY.

Bibliography

Hooglund, Eric. "Government and Politics." In *Turkey: A Country Study*, edited by Helen Chapin Metz. Washington, DC: U.S. Government Printing Office, 1996.

FRANK TACHAU
UPDATED BY M. HAKAN YAVUZ

TRUMAN, HARRY S.

[1884–1972]

Thirty-third president of the United States.

At the end of World War II, the Middle East was not among the United States' strategic priorities. Even after the Iranian crisis of 1945 and 1946 and following the promulgation of the Truman Doctrine in 1947, the American administration seemed reluctant to involve the United States in an area that had been part of the British, and partially French, sphere of influence. Indeed, Truman and his assistants hoped that, even after the British withdrawal from Greece and Turkey, London would be able to retain control of the Middle Eastern "inner core" and to resist any threat of Soviet infiltration into the area. Although members of the Truman administration held negative opinions about the effects of British (and French) colonialism on emerging

Arab nationalism, nevertheless geostrategic necessities led the United States to favor some continuation of British influence in the region.

This inconsistency also applied to American policy on the "Zionist question." The foundation of a Jewish state in Palestine became one of the main issues of Truman's worldview, although the U.S. president was annoyed by Zionist importunity and influenced by the State Department's negative opinion. However, advised above all by his special counselor, Clark Clifford, and by David Niles, Truman believed that the birth of Israel would represent a strategic asset for Washington's Middle East policy. So the United States favored the new Jewish state, with the negative repercussion that its relations with the Arab Middle East became problematic. Fearing that some Arab countries would be drawn into the Soviet orbit, Truman tried to implement a policy of appeasement toward the Arabs. In this connection, he attempted to find a solution (via the UN Conciliation Commission for Palestine) to the question of the Palestinian refugees of the 1948 Arab-Israel War. This issue was not resolved and, along with other unresolved questions, became the inheritance of Truman's successor, Dwight D. Eisenhower, and Secretary of State John Foster Dulles.

Bibliography

Cohen, Michael J. *Fighting World War Three from the Middle East: Allied Contingency Plans, 1945–1954.* London: Cass, 1997.

Cohen, Michael J. *Truman and Israel.* Berkeley: University of California Press, 1990.

Druks, Herbert. *The Uncertain Friendship: The U.S. and Israel from Roosevelt to Kennedy.* Westport, CT: Greenwood Press, 2001.

Lesch, David W., ed. *The Middle East and the United States: A Historical and Political Reassessment.* Boulder, CO: Westview Press, 2003.

ANTONIO DONNO

TRUMPELDOR, YOSEF

[1880–1920]

Zionist leader and military organizer in Palestine.

Born in the northern Caucasus in Russia, Yosef Trumpeldor served in the tsar's army during the Russo–Japanese War (1904–1905). He was wounded and lost an arm but returned to combat, which earned him decorations and promotion as the first Jewish officer in the Russian army.

Ardent about Zionism and an advocate of agricultural settlements, he organized Jewish self-defense groups in Russia (for emigration) and later in Ottoman Palestine, where he immigrated. During World War I he lobbied for the creation of a British-backed Jewish Legion, serving as second-in-command in what became the Zion Mule Corps. After the war he was affiliated with ha-Halutz (the agricultural pioneers) and encouraged Russian Jewish youth to go to Palestine to create agricultural and industrial settlements. Just before the British and French mandates took effect in the Middle East, he was sent to organize the defenses of Tel Hai, a pioneer Jewish settlement in northern Galilee. He died defending it on I March 1920. His last words, reported as "never mind, it is good to die for our country," initially became the motto of a nationalist myth and more recently have been material for humorous subversions of the legend that both signify and contribute to the erosion of classical Zionist ideology in Israel.

See also HA-HALUTZ; JEWISH LEGION; TEL HAI.

Bibliography

Zerubavel, Yael. "The Politics of Interpretation: Tel Hai in Israel's Collective Memory." *American Jewish Studies Review* 16 (1991): 133–160.

Zerubavel, Yael. *Recovered Roots: Collective Memory and the Making of Israeli National Tradition.* Chicago: University of Chicago Press, 1995.

DONNA ROBINSON DIVINE

TSEMEL, LEAH
[1945–]

Israeli lawyer and human rights activist.

Leah Tsemel was born in Haifa in 1945. Her mother and father were Jewish émigrés from Russia and Poland, respectively. Tsemel graduated from the Hebrew University of Jerusalem with a degree in criminal law in 1968. While at university she joined Matzpen, a radical left group a of the 1960s and 1970s that opposed Zionism and occupation.

Her distinguished legal career reflects a passionate and uncompromising commitment to human rights and progressive political positions, including support for establishing an independent state of Palestine with the 1967 Green Line as its borders, a unified Jerusalem as the capital of both Israel and Palestine, and the recognition in principle of the right of return of Palestinian refugees.

Since the 1970s, Tsemel has represented Palestinians in legal cases involving identity card confiscation, family reunification, house demolitions, deportations, political prisoners and administrative detainees, accused suicide bombers, and land confiscation. Her efforts to contest the use of torture on Palestinians are internationally recognized. In 1996, she received the Human Rights Award of the French Republic on behalf of the Public Action Committee against Torture in Israel. Tsemel was instrumental in a landmark Israeli Supreme Court decision of 6 September 1999 prohibiting the use of torture in interrogations by the Israeli General Security Services.

In 1972, Tsemel married Michael Warshavsky, a journalist and peace activist. They have two children.

See also GREEN LINE; REFUGEES: PALESTINIAN.

Bibliography

Salokar, Rebecca Mae, and Volcansek, Mary L., eds. *Women in Law: A Bio-Bibliographical Sourcebook.* Westport, CT: Greenwood Press, 1996.

MONA GHALI

TUBI, TAWFIQ
[1922–1994]

Israeli Palestinian politician.

Born in Haifa, Tawfiq Tubi was educated at the Mt. Zion school in Jerusalem. He joined the Palestine Communist party in 1941 and later was one of the founders of the League for National Liberation, which originally opposed partition of Palestine but later came to accept it, after the Soviet Union indicated that it would support partition. After the state of Israel was proclaimed (1948), he became a member of the Knesset on the Maki (Israel Communist

Party) list and a member of the Central Committee. In 1976, he was elected secretary general of the Hadash political faction. He was also the editor of *al-Ittihad*.

Bibliography

Rolef, Susan Hattis, ed. *Political Dictionary of the State of Israel*, 2d edition. New York: Macmillan, 1993.

BRYAN DAVES

TUDEH PARTY

The main orthodox Communist organization in contemporary Iran.

The Tudeh Party (Hezb-e Tudeh-ye Iran; the Party of the Iranian Masses) was formed in 1941 in Iran by members of the famous Fifty-three, who had been arrested in 1937 but were released immediately on the British-Soviet occupation of Iran during World War II. The Fifty-three were predominantly young, university-educated Marxist intellectuals from middle-class and Persian-speaking families. The Tudeh Party quickly grew to become the organization of the masses in reality as well as in name. It did so in part because its labor unions mobilized a significant portion of the wage-earning population; in part because it attracted many civil servants, professionals, and intellectuals; and in part because it successfully portrayed itself as the champion of patriotism and constitutional liberties against foreign imperialism and the threat of royal dictatorship. By 1945, the list of Tudeh sympathizers read like a Who's Who of Iran's intelligentsia.

After 1945, however, the Tudeh suffered a series of setbacks. Its patriotic credentials were undermined when it supported the Soviet-sponsored revolt in Azerbaijan, echoed the demands of the Soviet Union's Josef Stalin for an oil concession, and failed to give full backing to Mohammad Mossadegh's campaign to nationalize the petroleum industry. Its constitutional and democratic credentials were brought into question once it declared itself a Marxist-Leninist party and became a formal member of the Soviet-led Communist movement. Moreover, its ability to function was drastically curtailed—first in 1949, when the party was banned after an attempt was made on the life of Mohammad Reza Shah Pahlavi; and second after the 1953 coup, when SAVAK, the secret police, helped by the U.S. Central Intelligence Agency, vigorously unearthed its underground network. Over forty Tudeh members were executed in the 1950s.

The Tudeh was further weakened by two major internal disputes. In the aftermath of the Azerbaijan revolt, a number of intellectuals left the party and in later years joined Mosaddegh's National Front (Jebhe-ye Melli). In the 1960s, at the height of the Sino-Soviet dispute, a number of younger activists, denouncing the Tudeh leadership as reformist and revisionist, formed their own pro-Chinese Sazman-e Engelab-e Hezb-e Tudeh-ye Iran (Revolutionary Organization of the Tudeh Party of Iran).

By the time of the Iranian Revolution (1979), little remained of the Tudeh within Iran. Despite this, the party tried a comeback; it instructed its cadres to return and elected as its first secretary Nur al-Din Kianuri, the proponent of an alliance with Ayatollah Ruhollah Khomeini. The previous first secretary, Iraj Iskandari, had favored the secular liberals, especially the National Front. From 1978 until 1983, the Tudeh supported the Islamic Republic of Iran, even when much of the left denounced the regime as a medieval theocracy.

This support ended abruptly in 1983, in the midst of the Iran–Iraq War, after Khomeini ordered Iranian troops to cross the border into Iraq. As soon as the Tudeh criticized this action, most of the party's leaders and cadres were arrested and tortured into confessing that they were "spies and traitors plotting to overthrow the Islamic Republic." The most extensive recantation came from Ehsan Tabari, a member of the Fifty-three and the most important intellectual in the Tudeh leadership. Tabari died in prison from heart failure, but 163 of his colleagues were killed—some under torture, others by hanging. A few party leaders escaped to Western Europe, where they continue to be active. They publish a biweekly, *Nameh-ye Mardom* (People's newsletter) and a periodical, *Donya* (The world), and run a clandestine radio station. They held a party congress in 1998 in Germany and often send delegates to international communist meetings.

See also AZERBAIJAN CRISIS; IRANIAN REVOLUTION (1979); IRAN–IRAQ WAR (1980–1988); KHOMEINI, RUHOLLAH; KIANURI, NUR AL-

DIN; MOSSADEGH, MOHAMMAD; NATIONAL FRONT, IRAN; PAHLAVI, MOHAMMAD REZA.

Bibliography

Abrahamian, Ervand. *Iran between Two Revolutions.* Princeton, NJ: Princeton University Press, 1982.

Raffat, Donné. *The Prison Papers of Bozorg Alavi: A Literary Odyssey.* Syracuse, NY: Syracuse University Press, 1985.

Zabih, Sepehr. *The Communist Movement in Iran.* Berkeley: University of California Press, 1966.

ERVAND ABRAHAMIAN

TUHAMI AL-GLAWI
[1879–1956]

Pasha of Marrakech under the French protectorate in Morocco, 1912–1956.

The younger brother of Madani al-Glawi, who established the power of the family, Tuhami ibn Muhammad al-Mazwari al-Glawi first served as pasha of Marrakech under Morocco's Sultan Abd al-Hafid from 1908 to 1911. He then benefited from Madani's alliance with the protectorate government of France in 1912, and following Madani's death in 1918 Tuhami was named pasha of Marrakech. A staunch supporter of the French protectorate and a wily politician, he accumulated enormous wealth and power as viceroy of southern Morocco and gained a reputation of being greedy and oppressive. His leadership of the movement to depose Sultan Muhammad V (1953), part of a pro-French effort to prevent the collapse of the protectorate, gained him much notoriety among Moroccan nationalists. He died in 1956, after the independence of Morocco.

See also GLAWI FAMILY, AL-.

Bibliography

Pascon, Paul. *Capitalism and Agriculture in the Haouz of Marrakesh.* London: KPI; New York: Routledge and Kegan Paul, 1986.

EDMUND BURKE III

TUMAN BEY
[1473–1517]

The last independent Mamluk sultan of Egypt.

After the death of Qansuh al-Ghuri al-Ashrafi in the battle of Marj Dabiq near Aleppo (August 1516), the Mamluks selected his viceroy, Tuman Bey, to continue the struggle against the invasion of Sultan Selim the Grim.

Superior Ottoman tactics and weaponry forced the Egyptian ruler to hurriedly manufacture cannons and raise an infantry corps that used muskets similar to those used by the janissaries. He rejected an offer to submit to Ottoman suzerainty in exchange for being allowed to remain governor of Egypt. The two armies met in Raydaniyya, near Cairo, on 22 January 1517. The Mamluk cavalry again suffered defeat, and Selim entered the capital in triumph. On 28 January, Tuman Bey launched a surprise night attack against the Ottomans in Bulaq. The battle raged for four days, with both sides displaying extreme ferocity, but the Mamluks finally withdrew to the haven of Upper Egypt. There, Tuman Bey raised an army composed of a combination of Arab bedouins and Mamluks, and he returned, on 2/3 April, to attack Selim near Giza. After another defeat, Tuman Bey escaped north to a village near Damanhur, where he was captured by Ottoman troops. He was hanged a fortnight later in Cairo.

Bibliography

Glubb, John Bagot. *Soldiers of Fortune: The Story of the Mamlukes.* New York: Stein and Day, 1973.

BASSAM NAMANI

TUNB ISLANDS

Islands near the entrance to the Persian Gulf that are controlled by Iran and claimed by the United Arab Emirates.

The Greater and Lesser Tunbs are two small islands in the Persian (Arabian) Gulf close to the Strait of Hormuz. Greater Tunb, 17 miles (27 km) southwest of the large Iranian island of Qeshm, has a total area of about 3 square miles (7.5 sq. km). There are no permanent freshwater sources on the island and historically no permanent settlements, although it was occupied seasonally. Lesser Tunb, about 5 miles (8 km) east of Greater Tunb, is less than 2 square miles (5 sq. km) in area and has no fresh water or inhabitants.

Historical evidence for the ownership of the Tunbs prior to the mid-nineteenth century is sketchy, but by the mid-1880s, both Iran and the shaykhdom of Ra's al-Khayma were claiming sovereignty over the islands. Ra's al-Khayma was a British protectorate, and in 1904 Britain sided with its dependency by expelling the Iranian customs officers from Greater Tunb. Iran protested the action and periodically asserted its claim to the Tunbs, most notably in 1968 after Britain announced that it would recognize the full independence of its Persian Gulf protectorates. Britain mediated an agreement for shared sovereignty over the nearby island of Abu Musa, but the ruler of Ra's al-Khayma declined to accept such an arrangement for the Tunbs. Consequently, one day before the British treaty of protection with Ra's al-Khayma was due to expire, Iran forcibly occupied the Tunbs (30 November 1971); Britain took no action. After the shaykhdom joined the new United Arab Emirates (UAE), the dispute with Iran remained dormant for twenty years. The UAE raised the issue of Iran's occupation in 1992, in conjunction with the dispute over Abu Musa. Since then, the Tunbs have been a source of contention between Iran and the UAE.

Bibliography

Mirfendereski, Guive. "The Ownership of the Tonb Islands: A Legal Analysis." In *Small Islands, Big Politics: the Tonbs and Abu Musa in the Persian Gulf*, edited by Hooshang Amirahamdi. New York: St. Martin's Press, 1996.

MALCOLM C. PECK
UPDATED BY ERIC HOOGLUND

TUNIS

Capital of the Republic of Tunisia.

Tunis is the largest city in Tunisia. The population of the greater Tunis urban area is estimated at 2,083,000 (2001), more than one-quarter of the country's total population of 9,673,000. (In 1984 the population of the city itself was estimated at about 600,000.)

In 1160, Tunis became the provincial capital of the Moroccon-based Almohad dynasty. The Almohads built the qasba (citadel) that remained the seat of political power in the city until France's protec-

torate (1881). In the thirteenth century, under the Hafsid dynasty, Tunis became the national capital, a distinction it has retained ever since.

Tunis had only one congregational mosque, that of al-Zaytuna, until 1252, when the mosque of al-Tawfiq was constructed. Subsequently congregational mosques were built throughout the city. Following their seizure of Tunis in 1574, the Ottomans converted the mosques of the qasba and al-Qasr to follow the Hanafi usage, the school of Islamic law to which they adhered. In the seventeenth and eighteenth centuries, the Tunis skyline was altered by construction of new mosques, including those of Yusuf Dey (1612), Hammuda Pasha (1655), and Sidi Mahriz (1692), and the New Mosque of Husayn (1726).

Corsair wealth of the deys and beys transformed Tunis into a cosmopolitan complex dominated by mosques, madrasas (Islamic secondary schools), *zawiyas* (Islamic mystic centers), palaces, and elegant homes. The Turks also constructed a *maristan* (hospital) in the seventeenth century.

Prior to 1858, Tunis was organized into a quarter system centered on major mosques. The gates between quarters were locked at night and whenever public disturbances occurred. Each quarter was self-sufficient, with its own bread ovens, markets, bathhouses, wells, cisterns, Qur'anic schools (*kuttab*), and prayer mosques (*masjid*). Daytime security was provided by the *dawlatli* (a position directly descended from the dey). The *shaykh al-madina* (chief guild leader, akin to city mayor) controlled nighttime security patrols.

This loose administration ended in 1858, when Muhammad Bey established the City Council (*al-majlis al-baladi*). He appointed the shaykh al-madina to head this council of fifteen members. Today the shaykh al-madina is president of the City Council and is appointed by the country's president.

France's protectorate (1881–1956) brought changes to Tunis. A deep-water channel was constructed that made it possible for oceangoing vessels to dock in the port of Tunis, near the modern city's downtown area. A causeway beside this channel connects Tunis and its suburbs of La Goulette (now Halq al-Wadi), Carthage, Sidi Bou Said, and La Marsa. France also drained the swamp that separated the walled old city from the Lake of Tunis and built there a new European-style city with parks, broad avenues, cathedrals, an embassy, and modern housing.

In the twentieth century, Tunis became the major destination of rural-to-urban migration because of its being the political, social, educational, economic, and entertainment center of Tunisia. It is the seat of the national government and the national headquarters of the government party, the Constitutional Democratic Rally (Ralliement Constitutionel Démocratique; RCD), and the site of the national university.

LARRY A. BARRIE

TUNISIA

This entry consists of the following articles:

TUNISIA: OVERVIEW
TUNISIA: PERSONAL STATUS CODE
TUNISIA: POLITICAL PARTIES IN

OVERVIEW

Arab republic in central North Africa.

Tunisia is bordered by Algeria on the west, the Mediterranean on the north and east, and Libya on the southeast. It includes the Kerkenna Islands off the east coast and the island of Djerba in the southeast. In 1993, Algeria and Tunisia settled a border dispute that had been under negotiation since 1983.

Geography and Climate

Tunisia's landmass comprises 59,984 square miles (155,360 sq. km); the total area is 63,170 square miles (163,610 sq. km). The country has three distinct regions: the northern Tell or high plains; the central steppes; and the arid south, characterized by date palm oases and numerous *shatts* (salt marshes), the largest of which is the Shatt al-Jarid.

The Dorsale massif, an extension of the Atlas Mountains, limits rainfall on the central steppes. The highest point in the chain is Mount Chambi (1,544 meters; 5,066 feet). The mountains enter Tunisia northwest of Fernania and veer northeast across Cape Bon before plummeting into the Mediterranean near El Haouaria.

One of Tunisia's few perennial rivers, the Medjerda, rises in Algeria, crosses northern Tunisia, and empties into the Gulf of Tunis. Most other Tunisian streams, except the Miliana, dry up during the summer. Since antiquity the Medjerda valley has contained Tunisia's richest farmland.

The central steppes are high near the border with Algeria and low near the coast, then merge into the Sahel (coast), an area lying between Hammamet (near Cape Bon) and Sfax. Farther south lies the Sahara.

The north and the Sahel are the most urbanized and most densely populated regions of Tunisia. Tunis is the largest city and the national capital. The second largest city, Sfax, has half as many inhabitants as greater Tunisia (2 million). Other important cities are Qairawan (an important religious center and the first Arab town in the country, founded in 670 C.E.), Sousse, Gafsa, and Bizerte.

Tunisia's natural resources include phosphate mines near Gafsa and a developing natural gas and petroleum industry. Foreign companies compete for oil concessions and continue to explore for new fields. Tunisia also produces small quantities of iron ore, lead, zinc, and salt. The Sahel region is a rich olive-growing area, and the southern oases contain extensive date-palm groves.

Northern Tunisia has a Mediterranean climate with cool, damp winters and warm, humid summers. Precipitation declines south of the Dorsale along the coast and is minimal in the interior steppes and Sahara, where winter days are mild but nights can be bitterly cold. Summer daytime temperatures in the interior steppes and southern desert can be very high. Temperatures at Tunis range from 6°C (43°F) to 33°C (91°F). Precipitation averages 60 inches in the north and 8 inches in the Sahara.

The People, the Language, and Religion

Tunisia's 8.4 million people are concentrated in the north, in the Sahel, and in regional urban centers such as Qairawan and Gafsa. More than half the population lives in the northern Tell and the Sahel, on about 20 percent of Tunisia's total land surface. About 53 percent (4,452,000) of Tunisians live in cities. Population density is 133 persons per square mile. Family planning programs in the 1970s and 1980s managed to lower the population growth rate from over 3 percent to about 2.1 percent by 1992; 38 percent of Tunisians were under age fifteen in that year. Many Tunisians engage in agricultural pursuits, but a growing number are in the tourist industry, humanities and professions, commercial sector, and government.

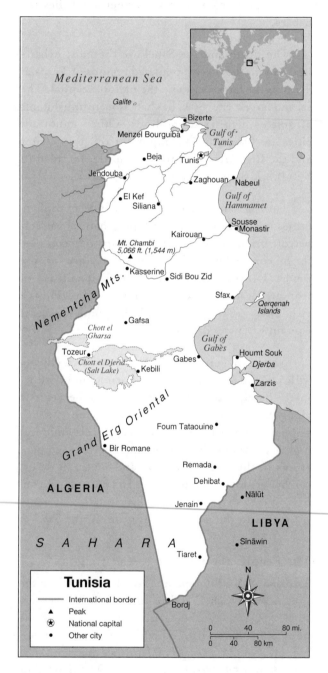

Tunisia's ethnic base is primarily mixed Arab-Berber or Arabized Berber. There are a few Berber speakers in isolated regions of the south. A tiny Jewish minority still exists; most Tunisian Jews left the country after 1957. Some European Christians live in Tunisia, primarily in the capital.

Tunisia's national language is Arabic (the first language of at least 98 percent of the people); French is the major second language as well as the dominant language of commerce and education. Although the print and audiovisual media use standard Arabic, most Tunisians speak their own dialect, which has three variations: an urban dialect, a rural village and small-town dialect, and a Bedouin dialect. Knowledge of the Egyptian dialect has been increasing since the 1970s because of Egypt's domination of the Arab cinema and television soap operas.

Islam is the official state religion. At least 98 percent of the population are Sunni Muslims. The island of Djerba harbors many Khariji Muslims. In the 1980s the Islamic Tendency Movement (Mouvement de Tendance Islamique; MTI) was formed, with Rached Ghannushi and Abdelfattah Mourou as its ideological leaders. Observance of Islamic rituals increased considerably in Tunisia during the 1980s and early 1990s. In recognition of this fact, and to thwart the designs of Islamists, the government sought to control all mosque appointments and to encourage moderation in religion. The government has grown more outwardly Islamic, following such traditional practices as waiting for the new moon before announcing the start of the Ramadan fast, and the firing of cannon to herald the first and last days of Ramadan.

The Economy

Tunisia's economy has improved due to good harvests (since 1990), economic restructuring, a growing manufacturing industry, a developing oil and gas sector, remittances from expatriates (an estimated 400,000 Tunisians work overseas), and a healthy tourist trade. Economic growth since 1988 has averaged about 4.2 percent, peaking at 8.6 percent in 1992. Unemployment ranges from the official 15 percent to a high of 20 to 50 percent in informal sectors of the economy. High rural unemployment has caused many young people to mi-

Habib Bourguiba is carried on the shoulders of his supporters as they celebrate the signing of the Franco-Tunisian Common Protocol in 1950. © Corbis. Reproduced by permission.

grate to urban centers in search of work, causing deterioration of public services and the taxing of city resources, especially in Tunis.

Tunisia's gross domestic product is about US$10 billion, and per capita income is about US$1,235. Agriculture comprises some 16 percent of the gross domestic product, and industry accounts for about 38 percent. The workforce is estimated at 2,250,000, with 34 percent in industry, 26 percent in agriculture, and 40 percent in services. Women make up just under 25 percent of the workforce (probably a much higher percentage of the rural "informal" sector). Labor unions have organized between 11 and 20 percent of the working class. The General Union of Tunisian Workers (Union Générale des Travailleurs Tunisiens; UGTT), headed by Ismail Sahbani, collaborates closely with the government and the Tunisian Union of Industrialists, Businessmen, and Artisans (Union Tunisienne des Industrialistes, Compagnies, et Artisans; UTICA).

History

Tunisia's geographic openness has made its history one of periodic invasions. Berber peoples settled the country in the fifth and fourth millennia B.C.E. The first outside civilization to make an impact came from Phoenicia, when émigrés from Tyre founded Carthage in 814 B.C.E. Carthage developed a maritime empire in the western Mediterranean and in the third century B.C.E. confronted Rome for control of the western Mediterranean. Three conflicts ensued that came to be known collectively as the Punic Wars. In the final battle of the Second Punic War (Zama, 202 B.C.E.), Rome's Scipio Africanus defeated Carthage's Hannibal. Rome now supplanted Carthage as mistress of the Mediterranean and dominated North Africa until the Vandal invasion of 429 C.E. Following the Vandals, the Byzantines in 533 extended their hegemony over Tunisia.

The most enduring historical legacy for Tunisia derives from the Arab invasions of the late seventh century. From 643 until 698, the Arabs struggled to defeat the Berbers and impose the Arabic language and Islam upon them. Qairawan was the capital for most medieval Tunisian dynasties. Founded in 670, it survived for centuries as the main garrison town and political and religious center.

The Aghlabid dynasty (800–909) ruled from Qairawan. The Shi'ite Fatimids (909–969) moved their capital to Mahdiya, then Egypt, founding a new imperial capital at Cairo. They left their lieutenants, the Zirids, in charge of North Africa. In 1049 the Zirids broke with the Fatimids who, in retaliation, unleashed the Banu Hilal nomads. They disrupted the countryside, intensified the renomadization of the steppes, and introduced a new dialect. Their defeat at Haidaran in 1052 and the sack of Qairawan in 1057 led the Zirids to move to Mahdiya.

The Almoravids, a Tuareg puritanical religious group, swept out of the western Sahara in the eleventh

century. In the middle of the twelfth century, the Berber Almohads came down from the High Atlas and extended their domains into Tunisia.

By 1250, Almohad power had waned to such a degree that a successor dynasty, the Hafsids, emerged in Tunisia to rule for the next three centuries with Tunis as their capital. In 1574, an Ottoman Turkish fleet under Sinan Pasha landed forces at La Goulette (now Halq al-Wadi). Following a brief siege, those forces seized Tunis and laid the foundations for Ottoman control that continued until the imposition of a protectorate by France in 1881. To collect taxes and to maintain security, the Ottomans established a rudimentary administration. Initially an Ottoman *bulukbash* (commander) was placed in charge of the janissary garrison *(ocak)*. In 1590, rebel janissaries formed a government dominated by the deys, who ran the country through the *diwan* (council). After 1640, an important tax-collecting official, the bey, emerged, and the powerful

Tunis, the capital of Tunisia. Tunis is built near the site of Carthage, an ancient enemy of Rome that was later incorporated into its empire. Buildings that date back to Carthage's time as one of the major cities of the Roman Empire can be seen here on Byrsa Hill. © LAURE COMMUNICATIONS. REPRODUCED BY PERMISSION.

Muradid family exercised considerable control over the government. During a civil war from 1702 to 1705, Ibrahim al-Sharif seized power. In 1705 an associate of al-Sharif, Husayn ibn Ali Turki, proclaimed himself bey of Tunis. In 1710 the Ottoman sultan officially recognized Husayn and legitimized his rule. The Husaynid dynasty ruled the country independently until 1881, and thereafter under France's control until 1956.

In the nineteenth century, the Husaynids accepted the suzerainty of the Ottoman Empire while pursuing their own reform agendas and independent foreign policies vis-à-vis Europe. Misguided military reforms in the 1840s, financial mismanagement in the 1860s, and increasing pressures from Europe in the 1870s culminated in France's protectorate based on the treaty of Bardo (1881) and the La Marsa Convention (1883).

The protectorate authorities speeded up the economic development of Tunisia, built a physical infrastructure, reformed the educational system, and imposed a political administration while retaining the bey as figurehead ruler. Simultaneously they heeded settler demands for land, sweeping aside informal tribal and village ownership agreements. Arabs were excluded from participation in politics. French settlers dominated the political structures, the courts, and the media.

Although there had been armed resistance to the French occupation from southern tribal elements, most of it was crushed by the end of 1883. The first stage of Tunisian nationalism was an intellectual elitist movement known as the Young Tunisians, which aimed to assimilate to the civilization of France so they could eventually rule their own country. They agitated for equal treatment because of their accomplishments, but the French did not take them seriously. A more serious stage in protonationalist agitation occurred just before and just after World War I in a movement led by Abd al-Aziz Thaalbi. The third stage came in the 1930s when a young lawyer, Habib Bourguiba, broke with the Destour Party and proclaimed the Neo-Destour.

World War II slowed the development of nationalism in Tunisia. After the war, however, Bourguiba followed a staged process, arguing that its cumulative effect would result in political independence. By late 1955, Algeria violently challenged France's rule through a war of national liberation. France therefore agreed to Tunisia's autonomy in 1955 and to its independence in March 1956. In 1957 the Republic of Tunisia proclaimed Bourguiba its first president.

In Tunisia's first decades of independence, continued dominance of the Neo-Destour, which became the Socialist Destour in 1964, and the government's antireligious attitude tarnished the nation's image. Police intimidated those who sought to chant the Qur'an in public, often beating and imprisoning them. In protest, pious intellectuals organized the Society for the Preservation of the Qur'an and, in the early 1980s, created the MTI.

Bourguiba's anti-Islam policies led to Zayn al-Abidine Ben Ali's palace coup of 7 November 1987. Ben Ali tried to co-opt the Islamists for the promised elections of 1989. To demonstrate his piety, he appeared on television participating in Ramadan rites at al-Zaytuna mosque in Tunis. In the spring of 1989, however, Ben Ali hedged on his promise to recognize the MTI if they removed religious terminology from their name. As the April elections approached and MTI changed its name to the Renaissance party, the government refused to recognize it.

Ben Ali's regime considers the Islamists to be the major challenge to its survival, equating them with terrorists. Ben Ali announced in late 1993 that national elections would be held in March 1994. He promised that seats would be set aside for minority party candidates. Ben Ali then announced his candidacy for a second presidential term.

Tunisia's "regime of change" has tamed the Islamist movement for the moment, has modestly improved its human-rights and democratic credentials, and has continued economic restructuring and privatization. The economy is functioning reasonably well, harvests continue to be good, tourism has rebounded dramatically, and the immediate prospects for the future appear good.

See also BEN ALI, ZAYN AL-ABIDINE; BERBER; BIZERTE; BOURGUIBA, HABIB; LA MARSA CONVENTION; QAIRAWAN; SFAX; SOUSSE; SUNNI ISLAM; THAALBI, ABD AL-AZIZ; TUNIS; UNION GÉNÉRALE DES TRAVAILLEURS

Tunisiens (UGTT); Union Tunisienne des Industrialistes, Compagnies, Artisans (UTICA).

Bibliography

Abun-Nasr, Jamil. "The Beylicate in Seventeenth Century Tunisia." *International Journal of Middle East Studies* 6 (1975): 70–93.

Anderson, Lisa. *The State and Social Transformation in Tunisia and Libya, 1830–1980.* Princeton, NJ: Princeton University Press, 1986.

Barrie, Larry A. "Tunisia: The Era of Reformism, 1837–1877." Master's thesis, Harvard University, 1966.

Entelis, John P. *Comparative Politics of North Africa: Algeria, Morocco, and Tunisia.* Syracuse, NY: Syracuse University Press, 1980.

Perkins, Kenneth J. *Tunisia: Crossroads of the Islamic and European Worlds.* Boulder, CO: Westview Press, 1986.

Valensi, Lucette. *On the Eve of Colonialism: North Africa before the French Conquest.* New York: Africana, 1977.

Zartman, I. William, ed. *Tunisia: The Political Economy of Reform.* Boulder, CO: L. Rienner, 1991.

Zussman, Mira. *Development and Disenchantment in Rural Tunisia: The Bourguiba Years.* Boulder, CO: Westview Press, 1992.

LARRY A. BARRIE

TUNISIA: PERSONAL STATUS CODE

Set of family laws that reduced gender inequality in Tunisia.

On 13 August 1956, less than five months after the proclamation of independence from French colonial rule, the Republic of Tunisia promulgated the Code of Personal Status (CPS). A set of laws regulating marriage, divorce, custody, and inheritance, the code profoundly changed family law and the legal status of women. Together with the Turkish civil code of 1926, the Tunisian CPS of 1956 represented a pioneering body of legislation that reduced gender inequality before the law in an Islamic country.

A reform from above, the CPS was initiated by the political leadership in the absence of a feminist grassroots mass movement. Although it expanded women's rights, the CPS should not be seen as a response from the state to pressures from women's protest groups. Individual women had participated in the struggle for national liberation and espoused a nationalist ideology, but no women's mass movement defending women's causes had developed in Tunisia in the 1950s. The initiators of the CPS described it primarily as an instrument of change, a way of bringing about a transformation in kinship patterns and family life, which they saw as a necessary condition for broader social, political, and economic changes.

The Tunisian code is called the *majalla* in Arabic. Several amendments further equalizing the legal status of men and women have been made and the text has been regularly updated since 1956. The CPS altered regulations on marriage, divorce, alimony, custody, adoption, and to a lesser extent inheritance, leaving few, if any, aspects of family life untouched. The best known and most daring reforms embodied in the CPS concern polygamy, or the man's right to have as many as four wives, and repudiation, or the unilateral right of the husband to end the marriage at will. The *majalla* outlawed polygamy altogether. It stated unequivocally that polygamy was forbidden. An attempt at marrying again while one was still married was punished with imprisonment of a year and a fine of approximately $500, which represented the equivalent of a year's income for many Tunisians when the CPS was promulgated in 1956. The CPS also abolished repudiation and changed regulations on divorce in fundamental ways. A divorce could now only take place in court. The wife and husband were equally entitled to file for divorce, and they could do so by mutual consent. One of them could also file alone, in which case the judge would determine whether compensation should be given by one spouse to the other and what the amount ought to be. A woman was liable to pay compensation to her husband if the judge estimated that it was the husband who had been wronged.

Among other innovations, the CPS made the wife responsible for contributing to the expenses of the household and to the financial support of children, if she had to means to do so. It expanded the right of mothers to have custody of their children. It made the registration of marriages and divorces mandatory, something that was not systematically the case earlier. It made adoption legally valid. It somewhat modified the rules on inheritance by favoring the spouse and female descendants over male cousins in some specific kinship configurations.

The CPS gave women greater rights by increasing the range of options available to them in their private lives. It also gave them greater obligations, as for example in the case of divorce and with respect to the financial responsibility for the household. Some aspects of the CPS overtly maintained gender inequality, however. The code left unaltered the general rule according to which women inherit half as much as men. The 1956 text required a wife to obey her husband; this was later debated and changed in the 1990s.

The reforms of the CPS can be seen as an effort to reshape kinship in Tunisian society in the aftermath of independence from colonial rule. The CPS replaced the vision of the family as an extended kinship group built on strong ties crisscrossing a community of male relatives with the vision of a conjugal unit in which ties between spouses and between parents and children are prominent. The elite in power in the 1950s treated family law reform as part of the transformation of society necessary for the development of a modern state.

See also GENDER: GENDER AND LAW.

MOUNIRA M. CHARRAD

TUNISIA: POLITICAL PARTIES IN

Tunisia has eleven active political parties.

There are eight legal political parties in Tunisia, including the government party. There are also three parties that have not been authorized: the Popular Unity Movement (Mouvement de L'Unité Populaire; MUP), a socialist party founded by Ahmed Ben Salah, former planning minister who fled Tunisia in 1973; the Tunisian Communist Workers Party (Parti Ouvrier Communiste Tunisien; POCT), a Maoist group; and the Renaissance Party (Hizb al-Nahda in Arabic), the party of Islamists, founded by Rashid Ghannushi. The legal parties are the Constitutional Democratic Rally (Ralliement Constitutionnel Démocratique; RCD), the Movement of Socialist Democrats (Mouvement des Dèmocrates Socialistes; MDS), the Popular Unity Party (Parti D'Unité Populaire; PUP), the Movement of Renewal (Harakat al-Tajdid), the Progres-

Tunisian president Zayn al-Abidine Ben Ali (b. 1936) came to power in 1987 when previous leader Habib Bourguiba was dismissed on grounds of failing mental capabilities. Once in power, Ben Ali changed the Destourian Socialist Party to the Democratic Constitutional Rally, and he easily retained his office in the country's first free elections in 1989. © AFP/CORBIS. REPRODUCED BY PERMISSION.

sive Democratic Party (Parti démocrate progressiste; PDP), the Unionist Democratic Union (Union Démocratique Unioniste; UDU), the Socialist Liberal Party (Parti Socialiste Liberale; PSL), and the Democratic Forum for Labor and Freedoms (Forum démocratique pour le travail et les libertés; FDTL).

RCD

The RCD has dominated all governmental institutions since Tunisia's independence in 1956. The party was founded by Habib Bourguiba and others in 1934 as the Neo-Destour. They broke away from the Destour (Constitution) Party, established by Abd al-Aziz Thaalbi in 1920. Bourguiba's group felt that the Destour had become too elitist and sought to build a grassroots party that could appeal to the rural and small-town folk that the Destour failed to represent. In 1964 the party changed its name to Socialist Destour Party (Parti Socialist Destourien; PSD). The party's final name change occurred in 1988, when the party congress adopted the name Constitutional Democratic Rally. This expressed the new direction of the government party following a coup that replaced Bourguiba with Zayn al-Abidine

Ben Ali. Moderate and pragmatic, the RCD has opened up the political system to multiple parties and has attempted to refashion a market economy to replace the earlier centralized socialist planning system. President Ben Ali is party president, and Ali Chaouch occupies the post of secretary-general. The party claims over 1.5 million members, distributed in thousands of cells nationwide. It controls the national parliament (Chamber of Deputies).

MDS

Ahmad Mestiri, formerly a member of the ruling party, founded the MDS in 1978 and welded the new party into the largest opposition to the RCD. With its forty thousand members, the MDS offers almost the same program as the RCD, except that it is more Arab nationalist and socialist. Ismaïl Boulahya is secretary-general.

PUP

Headed by Mohamed Belhaj Amor, the PUP offers a nationalist and socialist program. It splintered off from the MUP in 1981 and in 1985 it was renamed the Parti d'Unité Populaire (PUP). Amor was succeeded in 2000 by Mohamed Bouchiha.

Movement of Renewal

Secretary-General Mohamed Harmel is a longtime Communist Party activist. The Movement adopted the name Mouvement Ettajdid (Arabic, Harakat al-Tajdid) in 1993, dropping the name Tunisian Communist Party (Parti Communiste Tunisien; PCT). It now follows a leftist, non-Marxist ideology that offers an alternative for leftists and intellectuals. It remains a small party whose membership numbers somewhere in the low thousands.

PDP

Nejib Chebbi, a lawyer, heads the Progressive Democratic Party, the former Socialist Progressive Rally (RSP), which has a nationalist and socialist emphasis. PDP leaders are willing to accommodate all nonviolent political viewpoints in national elections. The PDP seeks a broader role for Tunisia in Arab politics. Regarded as the most critical of the opposition parties, it did not gain any seats to the Chamber of Deputies in the legislative elections of 1999.

UDU

Abderrahmane Tlili founded the Unionist Democratic Union (UDU). It has close ties with the Union Générale des Travailleurs Tunisiens (UGTT), the country's largest labor union. A high concentration of union members makes up UDU's constituency. UDU espouses both Arab nationalism and Israel-PLO peace talks.

PSL

In 1993 the Social Party for Progress (PSP) became the Socialist Liberal Party (PSL). Led by Mounir Beji, a lawyer, the PSL supports liberalism, economic privatization, and American foreign policy interests in the region. Despite being considered the weakest legal party, it obtained two deputies in the 1999 legislative elections.

FDTL

Founded in 1994, the Democratic Forum for Labor and Freedoms (FDTL) was legalized in 2002. Its secretary-general, Mustapha Ben Jaafar, a former leader of the MDS, defines its ideology as social-democratic.

Since 1993, new laws have been implemented aimed at encouraging political pluralism. Accordingly, and as of 2003, the legal opposition parties share 34 seats, out of 182, in the Chamber of Deputies. The results of the legislative elections of 1999 were as follows: RCD, 148 deputies; MDS, 13; PUP, 7; UDU, 7; Ettajdid, 5; PSL, 2; PDP, 0.

Bibliography

Murphy, Emma. *Economic and Political Change in Tunisia: From Bourguiba to Ben Ali.* New York: St. Martin's Press in association with University of Durham, 1999.

Nelson, Harold D., ed. *Tunisia: A Country Study,* 3d edition. Washington, DC: U.S. Government Printing Office, 1986.

Perkins, Kenneth J. *Historical Dictionary of Tunisia.* Metuchen, NJ: Scarecrow Press, 1989.

Zartman, I. William, ed. *Tunisia: The Political Economy of Reform.* Boulder, CO: L. Rienner, 1991.

LARRY A. BARRIE
UPDATED BY ANA TORRES-GARCÍA

TUNISI, BAYRAM AL-

[1893–1961]

Egyptian poet.

Born into a small merchant family in a popular quarter of Alexandria, Bayram al-Tunisi studied at religious schools but learned the form of poetry called *zajal* by memorizing oral poetry. In 1919, he began to publish poetry critical of Egypt's monarchy and of the British occupation, in the journal *Issues,* leading to a long period of exile in France and Tunisia. After his return to Egypt in 1938, al-Tunisi published poetry in various Egyptian newspapers.

DAVID WALDNER

TUQAN, FADWA

[1917–2003]

Palestinian poet.

Fadwa Tuqan was born to the eminent Tuqan family of Nablus, one of the leading traditional families of central Palestine, which produced several notable figures in Palestinian education, literature, and politics. Like her elder brother, Ibrahim, she became one of the most influential poets in modern Palestinian literature, publishing her first collection of poetry, *Wahdi ma al-Ayyam* (Along with the days), in 1952.

Her work is noted for having broken with traditional Arabic poetic styles, introducing, for example, free verse into modern Arabic poetry. Tuqan's poetry is also noteworthy for discussing sensual themes, as well as for depicting the social conditions facing Palestinians, especially Palestinian women. Her 1985 autobiography, *Rihla Jabaliyya, Rihla Sa'ba* (A mountainous journey, a difficult journey), provides a forceful discussion of the plight of women in Palestine prior to the first Arab–Israel War and the creation of Israel in 1948. Starting with the Israeli occupation of her native West Bank in June 1967, Tuqan also began writing poetry with nationalist themes. Some of her poems were printed in the underground nationalist publication *Filastin* in the mid-1970s. Israeli general and politician Moshe Dayan once remarked that the power of just one of her poems, like her famous "The Freedom Fighter and the Land," was equal to that of several Pales-

tinian guerrilla fighters. She was not above participating in secret Arab-Israeli contacts, however. Dayan met with her twice in late 1968, when he was Israel's defense minister, as part of his secret effort to strike up a dialogue with Arab leaders. Tuqan once passed along a message from Dayan to Egyptian President Gamal Abdel Nasser, and offered to contact Yasir Arafat, leader of the al-Fatah movement.

In 1990 she was awarded the Palestine Liberation Organization's Jerusalem Award for Culture and Arts, as well as the Honorary Palestine Prize for Poetry in 1996. Fadwa Tuqan died in Nablus, where she had lived all her life, on 13 December 2003. A line from one of her poems sums up her wish to be buried in her native Palestine: "Enough for me to die on her earth, be buried in her, to melt and vanish into her soil."

See also ARAFAT, YASIR; DAYAN, MOSHE; FATAH, AL-; NASSER, GAMAL ABDEL; WEST BANK.

Bibliography

Fischbach, Michael R. "Fadwa Tuqan." In *Encyclopedia of the Palestinians,* edited by Philip Mattar. New York: Facts On File, 2000.

Jayyusi, Salma, ed. *Anthology of Modern Palestinian Literature.* New York: Columbia University Press, 1995.

Tuqan, Fadwa. *A Mountainous Journey: An Autobiography,* translated by Olive Kenny and Naomi Shihab Nye. St. Paul, MN: Graywolf Press, 1990.

ABLA M. AMAWI
UPDATED BY MICHAEL R. FISCHBACH

TUQAN FAMILY

Prominent Palestinian family from Nablus.

Descended from an ancient Arabian tribe, the Tuqans settled in Nablus during the twelfth century. Through the nineteenth century, they were associated with other Qaysi tribes in rivalry with the local Yemeni federation. By the 1800s they had amassed great wealth, owning an imposing palace as well as a number of villas in Nablus. They shared the post of governor with the Abd al-Hadi family and used their land and tax-farm wealth to build up Nablus's famed soap and olive oil industries. Their political dominance in Nablus lasted through the

1970s as various family members gained posts under the rule of Jordan.

Prominent family members include Hafiz, a late-nineteenth-century banker; Ahmad (1903–1981), a Cambridge University graduate who was prominent in education under the British Mandate and Jordanian rule; Sulayman (1893–1958), mayor of Nablus from 1925 to 1948 and a leader of resistance to Zionism; Fadwa (1917–2003) and Ibrahim (1905–1941), sister and brother who became noted poets; Qadri (1911–1971), an educator and writer who sat in the Jordanian parliament from 1951 to 1955 and became Jordan's foreign minister in 1964; Baha al-Din (1910–1998), a historian and politician in the Jordanian government; and Aliya (1948–1977), daughter of Baha al-Din who became the third wife of Jordan's King Hussein ibn Talal from December 1972 until her death in a helicopter crash in February 1977.

See also ABD AL-HADI FAMILY; HUSSEIN IBN TALAL; NABLUS; TUQAN, FADWA.

Bibliography

Fischbach, Michael R. "Tuqan Family." In *Encyclopedia of the Palestinians,* edited by Philip Mattar. New York: Facts On File, 2000.

Muslih, Muhammad Y. *The Origins of Palestinian Nationalism.* New York: Columbia University Press, 1988.

ELIZABETH THOMPSON
UPDATED BY MICHAEL R. FISCHBACH

TURABI, HASAN AL-
[1932–]

Fundamentalist Islamic thinker.

Born in the city of Kasla in Sudan to a family of religious learning and traditions, Hasan al-Turabi earned a B.A. in law from the University of Khartoum, an M.A. in law from the University of London, and a doctorate in constitutional law from the Sorbonne in Paris. He became dean of the University of Khartoum Law School in 1964, then attorney general in 1979, and a member of the Sudanese parliament in 1965. In 1977 he became a minister of justice.

Turabi is the leader of the Sudanese branch of the Muslim Brotherhood, which was transformed into the National Islamic Front (NIF) in 1985 under his leadership. In 1988 the NIF joined the coalition government of Sadiq al-Mahdi, and Turabi served first as minister of foreign affairs and later as deputy prime minister. He was the ideological power behind the military regime of Hasan al-Bashir in Sudan in 1989. In 1996 Turabi became the speaker of the parliament, and his influence spread throughout the state organization and political parties. He fell out of favor with President al-Bashir's regime and since 2000 has been either in prison or under house arrest. However, Turabi's importance lies not in his statesmanship, but in his intellectual and ideological developments as well as his impact on Islamism in North Africa in particular and the Arab world in general.

Turabi is a fundamentalist Islamic thinker because he views Islam as the ultimate ideological and political authority for both the state and society. He views Islam as containing all the necessary elements for the creation of a viable and modern civilization and culture. Rather than a return to earlier Islamic social and political practices, Turabi advocates a progressive Islamic revival that incorporates into Islam the best of traditional Islam and Western culture. He argues that the state's only purpose is to set rules to enable society to conduct its affairs, and that it must allow society, the primary institution in Islam, to freely pursue its interests. The *shariʿa* and the Islamist jurists ensure that the role of the state remains limited. Because any society has the right to exercise *shura* (consultation) and *ijma* (consensus), and because this requires producing *ijtihad* (opinions), pluralism is necessary to enable society to identify which policies best serve its interests. As such, Turabi argues, *democracy* is simply a Western term identical to Islam's *shura* and *ijma*. Although ultimate sovereignty belongs to God, practical and political sovereignty belong to the people. Society, therefore, always remains free to choose its rulers and representatives. In this fashion, Islam can bring the best of its own civilization along with other civilizations.

Turabi distinguishes the conditions of contemporary life from those present during the rise of Islam in the seventh century. Because Muslims are living in a world much different from the one that Islamic jurisprudence legislated, they must look toward radical social and political reforms in order to

In 1964, Hasan al-Turabi participated in a revolt in Khartoum, the capital of Sudan, fighting for the formation of an Islamic government. He fought alongside, and became the leader of, the Muslim Brotherhood. He helped the group grow and gain power, and it eventually became the National Islamic Front. Turabi would then go on to help install President Omar Hassan al-Bashir, who vowed to rule the country under Islamic law. © AP/WIDE WORLD PHOTOS. REPRODUCED BY PERMISSION.

bring about the necessary Islamic revival. The historical development of Islamic jurisprudence must be rejected in favor of a process that depends on free thinking, and the state must establish a new circle of *ulama* (Islamic clergy) while continuing to derive its jurisprudence from the people. Any democratic developments in Islam must extend to the institutions of society and the family, each segment of which must work to further Islamic revival in both public and private life. Political freedom is an original part of creed and nature because freedom is what distinguishes man from animal. This includes the freedom of expression, which is stipulated in the *shari*ʿ*a*.

As for the individual, Turabi notes that man is not forced to worship God, but chooses to do so. Individual freedom is essential and cannot be taken away by the state, institutions, or society. This freedom, he argues, must be embodied in a constitution to ensure that the strength of any political leader may be checked by representative councils. Because institutionalization of freedom inevitably leads to its destruction, individual freedoms are bound and protected by Islam.

Turabi's views and writings on Islam seem to place him in the category of moderate Islamist thinkers, but the practice of his authority in Sudan suggests otherwise. Although he has called for freedom of association and multiparty representative bodies, the current Sudanese government has systematically destroyed most civic associations and remains one of the most oppressive regimes and egregious human-rights violators in the Middle East.

See also SUDAN.

Bibliography

El-Effendi, Abdelwahab. *Turabi's Revolution: Islam and Power in Sudan.* London: Grey Seal, 1991.

Moussalli, Ahmad. *Moderate and Radical Islamic Fundamentalism: The Quest for Modernity, Legitimacy, and the Islamic State.* Gainesville: University of Florida Press, 1999.

Turabi, Hasan al-. "Islam, Democracy, the State and the West: Summary of a Lecture and Roundtable Discussion with Hasan al-Turabi," prepared by Louis Cantori and Arthur Lowrie. *Middle East Policy* 1, no. 3 (1992): 52–54.

JILLIAN SCHWEDLER
UPDATED BY AHMAD S. MOUSSALLI

TURABI, WISAL AL-MAHDI
[?–]

Supporter of women's rights in Sudan.

Wisal al-Mahdi Turabi, a member of the large landowning al-Mahdi aristocracy, is the wife of Hasan al-Turabi, founder of the Sudanese Muslim Brotherhood and architect of the National Islamic Front (NIF) takeover of Sudan by military coup d'etat in 1989. Her brother, Sadiq al-Mahdi, is a leader of the influential Umma Party who has twice been prime minister of Sudan. Although the Umma Party and the NIF have been rivals, they both support Muslim women's activism, in which Wisel al-Mahdi has played a prominent role.

When the NIF seized power in 1989, the activist band of Islamists mobilized its female adherents. Wisal al-Mahdi became a spokeswoman for NIF policies such as mandatory veiling and the removal of women from "humiliating" public jobs, such as waitresses and gas station attendants. She upheld the right of women to hold high-status positions, such as judges and government ministers, and she supported *shariʿa* as state law.

Although a trained lawyer, Wisal al-Mahdi has not practiced law and appears to adhere to a conservative Muslim role for women, maintaining a proper *Shariʿ* home and providing support for her husband's national and international roles as a leading figure in the global Islamist movement. Nevertheless, some of her public comments reveal a radical Islamist feminism, blaming Arab patriarchy for the oppression of women in Sudan and elsewhere.

See also GENDER: GENDER AND LAW; GENDER: GENDER AND POLITICS; SUDAN; TURABI, HASAN AL-.

Bibliography

Hale, Sondra. *Gender Politics in Sudan: Islamism, Socialism, and the State.* Boulder, CO: Westview Press, 1996.

CAROLYN FLUEHR-LOBBAN

TURBAN

See CLOTHING

TÜRKES, ALPARSLAN

[1917–1997]

Turkish military officer and leader of the ultrapatriotic National Action Party.

Alparslan Türkes was born in Cyprus and graduated from the Turkish military academy. Due to his involvement in pan-Turkish propaganda during World War II, he was arrested in 1944 but released after an investigation. During the 1950s he served on the general staff and with NATO. He emerged as a key player in Turkey's 1960 military coup, and in its aftermath he was a member of the National Unity Committee (NUC) that was in charge of the government. Due to his radicalism, he was removed from the NUC in November 1960 and sent to New Delhi as a military attaché. After his return to Turkey in 1963 he became active in politics, eventually becoming the leader of the Republican Peasants Nation Party in 1965. He developed the doctrine of Nine Lights, which stressed nationalism and order in society. Under his leadership, the party transformed itself into the ultrapatriotic Nationalist Action Party (1969–1980). He served as vice-premier in Süleyman Demirel's National Front governments of 1975 and 1977. After the 1980 coup, Türkes was arrested and the party was banned; he reentered the political arena in 1983, became the leader of the Nationalist Worker Party, and entered parliament in 1991.

See also NATIONALIST ACTION PARTY.

Bibliography

Zürcher, Erik J. *Turkey: A Modern History,* revised edition. London: I. B. Tauris, 1997.

FRANK TACHAU
UPDATED BY M. HAKAN YAVUZ

TURKEY

Modern republic formed from the central regions of the Ottoman Empire.

The Republic of Turkey (Türkiye Cumhuriyeti) was established in 1923. Its government was an authoritarian, one-party state until 1946, when the first competitive elections were held. In subsequent decades there have been three military coups, and one instance of military pressure that forced a civilian government to resign.

According to the 2000 census, Turkey's population was 67,844,903, an increase of 18.34 percent over the population of 56,473,035 enumerated in October 1990. In 2000 the population distribution was 65 percent urban and 35 percent rural.

The total area of Turkey is 300,948 square miles (779,456 sq. km). The Asian portion of Turkey, Anatolia (historically Asia Minor), comprises 291,773 square miles (755,693 sq. km), or about 97 percent of the total; the section located on the European continent totals 9,175 square miles (23,763 sq. km). The European portion of Turkey is separated from the Asian by the Sea of Marmara, which in turn is connected to two larger bodies of water by two narrow straits. In the northeast, the Bosporus Strait connects the Sea of Marmara to the Black Sea, while in the southwest, the Dardanelles Strait connects it to the Aegean Sea. Turkey borders the Aegean Sea and Greece on the west, Bulgaria on the northwest, the Black Sea on the north,

Georgia on the northeast, Armenia on the east, Iran and Iraq on the southeast, and Syria and the Mediterranean Sea on the south.

The capital of Turkey, Ankara, is located in the central Anatolian plains; a small market town in 1923, Ankara today is home to more than 3.5 million people. The largest city, Istanbul, straddles the European and Asian sides of Turkey and has a population of 9.1 million. An important historical city, Istanbul (formerly Byzantium, then Constantinople) was first the capital of the Byzantine Empire and later the capital of the Ottoman Empire. Today, it is the cultural and business capital of Turkey. The third-largest city is İzmir (English, Smyrna), a major industrial center with a population of 2 million. Other major cities, each with populations over 1 million, include Adana, Bursa, and Konya.

Geographically, Turkey consists of a ring of mountains that enclose a series of plateaus that lie between 2,625 and 6,560 feet (800 and 2,000 m) above sea level. The highest mountains are in the east, with Mount Ararat reaching 16,945 feet (5,165 m). In the west, the highest mountain, Mount Erciyas, reaches 12,800 feet (3,900 m). The coastal regions on the south, west, and north are extremely narrow. Most of the coastal regions receive adequate rainfall; as much as 100 inches (254 cm) falls annually on the eastern Black Sea coast, and almost as much on the Aegean coast. The central plateau, on the other hand, is sheltered by its ring of mountains and receives little rainfall, generally under 10 inches (250 mm) annually. There are extensive expanses of arid steppe and even desert. Turkey's two major rivers, the Tigris and Euphrates, are both in the east. There are many lakes, both salt and freshwater; the largest is Lake Van, which covers 1,100 square miles (2,850 sq. km). Climate in the central plain ranges from severe winters with temperatures often dropping to minus 22 degrees Fahrenheit (minus 30 degrees Celsius) to hot and dry summers, with temperatures ranging from highs of 85 to 110 degrees Fahrenheit (30 to 43 degrees Celsius) in the southeast. In the western region, winters are relatively mild, hovering around freezing, and summers are hot. The Aegean coast is mild in winter and temperate in summer.

Turkey is divided into seventy-three provinces, each administered by a governor. According to the

Suleimaniye Mosque is one of the highlights of Istanbul. Turkey is overwhelmingly Muslim, but the military has determinedly kept religion out of government. Istanbul, formerly Constantinople, Turkey's largest city was the capital of the Eastern Roman, or Byzantine, Empire for more than 1,000 years and then of the Ottoman Empire for another 450 years. © CORBIS. REPRODUCED BY PERMISSION.

1982 constitution, legislative power is vested in a unicameral Grand National Assembly composed of 400 deputies elected by universal adult suffrage and serving five-year terms. In 1987 the number of deputies was raised to 450. Executive power is vested in the office of the prime minister and in the office of the president, who is elected to a seven-year term by the assembly. Although the prime minister heads the government, the president has the power to appoint a prime minister, senior civil servants, and senior members of the judiciary; submit constitutional amendments for popular referenda; challenge the constitutionality of laws by submitting them to the constitutional court; call for new elections; declare martial law; and order the armed forces into action domestically or internationally. In addition, the National Security Council—composed of the president; prime minister; chief of staff; heads of the army, navy, air force, and police; and

The ancient city wall still stands in Alanya, southern Turkey, along the Mediterranean Sea opposite Cyprus. A significant link between Europe and Asia, Turkey has roots dating back many millennia. © CORBIS. REPRODUCED BY PERMISSION.

ministers of interior, foreign affairs, and defense—has the power to present compulsory orders to the government in matters of national security.

There are no official census data on the ethnic, religious, and linguistic composition of the population of Turkey. The majority of Turks are native Turkish speakers. Ethnically, they trace their roots back to central Asia, although many Turks are Caucasians, particularly Circassians and Georgians. There is also a significant population of Kurds, a people of Indo-European descent who speak Kurdish, a language closely related to Persian. Kurds comprise an estimated 15 to 20 percent of Turkey's total population. Kurds are concentrated in the east and southeast and along the Syrian and Iraqi borders, but significant numbers have migrated to major cities in western Turkey. A large number of

Arabs inhabit the region of Hatay, a small territory formerly part of Syria but ceded by the French to Turkey in 1939. The large populations of Greeks and Armenians in the nineteenth century were reduced by war and deportations during and after World War I to relatively small numbers living in Istanbul: roughly 6,000 Greeks and 60,000 Armenians. The vast majority of Turkish citizens are Muslim. Most Kurds and Turks are Sunni Muslims, but an estimated 20 to 30 percent of the population are Shiʿite Muslims, primarily of the Alevi sect. There are also small numbers of Jews (22,000), Greek Orthodox, Armenian Orthodox, and Assyrian Christians.

Agriculture and Industry

Turkey's major agricultural products are cereals, cotton, tobacco, grapes, figs, olives, hazelnuts, oilseeds, and tea. Until 1980 agricultural products, particularly cotton, provided the bulk of exports. Despite continued government attention to raising agricultural output, growth has been slow, limited by the lack of irrigated land and the low rainfall on the central plateau. Only about one-third of all land is cultivated, mostly on family-size plots, with larger farms in the coastal regions. Agriculture provides about 20 percent of the gross national product.

The Turkish government initiated a strategy of state-led industrialization in the 1930s, when a series of public enterprises were established. After 1950 increasing support was given to the private sector, so that by 1970, private-sector industrial output and investment was almost equal to that of the public sector. In 1980 the government launched a program of liberalization, designed to diminish state economic intervention and increase the role of market forces. Since 1987 the government has been privatizing some state economic enterprises, though progress has been slow. The largest industry is textiles, providing about one-third of output and export earnings. Turkey's production and export of iron and steel have increased rapidly, as has production of cement and paper products. Motor vehicle production began in the 1950s but consists mostly of assembly industries; because production has been spread out over a large number of small plants, production costs are high and exports have been negligible. Turkey's petrochemical industry produces fertilizers and a range of industrial inputs.

MAP BY XNR PRODUCTIONS, INC. THE GALE GROUP.

Other manufacturing industries include tobacco, chemicals, pharmaceuticals, glassware, and engineering.

Turkey has a large mining industry, mostly in the public sector, employing over 200,000 workers. Important mineral resources include bauxite, borax, chromium, copper, iron ore, manganese, and sulfur. The center of coal mining is at Zonguldak, on the Black Sea coast. Oil was discovered in 1950 in the southeast, but production is limited, accounting for about 10 percent of domestic consumption; the remainder is imported. In 1990 petroleum products accounted for about 15 percent of all imports. Of Turkey's natural mineral resources, only borates and petroleum products are exported, in small quantities.

Imperial History

Urban culture in Asia Minor dates to the second millennium B.C.E. In 330 C.E., the Roman emperor Constantine founded the city of Constantinople (now Istanbul), which became the capital of the Eastern Roman, or Byzantine, Empire. In the eleventh century, Ghuzz Turks who had established the Seljuk empire in the area that is today Iran and Iraq began to migrate into Anatolia, conquering territory from the Byzantine Empire. By the thirteenth century, independent princedoms were established in Anatolia, including the principality of the House of Osman, or Othman, in the northwest. Over the next several centuries, the Ottoman (from Othman) Empire conquered all of the Byzantine Empire, capturing Constantinople in 1453, as well as much of eastern Europe and the Middle East.

By the year 1800, however, several European states as well as the Russian Empire had become stronger than the Ottoman Empire. Throughout the nineteenth century, the government undertook various reform efforts to strengthen the Ottoman military, administration, political organization, and economy in order to meet the competition presented by rivals.

In the course of the nineteenth century, a middle class emerged in the Ottoman Empire. Educated in the new schools of the empire, members of the middle class had a vision of a liberal society ruled by a constitutional government and formed movements to achieve their goal, such as the Young Ottomans and later the Young Turks. These groups alternately were supported by reformist governments or suppressed by autocratic governments. In 1908, the Committee of Union and Progress (CUP) overthrew Abdülhamit II and restored the constitution. The CUP government initially enjoyed widespread popular support. But subsequent opposition to its modernizing reforms, combined with foreign wars, led the CUP to establish its own dictatorship. In 1914 the CUP formed an alliance with the Central Powers and entered World War I. After four years of fighting a bitter defensive war against the Allies on many fronts, the empire was defeated; Allied armies captured the Middle Eastern territories of Palestine, Syria, and Iraq; and Allied forces occupied Istanbul. On 30 October 1918 the Turks signed an armistice at Mudros.

Birth of the Modern Republic

On 15 May 1919, Greek forces invaded western Turkey, triggering the formation of a new Turkish army that would defeat the Greeks and then establish the modern Turkish republic. The leader of the Turkish war of liberation was Mustafa Kemal, later given the name Atatürk (Turkish: "father of the Turks"). On 23 July 1919 Kemal convened a nationalist congress in Erzurum, delegates to which later issued the National Pact (Mithaq al-Watani), a declaration calling for the dissolution of the empire and control over non-Turkish provinces, the end of foreign occupation, and the independence of all areas inhabited by Turks. Pulling together an army, the independence movement succeeded in defeating the Greek army and negotiating a withdrawal of Allied forces. The Treaty of Mudanya recognizing Turkish sovereignty was signed on 24 July 1923. On 29 October 1923 Turkey was declared a republic with Kemal as its first president and Ankara as its capital.

Modernization

The next two decades were years of reform, as Kemal and his associates attempted to complete the now 100-year-old project of modernizing Turkey.

The 1924 constitution created an elected parliament as the sole repository of sovereignty and a presidency exercising executive power. In practice, however, Kemal's government was a dictatorship. A single party, the Republican People's Party (RPP), was formed as the agent of central government rule and control. In 1924 the caliphate, the highest religious office, was abolished, and in 1928 Turkey was declared a secular state. The old legal codes were annulled and replaced with civil and criminal codes adopted from Europe. The fez, the trademark Ottoman headgear adopted in the nineteenth century, was considered a symbol of the old order and was declared illegal, while the Arabic alphabet was replaced with a Roman one.

In 1929, with the onset of the Great Depression and the lapsing of the Treaty of Lausanne, which had imposed a laissez-faire trade policy on Turkey, Kemal launched a program of state-led economic development. Influenced by the Soviet experiment with its five-year development plans, in 1934 the government formulated its own five-year plan for industrial investment. Completed in 1939, the plan introduced heavy industry into Turkey while allowing the country to weather the depression with a trade surplus.

During the 1930s Kemal transformed the RPP on the model of European fascist parties. The distinction between party members and government officials was blurred, as all public officials were expected to work to implement the new ideology of the party. This ideology, officially adopted in 1931 and known as Kemalism, emphasized six themes: republicanism, nationalism, populism, statism, secularism, and *devrimçilik,* which was interpreted by moderates as reformism and by radicals as revolutionism. In 1938 Kemal Atatürk died and was replaced as president by his lieutenant, Ismet Inönü. Although Inönü kept Turkey neutral during World War II, a number of government policies on resource mobilization created widespread economic austerity, alienating large sectors of the population including those businessmen who opposed the policy of state-led economic development.

Political Reforms and Military Coups

The post–World War II period was a new era for the Turkish republic. Responding to the dissatisfaction of wartime economic policies and feeling the need to win American support against Soviet encroachments, Inönü announced the resumption of multiparty politics and competitive elections. There had been two experiments with a second party in the 1920s, but in both cases the opposition party was closed down after a short life. This time, the commitment to political pluralism was greater, and in the general elections of May 1950, the chief opposition, the Democrat Party (DP), won an overwhelming victory. The DP had campaigned on a platform of economic and cultural liberalism and increased political freedoms. Its new economic policies, based on import-substituting industrialization and the encouragement of agriculture, increased the standard of living of wide sectors of the population, particularly peasants. The DP permitted more freedom of religion than the Kemalists, who were militantly hostile to religion. But the DP increased the role of the state in the economy instead of reducing it; as the 1950s passed, the party showed signs of becoming dictatorial. A combination of incipient economic crisis and antidemocratic measures prompted a military coup on 27 May 1960.

The new military rulers formed a thirty-seven-member National Unity Committee (NUC) and convened a constitutional convention, dominated by supporters of the RPP. A new constitution was promulgated in 1961, and it included several liberal provisions. The NUC also allowed political parties to resume their activities. The two principal parties, the RPP—still led by Inönü—and the Justice Party (JP), the successor to the DP, formed a series of short-lived coalition governments, first together, and later between the RPP and several smaller parties, and then the JP with smaller parties. In October 1965 the JP, led by Süleyman Demirel, won a majority. The Turkish economy, now supervised by the State Planning Organization, which issued five-year development plans, grew at a rapid rate during the 1960s. But political instability came from two sources: numerous defections of members from existing parties and the proliferation of smaller parties; and the eruption of street violence as radical students and organizations on the left clashed with extremist students and organizations on the right.

On 12 March 1971 the military leadership accused the government of allowing the country to slip

Mustafa Kemal (who later took the name Atatürk, or "father of the Turks") led the Turkish war of independence in 1919, marking an end to the long-declining Ottoman Empire and the birth of the Republic of Turkey in 1923. As its first president, Kemal forcefully transformed the Islamic country into a modernized, secular, authoritarian state before his death in 1938. © BETTMANN/CORBIS. REPRODUCED BY PERMISISON.

into anarchy and called for the creation of a stable government. The Demirel government resigned, and subsequently martial law was declared. After martial law was finally lifted in September 1973, Turkey was ruled by a series of weak coalition governments as economic conditions deteriorated. By the end of the decade, the economy was in critical condition; beginning in 1978, political violence once again erupted in the streets. On 12 September 1980 the military intervened for the third time in two decades. All existing political parties were banned, and their members prohibited from engaging in politics. A new constitution, promulgated in 1982, reversed some of the liberal measures of the 1961 constitution by enhancing the authority of the president and the cabinet vis-a-vis parliament and placing restrictions on political activity.

Party Politics

In 1983 elections were held among three new parties. The winning party was the Motherland Party (Anavatan Partisi; ANAP), led by Turgut Özal, a technocrat who had designed the January 1980 measures. Özal formed a new government and accelerated the strategy of economic liberalization and encouraging exports. Despite some success at economic liberalization, persistent government deficits resulted in high inflation and eroded popular support for the government. New parties emerged to rival ANAP: the True Path Party (TPP; Doğru Yol Partisi), a continuation of the Justice Party, led by Süleyman Demirel after 1987; the Social Democratic Populist Party (Sosyal Demokrat Halkci Parti; SHP), a continuation of the RPP under the leadership of Erdal İnönü, the son of Ismet İnönü; and the Refah Party, the continuation of the National Salvation Party. In 1989 Özal was elected president. In the 1991 elections ANAP, now led by Mesut Yilmaz, came in third, and the top two parties, the TPP and the SHP, formed a coalition government. On 17 April 1993 Özal died, and Demirel replaced him as president. On 13 June 1993 Tansu Çiller, an American-trained economist and former professor at Bosporus University, became the new head of the TPP and prime minister. Çiller was the first woman to serve as prime minister of Turkey.

In the 1995 parliamentary elections, the Refah Party obtained the largest number, but not a majority, of parliamentary seats, the first time an avowedly religious party had done so well since the establishment of the republic more than seventy years earlier. In 1996 Necmeddin Erbakan formed a coalition government, but the military effectively forced him to resign one year later. During the next five years, a series of coalition governments that purposefully excluded Refah and its successor failed to implement programs to deal with the country's economic problems. In the fall 2002 elections, the Justice Party and the Development Party, one of the successor parties to Refah, won an overwhelming majority of parliamentary seats in an election that saw the virtual elimination of ANAP and TTP from politics.

> See also ABDÜLHAMIT II; ADANA; ALEVI; ANATOLIA; ANKARA; ATATÜRK, MUSTAFA KEMAL; BURSA; ÇILLER, TANSU; COMMITTEE FOR UNION AND PROGRESS; DEMIREL, SÜLEYMAN; DEMOCRAT PARTY; ERBAKAN, NECMEDDIN; ERZURUM; İNÖNÜ, ERDAL; İNÖNÜ, İSMET; ISTANBUL; İZMIR; KEMALISM; KONYA; KURDS; NATIONAL UNITY COMMITTEE (TURKEY); ÖZAL, TURGUT; YOUNG OTTOMANS; YOUNG TURKS.

Bibliography

Ahmad, Feroz. *The Making of Modern Turkey.* New York: Routledge, 1993.

Bianchi, Robert. *Interest Groups and Political Development in Turkey.* Princeton, NJ: Princeton University Press, 1984.

Findley, Carter V. *Bureaucratic Reform in the Ottoman Empire: The Sublime Porte, 1789–1922.* Princeton, NJ: Princeton University Press, 1980.

Fisher, W. B. *The Middle East: A Physical, Social, and Regional Geography,* 7th edition. London: Methuen, 1978.

Tapper, Richard, ed. *Islam in Modern Turkey: Religion, Politics, and Literature in a Secular State.* London: I. B. Tauris, 1991.

Waldner, David. *State Building and Late Development.* Ithaca, NY: Cornell University Press, 1999.

DAVID WALDNER
UPDATED BY ERIC HOOGLUND

TURKI, FAWAZ

[1940–]

Palestinian writer.

Fawaz (also Fawwaz) Turki was born in Haifa, Palestine, but grew up as a refugee in Beirut after his family fled Palestine during the Arab–Israel War of 1948. He later worked in Saudi Arabia, has taught in Europe and in Australia, and has traveled widely in India, the Middle East, and the United States. Turki has written several personal accounts dealing with aspects of Palestinian struggle and identity, including his acclaimed *The Disinherited: Journal of a Palestinian in Exile.* His later book, *Exile's Return,* was noteworthy for its criticism of Palestinian society.

His style is noteworthy for his exceptional and forceful command of English, and his ability to offer a penetrating view of Palestinian life for an English-speaking audience. His writings include poetry and newspaper columns as well as novels.

See also LITERATURE: ARABIC.

Bibliography

Turki, Fawaz. *The Disinherited: Journal of a Palestinian in Exile.* New York: Monthly Review Press, 1972.

Turki, Fawaz. *Exile's Return: The Making of a Palestinian American.* New York: Free Press, 1994.

JENAB TUTUNJI
UPDATED BY MICHAEL R. FISCHBACH

TURKISH–AFGHAN TREATY (1928)

Agreement between Turkey and Afghanistan designed to secure their independence from Soviet and British influence.

The Turkish–Afghan treaty, signed 28 May 1928, was the third in a series of bilateral agreements between Turkey and Afghanistan, non-Arab Muslim states bordering the Soviet Union. While the treaty did not include a mutual defense pact, it did proclaim peaceful relations between the two countries, barred either party from entering into a hostile alliance against the other, and called for mutual consultations in the event of threat of aggression from third parties.

Bibliography

Hurewitz, J. C. *The Middle East and North Africa in World Politics: A Documentary Record,* 2d edition. 2 vols. New Haven, CT: Yale University Press, 1975–1979.

DAVID WALDNER

TURKISH FILM

See FILM

TURKISH GRAND NATIONAL ASSEMBLY

The legislative body of Turkey.

The first parliament in Ottoman/Turkish history was convened in 1876 and was short lived. The second attempt, in 1908, also lasted for only a brief period. After the collapse of the Ottoman Empire, the Turkish Grand National Assembly (Türkiye Büyük Millet Meclisi) was founded on 23 April 1921, at the outset of the Turkish War of Independence; it proclaimed the republic on 29 October 1923. The assembly functioned as a legislature with one party until 1946; a transition to multiparty politics was initiated by the original party, the Republican People's Party (RPP; or Cumhuriyet Halk Partisi, CHP).

Two-Party Politics

According to the constitution, the assembly represented the expression of national sovereignty. Its function was to legislate, control the executive via the budget, and elect the head of state. From 1950 to 1957 the assembly was headed by the Democrat Party. In the 1950, 1954, and 1957 elections, the two major parties collectively received more than 90 percent of the total votes and controlled 98 percent of the parliamentary seats. The traditional center-periphery or elite-mass cleavage that the Turkish Republic inherited from the Ottoman Empire shaped the emerging political dualism. The Democrat Party projected the image of representing the interests of the periphery, including their religious aspirations, while the RPP was identified with the elitist and secularist orientation of the political center. Institutional factors also proved to be important. The simple plurality electoral system with multi-member districts worked to the advantage of the two strongest parties.

Financial and economic crises and the electoral losses of the Democrat Party in 1957 led to the adoption of authoritarian policies and laws, which brought about the military coup of 1960. The activities of the assembly were suspended for a year; all the deputies and cabinet members of the Democrat Party were prosecuted and parliament was dissolved.

1961 Constitution

The 1961 constitution, drafted by a constituent assembly, placed importance on the division of powers and broadened civil liberties. Broadcasting and higher education were granted autonomy. Numerous checks and balances were introduced, aimed at controlling arbitrary executive rule. A bicameral legislature was formed. The lower house, the National Assembly (Millet Meclisi), had 400 members elected for four-year terms. The upper house, the Republican Senate (Cumhuriyet Senatosu), consisted of 150 members elected for six-year terms, plus fifteen additional senators appointed by the president of the republic on the basis of merit, a varying number of ex-officio life members who belonged to the National Unity Committee of the interim military government, and former presidents of the republic. The legislative powers of the Senate remained limited and subordinate to the National Assembly. Joint sessions of the two assemblies constituted the new Turkish Grand National Assembly (TGNA). After the military coup of 1980, the Senate was abolished. On 12 September 1980, the legislature was dissolved and all political parties banned. The interim regime lasted two years. An appointed consultative assembly prepared a new constitution.

Yalim Erez (in the background, at left), the minister for industry and an independent deputy in the Turkish Grand National Assembly, formed a new Turkish government in 1998. It was one of several coalition governments established between 1996 and 2002 in an effort to deal with serious economic problems. © ABC AJANSI/CORBIS SYGMA. REPRODUCED BY PERMISSION.

1982 Constitution

The 1982 constitution was approved by a referendum on 9 November 1982. It vests legislative power in a unicameral assembly, elected by universal adult suffrage (the age at which one could vote was at first twenty-one but in 1995 was lowered to eighteen) for a maximum of five years. By-elections are to be held once between elections unless the number of vacancies reaches 5 percent of the parliament. The president of the republic is elected by the TGNA from among its members or from among candidates who have a higher education and are over forty. The president serves for a single term of seven years; a successor must be elected within thirty days. If no successor can be elected by the fourth ballot, parliament must dissolve itself. After the presidencies of Turgut Özal and Süleyman Demirel, in 2000 the TGNA elected Ahmet Necdet Nezer, former chair of the Constitutional Court. The prerogatives of the president are more extensive than in the previous constitution; they include the power to dissolve parliament. The 1987 elections enlarged the membership of the TGNA from 400 to 450; in 1995, the number of seats was raised to 550. The main functions of the TGNA are enacting, amending, and repealing laws; supervising the Council of Ministers; authorizing the Council of Ministers to issue governmental decrees that have the force of law; approving the budget; declaring war; ratifying international agreements; and proclaiming amnesties and pardons. Legislators exercise control in the form of written questions, investigation, and interpellation. Members of parliament are granted parliamentary immunity with regard to freedom of speech and, under certain circumstances, freedom from arrest.

As of 1993, constitutional amendments require a two-thirds majority. If no quorum is achieved, the president of the republic can return the amendment to parliament or refer the amendment to a popular vote. The state monopoly on television was eliminated, opening television to national and international channels; the right of government officials to organize unions was granted; prisoners were given the right to vote; political parties were permitted to establish women's and youth branches; discretionary power was allocated to the executive to declare early local elections or to postpone them. In the summer of 2002, new amendments legalized Kurdish-language radio and television, private-school education in Kurdish, and the abolition of capital punishment.

Under the current electoral rules, a party must receive 10 percent of the vote to gain representation in parliament. After 1987, this threshold was increased by adding a district-level quota (calculated by a simple proportion of the valid votes) to the parliamentary seats per district. This practice left a number of parties out of parliament. The Kurdish parties were eliminated despite their high regional return because their nationwide vote was less than 10 percent. Parties that do receive 10 percent of the national note win a proportionally higher share of parliamentary seats. For example, the Justice and Development Party (Adalet ve Kalkınma Partisi) under the leadership of Tayyip Erdoğan received 34.2 percent of the votes but 363 seats, eliminating all competing parties with the exception of the RPP, which received 19.3 percent of the votes and 178 seats. With the phasing out of sixteen political parties, 45.3 percent of the voters remained without representation. This brought Turkish politics back to a dual party system. In parliament, 89 percent of the members were newcomers. More than 80 percent of the parliamentarians had a higher education; they were predominantly lawyers, engineers, businessmen, and economists. The representation of women registered a slow gain. Despite the active support of women's organizations, the number of women parliamentarians registered only a slight increase, from 23 in 1999 to 24 in 2002.

Realignment

Looking at the political composition of the TGNA, a significant voter realignment can be seen, and high volatility in Turkey's major parties. Beginning in the 1980s and continuing in the 1990s, the moderate right parties registered a steady decline. Özal's party, the Motherland Party (Anavatan Partisi), winner of the 1983 elections, fell from having 292 representatives in 1987 to having 88 in 1999. On the moderate left, a similar phenomenon took place. The RPP was left out of parliament in 1999 with 8.7 percent of the votes and returned in 2002 with 19.3 percent; Bülent Ecevit's party, the Democratic Left Party (Demokratik Sol Partisi), gained 22.2 percent in 1999 but was eliminated with 1.2 percent in 2002.

This realignment pushed the extreme right, exemplified by the ultra-right-wing Nationalist Action Party (Milliyetçi Hareket Partisi) and the much smaller nationalist Great Unity Party (Büyük Birlik Partisi), into the political spectrum. The Islamist Welfare Party (Refah Partisi) and its successor the Virtue Party (Fazilet Partisi) also benefited from this realignment. The coalition governments of the 1990s were dominated by these political groups. The results of the 2002 election indicate that the center-periphery cleavage has lost its determining relevance. Instead, protest voting seems to have gained ascendancy.

The performance of Turkey's parliamentary system offers an important example of how electoral processes have played a critical role in opening the political system after each military intervention. Another new aspect of Turkish political life is the growing importance of local elections. With the increasing weight of large cities and metropolitan areas, urban problems influence electoral choice at the local and national level. The recent electoral success of the Justice and Development Party is partly due to the reputation Erdoğan, the former mayor of Istanbul, acquired. Major conflicts in national politics, such as those over secularism, affect voting patterns at both levels. Although Turkey's democratization started during the late 1940s, democracy has not been fully achieved, but the country's relatively long and continuous experience with democratic politics in twenty-two national elections represents a significant achievement.

See also AKP (JUSTICE AND DEVELOPMENT PARTY); DEMIREL, SÜLEYMAN; DEMOCRAT PARTY; ERDOĞAN, TAYYIP; MOTHERLAND PARTY; NATIONALIST ACTION PARTY; OTTOMAN EMPIRE; ÖZAL, TURGUT; REFAH PARTISI; REPUBLICAN PEOPLE'S PARTY (RPP).

Bibliography

Heper, Metin, and Evin, Ahmet, eds. *State, Democracy, and the Military: Turkey in the 1980s.* New York; Berlin: W. de Gruyter, 1988.

Özbudun, Ergun. *Contemporary Turkish Politics: Challenges to Democratic Consolidation.* Boulder, CO: Lynne Rienner, 2000.

Zürcher, Erik J. *Turkey: A Modern History,* new revised edition. New York and London: I. B. Tauris, 1998.

NERMIN ABADAN-UNAT

TURKISH HEARTH ASSOCIATION

Group formed to promote Turkish nationalism.

Toward the end of the Ottoman Empire, Ziya Gökalp and other Turkish intellectuals founded the Turkish Hearth Association (Türk Ocaği) in 1911 to promote nationalism, especially Gökalp's synthesis of Turkism, Islamism, and modernism. The association provided the Union and Progress political party with ideological direction. With government support, this private association sponsored nationalistic publications, speeches, sports, health, and economic development projects. By 1930, the association had 254 branches in cities and towns across Turkey. In 1931/32, the Republican People's party dissolved the association, took over its property, and established the People's Houses (*Halk Evleri*) in its place.

See also GÖKALP, ZIYA; PEOPLE'S HOUSES.

Bibliography

Lewis, Bernard. *The Emergence of Modern Turkey,* 3d edition. New York: Oxford University Press, 2002.

PAUL J. MAGNARELLA

TURKISH HISTORICAL SOCIETY

Academy dedicated to the study of Turkish history.

The forerunner to this society was the Turkish Historical Committee of the Turkish Hearth (Türk Ocaği Türk Tarih Heyeti) formed on 4 June 1930. This committee was reorganized as the Society for the Study of Turkish History (Türk Tarihi Tetkik Cemiyeti) on 12 April 1931 (officially recognized on 15 April 1931), and renamed the Turkish Historical Society (Türk Tarih Kurumu) on 3 October

1935. On 7 November 1982, the society was made subordinate to the Atatürk Kültür, Dil ve Tarih Yüksek Kurumu that now oversees the cultural, linguistic, and historical societies. The society has convened historical congresses (the first one, held 2-10 July 1932), publishes the journal *Belleten,* as well as monograph series devoted to all periods of the history of Turkey from the civilizations of ancient Anatolia to the modern day. It also serves as an academy for historical sciences honoring Turkish and foreign scholars.

ULI SCHAMILOGLU

TURKISH–ITALIAN WAR (1911–1912)

War launched by Italy against Turkey for control of Libya.

The Turkish–Italian War (29 September 1911 to 8 October 1912) was initiated by Italy in Libya as a step toward acquiring a modern empire. The diplomatic ground for this move was prepared by reaching secret bilateral agreements with Britain, France, Germany, Austria-Hungary, and Russia, all of which gave Italy a free hand in Libya in exchange for reciprocity elsewhere. This was in violation of the Congress and Treaty of Berlin (1878), in which the European powers guaranteed the sovereignty and territorial integrity of the Ottoman Empire.

Italy sent an ultimatum to the Ottoman government on 26 September 1911, declaring that it would occupy Libya within twenty-four hours unless the Ottoman Empire undertook immediate measures to protect the security of Italian citizens residing in Libya and also their property. Italy also said that Istanbul's dispatch of weapons to Libya was a provocation because these would be used against "peaceful" Italian colonists. When its demands were not met, Italy declared war against the Ottoman Empire (29 September), placed a blockade on the Libyan coast, and started landing in Tripoli (4 October). The conquest of the coastal towns was swift: Tripoli (12 October), Derna (18 October), Benghazi and Khoms (21 October), and the smaller towns soon after.

The Ottoman military force in Libya was small and much below standard. When war broke out, the Ottomans could not forward military support to

Libya due to the Italian sea blockade and the decision of Britain and France to prevent the passage of military reinforcements to the belligerents through Egypt or Tunisia.

As a result of these conditions, the Ottoman authorities in Istanbul allowed volunteers to infiltrate into Libya. (Among them were Enver Paşa, who later became the minister of war, and Mustafa Kemal Atatürk, the founder of the Turkish republic.) They left the actual direction of the war to the Ottoman military command in Libya, which decided to retreat from the coast—where the Italians had a clear military advantage owing to the size and quality of their forces. An Ottoman-Libyan force was established, composed of tribal soldiers, Ottoman professionals, and a mixed Ottoman-tribal command, which in Cyrenaica was connected with the Sanusi leadership and network of *zawiyas* (religious compounds).

The Italian invading forces were the first to make military use of airplanes (for reconnaissance and bombing). They made no meaningful gains after their initial conquests because they attempted to fight a trench war against the resistance, which engaged in guerrilla warfare and took advantage of the hilly or desert terrain and the support of the population. Failing to advance into the hinterland, the Italians widened the scope of the war to the eastern Mediterranean to put more pressure on the Ottomans. During April and May 1912, Italy occupied the Dodecanese islands, tried to enter forcibly the Dardanelles channel connecting Istanbul to the Aegean Sea, and bombarded some Ottoman ports, including Beirut. These operations caused the Ottomans heavy damage, aroused strong apprehension among the European powers, and provoked international efforts to solve the crisis.

In the Balkans, increasing unrest led to the outbreak of the first Balkan War on 8 October 1912. Unable to fight on two major fronts, and perceiving the Balkans as more important to the empire than Libya, the Ottoman government decided to end the war in Libya. The Treaty of Peace, concluded in October 1912, stipulated that Ottoman forces were to depart Libya, but that the Ottomans could send Muslim religious representatives there. The Ottoman withdrawal was to be followed by an Italian evacuation of the Dodecanese. The issue of sovereignty was not settled conclusively: Although Italy regarded Libya as part of the Italian homeland following its declaration on the extension of Italian law over Libya (5 November 1911, only one month after the war had started and before any peace treaty had been concluded), the Ottomans told the local population that they were being granted autonomy under Ottoman rule. Most Ottoman forces left Tripolitania, but many remained in Cyrenaica, and reinforcements also were sent later, especially during World War I. Until then, Italy managed to occupy most of Tripolitania and prevented the functioning of the Ottoman-chosen religious representation.

Bibliography

Childs, Timothy W. *Italo-Turkish Diplomacy and the War over Libya, 1911–1912*. New York; Leiden, Netherlands: Brill, 1990.

Simon, Rachel. *Libya between Ottomanism and Nationalism: Ottoman Involvement in Libya during the War with Italy (1911–1919)*. Berlin: K. Schwarz, 1987.

RACHEL SIMON
UPDATED BY ERIC HOOGLUND

TURKISH LANGUAGE

Türkçe; official language of the Republic of Turkey.

Turkish is one of the Turkic languages of the Altaic language family, one of the world's major language families. Turkic, Mongolian, and Manchu-Tungus constitute the Altaic language family, which originated around the Altai mountain ranges in central Asia, straddling Mongolia, China, and Russia. Altaic languages usually are grouped with the Uralic languages—for example, Samoyed, Finnish, and Hungarian. Debates continue about whether the typological and lexical similarities between the two language families signal a common ancestor language or prolonged contact.

The Turkic Languages

The Turkic language group includes most of the languages and dialects spoken along a wide Eurasian belt that extends from eastern Siberia to eastern Europe and the Balkans. The major representative Turkic languages are (starting in the east) Yakut, Altai, Khakas, Uygur, Kyrgyz, Kazakh, Uzbek,

Turkmen, Bashkir, Tatar, Chuvash, Azeri, and Turkish. With the exception of Turkish, all of these languages are spoken in the republics and territories of the former Soviet Union or in northwestern China.

Turkish, Azeri (also referred to as Azerbaijani Turkish), and Turkmen are the major members of the southwestern, or Oghuz, branch of the Turkic languages. In demographic terms, this branch is the most important Turkic group. The Azeri language is spoken in the Republic of Azerbaijan and in northwestern Iran. Turkmen is spoken in the Republic of Turkmenistan and in adjoining territories in northern Iran and Afghanistan, as well as in Iraq. Lesser-known members of the southwestern branch are Gagauz, spoken in the Balkan states of Bulgaria and Moldavia, and Qashqaʾi, spoken in parts of southwestern Iran. The languages of this branch are closely related and have a relatively high degree of mutual intelligibility. What interferes with the complete comprehension of written material is mainly vocabulary, which was developed or acquired by each language while functioning in different historical and cultural spheres, and the different alphabets they use (Arabic and Latin). In oral communication, differences in pronunciation slow down comprehension.

Turkish was introduced to the Middle East with the westward migration of various Turkish tribes, who had converted to Islam by the ninth century, from the western regions of central Asia. By the end of the eleventh century, these Muslim Turks had conquered Asia Minor, and the Turkish language began to be established in Anatolia. As the official administrative language of the Ottoman Turks, Turkish spread further with the continuing Ottoman conquests, into the Balkans and central Europe to the north and into the Arab lands and North Africa to the south. Turkish became the lingua franca in many of these regions, and the impact of Turkish on the indigenous languages after centuries of contact is clearly discernible today.

Old Anatolian, Ottoman, and Modern Turkish

The earliest written Anatolian Turkish materials are in Arabic script and date from the thirteenth century. Three basic periods are recognized for the historical development of the Turkish language, based on written data: (1) Old Anatolian Turkish for the thirteenth through fifteenth centuries; (2) Ottoman Turkish for the fifteenth through the early twentieth centuries; (3) Modern Turkish since 1928. The linguistic base remained remarkably stable, particularly for the spoken language, so that some poetry, including early hymns of Sufism and Sufi orders from the fourteenth century still can be understood and appreciated by a general audience. However, in the process of adapting to Islam and the Arab-Persian culture, Turkish gradually acquired many words and some syntactic elements from Arabic and Persian. As the Ottoman Turks became the standard-bearers for the Islamic world, borrowings from both Arabic and Persian accelerated to such an extent that by the nineteenth century an official or literary Ottoman Turkish text could be understood only by an educated elite conversant in Turkish, Persian, and Arabic.

By the start of the twentieth century—and hastened by the post–World War I disintegration of the Ottoman Empire—nationalistic notions about a distinct Turkish identity inspired moves to rid the language of excessive foreign elements. The Alphabet Reform of 1928 abandoned the Arabic script and mandated a phonetic Turkish script based on the Latin alphabet; this was a crucial factor in the emergence of Modern Turkish. The new writing system was tailored exclusively to the vowel-rich Turkish sound system, eventually setting up a well-defined modern national standard for Turkish based on the dialect of Istanbul, the old capital of the Ottoman Empire and the educational, cultural, and intellectual center of the country.

The Turkish language shares a core vocabulary with the other Turkic languages and exhibits characteristic common features: vowel harmony, agglutination, and, on the syntactic level, left-branching. Turkish has eight vowels, four pairs with corresponding front/back, high/low, and rounded/unrounded sounds, which form the basis for vowel harmony. According to vowel harmony rules, vowels of suffixes must have the same properties as the vowel in the last syllable: either front/back or rounded/unrounded. Twenty-one letters represent the consonants. Agglutination in Turkish takes the form of suffixes attached to the end of a word, whether noun or verb. Suffixes add to the word's meaning and/or mark its grammatical function. Turkish does not have a definite article, nor does it have gender pronouns (one word signifies *he, she, or it*). Sentence construction follows the subject-object-verb pattern. As a left-branching language, all modifiers precede the element modified.

A lexical inventory of Modern Turkish clearly shows that the Turkish language has enriched itself by borrowing freely from other languages and continues to do so. In 1931 the Turkish Linguistic Society undertook reforms that effectively resulted in eliminating Arabic and Persian words not fully assimilated into the Turkish language. However, these words were replaced with neologisms or borrowings from European languages.

See also ANATOLIA; AZERI LANGUAGE AND LITERATURE; ISTANBUL; LITERATURE: TURKISH; OTTOMAN EMPIRE; SUFISM AND THE SUFI ORDERS; TRIBES AND TRIBALISM: QASHQAʾI; TURKISH LINGUISTIC SOCIETY; TURKISH SCRIPT.

Bibliography

Boeschoten, Hendrik, and Verhoeven, Ludo, eds. *Turkish Linguistics Today.* New York; Leiden, Netherlands: E. J. Brill, 1991.

Kowalski, T. "Ottoman Turkish Dialects." In *Encyclopaedia of Islam,* Vol. 4. Leiden, Netherlands: E. J. Brill.

Lewis, G. L. *Turkish Grammar.* Oxford: Clarendon Press, 1967.

Slobin, Dan Isaac, and Zimmer, Karl, eds. *Studies in Turkish Linguistics.* Philadelphia; Amsterdam: J. Benjamins, 1986.

ERIKA GILSON
UPDATED BY ERIC HOOGLUND

TURKISH LAW ON THE PROTECTION OF THE FAMILY (1998)

Turkish law to protect women.

The Law on the Protection of the Family primarily aims to improve the handling of domestic violence cases. Before its enactment, such cases were tried in accordance with the Criminal Code, thus requiring victims to appeal to the police and to obtain a report from a state hospital. Women's organizations have claimed that such requirements inhibit women's appeal to legal recourse, because police and doctors are usually more interested in the "reconciliation" of spouses than in initiating legal action. With the introduction of the law, the complaint of the victim or the decision of the public prosecutor suffices to order immediate removal of the abuser from the domicile or imprisonment for up to six months.

The issue of domestic violence is central to Turkey's post-1980 feminism, and the enactment of the law illustrates a successful collaboration between activists and the state. Among many others, three organizations—the Purple Roof Foundation, the Altındağ Women's Solidarity Foundation, and Women for Women's Rights—have closely worked with the General Directorate on the Status and Problems of Women to secure support from parliamentarians, jurists, and the media.

The impact of the law on social attitudes is, however, questionable. The number of reported cases of domestic violence did not decrease significantly in the five years after passage of the law, and, according to a study conducted among college students, most males still approve of wife beating.

See also GENDER: GENDER AND LAW; GENDER: GENDER AND POLITICS; TURKEY.

Bibliography

Arat, Yeşim. "Feminist Institutions and Democratic Aspirations: The Case of the Purple Roof Women's Shelter Foundation." In *Deconstructing the Images of "The Turkish Woman,"* edited by Z. Arat. New York: St. Martin's Press, 1998.

Sakallı, Nuray. "Beliefs about Wife Beating among Turkish College Students: The Effects of Patriarchy, Sexism, and Sex Differences." *Sex Roles* 44, nos. 9–10 (2001): 599–610.

BURÇAK KESKIN-KOZAT

TURKISH LINGUISTIC SOCIETY

Organization devoted to the study of Turkish and the Turkic languages.

The Society for the Study of the Turkish Language (Türk Dili Tetkik Cemiyeti) was founded on 12 July 1932, on the model of a similar society that already existed for the study of Turkish history. In 1934, its name was updated to the Türk Dili Araştirma Kurumu reflecting the society's interest in purging the Turkish Language of its numerous borrowed Arabic and Persian words. In 1936, the name was changed again to the Turkish Linguistic Society (Türk Dil Kurumu). On 7 November 1982, the society was made subordinate to the Atatürk Kültür, Dil ve Tarih Yüksek Kurumu that now oversees the cultural, linguistic, and historical societies. The society has convened linguistic congresses (the first congress opened in 1932), publishes the journal *Türk Dili,* and publishes dictionaries and other works related to Turkish and all the other Turkic languages. In contrast to other such societies in Turkey, the activities of the Turkish Linguistic Society have not been led by scholars of the Turkish language, and one result has been that the society's activities have assumed a populist character. The society has also been at the center of recurring and intense national debates over language reform, most recently over the degree to which vast numbers of neologisms (new words or word forms adopted from foreign words) should be introduced into the Turkish language (often over the objections of many politicians and scholars).

See also TURKISH LANGUAGE.

Bibliography

Heyd, Uriel. *Language Reform in Modern Turkey.* Jerusalem: Israel Oriental Society, 1954.

ULI SCHAMILOGLU

TURKISH NATIONAL PACT

A resolution that stated the goal of political independence for Turkey.

This resolution adopted by the Ottoman parliament in Istanbul on 17 February 1920, declared support for the demands of the nationalist movement led by Mustafa Kemal Pasha (Atatürk). It included: the integrity of all territories inhabited by "an Ottoman Islamic majority"; popular plebiscites to determine the future of territories whose status was in doubt (Kars, Ardahan, and Batum in the Caucasus; western Thrace; and areas with Arab majorities); "protection" of the city of Istanbul and the Sea of Marmara and negotiation regarding trade and commerce in the Bosporus and the Dardanelles; recog-

nition of minority rights provided reciprocal rights were extended to Muslim minorities in other countries; and recognition of full independence and sovereignty for "the country." This was essentially the program implemented in the wake of the defeat of the Greek army in western Anatolia and the withdrawal of British power from Istanbul and its environment in 1922. Functionally, the national pact served as a declaration of independence by nationalist Turkey.

Bibliography

Shaw, Stanford J., and Shaw, Ezel Kural. *History of the Ottoman Empire and Modern Turkey,* Vol. 2: *Reform, Revolution, and Republic: The Rise of Modern Turkey, 1808-1975.* Cambridge, U.K., and New York: Cambridge University Press, 1977.

FRANK TACHAU

TURKISH NEWS AGENCY

See NEWSPAPERS AND PRINT MEDIA: TURKEY

TURKISH SCRIPT

Latin alphabet used predominantly in Turkey to write Turkish.

Contemporary Turkish is written in the Roman alphabet; the Turkish script is composed of eight vowels and twenty-one consonants, which are marked by various diacriticals. The first writings in Turkic language date to about 700 C.E. and use a runic alphabet. Later, Turkish came to be written in the Arabic alphabet. The earliest writings of Turkish in the Arabic script date to the thirteenth century and show strong Arabo-Persian linguistic influences. The fourteenth and fifteenth centuries show a boom in textual production. The literary Ottoman Turkish of this period was far removed from the spoken language. Beginning in the eighteenth century, with the decline of the Ottoman Empire, movements in favor of a language with stronger Turkish and less Ottoman characteristics gained momentum. In 1909, the Turkish Club began promoting a simpler Turkish, comprehensible across social strata. Mustafa Kemal Atatürk later founded the Turkish Language Academy. As part of Atatürk's sweeping reforms, the Turkish script was officially switched from the Arabic to the Roman alphabet in 1928.

See also ATATÜRK, MUSTAFA KEMAL; TURKISH LANGUAGE.

Bibliography

Campbell, George. *Compendium of the World's Languages,* vol. 2, 2d edition. London: Routledge, 2000.

NOAH BUTLER

TURKISH WORKERS PARTY

Turkish political party, 1961–1971.

This first avowedly socialist group to make a significant impact on the Turkish party system was founded in February of 1961. Its emergence signified the relative liberalism of the political order in the wake of the military intervention of 27 May 1960. The party competed successfully in the elections of 1965 and 1969, polling about 3 percent of the vote and gaining fifteen seats in the former and two in the latter election (the difference is attributable to changes in the electoral law). Its presence on the scene may have pulled the centrist Republican People's party (RPP) to the left. The party was subject to official and mob harassment, including violent attacks on its facilities and members. It was dissolved by order of the constitutional court in July 1971 on grounds that its leaders had encouraged communism and ethnic divisiveness (specifically, Kurdish separatism).

Bibliography

Ahmad, Feroz. *The Turkish Experiment in Democracy, 1950–1975.* Boulder, CO: Westview Press, 1977.

FRANK TACHAU

TURKISM

Political and cultural movement that emerged in the late nineteenth century and helped to form the new Turkish republic.

A movement of many tendencies, Turkism evolved largely in response to European nationalism and to the perceived failure of Ottomanism, as the empire was rocked by minority nationalist movements in the Balkans and Armenia. Sentiments of Turkish nationalist feeling can be traced to historical writings of the mid-nineteenth century, such as those of Ahmet Vefik Paşa (1823–1891). The first Ottoman Turcologist was Necib Asim (1861–1935). Politically, Turkism was most prominently expressed by the Young Turk movement, first in exile in the 1890s in Europe and Egypt and later in Anatolia after the 1908 Young Turk revolution. Competing tendencies included Anatolian nationalism, which traced Turkish roots in the territory to ancient times, and pan-Turkism, espoused especially by Turkish refugees from Russia and central Asia. The political manifesto of pan-Turkism is considered Russian-born Yusuf Akçura's 1904 essay, "Üç Tarz-i Siyaset" (Three Kinds of Policy), which rejected Ottomanism and Islam as bases of national identity and policy.

A major Turkish literary movement appeared in the early twentieth century, with groups like the Genç Kalemler (Young Pens) founded in 1911 in Salonika and the Türk Deneği (Turkish Society) founded in 1908 in Constantinople (now Istanbul). These and other groups were devoted to reviving Turkish folklore, studying the roots and branches of the various Turkic languages, and purifying the Ottoman language of non-Turkish words. The most important ideologue of the Young Turk era was the pan-Turkist writer and sociologist, Ziya Gökalp (1876–1924), who developed a populist vision of the rebirth of Turkish society. Eventually, Anatolian-based Turkism would prevail, with Mustafa Kemal's revolution and war of independence, beginning in 1919.

See also AHMET VEFIK; GENÇ KALEMLER; GÖKALP, ZIYA.

Bibliography

Lewis, Bernard. *The Emergence of Modern Turkey,* 3d edition. New York: Oxford University Press, 2002.

Shaw, Stanford J., and Shaw, Ezel Kural. *History of the Ottoman Empire and Modern Turkey,* Vol. 2: *Reform, Revolution, and Republic: The Rise of Modern Turkey, 1808–1975.* Cambridge, U.K., and New York: Cambridge University Press, 1977.

ELIZABETH THOMPSON

TURKMANCHAI, TREATY OF (1828)

Treaty by which Iran ceded its territories in the Caucasus to Russia.

The Treaty of Turkmanchai concluded a war between Iran and Russia that Iran initiated in 1826 with the aim of recovering territory in the Caucasus region that it had lost to Russia in 1813. The war went very badly for Iran, which was forced to accept unfavorable peace terms in the treaty signed in the village of Turkmanchai, about 80 miles southeast of Tabriz, on 21 February 1828. Under the treaty, Iran ceded its remaining provinces north of the Aras River (Yerevan and Nakhichevan) to Russia; extended preferential trade rights to Russian subjects; recognized Russia's exclusive naval rights in the Caspian Sea; accepted the application of Russian law to Russian subjects in Iran involved in civil or criminal legal cases; and agreed to pay Russia an indemnity of 20 million rubles.

Bibliography

Lambton, Ann K. S. "Persian Trade under the Early Qajars." In *Islam and the Trade of Asia: A Colloquium,* edited by D. S. Richards. Philadelphia: University of Pennsylvania Press, 1970.

FARHAD SHIRZAD
UPDATED BY ERIC HOOGLUND

TURKMEN

See GLOSSARY

TURKO–IRANIAN WAR (1821–1823)

The final war between the Qajar Persians and the Ottoman Turks.

This conflict began in 1821 when the Persian governor of Erzerum gave protection to tribes fleeing Azerbaijan. Actually, the conflict was instigated by Russia, which was anxious to weaken the Ottoman position in the Greek Revolution. The Russians induced Abbas Mirza, son of Fath Ali Shah Qajar, to invade Ottoman Turkey. He did, occupying Kurdistan and all the districts adjacent to Azerbaijan. As a counter move, the Ottoman viceroy of Baghdad invaded Persia but was defeated and chased back to Baghdad. In retaliation, Fath Ali Shah Qajar's oldest son, Mohammad Ali Mirza, laid siege to that city; his illness, and later death, lifted the siege, and the action shifted to the north. In the battle of Erzurum (1821) Abbas Mirza's army of 30,000 men defeated an Ottoman army of over 50,000. An epidemic of cholera precluded further action in the south, and the two powers ended hostilities with the Treaty of Erzurum on 28 July 1823. This treaty involved no change in territorial borders, but it did guarantee Persia access to the holy places in Iraq and Arabia; Ottoman suppression of Kurdish raids on Persian territory; release of the possessions of Persian merchants in Turkey; and an exchange of ambassadors.

Bibliography

Sykes, Percy Molesworth. *A History of Persia* (1915). London: Routledge and K. Paul, 1969.

DANIEL E. SPECTOR

TURKOLOGY

The academic study of the languages and civilization of the Turkic peoples with a traditional emphasis on sources written in Turkic languages.

The modern Turkic languages include Turkish, Uzbek, Kazakh, Azeri, Kazan Tatar, Turkmen, Kirghiz, Chuvash, Bashkir, Karakalpak, Yakut, Kumik, Crimean Tatar, Uighur, Tuvan, Gagauz, Karachay, Balkar, Xakas, Noghay, Altay, Shor, Dolgan, Karaim, and Tofalar. Native scholars have been writing descriptions of the Turkic dialects since the eleventh century. In the West, the earliest works on Turkey appeared in the fifteenth and sixteenth centuries, and the first descriptions of the Turkish language were published in the seventeenth century. The formal study of Turkish and other Turkic languages was introduced in Europe in the eighteenth century, and by the end of the nineteenth century, there were prominent centers of Turkology at universities in Paris, Moscow, Saint Petersburg, Kazan, Budapest, and Vienna. Today Turkology is widely taught in modern political units representing individual Turkic peoples: the Turkish republic, the Turkic republics of the former USSR, and the Uighur Autonomous Region in the People's Republic of China, where it is synonymous with the study of the local national culture. Turkology is also offered at major universities in Europe and North America, though the study of the language and civilization of the Turkish republic is far better represented than the study of the Turkic peoples as a whole.

Bibliography

Menges, Karl H. *The Turkic Languages and Peoples: An Introduction to Turkic Studies,* 2nd revised edition. Wiesbaden: Harrassowitz, 1995.

Poppe, Nicholas. *Introduction to Altaic Linguistics.* Wiesbaden: Harrassowitz, 1965.

ULI SCHAMILOGLU

TURKS

Ethnic group living in Turkey; also used to refer to Turkic-language speakers in Central Asia.

Turks are an ethnolinguistic group living in a broad geographic expanse extending from southeastern Europe through Anatolia and the Caucasus Mountains and throughout Central Asia. Thus Turks include the Turks of Turkey, the Azeris of Azerbaijan, and the Kazakhs, Kyrgyz, Tatars, Turkmen, and Uzbeks of Central Asia, as well as many smaller groups in Asia speaking Turkic languages. In a legal sense, however, *Turks* refers only to citizens of Turkey, even those (up to 20% of the population) who are not ethnically Turkish.

Nomadic Turks began infiltrating into Iran from Central Asia as early as the eighth century. Although the initial contacts generally were peaceful, by the tenth century large groups of Turks were invading Iran, and in the eleventh century they began invading Anatolia. First the Seljuk Turks and subsequently the Ottoman Turks established kingdoms in Anatolia. The Ottomans conquered the Byzantine imperial capital Constantinople (now Istanbul) in 1453, and this city then became the center of the Ottoman Empire, which at its height in the sixteenth and seventeenth centuries spanned three continents. Although the Ottoman Empire was multiethnic, Europeans often referred to its subjects as Turks and used "Ottoman Empire" synonymously with "Turkey."

During the nineteenth century, some Ottoman/Turkish intellectuals began to advocate pan-Turanism, a movement to unite all Turkic-language peoples under the Ottoman Empire. After the establishment of the Republic of Turkey in 1923, the government rejected pan-Turanism as an official policy. Nevertheless, interest in the cultural, if not political, unity of Turkic peoples has been a strong current among intellectuals in Turkey and has been revitalized since the collapse of the Soviet Union in 1991 and the emergence in Central Asia of several new Turkic-speaking countries.

See also ANATOLIA; ISTANBUL; TURKEY; TURKISH LANGUAGE.

Bibliography

Yavuz, M. Hakan. "Turkish Identity Politics and Central Asia." In *Islam and Central Asia: An Enduring Legacy or an Evolving Threat?* edited by Roland Sagdeev and Susan Eisenhower. Washington, DC: Center for Political and Strategic Studies, 2000.

ERIC HOOGLUND

TÜRK YURDU

See NEWSPAPERS AND PRINT MEDIA: TURKEY

TWAREG

Berber-speaking people of the Sahara, mostly in Algeria.

Twareg is an apparently non-Berber plural; the singular is *targui* or *targi.* Twareg (also Tuareg) call themselves, according to the region, *amahagh, amaiagh,* or *amashagh,* all reflexes of *amazigh,* the term more widely used for Berber in the rest of North Africa. It is estimated that there are 400,000 to 500,000 Twareg-language/dialect speakers. Most are fair-skinned Europids, although many are descendants of or mixed with negroid populations (of whom most were slaves). Twareg traditionally distinguish socially between the "noble" clans, camel nomads who in the past could range far and wide, wage war, and claim a share of the resources of groups they dominated (and whose protection they assured), and "vassal" clans, also nomadic but essentially herdsmen (mainly goats, but also camels belonging to the nobles, and cattle in some places), subjects of the noble clans. Other groups often are counted as Twareg, notably sedentary former slave populations (now primarily agriculturalists in the oases and artisans).

The requirements of modern states—fixed borders, schooling of children, control of territory and citizens—and the industrial exploitation of resources have placed extreme pressures on the nomadic existence and traditions dear to the Twareg. They nonetheless maintain such traditional cultural traits as a strong matrilineal principle (in much of their inheritance of property, succession to chieftainship, rights and obligations toward vassal groups, etc.) and the strict veiling of men (women, however, typically are not veiled).

See also BERBER.

THOMAS G. PENCHOEN

TWAYNI, GHASSAN
[1926–]

Lebanon's best-known journalist and publisher; former minister, ambassador, and representative from Lebanon to the United Nations.

A Greek Orthodox born in Beirut, Ghassan Twayni (also Tueni) has been one of the most influential figures in post–World War II Lebanon. His impressive and multifaceted career as academic, journalist, businessman, politician, diplomat, and man of letters has made him a prime shaper of public opinion in his country and one of the most respected commentators on Lebanese and Arab affairs throughout the United States and Europe.

He received a bachelor of arts degree in philosophy from the American University of Beirut (AUB) in 1945 and a master of arts degree in political science from Harvard University in 1947. After a year as a lecturer in political science at AUB (1947–1948), he became editor in chief of the daily newspaper *al-Nahar* in 1948, a position he occupied until he turned it over to his son, Jubran, in December 1999. He worked in journalism and publishing most of his life, and was active as the founder and chairman (from 1960 onwards) of Press Cooperative S.A.L. publishing group, editor-publisher of the *al-Nahar* S.C.P.A. Publishing Company after 1963, publisher and editor in chief of the French-language dailies *Le jour* (1965) and *L'orient-Le jour* (1970–1991), and chairman of the board of the Société Générale de la Presse et d'Edition (1985–1991).

In 1951, embarking on a political career, Twayni won a parliamentary seat after running successfully in Mount Lebanon as a candidate of the Socialist National Front, a loose coalition of politicians headed by Camille Chamoun and Kamal Jumblatt

that called for the resignation of President Bishara al-Khuri, whose second term in office had become tainted with charges of nepotism, administrative corruption, and heavy-handed tactics. Twayni was reelected in 1953 and 1957, both times as a representative for Beirut, and was deputy speaker of parliament between 1953 and 1957. By then, he had established himself as one of the most prominent and competent members of a new generation of young, well-educated, reform-minded professionals who had become active in politics in an effort to modernize the Lebanese state. It was this reputation that led to his appointment in October 1970 as deputy prime minister and minister of information and education in President Sulayman Franjiyya's first cabinet (the so-called Youth Cabinet, headed by Sa'ib Salam and composed predominantly of young technocrats recruited from outside parliament). Twayni resigned in January 1971, however, in protest against the president's and the prime minister's unwillingness to support the educational reforms he had proposed. He was subsequently appointed minister of labor and social affairs, tourism, and industry and oil in a cabinet headed by Rashid Karame (July 1975 to December 1976).

After the 1960s Twayni frequently represented his country abroad, both in official and unofficial positions. Following the Arab–Israel War (1967), he was ambassador-at-large and personal representative of President Charles Hilu on a special mission to the United States. In December 1976 he was President Ilyas Sarkis's special emissary to Washington, D.C. His diplomatic skills and achievements eventually led to his appointment in September 1977 as ambassador and permanent representative of Lebanon to the United Nations, a position he held until September 1982. Between 1982 and 1988 he served as special adviser to President Amin Jumayyil. His responsibilities during this period included coordinating negotiations for the withdrawal of foreign forces from Lebanon. In the early 1990s he was president of Balamand University, and he remains on the board of trustees of AUB. He continues to shuttle back and forth between Lebanon, Europe, and the United States.

See also AMERICAN UNIVERSITY OF BEIRUT (AUB); ARAB–ISRAEL WAR (1967); CHAMOUN, CAMILLE; FRANJIYYA, SULAYMAN; HILU, CHARLES; JUMAYYIL, AMIN; JUMBLATT,

KAMAL; KARAME, RASHID; KHURI, BISHARA
AL-; SARKIS, ILYAS.

Bibliography

Hudson, Michael C. *The Precarious Republic: Political Modernization in Lebanon.* Boulder, CO: Westview Press, 1985.

Petran, Tabitha. *The Struggle over Lebanon.* New York:
Monthly Review Press, 1987.

GUILAIN P. DENOEUX
UPDATED BY MICHAEL R. FISCHBACH

TWIN PILLARS POLICY

*U.S. policy to promote Iran and Saudi Arabia as local
guardians of U.S. interests in the Persian Gulf region.*

The decision by Great Britain in the late 1960s to
withdraw its military forces from the Persian Gulf
and to grant independence to its ten protectorates
along the east coast of the Arabian Peninsula confronted the United States with a strategic dilemma.
It was the height of Cold War rivalry with the Soviet
Union, and the United States was deeply involved
in Vietnam. Consequently, the United States decided instead of direct intervention to build up its
two regional allies, Iran and Saudi Arabia, as local
powers that could protect the region from the spread
of Soviet influence. As the "twin pillars" of U.S.
policy, both countries were encouraged to acquire
billions of dollars of the most advanced arms during the 1970s. Iran embraced the twin pillars policy more enthusiastically than Saudi Arabia and
intervened militarily, with U.S. approbation, in Iraq
and Oman. The policy collapsed suddenly in 1979,
when the shah (king) of Iran was overthrown in a
revolution that brought to power a republican
regime opposed to U.S. influence in the region.

See also UNITED STATES OF AMERICA AND THE
MIDDLE EAST.

Bibliography

Hooglund, Eric. "The Persian Gulf." In *Intervention into
the 1990s: U.S. Foreign Policy in the Third World,* edited by
Peter Schraeder. Boulder, CO: Lynne Rienner,
1992.

ZACHARY KARABELL
UPDATED BY ERIC HOOGLUND

TYRE

*Historic coastal city in south Lebanon on the Mediter-
ranean Sea.*

Throughout its history, Tyre (now Sur), which is
located fifty-two miles (83 km) from Beirut, has
known several invasions and occupations. In the
eighth century B.C.E., Tyre rebelled against the Assyrians, and in the sixth century B.C.E., the population of Tyre organized a revolt against the
Chaldeans. In 333 B.C.E., following his defeat of
the Persians, Alexander the Great was welcomed by
all Phoenician cities with the exception of Tyre.

Tyre has also had a golden age (especially under the Romans) because of its flourishing glass and
purple dye manufacturing. It was under the Romans
that Christianity reached Tyre in the person of Saint
Paul, who visited the city and stayed for ten days. In
638 C.E., Tyre fell under the control of the Fatimids, where it remained until 1124. In that year
Tyre was besieged by the Crusaders and was incorporated in the kingdom of Jerusalem, as a part of
which it grew prosperous. The city was recaptured
and destroyed by the Mamluks in 1291.

Oranges, citrus, bananas, and sugar cane are the
major fruits and vegetables produced in Tyre. Some
of the inhabitants of the city and the surrounding
region also make their living as fishermen. The old
Phoenician city today has a large number of banks
and financial institutions, several educational and
humanitarian institutions, and hospitals and health
centers to serve its population of 30,000 (1996).
In a city that also has an active sport life, soccer clubs
are especially popular.

GEORGE E. IRANI

TZOMET

See ISRAEL: POLITICAL PARTIES IN

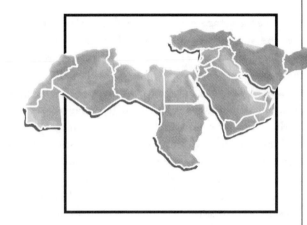

UGANDA PROJECT

Proposal for a Jewish state in British territory in East Africa.

In 1902 Theodor Herzl petitioned the Royal Commission for Alien Immigration in London for assistance in alleviating the plight of Jews. In the summer of 1903, the British colonial secretary informed the World Zionist Organization of Great Britain's agreement in principle that East Africa could serve as a potential Jewish homeland. The apparent motivation for this plan, which became known as the Uganda Project or Uganda Scheme, was a desire to help the Jews as well as to develop the area for further colonization and perhaps to minimize further Jewish immigration to Great Britain.

The Sixth Zionist Congress met shortly thereafter, and Herzl presented the Uganda Scheme (it was actually Kenya), urging its acceptance as a temporary measure. Max Nordau, Eliezer Ben-Yehuda, Nachman Syrkin, and Rabbi Yitzhak Yaacov Reines supported it, whereas Menachem Ussishkin and Ber Borochov, as well as Vladimir Ze'ev Jabotinsky, staunchly opposed it. The proposal became the subject of one of the fiercest debates in Zionist history. When Herzl won, and the Congress voted, 295 to 178, in favor of a proposal to investigate the plan's viability, the opposition stormed out and agreed to return only after Herzl assured them of his allegiance to Palestine as the ultimate objective of Zionism.

In spring 1904 the British government withdrew its offer. Herzl died before the Seventh Zionist Congress, in 1905, at which the scheme was overwhelmingly rejected by a majority of the 497 delegates.

See also HERZL, THEODOR; WORLD ZIONIST ORGANIZATION (WZO).

Bibliography

Heymann, Michael, ed. *The Uganda Controversy: Minutes of the Zionist General Council,* 2 vols. Tel Aviv and Jerusalem: Tel Aviv University, Institute for Zionist Research and the Zionist Library, 1970–1977.

Shimoni, Gideon. *The Zionist Ideology.* Hanover, NH: University Press of New England, 1995.

CHAIM I. WAXMAN

ULAMA

Muslim religious scholars.

The term *ulama* literally means those who possess knowledge (*ilm*), particularly of Islam. The *ulama* emerged as the first interpreters of the Qur'an and transmitters of *hadith*, the words and deeds of the prophet Muhammad. These scholars also became the first to outline and elaborate the basic principles of Islamic law (*shari'a*). The *ulama* were central to Islamic education in the premodern Middle East. They regulated instruction at all levels and were instrumental in the process of training Islamic scholars in *madrasas* (residential colleges), which were

Now under the leadership of Ayatollah Seyed Ali Khamenei, the Shi'ite *ulama*, or cultural elite acting as guardians and interpreters of Islamic faith, have exercised unequaled political as well as religious authority in Iran since the revolution of 1979. This is in contrast to the deep divides over the authority of the *ulama* in the Sunni world. © AP/WIDEWORLD PHOTOS. REPRODUCED BY PERMISSION.

established by the eleventh century. These medieval institutions developed a rigorous curriculum centered around instruction in the law, training future jurists, theologians, and state functionaries. This system of higher education was the first in a series of successful attempts to link the *ulama* to political authority in the Islamic world. Members of the *ulama* might also participate in Islamic mysticism as members—even leaders—of organized Sufi fraternities.

The *ulama* are often defined as a class when in fact the socioeconomic status of their membership remained quite varied. Lawyers and judges were key members of the *ulama*; their legal skills were critical to the regulation of Islamic society in social and commercial matters such as wills, marriage, and trade. The *ulama* also included theologians, prayer leaders, and teachers, many of whom continued to participate in the economy as traders or artisans. Until the mid-nineteenth century, state bureaucracies in the Middle East employed members of the *ulama* as tax collectors, scribes, secretaries, and market inspectors. The *ulama* formed a cultural elite and retained the admiration and respect of the Muslim masses because they, not the rulers, were perceived as the true guardians and interpreters of the Islamic faith. As long as the *ulama* remained independent of state control, they continued to represent a base of potential support or opposition to ruling elites.

The advent of secularism and nationalism in the Middle East aroused the resistance of the *ulama*, who, increasingly, were perceived as obstacles to modernism and reform. The traditional power of the Sunni *ulama* over law, education, and bureaucracy was stripped away in the nineteenth century throughout the Ottoman Empire and in Egypt. Confiscation of *Waqf* properties, the traditional means of economic support for the *ulama*, increased their reliance on government authority for economic maintenance and served to compromise the group's independent religious and political influence. In the late nineteenth century individual members of the *ulama*, such as Muhammad Abduh, directed their influence in educational and religious reform through Egypt's famed Sunni theological center al-Azhar. More recent twentieth-century Islamic political movements in Egypt, such as the Muslim Brotherhood, successfully circumvented what was perceived as the compromised model of the traditional *ulama*.

The problem for the contemporary Sunni *ulama* rests in the definition and scope of their authority. Challenges to the sole Sunni legal authority of al-Azhar have arisen in Saudi Arabia with its state-sponsored Permanent Council for Scientific Research and Legal Opinions. Hanbali jurists who issue *fatawa* (sing.: *fatwa*) through this medium are able to affect much of the Arabic-speaking world through the power of electronic communication. The tendency toward such authoritarian discourses in the Sunni world has been challenged by individuals who wish to assert the egalitarian possibilities of a more accessible *ulama*. Sudanese President Hasan al-Turabi has argued that the *ulama* should consist of all devout, educated Muslims, not only those strictly trained in legal and theological matters. Such populist assertions undermine premodern precedent and underscore the deep divide within Sunni Muslim society today over the definition of religious and legal authority. The continued power and legitimacy of the *ulama* as leaders for the Sunni Muslim majority worldwide remains a matter of heated debate.

In contrast, the role of the *ulama* in Shi'ite Iran has reached new heights of political and religious authority since the Iranian Revolution of 1979. Under the weak Safavid and Qajar dynasties the strength of the *ulama* increased. Beginning in 1925, despite the Pahlavi regime's attempts at secular government and bringing the *ulama* under state control, the scholars remained a potentially potent source of opposition. The *ulama* assumed leadership in the organized resistance to the shah, which culminated in the 1979 revolution and the formation of the Islamic Republic of Iran. The Shi'ite *ulama* in Iran successfully utilized their religious prestige as the only legitimate interpreters of Islam as a revolutionary weapon against a modern secular government.

See also Abduh, Muhammad; Azhar, al-; Iranian Revolution (1979); Muslim Brotherhood; *Shari'a*; Shi'ism; Sunni Islam; Waqf.

Bibliography

Abou el Fadl, Khaled. *Speaking in God's Name: Islamic Law, Authority, and Women.* London: Oneworld Press, 2001.

Mottahedeh, Roy P. *The Mantle of the Prophet: Religion and Politics in Iran.* New York: Pantheon, 1985.

Zaman, Muhammad Qasim. *The Ulama in Contemporary Islam: Custodians of Change.* Princeton, NJ: Princeton University Press, 2002.

DENISE A. SPELLBERG

UMAR, MADIHA
[1908–]

Syrian painter.

Madiha Umar was born in Syria. She is widely regarded as a pioneer in using the abstract elements of Arabic calligraphy in modernist painting. This innovation, turning an element of historical Islamic art into a recognized modernist form, was later to emerge as a major trend in contemporary art throughout the Arab world and in other majority-Muslim countries. Although some artists have focused on the Arabic word as communicative of spiritual power (a concept in Islam), Umar concentrates on the beauty of individual letters, including their formal possibilities and their figurative associations. This interest in letters originally stems from her early fascination with the Arabic calligraphy on mosque domes and minarets. During the 1930s, Umar trained in England and also spent time in Iraq, taking classes and teaching. She completed her M.F.A. at the Corcoran School of Art in Washington, D.C. Her works were exhibited in the United States as early as the 1940s.

See also ART.

Bibliography

Ali, Wijdan. *Modern Islamic Art: Development and Continuity.* Gainesville: University Press of Florida, 1997

JESSICA WINEGAR

UMAYYAD MOSQUE

Mosque established in Damascus by the Umayyad Caliph Walid ibn Abd al-Malik (705–715).

To construct and decorate the mosque, Walid employed the best craftsmen from Constantinople (now Istanbul) and from the Umayyad Empire. The design included a large open courtyard, a covered area on the side closest to the qibla (the direction of Mecca), and walls covered with elaborate mosaics. The mosque was one of the spectacular results of the building program of the Umayyads, who made Damascus the capital of their empire. The Umayyad mosque is one of the most monumental artistic structures in modern Syria.

MUHAMMAD MUSLIH

UMMA

See GLOSSARY

UMM AL-QAYWAYN

The emirate in the United Arab Emirates with the smallest population.

Umm al-Qaywayn lies south of Ra's al-Khayma, the northern-most emirate, and north of Sharjah on the coast of the Persian (Arabian) Gulf. It possesses the second-smallest territory, approximately 300 square miles, and its population was estimated in 1997 to be about 39,000. The capital town of the same name, which contains most of the emirate's population, was established on a sand spit for physical security. Only Abu Dhabi shares Umm al-Qaywayn's advantage of being located in a single contiguous territory.

Along with Ajman and Fujayra, Umm al-Qaywayn is one of the poorest of the United Arab Emirates and is heavily dependent on development funds from Abu Dhabi. It has very modest gas production, and few industries, the most important being cement production. Like Dubai, the emirate has established a free zone to attract overseas investment in manufacturing and trade. Nonetheless, much of Umm al-Qaywayn's population engages in the traditional pursuits of fishing and shipbuilding.

The ruling family is the Muʿalla, sometimes referred to as the Al Ali. The current amir, Shaykh Rashid ibn Ahmad, has ruled since 1981, when he succeeded his father, Shaykh Ahmad ibn Rashid al-Muʿalla, whose rule had begun in 1929.

See also MUʿALLA FAMILY, AL-; UNITED ARAB EMIRATES.

Bibliography

Anthony, John Duke. *Arab States of the Lower Gulf: People, Politics, Petroleum.* Washington, DC: Middle East Institute, 1975.

Ghareeb, Edmund, and Abed, Ibrahim al-, eds. *Perspectives on the United Arab Emirates.* London: Trident Press, 1997.

Metz, Helen Chapin, ed. *Persian Gulf States: Country Studies,* 3d edition. Washington, DC: Library of Congress, 1994.

Peck, Malcolm C. *The United Arab Emirates: A Venture in Unity.* Boulder, CO: Westview Press; London: Croom Helm, 1986.

Taryam, Abdullah Omran. *The Establishment of the United Arab Emirates, 1950–1985.* New York; London: Croom Helm, 1987.

MALCOLM C. PECK
UPDATED BY ANTHONY B. TOTH

UMM AL-QURA UNIVERSITY

Saudi Arabian university.

King Abd al-Aziz University was founded in Jidda in 1967 as a private college. Later taken over by the Saudi state, it opened branches in Mecca and Medina; the former became independent as Umm al-Qura ("The Mother of Villages," a name for Mecca) University in 1979. It opened another campus at al-Ta'if in 1981. Umm al-Qura University offers programs in the sciences, Islamic studies, Arabic language, education, and agriculture. Student enrollment numbers more than 20,000. King Abd al-Aziz University employs more than 2,000 teachers and has a student population of more than 39,000.

KHALID Y. BLANKINSHIP

UMMA PARTY

Political party in Sudan founded by Abd al-Rahman al-Mahdi in 1945.

Sayyid Abd al-Rahman al-Mahdi (1885–1959), the posthumous son of Muhammad Ahmad Abdullah al-Mahdi (1848–1885), used his wealth acquired by his loyalty to the British during World War I and his religious influence as the leader of the Ansar to enhance his political ambitions by launching a newspaper, *al-Umma.* Then, in February 1945, he mobilized his followers, the Ansar, to establish the Umma political party. The name refers to the community of Islam (*umma*). Its political platform, however, promotes a Sudan for the Sudanese, evoking the legacy of the Mahdist State, founded by his father, which was hostile to the imperial ambitions of Egypt. The founding members included prominent Mahdists. Although Abd al-Rahman publicly remained aloof, he provided the funds and spiritual guidance for the party, which alienated many non-Mahdist Sudanese who were deeply suspicious that he was using the party to further his monarchical ambitions. The opposition gravitated to the Ashiqqa (Brothers) Party founded by Isma'il al-Azhari (1900–1969), which advocated the union of the Nile Valley with Egypt.

Frequent attempts to reconcile the unionists and the Umma failed when Azhari broadened his narrow political base to found the National Unionist Party (NUP) with Sayyid Ali al-Mirghani and his Khatmiyya Brotherhood, bitter rivals of the Ansar and historically pro-Egyptian. The Umma lost the elections in 1952 to the NUP, and Azhari declared the Sudan independent on 1 January 1956. The Umma Party continued to play a powerful role in the first parliamentary government (1956–1958) and even under the military regimes of Major-General Ibrahim Abbud (1958–1964) and Colonel Muhammad Ja'far Numeiri (1969–1985), when political parties were officially proscribed. It sustained an intense rivalry with the Democratic Unionist Party (the former NUP), whose patrons, the Mirghani family, played a role similar to that of the descendants of Sayyid Abd al-Rahman—his son Siddiq al-Mahdi and grandson Sadiq al- Mahdi—in the Umma Party.

The Umma Party was not without internal rivalry, particularly among the more conservative Ansar, who were led by Imam al-Hadi until he was killed in the suppression of the Ansar by Numeiri in 1970. Since then, Sadiq al-Mahdi, the great-grandson of the Mahdi, has led the Umma Party. He served as prime minister in all the coalition governments between 1986 and 1989, after which he was placed under arrest by Brigadier Umar Hasan Ahmad al-Bashir, who seized control of the government in his coup d'état of June 1989. Although all political parties except Bashir's National Islamic Front (NIF) were proscribed, the organization of the Umma Party in the Sudan remained in place and its leadership joined the other opposition parties in exile who had formed the National Democratic Alliance (NDA) in Asmara, Eritrea.

In December 1996 Sadiq made a spectacular escape from house arrest to join the NDA in Asmara. Thereafter, he played an ambiguous role, seeking control of the NDA on the one hand and a rapprochement with the Bashir government on the other, both of which weakened the authority of the NDA. He failed to dominate the NDA; but when President Bashir permitted political parties to once again be openly active in Sudan, Sadiq signed the Djibouti Agreement with President Bashir in November 1999 and was able to return to lead the Umma as an opposition party. Although a body of the Umma leadership defected from the Umma to join the government, Sadiq remained in Khartoum and was confirmed leader of the opposition Umma Party in April 2003 at its first general conference in fifteen years.

See also ANSAR, AL-; AZHARI, ISMA'IL; *MAHDI*; MAHDIST STATE; SUDAN.

Bibliography

Khalid, Mansour. *The Government They Deserve: The Role of the Elite in Sudan's Political Evolution.* London: Kegan Paul, 1990.

Khalid, Mansour. *War and Peace in Sudan: A Tale of Two Countries.* London: Kegan Paul, 2003.

Mahjoub, M. A. *Democracy on Trial.* London: Andre Deutsch, 1974.

Niblock, Tim. *Class and Power in the Sudan: The Dynamics of Sudanese Politics, 1898–1985.* Albany: State University of New York Press, 1987.

Woodward, Peter. *Sudan: The Unstable State.* Boulder, CO: Lynne Rienner, 1990.

ROBERT O. COLLINS

UMM KULTHUM
[c. 1904–1975]

The most famous Arab singer of the twentieth century.

Umm Kulthum performed for more than fifty years, beginning in the villages and towns of the Egyptian delta in the early twentieth century and continuing until her final illness in 1973. In the course of her long career, Umm Kulthum recorded over three hundred songs and appeared in six films. She performed throughout the Arab world and is often considered the most accomplished singer of her time.

The Egyptian singer Umm Kulthum, photographed in Cairo in 1968, enjoyed immense popularity throughout the Arab world from the 1920s until her death in 1975. She supported Arab culture through her performances of populist songs derived from Arab music and poetry, as well as by speaking out for government support of such music and the musicians who played it. © BETTMANN/CORBIS. REPRODUCED BY PERMISSION.

She was born in the Egyptian village of Tammay al-Zahayra in the province of Daqhaliya to Shaykh Ibrahim al-Sayyid al-Baltaji (died 1932), the imam of the village mosque, and his wife, Fatima al-Maliji (died 1947). Her father augmented his income by singing religious songs for local celebrations. Umm Kulthum learned the songs while listening to him train her brother Khalid as his accompanist. Impressed with the power of his young daughter's voice, Shaykh Ibrahim eventually included her along with Khalid and their cousin Sabr in his performances.

The young girl with the very strong voice became the family's star attraction. To protect her reputation, the father had her wear a boy's coat and head covering, and he conducted all business on her behalf. By 1917, the family began to consider a serious singing career for Umm Kulthum and in about 1922 they moved to Cairo to launch her in the commercial music business. In Cairo, Umm Kulthum was not an immediate success. Compared with the women already established as successful performers and recording stars, including Munira al-Mahdiyya and Fathiyya Ahmad, she was viewed as unsophisticated and countrified. She engaged music teachers and endeavored to copy the manners of the elite women in whose homes she sang. Like other aspiring performers, she was aided and schooled by a number of mentors, including singer Shaykh Abu al-Ilah Muhammad, poet Ahmad Rami, and the amateur musician Amin al-Mahdi. By 1928, she surpassed the popularity of her competitors and remained at the top of musical society for the remainder of her career.

Umm Kulthum began to make commercial recordings in 1924. Although recording companies were usually conservative and disinclined to take a chance on an unknown singer, they vied with each other for the largest possible share of the market; as a result the relatively unknown Umm Kulthum was recruited by Odeon Records and recorded fourteen songs in 1924 and 1925. These were immediately successful, for, as she later explained, her long years of performing in the delta provided her with a larger audience outside Cairo than most other singers. This experience awakened Umm Kulthum to the nature of her potential audience. During the late 1920s and the 1930s she began her lifelong involvement with the mass media: commercial recording (1924), radio (1934), film (1934), and television (1960). Commercial recordings had been circulating in Egypt since about 1904 and, despite the relatively high cost of phonograph players and records, were widely accessible. They were installed in public places, such as coffee houses, where even those who could not afford the equipment could hear the records. (Later, radios, televisions, and cassette players were similarly shared.) From 1937 until her final illness, her concerts on the first Thursday of each month were broadcast live to an ever growing audience. These concerts were certainly her best-known professional activity and allowed Umm Kulthum to count among her audience millions of listeners beyond the ticket-buying audience in Cairo.

She started with a repertoire of traditional, predominantly religious songs as a child; in the late 1920s and 1930s, she began to sing new virtuosic songs, often composed for her by Muhammad al-Qasabji on the romantic poetry then in vogue by Ahmad Rami. During her golden age in the 1940s and 1950s, she sang colloquial songs of populist expression written by Zakariyya Ahmad and Bayram al-Tunisi and serious neoclassical songs by Riyadh al-Sunbati and Ahmad Shawqi; these have become her best known. In the late 1950s and 1960s, she commissioned new love songs by younger poets and composers and finally collaborated with her colleague and rival, Muhammad Abd al-Wahhab; they produced ten songs, which retain great popularity to the present day.

In her later years, she was recognized as an important public figure, in general, and a symbol of authentically Egyptian and Arab culture and art. She served seven terms as president of the musicians' union and as a member of the selection committee for radio and of several national commissions on the arts. After the Egyptian defeat in the Arab-Israel War (1967), she initiated a series of benefit concerts in Egypt and throughout the Arab world designed to replenish the Egyptian treasury. She appeared in Morocco, Libya, Sudan, Lebanon, Abu Dhabi, and Tunisia, and her trips to these countries took on the character of diplomatic visits.

Health problems that had plagued Umm Kulthum for much of her life worsened as she aged, and she spent most of the last year of her life under medical treatment. She died on 3 February 1975.

See also ABD AL-WAHHAB, MUHAMMAD; MUSIC; SHAWQI, AHMAD.

Bibliography

Awad, Mahmud. "Umm Kulthum: Allati la ya'rifuha ahad" (The Umm Kulthum Nobody Knows). In *Middle Eastern Muslim Women Speak,* edited and translated by Elizabeth Warnock Fernea and Basima Qattan Bezirgan. Austin: University of Texas Press, 1977.

Danielson, Virginia. "Shaping Tradition in Arab Song: The Career and Repertory of Umm Kulthum." Ph.D. diss., University of Illinois, 1991.

Danielson, Virginia. *The Voice of Egypt: Umm Kulthum, Arabic Song, and Egyptian Society in the Twentieth Century.* Chicago: University of Chicago Press, 1997.

VIRGINIA DANIELSON

UMM NA'SAN

Second largest of the thirty-three islands in the archipelago that constitutes the State of Bahrain.

Umm Na'san occupies some 8.5 square miles (22 sq. km) and lies approximately 2.5 miles (4 km) off the western coast of the main island of Bahrain, the largest in the archipelago. It is reserved for the private use of the ruler. Several small springs provide water for a limited pastureland, and date palm gardens grow along its western shore, gardens planted and stocked with deer and gazelle by Shaykh Hamad ibn Isa Al Khalifa during the 1930s. Ruins dot the surface of the island, lending credence to local legends that it was the seat of the ancient rulers. The causeway from Saudi Arabia to the main island, Bahrain, passes through Umm Na'san.

Bibliography

Cottrell, Alvin J., ed. *The Persian Gulf States: A General Survey.* Baltimore, MD: Johns Hopkins University Press, 1980.

FRED H. LAWSON

UNION DÉMOCRATIQUE DU MANIFESTE ALGÉRIEN (UDMA)

A moderate Algerian organization whose goals changed from autonomy within the colonial system to full independence.

The Union Démocratique du Manifeste Algérien (UDMA; Democratic Union of the Algerian Manifesto) was founded by Ferhat ABBAS during the spring of 1946 and ceased to exist in April 1956 when Abbas, in Cairo, announced his alliance with the Front de Libération Nationale (FLN; National Liberation Front). It grew out of the moderate wing of the Algerian political spectrum, which in the 1930s had sought reform within the colonial system. When the colons refused such reform, it moved in the 1940s toward Algerian autonomy.

Winning eleven of the thirteen Algerian seats in the second French Constituent Assembly in 1946, Abbas proposed an autonomous Algeria within the framework of the French Union. When this program failed to carry, the party was diminished considerably in influence. Representing mainly educated, middle-class levels of society, the party had some three thousand members by 1950 and participated actively in the Algerian Assembly established by the Organic Law in 1947.

After joining the FLN, Abbas and other UDMA leaders served in the Conseil National de la Révolution Algérienne (CNRA; National Council of the Algerian Revolution) and subsequently in the Provisional Government of the Algerian Republic (Gouvernement Provisoire de la République Algérienne; GPRA).

Bibliography

Quandt, William B. *Revolution and Political Leadership: Algeria, 1954–1958*. Cambridge, MA: MIT Press, 1969.

JOHN RUEDY

UNION GÉNÉRALE DES ÉTUDIANTS TUNISIENS (UGET)

See GENERAL TUNISIAN UNION OF STUDENTS (UGTE)

UNION GÉNÉRALE DES TRAVAILLEURS MAROCAINS (UGTM)

Moroccan labor union.

The Istiqlal Party founded the General Union of Moroccan Workers (UGTM) in 1959 to compete with the Moroccan Labor Union (Union Marocaine du Travail, UMT), then associated with the National Union of Popular Forces (Union Nationale des Forces Populaires, UNFP). The UGTM represents the labor branch of the Istiqlal Party, which emphasizes nationalistic, pro-Islamic, and pan-Arab policies. The UGTM takes a pragmatic stance toward the government, not hesitating to support its policies. This was particularly true when the Istiqlal Party was represented in the cabinet (1977–1984). During the 1980s the UGTM gained ascendancy within various sectors, but especially in the rural milieu and agriculture.

The UGTM competed with the UMT in the 1970s and with the Democratic Confederation of Labor (CDT), created in 1978, in the 1980s. However, in the 1990s the UGTM joined forces with the CDT. The socioeconomic situation of the country had been steadily worsening since the 1980s, and both unions called for strikes during the 1990s to force the government into a dialogue with labor representatives. Similar tactics were repeated in 2002 under the government of Abderrahmane Youssoufi. The strikes concluded the following month with a social pact negotiated by the government, the employers, the CDT, and the UGTM.

As of 2003, the modification of the current Labor Code, which could represent a limitation on the right to strike, is an issue of great concern to both unions. UGTM's secretary general is Abderrazak Afilal.

See also UNION MAROCAINE DU TRAVAIL (UMT); YOUSSOUFI, ABDERRAHMANE.

LARRY A. BARRIE
UPDATED BY ANA TORRES-GARCIA

UNION GÉNÉRALE DES TRAVAILLEURS TUNISIENS (UGTT)

Tunisian labor union.

The Union Générale des Travailleurs Tunisiens (General Union of Tunisian Workers) is the strongest labor union in Tunisia. Founded in 1946 by Ferhat Hached, the union was the first indigenous attempt to organize Tunisia's workers. Hached broke with the French, communist-led General Confederation of Workers (*Confédération Générale des Travailleurs*; CGT). The new union worked closely with the nationalist movement in Tunisia. Consequently, members of the French resistance organization Red Hand assassinated Hached in 1952.

From 1952 until 1969, the union was under the influence of Ahmed Ben Salah and his socialist economic policies. The fall of Ben Salah in 1970 led to its reorganization and reemergence in 1976 under the charismatic leadership of Habib Achour, who dominated the UGTT until 1989. From the late 1970s to the early 1980s, the union exerted a fierce opposition to the government. The UGTT tended to oppose economic liberalization because this would lessen its control of the labor movement and adversely affect workers. Achour signed the Social Contract of 1977, which stipulated that the union would control labor unrest. Deteriorating economic conditions, however, caused Achour to break this pact. A wildcat work stoppage at Qsar Hellal in October 1977 led to a confrontation between the army and striking workers, the first time the government had used the army to suppress labor. In early January 1978, the UGTT issued a resolution extremely critical of the economic policies of Habib Bourguiba's regime. On 26 January 1978, called "Black Thursday," a bloody clash left 150 people dead. The government declared a state of emergency and arrested UGTT leaders. Achour was tried for sedition and sentenced to ten years in jail. The regime imposed a new executive bureau on the union and weakened it as a force of opposition to the government's economic policies.

Pardoned in 1981, Achour returned to the post of UGTT president, with leftist Taieb Baccouche as secretary-general. Privatization measures of the mid-1980s eroded the UGTT's clout. In January 1984, riots broke out as a result of an increase in the price of bread. The ensuing violence led the union to harden its stance toward the government. By 1985, the UGTT had again run afoul of the government by threatening to strike if the decline in workers' real wages was not reversed. In December, the government again disbanded the union and jailed its leadership on various charges.

The 1987 palace coup of Zayn al-Abidine Ben Ali led to improved relations between the government and the UGTT. Internal dissent, exemplified by the split that in the early 1980s created the National Union of Tunisian Workers (*Union Nationale des Travailleurs Tunisiens*; UNTT), had weakened the organization as the main opposition force. The union, therefore, started to lose its role as the country's leading social movement to the Tunisian League for the Defense of Human Rights (LTDH).

In 1989, encouraged by the government, the reunification of the UGTT and the UNTT was made official and the union leaders were substituted. Achour was replaced by Ismail Sahbani and Ali Romdhane. In late December 1993, Sahbani consolidated his position and expelled his chief opponents from the UGTT's executive bureau.

The union's nineteenth congress, held in April 1999, elected Sahbani as secretary general for the third time. There was, however, increasing discontent among the UGTT membership over his authoritarian leadership style and his conciliatory attitude toward the regime. Forced to resign, Sahbani was replaced by Abdessalem Jerad in September 2000.

See also ACHOUR, HABIB.

Bibliography

Murphy, Emma. *Economic and Political Change in Tunisia: From Bourguiba to Ben Ali.* New York: St. Martin's Press in association with University of Durham, 1999.

Nelson, Harold D., ed. *Tunisia: A Country Study,* 3d edition. Washington, DC: American University, 1988.

LARRY A. BARRIE
UPDATED BY ANA TORRES-GARCIA

UNION MAROCAINE DU TRAVAIL (UMT)

Morocco's oldest trade union.

The Moroccan Labor Union (Union Marocaine du Travail, UMT) was formed in 1955 with the help of the nationalist Istiqlal Party. It reportedly had a membership of over 600,000 in the early years of Morocco's independence, becoming the nation's largest labor organization. It enjoyed a monopoly of Moroccan unionism until the Istiqlal Party founded the General Union of Moroccan Workers (Union Générale des Travailleurs Marocains, UGTM) in 1959, which took over 10 percent of its membership.

Although affiliated with the National Union of Popular Forces (Union Nationale des Forces Populaires, UNFP) from 1959 to 1962, the UMT declared its autonomy from political parties at its Third Congress (1963). In the 1960s the government declared a state of emergency, during which political and union activity was restricted for several years. During this period the UMT saw its membership decline sharply. The state of emergency ended in July 1970, prompting a rapid rise in labor unrest soon afterward. Nevertheless, the UMT remained weak, affected by organizational and leadership problems.

By the mid-1970s internal dissent had emerged within the organization. Some criticized the union leadership for inaction and subordination to the state. Mahjoub Ben Seddiq has been its secretary general since 1955. In 1978 the USFP founded the Democratic Confederation of Labor (Confédération Démocratique du Travail, CDT), an organization that soon attracted former UMT union members. In the 1990s UMT's political activism was surpassed by the CDT, which, in alliance with the UGTM, has become the leader of trade union militancy in Morocco.

See also UNION GÉNÉRALE DES TRAVAILLEURS MAROCAINS (UGTM).

Bibliography

Clement, Jean-François, and Paul, Jim. "Trade Unions and Moroccan Politics." *Merip Reports* 127 (October 1984): 19–24.

BRADFORD DILLMAN
UPDATED BY ANA TORRES-GARCIA

UNION NATIONALE DES ETUDIANTS MAROCAINS (UNEM)

Originally left-wing opposition group in Morocco that came to be dominated by Islamists in the 1990s.

The Union Nationale des Etudiants Marocains (UNEM), originally supported by teachers and high school students, was involved in extralegal and radical activities against the monarchy and its governments during the 1960s and 1970s, when it was associated with the progressive faction of the Istiqlal Party and the Union Nationale des Forces Populaires (UNFP). Its agenda was redress of political, social, economic, and educational grievances. In July 1963 Hamid Berrada, secretary-general of the UNEM, was condemned to death for allegedly plotting against the state in support of Mehdi Ben Barka. He fled the country and, with Ben Barka and Muhammad al-Basri, initiated a campaign to denounce the monarchy. One year later, UNEM's president, Muhammad Halaoui, was arrested for having criticized Berrada's sentencing. Between 1963 and 1973 UNEM leaders were repeatedly arrested and imprisoned for organizing strikes and engaging in subversion. The peak of the government's crackdown came in April 1972 with a mass trial of eighty-one student leaders on charges of treason. Twenty-eight received long jail sentences.

The UNEM was dissolved in 1973 and reconstituted in 1978. The new leadership initiated a number of demonstrations between 1979 and 1981 that resulted in further clashes with the authorities, but in general the political calm in Morocco during the 1980s was reflected in the UNEM's relatively low profile. In 1991 clashes on university campuses between leftists and Islamists were related, in part, to their respective attempts to gain control of the UNEM. Mostly affiliated with Jamiʿat al-Adl wa al-Ihsan (Justice and Charity Group), the leading Islamist extraparliamentary movement, Islamist students came to control most of the country's student organizations by the end of the decade, including the UNEM, and found themselves in periodic confrontations with the authorities.

See also BEN BARKA, MEHDI; ISTIQLAL PARTY: MOROCCO; UNION NATIONALE DES FORCES POPULAIRES (UNFP).

Bibliography

Waterbury, John. *The Commander of the Faithful.* London: Weidenfeld and Nicolson, 1970.

BRUCE MADDY-WEITZMAN

UNION NATIONALE DES FORCES POPULAIRES (UNFP)

One of Morocco's leading leftist political parties.

The Union Nationale des Forces Populaires (National Union of Popular Forces, UNFP) was founded in December 1959 by progressive and leftist elements of the Istiqlal Party, Morocco's most important nationalist force. Among its founders were Mehdi Ben Barka; Abdullah Ibrahim (prime minister from 1959 to 1960); Mahjoub Ben Seddiq (secretary-general of the Union Marocaine du Travail [Moroccan Labor Union], UMT); Abderrahmane Youssoufi; Mohamed Fqih Basri; and Abderrahim Bouabid. Following two failed coup attempts in 1971 and 1972, the government arrested many UNFP members and placed them on trial. In 1972, internal disputes led to the emergence of two blocs within the party: the Casablanca group led by Ibrahim, and the Rabat section led by Bouabid. During 1973, a series of detentions forced the Rabat group to put its activities on hold for a period of four months. The political turmoil led to severe divisions within the party, causing the UNFP section in the city of Rabat to split from the party and found a new party, the Union Socialiste des Forces Populaires (Socialist Union of Socialist Forces, USFP), in 1974. Because most of the UNFP's members joined the USFP, the remnant UNFP headed by Ibrahim became an insignificant party under the guidance of the UMT. The UNFP boycotted the 1977 elections and the municipal and parliamentary elections of 1983 and 1984.

The ideology of the UNFP was socialist, calling for a transformation of the social structure, nationalization of the means of production, greater rewards for workers, and land reform. It consistently opposed the leadership of King Hassan II and called for the creation of a representative democracy. In the international arena, the UNFP supported Arab unity within a socialist democratic framework, favored developing nation revolutionary movements, and opposed Western involvement in the national economy. Strongly nationalist, the party and its successor, the USFP, unconditionally supported the government line in Western Sahara and refused to agree to any form of settlement that would relinquish Moroccan sovereignty rights over the territory.

Ben Barka served as the UNFP's general secretary until his assassination in France in 1965. The party's principal leadership structure consisted of a central committee, an administrative commission, and a general secretariat. In 1967, the UNFP created a political bureau composed of Bouabid, Ibrahim, and Ben Seddiq, which the party's administrative commission dissolved in 1972. The leadership of the UNFP was often divided. The party held its second and last national congress in 1963. The UMT provided most of the party's infrastructure at the local level.

After briefly heading the government in 1959 and 1960, the UNFP joined the opposition. At the height of its power during the early 1960s, it won 414 out of 765 seats in the 1960 local elections and 28 out of 144 seats in the 1963 parliamentary elections. Severe repression after 1962 and a split with the UMT caused it to lose much of its strength during the late 1960s.

The UNFP had a diverse membership united more by a commonality of interests than a common ideology. Second-generation nationalists from the Istiqlal with modest family backgrounds and French educations held top positions. Professionals, teachers, and government workers composed much of the party's middle-level hierarchy. Rank and file members were largely trade union members and students. Wealthy members of the UNFP provided most of its financing. It had a diverse constituency, attracting its greatest support from workers living in Atlantic coast cities and from government cadres, students, and traders in the Sousse region.

See also BEN BARKA, MEHDI; BOUABID, ABDERRAHIM; IBRAHIM, ABDULLAH; ISTIQLAL PARTY: MOROCCO; UNION SOCIALISTE DES FORCES POPULAIRES (USFP); YOUSSOUFI, ABDERRAHMANE.

Bibliography

Waterbury, John. *The Commander of the Faithful: The Moroccan Political Elite—A Study in Segmented Politics.* New York: Columbia University Press; London: Weidenfeld & Nicolson, 1970.

BRADFORD DILLMAN
UPDATED BY VANESA CASANOVA-FERNANDEZ

UNION OF TUNISIAN WOMEN

The largest and oldest women's organization in Tunisia.

In 1956, L'Union Nationale des Femmes Tunisiennes (Union of Tunisian Women; UNFT) was formed with the explicit goal of elevating the cultural, social, economic, and political status of Tunisian women. As a women's auxiliary of the national Neo-Destour Party, the UNFT was primarily responsible for communicating, supporting, and implementing the Neo-Destour Party's initiatives and policies. Among its early initiatives were literacy and education campaigns and awareness-raising programs about the personal status code and women's rights. The UNFT became a prominent organization in the years after independence, with nearly 14,000 members in 1960 and more than 38,000 in 1969. By 2000, the UNFT had grown to a membership of more than 135,000, with regional offices and regional delegates in each of Tunisia's twenty-three governorates.

The UNFT has been primarily dedicated to women's advocacy at the national level, urging the implementation of state-sponsored programs. With the goal of promoting women's interests in all areas of society, the UNFT has sponsored and implemented projects relating to business, culture, science, health, and education. The social condition of women and the elimination of poverty continue to be of particular concern to the organization, and the UNFT works with both governmental and nongovernmental organizations to address women's needs and represent women's interests.

See also GENDER: GENDER AND EDUCATION; GENDER: GENDER AND LAW; GENDER: GENDER AND POLITICS; TUNISIA.

ANGEL M. FOSTER

UNION SOCIALISTE DES FORCES POPULAIRES (USFP)

Moroccan Socialist political party.

The Union Socialiste des Forces Populaires (Socialist Union of Popular Forces, USFP) was formed in 1974 by a large breakaway faction of the Union Nationale des Forces Populaires (National Union of Popular Forces, UNFP) led by Abderrahim Bouabid. A member of the Socialist International and strongly nationalist, the USFP supports the Moroccan government's stand on Western Sahara and it has consistently opposed the United Nations referendum plan for the region. The position of general secretary has been held by Bouabid (1974–1992) and Abderrahmane Youssoufi (1992–). Most of its members—primarily teachers, students, and government workers—come from urban middle-class backgrounds. During the 1990s the party, which in the past had a strong constituency among students, workers, and the unemployed, lost ground in favor of Morocco's Islamist parties, mainly the moderate Justice et Développement Party (Justice and Development, PJD) and the now illegal Al-Adl wa'l Ihsan (Justice and Charity Organization) headed by Abdessalam Yassine. The USFP is closely allied with the Democratic Labor Confederation, one of Morocco's leading trade unions.

Following the establishment of a bicameral system in 1997 and the elections that took place amid wide accusations of fraud, King Hassan II appointed Youssoufi prime minister in February 1998. Together with the Istiqlal Party, the USFP formed the core of the new government. The USFP won the legislative elections of 27 September 2002, which were marked by low participation (51.5%) and the success of the Islamist PJD. After the elections, the USFP announced that it would not form a cabinet with the PJD but would instead resuscitate its alliance with the Istiqlal Party. Despite the victory of the USFP, the king appointed Driss Jetou of the Istiqlal Party prime minister in October 2002, amid protests from the USFP and other parties. Differences over the USFP's role after 1998 have caused strains in relations with other member parties of the national democratic bloc, or Kutla. In the municipal elections of September 2003, which took place in the aftermath of bomb attacks that killed forty-five people in Casablanca and severely restricted the participation of Islamist parties, the USFP ranked second after the Istiqlal party, winning 14.2 percent of the vote and 3,373 of the total 23,689 local council seats.

See also ISTIQLAL PARTY: MOROCCO; UNION NATIONALE DES FORCES POPULAIRES (UNFP); WESTERN SAHARA; YOUSSOUFI, ABDERRAHMANE.

Bibliography

Hughes, Stephen O. *Morocco under King Hassan.* Reading, U.K.: Ithaca, 2001.

VANESA CASANOVA-FERNANDEZ

UNION TUNISIENNE DES INDUSTRIALISTES, COMPAGNIES, ARTISANS (UTICA)

Tunisian federation of employers.

The Tunisian Union of Industrialists, Businessmen, and Artisans (UTICA) was created during the third congress of the Neo-Destour Party on 17 October 1948. Initially called Union Tunisienne de l'Industrie et du Commerce (Tunisian Union of Industry and Commerce) and later the Union Tunisienne de l'Industrie, du Commerce, et de l'Artisanat (Tunisian Federation of Industry, Commerce, and Handicrafts), the union represents the interests of Tunisian employers as signatories of pacts regarding wages and work conditions in the Tunisian market. As of 2003, Hédi Djilani became the president of the union.

UTICA regularly negotiates wages and working conditions with the government and the Union Générale des Travailleurs Tunisiens (General Union of Tunisian Workers; UGTT). Based on these negotiations, the government sets annual wages for the labor force. The 1956 labor code guarantees a minimum wage, provides for arbitration to settle disputes, authorizes union membership, sets the work week and other labor standards, and provides for social security and disability insurance payments. The government also seeks to ensure that wages do not lag behind inflation. In May 1999, the Tunisian government increased minimum monthly wages in the public and private sectors by between 3.3 percent and 3.7 percent. Amendments to the labor code in 1994 and 1996 allowed firms to consider an employee's productivity when evaluating salary, to set working hours according to their needs, and to base part of an employee's salary on productivity; it also allowed layoffs based on economic or technological needs.

Since 1986, Tunisia's economic restructuring program has led to the privatization of a number of public conglomerates, the reduction of food subsidies, and a general liberalization of the economy. Tunisia's economic liberalization is linked to structural adjustment policies under the patronage of the International Monetary Fund and the World Bank, upon which the country depends for financial support. The liberalization of Tunisia's economy has taken place within the framework of a structural adjustment program (1986); adherence to the General Agreement on Terms of Trade (GATT) in 1989 and membership in the World Trade Organization since 1994; and the signing of a free-trade agreement with the European Union in 1995.

UTICA supported the construction in 1999 of the Elgazala Technology Park in Ariana (a city north of Tunis). The union views the transfer of technology and automation to Tunisia as a key to the country's economic diversification and a necessary step toward attracting foreign investment.

In the international sphere, UTICA has become prominent in strengthening economic ties between the Tunisian government and other developing nations. In March 2003, UTICA signed a series of agreements with its Moroccan counterpart, the Confédération Générale des Enterprises du Maroc

(General Confederation of Enterprises in Morocco), to promote the integration of both economic regions. The two organizations called for the implementation of the Moroccan-Tunisian free-trade agreement, the creation of a databank of joint industrial projects, and the deregulation of customs duties. Outside the Arab world, UTICA has played a prominent role in the strengthening of commercial ties between Tunisia and Pakistan. In October 2002, UTICA signed an agreement with its Pakistani counterpart to set up a joint business council between their respective national chambers of commerce.

See also UNION GÉNÉRALE DES TRAVAILLEURS TUNISIENS (UGTT).

Bibliography

Nelson, Harold D., ed. *Tunisia: A Country Study,* 3d edition. Washington, DC: U.S. Government Printing Office, 1988.

UTICA. Available from <http://www.utica.org.tn/>.

LARRY A. BARRIE
UPDATED BY VANESA CASANOVA-FERNANDEZ

UNITED ARAB EMIRATES

Federation of seven shaykhdoms at the southern end of the Persian Gulf.

The United Arab Emirates (U.A.E.) is bounded on the north by a small portion of Qatar, the Persian (Arabian) Gulf, and a detached segment of Oman. The country shares a long, undefined border with Saudi Arabia (west and south) and Oman (east). It has an area of just over 32,000 square miles, about the size of the state of Maine. Abu Dhabi occupies nearly 87 percent of the total; Dubai, less than 5 percent; and Sharjah, just more than 3 percent. The emirates of Ra's al-Khayma, Fujayra, Umm al-Qaywayn, and Ajman occupy the remainder. The country has a flat coastal plain; an interior desert, part of the Empty Quarter (Rub al-Khali); an elevated plateau; and the Hajar Mountains, shared with Oman. Principal oasis regions are Liwa and Buraymi. Rainfall is highly seasonal, localized, and scanty. Summer temperatures often reach 115°F on the humid coast, and higher in the dry interior. From October to March the weather is mild and pleasant.

The U.A.E.'s population has risen from about 180,000 in 1968 to approximately 3.1 million in 2000; the influx of expatriate workers and their dependents account for most of the growth and some 80 percent of the total population. The U.A.E. is overwhelmingly urban, and the largest cities are (in descending order) Dubai, Abu Dhabi, Sharjah, and Ra's al-Khaymah. Nearly all U.A.E. nationals and expatriates are Muslims; significant exceptions include some Indians, Filipinos, and Westerners. Sunnis account for about 85 percent of all Muslims. Tribal affiliation remains very important among Emiratis, whose rulers are drawn from the leading families of the dominant tribes.

History

Most of the current ruling families took power in the early part of the nineteenth century when Great Britain imposed a general truce after a series of violent clashes with the Qawasim seafaring forces who had opposed Britain's military and commercial ascendancy in the lower Persian Gulf. A series of treaties between these rulers and Britain codified Britain's predominant position and gave rise to the region being called the Trucial Coast or Trucial Oman. The area was known as Sahil Oman (Oman Coast) by Arabic-speakers. These treaties had a ten-

Traditions, including camel races in the desert, and tribal affiliations remain important elements of life in the United Arab Emirates, even as this federation of seven shaykhdoms experiences widespread change thanks to its oil wealth. © ALAIN LE GARSMEUR/CORBIS. REPRODUCED BY PERMISSION.

dency to reinforce the leading role of the local rulers and create a powerful political status quo. However, local politics, mainly in the form of family disputes and alliances, have resulted in some changes. For example, Dubai became independent of Abu Dhabi in 1833, Ra's al-Khayma seceded from Sharjah in 1869, and Fujayra gained independence from Sharjah in 1952. A treaty in 1892 further codified British power in the region, prohibiting rulers from engaging in diplomacy with non-British powers or ceding their territories to outsiders without British approval. In the nineteenth and early twentieth century, fishing, pearling, trade, and agriculture were the main sources of income for the inhabitants of the emirates. However, the world depression of the 1930s and the collapse of the Persian Gulf pearl market plunged the region into great poverty, forcing many to migrate elsewhere.

Britain instigated the first efforts at federation when it established the Trucial Council in 1952, an administrative body made up of the seven rulers. However, rivalries and philosophical differences prevented the rulers from joining in federation until 1971, when all but Ra's al-Khaymah formed the U.A.E. (Ra's al-Khaymah joined the federation the following year.) The ruler of Abu Dhabi, the largest and wealthiest emirate, Shaykh Zayid ibn Sultan al-Nahayyan, became president of the U.A.E., and Dubai's Shaykh Rashid ibn Sa'id al-Maktum became vice president. While much of the political history of the emirates has revolved around relations among the ruling families, it also has been affected by interactions with regional powers such as Oman, the rulers of Najd (later Saudi Arabia), Bahrain, Qatar, and Iran. At its inception Abu Dhabi's dispute with Saudi Arabia and Oman over the Buraymi (al-Ayn) Oasis remained unresolved; traditional rivalries among the seven amirs threatened the federation's viability; and Iran coerced Sharjah into a joint occupation of Abu Musa island (which contributed to a coup attempt that took the life of Sharjah's ruler, Shaykh Khalid ibn Muhammad), and forcibly seized the Tunb Islands from Ra's al-Khayma.

Economy

Since the early 1960s, when Abu Dhabi began exporting oil, the U.A.E. economy has been dominated by this sector. The country's proven oil reserves, 94 percent of which were located in Abu

Dubai, the largest city in the United Arab Emirates, has undergone considerable and almost continuous transformation since this late 20th-century photograph along Dubai Creek. Although Abu Dhabi has by far the most land and greatest amount of oil and natural gas reserves of the U.A.E.'s seven shaykhdoms, Dubai has a vital function with its extensive port facilities and free-trade zone. © Christine Osborne/Corbis. Reproduced by permission.

Dhabi emirate, amounted to some 98 billion barrels in 2001, more than 9 percent of the world's total. Dubai possesses 4 billion barrels; Sharjah, 1.5 billion; and Ra's al-Khayma, 100 million. Abu Dhabi also has the bulk of the country's 212 trillion cubic feet of natural gas reserves. The gap in economic development between Abu Dhabi, Dubai, and Sharjah, on the one hand, and the rest of the emirates is considerable, though it is moderated by federal government spending on infrastructure, with most of the funding from Abu Dhabi. Dubai, long the major trading center of the lower Gulf, is the region's leading entrepôt with the most extensive port facilities. Its Jabal Ali free zone has helped expand the U.A.E.'s nonoil sector to 60 percent of total GDP. Promotion of traditional economic activities, including agriculture and fishing, has created employment opportunities in the poorer emirates and achieved significant import substitution.

Government and Politics

The U.A.E.'s constitution provides for federal legislative, executive, and judicial institutions. The political system is a mix of presidential and parliamentary features, with the greatest power in the executive Federal Supreme Council, whose members are the rulers of the seven member states. Zayid has been president since independence, and Rashid served as both prime minister and vice president, posts assumed by his son Maktum in 1986, following Rashid's incapacitation. The legislature, called the Federal National Council, has only consultative powers, despite being given a somewhat greater role in the 1990s. Its forty members are appointed by the rulers: eight each from Abu Dhabi and Dubai,

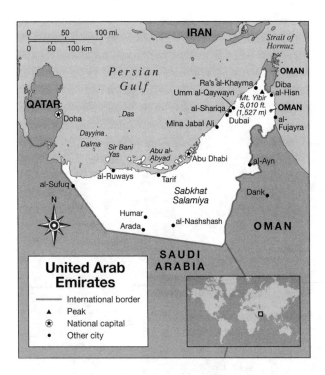

United Arab Emirates

— International border
▲ Peak
✪ National capital
• Other city

MAP BY XNR PRODUCTIONS, INC. THE GALE GROUP.

six each from Sharjah and Ra's al-Khayma, and four apiece from the remaining emirates. Real legislative authority resides in the Council of Ministers, which initiates most laws, oversees implementation of federal laws, and prepares the federal budget.

Considerable powers are left to the individual emirates, each governed in an essentially traditional manner by a hereditary ruler. Even in foreign affairs, defense, and finance, theoretically federal concerns under the constitution, the individual emirates act autonomously. Each emirate has pursued its own oil policy. Dubai and Sharjah maintained business as usual with Iran while the federal government tilted toward Iraq during the Iran-Iraq War (1980–1988). Zayid has championed a centralized U.A.E., whereas others, especially his former rival, Rashid, have favored the loose federal arrangement.

Foreign Relations

The U.A.E. maintains generally friendly relations with its neighbors, although these can be complicated by the independent actions of various emirates. It has played an active role in the Gulf Cooperation Council (GCC), which promotes economic and security ties to the other five conserva-

tive Gulf Arab states. Zayid has assumed a major role in the Arab world as a force for moderation, as in his efforts to promote Egypt's reintegration into the Arab League. Relations with the United States have been friendly, though sometimes strained because of what is seen as a one-sided American policy toward the Arab-Israel conflict. The United States, Japan, and the United Kingdom are the U.A.E.'s major trading partners. After the Iraqi occupation of Kuwait, the U.A.E. cooperated closely with the United States and other members of the anti-Iraq coalition. However, during the late 1990s the country modified its stance, sending food and medicine to Iraq, and opposing a U.S. attack on the country. In a dramatic break from precedent among countries in the Arab League, the U.A.E. suggested in early 2003 that Saddam Hussein step down as leader of Iraq as a way to avoid imminent war with the United States.

See also ABU DHABI; AJMAN; BURAYMI OASIS DISPUTE; DUBAI; FUJAYRA; RA'S AL-KHAYMA; RUB AL-KHALI; SHARJAH; TRUCIAL COAST; UMM AL-QAYWAYN.

Bibliography

Anthony, John Duke. *Arab States of the Lower Gulf: People, Politics, Petroleum.* Washington, DC: Middle East Institute, 1975.

Ghareeb, Edmund, and Abed, Ibrahim al-, eds. *Perspectives on the United Arab Emirates.* London: Trident Press, 1997.

Heard-Bey, Frauke. *From Trucial States to United Arab Emirates: A Society in Transition.* New York; London: Longman, 1982.

Lienhardt, Peter. *Shaikhdoms of Eastern Arabia,* edited by Ahmed Al-Shahi. New York; Houndmills, U.K.: Palgrave, 2001.

Metz, Helen Chapin, ed. *Persian Gulf States: Country Studies,* 3d edition. Washington, DC: Library of Congress, 1994.

Peck, Malcolm C. *The United Arab Emirates: A Venture in Unity.* Boulder, CO: Westview Press; London: Croom Helm, 1986.

Taryam, Abdullah Omran. *The Establishment of the United Arab Emirates, 1950–1985.* New York; London: Croom Helm, 1987.

MALCOLM C. PECK
UPDATED BY ANTHONY B. TOTH

UNITED ARAB REPUBLIC (UAR)

Union of Syria and Egypt, 1958–1961.

By the late 1950s, Egypt was the most powerful Arab state. Many Arabs were enamored of President Gamal Abdel Nasser's advocacy of pan-Arab unity under Egypt's leadership. Syria, which shared Egypt's anti-Western stance, was considerably weaker, facing both external threats and an unstable internal political situation. For some Syrians, particularly members of the Ba'th party, union with Egypt offered hope for resolving a host of problems. As early as November 1957, Syria's National Assembly called for union with Egypt. Nasser agreed, but only on his terms: full union (not a federation) under his leadership. On 1 February 1958, he joined Syria's president, Shukri al-Quwatli, in announcing the formation of the United Arab Republic (UAR). A referendum on union and Nasser's presidency was approved on 21 February.

New governmental institutions were created in March 1958. Four vice presidents were appointed: two Egyptians (Abd al-Hakim Amir and Abd al-Latif al-Baghdadi) and two Syrians (Akram al-Hawrani and Sabri al-Asali). Amir also was commander of the joint UAR military. A regional council of ministers was established for each province, as was a unified cabinet (whose members were appointed in October). In March 1960, a new National Assembly was created. Nasser appointed its delegates—a higher proportion of whom were Egyptians—who first met that July. He also imposed Egypt's one-party system on Syria. Only the National Union, established in Egypt in May 1957, was allowed to function.

Formation of the UAR threatened the West with the prospect of Arab unity under Nasser's leadership. That the UAR immediately tried to draw in other states furthered this perception. In March 1958, the United Arab States was forged with Yemen and would last until December 1961. More significantly, cooperation talks were held between the UAR and the government that came to power during the July 1958 revolution in Iraq. Although the two never unified, Britain and the United States were unsettled by the prospect. Formation of the UAR, the civil war in pro-Western Lebanon, and the revolution in Iraq, formerly the West's leading Arab client,

prompted the dispatch of U.S. troops to Lebanon and British troops to Jordan in July 1958, to bolster anti-UAR Arab governments.

Syria soon became disappointed with the UAR. Ba'thists were angered at being barred from power in a union that some Syrians felt more closely approached Egypt's occupation of Syria. By late 1959, major Ba'thists had been dismissed from the government. The powerful Syrian bourgeoisie was alienated by Nasser's state-managed economic policies, especially limits on landholdings and the 1961 socialist decrees. In August 1961, Nasser strengthened his centralized control by abolishing the two councils of ministers and the cabinet, and adding three new vice presidents, for a total of seven (only two of whom were Syrians).

Syria's units of the UAR army in Damascus launched a secessionist coup on 28 September 1961. Following limited fighting, Nasser decided against enforcing union militarily. The breakup of the UAR was a tremendous blow to Nasser's prestige and the dream of pan-Arab unity. Egypt used the name United Arab Republic until 1971, when it became the Arab Republic of Egypt.

See also Amir, Abd al-Hakim; Baghdadi, Abd al-Latif al-; Ba'th, al-; Hawrani, Akram al-; Nasser, Gamal Abdel; National Union (Egypt); Quwatli, Shukri al-.

Bibliography

Jankowski, James. *Nassers' Egypt, Arab Nationalism and the United Arab Republic.* Boulder, CO: Lynne Rienner Publishers, 2001.

MICHAEL R. FISCHBACH

UNITED JEWISH APPEAL (UJA)

The main organization through which U.S. Jews support Jews abroad.

In 1939 the United Palestine Appeal joined with the American Jewish Joint Distribution Committee and the National Refugee Service to form the United Jewish Appeal (UJA). Most of what it raises goes to what is now called the United Israel Appeal, which operates through the Jewish Agency in Israel. Funds are also given to support Jewish communities in other parts of the world. The UJA operates through hundreds of federations and welfare funds in the United States.

Between 1939 and 1967 the UJA raised an estimated $1.925 billion, including $147 million in 1948, the year that the state of Israel was created, and $250 million in 1967, when the 1967 War occurred. Nearly $1 billion was distributed to the UJA and its predecessor, the United Palestine Appeal (UPA).

In 1999 the UJA, the United Israel Appeal (UIA), and the Council of Jewish Federations merged to form the United Jewish Communities (UJC). In the same year the UJC was reported to have raised $524 million, making it the seventh-largest charity in the United States. The UJA Federation of New York was reported to have raised $157 million.

See also JEWISH AGENCY FOR PALESTINE.

Bibliography

American Jewish Yearbook, 2000. Scranton, PA: American Jewish Committee and Publication Society, 2000.

United Jewish Communities. Available from <http://www.ujc.org>.

PAUL RIVLIN

UNITED NATIONS AND THE MIDDLE EAST

The United Nations (UN) has played a prominent role in the Middle East, passing resolutions, facilitating negotiations, and organizing peacekeeping operations.

The world organization's most important contributions since 1948 are discussed in chronological order.

Arab–Israel War (1948)

The problem of Palestine was brought before the United Nations in April 1947. In May, the General Assembly set up the United Nations Special Committee on Palestine. In its August report, the majority recommended a plan of partition. On 29 November 1947, the General Assembly adopted one and decided that the British Mandate over Palestine should be terminated not later than 1 August 1948. The Jewish Agency accepted the partition plan, but the Arab Higher Committee and all Arab states rejected it.

On 14 May 1948, the British Mandate over Palestine expired. The Jewish Agency proclaimed the State of Israel on the territory allotted to the Jewish community under the partition plan. On the following day, the Arab states instituted armed action in Palestine. On 21 May, the Security Council appointed Folke Bernadotte the United Nations mediator for Palestine.

Fighting ended in June with a truce, which was followed by the dispatch of a military observer mission, the United Nations Truce Supervision Organization (UNTSO), the first UN peacekeeping operation. Bernadotte's mediation activities were cut short when he was assassinated in Jerusalem on 17 September 1948 by the Stern gang (LEHI). His work was immediately resumed by Ralph Bunche. On 11 December 1948, the General Assembly set up the UN Conciliation Commission for Palestine (France, Turkey, and the United States).

Between February and July 1949, Israel concluded armistice agreements with Egypt, Lebanon, Jordan, and Syria under Bunche's auspices; he was awarded the 1950 Nobel Peace Prize for his efforts. The agreements gave temporary control of the Gaza Strip to Egypt; of the West Bank, including East Jerusalem, to Jordan; and of the remaining parts of Palestine to Israel. With three of the four armistice agreements signed, Israel was admitted to the United Nations on 11 May 1949.

In December 1949, the General Assembly established the United Nations Relief and Works Agency to provide assistance to Palestinian refugees. The Trusteeship Council drafted a statute for the internationalization of Jerusalem in April 1950; it was rejected by Israel and Jordan.

After the conclusion of the armistice agreements, the responsibility for promoting a final settlement of the Palestine problem fell on the Conciliation Commission, but no progress was achieved. Despite the efforts of UNTSO, the situation along the armistice demarcation lines remained tense. Palestinian *fida'iyyun* (freedom fighters) carried out frequent raids against Israel, which were invariably followed by harsh retaliation by Israel's armed forces.

Suez Crisis

Tension in the region rose to a critical level in 1956, when Egypt's Gamal Abdel Nasser nationalized the Suez Canal Company, which was controlled by British and French interests. While UN secretary-general Dag Hammarskjöld endeavored to work out a compromise solution, Israel's troops invaded Egypt on 28 October 1956 and within a few days occupied the Gaza Strip and most of the Sinai Peninsula, while an Anglo-French force landed in the Suez Canal Zone. To help resolve the crisis, the Security Council established the United Nations Emergency Force (UNEF) to separate Egyptian and Israeli forces along the Gaza and Sinai frontiers.

Six-Day War

On 18 May 1967, UNEF was withdrawn at Egypt's request. Three weeks later, war broke out. Hostilities started on the Egyptian front on 5 June and soon thereafter spread to the Jordanian and Syrian fronts. The war ended on 10 June with a cease-fire. By that time, Israel had taken Sinai and the Gaza Strip from Egypt, the West Bank (including East Jerusalem) from Jordan, and the Golan Heights from Syria.

On 22 November 1967, the Security Council unanimously adopted Resolution 242, known as the land for peace resolution, which remains the basis for a negotiated settlement. It called on the parties to seek a comprehensive settlement in the Middle East and stipulated that the establishment of a just and lasting peace should be based on the withdrawal of Israel's armed forces from territories occupied in June 1967 and the recognition of the right of all states in the region to live in peace within secure boundaries. Gunnar Jarring, special representative of the secretary-general, began a mediation mission in December 1967, but little progress was made. The mission lapsed in early 1973.

October 1973 War

War broke out on 6 October 1973, when Egypt's and Syria's forces launched simultaneous attacks against Israel's posts in the Suez Canal Zone and on the Golan Heights in order to liberate their occupied territories. As fighting intensified, especially on the Egyptian front, the Security Council met on 22 October and adopted Resolution 338, which called on

Count Folke Bernadotte (1895–1948) was sent by the UN, in 1948, to the newly formed nation of Israel, in order to assist in mediating the conflict between Israel and surrounding Arab countries. While in Israel, Bernadotte was assassinated by Jewish terrorists. © NATIONAL ARCHIVES/USHMM PHOTO ARCHIVES. REPRODUCED BY PERMISSION.

belligerents to cease fighting and begin negotiations to establish a just and durable peace on the basis of Resolution 242.

But the fighting continued. At the request of President Anwar al-Sadat of Egypt, the Soviet Union agreed to send troops to the area, a move that the United States strongly opposed. On 25 October 1973, the Security Council ordered an immediate cease-fire and established the second United Nations Emergency Force (UNEF II) to supervise it.

A peace conference convened in Geneva under U.S. and Soviet sponsorship in December 1973. Chaired by UN secretary-general Kurt Waldheim, it was attended by Egypt, Israel, and Jordan. Syria refused to participate, and the Palestine Liberation Organization (PLO) was not invited. The conference lasted only two days, but it paved the way for U.S. mediation, which led to military disengagement agreements between Israel and Egypt and Syria.

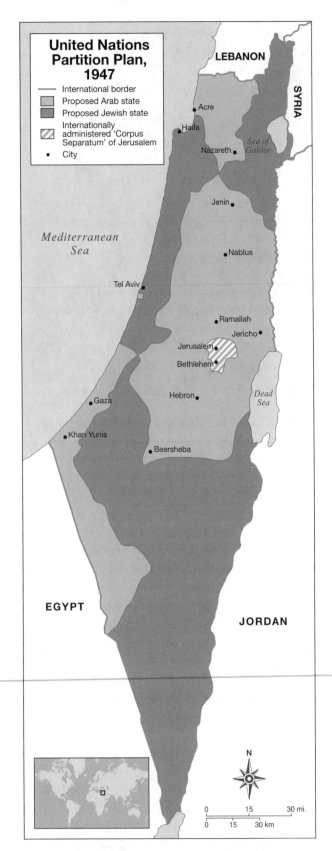

MAP BY XNR PRODUCTIONS, INC. THE GALE GROUP.

The Camp David Accords and the Egypt–Israel Peace Treaty

The peace process was revived in November 1977, when President Sadat traveled to Jerusalem. His visit was followed by direct negotiations between Egypt and Israel under U.S. auspices, which led to the Camp David Accords in September 1978 and the peace treaty between Egypt and Israel in March 1979. Sadat and Israeli Prime Minister Menachem Begin shared the 1978 Nobel Peace Prize.

It was the clear intention of the parties to the peace treaty to use UNEF II and UNTSO military observers for peacekeeping along the border, but the Soviet Union, which strongly opposed the peace treaty, made it clear that it would veto an extension of UNEF II. The Security Council therefore decided to let the UNEF's mandate lapse. The U.S. later organized and financed the Multinational Force and Observers to carry out the peacekeeping functions that the UNEF II had been expected to perform.

Israel's Invasions of Lebanon

Although relations between Egypt and Israel were normalized with the peace treaty, other aspects of the Arab–Israel conflict deteriorated after Israel's invasion of Lebanon in March 1978, following a terrorist raid against Israel by PLO fighters based in southern Lebanon. On 19 March, the Security Council called on Israel to withdraw from Lebanon's territory and established the UN Interim Force in Lebanon (UNIFIL) to confirm the withdrawal process. UNIFIL was unable to fulfill its mandate, however. In 1982, Israel again invaded Lebanon. In 1985, Israel's forces withdrew from most of the occupied territory but continued to hold a border area known as the security zone. UNIFIL remains in southern Lebanon.

Resumption of the Peace Process

The Madrid Peace Conference on the Middle East was convened in November 1991 by the United States and the Soviet Union to promote a comprehensive settlement of the Arab–Israel conflict on the basis of Security Council Resolutions 242 and 338. On 13 September 1993, Israel and the PLO signed the Declaration of Principles for interim self-government for the Gaza Strip and Jericho. Although the agreement is known as the Oslo Accord because of the secret negotiations held there, the PLO and Israel actually signed the text in Washington. The Oslo Accord was renegotiated in 1995 (known as Oslo 2). The United Nations played a marginal role in negotiating and implementing these agreements, but the world body's ability to continue virtually came to a halt during the second intifada early in September 2000 (see below). It has, however, been active in international assistance supporting the implementation of the declaration of principles.

The United Nations maintains three peacekeeping operations in the area: the UN Disengagement Observer Force on the Golan Heights, UNIFIL, and UNTSO. UNRWA assists about 3.2 million Palestinian refugees in Gaza, the West Bank, and neighboring Arab states.

The Rebellion in Lebanon

In May 1958, a rebellion by armed Muslims broke out in Lebanon when President Camille Chamoun, a Christian Maronite, announced his intention to seek a constitutional amendment that would enable him to stand for a second term. Lebanon's government brought the matter before the Security Council, charging that the United Arab Republic (formed temporarily by the union of Egypt and Syria under Nasser) was supporting the rebellion.

By Resolution 128 of 11 June 1958, the Security Council decided to dispatch the UN Observation Group in Lebanon (UNOGIL). By August 1958, General Fu'ad Chehab, the Maronite commander of the army, had been elected president of Lebanon, effectively removing the question of a second term for Chamoun. In November 1958, Lebanon's government informed the Security Council that cordial and close relations had been reestablished between Lebanon and the United Arab Republic. UNOGIL was terminated the following month.

Yemen

In September 1962, a rebellion led by the army overthrew Imam Muhammad al-Badr and proclaimed the Yemen Arab Republic. Following his overthrow, the imam rallied the tribes in the northern part of the country and, with financial and material support from Saudi Arabia, the royalists fought a fierce guerrilla war against republican forces. At the beginning of October 1962, Egyptian troops were dispatched to Yemen at the request of the revolutionary government. After the 1962 session of the General Assembly, UN Secretary-General U Thant undertook a peace initiative. In April 1963, Egypt, Saudi Arabia, and the Yemen Arab Republic accepted his disengagement plan. Saudi Arabia would terminate all support to the Yemeni royalists and Egypt would withdraw its troops from Yemen. A demilitarized zone would be established on each side of the border between Saudi Arabia and Yemen, and impartial observers would monitor the disengagement.

The UN Observation Mission in Yemen (UN-YOM) began operations in July 1963. Following the conference of Arab heads of state at Cairo in mid-January 1964, relations between Egypt and Saudi Arabia improved markedly. UNYOM was withdrawn on 4 September 1964.

Economic and Social Commission for Western Asia (ESCWA)

On 9 August 1973, Economic and Social Council (ECOSOC) Resolution 1818 established the Economic Commission for Western Asia as the successor to the United Nations Economic and Social Office in Beirut to facilitate development within and outside the region. Largely because of the awkwardness of excluding Israel from the "region," this was the last UN regional commission to be created (the first began in 1947), and on 26 July 1985 ECOSOC added social aspects to the commission's work and changed its title to the Economic and Social Commission for Western Africa (ESCWA). As a result of insecurity, the headquarters were relocated temporarily from Beirut to Amman, and then to Baghdad in 1982. After the beginning of the Gulf War, the headquarters were relocated to Amman once again in 1991. In July 1994, the General Assembly decided that the commission would return to Beirut; and UN secretary-general Kofi Annan inaugurated the permanent headquarters in March 1998.

Cyprus

Following the outbreak of fighting between the Greek and Turkish communities on Cyprus in December 1963, the conflict was brought before the

The United Nations grants admission to Israel, 1949. © HULTON-DEUTSCH COLLECTION/CORBIS. REPRODUCED BY PERMISSION.

Security Council. By Resolution 186 of 4 March 1964, the council established the UN Peacekeeping Force in Cyprus (UNFICYP) to prevent a recurrence of fighting and to return normal conditions to the island. UNFICYP became operational on 13 March. After August 1964, quiet was restored, and it lasted until July 1974, when supporters of *enosis* (union of Cyprus with Greece) staged a coup d'état against the Cyprus government. Turkey launched an extensive military operation on the island. The fighting ended in August 1974. By that time, Turkey's army controlled about 38 percent of northern Cyprus. To prevent a recurrence of fighting, UNFICYP established a zone across the island between the Cyprus National Guard to the south and the Turkish and Turkish Cypriot forces to the north.

Resolution 186 also asked the UN secretary-general to appoint a mediator to promote a peaceful settlement of the Cyprus problem. The first mediator, Galo Plaza Lasso, reported in April 1965 that a settlement could best be achieved on the basis of a unitary government with adequate protection and guarantees for individual and minority rights. His report was rejected by the Turkish side and Plaza Lasso resigned in December 1965. Intercommunal talks began in 1968 under the auspices of the UN secretary-general, but they made little progress.

In February 1975, the Turkish Cypriot leadership announced the establishment of the Turkish Federated State of Cyprus in the northern part of the island. Known after 1983 as the Turkish Republic of North Cyprus, it failed to receive international recognition. UN-sponsored intercommunal negotiations finally resulted, in February 2004, in an agreement to have a unified island become a member of the European Union in May 2004. UNFICYP, whose mandate has been repeatedly extended, continues to deploy military personnel.

Bahrain

Bahrain, which until 1970 had "special treaty relations" with the former colonial power, Britain, was claimed by Iran because the island had been under its sovereign jurisdiction before 1783. Britain announced its intention to withdraw from East of Suez in 1968, and in early 1969 Iran and Britain asked Secretary-General U Thant to help resolve the disputed territory. Following nearly one year of negotiations, an agreement was reached under which U Thant would appoint a personal representative to ascertain the wishes of the people of Bahrain.

A resulting April 1970 report affirmed that the overwhelming majority of the people of Bahrain wished it to be a fully independent and sovereign state. On 11 May 1970, the Security Council endorsed the findings. Shortly thereafter, Bahrain gained its independence; it became a UN member in September 1971.

Afghanistan

On 27 December 1979, the Soviet Union entered Afghanistan to assist the communist-led government in its fight against insurgent movements. It was soon embroiled in a guerrilla war with the fighters of the Afghan resistance, known as Mojahedin, who received substantial financial and material support from Pakistan and the United States. During the hostilities, some 3 million refugees fled to Pakistan and about 2 million to Iran.

On 14 January 1980, the General Assembly adopted a resolution that called for the withdrawal of all foreign troops from Afghanistan. In February 1981, UN secretary-general Kurt Waldheim appointed Javier Pérez de Cuéllar as his personal representative to deal with the situation. When Pérez de Cuéllar succeeded Waldheim as secretary-general in January 1982, the mission was taken over by Diego Cordovez.

Afghanistan and Pakistan agreed in 1982 to engage in indirect negotiations, with Cordovez as intermediary. Those negotiations led to the conclusion, in Geneva, of the April 1988 Agreements on the Settlement of the Situation relating to Afghanistan. Both Afghanistan and Pakistan undertook not to interfere in the internal affairs of the other state, and the Soviet Union and the United States agreed not

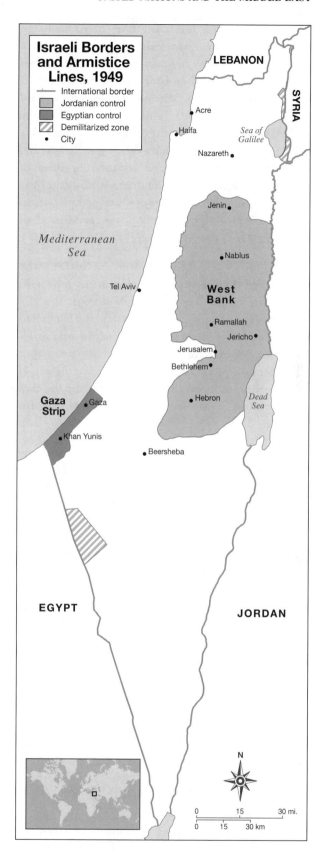

MAP BY XNR PRODUCTIONS, INC. THE GALE GROUP.

to interfere in the internal affairs of Afghanistan and Pakistan. The agreements also provided for a phased withdrawal of Soviet forces from Afghanistan by 15 February 1989 and for the establishment of the UN Good Offices Mission in Afghanistan and Pakistan (UNGOMAP), which was set up at the end of April 1988, to monitor implementation. Besides monitoring the withdrawal of the Red Army, UNGOMAP assisted in the voluntary return of refugees to Afghanistan. The final withdrawal of the Soviet Union's 100,300 troops was completed on 12 February 1989. UNGOMAP was terminated in March 1990.

The civil war continued after the Soviet withdrawal, and the two superpowers continued to send weapons until January 1991. In May 1991, the UN secretary-general proposed a peace plan that called for free and fair elections leading to the establishment of a broad-based government. In April 1992, the communist regime collapsed with the defeat of the government forces, but this did not stop the civil war; fighting continued between rival Mojahedin factions.

In September 1996, the Taliban, a group comprised of Afghans trained in religious schools in Pakistan and former Mojahedin fighters, captured Kabul with the stated aim of setting up a pure Islamic state. Following an American attack (see below), the Taliban was ousted from power on 17 November 2001, and in December the Afghan Interim Authority (AIA) was established after a number of prominent Afghans met under UN auspices in Bonn, Germany, led by Special Representative of the Secretary-General Lakhdar Brahimi. The AIA was inaugurated on 22 December 2001, with a six-month mandate, to be followed by a two-year transitional authority.

Iran–Iraq War

On 22 September 1980, the armed forces of Iraq invaded Iran and soon occupied a sizable portion of its territory. By Resolution 479 of 28 September 1980, the Security Council called upon Iran and Iraq to refrain from further use of force and to settle their dispute by peaceful means, but Iran rejected the resolution as one-sided. On 11 November, Secretary-General Waldheim appointed Olof Palme as his special representative to promote a

peace settlement. Palme made some initial progress, but a peace settlement remained elusive.

During the initial phase of the war, Iraq's forces advanced inside Iran. In December 1980, Iranian forces stopped the advance, and by late 1982 they had pushed the Iraqi troops back in some areas beyond the border. Then fighting settled into a stalemate. Both parties engaged in frequent air attacks against military and oil installations and urban civilian areas.

Facilitated by the waning of the Cold War, on 20 July 1987 the Security Council adopted Resolution 598, which demanded that Iran and Iraq observe an immediate cease-fire and withdraw their forces to the international border. Intensive diplomatic negotiations lasted until 8 August 1988, when both parties formally accepted the cease-fire arrangements.

The next day, the Security Council established the UN Iran–Iraq Military Observer Group (UNIIMOG) to supervise the cease-fire and the withdrawal process. The mission began operations in mid-August with 400 military observers and about 500 military support personnel. After the cessation of hostilities, Iran and Iraq began direct talks to settle outstanding issues. On 15 August 1990, shortly after its invasion of Kuwait, Iraq lifted its claim over the Shatt al-Arab, thus removing a major cause of conflict with Iran. UNIIMOG was terminated on 28 February 1991.

Following the war, Pérez de Cuéllar used the close relationship he had developed with Iran's leaders to obtain the release of hostages in Beirut. After securing Iran's cooperation in 1989, he asked Giandomenico Picco to deal with this matter in a one-man secret mission. Almost four years later, the mission resulted in the release of eleven Western hostages detained in Beirut and of ninety-one Lebanese held by kidnap groups.

Western Sahara

In 1985, Secretary-General Pérez de Cuéllar and the chairman of the Organization of African Unity sought to promote a peaceful settlement of the conflict between Morocco and POLISARIO (Frente Popular para la Liberación de Saguia al-Hamra y Río de Oro) over Western Sahara. In August 1988, the two warring parties accepted the settlement proposals in principle. Those proposals envisaged a

The United Nations tours the Jenin refugee camp in Palestine, surveying the damage from an Israeli military strike. © AP/WORLD WIDE PHOTOS. REPRODUCED BY PERMISSION.

cease-fire followed by a referendum that would enable the people of Western Sahara to choose between independence and continued union with Morocco.

In April 1991, the secretary-general submitted to the Security Council a detailed plan for implementing the settlement proposals. It provided for the establishment of the UN Mission for the Referendum in Western Sahara (MINURSO) and contained a tentative timetable for the operation, according to which the referendum would be held twenty weeks after the ceasefire. On 29 April 1991, the Security Council approved the implementation plan and established MINURSO, and on 24 May the secretary-general announced that the cease-fire would enter into effect on 6 September 1991. As an interim measure, military observers were sent to Western Sahara to monitor the ceasefire.

MINURSO's Identification Commission was established in May 1993, and registration of voters began in August 1994 and was completed in December 1999. A crucial issue in the process involved the identification of applicants from three contested tribal groups. Although divergent views still exist between the parties and elections are yet to be held, the situation in Western Sahara has been generally quiet.

The Gulf Crisis and its Aftermath

On 2 August 1990, Iraq invaded Kuwait, quickly occupied the country, and annexed it. On the same day, the Security Council condemned the invasion and demanded the immediate withdrawal of Iraq's forces. When Iraq failed to comply, the council met again on 6 August and imposed economic sanctions. On 29 November, it adopted Resolution 678, which authorized member states cooperating with Kuwait to use all necessary measures to implement its resolutions if Iraq failed to withdraw by 15 January 1991.

On 16 January 1991, coalition forces led by the United States launched military operations against Iraq. The United Nations was on the sidelines during the Gulf War, but it played a key role again after the military operations were suspended on 28 February. At that time, coalition forces had driven Iraq's troops from Kuwait and had occupied southern Iraq.

On 2 March 1991, the Security Council demanded that Iraq implement all its resolutions and specified the measures to be taken to end the hostilities. The next day, an informal cease-fire was signed by military commanders in the field. On 3 April 1991, the Security Council adopted Resolution 687, which laid down in detail the specific terms that Iraq must accept in order to obtain a formal cease-fire. After receiving Iraq's official acceptance, the Security Council established the UN Iraq-Kuwait Observation Mission to supervise the cease-fire and monitor a demilitarized zone between Iraq and Kuwait.

In the aftermath of the Gulf War, the Kurdish population in northern Iraq and the Shi'ites in the south rebelled against the government, which took harsh actions to suppress the rebellions. By Resolution 688 of 5 April 1991, the Security Council demanded that Iraq immediately end the repression and give international humanitarian organizations access to all those in need of assistance within its territory. A UN humanitarian operation to provide food and essential relief supplies in all parts of Iraq, especially in the northern Kurdish area, was launched. Indeed, this was the first in a series of military interventions in the 1990s to foster humanitarian values as the theme of "sovereignty as responsibility" gained resonance.

Sanctions were not lifted by the Security Council until May 2003 (see below) because Iraq under Saddam Hussein never fully complied with the conditions of the initial resolutions to end the war or with the thirteen subsequent ones passed by the Security Council between 1991 and 2002. The negative impact of sanctions on the lives of Iraqis became controversial even after the institution of an oil-for-food program. An innovation approved by the Security Council in Resolution 687 was the UN Special Commission (UNSCOM), which from 1991 to 1998 sought to find and eliminate Iraq's weapons of mass destruction. Iraq's lack of compliance and the eventual rejection of UNSCOM would later become an issue in the United States–United Kingdom invasion of Iraq in March 2003 (see below).

After 11 September 2001: Wars in Afghanistan and Iraq

The attack by al-Qaʿida operatives on the World Trade Center and on the Pentagon on 11 September 2001 altered substantially the security equation in the Middle East and around the world. On 12 September, the Security Council adopted the strong condemnatory Resolution 1368, which termed these assaults a threat to international peace and security and referred to the right of self-defense. Later that same month, Resolution 1373 obliged member states under Chapter VII of the UN charter to cooperate in the fight against terrorism and also created the Counter-Terrorism Committee. Also in September, the General Assembly condemned the devastating attacks. Citing the provisions for self-defense under UN Charter Article 51, the United States began military operations against Afghanistan on 7 October 2001 and overthrew the Taliban government in November (see above). With the United Nations playing a substantial role in helping to rebuild political structures, almost 10,000 U.S. troops remained in the country along with the UN-approved International Security Assistance Force (ISAF) under NATO auspices. ISAF maintained security around Kabul but resisted pressures to deploy elsewhere until late 2003, when a decision was made to do so. At the same time, the security situation remained tenuous, with al-Qaʿida's leader, Osama bin Ladin, apparently at large.

In the fall of 2002, the United States opened a new front in its war on terrorism and weapons of mass destruction with an attack on the regime of Saddam Hussein in Iraq. In December 1999, the Security Council had created the UN Monitoring, Verification, and Inspection Committee (UNMOVIC) to replace UNSCOM; in October 2002, resolution 1441, which had unanimous support, granted UNMOVIC unconditional and unrestricted access to locations in Iraq, including those previously termed sensitive sites. UNMOVIC's mandate was to disarm Iraq of its weapons of mass destruction and to mon-

A United Nations convoy travels through Lebanon. © AFP/CORBIS. REPRODUCED BY PERMISSION.

itor conformity with its obligations not to reacquire the weapons prohibited by the Security Council. Citing Iraq's lack of compliance with UN resolutions, the United States and the United Kingdom went to war in Iraq on 23 March 2003 without Security Council approval. They had withdrawn a draft resolution following a heated debate that reflected divisions not only among Western states but throughout the world. One of the main points of contention was the need to permit more time for inspections. Saddam Hussein's regime fell on 9 April 2003 and U.S. president George W. Bush declared victory on 1 May, although substantial resistance continued.

Security Council Resolution 1483 brought the United Nations back into the picture and led to the end of sanctions and the beginning of the world organization's involvement on the ground. U.S. insistence on maintaining political and military control inside occupied Iraq prevented a more diverse international presence. The attack on the UN's Bagh-

dad headquarters on 19 August 2003 led to the highest death toll in the history of the organization, killing twenty-two people, including the special representative of the secretary-general, Sergio Vieira de Mello.

The United States and the United Kingdom returned to the United Nations in the hope of securing more international military and financial support for the war's aftermath. The Security Council passed Resolution 1511 on 16 October 2003, which appeared to have been helpful in securing modest financial pledges at a donors' conference held shortly thereafter in Madrid. However, the resolution did not secure substantial military forces from other states, which sought a clearer role for the United Nations. At the outset of 2004, there was still no evidence that Iran had either weapons of mass destruction or links to al-Qaʿida, which were the main reasons the administrations of U.S. president George W. Bush and U.K. prime minister Tony Blair had cited for going to war.

Ongoing Israeli–Palestinian Conflict

The second armed intifada, or uprising, began in September 2000 after a near-breakthrough in the final days of the administration of President Bill Clinton, who had sought to bridge the divide between Israeli prime minister Ehud Barak and Palestine Authority president Yasir Arafat. Following the election of Ariel Sharon as prime minister of Israel, violence involving Palestinian suicide bombings of Israeli civilians and harsh Israeli repression and assassinations continued and worsened. A suicide bombing at a Netanya hotel during the Passover holiday led to a massive Israeli attack against the Jenin refugee camp in April 2002, and a fierce battle ensued. In response to Palestinian accusations of a massacre, the Security Council asked the United Nations to investigate the events in Jenin, but Israel, after having initially agreed to permit access, did not do so. Under pressure after widespread criticism of its unilateral approach to Iraq and to international relations more generally, in April 2003 the Bush administration published a "road map" to encourage a break in the violence and eventual political negotiations for the creation of a Palestinian state. The road map was created by a quartet, whose members were the United States, the United Nations, Russia, and the European Union.

See also AFGHANISTAN: U.S. INTERVENTION IN; ANNAN, KOFI A.; AQSA INTIFADA, AL-; ARAB HIGHER COMMITTEE (PALESTINE); ARAB–ISRAEL WAR (1948); ARAB–ISRAEL WAR (1967); ARAB–ISRAEL WAR (1973); BAHRAIN; BERNADOTTE, FOLKE; BIN LADIN, OSAMA; BUNCHE, RALPH J.; FIDA'IYYUN; GULF CRISIS (1990–1991); HAMMARSKJÖLD, DAG; IRAN–IRAQ WAR (1980–1988); JEWISH AGENCY FOR PALESTINE; MANDATE SYSTEM; OSLO ACCORD (1993); PAKISTAN AND THE MIDDLE EAST; PALESTINE LIBERATION ORGANIZATION (PLO); PARTITION PLANS (PALESTINE); PÉREZ DE CUÉLLAR, JAVIER; POLISARIO; QA'IDA, AL-; SANCTIONS, IRAQI; SUEZ CRISIS (1956–1957); TALIBAN; UNITED NATIONS EMERGENCY FORCE; UNITED NATIONS INTERIM FORCE IN LEBANON; UNITED NATIONS RELIEF AND WORKS AGENCY FOR PALESTINE REFUGEES IN THE NEAR EAST (UNRWA); UNITED NATIONS SPECIAL COMMITTEE ON PALESTINE, 1947 (UNSCOP); WAR IN IRAQ (2003); WESTERN SAHARA WAR; YEMEN CIVIL WAR.

Bibliography

Annual Report of the Secretary-General on the Work of the Organization. New York: United Nations.

Boudreault, Jody, ed. *United Nations Resolutions on Palestine and the Arab–Israeli Conflict,* Vol 4: *1987–1991.* Washington, DC: Institute for Palestine Studies, 1993.

Krasno, Jean E., and Sutterlin, James S. *The United Nations and Iraq: Defanging the Viper.* Westport, CT: Praeger, 2003.

Sherif, Regina S., ed. *United Nations Resolutions on Palestine and the Arab–Israeli Conflict Vol. 2, 1975–1981.* Washington, DC: Institute for Palestine Studies, 1988.

Simpson, Michael, ed. *United Nations Resolutions on Palestine and the Arab–Israeli Conflict Vol. 3, 1982–1986.* Washington, DC: Institute for Palestine Studies, 1987.

Tomeh, George J. *United Nations Resolutions on Palestine and the Arab–Israeli Conflict, 1947–1974.* Washington, DC: Institute for Palestine Studies, 1988.

United Nations. *The Blue Helmets: A Review of United Nations Peace-Keeping.* New York: United Nations, 1996.

United Nations Yearbook. New York: United Nations, 1947–1996.

Urquhart, Brian. *Ralph Bunche: An American Life.* New York: Norton, 1993.

Weiss, Thomas G.; Forsythe, David P.; and Coate, Roger A. *The United Nations and Changing World Politics,* 4th edition. Boulder, CO: Westview Press 2004.

F. T. LIU
UPDATED BY THOMAS G. WEISS

UNITED NATIONS CONCILIATION COMMISSION FOR PALESTINE (UNCCP)

Commission appointed to deal with the problem of dislocated Palestinians and to help reach a comprehensive peace settlement after the 1948 Arab–Israel War.

Following debate on the Bernadotte report, a UN General Assembly resolution on 11 December 1948 established the Conciliation Commission for Palestine, instructing it "to take steps to assist the parties concerned to achieve a final comprehensive peace settlement of all questions outstanding between them" and to facilitate the repatriation or resettlement with compensation of the Palestinian refugees. The commission was composed of representatives from France, Turkey, and the United States. The commissioners began with a round of shuttle diplomacy in Middle Eastern capitals, held a conference with Arab representatives in Beirut, and then convened a major conference, meeting separately with Arab and Israeli representatives, in Lausanne between April and August 1949. These meetings, along with a further series of discussions in Geneva in 1950, produced little apart from declarations of good intention (including the Lausanne Protocol), preparations to unblock frozen Arab bank accounts in Israel, and a scheme for family reunification.

At a conference of Arab and Israeli delegates in Paris in late 1951, the commission tried but failed to achieve agreement on specific proposals for a peace settlement. After the breakdown of the conference, the commission, convinced that the parties were not yet prepared to make peace, confined its efforts to dealing with the Palestinian refugee problem. Even then, it was able to make only limited progress, mainly on background studies of the technical aspects regarding future compensation. Despite the lack of progress, the commission still exists and the General Assembly still continues to pass annual resolutions calling on it to continue its efforts to carry out its original mandate.

See also LAUSANNE CONFERENCE (1949).

Bibliography

Azcárate, Pablo de. *Mission in Palestine, 1948–1952.* Washington, DC: Middle East Institute, 1966.

Caplan, Neil. *Futile Diplomacy,* Vol. 3: *The United Nations, the Great Powers and Middle East Peacemaking, 1948–1954.* Totowa, NJ, and London: Frank Cass, 1997.

Fischbach, Michael R. *Records of Dispossession: Palestinian Refugee Property and the Arab–Israeli Conflict.* New York: Columbia University Press, 2003.

Forsythe, David P. *United Nations Peacemaking: The Conciliation Commission for Palestine.* Baltimore, MD: Johns Hopkins University Press, 1972.

Hamzeh, Fuad Said. *United Nations Conciliation Commission for Palestine, 1949–1967.* Beirut: Institute for Palestine Studies, 1968.

Morris, Benny. *The Birth of the Palestinian Refugee Problem, 1947–1949.* New York; Cambridge, U.K.: Cambridge University Press, 1987.

FRED J. KHOURI
UPDATED BY NEIL CAPLAN

UNITED NATIONS ECONOMIC SURVEY MISSION (1949)

Mission to recommend effects of 1948 Arab–Israeli war and origins of UNRWA.

On 23 August 1949 the United Nations Conciliation Commission for Palestine (UNCCP) established the Economic Survey Mission, instructing it to recommend a program to assist in the recovery of the countries affected by the 1948 Arab-Israel War. The principal impetus for the creation of the mission was the failure of the UNCCP to make progress toward a political solution of the Palestinian refugee problem, but the UNCCP appointed Gordon R. Clapp, former director of the U.S. Tennessee Valley Authority, to chair the mission, thus focusing instead upon fostering the economic conditions requisite to a peace settlement. Within three months the mission concluded that the large-scale undertakings it hoped would fully reintegrate the refugees, such as Arab-Israeli cooperation in a development project for the Jordan River, were politically unfeasible.

In mid-November 1949 the mission recommended that the United Nations General Assembly both adopt a more circumspect program of public works as a first step toward rehabilitating the refugees, and assist needy individuals. On 8 December 1949 the General Assembly responded by passing Resolution 302, thereby creating the United Nations Relief and Works Agency. The agency coordinated its activities with the local governments and allocated $49 million for eighteen months of operations, but it continued to function after that in order to prevent a further deterioration of the refugees' conditions.

See also UNITED NATIONS AND THE MIDDLE EAST; UNITED NATIONS RELIEF AND WORKS AGENCY FOR PALESTINE REFUGEES IN THE NEAR EAST (UNRWA).

Bibliography

Fischbach, Michael R. *Records of Dispossession: Palestinian Refugee Property and the Arab–Israel Conflict.* New York: Columbia University Press, 2003.

Hurewitz, J.C. *The Struggle for Palestine.* New York: Greenwood Press, 1968.

Khouri, Fred J. *The Arab–Israeli Dilemma,* 2d edition. Syracuse, NY: Syracuse University Press, 1976.

ZACH LEVEY

UNITED NATIONS EMERGENCY FORCE

Peacekeeping operation established during the Suez crisis.

The Suez crisis, during which Israel, France, and Britain invaded Egypt and occupied sizable portions of its territory, was brought before the United Nations (UN) General Assembly in early November 1956. Secretary General Dag Hammarskjöld submitted a plan for setting up an emergency UN force to supervise the cessation of hostilities on 5 November. The General Assembly then authorized the establishment of the United Nations Emergency Force (UNEF), the first UN peacekeeping force.

UNEF was composed of contingents provided by member states. Troops from the five permanent members of the Security Council and any countries that might have a special interest in the conflict were excluded. UNEF's establishment in the conflict area required the consent of all parties concerned. Its soldiers had light defensive weapons but were not authorized to use force except in self-defense.

UNEF, operational by mid-November 1956, initially had about 6,000 troops from Brazil, Canada, Colombia, Denmark, Finland, India, Indonesia, Norway, Sweden, and Yugoslavia. Its first commander was Major General E. L. M. Burns of Canada. As the troops were deployed to supervise the cease-fire, negotiations were being carried out for the withdrawal of the occupation forces. A phased withdrawal began under the supervision and with the assistance of UNEF. The withdrawal of Britain's and France's forces was completed by 22 December 1956, and that of Israel's forces in March 1957.

After the withdrawal, UNEF was deployed along the Egypt–Israel border and maintained a post at Sharm al-Shaykh, which controlled access to the Gulf of Aqaba. By 1967 UNEF had been reduced to about 3,400 troops.

In May 1967, as tension arose again to a critical level in the Middle East and, despite Secretary General U Thant's appeal, President Gamal Abdel Nasser of Egypt requested the withdrawal of UNEF. UNEF therefore discontinued its operations on 18 May 1967. Three weeks later there was a new war in the Middle East.

See also ARAB–ISRAEL WAR (1956); HAMMARSKJÖLD, DAG; NASSER, GAMAL ABDEL; SUEZ CRISIS (1956–1957); UNITED NATIONS AND THE MIDDLE EAST.

Bibliography

Burns, E. L. M. *Between Arab and Israeli.* Toronto: Clarke, Irwin, 1962.

Thant, U. *A View from the UN.* Garden City, NY: Doubleday, 1978.

F. T. Liu

UNITED NATIONS INTERIM FORCE IN LEBANON

UN force in Lebanon to confirm Israeli withdrawal and assist the Lebanese government with restoring order and security.

Israel's invasion of southern Lebanon in March 1978, at a crucial stage in negotiations between Egypt and Israel, caused the United States to insist on rapid United Nations Security Council action. Resolution 425 of 19 March called on Israel to withdraw its forces and established a United Nations Interim Force in Lebanon (UNIFIL) to confirm Israel's withdrawal, restore peace and security, and assist the Lebanese government in regaining its authority. The force, initially 4,000 strong, later increasing to 6,000, began to arrive in early April 1978.

UNIFIL had no mandate to deal with the various Palestine Liberation Organization (PLO) groups and Israel's proxy South Lebanon Army, irregular forces that dominated the region. The Lebanese government had no wish to reestablish its authority in the area. Southern Lebanon was a peacekeepers nightmare.

Despite humiliations, including being swept aside during Israel's 1982 invasion, and sustaining almost 250 casualties, UNIFIL remained in place because it provided some measure of security, stability, and humanitarian protection in an extremely volatile border area. When Israel finally withdrew in May 2000, UNIFIL deployed to the border. The Lebanese government, deaf to all exhortations, left the radical Shiʿite movement Hizbullah in control of the border area, and many incidents resulted. In

2002 UNIFIL was restructured as a 2,000-strong armed observer force with contingents from France, Ghana, India, Italy, Nepal, Poland, and Ukraine. Its mandate ran to July 2003.

See also HIZBULLAH; PALESTINE LIBERATION ORGANIZATION (PLO); SOUTH LEBANON ARMY; UNITED NATIONS AND THE MIDDLE EAST.

Bibliography

Skogmo, Bjørn. *UNIFIL: International Peacekeeping in Lebanon, 1978–1988*. Boulder, CO: Lynne Rienner, 1989.

UNIFIL–United Nations Web site. Available from <http://www.un.org/depts/dpko/missions/unifil>.

AS'AD ABUKHALIL
UPDATED BY BRIAN URQUHART

UNITED NATIONS RELIEF AND WORKS AGENCY FOR PALESTINE REFUGEES IN THE NEAR EAST (UNRWA)

Organization that aids Palestine refugees.

The United Nations Relief and Works Agency for Palestine Refugees in the Near East (UNRWA) was created by UN General Assembly Resolution 302 (IV) on 8 December 1949, with the mandate to provide humanitarian assistance and emergency relief to Palestine refugees who had lost their homes and livelihood as a result of the Arab–Israel War of 1948. Palestine refugees within the purview of UNRWA are persons whose normal residences were in Palestine for a minimum of two years before the 1948 war, and their descendants. In 1949 UNRWA extended assistance to some 750,000 refugees, practically all of them Palestinian Arabs. By 2001 UNRWA had 3,874,738 registered refugees on its rolls, and was present in 59 refugee camps in the Middle East.

UNRWA's humanitarian activities have centered on three major programs: an educational program that ran 647 elementary and preparatory schools and vocational centers with 457,349 students in 1999; a health program with a network of units and medical staff that registered 7,163,056 patient visits in 1999; and a relief and social services program to assist disadvantaged groups. UNRWA also has set up special programs to improve the living conditions in refugee camps, especially housing and environmental sanitation, and to respond to emergencies. UNRWA has often had to carry out its mission in the midst of civil strife and military conflict. During the Arab–Israel War of 1967, more than 350,000 Palestinians fled from the territories seized by Israel; these included 200,000 refugees from the 1948 war, who were displaced for a second time. Later, the 1970 fighting between Jordan's army and the armed elements of the Palestine Liberation Organization (PLO) stationed in Jordan, another Arab–Israel War (October 1973), the Lebanese civil war that started in 1975, Israel's invasions of Lebanon in 1978 and in 1982, the Palestinian uprising (Intifada) and Israel's response to it, and more recently, Iraq's invasion of Kuwait and the Gulf Crisis (1990–1991) all had serious effects on the conditions of Palestine refugees and the work of UNRWA. The organization was long headquartered in Beirut, but due to the Lebanese civil war it moved to Vienna in 1978. In 1994 it announced that it was moving to Gaza, to territory controlled by the Palestinian Authority. The move was completed by July 1996.

UNRWA's budget is funded 95 percent by voluntary contributions. In 2002 the UN General Assembly approved a cash and in-kind budget of $326.2 million, of which UNRWA actually received $305.9 million. With the significant increases in costs associated with the wide-scale destruction wrought during the al-Aqsa Intifada that began in October 2000, the agency's budgetary needs have increased considerably. Yet the shortfall had to be made up by cutbacks. Actual expenditures during 2002 were $293.8 million, $32.3 million less than had been budgeted for by the General Assembly. By early 2003, UNRWA was facing a dire financial situation, and had made six emergency appeals for additional funding within a year.

See also AQSA INTIFADA, AL-; ARAB–ISRAEL WAR (1948); ARAB–ISRAEL WAR (1967); ARAB–ISRAEL WAR (1973); GAZA (CITY); GULF CRISIS (1990–1991); INTIFADA (1987–1991); PALESTINE LIBERATION ORGANIZATION (PLO); PALESTINIAN AUTHORITY; REFUGEES: PALESTINIAN.

Bibliography

UNRWA web site. Available from <www.un.org/unrwa>.

Viorst, Milton. *Reaching for the Olive Branch: UNRWA and Peace in the Middle East.* Washington, DC: Middle East Institute, 1989.

F. T. LIU
UPDATED BY MICHAEL R. FISCHBACH

UNITED NATIONS SPECIAL COMMISSION (UNSCOM)

Commission charged with eliminating Iraq's weapons of mass destruction.

After the end of the first Gulf War (1991), the United Nations Security Council passed several resolutions concerning Iraq. Resolution 687, which was passed on 3 April 1991, was the most important one. It set forth the continuation of the sanctions and the embargo on Iraq until it dismantled its weapons of mass destruction (WMD) program, which included all ballistic missiles with a range of 90 miles (150 km), and all chemical, biological, and nuclear facilities. Resolution 687 also banned the development of such weapons in the future. A related resolution, 715, adopted on 11 October 1991, called for the establishment of a long-term comprehensive monitoring system covering all current and future facilities related to weapons of mass destruction.

The United Nations Security Council created a special commission, the United Nations Special Commission (UNSCOM), which it charged with eliminating Iraq's nonnuclear WMD covered by Resolution 687. Also, UNSCOM would assist with the International Atomic Energy Agency (IAEA) inspections in the nuclear area. UNSCOM was given sweeping powers to do on-site inspections of Iraq's biological, chemical, and missile capacities, to remove and render harmless all chemical and biological weapons, to supervise the destruction of all ballistic missiles with a range exceeding 90 miles (150 km), and to verify Iraq's compliance with Resolution 687.

With a great deal of reluctance, the Iraqi government accepted Resolution 687 in May 1991. The government did not have much choice, as the resolution had passed the Security Council unanimously. Furthermore, the United States and Britain were ready to implement it and they were willing to use force if necessary.

UNSCOM operations lasted about eight years. The commission was first chaired by Rolf Ekeus, a Swedish career diplomat. From the beginning, the relationship between UNSCOM and Iraq was strained and shrouded in suspicion. On many occasions, Iraq acted in bad faith by delaying and hesitating to fulfill both the letter and the spirit of Resolutions 689 and 715. When Iraq tried to prevent UNSCOM inspectors from using their aircraft for security and political reasons, the UN Security Council adopted Resolution 707 on 15 August 1991, calling for Iraq to give full access to UNSCOM inspectors, full disclosure of weapons programs, and full disclosure of all suppliers' names. UNSCOM team members came from various countries, but the majority of the members were American and British.

The tension continued between Iraq and UNSCOM throughout the commission's operation in the country. Several confrontations between the parties prompted the United States to launch short military operations against targets inside Iraq. In July 1997 Ekeus was replaced by Richard Butler, an Australian disarmament expert who lacked diplomatic finesse, and who began to work more closely with the U.S. government. After a series of confrontations in 1997 and 1998 between Iraq and UNSCOM, the United States launched Operation Desert Fox in December 1998. The operation lasted for four days and consisted of aerial bombardments of military targets. It put an end to UNSCOM inspections, because Iraq refused further cooperation. The United Nations Security Council struggled for a year to come up with a new arms inspection formula that was acceptable to the members of the council. In January 2000 the UN adopted Resolution 1284, which formed a new commission, the United Nations Monitoring, Verification, and Inspection Commission (UNMOVIC). For two years Iraq refused to deal with the new commission.

Both Iraq and UNSCOM were responsible for confrontations. To Iraq, Resolution 687 and the commission it created impinged on Iraqi sovereignty, because Iraq's weapons program was one of the mainstays of Saddam's power, both domestically and regionally. Iraq accused the inspectors of trying to strip the nation of its industrial and technological capacity, and it objected to UNSCOM's intrusive and confrontational approach. In addition, Iraq accused the United States of using and subverting UNSCOM to gather intelligence in order to change the government in Iraq.

UNSCOM, on the other hand, allowed itself to be used by the United States government to collect intelligence data by the U.S. members of the inspection teams, according to Dilip Hiro (pp. 97, 107, and 119). The United States started to subvert UNSCOM operations as early as 1992 by using its intelligence agents and technicians trained in handling communications and bugging devices to intercept microwave transmissions sent by the Iraqi military. In the aftermath of Operation Desert Fox, several damaging revelations appeared in the U.S. press about the infiltration of UNSCOM by U.S. intelligence agencies.

By 1998, despite the tension between Iraq and UNSCOM, the commission had accomplished most of its job of discovering WMD, destroying them, and establishing a comprehensive remote monitoring system. According to Scott Ritter, the bulldog of UNSCOM, Iraq no longer possessed any meaningful quantities of chemical or biological agents, if it had possessed any at all (*New York Times,* 3 July 2000). In the spring of 2003 U.S. armed forces invaded and occupied Iraq; despite intense searching, as of the following spring they had failed to discover any weapons of mass destruction.

See also GULF WAR (1991); IRAQ; WAR IN IRAQ (2003).

Bibliography

Hiro, Dilip. *Iraq in the Eye of the Storm.* New York: Thunder's Mouth Press, 2002.

Ritter, Scott. *Frontier Justice: Weapons of Mass Destruction and the Bushwhacking of America.* New York: Context Books, 2003.

AYAD AL-QAZZAZ

UNITED NATIONS SPECIAL COMMITTEE ON PALESTINE, 1947 (UNSCOP)

Committee created in 1947 to deal with the future government of Palestine.

Following the end of World War II the Arab-Zionist conflict in Palestine was internationalized, and greater efforts were made to resolve it. After a few unsuccessful Anglo-American endeavors, in February 1947 the British handed over the Palestine problem to the United Nations.

In May 1947 the UN General Assembly created a Special Committee on Palestine (UNSCOP) with eleven members—Australia, Canada, Czechoslovakia, Guatemala, India, Iran, the Netherlands, Peru, Sweden (chair), Uruguay, and Yugoslavia. It was mandated to investigate all matters relevant to the Palestine problem and to submit a report, including proposals for a solution, to the General Assembly.

The committee visited Palestine and heard testimonies from Jewish representatives, and it witnessed the dramatic capture by the British of the ship *Exodus,* which carried 4,500 European Jewish refugees. The Palestinian Arab leadership refused to testify, but the committee nevertheless met in Lebanon with representatives of the Arab states. Members of the committee also met Jewish inmates of displaced persons camps in Europe.

The UNSCOP Report, submitted on 31 August 1947, unanimously supported the termination of the British mandate in Palestine. The representatives of Iran, India, and Yugoslavia supported a federal solution (known as the minority plan) that envisaged Arab and Jewish regions within a federal union with Jerusalem as its capital. The representatives of the other states (except Australia) favored a partition into two separate independent states (the majority plan) with Jerusalem as a *corpus separatum* under an international regime.

On 29 November 1947 the General Assembly adopted Resolution 181, based on the UNSCOP majority plan, by a 33–13 vote, with 10 abstentions. The Jewish Agency accepted the resolution, and the Arab Higher Committee rejected it.

See also EXODUS (1947).

Bibliography

Garcia-Granados, Jorge. *The Birth of Israel: The Drama As I Saw It.* New York: Knopf, 1948.

Louis, William Roger, and Stookey, Robert W., eds. *The End of the Palestine Mandate.* Austin: University of Texas Press; London: IB Tauris, 1986.

Wilson, Evan. *Decision on Palestine: How the U.S. Came to Recognize Israel.* Stanford, CA: Hoover Institution Press, 1979.

F. T. LIU
UPDATED BY JOSEPH NEVO

UNITED NATIONS TRUCE SUPERVISION ORGANIZATION (UNTSO)

United Nations (UN) peacekeeping machinery in Israel and neighboring Arab countries.

The United Nations Truce Supervision Organization (UNTSO) was created through several UN resolutions to oversee the Security Council truce agreement between Israel and the Arab states that went into effect on 11 June 1948. Unarmed UN military observers were first sent to Cairo and throughout Palestine. After hostilities in the 1948–1949 Arab-Israel war ended, UNTSO was expanded and charged with overseeing the signatories' application of the four armistice agreements. Its observers were stationed along armistice lines between Israel and Egypt, Syria, Lebanon, and Jordan. Observers remained in the region through the 1956 Suez crisis and were supported by the new and more broadly empowered UN Emergency Force. In June 1967 UNTSO demarcated the cease-fire lines between Israel and Syria, supervised the cease-fire, and oversaw renegotiations for observers along the Suez Canal. UNTSO observers assist other armed peacekeeping operations in the Middle East, such as the UN Interim Force in Lebanon. In March 1996 UNTSO had 178 observers, down from its maximum strength of 572 observers in 1948; 28 have died in service since 1948. UNTSO is headquartered in Jerusalem and has offices in Beirut and Damascus.

See also ARAB–ISRAELI GENERAL ARMISTICE AGREEMENTS (1949).

Bibliography

Burns, E. L. M. *Between Arab and Israeli.* New York: Ivan Obolensky, 1963.

Higgins, Rosalyn. *United Nations Peacekeeping: Documents and Commentary.* 4 vols. New York; Oxford, U.K.: Oxford University Press, 1969–1981.

United Nations. *The Blue Helmets: A Review of United Nations Peace-keeping,* 3d edition. New York: United Nations Deptartment of Public Information, 1996.

CHARLES U. ZENZIE
UPDATED BY NEIL CAPLAN

UNITED STATES OF AMERICA AND THE MIDDLE EAST

The Middle East has been an area of vital interest to the United States since World War II.

Although U.S. interest in the Middle East can be traced to the early years of the American republic, the region has been a principal focus of U.S. foreign policy since World War II. Oil investments and the special U.S. relationship with Israel were the chief reasons for U.S. involvement in that area of confrontation between the United States and the Soviet Union during the Cold War.

U.S.–Middle East Relations

U.S. contacts with the Middle East started in about 1800 in North Africa. U.S. naval forces defeated the Barbary pirates in 1816, but most relations in the nineteenth century were educational and commercial in nature. Protestant missionaries established several schools, medical facilities, and colleges in Egypt, Turkey, Syria, and Lebanon.

In 1919 President Woodrow Wilson sent the King–Crane Commission to inquire into the wishes of the Syrian and Palestinian people as to their political future. In the 1920s and 1930s U.S. oil companies invested heavily in Iran, Iraq, Bahrain, Saudi Arabia, and Kuwait. During World War II, the United States participated in the Allied battles for North Africa and established the Persian Gulf Command to transport lend-lease materials from the Gulf, through Iran, to the Soviet Union. By 1945 several U.S. air bases, supply depots, and transportation facilities were operating throughout the Middle East. From the end of World War II until the collapse of the USSR in the early 1990s, a major objective of U.S. foreign policy was to prevent Soviet penetration of the Middle East. When British political and military commitments in the area diminished, several Middle Eastern countries signed agreements with the United States, and the region became the recipient of the greatest portion of U.S. military and economic aid.

Soviet pressure on Turkey and Iran marked the beginning of the Cold War, and the Truman Doctrine of 1947 represented one of the first efforts in the new "containment" policy to halt Soviet expansion. Responding to feared Soviet encroachments in Greece, Turkey, and Iran, the United States, under the Truman Doctrine, sent $400 million in aid to Greece and Turkey, and helped modernize Turkey's armed forces. U.S. advisers were also sent to Iran.

Founded in 1948 with U.S. support and, by the 1960s, viewed as an important strategic asset, Israel became the largest single recipient of U.S. economic and military assistance. Close ties with Israel were reinforced by humanitarian impulses inspired by knowledge of the Holocaust. The assistance to Israel made it difficult for the United States to establish closer ties with the surrounding Arab nations. During the 1950s Egypt refused to join a Middle East defense organization proposed by the United States, Great Britain, and France. Instead, the Northern Tier or Baghdad Pact, which was based on a military alliance between Turkey, Iraq, Iran, and Pakistan, was devised. The pact was linked with other containment alliances through Turkey's membership in the North Atlantic Treaty Organization in the West and Pakistan's affiliation with the Southeast Asia Treaty Organization in the East.

Efforts by Western countries to keep Soviet influence out of the Middle East were undermined by the events leading up to the Arab–Israel War of 1956. Attempts by the United States to cultivate better relations with Egypt were subverted when the United States refused to provide Egypt with aid to construct the Aswan High Dam; as a consequence, President Gamal Abdel Nasser nationalized the Suez Canal in July 1956. Despite the strain in relations between the two countries, the Eisenhower administration strongly opposed the invasion of Egypt by Britain, France, and Israel in October 1956, and joined the Soviet Union in condemning the attack.

Following the war, unrest throughout the Middle East and the spread of nationalist doctrines that the U.S. government perceived as leftist led in January 1957 to the Eisenhower Doctrine, whereby military and economic assistance was dispensed to the Middle East and the use of U.S. forces was provided to protect countries in the region "against overt aggression from any nation controlled by international Communism." The doctrine was tested in April 1957 when the U.S. Sixth Fleet was sent to the eastern Mediterranean to support Jordan's King Hussein. After the 1958 revolution in Iraq, Lebanon's

U.S. secretary of state Madeleine Albright listened in as Palestinian leader Yasir Arafat talked with President William J. Clinton by telephone from Arafat's office in Gaza in September 1999. Despite initial progress toward final settlement of disputes about Palestine, Clinton's efforts to achieve Camp David Accords of his own in summer 2000 ultimately collapsed and were soon followed by a new and bloody Palestinian uprising against Israel. © REUTERS NEWMEDIA INC./CORBIS. REPRODUCED BY PERMISSION.

President Camille Chamoun also called on the United States for assistance to protect his regime from revolutionary forces, and President Eisenhower responded by sending 14,000 marines. They were withdrawn a few weeks after a truce was arranged, through intervention of the United States, between the various conflicting Lebanese parties.

The United States's efforts to resolve the Arab–Israel dispute during the Eisenhower administration centered on the Arab refugee problem and projects intended to achieve the economic reconstruction of the Middle East through cooperative development of the region's water resources. Although he was successful in achieving a de facto regional water-sharing accord, Eric Johnston, Eisenhower's special representative, failed to obtain agreement for proposals to resettle the refugees. During 1955 and 1956 the United States also joined Britain in a secret operation, code-named "Alpha," which was designed to coerce Egypt and Israel into direct talks. The operation ended in failure when another Eisenhower emissary, Robert Anderson, returned to Washington in March 1956 after a fruitless round of shuttle diplomacy. The Kennedy administration sought to promote good relations with

U.S. deputy secretary of defense Paul Wolfowitz, addressing a pro-Israel rally on 15 April 2002 in front of the U.S. Capitol, expressed President George W. Bush's "solidarity" with Israel. The United States supported the creation of Israel in 1948 and developed closer ties, including large amounts of economic and military aid, beginning in the late 1960s—which in turn often strained its relationship with Arab nations. © AFP/CORBIS. REPRODUCED BY PERMISSION.

"progressive" Middle Eastern countries concerning containment. Kennedy also approved the first U.S. sale of a major weapons system to Israel.

UN Resolutions

After the Arab–Israel War of 1967 between Israel and Egypt, Syria, and Jordan, UN Security Council Resolution 242, drafted with U.S. help, became the basis for U.S. policy in the Arab–Israel conflict. Its requirement that Israeli forces withdraw from territories occupied during the war hinged on the achievement of a comprehensive peace settlement. The Nixon administration's Rogers Plan, which was based on Resolution 242, called for Israel to withdraw to its pre-June 1967 borders (with minor exceptions). After the 1967 war, Egypt and Syria were

rearmed by the Soviet Union, with whom they signed defensive alliances. In 1968, when the British announced their planned withdrawal from the Persian Gulf, the United States decided to build up the military forces of Saudi Arabia and Iran. Ties between Israel and the United States were greatly strengthened after the 1967 war when Israel demonstrated its potential as a strategic ally by shipping great quantities of captured Soviet-made weapons to the United States for close analysis. Ties were also aided by a strong pro-Israel lobby that influenced Congress, the White House, and the media. During the Reagan administration a memorandum of understanding was signed between Israel and the United States calling for cooperation to "deter all threats from the Soviet Union to the region." The pact provided for joint military exercises and working groups for cooperation in development and in the defense trade. In 1987 the U.S. Congress formally designated Israel a "major non-NATO ally." Israel was considered a special case in U.S. efforts to curb the expansion of nuclear powers and was not pressured to join the Nuclear Nonproliferation Treaty.

During the 1973 October War between Israel and Egypt and Syria, U.S.–Soviet relations worsened. Moscow and Washington provided their respective clients with billions of dollars in arms; a threat by the Soviets to send troops to assist Egypt and nuclear alert by the United States brought the two countries to the brink of war. After the outbreak of the war in late October, the Arab oil-producing nations imposed an oil embargo that created an energy crisis in the United States and Western Europe. A peace conference at Geneva in December 1973 broke up after two days without settling the conflict, but Secretary of State Henry Kissinger subsequently initiated step-by-step negotiations that resulted in disengagement agreements between Israel, Syria, and Egypt and provided for Israel's withdrawal from parts of Sinai and the Golan area.

Relations between Egypt and the United States improved after 1973 as Egypt's President Anwar al-Sadat shifted from relying on Soviet aid to being receptive to U.S. influence. Hoping to capitalize on the improved diplomatic climate, President Jimmy Carter attempted to reconvene the Geneva Peace Conference in 1977, but Sadat flew to Jerusalem in November to start direct negotiations with Israel.

U.S. president Jimmy Carter (center) engaged in intensive diplomacy with President Anwar al-Sadat (left) of Egypt and Prime Minister Menachem Begin of Israel in 1978 to bring about the Camp David Accords, for which the two Middle Eastern leaders were awarded the Nobel Peace Prize. The agreement resulted in the Israeli return of the occupied Sinai Peninsula to Egypt and Egyptian recognition of Israel, but it did not lead to an overall settlement of the Arab–Israel conflict. COURTESY OF JIMMY CARTER LIBRARY.

Sadat's dramatic initiative began a new peace process based on direct bilateral contacts between Egypt and Israel. When bitter disagreements between the two adversaries threatened to disrupt negotiations, Carter intervened personally. He invited Sadat and Israel's Prime Minister Menachem Begin to Camp David, where two frameworks for peace were hammered out—one dealing with Egyptian–Israeli relations and the other with the Palestinian issue. Under Carter's guidance, the Camp David Accords were shaped into the Egyptian–Israeli peace treaty that was signed in Washington, D.C., in March 1979. At the Camp David summit Carter persuaded Begin to include establishment of a Palestinian "self-governing au-thority" in the final accords. "Palestinian home-land" and "Palestinian rights" were accepted for the first time as legitimate concepts by the U.S. government.

Elsewhere in the Middle East, Carter's policy of containing Soviet influence in the Persian Gulf was undermined when his close ally Mohammad Reza Pahlavi, the shah of Iran, was overthrown in 1979. The president's efforts to obtain the release of U.S. hostages held by the new revolutionary government in Tehran took over a year to resolve successfully, and this delay was a factor in his loss of the 1980 presidential election.

An American soldier in Baghdad, Iraq, looks for the enemy after a rocket-propelled grenade hit a U.S. Army vehicle, killing three other soldiers and a translator. U.S., British, and other forces rapidly took control of Iraq and ousted Saddam Hussein as its ruler in April 2003, but the occupation was marked by numerous daily attacks on American and coalition troops, as well as civilian supporters and aid workers, which continued after the capture of Saddam in December. © AP/WIDEWORLD PHOTOS. REPRODUCED BY PERMISSION.

Presidents Ronald Reagan and George H. W. Bush continued the containment policies of their predecessors and also became deeply involved in the Arab–Israel conflict. During the Lebanese war in 1982, Reagan sent the Sixth Fleet and the U.S. Marines to Beirut as part of a multinational peacekeeping force. Lebanese militias attacked the marines, inflicting heavy casualties, and the marines were withdrawn soon after. The Reagan plan for Middle East peace envisioned "self-government by the Palestinians . . . in association with Jordan" as the "best chance for a durable, just, and lasting peace." Bush's attempts to continue negotiations based on the Reagan plan and Resolution 242 were stymied until 1991, when the Madrid Conference convened. Cosponsored by the United States and Russia, the new peace process provided for bilateral talks between Israel and Syria, Lebanon, and joint Jordanian–Palestinian delegations. It also included a series of multilateral meetings on such substantive issues as security, environment, economic development, water, and refugees.

President Bush involved the United States in its largest foreign military operation since Vietnam when in 1991 he sent U.S. forces to drive Iraq from Kuwait. From a military perspective, the operation was a success because the United States and the allied forces sustained only minor casualties. Bush was sharply criticized, however, because Iraq's President Saddam Hussein remained in power despite his defeat on the battlefield.

Post–Cold War Policy

When the Soviet Union collapsed in 1991, a new phase of U.S. foreign policy began; containment was no longer the principal objective. Instead, Russia and the United States cooperated in regard to the Middle East. As Soviet influence in the region declined, the United States became the dominant power, and its influence was paramount. This situation greatly facilitated Washington's goal of maintaining the political status quo through its support of friendly regimes. It also made it easier to intervene when U.S. concerns such as assured access to oil and the security of Israel appeared to be threatened.

Initial attempts by President William J. Clinton to resolve the Arab–Israel conflict seemed encouraging, but the failure of an Israeli–Palestinian summit at Camp David in July 2000 contributed to a second Palestinian intifada (uprising) against Israel's occupation of the West Bank and Gaza. By 2003 hostilities degenerated into a low-intensity war between Israel and Palestinians that threatened U.S. policies aimed at maintaining stability in the region through support for the status quo.

An attack by Middle Eastern terrorists destroyed the World Trade Center in New York and severely damaged the Pentagon in Virginia on 11 September 2001, resulting in thousands of casualties. The September attack intensified President George W. Bush's war on terrorism, leading to a U.S.-led attack on Afghanistan. The war in Afghanistan resulted in expulsion of the Taliban government in Kabul and establishment of a new regime allied with the United States. Bush renewed efforts to overthrow Saddam Hussein in 2002 and 2003, charging that he was a threat to international peace and that he had developed weapons of mass destruction in violation of UN Security Council resolutions. U.S. forces were assembled in surrounding countries, and invaded Iraq in March 2003.

See also CAMP DAVID ACCORDS (1978); CAMP DAVID SUMMIT (2000); GULF CRISIS (1990–1991); KING–CRANE COMMISSION (1919); MADRID CONFERENCE (1991); TWIN PILLARS POLICY; WAR IN IRAQ (2003).

Bibliography

Bialer, Uri. *Oil and the Arab–Israeli Conflict, 1948–63.* London: Macmillan, and New York: St. Martin's Press, 1999.

Carter, Jimmy. *The Blood of Abraham.* Boston: Houghton Mifflin, 1985.

Clawson, Patric, and Gedal, Zoe Danon. *Dollars and Diplomacy: The Impact of U.S. Economic Initiatives on Arab–Israeli Negotiations.* Washington, DC: Washington Institute for Near East Policy, 1999.

Cristol, A. J. *The Liberty Incident: The 1967 Israeli Attack on the U.S. Navy Spy Ship.* Washington, DC: Brassey's, 2002.

Davidson, Lawrence. *America's Palestine: Popular and Official Perceptions from Balfour to Israeli Statehood.* Gainesville: University Press of Florida, 2001.

Gerges, Fawaz A. *America and Political Islam: Clash of Cultures or Clash of Interests?* Cambridge, U.K.: Cambridge University Press, 1999.

Hart, Parker T. *Saudi Arabia and the United States: Birth of a Security Partnership.* Bloomington: Indiana University Press, 1999.

Obenzinger, Hilton. *American Palestine: Melville, Twain and the Holy Land Mania.* Princeton, NJ: Princeton University Press, 1999.

Quandt, William B. *Peace Process: American Diplomacy and the Arab–Israeli Conflict,* revised edition. Washington, DC: Brookings Institution Press; Los Angeles: University of California Press, 2001.

Sick, Gary. *All Fall Down: America's Tragic Encounter with Iran.* New York: Penguin Books, 1985.

Spiegel, Steven. *The Other Arab–Israeli Conflict: Making America's Middle East Policy, from Truman to Reagan.* Chicago: University of Chicago Press, 1985.

Stein, Kenneth W. *Heroic Diplomacy: Sadat, Kissinger, Carter, Begin and the Quest for Arab–Israeli Peace.* New York: Routledge, 1999.

Telhami, Shibley. *The Stakes: America and the Middle East.* Boulder, CO: Westview Press, 2002.

Touval, Saadia. *The Peace Brokers: Mediators in the Arab–Israeli Conflict, 1948–1979.* Princeton, NJ: Princeton University Press, 1982.

DON PERETZ

UNITY PARTY

Turkish political party, active in the 1960s and 1970s.

The Unity party came to be identified with the Shiʿite Alevi minority community. It changed its name to the Turkish Unity party in November of 1971, perhaps to overcome this image. With the outlawing of the Turkish Workers Party, eight of its former members were allowed to run as independents on the Unity party's election list in 1973, giving it a distinct leftist inclination. It polled only 1 percent of the vote and gained only one seat, however, compared to nearly 3 percent and eight seats in 1969. In 1977 it did even less well, failing to win any seats at all.

See also ALEVI; TURKISH WORKERS PARTY.

Bibliography

Weiker, Walter F. *The Modernization of Turkey: From Ataturk to the Present Day.* New York: Holmes and Meier, 1981.

FRANK TACHAU

UNIVERSITY OF JORDAN

The main public university in Jordan.

The University of Jordan was established in 1962 on a picturesque hillside in the western outskirts of Amman that formerly was the site of an agricultural research station. The university comprises eighteen faculties, including arts, sciences, economics and commerce, *shariʿa* (Islamic law), medical sciences (including general medicine, nursing, and pharmacy), education, agriculture, engineering and technology, law, and physical education, and as of 2003 boasted 961 faculty members. It awards both undergraduate and graduate diplomas, and also has a teaching hospital. As with all public universities in Jordan, students pay nominal tuition and are able to buy books and materials at subsidized prices. In 2003, the university student population stood at 25,000, eighty-eight percent of which came from Jordan.

Bibliography

Gubser, Peter. *Jordan: Crossroads of Middle Eastern Events.* Boulder, CO: Westview, 1983.

JENAB TUTUNJI
UPDATED BY MICHAEL R. FISCHBACH

UNIVERSITY OF KHARTOUM

A Sudanese institution established in 1902.

Horatio Herbert Kitchener, Lord Kitchener of Khartoum, established the Gordon Memorial College in the memory of the British general Charles George Gordon, who died at Khartoum in 1885, to establish a formal seat of learning in the Sudan. Kitchener opened the college on 8 November 1902. During the first half of the twentieth century, Gordon Memorial College was transformed from a secondary school to a college with a more sophisticated curriculum and a more renowned faculty. Most graduates during these years became civil servants in the British administration of the Sudan.

Its function as a vocational training institute was substantively changed when the college was affiliated with London University in 1945 to grant equivalent degrees; in 1951 the Gordon Memorial College and Kitchener School of Medicine were combined to create the University College of Khartoum. Upon Sudan's independence in 1956 the University College abandoned its connections with the University of London to become the University of Khartoum. Since then it has expanded to include numerous research institutes and a variety of schools.

As the campus lies in the heart of Khartoum, the university's faculty, staff, and particularly its students have played a significant role in the political life of Sudan. Its graduates organized and led the Graduates' General Congress in 1938, which played a dynamic role in the evolution of Sudanese nationalism and in Sudan's governments after independence. After the coup d'état of 30 June 1989 by Umar Hasan Ahmad al-Bashir, the National Islamic Front (NIF) government reoriented the university's curriculum and purged the Western-educated Sudanese and expatriate faculty, replacing them with instructors more suitable to the NIF's Islamist ideology. At the same time the government launched a dramatic expansion of the university, so that in 2002 there were 17,000 undergraduates, 6,000 graduate students, and an academic staff of more than 1,000.

Bibliography

Beshir, Mohamed Omer. *Educational Development in the Sudan, 1898–1956.* Oxford, U.K.: Clarendon Press, 1969.

ROBERT O. COLLINS

UNIVERSITY OF TEHRAN

The first modern university in Iran.

In May 1934, the Majles (national assembly) passed a law to incorporate five existing public colleges as a new University of Tehran. The original faculties included law, literature, medicine, science, and technology (engineering). Reza Shah Pahlavi officially inaugurated the University of Tehran in February 1935 by laying the foundation stone for its campus in an area northwest of the then new administrative and commercial district. Subsequently, faculties of agriculture, fine arts, and theology were added, as well as a printing press and a central library.

In 1943, the university became independent of the ministry of education and a board of directors was organized. Elected by the faculty, the new governing body also elected the dean. This independence was undermined after 1953, when the election of the dean became a formality, since the new dean had to be approved by the shah. By the late 1960s, the shah was making appointments from among politicians instead of academics, further undermining the university's academic integrity. These efforts at political control, however, did not prevent the University of Tehran from becoming the nurturing ground for all the opposition movements against Mohammad Reza Shah Pahlavi's regime, including the opposition that eventually led to the Iranian Revolution (1979).

The 1979 revolution and the Iran–Iraq War slowed the development of the university, but since 1989 it has continued to develop and expand, adding several new faculties and institutes. Despite the establishment of other universities in both Tehran and other Iranian cities, the University of Tehran has an unrivaled reputation in the country for academic excellence. During the early 2000s, the annual enrollment was about 30,000 students, over 60 percent of whom were female; the faculty exceeded 1,500. The administration of the university is still based on the pattern established during the previous regime.

See also IRANIAN REVOLUTION (1979); IRAN–IRAQ WAR (1980–1988); PAHLAVI, MOHAMMAD REZA; PAHLAVI, REZA.

Bibliography

Banani, Amin. "Educational Reforms." In *The Moderniza-tion of Iran, 1921–1941.* Stanford, CA: Stanford University Press, 1961.

MANSOUREH ETTEHADIEH
UPDATED BY ERIC HOOGLUND

UQBI, TAYYIB AL-
[1888–1960]

Prominent member of the Algerian Association of Reformist Ulama.

Born near Biskra in Algeria, Tayyib al-Uqbi (also Tayeb el-Okbi) studied in Medina and was influenced by the Muwahhidun movement of Islam. He was known as an eloquent and controversial Islamic scholar. In 1936 al-Uqbi was accused of planning the murder of the *mufti* (canon lawyer) of Algiers but was acquitted in 1939. Al-Uqbi criticized Shaykh Abd al-Hamid Ben Badis's political involvements and left the association in 1938; he preferred discussion of religious and spiritual questions as disclosed by his journal, al-Islah.

See also MUWAHHIDUN.

Bibliography

Naylor, Phillip C., and Heggoy, Alf. *Historical Dictionary of Algeria,* 2d edition. Metuchen, NJ: Scarecrow Press, 1994.

PHILLIP C. NAYLOR

URABI, AHMAD
[1841–1911]

Egyptian nationalist leader and army officer.

Ahmad Urabi, the son of a village shaykh of Iraqi Arab origin, studied for two years at al-Azhar in Cairo and then entered the Cairo military academy at the behest of Sa'id Pasha in 1854/55 and soon earned his commission. After the deposition of Khedive Isma'il in 1879, he is said to have supported the emerging National Party of Egypt, but his first proven act was to represent a group of discontented ethnic Egyptian officers who were protesting against the favoritism shown to Turkish and Circassian officers by War Minister Uthman Rifqi. Khedive Taw-fiq and Prime Minister Riyadh intended to dismiss Urabi and his group for insubordination, but other Egyptian officers seized control of the war office and rescued Urabi in February 1881. Subsequently, the khedive agreed to replace Rifqi with Mahmud Sami al-Barudi as war minister. On 9 September fearing a khedival counterplot, the Egyptian officers surrounded Abdin Palace, confronted Tawfiq, and obliged him to set up a constitutionalist government with Muhammad Sharif as prime minister and to increase the size of the Egyptian army.

As Britain and especially France—concerned about the safety of the Suez Canal, their investments, and their citizens in Egypt—became increasingly hostile to the Urabist movement, the Nationalists replaced Premier Sharif with Mahmud Sami al-Barudi in February 1882, and Urabi became war minister. The Nationalists continued to fear a khedival counterplot and took steps to weaken the Turks and Circassians within the officer corps, also stirring up popular feeling against the European powers. Riots broke out in Alexandria in June 1882, and many European residents fled. Britain and France threatened military intervention to support the khedive (whose relationship with the Nationalists seems to have been ambivalent) and to protect their citizens. They demanded that the Egyptian army remove all fortifications from Alexandria, and, when Urabi did not comply quickly enough, British ships began bombarding them, leading to the outbreak of fires in Alexandria. British troops (unaided by France, which had withdrawn because of a ministerial crisis) landed at Alexandria and later at Isma'ilia to restore order. Urabi and the Egyptian army continued to resist the British, even after the khedive had gone over to their side, until their crushing defeat at al-Tall al-Kabir on 13 September 1882. Once the British entered Cairo, Urabi surrendered, was put on trial for treason against the khedive, but was not executed. He was exiled to Ceylon—until he was allowed by Khedive Abbas Hilmi II to return in 1901. He played no part in the later National party of Mustafa Kamil, died in obscurity, and was generally scorned by educated Egyptians until the 1952 revolution. Since then he has been rehabilitated by Gamal Abdel Nasser and his fellow officers—whose occupational and class backgrounds paralleled his own. Now he is generally considered a patriot who resisted the British, the khedive, and the aristocracy in favor of constitutional government and the welfare of Egypt's common people.

His writings include *Kashf al-Sitar an Sirr al-Asrar*, published in two volumes (Cairo, 1925).

Bibliography

Baring, Evelyn, Earl of Cromer. *Modern Egypt*. London: Macmillan, 1908; reprint, London and New York: Routledge, 2000.

Blunt, Wilfrid S. *Secret History of the English Occupation of Egypt*. London: Unwin, 1907.

Mayer, Thomas. *The Changing Past: Egyptian Historiography of the Urabi Revolt, 1882–1983*. Gainesville: University of Florida Press, 1988.

Schölch, Alexander. *Egypt for the Egyptians! The Socio-Political Crisis in Egypt, 1878–1882*. London: Ithaca Press, 1981.

ARTHUR GOLDSCHMIDT

URBANIZATION

The growth of cities and the social and physical transformations arising from this phenomenon.

The Middle East is home to the world's first cities as well as some of its most notable ones. The first cities, which developed in southern Mesopotamia (now in Iraq) about 3500 B.C.E., had small populations by modern standards—not exceeding about 20,000 inhabitants. By 3000 B.C.E. cities also grew along the Nile in Egypt. From these early centers, urban life spread throughout the world.

Until about 1800 most of the great cities such as Babylon, Alexandria, Ctesiphon, Constantinople (now Istanbul), Baghdad, and Cairo could grow large because they had access to water transport and income from an imperial tax base. Industry and trade were the main sources of income for smaller cities, including Tyre, Sidon, Beirut, Carthage, Tabriz, Palmyra, and Mecca. The development of some cities was heavily influenced by their religious significance; these include Jerusalem, Karbala, Mashhad, Mecca, Medina, and Qom. The proportion of the total population living in cities in what became known as the Middle East seldom exceeded 15 percent before the nineteenth century.

New factors contributed to the growth of cities after 1800, including modern transportation, new trade patterns, and European penetration. Following World War I and the fall of the Ottoman Empire, nationalist regimes were established, first in Iran and Turkey, later in Iraq, Jordan, and Syria. These focused development inward. East of Libya, the capitals of the large countries are all inland (Ankara, Cairo, Damascus, Baghdad, Riyadh, San'a, Tehran) and since their development policies were statist, these cities expanded. After World War II, rail and road networks that centered on the capitals were extended, facilitating migration to them. At the same time, rapid rural population growth and the mechanization of agriculture, largely implemented after 1945, pushed farmers from the land. Millions of people in the region moved to cities in search of jobs, education, and other services.

Israel was established in 1948 after a period of conflict, and its urban growth—mainly Tel Aviv and Haifa—was fueled by an influx of Jewish immigrants. Palestinians left or were expelled by Israeli forces in 1948, swelling cities in neighboring countries including Lebanon (Tyre, Sidon, and Beirut), Jordan (Amman), and Kuwait, as well as the territories of the West Bank and the Gaza Strip.

Oil boomtowns (Abadan, Abu Dhabi, Dhahran, Kuwait City) grew rapidly for short periods, but they never became as large as the major political and commercial centers. In the larger countries (Algeria, Egypt, Iran, Morocco, Turkey) close to 50 percent of the population was urban by the mid-1990s. In some of the smaller countries (Israel, Lebanon, Kuwait, the United Arab Emirates) the proportion is as high as 90 percent.

See also URBAN PLANNING.

Bibliography

Blake, G. H., and Lawless, R. I., eds. *The Changing Middle Eastern City*. New York: Barnes & Noble; London: Croom Helm, 1980.

Bonine, Michael, ed. *Population, Poverty, and Politics in Middle East Cities*. Gainesville: University Press of Florida, 1997.

Brown, L. Carl, ed. *From Madina to Metropolis: Heritage and Change in the Near Eastern City*. Princeton, NJ: Darwin Press, 1973.

Saqqaf, Abdulaziz Y., ed. *The Middle East City: Ancient Traditions Confront a Modern World.* New York: Paragon House, 1987.

JOHN R. CLARK
UPDATED BY ANTHONY B. TOTH

URBAN PLANNING

Effect on city organization of colonialism and petroleum wealth.

In the modern period two major influences have shaped contemporary urban planning in the Middle East: colonialism and petroleum. These two influences, and a host of other minor factors, have had different roles during three phases of constructing urban landscapes: the colonial period (c. 1800–1945), a transitional period (c. 1945–1972), and the oil-boom era (post-1972). Within these three stages, urban planning has shifted from being primarily involved in physical planning and urban design to integrating socioeconomic and physical planning.

The Colonial Period (1800–1945)

Although not all countries in the Middle East were colonized at the same time or in the same pattern, a common thread connects the urban-planning process. Europeans used urban planning successfully to establish and maintain the colonial extractive system. Physical segregation was the main tool used in implementing this policy. Urban planning in this period was dominated by physical land-use planning and urban design, which chiefly concerned the arrangement of urban infrastructure and land use. The colonial use of physical planning established and maintained a trading network and facilitated a suitable living environment for European colonial administrators, workers, and their households.

European colonialists built port cities to collect and ship goods (for example, Aden, Casablanca, Tunis, Suez, Hormuz, and Port Saʿid). They also built interior towns to serve as military centers, local administrative capitals, or collection points for regional resources, and they built infrastructure, such as roads and railways, to connect interior cities to ports. This trade-related settlement system became the new colonial urban hierarchy that is still common all over the Middle East.

Urban planning then played its second major role in this period by maintaining and servicing the influx of European military personnel, administrators, businesspeople, settlers, and fortune seekers. Planning was utilized to build the segregated city, in which a European, upper-class quarter was separated from the rest of the city. French Morocco offers the most vivid example of this kind of city planning: European quarters were built separate from the old medinas; important urban cultural sites were preserved; and the European part of the city utilized the most up-to-date urban-planning techniques. Similar practices were followed in Algeria, Tunisia, Libya, and Egypt. These urban plans segregated Europeans, along with some local resident minority groups (such as Coptic Christians and Jews) and a small community of the native rich, from the indigenous population, resulting in a dual city. A parallel but noninstitutionalized development in Palestine was the building of Tel Aviv as a Jewish city adjacent to Arab Jaffa.

In the dual city, a disproportionate share of the urban revenue was spent on the European quarters, even though taxes were raised mostly from the native quarters. As a result, the European neighborhoods had large residential plots, low densities of population, and broad tree-lined roads and streets. They were also better connected to urban amenities like water, electricity, and sewage facilities. These low-density residential quarters with their superior facilities and other urban benefits provided healthier environments for their residents. In addition, they provided the Europeans with a culturally familiar environment, making them more interested in working in colonies and thus maintaining the colonial system.

In countries where local rulers had more autonomy or colonialism was not officially present, rulers tried to copy European styles of design and urban planning. In Egypt before British control began in 1882, Khedive Ismaʿil (r. 1863–1879), influenced by his visit to Paris, tried to follow for Cairo the urban plans of Baron Georges-Eugène Haussmann. Later, in Iran, Reza Pahlavi Shah (r. 1925–1941) promoted a grid design for Tehran and constructed wide avenues through the old quarters of the city, and a "modern" city along the lines of the European model was built in north Tehran, where the rich began to reside. It was thought that copying Western urban form would lead to modernization, but the end result was the growth of dual cities similar to those that developed in colonized countries. Indeed, the internal structure of most Middle Eastern cities still can be traced back to this period.

The Transitional Period (1945–1972)

Urban planing assumed a lesser role in the Middle East during this politically active period. Since most of the countries in this region either had just become politically independent or were in the process of becoming so, urban planning was less important than ongoing political struggles and social movements. In the immediate postcolonial period, a spontaneous population movement occurred within some major Middle Eastern cities. In particular, the space formerly occupied by Europeans was taken over by the indigenous elites. In countries such as Morocco and Tunisia, this transition occurred in a peaceful and orderly fashion, but in a few countries, most notably Algeria, the rapid exodus of foreign settlers resulted in more diverse economic classes taking over the quarters formerly occupied by colonialists. Nevertheless, most Middle Eastern cities maintained their dual character.

Major concerns for urban planners were to provide housing for new migrants from rural areas and to bridge the gap between the former European and traditional quarters. To consolidate power, new rulers provided various social groups with land, housing, and urban amenities in return for their political support. In Israel, for example, the Labor Party provided temporary housing in the 1950s for Jews immigrating from postwar Europe and from other areas of the Middle East. Later, these immigrants were resettled in new urban neighborhoods and in newly established development towns in less populous areas.

Urban planning also began to develop in a new direction, emphasizing company-town building, master-plan technique, and economic development. This aspect was particularly evident in the Persian Gulf states of Iran, Iraq, Kuwait, Qatar, and Saudi Arabia. The steady growth of oil revenues beginning in the late 1950s encouraged governments to devise long-term economic development plans or to invest in industrial projects. These policies had a major impact on developing urban planning into an integrated physical-economic approach.

U.S. and British oil companies also established company towns for their workers. The Arabian-American Oil Company (ARAMCO), for example, used Western planners and engineers to lay out company towns such as Dhahran and Abqaiq using a system of blocks with a grid pattern. Similarly in Iran, British planners modeled the city of Abadan on the landscape of suburban England. Middle Eastern countries depended on the West for qualified planners and consultants to carry out urban planning. Consequently, a planning technique then common in the West, the master plan, was imported to the Middle East and soon became ubiquitous throughout the region. Most plans were end-state master plans, in that the ultimate look of the city in the future was already predetermined. Most plans were also unclear about the process of city planning or procedures for implementation. Additionally, the plans were usually static and design-oriented, with little consideration for the social and economic needs of the majority. Although very few master plans actually were implemented, the process of designing master plans proved to be a positive development for urban planning.

The Oil-Boom Era (1973 to the Present)

In the 1970s the role of urban planning underwent a rapid transformation, particularly in the oil-producing countries, where the rise in oil revenues enabled governments to embark on a variety of grandiose urban projects. A major focus was on comprehensive planning, which involved the private sector and considered spatial development concerns. The construction of new towns absorbed considerable investment. Three major goals prompted the building of new towns: to relieve the population pressures on the major cities by drawing migrants away from already overcrowded cities; to accommodate the growing population of industrial workers and to facilitate industrialization; and to accommodate military bases throughout the region. Primarily, Western firms have undertaken the planning of these new towns, especially those in oil-rich countries. Although efforts to incorporate aspects of indigenous culture into the design of these towns have been made, such efforts have not been fully successful. Most of these towns have used zoning to isolate economic activities, in contrast with the mixed-use tradition in the region, and their layouts are designed for the use of the automobile.

With the oil wealth–fueled economic growth of the Persian Gulf countries serving as a catalyst, the rejection of end-state master plans soon became common all over the Middle East in favor of new city plans that give more consideration to social and economic factors. In addition, the new plans were integrated into broader regional and national planning strategies based on large urban centers in such countries as Egypt, Iran, Morocco, and Saudi Arabia. The new dynamic style of planning is also evident in the use of Integrated Urban Development Projects (IUDPs) among local planners and planning consultants. The emphasis of IUDPs is on the sectoral and spatial integration of projects, operating alongside, although often effectively replacing, comprehensive master planning. For example, the IUDP for Baghdad consisted of three integrated plans for central Iraq, greater Baghdad, and Baghdad the city. Three models—urban corridors, growth poles, and dispersed settlements—were used to develop comprehensive alternative strategies based on future scenarios. After evaluating the scenarios, a hybrid of all three models applicable to Iraq's needs was adopted.

Although the focus of making plans had changed, the tools for implementing them remained inadequate in most Middle Eastern countries. The reasons include a lack of cooperation among decision makers, a lack of enforcement legislation, and the conflict between the beautification and modernization of the city and the meeting of basic needs of the inhabitants. Thus, urban planning in the Middle East still is grappling with numerous problems. One major issue in large cities of oil-rich countries is how to allocate resources between immigrants and the native population. These immigrants, often from other Middle Eastern countries, are not granted citizenship or the right to own property, placing a heavy burden on the rental markets. In addition, a new form of segregation is taking place: Housing estates are planned so as to minimize contact between immigrants and the indigenous population. For example, in the new towns of Jubail (Saudi Arabia) and Umm Said (Qatar), dormitory-style housing for single expatriate workers secludes them from the native population.

Perhaps the most important issue for city planning is rapid population growth and urbanization. At approximately 3 percent per annum, the region's population growth rate is higher than the figure for any other world region with the exception of sub-Saharan Africa. The urbanization rate, at more than 4.5 percent for most countries in the Middle East, is also among the fastest in the developing world. Most large cities of the region suffer from overcrowding; squatter settlements; housing shortages; poverty; unemployment; lack of adequate urban infrastructure, services, and amenities; and escalating environmental degradation, including unbearable pollution. These and other urban problems are placing increasing stress on the budgets, resources, and planning capacities of municipal governments, forcing planners and policy makers to seek new ways of managing urban growth. In fact, this need to cope with many intertwined urban problems often has led to planning being used as a tool to anticipate future problems and merely manage current ones, rather than solve them. A more preventive approach to urban planning must take the place of the existing curative approach.

See also ARCHITECTURE; COLONIALISM; URBANIZATION.

Bibliography

Abu-Lughod, Janet L. "Moroccan Urbanization: Some New Questions." In *Development of Urban Systems in Africa,* edited by R. A. Obudho and Salah El-Shakhs. New York: Praeger Publishers, 1979.

Amirahmadi, Hooshang. "Regional Planning in Iran: A Survey of Problems and Policies." *Journal of Developing Areas* 20, no. 4 (1987): 501–530.

Amirahmadi, Hooshang, and El-Shakhs, Salah S., eds. *Urban Development in the Muslim World.* New Brunswick, NJ: Center for Urban Policy Research, 1993.

Brown, Kenneth, et al., eds. *Middle Eastern Cities in Comparative Perspective: Points de vue sur les villes du Maghreb et du Machrek: Franco-British Symposium, London 10–14 May 1984.* Atlantic Highlands, NJ; London: Ithaca Press, 1986.

Denither, Jean. "Evolution of Concepts of Housing, Urbanism, and Country Planning in a Developing Country: Morocco, 1900–1972." In *From Madina to Metropolis: Heritage and Change in the Near Eastern City,* edited by L. Carl Brown. Princeton, NJ: Darwin Press, 1973.

Zaim, Sabahaddin. "Urbanization Trends in Turkey."
In *The Middle East City: Ancient Traditions Confront a Modern World*, edited by Abdulaziz Y. Saqqaf. New York: Paragon, 1987.

HOOSHANG AMIRAHMADI
UPDATED BY ERIC HOOGLUND

URF

See GLOSSARY

URWA AL-WUTHQA, AL-

Anti-British Muslim newspaper.

Edited from Paris by Jamal al-Din al-Afghani and Muhammad Abduh, *al-Urwa al-Wuthqa* was published between March and October 1884. The title, meaning "the firmest bond," alludes to the Qurʾan; it had been used by Afghani in 1883 to refer to the pan-Islamic caliphate of the Ottoman sultan. After eighteen issues had appeared in 1884, the paper suddenly ceased publication, probably owing to lack of funds. (The closing is usually atributed to the British banning the paper from entering India and Egypt, but since it was distributed free throughout the Muslim world, this measure should not have stopped it.) The financing of *al-Urwa al-Wuthqa* is unclear, although documents suggest that a Tunisian general, probably Wilfrid Blunt, and possibly the former Egyptian Khedive Ismaʿil were involved. Subsidization afforded wide distribution, which helped to enhance the reputation of the paper and its editors.

Most of the political articles in the paper championed the struggle against British imperialism in Muslim lands. The more theoretical articles were mainly devoted to an activist reinterpretation of Islamic ideas and to a call for unity among Muslims. *Al-Urwa al-Wuthqa*, which contributed to the fame of its editors in the Muslim world, was the first forum in which Afghani stressed Muslim unity, or pan-Islam, the ideology with which he is most associated.

See also ABDUH, MUHAMMAD; AFGHANI, JAMAL AL-DIN AL-.

NIKKI KEDDIE

UŞAKLIĞIL, HALIT ZIYA
[c. 1866–1945]

Turkish novelist, journalist, and poet.

Halit Ziya Uşakliğil was born in Istanbul, the son of a businessman from a prestigious İzmir family. When he was fourteen years old, the family returned to İzmir, where in 1884 he published the city's first daily newspaper, *Nevruz*. He started up other İzmir newspapers while working in Istanbul as a French teacher and bank employee. In the 1890s, he became active in the Servet-i Fünun (Wealth of Knowledge) literary movement and began writing novels. In 1909, he became a professor of literary history and aesthetics at Istanbul University.

Uşakliğil is considered a top Turkish novelist who bridged the nineteenth-century Tanzimat (reform) and twentieth-century republican periods, combining the complex storylines and heightened rhetoric of the former period with the cosmopolitan tastes and psychological realism of the later one. In the 1920s, he turned from novels to other forms, particularly short stories, and published about two hundred. He also published poetry, several plays, literary studies, and memoirs.

Bibliography

Mitler, Louis. *Ottoman Turkish Writers: A Bibliographical Dictionary of Significant Figures in Pre-Republican Turkish Literature.* New York: P. Lang, 1988.

ELIZABETH THOMPSON

ÜSKÜDAR

The oldest and largest district of Asian Istanbul.

Situated across the Bosporus from the walled city of Constantinople, Üsküdar was called Chrysopolis in ancient times and Scutari in the Byzantine era. In the period of Ottoman rule, Üsküdar became more integrated into the life of the capital city, as it became the center of several dervish orders and tekkes, military barracks, and, in the nineteenth century, textile and other factories. In the 1860s, it was formally incorporated into the municipal government of Constantinople (now Istanbul). It was in Üsküdar that Florence Nightingale set up her famed hospital during the Crimean War (1853–1856). And in the late nineteenth century, Russian Turks established the first center of Turkic studies in the empire in an Üsküdar *tekke*. The district, known for its fine gardens, in recent years has become a large residential quarter of the city with a population over 200,000.

See also TEKKE.

Bibliography

Shaw, Stanford J., and Shaw, Ezel Kural. *History of the Ottoman Empire and Modern Turkey*, Vol. 2: *Reform, Revolution, and Republic: The Rise of Modern Turkey, 1808–1975*. Cambridge, U.K., and New York: Cambridge University Press, 1977.

ELIZABETH THOMPSON

USS *COLE*

See COLE, USS

USSISHKIN, MENAHEM
[1863–1941]

Zionist leader.

Menahem Ussishkin, engineer and leader of the Russian-based Zionist movement Hibbat Zion, was a spokesman for a practical Zionism favoring land settlement, diaspora activities to aid distressed communities, and cultural autonomy, even after the World Zionist Organization insisted on suspending such actions until a political charter recognizing Jewish national rights in Palestine was secured. Ussishkin replaced Chaim Weizmann as head of the short-lived Zionist Commission after the end of World War I and later served as chairman of the Jewish National Fund until his death in 1941. A fervent advocate of expanding Jewish land ownership as a tool for strengthening Zionism's political claims, he was equally passionate about reviving Hebrew as a spoken language and expanding educational institutions in Palestine.

See also HIBBAT ZION.

Bibliography

Luz, Ehud. *Parallels Meet: Religion and Nationalism in the Early Zionist Movement (1882–1904)*. Philadelphia: Jewish Publication Society, 1988.

DONNA ROBINSON DIVINE

USS *LIBERTY*

See LIBERTY, USS

U.S.S.R.

See RUSSIA AND THE MIDDLE EAST

USTADH

See GLOSSARY

USULI

Philosophy of Islamic law.

The Usuli school of Shi'ite jurisprudence, developed in contrast to the Akhbari (traditionalist) school, argues for the primacy of the *ulama* as interpreters of Islamic law and prophetic and imami traditions. The Usulis favor the legitimacy of reasoning (*aql*) and interpretation (*ijtihad*) of traditions of the Prophet and the imams as sources for the derivation of Islamic law. Thus, they allow for the emulation of prominent Shi'ite *ulama* by the believers, who are incapable themselves of interpreting the Qur'an or the teachings of the Prophet and the imams. In addition, the Usulis believe in critical readings of the contents of major Shi'ite compilations of prophetic and imami traditions. They also prohibit the emulation of past masters of religion, so that the centrality of living *ulama* as interpreters of Shi'ite jurisprudence is preserved. Rivalry between the two schools heightened in the Safavid period, with the Usulis emerging as the ultimate victors by the eighteenth century.

Shi'ite *ulama* were able to play a prominent role in the constitutional movement of Iran (1905–1911), drawing on elements of Usuli thought to justify both the ratification of the constitution and the participation of clergymen in political affairs. The evolution of the Usuli doctrine of a hierarchical clerical establishment made for the creation of clerical ranks such as *hujjat al-islam, ayatollah*, and the *marja al-taqlid* (source of emulation) in contemporary Shi'ism. In addition, Usuli discourse made for the legitimation of the doctrine of *velayat-e faqih*, or governance of the jurisconsult, in post-1979 Iran.

See also SHI'ISM.

Bibliography

Amanat, Abbas. "In Between the Madrasah and the Marketplace: The Designation of Clerical Leadership in Modern Shi'ism." In *Authority and Political Culture in Shi'ism*, edited by S. A. Arjomand. Albany: State University of New York Press, 1988.

Hairi, Abdolhadi. *Shi'ism and Constitutionalism in Iran*. Leiden, Netherlands: Brill, 1977.

Newman, Andrew J. "The Nature of the Akhbari/Usuli Dispute in Late Safawid Iran." *Bulletin of the School of Oriental and African Studies* 55, 1–2 (1990): 22–51; 250–261.

NEGUIN YAVARI

UTAYBA TRIBE

See TRIBES AND TRIBALISM: UTAYBA TRIBE

UTAYBI, JUHAYMAN AL-

[c. 1940–1980]

Saudi ideologue and leader of the Mecca insurrection, 1979.

Utaybi was born in a bedouin settlement at Qasim in central Saudi Arabia. It is unclear whether he received any formal education during his childhood. Utaybi served in the National Guards for about eighteen years, and toward the end of this period he studied at the Islamic University in Medina.

The year 1974 seems to have marked Utaybi's break with formal state institutions. The circumstances under which he left the National Guards are unknown; his departure from the university resulted from his disagreement with his teachers' applied interpretation of Islamic law in relation to the Saudi regime. He began a period of self-education and preaching, drawing a circle of followers. His first *risala* (treatise), "Al-imara wa al-bay'a wa al-ta'a" (Rulership, allegiance, and obedience), appeared in 1974. Utaybi was arrested with ninety-eight others in 1978; all were released without trial.

At least eleven *risalas* by Utaybi were printed between 1974 and 1979. His writings combined a strict application of the Wahhabi (Muwahhidun) doctrine with widely accepted traditions having a messianic dimension. He accused the Saudi rulers of doctrinal deviation, greed, and corruption. He also accused the religious establishment of complicity and preached that it was the duty of Muslims to combat the evils of the regime.

Utaybi anticipated that the regime would pursue and persecute its puritan opponents, whose sole and ultimate refuge would be the Ka'ba (the holy shrine inside the Grand Mosque at Mecca). There, the *mahdi's* (messiah's) appearance would be established, armed resistance would start, and the Muslims would be victorious in the Arabian Peninsula and beyond. On 22 November 1979 Utaybi led a heavily armed group, estimated at between 500 and 2,000, who seized the Ka'ba. They were ousted two weeks later. For their crime, Utaybi and sixty-two others were beheaded on 9 January 1980.

See also IKHWAN; MUWAHHIDUN.

Bibliography

Kechichian, Joseph. "Islamic Revivalism and Change in Saudi Arabia: Juhayman al-Utaybi's 'Letters' to the Saudi People." *Muslim World* 80, no. 1 (1990): 1–16.

ABDEL AZIZ EZZELARAB
UPDATED BY ERIC HOOGLUND

UTHMAN, MUHAMMAD ALI

[c. 1908–1973]

North Yemen political leader.

Muhammad Ali Uthman was a Yemeni nationalist and republican, a strong supporter of both the 1962 revolution that resulted in the Yemen Arab Republic (YAP) and the 1967 coup that replaced the al-Sallal regime with that of Qadi Abd al-Rahman al-Iryani. He was a member of the Republican Council, the plural executive created by the al-Iryani regime, from 1967 until his assassination in 1973. His murder, the result of a local dispute, was at the time attributed wrongly to leftist dissidents supported by the revolutionary regime in South Yemen; it was seized upon by the government as an excuse to crack down on leftists. Uthman was a traditional local notable and landowner, and a Sunni Muslim of the Shafi'i sect, with much influence in part of the Hujariyya, Jabal Sabr, and the lower elevations south of Ta'iz City. He is memorialized in a very good English-language school in Ta'iz (grades I through 12), which was named after him shortly after his death.

See also PEOPLE'S DEMOCRATIC REPUBLIC OF YEMEN; TA'IZ; YEMEN; YEMEN ARAB REPUBLIC.

Bibliography

Bidwell, Robin. *The Two Yemens.* Boulder, CO: Westview; Harlow, U.K.: Longman, 1983.

ROBERT D. BURROWES

UTHMAN, UTHMAN AHMAD
[1917–1999]

Egyptian civil engineer, construction magnate, and cabinet minister.

Born in Isma'iliyya and educated at Cairo University, Uthman Ahmad Uthman founded a civil engineering company soon after graduation instead of entering government service. But he quickly discovered that the booming oil industry in Saudi Arabia offered him better opportunities for advancement than did Egypt. His construction firm, the Arab Contractors, founded in 1940, expanded until it was able to bid on multimillion-dollar projects in the United Arab Emirates (then called Trucial Oman), Iraq, Kuwait, and Libya. Although his company was sequestered by Gamal Abdel Nasser in 1961, Uthman remained in control and played a major role in constructing the Aswan High Dam.

He became highly visible in Egyptian public life during the period of the Infitah policy of Anwar al-Sadat, building a new bridge across the Nile River and various traffic flyways in downtown Cairo. His firm also deepened the Suez Canal and built the Dhahran International Airport, the Kuwait Municipal Building, the Benghazi (Libya) sewer system, the Kirkuk (Iraq) feeder canal, and a first-class hotel in Khartoum (Sudan). He became minister for reconstruction in 1973, adding housing to his portfolio in 1974. His son married one of Sadat's daughters.

During the Sadat era, Uthman accumulated power and wealth in ways that aroused widespread suspicion, in part by being both a minister who could issue tenders on contracts and a contractor who could bid on them. Under Husni Mubarak he became vulnerable to criticism by journalists, the Engineers' Syndicate, and even his son, but his firm has remained prominent in Egypt, other Arab states, and other African countries. Although he was a fervent advocate of free-enterprise capitalism, Uthman's personal success depended on his political connections as much as on his intelligence and hard work.

See also ASWAN HIGH DAM; INFITAH.

Bibliography

Baker, Raymond William. *Sadat and After: Struggles for Egypt's Political Soul.* Cambridge, MA: Harvard University Press, 1990.

Beattie, Kirk J. *Egypt during the Sadat Years.* New York: Palgrave, 2000.

Goldschmidt, Arthur. *Biographical Dictionary of Modern Egypt.* Boulder, CO: Westview, 2000.

Heikal, Mohamed. *Autumn of Fury: The Assassination of Sadat.* New York: Random House, 1983.

Springborg, Robert. *Mubarak's Egypt: Fragmentation of the Political Order.* Boulder, CO: Westview, 1989.

ARTHUR GOLDSCHMIDT

UZBEKS

A Central Asian people.

In the 1920s and 1930s, before the Soviet Union implemented language and nationalities policies, the Uzbek language, an eastern Turkic language of the Altaic family generally known as Turki (Chaghatai), was written in Arabic script and was the principal literary language for all Turkic-speaking central Asians. When they were forced to adopt Cyrillic script (i.e., the Russian and Slavic alphabet), Uzbeks and other central Asian Turks were denied easy access to their rich literary heritage, which dates to the fifteenth century.

Uzbeks practice Islam; they are Sunni Hanafi Muslims. Originally pastoral nomads, by the early part of the twentieth century they were predominantly sedentary subsistence farmers, herders, or inhabitants of small towns engaged in producing and marketing crafts. Until the mid-nineteenth century, the Uzbeks were politically the preeminent force in the region. From the 1860s to 1991, the Uzbeks and other central Asian Muslims suffered colonial occupation of their lands by czarist Russia and its successor, the Soviet Union. As of 2001, Uzbeks constitute more than 80 percent of the population of the independent state of Uzbekistan; about 15 million Uzbeks speak the Northern Uzbek language. Uzbeks are also one of the larger ethnic minority groups in neighboring Tajikistan and in the northern part of the Islamic State of Afghanistan, where Southern Uzbek, a related but distinct language, is spoken.

Bibliography

Allworth, Edward A. *The Modern Uzbeks: From the Fourteenth Century to the Present: A Cultural History.* Stanford, CA: Hoover Institution Press, 1990.

M. NAZIF SHAHRANI

UZI

See GLOSSARY

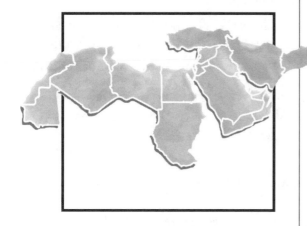

VA'AD LE'UMI

National Council of the Jews in Mandatory Palestine.

The Va'ad Le'umi (VL) was the supreme executive authority and representative organ of the Yishuv (Jewish community in Palestine) between 1920 and 1948. Functioning much like a cabinet, each Va'ad Le'umi was composed of members of an Asefat ha-Nivharim (elected assembly), and its day-to-day operations were largely in the hands of a chairman and a smaller executive committee. For most of the Mandate period the executive was headed by a praesidium of Yizhak Ben-Zvi, Yaakov Thon, and David Yellin.

One of the main functions of the VL was to act as official representative for the heterogeneous, highly politicized Jewish community in Palestine. The VL served as a high-level public forum for debating the divergent viewpoints and conflicting interests of religious versus secular Jews; farmers and employers versus organized labor; and native versus newly arrived immigrant groups having differing traditions (e.g., Sephardim versus Ashkenazim). The Palestine Royal Commission Report (1937) credited the VL and its local educational system with counteracting these divisive forces by the forging of a "national self-consciousness of unusual intensity."

The VL was frequently beset by organizational difficulties and jurisdictional squabbles with the Palestine Zionist Executive and the Jewish Agency Executive (both responsible to the World Zionist Organization). While most matters of high policy were decided by Zionist leaders and organs in Palestine and abroad, the VL was able to exercise its autonomy mainly in the spheres of education and local communal affairs. After 14 May 1948 the functions and departments of the VL and those of certain sections of the Jewish Agency came under the authority of a provisional state council of the State of Israel.

See also BEN-ZVI, YIZHAK.

Bibliography

Burstein, Mosh. *Self-Government of the Jews in Palestine since 1900.* Tel Aviv: Hapoel Hatzair, 1934.

Caplan, Neil. *Palestine Jewry and the Arab Question, 1917–1925.* London: Frank Cass, 1978.

Shaw, J. V. W., ed. *A Survey of Palestine: Prepared in December 1945 and January 1946 for the Information of the Anglo-American Committee of Inquiry* (1946), 2 vols. Washington, DC: Institute for Palestine Studies, 1991.

NEIL CAPLAN

VAKA-I HAYRIYE

Turkish for "the beneficial event"; the end of the janissary corps in 1826.

The term *vaka-i hayriye* has been used by Turkish historians to describe the government-ordered destruction of the Ottoman Empire's military unit, the janissary corps, on 15 June 1826. This momentous event resulted in considerable bloodshed (6,000 dead, according to conservative estimates) and was received with dismay and mixed emotions by large segments of the populace. In an attempt to gain public approval, Mahmud II's regime, using the services of the *ulama* (Islamic scholars), presented the incident as unavoidable and necessary to protect the very survival of Islam and the Ottoman Empire. Immediately following the destruction of the janissary corps, Mahmud II ordered the court chronicler, Mehmet Esad Efendi (c. 1789–1848), to record the official version of events, *Üss-i Zafer* (Foundation of victory), which was printed in Istanbul in 1828 and served as the main source for every other Ottoman account of this period.

See also JANISSARIES; MAHMUD II.

Bibliography

Levy, Avigdor. "The Ottoman Ulama and the Military Reforms of Sultan Mahmud II." *Asian and African Studies* 7 (1971): 13–39.

AVIGDOR LEVY
UPDATED BY ERIC HOOGLUND

VALENSI, ALFRED
[1878–1944]

Tunisian Zionist.

Alfred Valensi, a member of the Sephardic Jewish elite, was one of the founders and leaders of the Tunisian Zionist Federation. While still a law student in France, he became a disciple of Max Nordau. Valensi was a contributor to major European journals.

A brilliant theoretician and organizer, he represented Tunisian Zionists at international gatherings in London and Carlsbad with his associate Rabbi Joseph Brami. In 1926, he settled in Paris, where he was later arrested and transported by the Nazis in 1944 to his death.

See also NORDAU, MAX.

Bibliography

Stillman, Norman A. *The Jews of Arab Lands in Modern Times.* Philadelphia: Jewish Publication Society, 1991.

NORMAN STILLMAN

VALI

See GLOSSARY

VANCE, CYRUS
[1917–2002]

U.S. lawyer and government official.

Cyrus Vance, born in Clarksburg, West Virginia, received a bachelor of arts degree from Yale University in 1939 and a law degree in 1942. After serving as a junior naval gunnery officer in the Pacific Theater in World War II and practicing law, he served in a number of government positions, including general counsel for the Department of Defense (1961–1962), secretary of the army (1962–1963), deputy secretary of defense (1964–1967), and secretary of state (1977–1980). He continued to be active in international affairs after his resignation in 1980. His work with Middle Eastern and Eastern European problems included service as President Lyndon Baines Johnson's special representative on Cyprus in 1967, helping to ensure that Greece and Turkey would not be drawn into war over the conflict. He received the Medal of Freedom from the U.S. president for his work. Before returning to federal service, Vance and Daniel Yankelovich founded the respected Public Agenda, a nonprofit and nonpartisan research organization in New York. His most prominent role in the Middle East was as secretary of state under President Jimmy Carter, during which he had a leading role in the Camp David Accords: He held extensive consultations with Israeli prime minister Menachem Begin and Egyptian president Anwar al-Sadat at Camp

David, Maryland, which led to the September 1978 peace agreement between the two countries. Vance resigned from the Carter administration in 1980 because he disagreed with the president's decision to use force to rescue the U.S. citizens held hostage in Teheran. Widely respected for his integrity and range of international contacts, Vance worked with the United Nations to secure the cease-fire in Croatia in 1991, and later helped to resolve creditor claims in a real estate case in New York in 1993. Vance died in 2002 after an extended bout with Alzheimer's disease.

See also CAMP DAVID ACCORDS (1978).

Bibliography

McClellan, David S. *Cyrus Vance.* Totowa, NJ: Rowman and Allanheld, 1985.

Quandt, William B. *Camp David: Peacemaking and Politics.* Washington, DC: Brookings Institute, 1986.

Vance, Cyrus. *Hard Choices: Critical Years in America's Foreign Policy.* New York: Simon and Schuster, 1983.

DANIEL E. SPECTOR

VAN, LAKE

Salt lake in eastern Turkey.

Lake Van is the largest lake in Turkey, some 5,600 feet (1,600 m) above sea level, with a surface area of 1,400 square miles (3,700 sq. km). Having no outlet, its waters evaporate and concentrate salts, including carbonates and sulphates of soda; the resulting blue-green color creates a startling, austere beauty. Lake Van is stocked with darek, a herring-like fish consumed locally.

Bibliography

Fisher, Sydney N. *The Middle East: A History,* 3d edition. New York: Knopf, 1979.

JOHN R. CLARK

VANUNU AFFAIR

A controversy over divulging Israeli nuclear information to a British newspaper.

In October 1986, Mordechai Vanunu (1954–), a former employee of the Dimona nuclear reactor in Israel, provided the *Sunday Times* of London with in-

formation and photographs of the plant, claiming Israel was producing nuclear arms and that it had stockpiled between one hundred and two hundred nuclear weapons. Israel denied the charges and stated that it did not possess nuclear weapons and would not be the first Middle Eastern country to introduce nuclear arms to the region.

Vanunu was kidnapped in Italy by the Mossad and returned to Israel, where he underwent a seven-month-long secret trial for treason and espionage against the state. The three-judge court's sixty-page verdict was almost completely classified; only one sentence was made public: "We decided the defendant is guilty on all three counts." The three counts involved espionage, the unauthorized transmission of information, and helping Israel's enemies in a time of war.

Vanunu was widely portrayed in the Israeli press as a traitor and as mentally deranged. His prison sentence at times included solitary confinement, and his cause was taken up by human rights and disarmament groups and scientists around the world. European disarmament groups claimed that he was a hero and he was nominated for the Nobel Peace Prize. World opinion was that the bulk of Vanunu's story and data was accurate, demonstrating that Israel did indeed have a substantial nuclear arsenal.

See also DIMONA; MOSSAD; NUCLEAR CAPABILITY AND NUCLEAR ENERGY.

Bibliography

Gaffney, Mark. *Dimona, the Third Temple?: The Story behind the Vanunu Revelation.* Brattleboro, VT: Amana Books, 1989.

Israel's First Bomb, The First Victim: The Case of Mordechai Vanunu. Nottingham, U.K.: Bertrand Russell Peace Foundation, 1988.

"Israel: Vanunu Convicted, Given 18 Years." Facts On File. Available from <www.2facts.com/stories/temp/77635temp1988009410.asp>.

JULIE ZUCKERMAN
UPDATED BY GREGORY S. MAHLER

VARLIK VERGISI

Capital tax levied in Turkey during World War II.

Adopted in November 1942 to finance Turkey's emergency military expenditures during World War

II, the Varlik Vergisi was heavily criticized as confiscatory and discriminatory. It was abolished in March 1944. Justified as a social equalization measure against those who profiteered during the war, up to 75 percent of net profits were collected as tax from trade companies. Istanbul merchants and non-Muslims were taxed far more heavily than Muslims and farmers. The tax produced long-term political effects in the fear of government as a threat to private property and in highlighting the dangers of one-party rule.

Bibliography

Lewis, Bernard. *The Emergence of Modern Turkey,* 3d edition. New York: Oxford University Press, 2002.

ELIZABETH THOMPSON

VATAN

See NEWSPAPERS AND PRINT MEDIA: TURKEY

VATICAN AND THE MIDDLE EAST

The Roman Catholic Church struggles to maintain its presence in the Middle East.

The presence of the Roman Catholic Church in the Middle East goes back to the Roman and Byzantine empires, to the Crusades, and to European imperialism and colonialism. Following the Second Vatican Council (1962–1965), Vatican diplomacy in the Middle East focused on three goals: preserving Christianity and a Christian presence in what Christians term the Holy Land, fostering peace with justice between Israel and the Palestinians, and maintaining Lebanon as an example of coexistence between Christians and Muslims.

The Vatican faces problems of demographic changes in the Middle East, especially in Jerusalem and the West Bank, where Christian Arabs are leaving because of their minority status; the resurgence of Islamic and Jewish fundamentalisms; and unstable economic and political situations. The relationship between the Vatican and Israel is a mixture of theological prejudice and political pragmatism. In recent years, however, the Holy See has established diplomatic relations with Israel (December 1993) and with the Hashemite Kingdom of Jordan (April 1994), and in 2000 the Vatican signed a Basic Agreement with the Palestine Liberation Organization (PLO). This agreement called for the resolution of the Israeli-Palestinian conflict on the basis of the various relevant UN resolutions. In March 2000 Pope John Paul II undertook a historic trip to Israel and the Palestinian-controlled territories, only the second time since 1964 that a sovereign pontiff set foot in the Holy Land. Throughout the Oslo peace process and the al-Aqsa Intifada the Vatican used its influence to ensure that the papacy's concerns and interests in Jerusalem and Christian holy sites were taken into consideration by U.S. president Bill Clinton, Israeli prime minister Ehud Barak, and PLO chairman Yasir Arafat.

The Lebanese Civil War (1975–1989) was a major challenge to the papacy. Several mediation missions were dispatched by both Pope Paul VI and Pope John Paul II, and in 1995 the latter convened in Rome a synod of Roman Catholic bishops, with Muslim and Orthodox Christian observers, for the express purpose of addressing the Lebanese situation. It is clear that if Lebanon were to fail as an example of coexistence, the Vatican's position in the region would be weakened.

See also CHRISTIANS IN THE MIDDLE EAST; HOLY LAND.

Bibliography

Dumper, Michael. *The Politics of Sacred Space: The Old City of Jerusalem in the Middle East Conflict.* Boulder, CO: Lynne Rienner, 2002.

Irani, George E. *The Papacy and the Middle East.* South Bend, IN: University of Notre Dame Press, 1989.

GEORGE E. IRANI

VAZHAPETIAN, NERSES

[1837–1884]

Armenian patriarch of Istanbul, 1873–1884.

Born in Istanbul, Nerses Vazhapetian spent his entire life in or near the Ottoman capital. Although deprived of a formal education at the age of fifteen after the death of his father, Vazhapetian became a teacher and joined the clergy of the Armenian Apostolic Church. Anointed a celibate priest in 1858, he was a bishop by 1862. Active in the administrative affairs of the Armenian Millet, Vazhapetian had a hand in drafting the so-called Armenian national constitution by which the Armenian Church and millet were regulated in the Ottoman Empire. In 1873, at age thirty-seven, he was elected Armenian partiarch of Istanbul.

The Russo-Ottoman War of 1877–1878, partly waged over the Armenian-populated provinces of eastern Anatolia, brought the issue of the Armenians to the fore of the diplomatic contest for influence in the Ottoman Empire. When the extent of the Kurdish predations over the Armenian communities became known, Vazhapetian, who had issued an encyclical supporting the Ottoman war effort, was authorized by the Armenian national assembly to appeal to Grand Duke Nicholas at San Stefano for consideration of local self-government in the areas of Armenian concentration. In the formal Treaty of San Stefano, signed on 3 March 1878, by the Ottomans and Russians, Article 16 provided for reforms and security under Russian trusteeship in the so-called Armenian provinces.

While Russian withdrawal from these areas was conditional on implementation of the reforms, the Congress of Berlin revised the terms of the treaty. The Armenian delegation sent by Vazhapetian to Berlin received no hearing, and Article 61 of the Treaty of Berlin, signed 13 July 1878, provided only for reforms as those territories were returned to the Ottomans. Still Armenians expected an international treaty to prove more binding on the Ottomans than mere promises. The failure of the European powers to require Sultan Abdülhamit II to proceed with reforms became the source of disillusionment. By the time of Vazhapetian's death in Istanbul, small groups of provincial Armenians had began to resort to self-defense in the face of continued insecurity in what became known as the Armenian Revolutionary Movement.

See also ARMENIAN MILLET; BERLIN, CONGRESS AND TREATY OF; SAN STEFANO, TREATY OF (1878).

Bibliography

Nalbandian, Louise. *The Armenian Revolutionary Movement: The Development of Armenian Political Parties through the Nineteenth Century.* Berkeley: University of California Press, 1967.

Walker, Christopher J. *Armenia: The Survival of a Nation,* revised 2d edition. New York: St. Martin's, 1990.

ROUBEN P. ADALIAN

VAZIR AFKHAM, SOLTAN ALI KHAN
[1867–1918]

Iranian courtier of the Qajar period.

Soltan Ali Khan was in the service of Mozaffar al-Din Qajar from the time the latter became crown prince in Tabriz. Upon the shah's ascension to power, Soltan Ali Khan was first appointed head of the Royal Correspondence Office and then minister of revenues, and in 1901 he received the title Vazir Afkham. In 1907, he was made prime minister and minister of interior under Mohammad Ali Qajar and headed the first Iranian cabinet after the Constitutional Revolution. Opposed by the Constitutionalists, he was deposed in 1909 and died in 1918, the same year his oldest son was killed in a romantic feud.

See also CONSTITUTIONAL REVOLUTION; MOHAMMAD ALI SHAH QAJAR; MOZAFFAR AL-DIN QAJAR.

NEGUIN YAVARI

VAZIRI, QAMAR AL-MOLUK
[1905–1959]

Considered the first professional female singer in Iran.

Qamar al-Moluk Vaziri was born to a middle-class family in the city of Kashan, Iran, in 1905. Raised by her grandmother, a religiously inclined woman who performed as a eulogist in women's gatherings, Qamar accompanied her to these events, where she herself also performed eulogies. She later studied under masters of Persian classical music and acquired fame as a singer. Numerous recordings were made of her songs. The singer died in 1959 from heart disease and was buried in Dhahir al-Dowleh cemetery in northern Tehran.

PARVANEH POURSHARIATI

VELAYAT-E FAQIH

Theory of governance in Shi'ite Islam.

From the Arabic term for "the authority, or governance, of the jurist," the doctrine of *velayat-e faqih* was associated particularly with Iran's Ayatollah Ruhollah Khomeini. It holds that those scholars of Shi'ite Islam most qualified in terms of piety and erudition are to exercise the governmental functions of the Twelfth Imam during his major occultation (absence from the terrestrial plane), which began in 939 C.E. and still continues. Even before the occultation, the imams would delegate certain of their functions, particularly in the judicial sphere, to qualified members of the Shiʿite Islam community as a matter of practical necessity. It was therefore natural that after the beginning of the occultation, other executive functions of the imam also should be assigned to the Shiʿite jurists, including, for example, the collection and disbursement of religiously mandated taxes (zakat and khoms), but not the waging of offensive jihad (holy war) or (according to some jurists) the holding of Friday prayers. This led to the crystallization of the theory of the niyabat-e amma (general deputyship) of the jurists, a process that was complete by the middle of the sixteenth century. Already in the Safavid period (1501–1702) the general deputyship occasionally was interpreted to include all the prerogatives of rule that in principle had belonged to the imams, but no special emphasis was placed on this. Similarly, although velayat-e faqih began to be discussed as a distinct legal topic in the nineteenth century, against a background of enhanced social authority for the Shiʿite jurists, no concrete political conclusions were drawn from the concept.

It was left to Ayatollah Khomeini to claim, in typically radical and comprehensive fashion, the right or even duty of the leading Shiʿite scholars to rule. He did this in his first published work (Kashf al-Asrar, 1944), again in a technical work on Shiʿite jurisprudence, and most fully and importantly, in a series of lectures delivered in 1970 during his exile in Iraq; these lectures were published under the title Hokumat-e Islami (Islamic government).

Khomeini's arguments in the lectures are both scriptural and rational, traditional and revolutionary. Asserting that Islamic government differs from all other forms of rule by being based on the implementation of divine law, Khomeini attributes the disarray of the Islamic world in general and Iran in particular to the prevalence of arbitrary rule and its concomitant man-made laws. He then demonstrates the centrality of government to the Islamic worldview and ridicules the opinion that the validity of the laws contained in the Qurʾan (the holy book of Islam) and other sources should have been restricted

to the first few centuries of the Islamic era. Next, he reviews in great detail the Qurʾanic verses and traditions of the prophet Muhammad and the imams, which, in his estimation, support the thesis of velayat-e faqih; cites the opinions of previous, mostly recent, Shiʿite scholars on the subject; and reaches the conclusion that "the same governance that was exercised by the Most Noble Messenger and by the Imams is also the prerogative of the jurists" (Khomeini).

In the last of the lectures, Khomeini laments the prevalence of the "pseudo-saintly" in the religious institution, and it was indeed several years before a sizable number of Khomeini's colleagues came to accept his thesis. It was the repressive policies of the shah of Iran, Mohammad Reza Pahlavi (ruled 1941–1979), that impelled the religious scholars to conceive of broad and radical aims and enabled them to gain a favorable response from much of the Iranian public. Nonetheless, although by the autumn of 1978 a clear majority of Iranians had come to favor the institution of an Islamic government under the leadership of Khomeini, it cannot be said that velayat-e faqih was a prominent slogan of the Iranian Revolution. Khomeini himself made no mention of it in the proclamations he issued during the revolution.

Not until the constitution of the Islamic Republic of Iran was elaborated by the Assembly of Experts that convened in the fall of 1979 did velayat-e faqih emerge as the pillar of the new order. It was enshrined in the preamble to the constitution in Article Five ("During the Occultation of the Lord of the Age [that is, the Hidden Imam], the governance and leadership of the nation devolve upon the pious and just jurist who is acquainted with the circumstances of his age; courageous, resourceful, and possessed of administrative ability; and recognized and accepted as leader by the majority of the people"); and in Articles 107 to 112, which specify the procedure for selecting the leader and list his constitutional functions.

Khomeini's own view was that these provisions did not do justice to velayat-e faqih, and in February 1988 he propounded the theory of velayat-e motlaqa-ye faqih ("the absolute authority of the jurist"). He declared obedience to the ruling jurist to be as incumbent on the believer as the performance of prayer, and his powers to extend even to the temporary suspension of such essential rites of Islam as the hajj (pilgrimage to Mecca). Although this formulation of the theory might appear to be an ideal prescription for theocratic absolutism, in fact, Khomeini was not seeking to extend his control of Iranian affairs (which in any event was far less than absolute). Rather, he was seeking to provide theoretical justification for government attempts to break the stalemate on controversial items of social and economic legislation.

The actual implementation of *velayat-e faqih,* moreover, was destined to change in a quite different direction. When Ayatollah Hosainali Montazeri was compelled in March 1989 to resign as designated successor to Khomeini, none of the other senior religious scholars seemed qualified for the position. When Khomeini died on 4 June of the same year, it was therefore Hojjat al-Islam Ali Khamenehi—a relatively junior figure in the religious hierarchy, despite his political prominence—who was chosen as leader of the Islamic Republic. This necessitated the modification of Article 109 of the constitution to remove scholarly seniority from the qualifications of the leader, a change that was approved in a referendum held in August 1989. It has been argued credibly that the resulting disjunction of political leadership from seniority in the learned hierarchy of Iranian Shi'ism effectively brings the implementation of *velayat-e faqih* to an end. If this is true, *velayat-e faqih* must be designated as a theory that was, to a degree, workable only because of the unique qualities and appeal of Khomeini, and that falls short of being a permanent solution to the problem of governance in a Shi'ite Muslim society.

Bibliography

Khomeini, Ruhollah. *Islam and Revolution: Writings and Declarations of Imam Khomeini,* translated by Hamid Algar. Berkeley, CA: Mizan Press, 1981.

Sachedina, Abdulaziz Abdulhussein. *The Just Ruler in Shi'ite Islam.* Oxford, U.K.: Oxford University Press, 1988.

HAMID ALGAR
UPDATED BY ERIC HOOGLUND

VELAYATI, ALI AKBAR

[1945–]

Foreign minister of Iran, 1981–1997.

Born in Tehran in 1945, Ali Akbar Velayati received a doctorate in pediatrics from Tehran University in 1971. After completing postgraduate work, he left for further studies in the United States, where he joined the Organization of Iranian Moslem Students. Returning home, he taught at his alma mater and was appointed deputy health minister in the first government appointed by Ayatollah Ruhollah Khomeini in 1979. He also served in the first parliament in 1980.

Before the Iranian revolution, Velayati was a member of the Hojjatieh group, an anti-Bahai conservative group that eventually challenged the dominance of the Islamic Republican Party (IRP). He left the group in 1983 when Khomeini denounced its activities, and he joined the Jam'iat Motalefeh Islami (Islamic Society, or JME), a group very close to the conservative *ulama* and bazaari merchants. In 1980 the IRP and JME unsuccessfully had pressed Iran's current president, Abolhasan Bani Sadr, to appoint Velayati as a foreign minister. In 1981 President Hojatoleslam Seyed Ali Khamenehi nominated Velayati for premier but could not win support from the parliament. Khamenehi accepted the parliament's choice of Mir Hossein Mousavi as prime minister if Velayati were appointed as foreign minister—a position Velayati held for more than sixteen years and through four administrations until 1997.

Velayati is a conservative pragmatist who helped to move Iran out of its revolutionary isolation and temper its adventurist foreign policies of the early 1980s. However, he opposed ties with the United States as an archenemy of the Islamic Republic and regards Israel as an illegitimate state in the heartland of Islam. He helped Iran to join international organizations and favored developing ties with Europe and developing countries.

Internally, his tenure in the foreign ministry has been criticized for putting more emphasis on loyalty than on professional qualifications. He is regarded as a nonclerical protégé of the religious elite who owes his long presence in Iranian politics to his loyalty to the supreme leader, Ayatollah Khamenehi. In 1997 he was named by a German court as a member of the Special Operations Committee that approved the 1992 assassinations of three Kurdish

Democratic Party leaders in the Mykonos Restaurant in Berlin.

Since his departure from the foreign ministry, Velayati has been a member of the Expediency Council, serves as an adviser on international affairs to Ayatollah Khamenehi and conducts foreign policy assignments, and continues to teach in the university and write articles and books on the history of Iran and the Iranian revolution for government publication. He also serves as the secretary-general of the Ahlul Bayt World Assembly—a religious institution named after the descendants of the prophet Muhammad and established to advance the Shi'ite cause around the world.

See also IRANIAN REVOLUTION (1979); IRAN–IRAQ WAR (1980–1988); KHAMENEHI, ALI; KHOMEINI, RUHOLLAH.

Bibliography

Moslem, Mehdi. *Factional Politics in Post-Khomeini Iran.* Syracuse, NY: Syracuse University Press, 2002.

ALI AKBAR MAHDI

VERSAILLES, TREATY OF (1920)

Treaty ending World War I; it established the mandate system for the governance and eventual independence of the Central Powers' former colonies.

The armistices of October and November 1918 ending hostilities in World War I were followed by the Conference of Paris at which World War I victors and associated powers determined the terms for dealing with Germany and her allies during the war. The conference, which officially began on 18 January 1919, resulted in five treaties. The Treaty of Versailles, signed on 28 June at Versailles, France, and ratified on 20 January 1920, addressed the terms of peace with Germany. The treaties of Sèvres, Neuilly, St. Germain, and Trianon dealt with the Ottoman Empire, Bulgaria, Austria, and Hungary, respectively. Besides setting forth the terms for dealing with Germany after World War I, the Treaty of Versailles established the League of Nations and the mandate system for governing territories surrendered by Germany. This treaty included the Covenant of the League of Nations as Part I, with Article 22 giving the league the power to supervise mandated territories consisting of former German colonies. The other treaties included the covenant in their texts.

The armistice with Germany and the Conference of Paris were both predicated on U.S. President Woodrow Wilson's Fourteen Points for peace enunciated in his address to Congress on 8 January 1918. In addition to his vision of a League of Nations, these included an adjustment of all colonial claims giving equal weight to the interests of colonial populations and to those of countries with colonial claims. This led many to believe that the peace conference would lead to the independence of the Arab portions of the Ottoman Empire. Based on this, Prince Faisal I ibn Hussein arrived in Paris in January 1919 as head of the Hijaz delegation and with the objective of securing an independent Arab state. At first the French opposed recognition of the Hijaz delegation based on the fact that the Hijaz was not one of the Allied belligerent states. The British, however, intervened, and the Hijaz delegation was recognized. On 29 January Faisal submitted a statement to the conference defining Arab claims. He requested recognition as "independent sovereign peoples" for those Arab-speaking peoples of Asia from the Alexandretta–Diyarbekir line south to the Indian Ocean. Essentially, this included what is now Syria, Lebanon, Israel, Jordan, and Iraq. Faisal exempted the Hijaz as already independent, as well as British Aden. The prince addressed the conference on 6 February, stressing the principle of the consent of the governed. He then proposed a commission to visit Syria and Palestine and ascertain the wishes of the populace. The French were not inclined to support this, but pressure by Wilson resulted, on 25 March, in the approval of a commission, later known as the King–Crane Commission.

Despite the sincere desires of Wilson to forge a new world in which all peoples would be the ultimate determiners of their national destinies and the eloquent arguments of Faisal and others on behalf of the Arabs, the Conference of Paris yielded to the imperial interests of Britain and France and, to a lesser extent, to those of Italy and Japan. The colonial territories of Germany and the Arab portions of the Ottoman Empire were assigned to members of the League of Nations under the mandate system established in the covenant. In the case of the Middle East, agreements made during World War I played a large role in distribution of mandates. The secret Anglo–Franco–Russian agreement of 16 May 1916, commonly known as the Sykes–Picot Agreement, divided the Arab dominions of the Ottoman Empire between Britain and France. Britain received the areas that are now Iraq, Jordan, and Israel; France got what is now Syria and Lebanon. The Balfour Declaration of 2 November 1917, also played a role in the disposition of Arab territories by the Conference of Paris. This was a letter from Lord Balfour, British foreign secretary, to Lord (Edmond de) Rothschild, a prominent British Zionist, that supported the establishment of a national home for the Jewish people in Palestine. These two documents, more than anything else, shaped the fate of the Middle East in the post–World War I era. The San Remo Conference of April 1920 awarded Syria, including Lebanon, as a Class A mandate to France; Iraq and Palestine, including Transjordan, became Class A mandates under British supervision. The mandate for Palestine endorsed the provisions of the Balfour Declaration. In 1921 Britain separated Transjordan from Palestine, exempting it from the provisions of the Balfour Declaration. As Class A mandates, all three were to be given independence when it was determined that they were able to stand on their own. In the case of Iraq and Transjordan, Arab dignitaries were given royal status in preparation for the eventual independence of these areas. Prince Faisal became the king of Iraq, and Prince Abdullah I ibn Hussein became the amir of Transjordan. The League of Nations confirmed these mandates in 1922, some of which outlived the international organization under which they were formed. The first mandate to obtain independence was Iraq, in 1932, followed by Syria and Lebanon in 1941. Transjordan, now Jordan, gained its independence in 1946. Palestine, much of which is now Israel, gained independence in 1948.

See also ABDULLAH I IBN HUSSEIN; ALEXANDRETTA; BALFOUR DECLARATION (1917); DIYARBAKIR; FAISAL I IBN HUSSEIN; HIJAZ; KING–CRANE COMMISSION (1919); ROTHSCHILD, EDMOND DE; SAN REMO CONFERENCE (1920); SÈVRES, TREATY OF (1920); SYKES–PICOT AGREEMENT (1916); WILSON, WOODROW; WORLD WAR I.

Bibliography

Antonius, George. *The Arab Awakening: The Story of the Arab National Movement.* London: H. Hamilton, 1938.

Sontag, Raymond J. *A Broken World, 1919–1939.* New York: Harper and Row, 1971.

DANIEL E. SPECTOR

VICTORIA COLLEGE

British-style public school in Alexandria, Egypt.

Victoria College was founded in 1901 on the initiative of eight resident merchants, bankers, and shipping magnates, six of whom were British, one Syrian, and one the Austro-Hungarian president of the Jewish Community of Alexandria. The makeup of the entering classes of 1902 reflected the cosmopolitanism that was to characterize the institution up to the mid-1950s—eight of the students were Syrian, including George Antonius and his three brothers, three were Greek, three were Egyptian Muslims, one was English, and ten were identified in the language of the time as "Israelite." In those early decades the language of instruction was English, but the study of Arabic and French was mandatory. The school also placed a strong emphasis on cricket, soccer, and hockey. Under the leadership (1901–1922) of its first headmaster, Charles Lias of King's College, Cambridge University, Victoria adopted the Oxford and Cambridge Joint Board Examination, the qualifying exam for English medical and engineering schools as well as for Oxford and Cambridge. Victoria boys obtained outstanding exam results, and the school became a breeding ground for university education in England and elsewhere. For example, between 1908 and 1913, thirty-three Victoria graduates attended European or U.S. universities, including nine at Cambridge, four at Toulouse, and one at the University of Edinburgh Medical School.

In 1906 the campus moved from downtown to the city's eastern suburbs. There its stately buildings and spacious playing fields stood out as an Alexandrian landmark and were the envy of other, less privileged schools. For more than half a century, Victoria College played an important role in providing a first-rate European education along British public-school lines to successive generations of well-born Egyptians—Muslims, Copts, and Jews—as well as foreign residents in Egypt, whatever their race, color, or creed. Primary identification with the school blurred ethnic and religious differences and created an atmosphere of tolerance within the tightly knit student body. The school's prestige extended well beyond Egypt under its second headmaster, R. W. G. Reed of Oxford, and it began to attract the scions of the English-speaking ruling elite in the rest of the region: Thus, King Hussein ibn Talal of Jordan and his brother, Prince Hassan; the last Hashimite king of Iraq, Faisal II ibn Ghazi, and his uncle, the regent Abd al-Ilah; the former sultan of Zanzibar; and the king of Albania were students at Victoria.

Along with all other foreign schools, Victoria was nationalized by Gamal Abdel Nasser in the wake of the Suez War in 1956 and now survives as a pale reflection of its former self, under the label of Victory College. In the 1990s, as a coeducational institution, its 6,000 students were jammed into a campus originally built for 500.

Bibliography

Atiyah, Edward. *An Arab Tells His Story: A Study in Loyalties.* London: John Murray, 1947.

Hamouda, Sahar, and Clement, Colin, eds. *Victoria College: A History Revealed.* Cairo: American University in Cairo Press, 2002.

ALAIN SILVERA
UPDATED BY WILLIAM L. CLEVELAND

VILAYET

See GLOSSARY

VILLAGE INSTITUTES

Turkish institutes for training primary-school teachers.

The Village Institutes (Köy Enstitüleri) of Turkey represented a short-lived (1940–1950) but highly innovative experiment in primary-school teacher training. In the 1930s, over 75 percent of Turkey's people lived in some 35,000 villages, and over 80 percent of these villagers were illiterate. Only a small proportion of villages had primary schools, and most of their urban-born teachers had difficulty coping with rural conditions. After the dissolution of the Ottoman Empire and the establishment of the Republic of Turkey in 1923, Mustafa Kemal

(Atatürk) and his ruling Republican People's Party (RPP) planned to design a national system of compulsory secular education to enculturate a new generation of Turks in the principles of modern science and Turkish nationalism. Educational reform and a cadre of new, secular teachers were to spread Kemalism and lift the masses from the depths of poverty and ignorance. While impressive educational gains were achieved in the cities, most villages remained without schools.

Ismail Hakki Tonguç, the director general of primary education, and his colleagues designed a plan they hoped would produce teachers capable of living in the villages and able to make a comprehensive impact on them. The plan called for creating special teacher-training institutes, recruiting village students to them, teaching these students general subjects plus useful village technology, and then sending them back to the villages to teach in five-year primary schools.

Shortly after the Turkish Grand National Assembly passed the necessary legislation in 1940, fourteen Village Institutes opened their doors to eager recruits. Actually, many of the institutes' facilities were incomplete, so teachers and students worked side by side building classrooms, dining halls, and dormitories. In the process, students acquired useful carpentry, masonry, and other construction skills.

The ministry of education intentionally located the institutes in rural areas, so that students could practice farming, plant orchards, develop water and sanitation systems, and generally confront typical village problems with modern skills and science. Youths of both sexes, between the ages of twelve and sixteen, who were graduated by a five-year village primary school, qualified for admission to a village institute. The government offered this education free to students who pledged to teach in an assigned village for twenty years after graduation.

Twenty-five percent of the Institute's five-year curriculum was devoted to agriculture (crop production, zootechnology, apiculture [beekeeping], and silkworm culture); 25 percent was devoted to technology (carpentry, construction, blacksmithing, health, and childcare for female students); and 50 percent dealt with general education (the Turkish language, history, literature, geography, math, biology, and civics). In 1950, the curriculum was expanded to six years. As village teachers, institute graduates were expected to teach general education subjects to children, adult-literacy classes, scientific farming and animal husbandry, and handicrafts; they were obligated to play a central role in the community and generally awaken the civic conscience of the rural population.

The institutes provided some of the most idealistic and dedicated rural teachers in Turkey's history. These young men and women inspired many villagers to continue their educations beyond primary school; some even went to the university. A number of village teachers, such as Mahmut Makal (author of *Bizim Köy*, translated as *A Village in Anatolia*), became famous writers who pioneered a new literary genre that focused on peasant life.

From their inception, however, the Village Institutes were subject to controversy. Political opponents described them as indoctrination agencies of the ruling party. Some educators claimed they failed to prepare students adequately for their exhaustive duties as rural teachers. Very conservative villagers complained that institute graduates preached revolutionary and antireligious ideas in their villages. More extreme opponents accused the institutes of teaching communism.

When the new opposition party, the Democrat party (DP), came to power in 1950, they removed institute supporters from the ministry of education and abolished the twenty-one existing institutes by transforming them into ordinary teacher-training schools. Before their demise, the institutes had graduated 15,767 men and 1,395 women.

Bibliography

Stone, Frank A. "Rural Revitalization and the Village Institutes in Turkey: Sponsors and Critics." *Comparative Education Review* 18 (1974): 419–429.

Vexliard, Alexandre, and Aytac, Kemal. "The Village Institutes in Turkey." *Comparative Education Review* 8 (1964): 41–47.

PAUL J. MAGNARELLA

VIZIER

See GLOSSARY

VOICE OF LEBANON

See RADIO AND TELEVISION: ARAB COUNTRIES

VOICE OF PALESTINE

See NEWSPAPERS AND PRINT MEDIA: ARAB COUNTRIES; RADIO AND TELEVISION: ARAB COUNTRIES

VOLPI, GIUSEPPE

Governor of Libya from 1922 to 1925, after a short period as governor of Tripolitania.

Giuseppe Volpi abandoned the policy of trying to govern Libya through Libyan representatives in the aftermath of the first Italo–Sanusi War. This had involved recognizing a Sanusi amir in Cyrenaica or trying to use the leaders of the Tripolitanian republic in Tripolitania.

Instead, Volpi gave a free hand to the military commanders on the spot, Rodolfo Graziani and Pietro Badoglio. His new policy was enthusiastically endorsed by the Fascists when they came to power in October 1922. It had been signaled the previous April, when he sanctioned an attack on Misurata, and achieved its fullest expression with the outbreak of the second Italo–Sanusi War in early 1923.

Volpi's three-year tenure as governor also marked the introduction of an intensive colonization scheme. He sought to increase the amount of state funds made available for it, alienated to the state all uncultivated land and all rebel-held land, once it was conquered, and provided tax-relief schemes to attract investment funding. By doing this, he prepared the way for the legislation introduced by Emilio de Bono, who actually began the process of large-scale Italian peasant migration into Libya.

See also GRAZIANI, RODOLFO; ITALY IN THE MIDDLE EAST.

Bibliography

Lombardi, P. "Italian Agrarian Policy during the Fascist Per iod." In *Social and Economic Development of Libya*, edited by E. G. H. Joffe and K. S. McLachlan. Wisbech, U.K.: Middle East and North African Studies Press, 1982.

GEORGE JOFFE

VOZUQ AL-DOWLEH, MIRZA HASAN KHAN

[1873–1950]

Iranian politician.

Mirza Hasan Khan was the nephew of Mirza Ali Khan Amin al-Dowleh, the famous prime minister under Mozaffar al-Din Qajar, and he was also the brother of Ahmad Qavam al-Saltaneh. In 1892, he replaced his father as tax collector of Azerbaijan, and four years later he was granted the title Vozuq al-Dowleh. He was elected to the first parliament from Tehran (1906), and, after holding several ministerial posts, he was appointed prime minister and minister of foreign affairs (1916). In 1918, he was reappointed prime minister for the purpose of forming a cabinet, and he headed the ministry of the interior. It was during his tenure as premier that the infamous Anglo-Iranian Agreement of 1919, transforming Iran into a British protectorate, was ratified. Following the conclusion of the agreement, Vozuq al-Dowleh received 60,000 pounds from the British government, but he was forced to return the sum to the Iranian government after Reza Shah Pahlavi took office. In 1921, Vozuq al-Dowleh was appointed minister of finance by the prime minister. After Reza Shah was forced by the Allied powers to abdicate in 1941, Vozuq al-Dowleh returned to private life as a land speculator.

See also AMIN AL-DOWLEH, MIRZA ALI KHAN; ANGLO-IRANIAN AGREEMENT (1919); MOZAFFAR AL-DIN QAJAR; PAHLAVI, REZA.

NEGUIN YAVARI

WADI

See GLOSSARY

WADI HADRAMAWT

Great valley in eastern Yemen.

Wadi Hadramawt is a 400-mile-long (640 km), well-watered valley east of Aden that constitutes one of the most agriculturally rich areas in Yemen. It produces millet, cotton, wheat, qat, and a variety of fruits and vegetables. The wadi dissects and drains the high plateau of eastern Yemen and is at the center of the Hadramawt, a distinctive geographic and sociopolitical region that was a famous trading state in ancient, pre-Islamic times.

See also HADRAMAWT.

ROBERT D. BURROWES

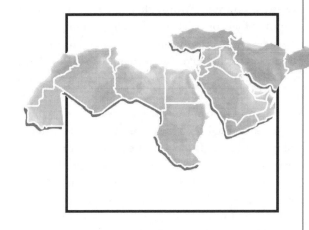

W

WADI NATRUN

Principal site of Coptic monasteries in Egypt.

Wadi Natrun is an elongated valley in Egypt's western desert near the Cairo-Alexandria road. As many as 500 Coptic monasteries, once housing up to 50,000 monks, were built there beginning in the fourth century, Four are currently in use: Dayr al-Baramus, Dayr Abu Maqar (St. Macarius), Dayr Anba Bishoi, and Dayr al-Surian. Dayr Anba Bishoi was the site of the enforced exile of Pope Shenouda III by President Anwar al-Sadat in 1981; he was released in 1985. Dayr Abu Maqar has witnessed a revival of Coptic monasticism since it was reopened by a dozen hermit monks in 1969. Since that date, rising numbers of Egyptian Christians have elected to spend part of their lives at Wadi Natrun's monasteries. Several are also open to tourism.

See also COPTS; SHENOUDA III.

Bibliography

Butler, Alfred J. *The Ancient Coptic Churches of Egypt,* 2 vols. Oxford: Clarendon, 1884; reprint, 1970.

Cannuyer, Christian. *Coptic Egypt: The Christians of the Nile.* New York: Abrams, 2000.

Evelyn-White, Hugh G. *The Monasteries of the Wadi 'n Natrun,*
3 vols. New York: Arno Press, 1973.

Kamil, Jill. *Coptic Egypt: History and Guide.* Cairo: American
University in Cairo Press, 1987.

Meinardus, Otto F. A. *Two Thousand Years of Coptic Christianity.* Cairo: American University in Cairo Press, 1999.

RAYMOND WILLIAM BAKER
UPDATED BY ARTHUR GOLDSCHMIDT

WAFD

Major Egyptian nationalist party organized in 1919.

The Wafd Party took its name from the delegation
(in Arabic, *wafd*) composed of Sa'd Zaghlul and
other notables who called for the complete independence *(istiqlal tamm)* of Egypt from the British immediately after World War I. When Britain refused

Mustafa al-Nahhas (right), seen here with President Giuseppe
Motta of Switzerland at a conference in 1937, was president of
the Wafd Party, which fought for years after World War I to
achieve Egyptian independence from Great Britain. He became
prime minister in 1941, but the Wafd lost popular support as he
worked with the British during World War II. © BETTMANN/
CORBIS. REPRODUCED BY PERMISSION.

to negotiate with the Wafd and exiled its leaders,
Egypt launched a full-scale rebellion in 1919. A sophisticated network of organizers in key cities and
villages allowed the Wafd to dominate the political
scene.

The Wafd did not become a formal political
party until 1924, six years after its inception. The
party was organized along hierarchical lines, with an
executive council. Although the party enjoyed the
support of a cross section of the Egyptian populace,
its leaders were predominantly urban, upper- and
middle-class, modern, and secular. The highly charismatic Zaghlul served as its president until his death
in 1927. The Wafdist leadership also included both
Muslims and Copts, notably Makram Ubayd. Women,
particularly Zaghlul's wife, Safiyya, and Huda al-
Sha'rawi, became leaders in the struggle for women's
voting rights, acting on the principle that the struggle against imperialism had to be accompanied by a
similar struggle for gender equality. Between the two
world wars, the Wafd engaged in a three-way struggle with the British and the Egyptian monarchy.
Seeking to undercut Egypt's demands for independence, Britain unilaterally declared Egypt independent in 1922 and promulgated a constitutional
monarchy in 1923. As the only party to enjoy widespread popular support for its anti-British stand,
the Wafd won the 1924 elections and all subsequent
elections that were not manipulated or rigged by
King Ahmad Fu'ad or his son Farouk.

Following Zaghlul's death, Mustafa al-Nahhas
became president of the party and continued its
struggle against the British. In 1936 he signed the
Anglo-Egyptian Treaty, which formalized Egyptian
and British relations but permitted both the continuation of a British military presence along the
Suez Canal zone and British control over the Sudan.

This failure to secure complete independence,
coupled with allegations of nepotism and corruption within the party, undermined some of its popular support. In the 1930s many Egyptian youths
joined various fascist and radical groups, and the
Wafd countered by creating the Blue Shirts, a paramilitary youth organization. In 1941, fearing a pro-
Nazi Egyptian government, Britain's ambassador
Miles Lampson (later Lord Killearn) forced King
Farouk to accept Nahhas as prime minister. Nahhas's willingness to work with the British throughout

World War II further undercut the Wafd's credibility as a nationalist and anti-imperialist party.

Following the 1952 military coup that deposed Farouk, the Wafd was formally disbanded (1953); some of its leaders were then tried for corruption and crimes against the state. In 1976, when Anwar al-Sadat announced the return to a multiparty system, the Wafd was revived under the leadership of Fuʾad Siraj al-Din. The New Wafd called for a parliamentary, multiparty system and the dismantling of socialist measures that had been enacted under Egypt's former president, Gamal Abdel Nasser. In a short time, the Wafd gathered a notable degree of support, particularly among Copts and in the richer urban areas. The Wafd voted to disband in reaction to Sadat's political crackdown in late 1978, but it was revived after Sadat's assassination by Islamists in 1981. In the 1984 elections the New Wafd cooperated with the Muslim Brotherhood and won 58 seats in parliament. By 1990 the New Wafd opposed the government and the continuation of the state of emergency, and it boycotted the 1993 elections. Its newspaper, *al-Wafd,* remained one of the few opposition publications. Following Siraj al-Din's death in 2000, Nʿuman Jumaʿa, a university professor, was elected the new leader in a notably open and transparent election. Representing the new generation, Jumaʿa pushed for political and economic changes; but without grassroots support, the Wafd remained a minority party in parliament.

See also NAHHAS, MUSTAFA AL-; NEW WAFD; SHAʿRAWI, HUDA AL-; ZAGHLUL, SAʿD.

Bibliography

Deeb, Marius. *Party Politics in Egypt: The Wafd and Its Rivals, 1919–1939.* London: Ithaca Press, 1979.

Terry, Janice J. *The Wafd, 1919–1952: Cornerstone of Egyptian Power.* London: Third World Centre for Research and Publishing, 1982.

JANICE J. TERRY

WAFDIST WOMEN'S CENTRAL COMMITTEE

Egyptian women's committee of the early Wafd party.

Early in the twentieth century Egypt took steps toward forming a *wafd,* or delegation, to demand independence from British rule. In 1910 the National Party (al-Hizb al-Watani) held a congress in Brussels, where Inshirah Shawqi's appeal for independence was read by a man because Egyptian gender conventions prevented her from speaking publicly. Later, Indian nationalist Bhikaji Cama confronted the Wafdist men on the issue of women's participation in the Egyptian nationalist movement. Women's participation in Egyptian civil society became a mobilizing component of the fight for independence, a struggle in which women played a key role.

As women began to enter the Egyptian public sphere, so too did they begin to enter the realm of politics. Wafd members' wives and other women took up the national cause and established the Wafdist Women's Central Committee (Lajnat al-Wafd al-Markaziyya lil-Sayyidat, WWCC) on 12 January 1920 in a meeting at St. Mark's Cathedral. When Wafd leader Saʿd Zaghlul was deported to the Seychelles in 1921, the WWCC continued to work for the nationalist cause in his absence. They coordinated embargoes against British goods and managed the financial side of the nationalist movement. Huda al-Shaʿrawi was elected president of the committee, and other founding members included Ulfat Ratib, Regina Habib Khayyat, Wissa Wasif, Ahmad Abu Usba, Sharifa Riyad, Ester Fahmi Wissa, Louise Majorelle Wasif Ghali, Ihsan al-Qusi, and Fikriyya Husni. Most came from large land-owning families, although some were middle-class Cairenes. The WWCC solidified links between various women's associations in Cairo in the nationalist cause, such as the New Women Society (Jamʿiyat al-Marʾa al-Jadida, founded by Shaʿrawi in 1919), the Society of the Renaissance of the Egyptian Woman (Jamʿiyyat Nahdat al-Sayyidat al-Misriyyat), and the Society of Mothers of the Future (Jamʿiyyat Ummuhat al-Mustaqbal). In addition, women from the WWCC helped to found women's organizations outside Cairo in Minya, Asyut, and Tanta.

Before the WWCC was a year old, members were bitterly disappointed when Saʿd Zaghlul and other Wafdist men did not consult them on a proposal for independence. They published a critique of the Wafdist men's actions and eventually founded the Egyptian Feminist Union (al-Ittihad al-Nisaʾi al-Misri). When Shaʿrawi left, other Wafdist women renamed their group the Committee of Saʿdist Women (al-Lajna al-Saʿdiyya lil-Sayyidat) and remained loyal to Zaghlul. Shaʿrawi and other women went on to dedicate their efforts to the feminist movement while the Wafd Party's role of serving as a vehicle for women's concerns diminished.

See also EGYPT; EGYPTIAN FEMINIST UNION; GENDER: GENDER AND LAW; GENDER: GENDER AND POLITICS; SHA'RAWI, HUDA AL-; WAFD; ZAGHLUL, SA'D.

Bibliography

Badran, Margo. *Feminists, Islam, and Nation: Gender and the Making of Modern Egypt.* Princeton, NJ: Princeton University Press, 1995.

Sharawi, Huda. *Harem Years: Memoirs of an Egyptian Feminist,* edited and translated by Margo Badran. London: Virago Press, 1986.

MARIA F. CURTIS

WAHDA DAM, AL-

See MAQARIN DAM

WAHHABI

See MUWAHHIDUN

WAHRHAFTIG, ZERAH

[1906–2002]

Israeli legal expert and politician.

Zerah Wahrhaftig (Warhaftig) was born in Belorussia and emigrated to Israel in 1947 via Poland, Lithuania, Japan, and the United States. Before his death in September 2002 at age 96 he was one of the last two living signers of the Israel's Declaration of Independence. As a young man he was active in the National Religious Front. He was a member of the Provisional Council of State, and after being elected to the first Knesset was continuously re-elected to the Knesset through the ninth Knesset in 1981. Wahrhaftig served as deputy minister of religious affairs from 1952 to 1958 and as minister of religious affairs in three governments, from 1961 to 1974. He was a member of the National Religious Party's moderate wing.

Wahrhaftig was an expert on the legal and constitutional system of Israel. As chairman of the Knesset Committee, he helped to draft legislation creating rabbinical courts and religious councils, enforcing sabbath law, the Israel Lands Law, and the 1950 Law of Return, which allowed Jews to settle in Israel. After the 1967 war, Wahrhaftig wrote a decree guaranteeing religious autonomy for Jews, Muslims, and Christians in the newly Israeli-administered Jerusalem, and drafted a constitutionally binding edict protecting respective holy sites.

See also ISRAEL: POLITICAL PARTIES IN.

BRYAN DAVES
UPDATED BY GREGORY S. MAHLER

WALLACH, YONA

[1944–1985]

Israeli poet.

Yona Wallach was born in Kiryat Uno, near Tel Aviv, to a veteran pioneer family. Her father was killed in the War of Independence when she was four, a trauma that haunted Wallach throughout her short life. Her widowed mother owned the only local cinema, where the impressionable Wallach absorbed the new-wave films that later echoed in her writing. A misfit in her small town and a high school dropout, Wallach, who wrote her first poem when she was seven, studied art, joined the Tel Aviv Circle of Poets, and published in their avant-garde periodicals.

Seeking relief from her emotional unrest, she turned to mental institutions and drugs, diving uninhibitedly into intense experiences. Life and writing became one, and when her first book, *Devarim* (Words, or Things, 1966), appeared, it shook the Israeli literary world with its inner demons, imaginary and absurd situations, surreal connections, bold depictions of sexuality, and fluid, violent, and seemingly unstructured diction.

In the five books that followed, Wallach took on the feminine revolution in Hebrew writing. She subverted religious and national preconceptions unprecedentedly and often used sexual encounters as the arena for examining issues of social injustice. Her poems blur boundaries between female and male, conscious and subconscious, horror and beauty, sensuality and spirituality. The self is shattered, and its components become separate entities.

Wallach, a precursor of postmodernism, led Israeli literature to uncharted lands. She died of cancer at the age of forty-one.

Bibliography

Kuvovi, Miri. "Violence in Wallach's Poetry." *Proceedings of the Eleventh World Congress of Jewish Studies,* Division C, vol. 3. Jerusalem: Ha-Igud ha-'olami le-madaè ha-Yahadut, 1994.

NILI GOLD

WAQF

An Islamic endowment created by its founder to dedicate specific property for the benefit of a particular public good (waqf khayri) *and/or the donor's family* (waqf ahli).

A *waqf* (Arabic plural, *awqâf*) may be composed of any kind of durable property whose use or income provides communal benefits, including mosques, hospitals, libraries, schools, canals, roads, and water fountains. The donor will write the charter for the administration of the *waqf* and appoint its initial trustees. The *ka'ba* in Mecca, the center of the Muslim pilgrimage, is the archetype of a *waqf.*

The first *waqf* established by Muhammad's community was the mosque at Quba in Medina. Charitable *waqfs* were established soon after when Muhammad dedicated seven orchards inherited from a follower to provide for the poor and needy. During the caliphate of Umar some donors established family *waqfs,* dedicating the income from their estates first to provide for their own descendents, with the surplus going to the poor. In the classical period of Islamic civilization the *waqfs* were an integral part of the economic and civil society infrastructure.

In the nineteenth and twentieth centuries, after the colonial powers had, to varying degrees, marginalized the *waqfs,* the secular states that succeeded them dismantled or appropriated them to a significant degree throughout most of the Muslim world. Motivations were partly economic (that the permanent nature of *waqfs* tied up resources that might be more effectively reallocated), but mainly political, aiming to increase state function, authority, and wealth at the expense of the civil (especially, the religious) sector. After appropriation of *waqf* lands for the benefit of multinational corporations by the shah of Iran, for example, migration of evicted tenant farmers to the cities contributed to the discontent leading to the revolution that established the Islamic Republic in 1979.

Despite the diminution in their properties, size, and autonomy, the *waqf* remains a significant element of Islamic society. In recent years they have experienced a resurgence, especially in Lebanon, Turkey, Jordan, and Algeria.

See also KA'BA.

Bibliography

Makdisi, George. *The Rise of Colleges: Institutions of Learning in Islam and the West.* Edinburgh, U.K.: Edinburgh University Press, 1981.

DENISE A. SPELLBERG
UPDATED BY IMAD-AD-DEAN AHMAD

WAR IN IRAQ (2003)

Controversial U.S.-led invasion and occupation of Iraq.

During the decade following the Gulf War of 1991, U.S.–Iraqi relations remained tense. At issue was the extent to which Iraq was cooperating with international monitors looking for evidence that the country was free of any weapons of mass destruction (chemical, biological, nuclear weapons). The United States was the leading force within the UN Security Council urging that the crippling international economic sanctions against Iraq that had been in place since August 1990 be continued until the United Nations Special Commission (UNSCOM) could certify Iraqi compliance. Several times during the administration of U.S. president William J. (Bill) Clinton, the situation deteriorated into crisis, including the December 1998 U.S. attack on Iraq known in the United States as Operation Desert Fox. Shortly thereafter, Iraq announced that UNSCOM's mission was over altogether.

Hardening of U.S–Iraq Relations under George W. Bush

The administration of President George W. Bush brought about a marked hardening of U.S. attitudes toward Iraq once he took office in January 2001. Bush, son of former president George H.W. Bush, who had led the 1991 Gulf War against Iraqi president Saddam Hussein, filled his administration with many veterans of his father's war with Iraq. These included Secretary of State Colin L. Powell, who had been chairman of the joint chiefs of staff of the U.S. military at the time of the Gulf War, and Vice President Richard Cheney, who had been secretary of defense for the elder Bush. The attacks carried out by al-Qaʿida on 11 September 2001, and Bush's decision to invade Afghanistan in October 2001, only hardened his resolve to confront Iraq. In his 30 January 2002 state of the union address, Bush included Iraq along with Iran and North Korea in what he called an "Axis of Evil." He pointed to what he claimed was evidence of Iraq's noncompliance with UN Security Council resolutions calling for disarmament, including a document purporting to show that Iraq had attempted to purchase 500 tons of uranium from Niger in 2000 (the International Atomic Energy Agency later proclaimed the document to be counterfeit). After months of claiming that Saddam Hussein constituted a clear threat to the United States, Bush convinced the U.S. congress to authorize him to use force against Iraq. The U.S. media offered no serious challenge to the administration's agenda.

Iraq agreed to allow UN weapons inspectors to return in September 2002, but an international debate over how to proceed ensued. The Bush administration encountered significant difficulties when it tried to convince other nations to support the use of force against Iraq if it failed to comply fully with UN resolutions. Not only did Bush face opposition from traditional rivals such as Russia and China, but he also had problems with longstanding U.S. allies within the North Atlantic Treaty Organization (NATO), including Germany and France. Those four nations, all of which sat on the UN Security Council at that time (Russia, China, and France as permanent members), remained adamant that the weapons inspectors be allowed to resume their activities before they would countenance any talk of war. Among U.S. allies, only Britain and Spain offered their full support to the U.S. hard line.

On 8 November 2002 the UN Security Council finally passed Resolution 1441, which demanded that Iraq allow the return of weapons inspectors. Iraq accepted, and officials of the United Nations

Monitoring, Verification, and Inspection Commission (UNMOVIC), created in December 1999 to replace UNSCOM, began their work on 27 November. In a 27 January 2003 report, chief inspectors Hans Blix and Muhammad El Baradei generally praised Iraqi cooperation and noted that they had not uncovered any evidence of weapons of mass destruction in the approximately 300 inspections that UNMOVIC had carried out to that date. The United States and Britain continued to make the case that Iraq had such weapons and constituted an immediate threat. On 3 February British prime minister Tony Blair posted a document on his official Web site that he claimed showed Iraqi weapons violations, based in part on British intelligence (parts of the document were later shown to have been plagiarized from open sources, not intelligence reports). U.S. secretary of state Colin Powell addressed the Security Council five days later, using props such as intercepted audiotapes of Iraqi military commanders' conversations, to convince the council that Iraq continued to disregard the international community. The U.S. administration also shifted its rationale for war during late 2002 and early 2003, mentioning banned weapons, then discussing possible Iraqi links to the al-Qaʿida network, then discussing the need to liberate Iraqis from Saddam's Hussein's dictatorial rule.

During the weeks of this debate there was unprecedented popular global opposition to waging war against Iraq. Demonstrations were held on all seven continents in early 2003, including at the McMurdo scientific research station in Antarctica. It has been estimated that 30 million people worldwide participated in antiwar demonstrations in 600 cities in dozens of countries during a weekend of global protest from 14 to 16 February. Countries whose governments supported the war—Britain, Spain, Italy, and the United States—were the scenes of what were perhaps their nations' largest ever public rallies. Huge demonstrations were held in Italy, where Pope John Paul II appealed for peace from the hawks. A January 2003 demonstration in freezing temperatures in Washington, D.C., was called the largest demonstration in the United States since the era of the Vietnam war protests.

Undeterred by such massive global opposition, including from longstanding U.S. allies, the United

States tried twice, in late February and early March, to convince the Security Council to adopt a resolution stating that Iraq had failed to comply with Resolution 1441 and calling for "serious consequences." These attempts failed. On 15 March UN Secretary-General Kofi Annan weighed into the debate by saying that an attack on Iraq absent a new resolution would constitute a violation of the UN charter. Bush, however, gave a televised speech the following day in which he demanded that Saddam Hussein and his sons Uday and Qusay leave Iraq within 48 hours or face attack. They refused. In Britain, the House of Commons voted two days after that, on 18 March, to support war.

The war commenced on 20 March with aerial bombing of Baghdad. Ground forces of a U.S.-led coalition invaded from Kuwait the next day while airborne troops based secretly in Jordan captured air bases in western Iraq. In addition to 255,000 Americans, this coalition eventually included 45,000 British troops, 2,000 Australians, and 200 each from Poland, Slovakia, and the Czech Republic. Fighting was fierce, but Iraqi forces were doomed from the start. By 6 April U.S.forces had captured Karbala and British troops had entered Basra. By 9 April U.S. forces had entered Baghdad as Saddam's regime crumbled. There were scenes of wild jubilation in parts of Baghdad at Saddam's downfall, as, for example, when crowds (and a U.S. tank) pulled down a huge statue of the deposed leader that had stood in Firdaws Square in downtown Baghdad. Tragically, the looting that swept through the city spread to some of Iraq's most important archaeological museums. The National Museum in Baghdad was sacked between 9 and 12 April, and both common pilferers and professional art thieves stole nearly 15,000 artifacts, some of them priceless treasures. Working with INTERPOL, U.S. officials worked to track down stolen artifacts that had been smuggled out of Iraq. By September 2003 more than 3,400 items from the National Museum had been recovered in Iraq, Jordan, Italy, and elsewhere. There was at least one case in which members of the U.S. forces themselves took an artifact from an Iraqi museum: The helmet of an Israeli aviator shot down over Iraq in June 1967 was taken from a display in a Baghdad military museum and given to Israeli authorities in Jordan in August 2003.

In the north, Kurdish forces joined the fight and helped to capture Mosul and Kirkuk. Saddam Hussein and other leading Iraqi officials went into hiding. The fighting was largely over by 16 April, and Bush declared on 1 May that "major combat operations" were over. At that point, U.S. and British military deaths in combat totaled 120. Iraqi deaths during that time, both civilian and military, were much more difficult to ascertain; estimates range from between 5,000 to 7,000 civilians killed, and 4,800 to 6,300 Iraqi soldiers. Saddam Hussein's sons Uday and Qusay were killed in a shootout with U.S. troops in Mosul on 22 July. Saddam himself was eventually captured by U.S. forces near Tikrit on 14 December.

Occupation of Iraq

To administer the occupied country, the United States created the Office for Reconstruction and Humanitarian Assistance. On 21 April 2003 former U.S. army general Jay Garner (1938–) was appointed as its head. Garner served as the civilian governor of occupied Iraq until he was replaced on 6 May by former U.S. State Department official L. Paul Bremer III (1941–). Bremer was named the administrator of the new Coalition Provisional Authority (CPA; in Arabic, Sultat al-I'tilaf al-Mu'aqqata), a division of the U.S. Department of Defense. As a result, Bremer became the civilian head of a U.S. military occupation administration. Through Security Council Resolution 1483 of 22 May 2003, the UN formally recognized the United States and Britain as occupying powers and lifted the sanctions imposed on Iraq, even though UNMOVIC had not yet certified Iraqi disarmament, as required by the sanctions resolutions. U.S. officials stated that the occupation was costing the United States approximately $1 billion per week, although some of those costs included items such as military salaries that would have been paid anyway. The United States also dispatched former secretary of state James Baker on an international campaign to convince Iraq's creditors to forgive the country's debts that had been accumulated by Saddam.

On 13 July 2003 Bremer created the Iraqi Governing Council (IGC) as an advisory body. The IGC included representatives from Iraq's main ethnic and religious groups, opposition politicians such as the Kurdish leaders Jalal Talabani and Mas'ud

Barzani, and returned exiles such as former diplomat Adnan Pachachi and Ahmad Chalabi, founder of the Iraqi National Congress. The IGC was allowed to form a cabinet, but final authority lay with Bremer, who retained veto powers over the IGC's decisions.

Armed resistance to the occupation escalated in the summer of 2003, as did attacks on a variety of Iraqi political and religious figures and foreign officials. On 19 August a car bomb at UN headquarters in Baghdad killed the top UN envoy to Iraq, Brazilian Sergio Vieira de Mello (1948–2003). Ten days later, on 29 August, leading Shi'ite cleric Ayatullah Muhammad Baqir al-Hakim (1939–2003) was assassinated in a massive bomb explosion in al-Najaf. By early 2004 guerrillas were carrying out increasingly more sophisticated bombings and other attacks on U.S. and other occupation troops, which had expanded by early 2004 to include combat and noncombat forces from thirty additional countries besides those that originally participated in the war. These attacks became an almost daily occurrence, not so much in the Shi'ite and Kurdish regions of Iraq as in the "Sunni Triangle" north of Baghdad, near towns such as Falluja and Tikrit. In addition, numerous car bombings killed scores of Iraqi civilians and officers of the reconstructed Iraqi police. On 2 March 2004, over 140 Iraqi Shi'a were killed during attacks in Baghdad and Karbala that came during the important Shi'ite religious celebration of Ashura. By late February 2004, 548 U.S. soldiers had died in Iraq since the beginning of the war, 337 as a result of hostile activity. Iraqi civilian deaths since the war began ranged somewhere between 8,000 and 10,000.

Controversy continued to swirl after the onset of the occupation. Although the presence of weapons of mass destruction was the major ostensible reason for going to war, by early 2004 occupation authorities had still not found any such stockpiles, a situation that eventually led President Bush, in January 2004, to call for a formal inquiry into prewar U.S. intelligence failures. In late 2003 in Britain, Prime Minister Blair was also engulfed in a controversy over the accuracy of his government's handling of intelligence. Paul Bremer was adamant by early 2004 that the CPA would turn over "sovereignty" to the Iraqi people on 30 June 2004, although

coalition troops would remain in the country. There were conflicting opinions about the shape of the new governmental system. Bremer's proposals for regional caucuses as the basis for constructing a new Iraqi legislature and interim government were rejected by most Iraqis, and he backed away from the idea in mid-February 2004. The leading Shi'ite cleric, Ayatullah Ali al-Husayni al-Sistani (1930–), wanted direct elections held as soon as possible. Iraq's Shi'ite Arabs and Kurds were much better organized politically than other ethnic and religious groups, including Sunni Arabs, Turkmen, Assyrians, and others, who were fearful that such quick elections could produce a Shi'ite-dominated country. In addition, the fact that al-Sistani is originally an Iranian (who came to Iraq decades ago) has raised some Sunni suspicions about Iranian influence. UN Secretary-General Kofi Annan sent special envoy Lakhdar Brahimi to Iraq to produce a recommendation for how to proceed, and stated in late February that it was not feasible to hold direct elections prior to the handover of sovereignty on 30 June. Fearing the possibility that Iraqis might draft a constitution that proclaimed *shari'a* to be the basis for legislation in the new Iraq, Bremer announced on 16 February that he would veto any such proposal coming from the IGC. On 8 March 2004, the IGC signed a provisional constitution for a federal Iraq that granted the Kurds a considerable voice in government. The constitution also called *shari'a* "a source" of legislation, as opposed to "the source."

See also ANNAN, KOFI A.; BAKER, JAMES A.; BARZANI FAMILY; BUSH, GEORGE HERBERT WALKER; BUSH, GEORGE WALKER; CHALABI, AHMAD; CLINTON, WILLIAM JEFFERSON; GULF CRISIS (1990–1991); GULF WAR (1991); HUSSEIN, SADDAM; IRAQ; IRAQI NATIONAL CONGRESS; POWELL, COLIN L.; QA'IDA, AL-; SANCTIONS, IRAQI.

Bibliography

Cordesman, Anthony H. *The Iraq War: Strategy, Tactics, and Military Lessons.* New York: Praeger, 2003.

Mahajan, Rahul. *Full Spectrum Dominance: U.S. Power in Iraq and Beyond.* New York: Seven Stories Press, 2003.

Official web site of the Coalition Provisional Authority: Authority. Official web site available from <http://cpa-iraq.org>.

Smith, Ray L., and West, Bing. *The March Up: Taking Baghdad with the First Marine Division.* New York: Bantam, 2003.

MICHAEL R. FISCHBACH

WARNIER LAW

Law passed by France's National Assembly in 1873 to establish individual titles on previously undivided lands held by families and tribes in Algeria.

The Warnier Law greatly facilitated land purchases by European settlers and appropriations by the state domain. It also hastened the appearance of small and dispersed properties insufficient to support the indigenous rural population.

PETER VON SIVERS

WAR OF ATTRITION (1969–1970)

Egypt's unsuccessful campaign to drive Israel back from the Suez Canal.

After the Arab–Israel War in 1967, fighting continued along the borders of the new territories captured by Israel, particularly along the Suez Canal. Violations of the cease-fire proliferated in September 1968, when Egypt concentrated some 150,000 troops along the west side of the canal. Heavy fighting took place on 8 and 9 March 1969, causing the death of Egypt's chief of staff, General Abd al-Munʿim Riyad. On 23 July of that year, President Gamal Abdel Nasser formally declared a war of attrition. He stated that, although his country was incapable of regaining the Sinai Peninsula by force, it could and would wear Israel out—hoping that Egyptian artillery barrages would make Israel withdraw its troops from the Suez Canal. Israel responded by building a system of thirty strongholds along the canal, known as the Bar-Lev Line.

On 31 October 1968 Israel had destroyed a power station at Naj Hamadi in upper Egypt, but it was not until July 1969 that it began regular aerial attacks that devastated Egyptian cities along the canal and turned their residents into refugees. In early 1970 Egypt received substantial amounts of Soviet military aid, including surface-to-air missile batteries that could down Israeli aircraft. After a number of aerial battles between Israeli planes and Russian-flown MiG fighters, the United States introduced its Rogers Plan and pressed Egypt and Israel for a new cease-fire, which went into effect on 7 August 1970.

Some controversy exists among military scholars as to which country actually won the war of attrition. Israel certainly proved its military superiority, especially in aerial dogfights with Egyptian pilots, but Egypt gained a diplomatic victory in persuading the Soviet Union to provide military assistance and in moving SAM missile batteries, which Egypt used in the 1973 Arab–Israel War, close to the Suez Canal. The long-term effect of the war of attrition has been to make Israel more suspicious of international peace proposals and Egypt more precise in its strategic military planning.

See also ARAB–ISRAEL WAR (1967); ARAB–ISRAEL WAR (1973); BAR-LEV, HAIM; ROGERS, WILLIAM PIERCE.

Bibliography

Bar-Siman-Tov, Yaacov. *The Israeli-Egyptian War of Attrition, 1969–1970: A Case Study of Limited Local War.* New York: Columbia University Press, 1980.

Herzog, Chaim. *The Arab–Israeli Wars: War and Peace in the Middle East,* revised edition. New York: Vintage, 1984.

Korn, David A. *Stalemate: The War of Attrition and Great Power Diplomacy in the Middle East, 1967–1970.* Boulder, CO: Westview, 1992.

BENJAMIN JOSEPH
UPDATED BY ARTHUR GOLDSCHMIDT

WATER

Because of its scarcity, water plays a central role in Middle Eastern politics and society.

Nowhere in the world is water more important than in the Middle East and North Africa. In no other region do so many people strive so hard for economic growth on the basis of so little water: here is found 5 percent of the world's population but only 1 percent of its fresh water. Of the ten nations with the least water per capita, six are in this region. No wonder that both Jewish and Muslim scriptures are full of references to water.

The Dead Sea is the lowest point on earth and the culmination of the Jordan River. Its high concentration of mineral salts makes this body of water lifeless but also makes its visitors buoyant, creating a popular tourist attraction along the border between Israel and Jordan. © RICHARD T. NOWITZ/CORBIS. REPRODUCED BY PERMISSION.

Role of Climate

The more heavily populated parts of the Middle East are semiarid, with rainfall of 10 to 29 inches (250 to 750 mm) per year. However, low rainfall is less of a problem than variability in rainfall. The great bulk of the rain falls in four winter months, with none falling during the rest of the year. Rainfall also changes rapidly with distance, from more than 20 inches (500 mm) on the coast of Lebanon to 8 inches (200 mm) in the Biqa, only an hour away by road but across the Lebanon mountains.

Seasonal and spatial variations in rainfall are sharp but predictable. What makes planning difficult is the sharp variation from one year to the next.

Reliable flow in the rivers (the flow that can be expected nine years out of ten) is only 10 percent of the average. In northern latitudes, water planning can be built around statistical averages; here, it must be built around extremes.

This already difficult water situation will likely get worse. Population growth rates are high, and most climate change models suggest higher temperatures, lower rainfall, and more frequent droughts for the region.

Role of History

Development in the Middle East and North Africa has always been more dependent on water than on any other resource, including oil. By the fourth millennium B.C.E., the Sumerians had built a paradise in what is now Iraq through intricate canals for irrigating crops; two millennia later it had largely collapsed because of salinization of the soil. Ancient cities, such as Palmyra in Syria, were possible only because of carefully engineered tunnels, called *qanats* (*foggaras* in Iran), to bring water from springs tens of kilometers away.

Over the years, the peoples of the Middle East have made water a preoccupation, and each nation has a central agency, typically a full ministry, to deal with water. Many of the principles for good water management were worked out in the Middle East—although just as often they were ignored for political, financial, or social reasons.

Water Sources

The Middle East includes two of the mightiest river systems in the world. The Nile has two main branches: The White Nile originates in Uganda, and the larger Blue Nile (together with the Atbara) originates in Ethiopia; they join near Khartoum and flow northward through Egypt to the Mediterranean. The Tigris and Euphrates both originate in Turkey and flow south-southeastward through Syria and Iraq before joining and flowing into the Persian Gulf via the Shatt al-Arab, at the Iranian border.

The region also includes numerous medium-sized rivers, such as the Jordan, which flows from three springs through the Sea of Galilee (one of the few natural lakes in the region) and into the Dead Sea, 415 meters below sea level. Only Turkey has an

Atatürk Dam, built across the Euphrates River in southeastern Turkey and in use since 1990, is one of the largest dams of its kind (earth and rock fill) in the world. Dams such as these are not only expensive but are also costly in terms of reducing the flow of water to countries lying downstream, contributing to a growing shortage of fresh water in much of the region. © ED KASHI/CORBIS. REPRODUCED BY PERMISSION.

abundance of river water, but its big rivers are only found in the eastern part of the nation. Finally, there are small coastal rivers (many of them ephemeral), and a few major wetlands, such as the marshlands in southern Iraq and the Sudd swamp in southern Sudan.

The construction of new dams and pipelines to deliver water from major rivers in the Middle East will cost two or three times as much per unit of water as current supplies, and if construction occurs in upstream countries, such as Ethiopia and Turkey, it will reduce flows downstream. Therefore, the region will increasingly shift toward the use of underground water, which has the great advantage of not evaporating. (Lakes and reservoirs in the region lose meters of water per year to evaporation.)

Historically, underground water was tapped by shallow wells dug in unconsolidated materials to get small flows of water. Today, much larger volumes of water are extracted from wells drilled tens to hundreds of meters into aquifers, which are rock layers with pores that contain water. Renewable aquifers are replenished (generally slowly) by rainfall; nonrenewable, or fossil, aquifers contain water trapped in sediments laid down millions of years ago.

Just more than 10 percent of the water supply for the region comes from aquifers, but in Israel and Jordan the share approaches 50 percent, and in Kuwait and parts of the Arabian Peninsula it approaches 100 percent (apart from desalination). Libya's Great Man-Made River pumps water from fossil aquifers in the south of the country and moves it 930 miles (1,500 km) to farms and cities in the north.

The third most important source of water in the Middle East is recycled sewage, which is treated and reused, mainly for irrigation. Despite common

Lake Van, a salt lake in eastern Turkey near the border with Iran, is the largest lake in the country. Turkey is the source of the Tigris and Euphrates as well as numerous lesser rivers, and it is one of only a handful of nations in the region where water is abundant. © ADAM WOOLFITT/CORBIS. REPRODUCED BY PERMISSION.

belief (shared by both Muslims and non-Muslims), there is no objection in Islamic law to the reuse of sewer water provided it is properly treated.

More than half of the world's desalination capacity is found in the region, mainly in the oil-producing nations of the Arabian peninsula with lots of by-product natural gas that was formerly flared. (Desalination is an energy-intensive process.) Costs for desalination have fallen to a level that makes it feasible as a source of potable water but still too expensive for irrigation.

Other sources of water are individually small but collectively provide sizable amounts of water. Water harvesting gathers rain that falls over a wide area and directs it to one field through small channels and micro-barrages. The technique can allow crops in areas where rainfall is only 4 inches (100 mm) per year. Rainwater is also collected from rooftops and stored in cisterns. If handled carefully, rooftop water can be used for drinking.

Uses of Water

By far the largest share of water in the region goes to agriculture—as much as 90 percent of total water use in some countries, and 60 percent in the more industrialized countries.

Drinking requires only a relatively small volume of water, but it must meet higher standards than that used for irrigation. Thirty liters of potable water per person-day is generally regarded as the minimum for drinking, cooking, and washing.

Industrial water use is low. Food and beverage processing are the largest industrial consumers. More is withdrawn for cooling but most of this water is recycled or returned to the watercourse.

A hidden but critical amount of water must be left in place to support fisheries and hydropower, as well as to protect habitat. This use is typically neglected by governments when they drain swamps, canalize rivers, or extend land. As a result, not only has the environment been degraded, but fish catches have declined and the salinity of groundwater has increased.

Problems

The nations of the Middle East all face three overlapping sources of stress in their water management: 1) quantity, which has been a source of stress since history began; 2) quality, which is a newer stress but increasingly important; and 3) equity, which occurs when the same water is subject to competing demands.

Quantity. Iran, Iraq, Lebanon, Sudan, Syria, and Turkey are fairly well endowed with water, with more than 1 million cubic meters (Mcm) per capita; Algeria, Egypt, Israel, Morocco, and Palestine form a middle group; and Jordan, Libya, Tunisia, and the countries of the Arabian Peninsula are least well endowed, with less than 500 Mcm per capita. However, water availability is declining in every nation, which means that current patterns of water use are not sustainable. Some projections for the Jordan River basin suggest that by 2025 household and industrial uses will require all the fresh water, leaving none for farmers. Most nations are also drawing down their renewable aquifers and mining fossil ones. Some have annual water deficits of several thousand Mcm.

Water quantity problems in the region can be resolved in small part by exploiting additional

Freshwater withdrawals by country and sector

Estimates for 2000

Country	Total	Per capita	Use (%)	(cubic km/a) Domestic	(cubic km/a) Industry	% with safe (cubic m/p) drinking water
Afghanistan	26.1	1,020	1	0	99	13
Algeria	4.5	142	25	15	60	94
Bahrain	0.2	387	39	4	56	100
Egypt	55.1	809	6	8	86	95
Iran	70.0	916	6	2	92	95
Iraq	42.8	1,852	5	3	92	85
Israel	1.7	280	36	11	51*	100
Jordan	1.0	155	22	3	75	96
Lebanon	1.3	393	28	4	68	100
Libya	4.6	720	11	2	87	72
Morocco	11.1	381	5	3	92	82
Oman	1.2	450	5	2	94	39
Saudi Arabia	17.0	786	9	1	90	95
Sudan	17.8	597	4	1	94	75
Syria	14.4	894	4	2	94	80
Tunisia	3.1	313	32	8	60	99
Turkey	31.6	481	16	11	72	83
Yemen	2.9	162	7	1	92	69

* Percentage by sector adjusted by author on basis of estimates by the Planning Department of the Israeli Water Commission. All data for Israel based on estimates by the author.

SOURCE: Gleick, Peter, et al, ed. *The World's Water: The Biennial Report in Freshwater Resources, 2002–2003* (Washington, D.C., Island Press, 2002).

TABLE BY GGS INFORMATION SERVICES, THE GALE GROUP.

sources of supply but in much larger part by better use of the water that is already available. People in the region use less water than those elsewhere in the world, but as a result of poor management and misguided economic policies conservation here (as in most other parts of the world) remains far short of its potential. Many nations lose half the water put into municipal systems to leaks, and they typically deliver piped water at low (or no) price. Cost-effective savings of 25 to 50 percent are possible in most uses.

Moreover, every country in the region provides water to farmers at highly subsidized prices. Under the influence of higher prices, Israeli scientists developed drip irrigation systems that have cut water use per hectare by 40 percent. However, drip irrigation is expensive and not appropriate for all crops. Lower-cost sprinkler systems, used at night to minimize evaporation, can also increase irrigation efficiency, as can irrigating only at times critical to plant growth.

Most analysts find that water is tens of times more valuable in industrial or household uses than in agriculture. Therefore, crops grown in the region will gradually be replaced by imports. It takes roughly a thousand tons of water to produce one ton of wheat. Using that ratio, Middle Eastern nations already import grains with a virtual water content equal to the flow of the Nile.

Quality. Much of the limited fresh water in the Middle East is polluted from growing volumes of human, industrial, and agricultural waste. Three problems stand out: 1) Overpumping of wells causes a decline in the water table—by as much as a meter a year in some areas. This decline adds to pumping costs and permits lower-quality water (or, if near the coast, seawater) to flow inward and contaminate the aquifer. The only way to avoid the problem is to match pumping rates to inflow. 2) Agricultural runoff is the major non-point source of water pollution—mainly sediment, phosphorus, nitrogen, and pesticides. Better farming methods, such as conservation tillage, contour planting, and terracing can control soil erosion and cut pollution by half or more. 3) Urban sewage systems have either begun to deteriorate or cannot handle the growing loads placed on them. Large investments are needed to improve their physical infrastructure.

Equity. Most of the larger rivers in the region cross an international border—some cross several borders—or form a border. No tabulation exists for aquifers that underlie national borders, but there are many.

Despite many statements suggesting that the next war in the Middle East will be over fresh water, there is little evidence for this. Not a single war has been fought over water for hundreds of years, but many treaties dealing with water have been signed. Water will be a source of conflict, but the conflicts will mainly be intranational rather than international. Likely sources of conflict include rural and urban users contending for the same water and rising demands from poor farmers, who are often disadvantaged in their access to water, and from women, who typically want more water for their households while men prefer to use it to grow cash crops. Israeli control of water in the West Bank is contentious, but even here experts have shown that compromise is feasible.

None of the three stresses on water in the Middle East will be easily resolved. Most of the nations in the region have already reached or are fast approaching the limits of their indigenous water supplies. Although higher prices for water and technological advances may defer the crisis, the only long-term solutions involve much greater efficiency in use, full reuse of wastewater, and gradual shifts of water from agriculture to other sectors. All of the nations of the Middle East and North Africa must revise their water policies to provide for a sustainable future, and they must find equitable ways to share water within and between nations.

Bibliography

Amery, Hussein A., and Wolf, Aaron T., eds. *Water in the Middle East: A Geography of Peace.* Austin: University of Texas Press, 2000.

Beaumont, Peter. "Water Policies for the Middle East in the Twenty-first Century: The New Economic Realities." *International Journal of Water Resources Development* 18, no. 2 (2002): 315–334.

Brooks, David B., and Mehmet, Ozay, eds. *Water Balances in the Eastern Mediterranean.* Ottawa: International Development Research Centre, 2000.

Kolars, John. "The Spatial Attributes of Water Negotiation: The Need for a River Ethic and River Advocacy in the Middle East." In *Water in the Middle East: A Geography of Peace,* edited by Hussein A. Amery and Aaron T. Wolf. Austin: University of Texas Press, 2000.

Lonergan, Stephen C., and Brooks, David B. *Watershed: The Role of Fresh Water in the Israeli–Palestinian Conflict.* Ottawa: International Development Research Centre, 1994.

Postel, Sandra. *Pillar of Sand: Can the Irrigation Miracle Last?* New York: Norton, 1999.

Rogers, Peter, and Lydon, Peter, eds. *Water in the Arab World: Perspectives and Prognoses.* Cambridge, MA: Division of Applied Sciences, Harvard University, 1994.

Shapland, Greg. *Rivers of Discord: International Water Disputes in the Middle East.* New York: St. Martin's Press; London: Hurst, 1997.

Waterbury, John. *The Nile Basin: National Determinants of Collective Action.* New Haven, CT: Yale University Press, 2002.

Wolf, Aaron T. "Transboundary Fresh Water Database." Department of Geosciences, Oregon State University. Available from <http://www.transboundarywaters.orst.edu>.

DAVID B. BROOKS

WATTAR, AL-TAHER
[1936–]

Algerian novelist, short-story writer, and journalist.

Al-Taher Wattar (also spelled Tahar Ouettar and Tahir Watter) was born in Sedrata (department of Souk Ahras, eastern Algeria). His studies, exclusively in Arabic schools, took him to the Ibn Badis Intitute of Constantine and then to the Zeitouna University of Tunis in 1954. In 1955–1956 he published his first short stories in newspapers and joined the Civil Organization of the FLN (Front de Libération Nationale). After the war, he edited two periodicals in Tunisia and Algeria: *al-Jamahir* (The masses) from 1962 to 1963 and *al-Ahrar* (Free people) from 1972 to 1974. He also served as a civil servant of the FLN and general director of Algerian Radio. Since 1989, Wattar has served as president of *al-Jahidhiya,* the Algerian literary and cultural association. An important figure in Algerian literature, he is one of the few novelists who have attempted to make up for the lack of conventional types in the Arabic novel.

His writings present a panorama of Algeria's postindependence history, with a look back at the Algerian War of Independence and a subtle treatment of postcolonial Algerian politics, culture, and society. His nationalistic works defend the socialist ideology and the role played by the communists in the Algerian War of Independence. His novel *L'As* (1974; The genius), in particular, reveals the communists' involvement in the fighting; Wattar used this book as a first step to indict those in power for their many failures. His *al-Sham'a wa ad-Dahalib* (1995; The candle and dark tunnels), addresses the fall of the Soviet Union and its aftermath.

The symbolic novel *al-Hawwat wa al-Qasr* (1980; The fisherman and the palace) reveals the disappointments of the people with the political agenda of independent Algeria. Another controversial subject Wattar raises is the abuses by the opportunists who benefited from both war and peace. His novels *al-Zilzal* (1974; The earthquake) and *Urs Baghl* (1978; A mule's wedding) are primarily allegorical writings with a deep vein of satire and provide insight into Algerian culture, politics, society, and psychology. His novel *al-Wali al-Tahir ya'ud ila Maqamihi al-Zaki* (1999; Saint Tahir returns to his holy shrine), deals with the Islamic renaissance. Wattar's *al-Shuhada Ya'udun Hatha al-Usbu* (1980; Martyrs come back this week), a collection of seven linked short stories, dramatically portrays the national betrayal of the memory of the martyrs of the War of Independence.

The novel *al-Ishq wa al-Mawt fi al-Zaman al-Harrashi* (1980; Love and death in the Harrashi time) expresses Wattar's great optimism during the rule of President Houari Boumedienne. But changes on the political scene ended his dreams, and the novel *Tajribatun fi al-Ishq* (1994; An experience in passion) is the cry of a disappointed man.

See also LITERATURE: ARABIC, NORTH AFRICAN.

Bibliography

Allen, Roger, ed. *Modern Arabic Literature*. New York: Ungar, 1987.

Cox, Debbie. "Marginality as Resistance to Incorporation in Algeria's Arabic Literature: An Approach to Tahar Wattar's 'Urs Baghal.'" *Journal of Algerian Studies* 1, no. 1 (1998).

Cox, Debbie. "The Novels of Taher Watter: Command and Critique?" *Research in African Literature* 28, no. 3 (fall 1997): 94–109.

Cox, Debbie. *Politics, Language and Gender in the Algerian Arabic Novel*. London: Edwin Mellen Press, 2002.

Granara, William. "Mythologising the Algerian War of Independence: Tahir Wattar and the Contemporary Algerian Novel." *Journal of North African Studies* 4, no. 3 (1999).

AIDA A. BAMIA
UPDATED BY AZZEDINE G. MANSOUR

WAUCHOPE, ARTHUR
[1874–1947]

British high commissioner in Palestine and Transjordan, 1931–1938.

Sir Arthur Grenfell Wauchope, a Scotsman, was a professional soldier who served in the Second Boer War and, from 1903 to 1914, in India. During the first two years of World War I he served on the western front. In 1916 he was transferred to Mesopotamia in command of the Highland Battalion and was wounded at the battle of Shaykh Sa'd. After the war he served in Germany, Great Britain, and Northern Ireland. He retired from the army as a lieutenant-general in 1931 and was appointed high commissioner of Palestine and Transjordan. The prime minister, Ramsay MacDonald, said that Wauchope was "a general who does it with his head, not his feet." As high commissioner, Wauchope compared the difficulty of dealing with the Arabs and Jews to that of a circus performer riding two horses at once. The early years of his tenure were marked by unprecedented levels of Jewish immigration and by growing political tension. Wauchope's proposal in 1935 for the establishment of an elected legislative council was rejected by Arabs and Jews as well as by the British parliament. In 1936 the three-year-long countrywide Palestine Arab revolt broke out. At first Wauchope urged restraint, but when clashes between British forces and Arab rebels intensified, he recommended the use of large-scale armed force to quell disorder. He retired on grounds of ill health in February 1938, before completing his second five-year term.

See also PALESTINE ARAB REVOLT (1936–1939).

Bibliography

Sykes, Christopher. *Cross Roads to Israel.* London: Collins, 1965.

KAREN A. THORNSVARD
UPDATED BY BERNARD WASSERSTEIN

WAVELL, ARCHIBALD PERCIVAL
[1883–1950]

Commander in chief of British forces in the Middle East; British general in World War II; Viceroy of India, 1943–1947.

Archibald Percival Wavell was born in Colchester, England, and graduated from Sandhurst, the British military academy. He served under General Edmund Allenby in Palestine in World War I. In 1937 he was again sent to Palestine to deal with the unrest between the Arabs and Jews. He successfully quelled the Palestine Arab Revolt and returned to Britain in 1938. In 1939, he became commander in chief for all British forces in the Middle East, where he defeated the Italian forces in North and East Africa (1940–1941). He was not successful in preventing the fall of Greece and Crete, and when he succumbed to General Erwin Rommel's Afrika Korps in 1941, he was reassigned to Southeast Asia. Wavell concluded his career as viceroy of India (1943–1947), the last viceroy before Lord Mountbatten, who helped ease India into independence from the British Empire.

See also PALESTINE ARAB REVOLT (1936–1939).

Bibliography

Collins, Robert J. *Lord Wavell.* London, 1947.

DANIEL E. SPECTOR

WAZIR, INTISAR AL- (UMM JIHAD)
[1941–]

Palestinian political figure.

Intisar al-Wazir was born in 1941 in Gaza city. In 1965 she married Khalil al-Wazir (Abu Jihad) a cofounder of al-Fatah and leader of the first Palestinian uprising, who was assassinated by Israeli commandos in Tunisia in early 1988. In 1965 she also participated in founding the General Union for Palestinian Women (GUPW) to support Palestinian

women socially, economically, and legally. She served as the secretary-general of the GUPW between 1980 and 1985.

Al-Wazir founded numerous centers for women that focused on literacy training and rehabilitation, including the Social Affairs Committee, the Martyrs' Families Organization, and the Committee for Prisoners and the Injured. Upon the creation of the Palestinian Authority, al-Wazir served as the first Palestinian minister for social affairs between 1996 and 2003.

In addition to her prominent role in social activism, al-Wazir has held important political positions since the early days of her public career. She joined al-Fatah in 1959 as its first female member. She has been a member of the Palestinian National Council since 1974 and a member of the Fatah Central Committee since 1987. In 1983 she served as the deputy secretary-general of the Fatah Revolutionary Council.

Al-Wazir lived in exile for thirty years, returning to the Gaza Strip in 1995. She was elected to the Palestinian Legislative Council (PLC) in 1996.

See also WAZIR, KHALIL AL-.

Bibliography

Kawar, Amal. *Daughters of Palestine: Leading Women of the Palestinian National Movement.* Albany: State University of New York Press, 1996.

KHALED ISLAIH

WAZIR, KHALIL AL-
[1935–1988]

Also known as Abu Jihad, one of the founding members of al-Fatah.

Khalil Ibrahim al-Wazir was born on 10 October 1935 to a Palestinian Sunni Muslim shopkeeper in Ramla in Mandatory Palestine. When its inhabitants were summarily expelled by Israeli forces in July 1948, al-Wazir made his way to Gaza City, where he resumed his education at a United Nations Relief and Works Agency school.

Al-Wazir first became politically active in 1953, covertly receiving military training in the Egyptian-administered Gaza Strip. Probably affiliated with the Muslim Brotherhood at this time, he formed his own commando unit, whose activities led to his brief imprisonment by the Egyptian authorities in 1954. In 1954 he also first met the future Palestine Liberation Organization (PLO) chairman, Yasir Arafat, beginning a lifelong partnership and friendship, which, in association with future PLO deputy chairman Salah Khalaf (Abu Iyad), was to form the resilient core leadership of the contemporary Palestinian national movement.

After completing his studies in Cairo, where he had moved in September 1956, al-Wazir left in 1957 for Kuwait as a schoolteacher. His meeting there with Arafat that fall, a meeting of minds regarding the need to establish an independent, armed Palestinian movement, sowed the seeds for the formation of the Palestine National Liberation Movement (al-Fatah) in 1959. Al-Wazir would serve on its Central Committee and the subsequently established Revolutionary Council for the rest of his life.

Among al-Fatah's founders, al-Wazir alone had prior experience in forming a guerrilla organization and played a leading role in its development. In 1963 he went to Algiers to open al-Fatah's first diplomatic mission and organize military training for its recruits. He used this post to establish relations with China (al-Fatah's first non-Arab source of arms), North Korea, and Vietnam; meet guerrilla theoretician Che Guevara; and participate in the 1964 Palestine National Council, which founded the PLO. During this period he also remained, with Arafat, the leading advocate within al-Fatah's Central Committee for an immediate start to military operations. When the debate was resolved in late 1964, al-Wazir was appointed deputy commander in chief of al-Fatah's military wing, al-Asifa (The Storm).

After the PLO came under the control of al-Fatah and other guerrilla organizations in 1968–1969, al-Wazir additionally assumed the post of deputy commander in chief of PLO military forces. Although this position gave him only limited authority over non-Fatah forces, al-Fatah's preponderance within the PLO ensured that he played a central role in PLO military affairs until his death. He firmly believed armed struggle was legitimate and consistently sought to escalate it. He also did not hesitate to attack or retaliate against civilian targets

Khalil al-Wazir (right) with George Habash at the 16th Palestinian National Council Meeting in 1983. Al-Wazir was one of the original members of the Palestinian Liberation Organization and played an important role in many of its operations up until his assassination in 1988. © ALAIN NOGUES/CORBIS SYGMA. REPRODUCED BY PERMISSION.

when he thought this necessary but opposed the use of violence outside the region.

Al-Wazir, who furthermore directed al-Fatah's Department of the Occupied Homeland, was also among the first of his colleagues to grasp the importance of complementing armed struggle in Gaza and the West Bank with political mobilization. Particularly after the PLO's evacuation from Beirut in 1982, he worked hard to develop al-Fatah's political infrastructure in the West Bank and Gaza Strip, thus helping prepare the ground for the popular uprising, or Intifada, which erupted in December 1987. It was primarily on account of his leading role in assisting the uprising's clandestine leadership and channeling support to the West Bank and Gaza that he was assassinated by an Israeli commando squad (which filmed the event) in Tunis on 16 April 1988. His death precipitated the most serious disturbances the West Bank and Gaza Strip had witnessed since 1967, and his funeral in Damascus was attended by hundreds of thousands, including representatives from all Palestinian factions. He is survived by his wife, prominent Fatah militant Intisar al-Wazir, and four of their five children.

Along with Khalaf, Khalil al-Wazir was the most important PLO and Fatah leader after Arafat and, in internal debates, consistently Arafat's closest ally. The achievements and failures of these organizations and of the Palestinian people generally during his time are therefore equally his.

A straightforward nationalist whose mind was attuned to practical action and organizational matters, al-Wazir was among Palestinians respected in life and venerated in death. Though denounced as a reactionary by more radical elements during the 1970s for his conservative positions, he enjoyed extensive contacts among other factions and later emerged as a prominent mediator. As with all Palestinian nationalist leaders during his lifetime, he was viewed by Israel as a terrorist, and Israel rejected his support of a negotiated settlement.

Neither an intellectual nor an orator, al-Wazir does not have any writings to his name and gave fewer press statements than his colleagues.

See also ARAFAT, YASIR; FATAH, AL-; INTIFADA (1987–1991); KHALAF, SALAH; MUSLIM BROTHERHOOD; PALESTINE LIBERATION ORGANIZATION (PLO); WAZIR, INTISAR AL- (UMM JIHAD).

Bibliography

Cobban, Helena. *The Palestinian Liberation Organisation: People, Power, and Politics.* Cambridge, U.K., and New York: Cambridge University Press, 1984.

Hart, Alan. *Arafat, Terrorist or Peacemaker?* London: Sidgwick and Jackson, 1984.

Sayid, Yezid. "Death of the 'Quiet Man.'" *Middle East International* 324 (30 April 1988):9.

MOUIN RABBANI

WAZZANI, MUHAMMAD HASSAN AL-
[1910–1978]

Moroccan nationalist.

In the early 1930s, Muhammad Hassan al-Wazzani, a native of Fez, was a leader of the Comité d'Action Marocaine (CAM). He was elected secretary-general of the Bloc d'Action Nationale in October 1936, but the following year founded the Parti Démocratique Constitutionnel (PDC). Wazzani was imprisoned for nine years (1937–1946) on political charges. Periodically, he cooperated with the Istiqlal, and from 1953 to 1954, he and his followers joined the National Front. Wazzani was named minister of state without portfolio in King Hassan's 1961 coalition government. He was among those wounded in 1971 in the attempted coup against the king.

See also PARTI DÉMOCRATIQUE CONSTITUTIONNEL (PDC).

BRUCE MADDY-WEITZMAN

WEIZMAN, EZER
[1924–]

Israeli politician and soldier; president of Israel (1993–2000).

Born in Haifa, Ezer Weizman is the nephew of Chaim Weizmann, Israel's first president. In 1942 Weizman joined the Royal Air Force and served in Rhodesia, Egypt, and India. In 1946 and 1947 he studied aeronautics in Britain. From 1946 to 1948 he was a member of the prestate underground Irgun Zva'i Le'umi.

Weizman was one of the founding fathers of the Israeli Air Force (IAF). Following the United Nations vote to partition Palestine, he worked in the Air Service, the IAF's predecessor, and during the 1948 war he commanded an IAF squadron. In 1950 he became IAF chief of operations, and in 1956 commander. In 1967 he became chief of the general staff.

In 1969 Weizman entered politics. He served as leader of the GAHAL Party and was minister of transportation in Levi Eshkol's Government of National Unity. He resigned from the government in 1970 and went into private business, but continued on the Herut Executive Committee. In 1977, when the Likud (formed from the merger of Herut, Gahal, and other right-of-center parties) won its first national election, Weizman was campaign manager.

Having been appointed minister of defense by the new prime minister, Menachem Begin, Weizman supervised the invasion of Lebanon in 1978; he also was a moderating influence in the Camp David peace talks in September 1978. Although he was perceived as a hawk when he joined the Begin government, Weizman increasingly argued for a more moderate approach; this led to conflicts with other members of the Likud. In May 1980 he resigned from the cabinet; six months later he voted against the government on a no-confidence vote, charging that Begin was intentionally frustrating the peace process.

In 1984 Weizman's political party, Yahad, won three seats in the Eleventh Knesset. Following the elections, Weizman was appointed minister of science in a National Unity government. In 1986 Yahad officially joined the Labor Party. In 1987 Weizman was the first member of the Labor Party in the Knesset to call for negotiations with the Palestine Liberation Organization (PLO). In 1990 he was accused of undertaking secret meetings with PLO officials (illegal at the time), but charges were never filed. He resigned his seat in the Knesset before the 1992 election, ostensibly because he was frustrated with the slow pace of peace negotiations, and in March 1993 the Labor Party nominated him as its candidate for president. He became the president of Israel on 14 May 1993 and was reelected to a second term as president in 1998.

Weizman introduced the modern presidency to Israel, breaking from the traditional model in which "nonpolitical" presidents avoided partisan politics. He was unapologetic about taking controversial positions, and on several occasions his actions caused political disruption. He resigned his presidency in July 2000. An investigation by the attorney general found that Weizman had received more than $300,000 from a French Jewish businessman between 1987 and 1993; the scandal resulted in his being the first Israeli president to be the subject of police investigation, and the first president to resign.

See also ISRAEL: POLITICAL PARTIES IN; WEIZMANN, CHAIM.

Bibliography

American-Israeli Cooperative Enterprise. "Ezer Weizman." In *Jewish Virtual Library.* Available from <http://www.us-israel.org/jsource/biography>.

State of Israel Ministry of Foreign Affairs. "Ezer Weizman." In *Personalities.* Available from <http://www.israel-mfa.gov.il/mfa>.

Weizman, Ezer. *The Battle for Peace.* New York: Bantam, 1981.

Weizman, Ezer. *On Eagles' Wings.* New York: Macmillan, 1976.

GREGORY S. MAHLER

WEIZMANN, CHAIM
[1874–1952]

Zionist leader; first president of Israel, 1948–1952.

Chaim (also Hayyim) Weizmann was born in the Jewish community of Motol, near Pinsk, in Belorussia, part of the Pale of Settlement, the region into which Jews were largely confined by the Russian empire. His father, a moderately prosperous timber merchant, educated his twelve children in the modern style. Chaim went to a Russian secondary school in Pinsk, studied in Germany, and earned his doctorate in chemistry in Geneva in 1899. From 1900 to 1904 he taught at the University of Geneva.

From his earliest youth Weizmann was a convinced Zionist. Committed to the promotion of Haskalah (secular modern Hebrew literature and culture), he encouraged a group of young Zionists, called the Democratic Fraction, to challenge the cautious policies of established Zionist leadership. Their initial project, the creation of a Jewish university in Palestine, widened the rift between secular and religious Zionists. In 1904 Weizmann took a position at the University of Manchester in England. He continued to participate in Zionist activities and, in the course of election campaigns in Manchester, met Arthur Balfour and Winston Churchill.

The outbreak of World War I dislocated the World Zionist Organization (WZO). Weizmann accepted a government appointment to supervise the synthetic production of acetone, a vital necessity for the production of mortar shells. As the war progressed, Weizmann's professional and political standing grew. Helped by C. P. Scott, editor of the *Manchester Guardian* and a sympathizer with Zionism, he met David Lloyd George, Herbert Samuel, and other Liberal ministers. Without the formal authorization of any official Zionist agency, Weizmann was instrumental in persuading British politicians to support Zionist aims. He argued that a British-sponsored Zionist entity in Palestine would enhance British strategic interests in the Middle East and secure imperial lines of communication to India. The Balfour Declaration of 2 November 1917, which promised British support for the establishment in Palestine of a Jewish National Home, was Weizmann's great diplomatic achievement and a turning point in modern Jewish history.

Chaim Weizmann (right) stands with U.S. president Harry Truman, holding the Torah, at the White House on 25 May 1948. Weizmann, serving as the president of the New Jewish State of Israel, met with the U.S. president to discuss Palestinian affairs. © BETTMANN/CORBIS. REPRODUCED BY PERMISSION.

In 1918 Weizmann headed the Zionist Commission, which visited Palestine and established a basis for cooperation with the British military administration there. He led the Zionist delegation to the Paris Peace Conference signalling the end of World War I 1919 and helped to secure confirmation of the British Mandate for Palestine. The terms of this document, which he negotiated in 1920 to 1922, established the legal basis for the Jewish National Home in Palestine. As president of the WZO from 1920 to 1931 and 1935 to 1946, Weizmann championed policies that strengthened the Jewish presence in Palestine without antagonizing the British. He called the alliance between Zionism and Britain the "Rock of Gibraltar" of his policy.

In spite of his diplomatic achievements, Weizmann was disappointed by the slow pace of Zionist development in Palestine in the 1920s. His energy was dissipated in quarrels with other Zionist leaders, in particular Louis D. Brandeis and Vladimir Ze'ev Jabotinsky, as well as in fundraising to meet the chronic financial difficulties of the WZO. Weizmann's Union of General Zionists adopted a moderate, centrist position on most issues. Although he was not a socialist, Weizmann formed an alliance with the more militant socialist-Zionists in

Palestine. He promoted pioneer agricultural communities as an effective way of attracting Jews to Palestine.

Increasingly concerned with the need to broaden the basis of the Zionist movement, Weizmann pushed through a proposal in 1929 to include leaders of non-Zionist organizations in the Jewish Agency, the official liaison with British authorities in Palestine. The Palestine riots of 1929 and the subsequent wavering in British support for Zionism led Weizmann to resign in protest from his joint presidency of the WZO and the Jewish Agency, but his skillful lobbying in London induced the prime minister, J. Ramsay MacDonald, to issue a clarifying letter in 1931 that reaffirmed Britain's commitment to the Balfour Declaration. Weizmann failed, however, to be reelected president of the WZO, which was headed from 1931 to 1935 by his close colleague Nahum Sokolow.

Weizmann returned to leadership of the movement in 1935. In the following year he gave powerful evidence to the Palestine Royal Commission, headed by Earl Peel. Weizmann's testimony and his subsequent private discussions with the commission helped bring about its recommendation for the partition of Palestine. In 1937 he succeeded in persuading a majority within a reluctant Zionist Congress to accept partition in principle. But the British government, which had initially approved the concept, changed its mind and in May 1939 issued a White Paper strictly limiting Jewish immigration and land purchase in Palestine.

Britain's shift in policy away from Zionism, and the consequent growth of Zionist hostility to Britain, weakened Weizmann's authority and diminished his stature. After the outbreak of World War II, the Palestinian labor-Zionist leader David Ben-Gurion superseded him as the dominant figure in the movement. By the end of the war Weizmann's paramount influence with the British and within Zionist circles was all but spent. His stern denunciation of Jewish terrorism earned him many enemies in the movement. Weizmann's tenure as president of the WZO ended in 1946, but out of respect for him no successor was named. He remained politically active and helped to persuade U.S. president Harry S. Truman to support the establishment of Israel upon the termination of the British Mandate in 1948. Weizmann served as first president of Israel, but he was frustrated by the largely ceremonial nature of the position. He lived on the grounds of the scientific institute at Rehovot, which was later named after him, until his death in November 1952.

See also BALFOUR DECLARATION (1917); CHURCHILL, WINSTON S.; HASKALAH; JABOTINSKY, VLADIMIR ZE'EV; JEWISH AGENCY FOR PALESTINE; LLOYD GEORGE, DAVID; PEEL COMMISSION REPORT (1937); SAMUEL, HERBERT LOUIS; SOKOLOW, NAHUM; WHITE PAPERS ON PALESTINE; WORLD ZIONIST ORGANIZATION (WZO); ZIONIST COMMISSION FOR PALESTINE.

Bibliography

Berlin, Isaiah. *Personal Impressions.* Oxford, U.K.: Oxford University Press, 1982.

Reinharz, Jehuda. *Chaim Weizmann: The Making of a Zionist Leader.* New York: Oxford University Press, 1985.

Weizmann, Chaim. *Trial and Error.* London: Hamish Hamilton, 1949.

BERNARD WASSERSTEIN

WEIZMANN INSTITUTE OF SCIENCE

A center of scientific research and graduate study in Israel.

Founded in 1934, the Weizmann Institute of Science is located in Rehovot, Israel. Dr. Chaim Weizmann, a world-renowned chemist, was the first president of the institute and later became Israel's first president. He organized the institute to pursue "pure" science while also dealing with practical problems facing the country and its economy. In the 1930s, Weizmann started work on projects relating to the citrus industry, dairy farming, and medicine. The institute was formally dedicated 2 November 1949.

The Weizmann Institute has nineteen departments grouped into five faculties: biology, biochemistry, chemistry, physics, and mathematics and computer science. It also encompasses several multidisciplinary research centers and institutes. In 2002, 2,500 scientists, technicians, and students were engaged in study and research at the Weizmann Institute.

See also WEIZMANN, CHAIM.

MIRIAM SIMON

WEST BANK

Territory disputed between Israel and the Palestinians, demarcated by the Green Line to the west and the Jordan River to the east.

The West Bank refers to the territory situated west of the Jordan River that was not included as part of Israel following the establishment of the state after the Arab–Israel War of 1948. The West Bank's total area is 2,270 square miles (5,880 sq. km), smaller than the area that was originally allocated to a future Arab state by the United Nations partition resolution of November 1947. It is demarcated by the Green Line (the armistice line set by the 1949 Jordanian-Israeli talks at Rhodes) in the west and the Jordan River in the east.

The West Bank occupies a place in the international consciousness far larger than its geography would suggest. The term acquired greater political significance and only came into common usage after the 1967 Arab-Israel War, when the area was separated from the rest of the Kingdom of Jordan (the East Bank). Many Israelis—and in particular the settlers—use the biblical term "Judea and Samaria" (Hebrew, Yehuda ve Shomron) to describe this region.

King Abdullah I ibn Hussein annexed the area to Jordan in April 1950 but, with only Great Britain and Pakistan recognizing this move, the region has remained without any clear status in international

At an Israeli checkpoint, Palestinians are held back while attempting to cross from Bethlehem into Jerusalem. © SHAUL SCHWARZ/CORBIS. REPRODUCED BY PERMISSION.

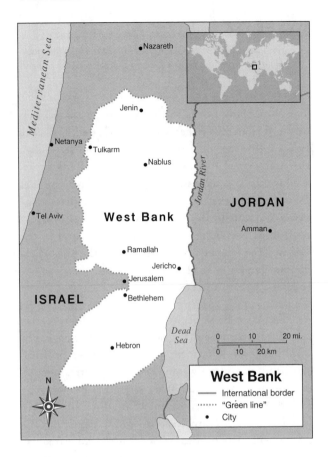

MAP BY XNR PRODUCTIONS, INC. THE GALE GROUP.

law. During the 1967 Arab-Israel War, Israel captured the region, occupying it fully until 1994, and parts of it thereafter. Since 1994, parts of the West Bank have been transferred to the Palestinian Authority under the terms of the 1993 Oslo Accord. The region forms the core of a possible future sovereign Palestinian state.

According to international law, Israel has administered the West Bank since June 1967 as a belligerent occupant. On 7 June 1967 Israel's area commander for the West Bank issued a military proclamation declaring the assumption by the Israel Defense Force (IDF) area commander of all governmental, legislative, appointive, and administrative power over the region and its inhabitants. Palestinian inhabitants of the West Bank continued until 1995 to be ruled under this system of military government. Municipal governments and village councils administered local services. As the occupying power, Israel both permitted and canceled scheduled elections for local governments and ap-

pointed and dismissed elected and appointed Palestinians as officials.

The region has been subject to widespread Israeli settlement activity since 1967. The settlements are administered under a municipal system separate from that of the Palestinian towns and villages. In 1992 the Israeli settlement of Maʿale Adumim, with a population of 15,000, became the first Israeli city in the West Bank.

On 27 June 1967 Israeli law, jurisdiction, and public administration were extended over a 28-square-mile (73 sq. km) area of the West Bank, including the 2.3 square miles (6 sq. km) that had constituted the municipal boundaries of East Jerusalem under Jordanian rule. This de facto annexation placed East Jerusalem and its Palestinian inhabitants under Israeli sovereignty. East Jerusalem is now considered by Israel an indivisible part of its capital city. Palestinians view East Jerusalem as the capital of their future state.

Other cities in the West Bank include Hebron, Bethlehem, Ramallah, Nablus, Jenin, and Jericho. The total population of the region in 2003 consisted of some 2 million Palestinians in the West Bank, with a further 180,000 Palestinians in East Jerusalem. Over 200,000 Israeli settlers lived in the West Bank and a further 170,000 Israelis in East Jerusalem.

In 1967 the Palestinian population of the region was largely agricultural, but under Israeli rule many left agriculture to find employment in the Israeli cities as menial laborers. Following the onset of the first intifada in 1987, most of the Palestinians were excluded from the Israeli labor market, giving rise to widespread unemployment and severe poverty. In early 2003 the economic situation of the population was worse than it had ever been since 1967.

In September 1993 the signing of the Oslo Accord marked the beginning of a transition to Palestinian self-rule. The West Bank was divided into Areas A, B, and C, with the Palestinian Authority taking over full administration in Area A, including all of the major urban centers, and partial control in Area B, including most of the Palestinian villages, while Israel retained full control in Area C, including most of the Jordan Valley, the areas in close proximity to the Green Line boundary, and around Jerusalem. Following the al-Aqsa Intifada, which began in September 2000, the Sharon government sent the IDF to reoccupy some Palestinian towns. The status of the West Bank was still awaiting resolution when a package of proposals, known as the "Road Map," was drawn up and sponsored by "the Quartet"—the United States, the European Union, Russia, and the United Nations—in 2003.

See also ISRAELI SETTLEMENTS; PALESTINIAN AUTHORITY.

Bibliography

Aronson, Geoffrey. *Israel, Palestinians, and the Intifada: Creating Facts in the West Bank.* London and New York: Kegan Paul, 1990.

Benvenisti, Meron. *The West Bank Data Project.* Washington, DC: American Enterprise Institute for Public Policy Research, 1984.

Benvenisti, Meron, and Khayat, Shlomo. *The West Bank and Gaza Atlas.* Boulder, CO: Westview Press, 1988.

Newman, David. "The Evolution of a Political Landscape: Geographical and Territorial Implications of Jewish Colonization in the West Bank." *Middle Eastern Studies* 21, no. 2 (1985): 192–205.

Newman, David. *Population, Settlement and Conflict: Israel and the West Bank.* Update Series in Contemporary Geographical Issues. New York: Cambridge University Press, 1991.

Shehadeh, Raja. *Occupier's Law: Israel and the West Bank.* Washington, DC: Institute for Palestine Studies, 1985.

Shehadeh, Raja, and Kuttab, Jonathan. *The West Bank and the Rule of Law.* Geneva and New York: International Commission of Jurists, 1980.

GEOFFREY ARONSON
UPDATED BY DAVID NEWMAN

WESTERNIZATION

The relatively uncritical adoption of first European and then North America cultural and sociopolitical attitudes and practices on the part of the non-European and non–North American world.

Westernization is sometimes inaccurately equated with modernization, and by extension with modernization theory, a construct very much in vogue in "development" and foreign aid circles between the 1950s and 1970s. In spite of a certain estrangement in the early modern period, and because of its geographical location, the Middle East never entirely lost the contacts that it had had with Europe in the high Middle Ages. However, the Arab, Iranian, and Turkish world did not experience the European humanist Renaissance, or any equivalent of the European Reformation, and by the sixteenth and seventeenth centuries had lost most of the preeminence in science and technology that it had enjoyed earlier.

More regular contacts between the West and the Middle East were reestablished at the end of the eighteenth century, partly as a result of Napoleon's expedition to Egypt in 1798, although the Ottoman Empire was probably as much if not more affected by the territorial losses inflicted upon it by Austro-Hungarian and Russian military superiority earlier in the century. By this time, the West was clearly "ahead" in economic, material, political, and scientific terms, so that the relationship became one of dependency, by the Middle Eastern "periphery" on the Western "center." Between 1798 and 1914, much of the region became politically subject to Britain and France (and to a lesser extent to Italy, Russia, and Spain), and the areas that were not directly colonized became part of the "informal empire," that is, part of the orbit of the capitalist West.

In the course of the nineteenth century, many of the states in the region, particularly Egypt, Qajar Iran, the Ottoman Empire, and Tunisia, underwent programs of administrative, educational, judicial, and finally constitutional reform. To some extent these programs reflected pressures from Europe and incorporated deliberate borrowings from European models, but they were also responses to widely felt local needs to achieve greater administrative efficiency and consistency, to reduce arbitrariness and despotism, and to introduce concepts of legal equality and citizenship into public life. Thus the *Hatt-i Şerif* of Gülhane of November 1839, one of the key texts of the Ottoman *Tanzimat* reforms, declares that all Ottoman subjects should have complete security for life, honor, and property, and that they shall be taxed and conscripted fairly and equitably, but also that "these imperial concessions extend to all our subjects, of whatever religion or sect they may be."

The extent and speed of the changes that took place in the nineteenth and twentieth centuries often introduced considerable confusion into the lives and thought of those involved. For example, the growing secularism of late nineteenth- and twentieth-century Europe has not been easily transposed to the Middle East, with the result that the relationship between Islam and modernity, or the West, has never been satisfactorily worked out. It has proved almost impossible for believing Muslims to apply the same critical-historical methodology to Islamic history as most Christians or Jews would apply to discussions of Christian or Jewish history. At the same time, some Western social attitudes, especially those concerned with consumerism, dress, the consumption of alcohol, and the social mixing of the sexes, have either been vigorously embraced or equally vigorously rejected by Middle Easterners. The Persian author Jalal Al-e Ahmad coined the phrase *Gharbzadagi*, or "Westoxification" to describe this awkward and often disturbing ambiguity. In general, the notion that the Middle East simply copied everything from the West is too simplistic; the reality is far more complex and nuanced.

Bibliography

Abrahamian, Ervand. *Iran between Two Revolutions.* Princeton, NJ: Princeton University Press, 1982.

Anderson, Lisa. *The State and Social Transformation in Tunisia and Libya, 1830–1980.* Princeton, NJ: Princeton University Press, 1986.

Deringil, Selim. *The Well-Protected Domain.* London: I. B. Tauris, 1998.

Hourani, Albert. *Arabic Thought in the Liberal Age, 1798–1939.* London and New York: Oxford University Press, 1962.

Hunter, F. Robert. *Egypt under the Khedives, 1805–1879.* Pittsburgh, PA: University of Pittsburgh Press, 1984.

Martin, Vanessa. *Islam and Modernism: The Iranian Revolution of 1906.* London: I. B. Tauris, 1989.

PETER SLUGLETT

WESTERN SAHARA

Former Spanish colony in northwest Africa; once called Spanish Sahara.

This area of some 102,700 square miles (266,000 sq km) is bordered by Morocco, Algeria, Mauritania, and the Atlantic Ocean. It has been the subject of a dispute involving the POLISARIO (Frente Popular para la Liberación de Saguia el-Hamra y de Río de Oro; Popular Front for the Liberation of Saguia el-Hamra and Río de Oro) independence movement, Morocco, Algeria, Mauritania, and Libya. In 2003 Western Sahara remained the last colonial territory on the African continent whose political status had not been definitively determined and legitimized by the international community. To rectify this, the United Nations has been attempting since 1986, when the Western Sahara War was still raging, to negotiate and implement a referendum among the inhabitants.

Geography and Population

The Western Sahara territory is part of the Sahara desert and consists of *hammada* (mostly barren rocky plateaus), coarse gravel, and sandy plains. It is extremely arid, receiving an average of less than 2 inches (5.1 cm) of rainfall annually, but rich in natural resources such as phosphates, minerals, and coastal fishing grounds. It is sparsely populated—Spain's 1974 census counted 73,497 persons, which was probably an underestimate; a U.S. Central Intelligence Agency publication placed the 1991 population at 196,737, including, presumably, the tens of thousands of Moroccans who have settled there since 1976. The annual growth rate was put at 2.6 percent. The capital is Laayoune (El-Aiun or al-Ayun).

The indigenous Sahrawi population is a mixture of Berber tribes (whose presence in the region dates from at least the first century B.C.E.) and thirteenth-century Arab migrants from southern Arabia. Until the twentieth century, social organization was tribal, along the lines of confederations, factions, and subfactions. Linguistically, the Hasaniyya dialect of Arabic, brought by the Arabian tribes, gradually supplanted Berber dialects. Economically and socially, the tribes were entirely nomadic. Calling themselves the "sons of the clouds," the Sahrawis roamed constantly in search of grazing land and water for their herds, traded with neighboring sedentary groups, engaged in livestock raiding from one another, and participated in the trans-Saharan caravan trade. Since the nineteenth century, the Reguibat have been the largest tribal grouping.

The nomadic way of life did not fit comfortably with European-introduced notions of fixed territorial delimitations. When coupled with twentieth-century events—prolonged droughts, fighting against French and Spanish colonialism, gradual sedentarization, economic change, and, finally, the outbreak of war following Spain's departure—probably as many Sahrawis came to live in neighboring countries (whose boundaries were themselves of twentieth-century origin) as within Western Sahara.

Political History

The political status of the area was rarely defined, since it belonged to what is known in Moroccan history as *bilad al-siba,* the lands of dissidence, as opposed to *bilad al-makhzan,* the areas of central, sultanic authority. (Ironically, the Almoravid Empire, the first dynasty to unite Morocco during the eleventh century, originated in Western Sahara and Mauritania.) Political linkages and affiliations with Moroccan sultans in the north varied, depending on the relative strength of the sultan and the various tribes, the relations between individual tribes and the government in the north, and relations among the tribes themselves.

Spain proclaimed a protectorate over part of the region in 1884. The Moroccan nationalist movement, which first emerged in the 1930s, claimed the area as part of its natural patrimony (along with Mauritania and parts of Algeria and Mali as well). The area's status was changed by Spain in 1958 from colony to overseas province. From the late 1950s, the newly emerging state of Mauritania also claimed it, partly to deflect Morocco's threat against Mauritania itself. POLISARIO's emergence in 1973 linked for the first time the notions of decolonization and independence for the territory, setting the stage for conflict. Spain agreed to relinquish the area in 1975, and it was divided between the two neighboring claimants, Mauritania and Morocco. Mauritania gave up its claim in 1979. Morocco has occupied the bulk of the territory since then.

In 1976, the POLISARIO established the Sahrawi Arab Democratic Republic (SADR) and organized a government-in-exile. During the following years, with Algeria's support, dozens of states, mainly developing and nonaligned countries, recognized the republic. After war broke out between Morocco and the POLISARIO, between 50,000

King Muhammad VI visited Western Sahara in 2001 to reassert Moroccan authority in the region. Morocco has occupied most of the disputed territory since Mauritania relinquished its claim on the southern portion in 1979. © AP/WIDEWORLD PHOTOS. REPRODUCED BY PERMISSION.

and 150,000 Sahrawi refugees fled to the Algerian Tindouf region, and as of 2003 remained there under the administration of the POLISARIO.

From the mid-1970s on, in his effort to fully integrate the Saharan provinces into Morocco, King Hassan II launched investment projects aimed at promoting the economic development of the territory and attracted settlement with special incentives. Civilian and military expenditures related to Western Sahara represented a considerable burden for Morocco's state budget, particularly from the late 1970s to the mid-1980s.

Morocco's claim over the Saharan territory helped King Hassan II build a national consensus in a period of internal instability. At the regional level, however, it has severely affected Moroccan relations with neighboring Algeria, which was a staunch supporter of the Sahrawis' right to self-determination. Consequently, the process of regional integration, which had been inaugurated with great fanfare in 1989 with the creation of the Arab Maghreb Union (UMA), remained stalled as of 2003.

Toward a Negotiated Settlement

It was not until 1991 that the parties officially accepted a UN-sponsored ceasefire, allowing it to set up MINURSO (United Nations Mission for the Referendum in Western Sahara). Besides monitoring the ceasefire, the objective of this UN mission was to prepare a list of people eligible to vote in the referendum on self-determination, which it would oversee, that would put an end to the conflict. According to the original settlement plan, the referendum should have taken place in 1992. Morocco and the POLISARIO, however, disagreed over voter eligibility criteria.

The situation remained deadlocked until 1997, when UN Secretary-General Kofi Annan, in an attempt to break the stalemate, appointed former U.S. Secretary of State James A. Baker as his personal envoy to try to settle the differences between the parties in conflict. After four rounds of negotiations, Baker managed to get an agreement between Morocco and the POLISARIO to resume the voter identification process, as well as a code of conduct to govern the parties during the referendum campaign.

However, the voter identification process still encountered serious difficulties, forcing continued postponement of the referendum and a continued presence for MINURSO in the disputed territories. When in early 2000 the UN mission finally made public the official list of voters, Morocco expressed its disagreement because a low percentage of its proposed candidates was accepted. The ensuing appeals process again delayed the referendum. The UN secretary-general subsequently concluded that the settlement plan was not a viable solution and suggested exploring other ways of ending the dispute.

Overall, the incompatibility of Morocco's discourse on territorial integrity and the POLISARIO's defense of the Sahrawi right to self-determination, coupled with geopolitical developments, had, as of 2003, left the dispute unresolved. Baker's latest UN-sponsored plan was to establish a transitional autonomous regime over a period of five years, at the end of which a referendum on self-determination would be scheduled. Participation was to include at least some of the Moroccans who had settled in the area. After considerable Algerian prodding, POLISARIO accepted the plan. Morocco, however, rejected the idea, fearing that its claim to sovereignty would be undermined.

See also BAKER, JAMES A.; POLISARIO; WESTERN SAHARA WAR.

Bibliography

Damis, John. *Conflict in Northwest Africa: The Western Sahara Dispute.* Stanford, CA: Hoover Institution Press, 1983.

Hodges, Tony. *Historical Dictionary of Western Sahara.* Metuchen, NJ: Scarecrow Press, 1982.

Hodges, Tony. *Western Sahara: The Roots of a Desert War.* Westport, CT: L. Hill, 1983.

Zoubir, Yahia H., and Volman, Daniel. *International Dimensions of the Western Sahara Conflict.* Westport, CT: Praeger, 1993.

BRUCE MADDY-WEITZMAN
UPDATED BY ANA TORRES-GARCIA

WESTERN SAHARA WAR

Conflict over control of Western Sahara, a former Spanish colony in northwest Africa.

Contention over the control of Western Sahara began on the eve of Spain's withdrawal in February 1976. The main protagonists were Morocco, which claimed the territory as an integral part of its historical patrimony, and the Algerian-backed POLISARIO independence movement. Algeria's patronage of POLISARIO was rooted in its larger geopolitical and ideological clash with Morocco. The dispute poisoned their bilateral relations and for a time held out the specter of Algerian–Moroccan fighting. Mauritania, the weakest of the states bordering Western Sahara, initially occupied part of the territory as well but was forced to disengage and then maintain a vulnerable neutrality.

Internationally, both the United States and France had strong strategic, political, and economic interests in North Africa. The conflict did not become an arena for Cold War competition because the Soviet Union adopted a low, pragmatic profile. The Organization of African Unity (OAU) was actively involved in attempting to mediate the dispute between 1976 and 1981 but then became an additional arena for it, resulting in temporary organizational paralysis. Beginning in the late 1980s, successive UN secretaries-general energetically promoted a diplomatic solution, albeit without success, as of 2003.

Outbreak of War

The parameters of the conflict took shape in the fall of 1975. The International Court of Justice issued an advisory ruling regarding the legal status of the territory that was ambiguous, but tilted away from Morocco's position. In response, Morocco's King Hassan II seized the initiative by dispatching hundreds of thousands of unarmed Moroccans in a great spectacle of nationalist and religious fervor across the Moroccan–Spanish Sahara frontier. This "Green March" catalyzed the transfer of Spanish control of the territory to Morocco and Mauritania, enshrined in the tripartite Madrid Accords of 14 November 1975. Spain's formal termination of control came on 26 February 1976. Moroccan troops immediately completed their takeover of the northern two-thirds of Western Sahara, and Mauritania took the southern third.

Meanwhile, fighting had already begun between Moroccan forces and POLISARIO units. On one occasion, Algerian forces assisting POLISARIO clashed with Moroccan troops. Concurrently, there was a large-scale civilian exodus (35–65% of the population) to camps in the Tindouf region of Algeria.

Militarily, POLISARIO's small units could not hope to block Morocco's advance. POLISARIO thus redirected its military efforts to focus on Mauritania, the weaker of its adversaries. Between 1976 and 1979, POLISARIO attacks helped to destabilize the regime of President Mokhtar Ould Daddah, who was overthrown in July 1978. After renewed pressure, the new Mauritanian military junta agreed in August 1979 to cede their portion of Western Sahara, Tiris al-Gharbia, to POLISARIO. However, the Moroccan army immediately preempted POLISARIO and took control itself.

The next few years witnessed fierce fighting. Morocco was on the defensive against highly motivated and tactically superior POLISARIO mobile units, which conducted a war of attrition against Moroccan forces within Western Sahara and southern Morocco. POLISARIO's goal was to render the economic and political cost too great for Morocco to bear. Morocco responded by tripling the size of its armed forces to approximately 150,000, stationing more than half of them in Western Sahara, and conducting large-scale sweeps of its own. It also threatened to invoke, but never implemented, the right of hot pursuit against POLISARIO sanctuaries situated in both Algeria and Mauritania.

In the fall of 1980 Morocco began constructing a system of defensive sand walls (berms) studded with fortified positions, observation points, and early warning equipment. By 1987 the sixth wall was completed, the network ran over 2,000 miles in length, and POLISARIO had been effectively closed off from 80 percent of the territory. No longer could its Land Rovers traverse the trackless territory from Algeria to the Atlantic; POLISARIO was increasingly limited to sporadic raids along the wall. Concurrently, Morocco poured hundreds of millions of dollars into the region, building schools, hospitals, and telecommunications facilities, staffed by tens of thousands of Moroccan civilians. Morocco's consolidation of its presence was made possible by generous military and civilian aid from France, the United States, and Saudi Arabia.

Whereas POLISARIO's military fortunes declined by the mid-1980s, politically it achieved a number of successes: diplomatic recognition from more than seventy countries for its government in exile, the Saharan Arab Democratic Republic (SADR), and full membership in the OAU. On the other hand, Algeria gradually reduced its aid to POLISARIO and retired to a mere supporting role for the UN secretary-general's renewed diplomatic efforts. The overall result by the late 1980s was a stalemated conflict, with neither side able to impose its will. By the beginning of 1990 POLISARIO was almost completely dependent on the UN-sponsored process. As of 2003 more than ten countries had withdrawn their earlier diplomatic recognition of SADR.

During the first years of the conflict POLISARIO had believed that time was on its side, and therefore refused to countenance any solution that fell short of full independence. King Hassan II, for his part, had staked his throne on the issue, making it the glue by which he consolidated and reinforced his political authority at home. Strategically, he never wavered in his goal to incorporate Western Sahara into his kingdom. Tactically, he showed great

A refugee camp, located at Polisario, houses 40,000 Sahrawi refugees. These people seek protection after having been displaced from their homes during the Western Sahara War. © NOGUES ALAIN/CORBIS SYGMA. REPRODUCED BY PERMISSION.

flexibility and skill. For example, in 1981, operating from a position of relative weakness, he demonstratively accepted the principle of a referendum among the Sahrawi population during an OAU summit at Nairobi and thus bought much-needed time. By 1990, while still negotiating the details of the proposed UN-sponsored referendum, Morocco was operating from a position of strength, as regional and international constellations had shifted in its favor.

UN Efforts at Diplomacy

In April 1991 the UN Security Council authorized the establishment of a combined military and civilian force, the United Nations Mission for t he Referendum in the Western Sahara (MINURSO), to organize and implement a referendum process between September 1991 and January 1992. Eligible Sahrawis were to choose between independence for the territory, necessitating immediate Moroc-

can withdrawal, and union with Morocco, necessitating the disbanding of POLISARIO. The 6 September 1991 cease-fire called for in the UN plan came into effect, but the timetable for full deployment of MINURSO and implementation of the referendum was repeatedly delayed. This was due to continuing disagreement over the question of voter eligibility. The Spanish census of 1974 served as the basis for the voter registration list—numbering around 74,000—prepared by UN officials. Morocco, however, insisted on major changes to include up to 150,000 persons who it said belonged to Western Saharan tribes but had migrated north during previous decades for economic or political reasons. POLISARIO wanted small-scale modifications to include more of its supporters.

The efforts of the UN secretary-general's personal representative, former U.S. secretary of state James Baker, generated renewed diplomatic momentum. In 1997 Baker hosted four separate rounds of talks between Moroccan and POLISARIO representatives, the last in Houston, Texas in September. A number of outstanding issues pertinent to the organization of the referendum were resolved, and the laborious process of identifying eligible voters was reinvigorated. However, by the beginning of 2000, hopes for holding the long-delayed referendum faded. The provisional list of eligible voters was approximately 90,000 only, while 140,000 other applicants, nearly all from the Moroccan side, had been rejected. Morocco, fearing electoral defeat, was determined to block the referendum and therefore insisted on appealing the rejections, a lengthy process that would take years. The UN Security Council, led by France and the United States, was unwilling to force Morocco to accept a UN *diktat*. Consequently, Baker floated variations of an old-new "third way" proposal that would bypass the referendum and create an autonomous Saharan entity federated to Morocco in all or part of the territory, or, alternatively, postpone the issue of sovereignty for anywhere between five and thirty years. The protagonists continued to meet periodically under Baker's good offices and even engaged in occasional confidence-building measures such as the release of prisoners of war. But as of 2003 a solution remained out of reach. SADR's political successes internationally had not paved the way to independence, marking a major departure from prevailing patterns of decolonization in developing nations. Morocco still desired de jure legitimation of its incorporation of Western Sahara, but its de facto rule there seemed to be accepted as unalterable by a large portion of the international community. The unresolved question continued to be the single most divisive issue between Morocco and Algeria.

See also BAKER, JAMES A.; DADDAH, MOKHTAR OULD; GREEN MARCH; ORGANIZATION OF AFRICAN UNITY (OAU); WESTERN SAHARA.

Bibliography

Damis, John. *Conflict in Northwest Africa: The Western Sahara Dispute.* Palo Alto, CA: Hoover Institution Press, 1983.

Damis, John. "Morocco and the Western Sahara." *Current History* 89 (April 1990): 165–168, 184–186.

Hodges, Tony. *Western Sahara: The Roots of a Desert War.* Westport, CT: Lawrence Hill, 1983.

Maddy-Weitzman, Bruce. "Conflict and Conflict Management in the Western Sahara: Is the Endgame Near?" *Middle East Journal* 45 (Autumn 1991): 596.

Maddy-Weitzman, Bruce. "Conflict Resolution in the New World Order: The UN and the Western Sahara." *Asian and African Studies* 26, no. 2 (July 1992).

Maddy-Weitzman, Bruce. "Inter-Arab Relations," and "Morocco." Annual chapters in *Middle East Contemporary Survey* (1977–2002).

Pazzanita, Anthony G., and Hodges, Tony. *Historical Dictionary of Western Sahara.* Metuchen, NJ: Scarecrow Press, 1982.

Zoubir, Yahia H., and Volman, Daniel, eds. *International Dimensions of the Western Sahara Conflict.* Westport, CT: Praeger Publishers, 1993.

BRUCE MADDY-WEITZMAN

WESTERN WALL

The extant part of the retaining wall surrounding the Temple of Solomon; a Jerusalem landmark and a holy prayer site for Jews.

The Hebrew Ha-Kotel Ha-Ma'aravi refers to the western retaining wall surrounding Jerusalem's Temple Mount. Sometimes called the "Wailing Wall," since Jews pray and cry near it, it is built of large limestones hewn for the Second Temple, which was enlarged during the reign of Herod (37–4 B.C.E.), king of Judea. It was destroyed by the Romans in 70 C.E.

Since then, the remaining wall has stood as a reminder and symbol of lost glory and the redemption to come; Jews turn toward it when they pray. By tradition, notes to heaven are placed in its cracks. During the British mandate, Jews had limited access in bringing religious appurtenances, which had to adhere to certain rules (e.g., using a curtain to separate men and women) or else were banned. During Jordanian rule, Jews' access to the wall was denied. After the reunification of Jerusalem in 1967, the area was excavated and became again a place of public prayer and assembly. The surrounding plaza is also the site of many national assemblies and civil religious events.

Bibliography

Heilman, Samuel. *A Walker in Jerusalem.* Philadelphia: Jewish Publication Society, 1995.

Meir, Ben Dov; Naor, Mordechai; and Aner, Zeev. *The Western Wall,* translated by Raphael Posner. Tel Aviv: Ministry of Defence, 1983.

SAMUEL C. HEILMAN

WESTERN WALL DISTURBANCES

A September 1928 dispute over Jewish religious rights at the Western Wall that led to political violence in August 1929.

The Western, or Wailing, Wall has been holy to Muslims because it is the western part of the Temple Mount and Haram al-Sharif where, Muslims believe, the prophet Muhammad tethered his "fabulous steed," al-Buraq, while on a nocturnal journey to heaven. The wall is also the holiest shrine of Judaism because it is the remnant of the western exterior of the Temple of Herod, built on the site of Solomon's temple. Jews placed a screen at the wall to separate men and women on 23 September 1928, the eve of the Day of Atonement. The Palestinians protested that the screen violated the status quo ante; the British authorities agreed and forcibly removed it. The incident was politicized by both communities over the next few months, a response that led to tensions and events such as a Revisionist Zionist demonstration on 15 August 1929 and a Palestinian counterdemonstration the following day.

Violence began in Jerusalem on 23 August when Palestinians attacked Jews in Meah She'arim. The rioters attacked the largely non-Zionist religious communities of Hebron and Safed, killing sixty-four and twenty-six people, respectively. Jewish rioters in turn killed Palestinians in a number of cities, but most were shot—some of them indiscriminately—by British troops and police suppressing the disturbances. The violence took the lives of 133 Jews and at least 116 Palestinians.

The Shaw Commission, which investigated the disturbances, determined that the immediate cause of the riots was the Jewish and Arab demonstrations of 15 and 16 August and that the ultimate cause was Palestinian fear that Jewish immigration and land purchase would lead to Jewish domination.

See also HARAM AL-SHARIF; SHAW COMMISSION; WESTERN WALL.

Bibliography

Mattar, Philip. "The Role of the Mufti of Jerusalem in the Political Struggle over the Western Wall, 1928–1929." *Middle Eastern Studies* 19, no. 1 (January 1983): 104–118.

Palestine Government. *A Survey of Palestine for the Information of the Anglo-American Committee of Inquiry.* 2 vols. Jerusalem, 1946. Reprint, Washington, DC: Institute for Palestine Studies, 1991.

PHILIP MATTAR

WEST GERMAN REPARATIONS AGREEMENT

Accord with Israel following World War II.

In September 1945 Chaim Weizmann, on behalf of the Jewish Agency, asked the governments that occupied Germany at the end of World War II—the United States, the Soviet Union, the United Kingdom, and France—to secure financial compensation for the Jewish people.

On 10 September 1952 the government of the Federal Republic of Germany (West Germany) agreed to pay 3.45 billion German marks ($845 million) in the form of goods to Israel, in installments between 1953 and 1966. The Conference on Jewish Material Claims against Germany was to allocate 450 million marks ($110 million). Thirty percent of the funds were allocated for the purchase of oil in the United Kingdom and 70 percent for goods bought directly by the Israeli government. These funds played an important role in the development of Israel's economy in the 1950s.

The agreement was the result of an Israeli claim for US$1 billion in compensation from West Germany (and a claim for $500 million from East Germany, which was never submitted because the powers occupying Germany refused to deal with the claim) to cover the cost of absorbing 500,000 victims of Nazi persecution, estimated at US$3,000 each.

The signing of the agreement led to serious political divisions in Israel; riots broke out on 7 to 9 January 1952 in Jerusalem outside the Knesset. The government favored a pragmatic policy toward Germany that would bring much-needed foreign currency to Israel; the opposition, led by Menachem

Begin, was ideologically opposed to reconciliation with Germany.

See also GERMANY AND THE MIDDLE EAST; WEIZMANN, CHAIM.

Bibliography

Brecher, Michael. *Decisions in Israel's Foreign Policy.* New Haven, CT: Yale University Press, 1975.

Deutschkron, Inge. *Bonn and Jerusalem: The Strange Coalition.* Philadelphia: Chilton Books, 1970.

Patinkin, Don. *The Israeli Economy in the First Decade.* Jerusalem: The Maurice Falk Project for Economic Research in Israel, 1959.

PAUL RIVLIN

WHEELUS AIR FORCE BASE

U.S. Air Force base located near Tripoli, Libya.

Wheelus was established as an American military installation in 1954. In return for base rights, the regime of King Idris received military assistance grants and the right to purchase excess stocks of U.S. weapons.

In 1964, Arab nationalism and anti-Western sentiment forced King Idris to call for a withdrawal of Britain's and America's forces. Following the overthrow of Idris in 1969, the United States completed its planned withdrawal and turned the facility over to Libya on 11 June 1970. Libyan pilots subsequently trained there under the guidance of French instructors. Since 1970, 11 June has been a national holiday in Libya.

Bibliography

Metz, Helen Chapin, ed. *Libya: A Country Study,* 4th edition. Washington, DC: U.S. Government Printing Office, 1989.

STUART J. BORSCH

WHITE FLAG LEAGUE

Sudanese nationalist movement founded in 1924.

Ali Abd al-Latif founded the White Flag League when the Sudan was governed by the Anglo-Egyptian Condominium Agreement. The group consisted of about 150 minor officials and junior officers in the Egyptian army. Representing an alliance of Sudanese and Egyptian nationalists, it advocated the union of the entire Nile valley under the Egyptian crown.

The White Flag League was largely responsible for the 1924 revolt against the British. Events reached a crisis following the assassination of Sir Lee Stack in Cairo; Britain's Field Marshal Edmund Allenby demanded the immediate withdrawal of Egyptian units from the Sudan. Refusing to obey the order to evacuate, the Egyptian and Sudanese league troops mutinied in Khartoum. When Egypt ordered its units to withdraw, however, they complied. The Sudanese were left to confront the British on their own; their defeat marked the end of the revolt and also that of the White Flag League.

See also CONDOMINIUM AGREEMENT (1899).

KENNETH S. MAYERS

WHITE PAPERS ON PALESTINE

British policy statements about mandatory Palestine issued from 1922 to 1939.

The British government, which ruled Palestine from 1917/1918 to 1948 under a League of Nations mandate, issued periodic policy statements called white papers that related to the tensions and recurring violence between the Arab and Jewish communities there.

Two precursors to the series of white papers on Palestine were the Palin Commission Report (1 July 1920) and Haycraft Report (Command 1540, 21 October 1921), which concluded that the Palestinian Arabs' feelings of "hostility to the Jews were due to political and economic causes, and connected with Jewish immigration and with their conception of Zionist policy" as leading to a Jewish state in which Palestinians would be subjugated.

Subsequently, the Churchill White Paper of June 1922 (Command 1700) attempted to placate both communities. It stated that the Jewish national home existed by right, but that the Palestinians should not be subordinated to the Jewish community. It declared that all Palestinians were equal before the law and described the Jewish national home as simply "a center in which the Jewish people as a whole may take, on grounds of religion and race, an interest and a pride." Jews would have the right to immigrate to Palestine, but their immigration must not exceed "the economic capacity of the country at the time to absorb new arrivals." Moreover, London aimed to establish full self-government in Palestine in "gradual stages" and would hold elections for a legislative council. The white paper thus reassured Arabs that they would have a political role and that Jewish im migration would be limited. Nonetheless, the Arab Executive objected to the reaffirmation of the Balfour Declaration (1917), which had supported the establishment of a Jewish home in Palestine, and rejected the legislative council as not guaranteeing majority rights. The World Zionist Organization criticized the limits on immigration and the proposed legislative council, which it wanted to postpone until the Jewish population was larger.

The colonial secretary issued the next white paper (Command 3229) on 19 November 1928, as Muslim-Jewish tension escalated over mutual claims at the Western (Wailing) Wall in Jerusalem. The white paper affirmed that no benches or screens could be brought to the wall by Jews, since they had not been allowed during Ottoman rule. Tension escalated, leading to Palestinian attacks against Jews at the wall and in several other towns in August 1929.

Four white papers issued in 1930 tried to defuse the conflict. The Shaw Commission of Inquiry (Command 3530, 30 March 1930) found that Jewish immigration and land purchases were immediate causes of "the Arab feeling of disappointment of their political and national aspirations and fear for their economic future," and that these were the underlying causes of the violence. The report declared that the government must issue clear statements safeguarding Arab rights and regulating Jewish immigration and land purchase. Another white paper (Command 3682, 27 May 1930) reaffirmed those findings, welcomed an investigation by an international commission of the conflicting claims to the Western Wall, and recommended appointing a special commission to assess the problems facing landless Palestinian peasants and the prospects for expanded agricultural cultivation.

Sir John Hope-Simpson's report, dated 30 August 1930 (Command 3686), was published simultaneously with the Passfield White Paper (Command 3692) of 21 October 1930. Hope-Simpson recommended a drastic reduction in the volume of Jewish immigration because of insufficient cultivable Palestinian land and widespread Palestinian unemployment. He criticized the Jewish National Fund, the Zionist Organization's land-purchasing agency, for forbidding Jews from reselling land to Arabs and banning Arab laborers on Jewish farms. The white paper concurred that stricter controls should be placed on Jewish immigration and land purchase, and asserted—for the first time—that the British government had obligations "of equal weight" to both communities and that it must renew the effort to establish the legislative council proposed in 1922.

The Arab Executive was pleased with these British policy recommendations because they acknowledged Arab concerns. But Chaim Weizmann, head of the Jewish Agency, resigned in protest when the Passfield White Paper was issued. London then backtracked. Zionist officials helped to draft a letter, signed by Prime Minister Ramsay MacDonald, to Weizmann on 14 February 1931 that expunged all damaging aspects of the Passfield White Paper and upheld the primacy of the government's promises to the Jewish community. Mollified, Weizmann withdrew his resignation, but the MacDonald "Black Letter," as it became known, infuriated the Arabs.

The white paper of 17 May 1939 (Command 6019) followed three years of Arab rebellion. The Peel Commission had recommended on 7 July 1937 that territorial partition between Arab and Jewish states was the only solution because Arab and Jewish aspirations were irreconcilable. Nonetheless, the Woodhead Partition Commission concluded on 9 November 1938 that partition was not feasible. The British government then convened the London Conference, which brought together the Jewish Agency, Arab governments, and Palestinian Arabs in lengthy but fruitless discussions. Afterwards, London issued a white paper that repudiated partition and proposed to create self-governing institutions over a ten-year period. Authority over the eventual independent state would be shared by its Arab and Jewish citizens. The white paper limited Jewish immigration to 75,000 over five years; subsequent immigration would require Arab approval. Jews' purchase of land would be limited in some parts of Palestine and forbidden in others.

Jewish and Palestinian Arab nationalisms were too intense and too antagonistic for this plan to succeed. The Zionists viewed the Balfour Declaration as a pledge to establish a Jewish state. When the white paper of 1939 withdrew the Peel Commission's partition proposal, their reaction was strongly hostile, particularly because the restrictions on immigration occurred just as Jews sought to flee Nazi persecution in Europe. Palestinians were relieved that London had set aside partition and would restrict Jewish immigration and land purchase, but were skeptical that London would fulfill its pledges. The MacDonald white paper remained mostly unimplemented, apart from the enforcement of immigration restrictions.

See also CHURCHILL WHITE PAPER (1922); HAYCRAFT COMMISSION (1921); MACDONALD, RAMSAY; PALIN COMMISSION REPORT (1920).

Bibliography

Government of Palestine. *A Survey of Palestine*, Vol. 1. Jerusalem: Government Printer, 1946.

Ingrams, Doreen. *Palestine Papers, 1917–1922: Seeds of Conflict.* New York: George Braziller, 1972.

Lesch, Ann Mosely. *Arab Politics in Palestine, 1917–1939: The Frustration of a Nationalist Movement.* Ithaca, NY: Cornell University Press, 1979.

Stein, Kenneth W. *The Land Question in Palestine, 1917–1939.* Chapel Hill: University of North Carolina Press, 1984.

ANN M. LESCH

WHITE REVOLUTION (1961–1963)

Program of reforms initiated by the shah of Iran in 1963.

Iran's ruler, Mohammad Reza Shah Pahlavi (r. 1941–1979), in January 1963 launched a series of reform policies that he called the White Revolution. The domestic aim was to undermine the political appeal of an influential but diffuse opposition movement by appropriating programs such as land tenure reform that it long had advocated. There also was an

international objective: to win favor with Iran's principal foreign ally, the United States, which then was a major source of economic and military assistance. During the administration of John F. Kennedy (1961–1963), U.S. policy supported economic and social reforms in countries such as Iran as a means of undercutting the appeal of antiregime movements that were perceived as being allied with the Soviet Union. Thus the major element of the shah's White Revolution was a land reform program (actually begun a year earlier) that eventually would redistribute about one-half of private agricultural land to peasants holding traditional sharecropping rights (approximately one-half of all village families).

Five other programs also comprised the White Revolution at its outset. These included the nationalization of forests; sales of shares in (some) government-owned industries; plans for workers to share in profits of large factories; voting rights for women; and the formation within the army of a literacy corps of draftees assigned to villages as teachers. Later, the literacy corps model was extended to a health corps (for draftees who had college-level training in medicine) and a development corps (for college graduate draftees). By the mid-1970s the White Revolution comprised a total of eighteen programs.

The results of the White Revolution were mixed. On the positive side, about half a million peasants obtained adequate land under the land reform program to engage in profitable farming, primary schools were established in several hundred villages that previously had none, and small towns and rural areas benefited from various government development initiatives. On the negative side, perhaps the most serious deficiency of the White Revolution was the raising of popular expectations that remained unfulfilled. With respect to land reform, for example, one-half of all rural families received no land at all; among those obtaining land, about 73 percent got less than six hectares, an amount sufficient only for subsistence farming. The net result was the creation of widespread disillusionment in villages. This pattern—some benefits accruing to a minority but overall disappointment for the majority—characterized many of the White Revolution programs by the early 1970s. At the same time, a class devoted to the White Revolution became part of the required curriculum in Iran's high schools. Criticism of the White Revolution—or any other policy of the shah—came to be regarded as a punishable political offense. As expressing praise for the White Revolution came to be associated with professing loyalty to the shah's regime, and, conversely, criticizing it came to be associated with opposition, any objective assessment of its actual achievements and failings in the years leading up to the 1979 Iranian Revolution became virtually impossible.

See also IRANIAN REVOLUTION (1979); KENNEDY, JOHN FITZGERALD; LAND REFORM; PAHLAVI, MOHAMMAD REZA.

Bibliography

Hooglund, Eric. *Land and Revolution in Iran, 1960–1980.* Austin: University of Texas Press, 1982.

ERIC HOOGLUND

WIFAQ, AL-

An organization formed in Morocco to cultivate Muslim–Jewish relations.

Al-Wifaq (French, *Entente*) was an organization founded under the aegis of the Istiqlal Party in Rabat in January 1956 to promote Muslim–Jewish rapprochement on the eve of Moroccan independence. The organizers included a number of Moroccan Jewish political activists, among them Marc Sabah, a protégé of Mehdi Ben Barka, and Albert Aflalo, Sabah's nephew and an employee of the U.S. embassy.

The movement enjoyed little success because of the indifference of the Muslim elite, the apprehensions of the Jewish community at large, and increased tensions caused by events in the Middle East.

See also BEN BARKA, MEHDI; ISTIQLAL PARTY: MOROCCO.

Bibliography

Stillman, Norman A. *The Jews of Arab Lands in Modern Times.* Philadelphia: Jewish Publication Society, 1991.

NORMAN STILLMAN

WIJDAN

See ALI, WIJDAN

WILLIAM FOXWELL ALBRIGHT INSTITUTE FOR ARCHEOLOGICAL RESEARCH IN JERUSALEM

See ARCHAEOLOGY IN THE MIDDLE EAST

WILSON, ARNOLD T.
[1884–1940]

British soldier, explorer, colonial administrator, oil company executive, author, and politician.

Sir Arnold Talbot Wilson spent the first part of his career in the Persian/Arabian Gulf and Mesopotamia (now Iraq), transferring from the Indian Army to the Indian Political Department in 1909. He was British consul in various parts of southwest Persia (now Iran) between 1907 and 1914 and carried out the earliest cartographic surveys of the area (*South-West Persia: A Political Officer's Diary, 1940*). He was also a member of the commission to delineate the frontier between the Ottoman Empire and Persia in 1913–1914.

For most of the next six years, Wilson was an administrator in Mesopotamia, first as deputy chief political officer to the Indian Expeditionary Force, then as deputy civil commissioner, serving under Sir Percy Cox in both capacities. In Cox's absence in Tehran between 1918 and October 1920, Wilson was appointed acting civil commissioner in Mesopotamia and the crown's political resident in the Gulf. Comparatively young for such responsibilities, Wilson proved an energetic and tireless administrator and inspired intense loyalty in his subordinates (although not in the Civil Commission's oriental secretary, Gertrude Bell). Nevertheless, a combination of temperament and political inclinations made it difficult for him to accept that Britain could not continue to exercise direct colonial control over Iraq as part of any postwar settlement. His refusal to make any concessions to nationalist sentiment was an important, though by no means the only, factor in precipitating the Iraqi revolution against British rule in the summer and autumn of 1920.

Wilson resigned from his post in Baghdad just before Cox's return to the city in October 1920 and spent the next twelve years working for the Anglo–Persian Oil Company, first in Persia and then in London. He was elected to Parliament as a Conservative in 1933 and 1935 and chaired several parliamentary committees. He published two books about his experiences in Iraq (*Loyalties: Mesopotamia, 1914–1917* [1930] and *Mesopotamia, 1917–1920: A Clash of Loyalties* [1931]). They were colored by his anger at what he saw as the failings of British policy and perhaps as the betrayal of his own ideals.

See also ANGLO–IRANIAN OIL COMPANY; BELL, GERTRUDE; COX, PERCY.

Bibliography

Marlowe, John. *Late Victorian: The Life of Sir Arnold Talbot Wilson.* London: Cresset, 1967.

PETER SLUGLETT

WILSON, WOODROW
[1856–1924]

U.S. president, 1913–1921.

Woodrow Wilson led the United States into World War I with his Fourteen Points as war aims. Among them was the promise of self-determination for the peoples of enemy states, including the Ottoman Empire. Self-determination reflected American idealism, but it conflicted with the imperial ambitions of Britain and France, the nation's wartime allies.

At the Paris Peace Conference held in 1919, the Hashimite leaders of Arabia sought a sovereign Arab state (including Palestine). This had been promised to them by the British in return for their revolt against the Turks. This state was supported by U.S. Protestant missionaries who had been resident for decades in the Ottoman territories. Also, the leaders of the Zionist movement sought access to Palestine for Jewish immigration based on a promise (the Balfour Declaration) made to them by the British in return for wartime support.

President Wilson led the U.S. delegation to the Paris Peace Conference. There he came under pressure from both Zionists and those supporting an Arab state. One result of this situation was the creation of the King-Crane Commission, the mission of which was to determine the popular will of the people of "Greater Syria." At the same time the president came under pressure to modify his support for self-determination so as to accommodate the imperial designs of his allies. The compromise realized here was a "mandate system" under the aus-

pices of the League of Nations. It was Wilson's belief in the "backward" nature of non-European populations that allowed him to accept the mandate system. The King-Crane Commission report was shelved, leaving imperialism triumphant in the guise of mandates.

Bibliography

Heckscher, August. *Woodrow Wilson.* New York: Scribner, 1991.

Schulte Nordholt, Jan Willem. *Woodrow Wilson: A Life for World Peace,* translated by Herbert H. Rowen. Berkeley: University of California Press, 1991.

ZACHARY KARABELL
UPDATED BY LAWRENCE DAVIDSON

WINGATE, CHARLES ORDE
[1903–1944]

British military officer who supported Zionism.

A Scot fluent in Arabic, Charles Orde Wingate was sent to Palestine in 1936 as an intelligence officer in the British army, where he translated his Protestant millenarian sentiments into support for Zionism. Ordered by the commander of British forces in Palestine, General Sir Archibald Wavell, to train mixed British and Zionist units in night fighting and guerrilla tactics during the Arab revolt (1936–1939), Wingate implemented the doctrine of "active defense." His "special night squads" were organized to protect the Iraq Petroleum Company pipeline. They inflicted casualties on the rebels and attacked guerrilla villages in Syria and Lebanon.

Heroic to the Zionists and ruthless to the Arabs, Wingate's actions appeared to cement a British–Zionist alliance. Wingate was removed from Palestine in 1939 by the British, who considered his Zionist sympathies an embarrassment. During World War II he served as a brigadier in Ethiopia and Burma. He died in an airplane crash in Burma.

See also IRAQ PETROLEUM COMPANY (IPC); PALESTINE ARAB REVOLT (1936–1939); WAVELL, ARCHIBALD PERCIVAL.

Bibliography

Bierman, John, and Smith, Colin. *Fire in the Night: Wingate of Burma, Ethiopia, and Zion.* New York: Random House, 2000.

Mead, Peter. *Orde Wingate and the Historians.* Braunton, U.K.: Merlin, 1987.

Rossetto, Arthur L. *Major General Orde Charles Wingate and the Development of Long-Range Penetration.* Lexington, VA: Military Affairs, 1982.

Royle, Trevor. *Orde Wingate: Irregular Soldier.* London: Weidenfeld and Nicolson, 1995.

Tulloch, Derek. *Wingate in Peace and War.* London: Macdonald and Co., 1972.

REEVA S. SIMON

WINGATE, REGINALD
[1861–1953]

Sirdar (commander in chief) and governor-general of the Sudan, 1899–1916; high commissioner in Egypt, 1916–1919.

Sir Francis Reginald Wingate was educated at the Royal Military Academy, Woolwich, England, and attained the rank of general in the British army. He served in India and participated as director of military intelligence in the campaign led by Lord Kitchener to conquer the Sudan (1896–1898).

During his seventeen-year term as governor-general of the Sudan, Wingate, who spoke Arabic and had detailed knowledge of the country, earned a reputation for competence and hard work. He was an ardent supporter of the Arab Revolt (1916) during World War I and consistently urged additional British monetary and military aid for the effort. In 1916, he was appointed high commissioner in Egypt.

With his extensive knowledge of the country, Wingate recognized the rise of Egyptian nationalism, caused in part by increased British military presence and controls during the war. Even before it ended, he advised the British Foreign Office and the British government to make some conciliatory gestures toward Egyptian nationalist feelings. After meeting with the nationalist delegation (Arabic, *wafd*), in November 1918, Wingate recommended that Wafd members be allowed to travel to London for direct negotiations; but Wingate lacked sufficient influence, and his recommendations were curtly rebuffed.

In the face of mounting violence and nationalist demonstrations in Egypt, Wingate was hastily removed from office while vacationing in Britain in 1919; he was replaced by the popular war hero Field Marshal Viscount Edmund Allenby.

See also ALLENBY, EDMUND HENRY; ARAB REVOLT (1916); KITCHENER, HORATIO HERBERT; WAFD.

Bibliography

Wingate, Ronald. *Wingate of the Sudan: The Life and Times of General Sir Reginald Wingate, Maker of the Anglo–Egyptian Sudan.* London: Murray, 1955.

JANICE J. TERRY

WISE, STEPHEN S.
[1874–1949]

U.S. Jewish leader.

Stephen S. Wise was born in Hungary and was brought to the United States as a small child. He received rabbinical training from Adolf Jellinek in Vienna and earned a doctorate at Columbia University. At the turn of the century, Wise was among a handful of card-carrying Zionists in the United States. In 1898 he served as a delegate to the Second Zionist Congress and subsequently helped to establish the Federation of American Zionists (later renamed the Zionist Organization of America [ZOA]). In 1907 Wise founded the Free Synagogue in New York City. Thereafter, his political activity brought him into close contact with U.S. Progressives and the left wing of the Democratic party. He developed close ties to Woodrow Wilson, Louis D. Brandeis, Felix Frankfurter, and Franklin D. Roosevelt.

Wise's public activity included the cofounding of the National Association for the Advancement of Colored People (1909); the establishment of the American Jewish Congress during World War I; securing U.S. support for the Balfour Declaration of 1917; serving as a Zionist spokesman at the Paris Peace Conference after World War I; cofounding the American Civil Liberties Union (1920); leading the ZOA, the United Palestine Appeal, and the American Zionist Emergency Council during the 1930s and 1940s; founding the Jewish Institute of Religion (1922); creating the U.S. anti-Nazi boycott of the 1930s and the World Jewish Congress (1936); and co-founding the American Jewish Conference (1943).

During World War II, Wise emerged as a champion of Roosevelt's wartime strategy. At Roosevelt's request, he even suppressed initial reports of the Holocaust. Wise's stance conflicted with Rabbi Abba Hillel Silver, a right-wing U.S. Jewish leader who advocated Zionist militancy and immediate U.S. intervention on behalf of European Jewry. In 1943 the Wise-Silver clash reached a climax, and Silver displaced Wise as American Zionism's undisputed leader.

See also SILVER, ABBA HILLEL.

MARK RAIDER

WIZO

See WOMEN'S INTERNATIONAL ZIONIST ORGANIZATION

WOLFF, HENRY DRUMMOND
[1830–1908]

British mission head who gained economic concessions from Iran.

Sir Henry Drummond Wolff was the head of a special British mission sent to Iran (then Persia) after 1881, when, under a conservative government, the British started actively to support concessions. He was instrumental in obtaining important economic and financial concessions from the Persian government and was sent to Persia in 1888 as British envoy. As a result of Wolff's pressure, the Qajar dynasty monarch, Naser al-Din Shah, opened Persia's only navigable river, the Karun, to international navigation. Wolff, with Baron Julius de Reuter's son, was instrumental in settling claims to the Reuter Concession obtained in 1872. One concession granted by Persia was the right to establish a national bank, the Imperial Bank of Persia, which gave the concessionaires exclusive rights to issue bank notes and other negotiable papers. In 1890, Wolff obtained from the shah for British financiers a monopoly over the production, sale, and export of Iranian tobacco. This concession triggered one of the first successful mass demonstrations in the modern history of Iran, the Tobacco Revolt, and so the concession was abandoned.

See also TOBACCO REVOLT.

Bibliography

Keddie, Nikki. *Roots of Revolution: An Interpretive History of Modern Iran.* New Haven, CT: Yale University Press, 1981.

PARVANEH POURSHARIATI

WOMEN AND FAMILY AFFAIRS CENTER

An independent Palestinian women's organization.

In 1988, empowered by the Palestinian women's movement during the first Intifada, the Women's Affairs Center was established at the initiative of the novelist Sahar Khalifa. Other independent women's organizations followed, staying outside the control of Palestinian political parties. The center's founding committee included Rita Giacaman, Rema Hammami, Islah Jad, Sahar Khalifa, and Amal Nashashibi. The board include some prominent educated women, mainly from Nablus city. The center was established as a women's research and training organization. In 1991, it opened a branch under the same name in Gaza City. In 1994, the steering committee formally separated the two centers and the Nablus center became the Women and Family Affairs Center. Another branch was opened in Amman (Jordan) but did not last long. The center produced a few issues of a journal, *Women's Affairs*, before it ceased publication. The center works to promote women's rights and gender equality within Palestinian society, and its main mandate is in the city of Nablus. It has no relations with Israelis. It focuses on training and advocacy to promote women's rights. It is difficult to measure the impact of its efforts due to the political instability of the times. The center coordinates some of its activities with other nongovernmental organizations in Nablus, but it has no formal links with the Palestinian Authority and depends on external funding.

See also GAZA STRIP; GENDER: GENDER AND EDUCATION; INTIFADA (1987–1991); OSLO ACCORD (1993); PALESTINE; PALESTINIAN AUTHORITY; WEST BANK.

ISLAH JAD

WOMEN IN BLACK

Israeli movement in support of the first Intifada (1987–1991), promoting a network of women's peace activities in Israel, the Occupied Territories, and the world.

In 1988, a small group of Israeli women responded to the outbreak of the first Palestinian Intifada by protesting in the streets of cities and towns across the country, dressed in black as a sign of mourning. Their regular vigils have inspired protest groups across the Western world. The Women in Black have worked together with other feminist and nonfeminist peace groups in protests against all aspects of the military occupation of the West Bank and Gaza and have given their name and support to groups of women opposed to engagement in other military conflicts as well. In Israel, they are opposed by Women in Green and other right-wing settler movements riled by the apparent success of the women's peace movements in capturing public attention.

The first Jewish Women in Black movement was organized against the oppression of Soviet Jews in the 1970s; it was, in turn, inspired by South African women who stood silently, wearing black sashes, in protest against apartheid. Both the Jewish and the South African groups, often made up of middle aged and middle-class women, successfully demonstrated the power of activism by women's groups standing against the compromise and complacency of the largely male establishments in South Africa and the Jewish community.

Israeli women's groups have drafted a series of peace platforms, formed committees to monitor the treatment of civilians, and engaged from the outset—at first illegally—in dialogues with Palestinian women. The Israeli Women in Black have sought to maintain the spontaneous nature of their demonstrations, aiming to draw together women of different political beliefs and from different organizations. Their efforts were reinvigorated in the late 1990s by the success of the Four Mothers movement in shifting public opinion in favor of Israel's withdrawal from South Lebanon. The Four Mothers movement was founded by four Israeli mothers who had sons serving in Lebanon in 1997, after a helicopter crash in that country that left seventy-three soldiers dead.

See also GAZA STRIP; INTIFADA (1987–1991); WEST BANK.

Bibliography

Women in Black. Available from <http://www.womeninblack.net>.

GEORGE R. WILKES

WOMEN'S AFFAIRS CENTER (GAZA)

A Palestinian women's organization in Gaza.

The Women's Affairs Center is a Palestinian non-governmental research and training center that promotes women's rights and gender equality within Palestinian society. It was established in Gaza City in August 1991; the founding committee included (alphabetically) Rita Giacaman, Rema Hammami, Sahar Khalifa, Islah Jad, I'timad Muhanna and Amal Nashashibi. In 1994, the center separated from a similar organization in Nablus and a change in the board followed to include prominent educated men and women, mainly from Gaza. In 1995, another change in board membership took place. The center aims at empowering women in Gaza through advocacy and research, and through training women in professional and technical skills in research, media, and management. Its goal is gender equity. It is difficult to assess its impact on women, but the center has managed to train some women in research and media skills. The center has no formal links with the Palestinian Authority and has wide networks of relations with other women's organizations in Gaza, the West Bank, and the Arab world; it has no relations with Israelis. The center depends on external nongovernmental funding and since the second Intifada, in September 2000, has faced financial difficulties.

See also AQSA INTIFADA, AL-; GAZA STRIP; GENDER: GENDER AND EDUCATION; INTIFADA (1987–1991); PALESTINE; WEST BANK.

ISLAH JAD

WOMEN'S CENTRE FOR LEGAL AID AND COUNSELING

Women's organization based in Jerusalem.

The Women's Centre for Legal Aid and Counseling was established in 1991, during the first Intifada, as a unit of the Women's Action Committee, a branch of the Democratic Front for the Liberation of Palestine, at the initiative of Siham Barghouthi, Amal al-Jua'aba, and Zahira Kamal. A board was formed, including Lamis Alami, Siham Barghouthi, Rawda el-Basir, Arham el-Damen, Samar Hawash, Zahira Kamal, Rana Nashashibi, Mukarram Qassrawi, and Lamia Quttineh. After a split with the

Popular Front, the center became an independent organization in 1992. It is based in Jerusalem, with one branch in the Old City of Jerusalem and one in Khalil/Hebron. It works to advance the legal and social status of Palestinian women through programs advocating women's legal rights, and through research and advocacy based on the international principles of human rights. The center's activities encourage the Palestinian Authority to adopt the Convention for the Elimination of All Forms of Discrimination against Women. The center has a wide network of relations with local, regional, and international organizations, including Israeli organizations, as well as with the Palestinian Authority.

See also GENDER: GENDER AND LAW; INTIFADA (1987–1991); POPULAR FRONT; WOMEN AND FAMILY AFFAIRS CENTER; WOMEN'S AFFAIRS CENTER (GAZA).

Bibliography

Women's Centre for Legal Aid and Counseling (WCLAC). *Annual Report*, 1999–2001.

ISLAH JAD

WOMEN'S FORUM FOR RESEARCH AND TRAINING (YEMEN)

A women's forum in Yemen.

The Women's Forum for Research and Training (Multaqa al-marʾa lil-dirasat, wa al-Tadrib, WFRT) was established in 2000 to mobilize women's and human-rights organizations to work together for empowering women. The forum's main objective is to advance the rule of law regarding women's issues and rights and to build consensus in society at large on the urgency of incorporating gender dimensions in all fields of development and law. The forum's work recognizes that even though Yemeni legislation on human rights is among the best in the Arab world, women's rights are regularly violated and women lack knowledge of their rights. To accomplish its goals, the forum works on several levels, including arranging workshops for state officials, introducing human-rights issues to key figures in nongovernmental organizations and development agencies, and arranging training courses for grassroots activists. The forum has its office in Taʿiz, and its staff includes very young people. The initiator

and manager of WFRT, Suʿad al-Qadasr is one of the most prominent Yemeni human rights activists. Prior to founding WFRT she was the chairperson of the Yemeni Women's Union Taʿiz branch and a leading figure in Human Rights Information and Training Centre. WFRT publications include research and surveys (*Street Children Phenomenon in Yemen*, 2003), the periodical *Multaqa* (Forum), and the leaflet "Suʾal wa jawab" (Questions and answers). WFRT is located on the Internet at <www.geocities.com/taralws/wfrt.htm>.

SUSANNE DAHLGREN

WOMEN'S INTERNATIONAL ZIONIST ORGANIZATION

Organization founded to address the needs of women immigrants in Palestine.

Established in London on 11 July 1920 by the Federation of Women Zionists of the United Kingdom, the Women's International Zionist Organization (WIZO) focused on agricultural training for women immigrants in Palestine, and on these women's role as citizens and as primary providers of education to children. The founders and leaders of the movement were Vera Weizmann, Edith Eder, Romana Goodman, Henrietta Irwell, and Rebecca Sieff, who served as the first president of WIZO until her death in 1966.

Initially headquartered in London, the organization established a network of federations throughout the world (except in the United States and the USSR). A member of both the World Zionist Organization and the World Jewish Congress, WIZO is now based in Israel, where it supports numerous institutions, such as baby homes for children of preschool age, youth clubs, summer camps and kindergartens for schoolchildren, secondary and agricultural schools, and community centers in border settlements and development towns.

See also WORLD ZIONIST ORGANIZATION (WZO).

Bibliography

Marder, Lucy, and Avner, Yossi. *Speaking for Women.* Tel Aviv, 1990.

SHIMON AVISH

WOMEN'S LIBRARY AND INFORMATION CENTER (ISTANBUL)

Istanbul foundation established for the preservation of the history of women.

The Women's Library and Information Center (Kadin Eserleri Kütüphanesi ve Bilgi Merkezi) was established in Istanbul as a foundation by Asli Davaz Mardin, Sirin Tekeli, Jale Baysal, Füsun Akatli, and Füsun Ertug-Yaras. It opened on 14 April 1990 in a historic building owned by the Istanbul municipality and overlooking the Golden Horn. The foundation declaration stated that the purpose of the library was "to gather knowledge about the history of women, to present this information in an organized way to those who do research today, and to preserve the written documents of the past and of today for future generations." A general board administers the library and an executive board, elected annually, directs its activities. The library has a collection of more than 8,500 books written by or about women; Ottoman, Turkish, and some foreign-language periodicals on women; more than 1,300 articles in women's studies; a collection of newspaper clippings since 1990; a collection of ephemera; a special collection to preserve the personal documents of women, including those presented by Hasene Ilgaz, Müfide Ilhan, and Süreyya Agaoglu; a collection on women artists and their works; a collection on women authors; an audio-visual collection; and an oral-history collection.

The library operates as a center of feminist activism, organizing women's exhibitions and special events, and cultivating international links to extend its feminist networks. It has helped to legitimize and institutionalize second-wave feminism in Turkey. In 1991 the library organized the First International Symposium of Women's Libraries in Istanbul. It has generated projects on women's oral history and women's publications.

The library is financed by donations made by its members and by the sale of its publications and annual diaries. It has cultivated amicable relations with different political parties that came to power in the Istanbul municipality, including the pro-Islamists, and has received some support on certain projects from the Turkish government and the Global Fund for Women.

See also GENDER: GENDER AND EDUCATION; TEKELI, SIRIN; TURKEY.

Bibliography

Davaz-Mardin, Asli. "The Women's Library in Istanbul." *Gender and History* 12 (2000): 448–466.

YESIM ARAT

WOMEN'S ORGANIZATION OF IRAN (WOI)

Iranian women's activist organization.

The Women's Organization of Iran (WOI) emerged in 1966, reflecting decades of Iranian women's activism. During the 1950s, as their awareness of progress elsewhere grew, Iranian women formed numerous organizations and sought the right to vote. Princess Ashraf Pahlavi, the shah's sister, bolstered these organizations, forming a committee in 1959 to prepare the articles of association for the High Council of Women's Organizations in Iran. An umbrella group, the high council coordinated the election of a 5,000-member assembly of women representatives approving the WOI's charter on 19 November 1966 in Tehran. A nonprofit institution run mostly by volunteers, the WOI had local branches receiving charitable donations and benefited from national fundraising. By 1975, the International Year of the Woman, the WOI had established 349 branches, 120 women's centers, and a center for research. The centers provided literacy classes and vocational training, family-planning information, and legal advice. The WOI supported the international feminist movement, formulating a national plan of action that resembled the United Nations General Assembly's World Plan of Action. Although anxious to avoid conflict with the religious authorities, the WOI with its successes nevertheless alienated senior clerics. Ironically, the political awareness gained through WOI projects enabled increased and effective women's participation in the Islamic revolution, which ultimately undid the WOI.

See also IRANIAN REVOLUTION (1979); PAHLAVI, MOHAMMAD REZA.

Bibliography

Afary, Janet. *The Iranian Constitutional Revolution, 1906–1911: Grassroots Democracy, Social Democracy, and the Origins of Feminism.* New York: Columbia University Press, 1996.

Afkhami, Mahnaz. "The Women's Organization of Iran: Evolutionary Politics and Revolutionary Change." 2003.

Najmabadi, Afsaneh. "Hazards of Modernity and Morality: Women, State and Ideology in Contemporary Iran." In *Women, Islam, and the State*, edited by Deniz Kandiyoti. Philadelphia: Temple University Press; London: Macmillan, 1991.

Nashat, Guity, ed. *Women and Revolution in Iran.* Boulder, CO: Westview Press, 1983.

Paidar, Parvin. *Women and the Political Process in Twentieth-Century Iran.* New York and Cambridge, U.K.: Cambridge University Press, 1995.

HALEH VAZIRI

WOMEN'S PEOPLE'S PARTY (1923)

The first and the only women's party founded in the Republic of Turkey.

The Kadinlar Halk Firkasi (Women's People's Party) was founded on 16 June 1923 in Istanbul. Among its founders were the leading feminists of the time, including Nezihe Muhittin (president), Nimet Remide (vice president), Şüküfe Nihal (general secretary), and Latife Bekir (party spokesperson). The Istanbul Provincial Administration rejected their petition for authorization, stipulating that women did not have the right to vote and hence could not establish a political party. The real reason for the rejection, however, was preparation for the Kemalist Republican People's Party (RPP), which was then being formed and which ruled the country single handedly until 1950.

Undiscouraged, the women established the Kadinlar Birliği (Women's Federation) on 7 February 1924, with the same leadership and objectives but a less political name, which did not intimidate the Kemalists. The federation intended to ameliorate rural women's conditions and, more importantly, to achieve woman suffrage. The latter was very much contingent upon the Kemalist cadre's wishes and did not happen until the eve of the twelfth congress of the International Women's Union, which was held in 1935 in Istanbul. Ten days after the congress, the federation dissolved itself under strong pressure from the RPP that it had fulfilled its primary task.

See also GENDER: GENDER AND LAW; GENDER: GENDER AND POLITICS; TURKEY.

Bibliography

Arat, Yeşim. "From Emancipation to Liberation: The Changing Role of Women in Turkey's Public Realm." *Journal of International Affairs* 54, no. 1 (2000): 107–125.

BURÇAK KESKIN-KOZAT

WOMEN'S RELIGIOUS RITUALS

In addition to observing their formal religious duties, women of various religious communities have developed their own rituals to meet their spiritual needs and personal aspirations.

Traditionally, women in all the major religious communities in the Middle East and North Africa have had less access to religious learning than have their male counterparts; they have been excluded from the formal clerical hierarchy, and their active role in official and public communal rituals has been, to different degrees, limited. Muslim women's access to the mosque has been restricted, as has that of Jewish women to the synagogue, and these restrictions are sometimes more the result of tradition than of religious law. At the same time, women have created their own rituals, which allow their active involvement in gender-segregated settings, often in the private sphere.

Rituals at Home and outside the Home

One woman-dominated activity is visiting neighborhood shrines and other holy sites—a practice common among Muslims, Jews, Christians, and Zoroastrians. Women use these occasions to pray, ask intercession, and find support from other pilgrims. Some of these shrines are dedicated to female holy figures, such as Rachel's tomb in Bethlehem and the shrine of Zaynab in Damascus; a number are guarded by women and visited solely by female believers. In North Africa, the veneration of *marabouts,* holy men and women, living and deceased, plays a central role. Their graves and their descendants are frequented by women for blessings (*baraka*) and guidance.

Many women's rituals take place at home, transforming domestic spaces into places of worship. In addition to individual prayers of petition (*du'a*), Muslim women sponsor collective rituals, like prayer meetings of gratitude or entreaty, and gatherings to

Women in chadors pass in front of a mosque in Iraq. As with other monotheistic religious faith communities in the Middle East, Muslim women—whose access to mosques have been restricted—have developed a variety of rituals, performed in the home and elsewhere. © PETER TURNLEY/CORBIS. REPRODUCED BY PERMISSION.

read the Qur'an, chiefly during the month of Ramadan. The Prophet's birthday is celebrated with the chanting of poems about his life. Shi'a women especially partake in a great variety of religious rituals. The days of birth and martyrdom of the imams, as well as significant dates in the lives of some of their female relatives, are commemorated with either festive gatherings or recitals about their sufferings and ritual crying. Women from Iran and Central Asia also prepare and offer a *sofreh*, a ritual meal dedicated to a holy figure.

For Christian women in the Arab world, the month of May is a special time of religious devotion, processions, prayer services, and reflection. This is the month of the Virgin Mary, a period during which women ask special favors, make pledges *(nadhr)*, and attend daily prayer gatherings and special masses in church. May is also a time of religious processions to shrines to Mary, in which members of other faith communities frequently participate, as in the procession to the church at Harissa in Jounieh, Lebanon.

Food and cooking play a central role in women's ritual activities throughout the Middle East. In addition to the religious obligation of lighting the Sabbath candles, Orthodox Jewish women are responsible for kosher cooking. Zoroastrian women prepare the food offerings for the religious cere-

monies, and during Ramadan Muslim women prepare special meals for their families and guests to share after sunset to break the daily fast. A common ritual is the distribution of votive dishes.

Vows, Cults, and Holy Women

Vows are an integral part of women's religious rituals. In personal or collective prayers, they ask God for favors, or petition a saint to intercede with God on their behalf, promising to fulfill some kind of return service—for example to help the poor. The assistance of supernatural forces is sought for problems over which women have little control: illness, infertility, the lost love of a husband, financial problems, or worries about children. In times of crisis women also contact local ritual experts—religious authorities, holy women and men, healers, midwives—for amulets, divination, and cures. Many rituals concern the individual life cycle. Prayers, recitations from the holy book, and amulets serve to ensure a quick conception, a safe pregnancy, or an easy delivery, or to ward off evil influences harmful to the mother and newborn child or to a newly married couple. Muslim women gather at weddings, chanting religious songs. They gather for the formal naming of a child and for a circumcision. They perform the lament for deceased family members at home and recite prayers for their souls.

Particularly in North Africa, Egypt, Sudan, the countries around the Persian Gulf, and Yemen, Muslim women also take part in spirit possession and healing cults, most commonly referred to as *zar*. Ritual masters, who are often women, try by means of trance and dance to pacify the spirits that have afflicted the women who consult them. They are sometimes also consulted by Christian women. By claiming to be possessed by a malevolent spirit, women can overstep the boundaries of acceptable behavior and demand, in the name of the spirit, concessions from their husbands.

Women may also become members of Sufi orders. Especially in North Africa, Turkey, and Pakistan the *zikr* (remembrance of God) includes ecstatic chanting, dancing, and drumming. These rituals are sometimes connected to a healing cult.

In addition to their religious importance, rituals serve to gain merit for a woman in the next world and to secure the well-being of women and their family members—living as well as deceased. The women sometimes perform the ritual in the name of a male relative or a child, acting as representatives to the supernatural. In all Middle Eastern religious communities, women have played a central role as preservers and transmitters of faith. Further, at collective rituals, women can establish emotional and supportive bonds with others not family members. For traditional women, these rituals often represent the only socially accepted activity outside the house. Excluded from the male religious hierarchy, women find in rituals the possibility of acting as religious experts, thereby gaining esteem, income, and mobility.

Women have developed a great variety of rituals, which differ from country to country and change with historical circumstances. Some are performed by women as well as men, others exclude men. Urban women generally have developed a richer religious life than village and nomad women. Popular rituals are the sphere in which the boundaries between the different religions are most fluid. Zoroastrian women display *sofreh* like Shi'a women, and in Egypt and Lebanon Muslim women may in times of crisis visit a church or consult a priest. Many women's religious rituals have an ambiguous status and are dismissed by the religious orthodoxy. In Saudi Arabia under the Wahhabis, most Muslim women's rituals have been forbidden. In Soviet Central Asia, women's domestic rituals played an important role in the survival of religious beliefs. With increasing literacy and access to religious learning, women have begun to renegotiate their role within the religious tradition and their activities have become more visible. At the same time Muslim women's less orthodox traditional rituals have become a point of attack by Islamic revivalists, male as well as female, who regard them as superstition.

See also GENDER: GENDER AND EDUCATION; MARABOUT; MUWAHHIDUN; SUFISM AND THE SUFI ORDERS.

Bibliography

Beck, Lois. "The Religious Lives of Muslim Women." In *Women in Contemporary Muslim Societies*, edited by Jane Smith. Lewisburg, PA: Bucknell University Press; London: Associated University Press, 1980.

Doumato, Eleanor Abdella. *Getting God's Ear: Women, Islam, and Healing in Saudi Arabia and the Gulf.* New York: Columbia University Press, 2000.

Fernea, R. and Fernea, E. "Variations in Religious Observances among Islamic Women." In *Women in the Muslim World*, edited by Lois Beck and Nikki Keddie. Cambridge, MA: Harvard University Press, 1978.

Hegland, Mary E. "Gender and Religion in the Middle East and South Asia: Women's Voices Rising." In *Social History of Women and Gender in the Modern Middle East*, edited by Margaret L. Meriwether and Judith E. Tucker. Boulder, CO: Westview Press, 1999.

Mazumdar, Shampa, and Mazumdar, Sanjoy. "Ritual Lives of Muslim Women: Agency in Everyday Life." *Journal of Ritual Studies* 13, no. 2 (1999): 58–70

Sered, Susan Starr. *Women as Ritual Experts: The Religious Lives of Elderly Jewish Women in Jerusalem.* New York and Oxford, U.K.: Oxford University Press, 1992

SABINE KALINOCK

WOMEN'S RENAISSANCE CLUB

The first women's association in Iraq.

The Women's Renaissance Club was established on 24 November 1923, mainly by wives of leading politicians and women from socially prominent families. Its aim was to promote women's welfare by emphasizing charity, education, and the arts. The club worked to increase the number of schools for girls, raise women's educational levels through literacy and sewing classes, and provide for the education and care for orphans. It worked to "combat unacceptable customs that are rejected by all God's precepts, and social customs that violate honor and goodness, and hinder the economy of the country."

The club was essentially a charitable organization to assist less fortunate women. Although it did not fight for the removal of the veil, it considered the veil an issue that could be resolved by social education. This incurred the wrath of conservatives, particularly Muslim conservatives, who felt that the club would corrupt family morals and bring Westernization. Although it was no more than a social club for upper-class women, its advocacy of education for girls was enough that it was forced to close in 1925 under pressure from conservatives.

See also ARAB NATIONALISM; ART; GENDER:
GENDER AND EDUCATION; GENDER: GENDER
AND LAW; GENDER: GENDER AND POLITICS.

JACQUELINE ISMAEL

WOMEN'S SERVICES

Services available to women in Turkey.

The Turkish parliament's confirmation of the United
Nations convention against discrimination based on
sex in October 1980 formed the legal basis for the
government's providing services to women. It started
with the establishment of a Women's Unit within
the State Planning Organization in 1985. It was followed by the creation of the General Directorate of
Women's Affairs (Kadının Statüsü ve Sorunları Genel
Müdürlüğü) within the Ministry of Labor and Social Security in 1990. This directorate was to collect data concerning the status of women in Turkey
and their major problems. It was transferred in 1991
to the office of the prime minister.

In 1993, an independent undersecretary for
women's affairs and social services (Başbakanlik
Kadin ve Sosyal Hizmetler Müsteşarlığı) was created
within the office of the prime minister, and the general directorate came under the supervision of this
undersecretary. In 1991, the directorate had a staff
of five; in 1994, the staff had grown to forty-two.
The provincial network has not yet been established.
In 1994, its budget was about 0.002 percent of the
national budget.

Special women's units have been set up in the
ministries of Health, Labor and Social Security, and
National Education. In 1993 the State Statistical Institute created a data bank for women's issues.

Several Turkish universities have established
women's studies centers that offer graduate courses
and M.A. degrees:

1. Istanbul University Women's Studies Center
   (Istanbul Üniversitesi Kadin Sorunları
   Araştırma ve Uygulama Merkezi), in 1990

2. Marmara University Women's Labor Force
   and Employment Center (Marmara Üniversitesi Kadin İşgücü İstihdamı Araştırma ve
   Uygulama Merkezi), in 1990

3. Ankara University Women's Studies Center
   (Ankara Üniversitesi Kadın Sorunları
   Araştırma ve Uygulama Merkezi), in 1993

4. The Middle East Technical University
   Women's Studies Graduate Program (ODTÜ
   Kadın Çalışmaları Yüksek Lisans Programı),
   in 1994

In 1980 local governments started to sponsor
literacy courses, legal-advice centers, and occupational orientation services for women. However,
these programs remained confined to municipali-
ties in the metropolitan areas. In 1993 labor unions
began to establish women's commissions in order
to acquaint female workers with their legal rights.
Almost all major political parties also have women's
commissions as well.

Nongovernment organizations concerned with
women's issues number 211. Their major endeavors
have been to increase women's visibility on the national level and create favorable public opinion regarding legislative and administrative initiatives that
benefit women. They are instrumental in raising consciousness and establishing various types of platforms, particularly combating sexual harassment and
violence in the family. The Women's Library and
Data Bank (Kadın Eserleri Kütüphanesi ve Bilgi
Merkezi Vakfi), which is supported by a foundation
and the city of Istanbul, has been active in collect-
ing oral histories of women leaders and artists and
creating an archive for historical records.

NERMIN ABADAN-UNAT

WOMEN'S STUDIES CENTER (JERUSALEM)

A women's organization in Jerusalem.

The Women's Studies Center was established at the
initiative of the Women's Action Committee (the
women's branch of the Democratic Front for the
Liberation of Palestine) in 1989. The founding
members were Siham Barghouthi, Penny Johnson,
Amal el-Juaʿabeh, Zahira Kamal, Randa Siniora,
and Lisa Taraki. In 1992, the center declared itself
an independent nongovernmental organization. It
works to promote women's rights and improve their
social status through research, training, advocacy,

and media research and training. The center has a wide network or relations with local, regional, and international women's organizations and was the coordinator for the Arab Women's Network for many years. It has no relations with Israelis. The center depends on external funding. Due to financial problems it was in the process of being integrated into the Palestinian Agricultural Relief Committees in 2003.

See also GAZA STRIP; GENDER: GENDER AND EDUCATION; INTIFADA (1987–1991); OSLO ACCORD (1993); PALESTINE; PALESTINIAN AUTHORITY; WEST BANK.

ISLAH JAD

WOODHEAD COMMISSION (1938)

British investigatory commission to Palestine.

The commission, led by Sir John Woodhead, was formed in March 1938 in response to dissension within the British government over the July 1937 Peel partition plan for Palestine and the re-ignition of the Arab revolt that had followed its promulgation. The new commission was instructed to gather evidence from the various parties and to recommend boundaries for two self-sufficient states, one Arab and one Jewish, to replace the British Mandate.

The Arab and Jewish positions were irreconcilable. All Palestinian Arab factions and the surrounding Arab states were unified in their opposition to partition and demanded the creation of an independent Arab state on the entire Mandate territory. The Jewish Agency proposed an increase in the territory designated for the Jewish state by Lord Peel. On 9 November 1938 the Woodhead Commission issued its report, which stated that two independent states would be impracticable on financial and administrative grounds. It called for a conference of all relevant parties in London to work out a compromise. The parties met at the St. James Round Table Conference in February/March 1939, which ended in deadlock. In order to enhance its security and improve its position with Arab states on the eve of war, the government then issued the MacDonald White Paper of 17 May 1939.

Bibliography

Galnoor, Itzhak. *The Partition of Palestine: Decision Crossroads in the Zionist Movement.* Albany: State University of New York Press, 1995.

BENJAMIN JOSEPH
UPDATED BY PIERRE M. ATLAS

WORLD BANK

The international organization lends to developing countries of the Middle East.

The World Bank is based in Washington, D.C. It includes the International Bank for Reconstruction and Development (IBRD) and the International Development Agency (IDA). IBRD has two affiliates, the International Finance Corporation (IFC) and the Multilateral Guarantee Agency (MIGA).

IBRD was established in 1945 and is owned by 152 countries. The bank's resources come from its capital, retained earnings, and very large loans from the world financial markets (US$8.9 billion in 1994). Its high creditworthiness allows it to borrow

Statement of subscriptions to the capital stock and voting power of Middle Eastern countries

Country	Capital subscribed*	Capital paid*	% of vote
Algeria	1,116.10	67.10	0.59
Bahrain	133.10	5.70	0.08
Egypt	857.50	50.90	0.46
Iran	2,857.42	175.80	1.48
Iraq	338.70	27.10	0.19
Israel	573.00	33.20	0.31
Jordan	167.40	7.80	0.10
Kuwait	1,602.00	97.40	0.84
Lebanon	41.00	1.10	0.04
Libya	945.80	57.00	0.50
Morocco	599.90	34.80	0.32
Oman	188.30	9.10	0.11
Qatar	132.20	9.00	0.08
Saudi Arabia	5,404.80	335.00	2.79
Syria	265.60	14.00	0.15
U.A.E.	287.70	22.60	0.16
Total	**15,539.50**	**926.60**	**8.20**

*In millions of dollars.

SOURCE: *World Bank Annual Report, 2001.* Washington, D.C.: World Bank, 2001.

TABLE BY GGS INFORMATION SERVICES, THE GALE GROUP.

<table>

Country	IBRD[†] loans	IBRD loan amounts*	IDA[‡] loan amounts*
Algeria	2	41.70	
Egypt	0	0	
Jordan	1	120.00	
Lebanon	1	20.00	
Morocco	2	97.60	
Tunisia	3	75.90	
Yemen			142.30
Total	9	355.20	142.30

Loans to Middle East Countries by the World Bank in 2001

*In millions of dollars
[†]International Bank for Reconstruction and Development
[‡]International Development Association

SOURCE: *World Bank Annual Report, 2001.* Washington, D.C.: World Bank, 2001.

TABLE BY GGS INFORMATION SERVICES, THE GALE GROUP.

Relative voting strength on the World Bank board of Middle East countries

Members on the executive board	% Votes in International Bank for Reconstruction and Development	% Votes in International Development Association
Algeria	.51	.21
Saudi Arabia	2.79	3.57
Kuwait	.84	.59
Total	4.14	4.37

SOURCE: World Bank, February 25, 2003.

TABLE BY GGS INFORMATION SERVICES, THE GALE GROUP.

at the most competitive rates. IBRD lends to the more advanced developing countries on creditworthy and productive projects. Pricing is based on the cost of funds to the bank. Loans are made to governments or are guaranteed by governments. Total IBRD loans made in 1994 totaled US$20,836 million. IFC, established in 1956, and MIGA, established in 1984, deal with the private sectors of the developing countries. MIGA is mandated to encourage private equity investments by providing noncommercial risk guarantees. IDA lends interest free to the very poor countries with an annual per capital GNP of US$650 or less per year. The loans have very long maturities and up to a ten-year grace period.

The World Bank's executive board is responsible for the general operations of the bank. The board approves projects, funding programs, and general management of both the IBRD and the IDA. The board is composed of twenty-four members. Each member represents and votes for his country as per its percentage contribution to the capital of either IBRD or IDA. Certain countries also will represent blocs of smaller members and vote on their behalf. The largest vote belongs to the United States, which contributes 17.42 percent of IBRD capital and 15.67 percent of IDA capital. Saudi Arabia has the largest single Arab state representation on the World Bank board with 2.79 percent of the votes of the IBRD.

In the Middle East, the World Bank's stated goals are "to emphasize sustained commitment to operations and analytical work, to promote employment-led growth, to foster human resources development, and to improve natural resource management." The bank provides support to countries that agree to implement stabilization and structural reform. These conditions imply substantial efforts to reduce budget deficits, cut subsidies, allow currencies to reach their market levels, and privatize the economy.

Bibliography

Kapur, Daves; Lewis, John P.; and Webb, Richard. *The World Bank: Its First Half Century.* Washington, DC: The Brookings Institute, 1997.

JEAN-FRANÇOIS SEZNEC

WORLD FEDERATION OF SEPHARDI COMMUNITIES

Organization to support Sephardic settlement in Palestine/Israel.

The organization was founded at a conference of Sephardic communities in Vienna in 1925, prior to the Fourteenth Zionist Congress. The creation of Sephardic settlements at Kfar Hittim, Tzur Moshe, and Bet Hannan followed. After the establishment of the State of Israel, the Sephardi World Congress was convened in Paris in 1951 to renew the organization's activities on behalf of the Sephardic population in Israel, in the areas of education, housing, welfare, and preservation of their heritage. A second congress was held in Jerusalem in 1954. Now known as The World Sephardi Federation, its activities in Israel have been concentrated in education and in helping economically underprivileged Sephardic communities. It also works to promote the bond between Diaspora and Israeli Sephardic communities.

Bibliography

World Sephardi Federation. Available from <http://www.jafi.org.il/wsf>.

MIA BLOOM

WORLD ORGANIZATION OF JEWS FROM ARAB COUNTRIES (WOJAC)

International organization created in 1975.

WOJAC's charter states that Jews from Arab lands can and should form a bridge of understanding between the Arab countries and Israel. Its spokesmen stress that United Nations Resolution 242, which spells out "the necessity for a just settlement of the refugee problem," refers to all refugees, Jews and Palestinian Arabs alike; thus the legitimate rights of post-1948 Jewish refugees from Arab countries will be acknowledged. These Jews or their descendants would then be entitled to indemnification for immovable assets they left behind in their former lands.

WOJAC credits the State of Israel for its efforts to absorb the Jews from Arab lands, despite the difficulties and discriminatory policies these refugees encountered, socially and economically, during their integration processes. On the other hand, it claims that, whereas Israel solved the problem of Jewish refugees from Arab lands, the Arab states are to be faulted for failing to rehabilitate the Palestinians after 1948, rendering the latter eternal refugees as well as political pawns in inter-Arab politics.

Until 1992, when Syria finally allowed Syrian Jews to emigrate freely, WOJAC actively supported Israel's and the Jewish Agency's position that the regime permit all Jews who wished to emigrate to do so. This was in accordance with the promise made by the late Syrian president Hafiz al-Asad to then–U.S. president Jimmy Carter at Geneva in 1977.

See also BEN-PORAT, MORDECHAI.

MICHAEL M. LASKIER

WORLD WAR I

War involving the Central powers (Germany, Austria-Hungary, Bulgaria, and the Ottoman Empire) against the Allies (Britain, France, Russia, Belgium, Greece, Romania, Italy, Portugal, Serbia, Montenegro, Japan, and the United States).

World War I (then called the Great War) began on 28 July 1914, when Austria declared war on Serbia (ostensibly because a Serbian nationalist assassinated the heir to the throne, Austrian Archduke Franz Ferdinand, and his wife on 28 June); on 1 August, Germany declared war on Russia; on 3 August, Germany declared war on France; on 4 August, Germany invaded Belgium.

In retaliation and to aid an ally, Britain declared war on Germany on 4 August. The Russians crossed their western border at the Ukraine to enter Austro-Hungarian Galicia and pressed on to battle Germany, losing the Battle of Tannenberg (26–30 August), on what came to be called the Eastern Front. Germany marched on France in late August but was stopped in the First Battle of the Marne (6–10 September) on what came to be called the Western Front; here trench warfare ensued until March 1918.

In the Middle East, the leadership of the Ottoman Empire was divided among those who desired neutrality, those who wanted to join the Allies, and those who preferred to join the Central powers. The last group, led by Minister of War Enver Paşa prevailed. The Ottoman cabinet signed a secret alliance with Germany on 2 August. The next week the Ottomans purchased the German cruisers *Goeben* and *Breslau,* replacing two Turkish ships (being built by Britain but confiscated by Britain at the outbreak of war). Renamed *Sultan Selim Yavuz* and *Midilli,* they shelled Sevastopol and Odessa, Russian cities on the Black Sea, 28 October, bringing the Ottoman Empire into the war; Russia declared war on the Ottomans 4 November; Britain and France declared war on them 5 November. Germany dominated Ottoman military actions, with General Otto Liman von Sanders directing the army and Admiral Wilhelm Souchon, the navy.

In November 1914, a British naval contingent bombarded the entrance to the Dardanelles, and in January 1915 the British organized to break through

An Australian soldier carries a wounded comrade to a field hospital on the beaches of Gallipoli, Turkey, during World War I (1914–1918). The Allies began an assault on the Gallipoli Penninsula in April 1915, as the first step in a plan to overtake the Ottoman Empire's capital, Constantinople. The plan failed and the Allies were forced to evacuate Gallipoli by the end of the year. © CORBIS. REPRODUCED BY PERMISSION.

the Turkish Straits (from the Mediterranean into the Black Sea at the Bosporus and Dardanelles). Britain's First Lord of the Admiralty Winston Churchill convinced the war cabinet that an amphibious attack could accomplish this, thereby taking the Ottomans out of the war and opening a supply route to Russia. Britain's War Secretary Lord Kitchener sabotaged the plan by refusing to send the necessary land troops. Britain's navy unsuccessfully attacked in February and March; in April an Anglo-French army landed on the Gallipoli peninsula, where the Ottoman Turks caused heavy casualties to the Allies, which by then included Italian forces. The British-French-Italian forces almost

broke through twice, but the lack of cooperation by the Russians at the Bosporus end of the Straits, faulty intelligence and, most of all, skillful tactics by the Turks and Germans led to a stalemate. The Allies withdrew from the Straits in January 1916.

Another area of major Middle Eastern hostilities was Egypt, under British protection since 18 December 1914. Khedive Abbas Hilmi II was deposed, and the British appointed Sharif Husayn ibn Ali to be sultan of Egypt. Cemal Paşa, Ottoman minister of marine, took over the Fourth Ottoman army—thereby controlling Syria, including Palestine. He sent his forces to make a surprise attack on the Suez Canal in February 1915; they crossed the Negev desert without detection. The Turkish forces could not hold the eastern bank of the canal and retired to the Sinai desert, maintaining bases in Maʿan, Beersheba, and Gaza. Cemal continued to raid the Suez Canal by air, forcing the British to keep a large force there, but in the end the British prevailed. A second assault on the canal was delayed until the summer of 1916 and failed totally. The Turco-German forces were on the defensive there until the end of the war, although in March and April 1917 they withstood a heavy British attack at Gaza, and moved to the offensive in the Yilderim Operation commanded by General Erich von Falkenhayn. But the Turko-German forces were defeated by a combination of factors, including the troops of British General Edmund Allenby (commander of the Egyptian Expeditionary Force), failure of some of their transport, and sabotage.

Major battles were fought in Russia, where in late 1914 the Turks attempted to take Kars and Batum. In the battles of 1915 and 1916 the Russians took Erzerum, Van, Trabzon, and Erzinjan. They were aided by Armenians—revolutionaries and irregulars. In 1916, Mustafa Kemal (Atatürk), commander of the Second Ottoman Army, joined the Third Army on the Caucasus front, but little was accomplished due to scarce ammunition, impossible conditions for transportation, and rampant disease. The two revolutions in Russia also affected the Caucasus front, as the Russian troops (except the Armenian and Georgian divisions) withdrew and went home to attend to domestic affairs in 1917. The Turks then occupied Kars, Ardahan, and Batum, but Georgian and German forces retook Batum. A Bolshevik-Armenian coup in Baku and the killing of ten thousand Turks there produced a Turkish drive to recapture the city in September 1918 and to kill many Armenians. At the end of the war, the Caucasus became the Allies' problem.

Iraq was the scene for the major hostilities of the Mesopotamia Campaign. British forces from India seized Basra before Turkey declared war. Traveling up to the confluence of the Tigris and Euphrates rivers, the Anglo-Indian forces under General Sir Charles Townshend took Kut al-Amara in 1915. In November, his army was defeated south of Baghdad and surrendered to the Sixth Turkish

Enver Pasha, Minister of War and Commander-in-Chief of the Ottoman military during World War I (1914–1918). Enver Pasha was instrumental in bringing the Ottoman Empire into the war on the side of the Central Powers, a decision that eventually led to his downfall and the end of the Ottoman Empire. COURTESY OF THE LIBRARY OF CONGRESS.

Army at Kut al-Amara in April 1916. Halil Paşa erred in allowing the Anglo-Indian forces to remain in the south, for they reestablished their hold there, built a railroad, and under Britain's General Sir Frederick Stanley Maude, retook Kut al-Amara in March 1917. Baghdad fell immediately after, and the Anglo-Indian forces headed north to Mosul (on the west bank of the Tigris), which they failed to reach by the time of the Mudros Armistice (30 October 1918).

Two national groups within the Ottoman Empire openly aided the enemy during the war: the Arabs and the Armenians. The Armenians followed the orders of the head of the Armenian Orthodox Church (who lived in Yerevan in the Caucasus) that the Russian czar was the protector of all Armenians. Some Armenians rebelled; in the region of Van and Erzurum, Armenians openly battled the Turks proclaiming an Armenian government in Van, April 1915—which touched off the Armenian deportations and the massive killing of Armenian civilians by the Turks in 1915/16.

Cemal Paşa's actions in Syria—in arresting and hanging about thirty Arabs in Beirut and Damascus 1915/16, many from prominent families, as well as his refusal to share grain with the starving Lebanese in 1916—pushed many Arabs to desire independence from Ottoman Turkey. This desire was furthered by the proclamation of Arab independence by Sharif Husayn ibn Ali of the Hijaz in June 1916. Husayn's action was part of the outcome of the secret Husayn-McMahon Correspondence.

Another secret negotiation over the division of the Arab Middle East was the Sykes-Picot Agreement between France, Britain, and Russia. An open negotiation between the Zionists and the British had led to the issuance of the November 1917 pro-Zionist Balfour Declaration, concerning a "Jewish national home" in Palestine.

The failure of the German-Turkish campaigns led to the buildup of British troops in Egypt and their move into Palestine. General Allenby led his Egyptian Expeditionary Forces west of the Jordan river, and Jerusalem fell to them in December 1917. Joined by French military detachments, he moved north to take Lebanon, while Hijazi forces, aided by Colonel T. E. Lawrence (of Arabia), Colonel C. C. Wilson, and Sir Reginald Wingate, paralleled Allenby's actions east of the Jordan River. Damascus fell in October 1918—and although Mustafa Kemal (Atatürk) and the Seventh Turkish Army held Aleppo, the armistice at Mudros ended all fighting, 30 October 1918.

Four years of war had devastated Ottoman Turkey, and the old order died. A new period for the Middle East began with the peace treaties, the rise to power in Turkey of Mustafa Kemal, the fall of empires, and the creation of new nation-states and spheres of influence.

See also BALFOUR DECLARATION (1917); HUSAYN–McMAHON CORRESPONDENCE (1915–1916); SYKES–PICOT AGREEMENT (1916).

Bibliography

Barker, A. J. *The Bastard War: The Mesopotamian Campaign of 1914–1918.* New York: Dial Press, 1967.

Kedourie, Elie. *England and the Middle East: The Destruction of the Ottoman Empire, 1914–1921.* Hassocks, U.K.: Harvester Press, 1978.

Lewis, Bernard. *The Emergence of Modern Turkey,* 3d edition. New York: Oxford University Press, 2002.

SARA REGUER

WORLD WAR II

War involving the Axis (Germany, Italy, Japan, Hungary, Romania, and Bulgaria) against the Allies (Britain, France, the United States, the Soviet Union, Australia, Belgium, Brazil, Canada, China, Denmark, Greece, the Netherlands, New Zealand, Norway, Poland, South Africa, and Yugoslavia).

When World War II began on 1 September 1939, the Middle East consisted of independent, semi-independent, and colonial states. From east to west they included the following: Iran and Turkey were independent, with Iran under Reza Shah Pahlavi and Turkey a republic. Syria and Lebanon were republics but under French control. Transjordan and Iraq were monarchies but under British control. Palestine was a League of Nations mandate under British control. The Arabian peninsula consisted of Saudi Arabia and Yemen, both independent, and Oman and a variety of Persian/Arabian Gulf states within the British sphere of influence. Egypt (with the strategic Suez Canal) and the Sudan were nominally independent but really under British control. Libya was an Italian colony. The French effectively controlled the rest of North Africa—Tunisia, Algeria, and Morocco—except for the western regions under Spanish rule.

In World War II, Britain and France were allied against Germany and Italy. All except Germany had significant imperial holdings and interests in the Middle East. Germany wanted not only the defeat of Britain and France, but German gains in this region. As the war began, the Axis powers controlled only a small part of the Middle East—Libya and some other Italian territory taken during the Ethiopian annexation in 1935. The fall of France to Germany in May 1940 and the establishment of the quasi-independent Vichy republic in June 1940 dramat-

British soldiers salute as the Union Jack is raised over Benghazi, Libya, after its capture from the Italians in 1943. North Africa was the scene of heavy fighting during the middle stages of World War II (1939–1945). © CORBIS. REPRODUCED BY PERMISSION.

ically altered the balance of power: In addition to Italy's territories being in their sphere of influence, the Axis powers had acquired France's territories.

North and East African Campaigns

The British initiated their first military action in the Middle East by an attack on French naval vessels at Oran, Algeria, 3 July 1940—which crippled the French fleet there (and resulted in 1,300 French dead). This was part of an effort to ensure that the Axis powers could not use the French fleet; the French squadron at Alexandria was disarmed while two French submarines in British ports joined the Free French forces fighting with the British. The next day, Italian forces from Ethiopia occupied border towns in the Sudan, and within six weeks they penetrated British Kenya and seized British Somaliland. On 13 September, Italian forces under Rodolfo Graziani invaded Egypt; they penetrated some sixty miles (90 km) within a week, and dug in along a fifty-mile (80 km) front from the coast to Sidi Barrani.

Since the threat to the Suez Canal was of primary importance, the British countered first against Graziani's army of 200,000. General Sir Archibald Wavell launched a surprise attack with an army of 63,000 on 6 December and drove through the Italian lines at Sidi Barrani, capturing 40,000 Italian troops by 12 December. The campaign continued for two months, ending with Italian surrender at Benghazi, Libya, on 7 February 1941. With advance units at al-Agheila, the British had advanced about five hundred miles (800 km), captured 130,000 Italian soldiers, and taken four hundred tanks and one thousand guns.

On 15 January 1941 the British launched an attack against Italian forces in East Africa, from the Sudan. Mogadiscio, capital of Italian Somaliland, fell on 26 February, followed by Neguelli in southern

Ethiopia on 22 March; the capital, Addis Ababa, fell on 6 April.

These British successes were soon to be reversed. Germany had not yet committed her forces to Operation Barbarossa, the invasion of Russia (22 June 1941), and in February and March was able to reinforce the Italians in western Libya with two divisions under General Erwin Rommel. In the meantime, the British had turned their attention to the defense of Greece, diverting troops from North Africa.

Rommel opened his attack on 3 April, and the British retreated from their recent gains in Libya. The Axis forces drove the British back to the Egyptian frontier by 29 May. The tables then turned when Germany diverted troops from North Africa for the invasion of Russia. The British launched an offensive on 11 December and were able to drive into Libya as far as Benghazi by 25 December. A reinforced Rommel was able to begin a drive on Egypt on 22 May 1942 that did not end until checked at al-Alamayn (El Alamein), just eighty miles (127 km) from Alexandria. General Montgomery's offensive

General Erwin Rommel with soldiers of the 15th Panzer Division in 1941, in Libya between Tobruk and Sidi Omar. Rommel earned the nickname "the Desert Fox" for his skillful leadership of Axis forces in North Africa during World War II (1939–1945). NATIONAL ARCHIVES—STILL PICTURE REFERENCE (NWCS-STILLS REFERENCE) NWDNS-242-EAPC-6-M713A. REPRODUCED BY PERMISSION.

from al-Alamayn began on 23 October, resulting in expulsion of Axis forces from Egypt by 12 November and the end of the threat to Egypt and the Suez Canal.

At about the same time, on 8 November, a British-American force under U.S. General Dwight D. Eisenhower began Operation Torch, the invasion of North Africa. Allied forces disembarking in French Morocco and Algeria faced some opposition from Vichy forces, but by 11 November, the two sides had reached an armistice. Pressed by Montgomery's Eighth Army in Libya and the new threat from the west, Rommel concentrated the Axis forces in Tunisia. Into 1943, bitter fighting continued, particularly at the Kasserine Pass, but by 12 May all German and Italian resistance had ended. The Axis powers had 950,000 men dead or captured and had lost 8,000 aircraft and 2.4 million tons of shipping.

Southwest Asia and Turkey

While the significant fighting of World War II in the Middle East was in Africa, the British still faced serious threats in Southwest Asia. The regimes in both Iran and Iraq flirted with support of the Axis powers as a means of diminishing British influence over their affairs. On 2 May 1941, pro-Axis sympathizers in Iraq tried to seize power. British forces intervened and put down all resistance by 31 May. Fearing that Reza Shah Pahlavi might take Iran into the German camp in the summer of 1941, British and Soviet forces entered Iran in late August and forced him to abdicate in favor of his son, Muhammad Reza Pahlavi, on 16 September. These actions effectively secured Iraq and Iran for the Allies.

The fall of France in June 1940 threatened to bring Syria and Lebanon into the Axis sphere of influence. Quick action by the British and Free French forces prevented this. On 8 June these forces occupied Syria and Lebanon. On 16 September Syria was proclaimed an independent nation, as was Lebanon on 26 November. Both remained loyal to the Allies during World War II, but soon after the end of hostilities they were able to assert their independence and obtain the withdrawal of Allied forces from their territory.

World War I had led to the disintegration of the Ottoman Empire and the creation of the Turkish republic under Kemal Atatürk. Turkey then faced pressure from both sides and from within as World War II loomed on the horizon. Atatürk and his successor, İsmet İnönü, favored the British as the power they believed would ultimately win. Other Turks feared Britain's ally, the Soviet Union, as a traditional enemy and realized that by June 1941 German troops were within 100 miles (160 km) of Istanbul. Still others remembered the disastrous decision of October 1914, when the Ottomans joined the Central Powers in World War I.

Shortly after the beginning of World War II, on 19 October 1939, Britain and France concluded a fifteen-year mutual assistance pact with Turkey. German success in 1940 and the invasion of Russia in 1941, however, led many Turkish leaders to favor the Axis. Thus, on 1 November 1940, İnönü declared it to be Turkish policy to remain a nonbelligerent in the war, while maintaining friendly ties with both Britain and the Soviet Union. The Allies, of course, continued to pressure Turkey for support, and on 3 December 1941, just before the United States declared war, the American Lend-Lease program was extended to Turkey. İnönü still pursued a neutral course but by 1943 realized that the Axis would lose. In August 1944, Turkey broke diplomatic relations with Germany, and on 23 February 1945 it formally declared war to comply with requirements for participation in the UN conference to be held in San Francisco in April.

Palestine

The Jewish and Arab populations of Palestine greeted World War II with mixed emotions. Neither was content with British rule. The Arabs resented the rule of their country by a European power pledged to uphold the Balfour Declaration (sanctioning Palestine as a haven for persecuted Jews from all parts of the world). The Jewish population, the Yishuv, suspected British commitment to the Balfour Declaration, especially since the British banned Jewish immigration into Palestine after 1939.

In light of the antisemitism of Nazi Germany and its extermination of European Jewry as a matter of state policy, the Yishuv had little recourse but to support the Allies. The resources of the Jewish community in Palestine were put at the disposal of the British, and efforts (often resisted by British authorities) were made to raise Jewish military units to support the war effort. Early in the war the Yishuv devised the Carmel Plan, to create a Jewish enclave on the Palestine coast, near Haifa, to resist a German landing and occupation. Fortunately, this never became necessary.

A small minority of Jews did continue to resist British control of Palestine. The LEHI (Stern Gang), under Abraham Stern, urged rebellion against the British and even approached the German representatives in Vichy-controlled Syria with an offer of support against the British in Palestine. Even after this offer was rejected and Stern killed in confrontation with British authorities in early 1942, this splinter group continued to resist the British; other Jewish groups then began to oppose the British as the war progressed, since British support of the Zionist cause seemed less than enthusiastic.

Some Arabs viewed Germany as an instrument to rid themselves of British rule. The mufti of Jerusalem, Hajj Amin al-Husayni, lent his support to the Nazi cause, and when fleeing from Jerusalem in 1937 and from Beirut in October 1939 to Baghdad, he established contact with the German ambassador to Turkey, Franz von Papen, offering Arab support. After an anti-British revolt in 1941, the British reestablished control of Iraq in May 1941. Hajj Amin, who participated in the revolt, left for Turkey and later for Rome and Berlin to support the Axis powers after they promised to free the Arab world and support its independence and unity. He was able to generate some support for the Axis among the Arabs, but the defeat of the Italians and Germans in North Africa prevented this from becoming a factor in the war.

The War's Effect on the Middle East

World War II ended with British and French control of most of the Middle East. The war did, however, shatter the aura of the invincibility of their arms. Consequently, rapid changes occurred in the region—Arab states asserted their independence, and the Jewish population of Palestine declared the State of Israel in 1948. Iran and Turkey insisted on full partnership in the international community. The European powers would no longer have undisputed control over the fates of the peoples in this region.

With the end of the war the United States emerged the premier Western power, but the challenge of the Cold War with the Soviet Union would soon have its own impact on the oil-rich Middle East.

See also ALAMAYN, AL-; ATATÜRK, MUSTAFA KEMAL; HUSAYNI, MUHAMMAD AMIN AL-; İNÖNÜ, İSMET; MONTGOMERY, BERNARD LAW; PAHLAVI, REZA; ROMMEL, ERWIN; STERN, ABRAHAM; WAVELL, ARCHIBALD PERCIVAL; YISHUV.

Bibliography

Hourani, Albert. A History of the Arab Peoples. Cambridge, MA: Belknap Press, 1991.

Keegan, John. The Second World War. New York: Penguin, 1990.

Lewis, Bernard. The Emergence of Modern Turkey, 3d edition. New York: Oxford University Press, 2002.

Peretz, Don. The Middle East Today, 6th edition. Westport, CT: Praeger, 1994.

Sachar, Howard M. A History of Israel: From the Rise of Zionism to Our Time, 2d revised and updated edition. New York: Knopf, 1996.

Time-Life Books. WW II: Time-Life Books History of the Second World War. New York: Prentice Hall, 1989.

DANIEL E. SPECTOR

WORLD ZIONIST ORGANIZATION (WZO)

Organization that transformed the Zionist idea of establishing a Jewish state into reality.

Founded in 1897 by Theodor Herzl at the first Zionist Congress in Basel, Switzerland, the Zionist Organization, as it was originally known, was created to serve as the organizational framework for the Zionist movement. It was to be composed of "all Jews who accept the Zionist program and pay the shekel (a nominal membership fee, differing from country to country)."

The Zionist Congress was established as the supreme governing body of the WZO. Before 1948 congresses were held in many European cities; thereafter, beginning with the twenty-third congress in 1951, all congresses were held in Jerusalem. At first they were held every one or two years; more recently they have been convened every four years.

Herzl, the first president of the WZO, chaired its first five congresses. After his death in 1904 the movement was headed by lackluster figures until the election of Chaim Weizmann as its president in 1920.

Between congresses, the movement was guided by a Greater Actions Committee, or General Council, and a Smaller Actions Committee, or Executive. Under the aegis of the WZO, the Jewish Colonial Trust was formed at the second Zionist Congress to serve as the bank of the Zionist movement. The Jewish National Fund was initiated at the fifth Zionist Congress to act as a land-purchasing agent in Palestine for the Jewish people.

Membership in the World Zionist Organization was initially on a regional basis, but as ideological differences emerged the membership structure splintered along ideological lines. Distinct political parties were formed, of which the most important were the Labor Zionists, the General Zionists (liberal centrists), the Mizrahi (religious Zionists), and (after 1925) the Revisionists (right-wing nationalists). The latter, led by Vladimir Ze'ev Jabotinsky, split from the WZO altogether in 1935 and formed the New Zionist Organization.

During the period of British mandatory rule in Palestine between 1920 and 1948 the WZO assumed many of the powers of a quasi-government of the Jewish community in the country. Article 4 of the Mandate provided for the establishment of a Jewish Agency, which "shall be recognized as a public body for the purpose of advising and cooperating with the administration of Palestine in such economic, social, and other matters as may affect the establishment of the Jewish national home and the interests of the Jewish population in Palestine." Until 1929 the WZO acted as the Jewish Agency for Palestine; thereafter, the agency was enlarged to include non-Zionists, but the WZO remained the dominant power within the new body. The political department of the Jewish Agency functioned, in effect, as the foreign ministry of the WZO throughout this period.

After the establishment of the State of Israel in 1948 the WZO gradually evolved into a foreign propaganda and political mobilization arm of the Israeli government. Many of the WZO's functions were assumed by the new government, but the Jewish Agency was not dismantled. In 1952 the Law of the Status of the WZO–Jewish Agency was promulgated whereby primary responsibility was assigned to the Jewish Agency for the development and settlement of the land and for the absorption of immigrants. In 1960 the WZO adopted a new constitution under which individuals were denied eligibility for membership, which was thereafter reserved for organizations.

See also HERZL, THEODOR; JABOTINSKY, VLADIMIR ZE'EV; JEWISH AGENCY FOR PALESTINE; JEWISH COLONIAL TRUST; JEWISH NATIONAL FUND; LABOR ZIONISM; WEIZMANN, CHAIM.

Bibliography

Laqueur, Walter. *A History of Zionism.* London: Weidenfeld and Nicolson, 1972.

BERNARD WASSERSTEIN

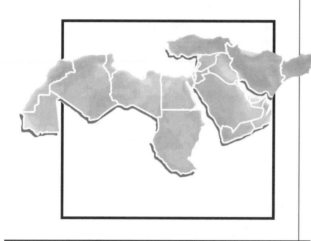

YA'ARI, ME'IR
[1897–1987]

Israeli political leader.

Born in Galicia, Me'ir Ya'ari was educated at the Vienna Academy of Agriculture and the University of Vienna. During World War I, he served as an officer in the Austro-Hungarian army. In Vienna, he was a leader of the ha-Shomer ha-Tzaʿir youth movement before emigrating to Palestine in 1919. Founder of the first kibbutz of ha-Shomer ha-Tzaʿir and the Histadrut, Ya'ari was also an early leader of the Kibbutz Artzi of the ha-Shomer ha-Tzaʿir movement in Israel and abroad. He was elected to the first Israeli Knesset, in which he remained until 1973, and served as general secretary of MAPAM. A prolific writer on Zionist ideology, Ya'ari was a principal intellectual force in the MAPAM movement.

See also ISRAEL: POLITICAL PARTIES IN.

BRYAN DAVES

YACINE, ABDESSALAME
[1928–]

Islamic intellectual and spiritual leader in Morocco.

Abdessalame Yacine is one of the foremost Islamic intellectuals in Morocco and the spiritual leader of the al-Adl wa al-Ihsan (Justice and Charity) movement. A former teacher and school principal, Yacine became an Islamic activist in the early 1970s after having been religiously awakened by an encounter with Sufism. Following his bold criticism of King Hassan II in an open letter entitled "Islam or the Deluge" in 1974, Yacine was jailed on a few occasions, and ultimately put under house arrest between 1989 and 2000. Besides this clash with the monarchy, he has mostly distinguished himself through a prolific literary production and the originality of his philosophy. Deeply influenced by his short Sufi experience, Yacine developed a nonviolent Islamism based on spiritual regeneration. His major works in Arabic and French underline the importance of spiritual guidance (*tarbiya*), proper companionship (*suhbah*), and prayer. In doing so, Yacine invites Muslims to reach a higher stage of consciousness called *ihsan* in order to become truly benevolent and build a better society. Yacine thus wishes to instill justice, honesty, and responsibility within various spheres, from family life to politics. His emphasis on spiritual growth, which he attempts to reconcile with the dryness of Islamic law, sets him apart from the more rigorist Islamists in Morocco and elsewhere. Nevertheless, al-Adl wa al-Ihsan, officially founded in 1987, is currently one of the most important Islamic organizations in the country. Although Yacine continues to criticize the Moroccan monarchy and government within acceptable limits, he has so far eschewed direct political involvement.

See also ADL WA AL-IHSAN AL-; HASSAN II; MOROCCO: OVERVIEW; MOROCCO: POLITICAL PARTIES IN; MUHAMMAD VI.

Bibliography

Shahin, Emad Eldin. "Secularism and Nationalism: The Political Discourse of ʿAbd al-Salam Yassin," in *Islamism and Secularism in North Africa,* edited by John Ruedy. New York: St. Martin's Press, 1994: 167–186.

HENRI LAUZIÈRE

YACOUBI, RACHIDA
[1946–]

Moroccan writer.

Rachida Yacoubi's first novel, *Ma vie, mon cri* (My life, my scream; 1995) described the poor condition of women in Moroccan society and caused a shock both in Morocco and abroad. Based partly on her own experience, the book tells the story of a woman whose husband is an alcoholic. She divorces him to stay alone with four children in a shantytown. This was almost the first time that a story so violently against male domination of society was published in Morocco. It was a great success and Yacoubi was invited to Europe on many occasions to speak about the condition of women.

Before Yacoubi's book, the condition of women in Morocco had been addressed only by male novelists (Tahar Ben-Jelloun, Driss Chraibi, Abdelhak Serhane) or by researchers (Souad Filal, Fatima Mernissi, Soumaya Naamane-Guessous). Following the publication of Yacoubi's novel, other Moroccan women published books about gender issues in Morocco. They include Halima Benhaddou (*Aïcha la rebelle,* 1982), Leila Houari (*Zeida de nulle part,* 1985), Nafissa Sbaï (*L'enfant endormi,* 1987), and Fatiha Boucetta (*Anissa captive,* 1991). In 2002, Yacoubi published an essay about the time she spent in prison ("Je dénonce"; I denounce), showing the inequality of men and woman before the judicial system in Morocco

See also HASSAN II; MOROCCO: OVERVIEW; MOROCCO: POLITICAL PARTIES IN; MOUDAWANA, AL-; MUHAMMAD VI.

RABIA BEKKAR

YADIN, YIGAEL
[1917–1984]

Israeli archaeologist, general, and politician.

Born in Jerusalem, the son of the archaeologist E. L. Sukenik, Yigael Yadin studied archaeology and Semitic languages at Hebrew University (1935–1945), later earning his Ph.D. (1955) studying the Dead Sea Scrolls. He joined the Haganah and adopted the personal code name Yadin, which later became his surname. Yadin was chief operations officer in the 1948 war and later chief of staff (1949–1952); he is credited with creating the principles of Israel's citizens' army reserve system. He resigned from the chief-of-staff position in 1952 because of budgetary disputes and joined the Hebrew University faculty in 1953, where he was appointed professor of archaeology in 1963. In 1976 he was a founder of the centrist Democratic Movement for Change, and from 1977 to 1981 he was a member of the Knesset and deputy prime minister. In 1981 he returned to Hebrew University. Yadin followed his father in studying the Dead Sea Scrolls. With Nahman Avigad, he published *Genesis Apocryphon* (1956), *Ben Sira from Masada* (1965), and *Temple Scroll* (1977). His most important archaeological achievements were the large-scale excavations at Hazor, the Cave of Letters in the Judaean desert, Masada, Megiddo, and Bet Sheʾan.

See also ARCHAEOLOGY IN THE MIDDLE EAST.

Bibliography

Astor, D.; Barnett, R. D.; Kane, J.; et al. "The Yigael Yadin Memorial Lecture." *Bulletin of the Anglo-Israel Archaeological Society* (1984–1985): 9–23.

Greenfield, J. "Bibliography of Yigal Yadin." *Journal of Jewish Studies* 33 (1982): 11–16.

Jerusalem Center for Public Affairs. "Yadin (Sukenik), Yigael." In *Glossary of Israeli Parties and Personalities: 1948–1981.* Available from <http://www.jcpa.org/art/knesset8.htm>.

Jewish Agency for Israel, Department for Jewish Zionist Education."Yigal Yadin." In *Our Gallery of People.* Available from <http://www.jajz-ed.org.il/100/PEOPLE>.

MIA BLOOM
UPDATED BY GREGORY S. MAHLER

YAD MORDEKHAI

Kibbutz that was the site of an important battle in the Arab–Israel War (1948).

Yad Mordekhai, named for Mordekhai Anilewitz, commander of the Warsaw Ghetto uprising, is located between Gaza and Ashkelon on the road to Tel Aviv. Founded in 1943, the kibbutz was attacked by Egypt's army on May 19, 1948. It held out for four days without relief; on the fifth day, the survivors broke through Egypt's lines to the settlement of Gvar Am. The attackers suffered 300 casualties.

Today the kibbutz has 700 inhabitants. The kibbutz supports itself through agriculture; industry, especially bee products from its apiary; and tourism, with visitors to a reconstructed battlefield from the 1948 war and a museum devoted to the Holocaust, Jewish resistance in Europe, the immigration of Holocaust survivors to Palestine during the British Mandate, and Israel's War of Independence.

Bibliography

Allon, Yigal. *Shield of David: The Story of Israel's Armed Forces.* New York: Random House, 1970.

Elon, Amos. *The Israelis: Founders and Sons.* New York: Penguin, 1983.

JON JUCOVY

YAD VASHEM

The Holocaust Martyrs' and Heroes' Remembrance Authority, as well as a site in Israel dedicated to commemorating the Jewish victims of Nazi persecution and extermination.

Established on the authority of the 1945 London Zionist Congress, Yad Vashem (from Isaiah 56:5) includes a museum of the Holocaust, facilities for conferences and memorial gatherings (Holocaust Remembrance Day ceremonies are held there on 27 Nisan), and a research institute. Yad Vashem is a feature of foreign dignitaries' official visits to Israel.

Yad Vashem's task is to perpetuate the legacy of the Holocaust to future generations so that the world never forgets the horrors and cruelty of the Holocaust. Its principal missions are commemoration and documentation of the events of the Holocaust; collection, examination, and publication of testimonies to the Holocaust; the collection and memorialization of the names of Holocaust victims; and research and education.

See also HOLOCAUST.

Bibliography

Young, James Edward. *The Texture of Memory: Holocaust Memorials and Meaning.* New Haven, CT: Yale University Press, 1993.

JON JUCOVY

YAHYA IBN MUHAMMAD HAMID AL-DIN
[1867–1948]

Imam of Yemen, 1904–1948; king of Yemen, 1918–1948.

Yahya ibn Muhammad Hamid al-Din took the patronymic al-Mutawakkil ala Allah on becoming imam in 1904. He succeeded to the imamate upon the death of his father Muhammad ibn Yahya, who had inaugurated a new period of rebellion against the rule of the Ottoman Empire in the highlands of Yemen in 1891.

Although Yahya was sometimes amenable to concessions and negotiations with the Ottoman authorities, he approved of the desire of the Zaydi people to be free of Ottoman rule. When Yahya received the *bayʿa* (oath of allegiance), he immediately called for a full-scale revolt against the Ottomans; his major motivation appears to have been the May 1904 boundary agreement about Yemen's southern borders, signed between the Ottomans and British, since he considered himself to be the legitimate ruler of both "north" Yemen and the territories held by the British in "south" Yemen.

Imam Yahya continued to lead the revolt against the Ottomans throughout the period before World

War I. His political shrewdness as well as his ability to wage irregular war against the Ottoman state forced it to negotiate with him, most importantly in the Treaty of Da'an in 1919, which granted most of his demands and gave him an almost free hand in matters of taxation, religious affairs, and judicial appointments.

During World War I, however, the imam sided with the Ottomans as fellow Muslims—the only Arab regime to do so. At the end of the war, the Ottomans departed Yemen and officially recognized Yahya as ruler there. For Imam Yahya, however, this was only the first step in creating the Yemen he perceived to be the patrimony of the Zaydi imams.

Yahya's primary policy objectives in the postwar period appear to have been: (1) to bring all of Yemen under his direct control; (2) to make Yemen completely independent of the influence and/or control of other states (to have complete autarky); (3) to weaken the cohesion and power of the tribes (to prevent them from developing a common front against the central government and resisting its policy objectives); and (4) to establish the ascendancy of Islamic law (Shari'a) throughout Yemen.

The methods Yahya employed to bring about his goals were diverse, and some were, in today's light, brutal. At first he paid subsidies and bribes to various tribal elements; later, when the treasury could clearly not support the demands of these payments, he sent military units to quell uprisings against his decisions, and also employed a traditional Yemeni technique—he took hostages from the tribes, typically the sons of the tribal Shaykhs. These hostages were kept in the imam's fortresses (where they were also educated) to guarantee the good behavior of their own tribes or tribal alliances. Yahya was assassinated in 1948.

Bibliography

Fisher, Sydney N. The Middle East: A History, 3d edition. New York: Knopf, 1979.

MANFRED W. WENNER

YAMANI, AHMAD ZAKI

[1930–]

Saudi official influential in world petroleum politics in the 1960s and 1970s.

Born in Mecca in 1930, Ahmad Zaki Yamani was educated at Cairo, New York, and Harvard universities. He began working for the government of Saudi Arabia in 1958 and rose to become minister of petroleum and mineral resources in 1962, a post he held until 1986. He is noted for his success in asserting Saudi control over the country's oil resources, helping to establish the Organization of Arab Petroleum Exporting Countries (OAPEC), and increasing the profits of oil-producing countries through asserting their rights to set production and pricing policies. He was instrumental in establishing the General Petroleum and Mineral Organization (PETROMIN), a Saudi company created to develop oil resources, and the College of Petroleum and Minerals in Dhahran. In response to Israel's victory in the October 1973 War, Yamani succeeded in leading an embargo of oil shipments by Arab producers to the United States and other supporters of Israel. He served as secretary-general of OAPEC in 1968 and 1969 and was seen as a prominent voice for moderation in the organization. In 1986 he established the Centre for Global Energy Studies.

See also ORGANIZATION OF ARAB PETROLEUM EXPORTING COUNTRIES (OAPEC).

ANTHONY B. TOTH

YANBU

A port on Saudi Arabia's Red Sea coast.

Located in the Hijaz region, Yanbu traditionally served the city of Medina. Originally Yanbu was divided into the port itself, Yanbu al-Bahr, and the inland agricultural settlement of Yanbu al-Nakhl. In the 1970s, along with al-Jubayl on the Persian Gulf, Yanbu became the center of a massive industrial development scheme that included oil refining, petrochemical industries, and heavy manufacturing complexes based on hydrocarbon fuels. Yanbu was planned as the smaller of the two sites, with two petroleum refineries, a natural gas processing plant, a petrochemical complex, other light industries, an industrial port, and a new city of 100,000 inhabitants. Energy for these projects was to be supplied via oil and gas pipelines from the Eastern Province, and the terminus of the Iraqi pipeline across Saudi Arabia was located nearby; the Iraqi pipeline was closed after Iraq's invasion of Kuwait in 1990, but the capacity of the Saudi east-west pipeline was later increased to nearly five million barrels per day. By 1999 Yanbu's population was about 70,000.

Bibliography

Farsy, Fouad al-. *Modernity and Tradition: The Saudi Equation.* London: Kegan Paul International, 1991.

J. E. PETERSON

YARIV, AHARON
[1920–1994]

Israeli career officer, cabinet minister and defense analyst.

Born in Russia in 1920, Aharon Yariv moved to Palestine at the age of fifteen and joined the Haganah in 1939. During World War II, Yariv fought in the British army, helping to liberate concentration camps. He was the first Israeli to attend the French Military Command and Staff School.

Yariv served in many positions in the Israel Defense Forces (IDF), including commander of the IDF Command and Staff School (1954), head of Central Command (1956–1957), commander of the Golani Brigade (1960–1961), and most significantly as chief of the Intelligence branch (Aman; 1964–1973) during which he provided the intelligence information responsible for the Israeli victory in 1967. From 1957 to 1960, he served as military attaché in Washington, D.C. Yariv left the Intelligence branch shortly before the 1973 Arab–Israel War, although he served as head of the Israeli delegation during the Kilometer 101 disengagement talks.

Elected to the eighth Knesset on the Labor Alignment ticket, Yariv became minister of transport under Golda Meir and later minister of information under Yitzhak Rabin. Together with another minister, Yariv wrote a formula for peace negotiations that recommended Israel carry out negotiations with any Palestinian faction that would recognize Israel's right to exist and that would not engage in terrorism. Yariv founded the Center for Strategic Studies at Tel Aviv University in 1977 and served as its head until his death.

See also ARAB–ISRAEL WAR (1973); HAGANAH; KNESSET; MEIR, GOLDA; RABIN, YITZHAK.

JULIE ZUCKERMAN

YARMUK RIVER

Tributary of the Jordan river.

The Yarmuk river forms boundaries between Jordan, Syria, and Israel, all of which have contested its use as a water source. About fifty miles (80 km) long, the Yarmuk rises in southern Syria and flows westward through a deep gorge along the Jordanian border of the Golan Heights region of Syria annexed by Israel in 1981. It empties into the Jordan river four miles (6.4 km) south of the Sea of Galilee. Although much smaller than the Euphrates (in Turkey, north Syria, and Iraq) or even the Litani (in Lebanon), the Yarmuk supplies up to 50 percent of the water flow in the lower Jordan river.

The Yarmuk shares a long and storied past with the Jordan river valley, as recounted in archaeological evidence, holy scripture and medieval chronicles. A Roman fortress town was built at the junction of the two rivers, and ruins of Roman- and Byzantine-era synagogues have been found nearby. In the early seventh century, it was through the Yarmuk gorge that Arab armies invaded the Jordan valley.

The Yarmuk's strategic importance has continued into the modern era. Today, it is the only undeveloped tributary of the Jordan river, in a region that now exploits the maximum capacity of existing water sources. Its only significant exploitation has been Jordan's East Ghawr Canal, built in 1964 to irrigate thirty thousand acres (12,150 ha) of farmland east of the Jordan river. Jordan plans to extend the nearly 50-mile (80-km) canal and build a 328-foot (100-m) dam at Maqarin to store the Yarmuk's waters for agriculture and for the cities of Irbid and Amman. Syria plans a series of small dams on the upper Yarmuk to benefit agriculture in the Hawran region.

But these plans require agreement from all parties enjoying riparian rights to the river—not just Syria and Jordan, but also Israel. Israeli interest in the Yarmuk began shortly after World War I, when Chaim Weizmann, later Israel's first president, proposed borders for Palestine that would include the river. In 1932, the Palestine Electric Corporation (now the Israel Electric Corporation) built a hydroelectric generating plant at the junction of the Yarmuk and Jordan rivers. It was destroyed by the Arab Legion in the 1948 war, but Israel has continued to claim the water rights to the Yarmuk granted by the British mandate.

Since 1948, the contest for the Yarmuk has at times been violent. Efforts in the 1950s to coordinate joint use of the Jordan river basin, like the 1953 Johnston Plan, failed to gain agreement from all sides. While Jordan pursued its unilateral East Ghawr Canal, Israel, between 1953 and 1964, built its National Water Carrier, which diverts the Jordan's water from north of the Sea of Galilee to Tel Aviv and the Negev desert. In response, the Arab League in 1960 coordinated a plan to develop the Yarmuk for the benefit of Jordan, Syria, and Lebanon. The project, begun in 1964, was to divert the Jordan's northern headwaters to the Yarmuk, where a dam on the Syrian-Jordanian border would also be built. In 1965 and 1966 Israel attacked bulldozers and facilities at construction sites in Syria. Israel's 1967 occupation of the Golan Heights put a final halt to the project. In 1969 Israeli raids destroyed part of Jordan's East Ghawr Canal, which was subsequently repaired.

After years of opposition, in 2003 Syria finally agreed to allow Jordan to begin construction of the Maqarin dam.

See also JOHNSTON PLAN (1953); MAQARIN DAM; WATER.

Bibliography

Farid, Abdel Majid, and Sirriyeh, Hussein, eds. *Israel and Arab Water: An International Symposium.* London: Ithaca Press, 1985.

Khouri, Fred J. *The Arab-Israeli Dilemma,* 3d edition. Syracuse, NY: Syracuse University Press, 1985.

Starr, Joyce R., and Stoll, Daniel, eds. *The Politics of Scarcity: Water in the Middle East.* Boulder, CO: Westview Press, 1988.

ELIZABETH THOMPSON

YARMUK UNIVERSITY

A public university in Jordan.

Established in 1976 on the outskirts of Irbid in northwest Jordan, Yarmuk University was the kingdom's second public university, opened in response to the rapidly increasing demands for higher education. The main campus of the university was built over a fifteen-year period and includes faculties of arts, economics, education and fine arts, engineering, Islamic studies, law, science, and an institute for archaeology and anthropology, as well as centers in various disciplines. At its inception, Yarmuk University pioneered new programs, including a center for Jordanian studies, a department of communications and journalism, a department of continuing education, a school for public health, and a department of computer science. In the 1999/2000 academic year, student enrollment was 17,800.

Bibliography

Gubser, Peter. *Historical Dictionary of the Hashemite Kingdom of Jordan.* Metuchen, NJ: Scarecrow Press, 1991.

JENAB TUTUNJI

YARMULKE

See GLOSSARY

YASAR KEMAL
[c. 1923–]

Long despised by Turkish intellectuals, who considered his "popular frescoes" as second-rate literature, Yasar Kemal is today Turkey's most famous living fiction writer.

Yasar Kemal's family was from Ercis, a small town near Van, in the Kurdish region of Turkey. During World War I, his father settled in the plain of Tchukurova, near Adana, where Yasar was born around 1923. He does not know his exact date of birth, but it was probably after 1923 because he was named Mustafa Kemal, after the founder of the Turkish Republic. During his childhood, he experienced considerable violence—an atmosphere that permeates his books, which are full of bandits and honor killings. Yasar Kemal's maternal uncle was one of Turkey's most renowned bandits, and Yasar Kemal himself was hardly five when his father was murdered in a mosque by his adoptive son.

After his father's death, his family was destitute and Yasar Kemal went to work on other people's land. During this time he observed nature, which he describes at length in his books. The land and its transformations as the seasons change are an important part of his novels. He also describes the poor peasants' fight for land that has been confiscated by rapacious *aghas* and *beys* (landowners)

At seventeen, Yasar Kemal became a leftist political activist. He was introduced to Marxism by Arif and Abidine Dino, two brothers who had been exiled to Adana, and he later became a member of the Central Committee of the Turkish Communist Party. After many menial jobs, he became a journalist, working for *Cumhuriyet* from 1951 to 1963 while writing his first three novels. From 1963 onwards he earned his living as a novelist, writing full-time.

Among his more than twenty-five books, the most famous are *Murder in the Ironsmith Market; Iron Earth, Copper Sky; The Wind from the Plain; The Undying Grass*; and his most famous, *Memed, My Hawk*. Most of them were translated into English by his wife, Thilda. During the early years of the twenty-first century, Yasar Kemal worked on a trilogy about the 1923 exchange of Greek and Turkish populations after the dismembering of the Ottoman Empire, and on his memoirs.

Although many of the secondary characters in his novels are Kurdish, Yasar Kemal used to deny that he was a Kurd. Since the 1990s, however, he has claimed his Kurdish identity, saying, "I am writing in Turkish, I never wrote a line in Kurdish, but I am a Kurd."

See also KURDS; LITERATURE: TURKISH.

KATHLEEN R. F. BURRILL
UPDATED BY CHRIS KUTSCHERA

YASHMAK

See CLOTHING

YASIN, AHMAD ISMA'IL
[1936–2004]

Founder of HAMAS.

Ahmad Isma'il Yasin was born in 1936 in the village of al-Jurah, south of Gaza. His family moved to the Gaza Strip after the 1948 Arab–Israel War. He had an accident in his youth (while playing sports) that resulted in his paralysis. He studied Arabic language and religion, became a teacher in both fields, and rose in prominence as a militant preacher in the mosques of Gaza. He headed the Islamic-oriented al-Mujamma al-Islami. In 1983 Yasin was arrested and charged with possession of weapons, then was released in 1985 during a famous prisoner exchange between Israel and the Popular Front for the Liberation of Palestine–General Command.

Yasin was the key founder and leader of HAMAS (acronym for the Arabic name of the Islamic Resistance Movement), which was officially begun in 1987. HAMAS's ideology is a militant and more violent version of the Muslim Brotherhood, and it analyzes the Arab–Israeli conflict in purely religious terms. Palestine is seen as a religious waqf land that belongs to Muslims, and enmity is expressed toward Jews. The movement calls for armed struggle, but unlike the secular Palestinian organizations of the 1960s and 1970s, it considers this struggle to be obligatory jihad. HAMAS played a key role in the Palestinian Intifada of 1987, and Yasin was arrested in 1989 and sentenced to life in prison. He was released in 1997, when Israel had a deal with Jordan's King Hussein after a failed assassination attempt in Jordan against the head of the Political Bureau of HAMAS, Khalid Mish'al. Despite Yasin's feeble physical state, he provided a strong leadership for the movement. He had a weak voice and a variety of ailments (some resulting from torture and mistreatment in Israeli jails), but he could inspire the masses. Although he left military decisions to the military branch of HAMAS, he legitimized the suicide attacks that characterized the second (al-Aqsa) Intifada of 2000. Yasin succeeded in turning HAMAS into the second most important Palestinian organization after Yasir Arafat's al-Fatah movement. His militancy did not prevent him from reaching pragmatic agreements with Palestinian organizations, including Marxist groups, and he had a large following in the Persian Gulf region, where he raised much of the money for HAMAS before U.S. pressures led Gulf governments to curtail fundraising for the movement. In 2003 Yasin survived an Israeli bomb attack on a house he was thought to inhabit. Yasin was assassinated outside a Gaza mosque on 22 March 2004 by a missile fired from an Israeli helicopter.

AS'AD ABUKHALIL

YATA, ALI
[1920–1997]

Moroccan journalist and left-wing politician.

Ali Yata was the first Muslim secretary-general of the Moroccan Communist Party. He served until it was banned in 1959. Later he established the party of Liberty and Socialism (1968) and the party of Progress and Socialism (1974, as its secretary-general). He also founded the newspaper *al-Bayane*. Yata was elected deputy in the 1977 elections saying that democratic progress had begun, but he demanded annulment of the 1983 local elections alleging fraud. He participated in the 1984 legislative elections. Yata supported Moroccan claims to the Sahara in the 1960s and to the Western Sahara in the 1970s and 1980s.

See also COMMUNISM IN THE MIDDLE EAST.

C. R. PENNELL

YAZD

Ancient Iranian city located in an oasis in the central desert region.

Yazd is the name of a province and its capital city in central Iran. The province, which extends over an area of 27,027 square miles (70,000 sq km), is largely desert, with the great salt desert known as the Kavir in the north merging into the great sand and stone desert (the Lut) of southeastern Iran. The province has lead and zinc deposits, many of which are sites of major commercial mining operations.

The city of Yazd was an important Zoroastrian religious center during the Sassanian dynasty (226–642 C.E.) and has remained a stronghold of Zoroastrianism up to the present, although adherents of this faith comprise less than 10 percent of the city's population. In the early 2000s, about one-half of all Zoroastrians in Iran lived in Yazd, and the fire temples there and in some surrounding villages had become historic pilgrimage sites. Between the thirteenth and nineteenth centuries, the city was internationally renowned for its silk, cotton, and woolen textiles, but these handicrafts declined dramatically after 1850 as the volume of European manufactured textiles imported into Iran increased. By the mid-twentieth century, entrepreneurs had established modern cotton and woolen textile mills in the city,

and Yazd gradually recovered its status as a regional commercial and production center. The railroad from Tehran to the Gulf of Oman port of Bandar-e Abbas, completed in 1995, passes through Yazd; its construction helped stimulate development in and migration to the city. Between 1976 and 1996, the population of Yazd increased more than 140 percent (an average of 7 percent per annum), from 135,925 to 326,776.

See also ZOROASTRIANISM.

Bibliography

Boyce, Mary. *A Persian Stronghold of Zoroastrianism.* Oxford, U.K.: Clarendon Press, 1977.

ERIC HOOGLUND

YAZDI, IBRAHIM
[1931–]

Iranian politician.

Born in Qazvin, where his father made his living as a retailer, Ibrahim Yazdi studied pharmacology at Tehran University and emerged as one of the leaders of the Muslim Student Association. In 1952 he galvanized student support in favor of Mohammad Mossadegh's oil nationalization platform. He co-edited two journals, *Forugh-e Elm* (The resplendence of knowledge) and *Ganj-e Shayegan* (The magnificent treasure), and was employed at the Worker Social Security Organization. Following the CIA-sponsored coup that ousted Mossadegh in 1953, Yazdi joined the newly formed National Resistance Movement. The movement was effectively crushed in 1957 but resurfaced in 1960 as the National Front, of which the Liberation Movement of Iran (formed in 1961 by the more religiously minded members of the original nationalist coalition) was a splinter group. Yazdi was a member of the nascent Liberation Movement of Iran, and after he left Iran for the United States in about 1960 was instrumental in organizing its opposition activities abroad, both in the United States and elsewhere. He also studied for his doctoral degree in the United States.

In 1978 he frequented Ayatollah Ruhollah Khomeini's headquarters in France. When he returned to Iran in 1979, he was appointed deputy prime minister, and in 1980 he became foreign minister in the cabinet of Mehdi Bazargan's provisional government. He was among the group of Bazargan's friends who constituted the nonclerical, moderate figures in the Islamic movement and who cooperated closely with the Revolutionary Guards. He also headed the nationalized Kayhan Publishing Group, which produced a daily newspaper whose circulation rate exceeded that of all the other Tehran dailies. He was elected to the Islamic parliament as a deputy from Tehran (1980–1984). In the falling-out between the moderates and the more radical Islamic Republican Party affiliates (1979–1981), the latter won. After falling from political favor, Yazdi devoted his energies to revitalizing the Liberation Movement of Iran, which now functioned as the only tolerated—albeit eventually officially banned—opposition party in the political landscape of Iran.

During the late 1980s and early 1990s, Yazdi's activities consisted primarily of criticizing the government's economic policies and its failure to deliver the political rights promised by the revolutionaries in 1979. Taking advantage of the liberalizing policies of President Ali Akbar Hashemi Rafsanjani, Yazdi in this period advocated—in various speeches, articles, and manifestos—fiscal reform, equitable distribution of income, and the normalization of ties with the United States. In 1995, after the death of Mehdi Bazargan, Yazdi emerged as the leader of the Liberation Movement of Iran. In 1996, he made an unsuccessful bid in the parliamentary elections as the Liberation Movement of Iran candidate for a seat from Tehran. In 1997 he was arrested for a short while after signing a letter protesting maltreatment by Ayatollah Khamenehi, the leader of Iran, of Grand Ayatollah Hosayn Montazeri, Ayatollah Khomeini's designated successor until he fell out with the regime in 1989, shortly before Khomeini's death. The judiciary arrested all senior members of the Liberation Movement of Iran in 2000, but Yazdi escaped arrest because he was in the United States undergoing treatment for prostate cancer. He was charged with antigovernment activity when he returned but was allowed to remain free after posting bail. His trial was still continuing at the end of 2003, although there were periods of several months' duration during which no court sessions were scheduled.

See also BAZARGAN, MEHDI; KHAMENEHI, ALI; MONTAZERI, HOSAYN ALI; MOSSADEGH, MO-

HAMMAD; RAFSANJANI, ALI AKBAR HASHEMI; REVOLUTIONARY GUARDS.

Bibliography

Chehabi, H. E. *Iranian Politics and Religious Modernism: The Liberation Movement of Iran under the Shah and Khomeini.* Ithaca, NY: Cornell University Press, 1990.

Milani, Mohsen M. *The Making of Iran's Islamic Revolution: From Monarchy to Islamic Republic,* 2d edition, Boulder, CO: Westview Press, 1994.

NEGUIN YAVARI

YAZIDIS

See TRIBES AND TRIBALISM: YAZIDIS

YAZIJI, IBRAHIM
[1847–1906]

A leading figure in the Arabic literary revival of the nineteenth century.

Ibrahim Yaziji was a Greek Catholic poet, grammarian, and man of letters from Mount Lebanon. Following in the footsteps of his father, Nasif, who had done pioneer work in rediscovering the Arabic literary heritage, he made a significant contribution to the Arab cultural and political awakening of the late nineteenth century. Like his father, he maintained a close relationship with the American and British Protestant missionaries in Beirut and played an important role in the revitalization of Arabic as a literary language. A member of the Syrian Scientific Society, an early secret society made up of Arab intellectuals and military officers who agitated for Arab independence from the Ottoman Empire, Yaziji is best remembered for an ode, first recited at a secret meeting of the society, which called upon Arabs to remember their past greatness and shake off Turkish rule. This ode and several other poems of his were memorized by a generation of Arab nationalists and inspired the incipient political movement for Arab independence.

See also ARAB NATIONALISM.

Bibliography

Antonius, George. *The Arab Awakening: The Story of the Arab National Movement.* London: H. Hamilton, 1938.

Salibi, Kamal. *A House of Many Mansions: The History of Lebanon Reconsidered*. Berkeley: University of California Press, 1988.

GUILAIN P. DENOEUX

YAZIJI, NASIF
[1800–1871]

Lebanese Christian scholar and author.

Nasif Yaziji played a significant role in revitalizing Arabic literary traditions. He was employed by Bashir Chehab, the amir of Lebanon, and moved to Beirut in 1840 to help U.S. missionaries prepare Arabic text-books for use in Christian mission schools. Yaziji appreciated classical Arabic literature and campaigned to eliminate the corruptions that had been absorbed into the language. His writings helped revive practices of classical scholarship and made classical literature important in contemporary Arab culture.

MARK MECHLER

YEHOSHUA, AVRAHAM B.
[1936–]

Israeli novelist, essayist, and professor of literature.

Avraham Yehoshua was born in Jerusalem into a fifth-generation Sephardic family and now lives in Haifa, where he teaches literature at the University of Haifa. A peace activist and a staunch defender of the Zionist project in his essays, he is best known as one of Israel's foremost novelists. Although he has published both plays and collections of short stories, the latter in his early writings, his greatest works are his seven novels, all of which have been translated into English. His novels are complex, full of humor and compassion, at times highly innovative in style, steeped in the classical modernist tradition, and always crafted with the highest literary skill. Recurrent themes in his novels are love and identity, history and choice, dialogue, and desire, all of which are embedded in the drama of the Jewish people and modern Israel. His masterpiece, *Mr. Mani*, highlights his skill at its finest, rivaling the best of world literature produced in the twentieth century. Israel's equivalent of U.S. novelist William Faulkner, Yehoshua has been the recipient of many prizes: the Brenner Prize in 1983, the Alterman Prize in 1986, the Bialik Prize in 1988, and the American Prize for the Best Jewish Book in 1990 and 1993. He was the inaugural winner of the Israeli Booker Prize in 1991 and in 1995 he received Israel's highest literary honor, the Israel Prize. His books have been translated into many languages. They have also been made into movies and adapted for the stage, television, and radio.

See also LITERATURE: HEBREW.

Bibliography

Yehoshua, A. B. *Between Right and Right*, translated by Arnold Schwartz. Garden City, NY: Doubleday, 1981.

Yehoshua, A. B. *Five Seasons*, translated by Hillel Halkin. New York: Doubleday, 1989.

Yehoshua, A. B. *A Journey to the End of the Millennium*, translated by Nicholas De Lange. New York: Doubleday, 1999.

Yehoshua, A. B. *A Late Divorce*, translated by Hillel Halkin. Garden City, NY: Doubleday, 1984.

Yehoshua, A. B. *The Liberated Bride*, translated by Hillel Halkin. Orlando, FL: Harcourt, 2003.

Yehoshua, A. B. *The Lover*, translated by Philip Simpson. Garden City, NY: Doubleday, 1977.

Yehoshua, A. B. *Mr. Mani*, translated by Hillel Halkin. New York: Doubleday, 1992.

Yehoshua, A. B. *Open Heart*, translated by Dalya Bilu. New York: Doubleday, 1996.

ANN KAHN
UPDATED BY STEPHEN SCHECTER

YELLIN-MOR, NATAN
[1913–1980]

Israeli underground leader.

Born Nathan Friedman-Yellin in Grodno, Poland, Yellin-Mor was an activist in the Polish branch of Betar and the Irgun Zva'i Le'umi. He was co-editor, along with Abraham (Yair) Stern, of *Di Tat*, the Irgun's Polish newspaper. He followed Stern to Palestine and became a major figure in Stern's virulently anti-British underground, Lohamei Herut Yisrael (LEHI: Freedom Fighters of Israel). In December 1941 he attempted to reach neutral Turkey via Syria to negotiate with Nazi representatives for a mass release of Jews from Eastern Europe in exchange for LEHI's cooperation in fighting Britain.

Upon his return he was imprisoned by the British but escaped in 1943. After Stern's death, Yellin-Mor became a member of the LEHI triumvirate, along with Israel Eldad and Yitzhak Shamir. In 1949 he was tried and convicted for the September 1948 assassination of United Nations emissary Count Folke Bernadotte, but the sentence was commuted in exchange for an oath to desist from any further violent activities. He led the left-wing faction of both LEHI and its post-statehood political entity, the Fighters Party, and he was elected to the First Knesset (1949–1951). In the ensuing years he moved increasingly to the left. He renounced Zionism and advocated a pro-Soviet foreign policy and the creation of a single Arab-Jewish socialist state in all of what had been Mandatory Palestine.

See also BERNADOTTE, FOLKE; SHAMIR, YITZHAK; STERN, ABRAHAM.

Bibliography

Heller, Joseph. *The Stern Gang: Ideology, Politics, and Terror, 1940–1949.* Portland, OR; London: Frank Cass, 1995.

BRYAN DAVES
UPDATED BY PIERRE M. ATLAS

YEMEN

A state on the southwestern corner of the Arabian Peninsula.

The Republic of Yemen was created in May 1990 as a result of the merger of the two previous states that used the name Yemen: the Yemen Arab Republic (YAR; often called North Yemen) and the People's Democratic Republic of Yemen (PDRY; often called South Yemen). The merger brought together two disparate political systems: the North had been governed by a military/tribal elite, which supported a free-market economy, whereas the South had been governed by a Marxist-Leninist political elite, which had introduced one of the most centrally directed economies in the modern world. After a transition period, the president of the North, Ali Abdullah Salih, was made president of the new unified state.

Population

In 2000, the population was estimated at 17.5 million, not including an indeterminate number of Yemenis living and working abroad, primarily in Arabian Peninsula states. Yemen has one of the highest birthrates in the world, as well as a high infant mortality rate; the net rate of annual increase is estimated at 3.6 percent.

Area and Borders

Since Yemen is one of the few states in the modern world without completely demarcated borders, it is not possible to give a precise figure for its total area. The northeast and east still have no internationally (or even locally) accepted borders. This has led to numerous border disputes and even wars between Saudi Arabia and both of the previously existing Yemens since the 1920s. The border with Saudi Arabia was demarcated as far as the Najran oasis after the Saudi-Yemeni War of 1934; this conflict also gave control of the Asir region to the Saudi state through a treaty renewed every twenty years, creating continued difficulties in relations between the two states. In the northeast, the generally recognized end of Yemeni sovereignty lies east of Ma'rib; with the discovery of oil and gas deposits in this area, however, new conflicts over the border between the two states arose in this area in the late 1980s and early 1990s. The demarcation of the border with Oman was officially completed in 1995, but despite repeated memoranda of agreement with Saudi Arabia in the 1990s, as well as a contract with a German firm to undertake its delineation in 2001, that process has yet to be completed. In the mid-1990s, a new set of border disagreements arose; these involved numerous islets in the Red Sea, the ownership of which was disputed with Eritrea as well as Saudi Arabia. A UN arbitration panel awarded the islands to Yemen in 1999, but the agreement specifically avoided defining the maritime boundary in a way that would offend the claims of Saudi Arabia. To the south, Yemen lies on the Gulf of Aden. The old border between the North and South—created by the Ottoman and the British empires in the early years of the twentieth century and technically abolished as a result of the union of 1990—nevertheless continues to be of some political importance.

Major Cities

San'a is the most important, largest, and probably the oldest city in Yemen—it is mentioned in the Bible under its old name, Uzal. By 2000, its population was considerably more than 1 million. It has been the capital city of Yemen for most of the past two millennia (with the exception of the reign of Imam Ahmad, 1948–1962, in which he moved the capital to Taʿiz) and became the administrative (political) capital of the new republic after unification. Its old city has been placed on the list of World Heritage Sites because of its unique architecture and historical importance; many of the buildings are more than 800 years old.

Aden, the capital of the former PDRY, has the best port on the Arabian Peninsula. For more than a century, until the late 1960s, it was a major British military and commercial possession. After unification, it was made the economic and commercial capital of the country, but its role in the civil war of 1994 and subsequent events caused it to lose some of its significance.

Hodeida (al-Hudayda) is the major port of the former North Yemen. Its facilities were extensively modernized by the Soviet Union in the 1960s. Consequently, it grew rapidly from a sleepy Red Sea fishing port handling primarily local trade to a major metropolitan area.

Taʿiz, the major city of the southern highlands of the former North Yemen, is located in one of the richest agricultural areas. Its population, predominantly of the Islamic Shafiʿi sect, had the longest and best-developed contacts with the outside world during the reigns of Imams Yahya and Ahmad in the twentieth century.

Although the country has a few smaller cities (e.g., Ibb, Dhamar, Saʿada and Zabid in the north, and Mukalla, Tarim, and Shibam in the south), the vast majority of the population lives in villages, each with an average population of fewer than 200 people. Yemen probably has the most decentralized population of any contemporary state.

Geography and Climate

Yemen's location, combined with its geographical characteristics, gives it the most favorable climate and agricultural resources of any country on the Arabian Peninsula. The country is divided into a number of relatively clear zones: The first of these, along the Red Sea and the Arabian Sea coasts, is hot and humid; from there, the land slopes upward into the first range of hills and low mountains, where the climate is considerably more temperate; eventually, after a series of high plains, the peaks of the cen-

MAP BY XNR PRODUCTIONS, INC. THE GALE GROUP.

The Qubbat Talha Mosque, which sits in Yemen's capital city of San'a. © CHRIS LISLE/CORBIS. REPRODUCED BY PERMISSION.

tral massif reach between 11,000 and 13,000 feet (3,355–3,965 m). These mountains have been terraced from time immemorial, and a vast array of fruits, vegetables, and grains (and the infamous qat plant) can be raised in the many microclimates created by this geography. In the central mountains, the humidity is low and the temperatures moderate, although in the winter it is not unusual to find temperatures below freezing and the occasional snow or ice storm. Over the centuries, the Yemenis have developed plant strains to occupy the many microclimates. On the other side of the central massif and away from the monsoons, which deliver the rain that makes extensive agriculture possible on the westward side, the land slopes away into the great central desert of Arabia, the Rub al-Khali, broken only by the great Hadramawt Valley, the home of numerous towns exploiting the limited water resources found there. The rainfall that the various mountain ranges wring out of the prevailing winds varies widely—from less than 3 inches (7.62 cm) per year in the deserts

and northern reaches of the country to about 38 inches (96.52 cm) per year in some of the areas around Ta'iz—about the same as in Seattle, New York, or Chicago.

Political Subdivisions

Administratively, the two preunification Yemeni states varied considerably. The units into which the two states were organized were frequently modified, sometimes as the result of political expediency and at other times due to the nature of the personnel available for major administrative duties. For example, in the PDRY, the first administrative reorganization sought to get rid of the old tribally organized political entities, which had been called the protectorates. Later, the state undertook to recreate some of these entities under new names to regain popular support. In the North, after the revolution, the number of administrative units (governorates) rose with the growth in the population as well as with the increasing number and variety of demands for governmental services. In the immediate aftermath of reunification, the number and characteristics of the administrative subunits within the two separate entities were largely retained. On the other hand, electoral districts have been substantially increased and modified over the years.

The Economy

The natural resource base of Yemen has begun to be developed, largely because it was not until the 1960s that either the North or the South had the opportunity to assess that base or attempt its development. The most important contemporary resources are oil and gas deposits, which were discovered in both North and South Yemen prior to unification and which contributed significantly to the push for unification. The majority of the population of Yemen continues to be employed in the agricultural sector, although productivity is not adequate to the requirements of the population. The multiplicity of microclimates makes it possible to grow just about any fruit or vegetable, from the citrus fruits, bananas, and cotton of the hot coastal plain, through the coffee, grains, and qat (a small tree valued for the alkaloids contained in its leaves) of the middle highlands, to the pears, grapes, and nuts of the high mountains.

Although industrial development has been a priority in both North and South Yemen since independence, it has not reached the stage where industry is a significant factor in the economy of either region. In fact, Yemen operates a monumental deficit in its current accounts because it has few exportable resources. Until 1991, the most important positive element in its balance of payments was the remittances of its large workforce in the various Gulf states and in other countries. Following the 1991 Gulf War, however, the majority of Yemenis abroad were forced to return home (some 800,000 from Saudi Arabia alone), creating a massive social and economic problem. Since then, a variety of international loans and development assistance funds have helped to ameliorate the continuing economic problems.

Culture

The population of Yemen is ethnically Arab, although of different origins. The majority is descended from the ancient south Arabian peoples, and the remainder immigrated from the Fertile Crescent area more than a thousand years ago.

Arabic is the official language. Although everyone speaks it, there are substantial differences in dialect from region to region. In some of the more remote areas of the island of Socotra (located in the Gulf of Aden) Mahri is still spoken.

The overwhelming majority of Yemenis are Muslims. They are, however, divided into different sects: In the northern areas, the Zaydis, members of a branch of Shiʿism, predominate; in the southern areas, the Shafiʿis, who follow a branch of Sunni Islam, are in the majority. There are, in addition, Ismaʿilis, members of another branch of Shiʿism, in the northern mountains; in and around Saʿada there are also small settlements of Jews.

The educational infrastructure is in a state of flux. Until the revolution of 1962, an insignificant number of people received any formal education. After the revolution, the government embarked on a major program to establish educational institutions, from primary schools to universities, of which there are several, including those at Sanʿa, Taʿiz, and Aden; these were, in the overwhelming majority of cases, coeducational. In the 1990s, however, Islamists gained increasing political power and began to impose their views on the educational establishment. Owing to several incidents in which the government saw the hand of Islamic extremists, the government began to implement earlier legislation intended to bring independent religious institutions under the control of the Ministry of Education, closing many, eventually even the private al-Iman University, operated by perhaps the most extreme Islamic leader in Yemen, Shaykh Abd al-Majid al-Zindani, and considered the center of Islamic extremism.

Government

Yemen is governed under a constitution that was approved by the parliaments of the two Yemens in 1990 and by popular referendum in 1991. This constitution declares Yemen to be a parliamentary democracy, with an executive appointed by and responsible to the parliament (the Council of Deputies). In 1994, Ali Abdullah Salih was elected by the coun-

A woman carries a child through an alley in San'a, Yemen. © CHRIS LISLE/CORBIS. REPRODUCED BY PERMISSION.

cil to a five-year term as president. In 1999, due to changes in the law, the first direct elections to the presidency were held; Salih was overwhelmingly elected to a seven-year term. His only real opponent was the son of the former leader of the PDRY, Najib Qahtan al-Sha'abi, although there were two additional candidates.

Elections to the new parliament were held in April 1993, with some eight parties and a sizable number of independents taking seats. Three parties dominated the outcome: the General People's Congress (GPC), formerly dominant in the North and associated with Ali Abdullah Salih; the Islah, now commonly referred to as the Yemeni Islah Party (YIP), a coalition of tribal and Islamic interests led by the second most influential political figure in the country, Shaykh Abdullah al-Ahmar of the Hashid Tribal Confederation; and the Yemeni Socialist Party (YSP), formerly dominant in the South and led by Ali Salim al-Baydh, who had become vice

president of the new state. Other parties exist, including a Nasserist party. The second election to the Council of Deputies took place in 1997; the aftermath of the 1994 civil war, however, meant that the role and influence of the YSP was considerably reduced, and the YSP boycotted the elections (al-Baydh went into exile). Consequently, the GPC gained 187 of the 301 seats, with its only serious competition, the YIP, gaining only 53. In the next round of elections, in April 2003, the GPC's margin of victory increased to 238 of 301 seats; the YIP could only manage 46 seats, and the YSP was reduced to 8 seats.

History

Some 2,000 years ago, Yemen (known as Arabia Felix to the Roman geographers) was famous and its city-states (e.g., Saba/Sheba, Ma'in), grew powerful and wealthy due to their monopoly over the trade in frankincense and myrrh. Once this monopoly was broken, Yemen retreated from the world stage. It was not until coffee became an important international trade commodity in the sixteenth through eighteenth centuries that Yemen once again achieved renown. However, its early monopoly over coffee was broken by foreign traders and governments, and it once again became a little-known province of various empires on the Red Sea.

The contemporary state of Yemen was created by two states with different historical experiences during the past two centuries. Although occasionally united in the past, they had not been so since 1728. Developments in the nineteenth century, however, are most important to an understanding of the events that led to the reunification of North and South Yemen in 1990.

In 1839, the British took the city of Aden in South Yemen in order to have a major port in the western Indian Ocean and to forestall further expansion by other parties in the Arabian Peninsula. Over the years, British interests continued to grow, and they eventually established extensive links with the multitude of principalities located in Aden's (Yemeni) hinterland.

Meanwhile, the Ottoman Empire, which had occupied Yemen for a variety of strategic and economic reasons but which had departed in the early seventeenth century, decided to return. One motive was to play a role in the Red Sea trade, as it had in the past, although there were other factors; this goal increased in importance with the completion of the Suez Canal in 1869. Eventually, British and Ottoman interests in southwestern Arabia clashed; the two powers decided to negotiate a frontier between their zones of influence and interest. Beginning in 1902, they agreed to demarcate a border between them; the agreement that was eventually signed in 1914 created the frontier between the Ottoman possession that became the Kingdom of Yemen (North Yemen) after World War I and the British Aden Protectorates, which became South Yemen.

Under the reigns of Imams Yahya and Ahmad (1918–1962), North Yemen remained largely cut off from the rest of the world, while Aden and the protectorates in the south received British subsidies and Aden developed into one of the world's busiest ports.

Both states, however, had political movements that sought change. In 1962, a revolution broke out in North Yemen, which sought to create a republic and remove the conservative Zaydi imam(s) from power. After an eight-year civil war, the two major factions compromised and created the Yemen Arab Republic. Imam Muhammad al-Badr, the titular head of the effort to restore the imamate, fled to Saudi Arabia and eventually died in exile in Great Britain. Shortly after the revolution broke out in North Yemen, various groups in South Yemen began to work for independence from Great Britain. After a lengthy and often violent conflict, the British agreed to withdraw from Aden and its protectorates in 1967. The group to which they ceded power, the National Front for the Liberation of South Yemen, created the People's Republic of South Yemen (later the People's Democratic Republic of Yemen).

Although both Yemens spoke of the goal of reunification, relations between them were often extraordinarily poor, due largely to their different economic and political systems. The North was governed by a military elite, which was tied to the West and permitted an almost unrestricted, though underdeveloped, capitalist economy to operate; in the South, a Marxist-Leninist political elite took power and tied the country to the communist bloc. Relations between the two states deteriorated into two separate wars—in 1972 and 1979.

In the late 1980s, oil (and later natural gas) was discovered in both Yemens; more importantly, it was found in the disputed border areas between them. The effort to develop these deposits without wasting further resources in fruitless wars largely overlapped with the decline of the Soviet Union (and some of its satellites that had provided important assistance to South Yemen). As a result, the potential benefits of a unified effort to develop their oil and gas deposits overcame the mutual suspicions and frictions that had characterized the previous twenty-five years, leading to the unity agreement of 1990. Friction between the North and the South did not disappear, however. Disputes within the original coalition government of the General People's Congress and the Yemeni Socialist Party led to a civil war from May through July 1994. The South suffered a complete defeat, which resulted in the forced exile of its leaders and the concomitant ascent of the Islah Party (YIP).

Perhaps the most important development of the 1990s, however, was the increase in Islamist sentiment and support. Fearful of its growing influence, the GPC (and Salih) undertook various measures to limit Islamist power, including seeking a rapprochement with a truncated YSP. The growing influence of the Islamists in Yemen was most dramatically illustrated by the attack, in 2000, by allies and supporters of al-Qaʿida against the USS *Cole* while it was refueling in Aden. Numerous incidents of political violence involving previously unknown groups (e.g., the Sympathizers of al-Qaʿida) heightened fears in Yemen and the West that the country had become a major breeding and training ground for radical Islamist groups. Salih's government had to walk a fine line between recognizing the increased Islamist sentiment in the population and accommodating the interests and concerns of its grantors of financial and political support, including the United States. The fact that the government did not control all of its territory and that its borders were porous did nothing to assuage the fears of the United States and Europe.

See also ADEN; *COLE*, USS; HADRAMAWT; HODEIDA; ISMAʿILI SHIʿISM; MAʾRIB; PEOPLE'S DEMOCRATIC REPUBLIC OF YEMEN; QAʿIDA, AL-; SALIH, ALI ABDULLAH; SANʿA; SOCOTRA; TAʿIZ; YEMEN ARAB REPUBLIC; YEMEN CIVIL WAR; YEMEN DYNASTIES; ZAYDISM.

Bibliography

Burrowes, Robert. *The Yemen Arab Republic: The Politics of Development, 1967–1986.* Boulder, CO: Westview Press, 1987.

Carapico, Sheila. *Civil Society in Yemen: The Political Economy of Activism in Modern Arabia.* Cambridge, U.K.: Cambridge University Press, 1998.

Dresch, Paul. *A History of Modern Yemen.* Cambridge, U.K.: Cambridge University Press, 2000.

Halliday, Fred. *Revolution and Foreign Policy: The Case of South Yemen, 1967–1987.* Cambridge, U.K.: Cambridge University Press, 1990.

Joffe, E.G.H.; Hachemi, M.J.; and Watkins, E.W. *Yemen Today: Crisis and Solutions: Proceedings of a Two-Day Conference Held at the School of Oriental and African Studies, University of London, November 25 and 26, 1995.* London: Caravel, 1997.

Wenner, Manfred. *The Yemen Arab Republic: Development and Change in an Ancient Land.* Boulder, CO: Westview Press, 1991.

MANFRED W. WENNER

YEMEN ARAB REPUBLIC

The official name of North Yemen from 1962 until its 1990 merger with South Yemen.

The emergence of North Yemen as a single political unit in modern times was largely a function of both the reoccupation of the country by the Ottomans in 1849 and the Yemeni resistance to this presence that coalesced around the imamate near the turn of the century. Defeat in World War I forced the Ottomans to withdraw in 1918, and a resurgent imamate state seized the opportunity. From 1918 until 1962, Yahya ibn Muhammad Hamid al-Din and his son Ahmad ibn Yahya Hamid al-Din acted to forge a monarchy much as the kings of England and France had done centuries earlier. The two imams strengthened the state, thereby securing Yemen's borders and pacifying the interior to degrees rarely known over the past millennium.

The imams used the strengthened imamate to revive North Yemen's traditional Islamic culture and society, this at a time when traditional societies around the world were crumbling under the weight of modernity backed by imperial power. They were aided in their efforts to insulate Yemen by the degree to which its agricultural economy was self-contained and self-sufficient. The result was a "backward" Yemen, though a small but increasing number of Yemenis exposed to the modern world wanted change and blamed the imamate for its absence. This produced a fateful chain of events: the birth of the Free Yemeni movement in the mid-1940s; the aborted 1948 revolution that left Imam Yahya dead; the failed 1955 coup against Imam Ahmad; and, finally, the 1962 revolution that yielded the Yemen Arab Republic (YAR).

Major Eras

In retrospect, the history of the YAR can best be divided into three periods. (1) The Sallal era (1962–1967), the wrenching first five years under President Abdullah al-Sallal, was marked by the revolution that began it, the long civil war and Egyptian

The Dar al-Hajar, or Rock Palace, in Wadi Dhahr, Yemen. This palace was built for Imam Yahya in the 1930s. After the fall of the Ottoman Empire in 1918, Imam Yahya assumed control over North Yemen. His family ruled the country until revolutionaries ended their authoritarian rule and created the Yemen Arab Republic in 1962. © EARL & NAZIMA KOWALL/CORBIS. REPRODUCED BY PERMISISON.

Of the many important changes that took place in the YAR since its birth in 1962, most of the positive ones have been compressed into the years since its fifteenth anniversary in 1977. Nevertheless, the previous decade was important, a transition in which much-needed time was bought by a few modest but pivotal acts and, most important, by economic good fortune. Global and regional economic events over which the YAR had no control facilitated a huge flow of funds into the country in the form of both foreign aid and remittances from Yemenis working abroad. This period of transition was necessary because the changes that had buffeted Yemen in the five years following the 1962 revolution had left it both unable to retreat into the past and ill-equipped to go forward. The ability to advance rapidly in the 1980s seems very much the result of the possibility afforded for a breather in the 1970s.

Establishing Sovereignty

Given the isolation and the decentralized nature of North Yemeni society, much of the YAR's first quarter-century was taken up with the effort to establish sovereignty over the land and people. The Yemenis who made the revolution in 1962 were preoccupied from the outset with the need to create a state with the capacity to maintain public security and provide services. The long civil war that came on the heels of the revolution both increased this need and interfered with meeting it. Yemeni state-building was more hindered than helped by the fact that the new state was largely built and staffed by Egyptians and by the fact that Egyptian forces did most of the fighting on behalf of the Yemenis.

The balance of power between the tribal periphery and the state at the center tipped back toward the tribes during the civil war. As a result, the reach of the YAR extended little beyond the triangle in the southern half of the country that was traced by the roads linking the cites of Sanʿa, Taʿiz, and Hodeida (al-Hudayda).

State-Building Efforts

The YAR created in 1962 lacked modern political organization. A major theme of its first twenty-five years consisted of attempts to fashion the ideas and organization needed to channel support and de-

intervention that quickly followed, and—above all—the rapid and irreversible opening of the country to the modern world. (2) A ten-year transition period (1967–1977) was marked by the end of the civil war, the republican-royalist reconciliation under President Abd al-Rahman al-Iryani, and the attempt by President Ibrahim al-Hamdi to strengthen the state and restructure politics. (3) The Salih era (1978–1990) is identified with both the long tenure of President Ali Abdullah Salih and the change from political weakness and economic uncertainty at the outset to relative political stability, the discovery of oil, and the prospect of oil-based development and prosperity in more recent years.

mands from society to the regime and, conversely, to channel information, appeals, and directives from the regime to society. The civil war strained and even deformed the new republic, deferring any major effort at political construction under President al-Sallal. Egypt's heavy-handed tutelage left little room for Yemeni national politics and politicians to develop.

As with other late-developing countries, the tasks of state-building in the new YAR went beyond the maintenance of order and security to include the creation of a capacity to influence, if not control, the rate and direction of socioeconomic change. The wrenching effects of the sudden end of isolation and of virtual self-sufficiency made it obvious that state-building in all of its aspects was desperately needed. No less than the viability and survival of Yemen in its new external environment depended upon it, just as the civil war and the political weakness of the YAR made it unlikely.

The Egyptian exodus in 1967 led to the quick overthrow of President al-Sallal and the republican-royalist reconciliation that finally ended the civil war in 1970. Some state-building of importance was achieved thereafter by the regime headed by President al-Iryani. A modern constitution was adopted in 1970, and some of the ministries and other agencies erected after the revolution were strengthened. Economic needs as well as political constraints caused Yemeni leaders during the al-Iryani era to focus on financial and economic institutions; only halting first steps were taken toward reform of the civil service and the armed forces, matters of great political sensitivity. President al-Hamdi, who forced President al-Iryani into exile in 1974, believed in the modern state and worked to realize it. He promoted efforts to build institutions at the center, initiated the first major reform and upgrading of the armed forces, and fostered the idea of exchanging the benefits of state-sponsored development for allegiance to the state.

The results of efforts by the Iryani and Hamdi regimes at political construction were modest. The price of the reconciliation was the first-time granting of office and influence in the state to leading tribal shaykhs and the expulsion of the modernist Left from the body politic—prices that weakened the position of all advocates of a strong state. The re-

sult was the narrowly based center-right republican regime, which, with changes, persisted from the late 1960s until at least the early 1980s. The chief institutional focus of politics during the Iryani era was the Consultative Council, which first convened after elections in early 1971. However, political parties were banned and, in the absence of explicit organizational and ideological ties, the council functioned as an assembly of local notables, especially the shaykhs.

President al-Hamdi was unable to strengthen his position by translating his great popularity into political organization. Indeed, his major political achievement actually narrowed the political base of his regime and shortened the reach of the state. Aware that the shaykhs were using their new positions to protect the tribal system, al-Hamdi moved swiftly to drive them from the Consultative Council and from other state offices. To this end, he dissolved the council and suspended the 1970 constitution. The tribes responded with virtual rebellion. Al-Hamdi's efforts to make up for this loss of support by reincorporating the modernist Left were hesitant. In addition to maintaining ties to old leftist friends, he launched both the Local Development Association (LDA) movement and the Correction movement. Despite their initial promise, al-Hamdi seems to have had second thoughts and to have pulled back from efforts to use these two initiatives as bases for a broad, popular political movement. His subsequent plans for a general people's congress ended with his assassination in 1977. Frustrated by his failure to grant them reentry into the polity, several leftist groups in 1976 created the National Democratic Front (NDF), which a few years later became the basis of the rebellion that challenged the Salih regime.

Socioeconomic Development of the 1970s

The civil war finally behind it, the YAR in the 1970s did undergo significant socioeconomic development based upon the rapid creation of a modest capacity to absorb generous amounts of economic and technical assistance from abroad and, most important, from the massive inflow of workers' remittances that fostered unprecedented consumption and prosperity. Whereas the remittances largely flowed through the private sector, the modest strengthening of state institutions and the increase in their capacities were the critical factors in Yemen's ability to absorb significantly increased foreign aid. By the late 1970s, work on a broad array of state-sponsored, foreign-assisted infrastructure, agricultural, and human resource development projects existed side by side with high levels of remittance-fueled consumption and economic activity in the private sector.

The Salih Regime

President Salih's long term in office, beginning in 1978, was witness to major gains in state-building. After a shaky start, the Salih regime slowly increased the capacity of the state in the provinces as well as in the cities, for the first time making the republican state more than just a nominal presence in the countryside. The armed forces were upgraded again in 1979 and, more recently, in 1986 and 1988. Modest efforts were made to improve the functioning of the civil service, ministries, and other agencies.

The Salih regime increased its dominance over lands controlled by the tribes, especially the large area that fans out north and east from San'a, the capital. However, the best evidence of the growing ability of the YAR to exercise power within its own borders was the political-military defeat of the NDF. With its origins in the expulsion of the Left from the republic in 1968, the NDF rebellion had finally burst into flame over a wide area by early 1980. This uprising was extinguished in 1982, and the state was able at last to establish a real presence in lands bordering South Yemen.

In 1979, the Salih regime had little political support outside the armed forces. After the failure of ad hoc efforts to change this, the regime put in place an impressive program of political construction during the first half of the 1980s. This phased, sequential program began in early 1980 with the drafting of the National Pact. The pact then became the subject of a long national dialogue and local plebiscites orchestrated by the National Dialogue Committee. Elections to the General People's Congress (GPC), and its several-day session, were held in mid-1982 to review and then to adopt the National Pact. This done, the GPC declared itself a permanent political organization, which would be selected every four years, meet biennially and be led by a seventy-five-member Standing Committee headed by President Salih.

The key to the success of the Salih regime's political effort lay in the flexible, step-by-step process by which it moved the Yemeni polity from where it was in 1979 to the holding of the GPC in 1982. By design and a bit of luck, moreover, this sustained initiative also provided a political process largely managed by the regime into which elements of the Yemeni left could be safely incorporated when, in 1982, the NDF rebellion was quelled. Two dialogues, the one between the regime and the NDF as well as the more public one between the regime and the rest of the nation, converged in a structure that facilitated a second national reconciliation.

Although President Salih insisted that the GPC was not a political party, its activities were clearly aimed at consensus-building, guidance, and control—typical functions of a party. In fact, the GPC did become an umbrella party, a loose organization of organizations in a society that was not well organized politically for many of the tasks of the modern world. The Salih regime was also buttressed by constitutional change during the 1980s. The 1970 constitution, suspended by al-Hamdi in 1974, had been reinstated confusingly in 1978 without its centerpiece, the Consultative Council, and with an amendment that formally created the presidency. Clarity and closure on a number of issues were not achieved until July 1988 when a new Consultative Council was finally chosen in accordance with the constitution. The council elections, the first since 1971, were hotly contested and relatively fair and open; despite the ban on parties, much partisanship was in evidence. In mid-July, the new council elected President Salih to a new term and then gave approval to the composition and program of the new government. As a result, for the first time since the Iryani regime was ousted in 1974, the head of state and the government were selected in accordance with the 1970 constitution, that is, by a properly chosen Consultative Council.

Oil and the Economy

The modest prosperity that the YAR enjoyed after the mid-1970s was paralleled by the modern sector's increasing vulnerability to negative economic and political forces, domestic and external. Political uncertainty early in the Salih era threatened the limited capacity of the state to foster and manage development, and this was followed by the fall in oil prices and worldwide recession that led to sharp drops in aid and remittances to Yemen. Faced with economic crises, the regime in the early 1980s adopted austerity measures, and these had some success in forcing the country to live within more modest means in a less generous world.

The YAR's long-term development prospects improved abruptly when oil was discovered in commercial quantities in 1984. This event also placed severe demands on the still very limited capacities of the state. With the oil find, the twin tasks facing the Salih regime were to maintain the new discipline and austerity of the past few years and to gear up to absorb efficiently the oil revenues that were expected to start flowing in late 1987. Despite the politically difficult combination of rising expectations and continued hard times, the regime during this period of transition was able to limit imports and government expenditures. Changes in organization and the appointment of top technocrats to key posts contributed to the modest success of the transition. Although oil for export did begin to flow in late 1987, the regime was forced in 1989 to reimpose austerity measures that it had relaxed prematurely the previous year. Nevertheless, at the same time that it wrestled with these politically hard choices, the government proceeded as fast as financing would allow with development of the oil and gas sector as well as with key infrastructure and agricultural projects.

Development in the 1980s

In the 1980s, the increasing capacity of the Yemeni state for development also helped it to perform its more traditional functions and was partly understood and justified in these terms. This was especially the case when the regime stepped up efforts to extend its reach into NDF-influenced and tribal areas. Certain development efforts made the periphery more accessible and made possible the delivery of basic services to places where the state was regarded with suspicion or scorn. Hence the emphasis on pushing roads into such areas as soon as they were pacified. President Salih came to justify development efforts in terms of nation-state building—in terms of national integration—as well as eco-

nomic gains. The development activities of the second half of the 1980s, as well as the content of the third Five-Year Development Plan adopted in 1988, reflected the continuing influence of these ideas.

This third period of YAR history, spanning the 1980s, ended with the creation of the Republic of Yemen, headed by President Salih. It was the political and economic turnaround of the YAR after the 1970s, as well as the sudden weakening of South Yemen in the late 1980s, that made possible the YAR-initiated merger.

See also AHMAD IBN YAHYA HAMID AL-DIN; FREE YEMENIS; YAHYA IBN MUHAMMAD HAMID AL-DIN.

Bibliography

Burrowes, Robert D. *Historical Dictionary of Yemen.* Lanham, MD: Scarecrow Press, 1995.

Burrowes, Robert D. *The Yemen Arab Republic: The Politics of Development, 1962–1986.* Boulder, CO: Westview Press, 1987.

Dresch, Paul. *Tribes, Government, and History in Yemen.* Oxford: Clarendon, 1989.

Stookey, Robert W. *Yemen: The Politics of the Yemen Arab Republic.* Boulder, CO: Westview Press, 1978.

Wenner, Manfred W. *The Yemen Arab Republic: Development and Change in an Ancient Land.* Boulder, CO: Westview Press, 1991.

ROBERT D. BURROWES

YEMEN CIVIL WAR

The long, bitter, and costly struggle in North Yemen fought by the republicans and royalists between 1962 and 1970.

The Yemen Civil War began with the 1962 revolution and dragged on intermittently until 1970. The second half of the war coincided with a long drought, and the two forces in combination caused hunger, economic hardship, social dislocation, and many deaths in most parts of the country. Without a doubt, the struggle remains as one of a few defining memories of one if not two generations of Yemenis.

In addition, the civil war forced the deferral of most major efforts at political and socioeconomic development in what would become the Yemen Arab Republic (YAR) until the 1970s. Indeed, it was not until after reconciliation that the Yemenis could really begin to take the destiny of Yemen into their own hands. At the height of the struggle, the republicans, who were committed to creating a modern state and using it to overcome the weakness and "backwardness" of Yemen, controlled little more than the third of the country defined by the triangle formed by the roads connecting San'a, Ta'iz, and Hodeida (al-Hudayda)—and much within the triangle was outside their effective control. Another third was controlled by the royalists and their tribal allies, and the last third by tribes and others either concerned with their own autonomy or willing to go either way if the price were right. If anything, the balance between the tribes and the state during these years was more in favor of the former than had been the case under the imamate just before the revolution.

The young imam Muhammad al-Badr survived the revolution on 26 September 1962, escaped from San'a, and went on to rally many of the northern tribes and other allies of the imamate for an assault upon the new republic. The civil war was quickly regionalized when Egypt came in strongly on the side of the republicans and Saudi Arabia sided with the imam and the royalists; it was internationalized when the Soviet Union and Eastern Europe supported Egypt and the new YAR, and the United States and the United Kingdom deferred to the Saudis and their interests. As a result, the Yemen Civil War became a microcosmic battleground for the "Arab cold war" between revolutionary Arab nationalist republicans and conservative monarchists and, to a lesser extent, between the Soviet Union and its socialist bloc and the Free World.

The Egyptians, who clearly saved the republic in those first years, took control of fighting the civil war and came to look over time more and more like an occupier; bogged down, they came to call the Yemeni civil war "our Vietnam." Seen as a puppet of Egypt's President Gamal Abdel Nasser, the regime headed by President Abdullah al-Sallal lost credibility and legitimacy. When Nasser withdrew his forces from Yemen on the occasion of the Arab-Israel War of 1967 (the Six-Day War), the Sallal regime collapsed in a matter of weeks, opening the way to the republican-royalist reconciliation that took another two years to consummate.

Although it put much state-building as well as socioeconomic development on hold and exacted a terrible price in human suffering, the civil war did open up an isolated and insulated Yemen to a flood of new ideas, institutions, and practices. The Yemen of the 1970s and later was able to grasp and utilize many of these new elements in a way that was impossible in the 1960s.

See also BADR, MUHAMMAD AL-; YEMEN; YEMEN ARAB REPUBLIC.

Bibliography

Burrowes, Robert D. *The Yemen Arab Republic: The Politics of Development, 1962–1986.* Boulder, CO: Westview Press, 1987.

Dresch, Paul. *Tribes, Government, and History in Yemen.* Oxford: Clarendon, 1989.

ROBERT D. BURROWES

YEMEN DYNASTIES

Ruling families of the area known today as Yemen.

The Zaydi imamate in Yemen has its origins in 897, when al-Hadi ila al-Haqq Yahya became the first Zaydi imam (with his seat in Sa'da). His fame as an intellectual as well as a leader led to the invitation to Yemen; there he developed a multitude of policies that eventually became the basic guidelines for the religious as well as political characteristics of Yemeni Zaydism.

Yahya, however, was not able to consolidate his rule in all of Yemen; there were revolts as well as segments of the population that did not accept his pretensions to religio-political rule. Although he did not succeed in establishing any permanent administrative infrastructure, Yahya's descendants became the local aristocracy, and it is from among them that the imams of Yemen were selected for the next one thousand years.

Yemen throughout most of that period was only rarely a unified political entity; in fact, what was included within its frontiers varied widely, and it has not been governed consistently or uniformly by any single set of rulers. It existed as a part of a number of different political systems/ruling dynasties between the ninth and sixteenth centuries, after which it became a part of the Ottoman Empire.

After Imam Yahya's death, a multitude of smaller dynasties and families established themselves in the Tihama (the low coastal plain) as well as in the highlands. Among the better known of these are the Sulayhids, the Hatims, the Zuray'ids, and the Yu'firids. It was during this period, when the Fatimid state was influential, that a portion of the population was converted to Isma'ili Shi'ism.

Beginning with the conquest of Yemen by the family of Salah al-Din ibn Ayyub (Saladin) in 1174, a series of dynasties exercised a modicum of control and administration in Yemen for roughly the next 400 years; these are, in chronological sequence, the Ayyubids, from 1173/74 to 1228; the Rasulids, from 1228 to 1454; the Tahirids, from 1454 to 1517; and the Mamluks, from 1517 to 1538, when the Ottoman Empire took the Yemeni Tihama.

During most of this period, the dynasties and their rulers were primarily engaged in familial, regional, and occasionally sectarian disputes. Ironically, the Sunni Rasulids, who eventually concentrated their rule in southern Yemen for precisely that reason, were the dynasty under which the region experienced the greatest economic growth and political stability.

Very little is known about the Zaydi imams and their efforts to establish themselves and develop some form of administration (including tax collection), or their success in promoting Zaydi goals during this period. From the available evidence, there was very little continuity and a great deal of competition among the Zaydi families and clans. For example, in a presumably representative two-hundred-year period from the thirteenth to the fifteenth centuries, there appear to have been more than twenty different candidates for the imamate, representing more than ten distinct clans.

Eventually, as the Europeans entered the Middle East, specifically the Portuguese and then others in the effort to control the Red Sea trade, Yemen and its Zaydi imams were increasingly unable to maintain their independence. It was not until the ascendancy of Imam Qasim ibn Muhammad and his son al-Mu'ayyad Muhammad in the early seventeenth century that the Zaydi Yemenis were able to resist the Ottoman Empire's forces and become an independent political entity.

See also ISMA'ILI SHI'ISM; ZAYDISM.

MANFRED W. WENNER

YEMEN HUNT OIL COMPANY

U.S. company that first discovered and developed oil in Yemen.

The Yemen Hunt Oil Company (YHOC), a subsidiary of the Hunt Oil Company of Dallas, was the first foreign company to discover and develop oil in North Yemen; the location was the Ma'ib al-Jawf basin, on the edge of the desert in the eastern part of the country, and the year was 1984. Partnering with Exxon and a Korean oil company, the company rapidly developed the production-for-export capacity of that basin and built a pipeline to a terminus on the Red Sea; crude oil began to flow in 1987. YHOC also discovered very sizable natural gas deposits in the area, as yet undeveloped. In addition, it was the operator in another consortium that discovered, developed, and then began producing oil during the 1990s in what, prior to Yemeni unification, was the neutral zone between the Ma'ib al-Jawf basin in North Yemen and the Shabwa region of South Yemen. Called the Jannah field, this area became an important contributor to oil production in unified Yemen. Hailed from the mid-1980s to the mid-1990s as the ally and economic savior of Yemen, the YHOC in recent years has become something of a whipping boy over such issues as "Yemenization" and allegedly questionable accounting procedures.

Bibliography

Burrowes, Robert. *Historical Dictionary of Yemen.* Lanham, MD: Scarecrow Press, 1995.

Burrowes, Robert. *The Yemen Arab Republic: The Politics of Development, 1962–1986.* Boulder, CO: Westview Press, 1987.

ROBERT D. BURROWES

YEMENI SOCIALIST PARTY

Yemeni political party.

Created in October 1978 as the "vanguard party" required by Marxist-Leninist theory, the Yemeni Socialist Party (YSP) superseded the United Political Organization of the National Front, which in turn had replaced the National Front for the Liberation of Occupied South Yemen (the National Front), created in 1963. The latter, which was made up of seven smaller groupings, including the Arab Nationalist movement, eventually emerged as the strongest and best organized of the various groups competing for leadership of Aden and the protectorates in opposition to the British presence.

As the sole party in the People's Democratic Republic of Yemen (PDRY), it was the organization that arranged the union of the People's Democratic Republic of Yemen with the Yemen Arab Republic (YAR) in 1990. Thereafter, it became one of the three major parties in the unified state. However, the elections of 1993 led to a civil war between the former PDRY and YAR, with the leaders of the YSP declaring a new Democratic Republic of Yemen in the South in May 1994. Soundly defeated by the central government, the party's leaders went into exile. Thereafter, the party's northern branch elected a new leadership, none of whose members had participated in the Democratic Republic of Yemen.

Tensions between the other two major parties in the unified Yemen, and the YSP's continued significant support in the South, resulted in a desire to return the YSP to some role in the central government in the late 1990s. Although the YSP boycotted the 1997 elections, some of its members were elected as independents. By the time of the 1999 presidential election, northern members of the YSP had been reintegrated into the political system, and although the actual head of the YSP was disqualified as a candidate, Najib Qahtan al-Shaʿabi, the son of the first president of South Yemen, was approved. In 2000, the YSP joined a bloc of opposition parties to create the Supreme Opposition Council, and in 2003 it participated in the parliamentary elections, gaining 8 percent of the seats.

See also PEOPLE'S DEMOCRATIC REPUBLIC OF YEMEN; YEMEN; YEMEN CIVIL WAR.

Bibliography

Gause, F. Gregory. *Saudi-Yemeni Relations, 1962–1982.* New York: Columbia University Press, 1990.

Halliday, Fred. *Revolution and Foreign Policy: The Case of South Yemen, 1967–1987.* Cambridge, U.K.: Cambridge University Press, 1990.

Joffe, E. G. H.; Hachemi, M. J.; and Watkins, E. W. *Yemen Today: Crisis and Solutions: Proceedings of a Two-Day Conference Held at the School of Oriental and African Studies, University of London, November 25 and 26, 1995.* London: Caravel, 1997.

Mundy, Martha. *Domestic Government: Kinship, Community, and Polity in North Yemen.* Cambridge, U.K.: Cambridge University Press, 1995.

Suwaidi, Jamal al-, ed. *The Yemeni War of 1994: Causes and Consequences.* Emirates Center for Strategic Studies and Research, 1996.

Wenner, Manfred. *The Yemen Arab Republic: Development and Change in an Ancient Land.* Boulder, CO: Westview Press, 1991.

MANFRED W. WENNER

YEMENI WOMEN'S UNION

Oldest women's organization in Yemen.

The Yemeni Women's Union (YWU; Ittihad Nisa al-Yaman) is the oldest women's organization in Yemen, with roots in the preindependence era. The present organization was formed in 1990 by combining the northern and southern branches following the unification of Yemen. In the north, the Yemeni Women's Association (YWA) was established in 1965 with branches in the biggest towns. Without official recognition, the main task of the YWA was to promote literacy and job skills among women. In the south, the General Union of Yemeni Women was formed in 1968 to continue the work of two women's organizations (the Arab Women's Club and the Aden Women's Association) established during the British colonial era. It played a vital role in empowering women and promoting the politics of women's emancipation. Soon after unification, the YWU lost official backing, its funding was minimized, and it faced problems in harmonizing its activities. Whereas the southern branch was dominated by socialists, the Sanaa branch in the north was run by women from the Islah Party. The membership of the united organization is around 4,000. The YWU aims at attaining rights and legitimacy for women, gender equity, and women's advocacy. The union has played an important role in promoting women's increased participation in elections. YWU branches are found today in most governorates, with projects funded by foreign donors. These include microcredit schemes, basic healthcare services, and job-skills training for women. The union is an active participant in fighting violence against women, the goal that unites most Yemeni nongovernmental organizations.

See also GENDER: GENDER AND EDUCATION; GENDER: GENDER AND POLITICS; YEMEN.

Bibliography

Dahlgren, Susanne. "Women in the Republic of Yemen." In *The Greenwood Encyclopedia of Women's Issues Worldwide,* Volume 4: *The Middle East,* edited by Bahira Sherif. Westport, CT: Greenwood Publishing, 2003.

SUSANNE DAHLGREN

YENI MECMUA

See NEWSPAPERS AND PRINT MEDIA: TURKEY

YESHIVA

A school in which the Talmud, Jewish legal codes, and rabbinic literature and commentaries are the primary subjects of study.

Although *semikha* (rabbinic ordination) may be an outcome of yeshiva study, yeshivas are institutions intended for all Jewish males who wish to advance their study of Judaism. Originally, it was the local place to sit and study texts. Yeshivas became places where scholars gathered, where each famous and learned teacher attracted his own students. In eighteenth-century Lithuania, where the modern form was developed, yeshivas drew students from a variety of European localities and provided the students with a formal curriculum, a place to stay, and often a stipend as well.

Yeshiva education consists of endless hours of vocal and intensive review of texts with fellow students *(khavruseh).* Usually once a day, after posting a bibliography and a series of textual glosses that students must explore in advance, a teacher will give a *shiur* (lesson in Talmud). Some modern yeshivas include secular studies as well (they are often called day schools in North America and *yeshivot tikhoniyot* in Israel).

In Israel, yeshivas are numerous; some embrace the ideals of religious Zionism, and some deny them. The former encompass *hesder* yeshivas, whose students combine military service with study; the latter have students who are exempted from military service. Among the most prominent of the former are the Etzion Yeshiva, Merkaz ha-Rav Kook, and Kerem b'Yavneh. Among the latter are the Ponovez Yeshiva, in B'nei B'rak, and the Mir Yeshiva, in Jerusalem. The greatest growth has been in yeshivas connected with Sephardim.

Bibliography

Helmreich, William B. *The World of the Yeshiva: An Intimate Portrait of Orthodox Jewry,* augmented edition. Hoboken, NJ: Ktav, 2000.

SAMUEL C. HEILMAN

YIDDISH

A vernacular language used by Ashkenazic Jews.

A language based on Germanic dialects infused with Hebrew and loanwords from areas in Europe in which it was spoken, Yiddish is the vernacular used by Ashkenazic Jews since the European Middle Ages. As Hebrew became primarily the language of liturgy and religious scholarship, Yiddish, by the end of the eighteenth century, emerged as the vehicle for the expression of secular literature, drama, poetry, and popular literature. By the nineteenth century, Yiddish was established as the la nguage of a secular European Jewish culture found mainly in Eastern Europe.

The Zionist ideology that stressed the return to Palestine and the use of Hebrew as the language of the Jewish nation was instrumental in the revival of Hebrew. In the language controversy that ensued in the early part of the twentieth century, Hebrew gained prominence over Yiddish and became the official language of the Yishuv and, later, the State of Israel. Yiddish increasingly became identified with Jews and Jewish culture of the diaspora. In response to the Holocaust and the liquidation of Yiddish culture under Soviet rule there has been a resurgent interest in the Yiddish language both in Israel and in North America. As a spoken language Yiddish has become the established vernacular of Orthodox Haredi and Hasidic Jews.

Bibliography

Rosten, Leo. *The Joys of Yiddish: A Related Lexicon of Yiddish, Hebrew and Yinglish Words Often Encountered in English . . . From the Days of the Bible to Those of the Beatnik.* New York: McGraw-Hill, 1968.

Weinstein, Miriam. *Yiddish: A Nation of Words.* South Royalton, VT: Steerforth Press, 2001.

REEVA S. SIMON
UPDATED BY NEIL CAPLAN

YILDIRIM ARMY

Special Ottoman strike force, also known as the Thunderbolt, or Seventh Army.

The army was organized in early 1917 by Enver Paşa to defend the Eastern Front in World War I. It comprised fourteen Ottoman divisions headed by German General Erich von Falkenhayn and included six thousand German soldiers and sixty-five top Ottoman officers, including General Mustafa Kemal (Atatürk). Enver Paşa had originally planned this special army to recapture Iraq but, in March 1917, sent it to block the new British and Arab campaign in Palestine, where they joined the Fourth Army at Gaza and won an initial victory.

The Ottoman-German effort, however, was weakened by conflicts over jurisdiction, by Turkish nationalist dissent toward the German leadership, and by matériel disadvantages. In the autumn of 1917, the British and Arab offensive forced an Ottoman withdrawal to Damascus, with heavy losses on 27 December. The Allied drive resumed the next autumn, and, on 1 October 1918, British General Edmund Allenby and the Arab nationalist revolt forced the Ottomans to evacuate the Syrian capital. Allenby's troops, aided by French forces landing at Beirut, nearly annihilated the Yildirim Army as the Ottomans were driven back to Alexandretta within two weeks. General Otto Liman von Sanders gave command of the Yildirim to Mustafa Kemal after the Mudros Armistice took effect 31 October, and Kemal surrendered at Adana on 13 November 1918.

Bibliography

Shaw, Stanford J., and Shaw, Ezel Kural. *History of the Ottoman Empire and Modern Turkey.* 2 vols. Cambridge, U.K., and New York: Cambridge University Press, 1976–1977.

ELIZABETH THOMPSON

YISHUV

The Jewish community in Palestine from the Ottoman period through the British Mandate.

Yishuv refers to the Jewish population—including the pre-Zionist Jewish community known as the Old Yishuv—living in Palestine before the State of Israel was proclaimed in 1948. The Old Yishuv had its roots in a religious revival among Jews in Eastern Europe at the end of the eighteenth century, which inspired increasing numbers to journey to Ottoman Palestine and settle in what they deemed the holy cities of Tiberias, Safed, Hebron, and Jerusalem. Motivated by a desire to observe Jewish religious commandments, scholars and pious men came to pray and study as preconditions to salvation. Palestine's Jewish population steadily increased from approximately 4,200 in 1806 to 26,000 on the eve of the first Zionist-sponsored immigration in 1882.

The Old and the New Yishuv

Concerned Jews in Europe sent financial aid to these pious communities as a way of sharing in the holiness of living and studying in the land of Israel. The collection and distribution of this aid (in Hebrew, *halukkah*) to support pious Jews and their religious institutions in Palestine was institutionalized in 1810 by a wealthy Dutch Jew, Rabbi Zvi Hirsch Lehren, who founded the Pekidim and Amarkalim of Eretz Yisrael (Officials of the Land of Israel) in Amsterdam.

Even with a sophisticated system of external funding, as the numbers of Jews in the Old Yishuv increased, their economic lot deteriorated. A few enjoyed economic security, but most lived in poverty. The religious schools (*kollelim*) provided their own subsidies, sometimes offering rent, health care, and support for widows and orphans, but all charitable services depended on budgetary circumstances and on the intellectual status of the scholars, with those from the wealthiest diaspora communities receiving the highest payments.

By 1882, Zionism had emerged in Europe, and Zionists began to sponsor immigration into Ottoman Palestine. Their goal was a self-supporting secular, egalitarian society based on productive labor and a Hebrew cultural renaissance; they named their community the New Yishuv. Proclaiming the need for social change, economic transformation, and

A ship filled with Jewish refugees docks in Haifa Port in 1945. Between 1945 and 1948, 69,000 Jews relocated from Europe to Palestine. Many did not successfully complete the journey and ended up in British detention camps in Cyprus. © PHOTOGRAPH BY ZOLTAN KLUGER. GOVERNMENT PRESS OFFICE (GPO) OF ISRAEL. REPRODUCED BY PERMISSION.

political reform, Zionist activities ruptured traditional patterns of pious Jewish life in Palestine and triggered intense competition for diaspora charity.

In Zionist historiography, the differences between Old and New Yishuv have been described as immense. In fact, there was some overlap. A generation of Jews who matured in Jerusalem during the Ottoman reform era of the 1860s responded to the challenge of meeting daily needs as well as to the spirit of the age by calling for the creation of a productive Jewish economy. Yosef Rivlin, Yoel Moshe Salomon, and Israel Dov Frumkin, prominent cultural and religious figures, became builders of new neighborhoods and founders of a new Jewish infrastructure. Among the housing projects outside the

Old City that they developed or supported were Nahalat Shiva, Mea Sheʿarim, Mishkenot Israel, Kiryah Neʾemana, and Bet Yaʿakov. By 1880, 2,000 Jews lived outside the Old City and 16,000 lived within the walls. A similar impulse drove Jaffa's Jewish leaders to establish the new suburbs of Neve Shalom, Yefe Nof, and Ahva. Some also advocated educational reform and contributed to the revival of Hebrew.

As for the Zionists, some came from traditional backgrounds and never gave up their faith or observance of religious ritual. Permanent alliances across the two communities were generally short lived, however; they often split over religious stipulations constraining the establishment of a modern Jewish society.

Zionism

Although immigrants driven by piety continued to arrive alongside Zionists, it was the Zionist vision that created Palestine's new institutions. Between 1882 and 1948, the Zionist movement established about 250 towns, villages, and cities designed by a corps of planners and officials pursuing national political goals. Schools, libraries, newspapers, workshops, and cultural and commercial enterprises were established—even in Jerusalem, the heart of the Old Yishuv.

After World War I and the dissolution of the Ottoman Empire, the British, under a mandate from the League of Nations, ruled Palestine. British doctrine recognized the Yishuv as one of Palestine's religious communities but in practice provided it with the opportunity to operate national-style institutions. Zionists brought their political parties with them to Palestine. From the early years of the twentieth century, a number of Zionist-Socialist parties (Poʿalei Zion, ha-Poʿel ha-Tzaʿir, Left Poʿalei Zion) as well as Mizrahi, the religious Zionist movement, had adherents and activists in Palestine. Political parties opened employment offices and founded agricultural collectives, soup kitchens, loan funds, newspapers, and schools. They provided recreational and cultural activities for members. Many of these activities were absorbed in 1920 by the Histadrut, which became one of the central vehicles of state-building for the Yishuv. Histadrut operations—labor exchanges, construction compa-

nies, and an underground army—were crucial in helping Jewish immigrants find work and community in their new homeland. The Histadrut became the base of power for David Ben-Gurion, who used his position as secretary-general to bring together several of labor's political parties in 1930 to form MAPAI, dominant in Yishuv politics and eventually in the World Zionist Organization. With backing from both the Histadrut and MAPAI, Ben-Gurion was able to outmaneuver political rivals such as Vladimir Zeʾev Jabotinsky and Chaim Weizmann.

Palestine's Jewish community organized itself in explicitly political structures, beginning with an assembly (Knesset Yisrael) elected by people who were more than twenty years old and had at least three months' residence in the region. Between sessions, the assembly delegated its powers to the Vaʿad Leʾumi (National Council), appointed from its ranks. The council nominated from among its members an executive charged with the actual administration of the community. Policies generated by the self-governing institutions of the Yishuv covered matters of health, social welfare, defense, and education. Without the authority to tax, however, Knesset Israel and its constituent institutions had limited power. Its funding depended on allocations from the World Zionist Organization. Some of Palestine's Orthodox Jewish residents remained aloof from the organization and did not participate in elections, since they objected to female suffrage and to the secular aims of Zionism. They insisted on their organizational separateness and retained an allegiance to the principles of the Old Yishuv.

Palestine was governed as a colony, but significant policies were often formulated by England's highest elected officials, including the prime minister and parliament. Yishuv politicians such as Ben-Gurion understood the pressing need to influence policymakers in London as well as those implementing regulations in Palestine. Hence, much power was assigned to international Zionist agencies and to their leaders, who attained global stature (e.g., Weizmann).

Until the creation of an expanded Jewish Agency in 1929, the Zionist executive's political department was also the central mechanism for creating contacts with Arab leaders within and outside of Palestine. Founded and directed by Chaim Kalvaryski, this department initiated contacts with Palestinian personalities willing to sit with Jews in institutions established on the basis of the Mandate's political framework. The department extended funds to village shaykhs, municipal leaders, newspapers, and movements deemed moderate on the issue of a Jewish national home in Palestine. In 1929, the Jewish Agency and the National Council set up the Joint Bureau to handle relations with the League of Nations and with Britain in both London and Palestine.

Two developments in the 1930s augmented the authority of Yishuv institutions. The first was an increase in the number of Jewish immigrants, who were now fleeing fascist Europe. This increased the number of people who participated in elections and other voluntary political activities. The second was the outbreak of the Arab Revolt in 1936 and the need for a larger Yishuv defense force. The Yishuv assumed responsibility for helping fund such a force through a voluntary tax levy. Yishuv institutions still drew their authority primarily from the networks created with various political movements and the leadership of the Jewish Agency, but as the legitimacy of these institutions strengthened they also began to function more effectively on their own.

When British rule began in Palestine, there were 56,000 Jews in a total population of 640,000. By the end of Britain's political tenure, the Jewish population had increased to 650,000, with substantial immigration occurring in the Mandate's last decade. Undoubtedly, the rise of Nazism and the threat of war expanded both interest in immigration and the actual numbers of Jewish immigrants, despite Britain's attempts to control the number of Jews entering Palestine.

The outbreak of the war in 1939 and the genocidal policies of the Nazis created enormous difficulty for the Yishuv. On the one hand, these policies substantiated the Zionist claim that diaspora Jewry lived in fragile, untenable conditions; on the other hand, by slaughtering the movement's potential population, they threatened the possibility of achieving the Zionist dream of sovereignty. However, World War II ended with the beginning of the Cold War, and the dramatic shift in the balance of world power helped the Yishuv win the international support necessary for Jewish statehood, especially from those interested in the dismantling of Great Britain's empire.

See also BEN-GURION, DAVID; ERETZ YISRAEL; HISTADRUT; ISRAEL: POLITICAL PARTIES IN; WEIZMANN, CHAIM; ZIONISM.

Bibliography

Caplan, Neil. *Palestine Jewry and the Arab Question, 1917–1925.* Totowa, NJ; London: Frank Cass, 1978.

Halper, Jeff. *Between Redemption and Revival: The Jewish Yishuv of Jerusalem in the Nineteenth Century.* Boulder, CO: Westview Press, 1991.

Halpern, Ben, and Reinharz, Jehuda. *Zionism and the Creation of a New Society.* New York: Oxford University Press, 1998.

Horowitz, Dan, and Lissak, Moshe. *Origins of the Israeli Polity: Palestine under the Mandate,* translated by Charles Hoffman. Chicago: University of Chicago Press, 1978.

Hurewitz, J. C. *The Struggle for Palestine.* New York: Norton, 1950.

McCarthy, Justin. *The Population of Palestine: Population History and Statistics of the Late Ottoman Period and the Mandate.* New York: Columbia University Press, 1990.

Parfitt, Tudor. *The Jews in Palestine: 1800-1882.* Wolfeboro, NH; Woodbridge, U.K.: Boydell Press; London: Royal Historical Society, 1987.

Troen, S. Ilan. *Imagining Zion: Dreams, Designs, and Realities in a Century of Jewish Settlement.* New Haven, CT: Yale University Press, 2003.

DONNA ROBINSON DIVINE

YIZHAR, S.
[1916–]

Israeli novelist.

The grandnephew of Israeli author Moshe Smilansky (1874–1953), S. Yizhar was born in 1969 in Rehovot, Israel. Yizhar's most famous novel, *Yeme Ziklag* (1958), is considered a work of great literary distinction. It describes seven days of battle during the Arab–Israel War of 1948 and underscores the burdens imposed on a society trying to fulfill the Zionist mission. His language and detailed descriptions of the land have influenced all subsequent generations of Israeli writers. His later novel, *Mikdamot* (Foretellings, 1992), views the Zionist pioneering enterprise through the eyes of a child. Yizhar served in the Knesset from 1949 to 1967 as a representative of the mainstream labor movement and also taught school for many years.

Bibiliography

Shaked, Gershon. *Modern Hebrew Fiction,* translated by Yael Lotan. Bloomington: Indiana University Press, 2000.

Yizhar, S. *Midnight Convoy and Other Stories.* Jerusalem: Institute for the Translation of Hebrew Literature, 1969.

BRYAN DAVES
UPDATED BY DONNA ROBINSON DIVINE

YÖN

See NEWSPAPERS AND PRINT MEDIA: TURKEY

YOSEF, OVADIAH

[1920–]

Israeli religious and political leader.

Ovadiah Yosef, Israel's most prominent Mizrahi religious leader, was born in Baghdad but has lived in Palestine since infancy. He was educated at the Sephardic Porat Yosef yeshiva in Jerusalem, and he was recognized as a brilliant scholar with a phenomenal memory from an early age. A rabbi by the age of twenty, he was deputy chief rabbi of Cairo when the state of Israel was founded in 1948. He returned to Israel in 1950, where he became a religious judge. In 1968 he was appointed chief rabbi of Tel Aviv. He served as the Sephardic chief rabbi of Israel from 1973 to 1983—a tenure marred by bickering with the Ashek021naic chief rabbi, Shlomo Goren. His religious authority and personal charisma led his followers to continue to accord him higher status than that given to the Sephardic chief rabbis who followed him in that post. His weekly Saturday night talks are broadcast by satellite around the world. These talks are followed closely by Israeli journalists, who are eager to report his often provocative and colorfully worded statements and rulings. These included his declaration that the six million Holocaust victims were "reincarnations of the souls of sinners. . . They had been reincarnated in order to atone."

Yosef's biography includes a series of frustrations and personal slights. He was never invited to join the Ashkenazic Council of Torah Sages of the Agudat Israel party—then the highest political and spiritual authority in the ultra-Orthodox world. In Ashkenazic circles he was dismissed as a person who memorized texts rather than an original thinker. His own religious mentor, Rabbi Eliezer Schach, announced that, because they still needed to follow Ashkenazic guidance, "the time has not yet come for Sephardim to take positions of leadership." Yosef was thus induced to support the first ultra-Orthodox Sephardi SHAS (derived from *Sephardim Shomrei Torah,* or Sephardi Torah Guardians) party, founded in 1983 by disaffected members of the Ashkenazic dominated Agudat Israel party. SHAS won 11 of the 120 parliamentary seats in the 2003 elections (down from 17 in 1999). Yosef's intended purpose is to restore the "crown of glory" to Sephardic Judaism—to reestablish the dominance of the Halakhah in accordance with Sephardic custom in Israel. He is now the ruling force behind the SHAS party, instructing the elected Knesset members how to vote in parliamentary issues.

Yosef's most famous work, *Yabiah Omer,* deals with halakhic problems in daily life. His religious rulings have been original, but also at times controversial, as when he recognized Ethiopian Jews as being fully Jewish during the 1970s. His leniency in religious ruling is sensitive to the diversity of religious observance among Sephardic Jews. He generally seeks accommodation rather than confrontation in Jewish-Arab issues, even as he sometimes uses abusive language (for example, "beasts of prey") to describe his enemies and those of Israel.

See also ADOT HA-MIZRAH.

JULIE ZUCKERMAN
UPDATED BY EPHRAIM TABORY

YOUNG ALGERIANS

A group of French-educated men who, early in the twentieth century, became the first Algerians to attempt reform within the colonial political system.

Estimated to number between 1,000 and 1,200, the Young Algerians (*Jeunes Algériens*) included intellectuals, members of the liberal professions, and individuals who had succeeded within French business circles. Most prominent among the group's members were Dr. Benthami Ould Hamida, Omar Bouderba, Fekar Ben Ali, Chérif Benhabylès, and—beginning in 1913—Khaled ibn Hashimi ibn Hajj Abd al-Qadir, grandson of Algerian patriot Abd al-Qadir.

While there were differences in the emphases of the Young Algerians, most were attempting to win for themselves rights approximating those of Frenchmen. Their agenda, before World War I, included exemption of at least some Algerians from the exceptive Code de l'Indigénat, more equitable distribution of taxes, easier access to French citizenship, and greater political participation for the educated. The agenda also included programs for the masses, including greater access to education, opening of grazing and forest lands, protections for property, and more careful monitoring of government abuse.

Despite support from many liberals in France, attempts to negotiate concessions failed in 1913 and 1914, largely because of colon opposition. During World War I, when thousands of Algerians served in the French armed forces, a grateful Prime Minister Georges Clemenceau promised reform. The resulting Jonnart Law of 4 February 1919, however, was viewed by most Young Algerians as being very far from what they had been promised. For a few years after the war, Khaled ibn Hashimi ibn Hajj Abd al-Qadir continued to lead the movement for reform within the system, but, by 1923, he gave up the effort and went into exile in the Near East.

See also CODE DE L'INDIGÉNAT.

JOHN RUEDY

YOUNG EGYPT

A patriotic association of Egyptian youth established in October 1933.

In 1937, Young Egypt (Misr al-Fatat) became a formal political party in Egypt; in 1940, the name was changed to the Islamic Nationalist party (al-Hizb al-Watani al-Islami); in 1949, it became the Socialist party of Egypt (Hizb Misr al-Ishtiraki).

The dominant figure in Young Egypt throughout its history was the lawyer/politician Ahmad Husayn. In the 1930s, the movement's program combined a vehement, anti-British Egyptian na-

tionalism, an antiparliamentary outlook, an emphasis on the paramilitary training and mobilization of youth, and a call for greater social justice. Politically opposed to the Wafd, Young Egypt aligned itself with the anti-Wafdist forces centered around the Egyptian palace; its paramilitary squads of Green Shirts periodically fought with the Blue Shirts of the Wafd.

Although it was suppressed during World War II, it afterward dropped its paramilitary features while retaining, but relabeling, much of its prewar populism. Like all Egyptian political parties, it was abolished in January 1953, after the Free Officers, led by General Muhammad Naguib, seized power from the monarchy of King Farouk.

Bibliography

Jankowski, James. *Egypt's Young Rebels: "Young Egypt," 1933–1952.* Stanford, CA: Hoover Institution Press, 1975.

JAMES JANKOWSKI

YOUNG OTTOMANS

Ottoman intellectuals and bureaucrats who constituted the first organized opposition to the pro-West modernizing elite of the Tanzimat.

Members of the group called themselves New Ottomans, while contemporary European observers referred to them as Young Turks. The latter term came to be used more specifically in reference to the next generation of liberal opponents of Sultan Abdülhamit as distinct from Young Ottomans, which has become the synonym of New Ottomans.

The Young Ottomans began their activities in Constantinople (now Istanbul). They faced repression and were forced into exile in Europe and other parts of the Ottoman Empire. Prominent Young Ottoman leaders were Namik Kemal (1840–1888), İbrahim Şinasi (1824–1871), Agha Efendi (1832–1885), Abdülhamit Ziya Paşa (1825–1880), and Ali Suavi (1838–1878). The group received important financial and moral support from a disaffected member of the Egyptian khedival family who had entered the Ottoman service, Mustafa Fazil Paşa (1829–1875). While these leaders were united in their opposition to the Tanzimat elite, and to the autocratic ministry of Paşas Fu'ad and Ali, they had hardly been bystanders to the Tanzimat. They had matured intellectually and professionally during the Tanzimat period. Many had served in the Translation Bureau, a breeding ground for Tanzimat bureaucrats. Some were stimulated by the frustration of their career ambitions under the Tanzimat regime.

The Young Ottomans differed in social and professional background. Ziya Paşa, the oldest in the group, was a writer and poet and had served as third secretary to Sultan Abdülmecit II. Namik Kemal, also poet and writer, came from a distinguished bureaucratic family. Şinasi, an army captain's son who held a post in the imperial arsenal before he was sent to Paris to study finance, was the most innovative and versatile from a literary point of view. Ali Suavi was a middle-school teacher and a religious-minded writer, even agitator.

The forerunner of the group was the Alliance of Fidelity or Patriotic Alliance, a loose group consisting of literary men and functionaries, which first met in Constantinople in June 1865. Organization was secret and conspiratorial, apparently modeled along the Carbonari of Italy, Spain, and France and led by a French-educated agitator, Mehmet Bey. The group did not publicize a program. The members were motivated by recent Ottoman setbacks in the Balkans and Lebanon and fear of disintegration. They felt constitutional government was necessary to preserve the empire and to ward off Europe's economic domination and diplomatic interventions. The group's expanding membership included bureaucrats, ulama (Islamic clergy), and army officers.

In 1866/67 Namik Kemal and Ali Suavi published newspapers (Tasvir-i Efkar and Muhbir) in which they vehemently criticized the government's policy regarding the insurrection in Crete and the impending surrender of Serbia. They published an open letter from Mustafa Fazil, who had left the empire over issues pertaining to his political ambitions in Egypt, which addressed the sultan and amounted to a liberal manifesto. The government ordered Namik Kemal, Ziya, and Ali Suavi to domestic exile and closed their newspapers. Instead, they accepted an invitation from Mustafa Fazil Paşa and fled to Paris. At this time, the government also un-covered the group's contacts with top security officials in preparation for a coup against Abdülaziz that was organized by Mehmet Bey.

The regrouping of the liberal-minded elements of the Patriotic Alliance as New Ottomans occurred in exile at the end of May 1867. In Paris and later London, they published the newspaper Hürriyet, edited by Namik Kemal and Ziya Paşa with financial support from Mustafa Fazil. They promoted liberal political principles and demanded a parliament. At the same time, they denounced liberal economic policies and advocated measures to buttress indigenous trade and to promote industry.

Despite considerable variation in their outlook on politics, society, and religion, the Young Ottomans projected an Islamic modernist synthesis. They opposed Western political and economic interference and wholesale adoption of Western thought and culture. Nevertheless, they were sympathetic to Western political institutions. Their thought was premised on the existence in Islamic political traditions of the concepts and institutions fundamental to a liberal political system based on representative principles. The Young Ottomans reinterpreted and popularized the concept of watan (homeland) to advance a political allegiance to the Ottoman state. They sought a contractual relationship between the subjects and the ruler, based on the Islamic principles of shura (consultation) and ijma (consensus), within the framework of an Ottoman watan. These views represented the first systematic expression of Islamic modernist ideas in the Muslim world.

The Young Ottoman movement was not the first expression of political protest against the Tanzimat. As early as 1859, a group of ulama and army officers had led a coup d'état aimed at Abdülmecit in resentment of Tanzimat policies that enhanced the status of the non-Muslim minorities vis-à-vis the Muslims, and—perhaps more importantly—had left the payment of officers in arrears (the Küleli Incident). The Young Ottomans constituted the first opposition group that attempted to offer alternative programs, inspired by Western thought but consistent with Islamic political ideals.

The movement signifies the beginnings of a campaign for social mobilization and the forging of a public opinion in the Ottoman Empire, even though the group's propaganda remained restricted to a literate Turkish-speaking intelligentsia. Their ideas appealed to disfranchised Westernized groups, students, Muslim commercial associations, and religious conservative opponents of the Tanzimat. They propagated their views through newspapers and literature utilizing a simplified Ottoman-Turkish. They were influenced by contemporary Turkish discoveries, which reinforced the Islamist and anti-imperialist outlook, especially in the pen of Ali Suavi.

The Young Ottomans pioneered journalism and introduced new genres and themes to Ottoman literature. Indeed, future members of the group began their oppositional activity in the first privately published Ottoman journals that appeared in the early 1860s (such as *Tercüman-i Ahval* and *Tasvir-i Efkar*). They introduced the genres of the novel and the drama to Ottoman literature, popularized them, and effectively used them as vehicles of political propaganda. The pioneer in this journalistic and literary activity was Şinasi. The Young Ottomans also translated into Turkish the works of European Enlightenment philosophers and authors such as Rousseau, Montesquieu, Voltaire, Molière, and Lamartine.

The Young Ottomans did not constitute a party organization despite their espousal of political propaganda and promotion of political agendas. After the early 1870s, the group lost its cohesion. Ideological and personal differences led to estrangement in European exile. Several leaders, including the benefactor Mustafa Fazil Paşa, accepted Abdülaziz's amnesty offer to return to Constantinople. Following the death of their nemesis, Ali Paşa, in 1871 the movement went into disarray in the capital. However, under the duress of the political and financial crises of the 1870s, progressive Ottoman statesmen started to look with favor upon Young Ottoman ideas about constitutional government. Midhat Paşa, known as the architect of the Ottoman constitution and parliament, emerged as the leading proponent of change and set out to give concrete expression to Young Ottoman ideas on constitutional government, drawing also on the services of Young Ottoman leaders. Namik Kemal and Ziya Paşa were members of the committee that drafted the Ottoman constitution of 1876. Namik Kemal's

long struggle to promote the Young Ottoman cause, his refusal to compromise, his passionately patriotic poetry and drama, and his lucid political writings stressing the notion of popular sovereignty gave him a reputation as the most influential Young Ottoman activist and author, as well as making him a source of inspiration for later constitutionalists.

Due to the absence of a party organization and their dependence on literary forms for the propagation of their ideas, the Young Ottomans had no direct impact on non-Turkish-speaking parts of the empire. For instance, their Islamic modernist ideas did not have an appreciable influence on later and similar currents in the Arab-populated areas. The Young Ottoman movement, however, was the ideological forerunner and inspiration of the later and more broadly based Young Turk movement. The Young Ottomans may not have offered a coherent political philosophy, but they were the precursors of most modern intellectual and political movements in the Middle East.

See also ALI SUAVI; MUSTAFA FAZIL; NAMIK KEMAL; ŞINASI, İBRAHIM; TANZIMAT; YOUNG TURKS; ZIYA, ABDÜLHAMIT.

Bibliography

Davison, Roderic H. *Reform in the Ottoman Empire, 1856–1876*. Princeton, NJ: Princeton University Press, 1963.

Mardin, Serif. *The Genesis of Young Ottoman Thought: A Study in the Modernization of Turkish Political Ideas*. Princeton, NJ: Princeton University Press, 1962.

HASAN KAYALI

YOUNG TUNISIANS

Tunisian reform movement that championed Tunisian rights during the French protectorate.

The imposition of the French protectorate over Tunisia in 1881 propelled a group of reform-minded urban elites, known as the Young Tunisians, to challenge the traditional order that it blamed for the country's economic and political misfortunes. The Young Tunisians initially acquiesced to French oversight as a practical step toward the modernization of state and society, but they were also intent on reforming native institutions in order to maintain and renew the Muslim heritage and identity of

Tunisia, and to this end, they founded the Khaldunniyya School in 1896. The nucleus of the Young Tunisian movement thus included modernists from the religious notability, such as Abd al-Aziz al-Thaalbi, as well as graduates of French universities or of the European-inspired Sadiqiyya College, such as Bashir Sfar, Ali Bash Hamba, and Hassan Gallati. By 1900, however, growing frustration with their political and economic marginalization was leading many Young Tunisians to intensify their criticism of the protectorate and its various forms of discrimination.

In 1907 Sfar, Bash Hamba, and al-Thaalbi launched French and Arabic editions of the journal *Le Tunisien* to promote and champion indigenous rights. The movement was radicalized further between 1911 and 1912 by the Italian invasion of Libya, and by the Protectorate's use of disproportionate military force against civilian demonstrators in November 1911 (the Jallaz Incident), and again in February 1912 against striking tramway workers. The authorities accused the Young Tunisians of instigating popular unrest, and deported al-Thaalbi, Sfar, Gallati, and Bash Hamba. Thus, on the eve of World War I, the Young Tunisian movement had been effectively decapitated and driven underground, but its popular anticolonial platform was soon resurrected in the 1920s by the Destour Party and its calls for Tunisian self-determination.

See also BOURGUIBA, HABIB; KHALDUNNIYYA; THAALBI, ABD AL-AZIZ; TUNISIA: POLITICAL PARTIES IN.

Bibliography

Abun-Nasr, Jamil. *A History of the Maghrib in the Islamic Period.* Cambridge, U.K.: Cambridge University Press, 1987.

O. W. ABI-MERSHED

YOUNG TURKS

Name given to groups in Ottoman society who demanded and strove for political and social change in the last several decades of the Ottoman Empire.

"Young Turk" is an expression coined in Europe that invokes three distinct phases of the Ottoman constitutionalist movement: the anti-Tanzimat cur-rent better known to historians as the "Young Ottoman" movement; the constitutionalist opposition to Sultan Abdülhamit; and the Second Constitutional Period introduced by the reinstitution of the constitutional regime in 1908. There was at no point a distinct organization called the Young Turks; nor did the groups recognized as Young Turks generally embrace this name. Nevertheless, historians identify the last three decades of the empire in reference to Young Turks, while "the Young Turk period" corresponds more precisely to the decade of their political predominance from 1908 to 1918.

Young Turk activity began in the late 1880s. Until the revolution of 1908, their opposition to Abdülhamit manifested itself both within the empire and abroad. The two spheres of activity were linked together only loosely. When a group of medical students in Constantinople (now Istanbul) founded in 1889 the secret cells of what would develop into the Committee for Union and Progress (CUP), individual intellectuals in exile had already launched a political and journalistic campaign against the Hamitian regime. The best known in the latter group was Khalil Ghanim, a Syrian Christian, who published a journal called *La jeune Turquie (Young Turkey).*

The Constantinople secret committee spread rapidly in the capital's higher schools and soon became known to the authorities. Reprisals forced many to exile, whereupon an expatriate liberal opposition came together around Ahmet Riza, a French-educated official in the Ministry of Agriculture. Influenced by European positivists, he failed to return from a mission in 1889 and turned into a vocal critic of the Hamitian regime. In 1895, he joined Khalil Ghanim, Alber Fua (a Jew), and Aristidi Paşa (a Greek) to publish *Meşveret*, which became the leading voice of Young Turks.

The next year, a member of the Constantinople secret committee, Murat Bey, fled to Cairo and later to Geneva. A Russian Turk who taught at the influential Mülkiye (civil service) school, Murat Bey was better connected with the liberal currents in Constantinople. His *Mizan* outshone *Meşveret*, both of which were smuggled into the empire. Murat was an Islamist-Turkist revolutionary, in contrast to Ahmet Riza's elitist and gradualist outlook. The two men were united in their anti-imperialism and denunciation of the Hamitian autocracy. Murat, however, joined Abdülhamit in 1897. Rivalries within the Young Turk movement in exile continued with the publication in Geneva of *Osmanh* by İshak Süküti and Ahmet Cevdet Paşa, founding members of the CUP in Constantinople. As repression increased in the empire, Young Turk activity shifted almost entirely to Europe and Egypt for a decade. The flight of Damad Mahmud Paşa, the brother-in-law of the sultan, to join the Young Turks in Europe opened a new phase in Young Turk activities.

Under the moral guidance and financial support of ailing Mahmud Paşa and the presidency of his son Sabahettin, the Young Turks held a conference in Paris in February 1902, which crystallized the divisions within the movement. Representatives of all major religious groups in the empire attended. The meeting revealed the separatist inclinations of Christian factions, while two groups around Ahmet Riza and Sabahettin divided over the suitability of centralist versus decentralist policies in achieving the ultimate aim of preserving the integrity of the empire. Subsequently, Sabahettin formed the Society of Administrative Decentralization and Private Initiative, modeled along the teachings of economist Frédéric Le Play and Edmond Demolins and as a rival to the CUP. A second conference in 1907 aimed at a reconciliation failed to bring Greek, Albanian, and some Armenian factions to the table.

Meanwhile, domestic opposition and conspiracy against the Hamitian regime regrouped in Macedonia. Different oppositional groups coalesced to revitalize the CUP, which in 1907 contacted the Ahmet Riza group in Europe. However, the exile communities had no role in the immediate circumstances that led to the Young Turk Revolution. If international events like the Japanese victory over Russia and the Russian and Iranian revolutions energized Young Turks everywhere, the nationalist activity among the Balkan peoples and the perceived threat to the empire by enhanced relations between Britain and Russia impelled the unionists in Salonika and Monastir to action.

Due to the role they played in the revolution, leaders of the Macedonian branches of the CUP eclipsed the other factions after 1908. They were, however, too inexperienced to take the helm of government and too insecure to embrace other Young

Ahmet Riza circa 1910. Riza was one of the leaders of the Committee for Union and Progress, one of several groups that collectively came to be known as the Young Turks. The Young Turks sought to reform and modernize the Ottoman Empire. They succeeded in taking control of the government in 1908 but fell from power after defeat in World War I (1914–1918). © RYKOFF COLLECTION/CORBIS. REPRODUCED BY PERMISSION.

Turk groups, including the CUP leadership in Europe. The differences within the Young Turk movement were now expressed in multiparty politics. The decentralists under Sabahettin formed the Liberal party before the 1908 elections. Even though they failed to block the election of a large majority of CUP candidates to parliament, the decentralists became an increasingly more potent opposition to the CUP, supported by autonomy-minded minority groups. Other parties that formed in 1910 and 1911 soon merged in the Ottoman Liberty and Entente party. The CUP's attempts to manipulate the elections to retain power undermined parliamentary rule, eliciting an ultimatum from a group of military officers called Saviors. Coupled with foreign pre-occupations such as the Italian and Balkan wars, the Young Turk governments gave way to governments led by old-school politicians in 1912. In 1913 the CUP wrested power with a coup d'état. Despite conciliatory measures to the liberals, the CUP remained as that faction within the Young Turk movement that dominated Ottoman politics until the end of the empire.

The Young Turks promoted the ideology of Ottomanism in an attempt to foster in all peoples of the empire a commitment to the Ottoman homeland within the framework of a constitutional government. There were organizational similarities, some ideological continuity, and shared political goals between the Young Ottomans and Young Turks. Despite what the ethnocentric term "Young Turk" suggests, the movement represented ethnically and religiously a much more diverse group than the Young Ottomans.

The Young Turk movement embraced varied ideological orientations (Westernism, Islamism, Turkism, positivism, centralism, decentralism), socio-economic backgrounds (lower middle-class students and officers, high officials, members of Ottoman and Egyptian royal households), and ethnic-religious affiliations. It was unified in the conviction for the necessity of reform designed to preserve the empire. The Young Turks were responsible for instituting the beginnings of modern politics in the Middle East, for expanding education and journalism, and for realizing economic, social, and administrative reforms. The movement provided the political nuclei for the successor states of the Ottoman Empire.

See also AHMET RIZA; COMMITTEE FOR UNION AND PROGRESS; OTTOMANISM; TANZIMAT; YOUNG OTTOMANS.

Bibliography

Ahmad, Feroz. *The Young Turks: The Committee of Union and Progress in Turkish Politics, 1908–1914.* Oxford: Clarendon, 1969.

Ramsaur, Ernest E. *The Young Turks: Prelude to the Revolution of 1908.* Princeton, NJ: Princeton University Press, 1957.

HASAN KAYALI

YOUSSEF, MULAY

Alawi sultan of Morocco, 1912–1927.

The ouster by France of Youssef's predecessor, Mulay Abd al-Hafiz, signaled the subordination of the Moroccan sultanate to French colonialism and a serious loss of prestige by the Moroccan ruling house. Mulay Youssef's reign was marked largely by the implementation of the Treaty of Fes (March 1912) and the aggressive administration of French rule by the resident general, Marshal Louis Lyautey, who held office from 1912 to 1925. The period of Youssef's reign also witnessed several significant movements against colonial rule, the most important of which was that of Abd al-Karim (al-Khattabi) in the Rif region from 1919 to 1926.

See also FES, TREATY OF (1912); KHATTABI, MUHAMMAD IBN ABD AL-KARIM AL-; LYAUTEY, LOUIS-HUBERT GONZALVE.

Bibliography

Burke, Edmund, III. *Prelude to Protectorate in Morocco.* Chicago: University of Chicago Press, 1976.

Rinehart, Robert, et al. *Morocco: A Country Survey.* Washington, DC, 1985.

MATTHEW S. GORDON

YOUSSOUFI, ABDERRAHMANE
[1924–]

Moroccan prime minister, 1998–2002.

Abderrahmane Youssoufi was the first opposition politician to occupy the position of Moroccan prime minister since 1958. Born into a Berber- and French-speaking family from the international zone of Tangiers, Youssoufi joined the Istiqlal Party when it was founded in 1944. His European education led him to cultivate personal and ideological ties with Mehdi Ben Barka and the leftist wing of the Istiqlal. In 1959, along with Ben Barka, Youssoufi became one of the founders of the socialist-oriented National Union of Popular Forces (Union Nationale des Forces Populaires, UNFP). Arrested in 1963 during the first major wave of repression against leftist militants, he served eighteen months in prison for his alleged participation in a plot against the monarchy. Pardoned, he left Morocco after the murder of Ben Barka in 1965. During his fifteen-year exile in

France, Youssoufi was a particularly active advocate for human rights. He returned to Morocco in 1980, resumed political action within the Socialist Union of Popular Forces (Union Socialiste des Forces Populaires, USFP), which was created in 1975, and became its secretary-general in 1992. To enhance the credibility of the kingdom's reforms, Hassan II named Youssoufi prime minister in 1998. Youssoufi uneasily presided over a coalition government whose key ministries were reserved for the king's collaborators. Such restrictions limited Youssoufi's capacity to further the democratization process and to address social issues. Priority was given to the creation of a suitable environment for private investors, particularly through a campaign against the corruption of civil servants and court officials. Accused of lacking initiative and compromising with the palace, Youssoufi was replaced by Driss Jettou in November 2002.

See also BEN BARKA, MEHDI; HASSAN II; MOROCCO.

HENRI LAUZIÈRE

YOUTH ALIYAH

Organization that benefits immigrant youth in Israel.

Even before Hitler became Germany's chancellor in 1933, Youth Aliyah (in Hebrew, *Aliyat ha-Noar*), a project that brought Jewish children to Palestine and provided them with vocational training, had been established by Recha Freier in response to the deteriorating condition of Jews in Germany. It was organized in Palestine by Henrietta Szold, with the cooperation of the Jewish Agency, the Va'ad Le'umi (National Council), and the kibbutz movement. Originally, parents paid for their own children's transportation to Palestine and their room and board. For a number of years, British authorities did not count these children in the official immigration quota for Palestine.

During the mid-1930s the organization expanded its activities and rescued increasing numbers of children from Nazi Germany and later from Austria. Starting in 1939 with the outbreak of World War II, Youth Aliyah brought children from the battle zones to Great Britain, Scandinavia, Belgium, the Netherlands, and even Palestine (such as the Polish children called "the Tehran children," who traveled in 1943 via the Soviet Union and Iran). From 1945 to 1948, Youth Aliyah located orphaned children of the Holocaust and brought some 15,000 to Palestine as "illegals." With the establishment of the State of Israel in 1948, Youth Aliyah focused on rehabilitating needy immigrant children from countries of the Middle East and on helping adolescents in distress and/or in dire poverty. Youth Aliyah programs, mostly financed by the Jewish Agency, have helped integrate more than 300,000 children into Israeli society.

Bibliography

Chinitz, Zelig. *Common Agenda: The Reconstitution of the Jewish Agency for Israel.* Jerusalem: Jerusalem Center for Public Affairs, 1985.

Gelber, Yoav. "The Origins of Youth Aliya." *Zionism* 9 (1988): 147–172.

DONNA ROBINSON DIVINE

YOUTH MOVEMENTS

Social and political groupings and organizations formed for Middle Eastern adolescents and young adults.

Youth movements have played an important role in Middle Eastern politics and society. Until the late nineteenth century, the defense of neighborhoods was frequently ensured by *futuwwa* and other informal associations of young men operating as local militias. These "gangs" provided internal order and protection against outside threats and were often engaged in welfare and charitable activities; however, they sometimes preyed on the people instead.

Although in the twentieth century most of these groups disbanded, new kinds of youth movements developed that transcended residential loyalties. Between the two world wars, scouting and Young Men's Muslim associations made their appearance in many Middle Eastern countries. These nonpolitical youth groups frequently provided the nucleus from which full-fledged political movements developed. Initially, for example, the Muslim Brotherhood relied heavily on the scouting movement to spread its religious message.

In the 1930s, several Middle Eastern countries spawned right-wing paramilitary youth associations and sporting clubs that were inspired by Hitler's

Germany, Mussolini's Italy, and Franco's Spain. These intensely nationalistic groups recruited primarily among newly educated middle-class students disillusioned with Western-style liberal democracy. They drew their appeal from an admiration of fascist discipline, unity, militancy, organization, and power—and from the hope that Germany and Italy might eliminate Franco-British influence in the Middle East. Members of these groups wore uniforms and followed rituals patterned after those of the Hitler Youth and Franco's Falange. The Phalange party (al-Kata'ib) and the Helpers (al-Najjada), in Lebanon, and Young Egypt (Misr al-Fatat) developed out of such paramilitary groups. The youth groups called Betar, which played an influential role in the development of revisionist Zionism in Europe and in Palestine under the British mandate, were also influenced in their organization and methods by the fascist youth movements.

In Palestine, from 1922 until the early years of the State of Israel, youth movements affiliated with the major Zionist political parties, the National Religious party (NRP) and the Histadrut (Israeli Federation of Labor Unions), played key roles as vehicles of socialization and integration into the Zionist polity and as agents of elite recruitment. Ha-Halutz (The Pioneer), a Zionist farming organization, trained young European Jews to join the agricultural movement in Palestine. The role of the youth branches of Israel's major political parties declined after the mid-1950s, except for B'nei Akivah, the NRP's youth branch, whose regular expansion since 1960 has contributed to the growth of religious nationalism in Israel.

In other Middle Eastern countries, governments have tried to prevent the development of autonomous youth movements. In one-party regimes, the ruling party usually has its own youth section. The most developed example of this is probably the Federation of Iraqi Youth, attached to the Iraqi Ba'th party. Under the auspices of athletic and cultural activities, the federation (which is itself divided into several programs catering to specific age groups) tries to diffuse the party's views among Iraq's younger generation.

Throughout the region, youth movements fueled by rapid population growth have played a leading role in antiregime activities. Student activism

was a recurrent feature of political life in the 1970s and 1980s in countries as different as Morocco, Egypt, Lebanon, Iran, Turkey, Sudan, and Tunisia, where student associations sometimes joined forces with other social groups to participate in riots against the government. In particular, through a variety of Marxist and Islamic-leftist organizations, young people were actively involved in the 1979 downfall of the shah of Iran. More generally, the Islamic resurgence of the 1970s and 1980s has been primarily a movement of disaffected youth (particularly high school and university students of provincial origins and middle- and lower-middle-class backgrounds) who have organized themselves through informal religious associations.

Youth associations also contributed to the turmoil of the 1970s in Turkey, where the ultranationalist far-right National Action party used youth groups to spread its message and carry out its actions. Similarly, some of the organizational roots of the Intifada, the uprising of Palestinians that broke out in December 1987 in the Israeli-occupied territories, can be found in youth clubs formed in the 1970s and 1980s. These groups were initially created for cultural, social, and athletic activities, but they rapidly developed into a political movement of resistance to Israel's administration. Youth associations enabled a new generation—often the youth of Palestinian refugee camps, who had known only Israeli rule but who, unlike their elders, could no longer bear to live under such control and felt they had little to lose—to vent its anger, frustration, and hatred.

Middle Eastern youth movements also include scouting and Young Men's/Women's Christian associations in Egypt, Lebanon, Jordan, and the Israeli-ruled territories. In Israel, a Young Men's/Women's Hebrew Association is similar. In the 1970s, a Young Men's and a Young Women's Muslim Association were formed in the West Bank. Like scouting, these associations are concerned with organizing social, cultural, self-help, charitable, skill-training, and athletic activities.

See also FUTUWWA; MUSLIM BROTHERHOOD; PHALANGE; YOUNG EGYPT.

Bibliography

Mardin, Serif. "Youth and Violence in Turkey." *European Journal of Sociology* 19 (1978): 229–254.

El-Messiri, Sawsan. *Ibn al-Balad: A Concept of Egyptian Identity.* Leiden: Brill, 1978.

Munson, Henry. *Islam and Revolution in the Middle East.* New Haven, CT: Yale University Press, 1988.

Peretz, Don. *Intifada: The Palestinian Uprising.* Boulder, CO: Westview Press, 1990.

GUILAIN P. DENOEUX

YÜCEL, HASAN ALI
[1897–1961]

Turkish educator, publisher, and writer.

Born in Istanbul, Hasan Ali Yücel obtained a degree in philosophy from Istanbul University in 1921. After teaching philosophy for a few years, he worked in the new Republic of Turkey's education directorate and published poetry and books on Turkish literature in the late 1920s and 1930s. He also joined the Turkish language-reform movement and eventually became a protégé of Atatürk. Yücel served as minister of education between 1938 and 1946, when he became known as an active reformer and supervised the publication of hundreds of translations of world classics. He also fostered the development of Village Institutes, which trained local teachers. President İsmet İnönü promoted his strict and controversial language reforms in school text-books.

In 1946, Yücel was accused by retired general Fevzi Çakmak of harboring communists in the Village Institutes. Although Yücel's name was cleared by a libel suit, during the trial accusations by Islam's religious right—that he supported subversive literature—cast a pall of self-censorship over public debate, and his successor undid many of his reforms. In the 1950s, Yücel worked for a publishing house and returned to writing, producing poetry and books of prose on citizenship, England, and Cyprus.

Bibliography

Heyd, Uriel. *Language Reform in Modern Turkey.* Jerusalem: Israel Oriental Society, 1954.

ELIZABETH THOMPSON

YÜKSEK ÖĞRETIM KURULU (YOK)

The Turkish Council of Higher Education, a policy-making and planning body.

The Yüksek Öğretim Kurulu originally was established in 1973, but in 1975 Turkey's Constitutional Court found its mandate to be incompatible with academic freedom and in conflict with the administrative autonomy of the universities. However, constitutional amendments after the 1980 military coup enabled its resurrection. Since then it has served as a liaison among the state, government, and universities. Its primary functions are to coordinate all resources allocated to higher education and to regulate academic activities. Its chairperson and some of its members are directly appointed by the president of the republic. The remaining members are appointed by the president from among candidates nominated by the government, the chief of the general staff, and the university senates.

Both in 1973 and much more urgently in 1981, the bureaucratic-military elite felt the need to depoliticize higher education. To this end, YOK ended the tradition of individual university senates electing deans and rectors. Instead, YOK gives the president a list of candidates it deems appropriate. Many political party leaders criticize YOK as an antidemocratic organization that restrains academic freedom, both directly and indirectly. Since the mid-1960s, numerous pieces of proposed legislation have sought to curb YOK's authority to intervene in academic issues.

YOK sought to standardize higher education in the early 1980s by determining the curricula to be followed in all universities, and soon became the target of widespread protests. Its position on the practice of veiling on university campuses also met with vociferous criticism. In 1983, it introduced the first nationwide prohibition against female students attending classes and taking examinations while wearing the veil. The Parliament overruled this ban in 1988 with a law that allowed "the covering of the head and the body on the basis of religious faith," but this law was annulled by the Turkish Constitutional Court. When the escalating Islamist mobilization in the 1990s rendered secularism the most crucial issue, and YOK its most reliable vanguard, the Council's authoritarian decisions went unobjected to by the state elites, despite vehement social opposition.

With the pro-religious Justice and Development Party's accession to the government in November

2002, a proposal to reform YOK's mandate was reinvigorated. This proposal endorsed a maximum of four years of service for Council members and rectors; selection of the chairperson by the Council; appointment of rectors by the President upon the recommendations by the university senates; nullification of all disciplinary charges against the faculty and students; and pardoning of students that dropped out because of academic absence. In this respect, the proposal attempted to restrict the YOK's administrative powers and to restore educational rights to veiled students who had been dismissed from the university. Although almost all social groups agree on the democratization of YOK's mandate, the proposal is regarded, especially by secularists, as hastily prepared and as an attempt to expel its current chairperson, Kemal Gürüz, rather than to initiate real reform.

See also TURKEY.

Bibliography

Bollag, Burton. "Clash of Turkish Leaders Stalls Higher-Education Reform." *Chronicle of Higher Education* 48, no. 45 (July 19, 2002): A 35.

Özdalga, Elisabeth. *The Veiling Issue: Official Secularism, and Popular Islam in Modern Turkey.* Richmond, U.K.: Curzon Press, 1998.

YOK. Available from <http://www.yok.gov.tr/english/index_en.htm>.

I. METIN KUNT
UPDATED BY BURÇAK KESKIN-KOZAT

YUNIS JABIR, ABU BAKR
[1940–]

Libyan general.

A brigadier general and de facto chairman of the joint chiefs of staff, Abu Bakr Yunis Jabir was born in 1940. Educated at the military college in Benghazi, he was a classmate of Muammar al-Qaddafi and a founding member of the Free Unionist Officers movement. Yunis Jabir participated in the September 1969 coup that overthrew King Idris and was one of the original members of the Revolutionary Command Council (1969–1977). He has served the Qaddafi regime in a variety of military positions since 1969, most recently as chief military commander.

See also LIBYA; QADDAFI, MUAMMAR AL-; REVOLUTIONARY COMMAND COUNCIL (LIBYA).

Bibliography

El-Kikhia, Mansour O. *Libya's Qaddafi: The Politics of Contradiction.* Gainesville: University Press of Florida, 1997.

St John, Ronald Bruce. *Historical Dictionary of Libya,* 3d edition. Lanham, MD: Scarecrow Press, 1998.

RONALD BRUCE ST JOHN

YURDAKUL, MEHMET EMIN
[1869–1944]

Turkish poet and politician.

Known as the "national poet" for his patriotic verses (he published a famous collection in 1897, *Türkçe Şiirler*), Mehmet Emin Yurdakul was born in Istanbul during the Ottoman Empire, the son of a ship captain. He entered the civil service and was appointed governor of the Hijaz.

In 1912, Mehmet Emin was a founding member of Türk Ocaği (Turkish Hearth), and during World War I he joined the National Turkish party. After the war he became a member of parliament in the new Republic of Turkey, taking the surname Yurdakul (slave to the homeland). Although he was an admirer of Atatürk, Mehmet Emin expressed several disagreements with the ideology of the new government. His poetry, still memorized today by Turkish schoolchildren, was characterized by an unadorned style and unabashed praise for the Turkish nation.

Bibliography

Mitler, Louis. *Ottoman Turkish Writers: A Bibliographical Dictionary of Significant Figures in Pre-Republican Turkish Literature.* New York: P. Lang, 1988.

DAVID WALDNER

YUSUFIAN, BOGHOS
[1775–1844]

Armenian minister of commerce and foreign affairs in Egypt in the 1820s and 1830s.

Boghos Yusufian, better known as Boghos Bey, was born in İzmir to a family well connected to the Armenian merchant class involved with overseas commerce. He made his money in Egypt as a customs official and trader. He was skilled in languages and served the British as an interpreter in the campaign against the French. He was first hired by Muhammad Ali as an interpreter and rapidly progressed to the position of personal secretary. Consolidating his rule in Egypt, Muhammad Ali found in Boghos an instrument for pursuing policies independent of his Ottoman sovereigns. Having earned Muhammad Ali's trust during his service in the palace in Cairo, Boghos was made minister of commerce in 1826. He ran his office from Alexandria and proved an adept intermediary between Egyptian economic policy and European commercial interests. In a reorganization of the government in 1837, Muhammad Ali created the joint ministry of commerce and foreign affairs and appointed Boghos Bey head of the department, leading many foreigners to assume that Boghos was the "prime minister" of Egypt.

To help modernize the administration of the country and improve its economy, Muhammad Ali became a great patron of the Armenians. In his early bid for power in Egypt, Muhammad Ali, then a small tobacco merchant of no military repute, had found an Armenian, Yeghiazar Amira, who was willing to give him a loan. Muhammad Ali repaid Amira many times over. He also encouraged Armenian settlement in Egypt. With Boghos Bey as its leading figure, the Armenian community in Egypt grew from a few dozen to two thousand. Among them were many relatives of Boghos whom he had brought over from İzmir, including the Nubar and Abro families. Arakel Bey Nubar (1826–1859) followed in his uncle's footsteps and became Egypt's minister of commerce. Boghos Bey's more famous nephew, however, was Nubar Pasha, who served three terms as prime minister of Egypt in the last quarter of the nineteenth century. Dicran Pasha d'Abro was minister of foreign affairs in the 1890s.

Among his many assignments, Boghos had also been entrusted by Muhammad Ali with training new and capable administrators. Charged with sending the most promising to Europe for further education with the approval of the pasha, Boghos also sponsored the education of the sons of many Armenian merchants in the service of Muhammad Ali. Among them was his successor to the ministry of commerce and foreign affairs, Artin Chrakian (1804–1859), whom Muhammad Ali appointed upon Boghos's death. It is reported that Boghos Bey died a man of modest means, all his resources having been placed in the service of his master.

See also CHRAKIAN, ARTIN; MUHAMMAD ALI.

Bibliography

Adalian, Rouben. "The Armenian Colony of Egypt during the Reign of Muhammad Ali, 1805–1848." *Armenian Review* 33, no. 2 (1980): 115–144.

Sayyid-Marsot, Afaf Lutfi al-. *Egypt in the Reign of Muhammad Ali.* Cambridge, U.K., and New York: Cambridge University Press, 1984.

ROUBEN P. ADALIAN

YUSUF, YUSUF SALMAN
[1901–1949]

Secretary-general of Iraq's Communist party, 1941–1949.

Yusuf Salman Yusuf, known as Comrade Fahd, was a Chaldean Christian. He attended the KUTV in Moscow (1935–1937). On his return to Iraq in 1938, he became a member of the Central Committee of the Communist party; he became its secretary-general in 1941. In 1947 he was condemned to death, but the sentence was commuted to penal servitude. He ran the party from prison until his retrial and execution in February 1949.

MARION FAROUK-SLUGLETT

YZERNITSKY, YITZHAK
See SHAMIR, YITZHAK

ZAB RIVERS

Great Zab of Turkey and Iraq and Little Zab of Iran and Iraq; major tributaries of the Tigris river.

The Great Zab rises in the mountains of southeast Turkey and runs for 260 miles (420 km), flowing southwest into the Tigris below Mosul, Iraq. The Little Zab rises in the Zagros mountains and flows for about 230 miles (368 km) southwest into the Tigris, some 50 miles (80 km) below the Great Zab. Their violent seasonal spring flow contributes about half the flood crest of the Tigris.

Bibliography

Fisher, Sydney N. *The Middle East: A History,* 3d edition. New York: Knopf, 1979.

JOHN R. CLARK

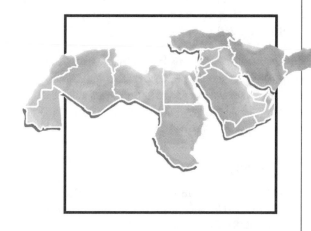

Z

ZABUL

Afghan province.

Zabul is the name of both a province in Afghanistan and an Iranian city. The Afghan province of Zabul is located in southeastern Afghanistan, bordering Pakistan on the south and the province of Kandahar on the west. Zabul province has a population of approximately 200,000, most of whom are Pushtun, though some Hazara live in the north. The provincial capital is Kalat, which lies along the main highway from Kabul to Kandahar. Zabul, which is famous for its almonds, is in a very dry and windy region, where agriculture is limited to a few irrigated valleys. The drought of the late 1990s and early 2000s hit this area particularly hard. Many of the tribes in Zabul province were strong supporters of the Taliban movement, and security remains problematic in this area.

The Iranian city of Zabul is in the Sistan-Baluchistan province and is situated near the Afghan border across from the Afghan city of Zaranj. The population of Zabul in 2001 was 126,000.

Bibliography

Adamec, Ludwig W. *Historical Dictionary of Afghanistan.* Metuchen, NJ: Scarecrow Press, 1991.

Iranian Statistical Year Book: 1380 (2001–2002). Tehran: Statistical Centre of Iran, 2002.

Rubin, Barnett R. *The Fragmentation of Afghanistan: State Formation and Collapse in the International System,* 2d edition. New Haven, CT: Yale University Press, 2002.

GRANT FARR

ZACH, NATAN
[1930–]

Israeli poet and critic.

Zach, one of the best known Israeli poets abroad, has been called "the most articulate and insistent spokesman of the modernist movement in Hebrew poetry." He had a profound influence on Israeli poetry and literature during the 1950s and 1960s. Zach was born in Berlin and emigrated to Palestine in 1935. He studied at the Hebrew University in Jerusalem and later at the University of Essex, England, where he wrote his doctoral dissertation. After returning to Israel, he lectured at Tel Aviv University and was later appointed professor at Haifa University. He also served as chairman of the repertoire board of two of Israel's leading theaters, the Ohel and the Cameri. In addition to his poems, Zach published critical essays and edited several literary publications. Nationally and internationally acclaimed, Zach was awarded the prestigious Bialik and Israel prizes as well as the Feronia Prize (Rome).

In 1967, together with the late Palestinian-Israeli poet Rashid Husayn, he assembled and translated the first collection of Palestinian folk poems. Individual poems of his have been published in Afrikaans, Arabic, Czech, Dutch, English, Estonian, French, German, Greek, Hungarian, Italian, Japanese, Polish, Portuguese, Russian, Serbo Croatian, Spanish, Yiddish, and Vietnamese.

One of Zach's most instrumental contributions to the national literature was his conscious rejection of the national symbolism and ethnic sentimentality of mainstream Israeli poetry prior to 1948. Zach's early poems, *First Poems* and *Different Poems* (in Hebrew), exhibit a marked disassociation with the specifics of time and place, expressing instead the voice of the individual. Through emphasizing the more morbid aspects of human existence, Zach sought to undermine both the form and content of traditional Is-

raeli poetry. To achieve that, he introduced new and unique poetic forms into Hebrew, including rhythm, rhyme, language, and metaphor. Other hallmarks of Zach's poetry are its intellectual detachment, emotional restraint, and subtle irony, all of which are employed against the excessive sentimentality and pathos of his predecessors. Zach influenced Hebrew poetry as well through his articulate and vociferous writings on its behalf. He published numerous essays promoting his modernist literary agenda both as a critic and as literary editor.

Zach's publications (in Hebrew) include *First Poems* (1955), *Other Poems* (1960), *All the Milk and Honey* (1966), *Northeasterly* (1979), *Anti-erasure* (1984), *Dog and Bitch Poems* (1990), *Because I'm Around* (1996), and *Death of My Mother* (1997).

Bibliography

Negev, Eilat, with an introduction by Risa Domb. *Close Encounters with Twenty Israeli Writers.* London and Portland, OR: Vallentine Mitchell, 2003.

YARON PELEG
UPDATED BY ADINA FRIEDMAN

ZAGHLUL, SA'D
[1857–1927]

Egyptian nationalist and leader of the Wafd, the nationalist party founded in Egypt in 1919.

A lawyer by profession, Sa'd Zaghlul served as Egypt's minister of education (1906), earning the praise of Lord Cromer. As vice-president of the Legislative Assembly (1913), Zaghlul attracted attention with his charismatic oratory. His wife, Safia, known in Egypt as "Mother of the People," was the daughter of Egypt's wealthy and pro-British prime minister, Mustafa Fahmi.

After World War I, Zaghlul led a delegation (Arabic, *wafd*) to Cairo to ask Britain's High Commissioner Reginald Wingate for permission to argue the case for Egypt's independence directly before the British government in London. Britain refused and in 1919 deported Zaghlul and other leading members of the wafd to Malta. The deportations precipitated the 1919 uprisings, when Egyptians of all classes, throughout the nation, boycotted British goods and sometimes violently attacked British installations and personnel. In an attempt to halt the rioting, the British reluctantly permitted Zaghlul and others to present the Egyptian nationalist case to the great powers attending the Paris Peace Settlements.

Although he enjoyed the support of the vast majority of Egyptians, Zaghlul failed to achieve independence from the British in these and subsequent negotiations. When he continued to demand the abolition of the protectorate over Egypt and nationalist agitation increased, the British deported Zaghlul again in 1921. The deportations only strengthened the Wafd and contributed to Zaghlul's popularity.

After the British had unilaterally declared the independence of Egypt in 1922 and King Fu'ad had signed the new constitution in 1923, Zaghlul was permitted to return to Egypt where he promptly resumed leadership of the Wafdist nationalist forces. Following the Wafd's overwhelming victory in free elections, Zaghlul became prime minister in 1924.

Zaghlul's triumph was short-lived, for in November 1924 Sir Lee Stack, *sirdar* (commander in chief of the Egyptian army) and governor-general of the Sudan, was assassinated while visiting Cairo. The assassination, coupled with Britain's demands for apologies and reparations, precipitated a government crisis and forced Zaghlul's resignation. Although Zaghlul remained the most popular Egyptian leader, he was prevented by the British from becoming prime minister in subsequent governments. In 1927, he died quietly in his home.

See also PARIS PEACE SETTLEMENTS (1918–1923); WAFD.

JANICE J. TERRY

ZAGROS

Mountain range in Iran.

The Zagros mountain range is the largest in Iran, stretching for 1,400 miles (2,253 km) from Armenia in the former U.S.S.R. in the northwest to the Persian Gulf in the south, and thence eastward to Baluchistan. It consists of a number of parallel ranges, the highest peak of which rises to 14,000 feet (4,270 m). It separates the Iranian plateau from the plains of Mesopotamia and Iraq in the west and the Persian Gulf in the south. Together with the Elburz (also known as Alborz) ranges in the north, the Zagros was formed from the Paleozoic to the Pliocene period.

Bibliography

Wilber, Donald N. *Iran: Past and Present—From Monarchy to Islamic Republic,* 9th edition. Princeton, NJ: Princeton University Press, 1981.

PARVANEH POURSHARIATI

ZAHAWI, JAMIL SIDQI AL-
[1863–1936]

Prominent Iraqi poet, philosopher, and educator, known for his defense of women's rights.

Jamil Sidqi al-Zahawi was born in Baghdad. During the Ottoman era, he held numerous positions: as a member of the Baghdad education council, where he championed education for women; as editor of the only newspaper in Baghdad, *al-Zawra*; as a member of the Supreme Court in Yemen and in Istanbul; as a professor of Islamic philosophy at the Royal University; and as a professor of literature at the College of Arts in Istanbul. After Iraq's independence in 1921, he was elected to parliament twice and appointed to the upper chamber for one term.

He was one of the leading writers in the Arab world, publishing in the major newspapers and journals of Beirut, Cairo, and Baghdad. Describing his life in a collection of his poems, he wrote, "In my childhood I was thought of as eccentric because of my unusual gestures; in my youth, as feckless because of my ebullient nature, lack of seriousness, and excessive playfulness; in my middle age as courageous for my resistance to tyranny; and in my old age as an apostate because I propounded my philosophical views" (Najim, p. 173, translated by author). In the 1930s, because of his political views, he was marginalized by the political establishment.

See also GENDER: GENDER AND EDUCATION; IRAQ.

Bibliography

Najim, Mohammed Yusif, editor. *Diwan Jamil Sidqi al-Zahawi,* Vol. 1. Beirut: Dar al-Kitab al-Arabi, 1971.

JACQUELINE ISMAEL

ZAHEDAN

Main city of southeastern Iran and administrative center of Sistan and Baluchistan province.

Zahedan occupies an upland plateau (4,718 ft./ 1,438 m in elevation) north of Mount Taftan, an active volcano in southeast Iran. It is just south of the area where the borders of Afghanistan, Iran, and Pakistan meet and 60 miles (96 km) northwest of Mirjaveh, the Iranian customs and passport control checkpoint on the border with Pakistan. Zahedan is a modern city that developed in the twentieth century. During the nineteenth century, the agricultural village of Duzhab occupied the site, one of the few areas in extremely arid Baluchistan with adequate groundwater for irrigated cultivation. During World War I, when Pakistan was part of British India, the British extended the imperial railway from Calcutta to Quetta westward to Duzhab. Later, during the reign of Reza Shah Pahlavi (r. 1926–1941), the village was officially renamed Zahedan after the medieval capital of Sistan, which had been destroyed by the Mongols, and the administrative center for Sistan and Baluchistan was moved here from Khash.

Zahedan had developed into a small town of 17,500 inhabitants by 1956. After Iran and Pakistan joined the U.S.-sponsored Central Treaty Organization in 1958, Zahedan, as a frontier town, became a site for military facilities and related infrastructure projects that spurred rapid growth. By 1976 the population had quintupled to 93,740. However, the ethnic composition of the population also changed, from a majority of local Baluchis and Persian-speaking Sistanis to a majority of migrants from the central areas of Iran. In the 1980s thousands of refugees from Afghanistan resettled in the city. By 1996 Zahedan's population had reached 419,500.

Population growth has spurred the establishment of small and medium-size businesses, including cotton textile manufacturing, woven and knotted carpet production, reed mat and basket making, leather processing, food processing, livestock feed production, ceramics, brick kilns, and grain milling. Zahedan is a large market for foreign goods, a significant proportion of which are smuggled over the border with Pakistan. Zahedan also is believed to be a major center for the illegal processing of opium—smuggled into Iran from Afghanistan and Pakistan—into illicit narcotics.

See also BALUCHIS; CENTRAL TREATY ORGANIZATION (CENTO); SISTAN AND BALUCHISTAN.

ERIC HOOGLUND

ZAHIR SHAH
[1914–]

King of Afghanistan, 1933–1973.

Born in Kabul, the capital of Afghanistan, Zahir attended Habibia and Istiqlal schools (1920–1924), then accompanied his father, Mohammad Nadir Khan, to France, where he continued his studies. Zahir's father was the second eldest and most influential of five Musahiban brothers, members of the Muhammadzai royal clan of the Barakzai Pashtun tribe, who enjoyed considerable power in court during the 1910s and 1920s. During the turbulent rule of the modernizing King Amanullah Barakzai (1919–1929), the Musahiban brothers fell into disfavor. In 1929, when popular rebellions forced Amanullah's abdication, followed by a nine-month interregnum of rule by a rural Tajik, Amir Habibullah, Zahir's father returned to eastern Afghanistan from France. With assistance from the British in India, Pashtun tribesmen, and religious leaders, Nadir Khan claimed the Afghan throne, declaring himself Muhammad Nadir Shah on 15 October 1929—thereby establishing the Musahiban dynasty.

Zahir returned to Kabul in October 1930 and attended the Infantry Officers School for one year. In 1931, he married the daughter of Ahmad Shah, a court minister. The only surviving son of Nadir Shah, Crown Prince Zahir at age seventeen was appointed assistant war minister (1932), then minister of education (1933). On 8 November 1933, following the assassination of his father, he was proclaimed King Mohammad Zahir Shah, with the religious title al-Mutawakkil ala Allah (he who puts his faith in Allah). To ensure the continuation of Musahiban rule, his accession to the throne was unopposed by his three surviving uncles. For the next thirty years, Zahir Shah simply reigned while two of his strong-willed and autocratic uncles held actual power as prime ministers—Sardar (Prince) Muhammad Hashim Khan (1933–1947) and Sardar Shah

Mahmud Khan (1947–1953), followed by Zahir Shah's cousin and brother-in-law, the dictatorial prime minister Sardar Muhammad Daud (1953–1963). During this period, although Afghanistan was officially a constitutional monarchy, power and decision making were monopolized by a few elder members of the Musahiban oligarchy; they maintained family unity through intermarriage, assuring continuation of their rule by stifling liberal expression and political freedoms with an oppressive police state.

Following a rift with Daud and his resignation as prime minister, Zahir Shah took power into his own hands in 1963 by appointing a nonrelative as prime minister. He then launched his program of Demokrasy-i Now (New Democracy)—a period of experimentation with democratic liberalization that lasted for a decade. During this decade, he encouraged the development of a new liberal constitution, supported relatively free elections, extended freedom of the press, and tolerated the formation of many political movements with diverse orientations. Indecisiveness and inaction on the passage of legislation governing political parties and his inability to prevent government interference by family members and friends undermined the democratic experiments. In 1973, while receiving medical treatment in Europe, Zahir Shah was overthrown in a military coup led by his paternal cousin (and sister's husband), Daud. Zahir Shah remained in foreign exile in Italy with his family, and Daud established a republic.

Zahir Shah is considered a mild-mannered, soft-spoken kindly gentleman who lacks energy and is devoid of initiative. He abdicated his throne and passively watched the people's struggles opposing Soviet occupation, communist rule, and civil strife that began in Afghanistan in 1978. Zahir Shah's written statement welcoming the initial fall of Mazar-e Sharif to Taliban in 1997 deeply saddened the peoples of northern Afghanistan. However, some of his former associates and officials also living in exile advocate his return to Afghanistan and possible restoration of the monarchy especially after the fall of the Marxist regime in 1992 and again after the fall of the Taliban regime in 2001. One of Zahir Shah's delegates to the Bonne Conference (December 2001), Hamid Karzai, was appointed chairperson of the interim post-Taliban govern-

Zahir Shah in his residence in Rome, 2001. Zahir was the last king of Afghanistan, reigning from 1933 until he was deposed in a bloodless coup in 1973. After more than 25 years in exile, he acquired a reputation as an elder statesman and was given the symbolic title "Father of the Nation" upon his return in 2002. © REUTERS NEWMEDIA INC./CORBIS. REPRODUCED BY PERMISSION.

ment. In April 2002 he ended his exile in Rome and returned to his palace in Kabul, renouncing all claims to the throne. The emergency Loya Jerga of June 2002, which he officially opened, gave him the title of "Father of the Nation." His title was reaffirmed by the Constitutional Loya Jerga of December 2003.

Bibliography

Dupree, Louis. *Afghanistan*. Princeton, NJ: Princeton University Press, 1980.

Shahrani, M. Nazif. "State Building and Social Fragmentation in Afghanistan: A Historical Perspective." In *The State, Religion, and Ethnic Politics: Afghanistan, Iran, and Pakistan,* edited by Ali Banuazizi and Myron Weiner. Syracuse, NY: Syracuse University Press, 1986.

M. NAZIF SHAHRANI
UPDATED BY ERIC HOOGLUND

ZAHLA

The capital of Lebanon's Biqa valley and the center of its economic activity.

Under the mandate, Zahla (also Zahleh) was a small town growing silkworms for export to France; it has developed into a major economic hub for the Biqa Valley, with a population of 55,000 (2002). The city's geographic location makes it an important station for commercial trucks coming into or leaving Lebanon. Zahla's main economic activity centers around the farming and poultry industries.

See also BIQA VALLEY.

GEORGE E. IRANI

ZAʿIM

See GLOSSARY

ZAʿIM, HUSNI AL-
[1894–1949]

Syrian military officer and politician.

Born in Aleppo to a Kurdish business family, Husni al-Zaʿim was captured by the British while serving in the Ottoman army and later joined the Troupes Spéciales in the French Mandate forces. Promoted to lieutenant colonel in 1941, he was charged with embezzlement by the Vichy government and was later arrested by the Free French. He was promoted from director of public security to chief of staff of the army in May 1948. As a precursor to his coup d'état, al-Zaʿim defied President Shukri al-Quwatli's order to arrest Col. Antoine Bustani, the scapegoat of a minor scandal, and gave him a position in the defense ministry instead. In the spring of 1949, Colonel al-Zaʿim overthrew the government of Khalid al-Azm and arrested President al-Quwatli.

Encouraged by the local representatives of U.S. intelligence in Damascus, and supported by the future Syrian president Adib Shishakli, the Zaʿim coup marked the first comprehensive takeover by the military in regional politics. The Syrian military would never be far from control of the political institutions. Al-Zaʿim's short rule sought to forcibly strip many traditional customs that appeared to in-

hibit progress. He even tried to explore the possibility of achieving a peace agreement with Israel. But his inconsistent foreign and domestic policy cost him the support of neighboring Arab regimes and of Syrian public opinion. His regime was overthrown on 14 August 1949 by Sami al-Hinnawi, and al-Zaʿim was executed. It is believed that Zaʿim paid with his life for his betrayal of Antun Saʿada, the leader of the Syrian Social Nationalist Party, whom al-Zaʿim backed at first but then handed over to the Lebanese authorities, who sentenced him to death in July 1949.

See also SAʿADA, ANTUN.

Bibliography

Rathmell, Andrew. *Secret War in the Middle East: The Covert Struggle for Syria, 1949–1961.* New York; London: I. B. Tauris, 1995.

Seale, Patrick. *The Struggle for Syria: A Study of Post-War Arab Politics, 1945–1958.* London: I. B. Tauris, 1986.

CHARLES U. ZENZIE
UPDATED BY EYAL ZISSER

ZAKAT

See GLOSSARY

ZAMIR, ZVI

See MOSSAD

ZAMZAM

The famous well of Mecca.

According to Muslim legend, Zamzam was opened by the angel Gabriel to provide for Hagar and Ismaʿil, who were in danger of dying of thirst after Abraham deposited them in what was then an unpopulated desert valley. History suggests that it was the coexistence of this well and the adjacent shrine (Kaʿba) that led to the emergence of Mecca as an important commercial and cultural center in pre-Islamic Arabia. For centuries Muslims have cherished the brackish water of Zamzam as sacred and have sought to benefit from its reputed blessings. To this day, pilgrims to the Meccan sanctuary descend the enclosed staircase to the well and either draw water for themselves to drink, or bottle it and take it home for a relative or friend who is ill.

See also KAʿBA.

SCOTT ALEXANDER

ZANA, LEYLA
[1961–]

Kurdish member of Turkey's parliament sentenced to jail for defending the rights of the Kurdish people.

Leyla Zana was born in 1961 in a Kurdish village near the town of Silvan in eastern Turkey. When she was fourteen her father married her to his cousin, Mehdi Zana, a political activist. In 1976 the couple moved to the Kurdish city of Diyarbakir, where Mehdi was elected mayor a year later. Arrested during the 1980 military coup d'état, he was sentenced to thirty years in prison.

Defending the rights of her husband as a political prisoner, Zana became an activist, and organized other women visiting their jailed family members. Meanwhile, she studied on her own, obtained a high school diploma, and engaged in journalistic and human rights activism, which led to her arrest in 1988.

In 1991 she became the first Kurdish woman elected to the parliament, and the first to break the ban on speaking in Kurdish in the parliament. She advocated in her native tongue for fraternal relations between Kurdish and Turkish peoples. Declared a "separatist," "traitor," and member of an illegal party, she was tried, convicted, and sentenced to fifteen years in jail in 1994. Since her imprisonment she has received several peace awards, including the European Parliament's Sakharov Prize for Freedom of Thought, and was nominated for a Nobel Peace Prize. In 1998 she was sentenced to two more years in jail for writing an article about the Kurdish new year (*Newroz*). In April 2003, a retrial convened under pressure from the European Union (which Turkey aspires to join) did not lead to her release.

Bibliography

Leyla Zana. Directed by Kudret Güneş. Artefilm, 2002.

Zana, Leyla. *Writings from Prison,* translated by Kendal Nezan and Harriet Lutzky. Watertown, MA: Blue Crane Books, 1999.

SHAHRZAD MOJAB

ZANAN MAGAZINE

An independent Iranian women's magazine.

The first issue of the monthly magazine *Zanan* (Women) appeared in February 1992 under the editorship and management of Shahla Sherkat. Fired after ten years of working in the editorial board of *Zan-i Ruz* (Today's woman) because of her "growing modernist, Western, and feminist tendencies" (Sherkat, 2003, p.4), Sherkat launched *Zanan* as an independent feminist journal. Although initially produced in a small room borrowed from the office of *Kian,* a reform-oriented journal, and with limited resources and the cooperation of only a couple of journalists, *Zanan* has grown into a professionally produced magazine with about thirty staff members and several freelance contributors; it has its office in an independent office building. *Zanan*'s survival (104 issues published as of December 2003) against financial odds and political pressures is a remarkable record of success in the history of Iran's usually short-lived independent publications in general and of its women's publications in particular.

Zanan represents a gradual shift among numerous Muslim women activists from radical Islamism or conservative patriarchal traditionalism to a liberal spiritualism and modernist egalitarian reformism that is described by some as Islamic feminism. This evolution, occurring within the context of widespread ideological disillusionment with militant and totalitarian Islamism, represents the gender dimension of a growing reform movement toward democracy, pluralism, secularism, and civil rights in Iranian society at large.

Zanan has played a pioneering role in Islamic women's rethinking of gender and reconstruction of womanhood. With significant contributions by Muslim feminist theologians such as Seyyed Mohsen Saʿidzadeh and secular lawyers such as Mehrangiz Kar, *Zanan* began challenging the patriarchal presuppositions that have shaped the dominant interpretations of Islam and the construction of *shariʿa* law and policy concerning women's rights, male-female relationships, sexual mores, and gender roles under the Islamic Republic of Iran.

Believing that *ijtihad* (reasoning from faith) is an obligation of every responsible adult, *Zanan* has expanded the domain of modern Islamic interpretation. It has embarked on a thorough and radical project aimed at "decentering the clergy and placing woman as interpreter and her needs as ground for interpretation" (Najmabadi, 1998, p. 71).

Zanan's agenda has not been limited to the reinterpretation of the Islamic canon. Each issue includes sections addressing social problems and contentious issues; theoretical debates, interviews, and cultural studies; critique of law and legal advice; feminist critique of literature and films; health issues, sports, and leisure; and new books and news. It also carries advertisements, which are not always free of stereotypical marketing techniques geared toward modern homemakers. Some *Zanan*'s writers, especially the younger ones such as Parastu Dokoohaki, Shadi Sadr, and Roya Karimi-Majd, have produced courageous and provocative reports highlighting not only oppressive and sexist traditions but also modern social ills affecting girls and the younger generation of women, including poverty, prostitution, drug abuse, addiction, and violence. Although it is circulated in different parts of Iran and in some diaspora circles, *Zanan*'s readers are primarily in the modern middle class and for the most part are middle-aged urban women.

In the 1997 presidential elections and the subsequent parliamentary elections, *Zanan* played a considerable role in mobilizing women's votes for Mohammad Khatami and moderate candidates for the Iranian parliament, the majlis. Yet through its critical monthly reports on the works of the majlis deputies and the policies of Khatami's government, and especially through challenging interviews and panel discussions, *Zanan* also took the reformers to task by highlighting their shortcomings and failures to safeguard women's rights and achieve progress on gender issues.

Adopting a nonviolent, spiritual, Sufi-like language in its editorials, *Zanan* has emphasized "autonomy and choice as the first pillar of freedom" (Sherkat, 1992, pp. 2–3). By inviting contributions from Iranian secular and Islamic feminists, living inside as well as outside the country, *Zanan* has provided a nonsectarian and inclusive forum for dialogue between secular and faith-based feminists. Its openness, however, is constrained by censorship as well as by the ideological and political constraints imposed by the regime. By introducing feminist theories, reports on women's status and movements

in other parts of the world, and translations of Western feminist literature, *Zanan* has avoided a reactive gender conservatism and a phobia about Western ideas, weaving textual, artistic, and intellectual connections between Muslim women and Western feminism. *Zanan* has altered the terms of the debate and dialogue not only among Islamic women activists, but also between Islamic and secular feminists.

See also KAR, MEHRANGIZ; SA'IDZADEH, SEYYED MOHSEN; *SHARI'A*.

Bibliography

Karimian, Ramim, and Bahrampour, Sha'banali. "Iranian Press Update." Middle East Report no. 212 (fall 1999). Available from <http://www.merip.org/mer/mer212/212_press-update.html>.

Najmabadi, Afsaneh. "Feminism in an Islamic Republic: 'Years of Hardship, Years of Growth.'" In *Islam, Gender, and Social Change*, edited by Y. Y. Haddad and J. L. Esposito. New York: Oxford University Press, 1998.

Tohidi, Nayereh. *Globalization, Gender, and Religion: The Politics of Women's Rights in Catholic and Muslim Contexts*, edited by Jane H. Bayes and Nayereh Tohidi. New York: Palgrave, 2001.

NAYEREH TOHIDI

ZAN-E RUZ

See NEWSPAPERS AND PRINT MEDIA: IRAN

ZANGWILL, ISRAEL
[1864–1926]

British novelist and playwright; early Zionist.

Israel Zangwill was a sophisticated British wit whose reputation was established with his novel *Children of the Ghetto* (1892), which depicted Jewish immigrant life in the East London ghetto. He joined in the Zionist cause of Theodor Herzl in 1895, arranging for Herzl a series of community meetings with prominent members of English Jewish society. He introduced Herzl to the Maccabeans, a society of Jewish authors, artists, and professionals, and helped organize the Maccabean Pilgrimage to Palestine in 1897. He also helped and employed the wandering Hebrew poet Naphtali Herz Imber, author of the

Zionist anthem "Hatikvah," during his stay in England (1889–1892) and made him famous as a character in his writings.

During the period of the Uganda Project, Zangwill founded and led the Jewish Territorial Organization for the Settlement of the Jews within the British Empire (1905–1925); it pursued the possibility of an East African province for a Jewish settlement, a so-called provincial Palestine. Zangwill felt that "any territory which was Jewish [and] under a Jewish flag, saves the Jew's body and the Jew's soul." Many Zionists broke with him over this issue, since his group did not acknowledge any organic connection between Zionism and Palestine.

During the early 1900s, Zangwill scored tremendous success as a playwright in England and in the United States. He also continued to write novels and produced his last play, *We Moderns* (1924), in New York City.

See also HERZL, THEODOR; UGANDA PROJECT.

Bibliography

Laqueur, Walter. *A History of Zionism.* New York: Holt, Rinehart, 1972.

Vital, David. *The Origins of Zionism.* Oxford: Clarendon Press, 1975.

Vital, David. *Zionism, the Formative Years.* Oxford: Clarendon Press, 1982.

MIRIAM SIMON

ZANZIBAR

Islands and coastal land in East Africa.

From the tenth century, many Arabs emigrated to Zanzibar, the 640-square-mile (1,658 sq. km) island of that name (also neighboring islands and the adjacent coast of East Africa). In 1698 Oman seized Zanzibar from the Portuguese, and in 1841 Oman's ruler, Shaykh Sayyid Sa'id, permanently moved his capital there from Muscat. Wealthy Omanis established an extensive plantation economy centered on clove production using African slave labor. After Sa'id's death in 1856, contention between his sons led to Britain's Canning Award (1861), splitting Oman and Zanzibar into separate sultanates. The latter declined, partly because of British suppression of the slave trade in 1873, and became a British protectorate in 1890.

Following Zanzibar's independence (1963) and union with Tanganyika (1964), the Arab population was severely mistreated by the Africans. Several thousand emigrated, mostly to the capital area of Muscat in Oman, after the accession of Sultan Qabus in 1970. In Zanzibar in 2000 and 2001, political tensions and violence followed elections that observers denounced as irregular. The major political parties signed an agreement in October 2001 calling for electoral reforms.

Bibliography

Bennett, Norman R. *A History of the Arab State of Zanzibar.* London: Methuen, 1978.

MALCOLM C. PECK

ZAQAZIQ UNIVERSITY

University in the eastern Nile delta.

Zaqaziq University was founded in 1974 in Zaqaziq, the capital of the eastern Nile delta province of Sharqiyya, from branch faculties of Ain Shams University in Cairo. In 2001, on its main campuses in Zaqaziq and its branch campus at Banha, the university had nearly 6,000 teaching staff and assistants and 146,816 students.

See also AIN SHAMS UNIVERSITY.

Bibliography

The World of Learning 2004. London: Europa Publications, 2004.

DONALD MALCOLM REID

ZARANIQ CONFEDERATION

Tribal grouping on North Yemen's largely nontribal coastal desert, the Tihama.

The Zaraniq, the largest and most formidable tribal grouping of the Tihama, stood in the way of efforts by Imam Yahya to extend control of the imamate state and were compelled to submit to the imam only after a savage two-year campaign in the late 1920s. An important part of the history of the Tihama for many centuries, the Zaraniq were known in the past as the Maʿaziba tribe and, like other tribes on the Tihama, claimed descent from the Akk tribe.

See also YAHYA IBN MUHAMMAD HAMID AL-DIN.

ROBERT D. BURROWES

ZARQA, AL-

Jordanian city.

Lying some 14 miles (23 km) northeast of Jordan's capital, Amman, al-Zarqa is Jordan's second-largest city (pop. 421,000 in 2002). The village witnessed tremendous growth beginning in the 1950s through the presence of a major military base, the development of industry and a free trade zone, and the influx of Palestinian refugees (who constitute some 60 to 70 percent of the population).

ABLA M. AMAWI

ZAWIYA

See GLOSSARY

ZAYDAN, JURJI
[1861–1914]

Early pan-Arab nationalist, author, and publisher.

Jurji Zaydan (also spelled Gurgi Zaidan) was born into a poor Greek Orthodox family in Beirut and, through self-education, obtained entry to the Syrian Protestant College in 1881. After a year in the medical school, he participated in a student strike and was expelled. As did many of his contemporaries, he went to Cairo, where he embarked on a career as a journalist, publisher, novelist, scholar, and pronationalist intellectual. He was a major contributor to Arab literature. During the thirty years of his life in Cairo, he produced twenty-one historical novels dealing with Arab history; a five-volume history of Islamic civilization (*Tarikh al-Tamaddun al-Islami,* Cairo, 1901–1906); a four-volume history of Arabic literature (*Tarikh Adab al-Lugha al-Arabiyya,* Cairo, 1910–1913); and a dozen other books on history, language, and literature. In 1892, he founded the magazine *al-Hilal,* which he authored, published, and distributed for the next twenty-two years practically single-handedly. With *al-Muqtataf,* it became the most important forum of the Arab Nahda (Re-naissance) for the discussion of history, nationalism, secularism, modern sciences, and political institutions. In addition, Zaydan was also the author of the first autobiography in Arabic, *Mudhakkirat Jurji Zaydan.*

At the end of the nineteenth century the European presence in the Middle East became ubiquitous and overwhelming in all its cultural, intellectual, political, and economic aspects. The task of the Arab intellectual was to respond to a twofold challenge: to adapt to life in the modern Europe-dominated world while continuing to assert the independent identity and viability of Arab society. It was exactly this twofold challenge that Zaydan made his life task to tackle. Less the political activist than the educator of the nation, he aimed at informing his Arab compatriots about the modern world as well as about their own past and national identity. Even as he familiarized his Arab readers with modern Europe and introduced them to European thought, he established the foundations for a pan-Arab national identity. He was the first to try in a scholarly and systematic fashion to reconstruct a history of the Arabs separate from Islamic history. By incorporating pre-Islamic Arabian and even Babylonian history into Arab history, Islam became only one phase. This perspective also made possible a future for the Arab nation independent from Islam. On the popular level, he tried to spread this idea along with national identity through his historical novels—a genre that he introduced to Arabic literature.

In addition to history, language assumed a central place in Zaydan's thinking. It was the symbol of national identity, a means of achieving such identity, and an expression of one's national culture and heritage. For him, the vitality of the language meant the viability of the nation. Drawing on concepts of evolution and progress, he attacked the classicist ideal and the religious rigor of archaic literary Arabic and insisted that developments and changes in the language were positive, proving its vitality. Especially through his magazine, *al-Hilal,* he contributed greatly to the simplification in style of formal literary Arabic and popularized new terms and concepts that reflected modern thought and knowledge.

His unceasing and successful effort to establish an Arab national identity defined by history and language created the foundations of political pan-Arab nationalism as it arose after the collapse of the Ottoman Empire.

Bibliography

Philipp, Thomas. *Gurgi Zaidan: His Life and Thought.* Wiesbaden, Germany: Steiner, 1979.

Zaydan, Jurji. *The Autobiography of Jurji Zaidan,* edited and translated by Thomas Philipp. Washington, DC: Three Continents Press, 1990.

THOMAS PHILIPP

ZAYDISM

The sect of Shiʿite Islam that prevails in the northern highlands of North Yemen and the political system that has existed to defend and advance that sect almost continuously since the late ninth century.

The Zaydi sect takes its name from Zayd ibn Ali Zayn al-Abidin, the fifth Shiʿite imam and the grandson of Husayn, who was one of the two sons of Ali and Fatima, the cousin and daughter of the prophet Muhammad. (Because Zayd was the fifth imam, Zaydis are sometimes called Fiver Shiʿa.) The doctrine of the sect as developed by Zayd and his followers was pragmatic, rational, and open to extension by critical examination and interpretation; and it rejected such features of other Shiʿite sects as the ideas of a "hidden" imam, an occult explanation of the Qurʾan, systematic dissimulation, and mysticism. Often referred to as the "fifth school" of Sunni Islam, Zaydism differs from Sunni orthodoxy primarily in its insistence on the institution of the imamate and the right of the descendants of Ali and Fatima to rule the world of Islam through that religio-political institution.

The founder of the Zaydi imamate in Yemen was al-Hadi ila al-Haqq Yahya ibn Husayn. He did so in the year 897 after being invited by tribes in the area around Saʿda to come from his native Medina to mediate their disputes and govern them. Al-Hadi's fourteen-year reign established in the highlands of North Yemen the Zaydi imamate, a state and political system that was to persist with numerous changes of fortune and breaks in continuity for over one thousand years into the 1960s, all the while maintaining many of the features that he and his immediate successors had decreed for it.

The strong imams of the first decades of the twentieth century, Imam Yahya and his son, Imam Ahmad ibn Yahya, served as the spiritual leaders, temporal rulers, and defenders of the community of Islam much as had their predecessors a millennium earlier. The Zaydi imamate was abolished on the occasion of the 1962 revolution that created the Yemen Arab Republic, but northern Yemen, and Saʿda in particular, is still known for its Zaydi population.

See also AHMAD IBN YAHYA HAMID AL-DIN; QURʾAN; YAHYA IBN MUHAMMAD HAMID AL-DIN.

Bibliography

Halliday, Fred. *Nation and Religion in the Middle East.* Boulder, CO: Lynne Rienner Publishers, 2000.

Serjeant, R. B. *Society and Trade in South Arabia,* edited by G. Rex Smith. Brookfield, VT: Variorum, 1996.

ROBERT D. BURROWES

ZAYTUNA UNIVERSITY

Prominent university in Tunis.

Built as a mosque in the eighth century, Zaytuna was enlarged by the Aghlabids in 864 when the Abbasid caliph al-Muʿtasim ordered the addition of a wing. It continues to serve as a school mosque and houses a huge library that in the fourteenth century was administered by the Malikite theologian Muhammad ibn Arafa. One of Zaytuna's students was Abd al-Rahman ibn Khaldun, the well-known Arab historian and philosopher. In modern times alumni include the leader of the Tunisian Destour party, Abd al-Aziz Thaʿlabi. In addition many Zaytuna graduates staffed the cadres of the Neo-Destour party.

Although at first traditional, teaching at Zaytuna was gradually modernized. The last reform came in 1933, at the hands of its students. Upon Tunisia's independence the Zaytuna became the *shariʿa* (Islamic law) school of the University of Tunis.

In 1945, Zaytuna had five branches in various cities of Tunisia and three thousand students in the secondary and college levels combined. The regional branches were not very active, and their ties with Tunis were very weak. With the appointment of al-Taher ben Ashour as the director of Zaytuna, new branches were opened in Tunisia and even in Algeria, raising their number to twenty-five. All became very active. The number of students in the main and the regional branches jumped to 20,000.

The growing national role of Zaytuna University in opposing French colonialism and the leadership of its graduates in the nationalist movement, caused it to become the target of the French colonial government. The university gradually found itself at odds with the political powers, and its activities were curtailed. The great cultural support Tunisia received from the Arab League allowed it to pursue the spread of Arabic culture and language teaching through Zaytuna University as well as other centers of learning, thus counteracting the colonial cultural policy of promoting French at the expense of Arabic. Zaytuna University was instrumental in safeguarding Arabic culture in Tunisia and also helped its neighbor Algeria, a country that did not have a similar cultural center.

See also LEAGUE OF ARAB STATES.

Bibliography

Abu-Nasr, Jamil M. *A History of the Maghrib.* Cambridge, U.K.: Cambridge University Press, 1971.

Hourani, Albert. *A History of the Arab Peoples.* Cambridge, MA: Belknap Press of Harvard University Press, 1991.

AIDA A. BAMIA

ZAYYAT, LATIFA
[1923–1996]

Egyptian university professor, literary critic, political activist, essayist, and fiction writer.

Latifa Zayyat was a cultural icon of nationalist and feminist commitment. Born in the Delta city of Dimyat (Damietta), she received her university education and in 1957 her doctoral degree in English literature from Ain Shams University, Cairo. She taught there from 1952 until her retirement and was briefly director of the Arts Academy in Cairo during the 1970s.

Throughout her life she remained politically active. Involved in nationalist and student politics in the 1940s, she was a leader of the National Committee of Students and Workers. From 1979 until her death she chaired the Committee for the Defense of National Culture, formed to counter the possible cultural effects of Anwar al-Sadat's normalization policy toward Israel and his *infitah* ("Open Door") economic policy; along with many other activist intellectuals, Zayyat was arrested in 1981—not her first experience as an Egyptian political prisoner.

The activism of the 1940s forms the historical backdrop to her novel *al-Bab al-maftuh* (*The Open Door*, 1960), a landmark work of Arab feminist literature, narrating the physical, social, and political awakening of a middle-class Egyptian girl. After a long hiatus, Zayyat published additional novels, short stories, and a play; her short story collection *al-Shaykhukha wa qisas ukhra* (Old age and other stories, 1986) was notable for its focus on aging and its cross-genre formal experimentation. She also published critical studies in Arabic and English, and translations into Arabic of T. S. Eliot's essays and other texts. In 1992, she published a controversially frank memoir, *Hamlat taftish: Awraq shakhsiyya* (Arrest/search campaign: personal papers). She was awarded Egypt's State Prize for Literature in 1996, a few months before her death.

See also BAKR, SALWA; GENDER: GENDER AND EDUCATION; GENDER: GENDER AND LAW; GENDER: GENDER AND POLITICS; LITERATURE: ARABIC.

Bibliography

Booth, Marilyn. "Translator's Introduction." In *The Open Door*, by Latifa al-Zayyat. New York; Cairo: American University in Cairo Press, 2000.

Zayyat, Latifa. *The Search: Personal Papers*, translated by Sophie Bennett. London: Quartet Books, 1996.

Zayyat, Latifa al-. *The Open Door*, translated by Marilyn Booth. New York; Cairo: American University in Cairo Press, 2000.

MARILYN BOOTH

ZBIRI, TAHAR
[1930–]

Algerian officer.

Born in the Annaba region, Tahar Zbiri supported Messali al-Hadj before joining the Armée de Libération Nationale (ALN). He had a distinguished record during the Algerian War of Independence (1954–1962), participating in the initial attacks of 1 November 1954, escaping with "historic chief" Moustafa Ben Boulaid from the French, and breaching the Morice Line in 1960. Although he served as chief of staff of the Armée Nationale Populaire (ANP) under President Ahmed Ben Bella, Zbiri's loyalties were to Houari Boumédienne, and he arrested Ben Bella during the June 1965 coup. Zbiri remained chief of staff but opposed Boumédienne's increasing authoritarianism. In 1967 he organized a military revolt that failed, resulting in his arrest and exile. President Chadli Bendjedid pardoned Zbiri in 1980 and he returned to Algeria. Immediately after the suppression of the October 1988 riots, Zbiri and other prominent veterans and ex-ministers urged Bendjedid to convene a national conference to organize a new, democratic Algeria. The president rejected this proposal and Zbiri aligned with the anti-Bendjedid faction within the Front de Libération Nationale (FLN). Zbiri was selected to preside over a commission to monitor the parliamentary elections of May 1997. He is also identified with Algeria's liberalizing economy as a supporter of the private Khalifa group, a controversial conglomerate that collapsed in 2003.

See also ALGERIAN WAR OF INDEPENDENCE; BOUMÉDIENNE, HOUARI.

Bibliography

Naylor, Phillip C. *The Historical Dictionary of Algeria,* 3d edition. Lanham, MD: Scarecrow Press, 2003.

PHILLIP C. NAYLOR

ZEID, FAHRALNISSA
[1901–1991]

Turkish artist.

Fahralnissa Zeid was the daughter of a prominent Turkish general. Like many Middle Eastern artists of the early twentieth century, she came from an elite family of politicians and intellectuals. Zeid studied under Namik Ismail at the Academy of Fine Arts in Istanbul and then at the Académie Ranson in Paris, starting in 1927. She later returned to Turkey to join the famed D Group of contemporary artists, who attempted to develop Turkish art along the European model in line with the new Turkish republic. Zeid married the Hashimite ambassador to Turkey and assisted him in diplomatic posts throughout Europe. She was one of the first Middle Eastern artists to show her work in the West, including exhibits in London, New York, and the Salon des Réalités Nouvelles in Paris as early as the 1940s. In the 1970s she went to Amman and founded the Fahralnissa Zeid Institute of Fine Arts, thereby influencing generations of future Jordanian and Palestinian artists. Zeid's work was influenced by Byzantine portraiture, medieval stained glass patterns, and the tradition of Turkish miniature paintings. Her cubist-inspired abstract art was the first art of its kind to gain wide exposure in Jordan, as her openings garnered extensive media coverage. She also did fanciful scenes and portrait painting, working in oil, collage, and stained glass.

Bibliography

Ali, Wijdan. *Modern Islamic Art: Development and Continuity.* Gainesville: University of Florida Press, 1997.

JESSICA WINEGAR

ZELDA
[1914–1984]

Israeli poet.

Born Zelda Shneurson and also known as Zelda Mishkovsky, she signed her poems with her first name only. A devout Hasidic Jew, she was well versed in ancient sacred and traditional Jewish texts. In 1926 she emigrated to Israel from her native Ukraine. Her first book, *Leisure,* was published in 1968. Zelda published six other volumes of poetry: *The Invisible Carmel, Be Not Far, Neither Mountain nor Fire, Tiny Poems, The Spectacular Difference,* and *Beyond All Distance.* Her work is acclaimed by secular Israeli readers for its gentle, transcendental, mystic quality. Her poem "Each Person Has a Name" describes the characteristics acquired by individuals through the names assigned them and has been embraced by Israelis as an expression of their own collective and personal experiences with trauma and loss. The melancholy underlying her worldview is lightened by a sense of acceptance, a faith in the possibility of glory, and an enchantment with the beauty and sanctity of life.

Bibliography

Carmi, T. *The Penguin Book of Hebrew Verse.* New York: Viking, 1981.

ZVIA GINOR
UPDATED BY DONNA ROBINSON DIVINE

ZELL AL-SOLTAN, MASʿUD MIRZA
[1850–1918]

The eldest son of Persia's Naser al-Din Shah.

Masʿud Mirza Zell al-Soltan (Shadow of the Sovereign) was excluded from succeeding Naser al-Din because his mother was not of the Qajar dynasty. He became governor of Isfahan in 1874 and from 1881 to 1887 was the powerful and oppressive ruler of much of southern Iran. He had a large private army and kept the local tribesmen under control, killing an important Bakhtiari chief in 1882. He had contempt for the *ulama* (Islamic clergy). The rival of his half-brother and future monarch, Mozaffar al-Din, governor of Azerbaijan, Zell al-Soltan was opposed at court in Tehran by Ali-Asghar Amin al-Soltan. In 1888, because of his excesses, his power was restricted to Isfahan. During the Constitutional Revolution, he hoped to replace Mohammad Ali as shah and, consequently, aided the revolutionaries by supplying some financial support.

Bibliography

Curzon, George Nathaniel. *Persia and the Persian Question* (1892). London: Cass, 1966.

LAWRENCE G. POTTER

ZEROUAL, LIAMINE
[1943–]

President of Algeria, 1994–1999.

Born in Batna, Liamine Zeroual (also al-Amin Zirwal) joined Algeria's National Liberation Army (ALN) at the age of sixteen. Later he attended a military school in the Soviet Union and France's Ecole de Guerre. Upon his return, he took over the military school of the National Popular Army (ANP) in Batna. Zeroual held various operational jobs within the ANP, including that of commander of the prestigious Military Academy in Cherchell. He earned the rank of general in 1988 and commanded the Land Forces. Zeroual resigned from the ANP in 1989 because of a conflict with President Chadli

Bendjedid about the restructuring of the military. He was appointed ambassador to Romania in 1990. In 1991 he retired to Batna.

After Bendjedid was deposed in 1992, Algeria was ruled by the High State Council. In 1993 General Khaled Nezzar, a powerful member of the Council, called Zeroual back from retirement as his replacement as minister of defense. In January 1994, with the dissolution of the Council, Zeroual was appointed president of Algeria. In November 1995 he was elected president with 60 percent of the popular vote in the country's first pluralist presidential election. His mission was to reestablish peace and security, to build legitimate state institutions, and to break with the old regime. Zeroual was able to build an institutional edifice. A political party, the Rassemblement National Démocratique (RND), was created in February 1997 to support his policies. The party obtained the majority in the June 1997 legislative elections. In a surprise move, Zeroual announced on 11 September 1998 that he would step down in February 1999. In April 1999 Abdelaziz Bouteflika, following a controversial election, became his successor.

See also ALGERIA: OVERVIEW; ALGERIA: POLITICAL PARTIES IN; BENDJEDID, CHADLI; BOUTEFLIKA, ABDELAZIZ; HIGH STATE COUNCIL (ALGERIA).

Bibliography

Quandt, William B. *Between Ballots and Bullets: Algeria's Transition from Authoritarianism.* Washington, DC: Brookings Institution Press, 1998.

Zoubir, Yahia H. "The Algerian Political Crisis: Origins and Prospects for Democracy." *Journal of North African Studies* 3, no. 1 (spring 1998).

Zoubir, Yahia H., and Youcef Bouandel. "Algeria's Elections: Prelude to Democratization?" *Third World Quarterly* 19, no. 2 (June 1998): 177–190.

MIA BLOOM
UPDATED BY YAHIA ZOUBIR

ZIADEH, MAY
[1886–1941]

Poet, translator, orator, essayist, and critic.

Marie Ziadeh (also Ziyada) was born in Nazareth to a Lebanese father and a Palestinian mother. After her family emigrated to Cairo in 1908, Ziadeh began her writing career, which was facilitated by her father becoming editor of the Cairo weekly *al-Mahrusa*. After initially writing under pseudonyms, she changed her name from Marie to May (or Mayy), and quickly distinguished herself as a prolific poet, translator, orator, essayist, and critic. She studied at the Egyptian University, mastered five languages, cooperated with early feminist groups such as the one led by Huda Shaʿrawi, and as early as 1913 started a literary salon in her parents' house.

Ziadeh's early work is characterized by romanticism, but increasingly her writing took on sociopolitical themes relating to socialism, colonialism, freedom of the press, and especially women's rights. Among her groundbreaking publications are her biographical accounts of the pioneer women writers Warda al-Yaziji, Aʾisha Taymur, and Bahithat al-Badiya. Ziadeh was also associated with the *mahjar* (émigré) Arab writers, particularly Kahlil Gibran, with whom she had an intense, lengthy correspondence. Although they never met, there has been much speculation on the nature of their relationship, and much written about her as his muse. Her articles on Gibran were widely read in the Arab world and helped make him famous, while also establishing her as a critic.

Ziadeh is most famous for her literary salon, which met weekly for over twenty years. Unlike other salons, hers was open to men and women of mixed religious, national, and social backgrounds. It drew some of the most prominent intellectuals of Egypt and provided her with a platform for both social acceptability and intellectual opposition.

After her parents died, the salon dissolved, and Ziadeh's final years were enmeshed in accusations of insanity and conjecture about her enigmatic life. In recent years, her work has received considerable attention, and she is now acknowledged to be one of the Arab world's most prominent emancipators.

See also EGYPT; GENDER: GENDER AND EDUCATION; LITERATURE: ARABIC; SYRIA.

ELISE SALEM

ZIKHRON YAʿAKOV

Village located 19 miles (31 km) south of Haifa.

In 1882, Romanian Jews founded Zikhron Yaʿakov, one of the early settlements of the Hovevei Zion (Hibbat Zion) movement. Financially supported in part by the Baron Edmond de Rothschild, the settlement, shortly after its founding, was given its present name in memory of the baron's father, Jacob (Zikhron Yaʿakov means "The Memory of Jacob"). Baron de Rothschild promoted the planting of grapes, and vineyards were established in the settlement as well as one of the largest wine cellars in Israel. In 1954, Baron de Rothschild and his wife were buried in Zikhron Yaʿakov. Located in the foothills of Mount Carmel, the village (pop. 12,000 in 2002) is a tourist site that draws visitors to the Rothschild mausoleum, botanical garden, and winery.

See also HIBBAT ZION.

Bibliography

Schama, Simon. *The Two Rothschilds and the Land of Israel.* New York: Knopf, 1978.

BRYAN DAVES

ZILI, RIDHA
[1942–]

Tunisian poet and photographer.

Ridha Zili was born in Monastir, Tunisia. He received a bilingual (Arabic and French) education but writes in French only. Zili's writing is greatly influenced by his work as a photographer, especially in his concept of the image. His only published collection of poetry, *Ifrikiya, ma pensée* (1967; Africa in my thoughts), describes his love of peace and his search for happiness. Zili rejects sadness and the nonsensical violence in the world and values his Tunisian African roots.

See also LITERATURE: ARABIC, NORTH AFRICAN.

AIDA A. BAMIA

ZIONISM

Movement for the establishment of an independent state in Palestine for the Jewish people.

Zionism may be seen as a national liberation movement for a Jewish homeland based on a nineteenth-century European political model. It defined Jews as a nation whose collective future depended upon the establishment of a national territorial entity in

Eretz Yisrael (in Hebrew, "the land of Israel"), from which most Jews had been dispersed by the Roman Empire at the beginning of the second century C.E. The movement's name was coined by the Viennese Jewish writer Nathan Birnbaum in 1885 and derives from *Zion,* one of the biblical names for Jerusalem, the focus of worldwide Judaism.

Zionists believed that antisemitism was endemic to the diaspora; thus, the achievement of national and civil rights in host nations, while desirable, was insufficient to secure economic and cultural interests for Jews in the long run. Few Zionists believed that the diaspora would be swept away (as was attempted a century later by Hitler's Nazi Germany), but a Jewish homeland—which would serve as a cultural and political model and as a magnet for its finest sons and daughters—could help to secure a future for Jews.

Foundations of Zionism

Through the centuries of exile, ritual, prayer, and the study of sacred texts preserved for Jews the knowledge that Judaism had developed in Eretz Yisrael and Zion. In nineteenth-century Europe during the Haskalah (the Jewish Enlightenment), revival of the Hebrew language as a nonreligious, literary medium transmitted secular works and secularized versions of sacred histories to assimilated generations losing faith in religion and religious authority. If Zionism were to ensure the survival of the Jewish people, it could do so only by going through the modern European Jewish experience, not by denying it. Zionists were Jews who believed that only in Zion could Jewish culture and the Jewish people be re-established and secure. At that time, however, Zion was located in Palestine, within the Ottoman Empire, and was populated by Arabs under Ottoman jurisdiction.

A "proto-Zionism" had existed in fact before it was fully defined or before the word itself was coined. As a way of helping the indigent and scholarly Jewish populations in Ottoman Palestine, Western European philanthropists such as Edmond de Rothschild and Sir Moses Montefiore proffered aid to projects that later would come to be associated with the Zionist movement—the purchase of land for settlements, farms, and businesses from Ottoman officials and Arab landlords; the building of schools

for vocational training; and the opening of medical facilities.

Jewish emigration to Eretz Yisrael also antedated the emergence of a Zionist movement. Jewish religious leaders had always endorsed the idea of living in the Holy Land as a means of discharging religious duties, and had actively promoted the expansion of Jewish communities in Safed, Tiberias, Hebron, and Jerusalem, creating financial mechanisms to meet the immigrants' material needs.

The wave of pogroms that followed the assassination of Russia's Czar Alexander II in 1881 turned an attachment for Zion into an ideology embraced by some of Russia's secular Jewish leaders and intellectuals. Newly promulgated regressive legislation and the resuscitation of antisemitic rhetoric dashed the hopes of those who had believed Russia's polity would evolve into a democracy, with basic rights granted to its population and the ideals of tolerance espoused. Although emigration to the United States and Britain was a popular way of escaping the immediate disabilities imposed by Russian policies, some educated Jews saw that moving to another land would neither end antisemitism nor secure a Jewish future. They argued that only a purposeful immigration with the goal of establishing a Jewish majority in a territory would achieve international respectability for Jewry and help protect Jews everywhere against discrimination. For those who called on Jews to liberate themselves, the Zionist idea supplanted the ideal of assimilation. Zionism was presented as resolving the Jewish problem by normalizing the conditions of Jewish existence.

Development of Zionist Organizations

Although many rabbinical authorities opposed Zionism for its secular and humanistic principles, many rabbis—most notably Samuel Mohilever and Isaac Jacob Reines—welcomed Zionism; they affiliated with Hibbat Zion, the first international Zionist organization to be founded, partly because they reasoned that in Eretz Yisrael a social and cultural environment could be created that was conducive to religious observance.

The Orthodox rabbinate did not, however, establish an entirely harmonious relationship with the secular leadership in Hibbat Zion. Many Orthodox

Theodor Herzl addresses a meeting of the Zionist Congress in Basel, Switzerland. The Zionist Congress was dedicated to establishing institutions necessary for the support of a Jewish state. © ISRAEL GOVERNMENT PRESS OFFICE (GPO) OF ISRAEL. REPRODUCED BY PERMISSION.

rabbis could not abide the dynamics of a political struggle that effected compromises between the demands of Zionism's secular and religious constituencies. Nor were the Orthodox entirely comfortable in an organization that did not acknowledge the primacy of religious law and rabbinic authority. The first nonsecular Zionist group, the Mizrahi, opened its office in 1893, but most rabbis, though comfortable with the nationalist claims of Zionism, were unwilling to accede to Zionist demands to share power and resources in local Jewish communities. As a consequence of the frustrating handicaps under which Hibbat Zion labored in the 1880s and 1890s, Zionism was at an impasse when Theodor Herzl undertook to lead the struggle for a Jewish state.

Unaware of developments in Eastern Europe, Herzl, a Viennese journalist, championed the idea of Jewish nationhood in response to the outbreak of antisemitism in France during the fraudulent espionage trial of Alfred Dreyfus (1894–1895). In 1896 Herzl published *Der Judenstaat (The Jewish State)*, a book that set forth the argument that both the world and the Jews needed a Jewish state. In 1897 Herzl succeeded in drawing together representatives from the local and regional Hibbat Zion organizations in eastern Europe and Jews from western Europe, establishing and becoming president of a new Zionist framework, the World Zionist Organization (WZO). Authorized by the WZO to secure international recognition for Zionist political goals, Herzl pursued in the capitals of Europe and in the Ottoman capital, Istanbul, official sanction for Jewish colonization in Palestine, but his efforts, albeit feverish and intense, were unsuccessful. The Ottoman sultan Abdülhamit II was not persuaded that a larger Jewish population in Palestine was consistent with his imperial political objectives or that such a population would promote economic development.

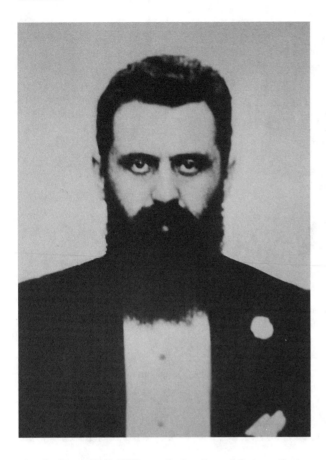

Theodor Herzl (1860–1904) was the founder and first president of the World Zionist Organization, a group whose purpose was to establish a Jewish homeland in Palestine. © LIBRARY OF CONGRESS. REPRODUCED BY PERMISSION.

Herzl's leadership did broaden the popularity of Zionism in western and eastern Europe and enlarge its Orthodox membership. Herzl focused the activities of the WZO on diplomacy and finances. This approach mobilized the support of a number of Orthodox rabbis concerned with easing the economic hardships in Palestine for eastern European immigrants and hopefuls, as well as with the creation of a hospitable political climate there. By permitting groups to shift the mode of their representation from regional affiliation to ideological, the WZO was also used advantageously by the Orthodox to influence the direction of policies and, for a number of years, to exclude Jewish culture from the scope of Zionist activities.

Zionism's preoccupation with political solutions and stratagems triggered opposition. Against the political orientation associated with the leadership of Hibbat Zion, the writer Ahad Ha-Am argued that the purpose of Zionism ought to be to revive a modern Jewish culture through the medium of the Hebrew language and a renewed interpretation of classic religious texts; a new Jewish state could only be founded with new artifacts of Jewish culture. Cultural Zionist Ahad Ha-Am's insights on the problems besetting the Jewish people and the Zionist movement helped to inspire a group opposing Herzl's leadership and political Zionism—the Democratic Faction. This group, led by the scientist Chaim Weizmann, did not repudiate political methods or consider them insignificant; rather, they insisted that just as legal titles (to land) could facilitate resettlement, so could settlement lead to concrete political gains. Insisting that the structure of the WZO must be reformed to increase popular participation and broaden its agenda, the Democratic Faction defined its own priorities as the investigation of the physical, political, and social conditions of Palestine for purposes of increasing Jewish immigration.

Creating a Jewish community in Palestine was not simply the solution to continuing antisemitism but also the opportunity to establish a whole and vigorous modern Jewish life. In the early years of the twentieth century, efforts to create a youth movement and to popularize Zionism among the young led several Zionist leaders to synthesize socialism with Zionism. No longer would Jews have to choose between socialism (popular in Russia and in the Pale of Settlement) and Zionism. Some Socialist-Zionists promoted a non-Marxist socialism, emphasizing social welfare and justice; others insisted that even the Marxist version of socialism could be combined with Zionism. Branches of the first Labor Zionist party, Po'alei Zion, founded in 1906, opened in many towns and cities of eastern Europe, attracting many educated Jewish teenagers. Ha-Halutz, the young pioneer farm movement, was nonpartisan and attracted many capable Austro-Hungarian Jewish youth, especially when it was funded by the WZO after World War I.

Before the conclusion of World War I, Zionists were unable to engage openly in mass mobilization in many countries. In the United States and western Europe, where organizations could operate freely, Zionism did not hold the imagination of most immigrants, who were struggling to work their way out of grinding poverty. In Russia, where the majority of Jews presumably felt sympathy with Zionist aims, Zionist activities were hobbled by the Russian Revolution, Soviet dictatorship, and persecution.

Establishment of the Jewish State in Palestine

With the issuance of the Balfour Declaration in 1917 and the Sèvres Treaty of 1920, Britain became formally committed to the establishment in Palestine of a Jewish national home. This gave Zionism its first major political victory. World War I had changed the map of Eastern Europe as well as that of the Middle East, thereby providing Zionists an opportunity to engage in grassroots political organization among previously isolated Jewish communities. Youth groups expanded, and camps were created to offer vocational and Hebrew-language training to prepare Jews for life and work in Palestine.

Throughout its history, the Zionist movement has had to make crucial choices among several options: Eretz Yisrael (Palestine) versus another territory, such as Uganda, Canada, Australia; a national home versus a cultural center for world Jewry; a Jewish nation-state versus a binational state in which Jews and Arabs might share political power; neutrality during World War I versus pro-British cooperation; high political profile versus quiet political lobbying; and uniformity versus diversity in political goals. Each decision was made after great debate during and outside of Zionist congresses, often triggering enmity, hard feelings, and the creation of new splinters and factions. One of the most serious splits occurred when Vladimir (Ze'ev) Jabotinsky left the WZO to create his own Revisionist Zionist movement.

With increasing knowledge of the extent of the Holocaust during World War II, the Zionist movement chose Jewish survival over acquiescence in British restrictions on immigration, which resulted in an anti-British militancy aimed at gaining free entry for Jewish refugees into Palestine from 1944 until 1948. With the establishment of the State of Israel in May 1948, the fulfilment of one of Zionism's goals was endorsed by international consensus—majority support at the United Nations, official recognition by many of the world's nations, and acceptance by most Jews (religious Jews excepted). The Arab and Muslim world remained outside this consensus. Post-1948 Zionism evolved into a movement dedicated to immigration (aliyah) for as many Jews as possible, land purchase for continued settlement, and political and economic support for Israel through institutionalized activity. Despite the recent "post-Zionist" intellectual trend that urges a redefinition of Israel as an inclusive state for all its citizens and detaches it from its special diaspora Jewish connections, many Jews continue to consider themselves Zionists in affirming this connection and the importance of Israel in sustaining their Jewish identity.

See also ABDÜLHAMIT II; AHAD HA-AM; ALIYAH; ANTISEMITISM; DIASPORA; DREYFUS AFFAIR; ERETZ YISRAEL; HA-HALUTZ; HASKALAH; HERZL, THEODOR; HIBBAT ZION; HOLY LAND; JABOTINSKY, VLADIMIR ZE'EV; JERUSALEM; LABOR ZIONISM; MIZRAHI MOVEMENT; MOHILEVER, SAMUEL; MONTEFIORE, MOSES; POGROM; ROTHSCHILD, EDMOND DE; WEIZMANN, CHAIM; WORLD ZIONIST ORGANIZATION (WZO); ZIONIST COMMISSION FOR PALESTINE; ZIONIST ORGANIZATION OF AMERICA; ZIONIST REVISIONIST MOVEMENT.

Bibliography

Avineri, Shlomo. *The Making of Modern Zionism: Intellectual Origins of the Jewish State.* New York: Basic Books, 1981.

Dowty, Alan. *The Jewish State: A Century Later.* Berkeley: University of California Press, 1998.

Halpern, Ben. *The Idea of the Jewish state.* Cambridge, MA: Harvard University Press, 1969.

Hertzberg, Arthur. *The Fate of Zionism: A Secular Future for Israel and Palestine.* San Francisco: HarperSanFrancisco, 2003.

Hertzberg, Arthur, ed. *The Zionist Idea: A Historical Analysis and Reader.* Philadelphia: Jewish Publication Society, 1997.

Laqueur, Walter. *A History of Zionism: From the French Revolution to the Establishment of the State of Israel.* New York: Schocken Books, 2003.

Rubinstein, Amnon. *From Herzl to Rabin: The Changing Image of Zionism.* New York: Holmes and Meier, 2000.

Sternhell, Zeev. *The Founding Myths of Israel: Nationalism, Socialism, and the Making of the Jewish State,* translated by David Maisel. Princeton, NJ: Princeton University Press, 1998.

Vital, David. *Zionism: The Crucial Phase.* Oxford, U.K.: Clarendon Press, 1987; New York: Oxford University Press, 1987.

DONNA ROBINSON DIVINE
UPDATED BY NEIL CAPLAN

ZIONIST COMMISSION FOR PALESTINE

Official representative of the World Zionist Organization in Palestine until 1921; a precursor of the Jewish Agency Executive.

The Zionist Commission was an informal group established by Chaim Weizmann as president of the World Zionist Organization (WZO) to advise the British on policies regarding the establishment of the Jewish national home. It carried out initial surveys of Palestine and aided the repatriation of Jews sent into exile by the Ottoman Turks during World War I.

It expanded the WZO's Palestine office (established 1907) into small departments for agriculture, settlement, education, land, finance, immigration, and statistics. In 1921, the commission became the Palestine Zionist Executive, which acted as the Jewish Agency, designated to advise the British mandate authorities on the development of the country in matters of Jewish interest.

See also JEWISH AGENCY FOR PALESTINE; WEIZMANN, CHAIM; WORLD ZIONIST ORGANIZATION (WZO).

Bibliography

Caplan, Neil. *Palestine Jewry and the Arab Question, 1917–1925.* London and Totowa, NJ: F. Cass, 1978.

DONNA ROBINSON DIVINE

ZIONIST ORGANIZATION OF AMERICA

U.S. organization supporting Zionism.

The Zionist Organization of America (ZOA) traces its origins to the 1898 founding of the Federation of American Zionists (FAZ) one year after Theodor Herzl created the World Zionist Organization (WZO). The FAZ sought to mobilize support for Herzl's plan "to create for the Jewish people a national home in Palestine secured by public law" (Basle Program, 1897). At first, the U.S. Zionist organization encountered great difficulty in attracting adherents within a mainly immigrant community concerned about its own integration into mainstream America. Indeed, in its early years, the FAZ, forerunner of the Zionist Organization of America, was perceived as a minor, fringe organization within the U.S. Jewish community. However, during World War I, a combination of factors—the plight of two-thirds of world Jewry in war-torn zones; the decision of the prominent U.S. Jew Louis Brandeis to head the FAZ; and the issuance of Great Britain's Balfour Declaration, which "view[ed] with favour the establishment in Palestine a national home for the Jewish people"—enabled the ZOA (FAZ's successor) to increase its membership from less than 12,000 in 1914 to 180,000 in 1918.

After unsuccessfully challenging the leadership and direction of the World Zionist Organization immediately following the war, the ZOA continued U.S. Zionists' erstwhile policy of loyally supporting the policies of the world Zionist movement and, since 1948, the State of Israel. At times, however, leaders emerged who challenged the policies and directions of the Zionist movement and Israeli government. During the Holocaust, ZOA leader Rabbi Abba Hillel Silver urged the WZO to stop trying to reach a modus vivendi with the British Mandate for Palestine and to seek instead to replace the Mandate Authorities with a Jewish State.

Led by its president Morton A. Klein, in 2003 the ZOA had 50,000 members in more than twelve local chapters. It actively advocates for Israel by combating what it views as "the anti-Israel bias of the media" and by promoting pro-Israel legislation on Capitol Hill. Sometimes, however, the Zionist Organization of America finds its advocacy at odds with the Israeli government itself; it opposes, for instance, former prime minister Yitzhak Rabin's signing of the Oslo Peace Process Agreement and Ehud Barak's negotiations with the Palestinian Authority.

See also BALFOUR DECLARATION (1917); HERZL, THEODOR; SILVER, ABBA HILLEL; WORLD ZIONIST ORGANIZATION (WZO); ZIONISM.

BRYAN DAVES
UPDATED BY JERRY KUTNICK

ZIONIST REVISIONIST MOVEMENT

The political party that represented the revisionist oppositional trend in Zionism; led by Ze'ev Jabotinsky from the 1920s through the 1940s.

The Zionist Revisionist Movement sometimes referred only to the political party (Ha-Zohar; Union of Zionist-Revisionists) and sometimes to various subsidiary bodies and institutions that expressed the revisionist ideology and accepted the leadership of Vladimir Ze'ev Jabotinsky, in particular the Betar youth movement, an avant-garde mass movement of youth and incipient army founded in 1923. Hence, a distinction must be made between, on the one hand, any discussion of the political history of the union and, on the other hand, the history of Betar, the National Labor Federation, and Brit ha-Hayyal (a union of Polish army veterans)—all of which were part of the Revisionist Movement (although they preferred to regard themselves as belonging to the "national movement" or to the "Jabotinsky movement").

The union itself was founded in 1925 in Paris by a group of veteran Zionists, most of them Russians, to propose a "revision" in the aims of Zionism, which basically meant a return to the principles of political Zionism espoused by Theodor Herzl. It found its greatest support among the Jewish communities of Eastern Europe (Poland and the Baltic states), but it had branches worldwide. It grew rapidly; in the elections for the 1927 Zionist Congress, it drew 8,446 votes and in the 1933 elections, 99,729 votes. Consequently, its representation grew at the Zionist Congress and in the Asefat ha-Nivharim (the parliament of the Jewish Yishuv in Palestine), and it became the major opposition party, taking on the image of the Zionist Right or even Zionist fascism, from the end of the 1920s. This electoral growth and development of revisionist institutions led to a number of controversies between the revisionists and the labor movement and the "official" Zionism. This division was often expressed in acts of violence, leaving a deep imprint on the political history and political culture of Zionism and the Yishuv. An internal conflict also existed between moderate elements that wanted to remain within the Zionist Federation and those that demanded that the union break away. It was resolved in 1933 when the moderates seceded from the union

Ze'ev Jabotinsky (bottom right) meets with Betar leaders in Warsaw, Poland, 1936. Jabotinsky founded the Zionist Revisionist Movement and its related organizations such as Betar in order to bring greater pressure to bear on Great Britain and mainstream Zionists to create a large and well-defended Jewish state in Palestine. © GOVERNMENT PRESS OFFICE (GPO) OF ISRAEL. REPRODUCED BY PERMISSION.

and founded a small independent party called the Jewish State Party.

A specific point of controversy with official Zionism was the union's "independent diplomacy." This was expressed in various activities, primarily in attempts to obtain the support of European countries, in particular of Poland, to pressure Britain in the Mandate Council of the League of Nations in Geneva. In 1934 the union organized a mass petition denouncing British policy, and after the rise of the Nazis to power, it organized a boycott against German goods. From the mid-1930s, it began disseminating propaganda (and engaging in clandestine activity) to encourage a mass emigration of 700,000 to 1.5 million Jews from Europe to Palestine within a ten-year period (the Evacuation Plan and the Ten-Year Plan). It also was active in organizing illegal immigration to Palestine.

In 1935, the union broke away from the Zionist Federation and set up the New Zionist Federation (NZO) that met with wide popular support. In 1945, it rejoined the Zionist Federation. The union maintained an extensive organizational system with centers in Paris, London, and Warsaw. In Palestine, the Ha-Zohar was the second-largest political party. After establishment of the state, the Irgun Zva'i Le'umi (IZL) founded an independent party while veteran members of the union had their own Revisionist Party, which never attained any representation, so most of its members finally joined the new party.

The movement's platform reflected Jabotinsky's program and ideology: the future establishment of a Jewish state on both sides of the Jordan river under Jewish sovereignty. As an interim measure, a colonization regime would be set up to create the conditions necessary to achieve a demographic Jewish majority—a prerequisite for a state. For this purpose, it called on the mandatory government to adopt an economic and settlement policy that would foster Jewish immigration and settlement. It also demanded that the Jewish Legion be reinstated, i.e., that Jewish military units be activated as an integral part of the British garrison in Palestine.

The official program relating to socioeconomic matters was a combination of etatism (state socialism) and liberalism: on the one hand, support for the private sector and on the other a demand for involvement by the mandatory government and the Jewish Agency in the creation of infrastructure, in providing assistance to the private sector, and in setting up legal arrangements to prevent strikes. The union viewed Palestinian Arabs as citizens with equal rights, on condition that they do nothing to impair the national character of the Jewish state. The revisionists believed that cooperation with the mandatory government and with Britain was essential. But to prevent Britain from reneging on its commitments, they thought it necessary to bring political and propaganda pressure to bear on Britain. In their view, the strategic cooperation in Palestine and Britain's readiness to help Europe's Jews in their distress were the basis for such cooperation. The party was not monolithic, and various views came to the fore. In the 1930s, its dominant mood was that of the "radical nationalists," who called for a more activist policy toward the British, beginning in 1930 but in particular after the events of 1936 (the revisionists opposed the partition plan recommended by the Peel Commission Report in July 1937).

As a result of the internal disputes, there was a great deal of tension in the movement, particularly between the union and Betar and various maximalist groups. This internal strife led to the creation of new organizations, weakly linked organizationally to the union (in particular, the IZL).

See also HERZL, THEODOR; IRGUN ZVA'I LE'UMI (IZL); JABOTINSKY, VLADIMIR ZE'EV; JEWISH AGENCY FOR PALESTINE; JEWISH LEGION; PEEL COMMISSION REPORT (1937); YISHUV; ZIONISM.

Bibliography

Jabotinsky, Vladimir. *The Political and Social Philosophy of Ze'ev Jabotinsky: Selected Writings,* edited by Mordechai Sarig; translated by Shimshon Feder. Portland, OR: Valentine Mitchell, 1998.

Katz, Shmuel. *Lone Wolf: A Biography of Vladimir (Ze'ev) Jabotinsky.* New York: Barricade Books, 1996.

Schechtman, J., and Ben Ari, Y. *History of the Revisionist Movement,* Vol. 1. Tel Aviv: Hadar, 1970.

Shavit, Yaakov. *Jabotinsky and the Revisionist Movement, 1925–1948.* London, U.K., and Totawa, NJ: Frank Cass, 1988.

YAAKOV SHAVIT

ZIWAJ MUT'A

Temporary marriage.

Temporary marriage (*ziwaj mut'a*), which was practiced in early Islamic Arabia, is a contract between a man and an unmarried woman for a particular duration of time. A man can marry numerous temporary wives in addition to his permanent wife or wives. Umar (r. 634–644), the second caliph, outlawed temporary marriage, but Shi'ites did not find his position legally binding because the Prophet and the Qur'an permitted *mut'a* marriage. Even a few Sunni societies continued to practice certain forms of *mut'a* marriage.

Social and economic circumstances shaping modern Shi'ite societies led to the emergence of new and at times arbitrary forms of temporary marriage. After the rise of the Iranian Islamic Republic in 1979, temporary marriage became popular, particularly among the urban lower classes. It also surfaced in Lebanon and other Arab Shi'ite communities. Shiʿite jurists debated several conditions relating to temporary marriage, but the law remained vague and ambivalent about women's rights. It is rare for a woman to negotiate a share of her husband's inheritance. A man is expected to provide for his children from a temporary marriage, but there are no institutional guarantees. A temporary marriage can be terminated by mutual consent before the end of the stipulated period. Overall, men have greater legal rights and control over the conditions of *mutaʿa* than women.

See also GENDER: GENDER AND HEALTH; GENDER: GENDER AND LAW; *SHARIʿA;* SHIʿISM.

Bibliography

Haeri, Shahla. *Law of Desire: Temporary Marriage in Shiʿi Iran.* Syracuse, NY: Syracuse University Press, 1989.

Khomeini, Ayatullah Ruhullah. "Non-Permanent Marriage." *Mahjubih* 2, no. 5 (1982): 38–40.

RULA JURDI ABISAAB

ZIYA, ABDÜLHAMIT

[1825–1880]

Young Ottoman writer.

The son of a customs clerk, Ziya Paşa was educated in one of the first secular Ruşdiye schools in Istanbul. He began work in the translation office and, through the support of Tanzimat reformer Reşit Pasa in 1854, became a secretary to Sultan Abdülmecit I. He lost his palace job in 1861 with the accession of Sultan Abdülaziz and held several minor posts in the 1860s. By 1866 he had joined the Young Ottoman Society in Europe and, with Namik Kemal and İbrahim Şinasi, became a leading intellectual of the period. Under Abdülaziz's rule, Ziya's political satires and other writings were banned as seditious, and he was posted as governor of Syria, in virtual exile.

Ziya Paşa's greatest influence was through his writings. He warned against blind imitation of Europe and criticized autocracy and poor policies such as the growing Ottoman debt. In 1868 he wrote a famous article, "Poetry and Prose" (Şiir ve Inşa), in which he criticized Ottoman literature as mere imitation of Arabic and Persian traditions and called on writers to seek inspiration in Turkish folk literature.

Bibliography

Davison, Roderic H. *Reform in the Ottoman Empire, 1856–1876.* Princeton, NJ: Princeton University Press, 1963.

Lewis, Bernard. *The Emergence of Modern Turkey,* 3d edition. New York: Oxford University Press, 2002.

Shaw, Stanford J., and Shaw, Ezel Kural. *History of the Ottoman Empire and Modern Turkey,* Vol. 2: *Reform, Revolution, and Republic: The Rise of Modern Turkey, 1808–1975.* Cambridge, U.K., and New York: Cambridge University Press, 1977.

ELIZABETH THOMPSON

ZOHAR, URI

[1935–]

Israeli actor and comedian who became a rabbi and teacher.

Uri Zohar began his professional acting career in 1953 and quickly rose to fame as a satirist and humorist. He starred in Israeli films in the 1960s, including *A Hole in the Moon* and *Every Bastard a King.* He was the first cinema artist to win the Israel Prize (which he refused), in 1976.

In the 1970s he became a sectarian Orthodox Jew and a rabbi and teacher in a yeshiva (religious school). He is active in the movement to attract secular Jews to religious orthodoxy, and uses his entertainment skills to promote this objective. He wrote an account of his religious transformation, *Ubaharta bahaim,* (1983)—which was subsequently translated as *Waking Up Jewish* (1985)—as well as several other volumes that espouse his views on secular Israeli society. In 1999 Zohar directed a widely distributed videotape and CD, titled *Ani Me-ashim* (I accuse) in which the former Shas political party leader Arye Deri alleged that the fraud charges of which he was accused (and for which he was imprisoned) were an Ashkenazic-elitist conspiracy against not only him but also the Sephardim as a group.

CHAIM I. WAXMAN

ZOHRAB, KRIKOR

[1861–1915]

Armenian writer and deputy in the Ottoman parliament.

Krikor Zohrab, also known as Grigor Zohrap, was born in Istanbul. He was educated in his birthplace and practicing law by 1883. He distinguished himself as an attorney who defended cases against the government until he was deprived of his license in 1905 and went abroad to France and Egypt. With the end of the Hamidian autocracy and the restoration of the Ottoman constitution, Zohrab returned to Istanbul. From 1908 to 1915, he was a member of the Armenian National Assembly. He also was elected a deputy to the Ottoman parliament where he defended the cause of universal social justice and gained distinction as an orator. Shocked by the 1909 mass killings of Armenians in Adana, he published his findings in Paris under the pseudonym of Marcel Leart as *La Question Arménienne à la Lumière des Documents*.

Zohrab also earned fame as an author of short stories and novellas in the realist style. The subjects of social inequality, injustice, and prejudice preoccupied him. His more important works include *Anhetatsads Serunt Me* (A vanished generation, 1887), *Khghjmdanki Tzayner* (Voices of conscience, 1909), *Kyanke Inchpes Vor e* (Life as it is, 1911), and *Lur Tsaver* (Silent sorrows, 1911). He also published essays on literature, politics, and the Armenian community. Before his own demise, he protested to Talat, the Young Turk minister of the interior, the summary arrest on the night of 24 April 1915, and subsequent execution of the Istanbul Armenian community leaders. His own immunity as a parliamentary deputy did not spare him from being arrested on 3 June, deported, and killed near Diyarbekir.

Bibliography

Baliozian, Ara. *The Armenians: Their History and Culture,* 2d edition. New York: Ararat Press, 1980.

ROUBEN P. ADALIAN

ZONNENFELD, YOSEF HAYYIM

[1849–1932]

Rabbi; leader of ultra-Orthodox Jerusalem community.

Yosef Hayyim Zonnenfeld was born in Verbo, Slovakia, and educated in the yeshiva in Pressburg. Settling in Jerusalem in 1873, he actively opposed secular Zionist educational activities and became a leader of the Old City Jewish community, assisting in the founding of the Meah She'arim community and others. A staunch sectarian, he opposed all co-operation between the Orthodox and non-Orthodox Jewish communities. He was one of the founders of the separatist rabbinic court in Jerusalem, and in 1920 he was elected rabbi of the separatist Orthodox community of Jerusalem. He was also a founder of the Agudat Israel in Palestine. Despite their warm personal relationship, he opposed Rabbi Abraham Isaac Hacohen Kook as rabbi in Jerusalem and, subsequently, as chief rabbi of Palestine. Nevertheless, Zonnenfeld was a strong supporter of Jewish settlement in Eretz Yisrael.

See also AGUDAT ISRAEL; ERETZ YISRAEL; KOOK, ABRAHAM ISAAC HACOHEN; MEAH SHE'ARIM.

Bibliography

Danziger, Hillel. *Guardian of Jerusalem: The Life and Times of Yosef Chaim Sonnenfeld.* Brooklyn, NY: Mesorah Publications, 1983.

CHAIM I. WAXMAN

ZOROASTRIANISM

Pre-Islamic religion founded by the Iranian prophet Zarathushtra (Zoroaster).

Founded as early as 1400 to 1200 B.C.E., Zoroastrianism spread from central Asia to Iran around the ninth century B.C.E., where it was propagated by priests called the *magi,* or *mobeds.* Zoroastrianism remained the major faith in Iran until the Sassanian state fell to the Arabs in 651 C.E. Thereafter, the religion lost many followers through conversion to Islam between the eighth and the thirteenth centuries. Zoroastrianism reached India in the tenth century, when some Zoroastrians migrated from Iran to avoid adopting Islam. Descendants of these immigrants are called the *Parsis* (Parsees). Those who remained behind sought refuge from Islam by moving to sparsely populated regions in central Iran. By the thirteenth century, extensive contact between Parsis and Persian Zoroastrians had recommenced. In 1854, when the Parsis sent an emissary to the Qajar court, the poll tax levied on Iranian Zoroastrians by the Muslim state was abolished. The community in India flourished, and in the mid-1990s it numbered around 72,000.

Zoroastrians in Iran encountered less success, though there was a respite from financial hardship and pressure to practice Islam during the Pahlavi dynasty (1925–1979). Since the Iranian Revolution, despite being recognized as an official minority of about 30,000, Zoroastrians are offered little protection from their Muslim neighbors, and many have fled Iran. International dispersion during the twentieth century has produced Zoroastrian communities in Pakistan (3,700), England (7,000), Australia (1,000), the United States and Canada (10,000), and other countries. By the early 1990s, low birthrates together with widespread nonacceptance of converts contributed to an overall decline in the number of Zoroastrians.

The faith's central canon is the Avesta (Pure instruction), a scripture that includes the Gathas (Songs), which were probably composed by Zarathushtra himself. Prayers recited by the laity in daily religious observances are compiled in a text known as the Khorde Avesta (Shorter Avesta). Next in importance are religious exegeses written in Pahlavi, a Middle Iranian language; among these are the Zand, a commentary on the Avesta, and the Bundahishn (Book of creation). There are more recent Zoroastrian texts in the New Persian, Gujarati, and English languages that transmit tenets of the faith and the meanings of rituals to believers who no longer understand the Avestan and Pahlavi languages.

The religion proposes an ethical dualism—which later became a cosmic dualism—between righteousness and falsehood, personified by a pair of primal spirits: Ahura Mazda (Ohrmazd), the Lord Wisdom, and Angra Mainyu (Ahreman), the Destructive Spirit. Ahura Mazda, the supreme deity, is believed to have created the spiritual and material worlds completely pure. Evil, disease, pollution, and death are attributed to Angra Mainyu, the devil. According to Zoroastrianism, Ahura Mazda created six *amesha spentas,* or beneficent spiritual beings, and other minor good spirits to assist him in protecting the material creations. Angra Mainyu produced numerous *daevas,* or demons, to defile the spiritual and material worlds. Zoroastrian texts claim that human beings were created by Ahura Mazda as allies in the struggle against Angra Mainyu, and that humans entered into a covenant with their creator to combat the forces of evil through daily good deeds.

Between the ages of seven and twelve, each Zoroastrian child undergoes initiation into the religion.

A Zoroastrian priest in London officiates at an initiation ceremony for children between seven and twelve years old. Founded more than 3,000 years ago in central Asia, Zoroastrianism was the major religion in Iran until the emergence of Islam. During the past 200 years, thousands of its adherents have established communities in India and, in much smaller numbers, in the West. © Tim Page/Corbis. Reproduced by permission.

The ritual, which symbolizes a spiritual rebirth, is termed *sedra pushun* in Iran and *navjote* in India. Every initiate dons a white undershirt called the *sedra,* or *sudra,* and ties a sacred girdle known as the *kashti,* or *kusti,* around the waist. The girdle, which most Zoroastrians continue to wear, should be untied and retied with the recitation of prayers on awakening each morning, and prior to performing worship. Many rituals, such as the *jashan,* or thanksgiving ceremony, are conducted within buildings known as fire temples. Fire is one of the seven sacred creations; the others are water, earth, metal, plants, animals, and human beings. Moreover, fire is believed to destroy evil, and thus it became the religion's icon. Sacred fires burn constantly in altars at major temples at Sharifabad, near Yazd, in Iran and at Surat, Navsari, and Bombay in India. Smaller temples in Iran and India and elsewhere do not maintain constantly burning fires; rather, a fire is lit in an altar prior to acts of worship. Because impurity is thought to arise from evil, Zoroastrians undergo elaborate rituals to ensure their spiritual purity. In addition to rituals of worship and purification, other acts of devotion include seven feasts, such as that celebrating Nav Ruz, the new year.

Zoroastrian doctrine holds that earth, fire, and water are polluted if a corpse is buried, cremated, or placed in water. Consequently, corpses are washed, then placed in a *dakhma* (funerary tower), which is open to the sky and accessible to birds of prey. Thereafter, the bones are collected and disposed of. Exposure of corpses has been phased out in Iran since the 1940s, replaced with interment (burial), but many Parsis in India and Pakistan continue the tradition of exposing bodies in funerary towers, particularly at Bombay and Karachi. Most Zoroastrians elsewhere follow their Iranian coreligionists' adaptation. Certain Zoroastrian communities, particularly those in North America, now perform cremation. Zoroastrians believe that after death each individual's soul is judged by a triad of gods—Mithra, the keeper of covenants; Rashnu, the judge; and Sraosha, the messenger—at the Bridge of the Separator, which connects earth to heaven over the pit of hell. If the soul's good deeds are greater than its evil deeds, it is led across the bridge into paradise. When its evil deeds outweigh the good, the soul is cast into hell until the day of universal judgment. In cases where a soul's good and evil deeds are equal, it is consigned to limbo. The faithful believe that at the end of time a savior (*saoshyant*) will resurrect the dead. Thereafter, Ahura Mazda will descend to earth and separate the righteous individuals from the evil ones. Each sinner will be purified of his or her transgressions and granted immortality. Then Angra Mainyu will be forced back into hell, and the world will become free of evil and impurity forever.

Bibliography

Boyce, Mary. *A Persian Stronghold of Zoroastrianism.* Oxford, U.K.: Clarendon Press, 1977. Reprint edition, Lanham, MD: University Press of America, 1994.

Choksy, Jamsheed K. *Purity and Pollution in Zoroastrianism: Triumph over Evil.* Austin: University of Texas Press, 1989.

Writer, Rashna. *Contemporary Zoroastrians: An Unstructured Nation.* Lanham, MD: University Press of America, 1994.

Zaehner, Robert C. *The Teachings of the Magi: A Compendium of Zoroastrian Beliefs.* New York: Macmillan; London: Allen and Unwin, 1956. Reprint, London: Sheldon, 1975.

JAMSHEED K. CHOKSY
UPDATED BY ERIC HOOGLUND

ZUBAYRI, QA'ID MUHAMMAD MAHMUD AL-
[1919–1965]

Yemeni political reformer.

Born in San'a, Qa'id Muhammad Mahmud al-Zubayri left North Yemen after a brief career as a government official. With Ahmad Muhammad Nu'man, he began his lifelong effort to reform Yemen's imamic government. He participated in the founding of the Liberal party and the Free Yemeni movement. At this time, his poetry, in particular, earned him a literary reputation. Zubayri strongly supported the revolution of 1962 but quickly became disillusioned with the policies of Abdullah al-Sallal. He founded the "Third Force" as an alternative to the royalists and republicans but was assassinated in 1965.

MANFRED W. WENNER

ZU'BI, MAHMUD AL-
[1938–2000]

Syrian politician and long-serving prime minister.

Hailing from a Sunni family in the southern village of Khirbat al-Ghazala, al-Zu'bi was a Ba'th party member in high school and studied agronomy in Cairo. He ascended in the party's agricultural bureaucracy to become head of the general authority for development of the Euphrates river basin from 1973 to 1976 and, from 1980 to 1981, director of the *maktab al-fallahin* (the peasants' office). In January 1980 he became a member of the Ba'th Regional (Syrian) Command. Al-Zu'bi was continually responsive to agrarian concerns in his capacity as he rose in government, both as speaker of parliament (1981–1987) and, later, as long-time prime minister (1987–2000) during the presidency of Hafiz al-Asad. He was dismissed in March 2000 and accused of corruption, after which he committed suicide on 31 May 2000.

Bibliography

Batatu, Hanna. *Syria's Peasantry, the Descendants of Its Lesser Rural Notables, and Their Politics.* Princeton, NJ: Princeton University Press, 1999.

Hinnebusch, Raymond A. *Authoritarian Power and State Formation in Ba'thist Syria: Army, Party, and Peasant.* Boulder, CO: Westview Press, 1990.

CHARLES U. ZENZIE
UPDATED BY MICHAEL R. FISCHBACH

ZURAYK, CONSTANTINE
[1909–2000]

Syrian intellectual and educator.

Constantine Zurayk (also Qustantin Zurayq) was born in Damascus. He received a B.A. from the American University of Beirut (AUB) in 1928, an M.A. from the University of Chicago in 1929, and a Ph.D. from Princeton University in 1930. He was an assistant professor of history at AUB (1930–1945) and later distinguished professor (1958-1977). He also served as counselor to the Syrian legation and then as minister to the United States (1945–1947), AUB vice president (1947–1949, 1952–1954), rector of the Syrian University in Damascus (1949–1952), and AUB acting president (1954–1957).

Zurayk, a prominent Arab intellectual, wrote *Ma'na al-Nakba* (1948; The meaning of the disaster), the first substantial critique of Arab society in light of the 1948 defeat in Palestine. An advocate of rationalism, scientific and cultural progress, and secular nationalism, he produced many other influential works, including *Nahnu wa al-Ta'rikh* (1959; Facing history), *Fi Ma'rakat al-Hadara* (1964; In the battle for civilization), and *Nahnu wa al-Mustaqbal* (1977; Facing the future), as well as translations and editions of European and Arabic works on cultural history. In 1963 he helped found the Institute for Palestine Studies, and served as its chairman until 1984. Zurayk died in Beirut on 12 August 2000.

See also AMERICAN UNIVERSITY OF BEIRUT (AUB); DAMASCUS; INSTITUTE FOR PALESTINE STUDIES.

Bibliography

Atiyeh, George N., and Oweiss, Ibrahim M. *Arab Civilization—Challenges and Responses: Studies in Honor of Constantine K. Zurayk.* Albany: State University of New York Press, 1988.

Nashabé, Hisham, ed. *Studia Palaestina: Studies in Honour of Constantine K. Zurayk.* Beirut: Institute for Palestine Studies, 1988.

CHARLES U. ZENZIE
UPDATED BY MICHAEL R. FISCHBACH

SYNOPTIC OUTLINE OF ENTRIES

The synoptic outline of entries provides a general overview of the conceptual scheme of the encyclopedia. Because the section headings are not mutually exclusive, certain entries are listed in more than one section.

ARAB-ISRAEL CONFLICT

Acheson, Dean
Alpha, Operation
Anglo–American Committee of Inquiry (1946)
Aqsa Intifada, al-
Arab Boycott
Arab Bureau (Cairo)
Arab–Israel Conflict
Arab–Israeli General Armistice Agreements (1949)
Arab–Israel War (1948)
Arab–Israel War (1956)
Arab–Israel War (1967)
Arab–Israel War (1973)
Arab–Israel War (1982)
Arab League Summits
Arafat, Yasir
Ard, al-
Arms and Armaments in the Middle East
Avnery, Uri
Azzam, Abd al-Rahman al-
Baker, James A.
Barak, Ehud
Barghuthi, Marwan
Bar-Lev, Haim
Begin, Menachem
Ben-Gurion, David
Benvenisti, Meron
Bernadotte, Folke
Black September
Bunche, Ralph J.
Camp David Accords (1978)
Dahlan, Muhammad
Dayan, Moshe
Dayr Yasin
Eban, Abba (Aubrey)
Egyptian–Israeli Peace Treaty (1979)
Fahd Plan (1981)
Fatah, al-
Gaza (City)
Gaza Strip
Geneva Peace Conference (1973)
Green Line
Habib, Philip Charles
Hammarskjöld, Dag
Institute for Palestine Studies
Israel: Overview
Israel: Military and Politics
Israeli Settlements
Jarring, Gunnar
Jericho Congress (1948)

BIOGRAPHIES

Ahmar, Abdullah ibn Husayn al-
Ahmet Ihsan To'kgoz
Ahmet Izzet
Ahmet Riza
Ahsa'i, Ahmad al-
Akçura, Yusuf
Akhondzadeh, Mirza Fath Ali
Akkad, Mustafa
Al al-Shaykh Family
Al Bu Sa'id Family and Tribe of Oman
Al Bu Sa'id, Qabus ibn Sa'id
Al Bu Sa'id, Sa'id ibn Taymur
Al Khalifa Family
Al Nahayyan Family
Al Rashid Family
Al Sa'ud Family
Al Sa'ud, Sa'ud ibn Abd al-Aziz
Al Sabah Family
Al Sabah, Mubarak
Al Saqr Family
Al Sudayri Family
Al Sudayri, Hassa bint Ahmad
Al Thani Family
Al Thani, Hamad ibn Khalifa
Al Thunayyan Family
Ala, Hoseyn
Alam, Amir Asadollah
Alami Family, al-
Alavi, Bozorg
Al-e Ahmad, Jalal
Ali Nasir Muhammad al-Hasani
Ali Riza
Ali Suavi
Allon, Yigal
Alterman, Natan
Altinay, Ahmed Refik
Amanollah Khan
Amichai, Yehuda
Amin al-Dowleh, Mirza Ali Khan
Amin al-Soltan, Ali-Asghar
Amin al-Zarb, Mohammad Hasan
Amin, Hafizullah
Amini, Ali
Amini, Fatemeh
Amir Kabir, Mirza Taqi Khan
Amir-Entezam, Abbas
Amit, Meir
Amri, Hasan al-
Anawati, Georges Chehata
Andranik Ozanian
Annan, Kofi A.
Antar, Ali Ahmad Nasir
Antun, Farah
Aoun, Michel

Aql, Sa'id
Arafat, Yasir
Aral, &Obreveθz
Arens, Moshe
Arfa, Hasan
Arif, Arif al-
Arkoun, Mohammed
Arlosoroff, Chaim
Asad, Bashshar al-
Asad, Hafiz al-
Ashmawi, Muhammad Abd al-Rahman Salih al-
Ashmawi, Muhammad Sa'id al-
Askari, Ja'far al-
Asmar, Fawzi al-
Atasi, Nur al-Din al-
Atatürk, Mustafa Kemal
Atay, Salih Rifki
Attas, Haydar Abu Bakr al-
Attlee, Clement
Avnery, Uri
Awad, Louis
Ayn al-Dowleh, Abd al-Majid Mirza
Ayni, Muhsin al-
Aziz, Tariq
Azm, Sadiq al-
Azuri, Najib
Azzam, Abd al-Rahman al-
Badr, Muhammad al-
Baghdadi, Abd al-Latif al-
Bahar, Mohammad Taqi
Bakdash, Khalid
Baker, James A.
Bakhtiar, Shapur
Bakhtiar, Timur
Bakhtiari, Najaf Qoli Khan Samsam al-Soltaneh
Balyan Family
Bani Sadr, Abolhasan
Banna, Hasan al-
Banna, Sabri al-
Baraheni, Reza
Barak, Ehud
Barghuthi Family
Barghuthi, Marwan
Baring, Evelyn
Bar-Lev, Haim
Barzani Family
Basma bint Talal
Bayar, Celal
Bayat, Mortaza Qoli
Baydh, Ali Salim al-
Bayrakdar, Mustafa
Bazargan, Mehdi
Begin, Menachem
Behar, Nissim

Fahmi, Mahmud Pasha
Faisal ibn Abd al-Aziz Al Saʿud
Farhad, Ghulam Muhammad
Farmanfarma, Abd al-Hoseyn Mirza
Farrokhzad, Forugh
Fassih, Ismail
Fath Ali Shah Qajar
Faysal ibn Turki Al Saʿud
Ferit, Damat Mehmet
Flapan, Simha
Foroughi, Mirza Mohammad Ali Khan Zaka al-Molk
Franjiyya Family
Franjiyya, Sulayman
Gökalp, Ziya
Gülbenkian, Calouste
Gülen, Fetullah
Güney, Yilmaz
Gürpinar, Hüseyin Rahmi
Gürsel, Cemal
Gailani, Ahmad
Ganim, Halil
Ganji, Akbar
Garang, John
Gaspirali, Ismail Bey
Geagea, Samir
Ghali, Boutros
Ghanim, al-
Ghanim, Fathi
Ghashmi, Ahmad Husayn
Ghassemlou, Abdul Rahman
Ghazali, Muhammad al-
Ghorbal, Ashraf
Ghuri, Emile al-
Gilboa, Amir
Glubb, John Bagot
Goldberg, Leah
Goldmann, Nahum
Golestan, Ebrahim
Golshiri, Houshang
Gordon, Aaron David
Greenberg, Uri Zvi
Grivas, Georgios Theodoros
Gur, Mordechai
Guri, Chaim
Habash, George
Habib, Philip Charles
Habibi, Emile
Habibollah Khan
Ha-Cohen, Mordechai
Haddad, Wadi
Hafiz, Amin al-
Hajir, Abd al-Hoseyn
Hajri, Abdullah al-
Hakim, Adnan al-

Hamama, Faten
Hamdi, Ibrahim al-
Hammarskjöld, Dag
Hammer, Zevulun
Hanafi, Hasan
Hananu, Ibrahim
Harel, Isser
Hareven, Shulamit
Hariri, Rafiq Bahaʾuddin al-
Harkabi, Yehoshafat
Hasan, Hani al-
Hasan, Khalid al-
Hashemi, Faezeh
Hashim, Ibrahim
Hashimi, Yasin al-
Hashimite House (House of Hashim)
Hatim Sultans of Hamdan
Hawatma, Nayif
Haykal, Muhammad Hasanayn
Hazaz, Hayyim
Hedayat, Sadegh
Hekmatyar, Golbuddin
Herzl, Theodor
Herzog, Chaim
Herzog, Yaʿacov David
Heskayl, Sasson
Hess, Moses
High Commissioners (Palestine)
Hillel, Shlomo
Hilmi, Ahmad
Hilu, Pierre
Hirawi, Ilyas al-
Hobeika, Elie
Hoffman, Yoel
Hoss, Salim al-
Hourani, Albert
Hoveyda, Amir Abbas
Husari, Sati al-
Husayn ibn Ali
Husayni, Husayn al-
Husayni, Jamal al-
Husayni, Muhammad Amin al-
Husayni, Musa Kazim al-
Hussein ibn Talal
Hussein, Saddam
Hut, Shafiq al-
Ibrahim, Saʿad al-Din
Ilaysh, Muhammad
İnönü, Erdal
İnönü, İsmet
İpekci, Abdi
Iqbal, Muhammad
Iryani, Abd al-Rahman al-
Ismaʿil, Abd al-Fattah

Jabotinsky, Vladimir Zeʾev
Jadid, Salah
Jamali, Muhammad Fadhil al-
Jamalzadeh, Mohammad Ali
Jarring, Gunnar
Jibril, Ahmad
Jinnah, Muhammad Ali
Joseph, Dov
Jumayyil, Amin
Jumayyil, Bashir
Jumblatt Family
Jumblatt, Walid
Kadivar, Mohsen
Kahane, Meir
Kalvaryski, Chaim Margaliut-
Kamal, Ahmad
Kamil, Kibrish Mehmet
Kanafani, Ghassan
Kaniuk, Yoram
Kar, Mehrangiz
Karacan, Ali Naci
Karbaschi, Gholamhosain
Karmal, Babrak
Karzai, Hamid
Kasap, Teodor
Kashani, Abu al-Qasem
Kasravi, Ahmad
Katznelson, Berl
Keinan, Amos
Kemalettin Bey
Kenaz, Yehoshua
Kennedy, John Fitzgerald
Kenter, Yildiz
Kessar, Israel
Khaddam, Abd al-Halim
Khalaf, Abdulhadi
Khalid ibn Abd al-Aziz Al Saʿud
Khalid, Khalid Muhammad
Khalidi, Ahmad al-Samih al-
Khalidi, Husayn Fakhri al-
Khalidi, Walid
Khamenehi, Ali
Kharrazi, Kamal
Khatami, Mohammad
Khazʿal Khan
Khomeini, Ruhollah
Khrimian, Mkrtich
Khuri, Bishara al-
Khyber, Mir Akbar
Kianuri, Nur al-Din
Kiarostami, Abbas
Kimche, David
Kirkbride, Alec Seath
Kisakürek, Necip Fazil

Kissinger, Henry
Koç, Vehbi
Kol, Moshe
Kollek, Teddy
Kook, Zvi Yehuda
Koprülü, Mehmet Fuat
Kovner, Abba
Kuchek Khan-e Jangali
Kudsi, Nazim al-
Lahad, Antoine
Lahhud, Emile
Lavon, Pinhas
Lawrence, T. E.
Leibowitz, Yeshayahu
Levin, Hanoch
Levinger, Moshe
Levy, David
Lloyd George, David
Luke, Harry
Luz, Kadish
Maʿrufi, Abbas
MacDonald, Malcolm
MacDonald, Ramsay
MacMichael, Harold
Madkour, Ibrahim
Magnes, Judah
Mahd-e Ulya, Malek Jahan Khanum
Mahfuz, Najib
Mahmud Durrani
Mahmud II
Mahmud, Muhammad
Mahmud, Mustafa
Maimon, Yehudah Leib Hacohen
Majali Family
Makhmalbaf Family
Makhmalbaf, Mohsen
Makki, Hasan Muhammad
Maksoud, Clovis
Maktum Family, al-
Malik, Charles Habib
Malkom Khan, Mirza
Maspéro, Gaston
Mawdudi, Abu al-Aʿla al-
Meged, Aharon
Mehmet Rauf
Mehmet V Reşat
Meir, Golda
Menderes, Adnan
Meushi, Paul Peter
Michael, Sami
Midhat Paşa
Millspaugh, Arthur
Minz, Benjamin
Modaʾi, Yitzhak

Mohajerani, Ataollah
Mohammad Ali Shah Qajar
Mohammadi, Maulawi Mohammad Nabi
Mojaddedi, Sebghatullah
Mojtahed-Shabestari, Mohammad
Mond, Alfred Moritz
Montazeri, Hosayn Ali
Mossadegh, Mohammad
Motahhari, Mortaza
Mozaffar al-Din Qajar
Muʿalla Family, al-
Muasher, Marwan
Mubarak, Husni
Muhammad, Aziz
Muhtar, Gazi Ahmet
Muhyi al-Din, Khalid
Muhyi al-Din, Zakariyya
Munif, Abdel Rahman
Musavi, Mir-Hosain
Musavi-Ardebili, AbdolKarim
Mustafa Reşid
Mustafa Suphi
Nabavi, Behzad
Nabi Salih, al-
Nabizade Nazim
Nadi, Yunus
Nadir Barakzai, Mohammad
Najibullah
Namik Kemal
Namir, Mordekhai
Naser al-Din Shah
Nashashibi Family
Nasir, Hanna
Nasrallah, Hasan
Nasser, Gamal Abdel
Nateq-Nuri, Ali Akbar
Navon, Yizhak
Nazif, Süleyman
Neʾeman, Yuval
Nerval, Gérard de
Nesin, Nüsret Aziz
Netanyahu, Benjamin
Nissim, Isaac
Nordau, Max
Nuʿaymi Family, al-
Numeiri, Muhammad Jaʿfar
Nuri, Abd al-Malik
Nuri, Fazlollah
Nursi, Said
Nusayba Family
Omar, Muhammad (Mullah)
Ormanian, Maghakia
Ormsby-Gore, William George Arthur
Oufkir, Muhammad

Ouled Sidi Cheikh
Ouziel, Ben Zion Meir Hai
Özal, Turgut
Oz, Amos
Pérez de Cuéllar, Javier
Pagis, Dan
Pahlavi, Mohammad Reza
Pahlavi, Reza
Palmerston, Lord Henry John Temple
Parsipur, Shahrnush
Peled, Mattityahu
Pelt, Adrian
Peres, Shimon
Pharaon, Rashad
Philby, Harry St. John
Plumer, Herbert Charles Onslow
Politi, Elie
Pollard Affair
Powell, Colin L.
Qabbani, Nizar
Qaddumi, Faruq
Qafih, Yihye ben Solomon
Qajar Dynasty
Qajar, Abdullah Mirza
Qajar, Agha Mohammad
Qaradawi, Yusuf al-
Qasimi Family of Raʾs al-Khayma, al-
Qasimi Family of Sharjah, al-
Qassam, Izz al-Din al-
Qotbzadeh, Sadeq
Qurai, Ahmad Sulayman
Qutb, Sayyid
Raab, Esther
Rabbani, Burhanuddin
Rabin, Yitzhak
Rabiyya Ali, Salim
Rafsanjani, Ali Akbar Hashemi
Rahnavard, Zahra
Rajavi, Masud
Rajub, Jibril
Ramadan, Taha Yasin
Ratebzad, Anahita
Ratosh, Yonatan
Ravikovitch, Dahlia
Reagan, Ronald
Recaizade Mahmud Ekrem
Richmond, Ernest T.
Rifaʿi, Zaid al-
Rogers, William Pierce
Roosevelt, Franklin Delano
Roosevelt, Kermit
Rubinstein, Amnon
Ruppin, Arthur
Rusk, Dean

Rutenberg, Pinhas
Sa'ada, Antun
Sa'edi, Gholamhossein
Sa'id, Nuri al-
Sa'id Pasha
Sa'idzadeh, Seyyed Mohsen
Saade, George
Saba Family
Sabbagh, Hasib
Sadat, Anwar al-
Sadat, Jihan al-
Sadr, Muhammad Baqir al-
Sadr, Muhsin
Safveti Ziya
Said, Edward
Salam Family
Salam, Sa'ib
Salih, Ali Abdullah
Salih, Teyib
Salim, Ali
Salim, Jawad
Sallal, Abdullah al-
Samuel, Herbert Louis
Sane'i, Yusef
Sapir, Pinhas
Sarid, Yossi
Sasson, Eliyahu
Saunders, Harold
Saygun, Ahmed Adnan
Sayyab, Badr Shakir al-
Sediq, Sohaila
Şeker Ahmet
Selçuk, Munir Nurettin
Selim III
Sepehri, Sohrab
Seri, Dan-Benaya
Şevket, Mahmut
Sezer, Ahmet
Sfeir, Nasrallah
Sha'bi Family
Sha'rawi, Muhammad Mutwalli al-
Sha'ul, Anwar
Shahada, George
Shahbandar, Abd al-Rahman
Shahin, Tanyos
Shahin, Yusuf
Shaltut, Muhammad
Shami, Ahmad Muhammad al-
Shami, Muhammad Abdullah al-
Shamir, Moshe
Shamir, Yitzhak
Shamlu, Ahmad
Shammas, Anton
Shapira, Hayyim Moshe

Sharabati, Ahmad al-
Sharef, Ze'ev
Sharett, Moshe
Shari'ati, Ali
Shariatmadari, Kazem
Sharif, Aziz
Sharif, Omar
Sharif-Emami, Ja'far
Sharon, Ariel
Sharqi Family, al-
Shawqi, Ahmad
Shenouda III
Shid, Nahid
Shiloah, Reuven
Shirazi, Mirza Hasan
Shitreet, Bekhor
Shlonsky, Avraham
Shultz, George
Shuqayri, Ahmad
Shuster, W. Morgan
Silver, Abba Hillel
Simavi, Sedat
Şinasi, İbrahim
Sisco, Joseph
Sistani, Ali al-
Smilansky, Moshe
Sneh, Moshe
Sobol, Yehoshua
Soheyli, Ali
Sokolow, Nahum
Somikh, Abdullah
Soroush, AbdolKarim
Stark, Freya
Stern, Abraham
Storrs, Ronald
Suissa, Albert
Sulayman, Hikmat
Sulh, Rashid al-
Sulh, Taki al-Din al-
Sunay, Cevdet
Suwaydi Family
Suwayhli, Ramadan al-
Sykes, Mark
Türkes, Alparslan
Tabataba'i, Mohammad
Tabataba'i, Ziya
Tahir, Kemal
Talabani, Jalal
Talal ibn Abdullah
Talat, Mehmet
Taleqani, Azam
Tall, Wasfi al-
Tamimi, Amin al-
Tamir, Shmuel

Tammuz, Benyamin
Tanburi Cemil
Taner, Haldun
Tanpinar, Ahmed Hamdi
Tantawi, Muhammad Sayyid al-
Taqla, Philippe
Tarhan, Abdülhak Hamit
Tariki, Abdullah
Tevfik Fikret
Tikriti, Hardan al-
Tlas, Mustafa
Truman, Harry S.
Trumpeldor, Yosef
Tsemel, Leah
Tuqan, Fadwa
Tuqan Family
Turabi, Hasan al-
Turki, Fawaz
Twayni, Ghassan
Uşakligil, Halit Ziya
Urabi, Ahmad
Ussishkin, Menahem
Utaybi, Juhayman al-
Uthman, Muhammad Ali
Uthman, Uthman Ahmad
Vance, Cyrus
Vanunu Affair
Vazir Afkham, Soltan Ali Khan
Vaziri, Qamar al-Moluk
Velayati, Ali Akbar
Volpi, Giuseppe
Vozuq al-Dowleh, Mirza Hasan Khan
Wahrhaftig, Zerah
Wattar, al-Taher
Wauchope, Arthur
Wazir, Khalil al-
Weizman, Ezer
Weizmann, Chaim
Wilson, Arnold T.
Wilson, Woodrow
Wingate, Charles Orde
Wise, Stephen S.
Wolff, Henry Drummond
Yücel, Hasan Ali
Yadin, Yigael
Yahya ibn Muhammad Hamid al-Din
Yamani, Ahmad Zaki
Yariv, Aharon
Yasar Kemal
Yasin, Ahmad Isma'il
Yazdi, Ibrahim
Yaziji, Nasif
Yehoshua, Avraham B.
Yellin-Mor, Natan

Yizhar, S.
Yosef, Ovadiah
Yunis Jabir, Abu Bakr
Yurdakul, Mehmet Emin
Za'im, Husni al-
Zach, Natan
Zahir Shah
Zana, Leyla
Zelda
Zell al-Soltan, Mas'ud Mirza
Ziya, Abdülhamit
Zohar, Uri
Zohrab, Krikor
Zu'bi, Mahmud al-
Zurayk, Constantine

COUNTRIES: AFGHANISTAN

Afghanistan: Overview
Afghanistan: Islamic Movements in
Afghanistan: Political Parties in
Afghanistan: Soviet Intervention in
Afghanistan: U.S. Intervention in
Amu Darya
Anglo–Afghan Treaty (1855)
Anglo–Afghan Wars
Bamyan
Barakzai Dynasty
Bost
Durand Line
Hazara
Helmand River
Herat
Kabul
Kandahar
Khyber Pass
Mazar-e Sharif
Omar, Muhammad (Mullah)
Pushtun
Refugees: Afghan
Shiberghan
Tajiks
Uzbeks

COUNTRIES: ARABIAN PENINSULA

Abu Dhabi
Abu Musa Island
Aden
Ajman
Al Bu Sa'id Family and Tribe of Oman
Anglo–Omani Treaties
Anjoman
Arabian Horses

Arabian Mission
Arabian Peninsula
As-Is Agreement
Ayn, al-
Baharina
Bahrain
Bahraini–Qatari Wars
Bahrain Order in Council
Bubiyan Island
Buraymi Oasis Dispute
Dammam, al-
Dhahran
Dhufar
Dhufar Rebellion
Doha
Dubai
Fao Peninsula
Free Officers, Yemen
Fujayra
Grand Mosque
Gulf Crisis (1990–1991)
Gulf of Oman
Hadramawt
Hamid al-Din Family
Hasa, al-
Hijaz
Hijaz Railroad
Hodeida
Jabal al-Akhdar, Oman
Jabal Shammar
Jazeera, al-
Jidda
Jubayl, al-
Khubar, al-
Kuwait
Kuwait City
Manama
Ma'rib
Maritime Peace in Perpetuity, Treaty of (1853)
Masira Island
Matrah
Mecca
Medina
Muharraq
Muscat
Nafud Desert
Najd
Neutral Zone
Oman
Persian (Arabian) Gulf
Protectorate States
Qatar
Ra's al-Khayma
Riyadh

Rub al-Khali
Saudi Arabia
Sharjah
Sib, Treaty of (1920)
Sitra
Socotra
South Arabian League
Ta'if, al-
Ta'if, Treaty of al-
Tiran, Strait of
Trans-Arabian Pipeline
Tribes and Tribalism: Yemeni
Trucial Coast
Tunb Islands
Umm al-Qaywayn
Umm Na'san
United Arab Emirates
Wadi Hadramawt
Yanbu
Yemen Arab Republic
Yemen Civil War
Yemen Dynasties

COUNTRIES: CENTRAL ASIA
Hindu Kush Mountains
Pamir Mountains

COUNTRIES: EGYPT
Alexandria
Alexandria University
American University in Cairo (AUC)
Aswan High Dam
Azhar, al-
Cairo
Cairo University
Coptic Museum
Damanhur
Dar al-Kutub al-Misriyya
Dar al-Ulum
Delta Barrages
Egypt
Egyptian Museum
Gezira Sporting Club
Infitah
Institut d'Égypte
Mahmudiyya Canal
Majlis Shura al-Nuwwab
Nasser, Lake
National Party (Egypt)
New Wafd
Nile River
Nubians

People's Assembly
Pharaonicism
Philae
Port Sa'id
Pyramids
Qusayr, al-
Saint Catherine's Monastery
Saint Mark's Cathedral
Satellite Cities Development
Sayyidna Husayn Mosque
Sharm al-Shaykh
Shepheard's Hotel
Sinai Peninsula
Siwa Oasis
Sphinx
Suez Canal University
Suez–Mediterranean Pipeline
Takfir wa al-Hijra, al-
Victoria College
Wadi Natrun
Wafd
Waqf
War of Attrition (1969–1970)
Zaqaziq University

COUNTRIES: IRAN

Abadan
Ahvaz
Algiers Agreement (1975)
Anglo–Iranian Agreement (1919)
Anglo–Iranian Oil Company
Anglo–Persian War (1856)
Anglo–Russian Agreement (1907)
Azerbaijan
Azerbaijan Crisis
Bakhtiari
Baluchis
Baluchistan
Bisitun
Constitutional Revolution
Cossack Brigade
Golestan Palace
Hamadan
Iran
Iran–Contra Affair
Iranian Revolution (1979)
Iran–Iraq War (1980–1988)
Iran Novin Party
Isfahan
Jangali
Jehad-e Sazandegi
Kerman
Kharg Island

Khorasan
Khuzistan
Kurdistan
Kurds
Lurs
Mashhad
Persian Cats
Qom
Revolutionary Guards
Shatt al-Arab
Shiraz
Sistan and Baluchistan
Social Democratic Party of Azerbaijan
South Persia Rifles
Students in the Line of the Imam
Tabriz
Tehran
Tobacco Revolt
Trans-Iranian Railway
Tripartite Treaty of Alliance
Turkmanchai, Treaty of (1828)
Turko–Iranian War (1821–1823)
White Revolution (1961–1963)
Yazd
Zabul
Zagros
Zahedan

COUNTRIES: IRAQ

Abd al-Ilah ibn Ali
Ahali Group
Askari, Ja'far al-
Assyrians
Aziz, Tariq
Baghdad
Barzani Family
Basra
Ba'th, al-
Bitar, Salah al-Din al-
Chalabi, Ahmad
Churchill, Winston S.
Cox, Percy
Gulf Crisis (1990–1991)
Hashimi, Taha al-
Husari, Sati al-
Husayn ibn Ali
Hussein, Saddam
Iran–Iraq War (1980–1988)
Iraq
Iraqi National Congress
Iraq Petroleum Company (IPC)
Jamali, Muhammad Fadhil al-
Kurdish Autonomous Zone

Mosul
Muhammad, Aziz
Najaf, al-
Patriotic Union of Kurdistan (PUK)
Ramadan, Taha Yasin
Refugees: Kurdish
Sa'id, Nuri al-
Salim, Jawad
Samarra
Sanctions, Iraqi
Sharif, Aziz
Somikh, Abdullah
Sulaymaniya
Talabani, Jalal
Tikrit
Tikriti Families

COUNTRIES: ISRAEL

Acheson, Dean
Aliyah
Allon, Yigal
Alpha, Operation
Alterman, Natan
American Israel Public Affairs Committee
American Jewish Committee
American Jewish Congress
Amichai, Yehuda
Amit, Meir
Arab Boycott
Arab–Israel Conflict
Arab–Israeli General Armistice Agreements (1949)
Arab–Israel War (1948)
Arab–Israel War (1956)
Arab–Israel War (1967)
Arab–Israel War (1973)
Arab–Israel War (1982)
Ard, al-
Arens, Moshe
Avnery, Uri
Barak, Ehud
Bar-Ilan University
Bar-Lev, Haim
Begin, Menachem
Ben-Aharon, Yitzhak
Ben-Gurion, David
Ben-Porat, Mordechai
Benvenisti, Meron
Ben-Zvi, Yizhak
Bialik, Hayyim Nahman
Black Panthers
Burg, Avraham
Burg, Yosef
Burla, Yehuda

Cohen, Ge'ula
Dayan, Moshe
Eban, Abba (Aubrey)
Egyptian–Israeli Peace Treaty (1979)
Eitan, Rafael
Entebbe Operation
Eretz Yisrael
Flapan, Simha
Galilee
Galilee, Sea of
Gilboa, Amir
Golan Heights
Goldberg, Leah
Goldmann, Nahum
Greenberg, Uri Zvi
Guri, Chaim
Gur, Mordechai
Gush Emunim
Haifa
Haifa University
Hammer, Zevulun
Harel, Isser
Hareven, Shulamit
Harkabi, Yehoshafat
Ha-Shomer Ha-Tza'ir
"Ha-Tikva"
Hazaz, Hayyim
Hebrew
Hebrew University of Jerusalem
Herzl, Theodor
Herzog, Chaim
Herzog, Ya'acov David
Heskayl, Sasson
Hillel, Shlomo
Histadrut
Hoffman, Yoel
Holocaust
Hula Swamps
Intifada (1987–1991)
Irgun Zva'i Le'umi (IZL)
Israel: Overview
Israel: Military and Politics
Israel: Overview of Political Parties in
Israeli Settlements
Jaffa
Jerusalem
Jewish Agency for Palestine
Jewish National Fund
Jews in the Middle East
Johnston Plan (1953)
Joint Distribution Committee
Jordanian Option
Joseph, Dov
Kafr Qasim

Kahan Commission (1983)
Kahane, Meir
Kaniuk, Yoram
Karp Report (1984)
Keinan, Amos
Kenaz, Yehoshua
Keren Hayesod
Kessar, Israel
Kibbutz
Kimche, David
King David Hotel
Kiryat Arba
Knesset
Kollek, Teddy
Kol, Moshe
Kook, Zvi Yehuda
Kovner, Abba
Labor Zionism
Land Day
Lavon Affair
Lavon, Pinhas
Law of Return
Leibowitz, Yeshayahu
Levinger, Moshe
Levin, Hanoch
Levy, David
Liberty, USS
Litani Operation (1978)
Litani River
Literature: Hebrew
London Conference (1956)
Luz, Kadish
Lydda
Maʿa lot
Maʿbarah
Madrid Conference (1991)
Magen David Adom (MDA)
Magic Carpet Operation
Maimon, Yehudah Leib Hacohen
Masada
Matzpen
Meah Sheʿarim
Meged, Aharon
Meir, Golda
Michael, Sami
Mimouna Festival
Minz, Benjamin
Modaʾi, Yitzhak
Moshav
Mossad
Nahalal
Namir, Mordekhai
National Water System (Israel)
Nazareth

Neʾeman, Yuval
Negev
Netanyahu, Benjamin
Neturei Karta
Newspapers and Print Media: Israel
Nissim, Isaac
Oslo Accord (1993)
Ouziel, Ben Zion Meir Hai
Oz, Amos
Oz ve Shalom (Netivot shalom)
Pagis, Dan
Palestinian Citizens of Israel
Palestinians
Palmah
Partition Plans (Palestine)
Peace Now
Peled, Mattityahu
Peres, Shimon
Petah Tikvah
Pollard Affair
Potash Industry
Raab, Esther
Rabin, Yitzhak
Radio and Television: Israel
Ramla
Ravikovitch, Dahlia
Refugees: Jewish
Rishon le-Zion
Rubinstein, Amnon
Sabra
Safed
Samaritans
Sapir, Pinhas
Sarid, Yossi
Sasson, Eliyahu
Seri, Dan-Benaya
Sèvres Protocol (1956)
Shamir, Moshe
Shamir, Yitzhak
Shammas, Anton
Shapira, Hayyim Moshe
Sharef, Zeʾev
Sharett, Moshe
Sharon, Ariel
Shaʾul, Anwar
Shekel
Shiloah, Reuven
Shin Bet
Shitreet, Bekhor
Shlonsky, Avraham
Silver, Abba Hillel
Sneh, Moshe
Sobol, Yehoshua
Suez Crisis (1956–1957)

Suissa, Albert
Taba
Tamir, Shmuel
Tammuz, Benyamin
Technion-Israel Institute of Technology
Tel Aviv
Tel Aviv University
Tel Hai
Terrorism
Tiberias
United Jewish Appeal (UJA)
United Nations and the Middle East
United Nations Emergency Force
United Nations Truce Supervision Organization
    (UNTSO)
Vaʿad Leʾumi
Wahrhaftig, Zerah
Weizman, Ezer
Weizmann, Chaim
Weizmann Institute of Science
West Bank
Western Wall
West German Reparations Agreement
World Federation of Sephardi Communities
World Organization of Jews from Arab Countries
    (WOJAC)
World Zionist Organization (WZO)
Yadin, Yigael
Yad Mordekhai
Yad Vashem
Yariv, Aharon
Yehoshua, Avraham B.
Yellin-Mor, Natan
Yishuv
Yizhar, S.
Yosef, Ovadiah
Youth Aliyah
Zach, Natan
Zelda
Zikhron Yaʿakov
Zionism
Zionist Organization of America
Zohar, Uri

COUNTRIES: JORDAN
Abdullah I ibn Hussein
Abdullah II ibn Hussein
Abu al-Huda, Tawfiq
Amman
Aqaba
Arab Legion
Basma bint Talal
Churchill, William

Circassians
Hussein ibn Talal
Hussein, Saddam
Irbid
Islamic Action Front
Jordan
Jordan River
Karak, al-
Majali Family
Muasher, Marwan
Petra
Rifaʿi, Zaid al-
Salt, al-
University of Jordan
Yarmuk River
Yarmuk University
Zarqa, al-

COUNTRIES: LEBANON
AMAL
American University of Beirut (AUB)
Antun, Farah
Aoun, Michel
Aql, Saʿid
Baʿalbak
Beirut
Berri, Nabi
Biqa Valley
Council for Development and Reconstruction (CDR)
Eddé, Raymond
Franjiyya Family
Franjiyya, Sulayman
Geagea, Samir
Hariri, Rafiq Bahaʾuddin al-
Hilu, Pierre
Hirawi, Ilyas al-
Hizbullah
Hobeika, Elie
Hoss, Salim al-
Husayni, Husayn al-
Jumayyil, Amin
Jumayyil, Bashir
Jumblatt Family
Jumblatt, Walid
Lahad, Antoine
Lahhud, Emile
Lebanese Forces
Lebanese University
Lebanon
Malik, Charles Habib
Nasrallah, Hasan
Parliamentary Democratic Front
Phalange

Phoenicianism
Progressive Socialist Party
Raad, In'am
Sa'ada, Antun
Saade, George
Salam Family
Salam, Sa'ib
Sfeir, Nasrallah
Shahada, George
Shuf
South Lebanon Army
Special Forces of the Levant
Sulh, Rashid al-
Sulh, Taki al-Din al-
Syrian Social Nationalist Party
Ta'if Accord
Twayni, Ghassan
Tyre
Yaziji, Nasif
Zahla

COUNTRIES: SUDAN
Khartoum
Nuer
Omdurman
Sudan
Sudanese Civil Wars
Sudd
Umma Party
University of Khartoum

COUNTRIES: SYRIA
Akkad, Mustafa
Asad, Bashshar al-
Asad, Hafiz al-
Atasi, Nur al-Din al-
Bakdash, Khalid
Ba'th, al-
Bitar, Salah al-Din al-
British–French Oil Agreement
Chehab, Bashir
Chehab, Fu'ad
Circassians
Damascus
Damascus Affair (1840)
Damascus University
Dayr al-Zawr Province
Hafiz, Amin al-
Hama
Hananu, Ibrahim
Husayn ibn Ali
Jadid, Salah

Khaddam, Abd al-Halim
Kudsi, Nazim al-
Latakia
National Bloc
National Progressive Front (Syria)
Qabbani, Nizar
Sa'ada, Antun
Shahbandar, Abd al-Rahman
Syria
Syrian Social Nationalist Party
Tlas, Mustafa
Zu'bi, Mahmud al-
Zurayk, Constantine

COUNTRIES: TURKEY
Alexandretta
Anatolia
Ankara
Ankara, Treaty of (1930)
Antakya
Ararat, Mount
Armenian Genocide
Armenian Millet
Black Sea
Bodrum
Bogazköy
Bursa
Caylak
Cilicia
Diyarbakir
Edirne
Ege University
Erzurum
Erzurum Congress (1919)
Euphrates Dam
Gecekondu
Genç Kalemler
Hacettepe University
Hürriyet
Istanbul
İzmir
İzmir Economic Congress
Justice Party
Kemalism
Konya
Kurds
Lausanne, Treaty of (1923)
People's Houses
Rumelia
Sivas Conference (1919)
Social Democratic Populist Party
Southeastern Anatolia Project
Trans-Turkey Pipeline

Turkey
Turkish–Afghan Treaty (1928)
Turkish Grand National Assembly
Turko–Iranian War (1821–1823)
Üsküdar
Van, Lake
Varlik Vergisi
Village Institutes

COUNTRIES: YEMEN

Islah Party
National Democratic Front (NDF)
National Front for the Liberation of South Yemen
People's Socialist Party
Perim
San'a
San'a University
Tribes and Tribalism: Yemeni
Yemen
Yemen Hunt Oil Company
Yemeni Socialist Party

CULTURE AND SOCIETY

Abu Zeid, Layla
Adham, Soraya
Adnan, Etel
Adot Ha-Mizrah
Agriculture
Akhavan-Saless, Mehdi
Akkad, Mustafa
Al-e Ahmad, Jalal
Algerian Family Code (1984)
Ali, Wijdan
Alizadeh, Ghazaleh
Alliance Israélite Universelle (AIU)
Al-Suswa, Amat al-Alim
Alterman, Natan
AMAL
Amichai, Yehuda
Amrouche, Fadhma At Mansour
Ani, Jannane al-
Anis Al-Jalis Magazine
Antisemitism
Arab College of Jerusalem
Arab Nationalism
Archaeological Museum (Istanbul)
Archaeology in the Middle East
Architecture
Art
Ashkenazim
Attar, Nejat al-
Attar, Suad al-

Avnery, Uri
Aya Sofya
Azeri Language and Literature
Ba'albak
Ba'albakki, Layla
Bahar, Mohammad Taqi
Ba'th, al-
Badr, Liana
Baghdad University
Bahithat al-Lubnaniyyat, al-
Bakkar, Jalillah
Bani-Etemad, Rakhsan
Banking
Baraheni, Reza
Bazaars and Bazaar Merchants
Behar, Nissim
Behbehani, Simin
Behrangi, Samad
Beirut College for Women (BCW)
Ben-Aharon, Yitzhak
Ben-Gurion University of the Negev
Ben-Yehuda, Eliezer
Berlin–Baghdad Railway
Bethlehem
Bialik, Hayyim Nahman
Bir Zeit University
Biret, Idil
Birth Control
Bitton, Simone
Brenner, Yosef Hayyim
Buber, Martin
Burla, Yehuda
Cairo Family Planning Association
Caland, Huguette
Camels
Ceramics
Chédid, Andrée
Chubak, Sadeq
Circumcision
Clothing
Colonialism in the Middle East
Crimes of Honor
Dance
Daneshvar, Simin
Dead Sea Scrolls
Dhow
Diaspora
Diseases
Djebar, Assia
Dönme
Dowlatabadi, Mahmoud
Economic and Military Aid
Economics
Education

Zelda
Ziadeh, May
Zionist Organization of America
Ziwaj Mutᶜa
Zohar, Uri

ORGANIZATIONS

Advisory Council (Palestine)
Afghan Women's Council
Ahram Center for Political and Strategic Studies, al-
AISHA: Arab Women's Forum
Alliance Israélite Universelle (AIU)
Al-Suswa, Amat al-Alim
AMAL
American Council for Judaism
American Israel Public Affairs Committee
American Jewish Committee
American Jewish Congress
Anglo–American Committee of Inquiry (1946)
Anglo–Iranian Oil Company
Ankara University
Arab Boycott
Arab Bureau (Cairo)
Arab Feminist Union
Arab Higher Committee (Palestine)
Arab League Summits
Arab Socialist Union
Arab Women's Association of Palestine
Arab Women's Congress
Arab Women's Executive Committee
Arab Women's Solidarity Association International
Arabian American Oil Company (ARAMCO)
Ard, al-
Association des Femmes Tunisiennes pour la
    Recherche et le Développement (AFTURD)
Association for the Protection of Women's Rights
    (Afghanistan)
Atatürk University
Awakened Youth
B'nai B'rith
Baᶜth, al-
Baghdad Pact (1955)
Bahithat al-Lubnaniyyat, al-
Bahrain Nationalist Movement
Bar-Ilan University
Beirut College for Women (BCW)
Ben-Gurion University of the Negev
Ben-Zvi, Rahel Yanait
Bilkent University
bin Ladin, Osama
Black Panthers
Bludan Conferences (1937, 1946)
Boğaziçi (Bosporus) University

Bouhired, Jamila
Brichah
Bund
Cairo Family Planning Association
Central Intelligence Agency (CIA)
Central Treaty Organization (CENTO)
Centre de Recherches, d'Études, de Documentation et
    d'Information sur la Femme (CREDIF)
Committee for Defense of Freedom and Human
    Rights
Committee for the Defense of Legitimate Rights
Confederation of Iranian Students
Confederation of Turkish Trade Unions
Council for Development and Reconstruction (CDR)
Dar al-Fonun
Dar al-Moᶜallamin
Democrat Party
Democratic Organization of Afghan Women (1965)
Democratic Party of Azerbaijan
Democratic Party of Kurdistan (Iran; KDP)
Democratic Women's Association (Tunisia)
Egyptian Feminist Union
Fatah, al-
Fedaᵓiyan-e Khalq
Fidaᵓiyyun
Foreign Office, Great Britain
Free Officers, Egypt
General Federation of Iraqi Women
General Union of Palestinian Women's Committees
    (GUPWC)
General Women's Union of Syria
Gezira Sporting Club
Gozanski, Tamar
Grossman, Haika
Gulf Cooperation Council
Gush Emunim
Haganah
Ha-Halutz
Haifa University
HAMAS
Ha-Shomer Ha-Tzaᶜir
Ha-Shomer
Hibbat Zion
Histadrut
Hizbullah
Husseini, Rana
İdadi Schools
Institut d'Égypte
Institute for Palestine Studies
International Monetary Fund
Iranian Bureau of Women's Affairs
Iraq Petroleum Company (IPC)
Iraqi Women's Union
Irbid

Taliban
Technion-Israel Institute of Technology
Tel Aviv University
Turkish Hearth Association
Turkish Linguistic Society
Umm al-Qura University
Umma Party
Union of Tunisian Women
United Jewish Appeal (UJA)
United Nations and the Middle East
United Nations Conciliation Commission for Palestine
    (UNCCP)
United Nations Economic Survey Mission (1949)
United Nations Emergency Force
United Nations Interim Force in Lebanon
United Nations Relief and Works Agency for Palestine
    Refugees in the Near East (UNRWA)
United Nations Special Committee on Palestine, 1947
    (UNSCOP)
United Nations Truce Supervision Organization
    (UNTSO)
University of Tehran
Va'ad Le'umi
Victoria College
Wafd
Wafdist Women's Central Committee
Weizmann Institute of Science
Women and Family Affairs Center
Women in Black
Women's Affairs Center (Gaza)
Women's Forum for Research and Training (Yemen)
Women's Library and Information Center (Istanbul)
Women's Organization of Iran (WOI)
Women's People's Party (1923)
Women's Religious Rituals
Women's Renaissance Club
Women's Studies Center (Jerusalem)
World Bank
World Federation of Sephardi Communities
World Organization of Jews from Arab Countries
    (WOJAC)
World Zionist Organization (WZO)
Yüksek Öğretim Kurulu (YOK)
Yarmuk University
Yemen Hunt Oil Company
Yemeni Socialist Party
Yemeni Women's Union
Yeshiva
Yishuv
Youth Aliyah
Youth Movements
Zaraniq Confederation
Zarqa, al-
Zionism

Zionist Commission for Palestine
Zionist Organization of America
Zionist Revisionist Movement

OTTOMAN EMPIRE

Bedel-i Askeri
Civil Service School (Ottoman)
Congress of Ottoman Liberals (1902)
Dardanelles, Treaty of the (1809)
Darülfünün
Dashnak Party
Dolmabahçe Palace
Dragomans
Erzurum, Treaty of (1823)
Galata
Galatasaray Lycée
Gallipoli
Greco–Turkish War (1897)
Hunkar-Iskelesi, Treaty of (1833)
Janissaries
Konya, Battle of
Land Code of 1858
Millet System
Musa Dagh
Nizip, Battle of (1839)
Ottoman Empire: Overview
Ottoman Empire: Civil Service
Ottoman Empire: Debt
Ottomanism
Ottoman Liberal Union Party
Ottoman Military: Army
Ottoman Military: Navy
Ottoman Parliament
Russian–Ottoman Wars
Salonika
San Stefano, Treaty of (1878)
Sèvres, Treaty of (1920)
Srvantziants, Garegin
Sublime Porte
Sultan
Tanzimat
Topkapi Palace
Turkish–Italian War (1911–1912)
Vaka-i Hayriye
Vazhapetian, Nerses
Yildirim Army
Young Ottomans
Young Turks

PALESTINE PROBLEM

Abbas, Mahmud
Abd al-Hadi Family

Advisory Council (Palestine)
Ahad Ha-Am
Alami Family, al-
Anglo–American Committee of Inquiry (1946)
Aqsa Intifada, al-
Arab Boycott
Arab College of Jerusalem
Arab Higher Committee (Palestine)
Arab–Israel Conflict
Arab–Israel War (1948)
Arab–Israel War (1956)
Arab–Israel War (1967)
Arab–Israel War (1973)
Arab–Israel War (1982)
Arab League Summits
Arafat, Yasir
Ard, al-
Attlee, Clement
Avnery, Uri
Azuri, Najib
Azzam, Abd al-Rahman al-
Balfour Declaration (1917)
Banna, Sabri al-
Barak, Ehud
Ben-Gurion, David
Bentwich, Norman
Benvenisti, Meron
Bernadotte, Folke
Bevin, Ernest
Biltmore Program (1942)
Binationalism
Bir Zeit University
Black September
Bludan Conferences (1937, 1946)
Bunche, Ralph J.
Camp David Summit (2000)
Cattan, Henry
Crossman, Richard
Darwaza, Muhammad Izzat
Dayr Yasin
Exodus (1947)
Fahd Plan (1981)
Fida'iyyun
Gaza (City)
Gaza Strip
Ghuri, Emile al-
Green Line
Gush Emunim
Habash, George
Haddad, Wadi
Haganah
HAMAS
Hasan, Hani al-
Hasan, Khalid al-

Ha-Shomer Ha-Tza'ir
Hawatma, Nayif
Haycraft Commission (1921)
Hebron
High Commissioners (Palestine)
Hope-Simpson Commission (1930)
Husayni, Jamal al-
Husayni, Muhammad Amin al-
Husayni, Musa Kazim al-
Husayn–McMahon Correspondence (1915–1916)
Hut, Shafiq al-
Intifada (1987–1991)
Islamic Jihad
Israeli Settlements
Jabal al-Khalil
Jabal Nablus
Jabotinsky, Vladimir Ze'ev
Jaffa
Jericho
Jericho Congress (1948)
Jerusalem
Jewish Agency for Palestine
Jews in the Middle East
Jibril, Ahmad
Jordanian Option
Kafr Qasim
Kahane, Meir
Kalvaryski, Chaim Margaliut-
Kanafani, Ghassan
Karama, Battle of (1968)
Karp Report (1984)
Khalidi, Ahmad al-Samih al-
Khalidi, Walid
King David Hotel
Kiryat Arba
Land Day
Lausanne Conference (1949)
Law of Return
Legislative Council (Palestine)
Levinger, Moshe
Lohamei Herut Yisrael
London (Roundtable) Conference (1939)
Luke, Harry
Lydda
Ma'a lot
MacDonald, Ramsay
MacMichael, Harold
Madrid Conference (1991)
Magnes, Judah
Meir, Golda
Mond, Alfred Moritz
Morrison–Grady Plan (1946)
Mossad
Nabi Musa Pilgrimage

Nablus
Nashashibi Family
Nazareth
Nusayba Family
Ormsby-Gore, William George Arthur
Oslo Accord (1993)
Oz ve Shalom (Netivot shalom)
Palestine
Palestine Arab Revolt (1936–1939)
Palestine Exploration Fund
Palestine Land Development Company
Palestine Liberation Organization (PLO)
Palestine National Charter (1968)
Palestine National Council
Palestine National Covenant (1964)
Palestine Research Center
Palestinian Arab Congresses
Palestinian Authority
Palestinian Citizens of Israel
Palestinians
Palin Commission Report (1920)
Partition Plans (Palestine)
Peace Now
Peel Commission Report (1937)
Peled, Mattityahu
Peres, Shimon
Permanent Mandates Commission
Philby, Harry St. John
Plumer, Herbert Charles Onslow
Popular Front for the Liberation of Palestine
Popular Front for the Liberation of Palestine—General
    Command
Qalqiliya
Qurai, Ahmad Sulayman
Rabin, Yitzhak
Ramallah
Ramla
Reagan Plan (1982)
Rejection Front
Richmond, Ernest T.
Roosevelt, Franklin Delano
Ruppin, Arthur
Rusk, Dean
Rutenberg, Pinhas
Sabbagh, Hasib
Sabra and Shatila Massacres
Safed
Saʿiqa, al-
Samuel, Herbert Louis
Sasson, Eliyahu
Saunders, Harold
Shamir, Yitzhak
Sharett, Moshe
Sharon, Ariel

Shaw Commission
Shuqayri, Ahmad
Silver, Abba Hillel
Stern, Abraham
Storrs, Ronald
Struma
Sumud
Sykes, Mark
Taba
Tamimi, Amin al-
Tel Hai
Terrorism
Tiberias
Truman, Harry S.
Trumpeldor, Yosef
Turki, Fawaz
United Nations and the Middle East
United Nations Conciliation Commission for Palestine
    (UNCCP)
United Nations Economic Survey Mission (1949)
United Nations Special Committee on Palestine, 1947
    (UNSCOP)
United Nations Truce Supervision Organization
    (UNTSO)
United States of America and the Middle East
Vaʿad Leʾumi
Wauchope, Arthur
Wazir, Khalil al-
Weizman, Ezer
Weizmann, Chaim
West Bank
Western Wall
White Papers on Palestine
Wilson, Woodrow
Wingate, Charles Orde
Woodhead Commission (1938)
Yehoshua, Avraham B.
Yellin-Mor, Natan
Zionism
Zionist Commission for Palestine

POLITICS

Adalat Party
Afghanistan: Political Parties in
AKP (Justice and Development Party)
Anglo–Egyptian Treaty (1954)
Arab Bureau (Cairo)
Arab Higher Committee (Palestine)
Arab League Summits
Arab Nationalism
Arab Socialism
Arab–Israel Conflict
Arab–Israeli General Armistice Agreements (1949)

Wazir, Khalil al-
Weizman, Ezer
Weizmann, Chaim
West German Reparations Agreement
White Revolution (1961–1963)
White Papers on Palestine
Wilson, Woodrow
Wise, Stephen S.
Woodhead Commission (1938)
World War I
World War II
World Zionist Organization (WZO)
Yadin, Yigael
Yellin-Mor, Natan
Yosef, Ovadiah
Za'im, Husni al-
Zionist Revisionist Movement

RELIGION

Afghani, Jamal al-Din al-
Afghanistan: Islamic Movements in
Ahl-e Haqq
Akhbari
Al al-Shaykh Family
Alevi
Allah
Arab Nationalism
Armenian Community of Jerusalem
Armenians in the Middle East
Assyrians
Bab, al-
Babis
Baha'i Faith
Bast
bin Ladin, Osama
Burg, Yosef
Caliphate
Christians in the Middle East
Copts
Damascus Affair (1840)
Dead Sea Scrolls
Druze
Feda'iyan-e Khalq
Forqan
Grand Mosque
Halakhah
Hammer, Zevulun
Hanafi School of Law
Hanbali School of Law
Haram al-Sharif
Hasidim
Hezb-e Islami
Hijab

Holy Land
Holy Sepulchre, Church of the
Husayni, Muhammad Amin al-
Ibadiyya
Ikhwan
İlmiyye
Jerusalem
Jews in the Middle East
Kahane, Meir
Kalemiyye
Kook, Zvi Yehuda
Law of Return
Leibowitz, Yeshayahu
Levinger, Moshe
Maimon, Yehudah Leib Hacohen
Maliki School of Law
Marja al-Taqlid
Meah She'arim
Mecca
Medina
Mevlevi Brotherhood
Milli Görüş Hareketi
Nabi Musa Pilgrimage
Nazareth
Neturei Karta
Ouziel, Ben Zion Meir Hai
Rabbi
Sabbath
Saint Catherine's Monastery
Saint Mark's Cathedral
Samaritans
Sayyidna Husayn Mosque
Shafi'i School of Law
Shapira, Hayyim Moshe
Shari'a
Sharif of Mecca
Shaykh al-Islam
Shaykhi
Shim'un, Mar
Shirazi
Shura
Sistani, Ali al-
Sunna
Supreme Muslim Council
Takfir wa al-Hijra, al-
Talmud
Taurus Mountains
Tekke
Templars
Vatican and the Middle East
Velayat-e Faqih
Yeshiva
Yosef, Ovadiah
Zamzam

Zaydism
Zoroastrianism

RELIGION: ISLAM

Afghanistan: Islamic Movements in
Alawi
Allah
Azhar, al-
Dar al Daʿwa wa al-Irshad
Dhimma
Druze
Fatwa
Fiqh
Hadith
Islam
Islamic Congresses
Islamic Salvation Army (AIS)
Jamiʿa al-Islamiyya, al-
Jihad
Kaʿba
Muwahhidun
Qurʾan
Shiʿism
Sufism and the Sufi Orders
Sunni Islam
Takfir wa al-Hijra, al-
Taliban
Ulama
Usuli
Waqf

WOMEN

Abu Zayd, Hikmat
Abu Zeid, Layla
Adham, Soraya
Adnan, Etel
Afghan Women's Council
AISHA: Arab Women's Forum
Algerian Family Code (1984)
Alia, Queen
Ali, Wijdan
Aliyer, Fatimah
Aloni, Shulamit
Al-Suswa, Amat al-Alim
Amari, Raja
Amer, Ghada
Amrouche, Fadhma At Mansour
Amrouche, Mary Louise (a.k.a. Marguerite Taos)
Ani, Jannane al-
Anis Al-Jalis Magazine
Arab Feminist Union
Arab Women's Association of Palestine

Arab Women's Executive Committee
Arab Women's Solidarity Association International
Araz, Nezihe
Ashour, Radwa
Association des Femmes Tunisiennes pour la
    Recherche et le Développement (AFTURD)
Attar, Nejat al-
Attar, Suad al-
Awadhi, Badria A. al-
Baʿalbakki, Layla
Badr, Liana
Bahithat al-Lubnaniyyat, al-
Bakkar, Jalillah
Bakr, Salwa
Bani-Etemad, Rakhsan
Barakat, Hoda
Baya
Behbehani, Simin
Behrouzi, Maryam
Beirut College for Women (BCW)
Ben Bouali, Hassiba
Ben-Zvi, Rahel Yanait
Biret, Idil
Birth Control
Bishara, Suha
Bitton, Simone
Bouhired, Jamila
Bouih, Fatna el-
Cairo Family Planning Association
Caland, Huguette
Centre de Recherches, d'Études, de Documentation et
    d'Information sur la Femme (CREDIF)
Chazan, Naomi
Chédid, Andrée
Constitutional Revolution, Impact on Women
Crimes of Honor
Dayan, Yael
Democratic Women's Association (Tunisia)
Djebar, Assia
Dorner, Dalia
Ecevit, Rahşan
Efflatoun, Inji
Egyptian Feminist Union
8 Mars Newspaper
Eskinazi, Roza
Faqir, Fadia
Faraj, Maysaloun
Farʾa, Wahiba
Farès, Nabile
Farid, Nagwa Kamal
Farmanfarmian, Settareh
Fawwaz, Zaynab
Fayruz
Faysal, Tujan

Saudi, Mona
School for Hakīmāt
Sebbar, Leila
Shalvi, Alice
Sha'rawi, Huda al-
Shawa, Laila
Shaykh, Hanan al-
Shihabi, Zlikha al-
Shochat, Manya
Sidera, Zineb
Sirry, Gazbia
Stanhope, Hester
Sudanese Women's Union
Sursock, Lady Cochrane
Taha, Mahmud Muhammad
Tallal, Chaibia
Tekeli, Şirin
Tlatli, Moufida
Toumi, Khalida
Tsemel, Leah
Tuqan, Fadwa
Turabi, Wisal al-Mahdi
Turkish Law on the Protection of the Family (1998)
Umar, Madiha
Union of Tunisian Women
Wafdist Women's Central Committee
Wazir, Intisar al- (Umm Jihad)
Women and Family Affairs Center
Women in Black
Women's Affairs Center (Gaza)
Women's Centre for Legal Aid and Counseling
Women's Forum for Research and Training (Yemen)
Women's Library and Information Center (Istanbul)
Women's Organization of Iran (WOI)
Women's People's Party (1923)
Women's Religious Rituals
Women's Renaissance Club
Women's Services
Women's Studies Center (Jerusalem)
Yemeni Women's Union
Zahawi, Jamil Sidqi al-
Zanan Magazine
Zayyat, Latifa
Zeid, Fahralnissa
Ziadeh, May
Ziwaj Mut'a

ZIONISM

Aaronsohn Family
Ahad Ha-Am
Aliyah
Alterman, Natan
American Council for Judaism

Arab–Israel Conflict
Arlosoroff, Chaim
Azuri, Najib
Balfour Declaration (1917)
Begin, Menachem
Ben-Aharon, Yitzhak
Ben-Gurion, David
Ben-Porat, Mordechai
Bentwich, Norman
Ben-Zvi, Yizhak
Bialik, Hayyim Nahman
Biltmore Program (1942)
Binationalism
Borochov, Ber
Brenner, Yosef Hayyim
De Haan, Ya'akov Yisrael
Dreyfus Affair
Eretz Yisrael
Exodus (1947)
Flapan, Simha
Goldmann, Nahum
Gordon, Aaron David
Ha-avarah Agreement
Ha-Cohen, Mordechai
Haganah
Ha-Halutz
Ha-Shomer
Ha-Shomer Ha-Tza'ir
Herzl, Theodor
Hess, Moses
Hibbat Zion
Hillel, Shlomo
Histadrut
Holocaust
Irgun Zva'i Le'umi (IZL)
Israel: Overview
Israeli Settlements
Jabotinsky, Vladimir Ze'ev
Jerusalem
Jewish Agency for Palestine
Jewish Brigade
Jewish Legion
Jewish National Fund
Jews in the Middle East
Joseph, Dov
Kahane, Meir
Kalvaryski, Chaim Margaliut-
Katznelson, Berl
Keren Hayesod
Kibbutz
Kiryat Arba
Kollek, Teddy
Kook, Zvi Yehuda
Kovner, Abba

Labor Zionism
Law of Return
Leibowitz, Yeshayahu
Literature: Hebrew
Lohamei Herut Yisrael
London (Roundtable) Conference (1939)
Magic Carpet Operation
Magnes, Judah
Masada
Matzpen
Meir, Golda
Mond, Alfred Moritz
Morrison–Grady Plan (1946)
Moshav
Mossad
Nahalal
Neturei Karta
Nordau, Max
Palestine Land Development Company
Palmah
Permanent Mandates Commission
Petah Tikvah
Ratosh, Yonatan
Rishon le-Zion
Rubinstein, Amnon
Ruppin, Arthur
Rutenberg, Pinhas
Sabra
Saison
Samuel, Herbert Louis
Sasson, Eliyahu
Shamir, Yitzhak
Shapira, Hayyim Moshe
Sharett, Moshe
Shiloah, Reuven
Shlonsky, Avraham

Silver, Abba Hillel
Smilansky, Moshe
Sneh, Moshe
Sokolow, Nahum
Stern, Abraham
Struma
Sykes, Mark
Tel Hai
Trumpeldor, Yosef
Uganda Project
United Jewish Appeal (UJA)
Ussishkin, Menahem
Va'ad Le'umi
Weizmann, Chaim
Western Wall
White Papers on Palestine
Wilson, Woodrow
Wingate, Charles Orde
Wise, Stephen S.
Women's International Zionist Organization
World Federation of Sephardi Communities
World Organization of Jews from Arab Countries
    (WOJAC)
World Zionist Organization (WZO)
Yadin, Yigael
Yehoshua, Avraham B.
Yellin-Mor, Natan
Yiddish
Youth Aliyah
Zelda
Zikhron Ya'akov
Zionism
Zionist Commission for Palestine
Zionist Organization of America
Zionist Revisionist Movement

LIST OF MAPS

LIST OF MAPS

LIST OF ENTRIES

Abd al-Quddus, Ihsan
David Waldner (1996)

Abd al-Rahman al-Mahdi
Robert O. Collins (1996)

Abd al-Rahman ibn Hisham
Edmund Burke III (1996)

Abd al-Rahman Khan
Ashraf Ghani (1996)

Abd al-Rahman, Umar
Ahmed H. Ibrahim

Abd al-Raziq, Ali
Arthur Goldschmidt (1996)

Abd al-Sabur, Salah
David Waldner (1996)

Abd al-Wahhab, Muhammad ibn
Ali Jihad Racy (1996)

Abdelghani, Mohamed Benahmed
Phillip C. Naylor

Abdesselam, Belaid
Phillip C. Naylor

Abduh, Muhammad
Arthur Goldschmidt (1996)

Abdülaziz
Justin McCarthy (1996)

Abdul-Aziz Bin Baz, Shaykh
Anthony B. Toth

Abdülhamit II
Justin McCarthy (1996)

Abdullah I ibn Hussein
Jenab Tutunji (1996)

Abdullah II ibn Hussein
Michael R. Fischbach

Abdullahi, Muhammad Turshain
Robert O. Collins (1996)

Abdülmecit I
Burçak Keskin-Kozat
I. Metin Kunt (1996)

Abdülmecit II
Eric Hooglund
Elizabeth Thompson (1996)

Abidin, Dino
David Waldner (1996)

Abu al-Huda, Tawfiq
Michael R. Fischbach
Jenab Tutunji (1996)

Abu al-Timman, Jaʿfar
Mahmoud Haddad (1996)

Abu Dhabi
Anthony B. Toth
Malcolm C. Peck (1996)

Abuhatzeira, Aharon
Martin Malin (1996)

Abu Himara
Edmund Burke III (1996)

Abu Musa Island
Eric Hooglund
M. Morsy Abdullah (1996)

Abu Nuwwar, Ali
Michael R. Fischbach
Jenab Tutunji (1996)

Abu Qir, Battle of (1798)
David Waldner (1996)

Abu Risha, Umar
Muhammad Muslih (1996)

Abu Zayd, Hikmat
Mona Russell

Abu Zeid, Layla
Marilyn Booth

Acheson, Dean
Zachary Karabell (1996)

Achour, Habib
Vanesa Casanova-Fernandez
Matthew S. Gordon (1996)

Adalat Party
Parvaneh Pourshariati (1996)

Adamiyat, Abbasquli
Mansoor Moaddel (1996)

Adamiyat, Fereydun
Mansoor Moaddel (1996)

Atabat
Neguin Yavari (1996)

Atasi, Hashim al-
Muhammad Muslih (1996)

Atasi, Jamal al-
George E. Irani (1996)

Atasi, Nur al-Din al-
Michael R. Fischbach
Muhammed Muslih (1996)

Atatürk, Mustafa Kemal
Ahmet Kuyas (1996)

Atatürk University
I. Metin Kunt (1996)

Atay, Salih Rifki
Elizabeth Thompson (1996)

Atlas Mountains
Will D. Swearingen (1996)

Atrash, Farid al-
Virginia Danielson (1996)

Atrash, Sultan Pasha al-
Muhammad Muslih (1996)

Attar, Nejat al-
Khalil Gebara

Attar, Suad al-
Jessica Winegar

Attas, Haydar Abu Bakr al-
Robert D. Burrowes

Attlee, Clement
Joseph Nevo
Jenab Tutunji (1996)

Austria–Hungary and the Middle East
Zachary Karabell (1996)

Avnery, Uri
Mordechai Bar-On
Martin Malin (1996)

Awadhi, Badria A. al-
Mary Ann Tétreault

Awad, Louis
Charles E. Butterworth
David Waldner (1996)

Awakened Youth
Grant Farr (1996)

Awali, al-
Emile A. Nakhleh (1996)

Ayan
Elizabeth Thompson (1996)

Aya Sofya
Zachary Karabell (1996)

Ayn, al-
Anthony B. Toth

Ayn al-Dowleh, Abd al-Majid Mirza
Neguin Yavari (1996)

Ayni, Muhsin al-
F. Gregory Gause, III (1996)

Ayn, Ras al-
Abdul-Karim Rafeq (1996)

Ayyub, Dhu al-Nun
Amatzia Baram (1996)

Ayyubi, Ali Jawdat al-
Ahmad Abdul A. R. Shikara (1996)

Azerbaijan
Neguin Yavari

Azerbaijan Crisis
Eric Hooglund (1996)

Azeri Language and Literature
Uli Schamiloglu (1996)

Azhar, al-
Donald Malcolm Reid
A. Chris Eccel (1996)

Azhari, Isma'il
Robert O. Collins (1996)

Azib
Rahma Bourqia (1996)

Aziz, Tariq
Michael R. Fischbach
Amatzia Baram (1996)

Azm, Sadiq al-
As'ad AbuKhalil

Azuri, Najib
Muhammad Muslih (1996)

Azzam, Abd al-Rahman al-
Mahmoud Haddad (1996)

B

Ba'albak
Guilain P. Denoeux (1996)

Ba'albakki, Layla
Laurie King-Irani

Bab, al-
Juan R. I. Cole (1996)

Bab al-Mandab
Robert D. Burrowes (1996)

Baban Family
Mamoon A. Zaki (1996)

Babis
Juan R. I. Cole (1996)

Baccouche, Hedi
Ana Torres-Garcia
Matthew S. Gordon (1996)

Badran, Mudar
Jenab Tutunji (1996)

Badr, Liana
George R. Wilkes

Badr, Muhammad al-
Emile A. Nakhleh (1996)

Baghdad
Ayad Al-Qazzaz

Baghdadi, Abd al-Latif al-
Donald Malcolm Reid
Arthur Goldschmidt (1996)

Baghdad Pact (1955)
William L. Cleveland
Zachary Karabell (1996)

Baghdad Summit (1978)
Michael R. Fischbach (1996)

Baghdad University
John J. Donohue (1996)

Baha'i Faith
Juan R. I. Cole (1996)

Baharina
Anthony B. Toth
Emile A. Nakhleh (1996)

Bahariya
Arthur Goldschmidt (1996)

Bahar, Mohammad Taqi
Michael C. Hillmann (1996)

Bahithat al-Lubnaniyyat, al-
Elise Salem

Bahrain
Fred H. Lawson

Bahraini–Qatari Wars
Fred H. Lawson

Bahrain Nationalist Movement
Fred H. Lawson (1996)

Bahrain National Oil Company (BANOCO)
Emile A. Nakhleh (1996)

Bahrain Order in Council
Emile A. Nakhleh (1996)

Bahr al-Abyad
Robert O. Collins (1996)

Bahr al-Arab
Robert O. Collins (1996)

Bahr al-Ghazal
Robert O. Collins (1996)

Bahr al-Jabal
Robert O. Collins (1996)

Baida
John L. Wright (1996)

Bakdash, Khalid
Garay Menicucci

Baker, James A.
Michael R. Fischbach (1996)

Bakhtiari
Eric Hooglund
Lois Beck (1996)

Bakhtiari, Najaf Qoli Khan Samsam al-Soltaneh
Neguin Yavari (1996)

Bakhtiar, Shapur
Ahmed H. Ibrahim

Bakhtiar, Timur
  Neguin Yavari (1996)

Bakil Tribal Confederation
  Manfred W. Wenner (1996)

Bakkar, Jalillah
  Laura Rice

Bakr, Ahmad Hasan al-
  Amatzia Baram (1996)

Bakr, Salwa
  Caroline Seymour-Jorn

Balaclava, Battle of
  Jean-Marc R. Oppenheim (1996)

Balafrej, Ahmed
  Matthew S. Gordon (1996)

Balbo, Italo
  George Joffe (1996)

Balfour Declaration (1917)
  Philip Mattar

Balkan Crises (1870s)
  John Micgiel (1996)

Balkans
  John Micgiel (1996)

Balkan Wars (1912–1913)
  Hasan Kayali (1996)

Balta Liman, Convention of (1838)
  Zachary Karabell (1996)

Baluchis
  Charles C. Kolb

Baluchistan
  Neguin Yavari (1996)

Balyan Family
  Rouben P. Adalian
  Aptullah Kuran (1996)

Bamyan
  Grant Farr

Bandung Conference (1955)
  Zachary Karabell (1996)

Bani-Etemad, Rakhsan
  Roxanne Varzi

Bani Sadr, Abolhasan
  Neguin Yavari

Banking
  Clement Moore Henry

Banna, Hasan al-
  Ahmad S. Moussalli
  Ali E. Hillal Dessouki (1996)

Banna, Sabri al-
  Michael R. Fischbach
  Steve Tamari (1996)

Bannis, Mohammad
  Aida A. Bamia

Baqri Family
  Norman Stillman (1996)

Baraheni, Reza
  Eric Hooglund
  Michael C. Hillman (1996)

Barakat, Hoda
  Elise Salem

Barak, Ehud
  Mordechai Bar-On

Barakzai Dynasty
  Eric Hooglund
  Ashraf Ghani (1996)

Barbary States
  Jerome Bookin-Wiener (1996)

Barbary Wars
  Jerome Bookin-Wiener (1996)

Barghuthi Family
  Michael R. Fischbach
  Steve Tamari (1996)

Barghuthi, Marwan
  Michael R. Fischbach

Bar-Ilan University
  Paul Rivlin
  Miriam Simon (1996)

Baring, Evelyn
  Arthur Goldschmidt
  Robert L. Tignor (1996)

Barkan, Ömer Lutfi
  I. Metin Kunt (1996)

Belkacem, Cherif
Phillip C. Naylor

Bell, Gertrude
Zachary Karabell (1996)

Bellounis, Muhammad
Phillip C. Naylor (1996)

Ben-Aharon, Yitzhak
Gregory S. Mahler
Zachary Karabell (1996)

Ben Ali, Zayn al-Abidine
Maria F. Curtis
Matthew S. Gordon (1996)

Ben Ammar, Tahar
Matthew S. Gordon (1996)

Ben Badis, Abd al-Hamid
Phillip C. Naylor (1996)

Ben Barka, Mehdi
Donna Lee Bowen (1996)

Ben Bella, Ahmed
Phillip C. Naylor

Ben Bouali, Hassiba
Rabia Bekkar

Ben Boulaid, Moustafa
Phillip C. Naylor (1996)

Bendjedid, Chadli
Phillip C. Naylor

Benflis, Ali
Phillip C. Naylor

Benghazi
John L. Wright (1996)

Ben-Gurion, David
Gregory S. Mahler

Ben-Gurion University of the Negev
Miriam Simon (1996)

Ben Jelloun, Umar
Bruce Maddy-Weitzman (1996)

Ben Khedda, Ben Youssef
Phillip C. Naylor (1996)

Ben M'hidi, Muhammad Larbi
Phillip C. Naylor (1996)

Bennabi, Malek
Yahia Zoubir

Ben-Porat, Mordechai
Gregory S. Mahler
Nissim Rejwan (1996)

Ben Salah, Ahmed
Emad Eldin Shahin
Kenneth J. Perkins (1996)

Ben Seddiq, Mahjoub
Bruce Maddy-Weitzman

Ben Simeon, Raphael Aaron
Norman Stillman (1996)

Bentwich, Norman
Bernard Wasserstein

Benvenisti, Meron
Zachary Karabell (1996)

Ben-Yehuda, Eliezer
Martin Malin (1996)

Ben Yousouf, Salah
Kenneth J. Perkins (1996)

Ben-Zvi, Rahel Yanait
Meron Medzini

Ben-Zvi, Yizhak
Donna Robinson Divine (1996)

Berber
Thomas G. Penchoen (1996)

Berber Dahir
Dale F. Eickelman (1996)

Berber Spring
Paul Silverstein

Berkowitz, Yizhak
Ann Kahn (1996)

Berlin–Baghdad Railway
Francis R. Nicosia (1996)

Berlin, Congress and Treaty of
Arnold Blumberg (1996)

Bernadotte, Folke
Amitzur Ilan

Berrada, Mohammed
Aida A. Bamia

Berri, Nabi
As'ad AbuKhalil

Bethlehem
Michael R. Fischbach
Benjamin Joseph (1996)

Bevin, Ernest
Lawrence Tal (1996)

Bevin–Sforza Plan
George Joffe (1996)

Beyoglu Protocol
Zachary Karabell (1996)

Bezalel Academy of Arts and Design
Ann Kahn (1996)

Bialik, Hayyim Nahman
George R. Wilkes
Nili Gold (1996)

Bidonville
Dirk Vandewalle (1996)

Bilhayr, Abd al-Nabi
George Joffe (1996)

Bilkent University
Burçak Keskin-Kozat
I. Metin Kunt (1996)

Biltmore Program (1942)
Neil Caplan

Binationalism
Neil Caplan

Bin Diyaf, Muhsen
Aida A. Bamia

bin Ladin, Osama
As'ad AbuKhalil

Bint al-Shati
Sabah Ghandour

Biqa Valley
Fred H. Lawson

Biret, Idil
Filiz Ali

Birth Control
Laurie King-Irani
Donna Lee Bowen (1996)

Bir Zeit University
Lawrence Tal (1996)

Bishara, Abdullah
Mary Ann Tétreault
Les Ordeman (1996)

Bishara, Suha
As'ad AbuKhalil

Bisitun
A. Shapur Shahbazi (1996)

Bitar, Salah al-Din al-

Bitat, Rabah
Phillip C. Naylor (1996)

Bittari, Zoubida
Aida A. Bamia (1996)

Bitton, Simone
George R. Wilkes

Bizerte
Kenneth J. Perkins (1996)

Bizerte Crisis (1961)
Kenneth J. Perkins (1996)

Black Panthers
Shlomo Deshen (1996)

Black Sea
Zachary Karabell (1996)

Black September
Michael R. Fischbach
Steve Tamari (1996)

Black Spring
Paul Silverstein

Black Thursday (1978)
Matthew S. Gordon (1996)

Bled al-Siba/Bled al-Makhzan
C. R. Pennell (1996)

Bliss, Daniel
Guilain P. Denoeux (1996)

Congress of Ottoman Liberals (1902)
David Waldner (1996)

Conseil National de la Révolution Algérienne
(CNRA)
John Ruedy (1996)

Constantine
Dirk Vandewalle (1996)

Constantinople
Paul S. Rowe

Constitutional Bloc
As'ad AbuKhalil (1996)

Constitutional Democratic Rally
Vanesa Casanova-Fernandez

Constitutional Revolution
Eric Hooglund (1996)

Constitutional Revolution, Impact on Women
Mangol Bayat

Coordination des Archs (Algeria)
Robert Mortimer

Coptic Museum
Donald Malcolm Reid
Donald Spanel (1996)

Copts
Milad Hanna
Gawdat Gabra
Donald Spanel (1996)

Corcos Family
Norman Stillman (1996)

Corsairs
Jerome Bookin-Weiner (1996)

Cossack Brigade
Jack Bubon (1996)

Cotton
Richard W. Bulliet (1996)

Council for Development and Reconstruction
(CDR)
As'ad AbuKhalil
George E. Irani (1996)

Cox, Percy
Michael R. Fischbach
Peter Sluglett (1996)

Crane, Charles R.
William L. Cleveland
Mia Bloom (1996)

Creech Jones, Arthur
Bernard Wasserstein

Crémieux Decree
Kenneth J. Perkins (1996)

Crimean War
C. Max Kortepeter (1996)

Crimes of Honor
Lynn Welchman

Crossman, Richard
Bernard Wasserstein

Curiel Family
Michael M. Laskier (1996)

Curzon, George Nathaniel
Eric Hooglund (1996)

Cyprus
Alexander Kitroeff (1996)

Cyprus Convention (1878)
Zachary Karabell (1996)

Cyrenaica
Ronald Bruce St John
John L. Wright (1996)

Cyril IV
Donald Spanel (1996)

Cyril V
Donald Spanel (1996)

Cyril VI
Donald Spanel (1996)

D

Dabbagh, Marzieh
Janet Afary

Dabbas, Charles
As'ad AbuKhalil (1996)

Daddah, Mokhtar Ould
Bruce Maddy-Weitzman

Daftari, Ahmad Matin
Neguin Yavari (1996)

Dağlarca, Fazil Hüsnü
Kathleen R. F. Burrill (1996)

Dahlan, Muhammad
Michael R. Fischbach

Damanhur
Arthur Goldschmidt (1996)

Damascus
Fred H. Lawson (1996)

Damascus Affair (1840)
Michael R. Fischbach
Jane Gerber (1996)

Damascus University
Abdul-Karim Rafeq (1996)

Dammam, al-
J. E. Peterson

Dance
Maria F. Curtis

Daneshvar, Simin
Eric Hooglund
Michael C. Hillmann (1996)

Dar al Daʿwa wa al-Irshad
Donald Malcolm Reid (1996)

Dar al-Fonun
Parvaneh Pourshariati (1996)

Dar al-Islam
Cyrus Moshaver (1996)

Dar al-Kutub al-Misriyya
Donald Malcolm Reid

Dar al-Moʿallamin
Grant Farr

Dar al-Ulum
Donald Malcolm Reid

D'Arcy Concession (1901)
Eric Hooglund
Daniel E. Spector (1996)

Dardanelles, Treaty of the (1809)
Daniel E. Spector (1996)

Darülfünün
Zachary Karabell (1996)

Darwaza, Muhammad Izzat
Michael R. Fischbach (1996)

Darwish, Ishaq
Elizabeth Thompson (1996)

Darwish, Mahmud
Robyn Creswell
Kamal Boullatta (1996)

Darwish, Sayyid
Virginia Danielson (1996)

Dashnak Party
Rouben P. Adalian

Dashti, Ali
Eric Hooglund
Michael C. Hillmann (1996)

Dates
Albertine Jwaideh (1996)

Daud, Muhammad
M. Nazif Shahrani (1996)

Daʾud Pasha
Asʿad AbuKhalil (1996)

Daʿwa al-Islamiyya, al-
Maysam J. al Faruqi

Dayan, Moshe
Nathan Yanai (1996)

Dayan, Yael
Meron Medzini

Dayr al-Zawr Province
Abdul-Karim Rafeq (1996)

Dayr Yasin
Don Peretz

Dead Sea
Peter Gubser (1996)

Dead Sea Scrolls
Mia Bloom (1996)

De Bunsen, Maurice
Zachary Karabell (1996)

Decentralization Party
Hasan Kayali (1996)

Declaration of La Celle St. Cloud
Zachary Karabell (1996)

Dede Zekai
David Waldner (1996)

Deedes, Wyndham
Elizabeth Thompson (1996)

De Gaulle, Charles
John P. Spagnolo (1996)

De Haan, Yaʿakov Yisrael
Bryan Daves (1996)

Dehkhoda, Ali Akbar
Michael C. Hillmann (1996)

Dellalzade İsmail
David Waldner (1996)

Delouvrier, Paul
Phillip C. Naylor

Delta
Arthur Goldschmidt (1996)

Delta Barrages
Gregory B. Baecher
David Waldner (1996)

De Menasce Family
Michael M. Laskier (1996)

Demetrius II
Donald Spanel (1996)

Demirel, Süleyman
Burçak Keskin-Kozat
Nermin Abadan-Unat (1996)

Democratic Organization of Afghan Women
(1965)
Senzil Nawid

Democratic Party of Azerbaijan
Audrey L. Altstadt (1996)

Democratic Party of Kurdistan (Iran; KDP)
Parvaneh Pourshariati

Democratic Party of Kurdistan (Iraq)
Chris Kutschera

Democratic Women's Association (Tunisia)
Angel M. Foster

Democrat Party
David Waldner (1996)

Denktash, Rauf
Pierre Oberling (1996)

Dentz, Henri-Fernand
George R. Wilkes

Derakhshandeh, Puran
Roxanne Varzi

Desalinization
Karim Hamdy
John F. Kolars (1996)

Deserts
John F. Kolars (1996)

Devrim, Izzet Melih
David Waldner (1996)

Dhahran
J. E. Peterson

Dhimma
Ilai Alon

Dhow
Malcolm C. Peck (1996)

Dhufar
Calvin H. Allen, Jr
Malcolm C. Peck (1996)

Dhufar Rebellion
Eric Hooglund
Malcolm C. Peck (1996)

Diaspora
Gabriel Sheffer

Diba, Farah
Haleh Vaziri

Dib, Mohammed
Phillip C. Naylor

Didouche, Mourad
Phillip C. Naylor (1996)

Dilmun
Emile A. Nakhleh (1996)

Dimona
Yehuda Gradus
Zachary Karabell (1996)

Dinka
Robert O. Collins (1996)

East India Company
Jenab Tutunji (1996)

Ebadi, Shirin
Ziba Mir-Hosseini

Eban, Abba (Aubrey)
Gregory S. Mahler (1996)

Ebtekar, Maʿsumeh
Nayereh Tohidi

Ecevit, Bülent
Burçak Keskin-Kozat
Nermin Abadan-Unat (1996)

Ecevit, Rahşan
Burçak Keskin-Kozat

Economic and Military Aid
Paul Rivlin
Marvin G. Weinbaum (1996)

Economics
Jean-François Seznec

Eddé, Emile
Sami A. Ofeish

Eddé, Raymond
Michael R. Fischbach
Guilain P. Denoeux (1996)

Eden, Anthony
Zachary Karabell (1996)

Edirne
Eric Hooglund

Education
Linda Herrera

Efflatoun, Inji
Jessica Winegar

Ege University
Burçak Keskin-Kozat
I. Metin Kunt (1996)

Egypt
Arthur Goldschmidt
Ali E. Hillal Dessouki (1996)

Egyptian Feminist Union
Marilyn Booth

Egyptian Geographical Society
Donald Malcolm Reid (1996)

Egyptian–Israeli Peace Treaty (1979)
Laurie Z. Eisenberg

Egyptian Museum
Donald Malcolm Reid

Egyptian Women's Union
Arthur Goldschmidt (1996)

8 Mars Newspaper
Laurie King-Irani

Eisenhower, Dwight David
Zachary Karabell (1996)

Eitan, Rafael
Martin Malin (1996)

Eldem, Sedad Hakki
Elizabeth Thompson (1996)

Elites
Donald Maolcolm Reid (1996)

Emergency Regulations
Benjamin Joseph (1996)

Entebbe Operation
Zev Maghen (1996)

Ente Nazionale Idrocarboni (ENI)
Dirk Vandewalle (1996)

Enver Paşa
Hasan Kayali (1996)

Eqbal, Manouchehr
Neguin Yavari

Erbakan, Necmeddin
M. Hakan Yavuz
Frank Tachau (1996)

Erbil, Leyla
David Waldner (1996)

Erdoğan, Tayyip
M. Hakan Yavuz

Eretz Yisrael
Chaim I. Waxman

Ersoy, Mehmet Akif
Elizabeth Thompson (1996)

Ertuğrul, Muhsin
Elizabeth Thompson (1996)

Farid, Nagwa Kamal
Carolyn Fluehr-Lobban

Farmanfarma, Abd al-Hoseyn Mirza
Mansoureh Ettehadieh (1996)

Farmanfarmian, Settareh
Cherie Taraghi

Farouk
Robert L. Tignor (1996)

Farrokhzad, Forugh
Michael C. Hillmann (1996)

Fashoda Incident (1898)
Zachary Karabell (1996)

Fasi, Allal al-
C. R. Pennell (1996)

Fasi, Muhammad al-
C. R. Pennell (1996)

Fassih, Ismail
Pardis Minuchehr (1996)

Fatah, al-
Michael R. Fischbach
Michael Dunn (1996)

Fatat, al-
Muhammad Muslih (1996)

Fath Ali Shah Qajar
Mansoureh Ettehadieh (1996)

Fatwa
Maysam J. al Faruqi
Wael B. Hallaq (1996)

Fawwaz, Zaynab
Marilyn Booth

Fayruz
Christopher Reed Stone

Faysal ibn Turki Al Saʿud
Malcolm C. Peck (1996)

Faysal, Tujan
Curtis R. Ryan

Fedaʾiyan-e Islam
Ervand Abrahamian

Fedaʾiyan-e Khalq
Ervand Abrahamian

Female Genital Mutilation
Carolyn Fluehr-Lobban

Feraoun, Mouloud
Phillip C. Naylor (1996)

Ferit, Damat Mehmet
Elizabeth Thompson (1996)

Ferman
Elizabeth Thompson (1996)

Fertile Crescent
Zachary Karabell (1996)

Fertile Crescent Unity Plans
H. G. Balfour-Paul (1996)

Fes, Treaty of (1912)
Matthew S. Gordon (1996)

Fez, Morocco
Donna Lee Bowen (1996)

Fezzan
John L. Wright (1996)

Fidaʾiyyun
Philip Mattar
Lawrence Tal (1996)

Film
Roxanne Varzi

Fiqh
Maysam J. al Faruqi

Fish and Fishing
Eric Hooglund

Flapan, Simha
Gregory S. Mahler
Zachary Karabell (1996)

Fly Whisk Incident (1827)
Kenneth J. Perkins (1996)

Food: Ash
Neguin Yavari (1996)

Food: Baklava
Clifford A. Wright (1996)

Food: Borek
Cyrus Moshaver (1996)

Food: Bulgur
Clifford A. Wright (1996)

Free Yemenis
Robert D. Burrowes (1996)

Freier, Recha
George R. Wilkes

French Foreign Legion
Kenneth J. Perkins (1996)

Frischmann, David
Ann Kahn (1996)

Front de Libération Nationale (FLN)
John Ruedy (1996)

Front for the Liberation of South Yemen
Robert D. Burrowes (1996)

Front Islamique du Salut (FIS)
Bradford Dillman (1996)

Front pour la Défense des Institutions
Constitutionelles (FDIC)
Bruce Maddy-Weitzman (1996)

Fu'ad
Robert L. Tignor (1996)

Fujayra
Anthony B. Toth
Malcolm C. Peck (1996)

Fujayra–Sharjah Conflict
Malcolm C. Peck (1996)

Fundamental Pact
Matthew S. Gordon (1996)

Futuwwa
Guilain P. Denoeux (1996)

G

Gafsa Incident (1980)
Matthew S. Gordon (1996)

Gailani, Ahmad
Grant Farr

Galata
Elizabeth Thompson (1996)

Galatasaray Lycée
Anthony B. Toth
I. Metin Kunt (1996)

Galilee
Zev Maghen (1996)

Galilee, Sea of
Bryan Daves (1996)

Gallei Tzahal
Ann Kahn (1996)

Gallipoli
Sara Reguer (1996)

Gamal, Samiyah
Roberta L. Dougherty

Ganim, Halil
Elizabeth Thompson (1996)

Ganji, Akbar
Babak Rahimi

Garang, John
Carolyn Fluehr-Lobban
Paul Martin (1996)

Gardanne Mission
Daniel E. Spector (1996)

Gaspirali, Ismail Bey
Uli Schamiloglu (1996)

Gaza (City)
Mallika Good

Gaza Strip
Sara M. Roy

Geagea, Samir
As'ad AbuKhalil
Guilain P. Denoeux (1996)

Gebeyli, Claire
Mona Takieddine Amyuni

Gecekondu
Eric Hooglund

Gencer, Leyla
Filiz Ali

Genç Kalemler
Elizabeth Thompson (1996)

Gender: Gender and the Economy
Khaled Islaih

Gender: Gender and Education
Rachel Christina

Giza
Arthur Goldschmidt (1996)

Glawi Family, al-
Rahma Bourqia (1996)

Glubb, John Bagot
Avi Shlaim (1996)

Gökalp, Ziya
Taha Parla (1996)

Golan Heights
Yehuda Gradus
Muhammad Muslih (1996)

Goldberg, Leah
Ann Kahn (1996)

Golden Square
Reeva S. Simon (1996)

Goldmann, Nahum
Gregory S. Mahler
Neil Caplan

Golestan, Ebrahim
Eric Hooglund

Golestan Palace
Parvaneh Pourshariati (1996)

Golpayagani, Mohammad Reza
Hamid Algar (1996)

Golshiri, Houshang
Eric Hooglund
Pardis Minuchehr (1996)

Golsorkhi, Khosrow
Afshin Matin-asgari

Gordon, Aaron David
Donna Robinson Divine

Gordon, Charles
Jean-Marc R. Oppenheim (1996)

Gorst, John Eldon
Peter Mellini (1996)

Government
Oliver Benjamin Hemmerle
Bernard Reich (1996)

Gozanski, Tamar
Laurie King-Irani

Grand Mosque
Anthony B. Toth
Malcolm C. Peck (1996)

Graziani, Rodolfo
George Joffe (1996)

Greater Syria
Abdul-Karim Rafeq (1996)

Greater Syria Plan
Zachary Karabell (1996)

Great Game, The
Zachary Karabell (1996)

Greco–Turkish War (1897)
Eric Hooglund
Alexander Kitroeff (1996)

Greeks in the Middle East
Alexander Kitroeff (1996)

Greek War of Independence
Alexander Kitroeff (1996)

Greenberg, Uri Zvi
Ann Kahn (1996)

Green Book
Lisa Anderson (1996)

Green Line
David Newman
Bryan Daves (1996)

Green March
Matthew S. Gordon (1996)

Griboyedov Incident
Parvaneh Pourshariati (1996)

Grivas, Georgios Theodoros
Zachary Karabell (1996)

Grobba, Fritz Konrad Ferdinand
Francis R. Nicosia (1996)

Grossman, Haika
George R. Wilkes

Gruenbaum, Yizhak
Zachary Karabell (1996)

Guest Workers
Eric Hooglund

Haggiag Family
Maurice M. Roumani (1996)

Ha-Halutz
Donna Robinson Divine

Haifa
Philip Mattar

Haifa University
Zachary Karabell (1996)

Haigazian College
George E. Irani (1996)

Haik
Rhimou Bernikho-Canin (1996)

Hajir, Abd al-Hoseyn
Neguin Yavari (1996)

Hajji Baba of Ispahan
Michael C. Hillmann (1996)

Hajri, Abdullah al-
Robert D. Burrowes (1996)

Hakim, Adnan al-
As'ad AbuKhalil (1996)

Hakim Family
Amatzia Baram (1996)

Hakim, Tawfiq al-
Roger Allen (1996)

Halakhah
Ephraim Tabory
Samuel C. Heilman (1996)

Halukka
Chaim I. Waxman

Hama
Geoffrey D. Schad
Abdul-Karim Rafeq (1996)

Hamadan
Parvaneh Pourshariati

Hamadi, Sabri
As'ad AbuKhalil (1996)

Hamama, Faten
Andrew Flibbert
David Waldner (1996)

Hama Massacre
Fred H. Lawson

HAMAS
Michael R. Fischbach

Hamas (Movement for a Peaceful Society)
Emad Eldin Shahin

Hamdi, Ibrahim al-
Manfred W. Wenner (1996)

Hamid al-Din Family
Robert D. Burrowes (1996)

Hamina, Mohammed Lakhdar
Phillip C. Naylor (1996)

Hammarskjöld, Dag
Brian Urquhart

Hammer, Zevulun
Gregory S. Mahler
Martin Malin (1996)

Hamra Riots
Michael R. Fischbach (1996)

Hamrouche, Mouloud
Phillip C. Naylor

Hamzawi, Rashid al-
Aida A. Bamia

Hanafi, Hasan
As'ad AbuKhalil

Hanafi School of Law
Wael B. Hallaq (1996)

Hananu, Ibrahim
Michael R. Fischbach
Muhammad Muslih (1996)

Hanbali School of Law
Wael B. Hallaq (1996)

Hand of Fatima
Laurence Michalak (1996)

Hanoune, Louisa
Robert Mortimer

Haq, al-
Michael R. Fischbach

Harel, Isser
Ian Black
Zev Maghen (1996)

Harem
Carolyn Fluehr-Lobban

Hareven, Shulamit
Adina Friedman
Nili Gold (1996)

Hariri, Rafiq Baha'uddin al-
As'ad AbuKhalil
Bassam Namani (1996)

Harkabi, Yehoshafat
Mordechai Bar-On
Martin Malin (1996)

Harkis
Phillip C. Naylor (1996)

Harratin
Rahma Bourqia (1996)

Harriman, W. Averell
Zachary Karabell (1996)

Hasa, al-
Anthony B. Toth
Malcolm C. Peck (1996)

Hasan, Fa'iq
Amatzia Baram (1996)

Hasan, Hani al-
Michael R. Fischbach
Lawrence Tal (1996)

Hasani, Taj al-Din al-
George E. Irani (1996)

Hasan, Khalid al-
Michael R. Fischbach
Lawrence Tal (1996)

Hashemi, Faezeh
Azadeh Kian-Thiébaut

Hashim, Ibrahim
Jenab Tutunji (1996)

Hashimi, Taha al-
Ayad al-Qazzaz (1996)

Hashimite House (House of Hashim)
Michael R. Fischbach

Hashimi, Yasin al-
Michael R. Fischbach
Mamoon A. Zaki (1996)

Ha-Shomer
Elizabeth Thompson (1996)

Ha-Shomer Ha-Tza'ir
Chaim I. Waxman

Hasidim
Chaim I. Waxman

Haskalah
Martin Malin (1996)

Hass, Amira
Khaled Islaih

Hassan I
Rémy Leveau (1996)

Hassan II
Rémy Leveau

Ha-Tikva
George R. Wilkes

Hatim Sultans of Hamdan
Robert D. Burrowes

Hatoum, Mona
Jessica Winegar

Hawatma, Nayif
Michael R. Fischbach

Hawi, George
Guilain P. Denoeux (1996)

Hawi, Khalil
Guilain P. Denoeux (1996)

Hawrani, Akram al-
Muhammad Muslih (1996)

Haycraft Commission (1921)
Philip Mattar

Hayim, Yusef
Sylvia G. Haim (1996)

Haykal, Muhammad Hasanayn
Ahmad S. Moussalli
Arthur Goldschmidt (1996)

Haykal, Muhammad Husayn
Arthur Goldschmidt (1996)

Haza, Ofra
Laurie King-Irani

Hazara
Grant Farr

Hazaz, Hayyim
Ann Kahn (1996)

Hazzan, Elijah Bekhor
Norman Stillman (1996)

Hebrew
Ruth Raphaeli (1996)

Hebrew University of Jerusalem
Pierre M. Atlas

Hebron
Michael R. Fischbach
Benjamin Joseph (1996)

Hedayat, Sadegh
Eric Hooglund
Michael C. Hillmann (1996)

Hekmatyar, Golbuddin
Grant Farr

Helmand River
Grant Farr

Herat
Grant Farr

Herzl, Theodor
Shimon Avish (1996)

Herzog, Chaim
Meron Medzini

Herzog, Izhak Halevi
Chaim I. Waxman (1996)

Herzog, Ya'acov David
Meron Medzini

Heskayl, Sasson
Sasson Somekh (1996)

Hess, Moses
Zachary Karabell (1996)

Hezb-e Islami
Grant Farr

Hibbat Zion
Donna Robinson Divine (1996)

High Commissioners (Palestine)
Philip Mattar

High State Council (Algeria)
John Ruedy

Hijab
Laurie King-Irani

Hijaz
Anthony B. Toth
Khalid Y. Blankinship (1996)

Hijaz Railroad
David Waldner (1996)

Hikma University, al-
John J. Donohue (1996)

Hilal, al-
Thomas Philipp (1996)

Hillel, Shlomo
Meron Medzini

Hilmi, Ahmad
Lawrence Tal (1996)

Hilu, Charles
As'ad AbuKhalil (1996)

Hilu, Pierre
As'ad AbuKhalil

Hindu Kush Mountains
Zachary Karabell (1996)

Hinnawi, Sami al-
Abdul-Karim Rafeq (1996)

Hirawi, Ilyas al-
As'ad AbuKhalil

Histadrut
Paul Rivlin (1996)

Historiography
John T. Chalcraft

Hizbullah
As'ad AbuKhalil

Hobeika, Elie
As'ad AbuKhalil
George E. Irani (1996)

Ibn Tulun Mosque
Jonathan M. Bloom (1996)

Ibrahim, Abdullah
Ana Torres-Garcia
C. R. Pennell (1996)

Ibrahim, Fatima Ahmed
Sondra Hale

Ibrahimi, Ahmed Taleb
Phillip C. Naylor

Ibrahimi, Bashir
Phillip C. Naylor (1996)

Ibrahim ibn Muhammad Ali
Ali E. Hillal Dessouki (1996)

Ibrahimi, Lakhdar al-
Ana Torres-Garcia
Elizabeth Thompson (1996)

Ibrahim, Izzat
Ayad al-Qazzaz (1996)

Ibrahim, Muhammad Hafiz
Kenneth S. Mayers (1996)

Ibrahim, Saʿad al-Din
Rita Stephan

İdadi Schools
Elizabeth Thompson (1996)

Idlibi, Ulfat al-
Marilyn Booth

Idlib Province
Abdul-Karim Rafeq (1996)

Idris al-Sayyid Muhammad al-Sanusi
Julie Zuckerman (1996)

Idrisids
Manfred W. Wenner (1996)

Idris, Yusuf
Roger Allen (1996)

Ifni
Bruce Maddy-Weitzman

Ignatiev, Nikolas Pavlovich
Zachary Karabell (1996)

Ikha al-Watani Party
Peter Sluglett (1996)

Ikhlassi, Walid
Sabah Ghandour (1996)

Ikhwan
Anthony B. Toth
Malcolm C. Peck (1996)

Ilaysh, Muhammad
Khalid Blankinship

İlmiyye
Elizabeth Thompson (1996)

Imperialism in the Middle East and North Africa
John Ruedy
Richard C. Bulliet (1996)

Incense
Malcolm C. Peck (1996)

Industrialization
Waleed Hazbun
Rodney J. A. Wilson (1996)

Infitah
Arthur Goldschmidt (1996)

İnönü, Erdal
M. Hakan Yavuz
David Waldner (1996)

İnönü, İsmet
Walter F. Weiker (1996)

Institut d'Égypte
Donald Malcolm Reid

Institute for Palestine Studies
Michael R. Fischbach (1996)

Institute for Women's Studies in the Arab World (Lebanon)
Mirna Lattouf

Institute of Women's Studies of Bir Zeit University
Mona Ghali

Intelligence Organizations
Maria F. Curtis
Dale F. Eickelman (1996)

International, Dana
Yael Ben-zvi

International Debt Commission
Donald Malcolm Reid (1996)

John XIX
Donald Spanel (1996)

Joint Distribution Committee
Paul Rivlin
Bryan Daves (1996)

Jordan
Michael R. Fischbach
Peter Gubser (1996)

Jordanian Civil War (1970–1971)
Michael R. Fischbach
Peter Gubser (1996)

Jordanian Option
Avi Shlaim (1996)

Jordan River
Curtis R. Ryan
Sara Reguer (1996)

Joseph, Dov
Chaim I. Waxman

Jubayl, al-
J. E. Peterson

Judaism
Samuel C. Heilman (1996)

Judeo-Arabic
Norman Stillman (1996)

Jumayyil, Amin
Michael R. Fischbach
Majed Halawi (1996)

Jumayyil, Bashir
As'ad AbuKhalil

Jumayyil, Pierre
Majed Halawi (1996)

Jumblatt Family
Michael R. Fischbach
As'ad AbuKhalil (1996)

Jumblatt, Kamal
As'ad AbuKhalil (1996)

Jumblatt, Walid
Michael R. Fischbach
As'ad AbuKhalil (1996)

Justice Party
David Waldner (1996)

K

Ka'ba
Maysam J. al Faruqi

Kabak, Aaron Abraham
Ann Kahn (1996)

Kabul
Grant Farr

Kabul University
Grant Farr

Kabylia
Vanesa Casanova-Fernandez
Thomas G. Penchoen (1996)

Kadivar, Mohsen
Farzin Vahdat

Kadri, Mufide
Jessica Winegar

Kafr Qasim
Elizabeth Thompson (1996)

Kahan Commission (1983)
Laurie Z. Eisenberg
Jenab Tutunji (1996)

Kahane, Meir
Gregory S. Mahler
Walter F. Weiker (1996)

Kaid, Ahmed
Phillip C. Naylor (1996)

Kalemiyye
Elizabeth Thompson (1996)

Kalischer, Hirsch
Martin Malin (1996)

Kalvaryski, Chaim Margaliut-
Neil Caplan

Kamal, Ahmad
Donald Malcolm Reid (1996)

Kamal, Zahira
Rachel Christina

Kamil, Kibrish Mehmet
David Waldner (1996)

Kamil, Mustafa
Arthur Goldschmidt (1996)

Kanafani, Ghassan
Lawrence Tal (1996)

Kandahar
Grant Farr

Kaniuk, Yoram
Stephen Schecter
Zeva Shapiro (1996)

Kan, Suna
Filiz Ali

Karacan, Ali Naci
Elizabeth Thompson (1996)

Karaites
Samuel C. Heilman (1996)

Karak, al-
Michael R. Fischbach
Peter Gubser (1996)

Karama, Battle of (1968)
Lawrence Tal (1996)

Karame, Abd al-Hamid
Guilain P. Denoeux (1996)

Karame, Rashid
Guilain P. Denoeux (1996)

Karam, Yusuf
George E. Irani (1996)

Karbala
Scott Alexander (1996)

Karbaschi, Gholamhosain
Ali Akbar Mahdi

Kariyuka, Tahiya
Roberta L. Dougherty

Karmal, Babrak
Grant Farr

Kar, Mehrangiz
Ziba Mir-Hosseini

Karnouk, Liliane
Jessica Winegar

Karp Report (1984)
Gregory S. Mahler
Martin Malin (1996)

Karzai, Hamid
Robert L. Canfield

Kasap, Teodor
David Waldner (1996)

Kashani, Abu al-Qasem
Hamid Algar (1996)

Kashif al-Ghita Family
Michael Eppel (1996)

Kashwar Kamal, Meena
Senzil Nawid

Kasravi, Ahmad
Eric Hooglund (1996)

Kassallah
Robert O. Collins (1996)

Kasztner Affair
Zev Maghen (1996)

Kateb, Yacine
Yahia Zoubir

Kattani, Muhammad ibn Abd al-Kabir al-
Edmund Burke III (1996)

Kattaniya Brotherhood
Dale F. Eickelman (1996)

Katznelson, Berl
Donna Robinson Divine (1996)

Kawakibi, Abd al-Rahman al-
Fred H. Lawson (1996)

Kaylani, Abd al-Rahman al-
Michael Eppel (1996)

Kaylani, Rashid Ali al-
Peter Sluglett (1996)

Keban Dam
Elizabeth Thompson (1996)

Keinan, Amos
Donna Robinson Divine
Ann Kahn (1996)

Kemalettin Bey
Eric Hooglund
David Waldner (1996)

Kemalism
Taha Parla (1996)

Kenaz, Yehoshua
Stephen Schecter
Zeva Shapiro (1996)

Kennedy, John Fitzgerald
Michael R. Fischbach
Zachary Karabell (1996)

Kenter, Yildiz
David Waldner (1996)

Keren Hayesod
Chaim I. Waxman

Kerman
Parvaneh Pourshariati

Kessar, Israel
Gregory S. Mahler
Martin Malin (1996)

KGB
Charles C. Kolb

Khaddam, Abd al-Halim
Michael R. Fischbach
Fred H. Lawson (1996)

Khader, Asma
Isis Nusair

Khalaf, Abdulhadi
Eric Hooglund
Emile A. Nakhleh (1996)

Khalaf, Salah
Elizabeth Thompson (1996)

Khaldunniyya
Kenneth J. Perkins (1996)

Khaled, Leila
Frances Hasso

Khal, Helen
Jessica Winegar

Khalidi, Ahmad al-Samih al-
Michael R. Fischbach

Khalid ibn Abd al-Aziz Al Saʿud
Anthony B. Toth
Malcolm C. Peck (1996)

Khalidi, Husayn Fakhri al-
Michael R. Fischbach
Muhammad Muslih (1996)

Khalidi, Wahida al-
Ellen L. Fleischmann

Khalidi, Walid
Muhammad Muslih (1996)

Khalid, Khalid Muhammad
Maysam J. al Faruqi

Khalifa, Sahar
Laurie King-Irani

Khalil, Samiha Salama
Laurie King-Irani

Khalis, Mohammad Unis
Grant Farr (1996)

Khal, Yusuf al-
Guilain P. Denoeux (1996)

Khamenehi, Ali
Roxanne Varzi
Hamid Algar (1996)

Kharg Island
Eric Hooglund
Neguin Yavari (1996)

Kharrazi, Kamal
Ali Akbar Mahdi

Khartoum
Ann M. Lesch

Khatami, Mohammad
Eric Hooglund

Khatibi, Abdelkabir
Aida A. Bamia

Khattabi, Muhammad ibn Abd al-Karim al-
C. R. Pennell (1996)

Khayr al-Din
Larry A. Barrie (1996)

Khazʿal Khan
John R. Perry (1996)

Khaznader, Mustafa
Larry A. Barrie (1996)

Khemir, Sabiha
Jessica Winegar

Khider, Mohamed
Phillip C. Naylor (1996)

Khidhir, Zahra
Jacqueline Ismael

Khomeini, Ruhollah
Eric Hooglund
Neguin Yavari (1996)

Khorasan
Parvaneh Pourshariati

Khraief, Bechir
Aida A. Bamia (1996)

Khrimian, Mkrtich
Rouben P. Adalian (1996)

Khrushchev, Nikita S.
Oles M. Smolansky (1996)

Khubar, al-
Eric Hooglund
Les Ordeman (1996)

Khuri, Bishara al-
Guilain P. Denoeux (1996)

Khutba
Elizabeth Thompson (1996)

Khuzistan
Parvaneh Pourshariati

Khyber, Mir Akbar
Grant Farr

Khyber Pass
Grant Farr

Kianuri, Nur al-Din
Ervand Abrahamian

Kiarostami, Abbas
Roxanne Varzi

Kibbutz
Chaim I. Waxman

Kibbutz Movement
Donna Robinson Divine (1996)

Kikhya Family
John L. Wright (1996)

Kikhya, Rushdi al-
George E. Irani (1996)

Kimche, David
Ian Black
Ann Kahn (1996)

King–Crane Commission (1919)
Philip Mattar (1996)

King David Hotel
Mordechai Bar-On

King Saʿud University
Anthony B. Toth

Kirkbride, Alec Seath
Joseph Nevo
Jenab Tutunji (1996)

Kirkuk
Reeva S. Simon (1996)

Kiryat Arba
David Newman
Elizabeth Thompson (1996)

Kisakürek, Necip Fazil
Elizabeth Thompson (1996)

Kisch, Frederick Hermann
Neil Caplan (1996)

Kissinger, Henry
Paola Olimpo
David Waldner (1996)

Kitchener, Horatio Herbert
Peter Mellini (1996)

Kléber, Jean-Baptiste
Zachary Karabell (1996)

Knesset
Gregory S. Mahler
Walter F. Weiker (1996)

Koç, Vehbi
Elizabeth Thompson (1996)

Kollek, Teddy
Gregory S. Mahler

Kol, Moshe
Gregory S. Mahler
Martin Malin (1996)

Konya
Eric Hooglund

Konya, Battle of
Elizabeth Thompson (1996)

Kook, Abraham Isaac Hacohen
Chaim I. Waxman (1996)

Kook, Zvi Yehuda
Chaim I. Waxman (1996)

Koor Industries
Paul Rivlin (1996)

Koprülü, Mehmet Fuat
Uli Schamiloglu (1996)

Kordofan
Robert O. Collins

Kosher
Zachary Karabell (1996)

Kovner, Abba
George R. Wilkes
Zev Maghen (1996)

Krim, Belkacem
Phillip C. Naylor (1996)

Kuchek Khan-e Jangali
Neguin Yavari (1996)

Kudsi, Nazim al-
Michael R. Fischbach
Muhammad Muslih (1996)

Kurd Ali, Muhammad
William L. Cleveland (1996)

Kurdish Autonomous Zone
Chris Kutschera

Kurdish Revolts
Amir Hassanpour

Kurdistan
Chris Kutschera

Kurdistan Workers Party (PKK)
Martin Van Bruinessen

Kurds
Chris Kutschera

Kütahya, Peace of
Zachary Karabell (1996)

Kut al-Amara
Karen Pinto (1996)

Kuttab
Elizabeth Thompson (1996)

Kuwait
Mary Ann Tétreault
Malcolm C. Peck (1996)

Kuwait City
Mary Ann Tétreault
Malcolm C. Peck (1996)

Kuwait Fund for Arab Economic Development
Mary Ann Tétreault
Emile A. Nakhleh (1996)

Kuwait Petroleum Corporation
Mary Ann Tétreault

Kuwait University
Anthony B. Toth
Malcolm C. Peck (1996)

L

Laabi, Abdellatif
Aida A. Bamia

Laayounne
Bruce Maddy-Weitzman

Labor and Labor Unions
Ellis Goldberg

Labor Zionism
Donna Robinson Divine

Lacheraf, Mostefa
Phillip C. Naylor

Lacoste, Robert
Phillip C. Naylor (1996)

Ladino
Norman Stillman (1996)

Lado Enclave
Robert O. Collins (1996)

Lebanese Women's Council
Lara Deeb

Lebanon
As'ad AbuKhalil

Lebanon, Mount
Guilain P. Denoeux (1996)

Legislative Council (Palestine)
Philip Mattar

Leibowitz, Yeshayahu
Chaim I. Waxman

Lemsine, Aicha
Aida A. Bamia

Lend-Lease Program
Zachary Karabell (1996)

Leskofcali Galip
David Waldner (1996)

Lesseps, Ferdinand de
David Waldner (1996)

Levantine
Philip Mattar
Jean-Marc R. Oppenheim (1996)

Levinger, Moshe
David Newman

Levin, Hanoch
Donna Robinson Divine
Ann Kahn (1996)

Levin, Shmaryahu
Martin Malin (1996)

Levin, Yizhak Meir
Ann Kahn (1996)

Levontin, Zalman
Bryan Daves (1996)

Levy, David
Gregory S. Mahler
Bryan Daves (1996)

Liberal Constitutionalist Party
David Waldner (1996)

Liberation Rally
David Waldner (1996)

Liberty, USS
Ian Black
Jenab Tutunji (1996)

Libya
Ronald Bruce St John
Lisa Anderson (1996)

LICA
Norman Stillman (1996)

Ligue Tunisienne pour la Défense des Droits de l'Homme (LTDH)
Ana Torres-Garcia
Larry A. Barrie (1996)

Likud
Walter F. Weiker (1996)

Lilienblum, Moses Leib
Walter F. Weiker (1996)

Litani Operation (1978)
Laurie Z. Eisenberg
Elizabeth Thompson (1996)

Litani River
Sara Riguer (1996)

Literature: Arabic
Pierre Cachia

Literature: Arabic, North African
Aida A. Bamia

Literature: Hebrew
Nili Gold (1996)

Literature: Persian
Eric Hooglund
Michael C. Hillmann (1996)

Literature: Turkish
Kyle T. Evered
Kathleen R. F. Burrill (1996)

Livnat, Limor
Meron Medzini

Lloyd George, David
Bernard Wasserstein

Lohamei Herut Yisrael
Pierre M. Atlas

Loi Cadre
Phillip C. Naylor (1996)

London Conference (1956)
Mordechai Bar-On

London Convention
Arnold Blumberg (1996)

London (Roundtable) Conference (1939)
Neil Caplan

London, Treaty of (1871)
Zachary Karabell (1996)

London, Treaty of (1913)
Zachary Karabell (1996)

Lotz, Wolfgang
Zev Maghen (1996)

Luke, Harry
Jenab Tutunji (1996)

Lurs
Eric Hooglund

Luxor
Paul Rowe
Arthur Goldschmidt (1996)

Luz, Kadish
Zev Maghen (1996)

Lyautey, Louis-Hubert Gonzalve
Remy Leveau (1996)

Lydda
Yehuda Gradus
Elizabeth Thompson (1996)

M

Ma al-Aynayn
Edmund Burke III (1996)

Maʿa lot
Yehuda Gradus
Zev Maghen (1996)

Maʿariv
Ann Kahn (1996)

Maʿbarah
Shlomo Deshen

Mabarrat Muhammad Ali
Nancy Gallagher

Maccabi
Norman Stillman (1996)

MacDonald, Malcolm
Joseph Nevo
Jenab Tutunji (1996)

MacDonald, Ramsay
Jenab Tutunji (1996)

MacMichael, Harold
Jenab Tutunji (1996)

Madani, Abassi al-
Robert Mortimer

Madani, Abdullah al-
Emile A. Nakhleh (1996)

Madani, Tawfiq al-
Phillip C. Naylor

Madkour, Ibrahim
Charles E. Butterworth

Madrasa
Denise A. Spellberg (1996)

Madrid Conference (1991)
Kenneth W. Stein

Magen David Adom (MDA)
Neil Caplan
Miriam Simon (1996)

Maghrib
Elizabeth Thompson (1996)

Magic Carpet Operation
Norman Stillman (1996)

Magnes, Judah
Chaim I. Waxman
Neil Caplan
Bryan Daves (1996)

Mahalla al-Kubra, al-
Ellis Goldberg (1996)

Mahalle Schools
Elizabeth Thompson (1996)

Mahdawi, Fadil Abbas al-
Louay Bahry (1996)

Mahd-e Ulya, Malek Jahan Khanum
Mansoureh Ettehadieh (1996)

Meddeb, Abdelwahhab
Aida A. Bamia

Medicine and Public Health
Evelyn A. Early (1996)

Medina
Anthony B. Toth

Mediterranean Sea
Vanesa Casanova-Fernandez
Elizabeth Thompson (1996)

Meged, Aharon
George R. Wilkes
Ann Kahn (1996)

Mehmet Rauf
David Waldner (1996)

Mehmet V Reşat
Eric Hooglund
Zachary Karabell (1996)

Meir, Golda
Zaki Shalom
Gregory S. Mahler (1996)

Meknes
Rahma Bourqia (1996)

Meknes, Treaty of (1836)
C. R. Pennell (1996)

Melilla
Bruce Maddy-Weitzman

Memmi, Albert
Stefanie Wichhart
Will D. Swearingen (1996)

Menderes, Adnan
Eric Hooglund
Walter F. Weiker (1996)

Menou, Jacques François
David Waldner (1996)

Mernissi, Fatema
Laura Rice

Mesopotamia Campaign (1914–1918)
Zachary Karabell (1996)

Messianism
David Waldner (1996)

Mestiri, Ahmad
Ana Torres-Garcia
Kenneth J. Perkins (1996)

Meushi, Paul Peter
George E. Irani (1996)

Mevlevi Brotherhood
Rita Stephan
Tayeb El-Hibri (1996)

MI-6
Zachary Karabell (1996)

Michael, Sami
Nancy Berg
Zvia Ginor (1996)

Middle East
Karen Pinto (1996)

Middle East Defense Organization (MEDO)
Zachary Karabell (1996)

Middle East Supply Center (MESC)
Daniel E. Spector (1996)

Middle East Technical University
Eric Hooglund
I. Metin Kunt (1996)

Midfaʿi, Jamil al-
Peter Sluglett (1996)

Midhat Paşa
Roderic H. Davison (1996)

Mihrab
Scott Alexander (1996)

Milani, Tahmineh
Roxanne Varzi

Military in the Middle East
Daniel E. Spector

Millet System
Benjamin Braude (1996)

Milli Görüş Hareketi
M. Hakan Yavuz
Nermin Abadan-Unat (1996)

Milli İstihbarat Teşkilati
Elizabeth Thompson (1996)

Morocco: Constitution
Henri Lauzière

Morocco: Political Parties in
Bruce Maddy-Weitzman

Morrison–Grady Plan (1946)
Zachary Karabell (1996)

Moshav
Paul Rivlin (1996)

Mosque
Scott Alexander (1996)

Mossad
Mordechai Bar-On

Mossadegh, Mohammad
Mansoor Moaddel (1996)

Mostaghanemi, Ahlam
Michelle Hartman

Mosul
Reeva S. Simon (1996)

Mosul, Anglo–Turkish Dispute over
Ayad al-Qazzaz (1996)

Motahhari, Mortaza
Hamid Algar (1996)

Motherland Party
M. Hakan Yavuz
Frank Tachau (1996)

Mou'awwad, Naila
Elise Salem

Moudawana, al-
Laura Rice

Mourou, Abdelfattah
Emad Eldin Shahin

Mouvement de l'Unité Populaire (MUP)
Ana Torres-Garcia
Larry A. Barrie (1996)

Mouvement National Algérien
John Ruedy (1996)

Mouvement Populaire (MP)
Bruce Maddy-Weitzman

Mouvement pour le Triomphe des Libertés
Démocratiques
John Ruedy (1996)

Movement for Unity and Reform (MUR)
Emad Eldin Shahin

Movement of Renewal
Vanesa Casanova-Fernandez
Larry A. Barrie (1996)

Mozaffar al-Din Qajar
Mansoureh Ettehadieh (1996)

M'Rabet, Fadela
Aida A. Bamia

Mu'alla Family, al-
Anthony B. Toth

Muasher, Marwan
Michael R. Fischbach

Mubarak, Husni
Arthur Goldschmidt

Mufide Kadri
David Waldner (1996)

Muhammad
Tayeb El-Hibri (1996)

Muhammad V
Rémy Leveau (1996)

Muhammad VI
Michael M. Laskier

Muhammad Ali
Fred H. Lawson (1996)

Muhammad Ali Mosque
Donald Malcolm Reid (1996)

Muhammad al-Sadiq
Larry A. Barrie (1996)

Muhammad, Aziz
Michael R. Fischbach
Michael Eppel (1996)

Muharram
Peter Chelkowski (1996)

Muharraq
Fred H. Lawson (1996)

Nadi, Yunus
Elizabeth Thompson (1996)

Nafud Desert
Eleanor Abdella Doumato (1996)

Naguib, Muhammad
David Waldner (1996)

Nahal
Zev Maghen (1996)

Nahalal
Donna Robinson Divine (1996)

Nahda, al-
Emad Eldin Shahin

Nahhas, Mustafa al-
Michael R. Fischbach (1996)

Nahnah, Mahfoud
Emad Eldin Shahin

Nahum, Halfallah
Maurice M. Roumani (1996)

Nahum, Hayyim
Michael M. Laskier (1996)

Najaf, al-
Michael R. Fischbach
Mamoon A. Zaki (1996)

Najd
Eleanor Abdella Doumato (1996)

Najibullah
Grant Farr

Najjada, al-
Elizabeth Thompson (1996)

Nakba, al- (1948–1949)
Philip Mattar

Namik Kemal
Eric Hooglund
Zachary Karabell (1996)

Namir, Mordekhai
Zev Maghen (1996)

Namir, Orah
Meron Medzini

Naqshbandi
JoAnn Gross (1996)

Naser al-Din Shah
Eric Hooglund

Nashashibi Family
Michael R. Fischbach
Muhammad Muslih (1996)

Nasir, Ahmed Sayf al-
John L. Wright (1996)

Nasir, Hanna
Michael R. Fischbach
Jenab Tutunji (1996)

Nasir, Najib
Elizabeth Thompson (1996)

Nasrallah, Emily
Elise Salem

Nasrallah, Hasan
As'ad AbuKhalil

Nasruddin Hoca
Burçak Keskin-Kozat
Kathleen R. F. Burrill (1996)

Nassar, Sadhij
Ellen L. Fleischmann

Nasser, Gamal Abdel
Raymond William Baker (1996)

Nasser, Lake
Gregory B. Baecher
Arthur Goldschmidt (1996)

Nassif, Malak Hifni
Caroline Seymour-Jorn

Nateq-Nuri, Ali Akbar
Farhad Arshad (1996)

National Bloc
Michael R. Fischbach
George E. Irani (1996)

National Congress Party
Lisa Anderson (1996)

National Democratic Front (NDF)
Robert D. Burrowes

National Democratic Front for the Liberation of
Oman and the Arab Gulf
Malcolm C. Peck (1996)

National Democratic Party (Iraq)
Reeva S. Simon (1996)

National Front for the Liberation of South
Yemen
Manfred W. Wenner

National Front for the Salvation of Libya
Lisa Anderson (1996)

National Front, Iran
Afshin Matin-asgari

National Front, Lebanon
George E. Irani (1996)

Nationalism
Richard W. Bulliet (1996)

Nationalist Action Party
M. Hakan Yavuz
Frank Tachau (1996)

National Liberal Party
George E. Irani (1996)

National Liberation Front (Bahrain)
Fred H. Lawson

National Oil Corporation (Libya)
Mary Ann Tétreault (1996)

National Pact (Lebanon)
As'ad AbuKhalil (1996)

National Party (Egypt)
Arthur Goldschmidt

National Party (Syria)
Mahmoud Haddad (1996)

National Progressive Front (Syria)
Khalil Gebara

National Progressive Unionist Party
Raymond William Baker (1996)

National Salvation Front (Lebanon)
As'ad AbuKhalil (1996)

National Salvation Party
Eric Hooglund
Nermin Abadan-Unat (1996)

National Security Council (Turkey)
M. Hakan Yavuz

National Union (Egypt)
Raymond William Baker (1996)

National Unity Committee (Turkey)
Frank Tachau (1996)

National Water System (Israel)
Sara Reguer (1996)

National Women's Committee (Yemen)
Susanne Dahlgren

Natural Gas: Economic Exploitation of
Mary Ann Tétreault

Natural Gas: Middle East Reserves of
Jean-François Seznec (1996)

Navon, Yizhak
Gregory S. Mahler
Miriam Simon (1996)

Nawfal, Hind
Marilyn Booth

Nazareth
Laurie King-Irani
Benjamin Joseph (1996)

Nazif, Süleyman
David Waldner (1996)

Nazmi, Ziya
David Waldner (1996)

Ne'eman, Yuval
Mordechai Bar-On

Negev
Yehuda Gradus
Elizabeth Thompson (Negev Desert) (1996)

Nerval, Gérard de
Maysam J. al Faruqi

Neshat, Shirin
Jessica Winegar

Nesin, Nüsret Aziz
Elizabeth Thompson (1996)

Netanyahu, Benjamin
Eric Silver
Julie Zuckerman (1996)

Neturei Karta
Chaim I. Waxman (1996)

Ouazzani, Mohamed Hassan
Bruce Maddy-Weitzman (1996)

Oufkir, Muhammad
Matthew S. Gordon (1996)

Oujda Group
John Ruedy (1996)

Ould Sid'Ahmed Taya, Ma'ouiya
Naomi Zeff

Ouled Sidi Cheikh
Phillip C. Naylor (1996)

Ouziel, Ben Zion Meir Hai
Chaim I. Waxman (1996)

OYAK (Ordu Yardimlasma Kurumu)
Elizabeth Thompson (1996)

Özal, Turgut
David Waldner (1996)

Oz, Amos
Adina Friedman
Zvia Ginor (1996)

Oz ve Shalom (Netivot shalom)
Mordechai Bar-On
Walter F. Weiker (1996)

P
Pachachi, Muzahim al-
Mamoon A. Zaki (1996)

Pagis, Dan
Adina Friedman
Julie Zuckerman (1996)

Pahlavi, Mohammad Reza
Ahmad Ashraf (1996)

Pahlavi, Reza
Ahmad Ashraf

Pakistan and the Middle East
Rasul Bakhsh Rais (1996)

Palestine
Neil Caplan
Ann M. Lesch
Don Peretz (1996)

Palestine Arab Revolt (1936–1939)
Rashid Khalidi (1996)

Palestine Economic Corporation
Elizabeth Thompson (1996)

Palestine Exploration Fund
Elizabeth Thompson (1996)

Palestine Land Development Company
Elizabeth Thompson (1996)

Palestine Liberation Organization (PLO)
Philip Mattar

Palestine National Charter (1968)
Muhammad Muslih (1996)

Palestine National Council
Maria F. Curtis
Mouin Rabbani (1996)

Palestine National Covenant (1964)
Muhammad Muslih (1996)

Palestine Research Center
Michael R. Fischbach
Jenab Tutunji (1996)

Palestinian Arab Congresses
Philip Mattar
Ann M. Lesch (1996)

Palestinian Authority
Michael R. Fischbach

Palestinian Citizens of Israel
Don Peretz

Palestinians
Philip Mattar
Muhammad Muslih (1996)

Palin Commission Report (1920)
Ann M. Lesch (1996)

Palmah
Pierre M. Atlas
Amos Perlmutter (1996)

Palmerston, Lord Henry John Temple
Eric Hooglund
Arnold Blumberg (1996)

Palmyra
Elizabeth Thompson (1996)

Pamir Mountains
Grant Farr

Pan-Arabism
Ronald Bruce St John

Pan-Turkism
Hasan Kayali (1996)

Parcham
Grant Farr (1996)

Paris Peace Settlements (1918–1923)
Eric Hooglund
Fawaz A. Gerges (1996)

Paris, Treaty of (1857)
Farhad Shirzad (1996)

Parliamentary Democratic Front
Michael R. Fischbach
As'ad AbuKhalil (1996)

Parsipur, Shahrnush
Michael C. Hillmann (1996)

Parti de l'Avant-Garde Socialiste (PAGS)
Yahia Zoubir
Phillip C. Naylor (1996)

Parti Démocratique Constitutionnel (PDC)
Bruce Maddy-Weitzman (1996)

Parti Démocratique de l'Indépendance (PDI)
Bruce Maddy-Weitzman

Parti d'Unité Populaire (PUP)
Ana Torres-Garcia
Matthew S. Gordon (1996)

Parti du Peuple Algérien (PPA)
John Ruedy (1996)

Parti National
Bruce Maddy-Weitzman (1996)

Parti National Démocratique (PND)
Bruce Maddy-Weitzman

Partition Plans (Palestine)
Avi Shlaim (1996)

Patriarch
Zachary Karabell (1996)

Patriarchs, Tomb of the
Chaim I. Waxman (1996)

Patriotic Union of Kurdistan (PUK)
Chris Kutschera

Peace and Amity, Treaty of (1805)
Larry A. Barrie (1996)

Peace Corps
Christopher Reed Stone
Zachary Karabell (1996)

Peace Now
Mordechai Bar-On

Peake, Frederick Gerard
Jenab Tutunji (1996)

Pearl Diving (Bahrain)
Fred H. Lawson (1996)

Peel Commission Report (1937)
Ann M. Lesch

Peled, Mattityahu
Mordechai Bar-On
Bryan Daves (1996)

Pelt, Adrian
Ronald Bruce St John

People's Assembly
Raymond William Baker (1996)

People's Democratic Party of Afghanistan
Grant Farr (1996)

People's Democratic Republic of Yemen
Robert D. Burrowes (1996)

People's Houses
Paul J. Magnarella (1996)

People's Socialist Party
Manfred W. Wenner

Pera
I. Metin Kunt (1996)

Peres, Shimon
Gregory S. Mahler

Pérez de Cuéllar, Javier
Ronald Bruce St John
Bryan Daves (1996)

Perim
Robert D. Burrowes

Permanent Mandates Commission
Elizabeth Thompson (1996)

Persian
M. A. Jazayary (1996)

Persian (Arabian) Gulf
Eric Hooglund
Elizabeth Thompson (1996)

Persian Cats
Eric Hooglund

Persian Script
Roxanne Varzi

Petah Tikvah
Chaim I. Waxman

Peter VII
Donald Spanel (1996)

Petra
Peter Gubser (1996)

Petrochemicals
Jean-François Seznec
Mary Ann Tétreault (1996)

Petroleum, Oil, and Natural Gas
Mary Ann Tétreault

Petroleum Reserves and Production
Jean-François Seznec

PETROMIN
Jean-Francois Seznec (1996)

Phalange
Michael R. Fischbach
As'ad AbuKhalil (1996)

Pharaonicism
James Jankowski (1996)

Pharaon, Rashad
George R. Wilkes
Les Ordeman (1996)

Philae
John Lundquist
David Waldner (1996)

Philby, Harry St. John
Neil Caplan
Benjamin Braude (1996)

Phoenicianism
As'ad AbuKhalil (1996)

Phosphates
Karim Hamdy

Pinsker, Leo
Martin Malin (1996)

Plague
Jenab Tutunji (1996)

Plumer, Herbert Charles Onslow
Ann M. Lesch (1996)

Pogrom
Jon Jucovy (1996)

Point Four
Elizabeth Thompson (1996)

POLISARIO
Bruce Maddy-Weitzman

Politi, Elie
George R. Wilkes
Michael M. Laskier (1996)

Pollard Affair
Ian Black

Polygamy
Jenab Tutunji (1996)

Popular Front
Charles U. Zenzie (1996)

Popular Front for the Liberation of Palestine
Maria F. Curtis
Mouin Rabbani (1996)

Popular Front for the Liberation of
Palestine–General Command
George R. Wilkes
Mouin Rabbani (1996)

Popular Front for the Liberation of the Occupied
Arabian Gulf
Malcolm C. Peck (1996)

Population
Paul Rivlin
Justin McCarthy (1996)

Port Sa'id
Charles C. Kolb
David Waldner (1996)

Postage Stamps
Donald Malcolm Reid

Potash Industry
Chaim I. Waxman
Peter Gubser (1996)

Potsdam Convention
Zachary Karabell (1996)

Powell, Colin L.
Michael R. Fischbach

Princess Basma Women's Resource Center
Isis Nusair

Progressive Socialist Party
As'ad AbuKhalil
George E. Irani (1996)

Protectorate States
Robert D. Burrowes (1996)

Protestantism and Protestant Missions
Eleanor Abdella Doumato

Protocols of the Elders of Zion
Michael R. Marrus
Jane Gerber (1996)

Pushtun
Eric Hooglund
Ashraf Ghani (1996)

Pyramids
Donald Malcolm Reid

Q

Qabbani, Nizar
Michael R. Fischbach
Bassam Namani (1996)

Qaddafi, Muammar al-
Ronald Bruce St John
Lisa Anderson (1996)

Qaddumi, Faruq
Michael R. Fischbach

Qadi
Scott Alexander (1996)

Qadiriyya Order
Laurence Michalak (1996)

Qafih, Yihye ben Solomon
Michael M. Laskier (1996)

Qaʿida, al-
Asʿad AbuKhalil

Qairawan
Matthew S. Gordon (1996)

Qajar, Abdullah Mirza
Mansoureh Ettehadieh (1996)

Qajar, Agha Mohammad
Mansoureh Ettehadieh (1996)

Qajar Dynasty
Eric Hooglund
John Foran (1996)

Qalqiliya
Michael R. Fischbach

Qanun
Elizabeth Thompson (1996)

Qaradawi, Yusuf al-
Abdin Chande

Qaramanli Dynasty
Rachel Simon (1996)

Qarawiyyin, al-
Rahma Bourqia (1996)

Qasim, Abd al-Karim
Louay Bahry (1996)

Qasimi Family of Raʾs al-Khayma, al-
Anthony B. Toth

Qasimi Family of Sharjah, al-
Anthony B. Toth

Qassam, Izz al-Din al-
Philip Mattar

Qatar
Anthony B. Toth
Malcolm C. Peck (1996)

Qatar Petroleum
Anthony B. Toth
Mary Ann Tétreault (1996)

Qaʿwar, Widad
Laurie King-Irani

Qawuqji, Fawzi al-
Ann M. Lesch (1996)

Qiyomijian, Ohannes
As'ad AbuKhalil (1996)

Qom
Parvaneh Pourshariati

Qotbzadeh, Sadeq
Neguin Yavari (1996)

Queen Surraya
Senzil Nawid

Qurai, Ahmad Sulayman
George R. Wilkes
Mouin Rabbani (1996)

Qur'an
Maysam J. al Faruqi
Elizabeth Thompson (1996)

Qusayr, al-
Donald Malcolm Reid
Arthur Goldschmidt (1996)

Qutb, Sayyid
Ahmad S. Moussalli
Jean-Marc R. Oppenheim (1996)

Quwatli, Shukri al-
Muhammad Muslih (1996)

R

Raab, Esther
Shibolet Zait (1996)

Raad, In'am
Michael R. Fischbach
George E. Irani (1996)

Rabat
Donna Lee Bowen (1996)

Rabbani, Burhanuddin
Grant Farr

Rabbi
Samuel C. Heilman (1996)

Rabi, Mubarak
Aida A. Bamia

Rabin, Yitzhak
Gregory S. Mahler

Rabiyya Ali, Salim
Robert D. Burrowes

Radio and Television: Arab Countries
William A. Rugh

Radio and Television: Israel
Dov Shinar

Radio and Television: Turkey
Brian Silverstein

Rafsanjani, Ali Akbar Hashemi
Eric Hooglund
Hamid Algar (1996)

Rahnavard, Zahra
Janet Afary

Rajavi, Masud
Ervand Abrahamian

Rajub, Jibril
Michael R. Fischbach

Ramadan, Taha Yasin
Michael R. Fischbach
Amatzia Baram (1996)

Ramallah
Michael R. Fischbach
Lawrence Tal (1996)

Ramgavar Azadagan Party
As'ad AbuKhalil (1996)

Ramla
Yehuda Gradus
Elizabeth Thompson (1996)

Ramses College for Girls
Linda Herrera

Rania al-Abdullah (Queen Rania)
Curtis R. Ryan

Rasafi, Ma'ruf al-
Sasson Somekh (1996)

Ra's al-Khayma
Anthony B. Toth
Malcolm C. Peck (1996)

Riyad, Mustafa al-
Arthur Goldschmidt (1996)

Rockefeller Museum
Michael R. Fischbach
Mia Bloom (1996)

Rogers, William Pierce
Ahmed H. Ibrahim
Zachary Karabell (1996)

Rolo Family
Michael M. Laskier (1996)

Roman Catholicism and Roman Catholic Missions
John J. Donohue (1996)

Romanization
Kathleen R. F. Burrill (1996)

Rome, Treaty of (1935)
Zachary Karabell (1996)

Rommel, Erwin
Daniel E. Spector (1996)

Roosevelt, Franklin Delano
Daniel E. Spector (1996)

Roosevelt, Kermit
Neguin Yavari

Rothschild, Edmond de
Reeva S. Simon (1996)

Royal Dutch Shell
Jean-François Seznec (1996)

Rub al-Khali
J. E. Peterson
Eleanor Abdella Doumato (1996)

Rubinstein, Amnon
Gregory S. Mahler
Bryan Daves (1996)

Rumelia
Karen Pinto (1996)

Ruppin, Arthur
Donna Robinson Divine (1996)

Ruşdiye Schools
Elizabeth Thompson (1996)

Rusk, Dean
Charles C. Kolb

Russia and the Middle East
Robert O. Freedman
Oles M. Smolansky (1996)

Russian–Ottoman Wars
Eric Hooglund
Oles M. Smolansky (1996)

Rutenberg, Pinhas
Neil Caplan
Sara Reguer (1996)

S

Saʿada, Antun
Sami A. Ofeish
Charles U. Zenzie (1996)

Saadawi, Nawal al-
Rita Stephan
David Waldner (1996)

Saade, George
Michael R. Fischbach
George E. Irani (1996)

Saba Family
Elizabeth Thompson (1996)

Sabah, Rasha al-
Mary Ann Tétreault

Sabah, Suad al-
Rita Stephan

Sabbagh, Hasib
George R. Wilkes
Mouin Rabbani (1996)

Sabbagh, Salah al-Din al-
Reeva S. Simon (1996)

Sabbath
Samuel C. Heilman

Sabra
Bryan Daves (1996)

Sabra and Shatila Massacres
Philip Mattar

Sabri, Ali
David Waldner (1996)

Sadat, Anwar al-
Fred H. Lawson (1996)

Salonika
Eric Hooglund
Elizabeth Thompson (1996)

Salt, al-
Jenab Tutunji (1996)

Samaritans
Benyamim Tsedaka

Samarra
Paul S. Rowe
Nazar al-Khalaf (1996)

Samar, Sima
Senzil Nawid

Samman, Ghada
Elise Salem

Samuel, Herbert Louis
Bernard Wasserstein

San'a
Robert D. Burrowes

San'a University
Robert D. Burrowes

Sanctions, Iraqi
Peter Sluglett

Sane'i, Yusef
Azadeh Kian-Thiébaut

San Remo Conference (1920)
Zachary Karabell (1996)

San Stefano, Treaty of (1878)
Oles M. Smolansky (1996)

Sant Egidio Platform
George R. Wilkes

Sanusi, Muhammad ibn Ali al-
Rachel Simon (1996)

Sanusi Order
Rachel Simon (1996)

Sanu, Ya'qub
David Waldner (1996)

Sapir, Pinhas
Martin Malin (1996)

Sarid, Yossi
Mordechai Bar-On
Bryan Daves (1996)

Sarkis, Ilyas
Bassam Namani (1996)

Sartawi, Issam
Benjamin Joseph (1996)

Sasson, Eliyahu
Itamar Rabinovich
Neil Caplan

Sassoon Family
Sylvia G. Haim (1996)

Satellite Cities Development
Maria F. Curtis
Hani Fakhouri (1996)

Saudi Arabia
J. E. Peterson

Saudi, Mona
Jessica Winegar

Saunders, Harold
George R. Wilkes

Saygun, Ahmed Adnan
David Waldner (1996)

Sayyab, Badr Shakir al-
Kamal abu-Deeb (1996)

Sayyida Zaynab Mosque
Raymond William Baker (1996)

Sayyidna Husayn Mosque
Raymond William Baker (1996)

School for Hakīmāt
Nancy Gallagher

Science and Technology
Antoine Benjamin Zahlan

Scouts
Guilain P. Denoeux (1996)

Sebastiani, Horace
Zachary Karabell (1996)

Sebbar, Leila
Aida A. Bamia

Shamlu, Ahmad
Eric Hooglund
Michael C. Hillmann (1996)

Shammas, Anton
Michael R. Fischbach
Ann Kahn (1996)

Shapira, Hayyim Moshe
Bryan Daves (1996)

Sharabati, Ahmad al-
Abdul-Karim Rafeq (1996)

Shaʿrawi, Huda al-
Marilyn Booth
David Waldner (1996)

Shaʿrawi, Muhammad Mutwalli al-
As'ad AbuKhalil

Sharef, Zeʾev
Gregory S. Mahler
Bryan Daves (1996)

Sharett, Moshe
Gregory S. Mahler (1996)

Shariʿa
Wael B. Hallaq (1996)

Shariʿati, Ali
Hamid Algar (1996)

Shariatmadari, Kazem
Neguin Yavari (1996)

Sharif
Scott Alexander (1996)

Sharif, Aziz
Michael R. Fischbach
Marion Farouk-Sluglett (1996)

Sharif-Emami, Jaʿfar
Neguin Yavari

Sharifian Dynasties
Edmund Burke III (1996)

Sharif of Mecca
Khalid Y. Blankinship (1996)

Sharif, Omar
Roxanne Varzi
David Waldner (1996)

Sharjah
Eric Hooglund
Malcolm C. Peck (1996)

Sharm al-Shaykh
Arthur Goldschmidt
Zachary Karabell (1996)

Sharon, Ariel
Eric Silver
Yaakov Shavit (1996)

Sharqi Family, al-
Anthony B. Toth
M. Morsy Abdullah (1996)

Shatt al-Arab
Neguin Yavari

Shaʾul, Anwar
Sasson Somekh

Shawa, Laila
Jessica Winegar

Shaw Commission
Philip Mattar (1996)

Shawqi, Ahmad
Irfan Shahîd

Shaykh
Marilyn Higbee (1996)

Shaykh al-Islam
Scott Alexander (1996)

Shaykh, Hanan al-
Elise Salem

Shaykhi
Juan R. I. Cole

Shazar, Shneour Zalman
Bryan Daves (1996)

Shazli, Saʿd al-Din
David Waldner (1996)

Shekel
Bryan Daves (1996)

Shenhar, Yitzhak
Bryan Daves (1996)

Shenouda III
Arthur Goldschmidt
Donald Spanel (1996)

Sumud
Elizabeth Thompson (1996)

Sunay, Cevdet
Elizabeth Thompson (1996)

Sun Language Theory
Elizabeth Thompson (1996)

Sunna
Maysam J. al Faruqi
Scott Alexander (1996)

Sunni Islam
Maysam J. al Faruqi
Tayeb El-Hibri (1996)

Suphi Ezgi
David Waldner (1996)

Supreme Muslim Council
Philip Mattar

Sursock, Lady Cochrane
Mona Takieddine Amyuni

Sursuq Family
Elizabeth Thompson (1996)

Suwaydi Family
Ayad al-Qazzaz (1996)

Suwaydi, Tawfiq al-
Ayad al-Qazzaz (1996)

Suwaydiya Oil Fields
Abdul-Karim Rafeq

Suwayhli, Ramadan al-
George Joffe (1996)

Sykes, Mark
Roger Adelson
Zachary Karabell (1996)

Sykes–Picot Agreement (1916)
Zachary Karabell (1996)

Syria
Ronald Bruce St John
Fred H. Lawson (1996)

Syrian Desert
Abdul-Karim Rafeq (1996)

Syrian Social Nationalist Party
Ronald Bruce St John

Syrkin, Nachman
Donna Robinson Divine (1996)

Szold, Henrietta
Mia Bloom (1996)

T

Taba
Philip Mattar
Ann M. Lesch (1996)

Taba Negotiations (1995, 2001)
Philip Mattar

Tabaqa Dam
John R. Clark (1996)

Tabataba'i, Mohammad
Eric Hooglund
Hamid Algar (1996)

Tabataba'i, Ziya
Hamid Algar (1996)

Tabriz
Neguin Yavari

Tabriz University
Parvaneh Pourshariati
Neguin Yavari (1996)

Tagger, Sioneh
Julie Zuckerman (1996)

Taha, Mahmud Muhammad
Carolyn Fluehr-Lobban

Tahir, Kemal
David Waldner (1996)

Tahtawi, Rifaʿa al-Rafi al-
Abdel Aziz EzzelArab (1996)

Taʾif Accord
George E. Irani
Bryan Daves (1996)

Taʾif, al-
J. E. Peterson

Taʾif, Treaty of al-
Anthony B. Toth
F. Gregory Gause, III (1996)

Taʿiz
Robert D. Burrowes

Umm al-Qaywayn
Anthony B. Toth
Malcolm C. Peck (1996)

Umm al-Qura University
Khalid Y. Blankinship (1996)

Umma Party
Robert O. Collins

Umm Kulthum
Virginia Danielson (1996)

Umm Naʿsan
Fred H. Lawson (1996)

Union Démocratique du Manifeste Algérien (UDMA)
John Ruedy (1996)

Union Générale des Travailleurs Marocains (UGTM)
Ana Torres-Garcia
Larry A. Barrie (1996)

Union Générale des Travailleurs Tunisiens (UGTT)
Ana Torres-Garcia
Larry A. Barrie (1996)

Union Marocaine du Travail (UMT)
Ana Torres-Garcia
Bradford Dillman (1996)

Union Nationale des Etudiants Marocains (UNEM)
Bruce Maddy-Weitzman

Union Nationale des Forces Populaires (UNFP)
Vanesa Casanova-Fernandez
Bradford Dillman (1996)

Union of Tunisian Women
Angel M. Foster

Union Socialiste des Forces Populaires (USFP)
Vanesa Casanova-Fernandez

Union Tunisienne des Industrialistes, Compagnies, Artisans (UTICA)
Vanesa Casanova-Fernandez
Larry A. Barrie (1996)

United Arab Emirates
Anthony B. Toth
Malcolm C. Peck (1996)

United Arab Republic (UAR)
Michael R. Fischbach (1996)

United Jewish Appeal (UJA)
Paul Rivlin

United Nations and the Middle East
Thomas G. Weiss
F. T. Liu (1996)

United Nations Conciliation Commission for Palestine (UNCCP)
Neil Caplan
Fred J. Khouri (1996)

United Nations Economic Survey Mission (1949)
Zach Levey

United Nations Emergency Force
F. T. Liu (1996)

United Nations Interim Force in Lebanon
Brian Urquhart
Asʿad AbuKhalil (1996)

United Nations Relief and Works Agency for Palestine Refugees in the Near East (UNRWA)
Michael R. Fischbach
F. T. Liu (1996)

United Nations Special Commission (UNSCOM)
Ayad Al-Qazzaz

United Nations Special Committee on Palestine, 1947 (UNSCOP)
Joseph Nevo
F. T. Liu (1996)

United Nations Truce Supervision Organization (UNTSO)
Neil Caplan
Charles U. Zenzie (1996)

United States of America and the Middle East
Don Peretz

Unity Party
Frank Tachau (1996)

University of Jordan
Michael R. Fischbach
Jenab Tutunji (1996)

University of Khartoum
Robert O. Collins

University of Tehran
Eric Hooglund
Mansoureh Ettehadieh (1996)

Urabi, Ahmad
Arthur Goldschmidt (1996)

Urbanization
Anthony B. Toth
John R. Clark (1996)

Urban Planning
Eric Hooglund
Hooshang Amirahmadi (1996)

Urwa al-Wuthqa, al-
Nikki Keddie (1996)

Uşakliğil, Halit Ziya
Elizabeth Thompson (1996)

Üsküdar
Elizabeth Thompson (1996)

Ussishkin, Menahem
Donna Robinson Divine

Usuli
Neguin Yavari

Utaybi, Juhayman al-
Eric Hooglund
Abdel Aziz EzzelArab (1996)

Uthman, Muhammad Ali
Robert D. Burrowes

Uthman, Uthman Ahmad
Arthur Goldschmidt

Uzbeks
M. Nazif Shahrani (1996)

V

Vaʿad Leʾumi
Neil Caplan

Vaka-i Hayriye
Eric Hooglund
Avigdor Levy (1996)

Valensi, Alfred
Norman Stillman

Vance, Cyrus
Daniel E. Spector

Van, Lake
John R. Clark

Vanunu Affair
Gregory S. Mahler
Julie Zuckerman (1996)

Varlik Vergisi
Elizabeth Thompson

Vatican and the Middle East
George E. Irani

Vazhapetian, Nerses
Rouben P. Adalian

Vazir Afkham, Soltan Ali Khan
Neguin Yavari

Vaziri, Qamar al-Moluk
Parvaneh Pourshariati

Velayat-e Faqih
Eric Hooglund
Hamid Algar (1996)

Velayati, Ali Akbar
Ali Akbar Mahdi

Versailles, Treaty of (1920)
Daniel E. Spector

Victoria College
William L. Cleveland
Alain Silvera (1996)

Village Institutes
Paul J. Magnarella

Volpi, Giuseppe
George Joffe

Vozuq al-Dowleh, Mirza Hasan Khan
Neguin Yavari

W

Wadi Hadramawt
Robert D. Burrowes (1996)

Wadi Natrun
Arthur Goldschmidt
Raymond William Baker (1996)

Wafd
J. Janice Terry

Wafdist Women's Central Committee
Maria F. Curtis

Wahrhaftig, Zerah
Gregory S. Mahler
Bryan Daves (1996)

Wallach, Yona
Nili Gold (1996)

Waqf
Imad-ad-Dean Ahmad
Denise A. Spellberg (1996)

War in Iraq (2003)
Michael R. Fischbach

Warnier Law
Peter von Sivers (1996)

War of Attrition (1969–1970)
Arthur Goldschmidt
Benjamin Joseph (1996)

Water
David B. Brooks

Wattar, al-Taher
Azzedine G. Mansour
Aida A. Bamia (1996)

Wauchope, Arthur
Bernard Wasserstein
Karen A. Thornsvard (1996)

Wavell, Archibald Percival
Daniel E. Spector (1996)

Wazir, Intisar al- (Umm Jihad)
Khaled Islaih

Wazir, Khalil al-
Mouin Rabbani (1996)

Wazzani, Muhammad Hassan al-
Bruce Maddy-Weitzman (1996)

Weizman, Ezer
Gregory S. Mahler

Weizmann, Chaim
Bernard Wasserstein

Weizmann Institute of Science
Miriam Simon (1996)

West Bank
David Newman
Geoffrey Aronson (1996)

Westernization
Peter Sluglett

Western Sahara
Ana Torres-Garcia
Bruce Maddy-Weitzman (1996)

Western Sahara War
Bruce Maddy-Weitzman

Western Wall
Samuel C. Heilman (1996)

Western Wall Disturbances
Philip Mattar (1996)

West German Reparations Agreement
Paul Rivlin

Wheelus Air Force Base
Stuart J. Borsch (1996)

White Flag League
Kenneth S. Mayers (1996)

White Papers on Palestine
Ann M. Lesch

White Revolution (1961–1963)
Eric Hooglund

Wifaq, al-
Norman Stillman (1996)

Wilson, Arnold T.
Peter Sluglett (1996)

Wilson, Woodrow
Lawrence Davidson
Zachary Karabell (1996)

Wingate, Charles Orde
Reeva S. Simon (1996)

Wingate, Reginald
Janice J. Terry (1996)

Wise, Stephen S.
Mark Raider

Wolff, Henry Drummond
Parvaneh Pourshariati (1996)

Women and Family Affairs Center
Islah Jad

Women in Black
George R. Wilkes

Women's Affairs Center (Gaza)
Islah Jad

Women's Centre for Legal Aid and Counseling
Islah Jad

Women's Forum for Research and Training
(Yemen)
Susanne Dahlgren

Women's International Zionist Organization
Shimon Avish

Women's Library and Information Center
(Istanbul)
Yesim Arat

Women's Organization of Iran (WOI)
Haleh Vaziri

Women's People's Party (1923)
Burçak Keskin-Kozat

Women's Religious Rituals
Sabine Kalinock

Women's Renaissance Club
Jacqueline Ismael

Women's Services
Nermin Abadan-Unat (1996)

Women's Studies Center (Jerusalem)
Islah Jad

Woodhead Commission (1938)
Pierre M. Atlas
Benjamin Joseph (1996)

World Bank
Jean-François Seznec

World Federation of Sephardi Communities
Mia Bloom (1996)

World Organization of Jews from Arab Countries
(WOJAC)
Michael M. Laskier

World War I
Sara Reguer (1996)

World War II
Daniel E. Spector (1996)

World Zionist Organization (WZO)
Bernard Wasserstein

Y

Ya'ari, Me'ir
Bryan Daves (1996)

Yacine, Abdessalame
Henri Lauzière

Yacoubi, Rachida
Rabia Bekkar

Yadin, Yigael
Gregory S. Mahler
Mia Bloom (1996)

Yad Mordekhai
Jon Jucovy

Yad Vashem
Jon Jucovy (1996)

Yahya ibn Muhammad Hamid al-Din
Manfred W. Wenner (1996)

Yamani, Ahmad Zaki
Anthony B. Toth

Yanbu
J. E. Peterson

Yariv, Aharon
Julie Zuckerman (1996)

Yarmuk River
Elizabeth Thompson (1996)

Yarmuk University
Jenab Tutunji (1996)

Yasar Kemal
Chris Kutschera
Kathleen R. F. Burrill (1996)

Yasin, Ahmad Isma'il
As'ad AbuKhalil

Yata, Ali
C. R. Pennell (1996)

Zabul
Grant Farr

Zach, Natan
Adina Friedman
Yaron Peleg (1996)

Zaghlul, Sa'd
Janice J. Terry (1996)

Zagros
Parvaneh Pourshariati (1996)

Zahawi, Jamil Sidqi al-
Jacqueline Ismael

Zahedan
Eric Hooglund

Zahir Shah
M. Nazif Shahrani

Zahla
George E. Irani (1996)

Za'im, Husni al-
Eyal Zisser
Charles U. Zeznie (1996)

Zamzam
Scott Alexander (1996)

Zana, Leyla
Shahrzad Mojab

Zanan Magazine
Nayereh Tohidi

Zangwill, Israel
Miriam Simon (1996)

Zanzibar
Malcolm C. Peck (1996)

Zaqaziq University
Donald Malcolm Reid

Zaraniq Confederation
Robert D. Burrowes (1996)

Zarqa, al-
Abla M. Amavi (1996)

Zaydan, Jurji
Thomas Philipp (1996)

Zaydism
Robert D. Burrowes (1996)

Zaytuna University
Aida A. Bamia (1996)

Zayyat, Latifa
Marilyn Booth

Zbiri, Tahar
Phillip C. Naylor

Zeid, Fahralnissa
Jessica Winegar

Zelda
Donna Robinson Divine
Zvia Ginor (1996)

Zell al-Soltan, Mas'ud Mirza
Lawrence G. Potter (1996)

Zeroual, Liamine
Yahia Zoubir
Mia Bloom (1996)

Ziadeh, May
Elise Salem

Zikhron Ya'akov
Bryan Daves (1996)

Zili, Ridha
Aida A. Bamia

Zionism
Neil Caplan
Donna Robinson Divine (1996)

Zionist Commission for Palestine
Donna Robinson Divine (1996)

Zionist Organization of America
Jerry Kutnick
Bryan Daves (1996)

Zionist Revisionist Movement
Yaakov Shavit (1996)

Ziwaj Mut'a
Rula Jurdi Abisaab

Ziya, Abdülhamit
Elizabeth Thompson (1996)

Zohar, Uri
Chaim I. Waxman

LIST OF CONTRIBUTORS

Nermin Abadan-Unat
Bogazici University, Istanbul
   Çiller, Tansu
   Civil Code of 1926
   Demirel, Süleyman
   Ecevit, Bülent
   Milli Görüş Hareketi
   National Salvation Party
   Refah Partisi
   Republican People's Party (RPP)
   State Planning Organization (SPO)
   Turkish Grand National Assembly
   Women's Services

M. Morsy Abdullah
Centre for Documentation and Research, Abu Dhabi
   Abu Musa Island
   Al Nahayyan Family
   Maktum Family, al-
   Sharqi Family, al-

O. W. Abi-Mershed
Georgetown University
   Clemenceau, Georges
   Young Tunisians

Rula Jurdi Abisaab
University of Akron, Ohio
   Sadr, Sitt Rabab al- (Charafeddine)
   Ziwaj Mutʿa

Ervand Abrahamian
City University of New York, Baruch College
   Fedaʾiyan-e Islam
   Fedaʾiyan-e Khalq
   Forqan
   Kianuri, Nur al-Din
   Mojahedin-e Khalq
   Rajavi, Masud
   Tudeh Party

Kamal Abu-Deeb
Centre of Near and Middle Eastern Studies
   Adonis
   Sayyab, Badr Shakir al-

Asʿad AbuKhalil
California State University, Stanislaus
   AMAL
   American University of Beirut (AUB)

Aoun, Michel
Arkoun, Mohammed
Arslan Family
Asʿad, Ahmad
Asʿad Family
Asʿad, Kamil
Asʿad Wali
Ashmawi, Muhammad Saʿid al-
Azm, Sadiq al-
Beirut
Berri, Nabi
Bin Ladin, Osama
Bishara, Suha
Chehab, Bashir
Chehab Family
Chehab, Fuʾad
Constitutional Bloc
Council for Development and Reconstruction
    (CDR)
Daʾud Pasha
Dabbas, Charles
Druze Revolts
Eddé, Emile
Fadlallah, Shaykh Husayn
Franjiyya, Sulayman
Geagea, Samir
Gibran, Kahlil
Hakim, Adnan al-
Hamadi, Sabri
Hanafi, Hasan
Hariri, Rafiq Bahaʾuddin al-
Hilu, Charles
Hilu, Pierre
Hirawi, Ilyas al-
Hizbullah
Hobeika, Elie
Hoss, Salim al-
Hunchak Party
Husayni, Husayn al-
Jumayyil, Bashir
Jumblatt Family
Jumblatt, Kamal
Jumblatt, Walid
Lahad, Antoine
Lahhud, Emile
Lebanese Arab Army
Lebanese Civil War (1975–1990)
Lebanese Forces
Lebanese University
Lebanon

Maronites
Nasrallah, Hasan
National Pact (Lebanon)
National Salvation Front (Lebanon)
Parliamentary Democratic Front
Phalange
Phoenicianism
Progressive Socialist Party
Qaʿida, al-
Qiyomijian, Ohannes
Ramgavar Azadagan Party
Saint Joseph University
Salam, Saʾib
September 11th, 2001
Sfeir, Nasrallah
Shabʿa Farms
Shahin, Tanyos
Shaʿrawi, Muhammad Mutwalli al-
Shuf
Special Forces of the Levant
Sulh, Sami al-
Trad, Petro
Yasin, Ahmad Ismaʿil

Rouben P. Adalian
Armenian National Institute
    Alishan, Ghevond
    Armenian Community of Jerusalem
    Armenian Genocide
    Armenian Millet
    Armenian Revolutionary Movement
    Armenians in the Middle East
    Balyan Family
    Cemal Paşa
    Chamchian, Mikayel
    Chrakian, Artin
    Dashnak Party
    Khrimian, Mkrtich
    Musa Dagh
    Ormanian, Maghakia
    Srvantziants, Garegin
    Vazhapetian, Nerses
    Yusufian, Boghos
    Zohrab, Krikor

Roger Adelson
Arizona State University
    Arab Bureau (Cairo)
    Foreign Office, Great Britain
    Sykes, Mark

Janet Afary
Purdue University
> Dabbagh, Marzieh
> Rahnavard, Zahra

Imad-ad-Dean Ahmad
Minaret of Freedom, Bethesda, MD
> Waqf

Karen Hunt Ahmed
University of Chicago
> Ajman

Kristian Alexander
University of Utah
> Iraqi National Congress

Scott Alexander
Catholic Theological Union
> Allah
> Jihad
> Karbala
> *Mihrab*
> Mosque
> Organization of the Islamic Conference
> Qadi
> Sharif
> Shaykh al-Islam
> Sunna
> Tekke
> Zamzam

Hamid Algar
University of California, Berkeley
> Akhondzadeh, Mirza Fath Ali
> Beheshti, Mohammad
> Golpayagani, Mohammad Reza
> Kashani, Abu al-Qasem
> Khamenehi, Ali
> Montazeri, Hosayn Ali
> Motahhari, Mortaza
> Nuri, Fazlollah
> Rafsanjani, Ali Akbar Hashemi
> Shariʿati, Ali
> Sufism and the Sufi Orders
> Tabatabaʾi, Mohammad
> Tabatabaʾi, Ziya
> Velayat-e Faqih

Filiz Ali
Mimar Sinan University
> Biret, Idil
> Gencer, Leyla
> Kan, Suna

Calvin H. Allen, Jr.
Shenandoah University
> Dhufar
> Oman
> Tamimahs

Roger Allen
University of Pennsylvania
> Hakim, Tawfiq al-
> Husayn, Taha
> Idris, Yusuf
> Mahir, Ahmad
> Mahir, Ali
> Mahmud, Muhammad
> Salim, Ali

Ilai Alon
Tel Aviv University
> Dhimma

Audrey L. Altstadt
University of Massachusetts, Amherst
> Democratic Party of Azerbaijan
> Social Democratic Party of Azerbaijan

Abla M. Amavi
Georgetown University
> Tuqan, Fadwa
> Zarqa, al-

Dina Amin
University of Pennsylvania
> Theater

Hooshang Amirahmadi
Rutgers University, New Brunswick
> Urban Planning

Mona Takieddine Amyuni
American University of Beirut
> Gebeyli, Claire
> Sursock, Lady Cochrane

Lisa Anderson
Columbia University
> Bourguiba, Habib
> General People's Committees
> General People's Congress (GPC)
> Green Book
> Jabha al-Wataniyya, al-
> Jallud, Abd al-Salam
> Jamahiriyya
> Libya

Mzali, Mohammed
National Congress Party
National Front for the Salvation of Libya
Qaddafi, Muammar al-

Yesim Arat
Bogaziçl University
Tekeli, Şirin
Women's Library and Information Center
(Istanbul)

Walter Armbrust
St. Anthony's College
Jabarti, Abd al-Rahman al-

Geoffrey Aronson
Hebrew University
West Bank

Farhad Arshad
Columbia University
Isfahan
Nateq-Nuri, Ali Akbar
Nuri, Abd al-Malik
Shirazi, Mirza Hasan

Ahmad Ashraf
Columbia University
Bazaars and Bazaar Merchants
Iran
Pahlavi, Reza

Pierre M. Atlas
Marian College
Haganah
Hebrew University of Jerusalem
Jabotinsky, Vladimir Ze'ev
Lohamei Herut Yisrael
Palmah
Saison
Sokolow, Nahum
Woodhead Commission (1938)
Yellin-Mor, Natan

Shimon Avish
Columbia University
Herzl, Theodor

Cemil Aydin
Ohio State University
Gülhane Imperial Edict (1839)
Islamic Congresses

Gregory B. Baecher
University of Maryland
Aswan High Dam
Delta Barrages
Nasser, Lake
Nile River

Louay Bahry
Washington, DC
Hussein, Saddam
Mahdawi, Fadil Abbas al-
Qasim, Abd al-Karim
Sa'id, Nuri al-

Raymond William Baker
Trinity College
Nasser, Gamal Abdel
National Progressive Unionist Party
National Union (Egypt)
New Wafd
People's Assembly
Saint Mark's Cathedral
Sayyida Zaynab Mosque
Sayyidna Husayn Mosque
Shaltut, Muhammad
Sultan Hasan Mosque
Wadi Natrun

H. G. Balfour-Paul
Devon, England
Fertile Crescent Unity Plans

Aida A. Bamia
University of Florida
Bannis, Mohammad
Berrada, Mohammed
Bin Diyaf, Muhsen
Chraibi, Driss
Ghallab, Abd al-Karim
Hacene, Farouk Zehar
Hamzawi, Rashid al-
Khatibi, Abdelkabir
Laabi, Abdellatif
Lemsine, Aicha
Literature: Arabic, North African
Mas'adi, Mahmoud al-
Meddeb, Abdelwahhab
M'Rabet, Fadela
Rabi, Mubarak
Sebbar, Leila
Sefrioui, Ahmed

Shukri, Mohammad
Tlili, Mustafa
Zili, Ridha

Mordechai Bar-On
Yad Itzhak Ben-Zvi Institute
    Anglo–Egyptian Treaty (1954)
    Arab–Israeli General Armistice Agreements
        (1949)
    Avnery, Uri
    Barak, Ehud
    Harkabi, Yehoshafat
    Israel: Military and Politics
    King David Hotel
    Lavon Affair
    London Conference (1956)
    Mossad
    Ne'eman, Yuval
    Oz ve Shalom (Netivot shalom)
    Peace Now
    Peled, Mattityahu
    Sarid, Yossi
    Shlonsky, Avraham
    Suez Crisis (1956–1957)

Larry A. Barrie
Fayetteville, NC
    Ahmad Bey Husayn
    Bayram V, Muhammad
    General Tunisian Union of Students (UGTE)
    Jalluli Family
    Khayr al-Din
    Khaznader, Mustafa
    Ligue Tunisienne pour la Défense des Droits
        de l'Homme (LTDH)
    Mareth Line
    Morocco: Overview
    Mouvement de l'Unité Populaire (MUP)
    Movement of Renewal
    Muhammad al-Sadiq
    Organisation Marocaine des Droits de
        l'Homme
    Peace and Amity, Treaty of (1805)
    Shabbi, Abu al-Qasim al-
    Tunis
    Tunisia: Overview
    Tunisia: Political Parties in
    Union Générale des Travailleurs Marocains
        (UGTM)
    Union Générale des Travailleurs Tunisiens
        (UGTT)

    Union Tunisienne des Industrialistes,
        Compagnies, Artisans (UTICA)

Michael L. Bates
American Numismatic Society, New York
    Numismatics

Vincent Battesti
Centre d'Études et de Documentation Économiques, Cairo,
Egypt
    Agriculture

Yehuda Bauer
Yad Vashem
    Holocaust

Mangol Bayat
Independent Scholar, Cambridge, MA, and Brauningshof,
Germany
    Constitutional Revolution, Impact on Women

Lois Beck
Washington University
    Marriage and Family

Joel S. Beinin
Stanford University
    Communism in the Middle East

Rabia Bekkar
Georgetown University
    Aicha, Lalla
    Algerian Family Code (1984)
    Arabization Policies
    Ben Bouali, Hassiba
    Bouhired, Jamila
    Mimouni, Rachid
    Yacoubi, Rachida

Yael Ben-zvi
Ben-Gurion University
    International, Dana

Nancy Berg
Washington University
    Michael, Sami
    Salim, Ali

Elizabeth M. Bergman
Columbia University
    Arabic Script

Rhimou Bernikho-Canin
Tarzana, CA
    Haik

Robert Betts
American University of Beirut
  Druze

Dale L. Bishop
National Council of the Churches of Christ in the USA
  Christians in the Middle East

Ian Black
Guardian Newspaper, *London*
  Harel, Isser
  Kimche, David
  Liberty, USS
  Pollard Affair
  Shiloah, Reuven
  Shin Bet

Khalid Blankinship
Temple University
  Hijaz
  Ilaysh, Muhammad
  Mecca
  Muslim World League
  Sharif of Mecca
  Umm al-Qura University

Jonathan M. Bloom
Boston College
  Ibn Tulun Mosque

Mia Bloom
Princeton University
  Algiers Agreement (1975)
  American Jewish Committee
  American Jewish Congress
  Camels
  Carter, Jimmy
  Crane, Charles R.
  Dead Sea Scrolls
  Diaspora
  Diwan
  Hadassah
  Rockefeller Museum
  Silver, Abba Hillel
  Szold, Henrietta
  World Federation of Sephardi Communities
  Yadin, Yigael
  Zeroual, Liamine

Arnold Blumberg
Towson State University
  Ashkenazim
  Berlin, Congress and Treaty of

  London Convention
  Palmerston, Lord Henry John Temple

Emma Aubin Boltanski
London, U.K.
  Nabi Musa Pilgrimage

Jerome Bookin-Wiener
Bentley College
  Barbary States
  Barbary Wars
  Corsairs

Marilyn Booth
University of Illinois, Urbana-Champaign
  Abu Zeid, Layla
  Ashour, Radwa
  Djebar, Assia
  Egyptian Feminist Union
  Fawwaz, Zaynab
  Ghazali, Zaynab al-
  Idlibi, Ulfat al-
  Nawfal, Hind
  Rauf Ezzat, Heba
  Sha'rawi, Huda al-
  Stanhope, Hester
  Zayyat, Latifa

Iris Borowy
University of Rostock, Historical Institute
  Alpha, Operation

Stuart J. Borsch
Columbia University
  Sidra, Gulf of
  Wheelus Air Force Base

Nabil Boudraa
Oregon State University
  Chédid, Andrée

Kamal Boullatta
Rabat, Morocco
  Darwish, Mahmud

Rahma Bourqia
Mohamed V University, Rabat
  Azib
  Gharb
  Glawi Family, al-
  Harratin
  Isawiyya Brotherhood
  Jma'a Tribal Council

Meknes
Qarawiyyin, al-
Shorfa
Tashilhit Language

Donna Lee Bowen
Brigham Young University
Alawite Dynasty
Ben Barka, Mehdi
Birth Control
Fez, Morocco
Rabat

Henry S. Bradsher
Arlington, VA
Afghanistan: Soviet Intervention in

Benjamin Braude
Boston College
Burckhardt, Johann Ludwig
Burton, Richard Francis
Canning, Stratford
Dönme
Doughty, Charles
Lawrence, T. E.
Millet System
Minorities
Philby, Harry St. John

David B. Brooks
Friends of the Earth, Canada
Water

Nathan J. Brown
George Washington University
Law, Modern

Jack Bubon
Fairfax, VA
Cossack Brigade
South Persia Rifles
Trans-Iranian Railway

Richard W. Bulliet
Columbia University
Alcohol
Cotton
Guilds
Historiography
Imperialism in the Middle East and North
    Africa
Nationalism

Orientalists, International Congress of
Terrorism

Martin Bunton
University of Victoria
Land Reform

Edmund Burke III
University of California, Santa Cruz
Abd al-Aziz ibn al-Hassan
Abd al-Hafid ibn al-Hassan
Abd al-Rahman ibn Hisham
Abu Himara
Ahmad Hibat Allah
Ahmad ibn Muhammad al-Raysuni
Kattani, Muhammad ibn Abd al-Kabir al-
Ma al-Aynayn
Marrakech
Moroccan Question
Sharifian Dynasties
Tuhami al-Glawi

Kathleen R. F. Burrill
Columbia University
Adivar, Abdulhak Adnan
Adivar, Halide Edib
Boratav, Pertev Naili
Dağlarca, Fazil Hüsnü
Literature: Turkish
Nasruddin Hoca
Ortaoyunu
Romanization
Yasar Kemal

Robert D. Burrowes
University of Washington
Abd al-Ghani, Abd al-Aziz
Ali Nasir Muhammad al-Hasani
Amri, Hasan al-
Antar, Ali Ahmad Nasir
Attas, Haydar Abu Bakr al-
Bab al-Mandab
Baydh, Ali Salim al-
Free Officers, Yemen
Free Yemenis
Front for the Liberation of South Yemen
Ghashmi, Ahmad Husayn
Hajri, Abdullah al-
Hamid al-Din Family
Hatim Sultans of Hamdan
Iryani, Abd al-Rahman al-
Islah Party

Isma'il, Abd al-Fattah
Ma'rib
Makki, Hasan Muhammad
National Democratic Front (NDF)
People's Democratic Republic of Yemen
Perim
Protectorate States
Rabiyya Ali, Salim
Sallal, Abdullah al-
San'a
San'a University
Shami, Ahmad Muhammad al-
Shami, Muhammad Abdullah al-
Socotra
South Arabian Armed Forces
Ta'iz
Treaty of Protection (1886)
Tribes and Tribalism: Yemeni
Uthman, Muhammad Ali
Wadi Hadramawt
Yemen Arab Republic
Yemen Civil War
Yemen Hunt Oil Company
Zaraniq Confederation
Zaydism

Noah Butler
Northwestern University
Alexandretta
Refugees: Balkan Muslim
Turkish Script

Charles Butterworth
University of Maryland, Department of Government and Politics
Anawati, Georges Chehata
Awad, Louis
Madkour, Ibrahim
Omar, Muhammad (Mullah)

Pierre Cachia
Columbia University
Literature: Arabic
Mahfuz, Najib

Robert L. Canfield
Washington University
Afghanistan: Soviet Intervention in
Karzai, Hamid

Byron Cannon
University of Utah
Abd al-Qadir

Neil Caplan
Vanier College
Antisemitism
Biltmore Program (1942)
Binationalism
Dulles, John Foster
Faisal–Weizmann Agreements
Jewish Legion
Kalvaryski, Chaim Margaliut-
Kisch, Frederick Hermann
London (Roundtable) Conference (1939)
Magen David Adom (MDA)
Mixed Armistice Commissions
Palestine
Philby, Harry St. John
Rutenberg, Pinhas
United Nations Conciliation Commission for Palestine (UNCCP)
United Nations Truce Supervision Organization (UNTSO)
Va'ad Le'umi
Yiddish
Zionism

Stephanie Capparell
The Wall Street Journal, *New York*
Hürriyet

Vanesa Casanova-Fernandez
Georgetown University
Achour, Habib
B'nai B'rith
Constitutional Democratic Rally
Habous
Jallud, Abd al-Salam
Kabylia
Lahouel, Hocine
Masmoudi, Muhammad
Mediterranean Sea
Movement of Renewal
Nuun Magazine
Organisation Marocaine des Droits de l'Homme
Organization of the Islamic Conference
Orientalists, International Congress of
Red Crescent Society
Sfar, Tahar
Spain and the Middle East
Union Nationale des Forces Populaires (UNFP)
Union Socialiste des Forces Populaires (USFP)

Union Tunisienne des Industrialistes,
Compagnies, Artisans (UTICA)

John T. Chalcraft
University of Edinburgh
Historiography

Abdin Chande
Sidwell Friends School
Qaradawi, Yusuf al-

Mounira Charrad
University of Texas, Austin
Tunisia: Personal Status Code

Peter Chelkowski
Kevorkian Center for Middle Eastern Studies
Muharram

Jamsheed K. Choksky
Indiana University, Bloomington
Zoroastrianism

Rachel Christina
RAND Education, University of Pittsburgh
Gender: Gender and Education
Kamal, Zahira

Kathleen M. Christison
Santa Fe, NM
Central Intelligence Agency (CIA)

John R. Clark
Columbia University
Adana
Aegean Sea
Alexandretta
Ankara
Euphrates Dam
Tabaqa Dam
Taurus Mountains
Tigris and Euphrates Rivers
Urbanization
Van, Lake
Zab Rivers

William L. Cleveland
Simon Fraser University
Antonius, George
Arslan, Shakib
Baghdad Pact (1955)
Crane, Charles R.

Kurd Ali, Muhammad
Victoria College

Juan R. I. Cole
University of Michigan
Ahsaʿi, Ahmad al-
Amin, Qasim
Bab, al-
Babis
Bahaʾi Faith
Shaykhi

Robert O. Collins
University of California, Santa Barbara
Abd al-Rahman al-Mahdi
Abdullahi, Muhammad Turshain
Azhari, Ismaʿil
Bahr al-Abyad
Bahr al-Arab
Bahr al-Ghazal
Bahr al-Jabal
Beja
Dinka
Kassallah
Kordofan
Lado Enclave
Nuer
Numeiri, Muhammad Jaʿfar
Omdurman
Sudd
Umma Party
University of Khartoum

Robyn Creswell
New York University
Darwish, Mahmud

Maria F. Curtis
University of Texas, Austin
Adham, Soraya
Arab Feminist Union
Bektashis
Ben Ali, Zayn al-Abidine
Bodrum
Bouih, Fatna el-
Central Intelligence Agency (CIA)
Communication
Dance
Intelligence Organizations
Jababdi, Latifa
Jamiʿa al-Islamiyya, al-

Muwahhidun
Palestine National Council
Popular Front for the Liberation of Palestine
Rateb, Aisha
Satellite Cities Development
Sistani, Ali al-
Wafdist Women's Central Committee

Susanne Dahlgren
University of Helsinki, Finland
Al-Suswa, Amat al-Alim
Far'a, Wahiba
National Women's Committee (Yemen)
Women's Forum for Research and Training
    (Yemen)
Yemeni Women's Union

Niyazi Dalyanci
Istanbul, Turkey
Istanbul Technical University
Trans-Turkey Pipeline

Virginia Danielson
Harvard University
Asmahan
Atrash, Farid al-
Darwish, Sayyid
Hafiz, Abd al-Halim
Music
Umm Kulthum

Bryan Daves
Columbia University
Ard, al-
Boutros-Ghali, Boutros
De Haan, Ya'akov Yisrael
Galilee, Sea of
Green Line
Iran–Contra Affair
Jewish Brigade
Jewish Colonization Association
Joint Distribution Committee
Levontin, Zalman
Levy, David
Oil Embargo (1973–1974)
Pérez de Cuéllar, Javier
Peled, Mattityahu
Ratosh, Yonatan
Rishon le-Zion
Rubinstein, Amnon
Sabra

Safed
Sarid, Yossi
Shapira, Hayyim Moshe
Sharef, Ze'ev
Shazar, Shneour Zalman
Shekel
Shenhar, Yitzhak
Shitreet, Bekhor
Sprinzak, Joseph
Ta'if Accord
Tiberias
Tubi, Tawfiq
Wahrhaftig, Zerah
Ya'ari, Me'ir
Yellin-Mor, Natan
Yizhar, S.
Zikhron Ya'akov
Zionist Organization of America

Lawrence Davidson
West Chester University
Wilson, Woodrow

Roderic H. Davison
Deceased
Midhat Paşa

C. Ernest Dawn
University of Illinois, Urbana
Aflaq, Michel
Arslan, Adil
Arsuzi, Zaki al-

Lara Deeb
Harvard University, Harvard Academy for International and Area Studies
Lebanese Women's Council

Richard Dekmejian
University of Southern California
Muslim Brotherhood

Walter Denny
University of Massachusetts, Amherst
Architecture
Art

Guilain P. Denoeux
Colby College
Aql, Sa'id
Ba'albak
Bliss, Daniel
Chamoun, Camille

Chamoun, Dany
Chehab, Khalid
Eddé, Raymond
Futuwwa
Geagea, Samir
Hawi, George
Hawi, Khalil
Karame, Abd al-Hamid
Karame, Rashid
Khal, Yusuf al-
Khuri, Bishara al-
Lahad, Antoine
Lebanon, Mount
Nimr, Faris
Scouts
Shader, Joseph
Shahada, George
Shidyaq, Ahmad Faris al-
Sulh, Kazem al-
Sulh, Rashid al-
Sulh, Riyad al-
Sulh, Taki al-Din al-
Taqla, Philippe
Twayni, Ghassan
Yaziji, Ibrahim
Youth Movements

Shlomo Deshen
Tel Aviv University
Black Panthers
Maʿbarah

Bradford Dillman
American University
Madani, Abassi al-
Mauritania
Union Marocaine du Travail (UMT)
Union Nationale des Forces Populaires (UNFP)

Donna Robinson Divine
Smith College
Ben-Zvi, Yizhak
Gordon, Aaron David
Ha-Halutz
Hibbat Zion
Hula Swamps
Jewish Agency for Palestine
Katznelson, Berl
Keinan, Amos
Kibbutz Movement
Labor Zionism

Levin, Hanoch
Nahalal
Ruppin, Arthur
Shamir, Moshe
Sobol, Yehoshua
Suissa, Albert
Syrkin, Nachman
Tel Aviv
Tel Hai
Trumpeldor, Yosef
Uganda Project
Ussishkin, Menahem
Yishuv
Yizhar, S.
Youth Aliyah
Zelda
Zionism
Zionist Commission for Palestine

Antonio Donno
Universita Degli Studi
Truman, Harry S.

John J. Donohue
University of Saint Joseph, Beirut
Baghdad University
Hikma University, al-
Missionary Schools
Roman Catholicism and Roman Catholic
Missions

Roberta L. Dougherty
Moreton-in-Marsh, U.K.
Gamal, Samiyah
Kariyuka, Tahiya

Eleanor Abdella Doumato
University of Rhode Island
Jabal Shammar
Nafud Desert
Najd
Protestantism and Protestant Missions
Rub al-Khali
Tribes and Tribalism: Arabian Peninsula

Michael Dumper
University of Exeter
Haram al-Sharif

Michael Dunn
International Estimate, Arlington
Arafat, Yasir
Fatah, al-

Ayse Durakbasa Tarhan
Mugla Universitesi, Sosyoloji Botl
 Aliyer, Fatimah
 Araz, Nezihe

Evelyn A. Early
U.S. Department of State
 Medicine and Public Health

Dale F. Eickelman
Dartmouth College
 Berber Dahir
 Intelligence Organizations
 Kattaniya Brotherhood
 Marabout

Laurie Z. Eisenberg
Carnegie Mellon University
 Camp David Accords (1978)
 Carter, Jimmy
 Egyptian–Israeli Peace Treaty (1979)
 Kahan Commission (1983)
 Litani Operation (1978)
 Reagan Plan (1982)
 South Lebanon Army

Emad Eldin Shahin
American University in Cairo
 Belhadj, Ali
 Ben Salah, Ahmed
 Hamas (Movement for a Peaceful Society)
 Mourou, Abdelfattah
 Movement for Unity and Reform (MUR)
 Nahda, al-
 Nahnah, Mahfoud
 Sahnoun, Ahmed
 Soltani, Abdellatif

Charles Enderlin
Jerusalem, Israel
 Shamir, Yitzhak

Michael Eppel
Haifa University
 Kashif al-Ghita Family
 Kaylani, Abd al-Rahman al-
 Muhammad, Aziz

Mansoureh Ettehadieh
University of Tehran
 Abbas Mirza, Na'eb al-Saltaneh
 Ahmad Qajar
 Bayat, Mortaza Qoli

 Farmanfarma, Abd al-Hoseyn Mirza
 Fath Ali Shah Qajar
 Mahd-e Ulya, Malek Jahan Khanum
 Malkom Khan, Mirza
 Mozaffar al-Din Qajar
 Qajar, Abdullah Mirza
 Qajar, Agha Mohammad
 Tehran
 University of Tehran

Kyle T. Evered
Illinois State University
 Literature: Turkish

Abdel Aziz EzzelArab
McGill University
 Tahtawi, Rifa'a al-Rafi al-
 Utaybi, Juhayman al-

Hani Fakhouri
University of Michigan, Flint
 Satellite Cities Development

Marion Farouk-Sluglett
Deceased
 Sharif, Aziz
 Yusuf, Yusuf Salman

Grant Farr
Portland State University
 Afghanistan: Political Parties in
 Afghanistan: U.S. Intervention in
 Ahmad Shah Mas'ud
 Amin, Hafizullah
 Amu Darya
 Anglo–Afghan Treaty (1855)
 Awakened Youth
 Bamyan
 Bost
 Dar al-Mo'allamin
 Dost Mohammad Barakzai
 Dubs, Adolph
 Durand Line
 Farhad, Ghulam Muhammad
 Gailani, Ahmad
 Habibollah Khan
 Hazara
 Hekmatyar, Golbuddin
 Helmand River
 Herat
 Hezb-e Islami
 Jami'at-e Islami

Kabul
Kabul University
Kandahar
Karmal, Babrak
Khalis, Mohammad Unis
Khyber, Mir Akbar
Khyber Pass
Mahmud Durrani
Mazar-e Sharif
Mohammadi, Maulawi Mohammad Nabi
Mojaddedi, Sebghatullah
Mojahedin
Nadir Barakzai, Mohammad
Najibullah
Pamir Mountains
Parcham
People's Democratic Party of Afghanistan
Rabbani, Burhanuddin
Ratebzad, Anahita
Refugees: Afghan
Shiberghan
Tajiks
Tarikh Tolana
Zabul

Maysam J. al Faruqi
Georgetown University
Ahmar, Abdullah ibn Husayn al-
Daʿwa al-Islamiyya, al-
Fahmi, Mahmud Pasha
Fatwa
Fiqh
Ghanim, Fathi
Hadith
Iqbal, Muhammad
Islam
Kaʿba
Khalid, Khalid Muhammad
Mawdudi, Abu al-Aʿla al-
Muhyi al-Din, Khalid
Muslim Brotherhood
Nerval, Gérard de
Qurʾan
Sufism and the Sufi Orders
Sunna
Sunni Islam

Elizabeth Fernea
Austin, TX
General Federation of Iraqi Women

Carter V. Findley
Ohio State University
Bureau of Translation
Cevdet, Ahmet
Ottoman Empire: Civil Service

Michael R. Fischbach
Randolph-Macon College
Abbas, Mahmud
Abdullah II ibn Hussein
Abu al-Huda, Tawfiq
Abu Nuwwar, Ali
Adenauer, Konrad
Ahali Group
Amman
Annan, Kofi A.
Antun, Farah
Aqaba, Gulf of
Aql, Saʿid
Arab Boycott
Arafat, Yasir
Archaeology in the Middle East
Ard, al-
Arif, Arif al-
Atasi, Nur al-Din al-
Aziz, Tariq
Baghdad Summit (1978)
Baker, James A.
Banna, Sabri al-
Barghuthi Family
Barghuthi, Marwan
Barzani Family
Basma bint Talal
Bethlehem
Black September
Bush, George Herbert Walker
Bush, George Walker
Clinton, William Jefferson
Cox, Percy
Dahlan, Muhammad
Damascus Affair (1840)
Darwaza, Muhammad Izzat
Eddé, Raymond
Fatah, al-
Franjiyya Family
Franjiyya, Sulayman
Habibi, Emile
Haddad, Wadi
Hafiz, Amin al-
HAMAS

Hamra Riots
Hananu, Ibrahim
Hasan, Hani al-
Hasan, Khalid al-
Hashimi, Yasin al-
Hashimite House (House of Hashim)
Hawatma, Nayif
Hebron
Holy Land
Holy Sepulchre, Church of the
Husayn ibn Ali
Husayni, Musa Kazim al-
Hussein ibn Talal
Institute for Palestine Studies
Irbid
Islamic Jihad
Jadid, Salah
Jamali, Muhammad Fadhil al-
Jarash
Jenin
Jerusalem
Jibril, Ahmad
Jordan
Jordanian Civil War (1970–1971)
Jumayyil, Amin
Jumblatt Family
Jumblatt, Walid
Karak, al-
Kennedy, John Fitzgerald
Khaddam, Abd al-Halim
Khalidi, Ahmad al-Samih al-
Khalidi, Husayn Fakhri al-
Kudsi, Nazim al-
Lausanne Conference (1949)
Lebanese Forces
Lebanese University
Majali Family
Malik, Charles Habib
Maqarin Dam
Muasher, Marwan
Muhammad, Aziz
Nablus
Nahhas, Mustafa al-
Najaf, al-
Nashashibi Family
Nasir, Hanna
National Bloc
Nusayba Family
Palestine Research Center
Palestinian Authority

Parliamentary Democratic Front
Phalange
Powell, Colin L.
Qabbani, Nizar
Qaddumi, Faruq
Qalqiliya
Raad, In'am
Rajub, Jibril
Ramadan, Taha Yasin
Ramallah
Reagan, Ronald
Rejection Front
Rifa'i, Zaid al-
Rockefeller Museum
Saade, George
Salam Family
Salam, Sa'ib
Shahada, George
Shammas, Anton
Sharif, Aziz
Shuf
Shuqayri, Ahmad
Somikh, Abdullah
Storrs, Ronald
Sulh, Rashid al-
Sulh, Taki al-Din al-
Tall, Mustafa Wahbi al-
Templars
Tikrit
Tikriti, Hardan al-
Tlas, Mustafa
Tuqan Family
Tuqan, Fadwa
Turki, Fawaz
Twayni, Ghassan
United Arab Republic (UAR)
United Nations Relief and Works Agency for
    Palestine Refugees in the Near East
    (UNRWA)
University of Jordan
War in Iraq (2003)
Zu'bi, Mahmud al-
Zurayk, Constantine

Ellen L. Fleischmann
University of Dayton
    Abd al-Hadi, Tarab
    Arab Women's Association of Palestine
    Arab Women's Congress
    Arab Women's Executive Committee

Husayni, Hind al-
Khalidi, Wahida al-
Mogannam, Matiel
Nassar, Sadhij
Shihabi, Zlikha al-

Andrew Flibbert
Trinity College
Hamama, Faten
North Atlantic Treaty Organization (NATO)

Carolyn Fluehr-Lobban
Rhode Island College
Arab
Farid, Nagwa Kamal
Female Genital Mutilation
Garang, John
Harem
Langer, Felicia
Muslim Sisters Organization
Nubians
Nuer
Republican Brotherhood
Taha, Mahmud Muhammad
Turabi, Wisal al-Mahdi

John Foran
University of California, Santa Barbara
Qajar Dynasty

Geremy Forman
University of Haifa
Jezreel Valley

Angel M. Foster
Ibis Reproductive Health
Birth Control
Cairo Family Planning Association
Democratic Women's Association (Tunisia)
Medicine and Public Health
Tunisia: Overview
Union of Tunisian Women

Steve Frangos
Round Lake, IL
Eskinazi, Roza

Robert O. Freedman
Baltimore Hebrew University
Communism in the Middle East
Russia and the Middle East

Adina Friedman
George Mason University
Guri, Chaim
Hareven, Shulamit
Hoffman, Yoel
Oz, Amos
Pagis, Dan
Zach, Natan

Nancy Gallagher
University of California, Santa Barbara
Diseases
Mabarrat Muhammad Ali
School for Hakīmāt

F. Gregory Gause, III
University of Vermont
Aden
Al Thani, Hamad ibn Khalifa
Ayni, Muhsin al-
Dual Containment
Ta'if, Treaty of al-

Khalil Gebara
University of Exeter
Attar, Nejat al-
International Monetary Fund
National Progressive Front (Syria)
Taqla, Philippe

Irene Gendzier
Boston University
Lebanese Civil War (1958)

Jane Gerber
City University of New York
Damascus Affair (1840)

Fawaz A. Gerges
Sarah Lawrence College
Paris Peace Settlements (1918–1923)

Mona Ghali
Richmond Hill, ON
Institute of Women's Studies of Bir Zeit
University
Tsemel, Leah

Sabah Ghandour
University of Balamand
Bint al-Shati
Ikhlassi, Walid

Zouhair Ghazzal
Loyola University, Chicago
    Alawi
    Lawrence, T. E.

Martin Gilbert
University of Oxford
    Churchill, Winston S.

Erika Gilson
Princeton University
    Turkish Language

Zvia Ginor
Jewish Theological Seminary of America
    Alterman, Natan
    Baron, Dvora
    Gilboa, Amir
    Michael, Sami
    Oz, Amos
    Seri, Dan-Benaya
    Suissa, Albert
    Zelda

Nili Gold
University of Pennsylvania
    Amichai, Yehuda
    Appelfeld, Aharon
    Bialik, Hayyim Nahman
    Hareven, Shulamit
    Hoffman, Yoel
    Literature: Hebrew
    Ravikovitch, Dahlia
    Wallach, Yona

Ellis Goldberg
University of Washington
    Labor and Labor Unions
    Mahalla al-Kubra, al-

Harvey E. Goldberg
Indiana University, Bloomington
    Jews in the Middle East
    Mimouna Festival

Arthur Goldschmidt
Pennsylvania State University
    Abbas Hilmi I
    Abbas Hilmi II
    Abd al-Maguid, Esmat
    Abd al-Raziq, Ali

    Abduh, Muhammad
    Arab
    Arab Socialist Union
    Aswan
    Baghdadi, Abd al-Latif al-
    Bahariya
    Baring, Evelyn
    Buhayra
    Communication
    Damanhur
    Delta
    Dinshaway Incident (1906)
    Drummond–Wolff Convention
    Dual Control
    Eastern Desert
    Egypt
    Egyptian Women's Union
    Ghali, Boutros
    Giza
    Gulf of Suez
    Haykal, Muhammad Hasanayn
    Haykal, Muhammad Husayn
    Infitah
    Isma'il ibn Ibrahim
    Kamil, Mustafa
    Luxor
    Mahmudiyya Canal
    Mahmud, Muhammad
    Mahmud, Mustafa
    Majlis Shura al-Nuwwab
    Mansura, al-
    Milner Mission
    Misri, Aziz Ali al-
    Mubarak, Husni
    Nasser, Lake
    National Party (Egypt)
    Nile River
    Nubar Pasha
    Nuqrashi, Mahmud Fahmi al-
    Qusayr, al-
    Riyad, Mustafa al-
    Sadat, Jihan al-
    Sharm al-Shaykh
    Shenouda III
    Siwa Oasis
    Suez Canal
    Urabi, Ahmad
    Uthman, Uthman Ahmad
    Wadi Natrun
    War of Attrition (1969–1970)

Mallika Good
Foundation for Middle East Peace
> Gaza (City)
> General Union of Palestinian Women's
>> Committees (GUPWC)

Jane E. Goodman
Indiana University
> Amrouche, Fadhma At Mansour
> Amrouche, Mary Louise (a.k.a. Marguerite
>> Taos)

Matthew S. Gordon
Miami University
> Achour, Habib
> Ahardane, Majoub
> Algiers, Battle of (1956–1957)
> Amin Bey, al-
> Arfa, Muhammad ibn
> Baccouche, Hedi
> Balafrej, Ahmed
> Ben Ali, Zayn al-Abidine
> Ben Ammar, Tahar
> Black Thursday (1978)
> Bouabid, Abderrahim
> Boucetta, Muhammad
> Bu Hamara
> Chenik, Muhammad
> Dlimi, Ahmed
> Fes, Treaty of (1912)
> Fundamental Pact
> Gafsa Incident (1980)
> Ghannouchi, Rached
> Green March
> La Marsa Convention
> Lamrani, Muhammad Karim
> Laraki, Ahmad
> La Tunisie Martyre
> Masmoudi, Muhammad
> Monastir
> Nouira, Hedi
> Oufkir, Muhammad
> Parti d'Unité Populaire (PUP)
> Qairawan
> Revolutionary Command Council (Egypt)
> Sfar, Tahar
> Sfax
> Sousse
> Suleiman, Mulay
> Youssef, Mulay

Yehuda Gradus
Ben-Gurion University
> Dimona
> Golan Heights
> Jabal al-Khalil
> Lydda
> Maʿa lot
> Negev
> Ramla
> Rishon le-Zion

JoAnn Gross
Trenton State University
> Naqshbandi

Peter Gubser
American Near East Refugee Aid, Washington, DC
> Amman
> Dead Sea
> Hussein ibn Talal
> Jordan
> Jordanian Civil War (1970–1971)
> Karak, al-
> Petra
> Potash Industry

David Gutelius
Stanford University
> Arab Maghreb Union
> Tindouf

Mahmoud Haddad
University of Balamund (Northern Lebanon)
> Abu al-Timman, Jaʿfar
> Ahd, al-
> Azzam, Abd al-Rahman al-
> Bustani, Sulayman
> National Party (Syria)
> Salafiyya Movement

Sylvia G. Haim
Middle Eastern Studies, England
> Farhud
> Hayim, Yusef
> Sassoon Family

Majed Halawi
New York, NY
> Alawi
> Jumayyil, Amin
> Jumayyil, Pierre

Sondra Hale
University of California, Los Angeles
Ibrahim, Fatima Ahmed
Sudanese Women's Union

Wael B. Hallaq
McGill University
Fatwa
Fiqh
Hadith
Hanafi School of Law
Hanbali School of Law
Maliki School of Law
Shafiʿi School of Law
Shariʿa

Karim Hamdy
Oregon State University
Chalabi, Ahmad
Desalinization
Jazeera, al-
Organization of Arab Petroleum Exporting
Countries (OAPEC)
Phosphates

Milad Hanna
al-Ahram *Newspaper*
Copts

Robert E. Harkavy
Penn State
Nuclear Capability and Nuclear Energy

Michelle Hartman
McGill University
Mostaghanemi, Ahlam

Khalid M. El-Hassan
University of Kansas
Beja
Omdurman
Salih, Teyib

Amir Hassanpour
University of Toronto
Ghassemlou, Abdul Rahman
Kurdish Revolts

Frances Hasso
Oberlin College
Khaled, Leila

Waleed Hazbun
Johns Hopkins University
Akkad, Mustafa
Industrialization

Samuel Heilman
City University of New York, Queens College
Halakhah
Judaism
Karaites
Rabbi
Sabbath
Western Wall
Yeshiva

Oliver Benjamin Hemmerle
Baden, Germany
Government
Iran–Contra Affair
Shultz, George

Clement M. Henry
University of Texas at Austin
Banking

Linda Herrera
Leiden University
Education
Musa, Nabawiyya
Ramses College for Girls
Saʿid, Amina al-

Tayeb El-Hibri
University of Massachusetts, Amherst
Ibadiyya
Islam
Lebanese Crises of the 1840s
Mevlevi Brotherhood
Muhammad
Shiʿism
Sunni Islam

Marilyn Higbee
Columbia University
Shaykh

Michael C. Hillmann
University of Texas, Austin
Al-e Ahmad, Jalal
Bahar, Mohammad Taqi
Baraheni, Reza
Carpets, Persian

Daneshvar, Simin
Dashti, Ali
Dehkhoda, Ali Akbar
Esfandiary, Fereydun
Farrokhzad, Forugh
Gharbzadegi
Ghassemlou, Abdul Rahman
Hajji Baba of Ispahan
Hedayat, Sadegh
Literature: Persian
Parsipur, Shahrnush
Shamlu, Ahmad

Eric Hooglund
Institute for Palestine Studies, Washington, DC
Abbas Mirza, Na'eb al-Saltaneh
Abdülmecit II
Abu Musa Island
Afghanistan: Islamic Movements in
Alavi, Bozorg
Algiers Agreement (1975)
Amir-Entezam, Abbas
Anatolia
Anglo–Iranian Agreement (1919)
Anglo–Persian War (1856)
Anglo–Russian Agreement (1907)
Ankara
Ankara University
Antakya
Arfa, Hasan
Azerbaijan Crisis
Bakhtiari
Baraheni, Reza
Barakzai Dynasty
Behrangi, Samad
Constitutional Revolution
Curzon, George Nathaniel
Daneshvar, Simin
D'Arcy Concession (1901)
Dashti, Ali
Dhufar Rebellion
Diyarbakir
Dowlatabadi, Mahmoud
Dual Containment
Edirne
Erzurum
Erzurum, Treaty of (1823)
Esfandiary, Fereydun
Fish and Fishing
Freedom Movement (Nezhat-e Azadi Iran)

Gecekondu
Golestan, Ebrahim
Golshiri, Houshang
Greco–Turkish War (1897)
Guest Workers
Hedayat, Sadegh
Hostage Crises
Iranian Revolution (1979)
Iran–Iraq War (1980–1988)
Isfahan
Istanbul
Istanbul University
Janissaries
Jehad-e Sazandegi
Kasravi, Ahmad
Kemalettin Bey
Khalaf, Abdulhadi
Kharg Island
Khatami, Mohammad
Khomeini, Ruhollah
Khubar, al-
Konya
Lausanne, Treaty of (1923)
Literature: Persian
Lurs
Ma'rufi, Abbas
Mahmud II
Majles al-Shura
Marja al-Taqlid
Mashhad
Mehmet V Reşat
Menderes, Adnan
Middle East Technical University
Mohammad Ali Shah Qajar
Montazeri, Hosayn Ali
Musavi-Ardebili, AbdolKarim
Namik Kemal
Naser al-Din Shah
National Salvation Party
Newspapers and Print Media: Iran
Palmerston, Lord Henry John Temple
Paris Peace Settlements (1918–1923)
Persian (Arabian) Gulf
Persian Cats
Pushtun
Qajar Dynasty
Rafsanjani, Ali Akbar Hashemi
Revolutionary Guards
Russian–Ottoman Wars
Salonika

Sepehri, Sohrab
Shamlu, Ahmad
Sharjah
Shiraz
South Persia Rifles
Students in the Line of the Imam
Tabataba'i, Mohammad
Tea
Tehran
Terrorism
Timar
Tobacco Revolt
Topkapi Palace
Treaty of 1815
Tripartite Treaty of Alliance
Tunb Islands
Turkey
Turkish–Italian War (1911–1912)
Turkish Language
Turkmanchai, Treaty of (1828)
Turks
Twin Pillars Policy
University of Tehran
Urban Planning
Utaybi, Juhayman al-
Vaka-i Hayriye
Velayat-e Faqih
White Revolution (1961–1963)
Yazd
Zahedan
Zoroastrianism

J. C. Hurewitz
Columbia University
Britain and the Middle East up to 1914
Eastern Question
Straits, Turkish

Ahmed H. Ibrahim
Southwest Missouri State University
Abd al-Rahman, Umar
Bakhtiar, Shapur
Rogers, William Pierce

Amitzur Ilan
Hebrew University
Bernadotte, Folke

George E. Irani
Royal Roads University
Arab Socialism
Atasi, Jamal al-

Beitaddin Declaration
Christians in the Middle East
Council for Development and Reconstruction
  (CDR)
Haigazian College
Hasani, Taj al-Din al-
Hobeika, Elie
Karam, Yusuf
Kikhya, Rushdi al-
Lebanese Front
Lebanese National Movement (LNM)
Maksoud, Clovis
Malik, Charles Habib
Ma'louf, Amin
Marine Barracks Bombing (Lebanon)
Meushi, Paul Peter
National Bloc
National Front, Lebanon
National Liberal Party
Progressive Socialist Party
Raad, In'am
Riyad, Mahmud
Saade, George
Sidon
Ta'if Accord
Tyre
Vatican and the Middle East
Zahla

Khaled Islaih
Jerusalem, Israel
Gender: Gender and the Economy
Hass, Amira
Wazir, Intisar al- (Umm Jihad)

Jacqueline Ismael
University of Calgary
Iraqi Women's Union
Khidhir, Zahra
Women's Renaissance Club
Zahawi, Jamil Sidqi al-

Charles Issawi
Princeton University
Manufactures
Modernization
Textile Industry
Trade
Transport

Islah Jad
London, U.K.
Women and Family Affairs Center
Women's Affairs Center (Gaza)
Women's Centre for Legal Aid and
    Counseling
Women's Studies Center (Jerusalem)

James Jankowski
University of Colorado, Boulder
Pharaonicism
Young Egypt

M. A. Jazayary
University of Texas, Austin
Persian

George Joffe
University of London
Aozou Strip
Balbo, Italo
Bevin–Sforza Plan
Bilhayr, Abd al-Nabi
Fourth Shore, The
Graziani, Rodolfo
Italy in the Middle East
Mukhtar, Umar al-
Muntasir Family
Suwayhli, Ramadan al-
Volpi, Giuseppe

Benjamin Joseph
Philadelphia, PA
Bethlehem
Emergency Regulations
Geneva Peace Conference (1973)
Haycraft Commission (1921)
Hebron
Jericho
Nabi Musa Pilgrimage
Nablus
Nazareth
Sartawi, Issam
Talmud
War of Attrition (1969–1970)
Woodhead Commission (1938)

Jon Jucovy
Ramaz Upper School
Agadir Crisis
Algeciras Conference (1906)

Allenby, Edmund Henry
Amiens, Treaty of
Bund
Dreyfus Affair
Masada
Pogrom
Yad Mordekhai
Yad Vashem

Sabine Kalinock
University of Frankfurt, Germany
Women's Religious Rituals

Zachary Karabell
Harvard University
Acheson, Dean
Adana Conference
Adenauer, Konrad
Ahmet Vefik
Alexandria Convention
Ali Suavi
Antun, Farah
Arish, Convention of al- (1800)
Austria–Hungary and the Middle East
Aya Sofya
Baghdad Pact (1955)
Balta Liman, Convention of (1838)
Bandung Conference (1955)
Behar, Nissim
Bell, Gertrude
Ben-Aharon, Yitzhak
Benvenisti, Meron
Beyoglu Protocol
Black Sea
British–French Oil Agreement
Bucharest, Treaty of (1812)
Budapest Convention (1877)
Burg, Yosef
Cairo Conference (1921)
Central Treaty Organization (CENTO)
Clark–Darlan Agreement (1942)
Clemenceau, Georges
Compagnie Française des Pétroles (CFP)
Cyprus Convention (1878)
Darülfünün
De Bunsen, Maurice
Declaration of La Celle St. Cloud
Dimona
Dragomans
Dulles, John Foster

Eden, Anthony
Eisenhower, Dwight David
Erzurum, Treaty of (1823)
Fashoda Incident (1898)
Fertile Crescent
Flapan, Simha
Franco–Tunisian Conventions
Greater Syria Plan
Great Game, The
Grivas, Georgios Theodoros
Gruenbaum, Yizhak
Gur, Mordechai
Habib, Philip Charles
Haifa University
Harriman, W. Averell
Hess, Moses
Hijab
Hindu Kush Mountains
Humphreys, Francis
Hunkar-Iskelesi, Treaty of (1833)
Husayn ibn Ali
Ignatiev, Nikolas Pavlovich
Ishaq, Adib
Jewish Legion
Johnson, Lyndon Baines
Kennedy, John Fitzgerald
Kléber, Jean-Baptiste
Kosher
Kütahya, Peace of
Lansdowne, Henry Charles Keith Petty
    Fitzmaurice
Lend-Lease Program
London, Treaty of (1871)
London, Treaty of (1913)
Maude, Frederick Stanley
Medina
Mehmet V Reşat
Mesopotamia Campaign (1914–1918)
MI-6
Middle East Defense Organization (MEDO)
Mission Civilisatrice
Mollet, Guy
Moltke, Helmuth von
Mond, Alfred Moritz
Montefiore, Moses
Montgomery, Bernard Law
Montreux Convention (1936)
Musa Kazim
Namik Kemal
Nixon, Richard Milhous

North Atlantic Treaty Organization (NATO)
Organization of African Unity (OAU)
Patriarch
Peace Corps
Potsdam Convention
Rogers, William Pierce
Rome, Treaty of (1935)
San Remo Conference (1920)
Sebastiani, Horace
Sharm al-Shaykh
Shepheard's Hotel
Şinasi, İbrahim
Soustelle, Jacques
Sublime Porte
Sykes, Mark
Sykes–Picot Agreement (1916)
Talat, Mehmet
Twin Pillars Policy
Wilson, Woodrow

Efraim Karsh
King's College
    Iran–Iraq War (1980–1988)

Hasan Kayali
La Jolla, CA
    Balkan Wars (1912–1913)
    Caliphate
    Cemal Paşa
    Committee for Union and Progress
    Decentralization Party
    Enver Paşa
    Ottomanism
    Ottoman Parliament
    Pan-Turkism
    Young Ottomans
    Young Turks

Benjamin Kedar
Institute for Advanced Studies, The Hebrew University of Jerusalem
    Masada

Nikki Keddie
University of California, Los Angeles
    Afghani, Jamal al-Din al-
    Anjoman
    Urwa al-Wuthqa, al-

Burçak Keskin-Kozat
University of Michigan, Ann Arbor
    Abdülmecit I
    Ankara, Treaty of (1930)

Bilkent University
Boğaziçi (Bosporus) University
Boratav, Pertev Naili
Bursa
Çiller, Tansu
Demirel, Süleyman
Ecevit, Bülent
Ecevit, Rahşan
Ege University
General Directorate on the Status and
     Problems of Women
Hacettepe University
İzmir
Marmara University
Nasruddin Hoca
Turkish Law on the Protection of the Family
     (1998)
Women's People's Party (1923)
Yüksek Öğretim Kurulu (YOK)

Nazar al-Khalaf
Montreal, Canada
Basra
Samarra
Sulaymaniya

Rashid Khalidi
University of Chicago
Arab Nationalism
Palestine Arab Revolt (1936–1939)

Fred J. Khouri
Villanova University
United Nations Conciliation Commission for
     Palestine (UNCCP)

Azadeh Kian-Thiébaut
University of Paris 8 and Monde Iraniene, CNRS
Amini, Fatemeh
Hashemi, Faezeh
Iranian Bureau of Women's Affairs
Sane'i, Yusef
Shid, Nahid
Taleqani, Azam

Carolyn Killean
University of Chicago
Arabic

Laurie King-Irani
University of Victoria
Ba'albakki, Layla
8 Mars Newspaper

Farès, Nabile
Gender: Gender and Law
Gozanski, Tamar
Haza, Ofra
Hijab
Khalifa, Sahar
Khalil, Samiha Salama
Masri, Mai
Nazareth
Qa'war, Widad

Alexander Kitroeff
New York University
Cyprus
Greco–Turkish War (1897)
Greeks in the Middle East
Greek War of Independence

John F. Kolars
University of Michigan, Ann Arbor
Climate
Desalinization
Deserts
Geography

Charles C. Kolb
National Endowment for the Humanities
Assyrians
Baluchis
Ceramics
KGB
Port Sa'id
Rusk, Dean
Sidon

C. Max Kortepeter
New York University
Capitulations
Crimean War

Martin Kramer
Tel Aviv University
Islamic Congresses

Wanda Krause
American University of Sharjah
Gender: Gender and Politics

P. R. Kumaraswamy
Jawaharlal Nehru University
China and the Middle East

I. Metin Kunt
Sabanci University
Abdülmecit I
Ankara University
Atatürk University
Barkan, Ömer Lutfi
Bilkent University
Boğaziçi (Bosporus) University
Bursa
Ege University
Galatasaray Lycée
Hacettepe University
Istanbul
Istanbul University
İzmir
Marmara University
Middle East Technical University
Osman, House of
Pera
Selim III
Sultan
Yüksek Öğretim Kurulu (YOK)

Aptullah Kuran
University of the Bosphorus
Balyan Family
Sultan Ahmet Mosque
Topkapi Palace

Jerry Kutnick
Gratz College
American Jewish Committee
American Jewish Congress
Zionist Organization of America

Chris Kutschera
Paris, France
Barzani Family
Kurdish Autonomous Zone
Kurdistan
Kurds
Mahmud of Sulaymaniya
Patriotic Union of Kurdistan (PUK)
Refugees: Kurdish
Talabani, Jalal
Yasar Kemal

Ahmet Kuyas
Galatasaray Üniversitesi
Atatürk, Mustafa Kemal

Lisa M. Lacy
University of Texas, Austin
Arabian Horses

Robert G. Landen
Virginia Polytechnic Institute
Anglo–Omani Treaties
Masira Island
Matrah
Muscat
Oman
Sib, Treaty of (1920)

Nico Landman
Universiteit Utrecht
Nursi, Said

Michael M. Laskier
Bar-Ilay University, Israel
Alawite Dynasty
Algeria: Political Parties in
Alliance Israélite Universelle (AIU)
Bourguiba, Habib
Curiel Family
De Menasce Family
Faraj, Murad
Farhi Family
Muhammad VI
Nahum, Hayyim
Politi, Elie
Qafih, Yihye ben Solomon
Refugees: Jewish
Rolo Family
Sagues, Albert
Suarès Family
World Organization of Jews from Arab
   Countries (WOJAC)

Mirna Lattouf
Arizona State University, Tempe
AISHA: Arab Women's Forum
Beirut College for Women (BCW)
General Women's Union of Syria
Institute for Women's Studies in the Arab
   World (Lebanon)

Henri Lauzière
Georgetown University
Adl wa al-Ihsan, al-
Bouyali, Moustafa
Morocco: Overview

Morocco: Constitution
Yacine, Abdessalame
Youssoufi, Abderrahmane

Fred Lawson
Mills College
Al Khalifa Family
Arab Academy of Damascus
Bahrain
Bahraini–Qatari Wars
Bahrain Nationalist Movement
Belgrave, Charles Dalrymple
Biqa Valley
Damascus
Free French Mandate
Hama Massacre
Homs
Kawakibi, Abd al-Rahman al-
Khaddam, Abd al-Halim
Manama
Maysalun
Muhammad Ali
Muharraq
Nabi Salih, al-
National Liberation Front (Bahrain)
Nizam al-Jadid, al-
Nizip, Battle of (1839)
Pearl Diving (Bahrain)
Sadat, Anwar al-
Sitra
Syria
Umm Naʿsan

Ann M. Lesch
Villanova University
Abbud, Ibrahim
Abd al-Hadi Family
Alami Family, al-
Ansar, al-
Arab Higher Committee (Palestine)
Gezira Scheme
Khartoum
Mahdist State
Palestinian Arab Congresses
Palin Commission Report (1920)
Peel Commission Report (1937)
Plumer, Herbert Charles Onslow
Qawuqji, Fawzi al-
Sudan
Sudanese Civil Wars

Taba
White Papers on Palestine

Rémy Leveau
Institut d'Études Politiques de Paris
Cambon–Lansdowne Agreement (1904)
Hassan I
Hassan II
Lyautey, Louis-Hubert Gonzalve
Muhammad V

Zach Levey
University of Haifa
Arms and Armaments in the Middle East
Northern Tier
Tripartite Declaration (1950)
United Nations Economic Survey Mission (1949)

Avigdor Levy
Brandeis University
Janissaries
Mahmud II
Ottoman Military: Army
Ottoman Military: Navy
Vaka-i Hayriye

Zafrira Lidovsky-Cohen
Stern College, Yeshiva University
Ravikovitch, Dahlia

F. T. Liu
International Peace Academy, New York
United Nations and the Middle East
United Nations Emergency Force
United Nations Relief and Works Agency for Palestine Refugees in the Near East (UNRWA)
United Nations Special Committee on Palestine, 1947 (UNSCOP)

John Lundquist
Asian and Middle Eastern Division, New York Public Library
Orientalism
Philae
Said, Edward

Charles G. MacDonald
Florida International University
League of Arab States

Bruce Maddy-Weitzman
Tel Aviv University
  Ben Jelloun, Umar
  Ben Seddiq, Mahjoub
  Comité d'Action Marocaine (CAM)
  Confédération Démocratique du Travail
    (CDT)
  Daddah, Mokhtar Ould
  Front pour la Défense des Institutions
    Constitutionelles (FDIC)
  Ibn Musa, Ahmad
  Ifni
  Istiqlal Party: Morocco
  Laayounne
  Melilla
  Morocco: Political Parties in
  Morrison–Grady Plan (1946)
  Mouvement Populaire (MP)
  Ouazzani, Mohamed Hassan
  Parti Démocratique Constitutionnel (PDC)
  Parti Démocratique de l'Indépendance
    (PDI)
  Parti National
  Parti National Démocratique (PND)
  POLISARIO
  Rassemblement National des Indépendants
    (RNI)
  Sahara
  Saharan Arab Democratic Republic (SADR)
  Spanish Morocco
  Tetuan
  Union Nationale des Etudiants Marocains
    (UNEM)
  Wazzani, Muhammad Hassan al-
  Western Sahara
  Western Sahara War

Zev Maghen
Bar-Ilay University, Israel
  Entebbe Operation
  Galilee
  Harel, Isser
  Kasztner Affair
  Kovner, Abba
  Landsmannschaften
  Law of Return
  Lotz, Wolfgang
  Luz, Kadish
  Maʿa lot
  Modaʾi, Yitzhak

  Nahal
  Namir, Mordekhai

Paul J. Magnarella
University of Florida
  People's Houses
  Turkish Hearth Association
  Village Institutes

Ali Akbar Mahdi
Ohio Wesleyan University
  Karbaschi, Gholamhosain
  Kharrazi, Kamal
  Mohajerani, Ataollah
  Musavi, Mir-Hosain
  Nabavi, Behzad
  Velayati, Ali Akbar

Gregory S. Mahler
Kalamazoo College
  Allon, Yigal
  Ben-Aharon, Yitzhak
  Ben-Gurion, David
  Ben-Porat, Mordechai
  Burg, Avraham
  Burg, Yosef
  Cohen, Geʾula
  Eban, Abba (Aubrey)
  Flapan, Simha
  Goldmann, Nahum
  Gur, Mordechai
  Hammer, Zevulun
  Israel: Overview of Political Parties in
  Israel: Political Parties in
  Kahane, Meir
  Karp Report (1984)
  Kessar, Israel
  Knesset
  Kol, Moshe
  Kollek, Teddy
  Levy, David
  Modaʾi, Yitzhak
  Navon, Yizhak
  Peres, Shimon
  Rabin, Yitzhak
  Rubinstein, Amnon
  Sharef, Zeʾev
  Sharett, Moshe
  Sneh, Moshe
  Tamir, Shmuel
  Vanunu Affair

Wahrhaftig, Zerah
Weizman, Ezer
Yadin, Yigael

Roshanak Malek
New York, NY
Tobacco Revolt

Hafeez Malik
Villanova University
Jinnah, Muhammad Ali
Taliban

Martin Malin
American Academy of Arts and Sciences
Abuhatzeira, Aharon
Alkalai, Judah ben Solomon Hai
Amit, Meir
Arens, Moshe
Avnery, Uri
Bar-Lev, Haim
Ben-Yehuda, Eliezer
Eitan, Rafael
Eshkol, Levi
Hammer, Zevulun
Haskalah
Kalischer, Hirsch
Karp Report (1984)
Kessar, Israel
Kol, Moshe
Levin, Shmaryahu
Mohilever, Samuel
Nordau, Max
Pinsker, Leo
Sapir, Pinhas

Sumit Mandal
Ithaca, NY
Hadramawt

Ruth Mandel
Bethesda, MD
Alevi

Azzedine G. Mansour
Laval University
Arch
Architecture
GIA (Armed Islamic Groups)
Lamari, Mohamed
Rassemblement National Démocratique
(RND)

Rassemblement pour la Culture et la
Démocratie (RCD)
Wattar, al-Taher

Abraham Marcus
University of Texas, Austin
Aleppo

Michael R. Marrus
University of Toronto, School of Graduate Studies
Ha-avarah Agreement
Protocols of the Elders of Zion

Paul Martin
Columbia University
Garang, John
Human Rights

Afshin Matin-asgari
University of California, Los Angeles
Confederation of Iranian Students
Golsorkhi, Khosrow
Hoveyda, Amir Abbas
National Front, Iran
Soroush, AbdolKarim

Philip Mattar
United States Institute of Peace
Advisory Council (Palestine)
Aqsa Intifada, al-
Arab College of Jerusalem
Arabic
Arab–Israel War (1982)
Arab League Summits
Asmar, Fawzi al-
Balfour Declaration (1917)
Camp David Summit (2000)
Cattan, Henry
Churchill White Paper (1922)
Fahd Plan (1981)
Fida'iyyun
Germany and the Middle East
Ghuri, Emile al-
Gulf Crisis (1990–1991)
Haifa
Haycraft Commission (1921)
High Commissioners (Palestine)
Hope-Simpson Commission (1930)
Husayni, Muhammad Amin al-
Husayn–McMahon Correspondence
(1915–1916)

Institute for Palestine Studies
King–Crane Commission (1919)
Legislative Council (Palestine)
Levantine
Nakba, al- (1948–1949)
Oslo Accord (1993)
Palestine Liberation Organization (PLO)
Palestinian Arab Congresses
Palestinians
Qassam, Izz al-Din al-
Refugees: Palestinian
Sabra and Shatila Massacres
Shaw Commission
Supreme Muslim Council
Taba
Taba Negotiations (1995, 2001)

Ann E. Mayer
Wharton School, University of Pennsylvania
Law, Modern

Kenneth S. Mayers
University of California, Los Angeles
Ibrahim, Muhammad Hafiz
White Flag League

Justin McCarthy
University of Louisville
Abdülaziz
Abdülhamit II
Population
Refugees: Balkan Muslim

Mark Mechler
Washington, DC
Yaziji, Nasif

Meron Medzini
Rothberg International School, The Hebrew University, Mt. Scopus
Aloni, Shulamit
Amit, Meir
Bar-Lev, Haim
Ben-Zvi, Rahel Yanait
Dayan, Yael
Dorner, Dalia
Herzog, Chaim
Herzog, Ya'acov David
Hillel, Shlomo
Jarring, Gunnar
Lavon, Pinhas

Livnat, Limor
Namir, Orah
Refugees: Jewish

Peter Mellini
Sonoma State University
Gorst, John Eldon
Kitchener, Horatio Herbert

Paul Mendes-Flohr
University of Chicago
Buber, Martin

Garay Menicucci
University of California, Santa Barbara
Bakdash, Khalid

John Micgiel
Columbia University
Balkan Crises (1870s)
Balkans
Bulgarian Horrors

Laurence Michalak
University of California, Berkeley
Djerba
Hand of Fatima
Jabal al-Akhdar, Libya
Qadiriyya Order
Sfar, Bashir
Tlemcen

Dan Michman
Bar-Ilan University
Holocaust

Pardis Minuchehr
Columbia University
Akhavan-Saless, Mehdi
Chubak, Sadeq
Fassih, Ismail
Golshiri, Houshang
Jamalzadeh, Mohammad Ali
Ma'rufi, Abbas
Sa'edi, Gholamhossein
Sepehri, Sohrab

Ziba Mir-Hosseini
University of London
Ahl-e Haqq
Ebadi, Shirin
Kar, Mehrangiz
Sa'idzadeh, Seyyed Mohsen

Mansoor Moaddel
Eastern Michigan University
    Adamiyat, Abbasquli
    Adamiyat, Fereydun
    Anglo–Iranian Agreement (1919)
    Anglo–Iranian Oil Company
    Bazargan, Mehdi
    Mossadegh, Mohammad

Shahrzad Mojab
Institute for Women's Studies and Gender Studies, University of Toronto
    Zana, Leyla

Robert Mortimer
Haverford college
    Coordination des Archs (Algeria)
    Hanoune, Louisa
    Madani, Abassi al-

Cyrus Moshaver
Columbia University
    Dar al-Islam
    Mashhad
    Sheshbesh

Ahmad S. Moussalli
American University of Beirut
    Ashmawi, Muhammad Abd al-Rahman Salih al-
    Banna, Hasan al-
    Haykal, Muhammad Hasanayn
    Qutb, Sayyid
    Takfir wa al-Hijra, al-
    Tantawi, Muhammad Sayyid al-
    Turabi, Hasan al-

Muhammad Muslih
C. W. Post College of Long Island University
    Abu Risha, Umar
    Arab Club
    Asad, Hafiz al-
    Atasi, Hashim al-
    Atasi, Nur al-Din al-
    Atrash, Sultan Pasha al-
    Azuri, Najib
    Fatat, al-
    Ghuri, Emile al-
    Golan Heights
    Hafiz, Amin al-
    Hananu, Ibrahim
    Hawrani, Akram al-
    Husayni, Abd al-Qadir al-
    Husayni Family, al-
    Husayni, Jamal al-
    Husayni, Musa Kazim al-
    Istiqlal Party: Palestine
    Khalidi, Husayn Fakhri al-
    Khalidi, Walid
    Kudsi, Nazim al-
    Mardam, Jamil
    Muntada al-Adabi, al-
    Nashashibi Family
    Palestine National Charter (1968)
    Palestine National Covenant (1964)
    Palestinians
    Quwatli, Shukri al-
    Umayyad Mosque

Amikam Nachmani
Bar-Ilan University
    Anglo–American Committee of Inquiry (1946)

Emile A. Nakhleh
Mount St. Mary's College
    Ahmar, Abdullah ibn Husayn al-
    Awali, al-
    Badr, Muhammad al-
    Baharina
    Bahrain National Oil Company (BANOCO)
    Bahrain Order in Council
    Bubiyan Island
    Dilmun
    Gulf Cooperation Council
    Khalaf, Abdulhadi
    Kuwait Fund for Arab Economic Development
    Madani, Abdullah al-
    Neutral Zone
    Organization of Arab Petroleum Exporting Countries (OAPEC)

Bassam Namani
Embassy of Lebanon, Washington, DC
    Beaufort, Charles-Marie-Napoléon d'Hautpoul de
    Dentz, Henri-Fernand
    Hariri, Rafiq Baha'uddin al-
    Murabitun
    Muwahhidun
    Qabbani, Nizar
    Sarkis, Ilyas
    Tuman Bey

Hisham Nashabi
Makassed Philanthropic Islamic Association, Beirut
    Arab College of Jerusalem

Senzil Nawid
Tucson, AZ

Afghan Women's Council
Association for the Protection of Women's
Rights (Afghanistan)
Democratic Organization of Afghan Women
(1965)
Esmati-Wardak, Masuma
Etemadi, Saleha Faruq
Irshad An-Niswaan
Kashwar Kamal, Meena
Ordinances on Veiling
Queen Surraya
Revolutionary Association of the Women of
Afghanistan (RAWA)
Samar, Sima
Sediq, Sohaila

Phillip C. Naylor
Marquette University

Abbas, Ferhat
Abdelghani, Mohamed Benahmed
Abdesselam, Belaid
Ait Ahmed, Hocine
Algeria: Constitution
Amis du Manifeste et de la Liberté
Amrouche, Jean
Argoud, Antoine
Belkacem, Cherif
Bellounis, Muhammad
Ben Badis, Abd al-Hamid
Ben Bella, Ahmed
Ben Boulaid, Moustafa
Ben Khedda, Ben Youssef
Ben M'hidi, Muhammad Larbi
Bendjedid, Chadli
Benflis, Ali
Bitat, Rabah
Blum–Viollette Plan
Boudiaf, Mohamed
Boudjedra, Rachid
Bouteflika, Abdelaziz
Brahimi, Abdelhamid
Bureaux Arabes
Camus, Albert
Catroux, Georges
Challe, Maurice
Code de l'Indigénat
Delouvrier, Paul
Dib, Mohammed

Didouche, Mourad
Evian Accords (1962)
Feraoun, Mouloud
Foucauld, Charles Eugène de
Ghozali, Ahmed
Haddad, Malek
Hadj, Messali al-
Hamina, Mohammed Lakhdar
Hamrouche, Mouloud
Harkis
Ibrahimi, Ahmed Taleb
Ibrahimi, Bashir
Kaid, Ahmed
Khider, Mohamed
Krim, Belkacem
Lacheraf, Mostefa
Lacoste, Robert
Lahouel, Hocine
Loi Cadre
Mimouni, Rachid
Moroccan–Algerian War
Nezzar, Khaled
Ouary, Malek
Ouled Sidi Cheikh
Parti de l'Avant-Garde Socialiste (PAGS)
Setif
Setif Revolt (1945)
Tripoli Programme (1962)
Uqbi, Tayyib al-
Zbiri, Tahar

Joseph Nevo
University of Haifa

Attlee, Clement
Bludan Conferences (1937, 1946)
Kirkbride, Alec Seath
MacDonald, Malcolm
United Nations Special Committee on
Palestine, 1947 (UNSCOP)

David Newman
Ben-Gurion University of the Negev

Green Line
Gush Emunim
Israeli Settlements
Kiryat Arba
Levinger, Moshe
West Bank

Francis R. Nicosia
Saint Michael's College

Berlin–Baghdad Railway
Grobba, Fritz Konrad Ferdinand

John D. Norton
University of Durham, England
Bektashis

Isis Nusair
Saint Mary's College
Husseini, Rana
Khader, Asma
Marʿi, Mariam
Princess Basma Women's Resource Center

Pierre Oberling
City University of New York, Hunter College
Denktash, Rauf

Sami Ofeish
University of Balamand
Eddé, Emile
Saʿada, Antun

Paola Olimpo
University of Lecce
Kissinger, Henry

Jean-Marc R. Oppenheim
Fordham University
Alexandria
Alexandria University
Balaclava, Battle of
Bonaparte, Napoléon
Gezira Sporting Club
Gordon, Charles
Levantine
Qutb, Sayyid

Les Ordeman
Columbia University
Bishara, Abdullah
Khubar, al-
Pharaon, Rashad
Tariki, Abdullah

Ibrahim M. Oweiss
Georgetown University
British–French Oil Agreement

Taha Parla
Bogazici University, Istanbul
Gökalp, Ziya
Kemalism

Malcolm C. Peck
Meridian International Center
Abd al-Aziz ibn Saʿud Al Saʿud
Abu Dhabi
Al al-Shaykh Family
Al Rashid Family
Al Saʿud, Saʿud ibn Abd al-Aziz
Al Sudayri Family
Al Sudayri, Hassa bint Ahmad
Al Thunayyan Family
Arabian Mission
Arab National Movement (ANM)
Buraymi Oasis Dispute
Dhow
Dhufar
Dhufar Rebellion
Doha
Dubai
Fahd ibn Abd al-Aziz Al Saʿud
Faisal ibn Abd al-Aziz Al Saʿud
Faysal ibn Turki Al Saʿud
Fujayra
Fujayra–Sharjah Conflict
Grand Mosque
Hasa, al-
Ikhwan
Incense
Khalid ibn Abd al-Aziz Al Saʿud
Kuwait
Kuwait City
Kuwait University
National Democratic Front for the Liberation
of Oman and the Arab Gulf
Popular Front for the Liberation of the
Occupied Arabian Gulf
Qatar
Raʾs al-Khayma
Sharjah
Trucial Coast
Tunb Islands
Umm al-Qaywayn
United Arab Emirates
Zanzibar

Yaron Peleg
Brandeis University
Agnon, Shmuel Yosef
Amir, Eli
Bejerano, Maya
Zach, Natan

Thomas G. Penchoen
University of California, Los Angeles
　Berber
　Djemaʿa
　Kabylia
　Mzab
　Twareg

C. R. Pennell
University of Melbourne, Victoria
　Bled al-Siba/Bled al-Makhzan
　Casablanca
　Ceuta
　Fasi, Allal al-
　Fasi, Muhammad al-
　Ibrahim, Abdullah
　Khattabi, Muhammad ibn Abd al-Karim al-
　Meknes, Treaty of (1836)
　Rif
　Rif War
　Yata, Ali

Don Peretz
State University of New York
　Arab–Israel Conflict
　Arab–Israel War (1948)
　Arab–Israel War (1956)
　Arab–Israel War (1967)
　Arab–Israel War (1973)
　Arab Revolt (1916)
　Camp David Accords (1978)
　Dayr Yasin
　Intifada (1987–1991)
　Palestine
　Palestinian Citizens of Israel
　Refugees: Palestinian
　United States of America and the Middle East

Kenneth J. Perkins
University of South Carolina, Columbia
　Ben Salah, Ahmed
　Ben Yousouf, Salah
　Bizerte
　Bizerte Crisis (1961)
　Bugeaud de la Piconnerie, Thomas-Robert
　Crémieux Decree
　Fly Whisk Incident (1827)
　French Foreign Legion
　Khaldunniyya
　Mestiri, Ahmad
　Tangier, Treaty of
　Thaalbi, Abd al-Aziz

Amos Perlmutter
American University
　Lavon Affair
　Palmah

John R. Perry
University of Chicago
　Browne, Edward Granville
　Khazʿal Khan

J. E. Peterson
Tucson, AZ
　Al al-Shaykh Family
　Al Bu Saʿid Family and Tribe of Oman
　Al Bu Saʿid, Qabus ibn Saʿid
　Al Bu Saʿid, Saʿid ibn Taymur
　Al Sudayri Family
　Al Thunayyan Family
　Dammam, al-
　Dhahran
　Gulf of Oman
　Jidda
　Jubayl, al-
　Riyadh
　Rub al-Khali
　Saudi Arabia
　Taʾif, al-
　Yanbu

Thomas Philipp
Friedrich-Alexander Universität, Erlangen
　Hilal, al-
　Zaydan, Jurji

Karen Pinto
American University of Beirut
　Archaeological Museum (Istanbul)
　Bliss, Howard
　Bodrum
　Kut al-Amara
　Middle East
　Opium
　Rumelia

Lawrence G. Potter
Columbia University
　Amin al-Dowleh, Mirza Ali Khan
　Amin al-Soltan, Ali-Asghar
　Amin al-Zarb, Mohammad Hasan
　Amir Kabir, Mirza Taqi Khan
　Zell al-Soltan, Masʿud Mirza

Parvaneh Pourshariati
Ohio State University
   Abadan
   Adalat Party
   Ahvaz
   Dar al-Fonun
   Democratic Party of Kurdistan (Iran)
   Democratic Party of Kurdistan (Iraq)
   Golestan Palace
   Griboyedov Incident
   Hamadan
   Iradeh-ye Melli Party
   Iran Novin Party
   Isfahan University
   Islah Taleban Party
   Kerman
   Khorasan
   Khuzistan
   Mardom Party
   Qom
   Shiraz University
   Sistan and Baluchistan
   Tabriz University
   Vaziri, Qamar al-Moluk
   Wolff, Henry Drummond
   Zagros

Crystal Procyshen
International Christian University
   Shaltut, Muhammad

Ayad al-Qazzaz
California State University, Sacramento
   Ahali Group
   Baghdad
   Bazzaz, Abd al-Rahman al-
   Daʿwa al-Islamiyya, al-
   Hashimi, Taha al-
   Ibrahim, Izzat
   Iraq
   Jabr, Salih
   Mosul, Anglo–Turkish Dispute over
   Sadr, Muhammad Baqir al-
   Suwaydi Family
   Suwaydi, Tawfiq al-
   Tikriti Families
   United Nations Special Commission
      (UNSCOM)

Donald Quataert
State University of New York, Birmingham

   Ottoman Empire: Overview
   Ottoman Empire: Debt
   Westernization

Mouin Rabbani
University of Oxford
   Habash, George
   Hut, Shafiq al-
   Palestine National Council
   Popular Front for the Liberation of Palestine
   Popular Front for the Liberation of
      Palestine–General Command
   Qurai, Ahmad Sulayman
   Sabbagh, Hasib
   Saʿiqa, al-
   Wazir, Khalil al-

Itamar Rabinovich
Tel Aviv University
   Sasson, Eliyahu

Ali Jihad Racy
University of California, Los Angeles
   Abd al-Wahhab, Humannad ibn

Abdul-Karim Rafeq
College of William and Mary
   Akrad, Hayy al-
   Ayn, Ras al-
   Damascus University
   Dayr al-Zawr Province
   Ghab, al-
   Greater Syria
   Hama
   Hinnawi, Sami al-
   Idlib Province
   Istiqlal Party: Syria
   Jabal, Badawi al-
   Jabal Druze
   Latakia
   Sharabati, Ahmad al-
   Syrian Desert

Babak Rahimi
Lake Forest, CA
   Alizadeh, Ghazaleh
   Ganji, Akbar

Mark Raider
State University of New York, Albany
   American Israel Public Affairs Committee
   Silver, Abba Hillel
   Wise, Stephen S.

LIST OF CONTRIBUTORS

Rasul Bakhsh Rais
Columbia University
    Pakistan and the Middle East

Ruth Raphaeli
Columbia University
    Hebrew

Sara Reguer
City University of New York, Brooklyn College
    Gallipoli
    Johnston Plan (1953)
    Jordan River
    Litani River
    National Water System (Israel)
    Rutenberg, Pinhas
    Sèvres, Treaty of (1920)
    World War I

Bernard Reich
George Washington University
    Government
    Israel: Overview

Donald Malcolm Reid
Georgia State University
    Adli
    Ahram Center for Political and Strategic
      Studies, al-
    Ain Shams University
    Alexandria
    Alexandria University
    American University in Cairo (AUC)
    Azhar, al-
    Baghdadi, Abd al-Latif al-
    Cairo
    Cairo University
    Champollion, Jean-François
    Coptic Museum
    Dar al Da'wa wa al-Irshad
    Dar al-Kutub al-Misriyya
    Dar al-Ulum
    Egyptian Geographical Society
    Egyptian Museum
    Elites
    Institut d'Égypte
    International Debt Commission
    Kamal, Ahmad
    Mariette, Auguste
    Maspéro, Gaston
    Mixed Courts
    Muhammad Ali Mosque

    Postage Stamps
    Pyramids
    Qusayr, al-
    Rida, Rashid
    Sa'id Pasha
    Salim Hasan
    Sphinx
    Suez Canal University
    Zaqaziq University

Nissim Rejwan
Hebrew University of Jerusalem
    Ben-Porat, Mordechai
    Ezra and Nehemiah Operations

Laura Rice
Oregon State University
    Amari, Raja
    Association des Femmes Tunisiennes pour la
      Recherche et le Développement
      (AFTURD)
    Bakkar, Jalillah
    Centre de Recherches, d'Études, de
      Documentation et d'Information sur la
      Femme (CREDIF)
    Gender: Study of
    Ghanmi, Azza
    Mernissi, Fatema
    Moudawana, al-
    Tlatli, Moufida

Paul Rivlin
Tel Aviv University
    Bar-Ilan University
    Economic and Military Aid
    Histadrut
    Jewish National Fund
    Joint Distribution Committee
    Koor Industries
    Moshav
    Na'amaat
    Population
    United Jewish Appeal (UJA)
    West German Reparations Agreement

Aleya Rouchdy
Wayne State University
    Nubians

Maurice M. Roumani
Ben-Gurion University of the Negev
    Ha-Cohen, Mordechai

Haggiag Family
Nahum, Halfallah
Nhaisi, Elia

Paul Rowe
University of Western Ontario
Constantinople
Luxor
Samarra
Sinai Peninsula

Sara M. Roy
Harvard University
Gaza Strip

Barnett R. Rubin
BESA Center for Stategic Studies
Ahmad Shah Mas'ud

John Ruedy
Georgetown University
Algeria: Overview
Algerian War of Independence
Algiers Charter
Arabization Policies
Armée de Libération Nationale (ALN)
Association of Algerian Muslim Ulama
(AUMA)
Colons
Comité de Coordination et d'Exécution
Comité Révolutionnaire d'Unité et d'Action
(CRUA)
Conseil National de la Révolution Algérienne
(CNRA)
Fanon, Frantz
Front de Libération Nationale (FLN)
High State Council (Algeria)
Imperialism in the Middle East and North
Africa
Manifesto of the Algerian Muslim People
Mouvement National Algérien
Mouvement pour le Triomphe des Libertés
Démocratiques
Organisation Armée Secrète (OAS)
Oujda Group
Parti du Peuple Algérien (PPA)
Star of North Africa
Union Démocratique du Manifeste Algérien
(UDMA)
Young Algerians

William A. Rugh
Georgetown University

Newspapers and Print Media: Arab Countries
Radio and Television: Arab Countries

Mona Russell
Massachusetts Institute of Technology
Abu Zayd, Hikmat
Anis Al-Jalis Magazine
Lata'if al-Musawwara Magazine

Curtis R. Ryan
Appalachian State University
Arab Legion
Faysal, Tujan
Islamic Action Front
Jordan River
Noor al-Hussein (Queen Noor)
Rania al-Abdullah (Queen Rania)

Elise Salem
Fairleigh Dickinson University
Adnan, Etel
Bahithat al-Lubnaniyyat, al-
Barakat, Hoda
Faqir, Fadia
Mala'ika, Nazik al-
Moghaizel, Laure
Mou'awwad, Naila
Nasrallah, Emily
Samman, Ghada
Shaykh, Hanan al-
Ziadeh, May

Ariel Salzmann
New York University
Tax Farming

Geoffrey D. Schad
Shippensburg University
Hama

Uli Schamiloglu
University of Wisconsin, Madison
Azeri Language and Literature
Gaspirali, Ismail Bey
Koprülü, Mehmet Fuat
Turkish Historical Society
Turkish Linguistic Society
Turkology

Stephen Schecter
Université du Québec à Montréal
Kaniuk, Yoram

Kenaz, Yehoshua
Yehoshua, Avraham B.

Jillian Schwedler
University of Maryland, College Park
Islah Party
Turabi, Hasan al-

Emanuela Trevisan Semi
Ca' Foscari University of Venice
Ethiopian Jews

Caroline Seymour-Jorn
University of Wisconsin, Milwaukee
Bakr, Salwa
Makdashi, Hesna
Munif, Abdel Rahman
Nassif, Malak Hifni
Rifaat, Alifa

Pamela Dorn Sezgin
Marietta, GA
Music

Jean-François Seznec
Lafayette Group
Economics
Natural Gas: Middle East Reserves of
Petrochemicals
Petroleum Reserves and Production
PETROMIN
Royal Dutch Shell
Stock Market
Suez Canal
Suez–Mediterranean Pipeline
World Bank

A. Shapur Shahbazi
Eastern Oregon State College
Bisitun

Irfan Shahîd
Washington, DC
Shawqi, Ahmad

M. Nazif Shahrani
Indiana University, Bloomington
Afghanistan: Overview
Afghanistan: Islamic Movements in
Daud, Muhammad
Uzbeks
Zahir Shah

Zaki Shalom
Ben-Gurion Research Center
Meir, Golda

Seteney Shami
Social Science Research Council
Circassians

Zeva Shapiro
New York, NY
Kaniuk, Yoram
Kenaz, Yehoshua

Yaakov Shavit
Tel Aviv University
Altalena
Cohen, Ge'ula
Irgun Zva'i Le'umi (IZL)
Shamir, Yitzhak
Sharon, Ariel

Gabriel Sheffer
The Hebrew University of Jerusalem
Diaspora

William Shepard
University of Canterbury
Amin, Ahmad

Dov Shinar
Ben-Gurion University of the Negev
Newspapers and Print Media: Israel
Radio and Television: Israel

Faegheh Shirazi
University of Texas, Austin
Clothing

Farhad Shirzad
New York, NY
Paris, Treaty of (1857)
Turkmanchai, Treaty of (1828)

Avi Shlaim
Oxford University
All-Palestine Government
Glubb, John Bagot
Jordanian Option
Partition Plans (Palestine)

Eric Silver
Jerusalem, Israel
Begin, Menachem
Netanyahu, Benjamin
Sharon, Ariel

Alain Silvera
Bryn Mawr College
  Victoria College

Brian Silverstein
University of California, Los Angeles
  Newspapers and Print Media: Turkey
  Radio and Television: Turkey

Paul Silverstein
Reed College
  Berber Spring
  Black Spring

Miriam Simon
Interreligious Coordinating Council in Israel
  Bar-Ilan University
  Ben-Gurion University of the Negev
  Exodus (1947)
  Ha-Tikva
  Magen David Adom (MDA)
  Navon, Yizhak
  Saison
  Struma
  Technion-Israel Institute of Technology
  Tel Aviv University
  Weizmann Institute of Science
  Zangwill, Israel

Rachel Simon
Princeton University Library
  Farhat al-Zawi
  Qaramanli Dynasty
  Sanusi, Muhammad ibn Ali al-
  Sanusi Order
  Turkish–Italian War (1911–1912)

Reeva S. Simon
Columbia University
  Arab–Israel War (1956)
  Archaeology in the Middle East
  Baʿth, al-
  Faisal I ibn Hussein
  Freemasons
  Germany and the Middle East
  Golden Square
  Holy Land
  Iraq
  Jaffa
  Jamali, Muhammad Fadhil al-
  Jerusalem
  Kirkuk
  Lavon, Pinhas

  Mosul
  National Democratic Party (Iraq)
  Rothschild, Edmond de
  Sabbagh, Salah al-Din al-
  Wingate, Charles Orde
  Yiddish

Peter von Sivers
University of Utah
  Ahmad Bey of Constantine
  Algiers
  Mukrani Family
  Oran
  Warnier Law

P. Oktor Skjaervo
Harvard University
  Iranian Languages

Peter Sluglett
University of Utah
  Abd al-Ilah ibn Ali
  Anglo–Iraqi Treaties
  Baʿth, al-
  Colonialism in the Middle East
  Cox, Percy
  Faisal II ibn Ghazi
  Ghazi ibn Faisal
  Hourani, Albert
  Ikha al-Watani Party
  Jawahiri, Muhammad Mahdi al-
  Kaylani, Rashid Ali al-
  Midfaʿi, Jamil al-
  Sanctions, Iraqi
  Shimʿun, Mar
  Sidqi, Bakr
  Sulayman, Hikmat
  Westernization
  Wilson, Arnold T.

Oles M. Smolansky
Lehigh University
  Brezhnev, Leonid Ilyich
  Khrushchev, Nikita S.
  Russia and the Middle East
  Russian–Ottoman Wars
  San Stefano, Treaty of (1878)
  Stack, Lee

Sasson Somekh
Tel Aviv University
  Heskayl, Sasson

Rasafi, Maʿruf al-
Salim, Jawad
Shaʾul, Anwar
Somikh, Abdullah

Tamara Sonn
The College of William and Mary
Alia, Queen

John P. Spagnolo
Simon Fraser University
De Gaulle, Charles
France and the Middle East

Donald Spanel
Credit Suisse First Boston
Coptic Museum
Copts
Cyril IV
Cyril V
Cyril VI
Demetrius II
John XIX
Mark VIII
Peter VII
Shenouda III

Daniel E. Spector
Troy State University
Alamayn, al-
Allied Middle East Command
D'Arcy Concession (1901)
Dardanelles, Treaty of the (1809)
Gardanne Mission
Gulf War (1991)
Lausanne, Treaty of (1923)
Mandate System
Middle East Supply Center (MESC)
Military in the Middle East
Millspaugh, Arthur
Rommel, Erwin
Roosevelt, Franklin Delano
Shuster, W. Morgan
Straits Convention
Tobruk
Vance, Cyrus
Versailles, Treaty of (1920)
Wavell, Archibald Percival
World War II

Denise A. Spellberg
University of Texas, Austin

Madrasa
Mahdi
Ulama
Waqf

Kenneth W. Stein
Emory University
Madrid Conference (1991)

Rita Stephan
University of Texas, Austin
Arab Women's Solidarity Association
  International
Husari, Sati al-
Ibrahim, Saʿad al-Din
Marriage and Family
Mevlevi Brotherhood
Saadawi, Nawal al-
Sabah, Suad al-

Norman Stillman
University of Oklahoma
Baqri Family
Ben Simeon, Raphael Aaron
B'nai B'rith
Busnach Family
Club National Israelite
Comité Juif Algérien d'études Sociales
Corcos Family
Dor Deʿa
Giado Concentration Camp
Hazzan, Elijah Bekhor
Jews in the Middle East
Judeo-Arabic
Ladino
LICA
Maccabi
Magic Carpet Operation
Valensi, Alfred

Ronald Bruce St John
Independent Scholar, Illinois
Asad, Bashshar al-
Asad, Hafiz al-
Cyrenaica
Libya
Maziq, Husayn
Pan-Arabism
Pelt, Adrian
Pérez de Cuéllar, Javier
Qaddafi, Muammar al-

Revolutionary Command Council (Libya)
Shamikh, Mubarak Abdullah al-
Stark, Freya
Syria
Syrian Social Nationalist Party
Tripolitania
Yunis Jabir, Abu Bakr

Christopher Reed Stone
Middlebury College
Fayruz
Peace Corps

Thomas Stransky
Tantur Ecumenical Institute, Jerusalem, Israel
Saint Catherine's Monastery

Samy S. Swayd
San Diego State University
Druze

Will D. Swearingen
Montana State University
Atlas Mountains
Memmi, Albert

Ephraim Tabory
Bar-Ilan University, Israel
Circumcision
Halakhah
Talmud
Yosef, Ovadiah

Frank Tachau
University of Illinois, Chicago
Confederation of Turkish Trade Unions
Erbakan, Necmeddin
Freedom Party
Free Republican Party
İzmir Economic Congress
Motherland Party
Nationalist Action Party
National Unity Committee (Turkey)
Social Democratic Populist Party
True Path Party
Türkes, Alparslan
Turkish National Pact
Turkish Workers Party
Unity Party

Kazuo Takahashi
University of the Air, Tokyo
China and the Middle East

Lawrence Tal
Admiral House, London, England
Bevin, Ernest
Bir Zeit University
Cattan, Henry
Fida'iyyun
Haddad, Wadi
Hasan, Hani al-
Hasan, Khalid al-
Hilmi, Ahmad
Jibril, Ahmad
Kanafani, Ghassan
Karama, Battle of (1968)
Land Day
Nusayba Family
Ramallah

Steve Tamari
Institute of Jerusalem Studies
Abbas, Mahmud
Ahmad al-Jazzar
Anglo–American Committee of Inquiry
    (1946)
Aqqad, Umar Abd al-Fattah al-
Arab Liberation Army
Arab Women's Congress
Arif, Arif al-
Banna, Sabri al-
Barghuthi Family
Beersheba
Black September

Cherie Taraghi
Üsküdar, Istanbul, Turkey
Behrouzi, Maryam
Farmanfarmian, Settareh
Islamic Countries Women Sport Solidarity
    Games (1992 and 1997)
Lahiji, Shahla

Abraham Terian
Andrews University
Armenian Community of Jerusalem

Janice J. Terry
Eastern Michigan University
Wafd

Wingate, Reginald
Zaghlul, Sa'd

Mary Ann Tetréault
Iowa State University
Al Sabah Family
Al Sabah, Mubarak
Al Saqr Family
Arabian American Oil Company (ARAMCO)
As-Is Agreement
Awadhi, Badria A. al-
Bishara, Abdullah
Ghanim, al-
Iraq Petroleum Company (IPC)
Kuwait
Kuwait City
Kuwait Fund for Arab Economic
    Development
Kuwait Petroleum Corporation
National Oil Corporation (Libya)
Natural Gas: Economic Exploitation of
Oasis Group
Occidental Petroleum
Organization of Petroleum Exporting
    Countries (OPEC)
Petrochemicals
Petroleum, Oil, and Natural Gas
Qatar Petroleum
Red Line Agreement
Sabah, Rasha al-
Trade
Trans-Arabian Pipeline

Elizabeth Thompson
University of Virginia
Abdülmecit II
Agop, Gullu
Ahmet Izzet
Ahmet Riza
Akçura, Yusuf
Altinay, Ahmed Refik
Ankara, Treaty of (1930)
Aqaba Incident
Arab Liberation Front
Aral, Oğuz
Arseven, Celal Esat
Atay, Salih Rifki
Bayrakdar, Mustafa
Bedel-i Askeri
Bludan Conferences (1937, 1946)

Bogazköy
Churchill, William
Cilicia
Darwish, Ishaq
Deedes, Wyndham
Diyarbakir
Dolmabahçe Palace
Eastern Orthodox Church
Eldem, Sedad Hakki
Ersoy, Mehmet Akif
Ertuğrul, Muhsin
Erzurum
Erzurum Congress (1919)
Esendal, Memduh Şevket
Eyüboğlu, Bedri Rahmi
Falconry
Ferit, Damat Mehmet
Ferman
Güney, Yilmaz
Gürpinar, Hüseyin Rahmi
Galata
Ganim, Halil
Genç Kalemler
Ha-Shomer
Ibrahimi, Lakhdar al-
İdadi Schools
İlmiyye
İpekci, Abdi
Isa Family, al-
Jabal al-Khalil
Jabal Nablus
Ja'bari Family
Jarallah Family
Jizya
Johnson–Crosbie Committee Report (1930)
Kafr Qasim
Kalemiyye
Karacan, Ali Naci
Keban Dam
Khalaf, Salah
Khutba
Kiryat Arba
Kisakürek, Necip Fazil
Koç, Vehbi
Konya, Battle of
Kuttab
Litani Operation (1978)
Lydda
Maghrib
Mahalle Schools

Mansure Army
Mediterranean Sea
Milli İstihbarat Teşkilati
Minaret
Muhsin, Zuhayr
Muhtar, Gazi Ahmet
Mustafa Fazil
Mustafa Suphi
Nadi, Yunus
Najjada, al-
Nasir, Najib
Negev
Nesin, Nüsret Aziz
Nizamiye Courts
Ormsby-Gore, William George Arthur
OYAK (Ordu Yardimlasma Kurumu)
Palestine Economic Corporation
Palestine Exploration Fund
Palestine Land Development Company
Palmyra
Permanent Mandates Commission
Persian (Arabian) Gulf
Point Four
Qanun
Qur'an
Ramla
Rejection Front
Ruşdiye Schools
Saba Family
Safveti Ziya
Sakakini, Khalil al-
Salonika
Şevket, Mahmut
Shumayyil, Shibli
Shuqayri Family
Shura
Silk
Simavi, Sedat
Sinai Peninsula
Şirket-i Hayriye
South Lebanon Army
Sultani Schools
Sunay, Cevdet
Sun Language Theory
Sursuq Family
Tamimi, Amin al-
Taner, Haldun
Tanzimat
Timar
Tripoli Conference (1977)

Tuqan Family
Turkism
Uşakliğil, Halit Ziya
Üsküdar
Varlik Vergisi
Yarmuk River
Yildirim Army
Yücel, Hasan Ali
Ziya, Abdülhamit

W. Kenneth Thompson
U.S. Department of State, Washington, DC
   Drugs and Narcotics

Karen A. Thornsvard
Madison, WI
   Amir, Abd al-Hakim
   Wauchope, Arthur

Robert L. Tignor
Princeton University
   Baring, Evelyn
   Farouk
   Fu'ad

Nayereh Tohidi
California State University, Northridge
   Ebtekar, Ma'sumeh
   Zanan Magazine

Ehud R. Toledano
Tel Aviv University
   Slave Trade

Ana Torres-Garcia
Universidad de Sevilla
   Ahardane, Majoub
   Baccouche, Hedi
   Bouabid, Abderrahim
   Ibrahim, Abdullah
   Ibrahimi, Lakhdar al-
   Lamrani, Muhammad Karim
   Ligue Tunisienne pour la Défense des Droits
      de l'Homme (LTDH)
   Mestiri, Ahmad
   Mouvement de l'Unité Populaire (MUP)
   Mzali, Mohammed
   Opium
   Ouary, Malek
   Parti d'Unité Populaire (PUP)
   SONATRACH
   Tunisia: Political Parties in

Union Générale des Travailleurs Marocains
(UGTM)
Union Générale des Travailleurs Tunisiens
(UGTT)
Union Marocaine du Travail (UMT)
Western Sahara

Anthony B. Toth
Arlington, VA
Abdul-Aziz Bin Baz, Shaykh
Abu Dhabi
Al Nahayyan Family
Al Rashid Family
Al Saʿud Family
Al Thani Family
Ayn, al-
Baharina
Buraymi Oasis Dispute
Committee for the Defense of Legitimate
Rights
Doha
Dubai
Fahd ibn Abd al-Aziz Al Saʿud
Fujayra
Galatasaray Lycée
Grand Mosque
Gulf Cooperation Council
Hasa, al-
Hijaz
Ikhwan
Islamic University of Medina
Jabal al-Akhdar, Oman
Jabal Shammar
Khalid ibn Abd al-Aziz Al Saʿud
King Saʿud University
Kuwait University
Maritime Peace in Perpetuity, Treaty of (1853)
Masira Island
Mecca
Medina
Muʿalla Family, al-
Muscat
Nuʿaymi Family, al-
Qasimi Family of Raʾs al-Khayma, al-
Qasimi Family of Sharjah, al-
Qatar
Qatar Petroleum
Raʾs al-Khayma
Sharqi Family, al-
Taʾif, Treaty of al-

Tariki, Abdullah
Tiran, Strait of
Tourism
Transport
Umm al-Qaywayn
United Arab Emirates
Urbanization
Yamani, Ahmad Zaki

S. Ilan Troen
Brandeis University
Ben-Gurion University of the Negev
Sèvres Protocol (1956)

Benyamim Tsedakah
Holon, Israel
Samaritans

Jenab Tutunji
George Washington University
Abdullah I ibn Hussein
Abu al-Huda, Tawfiq
Abu Nuwwar, Ali
Aqaba
Aqaba, Gulf of
Arab Legion
Asmar, Fawzi al-
Attlee, Clement
Badran, Mudar
Brookings Report (1975)
Clayton, Gilbert
East India Company
Fahd Plan (1981)
Guinness, Walter Edward
Hashim, Ibrahim
Holy Sepulchre, Church of the
Ismaʿili Shiʿism
Jericho Congress (1948)
Jewish Colonial Trust
Kahan Commission (1983)
Kirkbride, Alec Seath
Liberty, USS
Luke, Harry
MacDonald, Malcolm
MacDonald, Ramsay
MacMichael, Harold
Majali, Hazza al-
Nabulsi, Sulayman al-
Nasir, Hanna
Palestine Research Center
Peake, Frederick Gerard

Plague
Polygamy
Richmond, Ernest T.
Rifaʿi, Samir al-
Salt, al-
Talal ibn Abdullah
Tall, Wasfi al-
Transjordan Frontier Force
Turki, Fawaz
University of Jordan
Yarmuk University

Brian Urquhart
New York, NY
Bunche, Ralph J.
Hammarskjöld, Dag
United Nations Interim Force in Lebanon

Farzin Vahdat
Harvard University
Kadivar, Mohsen
Mojtahed-Shabestari, Mohammad

Martin Van Bruinessen
Universiteit Utrecht
Kurdistan Workers Party (PKK)

Dirk Vandewalle
Dartmouth College
Annaba
Bidonville
Boumédienne, Houari
Cantonnement/Refoulement
Constantine
Ente Nazionale Idrocarboni (ENI)
SONATRACH

Roxanne Varzi
New York University
Bani-Etemad, Rakhsan
Behbehani, Simin
Derakhshandeh, Puran
Film
Jihad
Khamenehi, Ali
Kiarostami, Abbas
Mahfuz, Najib
Makhmalbaf Family
Makhmalbaf, Mohsen
Milani, Tahmineh
Persian Script
Shahin, Yusuf
Sharif, Omar
Shiʿism

Haleh Vaziri
Intermedia Survey Institute, Washington, DC
Diba, Farah
Women's Organization of Iran (WOI)

Peter von Sivers
University of Utah
Algiers

David Waldner
University of Virginia
Abd al-Quddus, Ihsan
Abd al-Sabur, Salah
Abidin, Dino
Abu Qir, Battle of (1798)
Ahmet Ihsan To'kgoz
Ahmet Rasim
Akbulut, Ahmet Ziya
Ali Riza
Ararat, Mount
Aswan High Dam
Awad, Louis
Başiretci, Ali
Bekir, Fahri
Caylak
Çerkes Hasan Incident
Cevdet, Abdullah
Civil Service School (Ottoman)
Clot, Antoine Barthélémy
Commercial and Navigation Treaties
Congress of Ottoman Liberals (1902)
Dede Zekai
Dellalzade İsmail
Delta Barrages
Democrat Party
Devrim, Izzet Melih
Dufferin Report (1883)
Erbil, Leyla
Evren, Kenan
Gülbenkian, Calouste
Gürsel, Cemal
Ghanim, Fathi
Ghorbal, Ashraf
Haddad, Saʿd
Hamama, Faten
Hijaz Railroad
İnönü, Erdal
International Monetary Fund
Justice Party
Kamil, Kibrish Mehmet

Kasap, Teodor
Kemalettin Bey
Kenter, Yildiz
Khalid, Khalid Muhammad
Kissinger, Henry
Land Code of 1858
Leskofcali Galip
Lesseps, Ferdinand de
Liberal Constitutionalist Party
Liberation Rally
Maratghi, Mustafa al-
McMahon, Henry
Mehmet Rauf
Menou, Jacques François
Messianism
Mufide Kadri
Muhyi al-Din, Khalid
Muhyi al-Din, Zakariyya
Musa, Salama
Mustafa Reşid
Nabizade Nazim
Naguib, Muhammad
Nazif, Süleyman
Nazmi, Ziya
Özal, Turgut
Philae
Port Saʿid
Recaizade Mahmud Ekrem
Saadawi, Nawal al-
Sabri, Ali
Sanu, Yaʿqub
Saygun, Ahmed Adnan
Şeker Ahmet
Selçuk, Munir Nurettin
Semitic Languages
Shafiq, Durriyya
Shahin, Yusuf
Shaʿrawi, Huda al-
Sharif, Omar
Shazli, Saʿd al-Din
Shilluk
Sidqi, Ismaʿil
Southeastern Anatolia Project
Suphi Ezgi
Tahir, Kemal
Takfir wa al-Hijra, al-
Tanburi Cemil
Tanpinar, Ahmed Hamdi
Tarhan, Abdülhak Hamit
Tevfik Fikret

Tharwat, Abd al-Khaliq
Tunisi, Bayram al-
Turkey
Turkish–Afghan Treaty (1928)
Yurdakul, Mehmet Emin

Bernard Wasserstein
University of Chicago
Britain and the Middle East from 1914 to the
    Present
Bentwich, Norman
Colonial Office, Great Britain
Creech Jones, Arthur
Crossman, Richard
Lloyd George, David
Samuel, Herbert Louis
Wauchope, Arthur
Weizmann, Chaim
World Zionist Organization (WZO)

Chaim I. Waxman
Rutgers University
Aaronsohn Family
Agudat Israel
Aliyah
Arlosoroff, Chaim
Borochov, Ber
Bund
Dreyfus Affair
Eretz Yisrael
Halukka
Ha-Shomer Ha-Tzaʿir
Hasidim
Herzog, Izhak Halevi
Irgun Zvaʾi Leʾumi (IZL)
Joseph, Dov
Keren Hayesod
Kibbutz
Kook, Abraham Isaac Hacohen
Kook, Zvi Yehuda
Law of Return
Leibowitz, Yeshayahu
Magnes, Judah
Maimon, Yehudah Leib Hacohen
Meah Sheʿarim
Mizrahi Movement
Neturei Karta
Nissim, Isaac
Ouziel, Ben Zion Meir Hai
Patriarchs, Tomb of the
Petah Tikvah

Potash Industry
Salant, Samuel
Uganda Project
Zohar, Uri
Zonnenfeld, Yosef Hayyim

Walter F. Weiker
Rutgers University
Ahdut ha-Avodah
Bayar, Celal
İnönü, İsmet
Israel: Overview of Political Parties in
Kahane, Meir
Knesset
Likud
Lilienblum, Moses Leib
Menderes, Adnan
Oz ve Shalom (Netivot shalom)
Sneh, Moshe

Shalvah Weil
Hebrew University of Jerusalem
Ethiopian Jews

Marvin G. Weinbaum
University of Illinois, Urbana
Economic and Military Aid

Thomas G. Weiss
Graduate Center, City University of New York
United Nations and the Middle East

Rachel Weissbrod
Bar-Ilan University, Israel
Exodus (1947)

Lynn Welchman
School of Oriental and African Studies, University of London
Crimes of Honor
Human Rights

Manfred W. Wenner
Prescott, AZ
Ahmad ibn Yahya Hamid al-Din
Bakil Tribal Confederation
Hamdi, Ibrahim al-
Hodeida
Idrisids
National Front for the Liberation of South Yemen
Organization for the Liberation of the Occupied South
People's Socialist Party
Salih, Ali Abdullah
Shaʿbi Family

South Arabian League
Yahya ibn Muhammad Hamid al-Din
Yemen
Yemen Dynasties
Yemeni Socialist Party
Zubayri, Qaʾid Muhammad Mahmud al-

Stephanie Wichhart
University of Texas, Austin
Memmi, Albert

George R. Wilkes
University of Cambridge
American Council for Judaism
Badr, Liana
Bialik, Hayyim Nahman
Bitton, Simone
Brenner, Yosef Hayyim
Brookings Report (1975)
Burton, Richard Francis
Chazan, Naomi
Cole, USS
Dentz, Henri-Fernand
Freier, Recha
Ghazali, Muhammad al-
Ghorbal, Ashraf
Grossman, Haika
Habash, George
"Ha-Tikva"
Hut, Shafiq al-
Kovner, Abba
Marzouki, Moncef
Matzpen
Meged, Aharon
Moadda, Mohamed
Muhyi al-Din, Zakariyya
New Wafd
Pharaon, Rashad
Politi, Elie
Popular Front for the Liberation of Palestine–General Command
Qurai, Ahmad Sulayman
Sabbagh, Hasib
Saʿiqa, al-
Sant Egidio Platform
Saunders, Harold
Shalvi, Alice
Shochat, Manya
Sisco, Joseph
Smilansky, Moshe
Women in Black

Rodney J. A. Wilson
University of Durham, England
Industrialization

Jessica Winegar
New York University
Ali, Wijdan
Amer, Ghada
Ani, Jannane al-
Art
Attar, Suad al-
Baya
Caland, Huguette
Efflatoun, Inji
Faraj, Maysaloun
Ghoussoub, Mai
Hatoum, Mona
Ishaaq, Kamala Ibrahim
Jacir, Emily
Kadri, Mufide
Karnouk, Liliane
Khal, Helen
Khemir, Sabiha
Neshat, Shirin
Niati, Houria
Saudi, Mona
Shawa, Laila
Sidera, Zineb
Sirry, Gazbia
Tallal, Chaibia
Umar, Madiha
Zeid, Fahralnissa

Clifford A. Wright
Arlington, MA
Tea

John L. Wright
Surrey, England
Baida
Basic People's Congresses
Benghazi
Cyrenaica
Fezzan
Istiqlal Party: Libya
Kikhya Family
Nasir, Ahmed Sayf al-
Omar Mukhtar Club
Sadawi, Bashir
Tripoli

Nathan Yanai
Haifa University
Dayan, Moshe

Neguin Yavari
Columbia University
Akhbari
Ala, Hoseyn
Alam, Amir Asadollah
Amini, Ali
Amir-Entezam, Abbas
Atabat
Ayn al-Dowleh, Abd al-Majid Mirza
Azerbaijan
Bakhtiari, Najaf Qoli Khan Samsam al-
    Soltaneh
Bakhtiar, Timur
Baluchistan
Bani Sadr, Abolhasan
Bast
Borujerdi, Hosayn
Chamran, Mostafa
Committee for Defense of Freedom and
    Human Rights
Daftari, Ahmad Matin
Eqbal, Manouchehr
Forughi, Mirza Mohammad Ali Khan Zaka
    al-Molk
Freedom Movement (Nezhat-e Azadi Iran)
Hajir, Abd al-Hoseyn
Hoveyda, Amir Abbas
Jangali
Kharg Island
Khomeini, Ruhollah
Kuchek Khan-e Jangali
Majles al-Shura
Marja al-Taqlid
Mohammad Ali Shah Qajar
Musavi-Ardebili, AbdolKarim
Qotbzadeh, Sadeq
Roosevelt, Kermit
Sadr, Muhsin
Shariatmadari, Kazem
Sharif-Emami, Ja'far
Shatt al-Arab
Shiraz
Soheyli, Ali
Students in the Line of the Imam
Tabriz
Tabriz University
Usuli
Vazir Afkham, Soltan Ali Khan
Vozuq al-Dowleh, Mirza Hasan Khan
Yazdi, Ibrahim

M. Hakan Yavuz
University of Utah
   AKP (Justice and Development Party)
   Erbakan, Necmeddin
   Erdoğan, Tayyip
   Evren, Kenan
   Gülen, Fetullah
   İnönü, Erdal
   Milli Görüş Hareketi
   Motherland Party
   Nationalist Action Party
   National Security Council (Turkey)
   Nursi, Said
   Sezer, Ahmet
   Social Democratic Populist Party
   True Path Party
   Türkes, Alparslan

Shibolet Zait
Columbia University
   Raab, Esther

Muhammad Zakariya
Arlington, VA
   Calligraphy

Mamoon A. Zaki
LeMoyne-Owen College
   Baban Family
   Hashimi, Yasin al-
   Mandaeans
   Najaf, al-
   Pachachi, Muzahim al-

Naomi Zeff
Somerville, MA
   Mauritania
   Nouakchott
   Ould Sid'Ahmed Taya, Ma'ouiya

Ronen Zeidel
Haifa University
   Osirak

Charles U. Zenzie
U.S.-Indonesia Society, Washington, DC
   Popular Front
   Sa'ada, Antun
   Shahbandar, Abd al-Rahman
   United Nations Truce Supervision
      Organization (UNTSO)
   Za'im, Husni al-
   Zu'bi, Mahmud al-
   Zurayk, Constantine

Steven Zipperstein
Hebrew University of Jerusalem
   Ahad Ha-Am

Eyal Zisser
Tel Aviv University
   Za'im, Husni al-

Yahia Zoubir
Thunderbird Europe/Centre Universitaire
   Bennabi, Malek
   Islamic Salvation Army (AIS)
   Kateb, Yacine
   Parti de l'Avant-Garde Socialiste (PAGS)
   Sadi, Said
   Toumi, Khalida
   Zeroual, Liamine

Julie Zuckerman
Jerusalem, Israel
   Goldmann, Nahum
   Idris al-Sayyid Muhammad al-Sanusi
   Netanyahu, Benjamin
   Pagis, Dan
   Shin Bet
   Sobol, Yehoshua
   Stern, Abraham
   Tagger, Sioneh
   Tamir, Shmuel
   Vanunu Affair
   Yariv, Aharon
   Yosef, Ovadiah

GENEALOGIES

In the following genealogies and lines of succession, an asterisk preceding a name indicates that the Encyclopedia contains an entry for that individual. The names of those who ruled are indicated by boldfaced type. The following genealogies are not exhaustive, including only well-known figures and those in the direct line of succession. Where possible, the existence of additional family members has been indicated with arrows. With a few exceptions, female descendants are not included because they are typically denied inheritance of a throne and, consequently, little information is available about them.

FIGURE 1

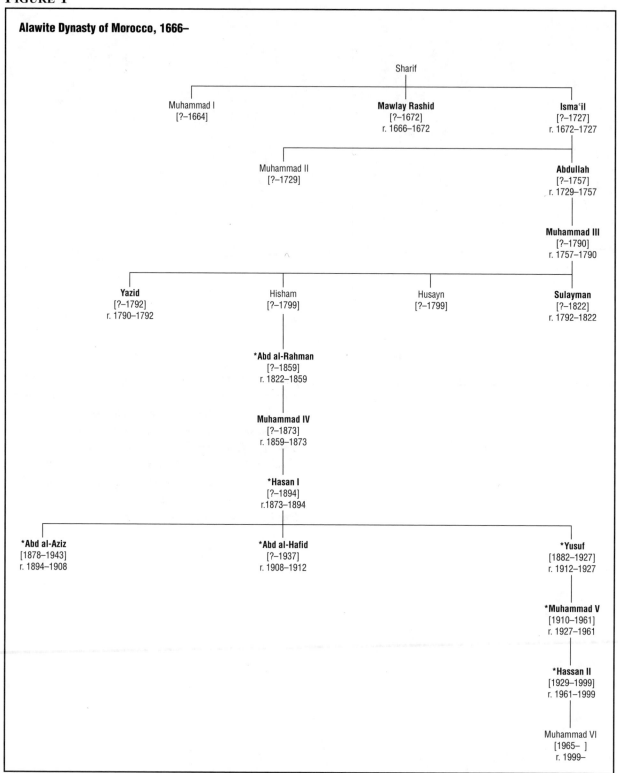

Alawite Dynasty of Morocco, 1666–

FIGURE 2

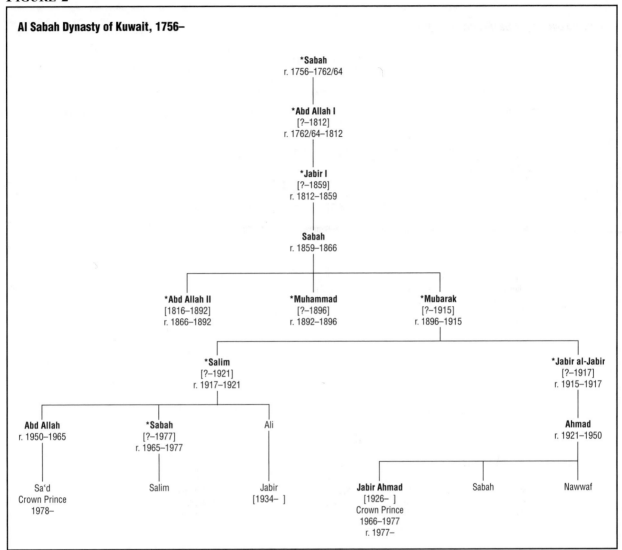

Al Sabah Dynasty of Kuwait, 1756–

FIGURE 3

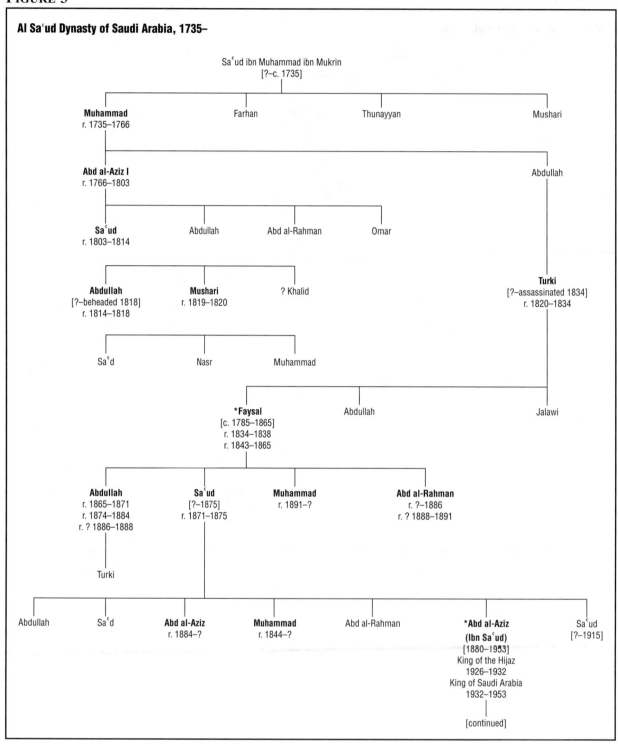

Al Saʿud Dynasty of Saudi Arabia, 1735–

FIGURE 3 (*continued*)

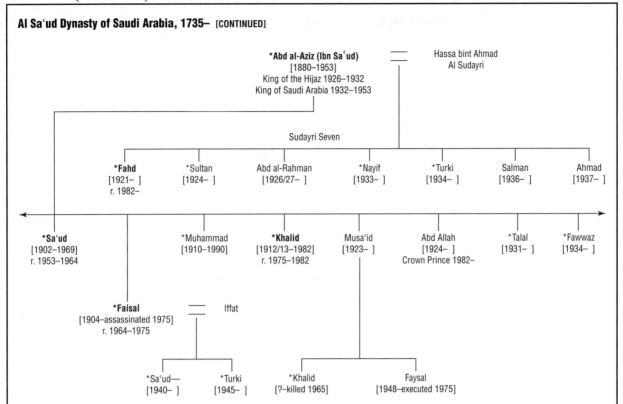

Al Saʿud Dynasty of Saudi Arabia, 1735– [CONTINUED]

Note: Abd al-Aziz ibn Saʿud Al Saʿud (1880–1953) fathered forty-five sons and as many daughters by at least twenty-three different women. His wife Hassa gave birth to seven sons known as the Sudayri Seven, a reference to Hassa's descent from the Al Sudayri tribe. The descendants of Muhammad ibn Saʿud, the founder of the Al Saʿud dynasty, number in the tens of thousands and include the current king, Fahd, one of the Sudayri Seven.

FIGURE 4

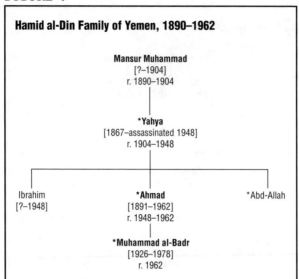

Hamid al-Din Family of Yemen, 1890–1962

Mansur Muhammad
[?–1904]
r. 1890–1904

*Yahya
[1867–assassinated 1948]
r. 1904–1948

Ibrahim
[?–1948]

*Ahmad
[1891–1962]
r. 1948–1962

*Abd-Allah

*Muhammad al-Badr
[1926–1978]
r. 1962

FIGURE 5

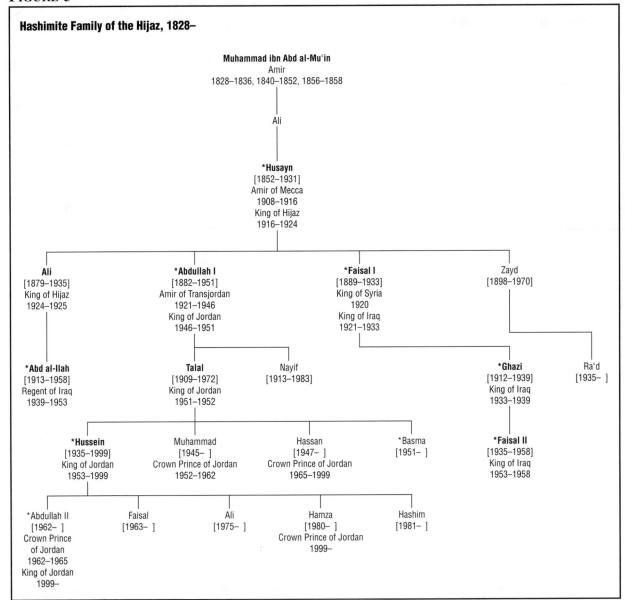

Hashimite Family of the Hijaz, 1828–

Muhammad ibn Abd al-Muʿin
Amir
1828–1836, 1840–1852, 1856–1858

Ali

*Husayn
[1852–1931]
Amir of Mecca
1908–1916
King of Hijaz
1916–1924

Ali
[1879–1935]
King of Hijaz
1924–1925

*Abdullah I
[1882–1951]
Amir of Transjordan
1921–1946
King of Jordan
1946–1951

*Faisal I
[1889–1933]
King of Syria
1920
King of Iraq
1921–1933

Zayd
[1898–1970]

*Abd al-Ilah
[1913–1958]
Regent of Iraq
1939–1953

Talal
[1909–1972]
King of Jordan
1951–1952

Nayif
[1913–1983]

*Ghazi
[1912–1939]
King of Iraq
1933–1939

Raʿd
[1935–]

*Hussein
[1935–1999]
King of Jordan
1953–1999

Muhammad
[1945–]
Crown Prince of Jordan
1952–1962

Hassan
[1947–]
Crown Prince of Jordan
1965–1999

*Basma
[1951–]

*Faisal II
[1935–1958]
King of Iraq
1953–1958

*Abdullah II
[1962–]
Crown Prince
of Jordan
1962–1965
King of Jordan
1999–

Faisal
[1963–]

Ali
[1975–]

Hamza
[1980–]
Crown Prince of Jordan
1999–

Hashim
[1981–]

FIGURE 6

Khalifa Family of Bahrain, 1782–

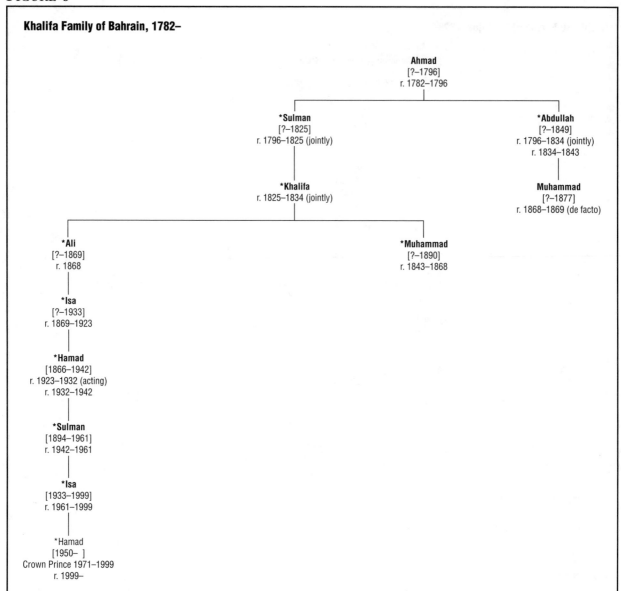

FIGURE 7

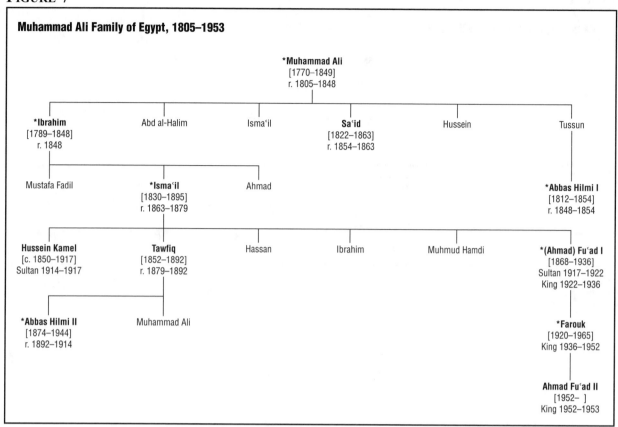

Muhammad Ali Family of Egypt, 1805–1953

FIGURE 8

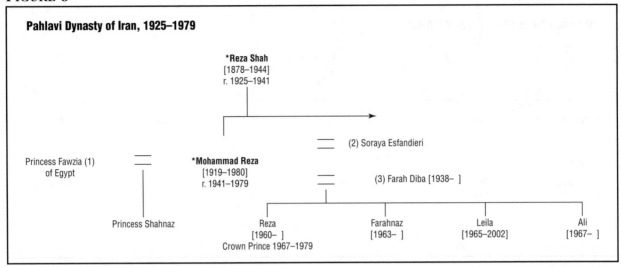

Pahlavi Dynasty of Iran, 1925–1979

FIGURE 9

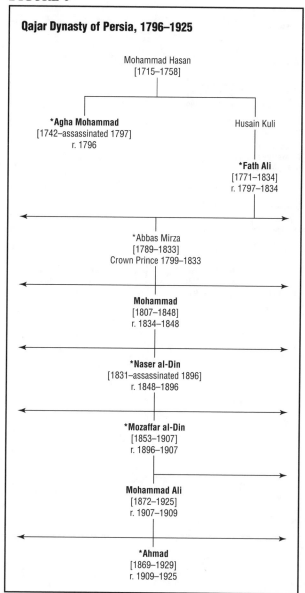

Qajar Dynasty of Persia, 1796–1925

Mohammad Hasan
[1715–1758]

*Agha Mohammad
[1742–assassinated 1797]
r. 1796

Husain Kuli

*Fath Ali
[1771–1834]
r. 1797–1834

*Abbas Mirza
[1789–1833]
Crown Prince 1799–1833

Mohammad
[1807–1848]
r. 1834–1848

*Naser al-Din
[1831–assassinated 1896]
r. 1848–1896

*Mozaffar al-Din
[1853–1907]
r. 1896–1907

Mohammad Ali
[1872–1925]
r. 1907–1909

*Ahmad
[1869–1929]
r. 1909–1925

FIGURE 10

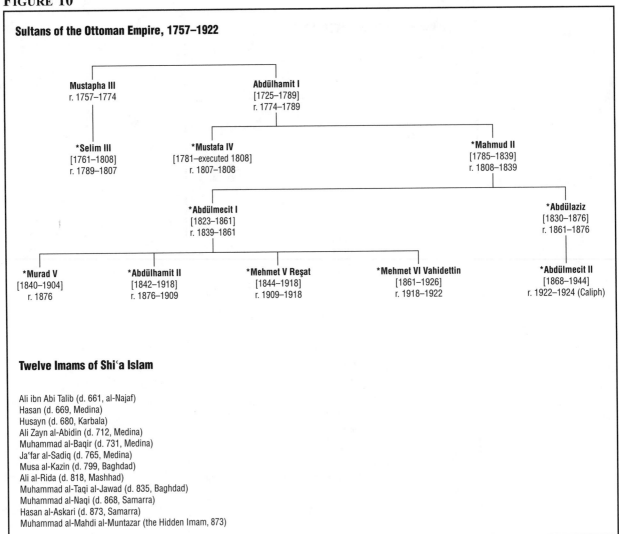

Sultans of the Ottoman Empire, 1757–1922

Mustapha III
r. 1757–1774

Abdülhamit I
[1725–1789]
r. 1774–1789

*Selim III
[1761–1808]
r. 1789–1807

*Mustafa IV
[1781–executed 1808]
r. 1807–1808

*Mahmud II
[1785–1839]
r. 1808–1839

*Abdülmecit I
[1823–1861]
r. 1839–1861

*Abdülaziz
[1830–1876]
r. 1861–1876

*Murad V
[1840–1904]
r. 1876

*Abdülhamit II
[1842–1918]
r. 1876–1909

*Mehmet V Reşat
[1844–1918]
r. 1909–1918

*Mehmet VI Vahidettin
[1861–1926]
r. 1918–1922

*Abdülmecit II
[1868–1944]
r. 1922–1924 (Caliph)

Twelve Imams of Shi'a Islam

Ali ibn Abi Talib (d. 661, al-Najaf)
Hasan (d. 669, Medina)
Husayn (d. 680, Karbala)
Ali Zayn al-Abidin (d. 712, Medina)
Muhammad al-Baqir (d. 731, Medina)
Ja'far al-Sadiq (d. 765, Medina)
Musa al-Kazin (d. 799, Baghdad)
Ali al-Rida (d. 818, Mashhad)
Muhammad al-Taqi al-Jawad (d. 835, Baghdad)
Muhammad al-Naqi (d. 868, Samarra)
Hasan al-Askari (d. 873, Samarra)
Muhammad al-Mahdi al-Muntazar (the Hidden Imam, 873)

GLOSSARY

A

Abd: *Arabic for "slave."* Abd means slave. It is also often seen as part of Islamic male names. In such cases, "abd" is always followed by one of the 99 names of God, and denotes "servant of." For example, Abd al-Rahman ("servant of the Forgiving One"), or Abd al-Jabbar ("servant of the Almighty"). Abdullah means "servant of God."

Abu: *Form of the Arabic word* ab *("father").* When it is followed by a first name—usually, the name of a man's first-born son—it means "father of ___." "Abu so-and-so" is used in lieu of calling a man by his first name.

Agha: *Socio-political title of authority.* Agha ("chief," "master") was associated with certain administrators in the Ottoman empire. It is also used in other settings, such as among Kurds.

Allah: *Arabic word for "God."* Allah is simply Arabic for "God"; It is not the name of God. Both Christian and Muslim Arabs use the word Allah in their scriptures.

Amir: *Political title.* Amir (also emir) is derived from the Arabic word *amara* ("to command"), and is a title given to a person of high political rank. It is often translated as "prince."

Ashur: *Islamic tithe.* Also called zakah or zakat, ashur (from the Arabic word for "ten") is a charitable tithe prescribed in Islam. In North Africa, ashur also denotes the tenth month of the Islamic calendar, Muharram.

Ayatullah: *Shi'ite religious title.* Ayatullah (also ayatollah) is a title denoting a very high level *mujtahid* cleric. It is the highest rank a Shi'ite cleric can attain. See also "mujtahid."

B

Baraka: *Arabic, "blessing."* Baraka means a blessing from God, and can also refer to good luck in general. It is also the spiritual benefit that can be bestowed on someone by a saintly figure, and can also refer to a donation to some charitable institution.

Bedouin: *Arab nomads.* The term comes from the Arabic word *badu,* meaning "those who live in the *badiya,* (desert)." Bedouin formerly lived as pastoral nomads in the desert regions of the Arab world, although by the twentieth century, few true nomads remained. The term is still used, however, to denote those tribes and families who are of bedouin origin.

Bey: *Political title.* Bey is a Turkish term often translated as "prince." In the Ottoman empire's administration and military, it was given to mid-level officers. In modern Turkey, it is often used as a suffix to a man's first name as a polite form of address.

Bilharzia: *See Schistosomiasis.*

Bint: *Arabic, "girl."* Female children in the Arab world sometimes are referred to by making reference to their father. Thus, "so-and-so, bint [daughter] so-and-so." See also "ibn."

C

Casbah: *Old quarters of an Arabic city.* From the Arabic *qasaba* ("divide," "cut up"; also, "citadel" or "capital"), it is a term often used by Europeans to denote the older, native quarters of a town, as distinct from the newer areas in which foreigners lived.

D

Derb: *Street or neighborhood.* Moroccan cities were made up of various streets and neighborhoods. Each of these was referred to as a derb, from the Arabic *darb* ("street" or "path").

Dey: *Political title.* The Turkish word for maternal uncle, the position of dey originally was military, but came to denote administrative power in as well. Deys were found in North Africa, especially Tunisia and Algeria, from the late seventeenth through the early nineteenth centuries.

Dinar: *Monetary unit.* Dinar is derived from the Greek "dinarion" and the Latin "denarius." During the early Islamic period, it was a type of gold coin. Currently it serves as the currency of Algeria, Bahrain, Iraq, Jordan, Kuwait, Libya, Tunisia, and parts of the former Yugoslavia.

Dirham: *Monetary unit.* During the early Islamic period, the dirham was a type of silver coin. Currently it is used in Morocco, Libya, the United Arab Emirates, and Jordan.

Dunum: *Unit of surface area.* The dunum is used to measure surface area in parts of the Fertile Crescent. During the late Ottoman period, it equaled 919 square meters. In the 1920s, it was enlarged to 1,000 square meters (about 0.25 acre) in Lebanon, Syria, Palestine, and Transjordan. In Iraq, the dunum is 0.618 acre.

E

Effendi: *Honorific title.* The origins of this title are Greek, and refer to a man of property or education. During the late Ottoman period, it was used as a sign of respect for middle class males as well as for some bureaucratic positions. Another form of the word, effendum, is still used in Egypt to mean "mister" or "sir."

F

Feddan: *Unit of surface area.* Deriving from an Arabic term for a yoke of oxen, it referred to the amount of land such animals could farm. Thus the actual surface area called a feddan varied from region to region. In Egypt, where it remains the standard unit of surface area today, it equals 4,200.883 square meters, slightly more than one acre.

Fellagha: *Term denoting outlaws.* Fellagha (also fallak) derives from colloquial Tunisian Arabic. It was widely used by the French press to refer to Tunisian guerrilla groups fighting colonial rule, and was eventually used by the fighters themselves. It was also used in reference to anti-French fighters during the early days of the Algerian war of independence.

Fellah: *Peasant.* Fellah (also fallah; plural: fallahun, but more commonly fallahin following colloquial usage) derives from the Arabic verb *falaha* ("cultivate"). It refers to small scale, subsistence level cultivators in Arab countries, but can be used, often derisively, by urbanites to refer to the rural population generally.

G

Ghazel: *Type of poetic form.* The word is Arabic (ghazal; "flirtation" or "love poem"), and is also seen as gazel or ghazal. A lyrical poetic mode often expressing romantic love or eroticism, the form passed into Turkish, Persian, and Urdu poetry as well.

Ghorfa: *Arabic for "room."* The Arabic ghurfa refers to a room. In southern Tunisia, seminomadic peoples, usually Berbers, built fortress-like, multistoried structures to store grain. Examples still exist near Tataouine, Ksar Haddada, and Médenine.

H

Hajj: *Islamic pilgrimage.* Hajj (with a short "a" sound) is one of the "Five Pillars of Islam," and refers to a Muslim's obligation to make a pilgrimage to the holy sites in the cities of Mecca and Medina, in today's Saudi Arabia. Islam requires all Muslims who are physically and financially able to make the hajj at least once in their lifetime. The title "hajj" or sometimes "hajji" (with a long "a" sound) is the title given to a man who has completed the hajj. The female equivalent is "hajja."

Halal: *Arabic for "lawful."* In Islamic usage, it refers to aspects of life that are religious acceptable or lawful. It is especially used to refer to meat that has been slaughtered and prepared in accordance with Islamic law. See also "haram."

Haram: *Arabic for "forbidden."* Haram refers to aspects of life, including acts, food, etc., that are forbidden by Islamic law. See also "halal."

Hezbollahi: *"One of the Party of God."* It comes from an Arabic term hizbullah, found in the Qur'an that stems from hizb ("party") and Allah ("God"). In Iran, a hezbollahi came to mean a zealous and sometimes violent supporter of the concept of an Islamic state.

Hoca: *Honorific title.* Hoca is a Turkish word derived from the Persian khwaja. In the Turkish speaking parts of the Ottoman empire, it denoted religious scholars and certain administrative bureacrats. It is still used in modern Turkey to refer to teachers and religious scholars. See also "khawaja."

Hosainiyeh: *Place of a certain type of religious ceremony.* In Iran, it is a place where the martyrdom of the Imam Husayn ibn Ali is commemorated, especially on Ashura, the tenth day of the Islamic month of Muharram. It refers to the death of Husayn, grandson of the prophet Muhammad, in 680 at the hands of the Umayyads at Karbala, in Iraq. Traditionally, a hosainiyeh was a different structure than a mosque, and was a populist institution rather than one under the control of the Islamic clerics.

I

Ibn: *"Son."* Male children in the Arab world sometimes are referred to by making reference to their father. Thus, "so-and-so, ibn [son] so-and-so." See also "bint."

Iltizam: *Tax farm.* The Arabic term iltizam refers to a duty or obligation. During the Ottoman empire, it referred to a type of taxation whereby the authorities auctioned the rights to collect taxes to an individual, who became known as a multazim. The multazim paid the auction amount to the government, and was free to extract as much in taxation as possible from those living within the iltizam. It usually denoted the right to collect taxes from a specific area, but sometimes referred to taxes collected from a certain trade or profession. It was also called muqataʿa in some areas. The Ottoman government tried on several occasions in the late nineteenth century to abolish the practice, but it remained in parts of the empire until the early twentieth century.

Imam: *Religious title.* The term derives from the Arabic amma, "to lead." Among Sunni Muslims, and imam refers to the leader of the prayers in a mosque. For Shiʿite Muslims, however, the term refers to the legitimate leader of the Muslim community, a position extending back to the first imam, Ali ibn Abi Talib, the cousin and son-in-law of the prophet Muhammad who also became the fourth caliph. Following Ali's death, the imamate devolved to his sons Hasan and Husayn, and thereafter to their descendants.

The Shi'ite concept of imam involves considerably greater power and influence than for Sunnis, for the Shi'ite imams possessed special spiritual powers to interpret the will of God.

Imamzadeh: *Persian term referring to the descendant of an imam or the tomb of such a person.* Among Twelver Shi'a in Iran, the term is used to denote the descendant of one of the first eleven imams, as well as the tomb built over the burial place of such a person. Visiting such tombs is considered a meritorious act than can impart a special spiritual blessing, or baraka, to the visitor. See also "baraka."

Inqilab: *Revolution or uprising.* In modern Arabic political usage, the term inqilab is usually used to connote a sudden seizure of political power, often via a military coup d'état. In Persian, the term means "revolution," such as the 1979 revolution in Iran.

Izlane: *Berber songs.* The singular is izli. These are short (usually no longer than two lines) poetic songs among Berbers in the Middle Atlas mountains. The songs are sung at festive occasions, accompanied by drums and clapping, and often speak of love. They are also a vehicle for social and political commentary.

J

Jihad: *"Struggle" in the service of Islam.* Jihad derives from the Arabic verb *jahada*, "to struggle" or "to endeavor." In Islam it can refer to a number of sacred endeavors, from an individual's personal attempts to live his/her life properly according to Islamic principles, to armed struggle in the defense of Islam or Islamic territory. The term mujtahid derives from *jahada* as well. See also "mujtahid."

K

Karakul: *Afghani sheep.* Karakul is the name of a breed of short-tailed sheep raised in northern Afghanistan, largely by Turkmen and Uzbeks. The fleece is used for making hats.

Kaza: *Ottoman administrative unit.* Kaza is a Turkish word derived from the Arabic *qada*. By the late Ottoman empire, a province (*vilayet*; Arabic: *wilaya*) was divided into governorates called *sanjaks* (Arabic singular: *sanjaq*) or *livas* (Arabic singular: *liwa*). These in turn were divided into smaller units called kazas. Kaza can also refer to the judgment of a *qadi*, or judge. See also "liwa," "qa'immaqam," and "vilayet."

Khan: *Highway inn for travelers, or a warehouse for merchandise.* Khans were built as rest stops for travelers and caravans. A khan was also an urban complex for storing merchandise and hosting merchants.

Khanjar: *Type of Arabic dagger.* A khanjar usually refers to a slightly curved, double edged dagger that tapers to a point. The hilt is often decorated.

Khatib: *Islamic preacher.* A khatib is the religious official who delivers the sermon during Friday prayers in a mosque, usually from a raised pulpit called a *minbar*. See also "minbar."

Khawaja: *Honorific title of Persian origin.* In Egypt and parts of the Fertile Crescent, khawaja was a title used to denote a non-Muslim, both foreigners as well as native Christians and Jews. The term comes from the Persian *khwaja*. See also "hoca."

Khawr: *Natural harbor; also part of place names.* The term is used in the Persian/Arabian Gulf region.

Khedive: *High-level title used in Egypt from 1867–1914.* Khedive is a Persian word for a high prince that was used by the governors of Ottoman Egypt from 1867–1914 to replace the title "pasha" carried by other governors in the empire. It was first used by Isma'il Pasha, grandson of Muhammad Ali, who secured this right from the Ottoman sultan in order to differentiate and elevate himself from other provincial governors. The term was replaced with "sultan" by the British, who occupied Egypt starting in 1882. See also "pasha" and "sultan."

Koran: *See Qur'an.*

Kochi: *Afghani pastoral nomads.* Derived from the Pushtu term koch ("pack"), kochi referes to pastoral nomads, mostly Baluchis and Pushtuns, in Afghanistan.

Komiteh: *Armed Islamic revolutionary group in Iran.* Prior to merging with the official armed forces in 1991, the Komitehs (Islamic Revolutionary Committees) developed out of mosque-based revolutionaries in Tehran in 1978. Ayatollah Ruhollah Khomeini gave them official status in 1979, as did the Iranian majles (legislature) in 1983. The Komitehs served as a type of police force, combating drug trafficking, "immoral" behavior, as well as working against groups opposing the new regime.

L

Laz: *Ethnic group in Turkey.* The Laz live on the Black Sea, near Turkey's border with Georgia. The Laz language belongs to the Kartvelian language family, and is related to Georgian.

Lazma: *Plot of land in Iraq.* Tribes living in Iraq would distribute irrigated land to cultivators, called lazma, who then obtained prescriptive rights to that land by virtue of their ongoing cultivation of it. This came despite the fact that the land was not formally registered to the tribe.

Leff: *Type of political coalition in North Africa.* Coming from the Arabic word *laffa* ("to wrap"), a leff refers to political coalition whose members assist one another during disputes with other leffs. It is also called *saff* in some parts of North Africa and the Fertile Crescent.

Lira: *Ottoman monetary unit.* The lira, or pound, was named after an Italian silver coin, and was the currency used in the Ottoman empire. Modern Turkey, Syria, and Lebanon continue to use the lira as their national currencies.

Liwa: *Ottoman administrative unit.* During the late Ottoman empire, a province (*vilayet*; Arabic: *wilaya*) was divided into liwas (called liva in Turkish). A liwa was also called a *sanjak* (Arabic: *sanjaq*). These in turn were divided into smaller units called qadas or kazas. See also "kaza," "mutassarif," and "vilayet."

Luti: *Term implying deviation from moral standards.* In Iran during the late nineteenth and early twentieth centuries, the term originally referred to a member of a chivalrous brotherhood. It later assumed more negative connotations implying drunkenness and moral deviation. In parts of the modern Arab world, luti is a term used for a homosexual. Some surmise that the term derives from the biblical figure Lot, son of Noah.

M

Madrasa: *Arabic for "school."* Madrasa is the Arabic word for school. In Sunni Islam it referred to a school for teaching Islamic law, or shari'a. It retains that meaning in parts of the contemporary Islamic world, although in modern Arab countries, the term is more broadly used to denote schools in general.

Majles: *Legislature or parliament.* Majles is the Persian form of the Arabic *majlis* (in Turkish, *meclis*), which is derived from the verb *jalasa* ("to sit"). It can mean a meeting, or sitting, in a number of senses, both private and public. In the public realm, it became the term used for legislatures in the Middle East and North Africa once these began to emerge in the nineteenth century. It can also refer to an appointed consultative body.

Malik: *"King" in Arabic.* Malik derives from the Arabic verb *malaka* ("to own"). It has been used in the modern Arab world to mean king.

Ma'palim: *Illegal Jewish immigrants to Palestine.* Ma'palim (Hebrew, "the daring ones") were Jewish immigrants who entered Palestine in violation of immigration quotas established by the British Mandate in Palestine, especially after the 1939 White Paper. The Zionist community in Palestine established the clandestine organization Mossad le-Aliyah Bet in 1938 to assist Jews fleeing Nazi persecution in Europe in reaching Palestine. British forces intercepted many ma'palim and interned them in camps in Cyprus, including the 4,515 passengers aboard the ship *Exodus*, whose detainment in 1947 helped turn international sentiment against British rule in Palestine.

Mellah: *Jewish quarter of Moroccan towns.* Mellah derives from the Arabic word for salt. It stems from the forced resettlement of the Jewish community in Fez to an outlying saline area, and came to denote Jewish areas throughout Morocco. In urban areas, mellahs were gated quarters of cities. In rural areas, they were separate Jewish villages.

Minbar: *Pulpit in a mosque.* In a mosque, the sermon (*khitab*) is delivered by the preacher (*khatib*) from a raised pulpit called a minbar, derived from the Arabic *nabara* ("to raise the voice"). See also "khatib."

Mizrahim: *Jews from Islamic countries.* Mizrahim means "the easterners" in Hebrew. It is a term used in modern Israel to denote Jews whose origins extend back to North African, Middle Eastern, and West or South Asian Jewish communities. Some of these communities were quite ancient, especially those in Iraq, Iran, Syria, and Yemen. Most of these communities moved to Israel after its creation in 1948. The term Mizrahim has started to replace "Sephardim," which for a long time was loosely used to denote all Jews who were not European ("Ashkenazim"), but which in a strict sense only refers to the Jews who were expelled from Spain in 1492. See also "Sephardim" and the encyclopedia entry "Adot ha-Mizrah."

Moslem *See Muslim.*

Muezzin: *The one who calls Muslims to pray.* A muezzin (Arabic: *mu'adhdhin*) calls the Muslim faithful to pray, usually from a minaret. The call to prayer must be in Arabic, even though most of the world's Muslims do not speak Arabic.

Mufti: *Type of Islamic cleric.* A mufti is an expert in Islamic law empowered to given religious opinions on various matters. Such an opinion is called a fatwa. See the encyclopedia entry "fatwa."

Mujtahid: *Type of Shi'ite Muslim cleric.* A mujtahid is a Shi'ite religious scholar who is authorized to practice *ijtihad,* or interpretation. While the "door of interpretation" was closed for Sunni Muslims approximately 1,000 years ago, high level Shi'ite clerics called mujtahids still practice *ijtihad.*

Mukhtar: *Chief or headman.* Deriving from the Arabic word *khatara* ("to choose" or "select"), a mukhtar ("selected one") was an official appointed by the Ottoman authorities to serve as a go-between between the government and a tribe, village, or urban quarter. The function was part of the Ottomans' centralization efforts, efforts that included attempts to undercut traditional religious figures who had maintained levels of local influence. The position is still found in parts of the Arab world.

Mulai: *Title and form of address.* In Arabic, "my lord." Also mawlai, mawlay. A form of address formerly used when speaking to a king, sultan, or caliph. It is still used in Morocco when referring to the crown prince.

Muslim: *Follower of the Islamic religion.* Muslim (sometimes rendered Moslem) is someone who follows the religion of Islam.

Mutasarrif: *Ottoman provincial official.* A mutasarrif was the recipient of taxes from sub-provincial governorates in the Ottoman empire. By the late Ottoman era, the term denoted the government-appointed head of a governorate, or sanjak (also liwa). See also "liwa."

N

Narghila: *Water pipe.* A narghila (also called *arghila, qalyan,* and *shisha*) is a water pipe used in the Middle East and North Africa to smoke tobacco, usually flavored tobacco called *tombac.* They are commonly seen in all-male coffee houses.

O

Oasis: *Watered area surrounded by desert.* An oasis is a fertile area, watered by wells, that is found in the midst of a desert. They can be small or large.

Oglu: *Turkish for "son of."* When used as part of a male name, it means "son of. . ." For example, Süleimanoglu ("son of Süleiman"). In 1935, the Turkish government obliged Turks to adopt Western-style last, or family, names. Many Turks used this form to create family names.

P

Pasha: *Ottoman administrative and military title.* The Ottomans introduced the title "pasha" (modern Turkish, *paşa*) in the fourteenth century. It was used for the governors of sanjaks, or liwas, but later was bestowed upon other men of high military or governmental rank. With the reorganization of the Ottoman administration in 1864, governors of provinces (vilayets) were given the title pasha. The term remained in use in Turkey and some Arab countries, although it was banned in most of these in the twentieth century. It is still sometimes used, but only to refer to a man in an honorific fashion. See also "liwa" and "vilayet."

Pesh Merga: *Kurdish, "those who face death."* Modern term used to denote armed Kurdish fighters. It first appeared during the Kurdish war against the Iraqi government that began in 1962.

Q

Qaʾid: *Arabic for "leader."* Arabic term denoting political leadership.

Qaʾimmaqam: *Ottoman provincial official.* The term itself is Arabic, and was the title given by Ottoman authorities to the official appointed to head a subgovernorate called a kaza (also qada). See also "kaza," "liwa," and "vilayet." It was also used to denote a low ranking military officer.

Qanat: *Canal.* A qanat (also qana) can mean an underground water channel for irrigating fields, but can also denote a surface level canal, both small and large (such as the Suez Canal).

Qat: *Plant with mildly stimulant effect.* The leaves of the qat (also khat) plant, Catha edulis, are chewed in southwestern Arabia and eastern Africa for their mildly stimulant effect. Similar to the stimulant qualities of caffeine, qat is chewed in the company of others as an important form of social gathering. In this regard, gathering together to chew qat is akin to gathering in a coffee house to drink coffee or tea. Qat chewing is a major activity in Yemen, whose economic as well as social impact on the country is profound. It is also chewed in African countries like Somalia.

Qibla: *Direction of Islamic prayer.* The qibla is the direction in which Muslims must pray. The first qibla was Jerusalem, but this was quickly changed in the seventh century to the direction of Mecca. Muslims around the globe all pray in the direction of Mecca.

Qirsh: *Monetary unit.* The Arabic word qirsh, and Turkish word ghurush or kuruş, is translated as piastre, itself the Italian name for the medieval peso duro. The qirsh was introduced into the Middle East in the early seventeenth century and became a unit of Ottoman currency equivalent to one-hundredth of a lira. It is still used as a small unit of currency in parts of the Middle East.

Qurʾan: *Holy book of Islam.* The Qurʾan (also Koran) is the holy book of Islam. It consists of *suras* (roughly, chapters) containing *ayas* (verses), and is believed by Muslims to be the literal word of God, as revealed in Arabic to the prophet Muhammad through the medium of the Angel Gabriel. The Qurʾan was redacted within several generations of the Prophet's death in 632, and is read and revered by Muslims worldwide as God's final and definitive message (Arabic: *risala*) to humanity.

R

Reʿaya: *Subjects of the Ottoman government.* Ottoman society was divided into two segments: rulers and ruled. The latter were called the reʿaya, from the Arabic word denoting "flock." The ruling institution—the sultan and his government—were obliged to protect the reʿaya, who in return paid taxes.

Reuter Concession: *Exclusive economic concession proposed by the Shah of Iran to Baron Julius de Reuter.* In July 1872, Nasir al-Din Shah, ruler of Iran, granted Baron Julius de Reuter, a British subject, a sweeping and exclusive seventy-year concession to carry out a number of business ventures within Iran. Among these were the construction of a railroad linking the Caspian Sea and the Persian Gulf, construction of streetcar lines, and operation of mines, among other ventures. Reuter, owner of a news agency, would have been granted an amazingly large amount of economic power with Iran. Opposition to the deal grew, both within Iran and in Europe (particularly Russia, which also had interests in Iran), and the concession was withdrawn in November

1873. Reuter did eventually maintain certain mining and banking rights in Iran, which led to the creation of the Imperial Bank of Persia.

Riyal: *Monetary unit.* The word *riyal* is of Spanish and French origin. The coin was introduced into the Ottoman empire in the nineteenth century, and first used in Iran in 1930, where it was popularly known as the kran. It is the basic currency unit of several Middle Eastern countries today, including Saudi Arabia, Iran, Oman, Yemen, and Qatar.

Roshanfekr: *Persian word for intellectuals.* Roshankekr (Persian, "enlightened thinker") is the Persian word for intellectual.

Ruzname: *Ottoman treasury offices and its registers.* The term comes from the Persian words *ruz* ("day"), and *name* ("book"). The Ottoman government used to term to denote a financial journal or ledger, and referred both to these and the Ottoman treasury offices as ruzname.

S

Salname: *Ottoman government yearbook.* Salname comes from the Persian words *sal* ("year"), and *name* ("book"). Salnames were statistical, geographical, and biographical yearbooks that were first published by the central Ottoman government in 1847 and later, beginning in 1865, by provincial authorities as well. Salnames contained information on population, expenditures, and education. They were discontinued after1922.

Sanjak: *See liwa.*

SAVAK: *Imperial Iranian intelligence agency.* SAVAK was the Persian acronym for the State Security and Intelligence Organization, and was formed by Mohammad Reza Pahlavi, Shah of Iran, in 1967. SAVAK was originally designed to ferret out communist activity, but grew to monitor all forms of internal dissent and external opposition and to censor the press. It was attached to the prime ministry. SAVAK became a feared organization within Iran and among Iranian exiles abroad, and was abolished after the 1979 revolution.

Sayyid: *Arabic word for "master," "lord," "chief," or "mister."* Prior to the coming of Islam, *sayyid* (plural: *sada* or *asyad*) was used in Arabia to denote a tribal chief. After the coming of Islam, it assumed a particular meaning: descendants and certain relatives of the prophet Muhammad. The term *sayyid* thereafter came to denote the direct descendants of the Prophet through his two grandsons, Hasan and Husayn, the sons of the union of the Prophet's daughter, Fatima, and his son-in-law (and cousin), Ali. In some part of the Arab world, notably in the Hijaz region of Arabia and parts of the Fertile Crescent, *sayyid* came to denote those who were part of the lineage of Husayn, while the term *sharif* denoted those descendant from Hasan. *Sayyids* were held in high social esteem. However, the terms *sayyid* or *sid* (also, "sidi": "my lord") have also been used in a variety of Islamic societies as a form of address for holy men and religious figures. It also is the modern Arabic equivalent of "mister." See also the encyclopedia entry "sharif."

Schistosomiasis: *Disease carried by small worms.* Also called bilharzia, the disease is spread by a small worm, known as the blood fluke, that attaches onto snails. Countries such as Egypt have witnessed the spread of the disease thanks to the development of dams, irrigation canals, and other such developmental projects. The medication that kills the snails that carry the disease is both expensive and unsuitable for use without close medical scrutiny. The result is that the disease has spread considerably, and constitutes one of the modern world's most significant parasitic infections.

Sefaretname: *Ottoman diplomatic report.* Derived from the Arabic word *safara* ("trip" or "journey") and the Persian word *name* ("book"), a sefaretname was a report written by an Ottoman diplomat upon his return from a foreign assignment.

Semites: *Members of the Semitic language family.* Semite (adjective: semitic) stems from the Hebrew *Shem*, the name of one of the sons of the Biblical figure Noah. Semites are peoples in the Middle East and Africa who speak one of the Semitic languages, which are branches of the Afro-Asiatic family. Examples of such languages are Amharic, Arabic, Aramaic, and Hebrew.

Sephardim: *Jews in medieval Spain and their modern descendants.* The term comes from the Biblical Hebrew word *Sepharad,* which while probably referring to the city of Sardis in Asia Minor, came to refer to the Iberian peninsula by the time of the Dark Ages in Europe. Sephardim thus referred to the Jews of Spain, who participated in the glittering civilization of Islamic Spain. However, with the Roman Catholic conquest of the final remaining Islamic part of Spain, Granada, in 1492, the Sephardim expelled or forced to convert. The exiles settled in a number of places, including the New World, European regions such as Italy and the Netherlands, and the Ottoman empire. In the latter, they established communities in the Balkans, Egypt, the Fertile Crescent, and North Africa. In their exile, they continued to speak Ladino, a form of medieval Castilian Spanish written in Hebrew letters. The term Sephardim eventually came to be used in an imprecise manner to mean all non-Ashkenazic Jews (Yiddish speaking Jews from central and eastern Europe), including those in Islamic regions like Iraq, Yemen, and Iran, whose ancestors never had lived in Spain. Increasingly, the term "Mizrahim" is being used to denote the Jews of North Africa, the Middle East, and west and south Asia, some of whom were descendants of the Spanish exiles but most of whom were not. See also "Mizrahim" and the encyclopedia article "Ashkenazim."

Serasker: *Highest Ottoman military rank in the nineteenth century.* Created in 1826, the officer of serasker represented the head of the Ottoman military. During the Tanzimat reorganization of government from 1839–1876, the serasker became a powerful figure, in control of his own treasury. The power of the serasker was reduced by Sultan Abdülhamit II, and was renamed minister of war in the early twentieth century. See also "seyfiyye."

Seven Sisters: *Group of Western oil companies in the Middle East.* The Seven Sisters were a cartel of Western oil companies that dominated the Middle Eastern oil industry from 1930–1970. They were: Standard Oil of New Jersey (Exxon), British Petroleum, Royal Dutch Shell, Chevron, Texaco, Mobil, and Gulf Oil. They increasingly lost power starting in the 1950s and 1960s as Middle Eastern countries began nationalizing their oil industries. With the merger of Chevron and Gulf in 1986, the number of "sisters" dropped to six, which remain important companies in the fields of oil refining and distribution.

Seyfiyye: *Ottoman military bureaucracy.* Derived from the Arabic term *sayf* ("sword"), the Ottomans used the term seyfiyye, "men of the sword," to refer to the various types of troops in the Ottoman military. The seyfiyye was replaced by the serasker in 1826, who unified the various types of military forces (with the exception of the navy). See also "serasker."

Shah: *Persian word for "king."* Shah is a title used by several different dynasties that ruled Iran.

Shuttle Diplomacy: *Term denoting a diplomatic intermediary shuttling back and forth between countries in an effort to arrange an agreement among contending countries.* The term was first raised to the level of public discourse to describe the efforts of American Secretary of State Henry Kissinger to bring about a disengagement of forces after the October 1973 Arab–Israeli war. Kissinger had to shuttle back and forth between the capitals of Egypt, Syria, and Israel, carrying his proposals, because the parties could not agree to meet together.

Sidara: *Type of cap used in Iraq.* The sidara was a type of cap introduced in Iraq in the 1920s that resembled a Western military cap that is called a variety of names, including side cap, for-and-aft cap, or overseas cap. Commonly black velvet, it became the emblem of the Iraqi governing and professional classes. It is no longer in use in Iraq, although a similar type of black cap is used by Muslims elsewhere, especially in south and southeast Asia.

Sitt: *Arabic for "lady."* Sitt is often used in female royal titles.

T

Taqlid: *Islamic legal term.* In Sunni Islam, the term taqlid came to mean "deference" or "imitation," in the sense that religious jurisprudents were obliged to defer to the doctrinal precedents of their respective schools of law (the

Shafi'i, Hanbali, Hanafi, and Maliki schools). This, then, reduces the realm of individual interpretation (*ijtihad*). In Shi'ite Islam, however, the position of marja al-taqlid is quite different, and denotes an elite jurist who is spiritually empowered to employ *ijtihad*. See the encyclopedia article "Marja al-Taqlid."

Tariqa: *Sufi order or brotherhood.* Tariqa is an Arabic word derived from the term meaning "the way." It is used to denote sufi mystical orders. See the encyclopedia entry "Sufism and the Sufi Orders."

Tell: *Hill or mound.* The Arabic word *tall* means a hill, and is used to describe such geographical features. In archeological parlance, however, it refers to a mound containing ancient archeological remains. Finally, it also refers to a large region of North Africa from Morocco to Tunisia.

Thalweg Line: *Maritime boundary.* The thalweg principle of international law, whereby a river or some other body of water constitutes an international border, was most notably used in the Middle East in the case of the border between Iraq and Iran. While at one point in history, the thalweg of the Shatt al-Arab river between the two left the entire river in Iraqi hands, a 1975 treaty moved the thalweg to the midpoint of the river. Overturning this treaty was one of the motivating factors that led Iraq to attack Iran in 1980.

Tishrin: *Arabic term for the tenth and eleventh months of the Gregorian calendar.* In the modern Arab world, Tishrin al-Awwal ("First Tishrin") refers to the Gregorian (Western) month of October, while Tishrin al-Thani ("Second Tishrin") refers to November. Some Arab countries, notably Saudi Arabia, do not use the Gregorian calendar but only the Islamic (hijri) calendar. It is also the name of a newspaper in Syria, named after the initial Arab victories in the October 1973 Arab–Israeli war.

Tiwizi: *Community agricultural support in Berber societies.* Tiwizi is a principle whereby Berbers provide agricultural workers to assist families who need more hands in the fields, and is a socially-mandated obligation.

Toman: *Iranian monetary unit.* Toman is a word of Tatar origin referring to a military unit of 10,000 men, and refers to a gold coin worth ten silver krans (riyals), or 10,000 dinars. It first appeared in Iran ca. 1600. See also "dinar" and "riyal."

Turkmen: *Turkic peoples in Turkmenistan, Iran, and Afghanistan.* The Turkmen are speakers of Western Oghuz Turkic, and were originally pastoral nomads. They lived east of the Caspian Sea and west of the Amu Darya (Oxus) River. In addition, Turkmen minorities today reside in Iraq, Syria, and Turkey.

U

Umma: *Arabic word for community, especially the Islamic community.* The Arabic word umma, derived from *umm* ("mother"), is a term used in Islam to denote the worldwide community of the faithful. In the twentieth century, the term was sometimes used by Arabs to mean "nation" in a political sense, both in global terms (the pan-Arab umma) and local terms (a specific nation).

Urf: *Arabic customary law.* Urf refers to largely unwritten tribal or customary codes that govern social relations, in contradistinction to Islamic law (*shari'a*) or state legal codes (qanun).

Ustadh: *Arabic for "teacher" or "master."* This term (also ostad or ustaz) is used to denote a teacher or professor, but can also be used as a polite form of address for any educated person.

Uzi: *Type of Israeli firearm.* The uzi is a short submachine gun designed by the Israeli army office Maj. Uziel Gal, after whom it is named.

V

Vali: *Ottoman provincial governor.* The term vali is the Turkish and Persian rendition of the Arabic *wali,* referring to someone who has been deputized to exercise authority. It meant "governor." The Mamluks assigned valis to their smallest administrative units, whereas in Iran and later in the Ottoman empire, a vali was the governor of the largest type of administrative unit. In the Ottoman empire, a vali was head of a *vilayet,* or province. See also "kaza," "liwa," and "vilayet."

Vilayet: *Ottoman Turkish term for province.* A vilayet, from the Arabic word *wilaya*, was the largest administrative unit within the Ottoman empire. See also "vali."

Vizier: *Type of government official; "minister."* Under the Ottomans, the vizier (Arabic: *wazir;* Turkish: *vezir*) served as a government minister. The vezir-i azam, or grand vizier, was the functional equivalent of a prime minister under the sultan. The Ottomans replaced the term with *vekil* (Arabic: *wakil*) in the 1830s, although *wazir* is still in use to denote a government minister in the Arab world.

Y

Yarmulke: *Jewish skullcap.* Jewish males have long worn a skullcap to indicate their submission to a higher authority, that is, God. The very religious wear one at all times, while more secular Jews only don them for religious ceremonies. The Hebrew term for this cap is *kippa.* Some speculate that the term yarmulke is an acronym for *yarai m'Elohim,* "one who is in awe of God."

Z

Za'im: *Arabic for "boss" or "leader."* Usually used in an informal manner to denote a strong leader. It is also used as a military rank in some Arab countries.

Zakat: *Islamic tithe, or almsgiving.* Zakat (also zaka) is one of the "Five Pillars of Islam," and is an important religious obligation for Muslims. It requires the giving of an individual's wealth. Historically, it was levied in Islamic countries as a tax upon adult Muslims.

Zawiya: *Islamic religious compound.* From the Arabic word for "corner" or "place of seclusion," a zawiya refers to the compound housing a Sufi brotherhood or the residence of a prominent Sufi master. See the encyclopedia article "Sufism and the Sufi Orders."

INDEX

A

AAC. *See* Anglo–American Committee of Inquiry
Aachen Congress (1818), 739
Aaronsohn, Aaron, 1–2
Aaronsohn, Alexander, 1
Aaronsohn, Ephraim Fishel, 1
Aaronsohn family, **1–2**
Aaronsohn, Malka, 1
Aaronsohn, Sarah, 1
Aba (garment), 611
Ababda clan, 433
Abadan (Iran), **2**
  Anglo–Iranian Oil Company in, 2, *201*, 518
  in Iran–Iraq War (1980–1988), 2, 1127
  urban planning in, 2300
Abadan Institute of Technology, 812
Abadan-Unat, Nermin, *as contributor*, 598, 601–602, 691–693, 745–746, 1545, 1665–1666, 1910–1911, 1918–1920, 2089–2090, 2243–2246, 2362
Aba Island
  Ahmad (Muhammad) on, 87
  Ansar on, 209, 210
Aba, Noureddine, 1426
Abasiyanik, Sait Faik, 784, 1437, 1440
Abassi, Madani. *See* Madani, Abassi al-
Abaya. *See* Aba
Abbas I (Safavi ruler), Isfahan under, 1141
Abbas, Ferhat, **2–4**, *3*
  in Amis du Manifeste et de la Liberté, 3, 189–190, 1804–1805
  Ben Badis (Abd al-Hamid) and, 441
  De Gaulle (Charles) and, Amrouche (Jean) as intermediary, 193
  in Front de Libération Nationale, 3–4, 2263, 2264
  and Hadj (Messali al-), 969
  Manifesto of the Algerian Muslim People by (1943), 3, 189, 1480
  "New Appeal to the Algerian People" by (1976), 4, 1365

  as president of provisional government, 3–4, 138
  in Union Démocratique du Manifeste Algérien, 3, 2263–2264
Abbas Hilmi I (viceroy of Egypt), **4–5**
  Chrakian (Artin) and, 588, 589
  deposition of, 2366
  government of, Clot (Antoine Barthélémy) in, 607
  and National Party, 1663
  Riyad (Mustafa al-) and, 1928
  uncle of, 1970
Abbas Hilmi II (viceroy of Egypt), *5*, **5–6**
  challenging British authority, 405
  court poet of, 2045
  and Gorst (John Eldon), 931
  government of, Ghali (Boutros) in, 6, 909
  Kamil (Mustafa) supported by, 1267
  Kawakibi (Abd al-Rahman al-) in service of, 1282
  Kitchener (Horatio Herbert) and, 5, 6, 1329
  removal of, 6, 509, 858
  and Urabi (Ahmad), 2297
Abbasi al-Mahdi, Muhammad al-, Ilaysh (Muhammad) opposition to, 1086
Abbas ibn Ali (imam), burial site of, as Atabat, 328
Abbasid dynasty, 662, 1131–1132, 2053
  decline of, 1132
  Islam under, 1147
  rise of, 1131–1132
  turbans during, 609
Abbas II (Baring), 407
Abbas, Ihsan, 1791
Abbas Khalili, 427
Abbas, Mahmud (Abu Mazin), **6–7**
  at Aqaba meeting (2003), 32
  Arafat (Yasir) and
    as political strategist, 6
    power struggle between, 7, 814, 997, 1900
  in al-Fatah, 6
  government of, Dahlan (Muhammad) in, 661
  at Oslo Accords (1993), 6
  in Palestinian Authority, as prime minister, 7, 1775, 1785

Alawite dynasty (Morocco) (continued)
Bu Hamara in, 542
corsairs used by, 643
Jews under, 1548
Marrakech under, 1493
Muhammad VI in, 1599–1600
political success of, 1549
al-Qarawiyyin under, 1871
as Sharifian dynasty, 2037, 2038

Alawite tribal confederation, 2212

Albania
Austro-Hungarian support for, 339
independence of, 384

Albanians, 383

Albayrak, Izzet, Kan (Suna) taught by, 1269

Albert Camus Prize, Gebeyli (Claire) awarded with, 872

Albert, Lake, 372

Albert Nile. See Bahr al-Jabal

Alborz. See Elburz Mountains

Albright, Madeleine, 2291

Albright, William Foxwell, 277

Al Bu Falasa dynasty (Dubai), 1474

Al Bu Saʿid dynasty, 107–108, 1710–1711
Dhufar under, 705–706
founder of, 107, 1710
Muscat under, 1616

Al Bu Saʿid, Faysal ibn Turki (sultan of Oman)
British relations with, 107, 204
Anglo–Omani treaties in, 204, 531–532
Cox (Percy) in, 645–646
reign of, 107

Al Bu Saʿid, Majid, 107

Al Bu Saʿid, Qabus (Qaboos) ibn Saʿid, 108, 1710, 1711
coup by (1970), 107, 108
NDFLOAG in, 1654
development under, 108
Dhufar under, 108, 705–706, 1842
foreign policy of, 108
Masira Island under, 1499
Muscat under, 1616
reign of, 108

Al Bu Saʿid, Saʿid ibn Sultan (sultan of Oman and Zanzibar), 107, 1710
emigration under, 2425

Al Bu Saʿid, Saʿid ibn Taymur (sultan of Oman), 109, 1710–1711

coup against (1970), 107, 108, 109, 705
NDFLOAG in, 1654
Dhufar rebellion against (1965–1975), 108, 109, 705, 1842
reign of, 108, 109, 1710–1711

Al Bu Saʿid, Tariq ibn Taymur, 107, 108

Al Bu Saʿid, Thuwayni, 107

Alcohol, 109–110

Al-e Ahmad, Jalal, 110, 668, 913, 1435, 1437, 2342
anti-Westernism of, 1091

Alef, Muhammad. See Atif, Muhammad

Aleichem, Sholem, 464

Alemdar. See Bayrakdar, Mustafa

Aleppine People's Party, 825

Aleppo (Syria), 111, 111–112
Armenian Catholics of, under millet system, 1544
commercial activity in, 111–112
French mandate in, 111
guilds in, 947
Hananu (Ibrahim) entry into, 989
music in, 112
in Ottoman Empire, 111–112
Sykes-Picot Agreement (1916) on, 2128

Aleppo College, 1551–1552

Alessandra, Jacques, 1356

Alevi sect of Shiʿism, 112–115
Bektashis and, 113, 435
beliefs of, 113, 114
language of, 113
origins of, 112–113
persecution of, 114
in Turkey, 2238
and Unity Party (Turkey), 2295

Alexander I (czar of Russia), and Bucharest Treaty (1812), 541

Alexander II (czar of Russia)
in Crimean War, 649
and London Treaty (1871), 1446
pogroms following assassination of, 2432
ultimatum of, after Bulgarian Horrors, 382

Alexander, Harold R. L. G., in Allied Middle East Command, 153

Alexander, Kristian P., as contributor, 1136–1137

Alexander, Scott, as contributor, 150, 1236, 1272, 1526, 1577,

1721–1722, 1863, 2036–2037, 2045–2046, 2122, 2171, 2422–2423

Alexander the Great (king of Macedonia)
Alexandretta founded by, 115
Alexandria Ariorum founded by, 1021
Alexandria founded by, 116
in Khorasan (Iran), 1312

Alexandretta (Turkey), 115–116
in French mandate, 115
in Ottoman Empire, 115
territorial conflict over, 115
Arslan (Adil) in, 306
Arsuzi (Zaki al-) in, 308
Turkish control of, 115

Alexandria (Egypt), 116, 116–118
Alexandria University in, 119
Arab League summit (1964) in, 1387
architecture of, 118, 282
banking in, 389
Bibliotheca in, 117, 118
B'nai B'rith lodge in, 489
British occupation of, 117, 118, 2297
commercial activity in, 116–117
De Menasce family in, 691
foreign population of, 117, 118
Institut Egyptien in, 1099
Jewish community in, 1016, 1930
patriarchate of
claims to, 590
Eastern Orthodox, 590–591
petroleum industry in, 1824
port of, 116, 117, 2206
textile mills in, 2181
Victoria College in, 118, 2315–2316
water supply of, 1468

Alexandria Ariorum, 1021

Alexandria Conference of Arab States. See League of Arab States

Alexandria Convention (1840), 118–119

Alexandria Protocol (1944), 1386. See also League of Arab States
Nahhas (Mustafa) and, 1636

Alexandria–Suez railroad, 528

Alexandria University, 119
Shahin (Yusuf) at, 2021–2022

Alexandria Why? (film), 2022

ALF. See Arab Liberation Front

Al Fahd (Sudayri Seven), 794
Al Sudayri family link to, 168

Algeria *(continued)*
  impact on Morocco, 1004
  movement leading to, 615
  Star of North Africa calling for,
    2089
  Tripoli Programme defining
    identity and direction for,
    2217
industrialization of, 1095
Italian relations with, Ente
    Nazionale Idrocarboni and,
    777–778
Jews in
  antidefamation organization for,
    619
  French citizenship for,
    Crémieux Decree on,
    647–648
  immigration to Israel, 1914
  during World War II, 1234
labor unions in, 1358
land purchases in, Warnier Law
    (1873) on, 2327
land reforms in, 1372
languages in, 121–122, 124 (*See also
    specific languages as subheads*)
in League of Arab States, 1387,
    1388
legal system of, 1382–1383
legislative body in, 932
literature of, 483, 496–497, 563,
    707, 715–716, 803–804,
    806, 822–823, 965, 1280,
    1403, 1422–1427, 2007
  in Arabic, 273, 1581
  Berber, 192, 193, 1426
  "Generation of 1954," 965
  novels and short stories, 1547,
    1581, 2332–2333
  poetry, 1581, 1687
  by women, 1581, 1687
local/provincial elections in
    (1990), 125, 133
mahdi-inspired uprising in
    (1849), 1463
manufacturing in, 127, 128
map of, *121*
marriage in
  Family Code on (1984), 136
  minimum age for, Khemisti Law
    on (1963), 132
Mauritanian relations with, Bend-
    jedid (Chadli) and, 444
military of
  coup by (1992), 126, 134
  elections influenced by, 126, 127
  equipment of, *1534*
  force levels of, *1528–1529*
  force structure of, *1532–1533*

in multiparty system, 132–133
revolt by (1962), 1537
Moroccan relations with (*See also
    Moroccan–Algerian War;
    Western Sahara War*)
  Ben Bella (Ahmed) and, 442
  Bouteflika (Abdelaziz) and, 503
  causes of strain in, 260
  POLISARIO and, 503,
    2190–2191
mountains of, 120, 335–336
Mukrani family in, **1610**
music of, 1617, 1714
National Assembly of, 127, 132
  elections to, 127
  power of, 129
  prime minister selected by, 128
nationalism in, 496, 497
  Boudiaf (Mohamed) and, 496
  Bouhired (Jamila) and, 497
  Hadj (Messali al-) and,
    968–969
  in literature, 1425–1426
  strains of, 124
natural gas in, 1671, *1671*
newspaper and print media of, 1678
  French-language, 1681–1682
  government-controlled, 1680
  transitional press, 1681
nuclear capability of, 1698
oil production in, 752
  Italian interest in, 777–778
in OPEC, 1719
in Ottoman Empire, 122, 1713
parliamentary elections in
  of 1991–1992, 95, 125–126,
    130, 134–135, 984
  of 1997, 1904, 2429
  of 2002, 135, 1904
phosphate industry in, 1834
poetry of, 193, 716
POLISARIO supported by, 503,
    1837, 2190–2191
political parties in, **131–135**, 1904
  Berber, 134
  dominant, 127, 134
  Islamist, 126, 133–134, 984
  multiple, legalization of, 125,
    130, 132–133
  number of, 133
  secular, 1905
  single-party system of, 125, 129
political system of, 127
population of, 120, 752, *753*
postage stamps of, 1850
presidential elections in
  of 1995, 127, 130, 135, 984,
    2430
  of 1999, 135, 984

presidential powers in, 127, 132
press freedom in, 125
provisional government of (*See
    Gouvernement Provisoire de
    la République Algérienne*)
radio and television in, 1894, *1895*
reforms in, 933
  under Bendjedid (Chadli), 445
regions of, 120, 1261
religions in, 122, 124
  Isawiyya Brotherhood, 1141
  Sunni Islam, 122
riots in (1988), casualties of, 132
Sahara in, *1963*
science and technology in, 2004
scout movement in, 2006
secularism in, 1965
socialism in
  Soltani (Abdellatif) criticizing,
    2079
  and SONATRACH, 2079–2080
Soviet relations with, 1943
steel industry in, 208
Tamazight language in
  after independence, 124
  as official language, 122, 130,
    1261
teachers in, foreign, 255, 256
terrorism in, 919
theater of, 1280
tourism in, 2196
in trade, 835
  Baqri family and, 396–397
  Busnach family and, 549–550
tribes in, 458, 459, 2253–2254
  political power of, 122
at Tripoli Conference, 2217
Tunisian relations with, 444
Twareg in, 2253–2254
water resources of
  freshwater withdrawals, *2331*
  quantity of, *2330*
Western Saharan relations with,
    1005, 1006, 1837
  Bendjedid (Chadli) and, 444
in Western Sahara War, Sahrawi
    exodus to, 1837
women in
  as artists, 1687, 2064
  constitution on, 129, 130
  economic status of, *877*
  Family Code on (1984), 130,
    136, 1905
  M'Rabet (Fadela) on, 1592
  as painters, 414
  as political activists, 990
  in politics, 443, 497, 892, 894,
    2195
  rights of, 892, 2195

Husayni (Muhammad Amin al-)
in, 1056
Husayn ibn Ali in, 221, 263–264,
324, 510, 1000, 1053, 2039,
2368
Lawrence (T. E.) in, 264, 324,
510, *511*, 513, 1384
McMahon (Henry) in, 1506
Midfaʿi (Jamal al-) in, 1524
Misri (Aziz Ali al-) in, 1550
nationalism in, 221, 262–264
Qawuqji (Fawzi al-) in, 1879
Quwatli (Shukri al-) in, 1885
Storrs (Ronald) in, 2092
Wingate (Reginald) in, 2354
Arab Revolts (1936–1939). *See* Palestine Arab Revolt (1936–1939)
Arab socialism, **265–266**
Hakim (Muhsin al-) on, 977
Hanoune (Louisa) and, 990
Arab Socialist Baʿth party (Syria),
1010
Arab Socialist List (Israel), 285
Arab Socialist Party
Baʿth party merging with, 412
in National Progressive Front,
1665
Arab Socialist Renaissance Party. *See*
Baʿth party
Arab Socialist Union (ASU) (Egypt),
266–267, 767
left faction of (National Progressive Unionist Party), 1665
Nasser (Gamal Abdel) and, 1650
Sabri (Ali) in, 1955
Sadat (Anwar al-) in, 1956
Sadat's (Anwar al-) dissolution of,
1665
as successor to National Union,
1667
Arab Socialist Union (Lebanon), in
National Front, 1656–1657
Arab Socialist Union (Syria)
Atasi (Jamal al-) in, 329
in National Progressive Front,
1665
Arab states, definition of, 221
Arab Studies Society, 1226
Arab summit conferences. *See* Arab
League summits
Arab theater. *See* Theater, Arabic
Arab Unified Military Command,
1387
Arab unity. *See* Pan-Arabism
Arab Woman and the Palestine Problem, The
(Mognnam), 1557

Arab Women's Association of Palestine (AWA), **267–268**
Arab Women's Executive Committee and, 268
Mogannam (Matiel) in, 1557
Arab Women's Conference (1944)
Abd al-Hadi (Tarab) at, 13
Shihabi (Zlikha al-) at, 2052
Arab Women's Congress (Palestine),
268
1929 meeting of, 268
Arab Women's Council, 1975
Arab Women's Development Society
(AWDS), 893
Arab Women's Executive Committee
(AWE) (Palestine), **268**
Abd al-Hadi (Tarab) in, 13
Khalidi (Wahida al-) in, 268,
1296
Mogannam (Matiel) in, 1557
Shihabi (Zlikha al-) in, 2051
Arab Women's Federation, 894
Arab Women's Forum. *See* AISHA
Arab Women's Network, Women's
Studies Center in, 2363
Arab Women's Solidarity Association
International (AWSA),
268–269
magazine published by, 1706
Saadawi (Nawal al-) in, 894,
1950
Arab Women's Summit, 1902
Arab Women's Union, 267
Nassar (Sadhij) in, 1648
Shihabi (Zlikha al-) in, 2051
Arab Women Writers, 805
Arafa, Muhammad ibn, 2427
Arafat Daily (Bitton), 483
Arafat, Yasir, **269–272**, *270*, *813*,
1784, *1861*
Abbas (Mahmud) under
as political strategist, 6
power struggle between, 7, 814,
997, 1900
as prime minister, 7
and Albright (Madeleine), *2291*
in Algeria, training for, 270
in Aqsa Intifada, 219, 272, 1727
in Arab–Israel War (1948), 269
in Arab–Israel War (1982),
270–271
Asad (Hafiz al-) in conflict with,
413
assassination of, attempted, by
PFLP–GC, 1842
authoritarian rule of, 1785

Avnery (Uri) meeting with, 340,
1187
Barghuthi (Marwan) in conflict
with, 402
Bush (George W.) refusing to deal
with, 549
at Camp David Summit (2000),
561–563, 606, 1775
blame attributed to, 562, 1168
offer rejected by, 399, 1727
clothing of, *kaffiya* in, 610
coalition building by, 271, 1774
Dahlan (Muhammad) and, power
struggle between, 661
daughter of, 272
decline in power of, 270, 271
education of, 269, 270
in Egypt, as youth, 269
Egyptian intelligence meetings
with, *1103*
engineering firm of, 270
in exile, 814
in al-Fatah, 270, 813, 814, 1773
vs. Habash (George), 962
Habib (Philip) meeting with, 1975
Hasan (Hani al-) and, 997
Hasan (Khalid al-) and, 998
Hawatma (Nayif) opposition to,
1009
headquarters of, moves of, 270, 271
Husayni (Abd al-Qadir al-) aided
by, 269
Hussein ibn Talal relations with,
1063
signing agreement with (1970),
2157
in Intifada (1987–1991), 271
Islamic Jihad and, 272, 1155
Israeli peace movement meetings
with, Peled (Mattityahu) in,
1812
Israeli rejection of, 1169
Israel recognized by, 271, 1725
in Jericho, 272, 1775
Jordanian peace accord with, 1247
and Karama, Battle of (1968),
1271
Khalaf (Salah) work with, 270,
1292
Khalil (Samiha Salama) run
against (1996), 1297
in Lebanese Civil War
(1975–1990), 270
in Muslim Brotherhood, 269, 272
Nobel Peace Prize to, *1817*
in Oslo Accords (1993), 271,
1725–1726
signing of, 271, 606, *1726*
terrorism renounced by, 219

Baghdad (Iraq) *(continued)*
  Jewish community in, 1023
  Jewish quarter of, in works by
    Michael (Sami), 1522
  location of, 359, 360
  Mamluk rulers of, 1478–1479
  marketplace in, *361*
  modern, 361–362
  origin of name of, 359
  under Ottoman rule, 360
    administration of, 173
    Midhat Paşa and, 1525
  under Persian rule, 360
  population of, 360, 361, 1131,
    1843
  as trade center, 360
  UN headquarters in, attack on
    (2003), 2283
  U.S. bombing of (1991), 362, *950*
  U.S. capture of (2003), 2325
  U.S. occupation of, 1070
  Women's Museum in, 898
  in World War I, 2367
  in World War II, 1968
Baghdad–Basra railroad, 533–534
Baghdad–Berlin railway. *See*
  Berlin–Baghdad Railway
Baghdad Club, 80
Baghdad–Damascus caravan, 2205
Baghdad Group for Modern Art,
  1978
Baghdadi, Abd al-Latif al-, **362–363**
  as vice president of UAR, 2273
Baghdad Law College
  Bazzaz (Abd al-Rahman al-) at,
    421
  Sharif (Aziz) at, 2037
Baghdad Military College, 1953
Baghdad Pact (1955), **363**, 826,
  1693, 1942
  Iran in, 363, 519, 1693
    Ala (Hoseyn) representing,
      100–101
  Iraq in, 363, 519, 1693
    under Qasim (Abd al-Karim),
      1872, 1969
    Sa'id (Nuri al-) supporting,
      363, 1969
    withdrawal of, 363, 573, 1133
  Jordan in, 1470, 1471
    refusing membership, 363
  Lebanon refusing membership to,
    363
  MEDO aspects included in, 1523,
    1693
  member states of, 363, 519
  opposition to, 363, 519

Pakistan in, 363, 519, 1693
  protests against, 1925
  renaming of (*See* Central Treaty
    Organization)
  Syria refusing membership to,
    363, 373
  Turkey in, 1693
    support for, 363, 519, 696
  U.S. support for, 2291
    Dulles (John Foster) in, 733
Baghdad Railway, Lansdowne (Lord)
  supporting, 1374
Baghdad Railway Company, 464
Baghdad Times (newspaper), 2088
Baghdad University, **364**, 1551–1552
Bagram (Afghanistan), U.S. military
  base in, 67
Baha al-Din al-Samuqi, 727, 728
Baha'i faith, **364–366**, *365*
  Abdu'l-Baha as leader of, 365
  Browne (Edward Granville) inter-
    ested in, 540
  on education, 365
  in Egypt, 365
  headquarters of, 365
  holy place for, *365*
  in Iran, 364, 365, 1548
  in Iraq, 365
  in Libya, 365
  persecution of
    by Islamic Republic of Iran, 365
    by Pahlavi regime, 365
    by Shi'ites, 365
  principles of, 364–365
  Rabbani (Shoghi Effendi) as leader
    of, 365
  stemming from Babi movement,
    356, 364
  on women, 365
Ba-Halomi (Tchernichovsky), 2168
Baharina, **366**
Bahariya, **366**
Bahar, Malek al-Shoara, 1757
Bahar, Mohammad Taqi, **366–367**,
  1436
  on universal male suffrage, 1144
Baha'ullah, Hosayn Ali
  and Babis, 364
  Baha'i faith founded by, 364
  beliefs of, 364–365
  in exile, 356, 364
Bahçeli, Devlet, in Nationalist Ac-
  tion Party, 1661
Bahithat (Lebanon), Moghaziel
  (Laure) in, 1557
Bahithat (publication), 367

Bahithat al-Badiya. *See* Nassif, Malak
  Hifni
Bahithat al-Lubnaniyyat al-, **367**
Bahonar, Mohammad Javad, bomb-
  ing against, 1119
Ba-Horef (Brenner), 507
Bahrain, *367*, **367–370**, *370. See also
  specific cities, organizations, people,
  and regions*
  Al Khalifa family in, 149–150,
    367–368, 369
  Arabian Mission in, 231
  Arab National Movement in, 262
  area of, 367
  Baharina in, 366
  banking in, 390, *393*
  border with Qatar, dispute over,
    370–371, 1877
  British military withdrawal from,
    521
  British protectorate in, 368
    Al Khalifa family in, 149–150
    Belgrave (Charles Dalrymple) as
      advisor in, 436
    nationalist opposition to, 368,
      371
    Order in Council establishing,
      372
    Zubara dispute, 370
  British treaties with, 149, 531, 614
  Catholics in, 1931
  cities of, 342, 1607
    capital, 367, 1479
  clothing in, women's, *610*
  constitution of (1973), 368–369
    revision of, 150
  defense costs as percentage of
    GNP or GDP, *1530*
  dhows in, 705
  Dilmun society in, 708
  economy of, 752, *753*
  education in, 436, 759
  elections in (2002), 370
  government of, 368–369
  in Gulf Cooperation Council, 949
  in Gulf Crisis (1990–1991), *950*
  higher education in, 1292
  human rights in, 1048
  independence of, 368, 371, 2219
    United Nations in, 2279
  Iranian Revolution (1979) sup-
    ported by, 368
  Islamic opposition movement in,
    369–370
  islands of, 2071, 2263
  labor unions illegal in, 368, 1358
  in League of Arab States, 1387,
    1388

Ben Saleh, Mohammad al-Hadi, 1429

Ben Seddiq, Mahjoub, **453**
imprisonment of, 453
in Union Marocaine du Travail, 453, 2266
in Union Nationale des Forces Populaires, 453, 1197, 2266, 2267

Ben Shaikh, Abdel Qader, 1429

Ben Simeon, Raphael Aaron, **453–454**

Bentwich, Norman, **454**, 2124

Benvenisti, Meron, **454**
Kollek (Teddy) criticized by, 1331

"Benvenisti Prognosis," 454

Ben Yahia, Habib, 440

Benyahia, Mohamed, 2217
death of, Ibrahimi (Ahmed Taleb) after, 1076

Ben-Yehuda, Eliezer, 427, **454–455**
and Hebrew revival, 1018
Uganda Project supported by, 2257

Ben Yizhak, Avraham, 1431

Ben Yousouf, Salah, **455–456**
assassination of, 455, 501
Ben Salah (Ahmed) and, 452
and beylicate, abolition of, 185
Bourguiba (Habib) and, 455, 501
exile in Egypt, 634
as justice minister, 455
in Neo-Destour Party, 455, 634

Ben-Zvi Institute, 457

Ben-Zvi, Rahel Yanait, **456**
as founder of Naʿamat, **1629**
and Ha-Shomer, 1001

Ben-Zvi, Yael, *as contributor*, 1105–1106

Ben-Zvi, Yizhak, **456–457**, *457*
Ben-Gurion (David) friendship, 446, 456, 457
in Jewish Legion, 457, 1230, 1281
presidency of, 457
in Vaʿad Leʾumi, 457, 2307
wife of, 456

Berats, 565

Berber(s), **457–463**, *458, 461, 462*, 1963–1964
agriculture of, 459
in Algeria, 121–122, 458, 459, 463–464 (*See also* Kabylia)
Ait Ahmed (Hocine) as leader of, 95
Algiers, 122, 139
censorship of, 1261

identity movement among, 192
in Mouvement pour le Triomphe des Libertés Démocratiques (MTLD), 969
in Mzab region, 1627
number of, 121
political parties supported by, 134
revolt by (1963), 95
Tamazight language of, 121–122, 638, 1261
youth killed in detention (2001), 96, 274, 638
art of, 459
in Atlas Mountains, 335, 336
rebellion against French protectorate, 1570
Braber, 458
Chawia, 458, 459
Chleuch, 458
on Djerba island, 717
Djerbi, 459
in Egypt, 458, 2071
emigration of, for work, 459
invading Iberian Peninsula, 2084
Jmaʾa tribal councils of, 1237
Kabyles, 458, 459
in Libya, 458
in Mauritania, 458–459
as minorities or subdominant group, 1549
in Morocco, 458, 459, 463, 487, 1567, 1569
under French protectorate, 1570
in Mouvement Populaire (MP), 1588–1589
under Muhammad VI, 1601–1602
music of, 193
Mzabi, 459
and nomadism, 459, *462*
origin of term, 457
religion of, 460
repression of, 463–464, 486 (*See also* Berber Spring; Black Spring)
sedentary, 459
social organization of, 459–460
Sousi, 459
Tuareg, 458, 459, *462*
in Tunisia, 458, 2226, 2227–2228
in Western Sahara, 2342
women, *458*, 463

Berber culture, 806, 1426
censorship of, in Algeria, 1261
official Moroccan recognition of, 1601–1602

Berber Dahir, **463**
Fasi (Allal al-) protesting against, 812
Free School campaign against, Arslan (Shakib) influence on, 307–308
Moroccan nationalism after, 1570, 1598

Berber festivals, *458, 461*

Berber languages, 457, 458, 460–463, 1567
alphabet of, 461–462
vs. Arabic
Arabization policies on, 255, 256
Kateb (Yacine) on, 1280
borrowing from Arabic language, 463
characteristics of, 460–461
dialects of
in Algeria, 458, 1422, 2253
in Morocco, 458, 2166–2167
Moroccan recognition of, official, 1601–1602
repression of, 463–464
Siwan dialect as, 2071
survival of, 463

Berber literature, 192, 462, 464, 1426

Berber music, 462

Berber Spring (1980) (Algeria), **463–464**
ban on Berber poetry and, 464
National Charter (1976) and, 444
Sadi (Said) in, 1959
start of, in Tizi-Ouzou, 1261
2001 commemoration of (*See* Black Spring)

Berdyczewski, Micah Joseph, 1430

Bergen-Belsen concentration camp, 1041

Berger, Elmer, in American Council for Judaism, 176

Berger, Joseph, 626

Berger, Morrow, 539

Bergman, Elizabeth M., *as contributor*, 234–235

Bergman, Samuel Hugo, 1461

Berg, Nancy, *as contributor*, 1521–1522, 1977–1978

Berihah. *See* Brichah

Berk, Ilhan, 1440

Berkowitz, Yizhak, **464**

Berlin–Baghdad Railway, **464–465**, 532–533
in Ankara, 207

construction of, 464–465
Deutsche Bank in, 464, 533, 904
international controversy over,
    2206
Potsdam Convention on (1911),
    1851
Berlin Conference (1885), 2085
Berlin, Congress of (1878), **465,**
    528
    Armenian delegation at, 2311
        Khrimian (Mkrtich) in, 1314
    Austro-Hungarian delegation at,
        339
    Ottoman Empire in, British sup-
        port for, 27
    San Stefano Treaty revised at, 27,
        654, 1989, 2311
Berlin Memorandum, 382
Berlin, Treaty of (1878), **465**
    on Armenians, 299, 2311
    and Austria-Hungary, 383, 465,
        528, 1989
    and Bosnia-Herzegovina, 383,
        1989
    cessions by Ottoman Empire in,
        26–27, 382–383, 465, 528,
        1989
    and Germany, 465, 528, 903
    and Greater Bulgaria, 382–383,
        1989
    and Montenegro, 383, 1989
    and Romania, 1989
    and Russian territories, 383, 465,
        528, 1989
    and Serbia, 383, 1989
Bernadotte, Folke, **465–466,** 2275
    in Arab–Israel War (1948), 2274
        at King David Hotel, 1324
    assassination of, 466, 1250, 1443,
        2026, 2274, 2385
    Bunche (Ralph J.) as assistant to,
        543
    Cattan (Henry) and, 570
Bernadotte Plan for Arab–Israeli set-
    tlement, 466
Bernikho-Canin, Rhimou, *as contribu-
    tor,* 975
Berque, Jacques, 2035
Berrada, Hamid, in Union Nationale
    des Etudiants Marocains,
    2266
Berrada, Mohammed, **466–467**
Berriane (Algeria), 1627
Berri, Nabi, **467–468**
    in AMAL movement, 174, 467,
        1037, 1647
    education of, 467

electoral success of, 467
vs. Husayni (Husayn al-), 1055
in parliament, 174
in "salvation committee," 1647
Besht (Ba'al Shem Tov), 1002
Bessarabia, Russian-Ottoman wars
    and, 1945
Beta Israel. *See* Ethiopian Jews
Bet al-Hakham family, 1012
Betar (youth movement), 1209
    Begin (Menachem) in, 424
    in Poland
        leaders of, 2437
        Yellin-Mor (Natan) in, 2384
    and revisionist Zionism, 2412,
        2437
Bet Hannan (Sephardic settlement),
    2364
Bet ha-Tefutsot (Tel Aviv), 928
Bethlehem (West Bank), **468,** *2339,*
    2340
    during Arab–Israel War (1948),
        468
    under British mandate, 468
    under Israeli control, 468
    Jordan annexing, 468
    location of, 468
    under Ottoman rule, 468
    pilgrims in, *1759*
    population of, 468
    sacred sites in, 468
Betts, Robert, *as contributor,* 726–730
Between Two Wars (Bitton), 483
Bet Zilkha (seminary), 2079
Beur (Sebbar), 2007
Beurs, 1427
Beverages, alcoholic, 109–110
Beverly Hills (Egypt), 1995
Bevin–Bidault agreement (1945),
    468
Bevin, Ernest, **468–469**
    and Anglo–American Committee
        of Inquiry, 198
        Crossman (Richard) in, 650
    as foreign secretary, 468–469,
        518, 647, 842
    Middle Eastern policy conducted
        by, 338
Bevin–Sforza Plan (1949), 468,
    469
Bevin–Sidqi agreement (1946), 468
Bewicke, Hilda, 286
Bey, 2622
Beyath, Yahya Kemal, 1439
Bey, Boghos. *See* Yusufian, Boghos

Beyoğlu, 864
Beyoğlu Protocol (1861), **469**
Beyzai, Bahram, 2186
Bezalel Academy of Arts and Design,
    469–470
Bezalel Museum, 470
BG militia (Lebanon), 1253
Bialik, Hayyim Nahman, **470,** 1164,
    1430–1431
    as Ahad Ha'Am's disciple, 470
    Alterman (Natan) compared with,
        171
    education of, 470
    Shlonsky (Avraham) rivalry, 2058
Bibby, Geoffrey, 708
Bible
    archaeological research on,
        275–276, 277–278
        Palestine Exploration Fund and,
            1771–1772
    Christian, 589
    Hebrew
        Dead Sea Scrolls and, 685
        kosher in, 1335
    Holy Land of, Palestine as, 1758
    Mount Ararat in, 274
    Tomb of the Patriarchs in, 1807
Biblical Hebrew (BH), 1017
Bibliotheca Alexandria, *117, 118*
Bibliothèque Nationale (Paris), Is-
    lamic coin collection of, 1702
Bicycle Run, The (Iranian film), 1473
Bid'a (religious innovation), muwah-
    hidun rejection of, 1625
Bidaya al-Mujtahid wa Nihaya al-Muqtasid
    (Hafid' al-), 1476
Bidonvilles, **470–471**
    in Casablanca, 569
    in Tripoli, 2216
Bidun, in Kuwait, 1347
Bieberstein, Marschall von, 904
Biggeh (Egypt), 1832
Bihayri, Ni'mat al-, 1924–1925,
    1994
Bilad, al- (newspaper), 1679
Bilad al-Sham. *See* Greater Syria
Bilad al-siba (lands of dissidence),
    Western Sahara as, 2343
"Biladi, Biladi" (Darwish), 675
Bilharzia. *See* Schistosomiasis
Bilhayr, Abd al-Nabi, **471**
Bilkent University, **472,** 491
Billah, Muhammad al-Baqi, 2114
Billets (Gebeyli), 872

Biltmore Program (1942), **472–473**

BILU. *See* Aliyah

Binationalism, **473**
 Anglo–American Committee of
  Inquiry on, 473
 Kalvaryski (Chaim Margaliut-)
  support for, 473, 1265

Bin Ayad, Mahmud, 389

Bin Diyaf, Muhsen, **474**

Bin Ladin, Osama, 474, **474–475**
 in Afghanistan, 474–475
 childhood of, 474
 in *Cole* attack (2000), 613
 education of, 474, 1865
 on Gulf Crisis, 475
 in Pakistan, 474
 in al-Qaʿida, 474–475,
  1865–1866
 Saudi support for, 164, 474
 and September 11th attacks, 475,
  2155, 2178
 in Sudan, 475
 Taliban and, 61, 475, 1712, 1865,
  2155
 U.S. attempts to capture, 1866
 U.S. support for (1980s), 2178
 wanted poster for, 2177

Bint, 2622

Bint al-Shati, **475–476**, 892

Binyamina (Israeli settlement), 1938

Biqa Valley (Lebanon), **476**, 901,
 2422

Bira, al- (Palestine), 893

Biʾr al-Qamh (Salim), 1978

Birds of Shade (Seri), 2012

Biret, Idil, **476–477**

"Bir içim su" (Tevfik Fikret), 2180

Birnbaum, Nathan, 2432

Birth control, **477–480**, 1510–1511
 advocates of, 477
 controversy over, 477
 cultural, political, and religious
  opposition to, 478–480
 manipulating population growth
  with, 477–478
 methods of, 480
 use of term, 478–479

Birth-control pills, 480

Birth of Israel, The: Myths and Realities (Flapan), 835

Birth rates, 1508

Bir Zeit University, **481**, 1901
 Aqqad (Umar Abd al-Fattah al-)
  support for, 219
 Barghuthi (Marwan) at, 402

gender studies at, 896
 Institute of Women's Studies
  (IWS) at, 1100–1101
 Matzpen beginnings at, 1500
 Nasir (Hanna) as founder of, 1646
 Nusayba (Sari) at, 1705

Bishara, Abdullah, **481**

Bishara, Azmi, in election of 2003,
 1788

Bishara, Suha, **481**

Bisharin clan, 433

Bishop, Dale L., *as contributor*,
 589–593

Bisitun (Iran), **481–482**

Bismarck, Otto von, at Berlin Congress, 465, 528, 903

Bistami, Abu Yazid al-, 2113

Bitar, Abd al-Razzaq al-, and Arab
 nationalism, 261

Bitar, Midhat al-, in Baʿth party, 69

Bitar, Salah al-Din al-, **482**
 Aflaq (Michel) and, 68–69, 482
 al-Tali published by, 68
 Arsuzi (Zaki al-) and, 308
 assassination of, 482
 in Baʿth party, 69, 412, 482
 in coup (1963), 482
 education of, 482
 in exile, 482
 as foreign minister, 482
 government of
  Atasi (Jamal al-) in, 329
  Hafiz (Amin al-) in, 971
 as prime minister, 482

Bitat, Rabah, **482–483**
 Ben Bella (Ahmed) and, 483
 under Bendjedid (Chadli), 483
 under Boumédienne (Houari),
  483
 in Comité Révolutionnaire d'Unité et d'Action, 137, 620
 French skyjacking of, 1309
 in Front de Libération Nationale,
  482

Bittari, Zoubida, **483**

Bitton, Simone, **483**

Bizerte (Tunisia), **483–484**, 2225

Bizerte Crisis (1961), **484–485**,
 501

Bizri, Afif al-, 2133

Blackboards, The (Iranian film), 1473

Black Box (Oz), 1748

Black Friday (Iran)
 casualties of, 1126
 public response following, 1126

Black, Ian, *as contributor*, 992,
 1322, 1409–1410, 1838,
 2055–2056, 2056–2057

Black Jews, in Dimona (Israel), Kahane (Meir) on, 1263

Black olives, *837*, 840

Black Panthers, 483, **485**
 protests in Israel, 1500

Black Saturday, Jumayyil (Bashir) in,
 1253

Black Sea, **485**, 2236
 area of, 485
 climate of, 605
 Ottoman access to, 485, 1446,
  2093–2094
 Russian access to, 739–740
  Kuçuk Kaynara Treaty (1774)
   and, 485, 739, 2094–2095
  London Treaty (1871) on, 1446
  Paris Peace (1856) on, 1446
  and relations with Ottoman Empire, 1945
  Straits Convention (1841) on,
   2092–2093, 2095
 Turkish control of, 485, 2095
 waterway joining Aegean Sea and
  (*See* Straits, Turkish)

Black September (1970), **485–486**,
 1063, 1245
 airplane hijackings by, 2176
 establishment of, 485
 hostages at Saudi embassy in Sudan by, 486
 Israeli athletes killed at Munich
  Olympics by, 485, 2176
 Khalaf (Salah) role in, 485,
  1292
 Majali (Habis) in, 1470
 name of, 485
 parties dissolved after, 1257
 Salama (Ali Hasan) in, 485
 Tall (Wasfi al-) assassinated by,
  485, 2157
 trigger for, 967

Black slaves, 2073, 2074

Black Spring (2001) (Algeria), 464,
 486
 Benflis (Ali) and, 445
 Bouteflika (Abdelaziz) and, 504
 casualties of, 274
 causes of, 1261
 Coordination des Arches created
  during, 274, 486, 638

Black Stone, 1259

Black Thursday (1978), **486–487**
 Union Générale des Travailleurs
  Tunisiens in, 41, 2265

Cemal Paşa, Ahmet *(continued)*
pan-Turkism of, 1800–1801
Syria under, 571–572, 2366, 2368
Damascus, 663
petition for independence of, 2202
Talat (Mehmet) and, 2153
in World War I, 905, 2366–2367, 2368

Cem, Cemil, 305

Censorship
in Algeria, of Berber culture, 1261
during conflicts, on all communications, 624–625
of education, 759, 761
in Egypt
of books, 1296
of Munif's (Abdel Rahman) books, 1611
of film industry, 98–99
in Iran, 1683
of education, 761
of film industry, 832
of literature, 1435, 1436–1437, 1803
of press, 1120, 1121, 1299
of theater, 2186
in Israel, 1683, 1897
in Ottoman Empire, 28
in Saudi Arabia, of books, 1611
in Turkey, of film industry, 832

Census. *See* Population

Center for Arab Women for Training and Research, 894

Center for Community Action, 489

Center for Community Medicine (Tunisia), 1496

Center for Human Rights and Public Policy (CHRPP), 489

Center for Islamic Study and Publication, 2036

Center for Jewish Identity, 489

Center for Muslim–Christian Encounter, 1953

Center for Senior Services, 489

Center for the Global South, Maksoud (Clovis) in, 1474

Center for Women's Participation (Iran), 1123

Center for Women's Studies and Research (Iran), 745

CENTO. *See* Central Treaty Organization

Central Bank of Tunisia, Nouira (Hedi) as head of, 1693

Central Committee of the Free Officers (Iraq), 1872

Central Conference of American Rabbis (CCAR), political Zionism affirmed by, opposition to, 176

Central Dialects, 1124

Central Intelligence Agency (CIA), 572–573
in Chilean coup, 1327
communist parties destroyed by, 627
in Egyptian–Israeli peace negotiations, 157, 573
failures of, 573
foreign intelligence organizations influenced by, 1102
functions of, 572
in Iranian coup (1953), 572, 1118, 1752
Iraqi National Congress funding from, 1137
KGB compared to, 1290
Mossad relations with, 1578
operations of, 572–573
organizational structure of, 572
Roosevelt (Kermit) in, 1937

Central Relief Committee, Joint Distribution Committee established by, 1239

Central Treaty Organization (CENTO), 363, 573–574. *See also* Baghdad Pact
Iran in, impact on country infrastructure, 2420
members of, 573

Central University (Madrid), 1951

Centre de Recherches, d'Études, de Documentation et d'Information sur la Femme (CREDIF) (Tunisia), 574

Centre for Global Energy Studies, 2378

Centre National de la Recherche Scientifique (Paris), 492

Century Corporation, 2063

Ceramics, 574–575

Cercle des représailles, le (Kateb), 1280

Ceride-i Havadis (newspaper), 1684
Churchill (William) at, 595
establishment of, 595

Ceriha (Mehmet Rauf), 1513

Çerkes Hasan incident (1876), 575

CESA. *See* Comité Juif Algérien d'Études Sociales

Ceuta (Spanish possession), 575–576, 1516, 1567, 2085

Cevdet, Abdullah, 576–577
Nizamiye courts organized by, 1690
in Ottoman Union Society, 622

Cevdet, Ahmet, 577–578
and Darülfünün university, 672
daughter of, Aliyer (Fatimah) as, 148
drafting Land Code of 1858, 1367
legal career of, 577–578
Osmanh published by, 2409

Ceylon, at Bandung Conference, 387

Ceyrekgil, Hasanzade Ibrahim, 872

CFP. *See* Compagnie Française des Pétroles

CFPA. *See* Cairo Family Planning Association

Chaabani, Mohammed, 442

Chabouti, Abdelkader, 919

Chad
Libyan border with, Aozou Strip in, 216
Libyan invasion of, CIA support for, 572

Chadirchi, Kamil, 1210
in Ahali group, 80–81
coup opposed by (1936), 80
as National Democratic Party leader, 1654–1655

Chador, 611

Chaghatai, descendants of, 1015

Chahine, Yusef, 497, 583, 832, 833

Chalabi, Ahmad, 578
exile of, 578
on Iraqi Governing Council, 2325–2326
in Iraqi National Congress, 578, 1137
return to Iraq, 578

Chalabi, Fadhil al-, 1720

Chalcedon, Council of (451), 589, 639

Chalcraft, John T., *as contributor*, 1035–1037

Chaldaean Catholic church, 592–593

Chalhoub, Michel. *See* Sharif, Omar

Challe, Maurice, 579
in Organisation Armée Secrète, 1715
and Sèvres Protocol (1956), 2109

Challe Plan, 579

Chamberlain, Neville, Eden (Anthony) in conflict with, 755

Chambi, Mount (Tunisia), 2225

Chamchian, Mikayel, 303, **579**

Chamedan (Alavi), 104

Chamoun, Camille, *580*, **580–581**
 attempt at monopolizing fishing in Lebanon, 1391
 as civil war (1958) catalyst, 1389–1391, 1399
 as Eisenhower Doctine (1957) advocate, 773, 1390
 election of, 580
 foreign policy of, 580
 government of
  Chehab (Khalid) in, 585
  Shader (Joseph) in, 2018
 in al-Hilf al-Thulathi, 1254
 Hilu (Charles) and, 1031
 Jumblatt (Kamal) opposing, 1255
 Karame (Rashid) opposing, 1271
 Khuri (Bishara al-) opposed by, 580, 1315
 in Lebanese Front, 1395
 Meushi (Paul Peter) opposing, 1520
 vs. al-Najjada, 977
 Nasser (Gamal Abdel) opposed by, 1399
 National Liberal Party of, 1661
 opposition to, 580–581
  Chehab (Fu'ad) response to, 585
 regime of, 1389–1391, 1399
 Salam (Sa'ib) opposing, 1975
 Sulh (Sami al-) supporting, 2119
 Syrian Social Nationalist Party supporting, 2137
 Taqla (Philippe) opposing, 2165
 Tigers militia of, in Lebanese Forces, 1394
 U.S. assistance to, 2291

Chamoun, Dany, **581**
 assassination of, 581, 871, 1661
 as leader of National Liberal Party, 1661

Chamoun, Jean Khalil, 1500

"Champagne spy." *See* Lotz, Wolfgang

Champollion-Figeac, Jacques-Joseph, 582

Champollion, Jean-François, 275, 492, **581–582**

Chamran, Mostafa, **582**
 Kharrazi (Kamal) and, 1300
 Khomeini (Ruhollah) supported by, 1311
 Qotbzadeh (Sadeq) and, 582, 1881

Chanak crisis (1922), 513, 1441–1442

Chancellor, John, 1402
 as high commissioner of Palestine, 1025

Chande, Abdin, *as contributor*, 1870

Chants anciens des femmes au Maroc (al-Fasi), 812

Chaouch, Ali, 2232

Chaouias, Berber language of, 122

Chapelet d'ambre, Le (Sefrioui), 2008

Characteristics of the Path Facing the Working Woman (report), 40

Charef, Mehdi, 1427

Charents, Yeghishe, 303

"Charge of the Light Brigade, The" (Tennyson), 379

Charitable organizations
 in Egypt, women's role in, 39–40
 in Iraq, for women, 2361–2362
 in United States, women's, 966

Charity. *See also* Philanthropy
 habous as, 964–965

Charles V (king of Spain), 2084

Charles X (king of France), 835

Charrad, Mounira M., *as contributor*, 2230–2231

Charter for National Action (Egypt), 1650

Châtillon, Renauld de, 1270

Chauvel, Harry, 510

Chawia, 458, 459

Chawqi Lycée, 497

Chazan, Naomi, **582**

Chebbi, Nejib, 2232

Chechens, *vs.* Circassians, in Jordan, 600

Checkbook diplomacy, in Kuwait, 1350–1351

Chédid, Andrée, **582–583**

Chédid, Louis, 582

Chefs historiques, 443, 451

Chehab, Bashir, **583–584**
 palace at Bayt al-Din, *583*

Chehab family, **584**
 Ahmad al-Jazzar and, 83, 583–584

Chehab, Fu'ad, **584–585**
 army under, 584
 Chamoun (Camille) opposing, 581
 domestic policies of, 585
 Eddé (Raymond) in conflict with, 754

election to presidency, 585, 1391
 government of, Karame (Rashid) in, 1271
 Hamadi (Sabri) and, 981
 al-Hilf al-Thulathi opposing, 581, 1254
 Hilu (Charles) and, 1031
 Jumayyil (Pierre) opposing, 1254
 as president, 1399
 as prime minister, appointment of, 584–585
 Salam (Sa'ib) criticizing, 1975
 Sarkis (Ilyas) under, 1991
 Taqla (Philippe) under, 2165

Chehabi dynasty, 1398
 Druze-Maronite conflict over, 1491

Chehabism, 585, 1399

Chehab, Khalid, **585–586**
 as prime minister, 585

Chelkowski, Peter, *as contributor*, 1605–1607

Chelow, 837

Chemical industry, 1483

Chemical weapons, 305
 in Iran, 1535
 in Iran–Iraq War, 1067, 1128, 1129, 1538
 in Iraq, 1535
 UN inspections for, 1539

Chemin des ordalies, Le (Laabi), 1355

Chemins qui montent, Les (Feraoun), 823

Cheney, Richard (Dick), in Gulf War (1990–1991), 2324

Chenik, Muhammad, **586**

Cherati, Ikhlef, 919

Cherbourg (France), Mossad operation in (1969), 1578–1579

Chercheurs d'os, les (Djaout), 716

Chérif, Hachemi, in Parti de l'Avant-Garde Socialiste, 1803

Cherifi, Hanifa, 289

Cherkes. *See* Circassians

Cheshmahayesh (Alavi), 104

Chevron Oil Company, 2099–2100

Chich Khan (film), 376

Chickpeas, 838, 839

Chicly, Shemama, 832

Chided, Andre, 2184

Chikhi, Omar, 918

Child custody. *See* Custody

Child labor, in Egypt, 1358

Children
 in cotton industry, *644*

Children *(continued)*
  health care for, 1509–1510
  importance in marriage and family, 1494
  in Iraq, impact of sanctions on, 1136
  preference for girls or boys, 1494
  as slaves, 2072
Children of Divorce (film), 1526
Children of Fire (film), 1500
Children of Gebalawi (Mahfuz), 1464
Children of Shatila (film), 1500
Children of the Ghetto (Zangwill), 2424
Child survival, 1509–1510
Chile, coup in, CIA role in, 1327
Chimères, Les (Nerval), 1675
China, **586–587**
  arms proliferation by, 586
  arms sales by, 750
    to Saudi Arabia, 1535
  Iraqi relations with, 586, 587
  Israeli relations with, 586–587
    Namir (Orah) and, 1641
  Middle East policy of, 586–587
  Naqshbandi in, 1642–1643
  Palestinian relations with, Wazir (Khalil al-) and, 2335
  Saudi relations with, 586, 587
  silk from, 2066
  U.S. relations with, Kissinger (Henry) in, 1327
  U.S. war in Iraq opposed by (2003), 2324
Chinese Gordon. *See* Gordon, Charles
Chirac, Jacques, *504*, 505
  Stasi Commission of, Arkoun (Mohammed) in, 289
Chirol, Valentine, Middle East designation and term popularized by, 1522
Chishti, Mu'in al-Din, 2113
Chishtiyya (Sufi order), 2113
Chleuh language, 1567
Chleuh people, 458
Choksy, Jamsheed K., *as contributor,* 2440–2442
Cholera, 711–712, 1508
  in Iraq, 714
  and population growth, 1843, 1845
"Cholera" (Iraqi poem), 1475
Chorasmian language, 1125
Chou En-Lai, 986
Chouf Le Look (Bitton), 483

Chraibi, Driss, **588,** 1423, 1427
  women in novels of, 588, 2376
Chrakian, Artin, **588–589**
  in educational reform, 588–589
  education of, 588
    Yusufian (Boghos) and, 2415
Chrakian, Khosrov, 588
Chrakian, Sukias, 588
Christ. *See* Jesus
Christian Democratic Union (Germany), Adenauer (Konrad) in, 43
Christianity. *See also specific denominations*
  antisemitism and, 211–212
  on birth control, 478, 479
  and education for women, 882–883
  Holy Land in, 1043
  in imperialism, 1089
  Jerusalem in, 1222
  messianism in, 1519
  in Ottoman Empire, 589–590, 1731
  Palestine in, 1758
  Sabbath in, 1954
  secular nationalism and, 590
  spread of, 589–590
  theology of, 589
Christian missions, schools of, 1550–1552
Christian–Muslim alliance, in Lebanon, 2116, 2118
Christians, **589–593**
  in Algeria, 122
  Arab
    in Jordan, 1242
    Protestant missionary work with, 1854
  in Arab nationalism, 1659
  in Barbary wars, fighting corsairs, 401
  in Bethlehem, 468
  in Damascus affair (1840), 664–665
  in Egypt, 1971 (*See also* Copts)
  emigration of, 590
  in Gaza Strip, 870
  in guilds, 947
  in Iran, 1548
  in Iraq, 738
  in Israel, 1163, *1164*
  in Lebanon (*See also* Maronites)
    in crises of 1840s, 1393–1394
    Lebanese Front of, 1395
    militias of, 1394
    Orthodox, 738
  as Levantines, 1405–1406

  as minorities or subdominant groups, 1548
  in nationalist movement, 1549
  number in Middle East, 590
  Orthodox
    number of, 738
    in Ottoman Empire, 738
  in Ottoman Empire
    and Balkan crises, 382–383
    and Bulgarian Horrors, 543
    millet system of, 1543–1545
    Orthodox, 738
  in Sudan, 523, 2099
  in Syria, 738, 2130
  in Tunisia, 2226
  women, religious rituals of, 2360
Christian Union Congregational Church in New Jersey, 488
Christina, Rachel, *as contributor,* 879–884, 1266
Christison, Kathleen M., *as contributor,* 572–573
Chronicle of a Disappearance (film), 833
Chroniques de la citadelle d'exil (Laabi), 1355
CHRPP. *See* Center for Human Rights and Public Policy
Chrysalide, La (Lemsine), 1403
Chubak, Sadeq, **593–594,** 1435
Churches for Middle East Peace, 1855
Churchill, Alfred, 595
Churchill White Paper (1922), **594,** 2349–2350
  Palestinian Arab Congress and, 1782
  Samuel (Herbert Louis) and, 1983
Churchill, William, **594–595**
  newspaper established by, 1684
Churchill, Winston S., **595–597,** *596*
  on Allied Middle East Command, 153
  at Cairo Conference (1921), 512, 554, 596, 617, 801, 1023, *1088*
  in Colonial Office, 617
  Egyptian policy of, *vs.* Allenby (Edmund Henry), 151
  foreign policy of, 595
  government of
    Attlee (Clement) in, 338
    Eden (Anthony) in, 755
    and Husayni (Amin al-), 1057
    and Jordan, Abdullah I ibn Husein in, 29, 1244

Chehab (Khalid) in, 585
establishment of, 633
Hamadi (Sabri) in, 981
Khuri (Bishara al-) in, 633–634, 1315
Taqla (Philippe) in, 2165
Constitutional Democratic Rally (RCD) (Tunisia), **634–635,** 2231–2232
  Ben Ali (Zayn al-Abidine) in, 439
  Bourguiba (Habib) in, 2231
  breaking away from Destour Party, 2231
  conflict within, 634–635
  foundation of, 2231
  leadership of, 634–635
  seeking control of LTDH, 1416
  size of, 615
Constitutional government, 932
Constitutional Liberty Party (Egypt), Haykal (Muhammad Husayn) and, 1013
Constitutional Revolution (Iran) (1905–1909), **635–637,** 2430
  Adamiyat (Abbasquli) in, 42
  Adamiyat (Fereydun) on, 42
  Akhbari school in, 98
  anjoman (assembly) in, 207
  Babis in, 356
  Baha'is in, 365
  Bakhtiari in, 374
  bast taken during, 411
  Bayat (Mortaza Qoli) in, 416
  bazaar as political base during, 419, 420
  Behbahani (Sayyed Abdollah) in, 2141–2142
  Browne (Edward Granville) supporting, 540
  constitution written during, 636, 1868
  dates of, disagreement over, 636
  Dehkhoda (Ali Akbar) in, 689
  guilds in, 947
  Jangali in, 1216
  journalistic writing by leaders of, 1435
  majles (parliament) formed in, 636, 1471–1472, 1868
  Malkom Khan's *Qanun* and, 1477
  Mossadegh (Mohammad) in, 1580
  Mozaffar al-Din Qajar in, 635–636, 1868
  newspapers and print media after, 1682
  opposed by Mohammad Ali Shar Qajar, 1559
  opposed by Nuri (Fazlollah), 1704

origins of, 635, 1868
political implications of, 1868–1869
protests in, 635–636
Sadr (Muhsin) in, 1960
Shaykhis in, 2047
Shi'ite *ulama* in, 2303
Tabataba'i (Mohammad) as leader of, 2141–2142
Tabriz during, 2144
women in, 891
  impact on, **637**
Construction Crusade. *See* Jehad-e Sazandegi
Constructive socialism, 1362
Containment policy
  Acheson (Dean) associated with, 40
  Carter's (Jimmy) rejection of, 567
Contes Fassis (al-Fassi), 812
Contes Turcs (Boratav), 492
Continental. *See* ConocoPhillips
Contraception, 480. *See also* Birth control
  rates of usage, 1844
Contra rebels (Nicaragua), in Iran–Contra affair, 1123
Convention Against Torture, 1048
Convention on the Elimination of all forms of Discrimination against Women (CEDAW) (1996), 887, 891, 896, 897, 912, 1048, 1396, 2357
Convention on the Rights of the Child (CRC), 1048
Conventions. *See under geographic term associated with the convention or under its popular name*
Conversos, 2084
Cooking, in religious rituals, 2360
Cook, Thomas, 2196
Cooperatives. *See* Agricultural cooperatives
Coordination des Archs (CADC) (Algeria), **638**
  establishment of, events leading to, 274, 486, 638
  platform of, 274, 638
Copeland, Miles, in Israeli–Egyptian peace negotiations, 573
Coptic Catholic Church, 592, 640
  under Mark VIII, 1490
Coptic Community Council
  Cyril V and, 656
  Cyril VI and, 657
  John XIX and, 1239

Coptic Evangelical Church, 640
Coptic language, 640
Coptic Legion, 1490
Coptic monasteries, in Wadi Natrun, 2319
Coptic Museum (Cairo), **638**
Coptic Orthodox Church
  establishment of, 639
  Ethiopic Orthodox Church and, 639, 657
  laity of, enfranchisement of, 656
  in Oriental Orthodox family, 591, 639
  patriarchs of, 656–657, 691, 1239, 2048–2049
  theology of, 639
Copts, **638–642**
  in al-Mansura, 1480–1481
  art of, 640
  definition of, 639
  in Egypt, 763–764, 1971–1972, 2048–2049
  language of, 640
  Milner Mission boycotted by, 1546
  Musa (Salama) on, 1614
  Muslim relations with, 640–642, 658
  Muslim violence against, 641–642, 2049
  in nationalist movement, 640–641, 1549
  in New Wafd, 2321
  New Wafd supported by, 1686
  number of, 638–639
  origin of term, 639
  under Ottoman rule, 1544
  in parliament, 641, 642
  Protestant missions and, 1854
  Saint Mark's Cathedral of, 1971–1972
  in Wafd, 2320
Corcos family, **642–643**
Cordova, 2084
Cordovez, Diego, 2279
Cornwallis, Kinahan, 808
  at Cairo Conference (1921), 554
Corpus Nummorum Saeculorun IX–XI (Tornberg), 1702
Correction Movement (Syria), National Progressive Front established after, 1665
Correction movement (Yemen), 2393
Corsairs, 401, **643**
  Aix-la-Chapelle Treaty (1821) outlawing, 401

Cultural elites, 775

Cultural identity, in art, 313

Cultural imperialism, 1090–1091

Cultural property
 in Armenian genocide, 295
 conflict over, 278–279
 ownership of, 279
 protection of, 278–279

Culture and Imperialism (Said), 1966

Cumali, Necati, 2187

Cumhuriyet (newspaper), 1633, 1685
 Yasar Kemal at, 2381

Cuneiform
 Egyptian, deciphering of, 276
 Persian, 1124

Cunningham, Alan Gordan, as high
 commissioner of Palestine,
 1025

Cuno, Kenneth, 1036, 1207

CUP. *See* Committee for Union and
 Progress

Curiel family, **651**

Curiel, Henry
 assassination of, 651
 communism of, 627, 651

Curtis, Maria F., *as contributor*, 43–44,
 227–228, 434–436,
 438–440, 490, 497–498,
 666–668, 1101–1105,
 1203–1204, 1214–1215,
 1625–1627, 1776–1781,
 1839–1841, 1905–1906,
 1994–1995, 2321–2322

Curzon, George Nathaniel, **651–652**
 Abdullah I ibn Hussein restrained
 by, 512
 as foreign secretary, 652, 842
 political career of, Kitchener (Horatio Herbert) and, 1329

Custody
 in Iran, 891
 personal status laws on, 887
 in Tunisia, 2230

Cyber AWSA, 269

Cyclist, The (Iranian film), 1473

Cyprus, **652–654**. *See also specific cities,
 organizations, people, and regions*
 in Arab–Israel War (1956), 245
 British rule in, 528–529,
 652–653
 Berlin Treaty (1878) and, 528,
 1989
 British military forces on, 519,
 521, 529
 Cyprus Convention on (1878),
 654

cities of, major, 652
constitution of, 697
economy of, 652
geography of, 652
independence of (1960), 652,
 653, 696–697, 943
legislative elections in, of 1960,
 653
in Ottoman Empire, 652, 653
Palestine Research Center move
 to, 1782
political system of, 652
population of, 652
presidential elections in, of 1959,
 653
Turkish–Greek dispute over,
 1531–1535
 Ecevit (Bülent) in, 1666
 Erbakan (Necmeddin) in, 1666
Turkish occupation of (1974–),
 652, 654
unification with Greece (enosis)
 internal conflict over, 653–654,
 697
 opposition to, 696
 support for, 653, 943
United Nations on, 653, 654,
 697, 2277–2278

Cyprus Convention (1878),
 654–655

Cyrenaica (Libya), **655–656**, 1410,
 2217
 cities of, 446
 Idris al-Sayyid Muhammad al-
 Sanusi as amir of, 655, 1081,
 1321
 independence for, 1321
 Italian occupation of, 655, 935,
 1321
 Mukhtar (Umar al-) in guerilla
 war against, 1609–1610
 Kikhya family in, 1321
 Sanusi order in, 446, 1609
 during World War II, 516

Cyrenaican National Congress, 1321

Cyrene (Libya), 655

Cyril I (Coptic patriarch), 657

Cyril IV (Coptic patriarch), **656**
 Coptic Church revival under, 640,
 656
 educational reforms of, 656
 murder of, Sa'id Pasha in, 656,
 691
 Peter VII and, 1822

Cyril V (Coptic patriarch), **656–657**
 educational reforms of, 656
 exile of, 656–657
 John XIX as successor of, 1239

Cyril VI (Coptic patriarch),
 657–658, 2048

Cyrillic alphabet, 235

Czechoslovakia, arms sales by
 to Egypt, 1650
 to Israel, 304

Czech Republic, in U.S. invasion of
 Iraq (2003), 2325

D

Da'an, Treaty of (1919), 2378

Dabbagh, Farajollah. *See* Soroush,
 AbdolKarim

Dabbagh, Marzieh, **659**

Dabbas, Charles, **660**
 presidency of, 660

Dabka. *See* Debka

"D'abord, ce n'est pas la guerre"
 (Sebbar), 2007

Dacians, 383

Daddah, Ahmed, 660

Daddah, Mokhtar Ould, **660**, 1503
 coup against (1978), 660
 POLISARIO and, 2345
 foreign policy of, 660
 presidency of, 660

Dafanna al-Madi (Ghallab), 910

Dafatir Thaqafiyya (periodical), 357

Daftari, Ahmad Matin, **660**

Daftari, Hedayatollah Matin, 660

Dagan, Meir, as Mossad director,
 1578, 1579

Daghestan, Naqshbandi in,
 1642–1643

Daghestani, Farah, in Princess
 Basma Women's Resource
 Center, 1852

Daghir, As'ad, in Istiqlal Party, 1198

Dağlarca, Fazil Hüsnü, **661**, 1437,
 1439

Dahab, Nefla, 1429

Dahlab, Saad, 788

Dahlan, Muhammad, **661–662**
 Arafat (Yasir) and, power struggle
 between, 661
 in Palestinian Authority, 1900
 in Preventative Security Forces,
 1785

Dahlgren, Susanne, *as contributor*, 169,
 806, 1669, 2357, 2398–2399

Dahna, al- (desert), 1638

Dahruj, Faruq, 1009

Decapolis, Irbid in, 1139

Decatur, Stephen, 2208

Decentralization Party (Ottoman Empire), **686–687**
Cevdet (Abdullah) in, 576

Declaration of Barcelona (1995), 1512

Declaration of La Celle St. Cloud (1955), **687**, 849

Declaration of Principles on Interim Self-Government Arrangements (DOP) (1993). *See also* Oslo Accords
Gulf Crisis and (1990–1991), 1792–1793
Palestine National Charter superseded by (1968), 1776
PFLP rejection of, 1840
provisions of, 1726, 1775
signing of, 1726

Declaration of the Establishment of the People's Authority (1977), 1413

Dedebaba, 435

Dede Zekai, **687**

Dédicace à l'année qui vient (Khatibi), 1304

Deeb, Katrin, in Arab Women's Executive Committee, 268

Deeb, Lara Z., *as contributor*, 1396

Deedes, Wyndham Henry, **687**
Kirkbride (Alec Seath) and, 1324
replacement for, 603
Richmond (Ernest T.) as assistant to, 1922

Defense Emergency Regulations, 777

Defense Regulations (Jordan, 1954), 35

Defensive Shield, Operation (Israel), 1169

Defterdar, 823

Defterhane, 1367

Deganya (kibbutz), 865, 1361
establishment of, 1319, 1320

De Gaulle, Charles, **688**
and Algerian independence, 138–139, 142, 848
Amrouche (Jean) as intermediary, 193
Algeria under, 688
Challe (Maurice) in, 579
Code de l'Indigénat in, 612
Delouvrier (Paul) in, 689
and Evian Accords (1962), 788
ordinance (7 March 1944) on, 3

and Free French mandate, 688, 851
Catroux (Georges) and, 570
government of
Delouvrier (Paul) in, 689
Soustelle (Jacques) in, 2081
on Hammarskjöld (Dag), 986
Loi Cadre discarded by, 1443
Muhammad V and, 1598

Degel HaTorah (Israel), 1180
break with Agudat Israel, 77
in United Torah Judaism, 1190

De Haan, Ya'akov Yisrael, **688–689**
anti-Zionism of, 688–689
assassination of, 688, 689

Dehkhoda, Ali Akbar, 540, **689**, 1435

Dehydration, with diarrhea in children, 1509–1510

"De la barbarie en général et de l'intégrisme en particulier" (Mimouni), 1547

Delcassé, Théophile, 119
and Moroccan Question, 1566

Delacroix, Eugène, Niati's (Houria) work as critique of, 1687

Dellalzade Ismail, **689**
Dede Zekai and, 687

Delouvrier, Paul, **689–690**

Delta Barrages, **690**

Delta, Nile, **690**
and disease, 710, 711

Demain (publication), 1717

Démantèlement, Le (Boudjedra), 497

De Menasce, Béhor Levi, 691

De Menasce family, **690–691**

De Menasce, Félix Béhor, 691

De Menasce, Jacob, 690–691

De Menasce, Jacques Béhor, 691

Demetrius II (Coptic patriarch), **691**
Cyril V compared with, 656

Demirel, Süleyman, **691–693**, *692*
as chief of state, 2219–2220
coup against (1980), 789
government of, 691–692, 1257, 2241
Çiller (Tansu) in, 598
Erbakan (Necmeddin) in, 780
İnönü (Erdal) in, 1097
National Salvation Party in, 1666
Türkeş (Alparslan) in, 2236
in Justice Party, 691, 1257, 2242
in Nationalist Front, 692, 1257

National Security Council banning from politics, 2219
Özal (Turgut) and, 692, 1584, 1746, 1747
presidency of, 692
as prime minister, 691–692, 1746, 1747, 2242, 2244
resignation of, 691, 1257
in True Path Party, 2219
True Path Party supported by, 1584

Demirjian, Stepan, 588

De Mirmono Tolena (Afghanistan), 786

Democratic Bloc (Morocco), 1574–1575

Democratic Constitutional Rally (RCD) (Tunisia). *See* Constitutional Democratic Rally

Democratic Faction (Zionist group), 2434
Weizmann (Chaim) and, 2337

Democratic Forum for Labor and Freedoms. *See* Forum Démocratique pour le Travail et les Libertés

Democratic Front for Peace and Equality (DFPE) (Israel), 1180–1181, 1183, 1673, 1787

Democratic Front for the Liberation of Palestine (DFLP), 1008, 1009
attack on Ma'alot by, 1452
Kamal (Zahira) in, 1266
Matzpen and, 1500
in PLO, 1773
split from PFLP, 1839

Democratic Left Party (Turkey)
Ecevit (Bülent) in, 746, 2245
Ecevit (Rahşan) in, 746, 747
Motherland Party in coalition with, 746
National Action Party in coalition with, 746

Democratic Movement for Change (DMC) (Israel), 1181
Amit (Meir) in, 190
and Citizens' Rights Movement, 1180
establishment of, 1181, 2376
foreign policy of, 1181
Free Center in, 1181
platform of, 1181
Rubinstein (Amnon) in, 1181
Shinui Party in, 1181, 1188
Yadin (Yigael) in, 1181, 2376

Economic and military aid *(continued)*
  from World Bank, 747, 749
  to Yemen Arab Republic, 749
Economic and Social Commission
    for Western Asia (ESCWA),
    878, 2277
Economic and Social Council
    (ECOSOC), 2277
Economic Community of West Africa
    (ECOWAS), Mauritania's
    withdrawal from, 1503
Economic Council, 1387
Economic elites, 775
Economic Independence: How? (Gozanski),
    934
Economics, **752–754**
  of imperialism, 1087, 1088–1090
  of industrialization, 1091–1094
Economic sanctions
  against Iraq, by United Nations
      (*See* Sanctions, Iraqi)
  against Libya
      by United Nations, 522, 1414,
        1415, 1707, 1708
      by United States, 1707–1708
Economic Support Fund (ESF), 748
ECOSOC. *See* Economic and Social
    Council
ECP. *See* Executives of Construction
    Party
Ecuador, in OPEC, 1720
Eddé, Carlos, 1653
Eddé, Emile, **754**
  Aoun (Michel) supported by, 754
  Khuri (Bishara al-) rivalry with,
      1315, 2202
  Muslim prime minister appointed
      by, 1653
  in National Bloc, 1653
  opposition to, in Constitutional
      Bloc, 634
  Phalange party and, 1254
  as president, 754
  as prime minister, 754
  son of, 754
  Sulh (Riyad al-) and, 2117
  Trad (Petro) supporting, 2202
Eddé, Raymond, **754–755**
  Chehab (Fu'ad) in conflict with,
      754
  exile of, 1653
  in al-Hilf al-Thulathi, 581, 1254
  Khuri (Bishara al-) opposed by,
      1315
  in Lebanese Civil War
      (1975–1990), 754

in National Bloc, 1653
in Socialist Front, 580
against Ta'if Accord, 754
Edebiyat-i Cedide, 1439
Eden, Anthony, **755**
  and Anglo–Egyptian Treaty
      (1936), 755
  in Arab–Israel War (1956), 755
  Chamberlain (Neville) in conflict
      with, 755
  under Churchill (Winston S.), 755
  and Fertile Crescent unity, 825
  as foreign secretary, 755, 842
  and "Gentlemen's agreement"
      (1937), 755
  Iranian oil nationalization op-
      posed by, 755
  and League of Arab States estab-
      lishment, 517
  at Montreux Convention (1936),
      755, 1565
  Nasser (Gamal Abdel) opposed by,
      755
  in Operation Alpha, 157
  as prime minister, 755
  resignation of, 520
  Sèvres Protocol shredded by, 2014
  on Suez Canal nationalization,
      520, 755, 2108
  on Suez Canal Users Association,
      1444
Eder, Edith, in Women's Interna-
    tional Zionist Organization,
    2357
Edip, Halide, 1800
Edirne (Turkey), **755–756**
  Balkan wars over, 384
  B'nai B'rith lodge in, 489
  foundation of, 755
  tourism in, 755
Edirne, Treaty of (1713), 739
Edot Ha-Mizrah. *See* Adot Ha-
    Mizrah
Educated Girls' Association (Sudan),
    2105
Education, **756–762**. *See also specific
    colleges, universities, and countries*
  in 9th–16th century, 756
  in 18th century, 756
  in 19th century, 757
  architecture, 284
  art, 312
  and "brain drain," 761
  censorship of, 759, 761
  centralization of, 759–760
  colonialism and, 758–759, 880
  European model and, 756, 757

in foreign schools, 758
gender and (*See* Gender, and edu-
    cation)
global policies on, 760–761
growth of press and, 759
madrasa system of, 1457–1458
in Mahalle Schools, 1461
missionary schools in, 1550–1552
modernization and, 880, 1556
nationalization and, 760
new schooling in (*See* New school-
    ing)
in private schools, 761
in religious schools, 756, 757,
    760, 761
vs. schooling, 756
in science and technology, 2004
upbringing aspect of, 759–760
of women, 760, 761, 879–884 (*See
    also* Gender, and education)
women's studies, 1100–1101
Education Regulation (1869) (Ot-
    toman Empire), 758
EEC. *See* European Economic Com-
    munity
Efendi, Agha, in Young Ottomans,
    2405
Efendi, Ali Riza, 330
Efendi, Mehmet Esad, on *vaka-i
    hayriye*, 2308
Efendi, Süleyman Fehim, and
    Cevdet (Ahmet), 577
Effendi, 2622
Efflatoun, Inji, **762**
Efrat, Yona, in Kahan Commission,
    1263
EFU. *See* Egyptian Feminist Union
Ege University, **762–763**
Egypt, **763–769**. *See also specific cities,
    organizations, people, and regions*
  20th-century achievements of,
      Haykal (Muhammad
      Hasanayn) on, 1013
  agriculture in, *753*, 754
      in Bahariya, 366
      child labor in, 1358
      cotton, 404, 405, 643–644,
        2180, 2181, *2181*
      and disease, 710
  alcohol in, 110
  All-Palestine Government sup-
      ported by, 154, 155, 156
  in Arab boycott against Israel, 224
  Arabia invaded by (1811–1818), 818
  Arabian horses in, 230, 231
  in Arab–Israel War (1948), 242,
      810, 1537

Russo–Persian wars under reign
of, 815–816
son of, Abbas Mirza (Na'eb al-
Saltaneh) as, 7
Tehran developing under, 2169
Fatherland and Freedom (Ottoman
Empire), Atatürk (Mustafa
Kemal) in, 331
Fatherland party (Afghanistan), 1813
Fatherland party (Iran), 1110, 2143.
See also Iradeh-ye Melli Party
Fathy, Hassan, 283
Fatima, as daughter of Muhammad,
1595, 1597
Fatimids
Cairo founded by, 551, 1158,
2054
Ibn Tulun Mosque restored by,
1074
as subdivision of Isma'ili Shi'ism,
1158
in Tunisia, 2228
in Tyre, 2255
Fatwa, 798, **816–817**
by Abd al-Rahman (Umar), 21
by Abdul-Aziz Bin Baz, 26
by Alusi (Mahmud Shukri al-), 173
on family planning, 1510
on female circumcision, 822
by Ilaysh (Muhammad), 1086
in Maliki school of law, 1476
muftis issuing, 816
against Rushdie (Salman)
by Khomeini (Ruhallah), 1300
Mohajerani (Ataollah) reaction
to, 1558
by Shaltut (Muhammad), 2022
Shaykh al-Islam issuing, 2045
by Shirazi (Mirza Hasan), 2057,
2193
by Tantawi (Muhammad Sayyid al-),
2161
Faust (Goethe), Nerval's (Gérard de)
translation of, 1675
Fava beans, 838–839
Fawda al-Ashya (Boudjedra), 497
Fawda al-Hawas (Mostaghanemi), 1424
Fawwaz, Zaynab, **817**, 890
Fawzia (princess of Egypt), marriage
to Pahlavi (Mohammad Reza),
1752
Fawzi, Husayn, 927
Fawzi, Mahmud
and Hammarskjöld (Dag), 986
in Suez Crisis (1956–1957), 2108
Fax services, 625

Fayd al-Khatir (Amin), 183
Fayruz, **817–818**, 1617
Faysal Bank, 2031
Faysal ibn Turki Al Bu Sa'id. *See* Al
Bu Sa'id, Faysal ibn Turki
Faysal ibn Turki Al Sa'ud (ruler of
central Arabia), **818–819**
and foreign affairs, 819
imprisonment of, 818
in Najd, Al Thunayyan (Abdullah
ibn Thunayyan) defeated by,
172
reign of, 819, 1999
in Wahhabi Islamic reform move-
ment, 819
Faysal, Tujan, **819–820**, 894
Fayum oasis, *1370*
Fayz, Mulla Muhsin, Ahsa'i (Ahmad
al-) on, 93
FAZ. *See* Federation of American
Zionists
Fazilet Partisi. *See* Islamist Virtue
Party
Fazy, Edmond, 352
FBI. *See* Federal Bureau of Investiga-
tion
FDA. *See* Front Démocratique Al-
gérien
FDIC. *See* Front pour la Défense des
Institutions Constitutionelles
FDTL. *See* Forum Démocratique
pour le Travail et les Libertés
Fecr-i Ati, 1439
Feda'iyan-e Islam (Iran), **820**
Ala (Hoseyn) assassination at-
tempted by, 101, 820
Borujerdi (Hosayn) denouncing,
494
Fatemi (Husayn) assassination at-
tempted by, 820
as fida'iyyun, 831
Hajir (Abd al-Hoseyn) assassinated
by, 976
Kashani (Abu al-Qasem) collabo-
ration with, 1277
Kasravi (Ahmad) assassinated by,
820, 1279
Muslim Brotherhood and, 820
Razmara (Ali) assassinated by,
100, 820
on *shari'a,* 820
Feda'iyan-e Khalq (Iran), **821**
Feddan, *1371*
Federal Bureau of Investigation
(FBI), in Pollard affair, 1838

Federal Republic of Germany. *See*
West Germany
Fédération de France du Front de
Libération Nationale (FF-
FLN) (Algeria), Ibrahimi
(Ahmed Taleb) in, 1076
Fédération des Elus indigènes (Alge-
ria), 3
Federation of American Zionists
(FAZ), 2436
Magnes (Judah) in, 1460
Wise (Stephen S.) in, 2354
Federation of South Arabia, army of,
2081
Federation of Turkish Cypriot Asso-
ciations, 696
Feis, Herbert, 229
Felafel, 838
Felicity Party (Turkey), establishment
of, 99, 1911
Fellagha, 2622
Fellah, 2622
Fellata, 2099
Feluccas (sailboats), *605*
Female genital mutilation (FGM),
600–601, **822**, 1511
in Egypt, 822
in Ethiopia, 822
opposition to, 601
by Cairo Family Planning Association, 555
origins of, 601
Tantawi (Muhammad Sayyid al-)
on, 2161
women's rights movement protesting, 822
Feminism
in Algeria, 894, 2195
M'Rabet (Fadela) and, 1592
colonial, 1037
in Egypt, 227, 2321–2322 (*See also*
Egyptian Feminist Union)
Amin (Qasim) as father of, 875,
890
among communists, 43, 44
Islamic, 892
leading figures of, 890–891,
1958, 1965–1966, 2019,
2030–2031
Musa (Nabawiyya) in, 1614
Nassif (Malak Hifni) in, 1652
and historiography, 1037
in Iran, 428, 745, 892
Women's Organization of Iran
in, 2358
in Iraq, 892

Foote, Hugh, 653

For and Against (Shamir), 2025

Foran, John, *as contributor,* 1868–1869

For Bread Alone (Shukri), 2060

Force et Matière (Buchner), 576

Forces of the Thunderbolt. *See*
    Sa'iqa, al-

Ford Foundation, 432

Ford, Gerald, government of,
    Kissinger (Henry) in, 1328

Ford, Henry, *Protocols of the Elders of Zion*
    and, 1856

Foreign Affairs (journal), "The Clash of
    Civilizations" (Huntington)
    in, 1091

Foreign Office (Britain), 514,
    841–842
  in Aden, 534
  Bevin (Ernest) in, 468–469, 647,
    842
  vs. Colonial Office, 617
  in Persia, 526
  salaries paid by, 525
  in Sudan, 530
  Trucial States as responsibility of,
    532, 2219

Forgotten Queens of Islam (Mernissi), 1518

Forman, Geremy, *as contributor,*
    1234–1235

Forqan (Iran), **842**

Forqan (journal), 842

Forster, E. M., Antonius (George)
    and, 213

Forsyth, John, in Damascus affair
    (1840), 664

Fortna, Benjamin, 756–757

Forty Days of Musa Dagh (Werfel), 1613

Forugh—e Elm (journal), 2382

Foroughi, Mirza Mohammad Ali
    Khan Zaka al-Molk, **842**

Forum Démocratique pour le Travail
    et les Libertés (FDTL)
    (Tunisia), 2231, 2232

Foster, Angel M., *as contributor,* 555,
    695, 2267–2268

Foucauld, Charles Eugène de, **843**

Foucault, Michel, 289
  and historiography, 1037

Fou de Shérazade, Le (Sebbar), 2007

Fou d'espoir, Le (Laabi), 1355

Foule, la (Chraibi), 588

Fountain of Orthodoxy (journal), 782

Four Mothers movement (Israel),
    2356

Fournier, Piérre, Kan (Suna) per-
    formance with, 1269

Fourteen Points, 2014, 2314, 2353

Fourth Shore, The, 380, **843**

Fraehn, C. M. (numismatic scholar),
    1702

France, **843–849**. *See also* Franco *en-
    tries;* French foreign legion;
    Vichy government; *specific cities,
    organizations, people, and regions*
  Algerian independence from (*See*
    Algerian War of Indepen-
    dence)
  Algerian occupation by (*See under*
    Algeria)
  Algerian relations with
    Bendjedid (Chadli) and, 444
    Bouteflika (Abdelaziz) and, *504,*
      505
    Evian Accords (1962) and,
      788–789
  Algerians in (*harkis*), 995
  antisemitism in, 1021, 2433
    Dreyfus affair and (1894), 723
  in Arab–Israel conflict, 846–847
    and Tripartite Declaration
      (1950), 2215
  in Arab–Israel War (1956),
    244–246
  Arab nationalism supported in,
    1839
  archaeological research by, 275,
    276, 277
  arms sales by, 750
    to Irgun Zva'i Le'umi, 170
    to Israel, 304, 2109
    NEACC and, 2215
  bled al-siba/bled al-makhzan theory of,
    487
  Bonaparte (Napoléon) ventures
    (*See* Napoleonic Wars)
  British relations with
    Berlin Treaty (1878) and, 528
    Cambon–Lansdowne Agreement
      in (1904), 529, 559–560,
      1374
    Egyptian occupation supported
      in, 119
  British rivalry with, 524, 846
    and Lebanese independence,
      1399
    over Egypt, 527–528, 529, 742
    over India, 525, 526
    over Iraqi oil, 2199
    over Lado Enclave, 1363
    over Trucial Coast, 531
  colonialism of, 613–616, *1087*
    habous under, 964

  mission civilisatrice of, 1552
  in Crimean War, 649, 739, 846
  in Dardanelles Treaty (1809),
    671–672
  Dreyfus affair, 846
  in Eastern Question, 739–743,
    846
  economic and military aid from,
    747
  education in, religious symbols
    banned in (2003), 289
  Egyptian relations with, Suez
    Canal and, 2014
  Egypt invaded by (*See under* Egypt)
  Faisal I ibn Hussein ejected by,
    801
  Free French mandate, 570, 688,
    851, 856, 2086
  Golan Heights mandate of, 925
  in Greek War of Independence
    (1821–1930), 940
  guest workers in, 945, 946
  in Gulf War (1991), 953
  imperialism of, 1090
  intelligence services of, 1101
  Iranian relations with, Gardanne
    Mission and, 869
  in Iraq, Faisal I ibn Hussein
    ejected by, 1244
  Iraqi relations with
    under Hussein (Saddam), 1066
    in World War II, 697
  Israeli relations with, 847
    and Dimona reactor, 1696
    in Sinai campaign of 1956, 1817
  Italian agreements with
    on Libya, 1200
    Treaty of Rome, 1933
  Jewish organizations in, 151
  in Lebanese Civil War
    (1975–1990), 1393
  Lebanese expedition (1860–1861),
    423
  Lebanese mandate of (*See under*
    Lebanon)
  legal system of, influencing law in
    Middle East, 886, 1380,
    1382–1383
  Libyan relations with, Aozou Strip
    in, 216
  mandates of, 614, 1479–1480 (*See
    also specific countries*)
    education in, 758
    King–Crane Commission on
      (1919), 1323
    Paris peace settlements on,
      1802
    San Remo Conference (1920)
      on, 1988

in Israel, 876–877, *877*
in Jordan, *877*, 877–878, *878*
in Kuwait, *877*
in Lebanon, *877*
modernization and, 874–876,
    883, 885–886
in Morocco, 874, *877*
oil boom and, 874
private sector, 878
public sector, 878
restrictive environment and,
    873–874
in Saudi Arabia, *877*
status of women, 876–878, *877*
in Syria, *877*
textile industry and, *875*, *876*
in Tunisia, 874, *877*
in Turkey, 877, *877*
in United Arab Emirates, 877
urbanization and, 875–876
in Yemen, 877, *877*
and education, 760, 761,
    879–884
in Afghanistan, 880
in Bahrain, 759
Christian influence, 882–883
curriculum, 880
in Egypt, 757, 761, 2003
Fawwaz (Zaynab) on, 817
fields of study, 878, 880
formal schooling, 880, 881, 882
illiteracy, 880
importance of, 879
improvements in, 876
informal schooling, 880,
    881–882
initiatives, 883
international comparisons, 880
in Iran, 761, 880, *882*
Islamic influence, 880–882
in Israel, 880
in Kuwait, 761
participation, 880
in Qatar, 761
in Saudi Arabia, 759, 761
in Turkey, 880
and women in labor force, 875
and health
birth control, 477–480
improvements in, 876
and historiography, 1037
and law, **884–890** (*See also*
    Women's rights)
citizenship rights, 874, 884, 887
colonialism and, 885–886
gay, lesbian, and transgendered
    rights, 888
in Iran, 1970
in Israel, 887

in Jordan, 887
in Kuwait, 884
in Lebanon, 884, 887, 1396
patriarchy and, 886
personal status laws, 874,
    886–888
regional and international per-
    spectives, 888–889
right to vote (*See* Suffrage)
in Saudi Arabia, 884
in Tunisia, 325, 2230–2231
in Turkey, 2249
in United Arab Emirates, 884
and literature, 1472–1473, 1475
and politics, **890–895** (*See also*
    Feminism)
in Afghanistan, 786, 894,
    1981–1982
in Algeria, 443, 497, 892, 894,
    2195
in Egypt, 762, 890–891, 892,
    894, 914–915, 1950–1951,
    1958, 1965–1966, 2019,
    2030–2031
in Iran, 428, 745, 891, 892,
    894, 1364–1365, 2153
in Iraq, 892
in Israel, 893, 934–935, 1440,
    1441, 2023, 2059
in Jordan, 819–820, 893,
    894
in Kuwait, 1951–1952
in Lebanon, 481, 894, 1396,
    1960–1961, 1975
in Morocco, 497–498, 894
nationalism and, 892–893
in Palestine, 893, 899,
    2051–2052
reforms, 890–891
right to vote (*See* Suffrage)
in Sudan, 894
in Syria, 893, 899–900
in Tunisia, 894, 912
in Turkey, 747, 891, 892, 894,
    2170–2171
women's organizations in,
    893–894
preference for children, 1494
study of, **895–897** (*See also*
    Women's studies)
contemporary, 896
development of, 895–896
institutionalized, 895,
    896–897
international conferences on,
    895
passivity paradigm in, 896
religious paradigm in, 896
rescue paradigm in, 896

Gendzier, Irene, *as contributor,*
    1389–1391
General Directorate on the Status
    and Problems of Women
    (Turkey), **897–898,** 2249
General Education Law (Ottoman
    Empire, 1869), 24, 2162
General Federation of Iraqi Women,
    898
General Federation of Labor (Is-
    rael). *See* Histadrut
General Intelligence Service (Egypt),
    Muhyi al-Din (Zakariyya) as
    founder of, 1608
General People's Committees
    (Libya), **898–899**
General People's Congress (GPC)
    (Libya), 409, **899,** 1413
establishment of, 899
on jamahiriyya, 899, 1213
on al-Manghusha government,
    2024
Shamikh (Mubarak Abdullah al-)
    in, 2023–2024
General People's Congress (GPC)
    (Yemen), 806
in civil war (1994), 2390
crackdown on Islamists by,
    2391
electoral success of, 1977,
    2389
Islah Party coalition with, 1143
Islah Party opposing, 1143
leadership of, 2389
Salih (Ali Abdullah) in, 1976
in Yemen Arab Republic, 2394
General Petroleum and Mineral Or-
    ganization. *See* PETROMIN
General Petroleum Company, 2110
General Refugee Congress, at Lau-
    sanne Conference (1949),
    1375
General Security Service (GSS) (Is-
    rael). *See* Shin Bet
General Syrian Congress (1920),
    538
General Treaty of Peace (1820),
    526, 2040, 2218
General Tunisian Union of Students
    (UGTE), **899**
General Union for Palestinian
    Women (GUPW), Wazir (Inti-
    sar al-) in, 2334
General Union of Algerian Workers.
    See Union Générale des Tra-
    vailleurs Algériens

Great Britain. *See* Britain

Greater Bulgaria
  Berlin Treaty and, 382–383, 465, 1989
  San Stefano Treaty and, 382, 465, 1988–1989

Greater Israel. *See Eretz Yisrael*

Greater Land of Israel movement.
  See Eretz Yisrael ha-Shelema

Greater Lebanon
  Beirut in, 429
  creation of, 1398

Greater Morocco, 942

Greater Syria, **936**, 948

Greater Syria plan, 824–826, **936**
  by Abdullah I ibn Hussein, 936
  Quwatli (Shukri al-) opposing, 936
  Sa'ada (Antun) and, 936, 1950
  Sa'id (Nuri al-) supporting, 936
  Syrian Social Nationalist Party supporting, 2136–2137, *2137*
  Za'im (Husni al-) opposing, 936

Greater Tunb, 2223–2224

Great Game, The, **936–937**

Great Man-Made River (GMMR), *1412*, 2329

Great Mosque (Damascus), *2129*

Great September Revolution (Libya), Muntasir family after, 1612

Great Socialist People's Libyan Arab Jamahiriyya. *See* Jamahiriyya (Libya)

Great Unity Party (Turkey), 2245

Great Voices of Arabic Music: Um Kulthum, Muhammad Abdel Wahab, and Farid al-Atrache (Bitton), 483

Great Zab River, 2417

Greco–Turkish War (1897), **937**

Greece. *See also specific cities, organizations, people, and regions*
  Aegean Sea controlled by, 51
  in Balkan League, 384
  in Balkan Wars (1912–1913), 384, 939
  dragomans (translators) from, 723
  in Greco–Turkish War (1897), 937, *937*
  independence of (1830), 1466 (*See also* Greek War of Independence)
    Adrianople Treaty (1829) and, 940
    London Treaty (1827) and, 940
  İzmir (Turkey) occupied by, 1201
  music of, 785

nationalism in, 1657–1658
  Megali Idea in, 1657–1658
Ottoman war with (1897), 27
rebellion against Ottoman Empire, 1466
Turkey invaded by (1919), 2240
Turkish relations with
  Chanak crisis (1922), 513, 1441–1442
  in dispute over Cyprus, 1531–1535
  Treaty of Ankara in (1930), 208
  unification with Cyprus (enosis)
    opposition to, 696
    support for, 653, 943
  U.S. economic and military aid to, 1836

Greek Catholic church, 592

Greek Catholic Synagogue Church (Nazareth), 1673

Greek Cypriot National Guard, 943

Greek millet, 1543–1545
  Armenian millet compared to, 296

Greek Orthodox Church. *See* Eastern Orthodox Church

Greeks, **938–939**
  in Arabian Peninsula, 938
  in Egypt, 938–939
    influence of, 938, 939
    in mixed courts system, 939
  as entrepreneurs, 938
  in Palestine, 938
  in Sudan, 938
  in Turkey, 2238
    Atatürk (Mustafa Kemal) and, 1549

Greek War of Independence (1821–1930), **939–940**
  Britain in, 940
  and Eastern Question, 738
  Egypt in, 939, 940, 1077
  France in, 940
  Ipsilanti uprising (1821) in, 939
  janissaries in, 1217
  Mustafa Reşid influenced by, 1623
  nationalism as result of, 1657–1658
  Ottoman Empire in, 939–940, 2093
    dismissal of Greek translators during, 545
    Muhammad Ali supporting, 2093
  Ottoman navy in, 1741
  Peloponnese uprising (1821) in, 939–940
  Russia in, 940

Green Army, in Turkish war of independence, Nadi (Yunus) in, 1633

Greenberg, Uri Zvi, **940–941**, 1432

Green Bird (Badr), 357

Green Book (Qaddafi), **941**, 1413, 1860

Green, David. *See* Ben-Gurion, David

Green Line, 430–431, **942**
  closure of, 942
  map of, *942*
  opening of, 942
  Tsemel (Leah) supporting, 2221
  West Bank demarcated by, 2339, 2340

Green March, **942–943**, 2084, *2085*, 2086
  in Western Sahara War, 1566, 1571, 2345

Green Mosque (Fez), *829*

Green olives, *837*, *840*

Green perestroika (Libya), 1414

Green Place, The (Shamir), 2025

"Green Pol Pot." *See* Zitouni, Djamel

Greffe (Boudjedra), 497

Greki, Anna, 1424

Grey, Edward
  and Fashoda incident, 529
  as foreign secretary, 842

Griboyedov Incident, **943**

Grigor V (Armenian patriarch), 291

Grigor VI (Armenian patriarch), 291

Grinnell College, Garang (John) at, 868

Grivas, Georgios Theodoros (Dighenis), **943**
  British rule opposed by, 653, 943
  enosis movement supported by, 653, 654, 696, 943
  Makarios III opposed by, 654

Grobba, Fritz Konrad Ferdinand, 906, **943–944**

Gromaire, Marcel, 2069

Gross domestic product (GDP)
  of Algeria, 127, *753*
  of Bahrain, *753*
  of Egypt, *753*
  of Iran, *753*, 1115, *1753*
  of Iraq, *753*
  of Israel, *753*, 1162, 1169
  of Jordan, *753*
  of Kuwait, *753*
  of Lebanon, *753*

HADASH. *See* Democratic Front for
    Peace and Equality
Hadassah, **966**
    Szold (Henrietta) in, 2138
Hadda Agreement (1925), Clayton
    (Gilbert) in, 603
Haddadin tribe, 2212
Haddad, Mahmoud, *as contributor,*
    35–36, 81, 352, 550, 1664,
    1973–1975
Haddad, Malek, **967**
    in Generation of 1954, 707
Haddad, Robert, at American Uni-
    versity of Beirut, 181
Haddad, Sa'd, **967**
    Israeli authority over, 254
    South Lebanon Army after death
        of, 1364
    South Lebanon Army under,
        2083
Haddad, Wadi, **967–968**
    airplane hijacking by (1976), 777
Haddam, Anouar, in GIA, 1155
Haddam, Tedjini, in High State
    Council, 1026
Haddatha Abu Hurayra Qala . . . (Mas'adi),
    1498
Hadd punishments, Taha (Mahmud
    Muhammad) against, 2145
Hadendowa clan, 433
Hadha al-Wajh A'rafuhu! (Ghallab), 910
Hadha Huwa al-Dustur (Ghallab), 910
Hadi al-Mahdi, al- (Sudanese
    leader), 210, 2261
Hadi, Asi al-, 1981
Hadi Bey, Osman, 275
Hadid, Muhammad
    in Ahali group, 80–81
    coup opposed by (1936), 80
    in National Democratic Party,
        1654
Hadira, al- (newspaper), 2016
Hadith (Islamic traditions), **968,**
    1476, 2033
    Amin (Ahmad) questioning of,
        183
    on female circumcision, 822
    on *hijab* (veiling), 1026
    Muhammad in, 1597
    muwahhidun adherence to, 1625
    patriarchal interpretations of,
        Mernissi (Fatema) on, 1518
    in Shafi'i school of law, 2018
    in Sufism, 2112
    Sunna extracted from, 2122

in Taliban curriculum, 2154
on turbans, 609
Hadithat Sharaf (Idris), 1082
Hadith Isa ibn Hisham (al-Muwaylihi),
    1420
HADITU. *See* Democratic Movement
    for National Liberation
Hadj, Ali Ben, 1455
Hadjerès, Sadek, in Parti de l'Avant-
    Garde Socialiste, 1803
Hadj, Messali al-, **968–970**
    in Amis du Manifeste et de la Lib-
        erté, 3, 189–190
    banning from Algeria, 1589
    Bellounis (Muhammad) support-
        ing, 438
    Ben Badis (Abd al-Hamid) and,
        441
    Ben Boulaid (Moustafa) support-
        ing, 443
    Boudiaf (Mohamed) supporting,
        496
    Comité Révolutionnaire d'Unité et
        d'Action opposing, 620
    deportation of, 3
    and Setif Revolt (1945), 2013
    Front de Libération Nationale re-
        jected by, 138, 1587–1588
    imprisonment of, 1804, 1805
    in Mouvement National Algérien,
        131, 1587–1588
    in Mouvement pour le Triomphe
        des Libertés Démocratiques,
        1589, 1805
    in Parti du Peuple Algérien, 1589,
        1804
    in Star of North Africa, 2089
    and Zbiri (Tahar), 2428
Hadramawt (Yemen), **970**
    British governance of, 1853
    incense in, 1091
    Jewish exodus from, Magic Carpet
        Operation for (1948–1950),
        1460
    tribes in, 2215
Hadrumetum. *See* Sousse (Tunisia)
Ha'eri, Abd al-Karim, 929
    death of, 1310
    Khomeini (Ruhollah) under, 1310
Haffar, Lutfi al-, in National Party,
    1664
Hafid, Mulay. *See* Abd al-Hafid ibn
    al-Hassan
Hafiz, Abd al-Halim, **970–971**
Hafiz, Amin al-, **971–972**
Hafsid dynasty, 2224, 2228

Haganah (Zionist military group),
    972–973
    Allon (Yigal) in, 153
    Amit (Meir) in, 190
    in Arab–Israel War (1948), 242
    vs. Arab Liberation Army, 1052
    Begin (Menachem) issued ultima-
        tum by, 1973
    Ben-Porat (Mordechai) in, 452
    Ben-Zvi (Rahel Yanait) in, 456
    Dayan (Moshe) in, 681
    and Dayr Yasin massacre (1948),
        684
    in De Haan (Ya'akov Yisrael) as-
        sassination, 688
    elite forces of (*See* Palmah)
    Eshkol (Levi) in, 784
    Gur (Mordechai) in, 956
    Guri (Chaim) in, 955
    Harel (Isser) in, 992
    Hareven (Shulamit) in, 993
    Hillel (Shlomo) in, 1030
    illegal immigration sponsored by,
        147
    Irgun Zva'i Le'umi break from,
        1139
    Irgun Zva'i Le'umi opposed by,
        1140
    in Israel Defense Force, 972
    Kaniuk (Yoram) in, 1268
    leadership of, 1172
    LEHI members kidnapped by,
        1442
    as literary catalyst, 1432
    Lotz (Wolfgang) in, 1447
    military doctrine of, 972
    Najjada, al- as Sunni counterpart
        of, 1638
    Namir (Mordekhai) in, 1641
    Ne'eman (Yuval) in, 1674
    Palmach unit of, 153
    Peres (Shimon) in, 1817
    Qawuqji's (Fawzi al-) encounters
        with, 1879
    Sharef (Ze'ev) in, 2031
    Sharon (Ariel) in, 2041
    Shiloah (Reuven) in, 2055
    Shochat (Manya) in, 2059
    Sneh (Moshe) in, 2075
    Stern (Abraham) in, 2090
    Yadin (Yigael) in, 2376
    Yariv (Aharon) in, 2379
Haggiag family, **973–974**
Haggiag, Hmani (Rahmin), 973
Haggiag, Khalifa, 973
Haggiag, Nessim, 973
Haggiag, Simeone, 973
Hagia Sophia. *See* Aya Sofya

Lilienblum (Moses Leib) on, 1417
and literature, 1430
Weizmann (Chaim) in, 2337
Hasneh (insurance company), 1034
Hass, Amira, **1003**
Hassan (prince of Jordan)
education of, at Victoria College,
2316
removed from post of crown
prince, 31, 1246
Hassan I (sultan of Morocco),
1003–1004, 2038
Marrakech under, 1493
sons of, 8, 14
Hassan II (king of Morocco),
1004–1006, *1005*, 2039
in Alawite dynasty, 106–107
as *amir al-mu'minin* (commander of
the faithful), 1586
ascension to throne, 1570, 1599
attempted coup against (1971),
1374, 1570–1571, 1573
Ouazzani (Mohamed Hassan)
and, 1743
Oufkir (Muhammad) and, 1743
attempted coup against (1972),
1570–1571
authority over parliament,
1572–1573
Bouabid (Abderrahim) opposing,
495
coalition government of,
1573–1574, 1575
Ahardane (Majoub) in, 81
Aicha (Lalla) in, 94
Dlimi (Ahmed) in, 718
Ouazzani (Mohamed Hassan) in,
1743, 2336
Oufkir (Muhammad) in, 1743
Youssoufi (Abderrahmane) in,
1573–1574, 1575, 2268, 2411
constitutions influenced by,
1572–1573
domestic policies of, 107
economic adviser of, 1366
emergency powers of, 1572, 1588
foreign policy of, 107
Green March organized by,
942–943, 2084, *2085*
human rights under, 1573, 1716
Istiqlal Party and, 1197
moudawana reform under, 1203
Mouvement Populaire and, 1588
political opponents of, 1574–1575
punishment for, 107
political parties supporting, 1574
political reforms under, 1571,
1573, 1600

as prime minister, 1599
as prince, 1599
on reform of al-Moudawana, 1586
sister of, Aicha (Lalla) as, 94
tutor of, 812
Union Nationale des Forces Populaires opposing, 2267
Western Sahara expansion sought
by, 1571, 1574, 1600, 2343,
2345–2346
Yacine (Abdessalame) criticism of,
2375
Hassan II Mosque (Casablanca), *568,
570*
architecture of, 283–284
Hassan, Amal Muhammad, 808
Hassana tribe, 2212
Hassaniya dialect, 1503
Hassanpour, Amir, *as contributor,* 914,
1339–1342
Hassidic Jews (Hasidim), **1002**
in Jerusalem, 1223
literature of, *71, 79*
in Safed, 1962
Yiddish language of, 2399
Hasso, Frances, *as contributor,* 1293
Hasson, Israel, as director of Shin
Bet, 1579
Hassoun, Jacques, 1304
Hassuna, Abd al-Khaliq, as secre-
tary-general of League of Arab
States, 352, 1386
"Hasta çocuk" (Tevrik Fikret), 2180
Hatay province (Turkey), capital city
of, 210–211
Ha-Tehiyah. *See* Tehiyah party
"Ha-Tikva" (Zionist anthem), **1007,**
2425
Hatim dynasty (Yemen), 2397
Hatim Sultans of Hamdan (North
Yemen), **1007**
Hatiri, Rafiq, 2117
HATM (Movement for Reform and
Renewal in Morocco). *See*
Movement for Unity and Re-
form (MUR)
Hatoum, Mona, **1007–1008**
Hatt-i Hümayun (1856), 423, 823,
885, 1732–1733, 2162. *See also*
Tanzimat era
Hatt-i Serif of Gülhane (1839),
1732–1733, 2073, 2162, 2163,
2164. *See also* Tanzimat era
Hattushash. *See* Bogazköy (Turkey)
Hatzfeld, Baron, 903

Haussmann, Georges, 552
and urban planning, 2299
Haut Comité d'Etat (HCE) (Algeria)
Abdesselam (Belaid) appointed by,
23, 1026
and Bouteflika (Abdelaziz), 504
dissolution of, 130
elections canceled by (1992), 95,
126
establishment of, 126, 130, 1026
Ghozali (Ahmed) in, 917
Nezzar (Khaled) establishing, 1686
Zeroual (Liamine) appointed by,
130, 1026
Hawa (journal), 1965
Hawadith, al- (newspaper), 1681, 1982
Hawari, Muhammad Nimr al-, in
Najjada, al-, 1638
Hawar Islands, 370, 371
Hawash, Samar, in Women's Centre
for Legal Aid and Counseling,
2356
Hawatma, Nayif, **1008–1009**, 1452
in Democratic Front for the Lib-
eration of Palestine, 1773
influence on PLO, 1008, 1009
Marxist-Leninist faction led by,
962
Hawa wa al-wafa, al- (Fawwaz), 817
Hawi, George, **1009–1010**
Hawi, Khalil, **1010**
Shi'r and, 1298
Hawi, William, death of, 1253
Hawrani, Akram al-, **1010–1011**
in Ba'th party, 69, 412
as vice president of UAR, 2273
Hawwari, Muhammad Nimr al-,
1375
Hawwat wa al-Qasr, al- (Wattar), 2333
Hayal (magazine), 1277
Hayapatum (Alishan), 144
Hayat, al- (newspaper), 1681
Hayat, Nina, 1427
Haycraft Commission (1921),
1011–1012, 2349
Haycraft, Thomas, 1011
Haydari, Buland al-, 344
Haydar, Sa'id, in Istiqlal Party, 1198
Hayim, Yusef, **1012**
Haykal, Muhammad Hasanayn,
1012–1013
and Ahram Center for Political
and Strategic Studies, 92
Sabri (Ali) in conflict with, 1956

Haykal, Muhammad Husayn, **1013–1014**
Abd al-Raziq (Ali) supported by, 21
Zaynab by, 1420

Hayy al-Ashgar (Egypt), 1995

Haza, Ofra, **1014**

Hazara, **1014–1015**
in Afghanistan, language of, 55
in Bamyan, 387

Hazaragi language, 55

Hazarajat region (Afghanistan), political parties in, 63–64

Hazaz, Hayyim, **1015–1016**, 1431

Hazbun, Waleed, *as contributor*, 98–99, 1091–1096

Ha-Zohar, 2437, 2438. *See also* Zionist Revisionist Movement

Hazrat Ali, Shrine of (Najaf), *1147*

Hazzan, Elijah Bekhor, 453, **1016**

HCE. *See* Comité d'Etat; Haut Comité d'Etat

Headgear, *607*, 608–611
in Turkey, declared illegal, 2240

Heakhzuyot (holding settlements), 1634

Healing cults, 2360

Health barbers, 2003

Heath, Edward, 521

Heavily Indebted Poor Country Initiative, Mauritania qualified for relief under, 1503

Hebrew alphabet, in Judeo-Arabic language, 1252

Hebrew art, 469–470

Hebrew Authors' Association, 547

Hebrew Bible
Dead Sea Scrolls and, 685
language of, 1016

Hebrew education, 427

Hebrew Encyclopedia, 1403

Hebrew Gymnasium (Jerusalem), 456

Hebrew Immigrant Aid Society, Jewish Colonization Association and, 1229

Hebrew Israelites, in Dimona (Israel), 708

Hebrew language, **1016–1018**
alphabet of, *1017*
Arabic relationship to, 232
vs. Arabic script, 232, 234
Ashkenazic use of, 321
Behar (Nissim) and, 427
Biblical, 1017

Haskalah movement and, 1003, 1018
Institute for Palestine Studies promotion of, 1099
in Israel, 1163
modernization of, 1556
poetry in, 1252
on postage stamps, 1850
preservation and growth of, 1017–1018
Rabbinic, 1017
revival of, 2399, 2432
Ben-Yehuda (Eliezer) and, 454–455
Bialik (Hayyim Nahman) and, 470
as Semitic language, 2010
Sephardic use of, 321
as symbol of Jewish independence, 1430
in Yiddish language, 2399

Hebrew literature. *See* Literature, Hebrew

Hebrew press, 1683–1684

Hebrew Resistance Movement
Begin (Menachem) in, 425
Haganah in, 973
Lohamei Herut Yisrael in, 1443

Hebrews, in Palestine, 1758

Hebrew theater. *See* Theater, Israeli

Hebrew Union College, Silver (Abba Hillel) at, 2066

Hebrew University of Jerusalem, **1018–1019**, 1224
archaeological department of, 277
Barak (Ehud) at, 398
Bentwich (Norman) at, 454
binationalism supported by, 473
bombing of student cafeteria in (2002), 1018
Burg (Yosef) at, 546
Goldberg (Leah) at, 927
Gur (Mordechai) at, 956
Guri (Chaim) at, 955
and Haifa University, 975
Harkabi (Yehoshafat) at, 995
Leibowitz (Yeshayahu) at, 1403
Magnes (Judah) as first president of, 1460–1461
Shamir (Yitzhak) at, 2025
Shammas (Anton) at, 2029
Stern (Abraham) at, 2090
Tsemel (Leah) at, 2221
Zach (Natan) at, 2418

Hebrew University of Tel Aviv, Ben-Porat (Mordechai) at, 452

Hebrew Writers Union, 470

Hebron (West Bank), **1019**, 2340
Israeli settlements in, 1019, 1325
expansion of, 2432
Gush Emunim movement and, 1019
Levinger (Moshe) leading, 1325, 1407
violence associated with, 1325
Israeli withdrawal from, 1677
Jabal al-Khalil mountains around, 1204–1205
Ja'bari family in, 1206
massacre in (1929), 2159
massacre of Palestinians in (1994), 1325
Tomb of the Patriarchs in, 1807
in Western Wall disturbances (1929), 2348

Hebron Agreement (1997), Kiryat Arba settlement in, 1325

HEC. *See* Higher Executive Committee; High Executive Council

Hedayat, Sadegh, **1019**
Alavi (Bozorg) and, 104
Pahlavi (Reza) alienating, 1757
plays by, 2186
short stories by, 1435

Hefetz (Levin), 1407

Hegel, Georg Wilhelm Friedrich, 1110

Heidelberg University
Goldmann (Nahum) at, 927
Taner (Haldun) at, 2160

Heikal, Muhammad Hasanayn. *See* Haykal, Muhammad Hasanayn

Heilman, Samuel C., *as contributor*, 979–980, 1250–1252, 1269–1270, 1889–1890, 1953–1954, 2347–2348, 2399

Hejaz Railway (Palestine/Israel), 974

Hekmatyar, Golbuddin, *60*, **1020**
in Afghan Interim Government, 63
communists opposed by, 61
and Hezb-e Islami, 1024
in Hezb-e Islami, 63, 1298
Kabul attacked by, 59
in Kashwar Kamal (Meena) assassination, 1279

Heliographs, 624

Hellenism, *vs.* Islam, 1148

Helmand-Arghandab River, 54

Helmand River, **1020**, 2070

Helmand Valley Project, 494

Helwan Railway (Egypt), 1930

Hijazi school, 1476

Hijaz, Kingdom of, 1507

Hijaz Railroad, 904, *1028*, **1028–1029**, 2206
  in Amman, 190–191
  southern terminus of, 1511

Hijra, al-, 2151

Hijra (migration)
  of Ikhwan, 1085, 1626
  of Muhammad, 1511, 1596, 1597
  and Wahhabi movement, 1626

Hikayat Zahra (Shaykh), 2046

Hikma University, al-, **1029**

Hikmet, Nazim, 1437, 1439, 2145

Hilal, al- (magazine), **1029–1030**, 1420
  Zaydan (Jurji) and, 2426

Hilf al-Thulathi, al- (Lebanon), 581, 1254
  Eddé (Raymond) in, 754

Hillel, Ayin, 1432

Hillel, Shlomo, **1030**

Hillmann, M., on Al-e Ahmad (Jalal), 110

Hillmann, Michael C.
  as contributor, 110, 366–367, 397, 566–567, 668–669, 678, 689, 784, 811, 913, 976, 1019, 1434–1437, 1802–1803, 2027
  on Parsipur (Shahrnush), 1803

Hilmi (Abd al-Baqi), Ahmad, **1030–1031**
  in All-Palestine Government, 154

Hilu, Charles, **1031**
  amnesty by, 1888
  government of, Karame (Rashid) in, 1271
  Jumayyil (Pierre) and, 1254
  as Phalange Party founder, 1031, 1400
  as president, 1399–1400
  Sarkis (Ilyas) under, 1991–1992
  Taqla (Philippe) under, 2165
  Twayni (Ghassan) under, 2254

Hilu, Henri, 1032

Hilu, Pierre, **1031–1032**

Hilu, Radwan al-, in Communist Party of Palestine, 626

Himmish, Bensalem, 1425, 1428

Hindiya River, 1316

Hindu Kush Mountains, 53, **1032**

Hinnawi, Sami al-, **1032**, 2422
  coup against (1949), 329
  government of, Aflaq (Michel) in, 69

Hira, Muhammad's retreats in, 1595

Hirawi, Ilyas al-, **1032–1033**
  government of, Hoss (Salim al-) in, 1045
  as president, 1400–1401

Hirfa, 947

Hiro, Dilip, 2289

Hirsch, Maurice de, 1229

Hirsch, Samson Raphael, followers of, in Agudat Israel, 77

Hirshfeld, Yair, in Oslo negotiations, 1725

Hisad al-Awwal, al- (Sha'ul), 2043

Histadrut (labor organization), **1033–1035**
  Ben-Aharon (Yitzhak) in, 438
  Ben-Gurion (David) in, 447
  Brenner (Yosef Hayyim) in, 507
  Burla (Yehuda) in, 547
  controlling economic resources, 1358
  elections in, 1176
  foundation of, 1361
  Haganah under, 972
  headquarters of, *1033*, 2172
  Katznelson (Berl) in, 1281
  Kessar (Israel) in, 1290
  Kol (Moshe) in, 1332
  Koor Industries founded by, 1334
  Labor Zionism as basis of, 1357
  Lavon (Pinhas) as secretary-general of, 1377, 1378
  Luz (Kadish) in, 1448
  Meir (Golda) in, 1513
  military controlled by, 1172
  Na'amat's affiliation with, 1629
  Shazar (Shneour Zalman) in, 2047
  Sprinzak (Joseph) in, 2087
  state-building by, 2402

Histoire, culture et société (Lacheraf and Djeghloul), 1362

Histoire des Musselmans (Dozy), 576

Historical Society of Afghanistan. *See* Tarikh Tolana

Historiography, **1035–1037**
  Hourani (Albert) and, 1035, 1046–1047
  Marxism and, 1036
  nationalism and, 1035, 1036–1037
  women and, 1037
  Zaydan (Jurji) and, 1035, 2426

History (Cevdet), 577, 578

History of the Arab Peoples, A (Hourani), 1047

Hitler, Adolf
  on al-Alamayn battle (1942), 102
  Atatürk (Mustafa Kemal) compared to, 333–334
  and Holocaust, 1040
  Husayni (Amin al-) and, 1042
  and Jewish immigration to Palestine, 961
  opposing Jewish immigration to Palestine, 906
  Philby (Harry St. John) praise for, 1833
  Protocols of the Elders of Zion and, 1856
  and Rommel (Erwin), 1934

Hitti, Philip, 488, 1397

HIV. *See* AIDS/HIV

Hizb al-Ahd al-Urdunni. *See* Jordanian Covenant Party

Hizb al-Ahrar al-Dusturiyyin (Egypt). *See* Constitutional Liberty Party (Egypt)

Hizb al-Islah (Palestine). *See* Reform Party

Hizb al-Istiqlal (Palestine). *See* Istiqlal Party

Hizb al-Nahda (Tunisia). *See* Renaissance Party

Hizb al-Sha'b. *See* People's Party (Syria)

Hizb al-Tahrir (Syria), 998

Hizb al-Umma al-Ishtiraki (National Socialist Party) (Iraq), establishment of, 1210

Hizb al-Watani, al- (Egypt). *See* National Party

Hizb En Nahda. *See* Renaissance Party (Tunisia)

Hizb-e Wadat, 387

Hizb-i I'tidal (Iraq), Mossadegh (Mohammad) in, 1580

Hizb Misr al-Ishtiraki. *See* Socialist party (Egypt)

Hizbullah (Lebanon), **1037–1038**
  vs. AMAL, 174, 1037, 1038
  CIA attack against leadership of, 573
  and al-Da'wa al-Islamiyya, 793
  Fadlallah (Shaykh Husyan) as spiritual guide of, 793, 794
  formation of, 2177
  Iran supporting, 2175
  on Israeli withdrawal from Lebanon, 2017
  lack of superpower patron for, 2177
  Lahhud (Emile) supporting, 1364

Husayni, Amin al-. *See* Husayni, Muhammad Amin al- (Hajj Amin)

Husayn ibn Ali (Hashimite leader), **1052–1053**, 2052–2053
Abd al-Aziz ibn Sa'ud Al Sa'ud conflict with, 646
Arab Bureau collaboration with, 225
in Arab Revolt (1916), 221, 263–264, 510, 1000, 1506, 2039, 2368
Askari (Ja'far al-) under, 324
Hijaz Railroad in strategy of, 1029
Arslan (Shakib) criticism of, 307
as caliph candidate, 557
death in Karbala, 1272
al-Fatat and, 815
in Hashimite family, 1000
Islamic congress held by, 1152
martyrdom of, plays on, 2186
and McMahon, correspondence with, 263–264, 1053, 1059–1060, 1506
overthrown by Al Sa'ud (Abd al-Aziz) (1924), 1625–1626
Sa'id (Nuri al-) supporting, 1967
sons of
Abdullah I ibn Hussein as, 29
and Arab nationalism, 1053
tomb of, as Atabat, 328, 1131, 1272
in World War I, 2366

Husayn ibn Ali Turki (bey of Tunisia), 2229

Husayni, Da'ud al-, 1054

Husaynid dynasty, 2229

Husayni family, al-, **1053–1054**
in Arab Club, 225–226
influence of, 1053
Jarallah family rivalry with, 1218
Nashashibi family rivalry with, 1224, 1644–1645, 1764, 1766
wealth of, 1053

Husayni, Faysal al-, 1054
and Arab Studies Society, 1226
secret talks with Israelis, 1705–1706

Husayni, Hind al-, **1055**

Husayni, Husayn al-, **1055**, 1058
in AMAL movement, 174
in parliament, 320

Husayni, Ishaq Musa al-, 1053–1054

Husayni, Jamal al-, 1053, **1055–1056**
Alami (Musa al-) and, 103

in All-Palestine Government, 154, 1030
in Arab Executive, 1783
in Arab Higher Committee, 1766
at London Conference (1939), 1766
Muslim–Christian Association guided by, 1761
in Palestine Arab Party, 1765, 1766

Husayni, Muhammad Amin al- (Hajj Amin), 1053, *1054*, **1056–1058**
in All-Palestine Government, 154, 155
antisemitic statement by, 212
Antonius (George) as advisor to, 214
appointment as mufti of Jerusalem, 1922
in Arab Club, 226
in Arab Higher Committee, 228
Arslan (Adil) opposition to, 306
assassination of, plans for, 1947
and Bludan Conferences, 488
under British mandate, 1056–1057
British relations with, 1764
Darwish (Ishaq) as nephew of, 673
exile of, 1057
German support for, 906, 944
Ghuri (Emile al-) supporting, 917
Golden Square supporting, 927
Husayni (Jamal al-) and, 1055, 1056
Islamic congress held by, 1152
as Jerusalem mufti, 1218, 1224, 1764
on Jews during World War II, 1234
Kaylani revolt (1941) supported by, 516
Muslim Brotherhood meeting with, 1621
Mussolini (Benito) supporting, 515
Nabi Musi Pilgrimage led by, 1630
Nashashibi family rivalry with, 1644–1645
and Nazi Germany, 1042, 1057
power of, 1764
revolt suggested to, by Qassam (Izz al-Din al-), 1874
Sabbagh (Salah al-Din al-) and, 1953
Samuel (Herbert Louis) supporting, 1983
in Supreme Muslim Council, 1011, 1224, 1764, 2124–2125

in Syria, Arif (Arif al-) with, 288
on UN Resolution 181, 1057, 1058
in World War II, 2371

Husayni, Munif al-, 1053

Husayni, Musa Kazim al-, 1053, **1058–1059**
antisemitism of, 212
in Arab Executive, 1224, 1764, 1782, 1783
death of, 1764, 1783
as Jerusalem mayor, 1224
dismissal of, 1645
Storrs (Ronald) dismissing, 2092
in Muslim–Christian Association, 1761
son of, 1052, 1054

Husayni, Raja al-, 1053
in All-Palestine Government, 154

Husayni, Rana. *See* Husseini, Rana

Husayni, Tahir Shuqri al-, daughter of, 1055

Husayniyya (place for storyteller), 1606

Husayn, Kamal al-Din, 853

Husayn Kamil, 509, 858

Husayn–McMahon correspondence (1915–1916), 263–264, 1053, **1059–1060**, 1506, 2368
Abdullah I ibn Hussein in, 29
in *The Arab Awakening* (Antonius), 214
British promise of support of Arab nation in, 380, 511, 742–743
Clayton (Gilbert) and, 603
conflicting interpretations of, 264
London Conference (1939) on, 1445

Husayn Mosque, al- (Karbala), *1131*

Husayn Muslim, Abu al-, *Sahih* of, 968

Husayn, Rashid, 2418

Husayn, Sharif, 511, 514–515

Husayn, Taha, **1060–1061**, 1419, 1420
Abd al-Raziq (Ali) supported by, 21
Amin (Ahmad) compared to, 183
at Cairo University, 556
on pre-Islamic Arabic poetry, 1923

Hüseyinzade, Ali, 1800

Husn al-awaqib aw Ghada al-zahira (Fawwaz), 817

Husni, Daud, 324, 336

Husni, Fikriyya, on Wafdist Women's Central Committee, 2321

Internet access, 625

"In the City of Slaughter" (Bialik), 470

In the House of Silence: Autobiographical Essays by Arab Women Writers (Faqir), 805

In the Shadows of the City (film), 1500

Intifada (1987–1991), 871, **1106–1109**, *1107, 1108. See also* Aqsa Intifada, al-
Arafat (Yasir) in, 271
Bir Zeit University during, 481
casualties of, 1108
causes of, 238, 1107, 1792
escalation of, 238, 1108
al-Fatah role in, 814, 1108
and Gaza City's economy, 869
and Gaza Strip's economy, 870
and Green Line closure, 942
HAMAS in, 2177, 2381
creation of, 983
Hareven (Shulamit) in, 993
impact on Israel, 1108
Islamic Jihad in, 1108, 1155, 2177
League of Arab States on, *1387*
objectives of, 1108
PFLP in, 1108, 1840
PLO coordination of, 2177
Dahlan (Muhammad) in, 661
Rajub (Jibril) in, 1900
Shamir (Yitzhak) opposing, 2026
start of, 1107
PFLP–GC in, 1235
tactics used in, 1107, 1108
Wazir (Khalil al-) and, 2335
in West Bank, 2340
Women in Black protests in, 2355–2356
youth movements in, 1108, 2412

Intifada 2000. *See* Aqsa Intifada, al-

Intisar al-Shabab (film), 324

Intrauterine devices (IUDs), 480

Introduction to Muslim Theology (Anawati and Gardet), 194

Invention du désert, l' (Djaout), 716

Investment, foreign
in Egypt, infitah policy promoting, 1096
industrialization limited by, 1093

IOCs. *See* International oil companies

Iowa State University, Garang (John) at, 868

IPC. *See* Iraq Petroleum Company

İpekci, Abdi, **1109**
in *Milliyet*, 1109, 1269

IPRP. *See* Islamic People's Republican Party

Ipsilanti, Alexander, 939

Iqbal, Muhammad, **1109–1110**
in modernist movements, 1150
two-nation theory of, 1109
and Jinnah (Muhammad Ali), 1236

Iqta, 2167

IRA. *See* Irish Republican Army

Irada, 479

Irade (sultan's will), 823

Iradeh-ye Melli Party (Iran), **1110**

Irak (Grobba), 944

Iran, **1110–1122**. *See also specific cities, organizations, people, and regions*
Abu Musa Island claimed by, 37–38, 2040
Afghanistan invaded by (1857), 204, 1117
Treaty of Paris on, 1802
and Afghan political parties, 64
Afghan refugees in, 1912
agriculture in, 902, 1115
alcohol in, 110
Anglo–Russian Agreement on (1907), 205
archaeology in, 276, 277, 481–482
architecture in, 282
arms sales to, 2201
from Britain, 523
by China, 586
by United States, 304, 1119, 1122–1123, 1689
art of, 566, 1615–1616, 1676, 2011
multimedia, 1676
Musavi (Mir-Hosain) and, 1615–1616
by women, 1676
in Baghdad Pact (1955), 363, 519, 1693, 2291
Baha'is persecuted by, 365
Bahrainis supporting, 369
Bakhtiari in, 374
Baluchis in, 385–386
banking in, 390, 392, *393,* 535–536
Wolff (Henry Drummond) and, 2355
bast in, 411–412
bazaars in, 419–421
blood money law in, 998
border with Iraq, 140–141, 2043
British relations with, 1117 (*See also* Anglo–Persian War (1856))
Curzon (George Nathaniel) in, 651–652

East India Company and, 526
economic privileges in,
Anglo–Iranian Agreement on (1919), 200
Jangali and, 1216
under Mozaffar al-Din Qajar, 1591
under Naser al-Din Shah, 1644
oil nationalization and, 518
Russian rivalry in, 88, 205, 535–536, 1942
Shuster (W. Morgan) as financial adviser and, 2063–2064
Tabataba'i (Ziya) supporting British policies, 2142, 2143
Tobacco Revolt (*See* Tobacco Revolt)
Tripartite Treaty of Alliance (1942) and, 2216
Wilson (Arnold T.) and, 2352–2353
during World War I, 809
British sphere of influence in, 205, 1118
bureaucracy of, 1119
carpets in, 566–567
Catholics in, 1932
censorship in
of education, 761
of film industry, 832, 833
of literature, 397, 1435, 1436–1437, 1803
of press, 1120, 1121, 1299
of theater, 2186
in Central Treaty Organization, 573
chemical and biological weapons of, 1535
Christians in, 1548
cities of, 2, 1498, 2070, 2420
capital, 2169–2170
desert, 2382
provincial capitals, 93, 1289–1290, 2057, 2143–2144
shrine, 1880
climate of, 902, 1110–1111
clothing in
aba, 611
turbans, 609, 610
colonialism in, 614
communication in, 624, 625
communism in, 41, 625, 626–627
constitutional revolution in (*See* Constitutional Revolution)
constitution of (1876), 758
constitution of (1906), 1383, 1435
drafting of, 636, 1868
signing of, 636, 1118

Muharram rites in, 1605–1606

music of, 1617–1618, 1619, 2311

in Napoleonic Wars, 816

Naqshbandi order in, 1642

national assembly of (*See* Majles)

nationalism in, 1659–1660

anti-Western aspect of, 205

under Mozaffar al-Din Qajar, 1591

national referenda in, 1118–1119

natural gas production in, *1671*

natural gas reserves in, 1115, *1671*

needle exchange programs in, 714

newspapers and print media of, 1682–1683

newspapers of, 867, 2142, 2143

in Northern Tier, 1692–1693

nuclear capability of, 1698

Pakistan and, 1696

U.S. accusations regarding, 1121

oil nationalization in, 100, 202, 1118, 1752

foreign response to, 1825

Kuwaiti oil after, 1349

Mossadegh (Mohammad) and, 1581

National Front and, 1655–1656

nullification of, 186

oil production in, 752, 1482

by Anglo–Iranian Oil Company, 200–202, 518, 742

Compagnie Française des Pétroles in, 628

Consortium Oil Agreement on (1954), 186

D'Arcy Concession for, 200, 536–537, 671

economic role of, 1115

in Mosul, Anglo–Turkish dispute over (1920–1928), 1582–1583

start of, 2199

oil reserves in, 1115

Oman and, in Dhufar rebellion, 705, 1842

in OPEC, 1719, 1720

opium production in, 725

Ottoman relations with, Zuhab region and, 783

Pakistani alliance with, 1758

parliament of (*See* Majles)

Peace Corps in, 1808

Persian cats in, 1821

and Persian Gulf States, current strains between, 1903

PFLP–GC links with, 1841

PFLP supported by, 1840

poetry of, 97

political ideologies in, 1116–1117

political parties in

suppression of, 1117

women in, 1129

political system of, 1115–1117

clergy in, criticism of, 1262

population growth in, 1111, 2420

population of, 752, *753*, 1110, 1111, 1844, 1845–1846

postage stamps of, 1849, 1850

presidential elections in, 1119, 1120, 1121, 2424

pronatalist policies of, 478, 479

Protestant missions in, 1854

provinces of, 345–346, 1116, 1289–1290, 1312–1313, 1316–1317, 2070

Prussian relations with, 903

Qajar dynasty in (*See* Qajar dynasty (Iran))

radio and television in, *1896*

railways in, *2206*

reform movement in, 1117, 1119–1122, 1303

religions in, 1112 (*See also* Shi'ite Islam *subhead*)

Babi movement, 354–356

Baha'i faith, 364, 365

Islam, 1111, 1112

Isma'ili Shi'ism, 1159

revolutions in (*See* Constitutional Revolution; Iranian Revolution)

riots in (1963), 1118, 1753

riots in (1999), 1120–1121

rivers of, 1316, 2417

rural development in, by Jehad-e Sazandegi, 1220

Russian relations with, 1117 (*See also* Russo–Persian treaties; Russo–Persian wars)

British rivalry in, 88, 205, 535–536

Griboyedov Incident and, 943

under Mozaffar al-Din Qajar, 1591

under Naser al-Din Shah, 1644

post-Soviet, 1944

Shuster (W. Morgan) and, 2063–2064

Turkmanchai Treaty (1828) and, 2251–2252

Russian sphere of influence in, 205, 1118

Saudi relations with, 1999–2000

Mecca riots (1988) and, 1627

science and technology in, 2004, 2005, 2006

secularization in, 891, 1756

Shaykhis persecuted in, 2047

Shi'ite Islam in, 2052, 2054

Akhbari school of, 97–98

conflict with Sunni Islam, 1548

during Ottoman Empire, 1548

as unifying force, 1549

social services in, 809–810

Soroush (AbdolKarim) as advocate of, 2080

Soviet invasion of (1920), 1216

Soviet invasion of (1941), 516, 2144

Soviet occupation of (1941–1946), 346, 1118, 1752

Azerbaijan crisis in, 346

end of, 346, 1118

Soviet relations with

during Cold War, 517

and Iran–Iraq War, 1127

Tripartite Treaty of Alliance (1942) and, 2216

Tudeh Party supported by, 2222

as state sponsor of terrorism, 2175

stock market in, 2091, *2091*

student activism in, 630–631, 1120

suffrage in, universal male, 1144

Syrian relations with, 318, 1291

temporary marriage (*ziwaj mut'a*) in, 2438

textile industry in, 2066, 2180, 2181, *2181*

theater in (*See* Theater, Persian)

Tobacco Revolt in (*See* Tobacco Revolt)

in trade, 1115, 2198, 2199, *2200*

concessions for, 1117–1118

East India Company and, 525

Trans-Iranian railway in, 2057, 2203–2204

transport in, modern means of, *2207*

tribes in, 374, 385–386, 2213

Tudeh Party supporting, 2222

Tunb Islands controlled by, 2223–2224

ulama in, 2259

United Arab Emirates relations with, 38

Tunb Islands and, 2223–2224

U.S. military personnel in, diplomatic immunity for, 1310–1311

U.S. policy toward

as "Axis of Evil," 1121

dual containment as, 730

Dulles (John Foster) and, 733

under Nixon (Richard Mihous), 1689

Truman Doctrine and, 2291

Iraq *(continued)*

communication in, 624, 625

communism in, 625, 626, 627

constitution of, provisional
(2004), 2071, 2326

cotton industry in, *2181*

coup in (1936), 35, 776, 999,
2065, 2115

Ahali group in, 80

coup in (1941), 35–36, 999

coup in (1958), 15, 288, 413,
520, 776, 1133, 1872, 1969

Hashimite monarchy overthrown
in, 1000

Mala'ika (Nazik al-) on, 1475

National Democratic Party in,
1654

coup in (1959), attempted, 1133,
1873

coup in (1963), 288, 377, 412,
413, 422, 1134, 1873, 2189

coup in (1968), 377, 413, 1134,
2189

coup in (1979), 378

debt of, after Iran–Iraq War
(1980–1988), 949

defense costs as percentage of
GNP or GDP, *1530*

disease in, 714

economic and military aid to, 748

economy of, 752, 753

Bazzaz (Abd al-Rahman al-)
and, 422

Iran–Iraq War and, 1134

Sa'id (Nuri al-) and, 1968

sanctions and, 1987

statistics on, *753*

during World War II, 1968

education in

economic sanctions and, 1986

expansion of, 1132, 1133

under Faisal I ibn Hussein, 801

missionary schools in, 1552

Sa'id (Nuri al-) and, 1968

for women, 1310

Egyptian relations with, Qasim
(Abd al-Karim) and, 1872

Egyptian unification with, agreement on, 288

elites in, 776

emigration from, 1068

establishment of, after World War
I, 1129

ethnic groups in, 1130–1131

family planning in, 478

feminism in, 892

foreign policy of, 1872

nonalliance, 1133

French relations with, 1066

futuwwa in, 860–861

geography of, 902–903, 1130

German relations with

German support for pan-Arab
groups, 906

Grobba (Fritz Konrad Ferdinand) and, 944

Jamali (Muhammad Fadhil al-)
and, 1213

in Greater Syria plan, 824–826

guest workers from, 946

in Gulf Crisis (1990–1991) *(See
Gulf Crisis)*

in Gulf War (1980–1988) *(See
Iran–Iraq War)*

Hashimite monarchy in, 1000

higher education in, 1029

at Baghdad University, 364

in *madrasa* system, 1458

human rights in, 1048

immunization rate in, 1510

independence of (1932), 515,
802, 1132, 1480, 1967

industrialization of, 1094–1095

infant mortality rate in, 1509

infrastructure of, 1134

after Gulf War (1990–1991),
1135

inheritance in, 898

intelligence services of, 1102

Iranian relations with

Algiers Agreement on (1975),
140–141, 1066–1067, 1119

Bazzaz (Abd al-Rahman al-)
and, 423

war *(See Iran–Iraq War
(1980–1988))*

in Iran–Iraq War *(See Iran–Iraq
War)*

irrigation in, 74

Tharthar project for, 2182–2183

Islamic movement in, 1068

Israeli relations with

Hussein (Saddam) threatening
Israel (1990), 949–950

Osirak reactor destruction and,
426

Jesuits in, 1029

Jews in, 1232, *1232*, 2079

immigration to Israel, 49, 188,
790, 1030, 1913

leadership of, 1023

during World War II, 807–808,
1233

Jordan federation, 826, 999,
1925, 1969

Jordanian relations with

Aqaba in, 217

Badran (Mudar) and, 357

Kurdish revolts in, 1134,
1340–1341

by Barzani (Mustafa), 1341, 1873

Talabani (Jalal) in, 2151

Kurds in *(See under Kurd(s))*

Kuwait claimed by

British troops as deterrent
against, 520

Bubiyan Island, 541, 949

under Qasim (Abd al-Karim),
1873

al-Warba Island, 541, 949

Kuwaiti negotiations with, Ibrahim
(Izzat) in, 1078

Kuwait invaded by *(See Gulf War
(1990–1991))*

labor unions in, 1358

land mines in, 1510

land reforms in, 1372

languages in, 1131

Arabic, 233

Iranian, 1124

Turkmen, 2248

in League of Arab States, 1386,
1387, 1388

in League of Nations

admission of, 35, 802, 1132

and Anglo–Iraqi treaties, 203

in Lebanese Civil War
(1975–1990), 1391

legal system of, 886

civil code, 1382

French influences on, 1380

Majalla, 1381, 1382

legislative body in, 932

literature of, 344, 416,
1421–1422, 1475, 1703–1704,
1903, 2002, 2043–2044,
2419

at London Conference (1939),
1445

malnutrition in, due to economic
sanctions, 1136, 1986

Mamluk rulers of, 1478–1479

manufacturing in, 1481–1483,
1483

map of, *1133*

Marsh Arabs of, 1496

Mauritania and, 1744–1745

as Mesopotamia, 1129–1130

military of, 949, 953, *1527*

equipment of, *1534, 1535*

force levels of, *1528–1529,
1530–1531*

force structure of, *1532–1533*

in internal conflicts, *1530–1531,
1536*

Jordanian civil war and, 1246,
1247

Israel *(continued)*
  port, 1211–1212
  Zionist, 1927
citizenship in, laws on, 1162
climate of, 1160–1161, 1668
clothing in, yarmulke *(kippah)*, 611
during Cold War, 2033
collective communities in (*See* Kibbutz)
communism in, 628, 963, 1182–1183, 1373
confiscating Arab land in Palestine, Land Day as answer to, 1369
constitution of, 448
  lack of written, 1164
cotton industry in, 644, 2180
currency of (*See* Shekel)
dance in, 667–668
Dead Sea and, 684–685
Declaration of Independence, Wahrhaftig (Zerah) as signer of, 2322
defense costs as percentage of GNP or GDP, *1530*
deserts of, 1160
divorce in, 887
Druzes in, 729
economic and military aid to, 747
  in Arab–Israel War (1973), 748
  Camp David Accords (1978) and, 748
  from United States, 748–749, *749, 750, 750*
economy of, *753*, 1161–1162, 1169
  Arab boycott and, 224
  growth in, 1162, 1169
education in, 1163
  in religious schools, 760, 761
  at Tel Aviv University, 2172
Egyptian peace negotiations with, 1166 (*See also* Egyptian–Israeli Peace Treaty (1979))
  after Arab–Israel War (1973), 251–252, 1166, 1328
  Boutros-Ghali (Boutros) and, 505
  at Camp David Accords (1978), 363, 560–561, 2293
  Carter (Jimmy) in, 539, 567, 770
  CIA in, 157, 573
  Crossman (Richard) in, 650
  in General Armistice Agreements (1949), 239–240
  Israeli peace movement's impact on, 1809
  Jarring (Gunnar) in, 1219
  Kissinger (Henry) in, 1328

  in Operation Alpha, 157
  opposition to, 363, 561, 2428
  Sadat (Anwar al-) and, 426, 770, 1957
  Saunders (Harold) and, 2001
Egyptian relations with
  arms race in, 236
  deterioration of, 236
  Lavon affair and, 449, 785, 1377–1378
  under Mubarak (Husni), 1593–1594
  under Nasser (Gamal Abdel), 1649–1650
  Sinai peninsula and, 1957, 2068
  Suez Canal and, 2014
  Taba dispute, 2139, 2140
  Tiran Strait blockades and, 2191
electoral system of, 1164, 1175–1176
  changes to, 1168, 1170, 1175
emergency regulations issued by, 776–777
espionage by, against U.S., in Pollard affair, 1838
espionage of, Mossad in, 1577–1579
establishment of state, 2435
  Balfour Declaration (1917) and, 380–381, 381, 511
  Bevin (Ernest) on, 468–469
  Biltmore Program (1942) on, 472
  Bludan Conferences against, 488
  British mandate ending and, 517–518, 616
  Churchill (Winston S.) on, 596, 597
  Churchill White Paper on (1922), 594
  as fundamental cause of Nakba, al, 1639–1640
  Guinness (Walter Edward) on, 948
  Holocaust and, 1042
  international support for, 1165
  Jericho Congress after (1948), 1221–1222
  Lloyd George (David) supporting, 1441
  Neturei Karta opposing, 1677
  Roosevelt (Eleanor) support for, 1935
  Sharett (Moshe) lobbying for, in United Nations, 2032
  Stalin (Joseph) support for, 1943
  Truman (Harry S.) supporting, 2220

  United Nations and, 518, 1165
  U.S. supporting, 517
  white papers on Palestine (1939) on, 515
  World Zionist Organization and, 2372–2373
Ethiopian Jews airlifted by (1991), 786, 1239
ethnic groups in, 1162–1163
feminism in, 2023
film industry of, 483, 833, 956
fishing in, 865
foreign policy of, Jordanian Option in, 1247
French relations with, 847
  and Dimona reactor, 1696
Gaza City occupied by, 869
Gaza Strip occupied by, 870, 871
at Geneva Peace Conference (1973), 900
geography of, 902–903, 1159–1160
government of, 932, 933
in Gulf War (1991), 951
Halakhah in, 979
higher education in, 975, 1018–1019, 1163
  Bar-Ilan University, 402–403
  at Ben-Gurion University of the Negev, 449–450
  at Bezalel Academy of Arts and Design, 469–470
  Magnes (Judah) in, 1460–1461
  at Technion-Israel Institute of Technology, 2169
history of, Flapan (Simha) challenging myths about, 835
human rights in, 2221
independence of (1948), 1362
  Ben-Gurion (David) proclaiming, 448, 2172
  as literary catalyst, 1432
industrialization of, 1095
intelligence agencies of (*See* Mossad)
in Iran–Contra affair, 1322
Iraqi Jews in, emigration of, 1030
Iraqi relations with
  Hussein (Saddam) threatening Israel (1990), 949–950
  Osirak reactor destruction and, 426
irrigation in, 1248
Jewish immigration to, *1231, 1234* (*See also* Aliyah; Jew(s), immigration of)
  from Arab countries, 2365
  Law of Return allowing citizenship for, 787, 1384

Magic Carpet Operation for
(1948–1950), 1460
residential transit camps for,
1452
from Soviet Union, 1943
Jewish refugees in, 1913–1914
Jews in
number of, 1162, *1164*
religious practices of, 1163
Jezreel Valley in, 1234–1235
Jordan and
attempted assassination of
Mashʿal (Khalil al-) and, 1579
General Armistice Agreement
between (1949), 240–241
Jordanian Option and, 1247
peace negotiations with, Khalidi
(Walid) in, 1296
peace treaty between (1994) (*See*
Jordanian–Israeli peace treaty)
journalism in, by women, 1003
Karaites in, 1270
Kasztner affair in (1954–1955),
1280
kibbutzim of, 2377
establishment of first, 855, 1361
Kurdish revolts supported by, in
Iraq, 1134
labor and labor unions in, 1357,
1358, 1361, 1362 (*See also* Histadrut; Labor Zionism)
umbrella organization for,
1033–1035
landsmannschaften in, 1373
languages in, 1163
Arabic, 1163
Hebrew, 1163
at Lausanne Conference (1949),
1375–1376
Lavon affair in, 449, 785,
1377–1378, 1577–1578, 1991
League of Arab States on, boycott
by, 224–225
in Lebanese Civil War
(1975–1990), 1103, 1391,
1393, 1400
as Lebanese Forces ally, 1393, 1394
Lebanese Front collaborating with,
1395
Lebanese internal security maintained by, 1536
Lebanese occupation by, withdrawal from (2000), 254,
1168, 2017
Lebanon and, 1166–1167
agreement with Jumayyil (Amin)
(1983), 1665
General Armistice Agreement
between (1949), 240

peace treaty between (1983),
318, 1393
security agreement between,
254, 1253
Lebanon invaded by (1978), 240,
1166, 1417–1418
and Beitaddin Declaration
(1978), 432
League of Arab States on, *1387*
PLO and, 2176
UN response to, 1393, 1400,
1417–1418
Lebanon invaded by (1982) (*See*
Arab–Israel War (1982))
legal system of, 886, 1383
Halakhah in, 1890
legislative body of, 933 (*See also*
Knesset)
literature of, 188, 408, 434, 547,
834–835, 855, 920–921,
926–927, 940–941,
955–956, 1164, 1268, 1288,
1407, 1432–1434, 2012,
2024–2025, 2029,
2058–2059, 2060, 2075,
2076, 2114–2115, 2159–2160,
2384, 2403, 2418, 2429 (*See
also* Literature, Hebrew)
Arabic-language, 963
avant-garde, 1040
"Generation of the State" revolution in, 182, 1040
maʿbarah experiences in, 1452
novels and short stories,
1521–1522
poetry, 2322–2323
satire, 1284
by women, 993, 1907
Lotz (Wolfgang) as espionage agent
of, 1446–1447
manufacturing in, *1162*, 1483, *1483*
medicine and public health in,
1459
military of (*See* Israel Defense
Force)
Mizrahi Jews in, 1162
modern means of transport in,
2207
and Morocco, 1006
moshavim of, 1576–1577
mountains of, 1160, 1206
museums of, 1164
music of, 1014, 1105–1106, 1164,
1618
Muslims in, 1163, *1164*
national identity in, Holocaust
and, 1042
newspapers and print media of,
1164, *1679*, 1683–1684

English-language, 1683
German-language, 1683
Hebrew, 1683
party-owned, 1683
privately owned, 1683
nuclear capability of, 1696–1698,
1697
Dimona reactor in, 708, 1288,
1697, 2309
rationale for, 1697–1698
occupied territories of (*See* Occupied territories)
and oil embargo (1973–1974),
1709
Orthodox Jews in, 1163
in Oslo Accord, 1724–1727
in Oslo II Interim Agreement
(1995), 1726, 1775, 1784
Palestinian citizens of (*See* Palestinian citizens of Israel)
peace movement in (*See* Peace
movement; *specific groups*)
"periphery doctrine" of, 992
Phalange Party supported by,
1954
plains of, 1234–1235
PLO cease-fire with (1981), 252,
1166
PLO mutual recognition with, 271,
928, 1167, 1725–1726, 1775
PLO negotiations, 2177–2178
PLO proclaimed as terrorist group
by, 2176
political parties of, **1175–1190** (*See
also specific parties*)
center/right, 1176
in coalition governments, 1164,
1175
electoral system and, 1175–1176
far left, 1177
influence of, 1176
left, 1176
Palestinian, 1178–1180, 1787,
1788
political issue complexity and,
1176–1177
reform, 1177
religious, 1176–1177, 1186
role of, 1175–1177
single-issue, 1177, 1182
political system of, 1164–1165
population of, 426, *753*, 1159,
1162–1163, 1844
by religion, 1162–1163, *1164*
postage stamps of, 1850
potash industry in, 1851
press control by, *1679*, 1681
prime minister of
cabinet of, 1164, 1330

Italo–Sanusi wars
first
Mukhtar (Umar al-) in, 1609
Treaty of Akrama ending (1917),
1609
second, Mukhtar (Umar al-) in,
1609–1610
Italy, **1199–1201**
Algerian relations with, Ente
Nazionale Idrocarboni and,
777–778
as British threat, 515
in Eastern Question, 739, 742
empire sought by, 1199–1200
Ethiopia conquered by (1935),
515
Fezzan occupied by, 830, 935
and France, Treaty of Rome between, 1933
French relations with, 1200
legal system of, influencing law in
Middle East, 1382
Libyan colonization by (*See under*
Libya)
Libyan relations with, 1415
masonic lodges set up by, 852
Ottoman relations with (*See* Turk-
ish–Italian War (1911–1912))
Sykes–Picot Agreement (1916) on,
742
Tripolitania occupied by, 935,
2218, 2247
Tunisia claims of, 1199
in World War I, 742
Gallipoli campaign, 866
and London Treaty (1913),
511
in World War II, 906, 1200,
2368–2372
Kaylani revolt (1941) supported
by, 516
Ittihad, al- (periodical), 2222
Darwish (Mahmud) in, 674
Habibi (Emile) and, 963
Ittihad al-nisa'i al-misri al-. See Egyptian
Feminist Union
Ittihad-e Islami (Afghanistan), 63
in mojahedin resistance, 1561
Ittihad Nisa al-Yaman. *See* Yemeni
Women's Union
*Ittijahat al-Tarbiyya wa al-Ta'lim fi Al-
maniya wa Inkiltira wa Faransa* (Ja-
mali), 1213
ITU. *See* Istanbul Technical Univer-
sity
I Want the Day (Badr), 357
IWS. *See* Institute of Women's Studies

IWSA. *See* International Woman Suf-
frage Alliance
IWSAW. *See* Institute for Women's
Studies in the Arab World
IZL. *See* Irgun Zva'i Le'umi
Izlane, 2624
İzmir (Turkey), *1201*, **1201–1202**,
2237
banks in, 389
Catholics in, 1932
Ege University in, 762–763
gecekondus on outskirts of, 872
Greek occupation of, 1201
Lausanne Treaty (1923) and, 1376
newspapers of, 2302
origins of, 1201
in Ottoman Empire, 1201
Kamil (Kibrish Mehmet) as gov-
ernor of, 1266
population of, 1201, 1202
port of, 194, 1201, 2206
Protestant missions in, 1854
Sèvres Treaty (1920) and, 1376
textile mills in, 2181
trade in, 1201
İzmir Economic Congress (1923),
1201, **1202**
and Turkish alphabet, 1933
Izmirlian, Matteos, 298
Izz al-Din, 2019

J

Jaafari, Shaban, Arfa (Hasan) and,
286
Jababdi, Latifa, 497, 498, **1203–1204**
imprisonment of, 1203
and moudawana reform,
1203–1204
Jabal, al- (Ghanim), 911
Jabal al-Akhdar (Libya), 655, **1204**
Jabal al-Akhdar (Oman), **1204**
Jabal al-Ansariyya, 909
Jabal Ali (Saudi Arabia), 1094
Jabal Ali Port, *2198*
Jabal al-Khalil (West Bank),
1204–1205
Jabal al-Zawiya, 909
Jabal Awliya Dam, 372
Jabal, Badawi al-, **1205**
Jabal Druze (Mount Lebanon),
1205
Jabal Druze (Syria), **1205–1206**
revolt in (1925–1927), 337, 729,
1206

Jabal Hafit (United Arab Emirates),
343
Jabali, Tahani al-. *See* Gebali, Tahani
al-
Jaballah, Abdallah, as founder of
Nahda, al-, 1635
Jabal Nablus (Israel), **1206**
Jabal Nafusa (Libya), 2218
Jabal Nuqum, 1983
Jabal Shammar (Saudi Arabia),
1206, 1638
Al Rashid family in, 818
tribes in, 2214
Ja'bari family, **1206**
Ja'bari, Muhammad Ali, at Jericho
Congress (1948), 1221
Jabarti, Abd al-Rahman al-,
1206–1207
Jabha, al- (periodical), 1842
Jabha al-Wataniyya, al- (United Na-
tional Front) (Tripolitania),
1207
Jabhat al-Amal al-Islami. *See* Islamic
Action Front
Jabiri, Ihsan al-, 307
Jabotinsky, Vladimir Ze'ev, *1208*,
1208–1209, 1432, 2437
Altalena named after, 170
Begin (Menachem) and, 424,
1181, 1209
and Ben-Gurion (David), 1209,
1947
death of, 1209
Irgun Zva'i Le'umi agreement
with, 1139
in Jewish Legion, 1208, 1230
Netanyahu (Benzion) as disciple
of, 1676–1677
in New Zionist Organization,
2372
program and ideology of, 2438
Revisionist movement formed by,
1362
and Rutenberg (Pinhas), 1946
on Tel Hai, 2173
Uganda Project opposed by, 2257
Weizmann's (Chaim) quarrel with,
2338
in Zionist Revisionist Movement,
1208–1209, 2372, 2435,
2437, 2438
Jabri, Ihsan, 103
Jabr, Salih, **1209–1211**
in Anglo–Iraqi treaty negotiations,
203, 1210

decline of, 1216–1217
end of (*vaka–i hayriye*) (1826), 1217,
    1467, 2308
establishment of, 1216
rebellions by, 417, 1217
    under Mahmut II, 1466–1467
recruiting for, 1216
reform of, 1217

Jankowski, James, *as contributor*,
    1831–1832, 2405

Jansen, Hermann, 207

Japan
    in Arab boycott against Israel,
        224, 225
    economic and military aid from,
        747
    in World War II, 1935

Japanese Red Army, PFLP ties with,
    1839

Jarallah family, **1218**

Jarallah, Hasan, 1218

Jarallah, Husam al-Din, 1218

Jarash (Jordan), **1218**
    ruins at, 1218

Jarash Festival, 1218
    Noor al-Hussein and, 1691

Jarba. *See* Djerba

*Jardin des sortilèges ou le parfum des légendes,
    Le* (Sefrioui), 2008

Jarida, al- (newspaper), 805

Jarra, Abu Ubayda ibn al-, 662

Jarring, Gunnar, **1218–1219**
    and UN Resolution 242, 1166,
        1219, 2275

Jasha'am tribe, 2212

Jasmund, A., 1285

Jassy Peace (1792), 739

Jauziyya, Ibn Taimiyya Ibn Qayim al-,
    436

Javanan-e Muslimin (Afghanistan),
    63

Jawahiri, Muhammad Mahdi al-,
    1219

Jawa'ib, al- (newspaper), 2051

*Jawlatun bayna Hanat al-Bahr al-Abyad al-
    Mutawassit* (Dou'aji), 721–722

Jayyusi, Salma al-Khadra, 1792

Jaza'iri, Ahmad al-, al-Takfir wa al-
    Hijra led by, 2151

Jaza'iri, Tahir al-
    and Arab nationalism, 261
    Kurd Ali (Muhammad) studying
        under, 1338

Jazayery, M. A., *as contributor*,
    1819–1820

Jazeera, al- (TV station),
    1219–1220, *1894*, 1896
    and Arab nationalism, 223
    criticism of, 1219
    establishment of, 1219, 1877
    expansion of, 1219–1220
    al-Qaradawi (Yusuf) on, 1870

Jazira, al- (newspaper), 1679

Jazrawi, Taha al-. *See* Ramadan, Taha
    Yasin

JCT. *See* Jewish Colonial Trust

JDC. *See* Joint Distribution Com-
    mittee

JDL. *See* Jewish Defense League

Jean Genet et Tennessee Williams à Tangier
    (Shukri), 2060

Jebana, 433

Jebhe-ye Melli. *See* National Front
    (Iran)

Jebhe-ye Nejat-e Milli (Afghanistan)
    Mojaddedi (Sebghatullah) in, 1561
    in mojahedin resistance, 1561

Jebhe-ye Nejat Milli (Afghanistan),
    63

Jebusites, in Jerusalem, 1222

Jehad-e Sazandegi (Iran), **1220**
    Nateq-Nuri (Ali Akbar) in, 1653

Jelve, Mirza Abul-Hasan, 2141

Jenin (West Bank), **1220–1221**,
    2340
    agriculture in, 1220, 1221
    in Arab–Israel War (1948),
        1220–1221
    Israeli occupation of, 1221
    refugee camp near
        Israeli assault on (2002), 1221,
            2284
        UN tour of, *2281*

Jerad, Abdessalem, in Union
    Générale des Travailleurs
    Tunisiens, 2265

Jericho (West Bank), **1221**, 2340
    Arafat (Yasir) return to, 272, 1775
    Biblical accounts of, 1221
    British rule in, 1221
    Jordanian rule in, 1221
    Palestinian refugee camps near,
        1221
    Palestinian self-rule in, 1221,
        1726, 1775

Jericho Congress (1948), 31,
    1221–1222

Jeroboam's Rebellion, 1631

Jerusalem, 1160, **1222–1227**. *See also*
    East Jerusalem; West
    Jerusalem
    al-Alami family in, 103
    Arab Club in, 225–226
    Arab College of, 226–227
    in Arab–Israel War (1948), 31,
        681, 1224
    in Arab–Israel War (1967), 249,
        1224–1225
    Arab Women's Association of
        Palestine in, 267
    archaeology in, 275, 278–279,
        1226
    Armenian community of, 290–292
    Armenian patriarchate of,
        291–292
    Bezalel Academy of Arts and De-
        sign in, 469–470
    during British mandate,
        1223–1224
    British occupation of (1917),
        509–510, 1223
    in Camp David Summit (2000),
        561
    as capital of Israel, 1224, 1225
    as capital of Palestine, 1223, 1226
    in Christianity, 1222
    Christian Quarter of, *1223*
    Christians in
        institutions of, 590
        number of, 590
    Church of the Holy Sepulchre in,
        1043–1044
    city plan of, 1222–1223
    Crusaders' conquest of, 1930
    division of (1948), 1224
    Eastern Orthodox patriarchate of,
        590–591
    expansion of, 1223, 1225
    expansion of Jewish community in,
        2432
    Hadassah Hospital in, 1224
    Haram al-Sharif (Temple Mount)
        in, *991*, 991–992
    Hebrew University in, 1224
    in Holy Land, 1043
    al-Husayni family in, 1053–1054
    infrastructure of, 1223
    Islamic Jihad attacks in, 1155,
        1226, 1227
    Israeli jurisdiction over, Neturei
        Karta opposing, 1677
    Israeli seizure of, in Arab–Israel
        War (1967), 1651
    Jarallah family in, 1218
    Jewish immigration into, 1223
    Jewish Quarter of, 1224, 1225,
        1225

Jerusalem *(continued)*
  Jews in
    Arab attacks on (1920), 1794
    as Yishuv, 2401–2402
  in Judaism, 1222, 1226, 1251
  Khalidi (Husayn Fakhri al-) as
    mayor of, 1224, 1295
  King David Hotel in, 1323–1324
  Kollek (Teddy) as mayor of, 1225,
    1331–1332
  Mandelbaum Gate in, 1224
  mayors of, 1224, 1225, 1226
  Mount Scopus in, 966
  Nashashibi family in, 1644–1645
  Nusayba family in, 1705–1706
  Orthodox quarter of, 1506
  Oslo Accord and, 1226
  in Ottoman Empire, 1222–1223
    British citizens in, 1796
  in Palestine Arab Revolt
    (1936–1939), 1224
  Palestinian Arab Congress in
    (1919), 1782
  Palestinian nationalism in, 1224
  Palestinians in
    residency status of, 1225, 1226
    threats to, 1226
  Pisgat Ze'ev settlement in, 1225
  population of, 1223–1224, 1225
  religious-secular competition
    among Jews in, 1225–1226
  riots in (1929), 235
  Roman destruction of, 1165
  Sadat (Anwar al-) visit to, 238
  Saint James Monastery in,
    291–292
  suicide bombings in, 1226
  Templars in, 2173
  unification by Israel (1967), 1225
  UN Resolution 181 (II) on, 1224,
    1225
  violence in, 1226
  wall dividing (2004), 1227
  Western Wall in (*See* Western Wall)
  in World War I, 151, 1223, 2368
  Zionism in, 1224
Jerusalem Center for Performing
  Arts, *2185*
Jerusalem Foundation, 1331
Jerusalem Girls College (JGC), 1055
Jerusalem Link, 1266
Jerusalem Post, 1683, 1684
  Kimche (David) in, 1322
Jerusalem Star (periodical), 1141
Jerusalem Symphony, 1164
Jerusalem Talmud, 2158
Jervis, Ludmilla, 285

Jesuits
  in Iraq, 1029
  in Ottoman Empire, 1931
  and Saint Joseph University,
    1971
Jesus, 1519
  in Christianity, 589
  Qur'an on, 1145
  tomb of, 1043
Je t'aime au gré de la mort (al-Qassim),
  1356
Jettou, Driss
  Istiqlal Party and, 1198
  as prime minister,1575, 2268,
    2411
Jeune Algérien, le: De la colonie vers la province
  (Abbas), 3
Jeune Turquie, La (newsletter), 867
Jew(s), **1231–1234**. *See also* Antisemitism; Judaism
  Aaronsohn family of, 1–2
  in Algeria
    antidefamation organization for,
      619
    French citizenship for,
      Crémieux Decree on,
      647–648
    during World War II, 1234
  Ashkenazic (*See* Ashkenazic Jews)
  benevolent associations of, 1373
  Biblical accounts of, 1231
  circumcision among, 601
  citizenship status of, 1232
  clothing of, yarmulke (*kippah*), 608,
    611
  communism among, 626, 627
  in Damascus affair (1840),
    664–665
  definition of, 1251
  diaspora of, 706
  economic mobility of, 1232
  education of
    Dor De'a movement in, 720
    opportunities for, 1231–1232
    at yeshivas, 2399
  in Egypt, during World War II,
    1234
  European, Haskalah movement
    among, 1002–1003
  in France
    denial of protection to, under
      Vichy government, 846
    organizations for, 151
  French language among, 1252
  in Germany, Haskalah movement
    among, 1002–1003
  in guilds, 947

immigration of
    to Balkan Peninsula, 383
    from Ethiopia, 786
    from Iraq, 790
    to Palestine (*See* Aliyah)
  in Iran, 1234
  in Iraq, 1232, *1232*, 2079
    during World War II, 807–808,
      1233
  in Jerusalem, as Yishuv,
    2401–2402
  Judeo-Arabic language of, 1252
  Karaites as, 1270
  Ladino language used by, 1363
  in Libya, 1410
    in Giado concentration camp,
      920
    during World War II, 1233
  of Middle Eastern origin (*See* Adot
    ha-mizrah)
  migration of, 1232, 1234, 1847
    into Israel, *1231*, 1234
    into Jerusalem, 1223
    into Palestine, 1233
  as minorities or subdominant
    groups, 1548
  in Morocco, 1234
    Corcos family of, 642
  under Muslim rule, 1231–1232
  in nationalist movement, 1549
  newspapers of, 1233
  origins of, 1231
  Orthodox (*See* Orthodox Jews)
  in Ottoman Empire, 383,
    1231–1232
    British support of, 1544
    as financiers, 807
    Herzl (Theodor) proposal re-
      garding, 1021
    millet system of, 1543–1545
  in Palestine (*See* Yishuv)
    immigration to (*See* Aliyah)
  political activism among, before
    Zionism, 1233
  Protestant missions targeting, 1854
  refugees, 1913–1914
    on *Exodus*, 2289
    Roosevelt (Franklin Delano)
      policies toward, 1935, 1936
  in Russia, 1360
  Sabras as, 1954
  vs. Samaritans, 1980
  Soviet, immigration to Israel, 48,
    147, 1162, 1163, 1169
  in Spain, converting to Christian-
    ity (*conversos*), 2084
  Spanish expulsion of (*See*
    Sephardim)
  in Syria, *1233*, 2129

in Tunisia, 1234, 2226
  Djerba, 718
in Turkey, 1233, 1234, 2238
in U.S., organizations for,
  176–179, 2273–2274
during World War II (*See also*
  Holocaust)
aliyah by, 147
  in Giado concentration camp,
  920
  Joint Distribution Committee
  aid to, 1239
  Levin (Yizhak Meir) rescuing,
  1408
  in Middle East, 1233–1234
  Shapira (Hayyim Moshe) rescuing, 2030
  Youth Aliyah aid to, 2411
in Yemen, 1231, 2388
Yiddish language of, 2399
Jewelry, Berber, 459
Jewish Agency for Palestine,
  1227–1228
and Abdullah I ibn Hussein,
  agreement between, 1058
Agudat Israel agreement with, 77
airlift operations of, 1913
Arlosoroff (Chaim) in, 289–290
Ben-Gurion (David) in, 447
Biltmore Program (1942) on, 472
Burg (Avraham) in, 546
Eban (Abba) in, 744
elections in, 1176
Eshkol (Levi) in, 784
establishment of
  American Jewish Committee in,
  178, 1227
  call for, 1227
  Churchill (Winston S.) on,
  596
  World Zionist Organization in,
  178
Goldmann (Nahum) in, 927
Gruenbaum (Yizhak) in, 945
and Haganah, 972
headquarters in Jerusalem, 1224
on Israeli immigration from Arab
  countries, 2365
Joseph (Dov) in, 1250
and Keren Hayesod, 1289
Kol (Moshe) in, 1332
Kollek (Teddy) in, 1331
leadership of, 1227
MacDonald (Malcolm) as liaison
  to, 1453
MacDonald (Ramsay) Letter to
  (1931), 1454, 2350
MacMichael (Harold) on, 1455

Magic Carpet Operation run by
  (1948–1950), 1460
Maimon (Yehudah Leib Hacohen)
  in, 1470
Meir (Golda) in, 1513
members of, 1227–1228
military controlled by, 1172
Nashashibi family and, 1644
non-Zionists in, 1227–1228
offices of, 1224, 1228
on Peel Commission partition
  plan, 1811
precursor of, 2436
Rothschild (Edmond de) as honorary president of, 1938
Samuel (Herbert Louis) and, 1983
Sasson (Eliyahu) in, 1993
Sharef (Ze'ev) in, 2031
Shazar (Shneour Zalman) in,
  2047
Shiloah (Reuven) in, 2056
Sneh (Moshe) in, 2075
status of, law on (1952), 2373
and Supreme Muslim Council,
  1922
United Hebrew Resistance Movement arranged by, 1140
on UN partition plan (1947),
  2274
Weizmann's resignation from
  presidency of, 1454, 2338
West German reparations sought
  by, 2348
World Zionist Organization and,
  2372–2373
and Youth Aliyah, 2411
Zionist Revisionist Movement and,
  2438
Jewish Brigade, **1229**
Amichai (Yehuda) in, 182
Holocaust and creation of, 1041
in World War II, 1540
Jewish Chronicle, 152
Jewish Colonial Trust (JCT), **1229,**
  2372
Levontin (Zalman) as director of,
  1408
Jewish Colonization Association
  (ICA), **1229–1230,**
  1937–1938
establishment of, 1229, 1937
Kalvaryski (Chaim Margaliut-) in,
  1265
Nasir (Najib) in, 1646
Jewish Colonization Corporation,
  donation from Mond (Alfred
  Moritz), 1564
Jewish Cultural Club (Libya), 1686

Jewish Defense League (JDL), Ka-
  hane (Meir) in, 1263
Jewish Enlightenment. *See* Haskalah
Jewish Institute of Religion, Wise
  (Stephen S.) as founder of,
  2354
Jewish Legion, **1230**
Ben-Gurion (David) in, 447, 1281
Ben-Zvi (Rahel Yanait) and, 456
Ben-Zvi (Yizhak) in, 457, 1230,
  1281
disbanding of, 1208, 1230
establishment of, 1208, 1230
Ha-Shomer members in, 1001
Jabotinsky (Vladimir Ze'ev) in,
  1208, 1230
Joseph (Dov) in, 1250
Katznelson (Berl) in, 1230, 1281
Trumpeldor (Yosef) lobbying for
  creation of, 2221
Zionist Revisionist Movement and,
  2438
Jewish Legion, The: Letters (Ben-Zvi), 457
Jewish Material Claims Against Ger-
  many, Conference on, 2348
Jewish Mule Corps, at Gallipoli,
  1540
Jewish National Fund (JNF), **1230,**
  2372
establishment of, 1230
Hope-Simpson's (John) criticism
  of, 2350
and Hula swamps, restoration of,
  1047
land purchased by, 616, 1229,
  1230
Palestine Land Development
  Company funded by, 1772
Ussishkin (Menahem) in, 2303
Jewish National Home, 2172
Jewish nationalism. *See* Zionism
*Jewish Peril, The. See Protocols of the Elders of
  Zion*
"Jewish Problem and the Socialist
  Jewish State, The" (Syrkin),
  2138
Jewish religious schools, 760, 761
Jewish settlements. *See also* Israeli set-
  tlements
  in South America, 1229
Jewish State, The (Herzl). *See Judenstaat,
  Der* (Herzl)
Jewish State Party, 2437
Jewish Territorial Organization for the
  Settlement of the Jews within
  the British Empire, 2425

Kirkbride (Alec Seath) in,
1324–1325
map of, *1762*
monarchic form of government
during, 933
Peake (Frederick Gerard) in,
257, *1810*
Transjordan Frontier Force defending, 2204
under Wauchope (Arthur), 2333
cabinet of ministers in, first, 35
and Camp David Accords (1978),
561
Catholics in, 1932
charitable *waqfs* in, 2323
children in, health care for, 1510
Circassians in, 600, 1218
cities of, 1218, 1243, 1979–1980
ancient, 1822–1823
capital, 190–192
northern, 1139
port, 217
provincial capital, 1270
civil war in (*See* Jordanian Civil
War)
climate of, 1240–1241
constitution of (1952), 35, 2152
coup in (1957), 1925
attempted, 39, 258, 1632–1633
currency of (dinar), devaluation
of, 1243
Dead Sea and, 684–685
defense costs as percentage of
GNP or GDP, *1530*
democratization in, 1245
Hussein ibn Talal and, 1063
deserts of, 1240
East Jerusalem controlled by, 1224
economic and military aid to, 747
from Arab countries, *748, 749*
dependence on, 751
from IMF, 749
from United States, 748, 749,
750
economy of, 752, *753*, 753–754,
1243–1244
education in, in religious schools,
761
Egyptian relations with
Palestinian claims in, 154, 155
pledge of financial aid (1957),
1632
elites in, 776
and al-Fatah, 2156
feminism in, 819
at Geneva Peace Conference
(1973), 900
geography of, 902–903, 1240
government of, 933

during Gulf Crisis (1990–1991),
951, 1064
Gulf of Aqaba in, 217
higher education in, 761, 2295
at Yarmuk University, 2380
honor killings in, 649, 887, 894
Noor al-Hussein in campaign
against, 1691
women's activism against, 1065,
1902
human rights activism in,
1291–1292
human rights in, 1065
under Hussein ibn Talal,
1061–1065
immunization rate in, 1510
independence of, 30, 518, 1480
industrialization of, 1095
in Iran–Iraq War (1980–1988),
357
and Iraq, federation of, 999, 1925
Iraqi federation, 826, 1969
Iraqi relations with, 217
Badran (Mudar) and, 357
Islamic coin collections in, 1703
Islam in, 1242–1243
Islamism in, electoral success of,
1151
Israel and
attempted assassination of
Mash'al (Khalil al-) and,
1579
General Armistice Agreement
between (1949), 240–241
Jordanian Option and, 1247
Khalidi (Walid) and, 1296
Mossad and, 1579
peace treaty between (1994) (*See*
Jordanian–Israeli peace treaty)
Jericho under, 1221
journalism in, 1065
labor unions in, 1358
land ownership in, 1371
languages in, 1242
at Lausanne Conference (1949),
1375
in League of Arab States, 1386,
1388
legal system of, 886
civil code, 1382
French influences on, 1380
Majalla, 1381
legislative body in, 932
literacy in, 1291
literature of, 804–805, 1422,
2001, 2156
at London Conference (1939),
1445
Majali (Rufayfan) in, 1470

Majali family in, 1470–1471
manufacturing in, 1483, *1483*
military of (*See* Arab Legion)
minorities in, 1242
modern means of transport in,
2207
Nabi Musi Pilgrimage banned by,
1630
national charter of, 1245
nationalism in, 520
nationalist movement in, 520
natural resources of, 1240
newspapers and print media in,
transitional press, 1681
and Oman, in Dhufar rebellion,
705–706
in Ottoman Empire, 1244
overpopulation in, 1243
and Palestine Liberation Organization, 1063
Palestinians in, 1241–1242,
1916
activists, 1008
civil war by, 1246–1247
from Nakba, al-, 1639
number of, 1241
and population growth, 2426
refugee camps for, *1245*
parliament of
dissolution of (1954), 35
elections for, 1151, 1245
Palestinians in, 1222
recalling of (1984), 1245
in peace process, 1245–1246
PFLP in, 1840
airplane hijackings by (1970),
270, 1246, 1840
government challenged by,
1773
philanthropy in, 409
phosphate industry in, 1834–1835
and PLO, 270, 2156
political system of, 30
population of, *753*, 1844
postage stamps of, 1849
potash industry in, 1851
prime minister of, 999, 1925
radio and television in, *1895*
railways in, *2206*
religious freedom in, 1242
rivers of, 1248–1249, 2379–2380
development of, 1238, 1248
Saudi Arabian relations with
Hussein ibn Talal and, 2156
pledge of financial aid (1957),
1632
Talal ibn Abdullah and, 2152
security in, 357
stock market in, 2091, *2091*

in Diaspora, 1251
vs. Ethiopian Jews, 787
future of, 1252
Halakhah, 979
Hasidim in, 1002
Holy Land in, 1043
Jerusalem in, 1222, 1226, 1251
kosher in, 1335–1336
messianism in, 1519
origins of, 1250–1251
Palestine in, 1758
principles of, 1251–1252
Sabbath in, 1954
Talmud and, 2157–2158
Judea and Samaria. *See* West Bank
Judenstaat, Der (Herzl), 1021, 2433
Judeo-Arabic language, **1252–1253**
Judeo-Spanish language. *See* Ladino
Judezmo. *See* Ladino
Jufayr, al- (Bahrain), 369, *370*
Juha (Arabic character), 1648
Julien, Charles-André, 489
July Revolution (Egypt), 1465
Juma²a, Nu²man, as New Wafd
  leader, 1686, 2321
Jumani, Dafi, 1972
Jumayyil, Amin, **1253**
  appointing Aoun (Michel) as in-
    terim president, 1394
  Geagea (Samir) challenging, 871
  government of
    Aoun (Michel) in, 215
    Hoss (Salim al-) in, 1045
    Karame (Rashid) in, 1272
  vs. Hobeika (Elie), 1039
  Israeli agreement of (1983)
    nullification of, 1665
    opposition to, 1665
  Jumblatt (Walid) and, 1253, 1256
  Karame (Rashid) opposing, 1272
  National Salvation Front oppos-
    ing, 1665
  in parliament, 1253, 1831
  in Phalange Party, 1400, 1831
  presidency of, 1253, 1400, 1831
  successor to, 1031
  against Tripartite Declaration
    (1950), 1394
  Twayni (Ghassan) under, 2254
  U.S. support for, 1488
Jumayyil, Bashir, **1253**
  in Arab–Israel War (1982), 253,
    254
  assassination of, 254, 1253, 1393,
    1394, 1400, 1831, 1908, 1954
  election of, 254, 1393, 1400

Franjiyya family rivalry, 849, 1394
Geagea (Samir) supporting, 871
Hirawi (Ilyas al-) and, 1033
Hobeika (Elie) and, 1038
Israeli support for, 253, 254, 1831
Israeli treaty rejected by, 254, 1103
in Lebanese Civil War, 581, 1253,
  1661
in Lebanese Forces, 1253, 1393,
  1394, 1400, 1831
presidency of, 1253, 1831
on "salvation committee," 1647
under Sarkis (Ilyas), 1992
Jumayyil, Nadim, 1253
Jumayyil, Pierre, **1253–1254**
  death of, 1831
  in al-Hilf al-Thulathi, 581, 1254
  Khuri (Bishara al-) opposed by,
    1315
  in Lebanese Front, 1395
  on National Pact, 1399
  in Phalange party, 1254, 1831
  Saade (George) as adviser of, 1951
  in Socialist Front, 580
Jumblatt, Bashir, murder of, Chehab
  (Bashir) in, 584
Jumblatt family, 729, **1254–1255**
  Arslan rivalry with, 307, 1255
  Chehab (Bashir) crackdown on,
    584
Jumblatt, Fu²ad, 1255
Jumblatt, Kamal, 729, **1255–1256**
  assassination of, 729, 1255, 1256,
    1853
  Khuri (Bishara al-) opposed by,
    1255, 1315
  in Lebanese Civil War, 1255,
    1256, 1853
  in Lebanese National Movement,
    1255, 1395, 1853
  in Parliamentary Democratic
    Front, 1802
  political power of, 1255–1256
  in Progressive Socialist Party,
    1255, 1852–1853
  in Socialist Front, 580
  Sulh (Rashid al-) and, 2117
Jumblatt, Nazira, 1255
Jumblatt, Walid, *727*, **1256**
  attempted assassination of, 1256
  and Damascus Tripartite Agree-
    ment, 1039
  as Druze leader, 2059–2060
  as family leader, 729, 1255, 1256
  Jumayyil (Amin) and, 1253, 1256
  in Lebanese National Movement,
    1395

in National Salvation Front, 1665
in Progressive Socialist Party,
  1256, 1853
Jumhuriyya, al- (newspaper), 911, 1678,
  1956
  Idris (Yusuf) in, 1082
Junayd, Abu al-Qasim al-, 2113
Jundi, Ahmad Sidqi Bey al-, in
  General Armistice Agreement
  (1949), 240
Jung, Eugène, 352
Junun (Bakkar), 376
Jurnal al-Iraq (newspaper), 1678, 1680
Jurnal al-Khadyu (newspaper), 1680
Jurshi, Salah Eddin al-, in Islamic
  Tendency Movement, 1586
Justice and Benevolence. *See* Adl wa
  al-Ihsan, al-
Justice and Charity. *See* Adl wa al-Ih-
  san, al-
Justice and Development Party
  (AKP) (Turkey), **99–100,**
  2236
  electoral success of, 99–100, 2245
  Erdoğan (Tayyip) in, 781, 2245
  establishment of, 99, 1911
  ideology of, 100
Justice and Development Party (PJD)
  (Morocco), 2268
Justice Party (Iran), Dashti (Ali) in,
  678
Justice Party (JP) (Turkey),
  1257–1258
  coalition governments formed by,
    2241
  Confederation of Turkish Trade
    Unions relations with, 631
  Demirel (Süleyman) in, 691, 1257,
    2242
  electoral success of, 691, 1257
  establishment of, 1257
  Gümüspala (Ragip) in, 1257
  Nationalist Action Party and, 1257
  organization of, 1257
  Republican People's Party coali-
    tion with, 1257, 2241
  State Planning Organization op-
    posed by, 2089
  True Path Party established by for-
    mer members of, 2219
*Justice sociale et développement en économie is-
  lamique* (Brahimi), 506
Justinian
  Aya Sofya (Hagia Sophia) rebuilt
    by, 342, 633
  Constantinople under, 632–633

Juwayni, Abu Muhammad al-, 2019

Jwaideh, Albertine, *as contributor*, 678–679, 732–733, 804, 1478–1479, 1496, 1961–1962, 2182–2183, 2213

K

Kaʿba (Mecca), 935, **1259–1260**, 1507, 1595, 1597, *1997*, 2422
   Utaybi (Juhayman al-) occupation of, 2304
   as *waqf*, 2323

Kabaağaçlu, Cevatsakir, 490

Kabak, Aaron Abraham, **1260**

Kabediya, Abd al-Rahman, in coup (1958), 1699

Kabir, Maliki al-Amir al-, 1086

Kabir, Saʿud al-, Abd al-Aziz ibn Saʿud Al Saʿud treatment of, 10

Kabir, Sulayman Pasha al-. *See* Abu Layla

Kabul (Afghanistan), **1260**
   in Anglo–Afghan wars, 196–197
   as capital, 53, 56, 1260
   in civil war, 59, 1260
   Kabul University in, 1260
   under Karzai (Hamid), 1260
   mayor of, 807
   population of, 1260
   refugees in, 1260
   Taliban capture of, 1561
   Taliban in, 61
   Taliban occupying (1996), 2154
   Timur Durrani in, 56

Kabul River, 54

Kabul University, **1260–1261**
   Islamic movements at, 60, 63
   political parties at, 62, 1260
   Samar (Sima) at, 1981

Kabul Women's College, 786

Kabyle Revolt (1963), 442

Kabyles, 458, 459

Kabyle unrest (1980). *See* Berber Spring

Kabyle unrest (1985), 444

Kabyle unrest (2001). *See* Black Spring

Kabylia (Algeria), 458, **1261**
   agriculture in, 1261
   Arch tribal structure in, 274
   Berbers in, 121–122
      disorders among (2001), Coordination des Archs in, 638

literature of, 192
   number of, 1261
   Tamazight language of, 121–122, 1261
   youth killed in detention (2001), 96, 274, 638
   disorders in (2001), Sadi (Said) resignation due to, 1960
   elections boycott in (2002), 1261
   Guenzetin assault (1955) in, 438
   population of, 1261

Kacemi, Abdel Hamid, 1904
   in Parti National Démocratique, 1805

Kach Party (Israel), 1184
   attacks by, 1264
   banned for racism, 1184, 1263
   Kahane (Meir) in, 1184, 1263
   in Kiryat Arba settlement, 1325

KADEK. *See* Freedom and Democracy Congress of Kurdistan

KADER (Turkey), 2171

Kadesh, Operation (Israel), 245

Kadha Ana Ya Dunya: Yawmiyyat Khalil Sakakini (al-Sakakini), 1973

Kadi-asker, 823

Kadiköy Girls School, 780

Kadın Adayları Destekleme ve Eğitme Derneği, 2171

Kadıncık Ana, 434

Kadin erenler (Araz), 274

Kadın Eserleri Kütüphanesi ve Bilgi Merkezi. *See* Women's Library and Information Center (Istanbul)

Kadinlara Mahsus Gazete (newspaper), 148

Kadınlar Halk Firkasi. *See* Women's People's Party (Turkey)

Kadinlar ve Siyasal-Toplumsal Hayat (Tekeli), 2170

Kadivar, Mohsen, **1261–1262**

Kadri, Mufide, **1262**

Kaffiya, 610–611

Kafi, Ali, in High State Council, 1026

Kafka, Franz, 216

Kafr Qasim (Israel), **1262**
   massacre of Palestinians in (1956), 1262

Kahana-Carmon, Amalia, 1433, 1434

Kahan Commission (1983), **1262–1263**
   on Eitan's (Rafael) role in Sabra and Shatila massacres, 774

findings of, 254, 1263
   Shamir (Yitzhak) reprimanded by, 1263, 2026
   on Sharon's (Ariel) role, 254, 1263, 2026

Kahane, Binyamin, 1263–1264

Kahane Hai (Israel), 1263–1264

Kahane, Meir, **1263–1264**
   assassination of, 1263
   in Kach Party, 1184, 1263

Kahan, Yitzhak, 1954
   in Kahan Commission, 1263

Kahil, Mary, 1453

Kahn, Ann, *as contributor*, 70–71, 464, 469–470, 506–507, 508–509, 547, 856, 866, 926–927, 940–941, 955–956, 1015–1016, 1260, 1284–1285, 1322, 1407–1408, 1452, 1512–1513, 1550, 2024–2025, 2029, 2060, 2075, 2159–2160, 2168–2169, 2384

Kaid, Ahmed, **1264**
   in Oujda Group, 1743, 1744

Kairouan. *See* Qairawan

Kalam schools, 1148

Kalat (Afghanistan), 2417

Kalbiyya tribe, 2212

Kalem (magazine), Arseven (Celal Esat) in, 305

Kalemiyye (Ottoman Empire), **1264–1265**

Kalimat ala Jidar al-Samt (Bin Diyaf), 474

Kalimat Haqq (Abd al-Rahman), 21

Kalinock, Sabine, *as contributor*, 2359–2361

Kalischer, Hirsch, **1265**

Kalvaryski, Chaim Margaliut-, **1265**
   binationalism supported by, 473, 1265
   Kisch (Frederick Hermann) support for, 1326
   in Zionist Executive, 1265, 2402–2403

Kamal, Ahmad, **1265–1266**
   in Egyptology, 276, 1265–1266

Kamal, Zahira, **1266**
   at Madrid Peace Conference (1991), 1266
   in Women's Centre for Legal Aid and Counseling, 2356
   in Women's Studies Center, 2362

Kaza (Ottoman court), 1690, 2624

Kazakh language, 2247, 2252

Kazakhs, 2253

Kazan Tatar language, 2252

Kazimayn Mosque (Baghdad), *359*

Kazim Paşa, and Hijaz Railroad, 1029

Kazim, Safinaz, 1907

KDP. *See* Democratic Party of Kurdistan; Kurdistan Democratic Party

KDPI. *See* Kurdish Democratic Party of Iran

Keban Dam, 788, **1284**, 2082, 2141

Kedar, Benjamin, *as contributor*, 1497

Keddie, Nikki, *as contributor*, 51–53, 206–207, 2302

Kedourie, Elie, 1406

Kefar (Sobol), 2076

Kéfi, Ridha, 1429

Keightley, Charles, 2108

Keilberth, Joseph, 476

Keinan, Amos, **1284–1285**

Kemalettin Bey, **1285**
  Ottoman Revival style of, 282, 1285

Kemalism, **1285–1288**
  Atatürk (Mustafa Kemal) rejection of concept, 333
  definition of, 1285, 1815
  Gökalp's (Ziya) thoughts in, 924
  ideology of, 1286, 1287–1288
  and National Security Council, 1666–1667
  Ottoman opposition to, 823
  in People's Houses, 1815
  reforms of, 1286
  repression in, 1286–1287
  secularization in, 1286, 1287
  six principles of, 1918
  themes of, 2240
  Westernization in, 1285–1286
  and women's rights, 2359

Kemal, Namik. *See* Namik Kemal

Kemal, Orhan, 2160

Kemal, Yahya, 2160

Kemençe, 2160

Kempff, Wilhelm, 476

Kenaz, Yehoshua, **1288**, 1433

Kenen, Isaiah L., in American Israel Public Affairs Committee, 177

Keneset (periodical), 470

Kenitra (Morocco), 913, 1567

Kenitra Civil Prison, 497

Kennedy, John Fitzgerald, **1288–1289**
  American Israel Public Affairs Committee work for, 177
  Egyptian relations with, 1288
  "flexible response" strategy of, 1327
  government of, Kissinger (Henry) in, 1327
  Iranian relations with, 1118, 1753, *1753*
  Middle East policy under, 2291–2292
  Peace Corps established by, 1808
  presidency of, 1288–1289
  and White Revolution in Iran, 2351

Kent Actors, 1289

Kenter, Musfik, 1289

Kenter, Yildiz, **1289**

Kenuz (Nubian dialect), 1696

Kenya
  in Uganda Project, 2257
  U.S. embassy bombing in, 1865, 2177

Kenyon, Kathleen, 277
  Palestine Economic Corporation funding for, 1772

Kerakanutiun Haykazian Lezvi (Chamchian), 579

Kerem (opera), 782

Kerem (Saygun), 2002

Keren Hayesod (World Zionist Organization), **1289**

Keren Kayemet le-Yisrael. *See* Jewish National Fund

Kerensky, Aleksandr, 1946

Kerman (Iran), **1289–1290**
  bazaars of, 420
  carpet weaving in, 566, 1290

Kermani, Karim Khan, 2047

Kermanshah (Iran), bazaars of, 420

Kerman Shaykhis, 2047

Kerr, Malcolm, assassination of, 181

Keskesi, 838

Keskin-Kozat, Burçak, *as contributor*, 33–34, 208, 472, 490–491, 492–493, 547–548, 598, 691–693, 745–746, 747, 762–763, 897–898, 965–966, 1201–1202, 1491, 1648, 2249, 2359, 2413–2414

Kesksou, 838

Kessar, Israel, **1290**

Ketabcheh-ye Ghaybi (Malkom Khan), 1477

Ketab-e Jom'eh (weekly), 2027

Ketuvim, 2058, 2157

Keyhan Publishing Company, Khatami (Mohammad) in, 1303

KFAED. *See* Kuwait Fund for Arab Economic Development

Kfar Habad (Israel), Lubavitcher Hasidim in, 1002

Kfar Hittim (Sephardic settlement), 2364

KGB (Soviet Union), **1290**
  functions of, 1290
  organization of, 1290

Khabur River, 344, 2129

Khad (Afghanistan secret police), Najibullah (Mohammed) as president of, 1638

Khaddam, Abd al-Halim, **1290–1291**

Khader, Asma, 894, **1291–1292**

Khadija (wife of Muhammad), 1595–1596

Khadiri, 2209

Khaiber, Mir Akbar, 1801

Khair-Eddine, Mohammed, 1355, 1427–1428

Khakas language, 2247

Khalaf, Abdulhadi (Abd al-Hadi), **1292**

Khalaf, Muna, in Institute for Women's Studies in the Arab World, 1100

Khalaf, Nazar al-, *as contributor*, 410–411

Khalaf, Rima, 820

Khalaf, Salah (Abu Iyad), **1292–1293**
  as aide to Arafat (Yasir), 270
  Arafat (Yasir) work with, 1292
  assassination of, 814, 1292
  and Black September, 485, 1292
  as al-Fatah founder, 813, 1292, 1773
  Hasan (Hani al-) and, 997
  in PLO, 814, 1292, 2335

Khalas fi al-Mafhum al-Urthuduksi, al- (Shenouda III), 2049

Khaldunniyya (Tunisia), **1293**
  establishment of, 1293, 2408

Khomeini, Ruhollah *(continued)*
regime of, 934
return to Tehran (1979), 1119,
1126, 1311
Sane'i (Yusef) as student of, 1987
Shariatmadari (Kazem) opposing,
2036
Students in the Line of the Imam
supporting, 2096
successor to, 1312
velayat-e faqih doctrine of, 793, 1311,
2311–2313
wife of, 1310
women's rights under, 892
Yazdi (Ibrahim) and, 2382, 2383
Khorasan (Iran), **1312–1313**
climate of, 1312
Naqshbandi in, 1642
population of, 1313
Khorasani, Akhund Molla Mohammad Kazem, 494
Khorde Avesta (Zoroastrian text),
2441
Khorramshahr (Iran), 1307–1308,
1317
in Iran–Iraq War (1980–1988),
1127
Khorvirap cathedral (Turkey), 297
Khotanese language, 1125
Khouri, Fred J., *as contributor*,
2284–2285
Khraief, Bechir, **1313–1314**
Khrimian, Mkrtich (Armenian patriarch), 298, **1314**, 2087
at Congress of Berlin (1878),
1314
influence of, 303, 1314
Khrushchev, Nikita S., **1314**
Brezhnev (Leonid Ilyich) under,
507
on Hammarskjöld (Dag), 986
Mossad acquisition of speech delivered by, 1578
Khubar, al- (Saudi Arabia), **1315**
U.S. military apartments attacked
in (1996), 1315
Khubz al-Hafi Sira Riwa'iyya, 1935–1956,
al- (Shukri), 2060
Khufu, pyramids of, 1857
Khurasani, Akhund, 977
Khuri, Bishara al-, **1315**
and Christian–Muslim alliance,
2118
in Constitutional Bloc, 633–634,
981, 1315
Eddé (Emile) in feud with, 2202

Eddé (Emile) rivalry with, 1315
government of
Chamoun (Camille) in, 580
Chehab (Khalid) in, 585
Karame (Abd al-Hamid) in,
1271
Sulh (Riyad al-) in, 1315
and Hamadi (Sabri), 981
and National Pact, 1315,
1662–1663
opposition to, 1315
Chamoun (Camille) in, 580,
1315
Chehab (Fu'ad) response to,
584
Jumblatt (Kamal) in, 1255,
1315
Karame (Abd al-Hamid) in,
1271
Shader (Joseph) in, 2018
by Socialist Front, 580
Phalange party and, 1254
as president, 1315, 1399
as prime minister, 1315
resignation of, 580, 1315
Sulh (Kazem al-) and, 2116
and Sulh (Riyad al-), 1315, 2118
Khuri, Faris al-
in Arab Academy of Damascus,
223
in National Party, 1664
Khuri, Khalil al-, in Constitutional
Bloc, 634
Khuruj al-Arabi, al- (Khalidi), 1295
Khusraw, Mulla, 988
Khutba, **1315–1316**
Khuzistan province (Iran),
1316–1317
cities of, 2
capital, 93
climate of, 1316
in Iran–Iraq War (1980–1988),
1317
Khaz'al Khan in, 1307
map of, 1317
population of, 1317
tribes in, 1316
Khyber, Mir Akbar, **1317**
Khyber Pass (Pakistan), 536,
1317–1318
Kian (magazine), 1630, 2423
Kian-Thiébaut, Azadeh, *as contributor,*
187, 998–999, 1123,
1987–1988, 2051, 2153
Kianuri, Nur al-Din, **1318**
in Tudeh Party, 2222

Kiarostami, Abbas, *831, 833,* **1318,**
1473
Kibbutz, **1318–1320**
age segregation in, 1319
agriculture in, 1319, *1319,* 1320
dance in, 668
decline of, 1320
education in, 1320
elite status of, 1319, 1320
establishment of first, 855, 1319,
1320, 1361
jobs in, 1319, 1320, *1320*
as literary catalyst, 1432
Meir (Golda) and, 1513
Mizrahi movement and, 1554
Nahal and, 1634
origins of, 1320–1321
population of, 1319
age structure of, 1320
tenets of, 1319, 1320
Youth Aliyah and, 2411
Kibbutz Artzi movement, 1319
Kibbutz En Gev, Kollek (Teddy) in,
1331
Kibbutz Ha-Dati, 1321
Kibbutz ha-Me'uhad movement,
1178, 1319
Kibbutz movement, 1319–1320,
1320–1321
establishment of, 1319
federations included in, 1319,
1320
and Histardut, 1034
Luz (Kadish) as leader of,
1448
number of kibbutzim in, 1319
religious, 1319–1320
secular, 1319
Shochat (Manya) in, 2059
Kidnappings, by al-Takfir wa al-
Hijra, 2150
Kifak inta? (record), 818
Kikhya family, **1321–1322**
Kikhya, Fathi, 1321
Kikhya, Rashid al-, 1321
Kikhya, Rushdi al-, **1322**
in People's Party, 1322
Kikhya, Umar Mansur al-, 1321
Killean, Carolyn, *as contributor,*
232–234
Kilometer 56 (Shamir), 2024
Kimche, David, **1322**
King Abd al-Aziz University. *See*
Umm al-Qura University

Kuhgiluyeh, 1447

Kuh-i Taftan (volcano), 385

Kulayni, Abu Ja'far al-, 2055

Kul system, 2072

Kultermann, Udo, 280

Kumaraswamy, P. R., *as contributor,*
586–587

Kumidiya Udib: Int Illi Qatalt al-Wahsh
(Salim), 1978

Kumik language, 2252

Kumkapi French School (Istanbul),
492

Kum Ombo (Egyptian agricultural
company), 1930

Kunt, I. Metin, *as contributor,* 33–34,
208, 334, 407, 472,
490–491, 547–548, 762–763,
864–865, 965–966,
1193–1196, 1201–1202, 1491,
1524, 1728, 1816–1817,
2009–2010, 2120,
2413–2414

Kupat Holim Kelalit (health fund),
1034

Kuran, Aptullah, *as contributor,* 386,
2120, 2194

Kurashi, Muhammad Abdullah al-,
at al-Azhar, 347

Kurd(s), *1341,* **1344–1346**
in cities, 1345
culture of, 1344–1345
international concern for,
1342
in Iran, 694, 914, 1111–1112
autonomy movement of, suppression of, 1922
Azerbaijan province of, 345
military action against, 1536
Sunni faith of, 1548
in Iraq, 1130
Ba'th Party and, 1066
CIA support for, 572
after Gulf War, 1068
Iranian support for, 1066
during Iran–Iraq War, 1129,
1130
Iraqi military action against,
1530, 1536, 1539
Kirkuk, 1325
Kurdish Autonomous Zone of,
1135, 1339
in Mosul, 1469–1470, 1582
no-fly zones and, 1069
political parties of, 1807
resistance in aftermath of
Iran–Iraq War, 1915

twelve-point agreement with,
422–423
United Nations on, 1339, 2282
U.S. invasion (2003) supported
by, 2325
in U.S. occupation, 2325–2326
U.S. supporting, 2174
in U.S. war (2003), 1339, 1341
languages of (*See* Kurdish languages)
literature of, 1345
as minorities or subdominant
group, 1549
music of, *1618*
in Naqshbandi, 1642–1643
nationalism of, 1659
number of, 1342, 1344
origins of, 1344
refugees, 1914–1915
religion of, 1345
revolts by (*See* Kurdish revolts)
society of, 1345
in Syria, Hayy al-Akrad quarter,
100
in Turkey, 2238
Atatürk (Mustafa Kemal) and,
1549
Diyarbakir, 715
imprisonment of political activists, 2423
infiltration of, 1545
military action against, 1536
pocu of, 610–611
and Refah Partisi, 1911
Republican People's Party and,
1919
revolt of 1922-1925, 1914
Yasar Kemal as, 2381
Yazidis as, 2214

Kurd Ali, Muhammad, **1338**
in Arab Academy of Damascus,
223, 1338
education of, 1338

Kurdish Autonomous Zone (Iraq),
1339, 2151
establishment of, 1135
Patriotic Union of Kurdistan in,
1807
power sharing in, 1339, 1807
regional division of, 1339
Washington Agreement on (1998),
1339, 1807

Kurdish Democratic Party of Iran
(KDPI), 914

Kurdish languages, 1344, 2238
in Alevi Shi'ism, 113
dialects of, 1124, 1342, 1344
written, 1344

Kurdish nationalism, 1340. *See also*
Kurdish revolts

Kurdish Regional Government, 2151

Kurdish revolts, **1339–1342**
foreign intervention in, 1340
in Iran, 1340, 1341
in Iraq, 1134, 1340–1341
Arif (Abd al-Salam) failure to
end, 288
Barzani (Mustafa) in, 1341, 1873
Hussein (Saddam) and, 1134,
1135
international support for, 1127,
1134
Mossad support for, 1578
Pahlavi (Mohammad Reza) supporting, 1127
Talabani (Jalal) in, 2151
in Turkey, 1340, 1341
by Kurdistan Workers Party,
1341, 1342, 1343

Kurdish Workers Party (Turkey),
1944

Kurdistan, **1342**
autonomy movement of,
1469–1470
Barzani family in, 408–409
boundaries of, 1342
cities of, 1342, 2115
Iranian, 1342
Iraqi, 1339, 1342
Lausanne Treaty (1923) and, 1376
mountains of, 1342
rivers in, 1342
Sèvres Treaty (1920) and, 1376
Shi'ite Islam in, Ahl-e Haqq sect
of, 82
Turkish, 1342

Kurdistan Democratic Party (KDP),
1642, 2151

Kurdistan Front of Iraq, 1339, 1807

Kurdistan Workers Party (PKK)
(Turkey), **1342–1344**
Alevis in, 114
dissolution of, 1344
establishment of, 1343
ideology of, 1342, 1343
origins of, 1342–1343
revolt by (1984–1999), 1341, 1342,
1343
violent tactics of, 1342, 1343

Kurdufan. *See* Kordofan

Kuria Muria islets, 527

Kurmandji dialect, 1344

Kush (Nubian kingdom), 1695

Kütahya Convention (1833), 2093

Kütahya, Peace of (1833), **1346**
  Syria in, 1077

Kut al-Amara (Iraq), **1346**
  battle of (1916), 1346
    British surrender at, 509, 1346
    Kashani (Abu al-Qasem) in, 1277
    Maude (Frederick Stanley) at, 1501, 2367
    World War I battles for, 1519, 2367

Kutan, Recai, 1911

Kutaysh, Umar, in PFLP, 1840

Kutla, al- (Morocco), 1574–1575

Kutla al-Wataniyya, al- (Libya), in national movement, 615–616

Kutnick, Jerry, *as contributor,* 177–179, 2436

Kutschera, Chris, *as contributor,* 408–409, 694–695, 1339, 1342, 1344–1346, 1469–1470, 1807, 1914–1915, 2151, 2380–2381

Kuttab, 475, 756, **1346–1347,** 2224

Kuttab, Eileen, 1100

Kuttab, Jonathan, 991

Kutubchi, Mullah Khidhir al-, 1309

Kutubiyya mosque (Morocco), 1568

Kuvayi milliye kadinlari (Araz), 274

Kuwait, **1347–1351.** *See also specific cities, organizations, people, and regions*
  Abd al-Aziz ibn Saʿud Al Saʿud in exile in, 9, 10
  Al Sabah family in, 158–160, 1348
  Al Saqr family in, 161–162
  Arabian Mission in, 231
  archaeological artifacts taken from, 279
  architecture of, *1350*
  banking in, 159, 162, *393*
  and Beitaddin Declaration (1978), 432
  borders of
    ambiguity of, 1349
    Anglo–Turkish convention on (1913), 159, 1678
    with Saudi Arabia, 1678
    Uqayr Treaty on (1922), 159, 1349
  Britain and, bond between, 1348–1349
  British control of, in foreign policy, 160

British protectorate in, 534
British treaty with (1899), 531, 614, 1348
cities of, capital, 1351–1352
citizenship in, 1351
climate of, 1347
constitution of, 159, 160, 162
  mineral resource ownership in, 1353
constitution of (1962), 1350
defense costs as percentage of GNP or GDP, *1530*
economic aid from, 749, 1349–1350, 1352
economy of, 752, *753,* 1349–1350, 1352
family planning in, 478
foreign policy of, 1350–1351
  economic aid in, 1350–1351, 1352
geography of, 1347
in Gulf Cooperation Council, 949
in Gulf War (1990–1991), economic impact of, 1349
higher education in
  at American University of Kuwait, 181
  at Kuwait University, 1353–1354
  women in, 1353–1354
immigrants in, 1347
independence of, 520
infant mortality rate in, 1509
Iraqi claim to
  British troops as deterrent against, 520
  Bubiyan Island, 541, 949
  Qasim (Abd al-Karim) on, 1873
  al-Warba Island, 541, 949
Iraqi invasion of (*See* Gulf Crisis (1990–1991))
Iraqi negotiations with, Ibrahim (Izzat) in, 1078
labor unions in, 1358
in League of Arab States, 1387, 1388
legal system of
  civil code, 1382
  French influences on, 1380
  Majalla, 1382
  reforms in, 1380
legislative body in, 932
liberation of (1991), 951
literature of, 1952
manufacturing in, 1483, *1483*
map of, *1347*
merchant opposition in, 159, 161
military of
  equipment of, *1534*
  force levels of, *1528–1529*

force structure of (army, air force, and navy), *1532–1533*
modern means of transport in, 2207
natural gas production and reserves in, *1671*
neutral zone shared with Saudi Arabia, 1678
newspapers and print media in, 1679
  diversity in, 1681
  English-language, 1681
oil in, 537, 2199
oil nationalization in, 1349
oil production in, 752, 1349
  concessions for, 1349
  al-Ghanim family in, 911
  after Iranian nationalization, 1349
  by Kuwait Oil Company, 1349, 1824–1825
  by Kuwait Petroleum Corporation, 1352–1353
oil revenues in, 1349
in OPEC, 1349, 1719
Ottoman alliance with, 158, 160, 161
Palestinians in, 1793
  number of, 1347
  persecution of, after Gulf War, 952
parliament of, 159, 160, 162
  architecture of building, *1350, 1351*
  elections for, 1350
  power of, 1350
  suspension of, 1350
political parties in, 1350
political system of, 1350
population of, *753,* 1347, 1844
prime minister of, monopoly on, 1350
Protestant missions in, 1854
radio and television in, *1895*
religion in, 1348
ruler succession in, 1350
Sanʿa University (Yemen) supported by, 1985
science and technology in, 2005
Shiʿism in, 2052
social services in, 1349
stock market in, 2091, *2091*
in trade, 2200
tribes in, 2213
U.S. support for, dependence on, 1351
water resources in, 1347
women in
  economic status of, *877*

higher education for, 1353–1354
in politics, 1350, 1951–1952
as writers, 1952
women's rights in, 884, 1951–1952
World Bank and
capital stock and voting power
in, *2363*
relative voting strength in, *2364*
Kuwait: Anatomy of a Crisis Economy (al-Sabah), 1952
Kuwait, Bay of, 1347
Kuwait City, **1351–1352**
architecture of, 1351
in Gulf War (1990–1991), 1351
National Assembly building in, *1350*, 1351
population of, 1352
traffic in, 1352
urban sprawl in, 1351–1352
walls around, 1351
Kuwait Foreign Petroleum Exploration Company, 1353
Kuwait Fund for Arab Economic Development (KFAED), 1349, **1352**
recipients of, 1352
Kuwait Museum, 1351
Kuwait Natural Petroleum Company, 1353
Kuwait Oil Company (KOC), 1349, 1824–1825
al-Ghanim family in, 911
as Kuwait Petroleum Corporation subsidiary, 1353
Kuwait Oil Tanker Company, 1353
Kuwait Petroleum Corporation (KPC), **1352–1353**
establishment of, 1349, 1353
Kuwait Petroleum International (KPI), 1353
Kuwait Stock Exchange, 1952
Kuwait University, **1353–1354**
Awadhi (Badria A. al-) at, 341
in Gulf War (1990–1991), 1353
Sabah (Rasha al-) at, 1952
vs. San'a University, 1985
Kuyas, Ahmet, *as contributor*, 330–334, 2071
Kvergic, H. F., 2122
Kwanyin, Kerubino, 868
Kyle, Ella, 1902
Kyprianos (Eastern Orthodox archbishop), 652
Kyprianou, Spyros, presidency of, 654, 697

Kyrgyz language, 2247
Kyrgyz people, 2253

L

Laabi, Abdellatif, **1355–1356**, 1428
Laayounne (Western Sahara), **1356**, 2342
Labor Alignment (Israel)
MAPAI in, 1185
MAPAM in, 1185
Labor and labor unions, **1357–1359**.
See also Child labor
in Algeria, 1358
development of, 1357
in Djibouti, 1358
in Egypt, 1358
illegal, 1358
imperialism's impact on indigenous, 1088–1089
in Iran, 1359, 2222
in Iraq, 1358
in Israel, 1357, 1358, 1361, 1362
(*See also* Histadrut; Labor Zionism)
in Jordan, 1358
in Kuwait, 1358
in Lebanon, 1358
in Libya, 1358
Marxism and "scientific socialism" and, 1357
in Mauritania, 1358
in Morocco, 453, 1358, 2264, 2265–2266
confederation of, 629–630
strikes by, 2264
privatization creating conflicts with, 1359
in Somalia, 1358
structure of, 1358
in Syria, 1358
in Tunisia, 41, 486, 1358, 2227, 2264–2265
for employers, 2268–2269
strike by, 2265
in Turkey, 1358–1359, *1359*
confederation of, 631, 1358–1359
Koç (Vehbi) on, 1331
women in (*See* Gender, and economy)
in Yemen, 1358
Labor Party (Israel). *See* Israel Labor Party
Labor rights, films on, 832
Labor Zionism, **1359–1362**, *1360*, *1361*, 2372, 2434

as basis of Histadrut, 1357
Ben-Zvi (Yizhak) supporting, 456, 457
Borochov (Ber) and, 493
Gordon (Aaron David) as philosopher of, 930
origins of, 1359–1360
in Palestine, 1357, 1360–1362
Revisionist Movement's conflict with, 1209, 1973
spread of, 1361
Lacheraf, Mostefa, **1362**
Lacoste, Robert, **1362–1363**, 1443
as Catroux (Georges) replacement, 570
Lacy, Lisa M., *as contributor*, 230–231
LADH. *See* Ligue Algérien des Droits de l'Homme
Ladino language, 1231, **1363**
Lado Enclave, **1363**
Laenser, Mohand, in Mouvement Populaire, 1588
Lagaillarde, Pierre, in Organisation Armée Secrète, 1715
Lagin (Mamluk sultan), 1074
La Guera, under Spanish control, 2085
Lahad, Antoine, **1364**
attempted assassination of, 481
as South Lebanon Army leader, 1364, 2083
Lahathat min Umri (al-Sabah), 1952
Lahhud, Emile, **1364**
government of, Hoss (Salim al-) in, 1045
Hariri (Rafiq) in conflict with, 994, 1364, 1401
as leader of Lebanese Army, 1364
as president, 1364, 1401
supporting Hizbullah, 1364
Lahiji, Shahla, 894, **1364–1365**
Lahm mishwi, 841
Lahouel, Hocine, **1365**
"New Appeal to the Algerian People" by (1976), 4, 1365
Lahrani, Sid Ahmed, 918
Lakes. *See specific lakes*
Lalluh, Abd al-Rahim, in PFLP, 1840
Lamari, Mohamed, **1365–1366**
La Marsa Convention, **1366**, 2229
French protectorate over Tunisia confirmed by, 1604
Lamartine, Albert, 2068
Lamartine, Alphonse de, 1421, 2088

Maddy-Weitzman, Bruce, *as contributor*, 450, 453, 618–619, 629–630, 660, 858, 1074, 1083, 1196–1198, 1356, 1588–1589, 1743, 1803–1804, 1805, 1836–1838, 1904–1905, 1963–1965, 2085–2086, 2179, 2266, 2336, 2342–2344, 2344–2347

Madhhab, 2018
    muwahhidun as followers of, 1625

Madina, al- (Saudi Arabia), 1995

Madina, al- (newspaper), 1679

Madinat al-Salam (Egypt), 1995

Madinat Nasr (Egypt), 1994–1995

Madkour, Ibrahim, **1456–1457**

Madrasa, 360, 756, **1457–1458**, 2154, 2192, 2625
    and Istanbul University, 1196
    ulama teaching at, 2258

Madrasat al-Alsun, 2146

Madrasat al-Jam'iyya al-Khayriyya al-Islamiyya bi al-Iskandariyya, 759

Madrasat al-Mushaghibin (Salim), 1978

Madrid Accords (1975), Spanish protectorate in Western Sahara ended by, 2345

Madrid Agreements (1975), 942, 943, 2084, 2086

Madrid Conference (1880), 1004

Madrid Peace Conference (1991), 238, **1458–1459**, 1725, 2084, 2294
    bilateral negotiations at, between Palestinians and Israel, 1768
    Bush (George H. W.) at, 549
    failure of, 1775
    framework for, PLO rejection of, 1775
    Hawatma (Nayif) opposition to, 1009
    Intifada as catalyst for (1987–1991), 1107
    Netanyahu (Benjamin) at, 1677
    Nusayba (Sari) at, 1706
    and Oslo Accord (1993), 1793
    Palestinian delegation at
        Abd Rabbo (Yasir) in, 1266
        Kamal (Zahira) in, 1266
    PLO representatives at, 271, 1458–1459
    refugee issue at, 1916
    Shamir (Yitzhak) at, 2026

Syria at, 319, 2135
U.S. role in, bias in, 1775

Mafdal (Israel). *See* National Religious Party

Maftul, 838

Magarief, Yusuf al-, as leader of National Front for the Salvation of Libya, 1655

Magazines, 1682. *See also* Newspapers and print media; *specific magazines*

Magen David Adom (MDA), **1459**

Maghariba tribe, 2023

Maghen, Zev, *as contributor*, 777, 865, 992, 1280, 1336, 1373, 1446–1447, 1448, 1451–1452, 1555, 1634, 1641

Maghreb pluriel (Khatibi), 1303

Maghrib, **1459–1460**
    labor unions in, 1358
    literature on, 588 (*See also* Literature, North African)
    Union of the Maghrib treaty, 1006

Maghrib (periodical), 379
    Comité d'Action Marocaine platform in, 618

Magic Carpet Operation, **1460**, 1913

Magiciens (film), 376

Magnarella, Paul J., *as contributor*, 1815–1816, 2246, 2316–2317

Magnes, Judah, 540, **1460–1461**
    Ahad Ha-Am and, 78
    binationalism supported by, 473
    and Hebrew University of Jerusalem, 1018
    Philby (Harry St. John) and, 1833

Magsaysay Award for Community Leadership, Samar (Sima) awarded with, 1982

Mahabad (Iran), in Azerbaijan crisis (1945–1946), 346

Mahalla al-Kubra, al-, **1461**

Mahalle Schools, **1461–1462**
    Tunisian abolition of, 1604

Mahan, Alfred Thayer, Middle East designation and term used by, 1522

Mahaz-e Islami (Afghanistan), 63
    in mojahedin resistance, 1561

Mahaz-e Milli-e Islami-e Afghanistan, 863

Mahbubi, Sadr al-Shari'a al-Thani al-, 988

Mahbusa, 2050

Mahdawi, Fadil Abbas al-, **1462**

Mahd-e Ulya, Malek Jahan Khanum, **1462**
    son of, Naser al-Din Shah as, 1462, 1643

Mahdi, **1462–1463**, 1519, 2123

Mahdi, al. *See* Ahmad, Muhammad

Mahdi, Ali Akbar, *as contributor*, 1273, 1300–1301, 1558, 1615–1616, 1629–1630, 2313–2314

Mahdi, Amin al-, 2262

Mahdi, Sadiq al-, Numeiri (Muhammad Ja'far) and, 1700–1701

Mahdist(s), Numeiri (Muhammad Ja'far) opposed by, 1699–1701

Mahdist movement, in Sudan, 404–405
    Khartoum, 1301
    in Umma Party, 2261

Mahdist state, **1463–1464**
    under Abdullahi (Muhammad Turshain), 32–33, 87
    under Ahmad (Muhammad), 87
    defeat of
        in Karari, Battle of (1898), 1712
        Kitchener (Horatio Herbert) in, 1329, 1712
        Omdurman as capital of, 1301, 1712

Mahdiya (ancient city), 2228

Mahdiyya, Munira al-, 2262

Mahfuz, Isam, 2184

Mahfuz, Najib, 553, 1420, *1420*, **1464–1465**
    Khemir (Sabiha) art on covers of, 1309

Ma Himar al-Hakim (Huhu), 1423

Mahir, Ahmad, 1465, **1465**
    government of, Misri (Aziz Ali al-) in, 1550
    Nuqrashi (Mahmud Fahmi al-) and, 1701

Mahir, Ali, **1465–1466**
    Azzam (Abd al-Rahman al-) support for, 352
    Mahmud (Muhammad) and, 1468–1469

Mahjar (émigré) writers, Ziadeh (May) and, 2431

Mahjub, Abd al-Khaliq, Ibrahim (Fatima Ahmed) influenced by, 1075

Mahjub, Rif'at al-, assassination of, 1215

Mandate system (continued)
  San Remo Conference (1920) on, 1988
  Sèvres Treaty (1920) and, 2015
  Sykes–Picot Agreement (1916) on, 2128
  Wilson's (Woodrow) acceptance of, 2353

Mandelbaum Gate, 1224

Mandel, Ruth, *as contributor*, 112–115

Mandub, 2033

Mandur, Muhammad, 1061

Manescalo, Alfonso, 282

Manetti, Fernando, 556

Manfaluti, Mustafa Lutfi al-, 1419

Manghusha, Muhammad Ahmad al-, 2024

Ma'nids, 2059

Manifesto of the Algerian Muslim People (1943), 3, **1480**
  Abbas (Ferhat) writing of, 3, 189, 1480
  Parti du Peuple Algérien approval of, 1804
  supplement to, 3

Ma'nis, 728

Mankur Palace, al- (Samarra), 1981

Männer und Mächte im Orient: 25 Jahre diplomatischer Tätigkeit im Orient (Grobba), 944

Manning, Olivia, 908

Manoogian, Aram, 676

Manor, Amos, 2056

Mansaf, 839

Mansour, Azzedine G., *as contributor*, 274, 280–284, 917–920, 1365–1366, 1904, 1905, 2332–2333

Mansur, al-, 359–360

Mansura, al-, **1480–1481**

Mansur, Abu Ja'far al- (Abbasid caliph), 1131–1132, *1132*

Mansur, Ahmad al-, 2038

Mansure Army, **1481**

Mansur, Hamza, 1151

Mansur, Hasan Ali
  assassination of, 1129, 1898
  and Iran-e Novin Party, 1047
  in Iran Novin Party, 1129

Manufacturers-Hanover Trust, 2082

Manufactures, **1481–1485**, 1555
  low productivity in, factors for, 1484
  1900-1945, 1481–1482

post-1945, 1482–1484
pre-1900, 1481

Manufacturing. *See also* Industrialization
  in Algeria, 127, 128
  in Iran, Isfahan, 1093, 1142
  in Israel, *1162*
  preindustrial, 1092–1093
  in Turkey, Bursa, 194

Manukian, Aram, 303

Man Who Lost His Shadow, The (Ghanim), 911

Many, Moshe, Middle Eastern origin of, 49

MAPAI (Israel), 1185
  Ahdut ha-Avodah in, 82, 1178, 1185
  Arlosoroff (Chaim) in, 289
  Ben-Gurion (David) in, 447, 1185, 2402
  Dayan (Moshe) in, 681–682
  establishment of, 1185
  foundation of, 1362
  Gruenbaum (Yizhak) supporting, 945
  Ha-Po'el ha-Tza'ir in, 1185
  in Israel Labor Party, 1185
  Katznelson (Berl) in, 1185, 1281
  Lavon affair and, 1185, 1188
  Lavon (Pinhas) as ideologist of, 1378
  Luz (Kadish) in, 1448
  and Palestinian citizens' political parties, 1786
  platform of, 1185
  prime ministers from, 1185
  RAFI Party split from, 1187–1188
  Shazar (Shneour Zalman) in, 2047
  Shitreet (Bekhor) in, 2058
  Sprinzak (Joseph) in, 2087

MAPAM (Israel), 1185
  Ahdut ha-Avodah in, 82, 1178
  Arab members of, 1185
  Ben-Aharon (Yitzhak) in, 438
  establishment of, 1185
  Flapan (Simha) in, 835
  and Ha-Shomer ha-Tza'ir, 1002
  in Labor Alignment, 1185
  in Meretz Party, 1185, 1186
  military influenced by, 1173
  Mossad surveillance of, 1578
  platform of, 1185
  Sneh (Moshe) in, 2075
  split in, 1185
  Ya'ari (Me'ir) in, 2375

Ma'pilim, 2625

Mapu, Abraham, 1430

Maqam (music), 1617, 1618

Maqama, 1420, 2184

Maqamat, 2113

Maqam, Mirza Bozorg Qa'em, 7

Maqarin (Widha) Dam, 1249, **1485**, 2379, 2380

Maqasi College al-, 2116

Maqasid al- schools, 759

Maqasid al-Shari'a, 834

Maqasid School of Maqasid Benevolent Society, 759

Maqrizi, al- (numismatic scholar), 1701

Maqwar, Ahmad, in Parti National, 1805

Mar'a al-Jadida, al- (Amin), 187

Mar'a al-Misriyya min al-Fara'ina ila al-Yawm, al- (Shafiq), 2019

Mara'a wa al-Amal, al- (Musa), 1614

Marabout (saint or holy person), **1485**, 2359

Maraboutic traditions, in Algeria, 122

Maraboutism, 460

Marabtin al-sadqan (clients for protection), 1609

Marada Brigade, 1394

Ma'rakatuna al-Arabiyya fi Muwajahat al-Isti'mar wa al-Sahyuniyya (Ghallab), 910

Maratghi, Mustafa al-, **1485–1486**

Marathon, in Oasis Group, 1707–1708

Marchand, Jean-Baptiste, 405, 529–530, 811

Marconi Company, 1893

Marcus, Abraham, *as contributor*, 111–112

Mardam, Jamil, **1486**
  in National Party, 1664

Mardin, Asli Davaz, in Women's Library and Information Center, 2358

Mardom Party (Iran), **1487**
  Alam (Amir Asadollah) in, 102, 1487

Mareth Line, **1487**

Margalit, Dan, 1452

Marghinani, al-, 988

"Marginal Notes on the Book of the Relapse" (Qabbani), 1859

Marguerite Taos Kabyle. *See* Amrouche, Mary Louise

Maude (Frederick Stanley) in, 1501, 2367

Mesopotamia, 1917–1920: A Clash of Loyalties (Wilson), 2353

Message, The (film), 98–99

Messaoudi, Khalida. *See* Toumi, Khalida

Messiah, 1519

Messianic Regime: The End of the Road (Ben-Aharon), 438

Messianism, **1519**

Messick, Brinkley, 756

Mestiri, Ahmad, **1519–1520**
   in Mouvement des Démocrates Socialistes, 2232

Meşveret (journal), 867
   Ahmet Riza at, 91, 623, 2408

Metaphysics (Avicenna), 1457

"Metei Midbar" (Bialik), 470

Métier à tisser, Le (Dib), 1426

Metropolitan Museum of Art (New York), 279

Metruk, 1368

Metternich, Klemens von
   in Damascus affair (1840), 664
   and Mustafa Reşid, 1624
   territorial expansionism under, 339

Me'uharim (Guri), 956

Meushi, Paul Peter, **1520–1521**

Mevat, 1368

Mevlevi Brotherhood, **1521**
   Atatürk (Mustafa Kemal) closing, 2171
   vs. Bektashis, 435

Mevlevis, 2113

Mezrag, Madani, in Islamic Salvation Army, 1155, 1156

MFO. *See* Multinational Force and Observers

M'hammas, 838

MHP. *See* Nationalist Action Party (Turkey)

MI-5, 1521

MI-6 (Britain), **1521**
   in Iranian coup (1953), 1118, 1752
   KGB compared to, 1290

MIA. *See* Mouvement Islamique Armé

Mi'ari, Muhammad
   in al-Ard movement, 285
   in Progressive List for Peace, 1187

Michael, Sami, 1452, **1521–1522**

Michalak, Laurence, *as contributor*, 717–718, 990, 1204, 1863–1864, 2015–2016, 2192

Michman, Dan, *as contributor*, 1040–1043

Middle East, as designation and term, **1522–1523**

Middle East Airlines, 1975

Middle East Broadcasting (MBC), 1895

Middle East Command (1951), 1692–1693

Middle East Defense Organization (MEDO), 519, **1523**, 1692–1693

Middle Eastern Jews. *See* Adot hamizrah

Middle East Society of Associated Accountants, 1951

Middle East Supply Center (MESC), **1523–1524**

Middle East Technical University, 491, **1524**
   Women's Studies Graduate Program of, 2362

Midfa'i, Jamil al-, 927, **1524**, 1968
   opposition to, 1283

Midhat, Ahmed, on Aliyer (Fatimah), 148

Midhat Paşa, **1524–1526**, 2407
   Baghdad improved by, 360
   in Çerkes Hasan incident (1876), 575
   Damascus under, 663
   Iraq improved by, 1132
   and Kuwait alliance, 158
   Namik Kemal and, 1641

Midrash, Rabbinic Hebrew in, 1017

Midwives, 2003

Miflagah Komunistit Yisraelit. *See* Israel Communist Party (MAKI)

MIFTAH. *See* Palestinian Initiative for the Promotion of Global Dialogue and Democracy

Miggiel, John, *as contributor*, 382–384, 542–543

Migration, 1846–1847

Mihrab, 1074, **1526**, 1577

Mikayelian, Kristapor, 676

Mikdamot (Yizhar), 2403

Miklat (newspaper), 464

Mikou, Mohamed, 1716

Mikoyan, Anastas, *1942*

Mikunis, Shmu'el, in Communist Party of Palestine, 626

Milani, Tahmineh, **1526**

Miles, George, in Islamic numismatics, 1702

Miliana River, 2225

Miliani, Mansouri, 918

Militant Clergy Association (MCA) (Iran), Karbaschi (Gholamhosain) opposing, 1273

Military, **1526–1543**
   active force levels of, *1528–1529*, *1529–1531*
   in arbitrator regime, *1536*
   in conflict between states, 1537–1540
   in conflicts with and among Great Powers, 1540
   defense costs as percentage of GNP or GDP, *1529–1530*, *1530*
   equipment of, *1534*, 1535
   force structure of (army, air force, and navy), *1532–1533*, 1535
   future of, 1541
   in internal affairs of other countries, 1530–1531
   in internal conflicts, 1530–1531, 1536–1537
   modernization of, 1535
   nontraditional, 1535
   organization of, 1527–1535
   participation in revolutions and coups, 1536–1537
   role of, 1540–1541
   in ruler regime, *1539*
   as school of nation, 1541
   Westernization of, 1527–1528

Military-administrative slaves, 2072–2073

Military aid. *See* Economic and military aid

Millat (Afghanistan), 62

Millet, 886

Millet Meclisi. *See* National Assembly

Millet system. *See also* Armenian millet
   missionaries under, 1551
   in Ottoman Empire, 1461, **1543–1545**, 1548, 1732 (*See also* Armenian millet)
   Christians in, 590, 1543–1545
   Cyprus in, 652
   in eighteenth–nineteenth century, 1544–95
   in fifteenth–seventeenth century, 1543–94

Milli Birlik Komitesi. *See* National Unity Committee (Turkey)

Po'alei Mizrahi and, 1186, 1187
in United Religious Front, 1190

Mizrahi, Tawfiq, in Club National Israélite, 612

MNA. *See* Mouvement National Algérien

MNR. *See* Mouvement National pour la Réforme

Moadda, Mohamed, **1554–1555**
as successor to Mestiri (Ahmad), 1520

Moaddel, Mansoor, *as contributor,* 41–42, 200–202, 421, 1580–1581

"Mobile Identity and the Focal Distance of Memory" (Khemir), 1309

Mobilization press, 1680, 1685

Moda'i, Yitzhak, **1555**
in Liberal Party, 1184

Modarres, Hasan, 1757

Moderate Liberal Party (Jordan), founder of, 1470

Modern Egypt (Baring), 406–407

Modernization, **1555–1556**. *See also* Industrialization
and decline of bazaars, 419, 420
economic aspects of, 1555
and education, 880
in Egypt, 1157–1158
and decline of bazaars, 419
under Muhammad Ali, 766
France and, 844
intellectual/psychological aspects of, 1556
in Iran, 1756
of law (*See* Law, modern)
in Morocco, Lyautey (Louis-Hubert Gonzalve) and, 1448
Persian, under Fath Ali Shah Qajar, 816
political aspects of, 1556
social aspects of, 1556
in Syria, 315
in Turkey, 2240
vs. Westernization, 2341
and women's status, 874–876, 883, 885–886

Modern Language Association, 1966

Mo'ed, 2157

Mofaz, Sha'ul, *750*
as defense minister, 1174

Mogannam, Matiel, **1556–1557**
in Arab Women's Executive Committee, 268

Moghaizel Foundation (Lebanon), 1557–1558

Moghaizel, Laure, 894, 1396, **1557–1558**

Mogul Empire, 525, 526

Mohajerani, Ataollah, **1558**

Mohamed Khan, 833

Mohammad VI (king of Morocco), 933

Mohammad Ali Shah Qajar (ruler of Iran), **1558–1559**
abdication of, 1559
constitutional supplement signed by, 636
constitution opposed by, 636–637, 1559
coup against, 1868, 2430
as crown prince, 7, 1559
deposition of, 88, 374, 637
father of, Mozaffar al-Din Qajar as, 1592
government of, Amin al-Soltan (Ali-Asghar) in, 184
Kuchek Khan-e Jangali opposing, 1337
majles opposed by, 636–637, 1559
reign of (1907–1909), 636–637, 1868–1869
masonic lodges allowed under, 852
Sadr (Muhsin) supporting, 1960
son of
Ahmad Qajar as, 88, 637
Naser al-Din Shah as, 1643
Vazir Afkham (Soltan Ali Khan) under, 2311

Mohammadi, Maulawi Mohammad Nabi, **1559–1560**
in Harakat-e Inqilab-e Islami, 63, 1561
in mojahedin resistance, 1561

Mohammad Shah Qajar (ruler of Iran)
reign of (1834–1848), 1868
wife of, Mahd-e Ulya, Malek Jahan Khanum as, 1462

Mohammadzai dynasty, 721, 2007

Mohilever, Samuel, **1560**
and Zionism, 2432

Mohseni, Asaf
in Harakat-e Islami, 63, 1561
in mojahedin resistance, 1561

Mojab, Shahrzad, *as contributor,* 2423

Mojaddedi, Sebghatullah, **1561**

election as president, by Afghan Interim Government, 63, 1561
in Jebhe-ye Nejat-e Milli, 63, 1561
in mojahedin resistance, 1561

Mojahed (newspaper), 1562

Mojahedin (Afghanistan), *1561,* **1561–1562**
communists opposed by, 53, 1561
coup by (1992), 66, 1561
external support for, 59
government of, 1561
Hazara and, 1015
infighting among, 1561
in Karzai interim government, 1561
Najibullah opposed by, 59, 66, 1561
under Omar (Muhammad), 1712, 1713
origins of, Islamic movement in, 61
parties involved in, 1561
in resistance war, 1561–1562
Saudi Arabian aid to, 1627
Soviet intervention opposed by, 53, 59, 65–66, 474
Taliban opposition to, 61, 1561
U.S. supporting, 2174

Mojahedin-e Khalq (Iran), **1562–1563**
alliance with Iraq, 1562
Bani Sadr (Abolhasan) in, 389
categorized as terrorist organization, 1562
Feda'iyan-e Khalq influence on, 821
Rafsanjani (Ali Akbar Hashemi) and, 1899
Rajavi (Masud) in, 1900
uprising by, suppression of, 1922
U.S. occupation of Iraq and, 1562

Mojtahed-Shabestari, Mohammad, **1563**

Moked (Israel)
Israel Communist Party in, 1182, 1188
RAKAH in, 1182, 1188

Moldavia, languages of, 2248

Moldavian Soviet Socialist Republic, 507

Moledet Party (Israel), 1186
electoral success of, 1186
in National Union, 1187
platform of, 1186
Ze'evi (Rehavam) in, 1186

Molière, 1421
Kasap (Teodor) plays based on, 1277
translation of, 92, 171

Mollet, Guy, **1563**
in Arab–Israel War (1956), 245
and Sèvres Protocol (1956), 2109
in Suez Crisis (1956–1957), 2108
visit to Algeria, French riots protesting (1956), *137*

Moltke, Helmuth von, 903, **1563–1564**

Moment of Innocence (Iranian film), 1473

Monarchic form of government, 933

Monastero, Alberto, and Jewish community in Tripoli, 974

Monasticism, 787
Coptic, 640, *641*

Monastir, **1564**

Mond, Alfred Moritz, **1564**

Monde, Le (newspaper), 477

Monnet, Jean, 689

Monnot, Georges, 1457

Monophysite, 639

Monophysite churches, 738

Monotheism, of Islam, 1596, 1597

Monroe, Elizabeth, 1323

Monsieur Bob'le (Shahada), 2020

Montagne du lion, La (Tlili), 2193

Montazeri, Hosayn Ali, **1564–1565**
Kadivar (Mohsen) studying under, 1262
Khamenehi's mistreatment of, Yazdi (Ibrahim) on, 2383
religious qualifications of Khamendi as *faqih* questioned by, 1564
as successor-designate to Khomeini
confirmation of, 1564
resignation of, 1564
as successor to Khomeini (Ruhollah), 1312

Montefiore, Moses, **1565**, 1976
in Damascus affair (1840), 664–665
and expansion of Jerusalem, 1223
and Zionism, 2432

Montenegro
in Balkan League, 384
Balkan refugees fleeing to, 382
in Balkan wars, 384
independence of
Berlin Treaty (1878) and, 383, 1989
San Stefano Treaty (1878) and, 382, 1988
nationalist movement in, 542

Monteux, Pierre, 477

Montgomery, Bernard Law, **1565**, 2194
at al-Alamayn battle (1942), 102, 516, 1565, 2370

Montjoie Palestine (Aba), 1426

Montreux Convention (1936), 485, **1565**
capitulations under abandoned (1939), 1636
Eden (Anthony) at, 755
mixed courts ended by, 1553
on Turkish Straits, Turkish control of, 621, 743, 2095

Moore, Clement Henry, 450

Moore, Henry, 1978

Moors, 1964

Morad, Gowhar, 1962

Morashah Party (Israel), 1186

Mor Çatï Kadïn Sïǧïnaǧï, 2171

Morgenthau, Henry, Jr., 1936

Morier, James Justinian, 976

Moriscos, 2084

Morley College (London), Ghoussoub (Mai) at, 916

Morning Herald (newspaper), 594

Moroccan–Algerian War, **1566**

Moroccan Association of Human Rights. *See* Association Marocaine des Droits de l'Homme

Moroccan crises (1905–1906, 1911)
Act of Algeciras on (1906), 8
Agadir crisis (1911), 70
Algeciras Conference on (1906), 119–120
British support for, 119–120
Cambon–Lansdowne Agreement on (1904), 559–560
financial aspect of, 14
German opposition to, 8, 70, 119–120

Moroccan Family Legal Code. *See* Moudawana, al-

Moroccan folk culture, 2008

Moroccan–Franco agreement. *See* Tangier, Treaty of (1844)

Moroccan Free Schools, 759

Moroccan Human Rights Organization. *See* Organisation Marocaine des Droits de l'Homme (OMDH)

Moroccan Institute of Higher Studies. *See* Institut des Hautes Études Marocaines

Moroccan Labor Union. *See* Union Marocaine du Travail

Moroccan League for the Defense of Human Rights. *See* Ligue Marocaine de Défense des Droits de l'Homme

Moroccan National Front
Parti Démocratique Constitutionnel in, 1803
Parti Démocratique de l'Indépendance in, 1804

Moroccan Observatory of Prisons (OMP), 498

Moroccan Question (1900–1912), **1566**, 2038
Abd al-Aziz ibn al-Hassan policies in, 8, 14
Abd al-Hafid ibn al-Hassan on, 14
Abu Himara's rebellion and, 37
Marrakech during, 1493

Morocco, **1567–1575**. *See also specific cities, organizations, people, and regions*
agriculture in, *753, 754*, 913
drought and, 1569
tax on *(tartib)*, 8
AIDS action plan in, 713–714
Alawite dynasty in, 105–107, 1569
Algerian relations with (*See also* Moroccan–Algerian War; Western Sahara War)
Ben Bella (Ahmed) and, 442
Bouteflika (Abdelaziz) and, 503
causes of strain in, 260
POLISARIO and, 503, 2190–2191
Arabic language in, 1422, 1567
Arabization policies on, 254–256
Arabization policies in, 254–256
in Arab Maghreb Union, 260, 1566
architecture in, 282, 283–284
art in, 2155
banking in, 389, 390, *393, 394*
as Barbary state, 401
Berber dialect in, 2166–2167
Berbers in, 458, 459, 463, 487
border with Algeria
conflict over, 1566
dispute settled in, 4
Britain and, 1569

Daftari (Ahmad Matin) as son-in-
law of, 660
fall of, 518
CIA in, 1937
government of
Amini (Ali) in, 186
Bakhtiar (Shapur) in, 375
Bakhtiar (Timur) in, 375
Bazargan (Mehdi) in, 421
guilds supporting, 947
Harriman (W. Averell) negotiations with, 996
imprisonment of, 1580, 1581
Kashani (Abu al-Qasem) and,
1277
in National Front, 1118, 1581,
1655–1656
in nationalism movement, 1660
negotiations with, Acheson (Dean)
in, 40
oil nationalization by, 202, 417,
518, 1118, 1581, 1752
Eden (Anthony) opposing,
755
foreign response to, 1825
Kashani (Abu al-Qasem) in,
1277
Kuwaiti oil after, 1349
Yazdi (Ibrahim) on, 2382
Pahlavi (Reza) opposed by,
1580–1581
Pahlavi (Mohammad Reza) power
struggle with, 1118, 1752
as prime minister, 1118
Tabataba'i (Ziya) opposing,
2143
Tudeh Party opposition to, 1118
Mossad Harav Kook, 1470
Mossad le-Ailiya Bet
airlift operations of, 1913
Hillel (Shlomo) in, 1030
Mosseri, Ezra, King David Hotel es-
tablished by, 1323
Mossinsohn, Yigal, 1432, 2185
Mostaghanemi, Ahlam, 1424, **1581**
Mostashar al-Dowleh, Mirza Yousuf
Khan, Adamiyat (Abbasquli)
work with, 42
Mosul (Iraq), **1582**
British control of, under San
Remo Conference, 1582
as French zone, under Sykes-Picot
Agreement (1916), 1582
inclusion in Iran *vs.* Turkey,
1582–1583
Kurds in, 1582
autonomy movement of,
1469–1470

oil deposits in
Anglo–Turkish dispute over
(1920-1928), **1582–1583**
royalties from given to Turkey,
1583
oil production in, 1138
population of, 1131
U.S. capture of (2003), 2325
in World War I, 2367
Motahhari, Mortaza, **1583**
Khomeini (Ruhollah) supported
by, 1311
Motherland Party (Turkey),
1583–1584, 2241–2242
Democratic Left Party in coalition
with, 746
electoral success of, 2245
establishment of, 1746
Özal (Turgut) in, 1583–1584,
1746–1747, 2241
Social Democratic Populist Party
opposing, 2077
True Path Party challenge to, 1584
True Path Party coalition with,
598, 1584, 2220
Yilmaz (Mesut) in, 746, 2242
Mother of the Prophet, The (Bint al-Shati),
476
Mothers (Bitton), 483
Mother State (Tahir), 2145–2146
Motor vehicles, 2207, 2207
Mottahedeh, Roy, 756
Mouʿawwad, Naila, **1584–1585**
Mouʿawwad, René
assassination of, 1584
wife of, 1584–1585
Moudawana, al- (Moroccan family
legal code), 1518, **1585–1586**
reform of, 1585–1586
Bouih (Fatna el-) in, 498
8 Mars newsletter on, 772–773
Jababdi (Latifa) in, 1203
on women, 94, 1585–1586, 1601
Moudjahid, al- (newspaper), 450, 804
Djebar (Assia) at, 716
Mountain River. *See* Bahr al-Jabal
Mount Lebanon. *See* Lebanon,
Mount
Mount Scopus (Jerusalem), 966
Mount Tubkal (Morocco), 1567,
1568
Mt. Zion School (Jerusalem), 2221
Mourners of Siyavosh (Daneshvar). *See*
Savushun
Mourning, Muharram as period of,
1605–1606

Mourou, Abdelfattah, **1586–1587,**
2226
defamation campaign against,
1587
in Islamic Tendency Movement,
1586–1587
Mousa, Amr
on late member-state dues to
League of Arab States, 1387
as secretary-general to League of
Arab States, *1385, 1386, 1387,
1388–1389*
Mousavi, Mir Hossein, government
of, Nabavi (Behzad) in, 1630
Moussalli, Ahmad S., *as contributor,*
321–322, 394–395,
1012–1013, 1884–1885,
2150–2151, 2161, 2234–2235
Mouvement de la Réforme Nationale
(MRN) (Algeria)
electoral success of, 135
platform of, 134
Mouvement de la Société pour la
Paix (MSP) (Algeria), 1636
electoral success of, 127, 135
platform of, 134
Mouvement de l'Unité Populaire
(MUP) (Tunisia), **1587,**
2231
Ben Salah (Ahmed) in, 452,
1804
Parti d'Unité Populaire branch of,
1804
Mouvement des Démocrates Social-
istes (MDS) (Tunisia), 2231,
2232
as Ben Ali (Zayn al-Abidine) op-
position, 439
Mestiri (Ahmad) in, 1520
Moadda (Mohamed) in, 1554
Mouvement de Tendance Islamique
(MTI) (Tunisia), 2226,
2229
Ben Ali (Zayn al-Abidine) against,
439
and General Tunisian Union of
Students, 899
Ghannouchi (Rached) in, 912
loosening restrictions on, by Ben
Ali government, 356–357
Mouvement Ettajdid (Tunisia), 2232
Mouvement Ettajid. *See* Movement of
Renewal
Mouvement Islamique Armé (MIA)
(Algeria), Bouyali (Moustafa)
in, 505–506, 918

Muscat (Oman), **1616**
  British influence in, 204, 1710
  Protestant missions in, 1854

Muscat and Oman. *See* Oman

Museum of Islamic Art (Cairo),
    Islamic coin collection of,
    1702

Museum of the Jewish diaspora (Tel
    Aviv), 928

Musha'sha tribe, 1316

Music, **1617–1620**, *1618, 1619*. *See also*
    Dance
  Arabic, 324, 336
  of Beja, 433
  Berber, 193, 462
  East West Divan and, 1966
  Egyptian, 22, 324, 336, 675,
    970–971, 2261–2263
  at Fez Festival of World Sacred
    Music, 667
  Greek, 785
  Iranian, 2311
  Israeli, 1014, 1105–1106, 1164
  Lebanese, 817–818
  overarching genres of, 1617
  processes and issues in, 1619–1620
  regional distinctions in, 1617–1618
  religious, of Alevis, 113–114
  Sufism and, 2113
  Syrian, 112
  Turkish, 476–477, 687, 689,
    872–873, 1269, 2002, 2009,
    2124, 2160
  Western influences on, 1619

Musical instruments, 1617

Musical occasions, 1619

Musketeer, Operation (Britain),
    245, 2108–2109

Muslih, Muhammad
  as contributor, 39, 225–226,
    316–320, 328–330, 337,
    351–352, 815, 917, 925–926,
    971–972, 989, 1010–1011,
    1052, 1053–1054, 1055–1056,
    1058–1059, 1198, 1295–1296,
    1296, 1337, 1486, 1611,
    1644–1645, 1758–1769, 1776,
    1781, 1788–1794, 1885–1886,
    2259–2260
  on Palestinian Arab Congress of
    1920, 1782

Muslim, 2626

Muslim Brotherhood, **1620–1622**
  against Anglo–Egyptian Treaty
    (1936), 766
  in Arab–Israel War (1948), 395,
    1621

Banna (Hasan al-) as founder of,
    1620–1621, 1924
  organization after assassination
    of, 1621–1622
in Egypt, 768, 1620–1622
  abolition of, 767
  and Afghan Islamic movements,
    60, 63
  alliance with Socialist Labor and
    Liberal parties, 1622
  alliance with Wafd, 1622
  Arafat (Yasir) in, 269, 272
  armed wing of, 1214
  Ashmawi (Muhammad Abd al-
    Rahman Salih al-) in, 321
  assassinations by, 1214
  Banna (Hasan al-) in, 394–395
  clash with Liberation Rally,
    1409
  in coup (1952), 1621
  Farouk opposing, 810
  Free Officers and, 853
  Ghazali (Muhammad al-) in,
    914
  and Hamas (Movement for a
    Peaceful Society), 984
  Hudaibi (Mamoun al-) as leader
    of, *1621*, 1622
  Hudaybi (Hasan al-) in, 321
  and Islamic Jihad, 1154
  vs. al-Jami'a al-Islamiyya, 1214
  Khalid (Khalid Muhammad)
    opposing, 1297
  Mubarak (Husni) and,
    1621–1622
  Nasser (Gamal Abdel) and,
    1621, 1649, 1650
  New Wafd and, 1685–1686,
    2321
  Nuqrashi (Mahmud Fahmi al-)
    and, 1701
  outlawed by Nasser (Gamal Ab-
    del), 987, 1214
  outlawed for opposing Palestine
    partition plans (1948), 1621
  parliament seats held by, 1622
  al-Qaradawi (Yusuf) in, 1870
  Qutb (Sayyid) in, 321, 1884
  vs. Revolutionary Command
    Council, 1921
  Sadat (Anwar al-) and, 321,
    1214, 1621, 1955–1956
  schools established by, 759
  Tilmisani (Umar al-) in, 321,
    1621
  Feda'iyan-e Islam and, 820
  Ghazali (Zaynab al-) in, 914
  and HAMAS, 982–983
  Hanbali School of Law and, 990

headquarters of, 395
influence of
  on Nahda, al-, 1635
  on Nahnah (Mahfoud), 1636
  in Iraq, 395
Jami'at-e Islami and, 1215
and jihad, 983
in Jordan
  electoral success of, 1150–1151
  and Islamic Action Front,
    1150–1151
  murshid amm (supreme guide) of,
    1621
objective of, 395
in Palestine Arab Revolt
  (1936–1939), 1620–1621
vs. PLO, 983
radical Muslim defectors from,
  1621
Society for Islamic Culture merging with, 395
spread of, youth movements and,
  2411
in Sudan, 395
  Turabi (Hasan al-) in, 2234
  women's participation in,
    1622–1623
in Syria, 357, 395
  amnesty for members of, 315
  Attar (Isam al-) in, 337
  and Hama rebellion, 980–981
  suppression of, 317, 2135
  Wahhabi influence on, 1626
  Wazir (Khalil al-) and,
    2334–2335
in Yemen, in Islah Party,
  1143

Muslim–Christian Association
    (Palestine)
  Arab Club and, 226
  Darwish (Ishaq) in, 673
  establishment of, 1761
  leadership of, 1761
  Palestinian nationalism promoted
    by, 1761–1762
  Zionism opposed by, 1761

Muslim Sisters Organization,
    1622–1623

Muslim Students Association
  Amir-Entezam (Abbas) in,
    188
  establishment of, 582
  Kharrazi (Kamal) in, 1300

Muslim Women's Association, 892,
    914

Muslim (Islamic) world, *vs.* Middle
    East, 1523

Muslim World League, **1623**

Natural gas, **1669–1671,**
    1824–1827
associated, 1669
demand for
    vs. coal, 1670
    vs. oil, 1670
for desalinization process, 2330
economic exploitation of,
    1669–1671
exporters of, 1670
future of, 1827
liquefaction process for, 1671
modern uses of, 1670
OPEC policies on, 1670
Natural gas deposits
in Afghanistan, 2050
in Sahara, 1963
in Tunisia, 2225
in United Arab Emirates, Sharjah,
    2040
in Yemen, 2390
Natural gas liquids, 1669
Natural gas production
in Middle East, 1671, *1671*
in Qatar, 1876
    North Field of, 1876, 1878
Natural gas reserves
in Iran, 1115
in Middle East, 1671, *1671*
in Qatar, 1875
in United Arab Emirates, 2271
Natzerat Illit (Jewish development
    town), 1673
Navarino, Battle of (1927), 940
Navarra, André, Kan (Suna) perfor-
    mance with, 1269
Navigation treaties. *See* Commercial
    and navigation treaties
Navon, Yizhak, **1671–1672**
as first modern Israeli president,
    1672
Middle Eastern origin of, 49, 1671
in RAFI Party, 1188
Sabra and Shatila massacre inquiry
    requested by, 1672
as Sephardic spokesman, 1672
Nawal El Saadawi Reader, The (al-
    Saadawi), 1950
Nawawi, Muhyi al-Din al-, 2019
Nawba (musical genre), 1617
Nawfal, Hind, **1672**
Nawfal, Maryam Nahhas, 1672
Nawfal, Nasim, 1672
Nawfal, Sara, 1672
Nawid, Senzil, *as contributor,* 68,
    325–326, 693, 786, 1140,

1278–1279, 1715, 1881, 1920,
    1981–1982, 2007–2008
Naylor, Phillip C., *as contributor,* 2–4,
    22–23, 95–96, 128–131,
    189–190, 193, 287, 437–438,
    440–441, 441–443, 443–445,
    450–451, 482–483, 489,
    495–497, 503–505, 506,
    545–546, 563, 570, 579, 612,
    689–690, 707–708,
    788–789, 822–823, 843,
    916–917, 967, 968–970, 985,
    987, 995, 1076, 1264, 1309,
    1336–1337, 1362–1363, 1365,
    1443–1444, 1456, 1547, 1566,
    1686, 1743, 1745, 2013, 2217,
    2297, 2428–2429
Nazareth (Israel), **1672–1673**
in Arab–Israel War (1948),
    1672–45
under British mandate
    (1922–1948), 1672
as capital of Arabs in Israel, 1673
conflict with Natzerat Illit, 1673
as only all-Arab city in Israel,
    1672–45
as site of Annunciation, 1673
Nazari ve ameli Türk musikisi (Suphi),
    2124
Nazariyeha-ye Dulat dar Fiqh-e Shi (Kadi-
    var), 1262
Nazerbekian, Avetis, in Armenian
    Social Democratic Party, 299
Nazerbekian, Maro, in Armenian
    Social Democratic Party, 299
Nazif, Süleyman, **1673–1674**
Nazi Party
Silver (Abbas Hillel) denouncing,
    2067
Templars supporting, 2173
Nazir, al- (journal), Ashmawi
    (Muhammad Abd al-Rahman
    Salih al-) in, 321
Nazmi, Ziya, **1674**
NDA. *See* National Democratic Al-
    liance
NDF. *See* National Democratic Front
NDFLOAG. *See* National Democratic
    Front for the Liberation of
    Oman and the Arab Gulf
NEACC. *See* Near East Arms Coor-
    dinating Committee
Near East, *vs.* Middle East,
    1522–1523
Near East Air Transport Company,
    1460

Near East Arms Coordinating Com-
    mittee (NEACC), 304, 2215
Near East Report (bulletin), 177
Neda-ye Iran-e Novin (periodical),
    1129
Nedim, Mahmut, 25
Nedjma (Kateb), 1280
Needle exchange programs, 714
Ne'eman, Yuval, **1674–1675**
Lavie File written by, 1674
as nuclear scientist, 1674–1675
Nefertari (queen of Egypt), tomb of,
    276
Negev (Israel), 1160, **1675**
in Arab–Israel War (1948), 243
climate of, 1161
Israeli settlements in, 1675
proposed Jewish settlement in,
    Churchill (Winston S.) on,
    595
Negev Desert, 1248, 1758
Negev Hills (Israel), 1675
Negev Institute for Arid Zone Re-
    search, 424
Nehar Mitzrayim (Ben Simeon), 454
Nehemiah Operation, 790
Nehru, Jawaharlal, at Bandung Con-
    ference, 387
Nelson, Horatio, in Battle of Abu
    Qir (1798), 39
Neo-Ba'th party (Syria)
in coup (1966), 482
leadership of, 330
Neo-Destour Party (Tunisia),
    634–635, 2427. *See also* Con-
    stitutional Democratic Rally
Baccouche (Hedi) in, 356
Ben Yousouf (Salah) in, 455
Bourguiba (Habib) in, 501, 502,
    2229
labor union links to, 1358
Masmoudi (Muhammad) in, 1499
Mestiri (Ahmad) in, 1519–1520
monopoly held by broken, 1627
Sfar (Tahar) in, 2016
and Tunisian independence, 849
Union of Tunisian Women and,
    2267
Neolithic cave paintings, *830*
Nerval, Gérard de, **1675–1676**
Neshat, Shirin, **1676**
Nesher, 1334
Nesin, Nüsret Aziz, 1437, 1440,
    1676
Nestorian Church, 738

Nestorians, 2056
  in Iran, 1548
  under Ottoman rule, 1544
Nestren (Tarhan), 2165
Netanyahu, Benjamin, **1676–1677**
  Barak (Ehud) and, 1677
  coalition government of, 1168
  election of, 1168, 1184, 1727
    HAMAS suicide bombings and,
      983
  in Hebron Agreement (1997),
    1325
  Levy (David) and, 1408
  in Likud Party, 1184
  Livnat (Limor) supporting, 1441
  Lubavitcher Hasidim support for,
    1002
  at Madrid Peace Conference
    (1991), 1677
  Mash'al (Khalil al-) saved from as-
    sassination by, 1579
  Oslo Accord rejected by, 1677
  Palestinian "reciprocity" urged by,
    1677
  peace process under, 1168, 1727
    Oslo Accord rejected by, 1726,
      1793
    at Wye River Accords (1998),
      606, 1677
  political defeat of, 1168
  Sharon (Ariel) under, 2026
Netanyahu, Benzion, 1676–1677
Netanyahu, Yonatan, 777
Netherlands
  oil embargo against (1973–1974),
    1709
  and trade, 2197
Netivot Shalom. *See* Oz ve Shalom
Neturei Karta, **1677–1678**
Neutral Zone, **1678**
  oil production in, 1678
  partitioning of, 1678
Nevi'im, 2157
Nevo, Joseph, *as contributor*, 338, 488,
  1324–1325, 1453–1454,
  2289–2290
"New Appeal to the Algerian People"
  (1976), 4, 1365
New Communist List (Israel). *See*
  RAKAH
New Dawn group (Egypt), 627
New Democracy (Afghanistan). *See*
  Demokrasy-i Now;
  Demokrasy-i Now
  (Afghanistan)
New Group (artistic movement), 34

New International Economic Order,
  500
New Iran Party. *See* Iran Novin Party
New Islamic Jihad (Egypt), in al-
  Jami'a al-Islamiyya, 1215
New Islamic Mission, 1917. *See also*
  Republican Brotherhood
New Israeli shekel (NIS), 2048
Newman, David, *as contributor*, 942,
  957–959, 1191–1193,
  1325–1326, 1406–1407,
  2339–2341
New Ottomans. *See* Young Ottomans
New Palace. *See* Topkapi Palace
New Persian studies, 540
New schooling, 756–757
  administrative bodies of, 757–758
  in Egypt, 756, 757
  for ethnic minorities, 758
  in Iran, 757, 758
  in Ottoman Empire, 757, 758
  vs. religious schooling, 756, 757
  in Yemen, 756
Newspapers and print media,
  1678–1685
  in Afghanistan, 1140
  in Arab countries, **1678–1682**
    common characteristics of,
      1679–1680
    cultural content of, 1680
    diversity in, 1681
    economic base for, 1680
    first (*Jurnal al-Iraq*), 1678
    fragmentation of, 1680
    historical development of,
      1678–1679
    loyalist press, 1680–1681
    mobilization, 1680
    non-Arabic and specialized,
      1681–1682
    offshore publishing of, 1681
    organization of, 1680–1681
    political ties of, 1680
    transitional press, 1681
    UNESCO standard for, 1679
  Arab–Israel conflict coverage in,
    1679
  in Egypt, 206, 1012, 1013,
    1374–1375
  growth of, and education, 759
  Hebrew, 1431, 1683–1684
  in Iran, 867, 1682–1683, 2142,
    2143, 2423–2424
  in Iraq, 1525, 1678
  in Israel, 1164, 1683–1684
  in Lebanon, 2254
  in Ottoman Empire, 409

  in Tunisia, 439–440, 2016
  in Turkey, 1050–1051, *1684,*
    1684–1685, 2067
    Nadi (Yanus) and, 1633
New Valley Project (Egypt), 1652
New Wafd (Egypt), 768, **1685–1686,**
  2321
  election boycott (1990) by,
    1685–1686
  Mubarak (Husni) and, 1685–1686
  and Muslim Brotherhood,
    1685–1686, 2321
  Sadat (Anwar al-) and, 1685
  secularism of, 1686
New Woman Research and Study
  Centre (Egypt), 894
New Women Society (Egypt), 2321
New York University Newman Prize,
  Gilboa (Amir) awarded with,
  920–921
New Zionist Organization (NZO),
  2372
  establishment of, 1209, 2437
Nezer, Ahmet Necdet, presidency of,
  2244
Nezhat-e Azadi Iran. *See* Freedom
  Movement
Nezib, battle of (1839), Moltke
  (Helmuth von) at, 1563
Nezikin, 2157
Nezzar, Khaled, **1686**
  Ait Ahmed (Hocine) opposed to,
    96
  attempted assassination of (1993),
    1686
  in coup deposing Bendjedid
    (Chadli) (1992), 1686
  defamation suit against Souaidia
    (Habib), 1686
  as defense minister, 1686
  Ghozali (Ahmed) supporting, 917
  in High State Council, 1026
  repression and torture charges
    against, 1686
  and Zeroual (Liamine), 1026,
    1365, 2430
Nhaisi, Elia, **1686–1687**
  power struggle with Nahum (Hal-
    fallah), 1636–1637
Niati, Houria, **1687**
Nicaragua, Contra rebels of, in
  Iran–Contra affair, 1123
Nicholas I (czar of Russia)
  British relations with, 648–649
  in Syrian War (1831–1833), 1346
  war against Ottoman Empire, 1945

Nicholas II (czar of Russia), 937

Nicolas Sursock Museum (Beirut), 2125

Nicosia (Cyprus), 652, 653

Nicosia, Francis R., *as contributor*, 464–465, 943–944

Nida al-Qawmi al- (Lebanon), 2116, 2119

Niebuhr, Karsten, 276

NIF. *See* National Islamic Front

Niger, Berbers in, 458

Niger River, 1963

Nightclubs, 1619

Nightingale, Florence, 649, 2302

Night of the Twentieth (Sobol), 2076

Nihal, Süküfe, in Women's People's Party, 2359

Nihayat al-Ijaz fi Sirat Sakin al-Hijaz (Tahtawi), 2148

Nihm tribe, 376

Nil, al- (newspaper), 817

Nile Basin, water availability in, 1687–1688

Nile River, **1687–1688,** 1963
 agriculture along, 690
 Alexandria linked to, by Mahmudiyya Canal, 116
 Aswan High Dam on (*See* Aswan
  High Dam)
 Bahr al-Abyad (White Nile), 372,
  373, 901–902
 Bahr al-Ghazal as tributary of,
  372
 Bahr al-Jabal as tributary of,
  372–373
 Blue Nile, 372, 902
 bridges across, at Cairo, 553
 Delta Barrages on, 690
 delta of, 690
  and disease, 710, 711
 Dinka people along, 709
 disease transmission through, 710,
  711
 drainage area of, 1687
 irrigation in Egypt from, 763
  Baring (Evelyn) developing,
   404, 405, 406
 Lado Enclave connecting Congo
  River with, 1363
 length of, 1687
 Philae island submerged in, 1832
 shipping on, 2205
 swamps of, 2105–2106
 as water resource, 1651–1652,
  1687, 2328–2329

Niles, David, 2220

Nile Valley, 763
 Nubians in, 1695–1696

NILI spy ring, 1

Niʿmatullah (Sufi order), 2113

Niʿmatullah bin ʿAbdullah, 2113

Nimr, Faris, **1688–1689**
 daughter of, 214

Nimrud, archaeological research in, 276

Nimsawi, Umar al-, 1394

Nimule, 372

Nine Lights, doctrine of, 2236

Nine Lights of Türkes, 1661

Nineveh, archaeological research in, 276

NIOC. *See* National Iranian Oil Company

NIS. *See* New Israeli shekel

Nisa, al- (Qurʾanic verse), 2153

NISAA Web site, 95

Nisaʾiyyat, al- (Nassif), 1652

Nisanit (Faqir), 805

Nissa (journal), 912

Nissaboury, Mustafa, 1355

Nissim and Cherie (Bitton), 483

Nissim, Isaac, **1689**

Nissim, Moshe
 in Liberal Party, 1184
 Middle Eastern origin of, 49

Nisvan-I Islam (Aliyer), 148

Nixon, John, 1518–1519

Nixon, Richard Milhous, **1689**
 and Arab–Israel War (1973), 799,
  1689
 Faisal ibn Abd al-Aziz Al Saʿud
  welcomed by, *1998*
 government of
  Kissinger (Henry) in,
   1327–1328
  Rogers (William Pierce) in,
   1929
  Shultz (George) in, 2061
 Middle East policy of, 1689,
  2292
 in OPEC oil embargo (1973),
  1689
 resignation of, 1689

Niyabat-e amma (general deputyship of jurists), 2312

Niyazi, Ghulam Muhammad
 in Afghan Islamic movement, 60
 in Jamiʿat-e Islami, 60

Nizam al-Jadid, al-, **1690**

Nizam al-Jadid program, 757

Nizam al-Mulk, 1457

Nizami (Tunisian military corps), 83–84

Nizam-i Cedit (Ottoman military corps), 1217

Nizamiye. *See* Ottoman military

Nizamiye courts, **1690**
 development of, Cevdet (Ahmed)
  in, 577

Nizamud-Din, Mullah, 2154

Nizari Ismaʿilis, 1158, 1159

Nizari tribe. *See* Adnan tribe

Nizat-i-Milli (Afghanistan), 64

Nizip, Battle of (1839), **1690–1691**

NLF. *See* National Liberation Front

NLL. *See* National Liberation League

NLP. *See* National Liberal Party

Nobel Peace Prize
 Annan (Kofi A.) awarded with,
  209
 Arafat (Yasir) awarded with, *1817*
 Begin (Menachem) awarded with,
  426
 Bunche (Ralph J.) awarded with,
  239, 543, 2274
 Ebadi (Shirin) awarded with, 1121
 Freier (Recha) nominated for, 855
 Ibrahim (Saʿad al-Din) nominated
  for, 1079
 Peres (Shimon) awarded with, *1817*
 Rabin (Yitzhak) awarded with, *1817*
 Sadat (Anwar al-) awarded with,
  426
 Zana (Leyla) nominated for, 2423

Nobel Prize for Literature
 to Agnon (Shmuel Yosef), 1164,
  1431
 to Mahfuz (Najib), *1420, 1420,*
  1464–1465

Noghay language, 2252

No, Lake, 372, 373

Nomadism, 902, 1410, 2209, 2211.
 See also Tribes and Tribalism
 in Algeria, 2253–2254
 Baluchis and, 385
 Berbers, 459, *462*
 in Eastern Desert, 737
 in Iran, 374, 2213
 Kurdish, 2214
 in Sahara, 1964
 in Saudi Arabia, 1996, 2213, 2214
 on Sinai Peninsula, 2068
 in Sudan, 433
 in Syrian Desert, 2136
 in Turkey, 2253
 in Yemen, 2209

Oil spills, 952

Oil tankers, 2107

Oil trade, 2199–2200, 2201
   Britain in, 517
      OPEC and, 522
   Persian Gulf in, 1820

Oil transport, 2207
   through pipelines (*See* Oil pipelines)
   in pricing, 1829
   Suez–Mediterranean Pipeline, 2110–2111
   Trans-Arabian Pipeline for, 2202–2203
   Trans-Turkey Pipeline for, 2208

Ojrat-ol misl, 2051

Okyar, Fethi, 854

Olam, ha- (newspaper), 2078

Olama, Mirza Mahmud Eftekhar, Khomeini (Ruhollah) taught by, 1310

Olam ha-Zeh, ha- (magazine), Avnery (Uri) in, 340

Old Lover, The (Erbil), 780

Olimpo, Paola, *as contributor*, 1327–1329

Olive oil, *837*, 840

Olives, *837*, 840

Olmert, Ehud, as Jerusalem mayor, 1332
   Haredi Jews and, 1226

OLOS. *See* Organization for the Liberation of the Occupied South

Olympic Games
   of 1972, Israelis murdered at, 1792
   of 1996, Palestinian Authority team at, 1784

Olympus, Mount, 937

Oman, **1709–1711**. *See also specific cities, organizations, people, and regions*
   agriculture in, 1204, 1711
   Al Bu Saʿid dynasty in, 107, 1710–1711
   in Arab boycott against Israel, 224
   Baluchis in, 385
   banking in, *393*
   borders of, with Yemen, 2385
   British relations with
      Anglo–Omani treaties in, 203–204, 525–526, 531–532, 614
      Cox (Percy) in, 645–646
      as de facto protectorate, 204
      in Dhufar rebellion, 521, 705, 1842

military forces in, 521
   telegraph service and, 527
Buraymi oasis claimed by, 517, 544
cities of
   capital, 1616
   port, 1500, 1616
climate of, 705, 1710
coup in (1970), 107, 108
defense costs as percentage of GNP or GDP, *1530*
Dhufar rebellion in (1965–1975), 705–706
   Soviet Union supporting, 2174
economy of, 752, *753*
fishing industry of, 834, 1711, *1711*
governates of, 705
in Gulf Cooperation Council, 949
in Gulf Crisis (1990–1991), 950
human rights in, 1048
labor unions illegal in, 1358
in League of Arab States, 1388
legal system of
   British influences on, 1380
   reforms in, 1380
legislative body in, 932
manufacturing in, 1483, *1483*
military of
   equipment of, *1534*
   force levels of, *1528–1529*
   force structure of (army, air force, and navy), *1532–1533*
natural gas production and reserves in, 1671, *1671*
newspapers and print media of, 1678–1679
   loyalist approach of, 1681
oil production in, 752
political system of, 1711
population of, *753*, 1844
radio and television in, *1895*
regions of, 705
   mountainous, 1204
sand deserts of, 1938
Sib Treaty (1920) in, 2064
tamimahs in, 2158
in trade, East India Company and, 525
tribes in, 385, 2210
   Al Bu Saʿid family in, 107
water resources of, freshwater withdrawals, *2331*
World Bank and, capital stock and voting power in, *2363*
and Zanzibar, 2425
Oman, Gulf of, **952**, 2040

Omar Gatlato (film), 2192

Omar, Mohamed Bel Haj, 452

Omar, Muhammad (Mullah), **1711–1712**
   election of, 2155
   in Kandahar, 1711, 1712, 2974
   Mohammadi (Maulawi Mohammad Nabi) and, 1559
   in Taliban, 64, 1712, 1767

Omar Mukhtar Club, **1712**
   Kikhya (Umar Mansur al-) conflict with, 1321

Ombre de la terre, L' (film), 2192

Ombres japonaises (Khatibi), 1304

Ombre sultane (Djebar), 1424

OMDH. *See* Organisation Marocaine des Droits de l'Homme

Omdurman (Sudan), **1712–1713**, 2097, 2100
   Ahmad (Muhammad) in, 87, 1301, 1712
   architecture of, 1301–1302
   as Mahdist capital, 1301, 1712
   population of, 1301

Omdurman, Battle of (1898), Abdullahi (Muhammad Turshain) in, 33

Omega, Operation, 157

O Mes Soeurs Musulmanes, Pleurez! (Bittari), 483

Omid. *See* Akhavan-Saless, Mehdi

Omnium Nord-African (ONA), 1005

OMP. *See* Moroccan Observatory of Prisons

OMV, Occidental Petroleum and, 1708

ONA. *See* Omnium Nord-African

Onay, Gulsin, 477

Once upon a Time (collection), 1435

Once Upon a Time Cinema (Iranian film), 1473

Once upon a Time on the Nile (film), 2022

100 Soruda Türk Folkloru (Boratav), 493

100 Soruda Türk Halk edebiyata (Boratav), 493

One Israel Party, Meimad in, 1186

One Man with His Gun (Chubak), 593

One Nation. *See* Am Ehad Party

1001 années de la nostalgie, Les (Boudjedra), 497

Only in London (Shaykh), 2046

Only Yesterday (Agnon), 71

On the Bridge (Bint al-Shati), 476

Organization of Petroleum Exporting Countries (OPEC) *(continued)*
    sharing strategy for, 1719–1720
    Organization of Arab Petroleum
        Exporting Countries and,
        1718
    Pahlavi (Mohammad Reza) in, 1753
    and pan-Arabism, 824
    participation strategy of, 1719,
        1826
    political divisions within,
        1720–1721
    power of, 522
    prices under, 522, 1718–1721,
        1826, 2200, 2201
    Tariki (Abdullah) as cofounder of,
        2166
    trade influenced by, 2199–2200
    U.S. opposition to, 1719
    wealth generated by, and Islamic
        numismatics, 1703
Organization of the Islamic Confer-
    ence (OIC), 799, **1721–1722**
    and Cairo Convention of Human
        Rights in Islam, 1049
    charter of, 1153, 1721
    establishment of, 1153, 1721
    functions of, 1153
    goals of, 1721
    membership in, 1722
Organization of the Mujahedin of
    Islamic Revolution (Iran),
    1630
Organization of the Vanguards of the
    Popular Liberation War. *See*
    Sa'iqa, al-
Oriental, as designation and term,
    1522
Orientalism, 492, **1722–1723**
    in art, 311, 1722
    on collection of Qur'an, 1883
    in literature, 1675–1676
    origin of concept, 1722
    in postage stamps, 1850
Orientalism (Said), 1036, 1722, 1966
Orientalists, International Congress
    of, **1723**
Oriental Jews. *See* Adot ha-mizrah;
    Mizrahi Jews
Oriental Orthodox Churches,
    591–592
    member churches in, 591, 639
    theology of, 589
Oriental Studies, 1035
Orient Express (Vienna–Istanbul
    railway), 464, 2206
Orient House, 1226, 1227

Orient, L'-Le jour (newspaper), 872,
    2254
Orlogin (publication), 2058
Ormanian, Maghakia, 298, **1723**
Ormsby-Gore, William George
        Arthur, **1723–1724**
Orontes River, 909, 980, 2129
Orr, Akiva, 1501
Ortaoyunu, **1724**
    Kasap (Teodor) plays based on,
        1277
Ortaoyunus, 2187
ORTF. *See* Office de la Radiodiffu-
    sion-Télévision Française
Orthodox Christians
    number of, 738
    in Ottoman Empire, 738
Orthodox churches. *See* Eastern Or-
    thodox Church; Oriental Or-
    thodox churches
Orthodox Islam. *See* Sunni Islam
Orthodox Jews
    in Israel, 1163
    Neturei Karta of, 1677–1678
    in Palestine, in 19th century, 1760
    political party of, Agudat Israel as,
        77–78
    and Sabbath, 1954
Orwell, George, 46
Or Yehuda Local Council, 452
OS. *See* Organisation Spéciale
Osirak nuclear reactor, **1724**
    in Iraq, Israeli strike against, 1535,
        1698
    Israel destroying (1981), 426
Oslo Accord (1993), **1724–1728**.
        See also Declaration of Princi-
        ples
    Abbas (Mahmud) in, 6
    accomplishments of, 1727
    American Jewish Congress support
        for, 179
    archaeological sites in, 278
    Barak (Ehud) implementing, 398
    and Camp David Summit (2000),
        562
    collapse of, 1726–1727
        blame for, 1727
    context for, 1725
    al-Fatah and, 814
    on Gaza Strip, 871
    Habash (George) on, 962
    and Haram al-Sharif, future of,
        992
    Hawatma (Nayif) criticism of,
        1009

Hebron after, 1019
Hut (Shafiq al-) protest against,
    1071
Islamic Jihad opposing, 1155
Israeli settlements in, 1193
Israeli withdrawals in, 1768, 1784
and Jerusalem, 1226
Khaled (Leila) opposing, 1293
Likud Party rejecting, 1185, 1726,
    1727
Livnat (Limor) opposing, 1440
Madrid Peace Conference leading
    to (1991), 1793
mutual recognition in, 238, 1167,
    1725–1726, 1768, 1775
Palestinian Authority based on,
    1784
Palestinian self-rule in, 238, 1775,
    2340–2341
Peres (Shimon) in, 1725, 1818
PFLP opposing, 1840
Rabin (Yitzhak) legacy and, 1892
reception of, 1725–1727
Said (Edward) opposing, 1966
Salim (Ali) in, 1978
Sarid (Yossi) supporting, 1991
secret negotiations in, 1725
    Qurai (Ahmad Sulayman) at,
        1725, 1881–1882
Sharon (Ariel) opposing,
    2177–2178
signing of, 1726
    by Arafat (Yasir), 271, 606, *1726*
    Clinton (Bill) in, 606, *1726*
    by Rabin (Yitzhak), 271, 606,
        1726
terrorism renounced in, 219, 1167
United Nations in, 2276–2277
Vatican and, 2310
West Bank under, 2340–2341
Zionist Organization of America
    on, 2436
Oslo II Interim Agreement (1995)
    Israeli withdrawal in, from West
        Bank, 1727, 1775, 1784
    provisions of, 1727
    signing of, 1727
    United Nations in, 2277
Osman I (Turkish ruler), 1728
Osman, Ahmed, 1904
Osman, House of, **1728**
Osmanli (journal), 576
Osmanli Bankasi, 390
Ossetic language, 1124
Ostermann, Helmut. *See* Avnery, Uri
Ostrich (Bejerano), 434
Otayba tribe. *See* Utayba tribe

Other, The (Chédid). *See Autre, l'*

Ottoman Bank. *See Osmanli Bankasi*

"Ottoman Bill of Rights." *See Hatt-i Hümayun* (1856)

Ottoman Bureau of Translation. *See Bureau of Translation*

Ottoman Debt Commission, 2199

Ottoman Empire, **1728–1737**. *See also specific cities, organizations, people, and regions*

  Abd al-Hadi family in, 12–13

  administrative divisions of, 1729

  Aegean Sea in, 51

  agriculture in, 1729–1730

    after Land Code of 1858, 1367–1369

    before Land Code of 1858, 1367

    tax farming and, 1367, 2167–2168

  alcohol in, 109–110

  Algeria under, 122, 1713

  Anatolia in, Land Code of 1858 effects, 1368, 1369

  Arabian relations with, Faysal ibn Turki Al Saʿud and, 819

  Arab nationalism in, 261

    crackdown on, 264

  Arab Revolt against (1916), 262–264, 510, 799–800

    McMahon (Henry) in, 1506

  architects in, 386

  architecture in, 280, 281, 282

  archives of, 407

  Armenians in

    Dashnak Party and, 676–677

    genocide against (*See* Armenian genocide)

    millet of, 296–298, 1543–1545

    resistance by, 195, 299–301, 1612–1613

    revolutionary movement of, 299–301, 303

  art of, 143, 2008–2009

  Austria-Hungary and, 534

  Austro-Hungarian relations with, 339–340

  Balkans in, nationalist movement in, 382–383, 542–543, 2163–2164

  in bankruptcy, 2199

  banks in, 389, 740, 2163

  Bektashis in, 435

  Black Sea access of, 485, 1446, 2093–2094

  Britain and

    in Aqaba incident (1906), 218

    Berlin Treaty (1878) and, 528

    British–Ottoman alliance, 491, 527–528, 530, 740, 846

    Bulgarian Horrors and, 382

    Canning (Stratford) and, 563–564

    capitulations granted to, 565, 621

    commercial convention, 2163

    Drummond-Wolff Convention between (1885), 726

    East India Company and, 525–526

    Levant Company and, 525

    Persian Gulf politics and, 531

    Sinai Peninsula and, 2068

    during Tanzimat era, 2162–2163

    during World War I, 509–511

  and Bulgarian Horrors (*See* Bulgarian Horrors)

  in caliphate, 556

  capitulations, 564–566, 620–621, 844–845

  Catholic missionaries in, 1931

  censorship in, 28

  Çerkes Hasan incident in (1876), 575

  cholera in, 712

  Christians in, 589–590, 1731

    Orthodox, 738

  Circassians in, 599

  cities of, 1979

    capital, 547, 1729, 2253

  civil code in, 577–578, 601

  civil service in, **1734–1735**

    Civil Service School for, 602

  climate of, 1729

  commercial and navigation treaties of, 620–621

  communication in, 28, 624

  constitution of, 1742, 2407

    Midhat Paşa as father of, 1524–1526

  constitution of (1876), 27, 1381

    Namik Kemal as framer of, 1641

  constitution of (1908), 2240

  constitution of (1909), 1381

  corsairs in, 643

  coup in (1826), attempted, 1466–1467

  coup in (1878), attempted, 144

  coup in (1908), 1659, 2240

  coup in (1913), 384, 623, 778, 2410

    and Armenian genocide, 293

  court system of, Nizamiye, 1690

  in Crimean War, 739, 2162

  Cyprus in, 652, 653

  in Dardanelles Treaty (1809), 621, 671–672

  debt of, 25, 614, 1732, **1735–1737**

    under Abdülaziz, 25

    under Abdülhamit II, 27–28

    under Abdülmecit I, 33

    in Crimean War, 33

  decline of, 1466, 1728

    and Eastern Question, 738–743

  dissolution of, 1728, 2240, 2250

  Druze in, 469, 728–729, 1398

  economy of, 741–742, 1729–1730

    Germany and, 904

    reform of, 2162–2163

  education in

    administrative bodies of, 758

    for civil servants, 602

    European model in, 757, 864

    Gaspirali (Ismail Bey) and, 869

    at İdadi schools, 1079–1080

    in Mahalle Schools, 1461

    middle, 1940

    new schooling in, 757, 758

    primary, 1940

    reform of, 24, 92, 757, 758, 2162

    state schools in, 757

    sultani lycées in, 864, 2121

  Egypt in, 741

    Buhayra, 542

    in Convention of al-Arish (1800), 288–289

    defeat of Tuman Bey and, 2223

  Egypt invaded by, in Aqaba incident (1906), 218

  elites in, 775, *775*

  ethnic diversity in, 1731–1732, 2253

  vs. European imperialism, 1087–1089

  European imperialism in, 2162–2163

  European part of (Rumelia), 1939

  Fertile Crescent under, 824

  Fezzan occupied by, 830

  freemasonry in, 852

  French relations with

    Muhammad Ali and, 846

    Sebastiani (Horace) and, 2006–2007

    during Tanzimat era, 2162–2163

  Gaza Strip in, 870

  geography of, 1729

  German relations with

    Abdülhamit II and, 742, 903–904

    and Berlin–Baghdad railway, 464, 532–533

    concessions granted to Germany, 904

Özal, Turgut, *1746*, **1746–1747**
    death of, 692, 1747, 2219
    Demirel (Süleyman) and, 692,
        1584, 1746, 1747
    as deputy prime minister, 1746
    in Keban Dam project, 1284
    in Motherland Party, 1583–1584
    presidency of, 1747, 2241–2242,
        2244
    as prime minister, 1746–1747
    at State Planning Organization,
        1746
Oz, Amos, 1164, 1433, **1747–1748**
Ozanian, Andranik. *See* Andranik
    Ozanian
Ozpetek, Ferzan, 832
Oz ve Shalom (Netivot Shalom),
    1748–1749
    establishment of, 1748
    objectives of, 1748

P

PA. *See* Palestinian Authority
Pachachi, Adnan, 1751
    on Iraqi Governing Council,
        2325–2326
Pachachi, Muzahim al-, **1751**
Pact of Alliance. *See* Sened-i Ittafak
Pact of the League of Arab States,
    1385
Padishah, 2120
Pages from the Calendar (Ben-Aharon),
    438
Pagis, Dan, 1432–1433, **1751–1752**
PAGS. *See* Parti de l'Avant-Garde
    Socialiste
Pahlavi, Ashraf (princess of Iran),
    women's rights supported by,
    2358
Pahlavi Foundation, 2037
Pahlavi Guards Cavalry Regiment,
    Arfa (Hasan) in, 286
Pahlavi language
    alphabet of, 1124, 1821
    Zoroastrian texts written in, 1124,
        2441
Pahlavi, Mohammad Reza (shah of
    Iran), *1658*, **1752–1755**, *1753*,
    1754
    accession of, foreign intervention
        in, 1118, 1752
    administrative policies under, 2420
    Algiers Agreement (1975) signed
        by, 2043

Allies installing, 2370
archaeology under, 277
assassination of, attempted, 1118,
    1752
    Kashani (Abu al-Qasem) in,
        1277
autocratic rule by, 1119, 1753–1754
and Baha'i persecution, 365
Bakhtiar (Shapur) opposing, 375
Bakhtiar (Timur) opposing, 375
Bakhtiar (Timur) supporting, 375
bazaars under, 420
Beheshti (Mohammad) against,
    428
Borujerdi (Hosayn) opposing, 494
and censorship, 1436
character flaws of, 1754–1755
children of, 1752
after coup (1953)
    increased power of, 1118,
        1752–1753
    reinstatement of, 1752
coup reinstalling (1953),
    1655–1656
death of, 707, 1754
demonstrations against (1963),
    1119, 1753
demonstrations against (1978),
    1126
educational policies of, 760, 761
in exile, 707, 1119, 1126, 1752,
    1754
foreign relations under, 1119, 1753
Freedom Movement leaders im-
    prisoned by, 850
government of
    Alam (Amir Asadollah) in, 102,
        1753
    Amini (Ali) in, 186, 1118, 1753
    Arfa (Hasan) in, 286
    Arsanjani (Hassan) in, 1118,
        1753
    Soheyli (Ali) in, 2078
Hoveyda (Amir Abbas) and, 1047
human rights under, 622
Iran hostage crisis and, 1046
in Iranian Revolution (1979),
    1125–1126
    actions leading to, 1125
    fall of, 1125, 1311
    response to uprisings by, 1126
Iran Novin Party created by, 1129
Khomeini (Ruhollah) opposing,
    1125–1126, 1310–1311
Khomeini's (Ruhollah) criticism
    of, 1606
Kurdish revolts in Iraq supported
    by, 1127
land deeds granted by, *1371*

land reforms of, 1753
majles power over, 1118, 1752
Mossadegh (Mohammad) power
    struggle with, 1118, 1752
and National Front, 1655–1656
newspapers and print media un-
    der, 1682
oil pricing strategy under, 1719,
    1753
oil production under, 1825
opposition to
    Mardom Party and appearance
        of, 1487
    Mojahedin-e Khalq in, 1562
    Nabavi (Behzad) in, 1630
    Rafsanjani (Ali Akbar Hashemi)
        and, 1898–1899
    University of Tehran and,
        2296
overthrow of, 2293
Pakistani relations with, 1758
power of
    decline of, 1754–1755
    rise of, 1118, 1752–1753
price hikes by, Daftari (Ahmad
    Matin) opposition to, 660
regime of, as literary theme, 1435,
    1436
revolutionary coalition against (*See
    also* Iranian Revolution)
    formation of, 1119, 1754
Shariatmadari (Kazem) criticizing,
    2036
during Soviet occupation, 1752
student activists opposing,
    630–631
Students in the Line of the Imam
    demanding U.S. extradition
    of, 2096
traditional supporters of, 1119,
    1753–1754
ulama opposing, 2259
and University of Tehran, 2296
and urban planning, 2299
U.S. support for, 996, 1937
and *velayat-e faqih* (governance of
    jurists), 2312
Western support for, 1118, 1752
White Revolution of, 2351–2352
wives of, 707, 1752
Pahlavi, Reza (crown prince of Iran),
    1752
Pahlavi, Reza (shah of Iran),
    1755–1757
    abdication by, forced, 1118, 1752,
        1757
    accession of, 1756
    Allies removing, 2143, 2370

Anglo–Iranian Agreement nullified by, 200
and architecture, 282
Arfa (Hasan) and, 285–286
as army commander, 1755
    Cossack Brigade under, 643
army reforms of, 1756
and Baha'i persecution, 365
Baraheni (Reza) opposing, 397
Bayat (Mortaza Qoli) under, 417
British support for, 1755
and censorship, 1436
character flaws of, 1756–1757
communist movement and, 41, 626
in Cossack Brigade, 643, 1755
in coup (1921), 88, 1118, 1755, 1869
    Cossack Brigade in, 643
coup led by (1921), 1580, 2143
death of, 1757
Dowleh (Nosrat al-) executed by, 809
educational policies of, 760, 1756
as elite, 776
government of
    Ala (Hoseyn) in, 100–101
    Alam (Amir Asadollah) in, 102
    Arfa (Hasan) in, 286
    Daftari (Ahmad Matin) in, 660
    Dashti (Ali) in, 678
    Millspaugh (Arthur) as financial adviser to, 1546
    Tabataba'i (Ziya) in, 1110
guilds under, 947
Islah Taleban Party supporting, 1144
Jangalis destroyed by, 1216
Khaz'al Khan arrested by, 1307
Kurdish revolts against, 1340
legal reforms of, 1756
as minister of war, 88
modernization by, 1756
nationalism of, 1659–1660
newspapers and print media under, 1682
oil concession under, to
    Anglo–Iranian Oil Company, 202
opposition to, Mossadegh (Mohammad) in, 1580–1581
as prime minister, 88, 1755
pro-German sympathies of, 906
Qajar dynasty ended by, 1869, 2143
regime of
    Eqbal (Manouchehr) in, 779
    as literary theme, 1435, 1436
    Luri tribes during, 1447

Tabataba'i (Ziya) denouncing, 2143
secularization by, 1756
South Persia Rifles disbanded by, 2083
state feminism under, 892
surname chosen by, 1659–1660
Tabataba'i (Ziya) and, 1682
Tehran developing under, 2170
and theater, 2186
Trans-Iranian railway commissioned by, 2203
tribal opposition to, 1756
tribal policy of, 374
U.S. support for
    CIA in, 572
    Dulles (John Foster) in, 733
veiling banned by, 891
Vozuq al-Dowleh (Mirza Hasan Khan) under, 2318
Westernization by, 1118
Pahlavi, Shahnaz, 1752
Pahlavi University (Shiraz). *See also* Shiraz University
    Alam (Amir Asadollah) at, 102
PAI. *See* Po'alei Agudat Israel
Paicovitch, Yigal. *See* Allon, Yigal
Pakhtun. *See* Pushtun
Pakistan, **1757–1758**
    Afghani conflict with, United Nations in, 2279–2280
    Afghan refugees in, 1912
    Afghan Women's Council in, 68
    in Baghdad Pact (1955), 363, 519, 1693, 2291
    Baluchis in, 385–386
    at Bandung Conference, 387
    bin Ladin in, 474, 1865
    border with Afghanistan
        as Durand Line, 400, 536, 734
        pass between, 1317
    in Central Treaty Organization, 573
    establishment of state (1947)
        Iqbal (Muhammad) in, 1109
        Jinnah (Muhammad Ali) in, 1236, 1237
    guest workers from, 946
    in Gulf War (1990–1991), 1758
    India conflict over Kashmir, nuclear threat in, 1696
    Iranian alliance with, 1758
    Iran's border with, 2420
    Islamic state in, Mawdudi (Abu al-a'la, al-) as advocate of, 1503–1504
    Jami'at-e Islami headquarters in, 1215

languages in, Iranian, 1124–1125
Middle East policy of, 1757–1758
military of, 1758
mountains of, 1799
    pass through, 1317
Muharram rites in, 1606
in Northern Tier, 1692–1693
nuclear capability of, 1696
    as "Islamic bomb," 1696
    technology shared by, 1696
Palestinians supported by, 1758
Saudi relations with, 1758
Shi'ism in, 2052
Sunni Islam in, 2123
Taliban supported by, 64
in trade, with Tunisia, 2269
tribes in, 385–386
turbans in, 609
women in
    as head of state, 808, 875
    religious rituals of, 2360
workers from, 1758
Zoroastrianism in, 2441, 2442
Pakistan Resolution (1942), 1237
Pakradouni, Karim, in Phalange party, 1831
Palestine, **1758–1769**. *See also* Arab–Israel conflict; *specific cities, organizations, people, and regions*
before 20th century, 1758–1761
agriculture in, 1760
All-Palestine Government proposed for, 154–156, 1030
Anglo–American Committee of Inquiry on (1946), 198–199
antisemitism in, 212
archaeology in, 275–276, 277
art of, 1007–1008, 2044
banking in, Levontin (Zalman) and, 1408
at Bludan Conference (1937), 488
borders of
    1949, 1760
    2000, 1768
    under British mandate, 1758, 1762
Jews and Christians on, 1758
British administration and mandate in (1917–1948), 512, 514, 614, 616, 1441, 1480, 1761–1767
    Abd al-Hadi family in, 13
    advisory council during, 50, 1762
    Allenby (Edmund Henry) in, 151, 1761

Palestine *(continued)*

anti-Zionism in, 1761–1762, 1763

anti-Zionist violence during, 1011

Antonius (George) in, 213

Arabs in, 222, 1763, 1789–1790

Balfour Declaration in (1917), 538, 614, 743, 1763, 1802

Bethlehem, 468

Bevin (Ernest) in, 647

binationalism in, 473

Churchill (Winston S.) and, 595–597

Churchill White Paper on (1922), 594

collapse of, 517–518

Colonial Office administration of, 514, 518, 617

Creech Jones (Arthur) in, 647

dual obligation of, 1763

education in, 1294

emergency regulations issued in, 776–777

Galilee in, 865

Galilee Sea in, 865

Gaza City, 869

government system of, 1761, 1762–1763

Haifa during, 974

Hebrew literature in, 1431–1432

Hebrew name for, 781

high commissioner of, 1762

High Commissioners during, 1025

Hilmi (Ahmad) during, 1030–1031

Histadrut during, 1033

Hope-Simpson Commission during, 1044–1045

Husayni (Muhammad Amin al-) during, 1056–1057

Husayni (Musa Kazim al-) during, 1058–1059

al-Husayni family during, 1053

imperialism of, 1090

Irgun Zva'i Le'umi revolt against, 1139–1140

Jewish forces armed by, 1770, 1790

Jewish immigration to, 1057, 1361

Jewish political organization in, 1764

Jewish sports organizations in, 1453

Kisch (Frederick Hermann) in, 1326

legislative council, 1402

legislative council during, 50, 1762–1763

London Conference (1939) on future of, 1445

MacMichael (Harold) on, 1455

map of, *1762*

Nashashibi family in, 1644–1645

Palestinian Arab Congress opposition to, 1782–1783

Palestinian political organization in, 1761–1762, 1764–1765

Palin Commission report on (1920), 1794–1795

Pan-Arabism in, 1799

Plumer (Herbert Charles Onslow) in, 1836

population growth during, 1763–1764

Qassam (Izz al-Din al-) against, 1874

restrictions to Jewish immigration under, 1045

revolt during (*See* Palestine Arab Revolt)

Richmond (Ernest T.) in, 1922

riots in, 512, 1763

rivalries during, intercommunal, 1763–1764

Saison in, 1972–1973

San Remo Conference (1920) on, 1988

self-government in, failure of, 1762–1763

Sèvres Treaty (1920) on, 2015

Special Night Squads during, 972

Supreme Muslim Council in, 2124–2125

Sykes-Picot Agreement (1916) on, 2128

termination of, UNSCOP support for, 2289

Transjordan Frontier Force defending, 2204

under Wauchope (Arthur), 2333

Weizmann (Chaim) and, 2338

Yishuv during, 1454, 1763–1764, 2402–2403

and Zionist movement, 2436, 2438

Zionist Revisionist Movement's policy regarding, 2438

British policy regarding

in Churchill White Paper (1922), 2349–2350

MacDonald Letter on (1931), 1454, 2350

in MacDonald White Paper (1939), 1454, 2350–2351, 2363

in Passfield White Paper (1930), 1453, 2350

white papers on, 2349–2351

Woodhead Commission (1938) on, 2350, 2363

in Christianity, 1758

civil administration in, temporary, 154

climate of, 1758

communism in, 626

constitution of (1988), 1966

cotton industry in, *2181*

dance in, 668

disease in, 714

Druze in, 729

economy of

19th-century, 1760

expansion of, 1789

education in, in religious schools, 761

fida'iyyun in, 831, 2176

film industry of, 833

flight and expulsion of Palestinians from (*See* Nakba, al-)

folk poems of, Hebrew translation of, 2418

Greeks in, 938

guest workers from, 946

higher education in, 1901

at Arab College of Jerusalem, 226–227

at Bir Zeit University, 481

as Holy Land of Bible, 1758

human rights organizations in, 991

hydroelectrification of, 1946

independence of, 801

in Islam, 1758

Israeli settlements in, Tel Hai, 2172–2173

Israeli statehood and status of, 1767

Jewish community in (*See* Yishuv)

Jewish immigration to, 2171 (*See also* Aliyah)

Anglo–American Committee of Inquiry on (1946), 198–199

Balfour Declaration (1917) on, 381, 614, 803, 1223, 1402

British limits on, 1011

by children through Youth Aliyah, 2411

Churchill White Paper (1922) on, 2350

Faisal–Weizmann Agreements on, 800, 803

legal aid and counseling for, 2357
organizations for, 2334, 2355, 2356, 2357
status in Israel, 1488
Zionism opposed by, origins of, 1789
Palestinian state
international support for, decline in, 1793
as PLO goal, 1775, 1791
PLO on
borders of, 1767
symbolic declaration of (1988), 1768, 1774, 1779–1780
in two-state solution
PFLP support for, 1840
public support for, 1793
UN support for, 1768
Palestinian Students Fund, 1953
Palestinian Talmud, 2158
Palin Commission report (1920), **1794–1795**, 2349
Palin, P. C., 1794
Palmah (Haganah elite force), **1795–1796**
Allon (Yigal) in, 153, 1795
Amichai (Yehuda) in, 182
British relations with, 1795
creation of, 972
Eitan (Rafael) in, 774
expansion of, 973
Guri (Chaim) in, 956
merged into Israel Defense Force, 1173, 1795–1796
Nahal as continuation of, 1634
Peled (Mattityahu) in, 1811
Rabin (Yitzhak) in, 1891
Shamir (Moshe) in, 2024
Palme, Olof, in Iran–Iraq peace settlement, 2280
Palmer, Sir Elwin, 931
Palmerston, Lord Henry John Temple, **1796–1797**
Asad (Hafiz al-) compared with, 320
and British–Ottoman alliance, 527–528, 530, 740, 1796–1797
and Crimean War, 648
in Damascus affair (1840), 664
delaying Suez Canal building, 528, 741
as foreign secretary, 527, 842, 1796
and international status of Bosporus and Dardanelles, 1444

at London Convention (1840), 2093–2094
and Muhammad Ali, 1346, 2007
and Mustafa Reşid, 1624
as prime minister, 527, 1796
Palmyra (Syria), **1797–1798**, *1798*
Stanhope (Hester) visit to, 275
Pamir mountains, **1799**
Pamuk, Orhan, 1437, *1438*
Panahi, Jafr, 833
Pan Am flight 103 bombing (Lockerbie), 522, 1414
and economic sanctions against Libya, 522, 1414, 1415
Libya failing to extradite defendants in, 522, 1414
Libyan compensation for, 1415, 1862
Libyan role in, Arab Maghreb Union on, 260
PFLP–GC in, 1841
Pan-Arab Feminist Union, 1965
Pan-Arabism, **1799–1800**. *See also* Arab nationalism; League of Arab States
of Aflaq (Michel), 68–69
archaeology and, 276–277
of al-Ard, 284–285
of Azzam (Abd al-Rahman al-), 352
of Bakr (Ahmad Hasan al-), 377
of Bazzaz (Abd al-Rahman al-), 421
of Darwaza (Muhammad Izzat), 673
decline of, 1799–1800
definition of, 1799
and education, 760
of Faisal I ibn Hussein, 800, 802, 824–825
Fertile Crescent unity and, 824–826
Germany supporting, 906
of Ghallab (Abd al-Karim), 910
of Ghanim (Fathi), 911
Hakim (Muhsin al-) reservations about, 977
Husari (Sati al-) conception of, 1051
Islamism supplanting, 1152–1153, 1799–1800
Nabulsi (Sulayman al-) in, 1632
of Nasser (Gamal Abdel), 1799
Nasser (Gamal Abdel) and, 1649, 1650–1651
of National Action League, 2030
vs. nation-state nationalism, 262
Numeiri's (Muhammad Ja'far) admiration for, 1699

OPEC and, 824
origins of, 1799
peak of, 1799
of PFLP, 1839
of PLO, 1781, 1791
of Quwatli (Shukri al-), 1885
of Sabbagh (Salah al-Din al-), 1953
of Sa'id (Amina al-), 1965
of Sa'id (Nuri al-), 825–826, 1967
of al-Sa'iqa, 1972
Salafiyya movement and, 1974
of Samman (Ghada), 1982
of Shawqi (Ahmad), 2045
of Shuqayri (Ahmad), 2061
Soviet support for, 517
of Zaydan (Jurji), 2426–2427
Paniagua, Valentín, 1818
Pan-Islamism
of Afghani (Jamal al-Din al-), 52, 2302
of Azzam (Abd al-Rahman al-), 352
Islamic congress promoting, 1152–1153
of Kuchek Khan-e Jangali, 1337
Panjah-o-seh nafar (Alavi), 104
Pan-Syrianism. *See* Syrian Social Nationalist Party
Panther (German gunboat), 70
Pan-Turanism, 1800, 2253
Pan-Turkism, **1800–1801**
of Akçura (Yusuf), 97, 1800
origins of, 1800
Papaver somniferum. See Opium
Papen, Franz von, 905
Paper trade, 2198
Pappé, Ilan, 1037
Paradise Lost (Milton), Armenian translation of, 144
Parallels and Paradoxes: Explorations in Music and Society (Said and Barenboim), 1966
Para Meselesi (Kasap), 1277
Paramilitary organizations, 1535
Para-statal foundations, in Iran, 1120
Parcham (Afghanistan), **1801**, 1813
collapse of government, 1801
in coup (1973), 57
in coup (1978), 1801, 1813
in coup (1979), 1801
Daud (Muhammad) and, 57, 58, 61, 679

Pitt, William, the Younger, 648

Piyano (journal), 434

PJD. *See* Justice and Development Party

PKK. *See* Kurdistan Workers Party

Plague, 710, **1835**
  and population growth, 1845

Plague, The (Camus), 563

Plakato, 2050

"Plan of Reforms" (manifesto), 812

Plants, in deserts, 604–605, 701–702

Plastics industry, in Saudi Arabia, 1094

Platform of Rome, 990

Playboys (Shamir), 2025

Plaza Lasso, Galo, in Cyprus problem, 2278

PLDC. *See* Palestine Land Development Company

PLF. *See* Palestine Liberation Front

PLFO. *See* Popular Front for the Liberation of Oman

PLF–PR. *See* Palestinian Liberation Front–Path of Return

PLO. *See* Palestine Liberation Organization

PLO: the Dialogue Desk (Bitton), 483

PLS. *See* Party of Liberation and Socialism

Plugot Mahatz. *See* Palmah

Plumer, Herbert Charles Onslow, **1835–1836**
  as high commissioner of Palestine, 1025, 2204

Plutoland (Awad), 341

PNC. *See* Palestine National Council

PND. *See* Parti National Démocratique

Pneumonic plague, 1835

Poaching, 834

Poʿalei Agudat Israel (PAI), 1187
  Agudat Israel and, 1187
  kibbutzim of, 1320
  Minz (Benjamin) in, 1550
  platform of, 1187
  in Torah Religious Front, 1178, 1189
  in United Religious Front, 1190

Poʿalei Mizrahi (Israel), 1187
  in National Religious Party, 1186
  in United Religious Front, 1190

Poʿalei Zion (Israel), 1361
  Ben-Gurion (David) in, 446

Ben-Zvi (Rahel Yanait) in, 456

Ben-Zvi (Yizhak) in, 456

binationalism supported by, 473

Shazar (Shneour Zalman) in, 2047

Poʿalei Zion (Labor Zionist party), 2434

POCT. *See* Parti Ouvrier Communiste Tunisien

Pocu, 610–611

Poʿel ha-Mizrahi, 1554, 2030

Poʿel ha-Tzaʿir, ha- (Israel)
  Ahdut ha-Avodah merging with, 1362
  Arlosoroff (Chaim) in, 289
  formation of, 1361
  in MAPAI, 1185

Poʿel ha-Tzaʿir, ha- (journal), 507

Poésie palestinienne de combat, La (Laabi), 1355

Poésies I (Shahada), 2020

Poetry. *See also* Literature; *specific poets*
  Algerian, 193, 716, 806, 1424, 1426
  Arabic, 1421–1422
    beliefs expressed in, 220–221
    modern, 1475
    pre-Islamic, Husayn (Taha) on, 1923
    symbolist movement in, 218
  Armenian, 144
  Egyptian, 22, 805, 1078–1079, 2044–2045
  Hebrew, 171, 182, 470, 920–921, 926–927, 941, 955–956, 1252, 1430–1432, *1433,* 1752, 1906, 2048, 2058–2059, 2418, 2429
    by women, 1887
  Iranian, 97, 2027
  Iraqi, 416, 1421–1422, 1475, 2002
  Israeli, 1336
  Kuwaiti, 1952
  Lebanese, 47–48, 307, 817, 872, 920, 1298–1299, 1421, *1421,* 2019–2021
  Moroccan, 396, 1355–1356, *1427,* 1428
  Ottoman, 1438, 1439, 1909, 2068
  Palestinian, 673–675, 1791, 1792, 2029, 2233, 2234
  Persian, 366–367, 397, 811, 929–930, *930,* 1435–1436
  resistance, 674
  Sufism and, 2113
  sung, 1617–1618

Syrian, 39

Tunisian, *1423, 1428, 1429,* 2017–2018

Turkish, 576, 661, 780, 782, 790, 1440, 2161, 2165–2166, 2179–2180, 2414

Yiddish, 941

Pogroms, **1836**
  aliyah caused by, 145–146
  definition of, 1836
  U.S. Jewish defense organizations after, 177
  and Zionism, 1024, 2432

Poindexter, John, in Iran–Contra affair, 1123

Point Four program (U.S.), **1836**

Poirier, Richard, 1966

Poland
  Betar in, leaders of, 2437
  Haskalah movement in, 1430
  Holocaust in, 1040
  Jews from, in Palestine, 146
  Jews immigrating from, 508–509
  Karlowitz Treaty (1699) and, 739
  in U.S. invasion of Iraq (2003), 2325

POLISARIO, 1005, **1836–1838**
  Algerian support for, 2343–2344, 2345
  Algeria supporting, 503, 1837, 2190–2191
  diplomatic recognition of, 2345
  establishment of, 1571
  executive committee of, 1964
  guerrilla war against Morocco (1976–1991), 1571, 1600, 2342, 2343–2347
    UN diplomatic efforts in, 2344–2345, 2346–2347
  League of Arab States not accepting, 1964
  Libya supporting, 1837, 2190–2191
  Mauritania territory ceded to, 2345
  SADR as government-in-exile of, 1964
  Sahrawi (Saharan) Arab Democratic Republic established by, 2343
  Spain opposing, 2084
  territory in Mauritania seized by, 1503
  war of national liberation against Spain, 1571, 2343
  in Western Sahara War, 1837

Political and Literary Essays (Baring), 407

Qiyomijian, Ohannes, **1880**

QIZs. *See* Qualified Industrial Zones

Qom (Iran), **1880**
 carpet weaving in, 566
 in Constitutional Revolution
  (1905–1909), 636
 in Iranian Revolution (1979),
  1119, 1126, 1880
 Montazeri (Hosayn Ali) at, 1564
 religious institution in, 929
 seminary for women in, 187
 as Shiʿite center, 2054–2055
 ulamas leaving Tehran for (1904),
  1591

Qom Law School, 1970

Qotbzadeh, Sadeq, **1880–1881**
 Chamran (Mostafa) and, 582, 1880
 Khomeini (Ruhollah) supported
  by, 1311

QP. *See* Qatar Petroleum

Qualified Industrial Zones (QIZs),
 in Jordan, 1244

Quandt, William, 539

Quarta Sponda. *See* Fourth Shore,
 The

Quataert, Donald
 as contributor, 1728–1734, 1735–1737
 as historiographer, 1036

Quba mosque (Medina), 2323

Qubbanji, Muhammad al-, 1618

Qubbat al-Sakhra (Jerusalem). *See*
 Dome of the Rock (Jerusalem)

Qubbat Talha Mosque (Sanʿa,
 Yemen), 2387

Quds al Arabi, al- (newspaper), 1681

Quds Committee, al-, Muhammad
 VI as chairman of, 1602

Qudsi, Nazim al-. *See* Kudsi, Nazim
 al-

Quds University, al-, Nusayba (Sari)
 as president of, 1705

Quduri, al-, 988

Queen Alia Fund for Social Development, 409

Queen Arwa University, Farʾa
 (Wahiba) founding, 806

Queen Surraya. *See* Surraya

Queen Zein Al-Sharaf Institute for
 Development, 409

*Quest for Identity: The Image of Iranian
 Women in Prehistory and History, The*
 (Lahiji and Kar), 1365

Question irakienne, La (Luizard), 1987

Quetta (Baluchistan), 385

Quetta (Pakistan), Revolutionary Association of the Women of
 Afghanistan (RAWA) in, 1920

Quinn, Anthony, 98

Qui se souvient de la mer (Dib), 1426

Qulaylat, Ibrahim, Murabitun
 founded by, 1612

Qum. *See* Qom

Qumisyun al-Taʿlim, 2146

Quneitra (Golan Heights), in
 Arab–Israel War (1973), *251*

Qurai, Ahmad Sulayman (Abu Ala),
 1784, **1881–1882**
 Arafat (Yasir) in power struggle
  with, 814
 in Oslo negotiations, 1725,
  1881–1882
 as PA prime minister, 1775, 1882
 as PA speaker of council, 1784
 in PLO, 1881–1882
 as prime minister, 2042

Qurʾan, **1882–1883**
 on alcohol consumption, 109
 on Allah, 1145
 and Arabic language, 232,
  233–234, 1419
 on birth control, 480
 calligraphy of, 558, *558*, 1883
 collection of, 1883
 definition of, 2627
 ethics in, 1145–1147
 fiqh derived from, 1148
 FIS on establishment of Islamic
  state based on, 857
 and *hadith*, 968
 on *hijab* (veiling), 1026
 Husayn (Taha) at, 1060
 interpretation of, 1882–1883
 on Jews, and antisemitism, 212
 in *madrasa* education system,
  1457–1458
 Mawdudi (Abu al-aʿla, al-) commentary on, 1504
 muwahhidun adherence to, 1625
 Nursi (Said) on, 1705
 on polygamy, 1839
 revealed by Muhammad,
  1595–1596, 1882
 role in Islam, 1145, 1883
 on *shariʿa*, 2033, 2034
 structure of, 1882
 Sufi interpretation of, 2111, 2112
 Sunna in, 2122
 themes of, 1882–1883
 on women, 808, 1987, 2153
  Mernissi (Fatema) on, 1518
 women's reading of, 2359–2360

Qurʾan and Issues of Human Condition, The
 (Bint al-Shati), 476

Qurʾanic Phenomenon, The (Bennabi), 451

Quray, Ahmad Sulayman. *See* Qurai,
 Ahmad Sulayman

Quraysh tribe, 2213
 and Hashimite house, 1000

Qurei, Ahmad Sulayman. *See* Qurai,
 Ahmad Sulayman

Qusaybi, Ghazi al-, 798

Qusayr, al- (Egypt), **1884**

Qusi, Ihsan al-, on Wafdist Women's
 Central Committee, 2321

Qutbiyyan, al- (Egypt), in al-Jamiʿa
 al-Islamiyya, 1215

Qutb, Sayyid, **1884–1885**
 and Afghan Islamic movements,
  60
 Belhadj (Ali) influenced by, 436
 bin Ladin studying works of, 474
 commentary on Qurʾan by, 1883
 execution of, 1215, 1621, 1884
 Islamic Jihad inspired by, 1154
 in Muslim Brotherhood, 1621,
  1884
  Ashmawi (Muhammad Abd al-
   Rahman Salih al-) and, 321
 Nasser (Gamal Abdel) and, 1884
 and al-Qutbiyyan, 1215
 Rida (Rashid) and, 1924
 in al-Takfir wa al-Hijra, 2150
 writings of, 1883, 1884–1885

Quttineh, Lamia, in Women's Centre for Legal Aid and Counseling, 2356

Qutuz (Mamluk sultan), 1044

Quwatli, Shukri al-, *1885,*
 1885–1886
 coup against (1949), 1886, 2422
 in exile, 1885–1886, 1886
 French occupation opposed by,
  1885
 government of, Arslan (Adil) in,
  306
 against Greater Syria plan, 936
 in National Bloc, 328, 1885
 in National Party, 1664
 presidency of, 1886, 2133
 United Arab Republic supported
  by, 1886, 2273

R

Raab, Esther, 1431, **1887**

Raʿad, al- (newspaper), 1682

Raad, Inʿam, **1888**, 2137

Raʿanan, Natan, at Merkaz ha-Rav, 1333

Rababa, 433

Rabat (Morocco), 828, 1567, *1570,* **1888**
  Arab League summit (1969) in, *1387*
  Arab League summit (1974) in, *1387*
  Catholics in, 1932
  numismatic center in, 1702–1703

Rabbani, Burhanuddin, **1888–1889**
  communists opposed by, 61
  coup against (1996), 61
  government of
    Ahmad Shah Masʿud in, 89
    Hekmatyar (Golbuddin) in, 1020
    Karzai (Hamid) in, 1276
  in Jamiʿat-e Islami, 60, 63, 64, 1215, 1561, 1888–1889
  in mojahedin resistance, 1561
  presidency of, 59, 1215, 1889
  veiling ordinances under, 1715

Rabbani, Mouin, *as contributor,* 961–963, 1070–1071, 1776–1781, 1839–1842, 1881–1892, 1952–1953, 1972, 2334–2336

Rabbani, Shoghi Effendi, 365

Rabbi(s), *1889,* **1889–1890**
  criteria for becoming, 1889
  women as, 1889
  and Zionist organizations, 1024–1025, 2432–2433

Rabbinic Hebrew (RH), 1017

Rabi, Mubarak, *1424, 1425,* **1890**

Rabinovich, Itamar
  as contributor, 1993
  in peace negotiations, 926

Rabin, Yitzhak, **1890–1892,** *1891*
  after Arab–Israel War (1973), 252
  and Arafat (Yasir), 1892
  assassination of, 403, 1168, 1726, 1793, 1892, 2177
  Barak (Ehud) under, 398
  election of, 1725
  financial scandal involving, 1891
  funeral of, Hussein ibn Talal at, 1246
  on Golan Heights, 926
  government of, 1891
    Allon (Yigal) in, 153
    Aloni (Shulamit) in, 157
    Gur (Mordechai) in, 956
    Hillel (Shlomo) in, 1030
    Namir (Orah) in, 1641

Peres (Shimon) in, 1818
  Sarid (Yossi) in, 1991
  Sharon (Ariel) in, 2041
  Yariv (Aharon) in, 2379
Harkabi (Yehoshafat) and, 995
and Hussein ibn Talal, *1063,* 1892
in Israel Defense Force, 1171, 1173
Israeli settlements under, 1192
Kissinger (Henry) and, *1328*
in Labor Party, 1167, 1183
legacy of, 1892
military career of, 1891
Nobel Peace Prize to, *1817*
in Oslo Accords (1993), 1725–1726
  signing of, 271, 606, *1726*
in Palmah, 1795
and peace agreements, 1892
Peres (Shimon) and, 1183, 1817, 1818
political career of, 1891
and Zionist Organization of America, 2436

Rabita al-Qalamiyya al- (Pen's League), 920

Rabiyya Ali, Salim, **1892**
  Ismaʿil (Abd al-Fattah) power struggle with, 1157, 1814
  Antar (Ali Ahmad Nasir) in, 211

Rachel's tomb (Bethlehem), 2359

Rachid, Ouakali, 919

Racine, translation of, 171

Racy, Ali Jihad, *as contributor,* 22

Raʾd (newspaper), 1110, 2142

Radd ala al-dahriyyin, al- (Afghani), 23

Raʾd-e Emruz (newspaper), 2143

Radfan Rebellion, Antar (Ali Ahmad Nasir) in, 211

Radif (Iranian music), 1617, 1618

Raʿd, Inʿam. *See* Raad, Inʿam

Radio and television, **1893–1898**
  in Algeria, MʾRabet (Fadela) on, 1592
  al-Jazeera, 1219–1220
  in Arab countries, 1893–1896
    audiences for, 1895
    ownership and control of, 1895–1896
  and Arab nationalism, 222–223
  Christian station, 1856
  in Egypt, 1469
  in Israel, 866, 1896–1897
  and music, 1619
  PFLP–GC radio stations, 1842
  Protocols of the Elders of Zion on, 1856
  in Saudi Arabia, 164, 798, 1894

spread of, 624–625, *625*
  in Turkey, 1897–1898, 2245
Radio Jerusalem. *See* Idhaʾat al-Quds
Radio Lebanon, 817, 818
Radubis (Mahfuz), 1464
Rafah, 870
Rafeq, Abdul-Karim, *as contributor,* 100, 344, 665–666, 683–684, 909, 936, 980–981, 1032, 1080–1081, 1198–1199, 1205–1206, 1375, 2030, 2126–2127, 2136, 2211, 2212
Rafiʿi, 2019
RAFI Party (Israel), 1187–1188, 1378
  Ben-Gurion (David) in, 1188, 1189
  Ben-Porat (Mordechai) in, 452
  Dayan (Moshe) in, 682, 1188
  establishment of, 1187–1188
  Kollek (Teddy) in, 1331
  on Lavon affair, 1188
  Navon (Yizhak) in, 1671
  Peres (Shimon) in, 1188, 1817
  platform of, 1188
Rafsanjani, Ali Akbar Hashemi, 1472, **1898–1899**
  Bani Sadr (Abolhasan) in conflict with, 388
  daughter of, 998
  election to presidency, 1120
  government of
    Mohajerani (Ataollah) in, 1558
    Musavi (Mir-Hosain) in, 1615
  and Iranian Bureau of Women's Affairs, 1123
  radicals' relationship with, 1120
  and Revolutionary Guards, 1922
  rural development under, 1220
  Tehran under, Karbaschi (Gholamhosain) as mayor of, 1273
Rafto Prize for Human Rights, to Ebadi (Shirin), 744
Rage aux tripes, La (Tlili), 2193
Raghib, Ali Abu al-, 820
Raghif Yanbud ka al-Qalb, al- (Samman), 1982
Rahbani, Asi al-, 817
Rahbani brothers, plays by, 1617
Rahbani, Mansur al-, 817
Rahbani, Ziyad al-, 818
Rah-e Now (journal), 867
Rahhal, Husayn al-, communism of, 625
Rahimi, Babak, *as contributor,* 148–149, 867

Rosen, Pinhas, in Lavon affair, 1377

Rosenthal, Joseph, in Socialist party, 625–626

Rosetta branch of Nile River, 1688

Rosetta Stone, 275, 276, 482, 492, 581

Roshanfekr, 2628

Roshangaran Publishing, 1364

Ross, Edward, in Anglo–Omani treaties, 204

Rotana (Nubian language), 1696

Rothschild, Edmond de, **1937–1938**
  as Balfour Declaration (1917) drafter, 380
  Behar (Nissim) and, 427
  Israeli settlements supported by, 145–146, 1822, 1927, 2431
  Jewish immigration to Palestine supported by, 1560
  response to *Der Judenstaat* (Herzl), 1021
  trying to regain Western Wall for Jewish community, 427
  and Zionism, 2432

Rothschild Foundation, and Israel Television, 1897

Rothschild-Hadassah University Hospital (Palestine), 966

Rothschild, James Armand de, 1937
  death of, 1938

Rouchdy, Aleya, *as contributor,* 1695–1696

Rouleau, Eric, 1292

Roumani, Maurice M., *as contributor,* 966, 973–974, 1636–1637, 1686–1687

Rousseau, Henri, 2044

Rowe, Paul S., *as contributor,* 632–633, 1447–1448, 1980–1981, 2067–2068

Royal Air Maroc (Morocco), 1569
  Ben Seddiq (Mahjoub) at, 453
  French skyjacking of, 1309, 1362
  Lamrani (Muhammad Karim) as director of, 1366

Royal Asiatic Society, 540

Royal Dutch Shell, **1938**
  in As-Is Agreement (1928), 323
  in price wars, 323
  and Turkish Petroleum Company, 1909

Royal Military College (England)
  Farouk at, 810
  Talal ibn Abdullah at, 2153

Roy, Sara M., *as contributor,* 870–871

RPN. *See* Rassemblement Patriotique National

RPP. *See* Republican People's Party

RSP. *See* Socialist Progressive Rally

Rub al-Khali (Saudi Arabia), 701, 1638, **1938,** 1995
  tribes in, 2213, 2215

Rubashov, Shneour Zalman. *See* Shazar, Shneour Zalman

Rub'e Rashidi (Tabriz), 2144

Rubin, Barnett R., *as contributor,* 89

Rubinstein, Amnon, **1938–1939**
  in Democratic Movement for Change, 1181

Rubiyya, Salim Ali. *See* Rabiyya Ali, Salim

Ruedy, John, *as contributor,* 120–128, 136–139, 142, 254–256, 290, 326, 617–618, 619–620, 632, 803–804, 857, 1025–1026, 1087–1091, 1480, 1587–1588, 1589–1590, 1715, 1743–1744, 1804–1805, 2089, 2263–2264, 2404–2405

Rugh, William A., *as contributor,* 1678–1682, 1893–1896

Ruhab (magazine), 434

Ruhafza, in *Irshad An-Niswaan,* 1140

Ruhi, Shaykh Ahmad, 891

Ruju ila al-tufula (Abu Zeid), 40

Ruman, Mikha'il, 2184

Rumaytha Rebellion (1935) (Iraq), 2065

Rumelia, **1939**

Rumi, Jalal al-Din, 434–435, 1149, 2113

Rumi, Mevlana Celalledina (Jalal al-Din), 1521

Runic alphabet, 2250

Ruppin, Arthur, 1461, **1939–1940**
  Palestine Land Development Company founded by, 1772

Ruqiyya, as daughter of Muhammad, 1595

Rüşdiye, 757

Ruşdiye Schools, 1461, **1940**

Rush, Alan, 158

Rushani, Laila Sarahat, in *Irshad An-Niswaan,* 1140

Rushdie, Salman, 351, 522
  fatwa against
    Kharrazi (Kamal) rejecting, 1300
    Mohajerani (Ataollah) reaction to, 1558

Rusk, Dean, **1940–1941**

Russell, Bertrand, 45

Russell, Francis, in Operation Alpha, 157

Russell, Mona, *as contributor,* 39–40, 206, 1374–1375

Russia, **1941–1944.** *See also* Russo *entries;* Soviet Union
  and Armenian revolutionary movement, 299, 300
  Armenians in
    Dashnak Party and, 676–677
    edict confiscating churches of, 300–301
  Black Sea access of, 739–740
    Kuçuk Kaynara Treaty (1774) and, 485, 739, 2094–2095
    London Treaty (1871) on, 1446
    Paris Peace (1856) on, 1446
  British relations with
    Constantinople and, 511, 528, 529
    Iran in, 88, 205, 651–652
    perceived threat to India and, 1941
    rivalry over Afghanistan, 536
    rivalry over Persia, 535–536
    rivalry over southern central Asia, 936–937
    Russo–Japanese War (1904–1905) and, 536
    spheres of influence, 1032, 1941–1942
    Suez Canal and, 529
    Turkish Straits and, 528, 529, 2093
  Circassians in, 599
  Cossacks of, and Iranian Cossack Brigade, 643
  cotton exported to, 644
  in Crimean War, 648–649, 739, 2162
  and Dardanelles Treaty (1809), 671, 672
  in Eastern Question, 739–742
  fishing industry of, 834
  French relations with,
    Russian–French alliance, 742
  German relations with, Potsdam Convention in (1911), 1851
  in Greek War of Independence (1821–1930), 940
  Haskalah movement in, 1430
  Hebrew literature from, 1015–1016
  Iranian relations with, 1117
    Griboyedov Incident and, 943
    under Naser al-Din Shah, 1644

Sabha (Libya), 1410

SABIC. *See* Saudi Basic Industries Corporation

Sabil al-Rashid (journal), 2182

Sabir, Mirza Ali-Ekber, 347

Sabkshenasi, 367

Sabra, **1954**

Sabra and Shatila massacres (Lebanon), 1774, **1954–1955**
  Eitan (Rafael) role in, 254, 774, 1263, 1954
  Hobeika (Elie) in, 1039
  investigation of (*See* Kahan Commission)
  Navon (Yizhak) requesting inquiry into, 1672
  Shamir (Yitzhak) role in, 1263, 2026
  Sharon (Ariel) role in, 254, 1039, 1263, 1954, 2026

Sabratah (ancient city), 2217

Sabri, Ali, **1955**
  Haykal (Muhammad Hasanayn) in conflict with, 1956

Sacred Things (section in Talmud), 2157

Sa'da (Yemen), Zaydi population in, 2427

Sa'd, Ahmad Sadiq, in New Dawn group, 627

Sadat, Anwar al-, *425,* **1955–1958,** *1956*
  Abd al-Rahman (Umar) granted amnesty by, 20
  and Ahram Center for Political and Strategic Studies, 92
  American University in Cairo and, 179
  in Arab–Israel War (1973), 250, 1957
  and Arab Socialist Union, 267, 1665
  army under, 767
  assassination of, 768, 771, –1593, 1957
    Abd al-Rahman (Umar) in, 20, 349
  Begin (Menachem) negotiating with, 1957
  Cairo University and, 556
  in Camp David Accords (1978), 426, 560, 567, 770, 1166, 1957, 2293, *2293*
    Boutros-Ghali (Boutros) and, 505
    PLO excluded by, 1774
    Vance (Cyrus) and, 2308

Copts under, 641–642

in coup (1952), 1956

education of, 1955

Egyptian–Israeli Peace Treaty (1979) signed by, 770

Faisal (ibn Abd al-Aziz Al Sa'ud) and, 1626

in Free Officers movement, 1956

and Gezira Sporting Club, 908

Ghorbal (Ashraf) as security adviser to, 915–916

Haykal (Muhammad Hasanayn) during regime of, 1012

imprisonment of, 1956

industrialization under, 1094

infitah economic policy of, 765–766, 1096, 1957

Jerusalem trip of, 238, 1957
  King David Hotel in, 1324
  Tripoli Conference as response to, 2217

Kissinger (Henry) meeting with, 1327

military experience of, 1537, 1540–1541

Mubarak (Husni) under, 1593

Muhyi al-Din (Khalid) opposing, 1608

Muhyi al-Din (Zakariyya) opposing, 1608

and Muslim Brotherhood, 1621, 1955–1956
  crackdown on, 321, 1956
  revitalization of, 1214

on Nasser (Gamal Abdel), 1649

Nasser (Gamal Abdel) friendship, 1955, 1956

as Nasser's (Gamal Abdel) successor, 1651

New Wafd under, 1685, 2321

normalization policy toward Israel, opposition to, 2428

ordering Soviet military advisers to leave, 508, 1957

in peace process, 2292–2293

and pension for Free Officers, 853

on postage stamps, 1850

as president, 767, 1956–1957

in Revolutionary Command Council, 1921

Sabri (Ali) and, 1955

satellite cities development by, 1994, 1995

Sha'rawi (Muhammad Mutwalli al-) under, 2031

Shazli (Sa'd al-Din al-) criticizing, 2048

Shenouda III accused by, 2048–2049

Sheounda III exiled by, 2319

Suez Canal University founded by, 2107

and U.S. relations, 2292

Uthman (Uthman Ahmad) and, 2305

as vice president, 1956

Wafd leadership arrested by, 1957

wife of, 1958

Sadat City (Egypt), 1995

Sadat, Jihan al-, **1958**

Sadawi, Bashir, **1958–1959**
  in National Congress Party, 1653

Sa'dawi, Nawwal al-, 875, 894

Sadd al-Wahda. *See* Maqarin (Widha) Dam

Saddam City. *See* Baghdad (Iraq)

Saddiq (holy person), 1485

Sadeh, Pinhas, 1433

Sadeh, Yitzhak
  in Haganah, 972
  in Palmah, 1795

Sadeq, Sayyed, 2141

Sa'dians, 2037–2038, 2059
  Marrakech under, 1493

Sadi family, 105

Sadiki College (Tunisia), Mourou (Abdelfattha) at, 1586

Sadiq al-Mahdi, al- (Sudanese leader), 210, 2103
  Baggara Arabs supporting, 1335
  imprisonment of, 2261
  in National Democratic Alliance, 2261
  as prime minister, 210, 2261
  sister of, 2235–2236
  Turabi (Hasan al-) under, 2234
  in Umma Party, 210, 2261

Sadiqi College (Tunis), 84, 1428, **1959**
  Ben Salah (Ahmed) at, 452
  Bourguiba (Habib) at, 500
  establishment of, 1307, 1604
  Sfar (Tahar) at, 2016
  vs. Zaytuna University, 1959

Sadiq, Isma'il al-, 2053

Sadiq, Jafar al-, 2053

Sadiq, Yusuf, as Free Officer, 853

Sadi, Said, **1959–1960**
  in Berber Spring (1980), 1959
  Bouteflika (Abdelaziz) supported by, 1960
  in Front des Forces Socialistes, 1959
  in Human Rights League, 1959

Volume 1: pp. 1–658; Volume 2: pp. 659–1354; Volume 3: pp. 1355–2028; Volume 4: pp. 2029–2632

Satmar Hasidim, 1002

Satmar Hassidic sect, Neturei Karta supported by, 1677

Saʿud family, al-. *See under* Al Saʿud

Saudi American Bank, 390

Saudi Arabia, **1995–2001**. *See also specific cities, organizations, people, and regions*

agriculture in, 1511, 1996

Al al-Shaykh family in, 101–102

alcohol in, 110

Al Rashid family in, 157–158

Al Saʿud family in (*See* Al Saʿud family)

Al Sudayri family in, 168–169

in Arab–Israel War (1948), 1626

in Arab–Israel War (1967), 799, 1626

in Arab–Israel War (1973), 251, 1626

Arab nationalism in, 799, 2166

archaeology in, 278

architecture in, 284

area of, 1995

armament levels of, 304

arms sales to, 796, 2201

by China, 586, 1535

by United States, 304

Asir region claimed by, 1081

banking in, 219, 390, *393*, 394

and Beitaddin Declaration (1978), 432

bin Laden (Osama) in, 474

bin Ladin (Osama) supported by, 164

at Bludan Conference (1937), 488

borders of, 1995

Anglo–Turkish convention on (1913), 1678

with Iraq, 10, 1678

with Jordan, 10

with Kuwait, 1678

with Qatar, 1877

Uqayr Treaty on (1922), 159

with Yemen, 10, 2385

British relations with

under Abd al-Aziz ibn Saʿud Al Saʿud, 515

under Faysal ibn Turki Al Saʿud, 819

Treaty of Protection (1886) and, 2208

Buraymi oasis claimed by, 517, 544

Camp David Accords (1978) and, 794, 796

Chinese relations with, 586, 587

cities of, 703, 1995, 2148–2149

capital, 1638, 1927–1928, 1995

holy, 1506–1507, 1511–1512, 1995, 1997, *1997*

port, 666, 1235–1236, 1250, 1315, 1995, 2378–2379

climate of, 1996

communication in, 625

Council of Ministers in, establishment of, 12

defense costs as percentage of GNP or GDP, *1530*

deserts of, 1938, 2136

economic aid from, 749

economy of, 752, *753*, 795, 1996–1997

education in, 759, 794, 798, 1997

Egyptian relations with, 795–796, 798

under Faisal (ibn Abd al-Aziz Al Saʿud), 1626

Sadat (Anwar al-) and, 1957

elites in, 776

establishment of, 9, 10–11, 515, 1998–1999

family planning in, 478

fishing in, 1996

German relations with, Grobba (Fritz Konrad Ferdinand) and, 944

government of, 934

in Gulf Cooperation Council, 949

in Gulf Crisis (1990–1991), 796, 950, 951, 953, 1067, 1538, 1627, 2000

Hanbali School of Law in, 990

higher education in, 1928, 1997

at Islamic University of Medina, 1156–1157, 1511

at King Faisal University, 666

at King Saʿud University, 1324

at Umm al-Qura University, 2260

women in, 1324

Hijaz in, 1028

human rights in, 1048

industrialization in, 752, 1094, 1997

in International Monetary Fund, 1106

Iranian relations with, 1999–2000

Mecca riots (1988) and, 1627

Iran–Iraq War (1980–1988) and, 795, 796, 2000

Iraqi relations with, 796

oil export, 2203

Islamic congresses held by, 1152–1153

Jordanian relations with

Hussein ibn Talal and, 2156

pledge of financial aid to Jordan (1957), 1632

Talal ibn Abdullah and, 2152

labor unions illegal in, 1358

languages in, 1997

in League of Arab States, 1386, 1387, 1388

Lebanese relations with, 795

legal system of, 1380–1381

reforms in, 1380

legislative body in, 932

literature of, 1611

location of, 1995

at London Conference (1939), 1445

malaria in, 711

manufacturing in, 1483, *1483*

map of, *1996*

military of

equipment of, *1534*, 1535

force levels of, *1528–1529*

force structure of, *1532–1533*

mountains of, 1995–1996

muwahhidun (Wahhabi followers) in, 1625–1627

natural gas production and reserves in, 1671, *1671*

neutral zone of

shared with Iraq, 1678

shared with Kuwait, 1678

newspapers and print media of, 1678–1679

loyalist approach in, 1681

offshore publishing of, 1681

oases in, 1995, 1996, 1997

in oil embargo (1973), 1626

oil production in, 752, 1995, 1996–1997, 2199

Abd al-Aziz (ibn Saʿud Al Saʿud) and, 1626

by Arabian American Oil Company, 229–230

and end of Red Line Agreement, 1910

nationalization of, 230

by Standard Oil of California, 11, 229

Tariki (Abdullah) and, 2166

U.S. companies favored in, 515

Yamani (Ahmad Zaki) and, 2378

oil revenues of, 795, 799

in OPEC, 1719

production quota for, 1720

in Ottoman Empire, 1999

Ottoman relations with, Faysal ibn Turki Al Saʿud and, 819

Pakistani relations with, 1758

Short stories *(continued)*
 in Persian literature, 1435,
  1802–1803
 of Syria, 1084
 of Tunisia, 1313
SHP. *See* Social Democratic Populist
 Party
Shuckburgh, Evelyn, in Operation
 Alpha, 157
Shuf (Lebanon), **2059–2060**
 Jumblatt family in, 1254
Shufman, Gershon, **2060**
Shuhada Foundation, 1982
Shuhuda Ya'udun Hatha al-Usbu (Wattar),
 2333
Shuja Durrani, 196, 735
 brother of, 1468
Shukri, Ibrahim, 768
Shukri, Mohammad, 1425, **2060**
Shulkhan Arukh (Karo), 979, 1962
Shultz, George, **2061**
 education of, 2061
 in Israeli–Lebanese security agreement, 254, 318
 at King David Hotel, 1324
 under Nixon (Richard M.), 2061
 and Reagan Plan (1982), 2061
Shumayyil, Shibli, **2061**
Shuqayri, Ahmad, **2061–2062**
 against Camp David Accords
  (1978), 2062
 education of, 2061
 in exile, 2062
 expulsion from Jordan, 2156
 vs. Hut (Shafiq al-), 1071
 in Istiqlal Party, 2061
 and Nasser (Gamal Abdel), 2062
 as PLO founder, 813, 1777, 2062
 as PLO leader, 814, 1767, 1772,
  1791, 2062
Shuqayri, Anwar al-, 2063
Shuqayri, As'ad al-, 2061,
 2062–2063
Shuqayri family, **2062–2063**
Shura, 1145, **2063**, 2234
 in Afghanistan, establishment of,
  63
 vs. anjoman (assembly), 207
 in Iran, 1359
Shura Council (Hizbullah,
  Lebanon), Nasrallah (Hasan)
  on, 1647
Shura-i Nizar (Afghanistan), in interim government, 64
Shura-i-Zanan-i-Afghanistan, 786

Shura-ye Ittifagh-e Islami
 (Afghanistan), 63
 in mojahedin resistance, 1561
Shuster, W. Morgan, **2063–2064**
 Russian demand for dismissal of,
  88
Shuttar, Al- (Shukri), 2060
Shutters (Freier), 855
Shuttle diplomacy, 2070
 definition of, 2629
 Kissinger (Henry) as architect of,
  1327–1328
Shu'un Filastiniyya (journal), 1782
 Darwish (Mahmud) as editor of,
  674
Siba'a tribe, 2212
Sibay tribe, 2209
Sibila, battle of (1929), 1085
Sib, Treaty of (1920), 1710, **2064**
Sidara, 611, 2629
Siddiq al-Mahdi (Sudanese leader),
 210
Siddiqi, al-Tayyib al-, 2184
Sidera, Zineb, **2064–2065**
Sidi Barrani (Egypt), 2369
Sidi Ifni (Morocco), 1083
Sidi Muhammad ibn Abdullah, fa-
 vorite son of, 1003
Sidi Muhammad ibn Abdullah Uni-
 versity, 828
Sidi Muhammad, Mulay (sultan of
 Morocco), Montefiore
 (Moses) and, 1565
Sidi Sliman (Morocco), 913
Sidi Yahya (Morocco), 913
Sidon (Lebanon), **2065**
 As'ad Wali in, 320–321
 fishermen strike (1975) at, 1391
 fishing in, 2065
 Hariri (Rafiq Baha'uddin al-) and,
  994
 Jewish financiers in, 807
Sidqi, Aziz, 1650
Sidqi, Bakr, **2065**
 in Ahali group, 80
 coup led by (1936), 999, 1001
  Abu al-Timman (Ja'far) sup-
   ported by, 35
  Ahali group in, 80
  crackdown on opposition by, 43
  Sulayman (Hikmat) friendship,
   2115
Sidqi, Isma'il, **2065–2066**
 in exile, 2065

 under King Fu'ad, 2065
 in Liberal Constitutionalist Party,
  2065
 Mahmud (Muhammad) and, 1468
 Maratghi (Mustafa al-) opposing,
  1486
 as prime minister of Egypt, 859,
  2066
 in Wafd, 2065
 Wafd opposing, 2066
 Zaghlul (Sa'd) and, 2065
Sidra, Gulf of, **2066**
Sieff, Rebecca, in Women's Interna-
 tional Zionist Organization,
 2357
Siemens, Georg von, 533
Sifr al-Naqla wa al-Tasawwur (Ben
 Saleh), 1429
Sifriyat ha-Po'alim (Shlonsky), 2058
Sihab, al- (turban of Muhammad),
 609
Silence (Iranian film), 1473
Silences du palais, Les (film), 2192
Silences of the Palace (film), 833
Silk, **2066**, 2180, 2197, 2198
Silk Road, 2066
Silo, Fawzi, in General Armistice
 Agreement (1949), 241
Silsila (initiatic chain), 1641, 2113
Silvera, Alain, *as contributor*,
 2315–2316
Silver, Abba Hillel, **2066–2067**
 during Holocaust, 2436
 Wise (Stephen S.) conflict with,
  2355
Silver, Eric, *as contributor*, 424–427,
 1676–1677, 2041–2042
"Silver Platter, The" (Alterman),
 171
Silverstein, Brian, *as contributor*,
 1684–1685, 1897–1898
Silverstein, Paul, *as contributor*,
 463–464, 485–486
Simaika, Marcus, Coptic Museum
 founded by, 638
"Siman-Tov's Thousand Wives"
 (Seri), 2012
Simavi, Erol, 1051, 2067
Simavi, Sedat, **2067**
 and *Hürriyet* (newspaper), 1051
Simeon bar Yohai, 717
Simit bread, *841*
Simko, Isma'il Agha, 1340, 1345
Simond, Paul Lewis, 710

Simon, Miriam, *as contributor*,
402–403, 449–450, 1459,
1671–1672, 2095–2096,
2169, 2172, 2339,
2424–2425

Simon, Rachel, *as contributor*, 807,
1870–1871, 1990,
2246–2247

Simon, Reeva S., *as contributor*,
244–246, 275–280, 412–414,
799–802, 852–853,
903–907, 927, 1043,
1211–1212, 1213–1214,
1222–1227, 1325, 1378, 1582,
1654–1655, 1937–1938, 1953,
2173, 2214–2215,
2353–2354, 2399–2400

Simoon wind, 605

Sinai (Israeli periodical), 1470

Sinai campaign of 1956, 681, 1537
Amit (Meir) in, 190
Anglo–Egyptian Treaty nullified
by, 200
Dayan (Moshe) in, 681
Israeli-French negotiations before,
Peres (Shimon) in, 1817
Operation Alpha and, 157

Sinai I disengagement agreement
(1974), Kissinger (Henry) in,
1328

Sinai II disengagement agreement
(1975), Kissinger (Henry) in,
1328

Sinai, Mount, 1971, 2067–2068

Sinai Peninsula, **2067–2068**
Bedouin tribes on, 2068
British occupation of, during
World War I, 509
British–Ottoman rivalry over,
2068
Camp David Accords (1978) on,
2068
climate of, 2067
Egyptian–Israeli Peace Treaty
(1979) on, 771, 2068
Egypt trying recapture of
(1972–1973), 1957, 2068
Israeli evacuation of (1982), 1166
military action against opponents of, 1536
Israeli seizure of, in Arab–Israel
War (1967), 249, 1537, 1651,
2068
location of, 763, 2067
London Treaty (1840) on, 2068
origin of term, 2067
under Ottoman control, 2068

withdrawal of UN forces from,
Nasser's (Gamal Abdel) request for, 1651

Şinasi, İbrahim, **2068–2069**
as pioneer of modernism, 1438
newspaper edited by, 1684
in Young Ottomans, 2069, 2405,
2406, 2407
and Ziya (Abdülhamit), 2439

Sinatra, Frank, 224

Sinekli Bakkal (Adivar), 46

Sinf, 947

Siniora, Randa, in Women's Studies
Center, 2362

Sion (journal), 292

Sion, Dov, 683

Sira al-Madhhab wa al-Aqida fi al-Qur'an
(Ghallab), 910

Siraj al-Akhbar (newspaper), 56
Young Afghan Party and, 62

Siraj al-Din, Fu'ad, as New Wafd
leader, 2321

Sirat al-Mustaqim, al- (Straight
Path), terrorist attack in
Casablanca, 1569

Sirhindi, Ahmad, 1642, 2114

Şirket-i Hayriye, **2069**

Sirry, Gazbia, **2069**

Sisakan (Alishan), 144

Sisco Associates, 2070

Sisco, Joseph, **2069–2070**

Sistan (Iran), **2070**

Sistani, Ali al-, **2070–2071**
al-Da'wa al-Islamiyya and, 681
direct elections urged by, 2326

Sistani language, 2070

Sistanis, in Zahedan (Iran),
2420

Sisters of Zion School (Jerusalem),
2051

Sisvan (Alishan), 144

Sitra (Bahrain), **2071**

Sitt, 2629

Sitt, al-. See Stanhope, Hester

Sitt Marie Rose (Adnan), 47

Siuni, Papken, 676

Sivas Conference (1919), **2071**
Atatürk (Mustafa Kemal) in, 331

Sivers, Peter von, *as contributor*, 85,
139–140, 1610, 1713–1715,
2327

Siwa oasis, **2071–2072**

Sixième jour, le (Chédid), 583

Six-Point Agreement (1973),
Kissinger (Henry) in, 1328

Six Points (Hammarskjöld), 2108

Sixth Day, The (Chédid). *See Sixième jour,
le*

Sixth of October City (Egypt), 1995

Siyah İnciler (Mehmet Rauf), 1513

Siyahkal incident (1971), 821

Siyasa, al- (journal)
Abd al-Raziq (Ali) in, 21
Haykal (Muhammad Husayn) and,
1013

Siyasa al-Dawliyya, al- (journal), 505,
1682

Skif, Hamid, 1426

Skin and the Gown, The (Appelfeld),
217

SLA. *See* South Lebanon Army

Slade School of Art (London)
Salim (Jawad) at, 1978
Sirry (Gazbia) at, 2069

Slave(s)
agricultural, 2072, 2073
black, 2073, 2074
Caucasian, 2073, 2074
children as, 2072
definition of, 2072
domestic, 2072, 2073
in Egypt, 2073, 2074
in harems, 2072, 2073, 2074
harratin as, 996
military-administrative,
2072–2073
social mobility of, 775
women as, 2072, 2073
in Yemen, 2073

Slave trade, **2072–2075**, 2197
Anglo–Egyptian convention (1877)
on suppression of, 2074
Brussels Act (1980) against,
2074
Christian sailors sold in, 542
Circassians in, 599, 2074
in Ottoman Empire, 2072–2074
abolition of, 2074
during Tanzimat era,
2073–2074
route of, 2073
in Tunisia, abolition of, 84
volume of, 2073

Slavic languages, in Ottoman Empire, 1731

Slavic nationalism, and Austria-
Hungary, 339

Slavs, 383

Slim, Fatima, 1429

Slouschz, Nahum, 277
  Haggiag (Khalifa) poems in books
    of, 973
Slovakia, in U.S. invasion of Iraq
    (2003), 2325
Slovenes, 383
Sluglett, Peter, *as contributor*, 14–16,
    202–203, 412–414, 613–617,
    645–646, 802, 915,
    1046–1047, 1084, 1219,
    1283–1284, 1524, 1985–1987,
    2056, 2065, 2115,
    2341–2342, 2352–2353
Smallpox vaccine, 1508, 2003
Smara, under Spanish control,
    2085
SMC. *See* Supreme Muslim Council
Smetana, Bedrich, and Zionist an-
    them, 1007
Smilansky, Moshe, **2075**, 2403
Smith, Sidney, 1330
Smithsonian Institution, 279
Smolansky, Oles M., *as contributor*,
    507–508, 1314, 1941–1944,
    1945–1946, 1988–1989,
    2087–2088
Smolenskin, Perez, 507
Smyrna. *See* İzmir
Sneh, Moshe, **2075**
Soap industry, in Idlib province
    (Syria), 1080
Sobhe Emruz (newspaper), 867
Sobol, Yehoshua, **2076**, 2186
SOCAL. *See* Standard Oil of Cali-
    fornia
Social and Democratic Movement
    (MDS) (Algeria), 1803
Social Democratic Party (Egypt),
    1957
Social Democratic Party (SDP)
    (Turkey)
  electoral success of, 1097
  establishment of, 1097
  İnönü (Erdal) in, 1097
  merger with Populist Party, in So-
    cial Democratic Populist
    Party, 1097
  Motherland Party challenged by,
    1747
Social Democratic Party of Azerbai-
    jan, **2076**
Social Democratic Populist Party
    (SHP) (Turkey), 1919,
    2076–2077, 2219, 2242
  establishment of, 1097, 2077

İnönü (Erdal) in, 1097,
    1098–1099, 2077
  Motherland Party opposition,
    2077
  Republican People's Party merging
    with, 2077
  True Path Party merging with,
    2077
Social Democratic Society
    (Afghanistan). *See* Afghan Na-
    tion
Social elites, 775
"Social idealism," 924
Social injustice, films on, 832
Socialism, 776
  in Afghanistan, 62
  in Algeria
    constitution on, 128, 130
    Soltani (Abdellatif) criticizing,
      2079
    and SONATRACH, 2079–2080
  Arab, 265
    Hakim (Muhsin al-) on, 977
    Hanoune (Louisa) and, 990
  and Arabic literature, 1422
  constructive, 1362
  in Egypt, 265, 266–267, 767
  and Hebrew literature, 1432
  and Labor Zionism, 1359–1360,
    1361–1362
  prudent, 422
  in Russia and Eastern Europe,
    1360
  "scientific," 1357
  and use of law for restructuring
    property rights, 1379
  and Zionism, 289, 1281, 2434
Socialist Destour Party (PSD)
    (Tunisia), 634, 2229, 2231
  Baccouche (Hedi) in, 356
  Ben Ali (Zayn al-Abidine) in, 439
  Ghannouchi (Rached) opposing,
    912
  and LTDH, 1416
  Mestiri (Ahmad) in, 1519–1520
Socialist Forces Front (Algeria). *See*
    Front des Forces Socialistes
Socialist Front (Lebanon)
  Chamoun (Camille) in, 580
  establishment of, 580
Socialist International, Republican
    People's Party in, 1919
Socialist Labor Party (Egypt), 768
  Muslim Brotherhood alliance with,
    1622
Socialist Liberal Party. *See* Parti So-
    cialiste Liberale

Socialist National Front (Lebanon),
    Twayni (Ghassan) as candidate
    of, 2254
Socialist Party (Egypt), 626, 2405
  Musa (Salama) on, 1614
Socialist Party (France), 1563
Socialist Party (Yemen). *See* Yemeni
    Socialist Party
Socialist People's Libyan Arab
    Jamahiriyya. *See* Jamahiriyya
    (Libya)
Socialist Progressive Rally (RSP)
    (Tunisia), 2232
Socialist Unionist Democratic Party
    (Syria), in National Progres-
    sive Front, 1665
Socialist Union of Popular Forces.
    See Union Socialiste des
    Forces Populaires
Socialist Union Party (Syria), in Na-
    tional Progressive Front, 1665
Socialist Vanguard Party (Algeria).
    See Parti de l'Avant-Garde So-
    cialiste
Socialist Workers Organization (Al-
    geria), 990
Social Party for Progress (PSP)
    (Tunisia), 2232
Social services
  in Iran, 809–810
  in Kuwait, 1349
Société Nationale de Transport et de
    Commercialisation des Hydro-
    carbures. *See* SONATRACH
Société Primitive (Jamaʿat al-
    Ruwwad), 997
Society for Islamic Culture (Egypt),
    395
  Muslim Brotherhood merger with,
    1620
Society for Protecting the Rights of
    the Child (Iran), 744
Society for the Defense of Liberty
    and National Sovereignty of
    the Iranian Nation, 1117
Society for the Preservation of the
    Qurʾan, 2229
  Ghannouchi (Rached) in, 912
Society for the Study of the Turkish
    Language. *See* Turkish Lin-
    guistic Society
Society for the Study of Turkish His-
    tory, 2246
Society for Women's Development
    (Sudan), 1622

Staff College, 1953

Stalin, Josef, 485
  ambitions in Middle East, 1942
  death of, MAPAM after, 1185
  vs. Khrushchev (Nikita S.), 1314
  and Palestinian partition, support
    for, 1943

Stampfer, Yehoshua, in Petah Tik-
    vah, 1822

Standard Oil of California
    (SOCAL)
  in Bahrain, 229
  in construction of Trans-Arabian
    Pipeline, 2202
  Red Line Agreement and, 1910
  in Saudi Arabia, 11, 229

Standard Oil of New Jersey. *See also*
    Exxon
  Arabian American Oil Company
    partnership with, 229
  in As-Is Agreement (1928), 323
  in construction of Trans-Arabian
    Pipeline, 2202
  Red Line Agreement and, 1910

Standard Oil of New York
  in price wars, 323
  Red Line Agreement and, 1910

Stanford University
  Barak (Ehud) at, 398
  Turkish collection at, 492

Stanhope, Hester, **2088**
  Palmyra visited by, 275

Stanley, Ethel, 404

Star Enterprises, 230

Stark, Freya, 513, **2088–2089**

Star of North Africa (Algeria),
    2089
  growth of, 1426
  Hadj (Messali al-) in, 969
  Khider (Mohamed) in, 1309
  Lahouel (Hocine) in, 1365
  Parti du Peuple Algérien as exten-
    sion of, 1804
  Parti du Peuple Algérien as suc-
    cessor of, 2089

Starrett, Gregory, 759

Stars of Jericho (Badr), 357

Stars Outside (Alterman), 171, 1432

Stasi Commission (France), Arkoun
    (Mohammed) in, 289

State feminism, 892–893

State List (Israel), 1188–1189
  Ben-Gurion (David) in,
    1188–1189
  in Likud, 1184, 1417

"Statement of Advice, The," 2079

State Planning Organization (SPO)
    (Turkey), **2089–2090**, 2241

Statue de sel, La (Memmi), 1423, 1517

Status of Women in Yemen, The (National
    Women's Committee), 1669

Stavsky, Avraham, 290

Steadfastness Fund. *See* Sumud
    Fund

Steamships, 2198, *2205*, 2205–2206

Steam: The Turkish Bath (film), 832

Steel industry
  in Algeria, 208
  in Turkey, 1482, 1484

Stein, Kenneth W., *as contributor*,
    1458–1459

Stekel, Wilhelm, Arabic translation
    of, 1294

Stephan, Rita, *as contributor*, 268–269,
    1051–1052, 1079, 1493–1496,
    1521, 1950–1951, 1952

Stephan, Stephen Hanna, 277

Stern, Abraham, *1442*, 1442–1443,
    2090
  and Bernadotte (Folke) assassina-
    tion, 1250
  CID killing, 1443
  Di Tat edited by, 2384
  in Haganah, 2090
  in Irgun Zvai Le'umi, *1442*, *1442*,
    2090
  in Lohamei Herut Yisrael, 972,
    1139, *1442*, 2090, 2384
  against white papers on Palestine
    (1939), 2090
  in World War II, 2371
  Yellin-Mor (Natan) and, 2384

Stern Gang. *See* Lohamei Herut Yis-
    rael

Stettinius, Edward, 1404

Stillman, Norman, *as contributor*,
    396–397, 453–454,
    549–550, 612, 619, 642–643,
    720, 920, 1016, 1231–1234,
    1252–1253, 1363, 1415–1416,
    1453, 1460, 2308, 2352

Stinger antiaircraft missiles, sold by
    U.S. to Afghan guerrillas,
    66

Stockholm (Sweden), Islamic numis-
    matics in, 1702

Stock market, **2090–2092**, *2091*
  in Bahrain, 2091
  in Egypt, 2091, *2091*
  foreign investors in, 2091
  in Iran, 2091, *2091*
  in Iraq, *752*

in Israel, 2090, 2091, *2091*
in Jordan, 2091, *2091*
in Kuwait, 2091, *2091*
in Lebanon, 2091
in Saudi Arabia, 2090, *2091*,
    2091–2092
size of, 2090
in Turkey, 2090, *2091*, 2092,
    2092

Stokes, C. B., 2063

Stone, Christopher Reed, *as contribu-
    tor*, 817–818, 1808

Stone on a Grave, A (Al-e Ahmad), 1437

Stories of Love and Pursuit (Badr), 357

Storrs, Ronald, 513, **2092–2093**
  Abdullah I ibn Hussein meeting
    with, 29, 2092
  in Arab Revolt, 2092
  and Balfour Declaration (1917),
    2092
  and Husayni (Musa Kazim al-),
    1058
  and Nashashibi (Raghib al-), 1645
  in Pro-Jerusalem Society, 2092
  Weizmann (Chaim) meeting with,
    2092

Story of a Warrior, A (Cohen), 613

Story of Tou, The (Ghanim), 911

Straight Path, The (journal), 782

Strait of Hormuz, 952

Straits Convention (1841), 1691,
    1945, **2093–2094**, 2095
  Turkish opposition to, 621

Straits, Turkish, 902, *2094*,
    2094–2095. *See also* Black
    Sea; Bosporus; Dardanelles
  and British–Russian relations,
    528, 529, 2093
  in Eastern Question, 739–740
  importance to Russia, 1945
  international control of, under
    Lausanne Treaty (1923), 1565
  passage through
    Dardanelles Treaty restricting,
      621
    Laussanne Treaty reestablishing,
      621
    Montreux Convention (1936)
      on, 743, 2095
    Soviet claim to, 621, 2095
    Straits Convention (1841) on,
      2093–2094, 2095
    Turkish control of, 621
  Turkish sovereignty over, under
    Montreux Convention (1936),
      1565
  in World War I, 2365–2366

"Stranger, The" (Bint al-Shati), 476

Stranger, The (Camus), 563

Strange Woman, A (Erbil), 780

Stransky, Thomas, *as contributor*, 1971

Stratétegies de développement pour l'Algerie: 1962-1991 (Brahimi), 506

Stratford de Redcliffe, Viscount. *See* Canning, Stratford

Street Children Phenomenon in Yemen (WFRT), 2357

Strike the Whore (film), 832

Strokes of Genius: Contemporary Iraqi Art (exhibition), 805

Struma (ship), **2095–2096**

Student activism. *See also* Youth movements
  in Afghanistan, Islamic movement in, 60, 63
  in Iran, 630–631, 1120
  in Lebanon, at American University of Beirut, 180
  for regime change, 2412

Students in the Line of the Imam, 850, **2096**

Sturgeon, 834

Suad al-Sabah Publishing and Distribution House, 1952

"Su'al wa jawab" (leaflet), 2357

Suarès della Pegna, Menachem, 2096

Suarès, Edgar, 2096–2097

Suarès family, **2096–2097**

Suarès, Félix, 2096

Suarès, Isaac, 2096

Suarès, Joseph, 2096

Suarès, Raphael, 2096

Suarès Square (Cairo), 2096

Subbi (baptizers), 1479

Sublime Porte (Ottoman Empire), **2097**
  fermans issued by, 823
  Mustafa Reşid as representative of, 1624

Succession ouverte (Chraibi), 588, 1423

Sudan, **2097–2102**. *See also specific cities, organizations, people, and regions*
  agriculture in, 2099
    dry-farming techniques of, 75
    Gezira Scheme and, 908
  area of, 2097
  art of, 1142
  assassination of Stack (Sir Lee) in (1924), 1465, 2349

banking in, *393*, 394

and Beitaddin Declaration (1978), 432

Beja in, 432–434, 2097

bin Ladin (Osama) in, 475, 1865

British–Egyptian dominion over, 529–530, 2100, 2102–2103
  Abd al-Rahman al-Mahdi in, 18–19, 209–210
  al-Ansar during, 209–210
  Baring (Evelyn) and, 405, 530
  Condominium Agreement on (1899), 405, 518, 530, 629, 1363, 2100, 2349
  education under, 2296
  fall of mahdist state to, 1463–1464
  Fashoda incident (1898), 405, 529–530, 811
  Foreign Office in, 530
  Gezira Scheme under, 908
  Kitchener (Horatio Herbert) in, 629, 1329
  Lado Enclave incorporated into, 1363
  Mahdist movement in, 404–405
  nationalist movement against, 2100
  revolt against (1924), 2349
  Wingate (Reginald) and, 2354

cities of, 1279–1280, 2100
  capital, 1301–1302, 1712

climate of, 2099

communism in, 627

constitution of (1999), 2101

cotton industry in, 644, 908, 2180

coup in (1958), 8, 2101
  Numeiri (Muhammad Ja'far) in, 1699

coup in (1964), 8, 1075, 2101
  Numeiri (Muhammad Ja'far) in, 1699

coup in (1969), 210, 2101, 2103
  Numeiri (Muhammad Ja'far) installed in, 1699

coup in (1985), 1075, 2101, 2103
  Numeiri (Muhammad Ja'far) deposed in, 1701

coup in (1989), 210, 2101, 2104, 2261, 2296

defense costs as percentage of GNP or GDP, *1530*

Dinka people of, 709, 867–868, 2098

economic aid to
  from Arab countries, 749
  from IMF, 749

economy of, 2099–2100, 2101

Egyptian invasion of (1822), 1077, 1602

Egyptian relations with, under Nasser (Gamal Abdel), 1649–1650

Egyptian union with, proposal for, 349

ethnic groups in, 2097–2099, 2103

Fur tribe in, 2098

geography of, 2099

Greeks in, 938

in Gulf Crisis (1990–1991), 951

higher education in, 2296

human rights in, 1048

independence of, 519, 1917, 2101, 2102
  declaration of, 349

irrigation in, 908

Islamic fundamentalism in, 2101, 2234–2235

languages in, 2099
  Arabic, 2099
  TaBedawie, 433

in League of Arab States, 1388

legal system of, 2104
  British influences on, 1380
  civil code, 1382

Libyan relations with, under Numeiri (Muhammad Ja'far), *1700*

literature of, 1977

location of, 2102

mahdist state in, 1463–1464

map of, *2098*

military of
  equipment of, *1534*
  force levels of, *1528–1529*
  force structure of, *1532–1533*

Muslim Brotherhood in, 395, 2234

nationalism in, 87, 2296

natural resources in, 2099–2100

newspapers and print media in, mobilization approach of, 1680

Nubians in, 1696, 2097–2098

Nuer in, 1699, 2098

October Revolution in (1964), 1917

oil production in, 2099–2100

parliament of, Ibrahim (Fatima Ahmed) in, 1075

political parties in, legalization of, 2261

population of, 2097

Protestant missions in, 1856

provinces of, administrative, 1335

pyramids in, 1857–1858

Suez Crisis (1956–1957) *(continued)*
  France in, 847, 2108–2110
    French foreign legion, 856
    Lacoste (Robert) supporting, 1363
    and London Conference (1956), 1444
    Mollet (Guy) and, 1563
    Nasser regime opposition and, 520
  Hammarskjöld (Dag) in, 1444, 2108
  Harkabi (Yehoshafat) during, 995
  international pressure for cease-fire in, 2109–2110
  Iraqi stand during, Bazzaz (Abd al-Rahman al-) critical of, 421
  Israel in, 520, 2108–2110
  Lloyd (Selwy) in, 2108
  London Conference (1956) in, 1444, 2108
  Mollet (Guy) in, 2108
  Musketeer Operation in, 2108–2109
  Nasser (Gamal Abdel) in, 1650, 2109, 2110
  Pineau (Christian) in, 2108
  Roosevelt (Kermit) involvement in, 1937
  Sèvres Protocol (1956) and, 520, 2013–2014, 2109
  United Nations in, 1444, 2108, 2109–2110, 2275
    Emergency Force of, 2275, 2286
  U.S. against use of force in, 2108
  U.S. response to, 2291
Suez, Gulf of, **952**
Suez, Isthmus of, 952
Suez–Mediterranean Pipeline (SUMED), 1830, **2110–2111**
Suffrage
  in Saudi Arabia, 884
  in United Arab Emirates, 884
  for women, 887
    in Bahrain, 893
    in Egypt, 891
    in Iran, *890*
    in Kuwait, 884, 893
Sufism, **2111–2114**
  Abd al-Wahhab (Muhammad ibn) criticizing, 2114
  abolishment of, in Turkey, 2171
  in Afghanistan, 863
  art influenced by, 312, 2113
  Banna (Hasan al-) and, 394, 1620
  Bektashis and, 434–436

interpretation of Qur'an in, 2111, 2112
  in Iraq, *2112*
  Kattaniya Brotherhood of, 1281
  Khalidi, 1642
  Mevlevi Brotherhood of, 1521
  Musa Kazim in, 1613
  mysticism of, 1149
  Naqshbandi in, 1641–1643
  orders of, 2113–2114 (*See also specific orders*)
    establishment of, 2113
    and spread of Islam, 1149, 2113, 2114
  origin of term, 2111
  orthodox opposition to, 1149
  philosophical expression of, 1149
  reform movements in, 1149
  restoring orthodoxy in, 1149, 2114
  and *shari'a*, 2112
  in Sharifism, 2037
  spread of, 1149
  in Sudan, 2099
  Suleiman (Mulay) suppressing, 2115
  tekke (headquarters) of, 2171
  theological and philosophical basis of, 2111–2113
  women in, 2360
  and Yacine (Abdessalame), 2375
Sufiyan tribe, 912
Sugar trade, 2198
Suha: Surviving Hell (documentary), 481
Suhravardi, and Ahsa'i (Ahmad al-), 93
Suhrawardi al-, 2113
Suhrawardi, Chihab al-Din Yahya: Récites de l'exil occidental (Meddeb), 1507
Suhrawardiyya (Sufi order), 2113
Suicide bombings
  in al-Aqsa Intifada, 219, 1169, 1793
    by al-Aqsa Martyrs Brigade, 219
  by al-Aqsa Martyrs of the World Islamic Front for Liberation, 814
  Arafat (Yasir) toleration for, 1793
  by HAMAS, 2177
  by Hizbullah, 2177
  by Islamic Jihad, 219, 1155, 1226, 1227
  in Israel, 2178
  Israeli response to, 1169
  in Jerusalem, 1226, 1227
  at Suez Canal, against British forces, 200
Suissa, Albert, **2114–2115**

Sukenik, E. L., 2376
  and Dead Sea Scrolls, 686
  at Hebrew University, archaeological department of, 277
Sukot (Nubian dialect), 1696
Suksukaniyya, 838
Süküti, İshak
  in Committee for Union and Progress, 2409
  in Ottoman Union Society, 622
Sulayhid dynasty (Yemen), 2397
  weakening of, 1007
Sulayman, Abdullah, oil concession by, 229
Sulayman Abu Layla (Mamluk ruler), 1478
Sulayman Agha (Sulayman the Great) (Mamluk ruler), 1478
Sulayman, Ali, 316
Sulayman, Hikmat, **2115**
  in Ahali group, 80
  in coup (1936), 80, 2065, 2115
  government of, Abu al-Timman (Ja'far) in, 35
  Hashimi (Yasin al-) and, 2115
  in Ikha al-Watani Party, 80, 1084
  Kaylani (Rashid Ali al-) and, 2115
  Sidqi (Bakr) friendship, 2115
Sulaymaniya (Iraq), **2115**
  Kurdish Regional Government established in, 2151
  as Kurdistan capital, 1342
  Mahmud of, 1469–1470
Sulayman, Omar, *1103*
Sulayman, Shakir Abu, 1395
Sulayman the Little (Mamluk ruler), 1478
Suleiman, Elia, 833
Suleimaniye Mosque (Istanbul), 2237
Suleiman, Mulay, **2115**
Süleyman I (the Magnificent), 1728
  Iraq under, 1132
  as Shaykh al-Islam, 2046
Süleymaniye Library. *See* Süleymaniye Mosque
Süleymaniye Mosque (Istanbul), *283*
  Aya Sofya as inspiration for, 342
Sulh, Kazem al-, **2115–2116**, 2118, 2119
  and National Pact, 1662–1663
Sulh, Rashid al-, **2116–2117**
Sulh, Riyad al-, *2117*, **2117–2119**
  assassination of, 2118
  daughter of, 165

Saʿada (Antun) in, 1949–1950, 2136–2137

Sulh (Riyad al-) assassinated by, 2118

Tall (Wasfi al-) supporting, 2156

Syrian University, 665, 666

Arab Academy of Damascus merger with, 223–224

Syrian War (1831–1833), 740–741, 2093

Battle of Konya in (1832), 1332–1333

Britain in, 1346

Egypt in, 740–741, 1346, 2093

France in, 740–741, 1346, 2093

Kütahya Convention (1833) ending, 2093

Ottoman Empire in, 740–741, 2093

Peace of Kütahya (1833) ending, 1346

Russia in, 740–741, 1346, 2093

Syrian War (1839), 740–741, 2093

Syris, Protestant missions in, 1854

Syrkin, Nachman, **2138**

Uganda Project supported by, 2257

Szold, Henrietta, **2138**

in Hadassah, 966, 2138

in Youth Aliyah, 855, 2138, 2411

T

TAʿAL (Israel), 1787, 1788

Taba (Egypt), **2139**

in Aqaba incident (1906), 218

Taba Accords. *See* Taba negotiations (1995, 2001)

Tabaʾi al-Istibdad wa Masariʿ al-Istiʿbad (Kawakibi), 1282

Tabaʿi, Muhammad al-, Asmahan and, 324

Taba incident. *See* Aqaba incident (1906)

Taba negotiations (1995, 2001), **2140**

Palestinian rights in, 1640

Tabaqa Dam, 788, 2129, **2140–2141**

Tabari, Ehsan, 2222

Tabatabaʾi, Mohammad, **2141–2142**

in Constitutional Revolution, 2141–2142

imprisonment of, 2142

studying under Shirazi (Mirza Hasan), 2141

Tabatabaʾi, Ziya, **2142–2143**

Anglo–Iranian Agreement nullified by, 200

coup by (1921), 88, 1118, 1682, 1755

denouncing Pahlavi dictatorship, 2143

in exile, 2143

Fatherland party of, 1110, 2143

in Iradeh-ye Melli Party, 1110

Mossadegh (Mohammad) opposed to, 1580

newspapers of, 1682, 2142, 2143

opposing Mossadegh (Mohammad), 2143

as prime minister, 2143

appointment of, 1755

Pahlavi (Reza) ousting, 1755

supporting British policy in Iran, 2142, 2143

Tabayniyy, Natila al-, 1429

Tabbe ot Ashan (Goldberg), 927

Tabbula, 841

TaBedawie language, 433

Tabenkin, Yitzhak, 956

Tabi, Shakir Sahib al-, 83

Tables reales, 2050

Tabory, Ephraim, *as contributor*, 600–601, 979–980, 2157–2158, 2404

Tabriz (Iran), **2143–2144**

in Azerbaijan crisis (1945–1946), 346, 693

bazaars of, 420

carpet weaving in, 566

in Constitutional Revolution, 636

industrial activity in, 345

in Russo–Persian wars, 7

Tabriz Shaykhis, 2047

Tabriz–Trabzon caravan, 2205

Tabriz University, **2144**

Eqbal (Manouchehr) at, 779

Tachau, Frank, *as contributor*, 631, 780, 851, 854–855, 1202, 1583–1584, 1657–1661, 1660–1661, 1667–1668, 2076–2077, 2219–2220, 2236, 2250, 2251, 2295

Tachelhit language, 1567

Tadiran, 1334

Tadja (in Muharram rite), 1606

Tadla plain (Morocco), 1567

Tadmur (Syria), 1797–1798

Tafakkuk, al- (Boudjedra), 497, 1426

Tafkir wa al-Hijra, al-. *See* Excommunication and Emigration

Tafna, Treaty of (1837), 17, 542

Tafsir, 2154

Tafsut n Imazighen. See Berber Spring

Tagger, Sioneh, **2144**

Tagger, Sulayman, in Club National Israélite, 612

Tahaddi, al- (Bin Diyaf), 474

Taha, Mahmud Muhammad, **2144–2145**

execution of, 1918

and Republican Brotherhood, 1917–1918

Taharut Sehiya (Tammuz), 2160

Tahdhib, al- (Baradhi, al-), 1476

Tahdid al-nasl. See Birth control

Taher, Abdal Hadi, in PETROMIN, 1830

Tahina, 841

Tahirid dynasty (Yemen), 2397

Tahiris, 2145

Tahir, Kemal, **2145–2146**

Tahkim, al-, 2052

Tahmasp, 2054

Tahrir al-Marʾa (Amin et al.), 187

Tahrira stitch, 1879

Tahtawi, Rifaʿa al-Rafi al-, 1419, **2146–2148**

in archaeology, 276

educational agenda and influence of, 2146–2147

education of, 2146

in Institut d'Égypte, 1099

institutional career of, 2146

on liberation of women, 890

political perspective of, 2147

Saʿid Pasha rehabilitating, 1970

as translation movement founder, 2146–2148

Taʾif, al-, **2148–2149**

Ikhwan occupation of, 1085

Muhammad's message rejected in, 1596

Taifa, 618, 947

Taʾif Accord (1989), **2148**

Council for Development and Reconstruction after, 645

Eddé (Raymond) opposing, 754

Geagea (Samir) supporting, 871

Hariri (Rafiq Bahaʾuddin al-) and, 994

Husayni (Husayn al-) and, 1055

National Pact revised by, 1663

Taʾif, Treaty of al- (1934), **2149**

on claims to Asir, 1082

TAMI (Israel), 1189
  Abuhatzeira (Aharon) in, 37
  electoral success of, 1189
  establishment of, 37, 1189
  in Likud, 1189
  National Religious Party criticized
    by, 1187
  platform of, 1189
Tamimahs, **2158**
Tamimi, Abdallah ibn Ibad al-Murri
  al-, Ibadiyya founded by, 1073
Tamimi, Adnan al-, 2158
Tamimi, Amin al-, **2158–2159**
Tamir, Shmuel, **2159**
  in Kasztner affair (1954–1955),
    1280
Tamir, Ya'el, in Peace Now, 1809
Tamiyya, 838
Tamkin, 2151
Tammuz, Benyamin, 1432,
  2159–2160
Tan (newspaper), 1676
Tanbur, 2160
Tanburi Cemil, **2160**
Taner, Haldun, **2160**, 2187
Tanganyika, and Zanzibar, union of,
  2425
Tangier (Morocco), 827, 1567, *1571*
  Catholics in, 1932
  under Spanish control, 2085
Tangier, Treaty of (1844), **2160**
Tangsir (Chubak), 593, 1435
Tanin (newspaper), 2180
Tannenberg, Battle of (1914), 2365
Tanpinar, Ahmed Hamdi, **2160–2161**
Tantawi, Muhammad Sayyid al-,
  2161
  on female circumcision, 822
Tanuhi, Izz al-Din al-, in Arab
  Academy of Damascus, 223
Tanukhis, 728
Tanzania, U.S. embassy bombing in,
  1865, 2177
Tanzim, al-, 1395
Tanzim al-usra. See Family planning
Tanzimatcilar (men of Tanzimat),
  1624
Tanzimat era (1839–1876) (Ottoman
  Empire), **2161–2165**
  administration during, 2063,
    2162, 2163, 2164
  Ahmet Vefik in, 92
  Armenian millet in, 298
  army in, 1737

assessment of, 2164
civil service in, Civil Service
  School and, 602
in Cyprus, 652
defense and international affairs
  during, 2162
design and implementation of reforms, 2164
dragomans in, 723
early opposition to, 2406
economy during, 2162–2163
education in, 757, 758, 2162
end of, 1735, 2164
and equal rights, 885
European influences and internal
  motivations of, 2163–2164
Gülhane Imperial Edict (1839)
  and, 954–955
Hatt-i Serif of Gülhane (1839) initiating, 2073, 2162, 2163, 2164
initiation under Abdülmecit I,
  33–34, 2161
and joint-stock companies, 2069
Land Code of 1858 in, 1366–1369
literature of, 1438–1439
Malkom Khan (Mirza) in, 1477
masonic lodges in, 852
millet system during, 1544
Mustafa Fazil in, 1623
Mustafa Reşid introducing,
  1623–1624
navy in, 1741
order and justice in, 2162
Ottomanism in, 1737
purpose of, 2161, 2164
rise of, 1735
slave trade during, 2073–2074
in Tunisia, 83
Westernization in, 2341
Young Ottoman opposition to,
  2163, 2405–2407
Tapline. *See* Trans-Arabian Pipeline
Taqaddum Party, al- (Iraq), 1961
Taqasim (music), 1618
Taqiyya (caution), 1548
Taqla, Philippe, **2165**
Taqla, Salim, 2165
Taqlid (imitation), 1149, 1504, 2022,
  2124, 2154, 2629–2630
  Iqbal (Muhammad) on, 1109
Taqrib bayna al-madhabib, al-, 2022
Taraghi, Cherie, *as contributor*, 428,
  809–810, 1154, 1364–1365
Taraki, Lisa
  in Institute of Women's Studies at
    Bir Zeit University, 1100
  in Women's Studies Center, 2362

Taraki, Nur Mohammed, 58
  assassination of, 58
  coup against (1979), 58, 186
  Durand Line challenged by, 734
  government of, Amin (Hafizullah)
    in, 186
  in People's Democratic Party of
    Afghanistan, 62, 1812
    Khalq faction of, 62, 1813
  presidency of, 186–187
  Soviet support for, 58, 65
Tarbiat Modarres University, Ebtekar
  (Ma'sumeh) at, 745
Tarbiya, 759–760
Tarbush, 611
Tarfaya (Morocco)
  under Moroccan control, 2086
  Spanish claim to, 1567
  under Spanish control, 2085
Tarhan, Abdülhak Hamit, 1438,
  2165–2166
  Cevdet (Abdullah) influenced by,
    576
Tarhan, Ayse Durakbasa, *as contributor*,
  148, 274
Tarifit language, 2167
Tarih-i Cevdet, 577, 578
Tarikh, al- (Algeria), 1456
T'arikh Muddah al-Faransis bi Misr
  (Jabarti), 1207
Tarikh Tolana, **2166**
Tariki, Abdullah, **2166**
Tariqa, 2630
Tariqa, 2099, 2113, 2114
Tariq al-Jadid, al- (journal), 1590–1591
Tariqa Muhammadiyya, 2114
Tarrifit language, 1567
Tarsus, 2167
Tartib (Moroccan tax on agriculture), 8
Tarzi, Mahmud, 1881
  in *Irshad An-Niswaan*, 1140
  Young Afghan Party and, 62
Tasarruf, 1367
TASE index, 2091
Tashilhit language, **2166–2167**
TASI index, 2092
Ta'silan likayan (Mas'adi), 1498
Taste of Cherry (film), 1318
Tasvir-i Efkar (newspaper), 1438,
  1640, 1673, 1684–1685,
  2068, 2406, 2407
  Karacan (Ali Naci) in, 1269
  Recaizade Mahmud Ekrem and,
    1909

Tripolitania (Libya) *(continued)*
population of, 2217
Qaramanli dynasty in, 1870–1871
Roman ruins in, 2218
Suwayhli (Ramadan al-) and, 2127
during World War II, 516

Tripolitanian National Congress
Party, 1959

Triptyque de Rabat (Khatibi), 1304

TRNC. *See* Turkish Republic of
Northern Cyprus

Troen, S. Ilan, *as contributor,*
2013–2014

Troupes Spéciales du Levant. *See*
Special Forces of the Levant

TRT. *See* Turkish Radio and Television

Trucial Coast, **2218–2219**
British control of, 531,
2218–2219, 2270
origin of name, 2219

Trucial Council, 2270

Trucial Oman Levies, 2219

Trucial States, 1489

Trucial States Council, 2219

Trucial States Rulers' Council,
Mu'alla (Ahmad bin Rashid
al-) on, 1592

True Path Party (DYP) (Turkey),
2219–2220, 2242
Çiller (Tansu) in, 598
in coalition government with
Motherland Party, 1584, 2220
in coalition government with Refah Party, 2220
in coalition government with SHP,
2219
Demirel (Süleyman) support for,
692, 1584
establishment of, 1257, 2219
Motherland Party challenged by,
1584, 1747
Social Democratic Populist Party
merging with, 2077

Truffaut, François, 175

Truman Doctrine (1947), 517, 1942,
2290–2291
Acheson (Dean) support for, 40
Point Four program under, 1836

Truman, Harry S, **2220**
American Israel Public Affairs
Committee work for, 177
and Anglo–American Committee
of Inquiry (1946), 338
and displaced persons after World
War II, 198

establishment of Israel supported
by, 2220
inaugural speech by (1949), Point
Four in, 1836
Middle East Defense Organization
supported by, 1523
on Palestine partition plans, Saudi
response to, 11
on Palestinian refugees of
Arab–Israel War (1948), 2220
Soviet containment strategy of,
2095
special envoy to Iran under, 996
Trans-Arabian Pipeline supported
by, 2202
Weizmann, Chaim and, 2338,
2338
during World War II, 1935

Trumpeldor, Yosef, **2220–2221**
assassination of, 1448, 2173
and ha-Halutz, 974, 2221
and Jewish Legion, 2221
in Russo–Japanese War
(1904–1905), 2220–2221
and Tel Hai defense, 2221

Tschernichovsky, Saul, 1431

Tsedaka, Benyamim, *as contributor,*
1980

Tsemel, Leah, 1501, **2221**

Tsirkas, Stratis, 938

Tuareg, 458, 459, 462

Tuareg language, 463
alphabet of, 461–462

Tuba and the Meaning of Night (Parsipur),
1436, 1803

Tubal ligations, 480

Tuberculosis, 712, 1508, 1510
vaccine for, 1508

Tübingen University (Germany), Islamic numismatics at, 1702

Tubi, Tawfiq, **2221–2222**

Tucker, Judith, 1037

Tudeh Party (Iran), **2222–2223**
Alavi (Bozorg) in, 104
Bakhtiar (Timur) supporting, 375
ban on, 779, 1118, 2222
CIA in destruction of, 627
Confederation of Iranian Students
and, 630
and Democratic Party of Azerbaijan, 693
establishment of, 627, 2222
and Feda'iyan-e Khalq, 821
Ghassemlou (Abdul Rahman) in,
914
Golestan (Ebrahim) in, 928

growth of, 2222
guild members in, 947
in Iranian Revolution, 2222
in Iran–Iraq War, 2222
Kianuri (Nur al-Din) in, 1318,
2222
oil nationalization opposed by,
1118
rise of, 627
setbacks suffered by, 2222
size of, 627
Soviet support of, 2222
Tabataba'i (Ziya) and, 2143
torture of members of, 2222

Tughra (signature), 823

Tuhami al-Glawi, **2223**
control of Marrakech, 1493
in rebellion (1907), 8, 14

*Tuhfa al-Maktabiyya li-Taqrib al-Lughat al-
Arabiyya, al-* (Tahtawi), 2148

Tujjar, 419

Tuman (section of Shammar tribe),
2214

Tuman Bey (sultan of Egypt), **2223**

Tunb Islands, **2223–2224**
Iran's occupation of, 1903

Tunis (Tunisia), **2224–2225**, 2225,
2228
Algerian government in exile in,
615
under Almohad dynasty, 2224,
2228
Arab League summit (1979) in,
1387
Arafat (Yasir) in, headquarters of,
271, 1774
as Barbary state, 401
Catholics in, 1932
corsairs in, 643
during French protectorate,
2224–2225
guest workers from, 946
under Hafsid dynasty, 2224, 2228
mosques in, 2224
newspapers of, 1678
under Ottoman control,
2228–2229
PLO in, after Arab–Israel War
(1982), 253
population of, 2224
quarter system in, 2224
Spanish occupation of, 2084
wealth of, 2224
Zaytuna University in, 1422

Tunisia, **2225–2230**. *See also specific
cities, organizations, people, and regions*

Union Marocaine du Travail (UMT)
(*continued*)
  Istiqlal Party affiliated with, 453,
    2265
  Union Générale des Travailleurs
    Marocains and, 453, 2264,
    2265
  Union Nationale des Forces Popu-
    laires affiliated with, 2265,
    2267
  Union Socialiste des Forces Popu-
    laires and, 453
Union Nationale de la Jeunesse Al-
  gérienne (UNJA), under
  Front de Libération Nationale
  control, 131
Union Nationale des Etudiants Al-
  gériens (UNEA)
  dissolution of, 131
  under Front de Libération Na-
    tionale control, 131
Union Nationale des Etudiants
  Marocains (UNEM), **2266**
  agenda of, 2266
  government crackdown on, 2266
  Islamists in, 2266
Union Nationale des Femmes Al-
  gériennes (UNFA), under
  Front de Libération Nationale
  control, 131–132
Union Nationale des Femmes
  Tunisiennes (UNFT). *See*
  Union of Tunisian Women
Union Nationale des Forces Popu-
  laires (UNFP) (Morocco),
  1574, **2266–2267**
  Basri (Muhammad al-) in, 1197,
    2266
  Ben Barka (Mehdi) in, 441, 1197,
    2266–2267
  Ben Jelloun (Umar) in, 450
  Ben Seddiq (Mahjoub) in, 453,
    1197, 2266, 2267
  Bouabid (Abderrahim) in, 495,
    2266, 2267
  Casablanca section of, 2266
  conflicts within, 2266–2267
  constitution boycotted by (1962),
    1572
  elections of 1963 boycotted by,
    1588
  establishment of, 1570
  FDIC opposing, 858
  government crackdown on, 2266
  Ibrahim (Abdullah) in, 1075,
    1197, 2266–2267
  leadership structure of, 2267
  platform of, 2267

Rabat section of, 2266–2267
split with Istiqlal Party, 812, 1197,
  2266
Union Marocaine du Travail and,
  2265, 2267
Union Nationale des Etudiants
  Marocains and, 2266
Youssoufi (Abderrahmane) in,
  2266, 2410
Union Nationale des Musulmans
  Nord-Africans, 969
Union Nationale des Travailleurs
  Tunisiens (UNTT), Union
  Générale des Travailleurs
  Tunisiens and, 2265
Union of Academies of Arabic Lan-
  guage, 1457
Union of General Zionists, 2338
Union of Moroccan Writers, 467
Union of Palestinian Medical Relief
  Committee, 402
Union of Palestinian Students
  (Egypt), Arafat (Yasir) in, 269
Union of the Daughter of the Nile,
  2019
Union of the Maghrib treaty, 1006
Union of Tunisian Women (UNFT),
  2267–2268
  membership of, 2267
  objectives of, 2267–2268
Union of Zionist Revisionists. *See*
  Zionist Revisionist Movement
Union Populaire Algérien (UPA), 3
Union Socialiste des Forces Popu-
  laires (USFP) (Morocco),
  1574–1575, 1601, **2268**
  Bouabid (Abderrahim) in, 495,
    2268
  electoral success of, 2268
  establishment of, 2267, 2268
  government led by, 1904
  human rights organization of, 1716
  Ibrahim (Abdullah) in, 1075
  Islamists role in government op-
    posed by, 1601
  Istiqlal Party and, 1197–1198, 2268
  platform of, 2268
  Union Marocaine du Travail and,
    453
  Youssoufi (Abderrahmane) in,
    2268, 2411
Union Theological Seminary, Bliss
  (Howard) at, 487
Union Tunisienne des Industrial-
  istes, Compagnies, Artisans
  (UTICA), 2227, **2268–2269**

Union Universelle de la Jeunesse
  Juive, 1453
Unit 101 (Israel), 2041
Unitarians. *See* Muwahhidun
United Arab Emirates (UAE),
  2269–2272. *See also specific cities,
  organizations, people, and regions;
  specific emirates*
  Abu Musa Island claimed by,
    37–38, 2040
  Al Nahayyan family in, 156
  archaeology in, 343
  assassination of Majali (Hazza al-)
    by, 1470–1471
  Baluchis in, 385
  banking in, *393*
  and Beitaddin Declaration (1978),
    432
  borders of, 2269
  British control of, 36, 2270
    Abu Musa Island dispute in, 38
    treaties on, 36, 614, 2270
  Catholics in, 1931
  cities of, 36, 343, 2270
  climate of, 2269
  constitution of, 2271
  defense costs as percentage of
    GNP or GDP, *1530*
  economic aid from, 749
  economy of, 752, *753*, 2270–2271
  education in, upbringing aspect
    of, 760
  emirates of, 36, 96, 731, 1903,
    2219, 2260 (*See also specific emi-
    rates*)
  establishment of, 36, 521, 2219
  fishing industry of, 834
  foreign relations of, 2270, 2272
  Fujayra–Sharjah conflict in (1972),
    859–860
  geography of, 2269
  in Gulf Cooperation Council, 949
  in Gulf Crisis (1990–1991), 950
  human rights in, 1048
  industrialization in, 752
  Iranian relations with, 38
    Tunb Islands and, 2223–2224
  on Iraq, 2272
  Islam in, 2270
  labor unions illegal in, 1358
  in League of Arab States, 1387,
    1388
  legal system of
    Majalla, 1382
    reforms in, 1380
  legislative body in, 932
  manufacturing in, 1483, *1483*
  map of, 2272

journals for, 1140
organizations for, 68, 325, 693
in politics, 786, 894, 1981–1982
Queen Surraya's impact on,
　1881
veiling for, *61*, 1715
in Alevi Shi°ism, 114
in Algeria
　as artists, 1687, 2064
　constitution on, 129, 130
　economic status of, *877*
　Family Code on (1984), 130,
　　136, 1905
　M'Rabet (Fadela) on, 1592
　as painters, 414
　as political activists, 990
　in politics, 443, 497, 892, 894,
　　2195
　under single-party system,
　　131–132
　as writers, 483, 1424, 1425,
　　1425, 2007
in Arab theater, 2184
Baha'i faith on, 365
in Bahrain, as students, 759
in Bangladesh, as head of state,
　808, 875
bank accounts of, 874, 878
Bektashi, 435
Berber, *458*, 463
birth control for (*See* Birth con-
　trol)
blood money for, 1987, 2051
Circassian, in slave trade, 599
clothing for, 607–611
　haik, 975
　hijab, 1026–1027
crimes of honor against,
　649–650, 887, 1495
　Noor al-Hussein in campaign
　　against, 1691
dance by, 667
dependence on men, 874, 888
education for, 760, 761
　through Protestant missions,
　　1855
in Egypt
　as activists, 1906–1907
　activists and advocates for, 1614,
　　1652
　as artists, 762, 2069
　birth control clinic for, *479*
　as cabinet members, 39
　charitable organizations run by,
　　39–40, 1452–1453
　as communists, 43–44
　as dancers, 866
　economic status of, 877, *877*
　education for, 1902

as judges, 808, 1905
in labor force, 874, 875, 878
as landholders, 878
magazine on, 206
participation in civil society,
　1905
physicians for, 2003
in politics, 762, 890–891, 892,
　894, 914–915, 1950–1951,
　1958, 1965–1966, 2019,
　2030–2031
as students, 761
in Wafd party, 2320,
　2321–2322
as writers, 378–379, 475–476,
　914–915, 1924–1925,
　1950–1951, 2019, 2431
as elites, 775
as explorers, 437
in family life, 1493–1496
fertility of, 1844
in *harem,* 992–993
health care for, 1509–1510
and historiography, 1037
in Indonesia
　as head of state, 808
　as judges, 808
in Iran
　activist organizations of, 2358
　as artists, 1676, 1899
　Constitutional Revolution im-
　　pact on, 637
　economic status of, *877*
　education for, 637, 880, *882,*
　　1113, 1114
　as filmmakers, 387–388
　government bureau on, 1123
　higher education for, 2296
　hijab (veil) worn by, 1027
　Islamic Revolution and, 1922
　as judges, 744
　as lawyers, 2051
　magazine for, 2423–2424
　in political parties, 1129
　in politics, 428, 745, 891, 892,
　　894, 1364–1365, 2153
　seminary for, 187
　in sporting events, 1154
　as students, 761
　suffrage for, 1471
　as writers, 427, 811, 1435,
　　1899
in Iraq
　charitable organization for,
　　2361–2362
　economic status of, *877*
　education for, 1310
　improving situation of, 898
　as judges, 808

umbrella organization for,
　1137–1138
UN economic sanctions and,
　1510
Islamic law regarding, Republican
　Brothers' call for reform in,
　1917–1918
in Israel
　economic status of, 876–877,
　　877
　education for, 880
　as head of state, 875, 891
　journalists, 1003
　in labor force, 877
　peace activities of, 2355–2356
　as poets, 2429–2430
　in politics, 893, 934–935,
　　944–945, 1440, 1441, 2023,
　　2059
　as writers, 408, 434, 926–927,
　　1433, 1887, 1907
Jewish, as rabbis, 1889
in Jordan
　as activists, 1065
　economic status of, *877*
　in labor force, 877–878
　literature on, 805
　Noor al-Hussein as advocate
　　for, 1691
　in politics, 819–820, 893, 894
　resource center for, 1852
　as students, 878
　as writers, 804–805, 2001
in Kuwait
　economic status of, *877*
　higher education for, 1353–1354
　in politics, 1350, 1951–1952
　as students, 761
　as writers, 1952
in labor force (*See* Gender, and
　economy)
in Lebanon
　activists and advocates for, 1557,
　　1584–1585
　as artists, 916
　college for, 431–432
　as cultural officials, 2125
　disease and, 714
　economic status of, *877*
　in labor force, 875
　as political activists, 481
　in politics, 894, 1960–1961,
　　1975
　religious rituals of, 2360,
　　2361
　as scholars, 367
　as writers, 397–398, 817, 872,
　　916, 1646–1647, 1975, 1982,
　　2046

Young Tunisians, 2229,
  2407–2408
  education at military academy, 84
  Khaldunniyya founded by, 1293,
    2408
  Thaalbi (Abd al-Aziz) in, 2182
Young Turks, 776, 2240,
  2408–2410
  Ahmet Riza in, 91, 623, 2408
  vs. Arab nationalism, 261, 263
  in Armenian genocide, 294
    Musa Dagh resistance of,
      1612–1613
  army under, 1739
  Bekir Fahri in, 434
  Cemal Paşa and, 571
  Committee for Union and
    Progress of, 622–623,
    2408–2410
  at Congress of Ottoman Liberals
    (1902), 631
  constitution under, 1742
  definition of, 2408
  Egyptian National Party support-
    ing, 1664
  freemasonry and, 852
  Ganim (Halil) in, 867
  Husari (Sati al-) and, 1051
  and Husayn ibn Ali, 1052, 1053
  ideology of, 2410
  İlmiyye decline under, 1086–1087
  and Jewish settlement in Palestine,
    1940
  Mehmet V as figurehead for, 1513
  Misri (Aziz Ali al-) in, 1550
  Nahum (Hayyim) and, 1637
  navy under, 1741
  Nursi (Said) and, 1704
  origins of, 2408
  Ottomanism of, 1737, 2410
  Paris conference of (1902), 2409
  parliament under, 1742
  revolution of (1908), 384, 2251
    Churchill (Winston S.) and, 595
    and civil service, 1735
    Enver Paşa in, 778
    newspapers and print media af-
      ter, 1685
    Ottoman army in, 1739
    Talat (Mehmet) in, 2153
  before revolution of (1908),
    2408–2409
  rivalries within, 623, 2408–2409
  in Salonika, 1979
  Shumayyil (Shibli) supporting,
    2061
  Turkism of, 2251
  vs. Young Ottomans, 2405, 2408,
    2410

Young, William Tanner, 1796
Young Women's Muslim Association
  (YWMA), Khidhir (Zahra) in,
  1310
Young Worker, The. *See* Po'el ha-
  Tza'ir, ha-
Youssef, Mulay (sultan of Morocco),
  1449, 2038, **2410**
  French selection of, 14
  Glawi (Madani al-) under, 921
  Lyautey (Louis-Hubert Gonzalve)
    putting on throne, 827, 1448
  al-Qarawiyyin university under, 1871
Youssoufi, Abderrahmane,
  2410–2411
  exile of, 2410–2411
  Hassan II and, 1006, 1571,
    1573–1574
  labor strikes under, 2264
  as prime minister, 1573–1574,
    1575, 2268, 2411
  Spanish enclaves disputed by, 1516
  in Union Nationale des Forces
    Populaires, 2266, 2410
  in Union Socialiste des Forces
    Populaires, 2268, 2411
Youth Aliyah (Israel), **2411**
  establishment of, 855
  Kol (Moshe) in, 1332
  Szold (Henrietta) in, 855, 2138
Youth movements, **2411–2413**. *See
  also specific movements*
  in 19th century, 2411
  in 20th century, 2411–2412
  Iraqi *futuwwa*, 860–861
  as literary catalyst, 1432
  paramilitary, 2411–2412
  role of, 2411–2412
  scouting, 2006
  in Zionist Revisionist Movement,
    1209
YSP. *See* Yemeni Socialist Party
Yücel, Hasan Ali, **2413**
Yu'firid dynasty (Yemen), 2397
Yuhanna, Mikha'il. *See* Aziz, Tariq
Yüksek Öğretim Kurulu (YOK)
  (Turkey), **2413–2414**
  Afghani (Jamal al-Din al-) at, 51
Yunis Jabir, Abu Bakr, **2414**
Yunus Emre (Saygun), 2002
Yurdakul, Mehmet Emin, 1439,
  1800, **2414**
Yusab II (Coptic patriarch), 657
Yushij, Nima, 427, 1435–1436
  Alizadeh (Ghazaleh) compared
    with, 149

Yusuf (Ottoman grand vizier), in
  Convention of al-Arish
  (1800), 289
Yusuf (ruler of Lebanon), Chehab
  (Bashir) and, 583
Yusuf, Fatima al-, *Ruz al-Yusuf*
  founded by, 18
Yusufian, Boghos (Boghos Bey),
  2414–2415
  death of, successor after, 589
  nephew and protégé of, Nubar
    (Boghos) as, 1694
Yusuf, Muhammad, as prime minis-
  ter, 57
Yusuf, Mulay, son of, Muhammad V
  as, 1597–1598
Yusuf, Yusuf Salman (Fahd), **2415**
  in Communist Party of Iraq, 627,
    2415
  execution of, 627, 2415
YWA. *See* Yemeni Women's Associa-
  tion
YWMA. *See* Young Women's Muslim
  Association
YWU. *See* Yemeni Women's Union
Yzernitsky, Yitzhak. *See* Shamir,
  Yitzhak

Z

Za'ab tribe, 2209
Zaban-i Zanan (magazine), 891
Zabol (Iran), 2070
Zab Rivers, **2417**
  Dukan Dam on, 732–733
Zabul (Afghan province),
  2417–2418
Zabul (Iranian city), **2417–2418**
Zach, Natan, 1432, **2418**
Zadig (Voltaire), 1675
Za'farani, al-, 2019
Zafzaf, Mohammad, 1428
Zaghlul, Sa'd, **2418–2419**
  Abbas Hamli II and, 6
  Abduh (Muhammad) and, 24
  Adli and, 46
  Afghani (Jamal al-Din al-) and,
    51
  British opposition to, 46
  on Cairo University, 555
  Copts and, 640–641
  excluded from office, by Kitchener
    (Horatio Herbert), 1329
  exile of, and Wafd, establishment
    of, 640